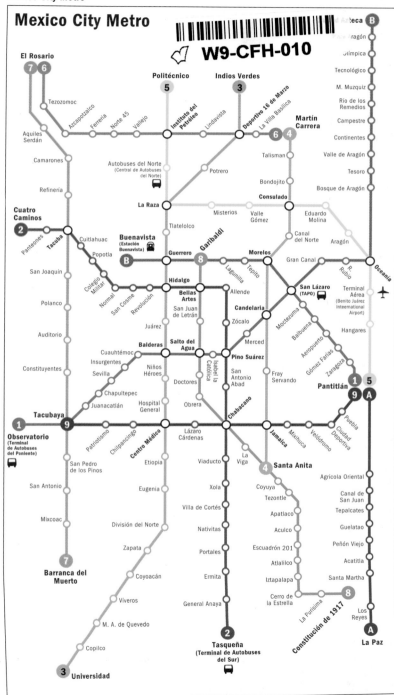

Mexico City Metro

W9-CFH-010

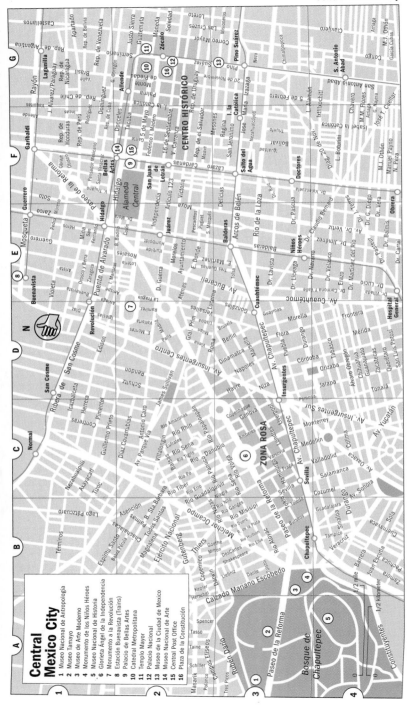

Central Mexico City

1 Museo Nacional de Antropología
2 Museo Tamayo
3 Museo de Arte Moderno
4 Monumento de los Niños Héroes
5 Museo Nacional de Historia
6 Glorieta Ángel de la Independencia
7 Monumento a la Revolución
8 Estación Buenavista (Trains)
9 Palacio de Bellas Artes
10 Catedral Metropolitana
11 Templo Mayor
12 Palacio Nacional
13 Museo de la Ciudad de Mexico
14 Museo Nacional de Arte
15 Central Post Office
16 Plaza de la Constitución

Let's Go Publications

Let's Go: Alaska & the Pacific Northwest 2001
Let's Go: Australia 2001
Let's Go: Austria & Switzerland 2001
Let's Go: Boston 2001 **New Title!**
Let's Go: Britain & Ireland 2001
Let's Go: California 2001
Let's Go: Central America 2001
Let's Go: China 2001
Let's Go: Eastern Europe 2001
Let's Go: Europe 2001
Let's Go: France 2001
Let's Go: Germany 2001
Let's Go: Greece 2001
Let's Go: India & Nepal 2001
Let's Go: Ireland 2001
Let's Go: Israel 2001
Let's Go: Italy 2001
Let's Go: London 2001
Let's Go: Mexico 2001
Let's Go: Middle East 2001
Let's Go: New York City 2001
Let's Go: New Zealand 2001
Let's Go: Paris 2001
Let's Go: Peru, Bolivia & Ecuador 2001 **New Title!**
Let's Go: Rome 2001
Let's Go: San Francisco 2001 **New Title!**
Let's Go: South Africa 2001
Let's Go: Southeast Asia 2001
Let's Go: Spain & Portugal 2001
Let's Go: Turkey 2001
Let's Go: USA 2001
Let's Go: Washington, D.C. 2001
Let's Go: Western Europe 2001 **New Title!**

Let's Go *Map Guides*

Amsterdam	New Orleans
Berlin	New York City
Boston	Paris
Chicago	Prague
Florence	Rome
Hong Kong	San Francisco
London	Seattle
Los Angeles	Sydney
Madrid	Washington, D.C.

Coming Soon: *Dublin* and *Venice*

Let's Go

▚ Let's Go writers travel on your budget.

"Guides that penetrate the veneer of the holiday brochures and mine the grit of real life."

—The Economist

"The writers seem to have experienced every rooster-packed bus and lunar-surfaced mattress about which they write."

—The New York Times

"All the dirt, dirt cheap."

—People

▚ Great for independent travelers.

"The guides are aimed not only at young budget travelers but at the independent traveler; a sort of streetwise cookbook for traveling alone."

—The New York Times

"Flush with candor and irreverence, chock full of budget travel advice."

—The Des Moines Register

"An indispensible resource, *Let's Go*'s practical information can be used by every traveler."

—The Chattanooga Free Press

▚ Let's Go is completely revised each year.

"Only *Let's Go* has the zeal to annually update every title on its list."

—The Boston Globe

"Unbeatable: good sightseeing advice; up-to-date info on restaurants, hotels, and inns; a commitment to money-saving travel; and a wry style that brightens nearly every page."

—The Washington Post

▚ All the important information you need.

"*Let's Go* authors provide a comedic element while still providing concise information and thorough coverage of the country. Anything you need to know about budget traveling is detailed in this book."

—The Chicago Sun-Times

"Value-packed, unbeatable, accurate, and comprehensive."

—Los Angeles Times

MEXICO
2001

Maya Sen editor
Alexander Kaufman associate editor
Jane Lupe Lindholm associate editor

researcher-writers
Jeremy Martinez
Tom Malone
Cristina Nelson
Abby Schlatter
Kenan Stem
Angie Chen
Corey O'Hara
Elizabeth Holt
Alex Ros

Daisy Stanton map editor

St. Martin's Press ≈ New York

HELPING LET'S GO If you want to share your discoveries, suggestions, or corrections, please drop us a line. We read every piece of correspondence, whether a postcard, a 10-page email, or a coconut. Please note that mail received after May 2001 may be too late for the 2002 book, but will be kept for future editions. **Address mail to:**

> **Let's Go: Mexico**
> **67 Mount Auburn Street**
> **Cambridge, MA 02138**
> **USA**

Visit Let's Go at **http://www.letsgo.com,** or send email to:

> **feedback@letsgo.com**
> **Subject: "Let's Go: Mexico"**

In addition to the invaluable travel advice our readers share with us, many are kind enough to offer their services as researchers or editors. Unfortunately, our charter enables us to employ only currently enrolled Harvard students.

HOW TO USE THIS BOOK

First, find a quiet spot, perhaps a shady *zócalo* bench somewhere in Genérico, Mexico. Take this book in your lap and open it. Carefully and lovingly turn the pages until you come, at last, to **How to Use This Book.** Here is what you might find:

WHAT IS IN THIS BOOK? Our first chapter, **Discover Mexico**, speaks of Mexico in sweeping (some might say clichéd) terms. It has a good friend called **Suggested Itineraries.** Suggested Itineraries suggests where and in what order one might Discover Mexico, and about how long the discovery might take. Our next chapter, the lively **Life and Times,** provides first-timers with a crash course in the art, culture, and history of Mexico—all in thirty pages. Its partner in crime, **Essentials,** does the dirty work, outlining all the information you might need to get yourself to Mexico, poke around a bit, and come back. The next part of the book, what some like to call **"The Meat,"** is chuck full of information on cities, hotels, restaurants, museums, ruins, and churches. It is divided by region: first Mexico City, then a rough trek northwest to southeast "from the deserts of Baja California to the jungles of the Yucatán," as our back covers have been known to exclaim. The mighty **Appendix** rounds out the rear, virtually rupturing with helpful supplements such as measurement conversion tables, temperature and rainfall statistics, a phrasebook of mildly useful sayings, times and mileages from city to city, a glossary, and a Spanish pronunciation guide written by a certified linguist.

HOW ARE LISTINGS ORGANIZED? Excellent question! Let's say you're in fair Genérico. After weathering the **Introduction** (our attempts at an overview), you will be accosted by **Transportation,** where, if we have done our job right, you will learn how to get yourself to and from town, and how to navigate from its transportation centers (the bustling Central de Áutobuses and the esteemed Aeropuerto Benito Juárez) to its heart, the *centro.* The dynamic duo of **Orientation** and **Practical Information** come next, providing you, eager reader, with a word or two about the neighborhoods of Genérico, and information on the tourist office, police station, hospitals, Internet service providers, and nearly every laundromat in town. Our researchers' thoughtful reviews of **Accommodations** and **Food** are next, listed in order of preference. These sections are followed by our favorite, **Sights**—an opportunity to discuss at length the Baroque facade of Iglesia Santo Domingo, and the reclining *chac-mools* of Pirámide Xtlactitxa. Sights are followed by the **Entertainment** and **Nightlife** sections, which tell you how to get your booty shaking on the most sizzling of Genérico dance floors. Finally, we follow up with suggested **Daytrips** to nearby attractions. As always, our favorites are marked with our corporate icon and shameless publicity device, the *Let's Go* thumbpick (◪).

WHAT ARE THESE BOXES FOR? We have two sorts of boxes. Boxes that are grey are called **greyboxes** (the audacity!) and provide witty, irreverent insight into the slim slice of Mexican life left uncovered by our comprehensive laundromat listings. The white boxes, called **whiteboxes,** have slightly more practical information (border crossings, dangerous highways, etc.) and are adorned by friendly icons.

SO WHAT? So what?! You sit on your bench in the shade, watching schoolchildren pass and old men gossip, and in your lap is the key to a country. Get up from your bench, walk across the *zócalo*, and strike into the heart of Mexico.

A NOTE TO OUR READERS The information for this book was gathered by *Let's Go* researchers from May through August of 2000. Each listing is based on one researcher's opinion, formed during his or her visit at a particular time. Those traveling at other times may have different experiences since prices, dates, hours, and conditions are always subject to change. You are urged to check the facts presented in this book beforehand to avoid inconvenience and surprises.

CONTENTS

MAPS

LEGEND

✚ Hospital	✈ Airport	✝ Church
🚓 Police	🚌 Bus Station	🏛 Museum
✉ Post Office	🚂 Train Station	🏠 Hotel/Hostel
ⓘ Tourist Office	Ⓜ METRO STATION	⛺ Camping
$ Bank	(184) Interstate Highway	Food & Drink
🏴 Embassy/Consulate	(207) Highway	Shopping
▪ Site or Point of Interest	⚓ Ferry Landing	♪ Arts & Entertainment
☎ Telephone Office	⚠ Archaeological Site	Nightlife
Theater	▲ Mountain	Internet Café

Pedestrian Zone

Park

Beach

Water

The Let's Go thumb always points NORTH.

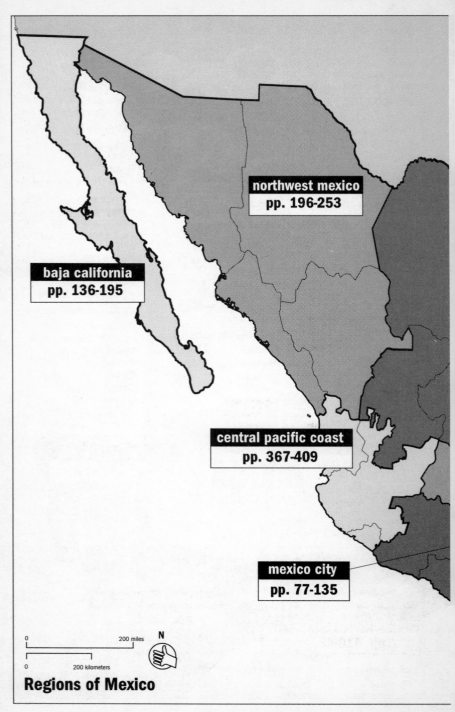

0   200 miles   N

0   200 kilometers

Regions of Mexico

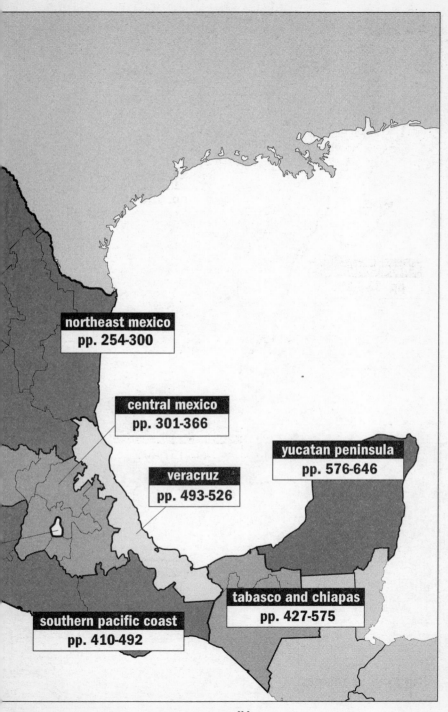

CALIF.
Tijuana
Mexicali
Ensenada
San Felipe
Puerto Peñasco
El Rosario
BAJA CALIFORNIA
SIERRA SAN PEDRO MARTIR
Bahía de Sebastián Vizcaíno
Guerrero Negro
San Ignacio
Santa Rosalía
SIERRA DE SAN FRANCISCO
Mulegé
BAJA CALIFORNIA SUR
Loreto
La Paz
Todos Santos
Cabo San Lucas
San José del Cabo
Topolobampo

ARIZONA
Tucson
Nogales
Santa Ana
SONORA
Hermosillo
Bahía Kino
Guaymas
Ciudad Obregón
Sea of Cortés

UNITED
NEW MEXICO
El Paso
Ciudad Juárez
Nuevo Casas Grandes
CHIHUAHUA
Chihuahua
Creel
SIERRA MADRE OCCIDENTAL
Hidalgo del Parral
Jiménez
COAHUILA
Gómez Palacios
Torreón
Los Mochis
Culiacán
SINALOA
DURANGO
Durango
ZACATECAS
Mazatlán
Fresnillo
Zacatecas
NAYARIT
Tuxpan
Tepic
AGUAS-CALIENTES
Aguas-calientes
León
Guanajuato
Puerto Vallarta
Guadalajara
JALISCO
Bahía de Navidad
Manzanillo
Colima
COLIMA
Morelia
Pátzcuaro
Uruapan
MICHOACÁN DE OCAMPO
Zihuatanejo/ Ixtapa

PACIFIC OCEAN

0   200 miles
0   200 kilometers
N

Mexico

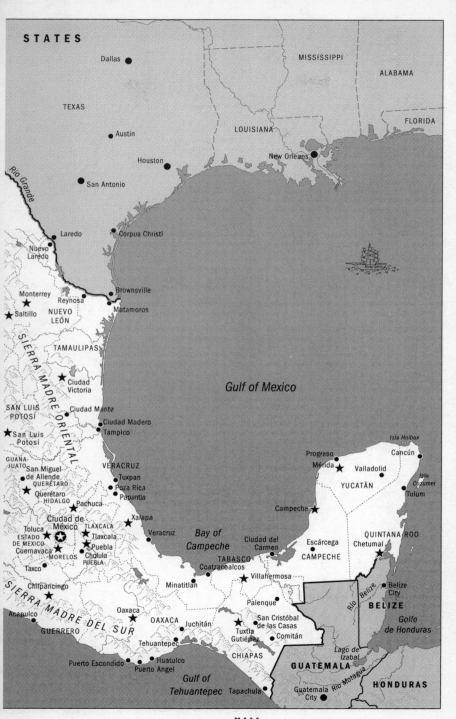

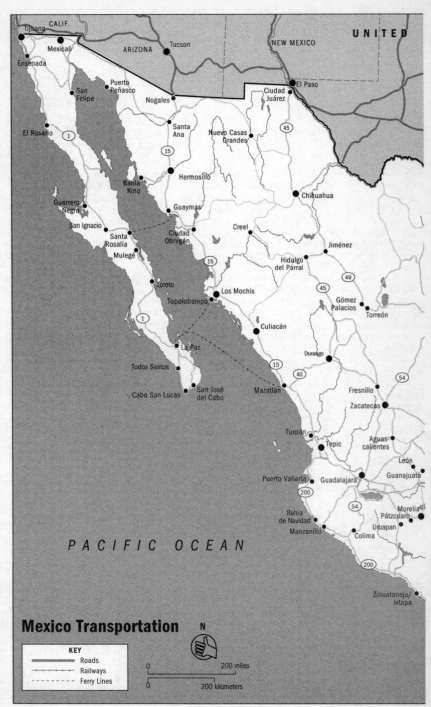

Mexico Transportation

KEY
Roads
Railways
Ferry Lines

0   200 miles
0   200 kilometers

N

PACIFIC OCEAN

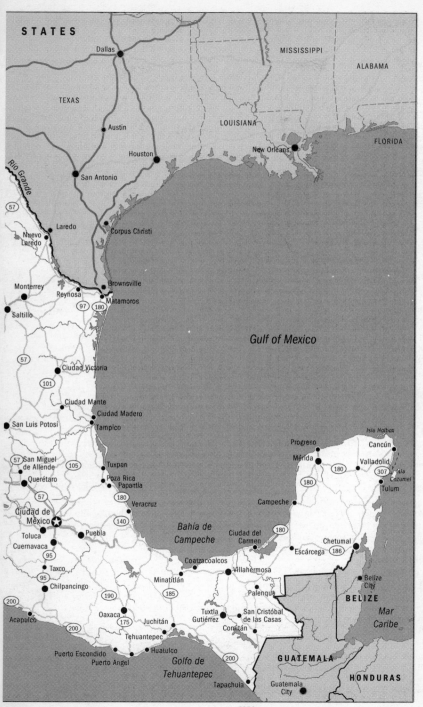

RESEARCHER-WRITERS

Jeremy Martinez   *Northwest Mexico*

While we were gnawing our knuckles over the latest flood or missed paycheck, Jeremy remained 100% chill, perhaps too busy befriending Mexican families, graphically describing stinky hotels, and ordering *all* his food spicy. Jeremy single-handedly crossed almost half the country, all the while sending us back the most disgusting candies imaginable. What's next for this all-around nice guy? China.

Tom Malone   *Northeast Mexico and Mexico City*

Tom was unquestionably a man's man—he liked his *cervezas* chilled, his bull-fights brutal, and, he soon discovered, his go-go dancing midget drag queens shimmying until dawn. The big-city *conquistador* of Team Mexico, Tom gleefully charged past the border, down the Gulf, and into *el D.F.*, turning out batches of thorough copy and making friends left and right.

Cristina Nelson   *Central Mexico and the Southern Pacific Coast*

As Mexican as her native Brownsville, street-savvy, wise-cracking Cristina dove into the southern Pacific coast and hit the *gringo* trail running. Slicing through the fluff like a master chef slicing through a tomato, this future UT lawyer wrote clear, thoughtful copy, spiced with the occasional garnish of sarcasm that left us cynics in the office smirking with mutual world-weariness.

Abby Schlatter   *Gulf Coast, Western Chiapas, and Oaxaca*

Abby was a big fan of Mexico—we were big fans of Abby. This champion corn-detasseler wowed us with her stamina, ingenious organizational schemes, and mind-boggling ability to simply *like* everything. Her copy—oh, what copy!—sung praises of even the most dismal pit, and her loving scrawls pointed out the subtle humour in the most boring of encounters. Abby, you have detasseled our hearts.

Kenan Stern   *Yucatán Peninsula and Eastern Chiapas*

Fresh from his last final (toast, anyone?), this Manhattanite tore through the Yucatán like seven rows of serrated teeth through a boogie-boarder's calf. Running down buses to rescue his backpack, rubbing elbows with Ernesto Zedillo, stealing the hearts of *yucateca* schoolgirls—just another day in the life of *El Tiburón*. Kenan expanded our already formidable Yucatán Armada, adding the newly-excavated ruins of Río Bec and shoring up shore coverage peninsula-wide.

Angie Chen   *Sonora and Northern Baja California*

Angie seduced a lot of things. First, our book. Reams of limp copy were massaged under her practiced hand into polished masterpieces. Second, our hearts. We wept with sadness when, while crossing a street in Rosarito, Angie broke her ankle. May this globe-trotting former Yosemite ranger grace *Let's Go* again.

Corey O'Hara   *Baja California Sur*

In the midst of despair, we saw an image. That image was sweet, sweet Corey O'Hara, former *Let's Go* RW and editor, who met our call with a four word answer: I can leave tomorrow. Corey manhandled the Cape, firing back stellar copy and even better marginalia. How he found time to go snorkeling we'll never know.

Elizabeth Holt   *Northern Baja California*

Bravely picking up where she left off last summer, this *Let's Go: Italy 2000* RW marauded the northern peninsula with pluck and vigor. Going back and forth in under ten days, Beth was the saving grace of Team Mexico.

Alex Ros   *Guatemala*

ACKNOWLEDGMENTS

WE THANK: Our RWs for their enthusiasm and dedication. Anne Chisholm for crisis management. Michal ("Typist") for fitting in perfectly. Daisy for her stellar mapwork. Visel for unofficial counsel. The basement for good times and solidarity. María for unflagging effort. And, of course, Olivia for everything (and late-night delirious dancing).

MAYA: My AEs, who (objectively) made this the Most Improved book in the series: Alex for his humour, patience, and defluffing prowess, and Jane for refusing to let jaded Team Mexico get her down. Matt, Hetty, Evan, and the Coöp. The friends away (Nadia, Michael, Adam) and the friends-for-life (Kenney, Large, Pops). Dan (Visel) for mid-afternoon wake-up calls. Dan (Zweifach) for late-night chats, good-natured ribbing, and making the leap from colleague to friend. Janson for attempts to drag me away and for so many other reasons. *Toda mi familia*, especially Papá, Mamá, and Dada to whom I owe my love for Mexico *and* for traveling. Now—Stanford ho!

ALEX: Maya being a good friend, making this book so good **Jane** being playfully secretive **Daisy** being fucking insane **Olivia** shaking it **Visel** sageness **Typist** typing **Gustavo** movies **Brendan** good roommatesmanship **Mindlin** mindlin! **Seth** being my best friend **Thea** the dogs balloons and beasts, the I don't know what to write, you're the best **My Parents** everything, no kidding **Kashi** poo-o-ochie **Coöp** being my home, containing my friends **Those Friends** Andrew Angie Charles Dave Derika Eddie Michelle Sarah Talya others others—

LUPE: Congrats to my *sótano salsa hermanos* for making it through. Alex and Maya: yeehaw! See you in Genérico. RW's: you made this book what it is. Olivia, Olivia: but for thee the ship would be sunk. Dan and Haley: thanks for allowing me to sneak across the border. MJ, Mardog, and KKW: your keen sense of what I needed kept me sane, much love. And a big thanks, as always, to my family, my inspiration and support.

Editor
Maya Sen
Associate Editors
Alexander Kaufman and Jane Lupe Lindholm
Managing Editor
Olivia L. Cowley
Map Editor
Daisy Stanton

Publishing Director
Kaya Stone
Editor-in-Chief
Kate McCarthy
Production Manager
Melissa Rudolph
Cartography Manager
John Fiore
Editorial Managers
Alice Farmer, Ankur Ghosh,
Aarup Kubal, Anup Kubal
Financial Manager
Bede Sheppard
Low-Season Manager
Melissa Gibson
Marketing & Publicity Managers
Olivia L. Cowley, Esti Iturralde
New Media Manager
Daryush Jonathan Dawid
Personnel Manager
Nicholas Grossman
Photo Editor
Dara Cho
Production Associates
Sanjay Mavinkurve, Nicholas
Murphy, Rosalinda Rosalez,
Matthew Daniels, Rachel Mason,
Daniel Visel
Some Design
Matthew Daniels
Office Coordinators
Sarah Jacoby, Chris Russell

Director of Advertising Sales
Cindy Rodriguez
Senior Advertising Associates
Adam Grant, Rebecca Rendell
Advertising Artwork Editor
Palmer Truelson

President
Andrew M. Murphy
General Manager
Robert B. Rombauer
Assistant General Manager
Anne E. Chisholm

DISCOVER MEXICO

Words cannot do justice to Mexico's *sabor*. Something so unique and so pervasive, so subtle and so striking can't be found in any museum or beach or ruin, and it certainly can't be found in any guidebook, no matter how solid the research, witty the prose, or keen the insight. Mexico's *sabor* is revealed only at rare times; when walking down the street, for example, you stop, look up from your worn and tattered map, and realize that all around you children are laughing and playing *fútbol*, elderly couples are engrossed in conversation, and young men are sitting outside a corner *taquería* just enjoying the air. The *sabor* is in the laughs, the smiles, and the humor of Mexico. This is the unexplainable element that defines Mexican life and its people. This is the unnameable thing that makes Mexico just *feel* different than any other country. The traveler who finds Mexico's *sabor* is sure to fall in love with the place, and in falling in love, realize that this is how Mexico somehow manages to embrace and transcend its beaches, its ruins, and its stereotypes of men in sombreros tipping back on *cantina* porches. Take a good look around you, smell the smells, see the sights, climb the ruins. But once in a while, put the book down and truly discover Mexico.

WHEN TO GO

Mexico has two seasons: rainy and dry. While it seldom rains in the northern half of the country, rainfall is both plentiful and variable in the southern half, ranging from zero to 15cm per month. Chiapas, the Yucatán Peninsula, and the Gulf Coast combined have the dubious distinction of being the soggiest parts of the country, and humidity there can reach uncomfortable levels in midsummer. Other parts of the southern half of the country are drier but experience predictable afternoon rainstorms. Pack a poncho or an umbrella—the rain is like clockwork. Temperatures fluctuate throughout the country; winters tend to be mild while summers vary from warm to excruciatingly hot. Temperatures soar both in the North and in the moist Gulf areas, rising by about 10-20°F. Exceptions to the rule are high altitude regions like the Valley of Mexico and the Valley of Oaxaca, which remain spring-like year-round.

You can't avoid the weather, but you can avoid traveling during peak tourist season, which encompasses December, late March and early April, and midsummer. Mexican families hit the road for Christmas breaks, *Semana Santa* (the week before Easter), and local festivals. For a list of national and regional festivals, see p. 647. Foreigners tend to visit mainly during their own national vacations in the winter, spring, and summer, often coinciding with Mexican holidays. Unless you want to spend your vacation rubbing elbows with hormone-charged, booze-seeking US college students, it's best to avoid resort towns such as Mazatlán, Cabo San Lucas, and Cancún during the waning weeks of March and the early weeks of April, traditional US Spring Breaks. Central Mexico and spots on the so-called *gringo* trail see the most tourist traffic during mid to late summer, when throngs of Spanish-language students hit the both the books and the trendy cafes in search of "Spanish immersion."

DISCOVER

THINGS TO DO

Mexico has no end of attractions. From climbing age-old Maya temples to haggling for silver trinkets in colonial open-air markets to diving through coral reefs to dancing the merengue with margarita in hand, each region has its own cultural allure and culinary appeal. See the **Highlights of the Region** section at the beginning of each chapter for specific regional attractions.

THE GREAT CIVILIZATIONS

A journey through Mexico is like a whirlwind through time. The ancient Olmecs—known world over for their colossal carved heads—were the first to call Mexico home, settling the villages of **San Lorenzo** (see p. 526), **La Venta** (see p. 532), and **Tres Zapotes** (see p. 521) in the lush and humid Gulf Coast around 1000 BC. Centuries later, during the Classic Period, a mighty empire rose in **Teotihuacán** (see p. 129), near modern-day Mexico City. The ruins left behind are so impressive that even the Aztecs thought that this city had been built by the gods. Farther south, the Zapotec capital **Monte Albán** (see p. 468) rivaled Teotihuacán in greatness, occupying a stately hillside position overlooking the verdant Oaxaca Valley. To the east, in the lowland jungles of the Yucatán Peninsula, the Classic Maya built decentralized cities such as **Palenque** (see p. 555), which continue to dazzle visitors with their distinct Classic architecture and jungle settings. Returning to Central Mexico, don't forget the Tlaxcalan civilizations that drew the breathtaking murals at **Cacaxtla** (see p. 350) and the Totonac civilization that carved the Pyramid of Niches at **El Tajín** (see p. 506). After the fall of the Classic civilizations, it was the Post-Classic powers like **Tula** (see p. 327), the birthplace of the feathered-deity Quetzalcóatl, and **Mitla** (see p. 465), whose intricate carvings and religious architecture are second to none, that kept Mesoamerican traditions alive. Head back into the Yucatán for a rendezvous with the warring Post-Classic Maya trio of **Chichén Itzá** (see p. 601), **Mayapán** (see p. 589), and **Uxmal** (see p. 586). Finally, witness the great end of Pre-Hispanic Mexico in the Aztec capital of **Tenochtitlán** (known to us as Mexico City. See p. 103). Climb in and around the **Templo Mayor** (see p. 105) in the shadow of the Spanish-built **Cathedral** (see p. 104), an unsubtle symbol of the Catholic Conquest.

SAND AND SURF

Who can resist miles and miles of sparkling golden and white beaches? Prefer the white sand? Strut your stuff in **Cancún** (see p. 613), the mother of all resorts. If the glam tourist scene isn't your style, ramble down the turquoise coast toward **Tulum** (see p. 637) for some beachside ruin cavorting. Of course, there are always the islands—**Isla Mujeres** (see p. 621), a small fishing village promising a quiet respite from nearby Cancún; **Isla Cozumel** (see p. 631), where coral is king and scuba is queen; and **Isla Holbox** (see p. 624), quiet keeper of the most splendid sunsets in the Western Hemisphere. Those preferring golden sand to the harsh white stuff might want to head to the Southern Pacific Coast. The surfing towns of **Puerto Escondido** (see p. 483), **Puerto Ángel** (see p. 477), **Zipolite** (see p. 479), and **Mazunte** (see p. 481) beckon with golden shores, formidable waves, and scantily clad beach bums. Those seeking less nudity and more pampering will want to head to the **Bahías de Huatulco** (see p. 470), scientifically calculated to be the next Cancún. Farther up the coast languidly sprawls the grand old dame of beach resorts, **Acapulco** (see p. 447), complete with men in tiny briefs plunging off high cliffs. The stately duo of **Ixtapa** and **Zihuatanejo** (see p. 441) keep visitors coming back, as do the resorts at **Puerto Vallarta** (see p. 387), **Manzanillo** (see p. 398), and **Mazatlán** (see p. 243). Bolder beachgoers might want to stray off the beaten track and head north to some of the most overlooked—and most spectacular—beaches in the country. Discover **San Felipe** (see p. 161), on the calm Sea of Cortés, or bask beneath the stars on the beautiful **Bahía de La Concepción** (see p. 171), one of the most pristine beaches in the world. For those who like things shaken—not stirred—no trip to Baja California would be complete without a quick jaunt farther down the peninsula to rocking **Los Cabos** (see p. 185).

COLONIAL LEGACIES

Mexico's rich history is mapped out on the land. If it could speak, each brick in each church in each city would tell stories of treason, murder, and conquest. History buffs will not be disappointed. The best place to explore is the very capital, **Mexico City** (see p. 77), the sprawling megalopolis with a population (almost 20 million) nearly equal to a medium-sized country. Check out the stately **Palacio Nacional** (see p. 104), home to Spanish viceroys and Mexican presidents. Stop by **Coyoacán** (see p. 101), where Hernán Cortés established his government and tortured the Aztec emperor Cuauhtémoc. Heading out of *el D.F.*, you'll come to **Cuernavaca** (see p. 335), former home of Cortés, and **Taxco** (see p. 435), the colonial silver town whose narrow, winding streets feel more like Spain than Mexico. Skip down south to the faded limestone streets of **Oaxaca** (see p. 453), birthplace of the nation's first president with indigenous roots, Benito Juárez. Swing by the meticulously planned city of **Mérida** (see p. 591), a large Maya center converted to a modern city by the Spanish. Frolic with the mummies in **Guanajuato** (see p. 303) and be sure to stop by the expat-populated **San Miguel de Allende** (see p. 309) and its friendly neighbor, **Dolores Hidalgo** (see p. 316), where you can sound the *Grito de Dolores* (the electrifying speech calling for Mexican Independence) for yourself. Cut up through **San Luis Potosí** (see p. 289), the nation's wealthy silver and gold capital, before coming back down through the steamy port of **Veracruz** (see p. 507). The first city founded by the Spanish, Veracruz is Mexico's port to the outside world and the site of numerous foreign invasions. Farther inland is **Tlaxcala** (see p. 343), the city-state that collaborated with Cortés to defeat the Aztecs. Neighboring **Puebla** (see p. 351) is the epitome of a colonial city, with its emphasis on order and rigidity embedded in the city's gridded streets and cobblestone walkways.

■ LET'S GO PICKS

BEST PLACE TO PROPOSE: On the shores of **Isla Holbox** (p. 624), watching the sunset, dressed in palm fronds, drunk.

BEST THIGH-MASTER SUBSTITUTE: Climbing the Pyramid of the Sun in **Teotihuacán** (p. 129)—guaranteed to leave you huffing and puffing.

MOST WORTHWHILE NEAR-DEATH EXPERIENCE: Driving in **Mexico City** (p. 77) can be hazardous to your health, but you'll learn to curse with the best of them.

BEST PLACE TO OBSERVE WILD ANIMALS IN THEIR NATURAL HABITATS: Spy on the *bronzus americanus* romping in the **Cancún** (p. 613), **Mazatlán** (p. 243), and **Cabo San Lucas** (p. 187) ecosystems.

BEST PLACES TO DE-STRESS: Zipolite (p. 479) and **Mazunte** (p. 481), where time slows and people are naked. **Real de Catorce** (p. 296), where the best mode of transportation is a horse.

BEST BAREFOOT CARMELITE CONVENT: Desierto de los Leones (p. 133), exciting self-flagellation just an hour out of Mexico City.

BEST PLACE TO THROW ONESELF OFF A CLIFF IN TINY BRIEFS: In **Acapulco** (p. 447). Duh.

BEVERAGES SURE TO WARM YOU UP: The steamy *café con leche* in **Veracruz** (p. 507)and the hot chocolate in **Oaxaca** (p. 453). To really, really warm up? Down a couple of shots in **Tequila** (p. 385).

SUGGESTED ITINERARIES

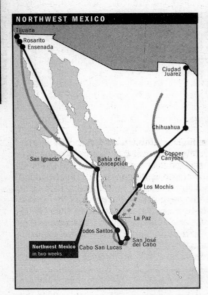

NORTHWEST MEXICO

Tijuana
Rosarito
Ensenada
Ciudad Juárez
Chihuahua
San Ignacio
Bahía de Concepción
Copper Canyons
Los Mochis
La Paz
Todos Santos
San José del Cabo
Cabo San Lucas

Northwest Mexico
in two weeks

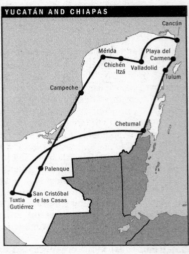

YUCATÁN AND CHIAPAS

Cancún
Mérida
Playa del Carmen
Chichén Itzá
Valladolid
Tulum
Campeche
Chetumal
Palenque
Tuxtla Gutiérrez
San Cristóbal de las Casas

NORTHWEST MEXICO (3 WEEKS)

Start things off in the den of debauchery—**Ciudad Juárez** (see p. 220). Make your next stop the Northwest metropolis, **Chihuahua** (see p. 225). From there, meander around the ruins at **Nuevo Casas** and **Paquimé** (see p. 224) before hopping on the next train to **Los Mochis** (see p. 239)—passing through the spectacular **Copper Canyons** (see p. 235), of course. From Mochis, hop on a ferry to **La Paz** (see p. 176) in Baja California Sur. Swing down into **San José del Cabo** (see p. 192) for a quick rest before partying with José's brother **Cabo San Lucas** (see p. 187) and his Spring Breaking chums. On your way back north, stop and say hello to the artsy expats in **Todos Santos** (see p. 182) and then trek over to **Mulegé** (see p. 169) and the spectacular **Bahía de la Concepción** (see p. 171). Heading northward, be sure to stop at **San Ignacio** (see p. 166), **Ensenada** (see p. 152), and **Rosarito** (see p. 145), home of *The Titanic* film remnants. Your heart will indeed go on...to **Tijuana** (see p. 139), the mother of all border towns and the end of the rollicking trip.

YUCATÁN AND CHIAPAS (3 WEEKS)

Start things off with some alcohol-drenched nights in **Cancún** (see p. 613). If funds run low, catch the next ferry to **Isla Mujeres** (see p. 621). Back on the peninsula, don't skip the cavernous *cenotes* of **Valladolid** (see p. 607) on your way to the Post-Classic ruins of **Chichén Itzá** (see p. 601). Relax those aching legs in the colonial hammock-filled city of **Mérida** (see p. 591). Cross through the **Ruta Puuc** (see p. 585) and then find yourself dancing in the plazas within the fortress walls of **Campeche** (see p. 578). Setting off south into the Chiapan jungle, hike the soaring temples of **Palenque** (see p. 555) and then discover the gem of **San Cristóbal de las Casas** (see p. 545), a backpacker's mecca. If you're in the mood to see wildlife of a different sort, head west to the sprawling capital **Tuxtla Gutiérrez** (see p. 539), home of the best zoo in Latin American and a base from which to explore the green walls of the **Sumidero Canyon** (see p. 543). Back through the Yucatán, **Chetumal** (see p. 642) is worth a visit for its world-class museum, while the mesmerizing beauty of **Tulum** (see p. 637) beckons. Toast the trip with a beer in the lively **Playa del Carmen** (see p. 626).

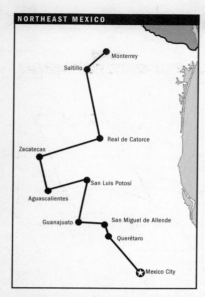

NORTHEAST MEXICO (2 WEEKS)
Start your journey off in eclectic **Monterrey** (see p. 267). After eating your fill of *cabrito*, head to **Saltillo** (see p. 275) before entering the realm that time forgot in **Real de Catorce** (see p. 296). No visit to the northeast is complete without stopping by the colonial cities of **Zacatecas** (see p. 277) and **Aguascalientes** (see p. 283). Afterwards, head back eastward into the plazas of **San Luis Potosí** (see p. 289) and then into the captivating former capital, **Guanajuato** (see p. 303). Share your travel anecdotes with the expats in **San Miguel de Allende** (see p. 309), pay your respects to Emperor Maximilian in **Querétaro** (see p. 318), and then head back to **Mexico City** (see p. 77) before trekking back home.

CENTRAL MEXICO (3 WEEKS) Start off your trip in **el D.F.** (see p. 77), but don't stay too long. **Puebla** (see p. 351), with its immense cathedral and colonial gridded streets, is calling. Don't forget to stop by its little neighbor with the big pyramid, **Cholula** (see p. 361). Head north toward the beautiful and peaceful city of **Tlaxacala** (see p. 343) before ascending the Sierra Madre Oriental and entering hilly **Xalapa** (see p. 493), known for its steamy beverages and culture. Turn the heat up in **Veracruz** (see p. 507) and mamba all night before catching the next bus to **Oaxaca** (see p. 453), where you can work your thighs by hiking the ruins at **Monte Albán** (see p. 468) and **Mitla** (see p. 465) and then kick back with a cup of *chocolate caliente*. Next, practice your haggling skills while you banter with silver vendors in **Taxco** (see p. 435), and then relive old memories in Cortés's palace in **Cuernavaca** (see p. 335) before heading northward into the stately colonial city of **Morelia** (see p. 425). Cap things off back in **Mexico City** (see p. 77), the biggest and baddest of them all.

DISCOVER

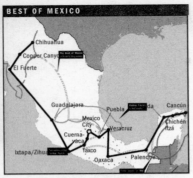

BEST OF MEXICO

THE BEST OF MEXICO (3-4 WEEKS)

Start things off in **Chihuahua** (see p. 225). Hop on the first train down the **Copper Canyons** (see p. 235) and into **El Fuerte** (see p. 238). After relaxing for a second or two, take off for Mexico's second largest city, **Guadalajara** (see p. 373), and then continue to **Ixtapa/Zihuatanejo** (see p. 441). Shop-till-you-drop in **Taxco** (see p. 435) and practice your Spanish in **Cuernavaca** (see p. 335). Stay for a couple of days in oh-so-exciting Mexico City (see p. 77) before hitting its smaller cousin **Puebla** (see p. 351). **Veracruz** (see p. 507), Mexico's steamy port, is next. If things get too hot, head to stately **Oaxaca** (see p. 453). Coming back north, stop by **Palenque** (see p. 555), en route to colonial **Mérida** (see p. 591). Finally, swing by **Chichén Itzá** (see p. 601) before engaging in some **Cancún** (see p. 613) mischief.

ESSENTIALS

FACTS FOR THE TRAVELER

DOCUMENTS AND FORMALITIES

> **ENTRANCE REQUIREMENTS**
>
> **Passport** (p. 8). Recommended for citizens of the US, Canada, and Japan. Required for citizens of Australia, Ireland, New Zealand, South Africa, the UK, and most other countries.
>
> **Visa** (p. 9). Visas are not required for citizens of the US, Canada, and most EU countries. Citizens of countries in Eastern Europe, Africa, and Asia need visas, as do individuals entering the country for work or extended study.
>
> **Inoculations:** (p. 18). None required, but some are recommended for travelers to more rural and humid parts of the country.
>
> **Driving Licences and Permits** (p. 9). All foreign licenses are accepted. Insurance is recommended. A **Vehicle Permit** is required to bring an automobile more than 22km into Mexico (p. 10).

MEXICAN SERVICES ABROAD

EMBASSIES AND CONSULATES

Embassies: Australia, 14 Perth Ave., Yarralumla, Canberra 2600 ACT (☎(06) 273 3905; fax 273 1190); **Canada,** 45 O'Connor St., #1500, KIP 1A4 Ottawa, ON. (☎(613) 233-8988, fax. 235-9123; www.embamexcan.com); **UK,** 42 Hertford St., Mayfair, W1Y 7TS, London (☎(44-20) 7499 8586; fax (44-20) 7495 4035; www.demon.co.uk/mexuk/); **US,** 1911 Pennsylvania Ave. NW, Washington, D.C. 20006 (☎(202) 728-1600; fax 728-1718; www.embassyofmexico.org).

Consulates: Australia, Level 1, 135-153 New South Head Rd., Edgecliff, Sydney 2027 NSW (☎(02) 326 1311 or 326 1292; fax 327 1110. **Canada,** Commerce Court West, 199 Bay St., #4440, M5L 1E9 Toronto, ON (☎(416) 368-2875; fax 368-0676; www.canada.org.mex); **UK,** 8 Halkin St., London SW1 X7DW (☎(020) 7235-6393; fax 7235-5480); **US,** 2827 16th St. NW, Washington, D.C. 20009 (☎(202) 736-1000; fax 797-8458).

TOURISM OFFICES

Chicago: 300 N. Michigan Ave., 4th fl., Chicago, IL 60601 USA (☎(312) 606-9252; fax 606-9012; email mgtochi@compuserve.com).

Houston: 10103 Fomdren St., #450, Houston, TX 77096 USA (☎(713) 772-2581; fax 772-6058; email mgtotx@ix.netcom.com).

London: Wakefield House, 41 Trinity Square, London EC# 4NDJ (☎(020) 7488 9392; fax 7265 0704; email mrc@jaruz.com).

Los Angeles: 2401 W. 6th St., 5th fl., Los Angeles, CA 90057 USA (☎(213) 351-2069; fax (213) 352-2074; email 104045.3647@compuserve.com).

Miami: 1200 NW 78th Ave., #203, Miami, FL 33126 USA (☎(305) 718-4091; fax 718-4098; email mgtomia@gate.net).

Montreal: 1 Place Ville Marie, #1931, Montreal, Québec H3B 2B5 (☎(514) 871-1052; fax 871-3825; email turimex@cam.org).

New York City: 21 E. 63rd St., 3rd fl., New York, NY 10021 USA (☎(212) 821-8314; fax 821-0367; email milmgto@interport.net).

Toronto: 2 Bloor St. W, #1502, Toronto, ON M4W 3E2 (☎(416) 925-2753; fax 925-6061; email mexto3@inforamp.net).

Vancouver (and Northwest US): 999 W. Hastings, #1610, Vancouver, BC V6C 2W2 (☎(604) 669-2845; fax 669-3498; email mgto@bc.sympatico.ca).

FOREIGN SERVICES IN MEXICO

EMBASSIES

Canada: Schiller 529, Col. Polanco, 11560 Mexico D.F. (☎5724 7900; fax 5724 7980).

UK: Rio Lerma 71, Mexico D.F. 06500 (☎5207 2449; fax 5207 7672).

US: Paseo de la Reforma 305, Colonia Cuauhtémoc, Mexico D.F. (☎5209 9100, 5207 2089, or 5207 2569; for visas 5208 8027).

US CONSULATES

Ciudad Juárez: López Mateos 924N (☎(1) 611 30 00).

Guadalajara: Progreso 175 (☎(3) 825 29 98; fax 826 65 49).

Hermosillo: Monterrey, 141 Poniente (☎(6) 217 23 75; fax 217 25 78).

Matamoros: Primera 2002 y Azaleas (☎(8) 812 44 02; fax 812 21 71).

Mérida: Paseo Montejo 453 (☎(9) 925 50 11; fax 925 62 19).

Monterrey: Constitución 411, Poniente 64000 (☎(8) 345 21 20).

Nogales: San José s/n, Fracc. Alamos (☎(6) 313 48 20; fax 313 46 52)

Nuevo Laredo: Calle Allende 3330, Col. Jardín (☎(8) 714 05 12; fax 714 79 84).

Tijuana: Tapachula No. 96, Colonia Hipódromo (☎(6) 681 74 00).

PASSPORTS

Citizens of Australia, New Zealand, South Africa, the UK, and most EU countries need valid passports to enter Mexico and to re-enter their own country. Mexico does not allow entrance if the holder's passport expires in under six months; returning home with an expired passport is illegal, and may result in a fine. It is recommended that citizens of the US, Canada, and Japan carry a valid passport, but proof of citizenship (such as an official birth certificate, naturalization certificate, consular report of birth abroad, or a certificate of citizenship) and a photo ID will also be accepted. A passport, however, carries much more authority than does a birth certificate, makes returning home by air easier, and is mandatory for anyone traveling from Mexico to Central America.

LOST PASSPORTS

Be sure to photocopy important documents: the front page of your passport, passport number, important IDs, visas, travel insurance policies, plane tickets, and traveler's check serial numbers. If you lose your passport, immediately notify the local police and your nearest embassy or consulate. To expedite replacement, you will need to know all information previously recorded and show ID and proof of citizenship. In some cases, a replacement may take weeks to process and may be valid for a limited time. In an emergency, ask for temporary traveling papers that will permit you to re-enter your home country.

NEW PASSPORTS

File any new passport or renewal applications well in advance of your departure date. Most passport offices offer rush services, but they come at a steep fee. Citizens living abroad who need a passport or renewal should contact their nearest consular service.

Australia: (Info ☎13 12 32; email passports.australia@dfat.gov.au; www.dfat.gov.au/passports.) Apply at a post office, passport office, or overseas diplomatic mission.

Canada: Canadian Passport Office, Department of Foreign Affairs and International Trade, Ottawa, ON K1A 0G3 (☎(613) 994-3500 or (800) 567-6868; www.dfait-maeci.gc.ca/passport). Applications available at passport offices, Canadian missions, and post offices.

ESSENTIALS

Ireland: Pick up an application from a *Garda* station, post office, or passport office and mail it to the Department of Foreign Affairs, Passport Office, Molesworth St., Dublin 2 (☎(01) 671 1633; fax 671 1092; www.irlgov.ie/iveagh), or the Passport Office, Irish Life Building, 1A South Mall, Cork (☎(021) 27 25 25).

New Zealand: Passport Office, Department of International Affairs, P.O. Box 10526, Wellington, New Zealand (☎(0800) 22 50 50 or (4) 474 8100; fax (4) 474 8010; www.passports.govt.nz; email passports@dia.govt.nz).

South Africa: Department of Home Affairs. Passports are issued only in Pretoria, but all applications must still be submitted or forwarded to the nearest South African consulate. Processing can take 3 months or more. For more information, check out http://usaembassy.southafrica.net/VisaForms/Passport/Passport2000.html.

United Kingdom: Info ☎(0870) 521 0410; www.open.gov.uk/ukpass/ukpass.htm. Get an application from a passport office, main post office, travel agent, or online at www.ukpa.gov.uk/forms/f_app_pack.htm.

United States: Info ☎(202) 647-0518; www.travel.state.gov/passport_services.html. Apply at any federal or state courthouse, authorized post office, or US Passport Agency.

OTHER FORMS OF IDENTIFICATION

When you travel, it's a good idea to carry two or more forms of ID on your person, including at least one photo ID. A passport combined with a driver's license or birth certificate is usually sufficient. Never carry all your forms of ID in the same place; split them up in case of theft or loss.

Although the **International Student Identity Card** (**ISIC;** www.isic.org) is the most widely accepted form of student identification, particularly in Western Europe, it is not particularly useful in Mexico; most student discounts, if any, are offered only to students at Mexican universities. If you're a smooth talker, though, and you have one, bring your **university ID,** and you might be able to sweet talk your way into free or discounted admissions.

VISAS AND PERMITS

Unless you're a North American tourist visiting for fewer than six months, it's a good idea to check with the nearest Mexican consulate or embassy for exact entry requirements. Checking beforehand is particularly important for those seeking to enter for human rights purposes; the political uprisings in Chiapas have made many Mexicans sensitive to meddling foreigners, and many have been detained, expelled, or deported for violating their tourist visa status or allegedly interfering in the country's internal politics. Also note that children traveling into Mexico may have to present special papers (see **Baby on Board,** p. 37).

TOURIST CARDS (FOLLETO DE MIGRACIÓN TURISTICA)

All persons, regardless of nationality, must carry a **tourist card** (**FMT,** for Folleto de Migración Turistica) on their person in addition to proof of citizenship. Most tourist cards are good for up to 180 days; some, however, are only good for 30 days or for a shorter pre-determined length. If you need to leave and re-enter the country during your stay, make sure your tourist card will enable you to do so; you might have to ask for a multiple-entry permit. US and Canadian citizens don't need the tourist card if they are staying in the country for less than 72 hours or intend to stay within the 22km US-Mexico border zone. When traveling into the country by plane, the US$18 tourist card fee is included in the airline ticket price, and the tourist card will be given to you to fill out during your flight. If driving into Mexico, you will be charged the fee at your point of entry. You can avoid any delays by obtaining one from a Mexican consulate or tourist office before you leave (see **Embassies and Consulates,** p. 7).

 DON'T LEAVE HOME WITHOUT IT. Because you may be asked to present your tourist card when leaving the country, you must keep it for the duration of your trip. Keep it along with your other valuables in a safe place.

TOURIST VISAS

Tourist visas are **not necessary** for citizens of Australia, Canada, New Zealand, the UK, the US, and most EU and Latin American countries for stays of up to 180 days; the tourist card is sufficient. Individuals with Eastern European, Asian, African, and Middle Eastern citizenship must procure a tourist visa from the nearest Mexican consulate before traveling; in order to do so, a valid passport, a valid I-94 form, three passport photographs, and evidence of a round-trip ticket are necessary. A consular fee of US$33 may also be charged, depending upon nationality.

BUSINESS VISAS

Under the North American Free Trade Agreement (NAFTA), US and Canadian citizens can enter Mexico to conduct business for up to 30 days with a **FM-N permit** (free). To do so, travelers must prove they are traveling on international business and that their pay is coming from a non-Mexican source; a letter from their company or firm in addition to a valid passport will suffice. Business travelers planning on staying longer than 30 days will have to apply for an **FM-3 permit** (consular fee of US$88), which is good for up to one year.

STUDENT VISAS

Students interested in studying in Mexico for longer than 180 days must obtain an **FM-3 permit** from their nearest Mexican consulate. In order to do so, they must submit the acceptance letter from the school they wish to attend along with several photographs, a statement proving economic solvency, and a certificate of good health. Those studying under a specific program must also submit a letter from the sponsoring organization. The consular fee depends on nationality and bureaucratic procedure; citizens of some nationalities might have to pay a US$28 fee. Note that students planning on studying for less than six months may enter the country with a normal tourist visa or tourist card.

RETIREMENT VISAS

Seeking a temperate climate and favorable exchange rates, many foreigners have chosen Mexico as their place of retirement. Those whose retirement income comes from abroad may seek the classification of **no immigrant-restista** (retired non-immigrant). Those interested in settling down in Mexico must contact the nearest consular office for an **FM-3 permit** (US$88) and present a valid passport, several photographs, proof of economic solvency, and other documents. The FM-3 visa will be good for 30 days, whereupon retirees must go to a immigration office in Mexico, prove solvency, and receive another stamp on their FM-3 permit, which must be renewed every couple of years. After 10 years, status changes to **FM-2** status, non-immigrant resident.

CUSTOMS

ENTERING MEXICO

BY CAR

Crossing into Mexico by land can be as uneventful or as complicated as the border guards want it to be. You may be waved into the country or directed to the immigration office to procure a tourist card (FMT) if you don't have one already. Make sure all papers are in order before proceeding; if there is anything amiss when you reach an immigration checkpoint 22km into the interior, you'll have to turn back.

If you plan on driving into Mexico, you will need to obtain a **vehicle permit** at the border. Permits are $12 when you pay with a valid credit card. Those without credit cards will have to provide a cash deposit or bond worth thousands of dollars, depending on the value of the car. Your deposit will be repaid in full when you return across the border, but paying the minimal fee by credit card is strongly advised. To extend a vehicle permit beyond its original expiration date and to avoid confiscation, contact the temporary importation department of Mexican customs. The maximum length granted to tourists is six months. A vehicle permit is valid only for the person to whom it was issued unless another driver is approved by the federal registry. Violation of this law can result in confiscation of the vehicle or heavy fines. In order to get a permit, you will need an original copy and a photocopy of several documents: a state vehicle registration certificate and vehicle title, a valid driver's license accompanied by either a passport or a birth certificate, and a Mexican insurance policy, which can be purchased at the border. If leasing a vehicle, you must provide the contract in your name (also in duplicate). **Vehicle permits are not needed if you do not plan to venture more than 22km over the border.** Furthermore, only legitimate drivers may purchase car-ferry tickets. Regulations change frequently; for updated information contact a consulate.

BY AIR

Entering Mexico by air is somewhat easier. Dash out of your plane as fast as possible to beat the rush to *aduana* (customs). Beware that agents randomly examine luggage using a press-your-luck light system; unless you want the entire airport to see that rhinestone g-string, leave it at home—or, better yet, wear it.

Mexican regulations limit the value of goods brought into Mexico by US citizens arriving by air or sea to US$300 per person and by land to US$50 per person. Amounts exceeding the duty-free limit are subject to a 32.8% tax.

HAPPINESS IS A WARM GUN. Mexico has severe penalties for those carrying weapons or firearms into the country, and many foreigners have been incarcerated for violating firearms regulations. If you are entering Mexico to hunt, you must contact the nearest Mexican consulate and your local police department *before* your visit to obtain written permission and proof of gun ownership. Trying to bring a weapon into Mexico is, however, more hassle than it's worth and can get you into big trouble. For the love of God, leave the gun at home.

LEAVING MEXICO

Upon returning home, you must declare all articles acquired abroad and pay a **duty** on the value of those articles that exceed the allowance established by your country's customs service. Goods and gifts purchased at **duty-free** shops abroad are not exempt from duty or sales tax at your point of return; you must declare these items as well. ("Duty-free" merely means that you do not have to pay a tax in the country of purchase.) To establish the value when you return home, keep receipts for items purchased abroad. Since you pay no duty on goods brought from home, record the serial numbers of any expensive items (cameras, computers, radios, etc.) you are taking with you before you begin your travels, and check with your country's customs office to see if it has a special form for registering them.

It's a very bad idea to take illegal drugs out of Mexico. If you have questions, call the **Mexican Customs Office** in the US (☎ (202) 728-1669) or contact your specific embassy or consulate for more information. In the north, especially along the Pacific coast, expect to be stopped repeatedly by burly, humorless troopers looking for contraband. That innocent-looking hitchhiker you were kind enough to pick up may be a drug peddler with a stash of illegal substances. If the police catch it in your car, the drug possession charges will extend to you, and your car may be confiscated. If you carry **prescription drugs** while you travel, it is vital to have a copy of the prescriptions themselves and a note from a doctor readily accessible at country borders.

Note that when entering the US, you may be hassled by immigration officers if you are a resident alien of the US or simply have a Latino surname.

MORE RESOURCES

Australia: Australian Customs National Information Line (in Australia call (01) 30 03 63, from elsewhere call +61 (2) 6275 6666; www.customs.gov.au).

ESSENTIALS

Canada: Canadian Customs, 2265 St. Laurent Blvd., Ottawa, ON K1G 4K3 (☎(800) 461-9999 (24hr.) or (613) 993-0534; www.revcan.ca).

Ireland: Customs Information Office, Irish Life Centre, Lower Abbey St., Dublin 1 (☎(01) 878 8811; fax 878 0836; taxes@revenue.iol.ie; www.revenue.ie/customs.htm).

New Zealand: New Zealand Customhouse, 17-21 Whitmore St., Box 2218, Wellington (☎(04) 473 6099; fax 473 7370; www.customs.govt.nz).

South Africa: Commissioner for Customs and Excise, Privat Bag X47, Pretoria 0001 (☎(012) 314 9911; fax 328 6478; www.gov.za).

United Kingdom: Her Majesty's Customs and Excise, Passenger Enquiry Team, Wayfarer House, Great South West Road, Feltham, Middlesex TW14 8NP (☎(020) 8910 3744; fax 8910 3933; www.hmce.gov.uk).

United States: US Customs Service, 1330 Pennsylvania Ave. NW, Washington, D.C. 20229 (☎(202) 354-1000; fax 354-1010; www.customs.gov).

MONEY

If you stay in cheap hotels, diet rigorously, and avoid sights and attractions, expect to spend US$6-15 per person per day. A less stingy (but substantially happier) traveler, depending on his or her level of extravagance, might expect to spend about US$20-35 traveling in less touristed areas and about US$35-50 near the US border or in resort areas. Prices for hotels start at about US$7 per night for a single and can increase dramatically. A basic sit-down meal will cost around US$3.

CURRENCY AND EXCHANGE

The currency chart below is based on August 2000 exchange rates. For the latest exchange rates, check a newspaper or consult the Internet (e.g. http://finance.yahoo.com, www.bloomberg.com, or www.letsgo.com/thumb).

PESO		
US$1 = 9.3 PESOS	1 PESO = US$0.11
CDN$1 = 6.3 PESOS	1 PESO = CDN$0.16
US£ = 13.8 PESOS	1 PESO = UK£0.07
AUS$1 = 5.4 PESOS	1 PESO = AUS$0.19
NZ$= 4.1 PESOS	1 PESO = NZ$0.24
SAR$1 = 1.3 PESOS	1 PESO = SAR$0.75

Changing money in Mexico is easy in all but the most rural areas, where banks might be scarce or might have very limited hours. The more money you change at one time, the less you will lose to commission. Also keep in mind that while all banks exchange dollars for pesos, some might not accept other currencies; foreign travelers of all nationalities would be wise to keep some US dollars on hand. **Casas de Cambio** (currency exchange booths) may offer better exchange rates than banks and are usually open as long as the stores near which they do business. In most towns, the exchange rates at hotels, restaurants, and airports are extremely unfavorable. Avoid them unless it's an emergency.

TRAVELER'S CHECKS

Traveler's checks are one of the safest means of carrying funds in Mexico. Travel agencies and banks will sell them for a small commission. Each agency provides refunds if your checks are lost or stolen, and many provide additional services, such as toll-free refund hotlines abroad, emergency message services, and stolen credit card assistance.

While traveling, keep check receipts and a record of which checks you've cashed separate from the checks themselves. Also leave a list of check numbers with someone at home. Never countersign checks until you're ready to cash them, and always bring your passport with you to cash them. If your checks are lost or stolen, immediately contact the company that issued your checks to be reimbursed; they may require a police report verifying the loss or theft. Less-touristed cities may not have refund centers at all, in which case you may have to wait to be reimbursed.

Exchanging traveler's checks in Mexico is fairly easy. Remember however, that some places (especially in northern Mexico) are accustomed to US dollars and will accept no substitute. It might also be difficult to exchange traveler's checks in the more rural parts of Mexico and other less touristed places. Finally, it's probably best to buy most of your checks in small denominations (US$20) to minimize your losses at times when you can't avoid a bad exchange rate. Purchase checks in US dollars; many *casas de cambio* refuse to change other currencies.

American Express: Call (800) 251 902 in Australia; in New Zealand (0800) 441 068; in the UK (0800) 521 313; in the US and Canada (800) 221-7282. Elsewhere call US collect +1 (801) 964-6665; www.aexp.com.

Citicorp: In the US and Canada call (800) 645-6556; in Europe, the Middle East, or Africa call the UK +44 (020) 7508 7007; elsewhere call US collect +1 (813) 623-1709.

Visa: In the US call (800) 227-6811; in the UK call (0800) 89 50 78; elsewhere call UK collect +44 (1733) 31 89 49. Call for the location of their nearest office.

CREDIT CARDS

Credit cards are accepted by all but the smallest Mexican businesses. **Visa** (US ☎(800) 336-8472) and **MasterCard** (US ☎(800) 307-7309) are the most readily accepted. **American Express** (US ☎(800) 843-2273) is also accepted; holders may cash personal checks at AmEx offices abroad, access an emergency medical and legal assistance hotline (24hr.; call collect to the US +1 (202) 554-2639), and enjoy American Express Travel Service benefits. All major cards can be used to get **cash advances,** which allow you to withdraw pesos from networked banks and ATMs throughout Mexico. Credit card companies get the wholesale exchange rate, which is generally 5% better than the retail rate used by banks and other currency exchange establishments. Transaction fees for all credit card advances (up to US$10 per advance, plus 2-3% extra on foreign transactions after conversion) tend to make credit cards a more costly way of withdrawing cash than ATMs or traveler's checks. In an emergency, however, the transaction fee may prove worth the cost. To be eligible for an advance, you'll need to get a Personal Identification Number (PIN) from your credit card company.

ATM CARDS

Automated Teller Machine (ATM) use is widespread in Mexico, and all but the smallest towns have ATMs in central locations, such as in the town *zócalo*, near commercial areas, or in large supermarkets. Most large banks (such as Bancomer and Serfín) also have ATMs outside their front doors or in their main lobbies. ATMs get the same wholesale exchange rate as credit cards, but there might be a limit on the amount of money you can withdraw per day (around US$500; check with your bank), and there is typically a surcharge of US$1-5 per withdrawal. Be sure to memorize your PIN in numeric form since machines in Mexico often don't have letters on their keys. Also, if your PIN is longer than four digits, ask your bank whether you need a new number. The two major international money networks are **Cirrus** (US ☎(800) 424-7787) and **PLUS** (US ☎(800) 843-7587). To locate ATMs around the world, call the above numbers, or consult www.visa.com/pd/atm or www.mastercard.com/atm.

 MONEY (THAT'S WHAT I WANT). While using ATMs is a convenient way to access money, travelers should take special care; thieves have been known to lurk around ATMs and then rob individuals either at the machine or shortly after they have used it. Exercise caution. Don't brandish your ATM card and use ATM machines during the day, inside commercial establishments or in a well-lit and busy areas. Transactions made outdoors or at night are much more likely to attract thieves.

GETTING MONEY FROM HOME

The cheapest way to receive money in Mexico is to have it sent through a large commercial bank with associated banks within Mexico. The sender must either have an account with the bank, or bring in cash or a money order. If the sender can supply the bank with exact information on the recipient's passport number and the Mexican bank address, the cabled money should arrive in one to three days; otherwise, there will be significant delays. Other options are listed below.

AMERICAN EXPRESS. Cardholders can withdraw cash from their checking accounts at any of AmEx's major offices and many representative offices (up to US$1000 every 21 days; no service charge, no interest). AmEx "Express Cash" withdrawals from any AmEx ATM in Mexico are automatically debited from the cardholder's checking account or line of credit. To enroll in Express Cash, card members may call (800) 227-4669 within the US; elsewhere call the US collect +1 (336) 668-5041. The AmEx national number in Mexico is (5) 326 26 26.

WESTERN UNION. Travelers from the US, Canada, and the UK can wire money abroad through Western Union's international money transfer services. In the US, call (800) 325-6000; in Canada (800) 235-0000; in the UK (0800) 833 833; in Mexico (5) 546-7361. The rates for sending cash are generally US$10-11 cheaper than with a credit card, and the money is usually available at the place you're sending it to within an hour. For the nearest location, consult www.westernunion.com.

FEDERAL EXPRESS. Some people choose to send cash abroad via FedEx to avoid transmission fees and taxes. In the US and Canada, call (800) 463-3339; in the UK (0800) 123 800; in Ireland (800) 535 800; in Australia 13 26 10; in New Zealand (0800) 733 339; in South Africa (021) 551 7610; and in Mexico (5) 228-9904. While FedEx is reasonably reliable, this method is illegal and somewhat risky.

US STATE DEPARTMENT (US CITIZENS ONLY). In dire emergencies only, the US State Department will forward money during normal business hours to the nearest consular office, which will then disburse it, according to instructions, for a US$15 fee. Contact the Overseas Citizens Service, American Citizens Services, Consular Affairs, Room 4811, US Department of State, Washington, D.C. 20520 (☎ (202) 647-5225; nights, Sundays, and holidays 647-4000; http://travel.state.gov).

TIPPING AND BARGAINING

It's the age old question: to tip or not to tip? In Mexico, it can be hard to know what to do. Over eager tipping can be offensive (never, for example, throw a couple of pesos at someone you just asked for directions), but many people make their livings assisting tourists in exchange for tips. In general, anyone who offers a service and then awkwardly waits around afterwards is expecting a tip. In a restaurant, waiters are tipped based on the quality of service; good service deserves at least 15%. Cab drivers are generally not tipped since they do not run on meters. Regardless of the quality of service, never leave without saying *gracias*.

In Mexico, skillful bargaining separates the savvy budget traveler from the timid tourist. If you're unsure whether bargaining is appropriate, observe the locals and follow their lead. A working knowledge of Spanish will help convince the seller that you are a serious bargainer, and you will be rewarded with a better deal. When hailing a cab, settle the price of the ride beforehand, lest you get pegged as a tourist and get charged exorbitantly.

 KNOW WHEN TO WALK AWAY, KNOW WHEN TO RUN. Buying quality crafts sometimes requires special knowledge. When buying **turqoise,** ask the vendor to put the rocks to the "lighter test." Plastic or synthetic material will quickly melt under the flame. When buying **silver,** examine the pieces closely and look for a stamp with the number **.925** on the underside. This stamp indicates that the silver is sterling (i.e., it has at least 925 parts in a 1000). If there's no number, the piece might be inferior silver—silver-plated or silver *alpaca* (nickel silver). If sterling's what you're looking for, walk away.

ESSENTIALS

 TRAVEL ADVISORIES. The following government offices provide travel information and advisories by telephone, by fax, or via the web.

Australian Department of Foreign Affairs and Trade: ☎(2) 6261 1111; www.dfat.gov.au.

Canadian Department of Foreign Affairs and International Trade (DFAIT): In Canada call (800) 267-6788, elsewhere +1 (613) 944-6788; www.dfait-maeci.gc.ca. Call for their free booklet, *Bon Voyage...But.*

New Zealand Ministry of Foreign Affairs: ☎(04) 494 8500; fax 494 8511; www.mft.govt.nz/trav.html.

United Kingdom Foreign and Commonwealth Office: ☎(020) 7238 4503; fax 7238 4545; www.fco.gov.uk.

US Department of State: ☎(202) 647-5225, auto faxback (202) 647-3000; http://travel.state.gov. For a copy of *A Safe Trip Abroad,* call (202) 512-1800. US citizens can also refer to the State Department's pamphlet *Tips for Travelers to Mexico,* which is available by mail from the Superintendent of Documents, US Government Printing Office, Washington, D.C. 20402, www.access.gpo.gov/su_docs, or via the Bureau of Consular Affairs home page at http://travel.state.gov.

SAFETY AND SECURITY

Mexico is relatively safe, although, like many other countries undergoing economic recessions, dire circumstances have led to increased crime, particularly against tourists. While most is of the petty and annoying variety—pick pocketings, purse-snatchings, etc.—violent and brutal attacks on tourists are reportedly on the rise. Exercise caution; common sense precautions and heightened alertness can help you avoid dangerous situations.

GENERAL SAFETY

VALUABLES. To prevent easy theft, don't keep all your valuables (money, important documents) in one place. **Photocopies** of important documents allow you to recover them in case they are lost or pilfered. Carry one copy separate from the documents and leave another at home. Carry as little money as possible, keep some aside to use in an emergency, and never count your money in public. **Don't put a wallet with money in your back pocket.** If you carry a purse, buy a sturdy one with a secure clasp, and carry it crosswise on the side, away from the street with the clasp against you. Secure packs with small combination **padlocks** which slip through the two zippers. A **money belt**, a nylon, zippered pouch with a belt that sits inside the waist of your pants or skirt, combines convenience and security; you can buy one at most camping supply stores. A **neck pouch** is equally safe, though far less accessible. Refrain from pulling out your neck pouch in public. Avoid keeping anything precious in a fanny-pack (even if it's worn on your stomach); your valuables will be highly visible and easy to steal.

ALCOHOL. Mexicans are fed up with foreigners who cross the border for nights of debauchery, so avoid public drunkenness—it is against the law and could land you in jail. Drinking is unsafe for other reasons. The US State Department warns of tourists—almost always traveling alone—at nightclubs or bars who have been drugged or intoxicated and then robbed and abducted.

DRUGS. Contrary to international opinion, Mexico rigorously prosecutes drug cases. A minimum jail sentence awaits anyone found guilty of possessing any drug, and Mexican law does not distinguish between marijuana and other narcotics. Even if you aren't convicted, getting arrested and tried will be long and incredibly unpleasant. The Mexican judicial process assumes you are guilty until proven innocent, and it is not uncommon to be detained for a year before a verdict is reached. Foreigners and suspected drug traffickers are never released on bail. Ignorance of Mexican law is no excuse, and a flimsy "Man, I didn't know it was illegal" won't get you out of jail. If you are arrested, there is little your embassy can do other than inform your relatives and bring care packages to you in jail. (For information on how to address those packages, see **Post and Communications,** p. 25.)

SAFETY WHILE GETTING AROUND

BY BUS. While bus travel is one of the safest ways to get around in Mexico, travelers should still exercise caution. Mexican highways have a reputation for being unsafe, and hijackings of buses, while fairly uncommon, do occur. **To minimize risk, take first-class buses rather than second-class buses.** First-class buses are more likely to take toll *(cuota)* roads instead of free *(libre)* highways, which have more reports of hijacking and incidences of crime. It is also a good idea to arrange your travel schedule so that any lengthy intercity bus travel is done **during daylight hours** when there is a lower chance of crime. Once on a bus—be it a local or intercity bus—keep your wits about you; stories abound about determined thieves who wait for travelers to fall asleep. Carry your backpack in front of you where you can see it or store it in the underside of the bus. In certain areas of the country, buses may be pulled over and boarded by humorless armed federal officials *(federales)* looking for drugs or illegal aliens. In such a situation, be quiet and cooperative.

BY CAR. Because the number of hijackings and robberies of non-Mexican drivers has increased, those who choose to drive on Mexican highways should be extremely careful. **Whenever possible, drive during daylight hours and with others.** Keep valuables out of eyesight, in your trunk if you can, and park your vehicle in a garage or well-traveled area. **Sleeping in your car** is not only often illegal, it is also extremely dangerous. If you absolutely must sleep in your car, do so as close to a police station or a 24-hour service station as possible.

Driving is unsafe for other reasons. Road conditions in Mexico are highly variable. The expensive *cuota* roads are not only the safest, but they provide the smoothest ride and the best road conditions. Free *(libre)* highways and local roads might have poor (or nonexistent) shoulders, few gas stations, and roaming animals. If you plan on spending a lot of time on the road, you may want to bring spare parts. Finally, it's always a good idea to use a little common sense and take extra preparation time. Learn local driving signals and customs, but keep in mind that they are frequently ignored by local drivers. Bring plenty of maps and have a good idea of the route you plan to take before you hit the road.

BY FOOT. To avoid unwanted attention, try to blend in as much as possible. Respecting local customs—in many cases, dressing more conservatively and avoiding obvious tourist paraphernalia—may divert attention. It also helps to familiarize yourself with your surroundings. When walking at night, stick to busy, well-lit streets and avoid dark alleyways and other large, deserted areas. Look for children playing, women walking in the open, and other signs of an active community. If you feel uncomfortable, leave as quickly and directly as you can. You may want to carry a **whistle** or another noise-making device to scare off attackers and attract attention. Memorize the emergency number of the city or area. If you are traveling alone, be sure that someone at home knows your itinerary and **never admit that you're traveling alone.** Whenever possible, *Let's Go* lists unsafe areas; it still helps to ask about safety at tourist offices or at hotel reception desks. For more information on safety for **Women Travelers,** see p. 33.

HIGHWAY TO THE DANGER ZONE. According to the US State Department, the following highways are particularly unsafe, and those traveling on them should exercise caution: **Highway 19** (Tuxtla to Tapachula), **Highway 19** (Tuxtla to Villahermosa), **Highway 186** (Chetumal to Villahermosa), **Highway 15** (Sinaloa), **Express Highway 1** (Sinaloa), the **Toluca Highway** (outside of Mexico City), and the highway connecting **Altamirano to Ixtapa/Zihuatanejo.**

OTHER AREAS OF CONCERN

Mexico is a fairly safe country, provided that you pay attention to your surroundings and take all common sense precautions. However, there are certain areas of the country where special care is advised.

MEXICO CITY. Mexico City, like most bloated metropolitan areas, has more than its share of crime; in fact it has the highest crime rate in the country. But before you cancel your visit to *el D.F.*, keep in mind that most crimes against tourists fall under the category of **petty street crime**—muggings, pick pocketings, and purse-snatchings. Although the government has prided itself on reducing crime in the city, visitors to the capital should still exercise extreme caution, particularly with transportation. For more information on safety in Mexico City, see p. 92.

CIUDAD JUÁREZ. Because of its position along the US border, the narcotic trade has flourished in Ciudad Juárez. Many foreigners involved in the trade have been kidnapped and/or murdered. The US State Department urges special caution for those visiting the entertainment district west of Av. Juárez.

CANCÚN. Cancún, an international tourist mecca, has drawn pickpockets and petty thieves from all over the country. Muggings, purse-snatchings, and hotel room thefts are on the rise. Use common sense and protect your valuables. A relatively new phenomenon are the sexual assaults and rapes that occur in the early morning hours in the Zona Hotelera. Intoxicated clubbers are separated from friends and then attacked. Such assaults, while few and far between, are on the rise. There have also been reports of increased police harassment and abuse.

CHIAPAS. Recent Zapatista activity has meant that tourists need to be especially careful when traveling in Chiapas. While the Mexican government has brought much of the area under control, armed rebels are occasionally active in the highlands north of San Cristóbal de las Casas, Ocosingo, and in the jungles east of Comitán. These rebels have in the past been openly hostile toward foreigners.

GUERRERO AND OAXACA. Because of political unrest in the rural parts of these states, visitors might encounter roadblocks and increased military presence. If your bus or car is pulled over, be prepared to show some sort of ID. There is no evidence, however, that the insurgent groups, the Popular Revolutionary Army and the Insurgent People's Revolutionary Army, have targeted tourists or will begin to do so.

BEACHES. Sadly, crime has infested even the most beautiful and pristine parts of the country, and tourists have not escaped attack. As tempting as it sounds, stay away from hidden or secluded beaches, unless they are known to be especially safe. If going to the beach, it's a good idea to go during the afternoon or during weekends, when families and visitors tend to be more numerous and beaches aren't so empty. Several US citizens have been killed while frolicking alone on beaches; some of these attacks happened during the morning hours. Exercise caution.

HEALTH

Before you can say "pass the jalapeños," a long-anticipated vacation can turn into an unpleasant study of the wonders of the Mexican health care system. While you can't foresee everything, some careful preparation can minimize trips to the clinic.

BEFORE YOU GO

In your **passport,** write the names of any people you wish to have contacted in case of a medical emergency and list any allergies or medical conditions of which you would want doctors to be aware. Carry up-to-date, legible prescriptions or a statement from your doctor stating the medication's trade name, manufacturer, chemical name, and dosage. While traveling, be sure to keep all medication with you in your carry-on luggage.

ESSENTIALS

INOCULATION REQUIREMENTS. Mexico does not require visitors to carry vaccination certificates nor does it require specific vaccinations for entry. It is advisable, however, to consult your doctor 4-6 weeks before departure. In addition to **booster shots for measles and tetanus,** consider the following vaccines and prescriptions:

Malaria Tablets: Chroloquinine is recommended for those traveling in rural and coastal areas in the southern half of the country.
Hepatitis A: Vaccine or immune globulin (IG)
Hepatitis B: Recommended for those planning long stays, those who might be exposed to blood, or those who plan on being sexually active.
Rabies: Recommended for those who might have contact with animals.
Typhoid Fever: Recommended for those traveling to rural areas only.

IMMUNIZATIONS AND PRECAUTIONS

Visitors to Mexico do not need to carry vaccination certificates, though anyone entering Mexico from South America or Africa may be asked to show proof of vaccination for yellow fever. Despite Mexico's lax attitude toward inoculation, all travelers over two years of age should have their standard vaccines up to date and should consult a doctor for any additional recommended inoculations.

USEFUL ORGANIZATIONS AND PUBLICATIONS

The US **Centers for Disease Control and Prevention (CDC;** ☎ (877) FYI-TRIP; www.cdc.gov/travel), an excellent source of information for travelers, maintains an international fax information service. The CDC's comprehensive booklet *Health Information for International Travelers*, an annual rundown of disease, immunization, and general health advice, is free on the website or US$22 via the Government Printing Office (☎ (202) 512-1800). The **US State Department** (http://travel.state.gov) compiles Consular Information Sheets on health, entry requirements, and other issues for various countries. For quick information on health and other travel warnings, call the **Overseas Citizens' Services** (☎ (202) 647-5225; after-hours 647-4000), contact a US passport agency or a US embassy or consulate abroad, or send a self-addressed, stamped envelope to the Overseas Citizens' Services, Bureau of Consular Affairs, #4811, US Department of State, Washington, D.C. 20520. For information on medical evacuation services and travel insurance firms, see http://travel.state.gov/medical.html. The **British Foreign and Commonwealth Office** also gives health warnings for individual countries (www.fco.gov.uk).

For detailed information on travel health, including a country-by-country overview of diseases, try the **International Travel Health Guide,** Stuart Rose, MD (Travel Medicine, US$20; www.travmed.com).

MEDICAL ASSISTANCE ON THE ROAD

The quality of medical care in Mexico often varies directly with the size of the city or town. The same also applies for the availability of English-speaking medical practitioners. Medical care in Mexico City is first-class, while care in more rural areas can be spotty and limited. Along with the town clinic (IMSS), local pharmacies can be invaluable sources of medical help. Most pharmacists are knowledgeable about mild illnesses—particularly those that typically plague tourists—and can recommend shots or medicines. Wherever possible, *Let's Go* lists pharmacies open for extended hours. If none are listed, ask a policeman or cab driver.

If you are concerned about access medical support while traveling, there are special support services you may employ. The *MedPass* from **Global Emergency Medical Services (GEMS),** 2001 Westside Dr., #120, Alpharetta, GA 30004, USA (☎ (800) 860-1111; fax (770) 475-0058; www.globalems.com), provides 24-hour international medical assistance, support, and medical evacuation resources. The **International Association for Medical Assistance to Travelers (IAMAT;** US ☎ (716) 754-4883, Canada ☎ (416) 652-0137, New Zealand ☎ (03) 352 2053; www.sentex.net/~iamat) has free membership, lists English-speaking doctors worldwide, and offers detailed info on immunization requirements and sanitation. If your regular **insurance** policy does not cover travel abroad, you may wish to purchase additional coverage (see p. 21).

ON THE ROAD

ENVIRONMENTAL HAZARDS

HEAT EXHAUSTION AND DEHYDRATION. Heat exhaustion, characterized by dehydration and salt deficiency, can lead to fatigue, headaches, and wooziness. Avoid it by drinking plenty of fluids, eating salty foods (e.g. crackers), and avoiding dehydrating beverages (e.g. alcohol, coffee, tea, and caffeinated soda). Continuous heat stress can eventually lead to heatstroke, characterized by a rising temperature, severe headache, and cessation of sweating. Victims should be cooled off with wet towels and taken to a doctor. The risk of heat exhaustion is greatest in Baja California and northern Mexico, where the combination of heat and dryness can result in rapid water loss.

SUNBURN. If you're prone to sunburn, bring sunscreen with you and apply it liberally and often to avoid burns and risk of skin cancer. Nowhere in Mexico are you safe from sunburn, though the risk increases as you travel toward the equator and as you go up in altitude. If you get sunburned, drink more fluids than usual and apply Calamine or an aloe-based lotion.

AIR POLLUTION. Mexico City has recently earned the distinction of having the worst air in the world for children. It's none too great for adults, either. Fortunately, many of the possible effects—wheezing, tightness in the chest, bronchitis-—tend to reverse themselves once exposure stops. Unfortunately, long-term exposure can result in serious problems such as lung cancer and heart disease. To protect yourself, heed daily pollution warnings. Pollution is usually worst during the winter and in the early morning hours.

ALTITUDE SICKNESS. Many places in mountainous Mexico, including Mexico City, are high enough for altitude sickness to be a concern. Symptoms may include headaches, dizziness, and sleep disruption. To minimize possible effects, avoid rapid increases in elevation, and allow your body a couple of days to adjust to a new elevation before exerting yourself. Note that alcohol is more potent and UV rays stronger at high elevations.

INSECT-BORNE DISEASES

Many diseases are transmitted by insects—primarily mosquitoes, fleas, ticks, and lice. Be aware of insects in wet or forested areas, while hiking, camping, or climbing around ruins. **Mosquitoes** are most active from dusk to dawn and are rampant along coastal areas. Use insect repellents which have a 30-35% concentration of DEET (5-10% is recommended for children). Wear long pants and long sleeves (fabric need not be thick or warm; tropic-weight cottons can keep you comfortable in the heat) and consider buying a **mosquito net** for travel in rural (especially coastal and humid) regions. Natural repellents can be useful supplements: taking vitamin B-12 pills regularly can eventually make you smelly to insects, as can garlic pills. Calamine lotion or topical cortisones (like Cortaid) may stop insect bites from itching, as can a bath with a half-cup of baking soda or oatmeal.

MALARIA. Transmitted by *Anopheles* mosquitoes that bite at night. The incubation period varies from 6-8 days to as long as months. Early symptoms include fever, chills, aches, and fatigue, followed by high fever and sweating, sometimes with vomiting and diarrhea. See a doctor for any flu-like sickness that occurs after travel in a risk area. Left untreated, malaria can cause anemia, kidney failure, coma, and death. If you are visiting coastal or rural areas of Campeche, Chiapas, Guerrero, Michoacan, Nayarit, Oaxaca, Quintana Roo, Sinaloa, Tabasco, and Yucatan, consider getting a prescription for **Chloroquine**. Chloroquine might have some side effects such as nausea, headaches, and vomiting; consult your doctor. Antimalarial drugs are not recommended for travelers to the major resort areas on the Pacific and Gulf coasts or travelers to the northern parts of the country.

OTHER INSECT-BORNE DISEASES. Filariasis is a roundworm infestation transmitted by mosquitoes. Infection causes enlargement of extremities and has no vaccine. **Leishmaniasis** is a parasite transmitted by sand flies. Common symptoms are fever, weakness, and swelling of the spleen. There is a treatment, but no vaccine. **CHAGAS disease (American trypanomiasis)** is another relatively common parasite transmitted by the cone nose and kissing bug, which infest mud, adobe, and thatch. Its symptoms are fever, heart disease, and later on an enlarged intestine. There is no vaccine and limited treatment. All three diseases are rare and limited in range to the tropical areas of Chiapas and the Yucatán.

FOOD- AND WATER-BORNE DISEASES

The biggest health threats in Mexico are food and water. ◪**Traveler's diarrhea,** known in Mexico as *turista*, often lasts two or three days. Symptoms include cramps, nausea, vomiting, chills, and fever. Scientifically speaking, *turista* is a temporary reaction to bacteria in new food ingredients. In plain speak, *turista* will blow your bowels inside out. **Watch what you drink and eat.**

Dirty water is enemy number one. Never drink water straight from the tap or from dubious sources, such as water fountains. Don't brush your teeth with tap water, don't rise your toothbrush under the faucet, and don't keep your mouth open in the shower. Be suspicious of the most clever disguise of impure water— the treacherous ice cube. **Drink only purified, bottled water (agua embotellada).** If you must purify your own water, bring it to a rolling boil (simmering isn't enough) and let it boil for about 30 minutes, or treat it with **iodine drops or tablets.**

If impure water is enemy number one, food is enemy number two. Stay away from those tasty-looking salads; eating uncooked vegetables (including lettuce and coleslaw) is a quick way to get *turista*. Other culprits include raw shellfish, unpasteurized milk and dairy products, and sauces containing raw eggs. Peel fruits and vegetables before eating them. Beware of food from markets or street vendors that may have been "washed" in dirty water or fried in rancid oil. Juices, peeled fruits, and exposed coconut slices are all risky. Also beware of frozen treats; they may have been made with bad water.

If you have the misfortune of developing *tourista*, try quick-energy, non-sugary foods with protein and carbohydrates to keep your strength up. Good things to eat are tortillas and salted crackers. Perhaps the most dangerous side effect of *turista* is dehydration and loss of electrolytes; drink lots of (pure) water with ½ tsp. of sugar or honey and a pinch of salt, uncaffeinated soft drinks, and bottled juices. If you develop a high fever or your symptoms don't go away after 4-5 days, consult a doctor; it might be more than just *turista*. More serious diseases with *turista*-like symptoms (diarrhea, nausea, and cramps) include:

CHOLERA. An intestinal disease caused by a bacteria found in contaminated food and water. Though most cholera outbreaks occur in developing countries in Asia and Africa, several outbreaks have been reported in Latin America. The early symptom of the disease is mild diarrhea; symptoms of more advanced stages include profuse diarrhea, dehydration, vomiting, and muscle cramps. See a doctor immediately; if left untreated, cholera may be deadly. Antibiotics are available, but the most important treatment is rehydration. The best way to avoid cholera is to be careful with water and food. A cholera vaccine (with 50% immunity) is available, but not recommended; see your doctor for more information.

THE GOLDEN RULE IN MEXICO. Beware of food and water. Drink only bottled water *(agua embotellada)* or purified water *(agua purificada)*. Eat food that has been boiled, peeled, or cooked. Otherwise, forget it. Remember: a careful tourist is a diarrhea-free tourist.

HEPATITIS A. A viral infection of the liver acquired primarily through contaminated water. Symptoms include fatigue, fever, loss of appetite, nausea, dark urine, jaundice, vomiting, aches and pains, and light stools. The risk is highest in rural areas and the countryside, but it is also present in urban areas. Ask your doctor about the vaccine (Havrix or Vaqta) or an injection of immune globulin (IG; formerly called gamma globulin).

TYPHOID FEVER. Caused by the salmonella bacteria; most common in villages and rural areas in Mexico. While primarily transmitted through contaminated food and water, it may also be acquired by direct contact with an infected person. Early symptoms include fever, headaches, fatigue, loss of appetite, constipation, and sometimes a rash on the abdomen or chest. Antibiotics are available, but a vaccination (70-90% effective) is recommended.

OTHER INFECTIOUS DISEASES

RABIES. Transmitted through the saliva of infected animals; fatal if untreated. By the time symptoms appear (thirst and muscle spasms), the disease is in its terminal stage. If you are bitten, wash the wound thoroughly, seek immediate medical care, and try to have the animal located. A rabies vaccine, which consists of 3 shots given over a 21-day period, is available but only semi-effective.

HEPATITIS B. A viral infection of the liver transmitted via bodily fluids or needle-sharing. Symptoms may not surface until years after infection. Vaccinations are recommended for health-care workers, sexually-active travelers, and anyone planning to seek medical treatment abroad. The 3-shot vaccination series must begin 6 mo. before traveling.

HEPATITIS C. Like Hepatitis B, but the mode of transmission differs. IV drug users, those with occupational exposure to blood, hemodialysis patients, and recipients of blood transfusions are at the highest risk, but the disease can also be spread through sexual contact

WOMEN'S HEALTH

Vaginal yeast infections can flare up in hot and humid climates. Wearing loosely fitting trousers or a skirt and cotton underwear will help, as will removing and thoroughly drying wet bathing suits after swimming. Over the counter remedies such as Monostat or Gynelotrimin are available in some parts of Mexico, but bring supplies from home if you are prone to infection or if you are traveling in more rural parts of the country. In a pinch, some travelers use a natural alternative such as a plain yogurt and lemon juice douche. While **maxi pads** are plentiful in Mexican pharmacies and supermarkets, **tampons** are harder to come by and, if available at all, come only in regular sizes. It might be wise to bring a supply along, especially if you are traveling to smaller cities. Contraceptive devices are also hard to find, with the exception of condoms, which are found in most large pharmacies.

Abortion remains illegal in Mexico. Women considering an abortion should contact the **International Planned Parenthood Federation (IPPF),** Regent's College, Inner Circle, Regent's Park, London NW1 4NS (☎ (020) 7487 7900; fax 7487 7950; www.ippf.org), for more information.

INSURANCE

Travel insurance generally covers four basic areas: medical/health problems, property loss, trip cancellation/interruption, and emergency evacuation. Although your regular insurance policies may well extend to travel-related accidents, you may consider purchasing travel insurance if the cost of potential trip cancellation/ interruption or emergency medical evacuation is greater than you can absorb. Prices for travel insurance purchased separately generally run about US$50 per week for full coverage, while trip cancellation/interruption may be purchased separately at a rate of about US$5.50 per US$100 of coverage.

Medical insurance (especially university policies) often covers costs incurred abroad; check with your provider. **US Medicare** covers travel to Mexico. **Canadians** are protected by their home province's health insurance plan for up to 90 days after leaving the country; check with the provincial Ministry of Health or Health Plan Headquarters for details. **Homeowners' insurance** (or your family's coverage) often covers theft during travel and loss of travel documents (passport, plane ticket, railpass, etc.) up to US$500.

ISIC (see p. 9) and its cousin, the International Teachers Identification Card, **ITIC**, provide basic insurance benefits, including US$100 per day of in-hospital sickness for up to 60 days, US$3000 of accident-related medical reimbursement, and US$25,000 for emergency medical transport. Cardholders have access to a toll-free 24-hour helpline for medical, legal, and financial emergencies overseas (US and Canada ☎ (877) 370-4742, elsewhere call US collect +1 (713) 342-4104). **American Express** (US ☎ (800) 528-4800) grants most cardholders automatic car rental insurance (collision and theft, but not liability) and ground travel accident coverage of US$100,000 on flight purchases made with the card.

INSURANCE PROVIDERS. Council and **STA** (see p. 29) offer a range of plans that can supplement your basic coverage. Other private insurance providers in the **US and Canada** include: **Access America** (☎ (800) 284-8300); **Berkely Group/Carefree Travel Insurance** (☎ (800)323-3149; www.berkely.com); **Globalcare Travel Insurance** (☎ (800)821-2488; www.globalcare-cocco.com); and **Travel Assistance International** (☎ (800)821-2828; www.worldwide-assistance.com). Providers in the **UK** include **Campus Travel** (☎ (01865) 258 000) and **Columbus Travel Insurance** (☎ (020) 7375 0011). In **Australia,** try **CIC Insurance** (☎ 9202 8000).

ACCOMMODATIONS

HOSTELS

The few hostels that exist in Mexico are youth-oriented, dorm-style accommodations, often having large single-sex rooms with bunk beds. Many have kitchens, laundry facilities, and storage areas, though may inconvenience their patrons with curfews and daytime "lock-out" hours. Perhaps most importantly, Mexican hostels tend to be run-down and far from town. Although a bit cheaper than hotels—around US$5-6 per person—the money you save usually doesn't make up for the inconvenience. For more information about Mexican hostels, contact the **Red Mexicana de Alojamiento para Jóvenes** (www.remaj.com or www.hostellingmexico.com; email hostellingmexico@remaj.com), a hostelling organization affiliated with Hostelling International.

HOTELS

Bargain-seekers will not be disappointed with Mexico's selection of hotels. Although some (particularly in resort towns) are among the world's most overpriced, the majority of Mexican accommodations are affordable and convenient. Usually located within a block or two of a city's *zócalo*, the cheapest hotels (about US$7-10 per night) rarely provide amenities such as air conditioning, though they usually have hot water and private bathrooms. Higher priced hotels (about US$20 per night) are often located in the same district but are much better equipped, with telephones and the occasional television. Before accepting a room, ask to see it, and always find out before paying whether the price includes any complimentary meals and if there are any extra surcharges.

All hotels, ranging from luxury resorts in Cancún to rent-by-the-hour joints in Tijuana, are controlled by the government's **Secretaria de Turismo (SECTUR).** This ensures that hotels of similar quality charge similar prices; you should always ask to see an up-to-date **official tariff sheet** if you doubt the quoted price. Many hotels post their official tariffs somewhere near the reception area. Although hotel prices are regulated, proprietors are not prohibited from charging *less* than the official rate. A little bargaining can work wonders, especially if you stay a number of days.

ESSENTIALS

YOU CAN CHECK OUT ANYTIME YOU'D LIKE. Reservations are almost always necessary during Christmas, *Semana Santa* (the week before Easter), and local festivals. At most other times, even during the summer season, you need not worry much about having to reserve rooms in budget hotels.

CAMPING

Travelers accustomed to clean and well-maintained campgrounds may be in for a few surprises. By and large, Mexican national parks exist only in theory. The "protected lands" are often indistinguishable from the surrounding countryside or city and may be dirty, unappealing, and overrun with amorous teenagers. Privately owned **trailer parks** are relatively common on major routes—look for signs with a picture of a trailer, or the words *parque de trailer, campamento,* or *remolques.* These places often allow campers to pitch tents or sling up a hammock.

For those budget-minded individuals traveling along the coast, the hammock is the way to go. Most beach towns in Mexico are dotted with **palapas** (palm-tree huts). For a small fee, open-air restaurants double as places to hang your hat and hammock when the sun sets. At beaches and some inland towns frequented by backpackers, **cabañas** (cabins, usually simple thatch-roof huts) are common. For the truly hard-core, camping on the beach can sometimes be an option. Lax permit laws and beach accessibility (every meter of beach in Mexico is public property) offer campers oodles of options.

BEYOND THE SEA. When camping on the beach, make sure safety is your number one priority. While all beaches in Mexico are public, not all of them are safe for camping. Hotel security in glitzy resort areas have a reputation for being unkind to beach campers. There have also been more serious reports of beach-side robberies, rapes, and assaults. It's a good idea to check in with the local tourist office or police department to see whether camping is safe or permitted. Use common sense: don't camp on very secluded beaches or beaches near unsafe urban areas.

USEFUL PUBLICATIONS AND WEB RESOURCES

BOOKS

Backpacking in Mexico, Tim Burford. Bradt Publishing, 1997 (US$17).

Baja Camping, Fred and Gloria Jones. Foghorn Outdoors, 1998 (US$15).

Mexico: A Hiker's Guide to Mexico's Natural History, Jim Conrad. Mountaineers Books, 1995 (US$17).

Mexico's Copper Canyon Country, John Fayhee. Johnson Books, 1994 (US$17).

Traveler's Guide to Mexican Camping, Mike Church. Rolling Home Press, 1997 (US$20).

For topographical maps of Mexico, write or visit the **Instituto Nacional de Estadísticas, Geografiá e Informática (INEGI),** Calle Patriotismo 711, Torre A, Del. Benito Juárez, Col. San Juan Mixcoac, Mexico, DF, (5) 598-8935. They are also available online at **Global Perspectives** (www.global-perspectives.com) and **Omnimap** (www.omnimap.com).

KEEPING IN TOUCH

MAIL

SENDING MAIL TO MEXICO

Mark envelopes "air mail" or "por avion" to avoid having letters sent by sea or by land.

Australia: Allow 3-4 weeks for regular airmail to Mexico. Postcards and letters up to 20g cost AUS$1; packages up to 0.5kg AUS$12, up to 2kg AUS$45.

Canada: Allow 2-3 weeks for regular airmail to Mexico. Postcards and letters up to 20g cost CDN$0.95; packages up to 0.5kg CDN$8.50, up to 2kg CDN$28.30.

UK: Allow 3-4 weeks for airmail to Mexico. Letters up to 20g cost UK£0.3; packages up to 0.5kg UK£2.22, up to 2kg UK£8.22. UK Swiftair is a day faster for UK£2.85 more.

US: Allow 2 weeks for regular airmail to Mexico. Postcards/aerogrammes cost US$0.55/0.60; letters under 1oz. US$1. Packages under 1lb. cost US$7.20; larger packages cost a variable amount (around US$15). **US Express Mail** takes 2-3 days and costs US$19/23 (0.5/1lb.).

Additionally, **Federal Express** (US and Canada ☎ (800) 247-4747; Australia ☎ 13 26 10; New Zealand ☎ (0800) 73 33 39; UK ☎ (0800) 12 38 00) handles express mail services from most of the above countries to Mexico. Note that Federal Express will not deliver to post offices in Mexico, only to businesses and residences.

RECEIVING MAIL IN MEXICO

There are several ways to arrange pick-up of letters sent to you by friends and relatives while you are abroad.

General Delivery: Mail can be sent to Mexico through **Poste Restante** (the international phrase for General Delivery; **Lista de Correos** in Spanish) to almost any city or town with a post office. Mail sent via *poste restante* will go to a special desk in the central post office, unless you specify a post office by street address or postal code. Letters should be marked *Favor de retener hasta la llegada* (Please hold until arrival); they will be held up to 15 days. It's probably not a good idea to send valuable items to a city's *Lista de Correos*.

 WITH LOVE, FROM ME TO YOU. Address *Poste Restante* letters to:
Vicente FOX (name)
Lista de Correos
Morelos 235 (street address for post office, or leave it blank)
San Luis Potosí (city), Morelos (state), 62001 (postal code)
MEXICO

ESSENTIALS

ESSENTIALS

American Express: AmEx's travel offices throughout the world offer a free **Client Letter Service** (mail held up to 30 days and forwarding upon request) for cardholders who contact them in advance. Address the letter in the same way shown above. Some offices will offer these services to non-cardholders (especially AmEx Travelers Cheque holders), but call ahead to make sure. *Let's Go* lists AmEx office locations for most large cities in **Practical Information** sections; for a complete list, call (800) 528-4800.

Packages sent via Express Mail International, FedEx, UPS, or other express services might be retained at a different office (often the MexPost office, see below). It's a good idea to not send anything particularly valuable via any sort of mail to Mexico.

SENDING MAIL HOME FROM MEXICO

Mexican mail service is painfully slow. **Airmail** from major cities in Mexico to the US and Canada takes anywhere from two weeks to one month; to Australia or New Zealand, one month; to the UK or Ireland, three weeks to one month; to South Africa, one to two months. Add another one or two weeks for mail sent from more rural areas. Mexican mailboxes are notorious for being infrequently picked up, but the bright plastic orange boxes labeled *Express* that have popped up around Mexico City and other large cities are quite reliable and are picked up every morning. Anything important, however, should be sent *registrado* (registered mail) or taken directly to the post office at the very least. To speed service, it's a good idea to write Spanish abbreviations or names for countries (i.e., EE.UU. for the US). Also write *Por Avión* on all postcards and letters, lest they sit on a boat in the Atlantic for two or three months.

Packages cannot weigh more than 25kg. Keep in mind that all packages are reopened and inspected by customs at border crossings; closing any boxes with string, not tape, is recommended. You may also have to provide several pieces of information: your tourist card data, contents, value and nature of the package ("Gift" works best), and your address and return address.

For the speediest service possible, **MexPost** works in collaboration with Express Mail International in the US and similar express mail services in other countries to deliver mail quickly and reliably. Three days is the official MexPost delivery time to the US, but allow up to a week. MexPost offices are usually found next to regular post offices, but if not, the post office staff can usually give you directions to the nearest MexPost office.

TELEPHONES

CALLING MEXICO FROM ABROAD

To call Mexico direct from home, dial:

1. The international access code of your home country. **International access codes** include: Australia 0011; Ireland 00; New Zealand 00; South Africa 09; UK 00; US 011. Country codes and city codes are sometimes listed with a zero in front (e.g., 033), but after dialing the international access code, drop successive zeros (with an access code of 011, e.g., 011 33).

2. 052 (Mexico's country code).

3. The city code (across from the city or town name) and local number.

CALLING ABROAD FROM MEXICO

The **LADATEL phones** that have popped up all over the country have revolutionized the way Mexico calls. To operate any LADATEL, you'll need a colorful pre-paid **phone card,** available at most *papelerías* (stationery stores) or *tiendas de abarrotes* (general stores)—look for the "De venta aquí LADATEL" signs posted in store windows. Cards come in 30, 50, and 100 peso increments. Once armed with your precious LADATEL phone card, calling using various methods can be a snap.

INTERNATIONAL CALLS WITH A CALLING CARD. A **calling card** is probably the cheapest way to make international calls from Mexico. To make a call with a calling card from Mexico, contact the operator for your service provider by dialing the appropriate toll-free Mexico access number. If your provider does not have a Mexico-specific access code, you should inquire beforehand as to the correct dialing procedures.

AT&T: ☎ 01 800 288 2872 (using LADATEL phones) or 001 800 462 4240.

Sprint: ☎ 001 800 877 8000.

MCI WorldPhone Direct: ☎ 001 800 674 7000 or ☎ 01 800 021 8000 (using Avantel phones).

DIRECT INTERNATIONAL CALLS. To call directly, insert your LADATEL card, dial 00 (to get an international line), the country code of the place you are calling, the area code, and phone number. You can then chat quickly (and nervously) while the seconds tick away. It is extremely expensive to make direct international calls. On average, 10-minute phone call to the US will exhaust a 100 peso phone card.

CALLING COLLECT. If you speak Spanish fluently and can't reach the international operator, dial 07 for the national operator, who will connect you (sometimes even a local operator can help). The term for a collect call is a *llamada por cobrar* or *llamada con cobro revertido*. Calling from hotels is usually faster but beware of exorbitant surcharges. Remember, however, that there can be a fee of 1-5 pesos for collect calls that are not accepted.

 CALLS MADE WITHIN MEXICO. The entire Mexican telephone system has been revamped and reorganized in the last two years. Before, numbers were listed as five or six digits accompanied by a two- or three-digit city code. Now, all local numbers are **seven digits** (with the exception of those in Mexico City, which are eight), and all city codes are one digit. *Let's Go* uses the new system, but, if you should encounter a five- or six-digit number written using the old system, add digits from the end of the old area code until you have seven digits. For example, if you see a number listed as ☎ 6 98 36, and you know the area code was 314, then the correct seven-digit number would be ☎ 146 98 36, which you should use to call locally. Add the city code and you've got ☎ (3) 146 98 36, the long-distance number, which you must dial in addition to an 01 prefix.

EMAIL AND INTERNET

With many Mexican businesses, language schools, and individuals now online, the Internet and the electronic communication it offers provide a cheap and accessible alternative to pricey phone calls and slow postal service. Cybercafes, included in the **Orientation and Practical Information** of most town listings, are perhaps the most prominent form of Internet access in Mexico. These cafes can be found in even some of the smaller Mexican towns; expect to compete for computers with gawky Mexican teenage boys and to pay US$2-10 per hour for access. For lists of additional cybercafes in Mexico, check out www.netcafeguide.com/mexico.htm or www.netcafes.com.

Some, but not all, Internet providers offer telnet, Internet Relay Chat (IRC, pronounced "eerk" in Spanish), and Instant Messenger (IM) programs such as America Online Instant Messenger or ICQ. All Internet providers maintain some sort of World Wide Web access, be it Netscape or Internet Explorer. Though in some places it is possible to forge a remote link with your home server, it is, in most cases, slower and more expensive than free **web-based email accounts** (such as Hotmail or Yahoo! Mail); it might be a good idea to sign up for one before your trip.

GETTING THERE

BY PLANE

When it comes to airfare, a little effort can save you a bundle. The key is to hunt around, to be flexible, and to ask persistently about discounts. Students, seniors, and those under 26 should never have to pay full price for a ticket.

DETAILS AND TIPS

Timing: The most expensive time to travel is between mid-June and August. Midweek (M-Th morning) round-trip flights run US$40-80 cheaper than weekend flights but are generally more crowded and less likely to permit frequent-flier upgrades. Traveling with an "open return" ticket can be pricier than fixing a return date when buying the ticket.

Route: Round-trip flights are by far the cheapest; "open-jaw" (arriving in and departing from different cities) tickets tend to be pricier. Patching one-way flights together is the most expensive way to travel.

Round-the-World (RTW): If Mexico is only one stop on a more extensive globe-hop, consider a RTW ticket. Tickets usually include at least 5 stops and are valid for about a year; prices range US$1200-5000. Try **Northwest Airlines/KLM** (US ☎(800) 447-4747; www.nwa.com) or **Star Alliance**, a consortium of 13 airlines including United Airlines (US ☎(800) 241-6522; www.star-alliance.com).

Gateway Cities: Flights between capitals and regional or tourist hubs will offer the cheapest fares. The cheapest gateway cities in Mexico are typically Mexico City, Guadalajara, and Cancún.

Fares: The cheapest round-trip fares to Mexico City from New York usually range from US$400-550; from London US$500-750; from Los Angeles US$280-350; from Sydney US$1400-1550; from Cancún US$200-400; from Monterrey US$180-250.

Taxes: Be prepared to add up to US$150 in taxes on a plane ticket to Mexico. Taxes average about US$80.

BUDGET AND STUDENT TRAVEL AGENCIES

While knowledgeable agents specializing in flights to Mexico can make your life easy and help you save, they may not spend the time to find you the lowest possible fare. Students and under-26ers holding **ISIC and IYTC cards** (see p. 9), respectively, qualify for big discounts from student travel agencies.

usit world (www.usitworld.com). Over 50 **usit campus** branches in the UK (www.usitcampus.co.uk), including 52 Grosvenor Gardens, **London** SW1W 0AG (☎(0870) 240 1010); **Manchester** (☎(0161) 273 1721); and **Edinburgh** (☎(0131) 668 3303). Nearly 20 **usit now** offices in Ireland, including 19-21 Aston Quay, O'Connell Bridge, **Dublin** (☎(01) 602 1600; www.usitnow.ie), and **Belfast** (☎(02890) 327 111; www.usitnow.com). Offices also in Athens, Auckland, Brussels, Frankfurt, Johannesburg, Lisbon, Luxembourg, Madrid, Paris, Sofia, and Warsaw.

Council Travel (www.counciltravel.com). US offices include: Emory Village, 1561 N. Decatur Rd., **Atlanta**, GA 30307 (☎(404) 377-9997); 273 Newbury St., **Boston**, MA 02116 (☎(617) 266-1926); 1160 N. State St., **Chicago,** IL 60610 (☎(312) 951-0585); 931 Westwood Blvd., Westwood, **Los Angeles**, CA 90024 (☎(310) 208-3551); 254 Greene St., **New York,** NY 10003 (☎(212) 254-2525); 530 Bush St., **San Francisco**, CA 94108 (☎(415) 566-6222); 424 Broadway Ave E., **Seattle**, WA 98102 (☎(206) 329-4567); 3301 M St. NW, **Washington, D.C.** 20007 (☎(202) 337-6464). **For US cities not listed,** call (800) 2-COUNCIL (226-8624). In the UK, 28A Poland St. (Oxford Circus), **London,** W1V 3DB (☎(020) 7437 7767).

CTS Travel, 44 Goodge St., **London** W1 (☎(020) 7636 0031; fax 7637 5328; email ctsinfo@ctstravel.com.uk).

STA Travel, 6560 Scottsdale Rd. #F100, Scottsdale, AZ 85253 (☎(800) 777-0112; fax (602) 922-0793; www.sta-travel.com). A student and youth travel organization with over 150 offices worldwide. Ticket booking, travel insurance, railpasses, and more. US offices include: 297 Newbury St., **Boston,** MA 02115 (☎(617) 266-6014); 429 S. Dearborn St., **Chicago,** IL 60605 (☎(312) 786-9050); 7202 Melrose Ave., **Los Angeles,** CA 90046 (☎(323) 934-8722); 10 Downing St., **New York,** NY 10014 (☎(212) 627-3111); 4341 University Way NE, **Seattle,** WA 98105 (☎(206) 633-5000); 2401 Pennsylvania Ave., Ste. G, **Washington, D.C.** 20037 (☎(202) 887-0912); 51 Grant Ave., **San Francisco,** CA 94108 (☎(415) 391-8407). In the UK, 11 Goodge St., **London** WIP 1FE (☎(020) 7436 7779 for North American travel). In New Zealand, 10 High St., **Auckland** (☎(09) 309 0458). In Australia, 366 Lygon St., **Melbourne** Vic 3053 (☎(03) 9349 4344).

Travel CUTS (Canadian Universities Travel Services Limited), 187 College St., **Toronto,** ON M5T 1P7 (☎(416) 979-2406; fax 979-8167; www.travelcuts.com). 40 offices across Canada. Also in the UK, 295-A Regent St., **London** W1R 7YA (☎(020) 7255 1944).

COMMERCIAL AIRLINES

Most major international airlines travel in and out of Mexico City. Popular Mexican carriers include **Aeroméxico** (☎(800) 237-6639; www.aeromexico.com), which flies to practically every Mexican city with an airport, and **Mexicana** (☎(800) 531-7921; www.mexicana.com), North America's oldest airline, which flies to most major US and European cities.

Taking **standby flights** requires considerable flexibility in arrival and departure dates and cities. Companies dealing in standby flights sell vouchers rather than tickets, along with the promise to get to your destination (or near your destination) within a certain window of time (typically 1-5 days). One established standby company in the US is **Airhitch,** 2641 Broadway, 3rd fl., New York, NY 10025 (☎(800) 326-2009; fax 864-5489; www.airhitch.org) and Los Angeles, CA (☎(888) 247-4482).

Another cheap option is to buy from **ticket consolidators,** or **"bucket shops,"** companies that buy unsold tickets in bulk from commercial airlines and sell them at discounted rates. The best place to look is in the Sunday travel section of any major newspaper (such as the *New York Times*), where many bucket shops advertise dirt cheap flights to popular Mexican destinations such as Acapulco and Cancún. Not all bucket shops are reliable, so insist on a receipt that gives full details of restrictions, refunds, and tickets, and pay by credit card (in spite of the 2-5% fee) so you can stop payment if you never receive your tickets. For more info, see www.travel-library.com/air-travel/consolidators.html or pick up Kelly Monaghan's *Air Travel's Bargain Basement* (Intrepid Traveler, US$8).

BY BUS OR TRAIN

Greyhound (☎(800) 229-9424 or (402) 330 8552; www.greyhound.com) serves many US-Mexico border towns, including El Paso and Brownsville, Texas. Schedule information is available at any Greyhound terminal, on the web page, or by calling the 800 number. Smaller lines serve other destinations. Buses tend not to cross the border, but at each of these stops you can pick up Mexican bus lines (among them Estrella de Oro, Estrella Blanca, ADO, and Transportes Del Norte) on the other side. Guatemalan bus lines operate at Guatemala-Mexico border towns, including Talismán and La Mesilla. Buses usually stop just short of the border, and you can walk across to Mexico and pick up a local bus to the nearest town. Buses also operate between Chetumal (see p. 642) and the capital of Belize, Belize City.

By train your options are limited to the US-Mexico border. You can take **Amtrak** (☎(800) 872-7245) to El Paso, walk across the border to Ciudad Juárez and use other forms of transportation to travel within Mexico. Amtrak also serves San Diego and San Antonio, where you can catch a bus to the border towns.

GETTING AROUND

BY BUS

Mexico's bus system never ceases to astound, amaze, and mystify. From most large cities, it is possible to get almost anywhere in the Republic, and companies like **Autotransportes del Oriente (ADO), Estrella Blanca,** and **Estrella de Oro** run cheaply and efficiently—as efficiently as is possible in Mexico, that is. Several types of bus services exist. Travel executive service, called **servicio ejecutivo,** and receive the royal treatment: plush reclining seats, sandwiches and soda, sometimes too frigid A/C, and movies galore. Slightly less fancy are **primera clase** (first-class) buses, which usually feature ridiculously bad movies and A/C. Significantly inferior in quality are **segunda clase** (second-class) buses, which are usually converted school buses or some variation thereof and are overcrowded, uncomfortable, and painfully slow. Because of safety concerns and because the slightly lower price seldom compensates for the inconvenience, it's a better idea to take first-class rather than second-class buses unless otherwise noted.

Buses are categorized as either *local* or *de paso*. **Locales** originate at the station from which you leave. **De paso** (in passing) buses originate elsewhere and pass through your station. Because they depend on the seating availability when the bus arrives, tickets cannot be purchased in advance. When *de paso* tickets go on sale, forget civility, chivalry, and anything which might stand between you and a ticket, or plan to spend the greater portion of your vacation in bus stations.

BY CAR

Driving in Mexico can be hazardous to your health. The maximum speed on Mexican routes is 100km per hour (62mph) unless otherwise posted, but, like most other traffic signs and regulations, it is often ignored. Mexicans are a rowdy bunch on the road. It's not unusual to hear drivers exchange such greetings as *"¡Baboso!"* (Drooling fool!), *"¡Eh, estupido!"* (Hey, stupid!), and, of course, the ubiquitous *"¿Donde apprendiste a manajar, menso?"* (Where did you learn how to drive, dumbass?). With enough practice, you'll be able to curse with the best Mexican driver. It's also not unusual for Mexican drivers to overuse their car horns; drive down any busy street, and you'll be serenaded by a harmonious chorus of horns, featuring everything from Beethoven's 9th to the opening refrains of *Dixie*, a la *Dukes of Hazzard*. In such a climate, it's best to drive defensively. If you're adventurous, though, join the fray and throw everything driver's education taught you out the window. Just be careful.

Driving norms aside, it's a good idea to avoid driving during the rainy season (May-Oct.), when road conditions deteriorate. If you are planning on driving extensively between cities, check with local authorities or with your nearest consulate for updates on potential danger. In general, it is a good idea to avoid less secure freeways *(libres)* in favor of toll *(cuota)* roads. Also avoid driving at night, when chances of hijacks and other criminal acts are higher. (For more information see **Traveling by Car,** p. 16.) While on the road, you may be stopped by agents of the Federal Public Ministry and the Federal Judicial Police for a search of your car and its contents. Be as cooperative as possible; they will usually just open your trunk, look around your car, and wave you through. For information about driving a car into Mexico and obtaining a **Vehicle Permit,** see **Entering Mexico By Car,** p. 10.

 FILL 'ER UP. Petroleos Mexicanos, more commonly, **PEMEX,** the national oil company, sells two types of gas: **Magna** (regular) and **Premium** (unleaded). Unleaded gas is now almost universally available in Mexico. Both *Magna* and *Premium* are extremely cheap by all but Saudi Arabian standards. PEMEX accepts cash and checks only.

If you're unlucky enough to break down on a major toll road between 8am and 8pm, pull completely off the road, raise the hood, stay with your car, and wait for the **Angeles Verdes** (Green Angels) to come to the rescue. These green-and-white emergency trucks, dispatched by radio and staffed by almost a thousand mechanics, are equipped for performing common repair jobs, towing, changing tires, and addressing minor medical problems. Your green saviors may take a while to show up, but the service (except for parts, gas, and oil) is free. Tipping is optional but a good idea. These guardian angels will assist you anywhere but in Mexico City, where you can contact the **Asociación Nacional Automovilística (ANA; ☎**5597 42 83).

Some credit cards cover standard **insurance.** If you rent, lease, or borrow a car, you will need a **green card,** or **International Insurance Certificate,** to prove that you have liability insurance. You can obtain it through the car rental agency; most include coverage in their prices. If you lease a car, ask the dealer for a green card. Some travel agents offer the card, and it may also be available at border crossings. Even if your auto insurance applies internationally, you will still need a green card to certify this to foreign officials. If you have a collision abroad, the accident will show up on your domestic records if you report it to your insurance company. Rental agencies may require you to purchase theft insurance in countries that they consider to have a high risk of auto theft. Ask your rental agency about rules applying specifically to Mexico.

BY TRAIN

The Mexican railroads are all owned by the government, with most lines operating under the name of **Ferrocarriles Nacionales de Mexico** (National Railways of Mexico, FFNN). The train system is not as extensive, punctual, cheap, comfortable, or efficient as the bus system and, assuming they are on time, even the "fast" trains can take twice as long as buses to reach their destination. Other than the spectacular ride through the **Copper Canyon** (**Los Mochis-Creel;** see p. 235) you probably won't want to rely on trains unless you really crave a leisurely crawl through the countryside.

BY PLANE

Flying within Mexican borders is a method of transportation usually overlooked by budget travelers. That said, time is money. As a general rule, whenever busing will take you longer than 36 hours, consider flying; chances are it will cost about the same or be only marginally more expensive, but save you many, many hours. If you are considering traveling by plane, visit one of the ubiquitous travel agencies that lurk on main streets; agents will be more than happy to help you find cheap, last minute fares. It's a good idea to mention whether you are a student or a senior citizen and ask about the possibility of stand-by seats. You can also check with Mexican airlines directly (See **Commercial Airlines,** p. 30).

BY THUMB

Mexicans who pick up tourists are often friendly, generous and well-meaning; in fact, people who *don't* pick you up will often give you an apologetic look or a gesture of explanation. However, you should always be careful. Women should never hitchhike, even when traveling in groups. Hitchhikers should size up the driver and find out where the car is going before getting in. Think twice if a driver opens the door quickly and offers to drive anywhere. Some bandit-ridden routes are par-

 COOL KIDS DON'T HITCHHIKE. Let's go strongly urges you to consider the risks before you choose to hitchhike and does not recommend hitchhiking as a safe means of transportation.

ticularly dangerous for hitchhikers (see **Traveling by Car,** p. 16). If you do decide to accept a ride, exercise caution and make sure you will be able to make a quick exit. Do not sit in the middle, for example, and try to keep all of your belongings easily accessible. If you have trouble getting out for any reason, affecting the pose of someone on the verge of vomiting has been known to work.

ADDITIONAL INFORMATION

SPECIFIC CONCERNS

WOMEN TRAVELERS

Mexico is not particularly friendly to women travelers. Mexican women seldom travel without the company of men. To find foreign women doing so, then, is somewhat surprising and draws attention. Moreover, Mexican men are notorious for their exorbitant *machismo,* a brand of Latin American chauvinism. For the woman traveler, this translate into whistles, catcalls, and stares. Persistent men will insist on joining you and "showing you the sights." If you're fair-skinned or have light-colored hair, *"güera, güera"* will follow you everywhere; if not, expect to hear the typical mating call, *"¿Donde vas, mamacita?"* (Where are you going, momma?). The best answer to this unwanted attention is to offer no answer at all. Ignore it and avoid making eye contact. *Machismo* is usually more annoying than dangerous, but in real emergencies yell for help or draw attention to yourself and the situation. It might be a good idea to bring a **whistle** or some sort of noise-making device and attach it to your keychain. Beware, however, that many police officers and uniformed officials are the biggest *machistas* of all; don't consider yourself safe from harassment just because men in uniform are nearby. Good allies are **local elderly women** or **nuns,** who command respect from men of all ages and may be able to help you in time of need.

There are preventative measures you can take to minimize unwanted attention, the first being awareness of Mexican social standards and dress codes. Mexican women seldom wear shorts, short skirts, tank tops, or halter tops. To do so—and to wear any sort of clothing without a supportive bra—is to ask for additional harassment and stares. The only times shorts and tank tops are condoned are in beach or resort areas or in towns with a high number of foreign students and tourists. More conservative areas of the country require even more conservative wear; bring a long skirt to wear in churches or in places like Chiapas, where locals are very religious. If you are traveling with a male friend, it may help to pose as a couple, no matter how distasteful it is to you and your friend; it will make it easier to share rooms and will also chill the blood of Mexican Romeos. Wearing a **wedding ring** on your left hand or a **Catholic cross** around your neck might also discourage unwanted attention, as can talking loudly and frequently about your muscular boyfriend *(novio muy fuerte)* or easily-angered husband *(esposo muy facilmente enojado);* some savvy women even carry pictures of these "boyfriends" and "husbands," and the beefier the man in the pictures, the better. Finally, look like you know what you're doing, even when you don't. Feigning confidence can scare away potential harassers or attackers.

FURTHER READING

A Journey of One's Own: Uncommon Advice for the Independent Woman Traveler, Thalia Zepatos. Eighth Mountain Press (US$17).

Adventures in Good Company: The Complete Guide to Women's Tours and Outdoor Trips, Thalia Zepatos. Eighth Mountain Press (US$7).

Active Women Vacation Guide, Evelyn Kaye. Blue Panda Publications (US$18).

Travelers' Tales: Gutsy Women, Travel Tips and Wisdom for the Road, Marybeth Bond. Traveler's Tales (US$8).

OLDER TRAVELERS AND RETIREES

Mexico's temperate climate, historical and architectural attractions, and favorable exchange rates lure older travelers and retirees alike. Thriving and tight-knit expatriate communities have popped up all over the country—in the center (San Miguel de Allende, Guadalajara, and Xalapa), north (San Carlos and Todos Santos), and south (Oaxaca, Puerto Escondido, and the breathtaking turquoise coast of Quintana Roo). For information on retiring in Mexico, see **Retirement Visas,** p. 10. Senior citizens just looking to travel in the country will be pleasantly surprised. Mexican conservative culture fosters respect of one's elders, and seniors will receive among the best service and treatment. Don't be surprised if young people embarrass you by offering you their seat on the Metro or on the bus. In addition to preferential treatment, seniors are eligible for a range of discounts, from transportation tickets to museums to accommodations. If you don't see a senior citizen price listed, ask and you may be rewarded. Many seniors also travel to Mexico to take advantage of the country's excellent language schools, many of which offer special discounts and programs for senior citizens (see **Studying Abroad,** p. 39).

Elderhostel, 75 Federal St., Boston, MA 02110, USA (☎(617) 426-7788 or (877) 426-2166; email registration@elderhostel.org; www.elderhostel.org). Organizes 1- to 4-week "educational adventures" in Mexico on varied subjects for those 55+.

The Mature Traveler, P.O. Box 50400, Reno, NV 89513, USA (☎(775) 786-7419, credit card orders (800) 460-6676). A magazine listing deals, discounts, and travel packages for the 50+ traveler. Subscription $30.

FURTHER READING

Living Well In Mexico: How to Relocate, Retire, and Increase Your Standard of Living, Ken Lubolt. John Muir Publications (US$15.95).

Chose Mexico for Retirement, John Howells and Don Merwin. Globe Pequot Press (US$14.95).

No Problem! Worldwise Tips for Mature Adventurers, Janice Kenyon. Orca Book Publishers (US$16).

A Senior's Guide to Healthy Travel, Donald L. Sullivan. Career Press (US$15).

BISEXUAL, GAY, AND LESBIAN TRAVELERS

Mexico's conservative and Catholic character makes homosexuality frowned upon at best, violently despised at worst. Intolerance is especially rampant in more rural areas of the country, where displays of gay or lesbian affection might be the quickest way to get harassed or beaten. More urban areas are generally more accepting of homosexuality; there is a fledgling gay-rights movement in Mexico City and a more rapidly growing movement in Monterrey. Sadly, however, the best rule of thumb is to avoid displays of homosexuality altogether—at least until you know you are in an safe and accepting environment, such as one afforded by gay and lesbian clubs and establishments (of which, interestingly enough, there are many). Whenever possible, *Let's Go* lists gay and lesbian establishments; there are, however, many more. The best way to find out about these establishments is to consult organizations, mail-order bookstores, and publishers which offer materials addressing specific gay and lesbian concerns. **Out and About** (www.planetout.com) offers a bi-weekly newsletter addressing travel concerns.

Gay's the Word, 66 Marchmont St., London WC1N 1AB (☎(020) 7278 7654; email sales@gaystheword.co.uk; www.gaystheword.co.uk). The largest gay and lesbian bookshop in the UK, with both fiction and non-fiction titles. Mail-order service available.

Giovanni's Room, 345 S. 12th St., Philadelphia, PA 19107, USA (☎(215) 923-2960; fax 923-0813; www.queerbooks.com). An international lesbian/feminist and gay bookstore with mail-order service (carries many of the publications listed below).

International Gay and Lesbian Travel Association, 4331 N. Federal Hwy., #304, Fort Lauderdale, FL 33308, USA (☎(954) 776-2626; fax 776-3303; www.iglta.com). An organization of over 1350 companies serving gay and lesbian travelers worldwide.

International Lesbian and Gay Association (ILGA), 81 rue Marché-au-Charbon, B-1000 Brussels, Belgium (☎/fax +32 (2) 502 24 71; www.ilga.org). Not a travel service; provides political information, such as homosexuality laws of individual countries.

WEBSITES

Aquí Estamos, www.aquiestamos.com. Chat, personals, and an online guide (still under construction) to over 30 Mexican cities.

Gay México, www.gaymexico.com.mx. An all-purpose informational site.

Ser Gay, www.sergay.com.mx. A Mexico City based site with chat forums and event listings in the D.F. area.

FURTHER READING

Spartacus International Gay Guide. Bruno Gmunder Verlag. (US$33).

Damron Men's Guide, Damron Road Atlas, Damron's Accommodations, and *The Women's Traveller.* Damron Travel Guides (US$14-19). For more info, call US ☎(415) 255-0404 or (800) 462-6654 or check their website (www.damron.com).

Gay Mexico, Ferrari Guides' Gay Travel A to Z, Ferrari Guides' Men's Travel in Your Pocket, Ferrari Guides' Women's Travel in Your Pocket, and *Ferrari Guides' Inn Places.* Ferrari Guides (US$14-16). For more info, call (602) 863-2408 or (800) 962-2912 or try www.q-net.com.

The Gay Vacation Guide: The Best Trips and How to Plan Them, Mark Chesnut. Citadel Press (US$15).

TRAVELERS WITH DISABILITIES

Mexico is becoming increasingly accessible to travelers with disabilities, especially in popular resorts like Cancún and Cabo San Lucas. Northern cities closer to the US also tend to be more accessible with Monterrey and Saltillo being the most wheelchair-friendly cities in the entire country. Money talks—the more you are willing to spend, the less difficult it is to find accessible facilities. Keep in mind, however, that most public and long-distance modes of transportation and most of the non-luxury hotels don't accommodate wheelchairs. Public bathrooms are almost all inaccessible, as are many ruins, parks, historic buildings, and museums. Still, with some advance planning, an affordable Mexican vacation is not impossible. Those with disabilities should inform airlines and hotels when making arrangements for travel; some time may be needed to prepare.

USEFUL ORGANIZATIONS

Mobility International USA (MIUSA), P.O. Box 10767, Eugene, OR 97440, USA (☎(541) 343-1284 voice and TDD; fax 343-6812; email info@miusa.org; www.miusa.org). Sells *A World of Options: A Guide to International Educational Exchange, Community Service, and Travel for Persons with Disabilities* (US$35).

Moss Rehab Hospital Travel Information Service (email netstaff@mossresourcenet.org; www.mossresourcenet.org). An information resource site on travel-related concerns for those with disabilities.

Society for the Advancement of Travel for the Handicapped (SATH), 347 Fifth Ave., #610, New York, NY 10016 (☎(212) 447-7284; www.sath.org). An advocacy group that publishes the quarterly travel magazine *OPEN WORLD* (free for members, US$13 for nonmembers). Also publishes a wide range of info sheets on disability travel facilitation and destinations. Annual membership US$45, students and seniors US$30.

TOUR AGENCIES

Directions Unlimited, 123 Green Ln., Bedford Hills, NY 10507, USA (☎(914) 241-1700 or (800) 533-5343; www.travel-cruises.com). Specializes in arranging individual and group vacations, tours, and cruises for the physically disabled.

FURTHER READING

Resource Directory for the Disabled, Richard Neil Shrout. Facts on file (US$45).

MINORITY TRAVELERS

The Mexican population is white, Indian, or a combination of the two. The homogeneity of the general populace means that any foreigner—regardless of skin color—is bound to stick out, particularly when traveling in rural or less touristed parts of the country. In general, the whiter your skin, the better treatment you'll receive. (Unfortunately, light-skinned travelers are often viewed as more wealthy and therefore are more likely to be the targets of crime.) This is not to say, however, that non-caucasian travelers will receive poor treatment. Rather, travelers of African or Asian ancestry will most likely receive attention from curious locals and their gawking children, who may giggle, point, and stare. Asians may find themselves called *chinos,* while African Americans are often called *morenos* or *negros.* None of these words is meant to be offensive; instead they are meant as descriptive terms. In many rural areas, non-Spanish speakers may be viewed as a threat. It helps to try to speak Spanish to help locals feel more at ease; a smile can work wonders. In larger cities and in cities catering to the tourist industry, speaking English might entitle you to better-than-average treatment.

TRAVELERS WITH CHILDREN

Mexicans love children and children love Mexico. Travel around the Republic and you'll see throngs of Mexican families on the beach, in museums, and in parks. Foreign families frequent beach and resort areas but are few and far between in the central parts of the country. Fear not, brave traveler! Traveling with children requires little more than added planning and a lot of extra patience. When deciding where to stay, for example, consider staying in more moderately-priced establishments. Unless you want your children rubbing elbows with questionable backpacker types, it's best to avoid the hard-core budget joints and hostels. It's also a good idea to call ahead to make sure your hotel welcomes children. In choosing a restaurant, make sure that the establishment offers food your child will like. Some children are finicky eaters, and the spicy (and sometimes unusual) food eaten by many Mexicans may seem strange to them; offer them simple and tasty *taquitos, quesadillas,* and *sopas de fideo* (yummy noodle soups). Unless your child has a particularly adventurous palate, stay away from the salsa *picante.* Finally, be extra careful with food and water safety, as children's digestive systems are generally more delicate than those of adults. Always give children plenty of *agua purificada* or *agua embotellada* to drink (especially if it's hot out), and take them to a doctor if they develop any abnormally severe diarrhea. When traveling by car between cities, make sure that your car has a seat for young children (if it doesn't, request one from your rental company). Also keep in mind that many Mexican highways—particularly those connecting Mexico City to the coasts—are hilly and windy and have a tendency to make children carsick. Plan accordingly and be prepared to pull over at a moment's notice, lest you want your vehicle decorated with fresh vomit.

Perhaps the only truly child-unfriendly part of the country might be Mexico City since the big city noise, congestion, and pollution tend to affect children more than adults. If staying in *el D.F.* with children, keep them indoors when pollution is at its heaviest—generally in early mornings during the winter. Stay alert for pollution index updates, frequently broadcast on radio and television. With the exception of Mexico City, the entire Republic is child-friendly, particularly the coastal

BABY ON BOARD. When entering Mexico, children traveling by themselves or with only one parent must present a parental consent form that has been signed, in the presence of a notary public, by both parents or by the parent not traveling. If the one parent is diseased, then a death certificate or court order must be presented. These rules are meant to curb the numbers of parents who try to flee with their children across international borders. Although the rules are seldom enforced, travelers have been turned away at the border for not providing proper documentation for their accompanying children.

regions, which offer children miles of golden and white beaches upon which to frolic and build sand castle after sand castle. Slather on the sunscreen, though— Mexico is good to children, but the Mexican sun isn't.

FURTHER READING

Let's Go Traveling in Mexico, Robin Rector Krupp. William Morrow Company, an illustrated journey through Mexico with the mythical Quetzalcóatl as guide. Ideal for children ages 4-8 years old. No relation to our favorite *Let's Go.* (US$16).

Backpacking with Babies and Small Children, Goldie Silverman. Wilderness Press (US$10).

How to take Great Trips with Your Kids, Sanford and Jane Portnoy. Harvard Common Press (US $10).

Tropical Family Vacations: In the Caribbean, Hawaii, South Florida, and Mexico, Laura Sutherland. Griffin Trade Paperback (US$17).

Family Travel and Resorts: The Complete Guide, Pamela Lanier. Ten Speed Press (US$20).

Have Kid, Will Travel: 101 Survival Strategies for Vacationing With Babies and Young Children, Claire and Lucille Tristram. Andrews and McMeel (US$9).

Adventuring with Children: An Inspirational Guide to World Travel and the Outdoors, Nan Jeffrey. Avalon House Publishing ($15).

Trouble Free Travel with Children, Vicki Lansky. Book Peddlers (US$9).

DIETARY CONCERNS

Vegetarians are rare in Mexico, and vegans are almost unheard of. You'll get long, incredulous stares not only from your waiters, but also from concerned patrons at nearby tables. Oftentimes, it's best to blame it on the weather ("It's so hot I only want to eat vegetables") or on illness ("I have *turista;* I will vomit on you if I eat lots of meat") rather than complicated ideology. A diatribe on animal rights will win you no converts and will raise more than a few eyebrows. With that said, the carnivorous nature of Mexicans can make it difficult for **vegetarian tourists** since most meals either feature meat dishes or are prepared using animal products. Some popular vegetarian dishes available in most restaurants include *quesadillas* (melted cheese wrapped in tortillas), *chilaquiles* (strips of fried tortillas baked in tomato sauce with cheese and fresh cream), *molletes* (french bread smothered with refried beans and cheese), and *frijoles* (beans). Beware that some types of *quesadillas* contain meat and that some types of beans are prepared with *manteca* (lard). **Vegan tourists** will have a harder go at it and may have to subsist on the old standbys of tortillas, beans, and rice. If you dislike beans and rice, it might be a good idea to bring high-energy protein snacks (such as granola bars and peanuts) to maintain your energy. Wherever possible, *Let's Go* includes vegetarian dining options, but if you have any doubts, check with your waiter to make sure that your food is completely meat-free. For **more information on vegetarianism abroad** contact the **North American Vegetarian Society,** P.O. Box 72, Dolgeville, NY 13329 (☎ (518) 568-7970; email navs@telenet.com; www.navs-online.org), which publishes *The Vegetarian Traveler: Where to Stay If You're Vegetarian,* a guide to international vegetarian-friendly restaurants and accomoda-

ESSENTIALS

tions(US$15.95). Also contact the **Asociación Mexicana de Vegetarianos,** c/o Alternative World, Apartido Postal WTC 031 World Trade Center, Mexico City, D.F. 03812 (☎5453 51 21; fax 5398 11 86; email mmobarak@nova.net.mx).

Despite the increasing number of Jews in Mexico (especially in Mexico City), keeping kosher can be difficult. Many large supermarkets sell kosher foods, but travelers will have less luck in restaurants and smaller towns. Those who keep kosher should contact synagogues for information on kosher restaurants. Your own synagogue or college Hillel should have access to lists of Jewish institutions across Mexico. **The Jewish Travel Guide,** which lists synagogues, kosher restaurants, and Jewish institutions in Mexico, is available in Europe from Vallentine Mitchell Publishers, Newbury House 890-900, Eastern Ave., Newbury Park, Ilford, Essex IG2 7HH, UK (☎(020) 8599 8866; fax 8599 0984) and in the US ($16.95 + $4 S&H) from ISBS, 5804 NE Hassallo St., Portland, OR 97213 (☎(800) 944-6190).

ALTERNATIVES TO TOURISM

STUDYING ABROAD

Mexico welcomes students of all ages and abilities with open arms. Before you hop on the next plane to Mexico, however, keep in mind that foreign study programs vary tremendously in expense, quality, living conditions, and degree of cultural exposure. Small, local schools and universities are generally cheaper, but international organizations may be better able to arrange academic credit at your home institution. As you can see, it's best to do your homework beforehand.

UNIVERSITIES AND UNIVERSITY PROGRAMS

Most undergraduates enroll in programs sponsored by US universities. Those relatively fluent in Spanish may find it cheaper to enroll directly in a local university, though getting credit may be more difficult. Applications to Mexican universities are usually due in early spring and require a transcript and a copy of your passport or birth certificate. Some schools that offer study abroad programs to foreigners

ESSENTIALS

are listed below. The first four listings are Mexican universities that accept foreign students for study abroad. The other listings are foreign schools with campuses or programs in Mexico.

Universidad Nacional Autonoma de Mexico (UNAM), Apdo. 70-391, Av. Universidad, Delegacion Coyoacán, Mexico, D.F. 04510 (☎5622 2470; fax 5616 2672; email cepe@sevidor.uman.mx; www.cepe.unam.mx), is the largest public university in Mexico with over 100,000 students. It operates the **Centro de Ensenanza para Extranjeros (CEPE)**, which provides semester, intensive, and summer programs in Spanish, art, history, and literature. The school also operates a satellite campus in Taxco.

Universidad de las Americas (UDLA), Santa Catarina Mártir, San Andrés Cholula, Puebla 72820, Mexico (http://info.pue.udlap.mx), is a private university that has the distinction of being the only Mexican university accredited in the US. Write to the Decanatura de Asuntos Internacionales (☎2229 3166; fax 2299 3169; email mexico@mail.udlap.mx) for information on becoming a visiting student.

Tecnológico de Monterrey (email study@itesm.mx; http://dir.sistema.itesm.mx/dial/proyectos/sim). One of the most prestigious private universities in the country, specializing in science, mathematics, and engineering. There are seven campuses across the country; each hosts its own international program.

Universidad Iberoamericana, Paseo de la Reforma No. 880, Col. Lomas de Santa Fe, Deleg. Alvaro Obregón, 01210 Mexico, D.F. (email international@uia.mx; www.uia.mx), or Ibero for short, is a private university that offers semesters abroad, summer programs, and intensive Spanish instruction. Its main campus is in Mexico City, but there are other satellite campuses.

Augsburg College Center for Global Education, 2211 Riverside Ave., Minneapolis, MN, 55454 USA (☎(800) 299-8889; fax (612) 330 1695; www.augsburg.edu/global/index.html). Semester-long programs, based in Cuernavaca, focusing on issues of gender, human rights, and ecology. Tuition $10,800; financial aid available.

Instituto Cultural Oaxaca

Your Gateway to Spanish

Beautiful Oaxaca beckons ... come learn Spanish in a charming colonial city at the crossroads of 16 cultures. Experience the most intensive folk-art scene, exquisite cuisine, and amazing archeological sites in all of Mexico. The Instituto Cultural Oaxaca offers ...

* All levels of Spanish including Literature
* 7 hour cultural immersion program
  - morning grammar and conversation classes
  - afternoon cultural workshops (folkloric dance, salsa, merengue, backstrap weaving, music, conversation, Oaxacan cooking, Mexican cinema, pottery)
  - Intercambio program (one-on-one conversation with a native Oaxacan)
* Enrollment any Monday
* Native Mexican, University-trained Professors
* Weekly concerts, lectures, and tours
* Family homestays/ Apartments/ Rustic Inns
* Credit accepted in many US, Canadian, and European Universities
* Costs US$450 for 4 weeks (Including lifetime registration)
* classes located in a gorgeous turn-of-the-century estate
* close to world class beaches on Oaxacan coast and outdoor activities in the towering Sierra Madre mountains

Visit us on-line at:

www.instculturaloax.com.mx

Reply to: Apartado Postal 340, Oaxaca, Oax., Mexico 68000
Street address: Avenida Juarez 909, Centro
E-mail: inscuoax@prodigy.net.mx
Telephone: 011-52-951-5-34-04 or 5-13-23
Fax: 011-52-951-5-37-28

Beaver College Center for Education Abroad, 450 S. Easton Rd., Glenside, PA 19038, USA (☎(888) 232-8379; www.beaver.edu/cea). Operates programs in Mexico. Costs range from $1900 (summer) to $20,000 (full-year).

Central College Abroad, Office of International Education, 812 University, Pella, IA 50219, USA (☎(800) 831-3629 or (515) 628-5284; studyabroad.com/central). Offers semester- and year-long programs in Mexico. US$25 application fee.

Colleges Abroad, 12130 N. Chickasaw Dr., Syracuse, IN 46567 USA (☎(219) 528 6120); www.collegesabroad.com/c-mexico.html). Programs ranging in length from summer- to year-long (US$2000-9000). Placements in Guadalajara, Mazatlán, Mexico City, Monterrey, and Querétaro.

Council on International Educational Exchange (CIEE), 205 E. 42nd St., New York, NY 10017 USA (☎(800) 407-8839; fax (212) 822-2699; www.ciee.org) sponsors a semester program at the University of Guadalajara. Contact program assistant Angela Munro (☎(212) 872 2762) or email studyinfo@ciee.org.

International Studies Abroad (ISA), 90 West 24th St., Austin, TX, 78705 USA (☎(800) 580 8826 or (512) 480 8522; fax 480 8866; www.studiesabroad.com). Offers programs at the University of Guanajuato. Prices range from US$2000-6000.

School for International Training, College Semester Abroad, Admissions, Kipling Rd., P.O. Box 676, Brattleboro, VT 05302 USA (☎(800) 336-1616 or (802) 258-3267; www.sit.edu). Semester- and year-long programs in Mexico run US$9500-12,900. Also runs the **Experiment in International Living** (☎(800) 345-2929; fax (802) 258-3428; email eil@worldlearning.org), 3- to 5-week summer programs that offer high-school students cross-cultural homestays, community service, ecological adventure, and language training in Mexico for US$1900-5000.

International Association for the Exchange of Students for Technical Experience (IAESTE), 10400 Little Patuxent Pkwy., #250, Columbia, MD 21044, USA (☎(410) 997-3068; www.aipt.org). Operates 8- to 12-week programs in Mexico for college students who have completed 2 years of technical study. US$50 application fee.

LANGUAGE SCHOOLS

Language schools, geared more toward high school students and older adults, concentrate in colonial cities, such as Cuernavaca, Puebla, and Oaxaca. Visitors to these cities can easily receive information directly from the schools. Programs generally cost anywhere from US$100 to US$500, depending on duration and whether the school is foreign or Mexican owned.

Centro Bilingue, Nueva Polonia #189, Lomas de Cortés, Cuernavaca, Morelos 62251 Mexico (☎(7) 311 30 72; www.spin.com.mx/~jmlozano/hola.html). Mailing address: Apdo. postal 38-3, Cuernavaca, Morelos 62251 Mexico. Intensive classes for US$190 per week. Also offers special language programs for children, executives, and nurses.

Instituto Falcon, Callejon de la Mora 158, Guanajuato, 36000 Mexico (☎(4) 731 10 84; fax (4) 731 07 45; www.institutofalcon.com). Offers a 16-week program in Mexican culture and Spanish language for US$395. Regular classes US$55-110 per week. Dorms and homestays US$4-19 per day. Senior discounts.

Instituto Habla Hispana, Calzada de la Luz 25, Apdo. 689, San Miguel de Allende, Gto., C.P. 37700 Mexico (☎(4) 152 07 13; fax 152 15 35). Send mail to c/o Kima Cargill, 814 E. 4th St., Austin, TX 78751 USA (email kcargill@mail.utexas.edu). Spanish courses for US$100 per week.

Language Immersion Institute, 75 South Manheim Blvd., The College at New Paltz, New Paltz, NY 12561, USA (☎(914) 257-3500; www.newpaltz.edu/lii). 2-week summer language courses and some overseas courses in Spanish. Program fees are about US$295 for a weekend or US$750 per 2 weeks.

Spanish Institute of Puebla, 15 Poniente #504, Puebla, Puebla 72420 Mexico (☎(2) 240 86 92; www.sipuebla.com). US$1400 for four weeks of intensive classes.

FURTHER READING AND RESOURCES
www.studyabroad.com

www.studyabroadlinks.com

Academic Year Abroad 2000/2001. Institute of International Education Books (US$45).

Vacation Study Abroad 2000/2001. Institute of International Education Books (US$43).

Peterson's Study Abroad 2001. Peterson's (US$30).

Peterson's Summer Study Abroad 2001. Peterson's (US$30)

WORKING ABROAD

The Mexican government is wary of giving up precious jobs to foreigners when so many Mexicans are unemployed. Previously, only 10% of employees of foreign firms located in Mexico could have non-Mexican citizenship; the limit now varies by sector. If you want to work in Mexico, you must secure a work visa (see **Business Visas,** p. 10).

TEACHING ENGLISH

International Schools Services, Educational Staffing Program, P.O. Box 5910, Princeton, NJ 08543, USA (☎(609) 452-0990; www.iss.edu). Recruits teachers and administrators for American and English schools in Mexico. US$150 application fee.

Office of Overseas Schools, US Department of State, Room H328, SA-1, Washington, D.C. 20522 (☎(202) 261-8200; fax 261-8224; www.state.gov/www/about_state/ schools). Keeps a comprehensive list of schools abroad and agencies that arrange placement for Americans to teach in Mexico.

World Teach, Center for International Development, 79 John F. Kennedy St., Cambridge, MA 02138, USA (☎(800) 483-2240 or (617) 495-5527; www.worldteach.org). Volunteers teach English, and environmental education for 6-12 months in Chiapas and the Yucatán. A bachelor's degree is required.

ARCHAEOLOGICAL DIGS

Archaeological Institute of America, 656 Beacon St., Boston, MA 02215, USA (☎(617) 353-9361; www.archaeological.org). The *Archaeological Fieldwork Opportunities Bulletin* (US$16 for non-members) lists field sites throughout Mexico. Purchase the bulletin from Kendall/Hunt Publishing, 4050 Westmark Dr., Dubuque, Iowa 52002, USA (☎(800) 228-0810).

VOLUNTEERING

Volunteer jobs are readily available, and many provide room and board in exchange for labor. You can sometimes avoid high application fees by contacting the individual workcamps directly.

AmeriSpan, PO Box 40007, Philadelphia, PA, 19106 USA (☎(800) 879 6640 or (215) 751 1100; www.amerispan.com). Internships and placements all over Mexico in the fields of education, public health, the environment, ESL, and social work.

Earthwatch, 680 Mt. Auburn St., Box 403, Watertown, MA 02272, USA (☎(800) 776-0188 or (617) 926-8200; www.earthwatch.org). Arranges 1-3-week programs in Mexico to promote conservation of natural resources. Programs average US$1700.

Explorations in Travel, Inc., 1922 River Rd., Guildford, VT 05301 USA (☎(802) 257-0152; fax (802) 257-2784; www.volunteertravel.com). Makes placements in organizations working on ecology and education, for a fee of US$750-950. Daily costs average US$5-10 during stay in Mexico.

Global Exchange, 2017 Mission, #303, San Francisco, CA 94110 USA (☎(415) 255-7296 ext. 239; email mexico@globale xchange.org; www.globalexchange.org/campaigns/mexico). Mexico campaigns focus on education, research, economic and human rights and aim to put activists in contact with Mexican grassroots movements. Also offers "Reality Tours" of local life and politics as an alternative to hotel tourism. Tours cost US$500-1000.

Habitat for Humanity International, 121 Habitat St., Americus, GA 31709, USA (☎(800) 334-3308; www.habitat.org). Offers opportunities to live in Mexico and build houses in a host community. Costs range US$1200-3500.

Volunteers for Peace, 1034 Tiffany Rd., Belmont, VT 05730, USA (☎(802) 259-2759; www.vfp.org). Arranges placement in workcamps in Mexico. Annual *International Workcamp Directory* US$20. Registration fee US$200. Free newsletter.

FURTHER READING

International Jobs: Where they Are, How to Get Them, Eric Koocher. Perseus Books (US$17).

How to Get a Job in Europe, Robert Sanborn. Surrey Books (US$22).

Work Abroad: The Complete Guide to Finding a Job Overseas, Clayton Hubbs. Transitions Abroad (US$16).

International Directory of Voluntary Work, Louise Whetter. Vacation Work Publications (US$16).

Teaching English Abroad, Susan Griffin. Vacation Work (US$17).

Overseas Summer Jobs 2001, Work Your Way Around the World, and *The Directory of Jobs and Careers Abroad.* Peterson's (US$17-18 each).

OTHER RESOURCES

Let's Go tries to cover all aspects of budget travel, but we can't put *everything* in our guides. Listed below are books and websites that can serve as jumping off points for your own research.

USEFUL PUBLICATIONS

Mexico Desconocido: These popular monthly travel magazines, in Spanish and English, describe little-known areas and customs of Mexico. Subscriptions to the US cost $50 (email mexdesco@compuserve.com.mx); subscriptions in Mexico cost 240 pesos. Online at www.mexdesco.com.

THE WORLD WIDE WEB

Almost every aspect of budget travel (with the most notable exception, of course, being experience) is accessible via the web. Even if you don't have Internet access at home, seeking it out at a public library or at work would be worth it; in less than 10 minutes at the keyboard, you can make a reservation at a hotel in the Yucatán, get advice on travel hotspots from travelers who have just returned from Baja California, or find out how much a bus from Ciudad Juárez to Guadalajara costs. Listed here are some budget travel sites to start off your surfing. Because website turnover is high, use search engines to strike out on your own. But in doing so, keep in mind that most travel websites simply exist to somehow get your money.

ON BUDGET TRAVEL

How to See the World: www.artoftravel.com. A compendium of great travel tips, from cheap flights to self defense to interacting with local culture.

Rec. Travel Library: www.travel-library.com. A fantastic set of links for general information and personal travelogues.

Shoestring Travel: www.stratpub.com. An e-zine focusing on budget travel.

INFORMATION ON MEXICO

The CIA World Factbook: www.odci.gov/cia/publications/factbook/index.html. has tons of vital statistics on Mexico. Check it out for an overview of Mexico economy and an explanation of its system of government.

Foreign Language for Travelers: www.travlang.com. Provides free online translating dictionaries and lists of phrases in Spanish.

MyTravelGuide: www.mytravelguide.com. Country overviews, with everything from history to transportation to live web cam coverage of Mexico.

Geographia: www.geographia.com. Describes the highlights and peoples of Mexico.

Atevo Travel: www.atevo.com/guides/destinations. Detailed introductions, travel tips, and suggested itineraries.

Columbus Travel Guides: www.travel-guides.com/navigate/world.asp. Helpful practical information.

LeisurePlanet: www.leisureplanet.com/TravelGuides. Good general background.

TravelPage: www.travelpage.com. Links to official tourist office sites throughout Mexico.

PlanetRider: www.planetrider.com/Travel_Destinations.cfm. A subjective list of links to the "best" websites covering the culture and tourist attractions of Mexico.

Foreign Language for Travelers: www.travlang.com. can help you brush up on your Spanish.

Mexico City Subway System: http://metro.jussieu.fr:10001/bin/select/english/mexico/mexico. An automated route-finder and map of the Mexico City Metro.

Mexico Reference Desk: www.lanic.utexas.edu/la/Mexico. A abundance of links to Mexico-related sites.

Microsoft Expedia: www.expedia.msn.com. This mega-site has everything you'd ever need to make travel plans on the web— compare flight fares, look at maps, and book reservations.

Travelocity: www.travelocity.com. Operates a comprehensive network of travel services.

US State Department Travel Advisory for Mexico: http://travel.state.gov/mexico.html. The word from above on travel safety and recommended precautions.

Yahoo! Mexico Links: www.yahoo.com/regional/countries/mexico. Well-indexed and searchable database of over 2000 links related to Mexico.

Zapatista Web Page: www.ezln.org. Provides up-to-the-minute information in English and Spanish about Mexico's most prominent rebel group.

AND OUR PERSONAL FAVORITE...

Let's Go: www.letsgo.com. Our recently revamped website features photos and streaming video, info about our books, a travel forum buzzing with stories and tips, and links that will help you find everything you could ever want to know about Mexico.

LIFE AND TIMES

THE LAND

Mexico is shaped like a horn-of-plenty. Its wide northern mouth runs more than 3000km along the US border, and its narrow southeastern tip just kisses Guatemala and Belize. In between, Mexico contains some two million sq. km of the world's most varied landscape. With parched scrub-brush deserts, jungle rainforests, mile-high volcanoes, temperate valleys, low coastal lagoons, and red canyon land, Mexico is one of the most physically and ecologically striking countries in the world.

GEOGRAPHY AND GEOLOGY

Mexico is situated at the eastern extremity of the "Ring of Fire," the region of tectonic activity encircling the Pacific Ocean that causes earthquakes and volcanic activity from Indonesia to Canada. These geologic forces have, over the millennia, shaped Mexico into a landscape of crags, valleys, and high mountain chains. Such variability in elevation and terrain make for a Mexican countryside that can change drastically over the span of just a few kilometers.

BAJA CALIFORNIA AND THE NORTH

Northern Mexico is by and large low, arid, and hot. The *noreste* (northeast) is dryer than the *noroeste* (northwest), and over time, periodically flooded rivers have carved much of the northwest into canyons. The **Barrancas del Cobre** (Copper Canyons) are the treasure of the region—five canyons converge to form one, covering an area four times the size of the Grand Canyon in the US.

The spur of the **Baja Peninsula** begins in Mexico's northwest corner and descends, dividing the **Gulf of California** (commonly called the **Sea of Cortés**) from the Pacific Ocean. The Peninsula is mountainous and scaldingly hot. A spine of mountains runs its dusty 1330km length and slopes gently to the eastern shore, but cuts sharply on the west to create a rocky coast. Those navigating the Sea of Cortés may find it difficult to land on the jagged eastern coast of Baja California.

THE CENTER

Two great mountain ranges, the **Sierra Madre Occidental** on the west and the **Sierra Madre Oriental** on the east, cut a V-shape through the heart of the country. The Sierra Madre Occidental is volcanic, with peaks nearly 3000m high, and the Sierra Madre Oriental reaches heights of nearly 4000m. Between the two ranges lies the **Altiplano**, a vast network of highlands stretching from the US border more than 2500km southward to the **Isthmus of Tehuantepec**, near the Guatemalan border. The hospitable southern Altiplano, including the Valley of Mexico, contains Mexico City and more than half of Mexico's entire population. The land just south of Mexico City at the base of the V, the **Cordillera Neovolcánica**, is the most volcanic in all of Mexico. The volcanoes **Citlaltépetl**, **Popocatépetl**, and **Iztaccíhuatl** all tower over 5000m above sea level, and smaller ones sprinkle the region. Though many of these volcanoes have lain dormant since the 1800s, Popocatépetl ("Smoking Mountain" in Náhuatl) erupted in 1994, spewing ash over the city of Puebla.

More southern still are the **Southern Highlands**, a series of mountain ranges, *mesas*, and valleys in the states of Guerrero and Oaxaca. The largest range is the **Sierra Madre del Sur**, which runs along the southwest coast of Mexico. Its feet reach into the sea, hiding resort towns like Acapulco along the craggy coast. The largest and most populous valley in the area is the verdant **Oaxaca Valley**.

The lands directly to the east and west of the area bounded by the Sierra Madre Occidental and the Sierra Madre Oriental are far less mountainous than the interior. Bordering the Sea of Cortez, the **Pacific Coastal Lowland,** east of the Sierra Madre Occidental is a dry, relatively flat region of *mesas* (coastal terraces). On the east side of the country, east of the Sierra Madre Oriental is the much wetter **Gulf Coastal Plain.** This is lagoon land, humid and swampy, running from the US border to the **Isthmus of Tehuantepec.** The Isthmus itself is a low stretch of land with hills rarely reaching higher than 300m. With the **Gulf of Campeche,** to its north, and the **Gulf of Tehuantepec** to its south, the Isthmus narrows to little more than 200km at its slimmest. Northeast of the Isthmus is the **Tabasco Plain,** and southeast are the **Chiapas Highlands,** an area of high mountains surrounding a large rift valley. The Highlands continue into Guatemala, forming the northern tip of the Central American ranges.

THE YUCATÁN PENINSULA

Northeast of the Highlands is the **Yucatán Peninsula.** An extremely flat region, the Peninsula is surrounded by the Gulf of Mexico to the west and north, and the Caribbean Sea to the east. The northern part of the Peninsula is much drier than the south, and the soil is high in porous limestone, absorbing moisture before it can consolidate into rivers. The only sources of fresh water are the *cenotes*, natural wells that pockmark the limestone bedrock. *Cavernas* (caverns) also dot the Peninsula; many were Maya cities and ceremonial sites. Some scientists believe the unusually high density of *cenotes* in the Yucatán is the result of the same **meteor impact** that might have killed the dinosaurs 65 million years ago. In the 1940s, an oil company drilling in the Yucatán uncovered evidence of what would later be known as the **Chicxulub Crater.** A gigantic bowl 180km across and more than 200km deep, buried half on land and half under the Gulf of Mexico, the crater cannot be seen without intricate instruments. A ring of caves on the perimeter of the crater suggests a link between *cenotes* and impact.

CLIMATE, FLORA, AND FAUNA

Mexico's climate runs from desert to rainforest with everything in between. There are two seasons: rainy (May-Aug., though a few regions receive rain year round) and dry (Sept.-April). Hurricanes and tropical storms are most likely to hit the coast between August and September. Mexico's patchwork landscape makes for a patchwork ecosystem, dependent more on altitude than latitude. In Mexico you will find cool coniferous forests, humid lagoons, luscious rainforests, icy mountain peaks, and arid cactus-covered big-sky country.

THE NORTH

Baja California and the north of the country most closely conform to the Mexican stereotype: dusty, bone-dry, and oppressively hot. Annual rainfall is often less than 25cm, and summer temperatures climb as high as 43°C (110°F). Travelers generally find Baja California to be the hottest place in all of Mexico. Though days may be broiling in these regions, be wary; once the scalding sun disappears for the night, cloudless skies allow the day's heat to escape, and temperatures fall dramatically.

The Sonoran and Chihuahuan deserts meet in the north of Mexico, and, together with the Mojave and Great Basin Deserts in the US, they comprise one of the world's largest desert regions. The **Chihuahuan Desert** is home to over 250 different kinds of cactus. Not to be outdone, the **Sonoran Desert** is the only place where one can find the tall, pillar-like varieties of cactus that resemble all-too-erect humans. The desert is also home to the unique **boojum tree,** a columnar succulent that can reach heights of over 15m. Larger **desert animals,** including armadillos, rabbits and other rodents, and lizards inhabit both deserts.

Baja California and the northern Pacific Coast are home to many large **aquatic mammals.** Those who yearn to swim with the dolphins *Flipper*-style will finally get their chance, while those who prefer to save the whales can treat themselves to an eyeful of over 15 different species. If your tastes run to the exotic and slightly grotesque, Baja California offers ample opportunity to view the mating of elephant seals. The seals mate up and down the coast, but **Bahía de Sebastián Vizcaíno,** near Guerrero Negro, is the best place to view the dirty deed—nearby islands are overrun with elephant seals, most in the process of making more elephant seals.

THE SOUTH

The southern climate varies greatly, mainly due to fluctuations in altitude. People often distinguish between *tierra caliente* (from sea level to an elevation of 1000m), *tierra templada* (1000-2000m), *tierra fria* (2000-3000m), and *tierra helada* (3000m and up). Both the Sierra Madre Occidental and Oriental receive rainfall year round. At lower elevations (300-1000m) the mountainsides are covered in deciduous forest. Trees and flowering plants such as orchids and bromeliads flourish during the summer, but most trees lose their leaves during the winter. Higher in altitude (1000-2000m), the forests become coniferous. Pines, junipers, and evergreen oaks are common. At the topmost levels (4000-5000m), trees cannot survive, and snow covers the ground year round. Between the two mountain ranges, the Altiplano is covered in grassland, punctuated by scrub brush and prickly-pear cactus. Many large mammals populate the highlands, among them foxes, mountain lions, pumas, and coyotes.

The states of **Tabasco** and **Campeche,** southwest of the Yucatán Peninsula, contain the only true **rainforests** in Mexico. Each rainforest is composed of several interlocking ecosystems—each level, from ground to canopy, is a system unto itself. Anteaters, tapirs (floppy-snouted, odd-toed beasties), and monkeys abound, as well as a seemingly endless variety of birds, lizards, frogs, and insects. At higher elevations, the rainforest becomes a **cloud forest.** Instead of periodic rainfall, moisture reaches the forest directly from standing clouds. The **Chiapas Highlands** are Mexico's most notable cloud forest. Those parts of the Gulf Coast that aren't rainforest are largely swamp and marshland. Mangrove trees densely line the sweltering shore, as fresh water mixes with salt in the region's many river deltas. Marshes, like rainforests, are frighteningly complex ecosystems containing an incredible diversity of plant and animal life. The disposition of the marsh varies greatly along the length of the Gulf Coast.

A "BRIEF" HISTORY

Over the span of 10,000 years, Mexico, the cross-roads of the American continent, has seen the rise and fall of mighty empires, the pain of conquest, three tumultuous revolutions, and the struggle to rebuild in the era of modern capitalism. Such incredible historical progress can hardly be condensed into a neat 19-page segment. Nonetheless...

PRE-HISPANIC SOCIETIES

Archaeologists generally categorize Mexican pre-Hispanic societies into five different time periods: **Pre-Agricultural** (or Paleoindian, 40,000-8000 BC), **Archaic** (8000-2000 BC), **Formative** (or Pre-Classic, 2000 BC-AD 200), **Classic** (AD 200-900), and **Post-Classic** (or Historical, AD 900-1521).

PRE-AGRICULTURAL AND ARCHAIC PERIODS

Most archaeologists believe that the first Mexicans arrived by crossing the **Bering Strait,** the stretch of dry land left by the receding ocean during the **Wisconsin (Pleistocene) Ice Age.** From about 50,000 BC to around 9000 BC a large scale migration took place as nomadic hunters followed game across the Bering Strait, from Rus-

50,000-9000 BC: Intrepid Mexicans-to-be cross a "land bridge" of sorts in the Bering Strait.

7500 BC: In a swift move, Mexicans switch from hunting to agriculture.

sia into Alaska. Archaeologists know very little about the lives of the early Mexicans; what has been uncovered indicates that they were most likely hunter-gatherers who used primitive tools to hunt large game such as hairy mammoths and giant armadillos. After 7500 BC, the climate became drier, causing the demise of the game that had long provided the hunter-gather with sustenance. It was around this time that the early Mexicans turned to agriculture, experimenting with such crops as maize and beans.

THE FORMATIVE PERIOD

This developing agricultural tradition gave birth to the great empires of Mesoamerica. Dominant culture during the Formative (or Pre-Classic) Period was characterized by dependency on maize and the linkage of religion with agricultural fertility.

THE OLMECS

1750-1350 BC: Olmecs "invent" Mesoamerican civilization and make large stone heads.

900 BC: Olmecs make the move to La Venta.

600 BC: La Venta is no more; the Olmecs are likewise.

The Olmec culture flourished in the warm, humid areas that today comprise the modern Mexican states of Veracruz (see p. 507) and Tabasco (seep. 528). The Olmec reign began in the farming and fishing village of **San Lorenzo** (see p. 526), first settled around 1700 BC. By 1350 BC, San Lorenzo had become increasingly complex, with large scale public works decorated with intricate artistic motifs including the trademark Olmec stone heads and the delicate jade figurines and masks. San Lorenzo was also home to the first ballcourt in the Americas. When San Lorenzo succumbed to invasion around 900BC, the site of **La Venta** (see p. 532), southeast of San Lorenzo, began to increase in importance. Archaeological evidence indicates that La Venta was a more sophisticated center, with both ceremonial and residential structures. Another important center was **Tres Zapotes** (see p. 521), a contemporary of La Venta. Perhaps the most important contribution of the Olmec culture was the development of **hieroglyphic writing,** influences of which are visible in the written works of other cultures, most noticeably the Maya. Of particular importance was the **long count system** of calculating dates, which used a system of dots and bars to represent days and months. After the demise of La Venta around 600 BC, the golden age of the Olmecs came to an end; they disappeared just as mysteriously as they had appeared.

THE CLASSIC PERIOD

AD 250-900: Classic Period. Swell times for everyone.

The Classic Period spanned about 1000 years, from AD 250 to AD 900. During this time, civilizations comparable to those of the great European empires developed in Mesoamerica, from Veracruz through Guatemala. The civilizations of the **Teotihuacanos, Zapotecs,** and **Maya** are considered the great civilizations of the time period, but other groups—such as those at **El Tajín** (see p. 506), **Cholula** (see p. 361), **Cacaxtla** (see p. 350), and **Xochicalco** (see p. 340)—were also formidable powers.

TEOTIHUACÁN

The city at **Teotihuacán** (see p. 129) was probably the most important and powerful of the great Classic civilizations. When the Aztecs settled the valley several centuries later, Teotihuacán seemed so impressive that it was believed only gods could have constructed it. They named it Teotihuacán, which means

"Place of the Gods" in Náhuatl, a reference to its overwhelming size. Evidence indicates that around 200 BC a civilization arose with advanced systems of urban design—Teotihuacán's complex road system was marked with ceremonial plazas, massive pyramids, and residential quarters. The influence of the Teotihuacanos spread well beyond the area of the central valley and evidence of trading is visible as far south as Guatemala.

AD 500: Mighty Teotihuacán is the most powerful Classic center. It is also very big.

MONTE ALBÁN AND THE ZAPOTEC EMPIRE

While Teotihuacán dominated the Valley of Mexico, **Monte Albán** (see p. 468), the Zapotec capital, dominated the Oaxaca Valley to the south. Between 500 BC and 100 BC the Zapotecs began settling this hilly region, just west of the modern-day Oaxaca de Juárez. The city rapidly grew from a small irrigated and terraced farming community to the largest power in the region. With a population hovering between 10,000 and 20,000, the city of Monte Albán was large enough to support a complicated social structure of nobles and priests. Between AD 400 and AD 700, however, the city began to lose its dominance, probably due to the rise of neighboring powers, such as the **Mixtec,** who ruled from the holy city, **Mitla** (see p. 465).

500-100 BC: Zapotecs make the scene in Monte Albán.

AD 400-700: Monte Albán is no more.

THE CLASSIC MAYA

The Maya civilization, unlike its contemporaries, had no one city of central power. The cities of **Palenque** (see p. 555), **Tikal** (p. 571), **Copán,** and others scattered throughout Chiapas and Central America served as regional capitals with peripheral towns subject to their rule. The Classic Period was a time of tremendous growth and advancement for the Maya, who became proficient in engineering, mathematics, art, architecture, and astronomy. They devised a method to predict the movement of celestial bodies with total precision, and were the first in the world to develop the mathematical idea of zero. The Maya dating system was also highly advanced. The Maya expressed themselves artistically through manuscripts, ceramics, murals, and reliefs. Their temples, still standing at many sites, were tall, steeply terraced pyramids with false fronts. Hardly the peaceful society of popular imagination, the Maya were a violent people. There is evidence of human sacrifice, intertribal warfare, and internal revolt. Perhaps this violence hastened the end of the Maya Classic Period around AD 900.

AD 100-900: The Maya are in their prime. They develop arts and sciences to a level never before seen in the Americas, and rarely before in the world.

AD 900: The Maya fall from grace.

THE POST-CLASSIC PERIOD

The Post-Classic period began with the demise of the great civilizations of Teotihuacán, Monte Albán, and the Maya around AD 900, continued with the rise of the Toltecs and eventually the Aztecs, and ended with the Spanish conquest of the Aztecs in 1521. The spread of the great Aztec empire facilitated long-distance trade, but made everything more militaristic and uniform—architecture and arts suffered considerably, and technological innovation slowed.

AD 900: Post-Classic Period begins. Everything goes awry.

THE TOLTECS

The Toltecs, originally known as the **Chichimeca** or the **Toltec-Chichimeca,** established their presence in central Mexico by about AD 800 in the modern-day states of Zacatecas and Hidalgo. The greatest Toltec leader was the benevolent and learned **Ce Acatl Topiltzin** (later known as **Topiltzin-Quetzalcóatl**)

AD 800-1100: The Toltecs have their day in Tula.

A VERY LONG COUNT

Even before they developed a writing system, the Maya used not one but *three* sophisticated, interlocking calendar systems. The basis of all three was a ritual count of 20 *k'in* (days), each of which was given a name and a glyph. A 20-*k'in* group was known as a *uinal* (month). From here the three systems diverge: there was the 13-*uinal* (260-day) ceremonial year and the 18-*uinal* and 5-*k'in* (365-day) secular year. These two calendars quickly got out of sync with one another, but would realign once every 52 years. The Maya bore witness to this convergence with enormous festivals, ceremonies, and sometimes massive destruction. The third way of measuring time was the Long Count. Not cyclical but linear, the Long Count reckoned all dates from the starting point 0.0.0.0.0, what scholars today believe was August 11th, 3314 BC. Besides the *k'in* and *uinal*, Long Count used the *tun* (18 *uinal*), the *k'atun* (20 *tun*), and the *baktun* (20 *k'atun*). Dates were written in the same manner that odometers show mileage, with the shortest periods, *k'in*, farthest right, and the longest, *baktun*, farthest left. August 24th, AD 2000 would correspond to 12.19.7.8.18—12 *baktun*, 19 *k'atun*, and so on. When 13 *baktun* have passed, the Maya believed, one Great Cycle would be done and the world would be reborn. Believe it or not, this is scheduled to happen on December 24th, AD 2011. Mark your calendars!

AD 987: Topiltzin-Quetzalcóatl leaves Tula, vowing to return in the year 1 Reed (AD 1519).

AD 1100: The Toltecs succumb.

AD 1050-1450: The Post-Classic Maya diaspora settles in the Yucatán, drinking from *cenotes* and exchanging culture with the similarly down-and-out Toltecs.

AD 1441: The Maya bicker and unceremoniously bite the dust.

who assumed the throne by killing his treacherous uncle. In AD 968, he founded the city of **Tula** (see p. 327), the splendid Toltec capital renowned for its agriculture and architecture. Tricked by his detractors, however, Topiltzin-Quetzalcóatl was shamed into leaving Tula in AD 987. Upon leaving, he promised that he would return in the next year of Ce Acatl, the year of **One Reed.** That year, for better or for worse, would eventually correspond with the year **1519** in the Christian calendar, the year of the Spanish invasion. The Toltec empire thrived into the 1100s, whereupon it was ravaged by drought and famine.

THE POST-CLASSIC MAYA

Whereas the Classic Maya civilizations occupied positions throughout parts of Mexico and Central America, the Post-Classic Maya settled almost exclusively in the Yucatán Peninsula around the **cenotes**, or sinkholes, that provide the only source of fresh water in the flat, limestone peninsula. Unlike the Classic Maya, whose artistic style had been relatively uninfluenced by other cultures, the Post-Classic Maya style was a mix of various styles, particularly Toltec. This influence is probably due to the extensive contact between Tula and the Post-Classic Maya. (Because of this influence, this time period in Maya history is sometimes referred to as the **Toltec Period.**) The three major city-states, **Chichén Itzá** (see p. 601), **Mayapán** (see p. 589), and **Uxmal** (see p. 586) together formed the **Mayapán League,** which Chichén Itzá dominated until its demise in the early 1400s. Mayapán then emerged as the most important Post-Classic Maya center. When Mayapán fell to a violent attack in 1441, it marked the end of a centralized Maya civilization. Independent city-states assumed control of the region.

THE AZTECS (THE MEXICA)

Perhaps no other group has captured the imagination as have the Aztecs, the violent and militaristic people who inhabited the central **Valley of Anáhuac** (the Valley of Mexico) from the late 1200s until the fall of their capital, Tenochtitlán, in 1521.

ORIGINS. The Aztec, then known as the **Mexica,** were a northern nomadic tribe that arrived in the fertile Valley of Anáhuac in the 13th century. From 1270 to 1319, the Aztecs lived at the mercy of the **Tepenec empire,** which occupied the Valley. Slowly, they began to acquire a foothold, trading and making strategic deals to win power. Under the rule of **Itzcóatl,** the Aztecs were finally able to win their independence and establish the city of **Tenochtitlán.** His successor, **Nazahualcoyótl** defeated the remaining city-states in the Valley, and the way was cleared for the mighty Aztec empire.

AD 1200-1521: The Aztecs, Mexico's bad boys, whip the region into shape.

> **EAGLE BITES SERPENT** Legend has it that the patron deity of the Mexica, the hummingbird god of sun and war **Huitzilopochtli,** revealed a vision to his people: they would see an eagle perched upon a cactus with a serpent in its talons, and when they did, they were to settle in that very spot. Having seen this vision by the side of Lago Texcoco, the ancient lake occupying the Valley of Mexico, the Mexica settled and built their mighty empire. The image was so enduring that the eagle and serpent can still be seen battling eternally on Mexico's flag.

SOCIETY. As the Aztec empire grew, its social hierarchy became more regimented and complicated. Tenochtitlán was at one point the largest and most magnificent city in the world, surpassing cities such as Paris and London, not only in population, but also in cleanliness, urban planning, and architecture. The royal family and nobles occupied the highest position in Aztec society, followed closely by the warring class. The Aztecs valued the art of war, and distinction on the battlefield was one of the few ways male citizens could enter the nobility. Traders, known as **pochteca,** were next in line. Their trade networks linked the entirety of Mesoamerica and formed the bedrock of the Aztec empire. Farmers, laborers, and artisans comprised the common class. Women in Aztec society enjoyed more rights than did their European counterparts and were active in religion, agriculture, and politics.

AD 1350: Tenochtitlán, the Aztec capital, is a model of good urban planning.

RELIGION. The Aztecs believed in cyclical time. The earth and sun had been recreated four times, and it was during the present time, the time of the fifth sun, that the earth would finally be destroyed. Because the Aztecs believed that their patron god Huitzilopochtli could sustain the cycles, pleasing him through human sacrifice was of utmost importance. Sacrifice was a solemn affair—the palpitating heart of the sacrificial victim would be removed with a sharp obsidian knife and then presented to the deity. Such a ceremony would take place in Tenochtitlán's main temple, the **Templo Mayor** (see p. 105). Other deities—such as the rain god **Tlaloc** and the feathered serpent **Quetzalcóatl**—comprised the extensive Aztec pantheon.

AD 1350: Aztecs swipe certain notions of time from the Maya, and busy themselves with gruesome human sacrifice.

LIFE AND TIMES

AZTEC RULE. The Aztec empire was the largest empire in Pre-Hispanic Mexico with over five million people. The Aztecs ruled by requiring townships to recognize Aztec sovereignty and contribute goods, land, and sacrificial victims to the empire. By the 16th century, the city and the empire were thriving and the Aztecs were at the peak of their power in the Valley of Mexico.

CONQUEST & COLONIZATION

With the arrival of the Europeans in the 16th century, the growth of the Aztec empire came to an abrupt end. The course of Mexican history radically changed, forging a new hybrid of native and Spanish cultures.

ENTER CORTÉS

ARRIVAL

1492: Columbus sails the ocean blue.

After **Christopher Columbus** inadvertently discovered the islands of the Caribbean in 1492, a wave of Europeans flocked to Mesoamerica and began to explore and exploit the new territories. In the early 16th century, the governor of Cuba, **Diego Velázquez,** launched numerous expeditions to search for slaves and gold. Because he had heard rumors of a mighty empire on the Mexican mainland, Velázquez knew that he had to send a particularly able leader to that area. For this mission, he chose thirty-four year old **Hernán Cortés,** a native of Extremadura in Spain. In 1519, Cortés began by landing on the island of **Cozumel.** It was here that he met **Jerónimo de Aguilar,** a Spaniard held captive by the Maya for eight years and who spoke Mayan.

1519: (1 Reed) Cortés picks a good moment to arrive in Mexico. Rumors spread that he is the returned deity-king Topiltzin-Quetzal-cóatl. He is, in fact, not.

Taking Aguilar with him, Cortés made his way up the Gulf Coast, toward Tabasco. After defeating the local natives, Cortés received a reward of twenty maidens. One of these was **Malintzin** (known to the Spanish as **Doña Marina** and to the Mexicans by the traitor appellation **La Malinche**), an Aztec who had been enslaved in the southern part of the country. La Malinche could speak both Náhuatl, the Aztec language, and Mayan. Using a these two interpreters (Náhuatl to Mayan by way of La Malinche, Mayan to Spanish by Aguilar), Cortés was able overcome the language barrier. La Malinche later became Cortés's mistress and adviser. Continuing up the coast, Cortés went to the Totonac capital of **Cempoala** (see p. 514) and eastward to **Tlaxcala** (see p. 343), persuading both the Totonecs and the Tlaxcalans to join him against the Aztecs. Cortés then proceeded to **Cholula** (see p. 361), where the combined army massacred 6000 of the Aztecs' allies; the bloody slaughter was named the **Cholula Massacre.**

FALL OF THE AZTECS

The mighty Aztec emperor **Moctezuma II** had been kept abreast of Cortés's progress. According to the legend, Quetzalcóatl had told that he would return in the year One Reed, which happened to correspond to the year of 1519. Moctezuma had to grapple with rumors that Cortés was the light-skinned Toltec ruler Topiltzin-Quetzalcóatl. When Cortés finally arrived at Tenochtitlán, Moctezuma had no choice but to greet him, inviting Cortés and his men to stay as royal guests. The initial period of peaceful, though tense, relations quickly soured when Moctezuma was kidnapped by the Spanish. In retaliation, Cortés was driven from Tenochtitlán. On the night of July 1,

1520, known to the Spanish as **La Noche Triste (the Sad Night),** the Spanish were expelled from the city. Nevertheless, Cortés quickly regrouped and the Aztecs—weakened by plagues and famine and overwhelmed by the Spaniards' technology—were unable to continue fending off the Spaniards. On August 13, 1521, the Aztecs, led by their new emperor **Cuauhtémoc,** were soundly defeated at **Tlatelolco.** Tenochtitlán had fallen.

THE COLONIAL PERIOD

Soon after the fall of Tenochtitlán, the Spaniards completely sacked the vestiges of the Aztec empire and rebuilt "New Spain" from the ground up.

EXPANSION OF CONTROL

Since the Aztec empire controlled much of central Mexico, most of that area was immediately brought under automatic Spanish control. It proved substantially more difficult to rein in the rest of Mesoamerica. A slew of *conquistadores* took up the task. Others were lured into the northern parts of the country by the search for the mythical cities of gold—the so-called **Northern Mystery.** Explorations led by **Francisco Vázquez de Coronado** and **Juan Rodríguez de Cabrillo** traveled as far north as Kansas and California; their search for the fabled cities, however, proved futile.

THE PLAGUES OF MESOAMERICA. As the Spaniards pushed through Mexico, they had a helpful friend clearing the way: disease. The everyday sicknesses Spaniards carried from the Old World turned into plagues that killed millions of Indians, who no natural immunities to the diseases. **Smallpox, typhoid, and dysentery** wiped out villages leaving behind empty tracts of land, called *tierras baldás*, which settlers grabbed eagerly. Disease is now recognized as being the most important factor in allowing Europeans to conquer the peop'es of the New World.

THE ENCOMIENDA SYSTEM. As the *conquistadores* began to realize that their appetite for gold and silver would go unfulfilled, they began to demand other forms of payments, mainly in the form of Indian labor and land. Villages had to send a quota of laborers to work on the Spaniards' farms, known as **encomiendas,** and in return, the **encomendero** was given the task of Christianizing and educating them. Reports of abuse, however, were rampant.

THE RELIGIOUS CONQUEST. As soon as the Spaniards took Tenochtitlán, they razed the Aztecs' central temple and built a cathedral—now Mexico's **National Cathedral** (see p. 104)—with the rubble. Some communities tried to defend their native religions but by the mid-1500s, missionaries had converted and baptized millions. Where Roman Catholicism gained a foothold, it was interwoven with traditional practices, creating the religious fusion that persists today in many rural areas.

> ## IT'S OVER THAT A-WAY! When gold-hungry Spaniards asked for directions, the natives' most common reply was "Mas Allá!" or "Over there!" They knew full well the search was futile, but at least by leading the Spanish astray they could keep them out of their hair.

1521: Cortés overstays his welcome. Tenochtitlán falls and Moctezuma is killed. **Dead Leader Meter: 1.**

LIFE AND TIMES

1521-1600: The Spanish take over, raping land and people in their quest for gold and power. The trend continues for quite some time.

1521-1600: Millions of indigenous people die from illnesses carried by the Spanish.

1521-1600: The *encomienda* system provides the Spaniards with cheap labor.

1521-1810: The Spanish convert millions to Catholicism.

THE DARK-SKINNED VIRGIN The Virgin of Guadalupe, patron saint of Mexico, embodies the religious hybrid that characterizes the nation. In 1531, an Indian peasant named Juan Diego was visited by the virgin four times. A sanctuary was built and as news of the story grew, Guadalupe quickly gained importance, aiding in the conversion of many Indians to Christianity. Often depicted as a dark skinned woman, she brings together native beliefs with the Catholic tradition.

RACE AND CLASS. Clear racial boundaries characterized colonial society. **Peninsulares,** whites born in Spain, were at the top of the social hierarchy. **Criollos (creoles),** Spaniards born in Mexico, were considered "second-class" citizens and were overlooked for high positions in the Church and government. **Indígenas** (or **Indios**) occupied the lowest position in colonial society. Complete segregation, however, was impossible, and, within a few generations, a huge new racial group had emerged—**mestizos,** children of mixed Spanish and *indígena* parentage. This group would eventually form nearly the entire racial fabric of Mexican civilization. Today, an overwhelming majority of the population is *mestizo*.

A COUNTRY IS BORN

THE STRUGGLE FOR INDEPENDENCE

"My children: a new dispensation comes to us today. Will you receive it? Will you free yourselves? Will you recover the lands stolen three hundred years ago from your forefathers by the hated Spaniards? Will you not defend your religion and your rights as true patriots? Long live our Lady of Guadalupe! Death to bad government!"
—Miguel Hidalgo, *El Grito de Dolores*

HIDALGO AND MORELOS

The rumblings of rebellion began with **Father Miguel Hidalgo y Costilla,** a quirky and rebellious priest in the small parish of Dolores (see p. 316). With friends **Juan de Aldama, Miguel Domínguez,** and the young priest **Ignacio Allende,** Hidalgo formed a "literary club," which soon turned its thoughts from literature to revolution. When Spanish officials got wind of the revolutionary plans, they arrested Allende. Alarmed, the rest decided to strike for independence at once. On the morning of **September 16, 1810,** Hidalgo ran to church of Dolores and rang the bells to summon the parishioners. He then delivered an electrifying call to arms—**El Grito de Dolores (The Cry of Dolores)**—to end Spanish rule, to promote the equality of races, and to demand a redistribution of the land. **Mexican Independence Day** commemorates this rebellion. Hidalgo's army quickly grew, capturing several major cities before its march was stopped by a Spanish ambush in March 1811 in the desert town of Monclova in Coahuila. Hildalgo was promptly tried for treason and heresy and executed by a firing squad. Nevertheless, the quest for independence had begun. After Hidalgo's death, another parish priest, **José María Morelos y Pavón** rose to lead the inde-

1910: Hidalgo and smoking-buddies kick off the revolution with the *Grito de Dolores.*

pendence movement. Under his command, the rebels captured Oaxaca, Orizaba, and Acapulco in attempts to cut off Mexico City from both coasts. Morelos was captured and, like his predecessor Hidalgo, was tried for treason and heresy and executed by a firing squad.

INDEPENDENCE WON

The five years following the Hidalgo and Morelos uprisings were chaotic. In the Mexican countryside, rebels such as **Vicente Guerrero** and **Guadalupe Victoria** kept the Spanish busy with guerilla skirmishes. Spain's **King Ferdinand VII,** under military pressure, had sworn allegiance to the Spanish Constitution of 1812, which professed popular sovereignty and other liberal provisions. Alarmed by this new radicalism in Spain and by the countryside rebels, many Mexican conservatives and clergy decided that the best way to preserve conservative ideals would be to join the revolution, and establish their own conservative government.

The most important convert was **Agustín de Iturbide,** a *criollo* loyalist who had led Spanish troops in battle against Hidalgo. In 1820, Iturbide was given several thousand men in order to fight Guerrero in southern Mexico. Rather than fight, however, Iturbide abruptly joined forces with the revolutionaries. Over several meetings the rebel and the traitor drafted the **Plan de Iguala.** Issued on February 24, 1821, it is most remembered for its three guarantees—the creation of an independent constitutional monarchy, the universalism of Roman Catholicism, and the establishment of equality before the law. **The Ejército de las Tres Garantías (the Army of the Three Guarantees)** was brought under the direction of Iturbide and grew significantly in both numbers and support, especially from conservative *criollos*. The new Spanish general, **Juan de O'Donoju,** knew Mexico was lost to the popular uprising and on August 24, 1821, Iturbide and O'Donoju signed the **Treaty of Córdoba** formalizing the principles set forth by the Plan de Iguala and establishing Mexico as an independent country.

THE NEW NATION

ITURBIDE'S EMPIRE

The national Congress, intimidated by both Iturbide and his supporters, almost immediately voted to name him the Emperor of Mexico, and on July 21, 1822, Iturbide was coronated. The victory was bittersweet: after the decade of war the economy was in shambles, the mining industry was in disarray, and commerce was at a standstill. These problems worsened as antagonism arose between the Emperor and members of Congress, many of whom disapproved of Iturbide's *criollo* origins. Rather than address the problems, Iturbide decided to do away with Congress altogether, disbanding the assembly on October 31, 1822. Reaction was swift and immediate, and those opposed to Iturbide summoned **Antonio López de Santa Anna** to head the rebel army. On December 1, 1822, Santa Anna officially launched his revolution and soon persuaded other rebel leaders to join him. After the unification of all anti-imperialist rebels under the **Plan de Casa Mata,** Iturbide took the hint and abdicated the throne in February 1823, immediately going into European exile.

1811: Hidalgo raises an army, is swiftly captured, and has his head removed. Morelos quickly does the same. **Dead Leader Meter: 3**

1812-20: People agree: Spain is terrible. Independence movement gains ground.

1821: Iturbide converts from loyalist to revolutionary.

Revolution #1 1821: Sensing defeat, Spain signs the Treaty of Córdoba. Mexico is now independent.

1822: In a great show of immodesty, Iturbide crowns himself Emperor of Mexico.

1822: Emperor Iturbide dissolves congress. People think this is a bad idea.

1822: Santa Anna launches his first rebellion.
1823: Iturbide is exiled.

LIFE AND TIMES

1832: Deprived of attention, Santa Anna gets bored and leaves.

Revolution #3
1832-35: Santa Anna gets bored again and comes back, leading yet another rebellion

1838: Pasty chef is attacked. Angry, France declares war. Mexicans are confused, but win.

> **ALL HAIL...THE LEG?** During the Pastry War, Santa Anna's left leg was severely wounded, and the limb had to be amputated. Not a man to take a lost limb lightly, Santa Anna had the leg transported to Mexico City whereupon, after an elaborate procession, it was given a formal burial. Entombed in an urn atop a pillar, the decayed limb was serenaded and applauded by important cabinet members and diplomats who were no doubt trying to muffle incredulous laughter.

THE ERA OF SANTA ANNA

In 1832 Santa Anna won the presidential election by the largest margin in Mexican history. The great general, however, was a man more interested in the pursuit of power rather than the actual attainment of it. He soon tired of the daily minutia of the office and left the presidency in the hands of his vice president, **Valentín Goméz Farías.** The pattern would be repeated many times in Santa Anna's lifetime. Goméz Farías, a true liberal, began his presidency with anti-Church reforms designed to revitalize the country. Outraged, clergy soon began to demand his removal and summoned Santa Anna out of his self-imposed retirement. Santa Anna answered the call and was soon leading another rebellion, this one on the conservative side.

Santa Anna's new regime, as such, was conservative instead of liberal. Mexico became a central militarized state, and the colonies grew rich on graft and bribery. As Santa Anna drained the state treasuries, Mexico became unable to pay off its foreign debt, causing tensions with foreign creditors to soar. In 1838, one of the infuriated creditor nations, France, attacked Veracruz and its defending fortress, San Juan de Ulúa. The conflict was dubbed the **Pastry War** in honor of a French pastry cook whose wares had been gobbled by marauding Mexican troops. The attacking French ships were driven back to sea and ultimately forced to accept the Mexican offer of 600,000 pesos in reparation.

THE GRINGO INTERVENTION

TEXAS SECESSION

1829-36: Texas itches to secede.

Throughout the early 1800s, American citizens had been colonizing the Mexican northern province of Texas. Concerned by the influx, the Mexican government tried to restrict immigration with the **emancipation proclamation of 1829** and the **colonization law of 1830.** It was too little too late. Incensed by the laws and by the under-representation of Texas in Mexican assemblies, Texans began to demand independence.

1836: Santa Anna gets back on the horse, attempting one last hurrah.

Never one to turn his back on a good fight, Santa Anna reprised his role as general and immediately marched north with an army of 6000. In February of 1836, his troops overwhelmed Texan rebels holed up in an old Franciscan monastery at the **Alamo.** The Mexicans triumphed, killing all 150 defenders of the fortress. The battle only spurred the Texans on as shouts of "Remember the Alamo!" became a universal battle cries. Under the leadership of **Samuel Houston,** the revitalized Texans captured Santa Anna and his army on April 21, 1836. Taken prisoner, the Mexican president was forced to sign a treaty pushing back Mexican control to the Río Bravo and granting Texas its independence. The humbled Santa Anna was

1836: Santa Anna is soundly defeated.

freed shortly after his capture, and Mexico made no further attempt to reconquer Texas. Still, the country refused to recognize Texas's newly won independence.

WAR WITH THE UNITED STATES

While the US had had its eye on the Lone Star Republic for some time, it was not until 1845 that the US Congress acted to annex newly independent Texas. The move enraged the Mexican government and tensions soon escalated. After some border skirmishes, the US formally declared war in May 1846. The issue was whether the US-Mexico border would be drawn at the Río Nueces as Mexico hoped or at the Río Bravo (known to US citizens as the Rio Grande) as the US wanted. US troops quickly made headway in the north, seizing control of New Mexico, California, and Chihuahua. Forces under future US President **Zachary Taylor** moved in a more central direction, capturing Nuevo León and its capital, Monterrey. On February 21 of the following year, Taylor and Santa Anna met head to head in the **Battle of Buena Vista.** Santa Anna proved unable to stall Taylor's forces, and he was ultimately defeated.

The most ambitious invasion, however, was led by general **Winfield Scott,** who, with his 10,000 men, landed on March 9, 1847 in Veracruz. For almost a month, the Americans held the city under siege; they plundered homes, raped women, and killed civilians. Moving onward, Scott defeated another army led by Santa Anna at **Cerro Gordo** and proceeded toward Mexico City. Despite valiant fighting, the Mexicans were unable to hold the Americans back. First to fall were the neighborhoods of **Contreras** and **Churubusco** and by September 7, only the **Castle of Chapultepec** (see p. 111) was left. Ardently protected by cadets from the Military Academy, the castle stood for several days before succumbing to the unceasing American barrage. Despite the defeat, the young cadets became known throughout Mexico as the **Niños Héroes (Boy Heroes)** for their bravery and for their refusal to surrender; particular impressive was the young **Juan Escutia,** the cadet who wrapped himself in the Mexican flag and threw himself from the roof of the castle in order to avoid American capture. The heroic actions of its soldiers notwithstanding, Mexico stood defeated and divided.

GREEDY GRINGOS

Signed on February 2, 1848, the **Treaty of Guadalupe Hidalgo** officially ended the war. With it, Mexico relinquished to the United States ownership of Texas at the Río Bravo border. In addition, Mexico was forced to sell California and New Mexico to the US for the paltry sum of $19 million. This was not to be the last of the US land grab. In 1853, five years later, Santa Anna returned from exile. To raise military funds, he sold what are today Arizona and southern New Mexico for $10 million in what Americans know as the **Gadsden Purchase.** Two thousand Mexicans had died in the battle for Mexico City—only to lose half the nation's territory.

REFORM

The Reform Era paved the way for the modern country of Mexico. This was, however, hardly a time of peace and prosperity; the country was bitterly divided between liberal reformers and the conservative Catholic Church.

1836: Texas wins. Mexico pretends not to notice.

1845: US annexes Texas. Mexico is furious.

1846: US declares war on Mexico over border disputes.

1847: Winfield Scott leads an ambitious and violent invasion of Mexico. Mexico is the big loser.

1847: Mexican youth hurl themselves off Chapultepec Castle. People think this was a good thing to do.

1848: US ends war and takes a lot of Mexican land.

1853: US takes a lot more Mexican land in Gadsden purchase. Mexico is kicked when it's down.

LIFE AND TIMES

JUÁREZ AND THE LIBERALS

Revolution #4
1855: Juárez and liberal buddies push for Santa Anna's removal. Santa Anna takes a look around and resigns for good.

Several intellectual liberals—among them **Melchor Ocampo, Santos Degollado, Guillermo Prieto,** and **Benito Juárez**—had begun tinkering with the possibility of revolution. Choosing **Juan Alvarez** as their leader, the liberal exiles banded together behind the **Plan de Ayutla,** which set forth grievances against Santa Anna and called for his removal. The movement slowly gained support and in 1855, Santa Anna stepped down from office, this time permanently.

1857: Juárez and his cohorts pass complicated liberal policies. Clergy become alarmed.

Under the leadership of new president **Ignacio Comonfort,** the new leaders and began to enact liberal change. As the Minister of Justice, Juárez passed the **Ley Juárez,** which abolished old regulations protecting the military and clergy from prosecution under civil laws. The new Constitution, the **Constitution of 1857,** reflected the liberal leanings of the new leadership by declaring Mexico to be a representative democracy and a republican nation with greater rights and liberty for its people. Conservatives and religious authorities were extremely alarmed by the new Constitution. By withholding sacraments and other Catholic rites for those who swore allegiance to the document, the Church was able to extort popular allegiance. The stage was set for yet another divisive confrontation.

WAR OF THE REFORM

Revolution #5
1858: Conservative general Félix Zuloaga disbands Congress and arrests Juárez.

The **War of the Reform,** the 1858 revolt of the conservatives against the liberal reformers, was Mexico's bloodiest war to date. Conservatives banded together behind the general **Félix Zuloaga,** proclaiming dissatisfaction with the increasingly secular state. With clerical support, Zuloaga disbanded Congress, arrested Juárez, and declared himself president. While Zuloaga busied himself with repealing the liberal *leyes,* Juárez escaped to Querétaro where he established a rival government. The tide turned in favor of the liberals in 1860 when their troops defeated a conservative army at **Silao.** Another victory shortly before Christmas in the town of San Miguel Calpulalpan ensured liberal victory.

Revolution #6
1860: Juárez escapes and starts rival government. He eventually regains power.

FRENCH INTERVENTION

THE INVASION

1861: Juárez becomes Mexico's first *indígena* president. Towns clamor to name their main streets "Juárez."

The Election of 1861 returned liberal reformers to power, with Juárez winning the presidency. However, the country was economically exhausted. Convinced that Mexico would be unable to pay the huge amount of foreign debt, Juárez declared a moratorium on debt payments, once again aggravating creditor nations. With the **Convention of London in 1861,** representatives of the Spanish, British, and French monarchs agreed to occupy Veracruz in order to forcibly extract dues. After a brief occupation, Spain and Britain soon pulled out, but **Napoleon III,** nephew of the great conqueror, had imperialistic ambitions in mind, and ordered his troops to march toward the capital. The first confrontation occurred on **May 5, 1862** when outnumbered Mexican troops under the command of general Ignacio Zaragoza successfully repelled the French soldiers from the city of Puebla (see p. 351). **Cinco de Mayo** is now a national holiday that commemorates this triumph. Despite the rousing victory, the French regrouped and came back a year later. With the subsequent fall of Puebla, Mexico City was doomed. On May 31, 1863, it surrendered to the French.

1862: Angry over unpaid debt, Napoleon III tries to be like his uncle.

CRAZY CARLOTA Maximilian was a sensible fellow, but his wife, Charlotte (in Spanish, Carlota) has gone down in Mexican history as a woman a few bolts short of a tool kit. In 1867, with the knowledge that her husband's regime was about to topple, Carlota left Mexico to appeal directly to Napoleon III. Her pleas were ignored and, guilt-ridden and depressed, the 26-year old Carlota really lost it. Convinced that Napoleon was trying to poison her, she tied up chickens in her room and refused to eat anything but the eggs they laid or drink anything but water fetched directly from the Trevi Fountain in Rome. Carlota was institutionalized soon thereafter, but survived to the ripe old age of 86. Dying in 1927, she survived nearly every other person involved in the French Intervention.

FRENCH RULE

To rule over Mexico, Napoleon chose the Austrian archduke **Ferdinand Maximilian** of Hapsburg, a man of noble birth and naïve ideologies. Maximilian was moderately liberal and anti-Catholic, but his policies angered conservatives, and what little popularity he had soon began to evaporate. Juárez was in the meantime looking for help from the US, which was eager to eliminate European imperialism in the western hemisphere. The US eagerly provided mercenaries and weapons, and the rebel army began to gain strength. Understanding the futility of his position, Napoleon withdrew his troops in 1867. Maximilian, left without French support, surrendered in Querétaro on May 15, 1867 and, like so many Mexican rulers before him, was executed.

1863-67: Maximilian is set up as emperor. He is somewhat inept.

RESTORATION

Juárez returned to the capital on July 15, 1867 and won a third term to the presidency. He set about improving the country's education and infrastructure; for the first time, education was made free and compulsory. Despite the progress, Juárez narrowly defeated **Sebastían Lerdo de Tejada** and the general **Porfirio Díaz** in the 1871 election. Díaz disputed the election of Juárez to a fourth term, but Juárez died shortly thereafter, automatically making Lerdo the next president. On November 16, 1876, Díaz made a grab at power, defeating federal troops at Tecoac in Tlaxcala. After Lerdo fled to the United States, Díaz triumphantly made his way to Mexico City, occupying the capital on November 21, 1876 and refusing to leave it for over 30 years.

Revolution #6 1867: Maximilian surrenders to Juárez. He is executed. **Dead Leader Meter: 4.**

1867-75: With Juárez back in power, times are good.

THE PORFIRIATO

Mexico flourished under the Díaz regime, known as the **Porfiriato** or the **Pax Porfirinana.** Transportation expanded, duties were slashed, the gold standard eliminated, and useless bureaucrats dismissed. Aided by Mexico's new railroad system, mining entered a golden age. Profitable ore and copper mines gave seed to the extravagant haciendas which still dot those regions. Many, however, grew increasingly discontent with the power of the Díaz dictatorship, which was hierarchical, corrupt, and oppressive. Díaz's personal army corps, the **rurales,** blanketed the countryside, enforcing Díaz's rule. Local governments were mere Díaz puppets; **jefes politicos,** Díaz's local bosses, had most of the true power. As industry prospered and land values sky-

1876: Porfirio Díaz grabs power. He will hold it for a very long time.

1876-1910: Porfiratorio. The country prospers, but people are oppressed and cynical.

rocketed, the gap between rich and poor widened. Indians suffered the most. Under a new law, they could be forced to sell their lands if they couldn't provide a legal title. By the turn of the century, most villages saw their land taken by wealthy individuals and companies. In addition, the **cientificos**—as Díaz's advisors were called—believed that the Indians were weak, immoral, and ineducable.

REVOLUTION

THE DÍAZ DOWNFALL

1910: Madero, like many others, is unhappy with Porfy. He calls for another revolution.

In the 1910 presidential election, Díaz faced a strong opponent. **Francisco Madero**, a wealthy *hacienda* owner from Coahuila, ran on an anti-re-election platform and was openly critical of the Díaz regime. Madero was soon apprehended and thrown into prison, and Díaz was declared landslide victor. After his family posted bail, Madero fled to Texas, where he came to the realization that only through force would any social change be enacted. On October 5, 1910, he issued the **Plan de San Luis Potosí,** proclaiming the time had come for a revolution.

1910: Aquiles Serdán is killed by Díaz's thugs. **Dead Leader Meter: 5.**

Madero was not, however, the first to strike. Two days earlier, the home of a Puebla leader, **Aquiles Serdán,** was discovered to house a large stash of artillery. Killed in an ambush, Serdán and his family became the revolution's early martyrs. While Díaz's minions cracked down, forces under the control of **Emiliano Zapata, Pascual Orozco,** and **Pancho Villa** used guerilla tactics to keep the revolutionary movement growing in the south and in the north. After the fall of Ciudad Juárez (see p. 220) on May 10, 1911, Díaz knew the jig was up, and resigned four days later.

REVOLUTIONARY GOVERNMENTS

MADERO

Revolution #7 (*The* Revolution) 1911: Madero, with the help of Orozco, Villa, and Zapata, forces Díaz out of power. The Porfiriato is through.

The Election of 1911 ushered in Madero and his vice president, **José María Pino Suárez.** In theory, the government tried to improve education, infrastructure, and labor regulation. In reality, Madero was sidetracked by rebel skirmishes and hostile politicians. Dissatisfied, on November 25, 1911, Zapata, the rebel from Morelos, proclaimed his own agrarian program, the **Plan of Ayala,** which disavowed Madero as president. Other revolts followed, most ending with the offending revolutionary tossed in jail.

On February 9, 1913, the tide changed permanently. **Manuel Mondragón,** a general in Madero's army, released two of the rebels, **Bernardo Reyes** and **Félix Díaz** (nephew of the former dictator), from prison; Reyes was promptly slain, but Díaz assumed control of the rebel forces. For the next ten days, known as the **Decena Trágica,** Mexico City was terrorized by fighting between Díaz and the federal general **Victoriano Huerta.**

1911: Madero takes power but is ineffective. Rebels cause trouble.

WHERE THE STREETS HAVE THOSE NAMES
Recognize most of these names? That's probably because nearly every Mexican city has an Av. Aquiles Serdán, a Calle Madero, a Blvd. Obregón, an Av. Benito Juárez, a Calle Zapata, a Calz. Orozco, and an Av. Pino Suárez.

On the tenth day, however, Huerta surprisingly switched sides, joining the rebels in the **Pact of the Embassy,** so called because of the US Embassy's role in organizing the agreement. The unified army then marched the National Palace (see p. 104) where Madero and vice-president Suárez were immediately taken as prisoners and shot. Huerta assumed the presidency that day.

THE HUERTA REGIME

The Huerta presidency was known for its cruelty and intolerance, and opposition rose quickly. Under the **Plan de Guadalupe, Pancho Villa, Alvaro Obregón,** and **Venustiano Carranza** joined forces. These **Constitutionalists** protested the illegal oust of Madero and Huerta's treachery. To the south, in the state of Morelos, forces under Zapata also fought Huerta; their primary grievance was Huerta's refusal to redistribute land to the Indians. Domestic pressures aside, it was foreign intervention that eventually caused Huerta's fall. After an international diplomatic *faux pas* involving American sailors in Veracruz, US President **Woodrow Wilson** ordered an invasion of the city. Huerta was forced to rush troops to Veracruz, leaving a military vacuum in the rest of the country. It was during this distraction that Pancho Villa captured the city of Zacatecas. Realizing his precarious position, Huerta resigned on July 8, 1914.

THE CARRANZA REGIME

REBEL CONTROL. Following Huerta's resignation, various civil wars played out over the entire country. Obregón held the capital, Carranza controlled Veracruz, Villa ruled the north, and Zapata held the south. Mexico was governed by four separate governments, all clamoring for official recognition. At the **Battle of Celaya,** Villa attempted to wrest control of the capital from Obregón. Obregón was ready, and 4000 Villistas were impaled or wounded on barbed-wire entrenchments. His reputation tarnished, Villa escaped toward the US-Mexico border where, angered by the American decision to recognize the Carranza government, he took his revenge on several US towns. (Some jokingly call these raids the only successful invasion of the US mainland by a foreign power.) In return, the US sent General **John J. Pershing** on a long and fruitless search for Villa.

THE CONSTITUTION OF 1917. The rebel fighting had left no clear victor, but Carranza was able to consolidate strength in the east and northeast parts of the country, and in 1917, he called for a new constitution. The remarkably liberal **Constitution of 1917** declared that private ownership of land was a privilege, not a right, and that lands seized from *pueblos* during the Porfiriato should be returned. Workers were guaranteed better conditions and the right to strike. Carranza won the special elections in held in March 1917, but failed to implement most of his radical document.

ZAPATA ASSASSINATED. In order to dispense with his most ardent critic, Carranza cooked up an elaborate scheme to assassinate Emiliano Zapata. On April 10, 1919, an unsuspecting Zapata walked into a presumed surrender only to be shot down in cold blood. Zapata was dispatched, but Obregón remained, still causing trouble in the northern states. He formed an alliance with **Adolfo de la Huerta** and **Plutarco Elías Calles,** and declared yet another revolt under the banner of yet another plan, this one the **Plan de Agua Prieta.**

Revolution #8 1913: Madero and his VP are killed. Huerta seizes power. **Dead Leader Meter: 7.**

1913-14: Huerta is not a nice man. Villa, Obregón, and Carranza unite against him.

Revolution #9 ...#9...#9 1914: Huerta's resources are diverted when the US invades Veracruz. The rebels take over.

1914-16: Four governments vie for control. Things are complicated.

1915-1916: Villa successfully "invades" the US. Americans are not amused.

1917: Carranza takes the helm.

1919: Carranza kills Zapata in a complex way. **Dead Leader Meter: 8.**

1919: Someone is named "Plutarco."

OBREGÓN AND CALLES

1924: In unprecedented fashion, Obregón willfully lets power pass to Calles. **Peacefully Retired Leader Meter: 1.**

Alarmed at the turn of events, Carranza fled the capital, but was killed while fleeing. Obregón took the helm. During his time, he poured his energies into a impressive expansion of the rural school system. Still, Obregón's most impressive achievement may have been his willingness to hand power over to Calles, who won the Election of 1924. Calles was succeeded by a line of puppet presidents completely under his control. Known during this time as the **Jefe Máximo,** Calles created the **Partido Nacional Revolucionario (PNR),** which in one form or another has run Mexico since 1929.

CÁRDENAS

1934: Cárdenas, supposedly a puppet of Calles, instead deports him.

1938: Cárdenas creates PEMEX. Foreign oil guzzlers are thwarted.

The Election of 1934 saw the coming of another great figure in Mexican history, **Lázaro Cárdenas.** Cárdenas, groomed to be one of Calles' puppets, won independent support and in 1936 had the *Jefe* deported to the US. Cárdenas then busied himself by redistributing some 44 million acres—twice as many as all of his predecessors combined—to thousands of Indians. Perhaps his most lasting accomplishment was the creation of a national oil company, **Petróleos Mexicanos (PEMEX),** as a means of regulating the industry and keeping it free from foreign pressures. While PEMEX was slow in accomplishing Cárdenas's economic goals, it did electrify Mexican national pride. Lastly, Cárdenas immeasurably strengthened the ruling party, which he renamed the **Partido de la Revolución Mexicana (PRM).**

POST-WWII

MID-CENTURY

CAMACHO, ALEMÁN, AND CORTINES

1940-58: A slew of uninteresting presidents are elected.

In 1940, **Avila Camacho,** an avid industrialist, followed Cárdenas. During the war, Camancho supported the Allied cause by pledging Mexican natural resources such as copper, lead, zinc, and human labor. He, like Cárdenas, also couldn't resist fiddling with the party's name, changing it to the **Partido Revolucionario Institucional (PRI),** the party's modern name. He was seceded in 1946 by **Miguel Alemán,** the first civilian president since Carranza. Alemán built dams and hydroelectric stations, and completed of Mexico's segment of the Pan-American highway. In addition, Alemán oversaw the completion of the modern campus of the **Universidad Autónoma Nacional de México,** (**UNAM,** see p. 120), a marvel of modern art and architecture. Alemán's successor, **Adolfo Ruiz Cortines,** was similar in ideology. Between 1952 and 1960, he pushed through public works projects begun by Alemán, and used the office to expand the social service clinics. It was also during his administration that women finally won the right to vote.

THOSE TURBULENT 60S

1958: Young, dashing Adolfo López Mateos is elected. A hippie before his time, he pushes government left.

The Election of 1958 saw the emergence of a different PRI candidate. **Adolfo López Mateos** was both younger and more energetic than any of his predecessors and approached the presidency with infectious enthusiasm. Stepping up land redistribution and using presidential power to support labor movements, López Mateos nudged the government slightly to the left. **Gustavo Díaz Ordaz,** a more conservative leader, presided over a troubled time. In the summer of 1968, rioting broke out in several of Mexico City's universities, most prominently at the UNAM. Things reached crisis levels in **Tlatelolco Plaza** (or **Plaza de las Tres Culturas,** see p. 114), where police killed an estimated 400 peaceful demonstrators and jailed another 2000 just 10 days before the 1968 Olympics were to open in Mexico City. The 1970 election of **Luis Echeverría** did little to relieve the dissatisfaction many Mexicans felt. Inflation skyrocketed and foreign debt hampered the growth of Mexico's economy.

1968: Police kill an estimated 400 student protestors in the Tlatelolco Massacre.
1970: Echeverría lets things get out of hand.

MEXICO IN MODERN TIMES

The Election of 1976 ushered in **José López Portillo,** who inherited a slew of economic problems. In an effort to slow the overheated economy, Portillo nationalized fifty-nine banks in 1982. Still, the economic woes spilled over into the presidency of **Miguel de la Madrid,** who was beleaguered by both economic and political problems. Foreign debt multiplied, and in response Madrid slashed thousands of government jobs. Perhaps the biggest blow to the Madrid administration was the **1985 Mexico City earthquake;** the quake, which registered an 8 on the Richter scale, killed thousands and left the country more shaken than the peso.

1976-88: López Portillo and de la Madrid try to bail out Mexico. They fail.
1985: An earthquake hits Mexico City, killing thousands.
2000: *Let's Go* makes a bad joke.

SALINAS

When the Harvard-educated **Carlos Salinas de Gortari** was elected in 1988, amid allegations of fraud, the country was faced with high unemployment, a drug crisis, and a $105 billion foreign debt.

1988: Salinas elected. He does his very best to save the economy, but people are too preoccupied with his bald head.

ECONOMIC REFORMS AND NAFTA. Salinas immediately tried to spur the economy, instituting wage and price controls, privatizing businesses, and halting land redistribution. In January 1992, Mexico agreed to enter into the **North American Free Trade Agreement (NAFTA),** which created a unified free trade zone between the US, Canada, and Mexico. The treaty attempted to attract foreign capital and to make Mexican industry more competitive by eliminating the tariffs, quotas, and subsidies that had existed since the 1940s. Whether NAFTA actually succeed in helping Mexican industry or whether it simply flooded the Mexican market with US goods remains to be seen.

1994: NAFTA. Everyone is confused.

REBELLION IN CHIAPAS. The economic reforms proposed by Salinas did not please all segments of the population. On January 1, 1994, the day NAFTA went into effect, a force of angry Maya rebels captured the city of San Cristóbal de las Casas (see p. 545) and held it in a twelve-day siege. Named the **Ejército Zapatista de Liberación Nacional (EZLN),** or the **Zapatista National Liberation Army,** the army was comprised of over 9000 Maya peasants and was led by the eloquent masked guerilla **Subcomandante Marcos**—later revealed to be **Rafael Sebastián Guillén Vicente,** a university-educated Marxist. The Zapatistas called for a complete government overhaul and free elections. Months of negotiations followed with the Bishop of Chiapas, **Samuel Ruiz,** eventually mediating a tenuous compromise.

1994: Displeased with NAFTA, Maya rebels in Chiapas hold San Cristóbal under siege.

ZEDILLO

The Zapatista uprising foreshadowed more problems to come. In March 1994, PRI presidential candidate **Luis Donaldo Colosio** was assassinated as he left a rally in Tijuana and his murder was never solved. To replace Colosio, the PRI chose reform-minded Budget Minister **Ernesto Zedillo Ponce de Léon.**

1994: Colosio assassinated, Zedillo takes charge. **Dead Leader Meter: 9.**

1994: The peso is in dire straits.

PESO CRISIS.

Just months into his presidency, Zedillo was faced with a precipitous drop in the value of the peso. Bailed out by a $20 billion loan from the US government, Mexico was salvaged from the depths of economic crisis. Nevertheless, interest rates soared and inflation accelerated, bringing the banking system to near collapse.

1994-97: Zedillo fights drugs and refuses to pick a successor.

1997: Cuauhtémoc Cárdenas, who has a fun name, becomes an important non-PRI governor.

REFORM AND CHANGE.

Undaunted, Zedillo moved from economic disaster to governmental reform. He formally ended the PRI tradition of the **degazo,** the practice of the incumbent president choosing his successor. Zedillo arrested several high-level officials on charges of conspiracy and murder, earning US endorsement as a "partner in the war on drugs." The July 1997 election provided evidence that the reforms were working. **Cuauhtémoc Cárdenas** of the **Partido de la Revolución Democrática (PRD)** won a landslide victory in the race for governorship of the State of Mexico, and the PRI lost its majority in the lower house of Congress for the first time in 68 years.

THE CHANGING OF THE GUARD

2000: Vicente Fox, who is very tall, is elected president. The PRI loses power for the first time since 1929. Zedillo retires peacefully . **Peacefully Retired Leader Meter: 2.**

The momentous reforms enacted by the Zedillo administration paved the way for the PRI's defeat. "A Crowning Defeat—Mexico as the Victor," cried the *New York Times* on July 4, 2000, a day after opposition candidate **Vicente Fox Quesada** defeated the groomed PRI candidate **Francisco Labastida Ochoa** 46% to 36%. The tall, bombastic Fox, a former Coca-Cola executive and Guanajuato governor, ran as a candidate of the conservative **Partido de Accion Nacional (PAN)** on the platform of opening trade, increasing wages and foreign investments, slashing bureaucracy, eliminating corruption, and returning the country to its Catholic roots. The contest, declared by many international observers as the cleanest Mexican election ever, was hard-fought with mud-slinging galore; Fox questioned his opponent's virility while Labastida ridiculed Fox's divorced status. When the dust settled, Fox emerged as the surprising victor, and the humbled PRI was forced out of power.

2000: *Let's Go* ponders the future.

Mexico continues to be plagued with problems, and only history will tell whether Fox will succeed in implementing his conservative agenda and getting the sluggish economy moving again. Legacy aside, though, history will never be able to erase Fox's most lasting legacy—breaking the longest hold one party has ever had on a modern government. And so, Mexico enters the 21st century with fresh leadership for a new century.

IT COULD HAVE BEEN TELENOVELA

Sex. Lies. Bad haircuts. Even the best *telenovela* screenwriters would have been hard pressed to come up with a plot as thick and intertwined as the one that enveloped the Salinas family in the mid-90s. In February 1995, it was revealed that **Raul Salinas de Gortari,** Carlos's brother, had been the mastermind behind the murder of their former brother-in-law, **José Francisco Ruiz Massieu.** Further investigations began to link Raul with drug cartels in the Gulf Coast, with large foreign bank accounts, and with presidential kickbacks. His reputation tarnished and his balding head mocked mercilessly, former president Carlos was forced into exile in Ireland. This is the stuff soaps are made of.

PEOPLE AND CULTURE

ETHNICITY AND LANGUAGE

Mexico's heterogeneity is largely grounded in history. The Spanish conquest was responsible for creating the nation's largest ethnic group, the **mestizos**—persons of mixed indigenous and European blood—who now comprise 60% of the population. The term *"mestizo,"* however, has come to have such varied meanings that the Mexican census no longer uses it as a category. **Criollos**—light-skinned Mexicans of pure European descent—make up around 9% of the population and are concentrated in urban areas and in the north. **Indígenas**—sometimes referred to by the politically incorrect appellation **Indios**—comprise about 25-30% of the population and to this day are the majority in most rural areas, particularly in the southern half of the country.

Mexico's official language is Castilian (Spanish), spoken smoothly and without the lisp that characterizes speakers from Spain. Large numbers of people, almost always *indígenas*, still speak some form of native language. In the Valley of Mexico, one can often hear the Aztec language, **Náhuatl;** in the Yucatán Peninsula and Chiapas, **Mayan** is frequently spoken in villages and markets; **Zapotec** is still spoken in the Oaxaca Valley. The 50 native languages, spoken by over 100,000 people in the country, are emblematic of Mexico's unique cultural identity.

FAITH AND RELIGION

Mexico is a Catholic country. Although religion is never explicitly mentioned in the Constitution, Mexico's Catholic consciousness permeates the country and unites the population. Walk around village streets, and you'll pass wooden crosses and roadside shrines dedicated to the Virgin. Ride in a Mexico City taxi cab (*sitio*, of course) and you might see a rosary hanging from the rearview mirror. Shop in the supermarket; you'll see polychrome candles depicting Christ and the saints. Step inside a parish church and discover dozens of devout Mexicans, crossing themselves and whispering. With around 90% of the population Catholic, Mexico is a country devoted to its faith. This faith, however, fused with native traditions, has created an altogether distinct flavor of Catholicism. The best example of this syncretism is the **Virgin of Guadalupe** (see p. 56), the dark-sinned apparition of the Virgin Mary that prompted the conversion of thousands of Indians in the 16th century. Moreover, recent years have seen a developing interest in native faiths, perhaps prompted by new archaeological research and a new embrace of Mexican indigenous identity. Aztec symbols have become synonymous with nationalism and Mexican pride. The famous Aztec **Sun Stone,** for example, adorns everything from belt buckles to soccer jerseys. Recent years have also seen the increasing presence of Protestantism. Although only about 6% of the population is Protestant, the numbers are on the rise, perhaps thanks to missionary activity. Other faiths—while not as well represented in Mexico as in the rest of the world—are increasing in numbers, particularly Judaism and Pentecostalism.

ART AND ARCHITECTURE

Mexican art is generally classified into three periods: the **Indigenous** (6000 BC-AD 1525), the **Colonial** (1525-1810), and the **Modern** (1810-present). Art created before the Spanish invasion is studied by archaeologists; for the most part, no written commentary on artistic expression exists from the time before the Conquest. With the arrival of the Spanish, Mexican art changed dramatically and was heavily influenced by new styles and interpretations, a trend that has endured through the Modern period.

THE PRE-HISPANIC ERA

Much of the art and architecture from this period has provided the basis for under-standing early Mexican history (see **Pre-Hispanic Societies,** p. 49). Some aspects of Pre-Hispanic styles were prevalent across Mexico. The use of **stone** is perhaps one of the most noticeable. The Olmecs shaped basalt into the colossal heads for which they are famous. The Maya used limestone and sandstone all over their cit-ies, as building blocks for palaces and temples, stelae (upright stone monuments often inscribed with glyphs and reliefs), and altars. Cities such as Teotihuacán, Tula, and Tenochtitlán show the continued use of monumental stone architecture in their buildings, carved reliefs, and statuary.

On a smaller scale, some of the most impressive pieces of Pre-Hispanic art would fit in your hand. **Carved jade** and **ceramic figurines** are plentiful from the very beginnings of Mexican culture through the Colonial period. Maya gods and nobil-ity are often depicted adorned with massive headdresses replete with lengthy feathers, necklaces of beads the size of eggs, and gold and copper bracelets to match the enormous bangles hanging from their earlobes. Much of the information gained from art such as stone monuments or small carved objects pertains only to the elite members of those societies; much less material has been recovered from the non-elite segments of these cultures.

Besides buildings and monuments, a final form of creative expression used by Pre-Hispanic peoples is **narrative depiction. Murals** such as those covering the walls at the Maya site of Bonampak reveal scenes of warfare, sacrifice, and celebration. **Frescoes** on interior walls of buildings at Teotihuacán depict, among other sub-jects, paradise scenes, floral arrangements, religious rituals, and athletic events. Scenes painted onto the **pottery** of all of these cultures depict mythological stories. Other reliefs and objects reveal calendrical events and dates—the famous **Aztec Sun Stone** is a prime example. This prophetic calender measures nearly four meters in diameter. Within its concentric rings are contained the four symbols of previous suns—rain, jaguars, wind, and fire—the plagues responsible for the destruction of earlier populations. The Aztecs believed that they were living in the period of the fifth sun, and they expected to be obliterated by an earthquake—the symbol for which also ominously appears on the stone.

THE ARCHITECTURE OF NEW SPAIN

Not surprisingly, the first examples of **colonial art** were created specifically to facil-itate religious indoctrination of the *indígenas* as quickly as possible. Churches were often constructed on top of pre-existing temples and pyramids. Volcanic stone, plentiful in most areas, was the main building material. Colonial architec-ture, recalling **Romanesque** and **Gothic** stylistic elements, is characterized by the use of huge buttresses, arches, and crenelations (indented or embattled mold-ings). An early architectural development was the open chapel *(capilla abierta)*, a group of arches enclosing an atrium.

Monasteries and churches under the direction of **Franciscan, Dominican,** and **Augustinian** missionaries were built according to climatic and geographic limita-tions. The Franciscan style tended to be functional and economic, while the Dominican style was more ascetic and harsh, due to earthquake danger and warm weather. Augustinian style was the most free-spirited and grandiose, and archi-tects indulged in gratuitous and excessive decoration whenever possible. Remark-able Augustinian buildings include the **Monastery of St. Augustín of Acolman** near Mexico City, and the **Monastery of Actopán** in Hidalgo.

A BLOSSOMING OF THE BAROQUE

The steady growth and spread of the Catholic Church throughout the 17th and 18th centuries necessitated the construction of cathedrals, parochial chapels, and convents. Moreover, this period brought the Baroque style to New Spain. Luxuri-ous **Baroque** facades, teeming with dynamic images of angels and saints, aimed to produce a feeling of awe and respect in the hearts of the recently converted *indí-*

genas. The narratives set in stone could be understood even by *los analfabetos* (the illiterate people) and easily committed to memory. A look at the cathedrals of Zacatecas and Chihuahua reveals the degree of artistry Baroque ideals encouraged. Baroque painting found its quintessential expression in the works of **Alonso López de Herrera** and **Baltazar de Echave Orio** (the elder).

Sumptuousness, frivolity, and ornamentation became more prevalent in the works of the late 18th-century artists and builders who couldn't get too much of a good thing. During this time, the **Churrigueresque** style was born and **Mexican High Baroque** was carried to the extreme. A hallmark of this style is the intricately decorated *estípites* (pilasters), often installed merely for looks, not support.

20TH CENTURY

As the Revolution reduced their land to shambles, Mexican painters developed an unapologetic national style. This success was made possible by **José Vasconcelos's** Ministry of Education program, which commissioned *muralistas* to create their art on the walls of hospitals, colleges, schools, and ministries. Vasconcelos also sent the artists into the countryside to teach and participate in rural life.

The Mexican **mural**, unequivocally nationalistic in its current form, dates back to the early days of the Conquest when Catholic evangelists, who could not communicate with the *indígenas*, used allegorical murals to teach them the rudiments of Christian iconography. **Diego Rivera**, the most renowned of the *muralistas*, based his artwork on political themes—land reform, Marxism, and the marginalization of *indígena* life. Rivera used stylized realism to portray the dress, action, and expression of the Mexican people, and natural realism (complete with ugly faces, knotted brows, and angry stances) to represent Spaniards and other oppressors of the *indígenas*. His innovative blend of Mexican history and culture reached a wide audience and embroiled him in international controversy.

Though Rivera is credited as the first to forge the path for *muralistas*, many other artists have contributed to the definition of the art form and have thus achieved national recognition. Some of the best-known *muralistas* include: **David Álfaro Siqueiros,** who brought new materials and dramatic revolutionary themes to his murals; the Cubism-influenced **Rufino Tamayo,** arguably the most abstract of the *muralistas*; and **José Clemente Orozco,** whose murals in Mexico City and lifelike plaster-of-paris skeleton characters have won him a great deal of fame.

Not all 20th-century Mexican artists have exchanged the traditional canvas for walls. **Juan Soriano,** by combining vanguard and traditional Mexican art, forged a name for himself as a painter and sculptor. Due in part to her incredible talent and **Hayden Herrera's** landmark biography, **Frida Kahlo** (1907-54) surpasses many Mexican artists in current worldwide recognition. Kahlo's paintings and self-portraits are icons of pain: the viewer is forced to confront the artist's self-obsession in its most violent and extreme manifestations.

LITERATURE

PRE-HISPANIC WRITING

As far as linguists and archaeologists have been able to tell, two languages were dominant in Mexico before the arrival of the Spanish: **Náhuatl** and **Mayan.** The earliest examples of writing are thought to be the glyphs inscribed at **San José Mogote** and **Monte Albán,** Oaxaca—two sites containing reliefs perhaps dating back to 600 BC. The destructiveness of the Conquest, particularly in its initial years, and the imposition of the Spanish language resulted in the loss of valuable information relating to *indígena* language. Considered a dangerous affront to Christian teachings, Maya and Aztec **codices** (unbound "books" or manuscripts) were fed to the flames. But due to the foresight of some indigenous leaders as well as a handful of missionaries, a number of Maya and Aztec codices did survive. Other historical works such as the **Books of Chilam Balam** (Books of the Jaguar Priest) and the

Annals of the Cakchiquel cover a range of topics. They are not exclusively historical works, but are instead narrative and poetic, laden with symbolism and lofty metaphor. The **Rabinal Achi** (Knight of Achi), the story of a sacrificed warrior, is considered to be the only surviving example of Pre-Hispanic drama.

COLONIAL LITERATURE

Surrounded by a New World, the Spanish were eager to send news home about the land they had conquered and the Mexican way of life. These letters home, among them Cortés' **Cartas de Relación** (Letters of Relation), were mainly Crown- and Church-flattering documents detailing the exhaustive ongoing efforts being undertaken to educate and Christianize *indígenas*. Other chronicles, such as the *Nuevo Mundo y Conquista* (New World and Conquest), by **Francisco de Terrazas,** and *Grandeza Mexicana* (Mexican Grandeur), by **Bernardo de Balbuena,** were written in rhyme in order to take the edge off the monotonous stream of facts.

Although historical texts dominated Mexico's literary output throughout much of the 16th and 17th centuries, poets made substantial achievements. **Sor Juana Inés de la Cruz** (1648-1695), a *criolla* of illegitimate birth who turned to the church to satisfy her intellectual curiosity, became a master lyricist known for her razor-sharp wit. Her most famous works are *Respuesta a Sor Filotea* (Response to Sor Filotea) and *Hombres Necios* (Injudicious Men). Her love poems display a passionate outlook, and many verses display a feminist sensibility ahead of their time.

STRUGGLING FOR A LITERARY IDENTITY

By the end of the 18th century, the struggle for independence became the singular social fact from which many Mexican texts grew. In 1816, **José Fernández de Lizardi,** a prominent Mexican journalist, wrote the first Latin American novel: **El Periquillo Sarniento** (The Itching Parrot), a tale that revealed Mexican society's displeasure with the status quo. His ideological, moralizing fiction was very influential. With the Spanish-American modernists of the 19th century, poetry reached a level it had not achieved since Sor Juana in **Manuel Gutierrez Nájera's** composition *De Blanco* (On Whiteness), a linguistic representation at its most distilled and self-contained.

Many romantic novels of the period used historical themes to introduce sweeping indictments of the military and clergy. Novelists sought to define Mexico's national identity, glorifying strength, progress, secularism, and education. Artists were didactic, producing works with such inspirational titles as *Triumph of Study Over Ignorance*. Whereas European Romanticism was an aesthetic challenge to Neoclassicism, Mexican Romanticism was an artistic response to the country's political and social realities. Shortly after the heyday of the Romantic novel came the popular novel of manners, most notably *El Fistol del Diablo* by **Manuel Payno,** and *Juanita Sousa* and *Antón Pérez* by **Manuel Sánchez Mármol.**

Literature during the **Porfiriato** (1876-1911) abandoned Romanticism for realism, and most writers expressed little sympathy for the poor. Others adopted a Modernist style, emphasizing language and imagery, and replacing didactic social themes with psychological topics. Visual artists, by contrast, began to reject the creed of the *científicos*. Many favored experimental techniques and chose to depict slums, brothels, and scenes from indigenous life. Their iconoclasm foreshadowed a growing dissatisfaction with the Díaz regime.

20TH-CENTURY GLOBAL PERSPECTIVES

Mexican literature in the Post-Revolutionary era is marked by a frustrated desire to forge a national tradition from the vestiges of pre-colonial culture. Nobel prize winner **Octavio Paz,** in such works as *El Laberinto de la Soledad* (The Labyrinth of Solitude), draws on Marxism, Romanticism, and post-Modernism to explore the making and unmaking of a national archetype. Paz, like his equally famous successor **Carlos Fuentes,** concerns himself with myths and legends in an effort to come to terms with Spanish cultural dominance. Fuentes published his first novel, *La region más transparente*, in 1958. Of late, the work of female writers, such as

Hollywood darling **Laura Esquivel** *(Like Water for Chocolate*, see p. 69), has been well received both nationally and internationally. **Elena Poniatowska,** the author of *Tinisma*—a novel about the life of another famous Mexican author, **Tina Modotti,** who was a secret agent for the Soviet Union during the Spanish Civil War—is making a name for herself in the world of Latin American writers. In the past two decades, a new literary movement has emerged from Mexico—the **Chicano movement.** Chicano literature describes the experiences of Latinos who come to the United States and must overcome numerous barriers to adapt to the new culture. Many Chicano authors are rapidly gaining respect in the international community. **Sandra Cisneros's** *House on Mango Street*—a novel narrated by an eleven-year-old girl who talks about her life on both sides of the Mexican border—has made Cisneros one of the most recognized Chicana authors today. Other Chicano writers such as **Américo Paredes** have used their status as Chicano authors to put traditional Mexican folklore into written form. In *With His Pistol in His Hands*, Paredes put into written form the story of **Gregorio Cortez,** a Mexican who was persecuted by the US judicial system for shooting a sheriff in self-defense. The ballad of Gregorio Cortez has since become an inspirational story to Mexicans.

POPULAR CULTURE

MUSIC

Every aspect of Mexican life is filled with music—in fine restaurants, at public events, on street corners where people gather around a local *gutarrista*. To understand Mexican music is to understand the heart of the nation, and when you feel moved by the spirit (or the tequila), stand with your legs shoulder-width apart, throw your head back, and cry "ay, ay, ay..." along with the music.

FOLK MUSIC

On the bus rides, in local bars, and on the street, you will hear three major types of traditional Mexican music:

CORRIDOS. Corridos, usually sung by guitar-plucking troubadours, remain truest to their folk origins. Grown out of oral storytelling, *corridos* recount the epic deeds of famous, infamous, and occasionally fictional figures from Mexico's past. A *corridista* may additionally function as a walking newspaper, singing songs about the latest natural disaster, political scandal, or any other decisive event.

RANCHEROS. Born in a fit of nationalistic fervor following the Revolution, **rancheras** were originally conceived as "songs of the people," dealing with matters of work, love, and land. Once performed with marimba and flute, *rancheras* are now more backed by the guitar and trumpets of *mariachi* bands. The songs are characterized by a passionate, sincere singing style, with final notes dragged out. Like American country/western music, today's *rancheras* are sentimental songs about down-and-out towns, faithful dogs, and love gone wrong. **Norteños** are a type of *ranchera* strongly influenced by polka, and *norteño* bands such as **Los Tigres del Norte** kick it accordion style. Some even feature utensil-based percussion.

MARIACHI. The black-and-red-clad men with bells and capes—the same ones that appear on tequila ads outside of Mexico—are **mariachis.** The most famous of Mexican music, *mariachi* music is lively and light-hearted, with bright guitar and energetic horn sections. Nowdays much of Mexican music, even lonesome *corridos*, are performed with *mariachi* backing. Wandering *mariachis* will strike up in front of restaurants and play at traditional *fiestas*. The world-famous tradition of women being serenaded by a group of *mariachis* in traditional Mexican garb is an almost obligatory supplement to a romantic evening—foreplay, if you will. Traditional *mariachi* music may deal with one or several of the following topics: being very drunk, loving a woman, being abandoned by a woman, wanting to get drunk, needing a woman, pondering the fidelity of one's horse, loving one's gun, and marveling at one's own stupefying virility. In their more somber (and sober) moments, *mariachis* have also been known to sing of death, politics, and revolutionary history.

OTHER MUSIC

In addition to the *corridos, rancheras,* and *mariachi,* Mexican music along the east-central coast and continuing into the Yucatán carries a strong dose of Afro-Caribbean **rhumba.** In states like Veracruz and Quintana Roo, drum-laden bands often strike up irresistible beats in the sea breeze and evening twilight of central plazas. The style has inspired countless **marimba** bands, whose popularized music can be found blasting in markets throughout the Republic. Imported from Colombia, **cumbia** has joined **salsa** as the dance music of choice across central and southern Mexico, inspiring young and old cut loose with the **merengue** dance step.

Mexico also knows how to rock. The latest alternative groups like **El Nudo** and **Caifanes** provide stiff competition to Spanish and American bands. Travelers from up north will feel at home, though, as American pop and hip-hop is ubiquitous in bars and *discotecas.* Striving to Mexicanize imports (and exports), Mexican artists often take American pieces and make them their own with altered lyrics or Latin beats.

TELEVISION

Mexican television can, for the most part, be broken down into four different categories: *telenovelas* (soap operas), comedies and variety shows, *noticias* (news shows), and imported American shows. Of these, *telenovelas* are second to none and occupy huge chunks of mid-afternoon airtime. The half-hour sitcoms that so central to American and European TV are not as popular in Mexico, though there are a few comedy and variety shows. Most of these feature some sort of sketch comedy, intermixed with musical numbers and audience participation contests. Popular variety shows include the Chilean *Sábado Gigante, Papá Soltero,* and the long-running *Chespirito,* whose characters are so popular, they are Mexican cultural icons. News and current events shows are popular in the late evenings, just around the time Mexicans are sitting in front of the TV after work, eating a quick supper. When the World Cup is raging, *fútbol* (football soccer) talk shows such as *Los Protagonistas* dominate the airwaves. The rest of Mexican television, sadly, is mostly American shows badly dubbed into Spanish.

There are about a dozen major national and regional networks that are most likely to appear on television sets throughout Mexico. The national networks include:

XEW 2: *Telenovelas* and old Mexican movies.

XHGC 5 (Televisa): Children's programming, late-night movies, and police, suspense, and horror shows.

Canal 7: Children's American shows dubbed into Spanish and some movies.

Canal 9: Mainly syndicated shows, including old Mexican comedy shows and movies, old *telenovelas,* and Mexican movies.

Canal 11 (Instituto Politécnico Nacional): culturally oriented shows and movies.

Canal 13 (Television Azteca): *Telenovelas* and news.

AND YOU THOUGHT SOAPS WERE BAD Love, sex, youthful rebellion, American economic hegemony. No subject is too racy (or too ridiculous) for a *telenovela.* So popular are these shows that it's not unusual to walk around during the midday in small towns and see locals hypnotized, drawn to TVs in restaurants, cafes, and store windows for their daily fix of lies and sex. Currently, *Las Soñadoras, Catalina y Sebastián,* and *Romántica Obsesión* are some of the favorite *telenovelas* in Mexico. Don't be surprised if a different group of *telenovelas* is on the air during your visit; the addictive hour-long examples of dramaturgy tend to run for four to six months before being ousted for a fresh group of characters.

In many regions, **Canal 22,** a cultural channel that airs movies and interviews with artists, and **Canal 40,** which airs news and music shows, have gained popularity.

SPORTS

Mexicans are never ones to pass up a good match-up. Although perhaps more frequently associated with Spain, **bullfighting**—the epic combat between man and large male cow—is Mexico's national sport. During the summer months, matadors and their entourages perform in packed bullrings all across the country, including Mexico City's **Plaza México,** the largest bullring in the world. James Michener's epic historical novel about the country, aptly titled *Mexico*, provides a detailed account of the history and practice of Mexican bullfighting.

Despite the popularity of publicly slaughtering cows, Mexico's heart belongs to **fútbol,** association soccer. Any unused patch of dirt, grass, or concrete is likely to be swarming with young boys (and the occasional brave girl) playing a rowdy pick-up game. (For your safety, it's best not to take sides; games can get vicious.) In addition to the informal street games, Mexico has a popular professional *fútbol* league with teams in most major cities. Guadalajara, for example, has arch-enemy teams—Las Chivas and Atlas—complete with rival fan bases. At the international level, the entire country cheers and jeers the **Mexican National Team,** the gang of green-clad flashy young men that always seems to be the underdog, and life comes to a standstill during important *fútbol* matches. Mexico played host to the all-important World Cup in 1970 and 1986 and holds important matches in the **Olympic Stadium** and the enormous **Estadio Azteca,** both in Mexico City.

Other sports coexist to a lesser degree with these two monoliths. Mexico has had its fair share of world **boxing** champions in the lighter weight divisions, and there have been some notable Mexican **marathon runners** in past years. **Baseball** is starting to attract players and spectators alike at all levels. Perhaps no discussion of sports can be complete without mention of Mexico's illustrious history in the Olympic event of **walking,** one of the only sports in which Mexico has medaled.

FOOD AND DRINK

Leave your preconceived notions of what constitutes "real Mexican food" behind and prepare your taste buds for a culinary treat. With some dedication (and at times, a little courage) the pleasures of Mexican cuisine can be yours.

THE STAPLES

Although there is a wide variety of regional cuisine and local favorites, **tortillas** are the unifying factor. This millennia-old staple is a flat, round, thin pancake made from either *harina* (wheat flour) or *maíz* (corn flour). Restaurants almost always give you a choice. *Arroz* (rice) and *frijoles* (beans) round out the triumvirate of Mexican staples. **Rice** is usually yellow Spanish or white Mexican rice and prepared with oil, tomato sauce, onions, and garlic. **Beans** can range from a thick paste to soupy "baked" beans. Expect to see these staples accompany almost every meal—breakfast, lunch, or dinner.

DESAYUNO (BREAKFAST)

Breakfast can range from a simple continental-style snack to a grand meal, rivaling the midday meal. Eggs are the mainstay of most Mexican breakfasts and are prepared in any and all combinations along with sides like *café con leche* (coffee with milk) and *pan dulce* (sweetened bread). **Scrambled eggs** (*huevos revueltos)* are usually prepared with *jamón* (ham), *tocino* (bacon), *machaca* (dried, shredded beef), or *nopalitos* (cactus). *Huevos rancheros* (fried eggs served on corn tortillas and covered with a tomato sauce), *huevos albañil* (scrambled eggs cooked in a spicy sauce), *huevos motuleños* (eggs served on a fried corn tortilla, topped with green sauce and sour cream), *huevos ahogados* (eggs cooked in simmering red sauce), and *huevos borrachos* (fried eggs cooked in beer and served with beans) are other common ways in which eggs are prepared. In more expensive restaurants omelettes are offered with any of the common meats plus *camarones* (shrimp) or *langosta* (lobster). To round out your *desayuno*, leave room for the tortillas and *frijoles*.

COMIDA (MIDDAY MEAL)

Mexicans have their big meal of the day—*la comida*—between 2 and 4pm. Both children and parents come home for an hour or two, eat, and relax afterwards, maybe endulging in a little *siesta*. Restaurants often offer *comida corrida* (sometimes called *la comida* or *el menú*), which is a fixed price meal including soup, salad, tea or *agua fresca*, a *plato fuerte* (main dish), and sometimes a dessert.

SOPA

Often a starting dish for the *comida*, Mexican soups come in two varieties: *sopas caldozas* (or *caldos*, water-based soups) and *sopas secas* (dry soups). *Sopas secas* are soups cooked to the point where the rice or pasta has absorbed the broth—hence the name *seca* (dry). *Caldos*, or normal *sopas*, are much more variable. One of the most popular is the *sopa de tortilla* (or *sopa Azteca*), a chicken-broth soup with strips of fried tortilla, chunks of avocado, and *chipotle* peppers. Another favorite is the *caldo tlalpeno*, which is a smoky blend of chicken broth and vegetables. Seafood also makes an appearance in Mexican soups. *Sopa de mariscos* features fish and shellfish. One of the most popular dishes in Mexico is **pozole**, a chunky soup with red, white, or green broth. Served with *tostadas* (fried tortillas) and lime wedges, *pozole* is made with large hominy kernels, radishes, lettuce, and some sort of meat, usually pork.

PLATO FUERTE

The main dish of any *comida* will usually feature some sort of meat platter (commonly beef, but fish is prevalent along the coasts) with sides of *frijoles*, *tortillas*, and *arroz*. *Platillos* vary throughout the Republic, and each area has its own specialties that have become known throughout the country and around the world.

THE NORTH. Happy and well-fed will be the carnivorous traveler, as meat dishes abound. One of the most famous is *cabrito*, a young goat roasted over hot embers, sometimes cooked in *adobo* (a red paste made from a mixture of garlic, cloves, peppers, oregano, and cumin) or in its own blood. Dried and shredded beef, called *machaca*, is used to make a variety of dishes, from eggs to *taquitos*. These beef dishes are frequently served with the popular *frijoles a la charra*, pinto beans cooked with onions, coriander, and tomatoes to the point where they attain a soup-like consistency.

PUEBLA. Anything ending in *"poblano"* stems from this state, rich in culinary history. A shiny, dark green variety of chile, the large *chile poblano* is used in a variety of Mexican dishes, mainly stuffed with ground beef or *queso fresco* (a soft, milky cheese) or smothered in walnut sauce to create another regional specialty, *chiles en nogada*. Perhaps the most famous dish from the area is bittersweet *mole poblano*, a rich chocolatey-brown sauce served with chicken and rice. Making *mole poblano* is not for the lazy chef; made with everything from chiles to raisins to peanuts to cinnamon to chocolate, *mole poblano* is one of the most complicated of Mexican dishes.

OAXACA AND THE PACIFIC COAST. Despite the popularity of *mole poblano*, Oaxaca is known as the land of **seven moles**: black, light red, green, yellow, *chichilo*, *manchamanteles*, and dark red *moles* all odiferously bubble in the region. Of these, the black Oaxacan *mole*—which uses the chilahuacle chile—is the most famous and is served over chicken, rice, or turkey. Almost as famous as Oaxaca's *moles* are its *tamales*, which are chicken and beef chunks imbedded in *masa* (dough) and then steamed in banana-leaf wraps.

VERACRUZ AND THE GULF COAST. In Veracruz and in most coastal areas, *marisco* is the word. Seafood dishes such as *cangrejo* or *jaiba* (crab), *ostiones* (oysters), and *camarones* (shrimp) are available everywhere, from world-class restaurants to beach-side shacks. Try the *huachinango* (wah-chee-NAAN-go) *a la vercrazuzana*, a snapper cooked with olive oil, garlic, tomatoes, and jalapeño peppers. Also try a *filete de pescado al mojo de ajo*, fish cooked or dressed with a garlic puree sauce. Finally, munch on the ubiquitous *tacos de pescado* (fish tacos), available at any self-respecting beach-side shack.

THE YUCATÁN. The most famous dish in the Yucatán Peninsula is the *cochinita pibil*, a pig seasoned with red paste and roasted and wrapped in banana leaves. Second to the *chochinita* are *papadzules*, tortillas dressed with pumpkin seed sauce and rolled with hard-boiled eggs. The *papadzules* are then served with a light tomato sauce. All food in the Yucatán is to a certain extent inspired by the famous *achiote* seasoning, made with annatto seeds and a mixture of other spices and herbs such as garlic, cumin, and oregano and sold in blocks called *recados*.

POSTRES Y DULCES (DESSERTS AND SWEETS)

Mexicans have an incurable sweet tooth. In addition to the ubiquitous junk food—the chocolates and pastries available on store shelves—traditional desserts include *flan*, a vanilla custard served over burnt sugar, *nieve* (ice cream), and *arroz con leche* (rice pudding). Puebla, recognized as the country's candy capital, is full of sweet shops selling *dulces de leche* (milk sweets) and *camotes* (candied sweet potatoes). Morelia and Michoacán specialize in *ates*, sticky sweet blocks of ground and candied fruit concentrate. San Cristóbal de las Casas and parts of Chiapas are well-known for their *cajetas* (fruit pastes) as well as coconut candies and cookies. In the Yucatán, you can buy types of pumpkin marzipan.

CENA (SUPPER)

Mexicans usually snack lightly before going to sleep, usually around 9 or 10pm. Found on almost any Mexican menu, *antojitos* (little cravings) are equivalent to a large snack or small meal. Tacos are small, grilled pieces of meat placed on an open, warm tortilla topped with a row of condiments. Burritos, popular in northern Mexico, are thin, rolled tortillas filled with meat, beans, and cooked vegetables. *Enchiladas* are rolled corn tortillas filled with meat or chicken and baked with sauce and cheese. *Quesadillas* are flat tortillas with cheese melted between them; *quesadillas sincronizadas* (sometimes called *gringas*) are filled with ham or gyro-style pork. *Tostadas* resemble flat, open tacos, topped with raw vegetables. *Chimichangas* are similar to burritos but are deep-fried, producing a rich crunchy shell. *Flautas* are similar to *chimichangas* but are rolled very thinly (like a cigar) before being deep-fried.

BEBIDAS (DRINKS)

BEERS AND LIQUORS

Along with tortillas, beans, and rice, *cerveza* (beer) could be considered a national staple. It is impossible to drive through any Mexican town without coming across a double-digit number of Tecate and Corona billboards, painted

---

HEY, DIDN'T I SEE THAT BACK THERE? Rest assured, it's not deja-vu. Nearly every single Mexican town has a **Sanborn's** or a **VIPS** restaurant. Sanborn's, easily distinguished by its owl logo and pretty waitresses dressed in traditional Mexican garb, is the classier of the two. Sit inside and sip your *chocolate caliente* with business clientele and hip urbanites. VIPS, on the other hand, caters more toward Mexican families with its special kids' menu. You'd be a fool not to try the *sopa de fideos* (noodle soup) and the french fries that come in the shape of letters. Don't shy away. Sanborn's and VIPS are beacons of hope, lighting the way toward something familiar and unchanging.

buildings, and cheap beer stores proudly selling their products. Popular beers in Mexico (listed roughly in order of quality) are **Bohemia** (a world-class lager), **Negra Modelo** (a fine dark beer), **Dos Equis** (a light, smooth lager), **Pacífico, Modelo, Carta Blanca, Superior, Corona Extra,** and **Sol** (watery and light). Mexicans share their love for bargain beer with the world, as demonstrated by the fact that the Mexican-made Corona Extra is a leading export and tops many international charts—including Canada, Australia, New Zealand, France, Italy, Spain, and most European markets—as one of the most popular beers.

Tequila is king when it comes to Mexican liquor. A more refined version of *mezcal*, tequila is distilled from the *maguey* cactus, a large, sprawling plant often seen by the side of Mexican highways. **Herradura, Tres Generaciones, Hornitos,** and **Cuervo 1800** are among the more famous, expensive, and quality brands of tequila. **Mezcal,** coarser than tequila, is sometimes served with the worm native to the plant—upon downing the shot, you are expected to ingest the worm. If you get a chance to sample **pulque,** the fermented juice of the *maguey*, don't hesitate—it was the sacred drink of the Aztec nobility for a reason. **Ron** (rum), while originally manufactured in the Caribbean, enjoys incredible popularity in Mexico and is manufactured in parts of the Valley of Mexico. Coffee-flavored **Kahlúa** is Mexico's most exported liqueur, but well-made **piña coladas** (pineapple juice, cream of coconut, and light rum) or **coco locos** (coconut milk and tequila served in a hollowed-out coconut) are much harder to find outside Mexico.

NON-ALCOHOLIC BEVERAGES

Plenty of popular beverage options don't include alcohol. Unique Mexican **refrescos** (sodas) out-taste their Coke and Pepsi counterparts. Try the *soda de fresa* (strawberry soda), *soda de piña* (pineapple soda), *toronja* (grapefruit soda), *manzanita* (apple soda), and Boing! (mango soda). If carbonation isn't your thing, try the traditional **aguas frescas,** which come in almost any imaginable fruit or vegetable flavor. Favorites are *agua de jamaica* (a red juice made from hibiscus) and *agua de horchata* (a sweet white rice milk).

For those desiring something warmer, Mexico is the land of plenty. Nearly every meal is capped off with a *taza de café* (cup of coffee) or *té* (tea). Coffee is nearly always drunk black or with cream *(con leche)*. For a truly unique Mexican experience, try coffee with steamed milk. Another hot favorite is *chocolate caliente* (hot chocolate). Far from the sticky sweet American variety, Mexican hot chocolate is dark and bittersweet with a rich aftertaste. For those chocolate lovers, the best place in all of the Republic to get this famous chocolate are the streets behind Oaxaca city's main market.

MEXICO CITY

The word "city" hardly does justice to this place. Encompassing over 1480 sq. km of sprawling humanity enshrouded in a semi-permanent yellow haze, the capital of the Republic appears to have no boundaries, no suburbs, no beginning, no end; skyscrapers and aluminum-covered shacks alike are embedded in the drained, saline lake-bed as far as the eye can see. Mexicans call this megalopolis **el D.F.** (deh-EFF-ay), short for **Distrito Federal** (Federal District). Others simply refer to it as **México**. Regardless of what you call it, Mexico City's staggering statistics speak for themselves. Depending on how you measure it, *el D.F.* is home to between 17 and 30 million people, one quarter of Mexico's entire population, in over 220 *colonias* (neighborhoods). Virtually the entire federal bureaucracy inhabits the D.F., including the Navy, paradoxically commanding the nation's fleet from 2240m above sea level. From the enormous central square to a sprawling governmental palace to the 40-story skyscrapers to Parque Chapultepec, the biggest city park in the Americas, everything here is larger than life. First-time visitors stop dead in their tracks when they realize the imposing three-story art-nouveau edifice across from the Palacio de Bellas Artes is simply the post office. No one here buries the ruins of the past nor apologizes for the excesses of the present. To be sure, the city isn't 100% shiny and happy. Torrents of problems have descended upon the city—earthquakes, volcanic eruptions, misery-induced crime, and naturally-exacerbated pollution have all collaborated to make the average *chilango* (the somewhat humorous, somewhat pejorative name given to D.F. natives) slightly cynical. Still, most do not see the city as an enemy—laments are grounded in an unconditional love for the apocalyptic metropolis. *Chilangos* are proud of their city's past, preoccupied with its present, and hopefully awaiting its future.

HIGHLIGHTS OF MEXICO CITY

WEAVE your way through Mexico City's **zócalo** (p. 98), the center of the country's capital, where ruins and cathedrals peacefully coexist, and government buildings are lovingly adorned with murals by Rivera, Siquieros, and Orozco.

LOSE yourself in the **Bosque de Chapultepec** (p. 111), the largest urban park in the Americas—it's got everything from panda bears to free concerts to the **Museo Nacional de Antropología** (p. 112), Mexico's biggest and best museum.

SUIT UP AND PARTY in the perennially packed bars and discos of the glamorous **Zona Rosa** (p. 99).

FLOCK with the devout to the **Basílica de Guadalupe** (p. 115).

NAP on the park benches of the gloriously green **Alameda** (p. 106), across from the French-inspired **Palacio de Bellas Artes** (p. 107).

VENTURE beyond the borders; some of Mexico City's most fabulous attractions aren't actually within the city proper—check out our suggestions for **daytrips** (p. 135), The nearby pyramids of **Teotihuacán** (p. 129), the most visited ruins in all of Mexico, deserve a special visit.

◣ A BRIEF HISTORY

Cities like this just don't happen. Centuries upon centuries have shaped the behemoth into what it is—the biggest, baddest city in the world.

ORIGINS 101: FACT AND FICTION

History of the Valley of Mexico begins with the arrival of the **Mexica** (mee-SHI-ka, later known as the **Aztecs**) in the 13th century AD. According to legend, the Aztecs arrived in the Valley of Mexico led by Huitzilopochtli, the hummingbird god of war, who had told

Central Mexico City

HOTELS

Casa de los Amigos, B
Hostel Catedral, J
Hostel Moneda, K
Hotel Antillas, I
Hotel Atlanta, H
Hotel Buena Vista, D
Hotel Buenos Aires, N
Hotel Edison, A
Hotel Hidalgo, F

Hotel Isabel, Q
Hotel Juárez, L
Hotel la Marina, G
Hotel Manolo Primero, S
Hotel Monte Carlo, P
Hotel Oxford, C
Hotel Principal, O
Hotel San Antonio, M
Hotel San Diego, R
Hotel Yale, E

SIGHTS

Casa de los Azulejos, 35
Catedral Metropolitana, 44
Centro Cultural José Martí, 23
Fonart, 26
Glorieta Ángel de la Independencia, 8
Glorieta Cristóbal Colón, 16
Glorieta Cuauhtémoc, 14
Iglesia de San Francisco, 37
La Lagunilla, 46
Mercado de Artesanías de la Ciudadela, 27

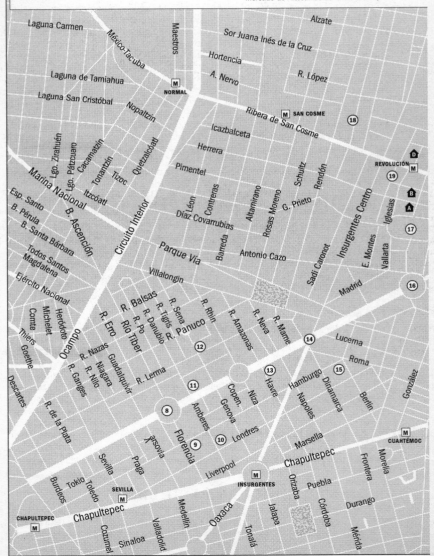

Mercado San Juan Artesanías, 28
Monumento a la Revolución, 17
Monumento de los Niños Héroes, 7
Museo de Arte Moderno, 6
Museo de la Charrería, 39
Museo de la Ciudad de México, 41
Museo del Chopo, 18
Museo Diego Rivera, 24
Museo Franz Mayer, 29
Museo Nacional de Antropología, 3
Museo Nacional de Arte, 34
Museo Nacional de Historia, 5

Museo Nacional de la Estampa, 30
Museo San Carlos, 20
Museo Siqueiros, 2
Museo Tamayo, 4
Palacio de Bellas Artes, 31
Palacio Iturbide, 38
Palacio Nacional, 43
Pinacoteca Virreinal de San Diego, 25
Suprema Corte de Justicia, 42
Templo Mayor, 45
Torre Latinoamericana, 36

SERVICES
American Express, 13
Biblioteca Ben Franklin, 15
Central Post Office, 32
Federal Tourist Office, 10
Ministry of Tourism, 1
Procedura General de Justicia, 9
Torre Medica, 19
Train Station, 21
U.S. Embassy, 11
U.K. Embassy, 12

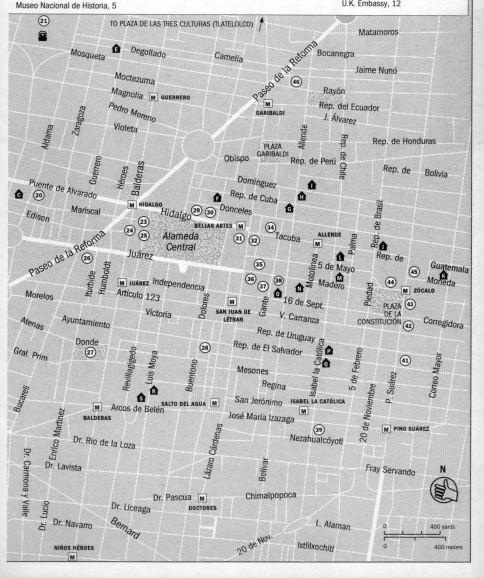

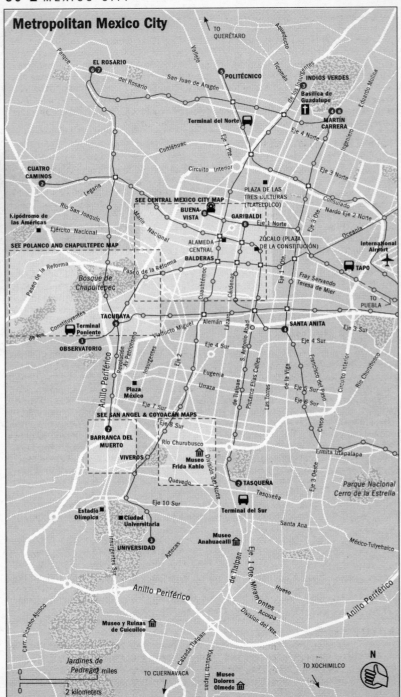

Metropolitan Mexico City

his chosen people to settle in the place where they saw an eagle with a serpent in its beak perched on a cactus. Lo and behold, the Aztecs witnessed this very sight at a spot just next to **Lake Texcoco** in the Valley of Mexico. The less glamorous reality is that the nomadic Aztecs simply knew a good place to settle when they saw one. Initially shunned by neighboring tribes as awkward and uncivilized, the barbaric Aztecs slowly but surely rose to power through trading and the formation of strategic alliances (as well as the occasional back-stabbing). At its height in the 15th century, the Aztec city, **Tenochtitlán,** was a wonder to behold. Its population (200,000) would have made it the sixth largest city in the world, and its complicated canals and drainage system would have made a city like London seem a filthy pit in comparison.

THE COLONIAL ERA

When **Hernán Cortés** arrived in Tenochtitlán in 1521, he could not believe his eyes. The city, gleaming with cleanliness, spread out before him for miles and miles, laid out in an inconceivably meticulous manner. Impressed, the Spaniard did what came naturally: he conquered the city. After the fall of Tenochtitlán, the triumphant conquistador busied himself in transforming the Aztec city into a capital for his new empire. Aztec temples were razed and the rubble was used to build new *palacios* and cathedrals, including those now seen in the city *zócalo*. The lovely grids of Aztec canals were drained and replaced with roads, some of which form the backbone of the city's modern infrastructure. Slowly, the city settled into a pattern. Spanish viceroys came and went, and the city, the bureaucratic center of the empire, thrived under Spanish control. By the time of Independence, Mexico City was the cultural capital of Latin America. Its consecration as a bishopric in 1533 ensured that it was the spiritual capital as well. The 18th century in particular was a time of great construction and renovations; an aqueduct was built linking the city to reservoirs in Chapultepec and the giant underground lake was finally drained, thereby opening up more of the Valley for settlement.

INDEPENDENT MEXICO

During most of the movements for Independence and, later, during Reform, Mexico City became something of a holy grail—the only goal for both revolutionary and foreign armies. No sooner had the *Grito de Dolores* left Hidalgo's lips than construction and sanitation fell by the wayside, and the city became booty traded back and forth between the Mexican people and US soldiers (in 1847), French interventionists (in 1863), and revolutionary armies (in 1821, 1867, and 1876). It was not until the dictatorship of Porfirio Díaz that the city regained some measure of stability. Construction resumed, and around the turn of the century buildings such as the magnificent Palacio de las Bellas Artes were built. The bustle and construction attracted countless immigrants seeking work and housing; by the mid-1930s, over one million people could identify themselves as *chilango*.

THE 20TH CENTURY

The wartime economic boom of the 1940s and 1950s gave way to stagnation and frustration in the 1960s, as Mexico, along with the rest of the world, fell upon times of despair. Perhaps emblematic of these sentiments were the student protests of 1968, when, during Olympic celebrations, innocent protestors were gunned down in places like the UNAM and in Tlatelolco. However, despite economic frustration, population growth was on the rise. Within a span of fifty years, the capital's population soared—from one million in 1930 to eight million in 1980. City planning, abruptly ceased, unable to handle the loads of domestic immigrants arriving to find work. This cessation paved the way for the rise of shanty-towns and slums, which can now be seen on the roads leading to the capital.

MODERN DAY

When it rains it pours. Amidst a stagnant economy and increasing frustration, a mighty 1985 earthquake sent both buildings and spirits tumbling to the ground. The June 1985 Popocatépetl eruption, mild as it was, was another lingering reminder of the city's precarious position atop a highly active geological area.

MEXICO CITY

Finally, to add insult to injury, the 80s and 90s saw air quality in the city deteriorate to dangerous levels; the city renowned for its cleanliness and breathable air has become one of the world's most polluted cities. But all is not lost in this mind-numbingly large city. The creation of the post of Governor of the State of Mexico in 1998 brought newfound hope to the millions who call this city home, along with the subsequent election of progressive leftist **Cuauhtémoc Cárdenas.** His promises have slowly started to materialize. Crime, made rampant by police abuses and corruption, is starting to plateau and may be descending from its notoriously high levels. The city has also begun to fight pollution in earnest, through educational campaigns and the use of strict controls. Perhaps most importantly, the city has become more sure of itself and of its complicated identity. The clearing of the Templo Mayor in the early 80s brought indigenous pride to the city, giving *chilangos* a newfound respect for the accomplishments of their Aztec forefathers. The city today is a sometimes terrifying mix of old and new, foreign and native. And, cynical and street-wise as *chilangos* are, most of them are head over heels in love with their city. Huitzilopochtli, wherever he is, is no doubt looking down at his beloved nomads, a smile on his face, knowing that he led them to the right place.

✈ GETTING THERE AND AWAY

All roads lead to Mexico City. Buses, trains, and planes from every town in the Republic haul passengers through the smoggy hyperactivity of the city's many temples of transport—the constantly-expanding Benito Juárez International Airport, the four crowded bus stations, the desolate train station, and the network of freeways. Fortunately for frazzled tourists, airports and stations have information booths with quasi-English-speaking personnel, official zone-rated taxi service, and nearby Metro stations. Except for the terrible train service, you might even be pleasantly surprised by how easy it is to get around.

BY AIR

The **Benito Juárez International Airport** (☎ 5571 3295; M: Terminal Aérea, Line 5) lies 6.5km east of the *zócalo*, the formal center of the city. **Blvd. Capitán Juan Sarabio** heads northeast to the airport from **Blvd. Puerto Aéreo,** one of the major roads circling the city. The surprisingly accessible airport is jam-packed with facilities, including **24-hour restaurants, cafeterias,** and **ATMs.**

GETTING TO AND FROM THE AIRPORT

Transportation into the city is uncomplicated. Buy a *transporte terrestre* ticket from the *venta de boletos* desk in the airport in Sala A or Sala E (right next to the arrival gate), and present it to any of the authorized taxis waiting outside. The price is determined by the zone to which you're traveling (73 pesos to the *centro*, 92 pesos to El Monumento a la Revolución or the Alameda Central.) Head straight for the ticket booths, avoiding the uniformed "taxi supervisors," who will try to get you on more expensive and unnecessarily large taxis. Also avoid unauthorized taxis—the potential savings are not worth the safety risk.

The Metro is by far the cheapest route to the city. The airport subway station, **Terminal Aérea,** Line 5, at the junction of Sarabio and Puerto Aéreo, is only a 5-minute walk from Sala A. Signs will point you in the right direction. Large bags are officially prohibited, but provided you avoid rush hour and can maneuver through the turnstile, a typical pack should not pose much of a problem. If returning to the airport by Metro, get off again at **Terminal Aérea,** Line 5. **Taxis** (☎ 5784 4811 or 5571 3600) will also take you to the airport from the city.

 GET OFF HERE. If traveling to the airport by Metro, **do not get off** at the Aeropuerto stop on Line 1 (also known as Blvd. Aeropuerto). The correct stop is **Terminal Aérea,** on Line 5.

FLIGHT INFORMATION

Flight Info Hotline and General Information: (☎5571 3600 or 5762 6773). Specify domestic or international flights.

Terminals: Sala A: All Aeroméxico, baby. **Sala B:** Mexicana, Aeromar, and Aerocalifornia. **Sala C:** Aerolineas Internacionales and AVIACSA. **Sala D:** ALLEGRO, TAESA, and charter flights. **Sala E:** International arrivals. **Sala F1:** Aeroméxico (international flights), America West, Avianca, Continental, Delta, Ecuatoriana, Lan Chile, and LAB. **Sala F2:** Air France, Aviateca, British Airways, Canadian, Copa, Cubana, ETA, JAL Japan, KLM, Malaysia, Miami Air, Northwest, and Taca. **Sala F3:** Air Canada, American Airlines, Argentinian Airlines, Iberia, Lufthansa, TWA, and United Airlines.

Domestic Carriers: Prices are roughly the same from airline to airline, but flight schedules and prices change frequently. Student discounts are usually not available, but always ask about *tarifas promocionales,* which may save you up to 50%. **Aerocalifornia,** Sala B, tends to be the most competitive. (☎5207 1392. Open daily 7am-7pm.) **Aeroméxico,** Paseo de la Reforma 445 at Mississippi (☎5726 0234; open M-Sa 9am-8:15pm), and Reforma 80 (☎5566 1078; open M-Sa 9am-6:15pm). At the airport, Sala A. (☎5133 4010. Open daily 4:30am-2am.) **Mexicana,** Reforma 312, at Amberes in the *Zona Rosa* (☎5726 0234; open M-F 9am-6pm), and Reforma 107 in the Hotel Sevilla Palace (open M-F 9am-6pm). At the airport, Sala B. (☎5448 0990. Open 24hr.) Many of these airlines also fly abroad.

International Carriers: Air France, Edgar Allen Poe 90, in Col. Polanco. (☎5627 6000. Open M-F 9am-2pm and 3-6pm.) At the airport, on the 3rd fl. above Sala F. (☎5627 6060. Open M 10am-2pm, Tu-Sa 10am-10pm, Su 1:30-10pm.) **American,** Reforma 314, 1st fl. Also at the airport in Sala F. (☎5209 1400. Open M-F 9am-6pm, Sa 9am-8:30pm.) **British Airways,** Balmes 8, Mez. office #6 (☎5785 8714), in Col. Polanco, and in the airport (☎5387 0300). **Canadian Airlines,** Reforma 390 (☎5208 1883). **Continental,** at the airport between Salas D and E. (☎5283 5500. Open M-F 9am-6pm, Sa 10am-2pm.) **Delta,** Reforma 381 (☎5202 1608 or 5207 3411). At the airport in Sala F. (☎5279 0909. Open daily 6am-6pm.) **Lufthansa,** Las Palmas 239, at Col. Lomas de Chapultepec. (☎5230 0000. Open M-F 9am-6pm.) At the airport. (☎5571 2702. Open daily 2:30-9:30pm.) **Swissair,** Hamburgo 66, 3rd fl., between Niza and Havre in the *Zona Rosa.* (☎5207 2455. Open M-F 9am-6pm.) **TWA,** in the airport in Sala F. (☎5627 0222 or toll-free 01 800 007 8000.) **United,** Hamburgo 213, ground fl. (☎toll-free 01 800 003 0777.) At the airport in Sala F. (☎5627 0222. Open daily 9am-noon and 3-5pm.)

AIRPORT SERVICES

Tourist Office: in Sala A (☎5786 9002), with the yellow signs. Hotel reservations available. Open daily 8am-8pm. Information kiosks in Salas A and F have flight info. Another tourist information booth in Sala A (☎5785 9542) has city tours for upwards of US$35, but no brochures. Open daily 7am-11pm.

Buses: The airport runs a convenient bus service which allows direct access to nearby towns from just outside Sala D. Buy tickets at the booth in front of where the buses park. Buses go to: **Cuernavaca** (21 per day 6:30am-11pm, 80 pesos); **Pachuca** (15 per day 7:15am-9:15pm, 100 pesos); **Puebla** (42 per day 6am-12:30am, 100 pesos); and **Querétaro** (14 per day 8:30am-9:15pm, 160 pesos).

Currency Exchange: Banks exchange currency and traveler's checks in almost all of the *salas.* **ATMs,** accepting a number of cards, are available in Sala A, directly under Sala B, and throughout Salas E and F. **Casas de cambio,** every foot or so, (open 6am to 8pm or later), and have rates comparable to what you'll find throughout the city.

Car Rental: In Sala E. Rates very similar at each company. Open until about 10:30pm.

Luggage Storage: In the corner of Sala A and in Sala E. 40 pesos per day per bag, 50-70 pesos per day for larger bags.

Police: (☎5599 0053 or 5599 0054), upstairs from Sala C. Also in Sala E1 (☎5599 0044). Open 24hr.

Pharmacy: Two locations. One in Sala C (open daily 6am-10pm) and another in Sala F (open daily 6am-11pm).

Medical Assistance: upstairs from Sala C, follow the red cross signs.

Fax: between Salas D and E. Open 24hr.

Internet Access: Axon Cyber Café, in Sala E (☎5786 9372). Fast. 1 peso per min.

Post Office: In Sala A. Open M-F 8am-7pm, Sa 9am-5pm.

BY TRAIN

Estación Buenavista (☎5547 1097; M: Buenavista, Line B) is north of the Monumento a la Revolución at the corner of Insurgentes and Mosqueta (Eje 1 Alzate). **Taxis** leave from the area, but these may or may not be *sitio* cabs. "Universidad" *peseros* run along Insurgentes regularly and will bring you to the Monumento a la Revolución neighborhood and the *Zona Rosa*. Mexican trains tend to be excruciatingly slow, and the system has essentially been phased out in favor of the bus system. One train leaves the station at 9am and goes to: **Querétaro** (M, W, F; 54 pesos), and **Apixaco** (Tu, Th, Sa; 30 pesos). Buy tickets for morning trains when the ticket booth (☎5547 1084 or 5547 1097) opens at 7am.

BY BUS

Mexico City's four main bus stations correspond to the cardinal directions and serve corresponding areas of the country.

Central de Autobuses del Norte (North Station): the Bajía, northern Veracruz, Jalisco, and all of northern Mexico.

Terminal Central de Autobuses del Sur (Tasqueña; South Station): Guerrero, Morelos, and Oaxaca.

Terminal de Autobuses de Pasajeros de Oriente (TAPO; East Station): Puebla, southern Veracruz, Oaxaca, Chiapas, and the Yucatán Peninsula.

Terminal de Autobuses del Poniente (West Station): Estado de México and Michoacán.

All stations are served by the Metro and offer 24-hour taxi service charging fixed rates. Buy your ticket inside to avoid being ripped off. *Peseros* (a.k.a. *colectivos*) also serve the four stations. Quality budget hotels near the bus stations are virtually nil—it's a much better bet to head toward the city center. The following bus prices change almost weekly, and listings are by no means comprehensive. Given the extensive network, it is possible to go almost anywhere at any time.

CENTRAL DE AUTOBUSES DEL NORTE

The Central de Autobuses del Norte, most commonly referred to as "Cien Metros" or "Mexico Norte," is on Cien Metros. (☎5587 1552. M: Autobuses del Norte, Line 5.) **Services include:** a hotel reservations service booth (open 7am-9pm) and a tourist information booth (open 9am-7pm) near the main entrance. A *casa de cambio,* also near the main entrance, offers poor rates. (Open daily 11am-6pm.) There is a Banamex ATM, restaurant, luggage storage (10-20 pesos per day), phone and fax offices, and a pharmacy (all open 24hr.), as well as a post office (open M-F 8am-7:30pm, Sa 9am-1pm) and telegram office (open M-F 9am-7:30pm, Sa 9am-4:30pm). From the **taxi stand,** rides to the *zócalo* or Revolución are 35 pesos. Many bus companies populate the station; prices are often suspiciously similar, and it's not uncommon for "competing" companies to share phone numbers. You've got an infinite but unvaried selection in this terminal/zoo.

ADO (☎5133 2424) goes to: **Oaxaca** (6hr., 7 per day 7am-12pm, 221 pesos); **Papantla** (5hr., 6 per day 10:30-12:30am, 119 pesos); **Puebla** (2hr., every 30min. 4am-10pm, 68 pesos); **Tuxpan** (6hr., every hr. 6am-midnight, 139 pesos); **Veracruz** (7hr., 6 per day 8am-12:15am, 189 pesos); and **Xalapa** (5hr., 3pm and 12:15am, 132 pesos). **ADO GL,** run by the same company, offers *ejecutivo* service to: **Oaxaca** (6hr., midnight, 261 pesos); **Tampico** (9hr., 10 and 11pm, 269 pesos); **Veracruz** (6hr., 11:30pm, 218 pesos); and **Villahermosa** (10hr., 10pm, 610 pesos). **UNO,** also run by ADO, goes super-deluxe to **Tampico** (9hr.; 9, 9:45, and 10:15pm; 380 pesos).

Elite (☎5729 0707). The name says it all. Posh service to: **Hermosillo** (30hr., every hr. 5:30am-1:15pm, 1234 pesos); **Puerto Vallarta** (14hr., 4 per day 5-11:45pm, 555 pesos); and **San Luis Potosí** (7hr., every hr., 221 pesos).

Estrella Blanca (☎5729 0707) goes to: **Chihuahua** (20hr., every hr. 6am-11:30pm, 778 pesos); **Durango** (12hr., 6 per day 5:30am-11:45pm, 481 pesos); **Torreón** (13hr., every hr., 540 pesos); and **Zacatecas** (7hr., every hr., 338 pesos).

Flecha Amarilla (☎5587 5222) goes to: **Guadalajara** (9hr., every hr., 280 pesos); **Guanajuato** (6½hr., 9 per day 11:45am-6:45pm, 233 pesos); **Morelia** (5hr., every 40min., 145 pesos); **Querétaro** (3½hr., every 15min. 4:20am-12:20am, 120 pesos); **San Luis Potosí** (7hr., every hr., 147 pesos); and **San Miguel de Allende** (4½hr.; 7:10, 11:15am, 5:40pm; 126 pesos).

Futura (☎5729 0707) goes to: **Acapulco** (5hr., every 1½hr. 6am-11:30pm, 220 pesos); **Aguascalientes** (6hr., every hr. 7:30am-12:30am, 287 pesos); **Chihuahua** (18hr., every hr. 8:50am-11:30pm, 778 pesos); **Matamoros** (14hr., 5 per day 2:15-10:30pm, 640 pesos); **Monterrey** (12hr., every hr. 7am-midnight, 495 pesos); and **Tampico** (9½hr., every 2hr., 286 pesos).

TERMINAL DE AUTOBUSES DE PASAJEROS DE ORIENTE

The Terminal de Autobuses de Pasajeros de Oriente (always called by its acronym, TAPO) is at General Ignacio Zaragoza 200. (☎5762 5977. M: San Lázaro, Line 1.) To get from the Metro to the station, carefully follow the "A TAPO" signs. Ignore the few signs to the **tourist information booth**; it no longer exists. **Services include:** 24hr. ATM, currency exchange (open daily 7am-11pm), a travel agency (☎5542 9092; open M-F 9:30am-6pm), food stands, a pharmacy, and luggage storage (10 pesos per 8hr., 15 pesos per 16hr., 20 pesos per day; 30 pesos more for larger bags). Helpful police booths are scattered throughout. **Taxi** ticket booths are near the Metro entrance (25 pesos to the *zócalo*, 35 pesos to Monumento a la Revolución).

ADO (☎5542 7192) goes to: **Campeche** (18hr., 6 per day 12:30-9:30pm, 544 pesos); **Cancún** (24hr., 5 per day 8:30am-6:45pm, 724 pesos); **Córdoba** (4½hr., 34 per day, 144 pesos); **Mérida** (20hr., 5 per day 12:30-9:30pm, 615 pesos); **Oaxaca** (6hr., 27 per day, 221 pesos); **Palenque** (12hr., 4 and 6:10pm, 431 pesos); **Veracruz** (5hr., 20 per day, 189 pesos); **Villahermosa** (10½hr., 22 per day, 376 pesos); and **Xalapa** (4½hr., 23 per day, 132 pesos). **ADO GL** offers *ejecutivo* service to all of the above locations, less frequently and at slightly higher prices.

Autobuses Cristóbal Colón (☎5133 2433) goes to: **Oaxaca** (6hr., 4 per day 12:30-11:30pm, 221 pesos); **San Cristóbal de las Casas** (18hr.; 2:30, 5:30, and 7:30pm; 455 pesos); **Tonalá** (13hr.; 5, 7:45, and 10pm; 403 pesos); and **Tuxtla Gutiérrez** (15hr., 5 per day 2:30-9:30pm, 440 pesos).

Autobuses Unidos (AU; ☎5133 2444) goes to: **Córdoba** (5hr., 21 per day, 130 pesos); **Oaxaca** (6-9hr., 11 per day, 198 pesos); **San Andrés Tuxtla** (8hr., noon and 9pm, 222 pesos); and **Xalapa** (5hr., 20 per day, 118 pesos).

Estrella Roja (☎5542 9200) goes to **Puebla** (2hr., every 30min. 4:30am-8:15pm, 53 pesos).

UNO (☎5522 1111). The lap of luxury. Service to: **Oaxaca** (357 pesos), **Veracruz** (200 pesos), **Villahermosa** (610 pesos), **Xalapa** (215 pesos), and other cities.

TERMINAL DE AUTOBUSES DEL PONIENTE

The Terminal de Autobuses del Poniente is on Av. Sur 122. (☎5271 4519. M: Observatorio, Line 1.) Follow signs to **Central Camionero Pte.** as you exit the Metro—a vendor-lined bridge leads to the terminal. From the terminal to the Metro, walk up the large staircase and make a left. The station is built in the shape of a "V" with the most important services clustered at the vertex. **Services include:** a restaurant (open 24hr.), luggage storage (small bags 2.5 pesos per 4hr., 5 pesos per 4-8hr., 7.5 pesos per 8-24hr.; 10 pesos per hr. for large bags), a pharmacy (open daily 7am-10pm), Telecomm fax services (open M-F

9am-8pm, Sa-Su 9am-5pm), a Western Union, and a long-distance caseta (open 24hr.). Buy **taxi** tickets from the authorized stand (to the *zócalo* 42 pesos, to the Monumento a la Revolución 35 pesos).

Autobuses del Occidente (☎5271 0106) goes to: **Guadalajara** (12hr., 4 per day 12:10am-10:20pm, 273 pesos); **Manzanillo** (16hr., 5 per day 1:10am-7:20pm, 410 pesos); **Morelia** (6hr., every 30min., 139 pesos); and **Tuxpan** (4hr., 5 per day 6:15am-11:50pm, 87 pesos).

Caminante goes to **Toluca** (1hr., every 5min. 5:50am-10:30pm, 28 pesos).

Elite (☎5729 0707 or 5729 0793) goes to **Chihuahua** (20hr., 2:30pm, 778 pesos) and **Morelia** (4hr., 3 per day 10:30am-5:30pm, 167 pesos).

ETN (☎5567 3102) goes to: **Guadalajara** (7hr., 7 per day, 445 pesos); **Morelia** (4hr., 34 per day, 220 pesos); **Toluca** (1hr., every 30min., 38 pesos); **Uruapan** (5½hr., 6 per day, 300 pesos); and many other cities.

Pegasso Plus (☎5277 7761) goes to **Morelia** (4hr., 36 per day, 175 pesos) and **Pátzcuaro** (5hr., 10 per day 6:30am-midnight, 195 pesos).

Servicios Coordinados goes to: **Morelia** (5½hr., 11 per day 8am-11:15pm, 139 pesos); **Querétaro** (6hr., 4 per day 7-10:45pm, 107 pesos); and other cities.

CENTRAL DE AUTOBUSES DEL SUR (TASQUEÑA)

The Tasqueña terminal is at Tasqueña 1320. (☎5689 9745. M: Tasqueña, Line 2). From the Metro, follow "Central" signs and exit through the market. **Services include:** a mini-travel agency for hotel reservations in select cities (open Su-F 9am-9pm, Sa 9am-3pm), a Telecomm and Western Union (☎5549 8015; open M-F 8am-7:30pm, Sa-Su 9am-6pm), a pharmacy (☎5689 0883; open 24hr.), and a cafeteria. Luggage lockers (small 10 pesos per day, large 20 pesos per day) are near Exit 3. Get a cab from the **taxi stand** (42 pesos to the *zócalo*, 32 pesos to the Monumento a la Revolución).

ADO, Cristóbal Colón, and **Estrella Roja** go to: **Oaxaca** (6hr.; 7:30am, 4pm, and midnight; 221 pesos) and places on the **Gulf Coast** and **Yucatán**.

Estrella de Oro (☎5549 8520) goes to: **Acapulco** (5hr., every hr. 6am-10pm, 220 pesos); **Cuernavaca** (1½hr., 4 per day 12:50-8:40pm, 43 pesos); **Ixtapa/Zihuatanejo** (9hr.; 8:20am, 8:40, and 10:40pm; 295 pesos); and **Taxco** (2hr., 6 per day 7:40am-8:10pm, 78 pesos).

Futura and **Turistar** (☎5628 5739 or 5628 5740) go to **Acapulco** (5hr., 38 per day, 220 pesos) and **Ixtapa/Zihuatanejo** (9hr., every 30min., 359 pesos).

Pullman de Morelos (☎5549 3505) goes to **Cuernavaca** (1¼hr., every 15min. 5:30am-midnight, 44 pesos).

BY CAR

Few car-related experiences can match the shock of driving into Mexico City. Serene mountain roads slowly metamorphose into blaring, bumper-to-bumper, multi-lane highways. Traffic keeps the city crawling from 9 to 11am and 3 to 7pm. Don't expect anyone to drive defensively—welcome to a city where stoplights are often considered optional (see **Getting Around,** p. 87). Several major roads lead into the city and intersect with the **Circuito Interior,** the route that rings the city, at which point they change names. **Route 57,** from Querétaro and Tepotzlán, becomes **Manuel Avila Camacho** just outside the Circuito. **Route 15,** from Toluca, turns into **Reforma** as it enters the city. **Route 95,** from Cuernavaca and Acapulco, becomes **Insurgentes,** which enters the city from the south side. **Route 150,** from Puebla and Texcoco, becomes **Ignacio Zaragoza,** which begins on the city's east side. **Route 85,** from Pachuca, Teotihuacán, and Texcoco, also becomes **Insurgentes** when you reach the northern city limits. Remember that as part of a desperate attempt to control congestion and contamination, one day of each week your car is not allowed to be driven in the city during the day. This is determined by the last number on your license plate; no one is exempt.

▣ GETTING AROUND

While most neighborhoods are easily traversed by foot, public transportation is necessary to travel between different areas of this spread-out city. The **Metro** is the fastest, cleanest, and quickest mode of transportation. Unfortunately, it becomes inhumanely crowded during rush hour (daily 7:30-9:30am and 6-9pm) and doesn't reach all parts of the city. More extensive are the thousands of white and green minibuses known as **peseros, micros,** or **colectivos** (1-3 pesos depending on the distance), with stickers marking the route on front. *Peseros* are particularly fast and easy to catch along Insurgentes. Taxis, while more expensive, are especially handy for traversing the city late at night and for women traveling alone. If you want to be safe, however, do not ever hail cabs on the street. **Sitio cabs** can be found at official stands or reached by phone. Use them and them only. Though a taxi may appear safe, you may be flagging down a mugging.

BY METRO

The Metro never ceases to amaze. The fare is cheap, the crowds enormous, the ride smooth and efficient, the service extensive, and the stations immaculate. Built in the late 1960s, the Metro now transports five million people per day, making the equivalent of two and a half trips around the world. On top of this, new tracks are laid daily. Mexico's Metro system knows no bounds.

Metro tickets (1.5 pesos, including transfers) are sold in *taquillas* (booths) at every station. Directions are stated in terms of the station at either end of a given line, and each of the two *andenes* (platforms) has signs indicating the terminus toward which trains are heading. For example, if you are on Line 3 between Indios Verdes and Universidad, you can go either "Dirección Indios Verdes" or "Dirección Universidad." Trains run M-F 5am-midnight, Sa 6am-1am, and Su 7am-midnight. Try to avoid the Metro from M-F 7:30 to 9:30am and 6 to 9pm, when commuters pack the cars like sardines. Lunch break (M-F 2-4pm) is also crowded. Cars at either end of the train tend to be slightly less crowded.

Theft is one of the biggest problems with riding the Metro. To avoid hassles, it's a good idea to carry any bags in front of you or on your lap. The safest place in a crowded car is with your back against the wall and your belongings in front of you. Remember that rear pockets are easy to pick, front pockets are safer, and empty pockets are best. Because of overcrowding, large bags or suitcases are sometimes not allowed on the Metro. If you are intent on taking the Metro with that overstuffed pack, come very early or after 10:30pm, when the Metro is fairly empty and guards are more likely to look the other way.

Women traveling alone on the Metro may receive even more unwanted attention, and the horrible experience of being groped is a distinct possibility. Do not hesitate to call attention to the offender with a loud *"¿No tiene vergüenza?"* (Don't you have any shame?) or, *"¡Déjame!"* (Leave me alone!). During rush hours, many lines

ME SO HORNY In the survival-of-the-fittest world of Mexico City driving, patience is not a virtue—it's a sure-fire way to go nowhere. This in mind, *chilangos* are among the world's quickest to blast their car horns: at each other, at pedestrians, at birds, at the world in general. The noise during rush hour can become almost unbearable, so much so that horns are banned in front of hospitals and in certain city neighborhoods. Still, in such an expressive culture, the horn can convey far more than simple frustration. A quick toot can say hello to a friend, or serve as a ready-made pickup line. Victorious soccer fans often drive home from the stadium beeping their victory honks in unison. Five short toots, directed at another car or person, can signify a certain five syllable Mexican insult suggesting an inappropriate relationship between the target and his mother. So if you do try driving in Mexico City—or even crossing the street—you better learn the language of horns.

EL METROPOLITAN

Some Metro stops are sights in their own right. In fact, nearly every Metro transfer stop has some kind of exhibit, from elementary school drawings of the subway system to a re-creation of a London theater. Here are some notable stops:

Pino Suárez, Lines 1 and 2: a small Aztec building at mid-transfer.

La Raza, Lines 3 and 5: the Tunel de la Ciencia (science tunnel) in the marathon transfer. Marvel at nifty fractals or wear your whites and glow in the dark under a map of the constellations. The stop even has a small science museum (open M-Sa 10am-6pm).

Zócalo, Line 2: scale models of the *zócalo* as it has appeared throughout its history.

Copilco, Line 3: the platforms are lined with murals.

Bellas Artes, Lines 2 and 8: Aztec statuettes, replicas from the nearby Templo Mayor.

have cars reserved for women and children, usually at the front and ends of the train and designated by a partition labeled *Mujeres y Niños.* Look for women and children gathering on a separate part of the platform for the reserved car.

Most transfer stations have information booths to help clueless travelers and provide invaluable color-coded subway guides, also available at the tourist office. You can also contact **COVITUR** (Comisión de Vialidad y Transporte Urbano del D.F.; Public Relations), Felicia 67 (☎5709 8036 or 5709 1133), outside the Salto de Agua Metro station (Lines 1 and 8). Nearly all stations have guards and security offices, and all are required to have a *jefe de la estación* (chief of station) in a marked office. They are ready to deal with questions, complaints, panic attacks, and just about anything else. Lost belongings can be reported to the **Oficina de Objetos Extraviados,** in the Candelaria station (Lines 1 and 4), but don't hold your breath waiting to get anything back. (☎5542 5397. Open M-F 9am-8pm.)

BY PESERO

The name *pesero* comes from the time when riding these green and white minibuses used to cost one old peso, equivalent to about US$0.01 today. Although not quite the steal they used to be, *peseros* are still extremely affordable and— though crowded—excellent ways to make short, direct trips around town. No printed information is available, though destinations are posted on the front window. If you are unsure, don't be shy about asking the driver personally: *"¿Se va a...?"* ("Are you going to...").

In 1997, a great effort was made to establish set *pesero* stops. Look for the traditional bus stand or a little blue sign with a picture of a *pesero.* Note that *peseros* still need to be hailed even from designated stops; a hardy wave will do the trick. Most *peseros* now only let you on and off at these stops, but some will still slow down at any corner. To get off, ring the bell (if there is one) or simply shout loudly *¡Bajan!* (Coming down!). To prevent a missed stop, tell the driver your destination. Drivers will honk horns (often rigged to play such cute tunes as "It's a Small World" and the theme from *The Godfather*) to signal availability during rush hour.

Peseros cost 2-3 pesos for cross-city rides and 5 pesos for trips over 17km (10% more 10pm-6am). Some *peseros* only run until midnight, but the major routes—on Reforma, between Chapultepec and San Angel, and along Insurgentes—run 24 hours. Other well-traveled *pesero* routes are M: Hidalgo to Ciudad Universitaria (via Reforma, Bucareli, and Cuauhtémoc); La Villa to Chapultepec (via Reforma); Reforma to Auditorio (via Reforma and Juárez); the *zócalo* to Chapultepec (via 5 de Mayo and Reforma); San Angel to Izazaga (via 5 de Mayo and Reforma); Bolívar to Ciudad Universitaria/Coyoacán (via Bolívar in the *centro*); and San Angel to M: Insurgentes (via Av. de la Paz and Insurgentes Sur). Many depart from M: Chapultepec to San Angel, La Merced, and the airport.

BY TAXI

 BABY, YOU CAN'T DRIVE MY CAR. Because of increased hijackings, robberies, and rapes, the US State Department issued a warning against hailing cabs off the street—including those delicious lime-green Volkswagen bugs. If you simply must travel by taxi, consider getting a cab from a hotel taxi stand or summoning a **sitio taxi** (radio taxi). *Sitios* are much safer, but cost about twice as much as regular taxis. Travelers should weigh risk against cost. When traveling from the bus station or the airport, head straight to the nearest taxi stand, where you can pay a fixed rate. As tempting as it might be, just say no to the bugs.

Mexico City has more taxis whizzing around its streets than any other city in the world. It's hard to cross the street without having to dodge yet another lime-green Volkswagen bug. For safety reasons, it's a good idea to avoid hailing taxis off the street, especially at night. If push comes to shove, and you simply *must* hail a taxi, make sure to check the driver's credentials (all legitimate drivers will have photo ID badges). Carry small denominations, as drivers will often cite a lack of change as a reason to pocket some extra pesos. Base fares typically begin at 5 pesos, and at night, drivers will add 20% to the meter rate.

If you choose to get around by taxi, the best option is to use **sitio taxis.** There are several *sitios* (taxi bases) in every neighborhood. All restaurants and hotels, as well as most locals, will know the local number. *Sitios* will respond to your phone call by sending a car to pick you up. If you're near the *sitio*, walk up to the first cab in line. Since *sitio* taxis don't use meters, ask the operator what the trip will cost; prices are set by the zone. Operators will always give you the right price, and drivers very rarely overcharge. Official *sitio* cabs cost up to twice as much as taxis hailed off the street, but the assured safety is worth the extra cost. Other options are hotel cabs and *turismo* taxis, which are equally safe, but charge even more than the sitio taxis. If you can't locate a *sitio* number or a hotel cab, try **Servi-taxi** (☎ 5271 2560). They offer safe service at *sitio* prices. To get to the airport in a pinch, call **Transportación Terrestre al Aeropuerto** (☎ 5571 4193). It is appropriate to tip in any type of taxi.

BY CAR

Driving is the most complicated and least economical way to get around the city, not to mention the easiest way to get lost. Mexico City's drivers are notoriously reckless and aggressive; they need to be to survive on the over-trafficked and confusing roads. Yellow lines are often absent, pedestrians pounce on any sign of hesitation, and stop signs are planted midstream. Red lights are so routinely defied that, on busy intersections, police officers must be summoned to direct traffic. If your car should break down within city boundaries, call the **Asociación Nacional Automovilística (ANA;** ☎ 5292 1970 through 5292 1977) and request assistance. Wait for them beside your car, with the hood raised. If you leave your car alone, give it a goodbye kiss before you go.

Parking within the city is seldom a problem; parking lots are everywhere (4-8 pesos per hr., depending on location and condition of lot). Street parking is difficult to find, and vandalism is extremely common. Police will put an *inmobilizador* on your wheels if you park illegally; alternatively, they'll just tow your car. If you return to an empty space, locate the nearest police depot (not station) to figure out if your auto has been towed—if it's not there, it was stolen. If anything is missing from your car and you suspect that the police tampered with it, call the English-speaking **LOCATEL** (☎ 5658 1111).

Car rental rates are exorbitant, driving is a hassle, and the entire process is draining. Still interested? To rent a car you must have a valid driver's license (from any country), a passport or tourist card, and be at least 25 years old. Prices for rentals at different agencies tend to be similar: a small VW or Nissan with unlimited kilometers, insurance, and tax (known as IVA) costs about 350-450 pesos per day or 3000-3500 pesos per week. Most agencies have offices at the airport or in

AND ON THE SEVENTH DAY... All vehicles, even those of non-Mexican registration, must follow Mexico City's strict anti-smog regulations. Restrictions apply M-F 5am-10pm, and penalties for violations are stiff. Every vehicle must "rest" one day per week and cannot be driven. The day of the week is dependent on the last digit of the license plate. Note that some cars manufactured after 1995 may be exempt from the limitations.
Monday: 5 or 6
Tuesday: 7 or 8
Wednesday: 3 or 4
Thursday: 1 or 2
Friday: 9 or 0

the *Zona Rosa.* **Avis,** at the airport (☎5588 8888 or toll-free 01 800 70 777; open daily 7am-11pm) and at Reforma 308 (☎5533 1336; open M-F 7am-10:30pm); **Budget,** at the airport (☎5271 4322; open 24hr.) and at Hamburgo 68; **Dollar,** at the airport (☎5207 3838) and at Chapultepec 322 (open daily 7am-8pm); **Hertz,** at the airport (☎5592 2867; open 7am-10:30pm).

✷ ORIENTATION

Mexico City extends outward from the *centro* roughly 20km to the south, 10km to the north, 10km to the west, and 8km to the east. There is much debate about where the city actually begins and ends. Because of the central location of most sights, few tourists venture past the Bosque de Chapultepec to the west, La Basílica de Guadalupe to the north, the airport to the east, or San Angel and the UNAM to the south. A rectangular series of routes (the **Circuito Interior**) and a thorough thoroughfare system (**Ejes Viales**) help to make cross-city travel manageable. Of these, the *Eje Central*, commonly known as Lázaro Cárdenas, is the central north-south route. At a more local level, the city is difficult to know well; even most *chilangos* (Mexico City residents) don't have it all down pat. What's more, many different neighborhoods use the same street names; the city has more than 300 Benito Juárez streets. Still, it is only a matter of cardinal directions and good ol' trial and error before you've mastered the basics of this megalopolis. The most important thing is to know the name of the **colonia** (neighborhood). Mexico City has over 350 *colonias;* Col. Polanco, *Zona Rosa*, Col. Roma, and Col. Juárez are some of the most touristed. Because street numbers aren't as important, try to locate nearby monuments, museums, *glorietas* (traffic circles), cathedrals, and skyscrapers. It shouldn't be hard—there are loads of them. Street names tend to be clustered systematically. Streets in the *Zona Rosa* are named after European cities, those directly across Reforma are named after large rivers of the world, and the ones in Polanco are named after famous philosophers. If you are sufficiently insane to drive around the city, a good map of the outer routes is essential. **Guía Roji Ciudad de México** (90 pesos), a comprehensive street atlas, is a valuable aid for anyone planning to stay in the city for some time. You can also pick up its little sibling, the abridged **mini-Guía Roji** (40 pesos).

CIRCUITO INTERIOR AND EJES VIALES

Aside from the large thoroughfares—Insurgentes, Reforma, Chapultepec, and Miguel Alemán—a system of *Ejes Viales* (axis roads) conducts the majority of traffic within the Circuito Interior, a rectangular artery made up of several smaller connected routes. *Ejes* either run north-south or east-west, and together make a sort of super-grid of faster roads laid over the city. *Ejes* numbers increase heading away from the *zócalo*. Theoretically, using the *Ejes* together with the Circuito, any general area of the city can be reached without much delay. Unfortunately, because of heavy traffic zipping around gleefully is not the norm.

CITY CENTER

As huge as Mexico City is, almost everything of interest to visitors lies within easy reach of the city center. Many attractions are on or just off **Paseo de la Reforma,** the broad thoroughfare that runs southwest-northeast, or **Insurgentes,** the boulevard running north-south through the city. These two main arteries intersect at the **Glorieta Cuauhtémoc.** From **Bosque de Chapultepec,** Reforma proceeds northeast, punctuated by *glorietas* (traffic circles), each with a monument in the center. Some of the more famous ones, in southwest-to-northeast order, include: Glorieta Angel de la Independencia, Glorieta Cuauhtémoc, and Glorieta Cristóbal Colón.

Our accommodations and food listings for Mexico City are divided according to the four areas of most interest to tourists. Moving northwest on Reforma from Chapultepec, the **Zona Rosa** is followed by the area **near the Monumento a la Revolución,** the **Alameda,** and, east of the Alameda, the **Centro Histórico.**

CENTRO HISTÓRICO. The *centro histórico* contains the *zócalo,* most of the historic sights and museums, extensive budget accommodations, and lively inexpensive restaurants. The area is bounded by Cárdenas to the west, El Salvador to the south, Pino Suárez to the east, and Rep. de Perú to the north. **Metro stops: Allende,** Line 2 (closer to the accommodations and the Alameda) and **Zócalo,** Line 2 (literally the center of the city).

THE ALAMEDA. The Alameda, the central city park and its surroundings, contains many restaurants and many of the city's most attractive sights. The area is bounded by Eje 1 Pte. (known as Rosales, Guerrero, and Bucareli) to the west, Arcos de Belén to the south, Lázaro Cárdenas to the east, and Pensador Mexicano to the north. The **Plaza Garibaldi** is approximately a half-kilometer northeast of the Alameda. **Metro stops: Hidalgo,** Lines 2 and 3, **Bellas Artes,** Lines 2 and 8 (closer to the park, the Palacio de Bellas Artes, the Plaza Garibaldi, and the post office), and **San Juan de Letran,** Line 8 (closer to most food and accommodations).

NEAR THE MONUMENTO A LA REVOLUCIÓN. The Monumento a la Revolución area (also known as **Buenavista**) contains perhaps the most copious supply of inexpensive hotels and eateries, though considerably fewer glitzy attractions than other neighborhoods. It is bounded by Insurgentes Centro to the west, Reforma to the south and east, and Mosqueta to the north. **Metro stop: Revolución,** Line 2.

ZONA ROSA. The *Zona Rosa* (Pink Zone) is the capital's most touristy, commercial district, home to some of the country's most exciting nightlife. It is bounded by Reforma to the north and west, Chapultepec to the south, and Insurgentes to the east. A few of the area's listings lie just east of Insurgentes, and a string of clubs spills south past Chapultepec along Insurgentes Sur. The **Bosque de Chapultepec** is just west of the *Zona Rosa.* **Metro stops: Insurgentes,** Line 1 (right in the middle of the action), and **Sevilla,** Line 1 (further west toward Angel de la Independencia).

FARTHER FROM THE CENTER

THE NORTHERN DISTRICTS. Approximately 3km north of the *zócalo* is the district of **Tlatelolco** (**M: Tlatelolco,** Line 3.) famous for its pyramid and the Plaza de las Tres Culturas. Approximately 4km farther north lies **La Villa Basílica** (**M: La Villa Basílica,** Line 6), home of the Basílica de Guadalupe.

THE SOUTHERN DISTRICTS. Several important southern districts are strung along Insurgentes Sur, 10-15km southwest of the *zócalo.* In rough order from southwest to northeast is **Ciudad Universitaria** (M: Universidad, Line 3), the suburb of **San Angel** (**M. A. Quevedo,** Line 3), and posh **Coyoacán** (**M: Coyoacán,** Line 3). Approximately 20km southeast of the *zócalo* is **Xochimilco** (**M: Tasqueña,** Line 2), the Venice of Mexico City.

MEXICO CITY

🛂 SAFETY AND HEALTH

Mexico City, like most bloated metropolitan areas, has more than its share of crime. Before you go cancel your visit to the D.F., however, keep in mind that most crimes perpetrated against tourists fall under the category of petty street crime—muggings, pick pocketings, and purse-snatchings. Mexico City also has a fair number of con artists, who concentrate in highly touristed areas and send teary-eyed children armed with sob stories to extract funds from kind-hearted tourists. It's best to shake your head and avoid eye contact. In addition, some tourists have been the targets of crime perpetrated by men in uniform. Just because someone is dressed as a figure of authority doesn't mean they won't rob you blind. Foreigners are particularly vulnerable near obvious tourist areas, such as the Zona Rosa and the *zócalo*. In general, the downtown area, where most sights and accommodations are located, tends to be safer, though the back streets near Buenavista and the Alameda are significantly less so.

In addition to petty crime, violent crime against tourists has been on the rise. To avoid becoming the next victim, stay away from untouristed streets and areas, particularly at night or when traveling alone. Refrain from ostentatious displays of wealth and avoid obvious marks of foreignness such as shorts, baseball caps, fanny packs, and cameras. Never display your cash, and visit ATMs discreetly and in well-lit places. Speaking in Spanish makes would-be attackers far less likely to bother you. Never follow a vendor or shoeshiner out of public view. Car hijackings are on the rise, especially at night. Avoid driving at night anywhere in Mexico City, and drive with others if you can. Lock your doors and keep your windows rolled up. For more information about general safety, see **Safety and Security,** p. 15.

Women are, unfortunately, at higher risk of attack. Mexican culture fosters *machismo*, which mainly manifests itself through insistent stares, provocative smiles, whistling, cat-calling, and vulgar propositions. Having light-colored hair or skin might lead to even more unwanted attention. These displays are generally more annoying than dangerous, and it's best to ignore it and avoid making eye contact. To avoid unwanted attention, do as Mexican women do—dress conservatively and avoid wearing shorts, tank tops, and short skirts. For more information on women traveling alone, see **Women Travelers,** p. 33.

In addition to the usual slew of health hazards faced by travelers to Mexico, Mexico City poses the additional problem of pollution. The city that used to be known as *la región más transparente del aire* (the region with the most transparent air) is now the most polluted in the world, and the layer of smog that blankets the city can cause problems for contact-lens wearers, those with allergies, the elderly, and small children. Travelers may want to bring eye-drops or throat spray, and asthmatics would be smart to bring along an extra inhaler. Pollution is particularly bad during the winter due to "thermal inversion," a phenomenon that occurs when warm air passing above the city traps the colder polluted air in the Valley of Mexico. The summer rainy season, on the other hand, does wonders for air cleanliness, and from May to October the air is quite breathable, posing few problems for most people. Newspapers and news programs often provide pollution indices, handy for determining whether pollution levels are unsafe.

🛈 PRACTICAL INFORMATION

TOURIST SERVICES

City Tourist Office: Infotur, Amberes 54 (☎5525 9380), at Londres in the *Zona Rosa*. (M: Insurgentes, Line 1). Helpful and friendly staff speaks some English. Excellent free city and Metro maps available on request. Lists hotels and restaurants grouped by region and price range, as well as upcoming events. Open daily 9am-9pm. The office operates information booths at the airport and the Cien Metros bus station. Other offices at San Angel, at the corner of Revolución and Madero (☎5616 4252), and Juárez 66 (☎518 10 03) near the Alameda at the corner of Revillagigedo.

WHEN THE RAIN COMES... If you come during the summer, keep a light poncho or umbrella handy. The rainy season (May-Oct.) brings daily 1-2hr. rain storms in the late afternoon or early evening. Otherwise, sunny and moderate weather prevails year-round.

Tourist Card (FMT) Info: Secretaría de Gobernación, Dirección General de Servicios Migratorios, Homero 1832 (☎5626 7200 or 5206 0506), in Col. Palanco. Take the Metro to Chapultepec, then catch a "Migración" *pesero.* The last stop is at the office. Come here to extend your FMT or clear up immigration problems. Arrive early to avoid long lines and prepare yourself for Mexican bureaucracy. Open M-F 9am-12:30pm.

Embassies: Visa processing can take up to 24hr. If you find yourself in an emergency after hours, still call—recorded messages provide important information.

Australia, Rubén Darío 55 (☎5531 5225), at Campos Eliseos in Col. Polanco. M: Auditorio, Line 7. Open M-Th 8:30am-2pm and 3-5:15pm, F 8:30am-2:15pm.

Belize, Bernardo de Galvez 215 (☎5520 1274), in Col. Lomas de Chapultepec. M: Observatorio, Line 1. Open M-F 9am-1:30pm.

Canada, Schiller 529 (☎5724 7900; www.canada.org.mx; email www@canada.org.mx), in Col. Polanco. M: Polanco or Auditorio, Line 7. Open M-F 9am-1pm and 2-5pm.

Costa Rica, Río Po 113 (☎5525 7764, 65, or 66), between Río Lerma and Río Panuco, behind the US Embassy. Open M-F 9am-5pm.

Guatemala, Explanada 1025 (☎5540 7520). M: Auditorio, Line 7. Open M-F 9am-1:30pm.

Honduras, Alfonso Reyes 220 (☎5211 5747), between Saltillo and Ometusco in Col. Condesa. Open M-F 10am-2pm.

New Zealand, Lagrange 103, 10th fl. (☎5281 5486). M: Polanco, Line 7. Open M-Th 9am-1pm and 3-5:30pm, F 9am-2pm.

UK, Río Lerma 71 (☎5207 2149). Open M-F 8:30am-3:30pm. Operators available 24hr.

US, Reforma 305 (☎5209 9100), at Glorieta Angel de la Independencia. Open M-F 9am-5pm. Operators available 24hr.

FINANCIAL SERVICES

Currency Exchange: Exchange rates in the city tend to be mediocre at best. *Casas de cambio* keep longer hours than banks, give better exchange rates, exchange non-US currencies, and sometimes stay open Su. Banks, on the other hand, offer one exchange rate and usually charge commission. Many *casas de cambio* are in the *centro,* along Reforma, and in the *Zona Rosa.* Call the **Asociación Mexicana de Casas de Cambio** (☎5264 0884 or 5264 0841) to find the exchange bureau nearest you. **Casa de Cambio Tíber** (☎5514 2760), on Río Tíber at Papaloapan, one block from the Angel. Open M-F 8:30am-5pm, Sa 8:30am-2pm. On the south side of the Alameda: **Casa de Cambio Plus,** Juárez 38 (☎5510 8953). Open M-F 9am-4pm, Sa 10am-2pm. Near the Monumento a la Revolución/Buenavista: **Casa de Cambio Catorce,** Reforma 51, 4th fl., near the Glorieta de Colón. Open M-F 9am-4pm.

ATMs: Lost or stolen cards can be reported 24hr. (☎5227 2777). **Citibank,** Reforma 390 (☎5258 3200 or 5227 2727; open 24hr.), and **Bank of America,** Reforma 265, 22nd fl. (☎5230 6400; open M-F 8:30am-5:30pm), can also help in an emergency.

American Express: Reforma 234 (☎5207 7282 or 5208 6004), at Havre in the *Zona Rosa.* Cashes personal and traveler's checks and accepts customers' mail and money wires. Report lost credit cards to the main office at Patriotismo 635 (☎5326 2666) and lost traveler's checks to either office. Open M-F 9am-6pm, Sa 9am-1pm.

LOCAL SERVICES

English Bookstores: American Bookstore, Madero 25 (☎5512 0306), in the *centro,* has extensive fiction, travel, and Latin American history books. Also a branch at Insurgentes Sur 1188 (☎5575 2372), in San Angel. Both branches open M-Sa 9:30am-8pm; *centro* store also open Su 10am-3pm. **Pórtico de la Ciudad de México,** Central 124 (☎5510 9683), at Carranza. English and Spanish books on Mexican history and archaeological sites. Open M-F 10am-7pm, Sa 10am-5pm. Also popular is **Librería Gandhi** (☎5510 4231), on Juárez along the Alameda. Open M-Sa 10am-9pm, Su 11am-8pm. Another at M.A. de Quevedo 128 (☎5661 0911) in San Angel.

English Library: Biblioteca Benjamin Franklin, Londres 16 (☎5209 9100), at Berlín, 2 blocks southeast of the Cuauhtémoc monument. Books, newspapers, and periodicals. Open M and F 3-7:30pm, Tu-Th 10am-3pm.

Cultural and Arts Info: Palacio Nacional de Bellas Artes (☎5521 9251, ext. 152 and 159), Juárez and Eje Central, for Bellas Artes info and reservations. Open M-Sa 11am-7pm, Su 9am-7pm. Check *Tiempo Libre* for city-wide listings.

Gay, Lesbian, and Bisexual Information: Colectivo Sol, write to Apdo. 13-320 Av. México 13, D.F. 03500. Has info on upcoming political and social events. Gay bars and clubs publicize events in *Tiempo Libre* and *Ser Gay.* Lesbians and bisexual women can contact **LesVoz** (☎5399 6019; email lesvoz@laneta.apc.org), the lesbian journal at Apartado Postal 33-091 México, D.F. 15900. Open M-Th 9am-1pm. Another resource is **El Closet de Sor Juana,** Xola 181, 2nd fl. (☎5590 2446), in Col. Alamos, a lesbian and bisexual group that organizes daily activities.

Women's Advocacy: Organización Nacional Pro-Derechos Humanos de las Mujeres y las Lesbianos (☎5399 6019; email proml@laneta.apc.org), gives free legal advice and support to women in cases of sexual discrimination or harassment. Open M-Th 8am-1pm.

LOCATEL: (☎5658 1111). The city's official lost-and-found hotline. Call if your car (or friend) is missing. Some English spoken.

Supermarkets: Most supermarkets are far from the *centro,* at residential Metro stops. Prices in supermarkets are higher than in *mercados* but lower than in corner stores. **Mega,** on the way to Tlatelolco from M: Tlatelolco, Line 3. Take the González exit, turn right on González, and walk 3 blocks; it's at the intersection with Cárdenas. Open daily 8am-10pm. **Aurrera,** 5 blocks north of Puente de Alvarado, on Insurgentes Nte. M: Revolución, Line 2. Also in San Angel, just outside M: M.A. Quevedo, Line 3. Open daily 7am-11pm. **Superama,** Río Sena and Balsas, in the *Zona Rosa,* directly outside M: Polanco, Line 7. Open daily 8am-9pm.

EMERGENCY

Emergency: ☎060

Information: ☎040

Police: Secretaría General de Protección y Vialidad (☎5588 5100). Open 24hr. In case of emergency, dial ☎08 for the Policía Judicial. No English spoken.

Tourist Police: Seguridad y Información Turística, in marked vans in the *Zona Rosa* near el Angel and in the *zócalo.* English spoken. Available 8am-8pm. **Patrullas de Auxilio Turistico,** is an auto service for tourists. Deals primarily with accidents, break-downs, and thefts. Little English spoken. **Procuradura General de Justicia,** Florencia 20 (☎5625 7692 or 5625 7696), in the *Zona Rosa.* A department of justice catering especially to tourists. File reports on anything—minor robberies, major abuses of power, or lost or stolen tourist cards. Some English spoken. Staffed 24hr.

Emergency Shelter: Casa de Asistencia Social (☎5744 8128 for women, 5530 4762 for men), on Calle Santanita in Col. Viaducto Pietá, near the treasury building.

Rape Crisis: Hospital de Traumatología de Balbuena, Cecilio Robelo 103 (☎5552 1602 or 5764 0339; M: Moctezuma, Line 1). Also dial ☎060.

Legal Advice: Supervisión General de Servicios a la Comunidad, Fray Servando 32 (☎5625 7208 or 5625 7184; M: Isabel la Católica, Line 1), south of the *centro* on José Maria Izagaza, 2 blocks south of the Metro stop. Call if you are the victim of a robbery or accident and need legal advice. Little English spoken. Open daily 9am-9pm.

Sexually Transmitted Disease Information and Innoculation Information: Secretaría de Salud, Benjamin Gil 14 (☎5277 6311; M: Juanacatlán, Line 1), in Col. Condensa. Open M-F 8am-7pm, Sa 9am-2pm.

AIDS Hotline: TELSIDA/CONASIDA, Florencia 8 Calzada de Tlalpan, 2nd fl. (☎5207 4143 or 5207 4077), at Col. Torielo Guerra. From M: General Anaya, Line 2, take a *micro* headed for *Zona de Hospitales.* Runs AIDS tests, provides prevention information, and serves as a general help center. Open M-F 9am-9:30pm.

Red Cross: Ejército Nacional 1032 (☎5395 1111), at Polanco. Open 24hr.

Pharmacies: Small *farmacias* abound on almost every street corner. In addition, all **Sanborn's** and supermarkets have well-stocked pharmacies.

Medical Care: The **US Embassy** (see p. 93) has a list of doctors with their specialties, addresses, phone numbers, and English-language abilities. In an emergency, ask for the nearset **IMSS** (Social Security) clinic; there is usually one in every neighborhood.

Dirección General de Servicios Médicos (☎5518 5100) has information on all city hospitals. Open M-F 9am-5pm.

American British Cowdray (ABC) Hospital, Calle Sur 136 (☎5227 5000), at Observatorio Col. Las Américas is expensive but trustworthy and excellent. No foreign health plans valid, but major credit cards accepted. Open 24hr.

Torre Médica, José Maria Iglesias 21 (☎5705 2577 or 5705 1820; M: Revolución, Line 2), has a few doctors who speak English.

COMMUNICATIONS

Fax: Tacuba 8 (☎5521 2049; fax 5512 1894), at the Museo Nacional de Arte in the right wing of the building, behind the central post office. Also has **telegram** and **Western Union** service. Open M-F 9am-11:30pm, Sa 9am-10:30pm, Su 9am-4:30pm. Many *papelerías* (stationery shops) also offer fax service.

Internet Access: Mexico City is wired. Here are a few recommended establishments.

Cyber Club, Edison 92 (☎5703 0111), near the Monumento a la Revolución. 12 pesos per 30min., 20 pesos per hr.; students 9 pesos per 30min., 15 pesos per hr. Open daily 10am-9pm.

Java Chat, Genova 44K (☎5525 6853), in the *Zona Rosa.* Enjoy coffee, soda, and the fast T1 connection. 39 pesos per hr. Open M-F 9am-11:30pm, Sa-Su 10am-midnight.

Conecte Café, Genova 71, on the 2nd fl. Ring the bell to get in. Connection could be faster for 20 pesos per hr. Open Su-Th 10am-10pm, F-Sa 10am-1am.

Lafoel, Donceles 80 (☎5512 5835), at the corner of Rep. de Brasil in the *centro,* has reasonably fast computers, a printer, and a scanner. 30 pesos per hr. Open M-Sa 9am-8pm, Su 10am-5pm.

Mini-Super Mas Por Menos, Lázaro Cárdenas 23, 1 block from the Palacio de Bellas Artes near the Alameda Central, has possibly the best name. 3 slow computers. 25 pesos per hr. Open daily 8am-midnight.

Courier Services: UPS, Reforma 404 (☎5228 7900). Open M-F 8am-8pm. **Federal Express,** Reforma 308 (☎551 09 96), in Col. Juárez near the Glorieta Angel de Independencia. Open M-F 8am-7pm, Sa 9am-1:30pm.

MEXICO CITY PUBLICATIONS

Tiempo Libre: the best resource for getting down and dirty in the city. The phenomenal weekly paper is on sale at most corner newsstands and covers movies, galleries, restaurants, dances, museums, and most cultural events. Every Th. 7 pesos.

El M (the Metro): an informative and professional newspaper featuring both national and international news. It's available at most Metro stops. Pick one up early—they tend to go fast. Free.

The Mexico City News: an English-language daily with film and theater listings. Extensive international news as well, in case you miss gossip from the home front. 7 pesos.

La Jornada: a top national newspaper, with international news and event listings. 6 pesos.

Ser Gay: available at newsstands and most gay bars, is not widely distributed but has a complete listing of gay and lesbian nightlife options.

Central Post Office: (☎ 5521 7394). On Lázaro Cárdenas at Tacuba, across from the Palacio de Bellas Artes. Open for stamps and *lista de correos* (window 3) M-F 8am-6pm, Sa 9am-4pm, Su 9am-noon. **Mexpost** inside. Open M-F 9am-4pm, Sa 9am-2pm. Postal museum upstairs with turn-of-the-century mailboxes and other old-school gear. Currently closed for renovations, but usually open M-F 8am-10pm, Sa 8am-8pm, Su 8am-4pm. **Postal Code:** 06002.

▐ ACCOMMODATIONS

To give you an idea of the size of this city, more than 1000 hotels exist within its expanse. Rooms abound in the *Centro Histórico* and near the Alameda Central. The best budget bargains are found near the Monumento a la Revolución on the Plaza de la República. Avoid the filthier sections around the Alameda and any area that makes you uncomfortable. Beware of any place where the hotel itself (and not the parking lot) is marked "Hotel Garage." These rooms are frequented by businessfolk "working late at the office" and allow entry directly from garage to room for some illicit lovin' on the sly. Also note that, in an attempt to cut down on prostitution, many budget establishments have adopted "No Guests Allowed" policies. Rooms, priced at 100 to 150 pesos for one bed and 150 to 200 pesos for two beds, should be clean and have carpeting, a TV, and a telephone. Some budget hotels charge according to the number of beds, not per person; beds tend to be large enough for two. If you don't mind snuggling (or simply want an excuse to do so), sharing a bed can save major pesos. Finally, always ask to look at a room before you accept it; this is easier to do after check-out time (noon-3pm).

The shabby neighborhoods around the four bus station stations generally offer expensive rooms. Even if you arrive late at night, it is not safe to walk even the few blocks to your hotel—you'd do best to make the trip by taxi. Once in a taxi, why not head to the center of town? Better yet, take the Metro if possible. For travelers arriving at the **Central de Autobuses del Norte (Cien Metros)** who insist on rooms close to the station, the pricey but comfy **Hotel Brasilia**, Av. de los 100 Mts. 4823, is a fair option, three blocks to the left along the main thoroughfare as you exit the bus station. Rooms are carpeted and clean, with TV, phone, and private safe. (☎ 5587 8577. Singles 180 pesos; doubles 240 pesos.) Both the **TAPO** and **Poniente** stations are in especially unsafe neighborhoods. If you arrive at either, take the Metro or a taxi to safer accommodations.

CENTRO HISTÓRICO

Situated between the *zócalo* and Alameda Central, hotels in the *Centro Histórico* are reasonably priced and fairly safe, though the streets empty out once locals head home. During the day, the action inevitably brings noise and congestion; if you prefer quieter surroundings, consider the Alameda or Revolución areas. Many of the hotels listed below are north of Madero and 5 de Mayo, the parallel east-west streets that connect the Alameda with the *zócalo*, and east of Lázaro Cárdenas, the north-south Eje Central that runs one block east of the Alameda. Street names change north of Tacuba: Isabel la Católica becomes República de Chile, and Bolívar turns into Allende. **Metro stops: Bellas Artes,** Lines 2 and 8; **Allende,** Line 2. Hotels on 5 de Mayo, Isabel la Católica, and Uruguay are better served by Metro stops **Zócalo,** Line 2, and **Isabel la Católica,** Line 1.

▨ **Hostal Catedral,** Guatemala 4 (☎ 5518 1726; email hostellingmexico@remaj.com), directly behind the Cathedral. With its grand opening in the fall of 2000, backpackers finally have a wonderful hostelling option in the heart of Mexico City. Services include laundry, restaurant, kitchen, cable TV lounge, pool table, and Internet access. Terrace and sunning area has an amazing view of the cathedral and the Torre Latinoamerica. Each bed comes with a big locker for luggage storage. Breakfast included. Dorm rooms 100 pesos; private doubles 250 pesos.

■ **Hotel Catedral,** Donceles 95 (☎5518 5232), a half-block north of the cathedral. Quiet, luxurious rooms with big cable TVs, phones, and access to 2 large balconies with views of the cathedral. Travel agent and restaurant in lobby. Singles 280 pesos; doubles 400 pesos; triples 540 pesos; 40 pesos per additional person.

■ **Hotel Isabel** (☎5518 1213), on the corner of El Salvador and Isabel la Católica. Palatial rooms with TV and phone branch off an inner and outer courtyard. Singles 95 pesos, with bath 150 pesos; doubles 110 pesos, with bath 190 pesos; triples 210 pesos; quads 300 pesos.

■ **Hotel Antilles,** Domínguez 34 (☎5526 5674), between Allende and República de Chile. In the castle-like lobby, a winding staircase leads to newly renovated rooms. Full amenities (TVs, bottled water, and phones) and an eager staff. Ask for a room with a balcony. Singles 190 pesos; doubles 250 pesos; triples 380 pesos; quads 400 pesos.

Hostal Moneda, Moneda 8 (☎5522 5821; www.hostelmoneda.com.mx; email info@hostamoneda.com.mx), on the street between the Palacio Nacional and the Templo Mayor. Another new hostel just off of the *zócalo*. Kitchen, TV lounge, and computer. The upstairs terrace has a nice view. Relatively big dorm rooms with 3 or more beds. 10% HI discount. 90 pesos per person includes breakfast and 10min. of Internet access.

Hotel Principal, Bolívar 29 (☎5521 1333), by the Parilla Leonesa restaurant, which offers room service. All rooms have high ceilings, TVs, phones, safes, and bottled water, but only 12 have windows. Helpful staff. Singles 155 pesos; doubles 210 pesos; triples 265 pesos; quads 330 pesos.

Hotel San Antonio, on the alleyway off 5 de Mayo called 2 Callejón de 5 de Mayo, between Isabel la Católica and Palma. The hotel is #29; knock on the door under the flags to be buzzed in. Off-the-beaten-path location affords a bit of peace. Clean, bright, and well-maintained. Rooms have TV and phone. Request a room with a bigger window to get more light. Singles 140 pesos; triples 200 pesos.

Hotel Monte Carlo, Uruguay 69 (☎5521 2559). Large, lovingly mismatched rooms have balconies, red carpets, yellow satin furniture, and clean tiled bathrooms. Relaxing lounge and top floor skylight. Sharing a bath saves 20-30 pesos. Singles 130 pesos; doubles 160 pesos; triples 210 pesos; 10 pesos per additional person.

Hotel Juárez, 1A Cerrada de 5 de Mayo 17 (☎5512 6929 or 5518 4718), between Isabel La Católica and Palma. Keep your eyes peeled for the elusive sign. Small and comfortable rooms, dark lobby, and good location, just off the main strip. Rooms have TV, radio, and phone, but only half have windows. Singles 110 pesos; doubles 130 pesos; 10 pesos per additional person.

Hotel Buenos Aires, Motolinia 21 (☎5518 2104 or 5518 2137), near the corner of Madero. Lively, if a bit run-down, with a tangerine courtyard. Near both the Alameda and the *zócalo*, each room has carpeting, soft beds, TV. Ask for a room with a window; most don't have them. Singles 95 pesos; doubles 130 pesos.

Hotel Atlanta, Domínguez #31 (☎5518 1200), Bright rooms with small, sparkling baths, cable TV, and phones. Singles 120 pesos; doubles 170 pesos; triples 230 pesos.

THE ALAMEDA

The expansive Alameda is always throbbing with activity, but its greenery and charm are replaced with dirt and danger as you wander into the surrounding streets. For the most part, try to avoid staying in this area—there are nicer parts of the city. The more viable hotels are south of Alameda Central. **Metro Stops: Balderas,** Line 1; **Salto de Agua,** Line 8; and **San Juan de Letran,** Line 8.

■ **Hotel Manolo Primero,** Moya 111 (☎5521 7309), near Arcos de Belén, halfway between M: Balderas, Line 1, and M: Salto del Agua, Line 8. Spacious blue hallways and a cavernous, jungle-like lobby. New rooms with king-sized beds, TV, lounge chairs, and clean, large bathrooms with gigantic mirrors. Singles 140 pesos.

Hotel San Diego, Moya 98 (☎5512 2653), between Pugibet and Delicias, 6 blocks south of the Alameda. This is a safe bet if its neighbor Manolo Primero is full. Mid-size rooms have TVs, but, alas, no shower curtains. Singles 120 pesos; doubles 160 pesos.

NEAR THE MONUMENTO A LA REVOLUCIÓN

Hotels near the Monumento a la Revolución are cheaper and quieter than their counterparts in the *centro* or the Alameda. Backpackers tend to congregate here, particularly in the hotels on Mariscal and Edison. **Metro stops: Revolución,** Line 2, serves hotels south of Puente de Alvarado/Hidalgo; **Guerrero,** Line 3, serves those to the north, near the train station.

▨ **Casa de Los Amigos,** Mariscal 132 (☎5705 0521 or 5705 0646), M: Revolución, Line 2. Originally the home of painter José Clemente Orozco, the Casa now houses tourists and social activists. The 4-day minimum stay is designed to promote involvement and understanding. Backpackers, grad students, eco-warriors, and other fascinating people from all over the world congregate here. A well-stocked library, lively lounge, a kitchen, and laundry facilities are all available in this cooperative atmosphere. Quiet hours 10pm-8am. No drugs or alcohol allowed in the house. Breakfast 15 pesos. Dorm rooms 60 pesos; private rooms 65-70 pesos; doubles 110-150 pesos.

Hotel Yale, Mosqueta 200 (☎5591 1545), M: Buenavista, Line B, between Zaragoza and Guerrero, to the left as you exit the Metro station. Recently remodeled rooms and baths, full-length mirrors, TVs, phones, and colorful unmatching furniture all make for an endearing hotel. Singles and doubles 90 pesos; triples and quads 160 pesos.

Hotel Edison, Edison 106 (☎5566 0933), at Iglesias. The luxury is worth the splurge. Enormous rooms with full amenities surround a shrubbery-filled courtyard. Singles 170-190 pesos; doubles 210 pesos; triples 240 pesos; quads 260 pesos.

Hotel Ibiza, Arriaga 22 (☎5566 8155), between Edison and Mariscal, keeps it simple, with about 20 identical rooms. Each one is small, with 1 bed, phone, and TV. Singles 100 pesos; doubles 150 pesos.

Hotel Oxford, Mariscal 67 (☎5566 0500), M: Revolución, Line 2, at Alcázar, next to the small park. Large, colorful rooms have TVs, phones, and views of the park. Bathrooms with huge sinks ideal for laundry. At night, the adjoining bar attracts a lively local crowd. Singles 85-105 pesos; doubles 115 pesos; triples 150 pesos; quads 200 pesos.

ZONA ROSA

The *Zona Rosa* is really posh—that's why you can't afford to stay there. Confine your *Zona* excursions to shopping, eating, and clubbing.

◖ FOOD

Options for meals fall into six basic categories: the very cheap (and sometimes risky) vendor stalls scattered about the streets; fast, inexpensive, and generally safe *taquerías;* slightly more formal *cafeterías;* more pricey and decorous Mexican restaurants; locally popular US-style eateries; and expensive international fare. In addition, US fast-food chains mass-produce predictable fare for the timid palate. **VIPS** and **Sanborn's** run hundreds of restaurants throughout the capital that are very popular with middle-class Mexicans; some are open 24 hours and have adjacent stores. If you're preparing your own food, local neighborhood markets and supermarkets stock almost anything you could need. For fresh produce and meats, try **La Merced** market (see p. 127), the mother of them all.

CENTRO HISTÓRICO

The historic downtown area of Mexico City has a wide selection of food at low prices, with slick US fast-food establishments, enormous *cafeterías,* and countless small eateries. Motolinia and Gante host a high concentration of eateries; there's plenty of good fare for vegetarians. **Metro stops: Zócalo,** Line 2; **Bellas Artes,** Lines 2 and 8; **Allende,** Line 2; and **Isabel la Católica,** Line 1.

▨ **Café Tacuba,** Tacuba 28 (☎5512 8482), M: Allende, Line 2. Excellent food and engaging conversation since 1912. Everyone who's anyone has been here. An amazing combo of camp and class, men in colonial garb may greet you or a *mariachi* band may serenade you. All dishes are made from scratch and worth the wait. *Antojitos* 15-42 pesos, entrees 50-80 pesos. Open daily 8am-11:30pm.

Restaurantes Vegetarianos del Centro, Mata 13 (☎5510 0113), between 5 de Mayo and Madero. Happy, healthy, sunshine-yellow eatery filled with an eclectic group of veggie lovers. *Comida corrida* 38 pesos, with salad 43 pesos. Open daily 8am-8pm.

Café Dayi, Isabela la Católica 9-11 (☎5521 6203), near Tacuba. Kitschy pseudo-Chinese decor, but the food—both Chinese and Mexican—is excellent. Crane your neck to watch the *fútbol,* as aproned waitresses refill your *agua de sandía* (watermelon juice). Chicken and duck dishes 35 pesos, *comida corrida china* and *mexicana* 31 pesos and 27 pesos respectively. Open daily 8am-11pm.

Restaurant Danubio, Uruguay 3 (☎5512 0912), east of Lázaro Cárdenas. If you won't miss the extra pesos, the stately seafood restaurant's good food and drinks make for a nice night out. Famous artsy types have left their scribblings framed on the walls. Entrees (70 pesos) and specials (100 pesos) big enough for two. Open daily 1-10pm.

Café El Popular, 5 de Mayo 10 (☎5510 9176). The simple red and yellow cafe attracts plenty of locals with its *menu del día (*30 pesos). Good, basic food and friendly staff. Entrees 34-40 pesos. Open daily 7am-1am.

Vitamex, Tacuba 66 (☎5512 9460), and several locations throughout the *centro*. A wildly colorful grocery store/cafe/yogurt stand sells veggie burgers (14 pesos), entrees (20-30 pesos), and an incredible variety of *licuados* (14 pesos). The vitamin counter has remedies for everything from ulcers to impotence. Open daily 10am-8pm.

THE ALAMEDA

The lively Alameda atmosphere happily infects the restaurants peppering the area. You'll find good, back-to-basics food. Prices are on the high side, but portions are large. For something different, try one of the Chinese restaurants on Dolores, two blocks west of Cárdenas and one block south of the Alameda. Cheap, small eateries line Independencia, one block south of the Alameda. **Metro stops: Hidalgo,** Line 2; **Bellas Artes,** Lines 2 and 8; **Juárez,** Line 3; and **San Juan de Letran,** Line 8.

▨ **El Moro,** Cárdenas 42 (☎5512 0896), outside M: San Juan de Letran, Line 3. Mexico's richest and most amazing hot chocolate this side of Oaxaca. The *chocolates* (25 pesos) come in 4 varieties: *mexicano* (light), *español* (thick and sweet), *frances* (medium thickness and sweetness) and *especial* (slightly bitter). Each comes with 4 churros, a recipe for sugar overload. Milk and soda (8 pesos) help wash it all down. Open 24hr.

▨ **Fonda Santa Anita,** Humboldt 48 (☎5518 4609), M: Juárez, Line 3. Go a block west on Artículo 120, turn right on Humboldt, and continue a half-block. The restaurant has represented Mexico in 5 World's Fairs and feels no need to dispel stereotypes—the tablecloths are bright pink and colorful depictions of bullfights and busty women cover the walls. Incredible versions of old standards and regional specialties from all over the country. *Comida corrida* 40 pesos. Open M-F 1-10pm, Sa-Su 1-8pm.

Oriental (☎5521 3099), on a pedestrian walkway at Dolores and Independencia, on a block of Chinese restaurants. The prices here are slightly lower (*comida corrida* 45 pesos), and there's a huge bronze Buddha at the entrance. Open daily 10am-11pm.

Energía Natural (☎5521 2015), at the corner of 16 de Septiembre and Dolores. The brightest and most beautiful of the bunch, with healthful touches such as whole wheat bread. Sandwiches and burgers 9-20 pesos. Open daily 8am-7pm.

NEAR THE MONUMENTO A LA REVOLUCIÓN

Without many affluent residents or big tourist draws, this area lacks the snazzy international cuisine of other areas. Instead, homey cafes, *torterías*, and *taquerías* dominate the scene. For hearty portions and low prices, this is the spot. **Metro stops: Revolución,** Line 2; and **Guerrero,** Line 3.

■ **La Especial de París,** Insurgentes Centro 117 (☎5703 2316). This *nievería* (ice cream place) has been scooping frozen wonders since 1921. 100%-natural treats, from *malteadas* (milkshakes) to *frutas glacé* (fruit ices). Double scoop 16 pesos, triple scoop 23 pesos, quadruple scoop 28 pesos. Open daily noon-9pm.

El Tigre, at Mariscal and Arrispe, is home of the formidable *Super Torta Gigante*. The friendly guys behind the counter will make you a big, big *torta* (13 pesos), such as the *española*, with ham, *chorizo* (spicy sausage), and cheese, or the *milchory*, with *chorizo*, cheese, and *milanesa* (breaded steak). Open daily 10am-8:30pm.

La Taberna (☎5591 1100), Arriaga at Ignacio Mariscal, below street level next to Hotel Pennsylvania. The service is fast and *comida corrida* (25 pesos) sure to please. Also has a relaxed and friendly bar. Open M-Sa 1pm-late.

Super Cocina Los Arcos, Ignacio Mariscal at Iglesias. Bright orange furnishings and a homey, cozy atmosphere. Service is a little slow, but it's all right—their chicken soups (16 pesos) and *alambres con queso* (22 pesos) are the best around. *Comida corrida* 16 pesos. Most dishes 12-30 pesos. Open M-Sa 8am-10pm.

Restaurant El Paraíso, Orozco y Berra at Gonzales Martínez, across the street from Museo del Chopo. Offers vegetarian *comida corrida* (18 pesos) in a friendly, family atmosphere. Open daily 8am-midnight.

ZONA ROSA

With its reputation as the city's glam tourist center, budget travelers might assume that only loaded tourists can eat here. Yet the reality is that although the area has some of the city's more expensive restaurants, many eateries cater to the clerks and office workers from the scores of surrounding office buildings. Still, you will see more tourists (and fast food joints) here than anywhere. If you're more interested in the *Zona Rosa's* slick party atmosphere than in filling your stomach, skip dinner in favor of a drawn-out evening appetizer. **Metro stops: Insurgentes**, Line 1; and **Sevilla,** Line 1.

■ **Cantina Las Bohemias,** Londres 142 (☎5207 4384). The intimate *cantina* will put you in the mood for love with tables for two, soft lighting, and romantic Spanish music. The impressive bar, however, makes this a good choice for anyone, romantic sap or not. *Antojitos* 25 pesos, entrees 70-80 pesos. Open M-Sa 1pm-1am.

■ **Saint Moritz,** Genova 44, next to Java Chat. Sure, maybe this tiny, lively restaurant doesn't have the flashy decor of the typical *Zona Rosa* eatery, but it is far and away the neighborhood's best value. *Menú del día* 16 pesos. Open M-Sa 10am-6pm.

■ **La Luna,** Oslo 11 (☎5525 0381), on the narrow walkway between Niza and Copenhagen. Beautiful sketches of *indigenas* grace the walls of this cozy, popular restaurant. The *comida corrida* (24 pesos) includes soup, a small and large entree, and a beverage. Avoid the 2-3pm lunch rush. Open M-Sa 8am-9pm.

Ricocina, Londres 168 (☎5514 0648), east of Florencia. Once the *Zona Rosa's* best-kept secret, the wonderful, family-owned restaurant has become one of the area's most popular lunch joints thanks to its straightforward, authentic dishes. Soft peach surroundings help you enjoy a delicious *menú del día* (30 pesos). Open daily 9am-6pm.

Vegetariano Yug, Varsovia 3 (☎5526 5330), near Reforma. Dig the classy Indian paintings, plants, and erotic Hindu sculpture, then try the *carnitas vegetarianas* (vegetarian "meats"; 39 pesos). The veggie buffet is Indian and French (45 pesos). Open M-F 7am-10pm, Sa 8:30am-8pm, Su 1-8pm.

Coffee House, Londres 102 (☎5525 4034). The ideal place to sip cappuccino (16 pesos), munch on a baguette sandwich (40 pesos), salad, or pastry (both 25 pesos), and partake in some serious people-watching. Open daily 8am-9pm.

Kam Ling, Londres 114 (☎5514 5837). This homey restaurant serves both Mexican (*comida corrida* 27 pesos) and Chinese (22-38 pesos) food. Open doors and location make it a good place to relax. Open daily 8am-10:30pm.

NEAR CHAPULTEPEC

Inside the Bosque de Chapultepec, sidewalk stands offer an enormous variety of snacks. Should you want a sit-down eatery, the area around the Chapultepec Metro station, just outside the park, is cluttered with vendors and small restaurants. **Metro stops: Chapultepec,** Line 1. A bit farther east, however, lie a few more restaurants, easily accessible by **M: Sevilla,** Line 1. A ritzier alternative are the *antojitos* in beautiful Colonia Polanco, north of the Museo de Antropología, accessible by **M: Polanco,** Line 7.

Los Sauces, Av. Chapultepec 530 (☎5528 6705), at Acapulco Roma, 1½ blocks east of M: Chapultepec, Line 1. The uniquely tiled bar and grill is cluttered with pictures of Mexican politicians and stars. Zone out to *telenovelas,* listen to the radio, or watch chefs chopping onions and peppers for your meal (18-25 pesos). Open daily 9am-9pm.

El Kioskito (☎5553 3055), on Chapultepec, at the corner with Sonora, serves succulent *antojitos* (12-20 pesos) and specialties (32-40 pesos) in a classy, relaxed atmosphere with tiled fountain and old photos of the city. The guacamole (11 pesos) has pizzazz. Open daily 8am-9pm.

COYOACÁN

The southern suburb of Coyoacán attracts students, young couples, and literati to its somewhat upscale restaurants. If you crave great coffee, cheesecake, or pesto, this is the place to spend an afternoon. Outdoor cafes and ice cream shops line the cobbled streets. For some sweet scoops, try **Santa Clara,** at Allende and Cuauhtémoc (18 pesos per scoop), or **Las Nieves de Coyoacán,** on Plaza Hidalgo (12 per scoop). For a cheap, excellent meal, try the **food court** on Hijuera, just south of Plaza Hidalgo. Frequented almost exclusively by locals, these tiny restaurants have home-cooked food at un-Coyoacán-like prices. (Open M-Sa 9am-9pm.) **metro stop: Coyoacán,** Line 3.

El Guarache (☎5554 4506), on the south side of Jardín Centenario. Take in the beauty of downtown Coyoacán and the nearby coyote fountain from a *jardín*-side table at this classy cafe. *Menú del día* comes with everything: drink, flavored coffee, and dessert (28 pesos). Entrees 32-50 pesos. Open daily 9am-10pm.

Café El Parnaso, Carrillo Puerto 2 (☎5554 2225 or 5658 3195), on Jardín Centenario, diagonally across from the cathedral. A celebrated book and record store with an outdoor cafe, all on the plaza's edge. Though the food is a bit pricey, the people-watching and eavesdropping are unbeatable. Coffee and cheesecake with strawberries 20-30 pesos. Open Su-Th 8am-midnight, F-Sa 8am-late.

El Jarocho (☎5568 5029), on Allende and Cuauhtémoc, 1 block north of Pl. Hidalgo. Follow the smell of freshly ground coffee to this legendary corner stand, or just look for the line of customers overflowing into the street. Straight out of Veracruz, the Jarocho has been serving some of the best java in the city since 1953. Cappuccino, mocha, and hot chocolate for under 6 pesos each. Open daily 7am-midnight.

Casa de los Taquitos (☎5554 8039), at the corner of Carillo Puerto and Ortega, 1 block south of the Jardín Centenario. All the taste and value of a great taco stand, in a more charming atmosphere. The bright yellow restaurant's flower-painted walls display a few prints by local favorite Frida Kahlo. Specialty tacos 5-36 pesos.

SAN ANGEL

The chic restaurants and *típico* taco stands of San Angel pack 'em in, especially on Saturdays, when crowds of well-to-do tourists and Mexicans are drawn to the booths of overpriced art in the Bazaar Sábado. If you want to dine in style, Plaza **San Jacinto** is the place to be. **Metro stop: M. A. Quevedo,** Line 3.

La Mora, Madero 2 (☎5616 2080), has a great view of the plaza from its upstairs patio. Flowers and cati adorn the walls, and the food is almost as good as the location. *Comida corrida* 30 pesos, including *agua purificada* and dessert. Open daily 8am-7pm.

Chucho el Roto, Madero 8 (☎5616 2041). A simple, deliciously inexpensive spot just steps from the action. This daytime diner, named for a notorious Mexican bandit and expert pickpocket of the late 19th century, serves a *menú del día* of soup, rice, entree, and dessert (22 pesos). Unlike its namesake, the open-air restaurant won't rob you blind. Breakfast specials 20 pesos. Open daily 9am-5:30pm.

El Rincón de La Lechuza, Miguel Ángel de Quevedo 34 (☎5661 0050), down from M: M. A. Quevedo, Line 3, just past La Paz. Remains joyfully crowded and decorated in yellow and white, with wood tables. Tasty tacos grilled over a fire 20-35 pesos; specials 35-45 pesos. Open Su-Th 1-11:30pm, F-Sa 1pm-1:30am.

La Finca Café de Dios (☎5550 9482), on Madero right off the Pl. de San Jacinto. This hole-in-the-wall coffee stand only serves 100% Mexican grown beans. All mocha, espresso, and piping hot treats under 6 pesos. If you're serious about your coffee, kilos of Chiapan coffee beans start around 60 pesos. Open daily 8am-8pm.

☉ SIGHTS

Overflowing with history, culture, and entertainment, Mexico City truly has something for everyone. A well-rounded picture of its sights will require a week at the very least, and even lifetime natives are always finding something knew. Most major museums and sights are open seven days a week, and smaller museums and attractions closed only on Mondays. Admission is almost always free for national students and teachers; oftentimes, smooth talking with enable you to enter free with an international student or teacher ID. There is often a fee for those who wish to carry cameras or videocameras.

CENTRO HISTÓRICO

*To reach the centro histórico by Metro, take Line 2 to **M: Zócalo.** The station's exit is on the east side of the square, in front of the Palacio Nacional. The Catedral Metropolitana lies to the north, the Federal District offices to the south, and the Suprema Corte de Justicia (Supreme Court) to the southeast. Some sights south of the zócalo can be better accessed by **M: Isabel La Católica,** Line 1, or **M: Pino Suárez,** Line 2.*

Mexico City spans thousands of kilometers and thousands of years, but it is all drawn together in the *centro.* On the city's main plaza, known as the **zócalo,** the Aztec **Templo Mayor,** the gargantuan **Catedral Metropolitana,** and the **Palacio Nacional** sit serenely side by side. It's not just the architecture that's eclectic; the space is shared by street vendors hawking everything from hand-woven bags to used-looking razors, AK-47-sporting soldiers reading adult comic books, permanent political protestors, homeless people, and hordes of picture-snapping tourists. The tourist crowds don't even begin to compare to the number of Mexicans who daily pass through or work in this center of the centers. If you have time to visit only one area in Mexico City, this is the place.

THE ZÓCALO

Officially known as the **Plaza de la Constitución,** the *zócalo* is the principal square of Mexico City. Now surrounded by imposing colonial monuments, the plaza was once the nucleus of **Tenochtitlán,** the Aztec island-capital and later the center of the entire Aztec empire. Cortés leveled the city and, atop the ruins, built the capital of the New Spain. Southwest of the **Templo Mayor**—the Aztecs' principal place of worship, which they called the *teocalli*—was the Aztec marketplace and major square. The space was rebuilt and renamed several times, becoming the Plaza de la Constitución in 1812. In 1843, the dictator Santa Anna ordered that a monument to Mexican Independence be constructed in the center of the square. Only the monument's *zócalo* (pedestal) was in place when the project was abandoned. The citizens of Mexico City began to refer to the square as the *zócalo*, a term which has since become the generic name for the central plazas that mark most of the cities and towns in Mexico.

PALACIO NACIONAL. Stretching the entire length of the enormous *zócalo*, the Palacio Nacional is as over-the-top as Mexico City itself. The building occupies the spot of Moctezuma's palace. After Tenochtitlán fell in 1521, the King of Spain granted the land to Hernán Cortés, who constructed his own home here using stones from the original palace. In 1562, the King of Spain bought back the house from Martín Cortés, the illegitimate son of the *conquistador*, in order make it a palace for the royal viceroys. It was destroyed by a riotous mob in 1692 and rebuilt a year later with the same stones. In the 1930s, the building was restored and a third story added under the direction of architect Augusto Petriccioli. Today, it no longer serves as the residence of Mexico's presidents; rather, it is the headquarters of the president's administration and other federal bureaucracies.

On your way into the *palacio*, note the large bell above the Baroque facade. It is the **Bell of Dolores,** which was which was brought to the capital in 1896 from the village of Dolores Hidalgo (see p. 316). It was this bell that Miguel Hildalgo rang on the morning of September 16, 1810, summoning Mexicans to fight for their independence. Every year the bell is rung again as the president repeats the inspiring speech delivered by Hidalgo—the *Grito de Dolores*.

The *palacio's* biggest attractions are the **Diego Rivera murals** on the main staircase and the western and northern walls. Rivera spent the years from 1929 to 1951 sketching and painting the frescoes, entitled *Mexico Through the Centuries*. The mural is divided into eight smaller scenes, each of which depicts an event in the social history of Mexico. Considering it was commissioned by the government, the murals are shockingly honest, making no attempt to sugar-coat the atrocities of Mexico's past. On the east side of the *palacio's* second floor is the **Museo del Recinto de Homenaje,** dedicated to revered Mexican president Benito Juárez. The museum occupies the very room in which Juárez died and displays an interesting—albeit small—collection of his personal artifacts.

Don't leave the *palacio* without visiting the newly restored **gardens,** in the far end of the palace, straight ahead from the entrance. Immaculate landscaping displays flowers and cacti from all of Mexico's regions. In 1999-2000, in honor of the 80th birthday of the brilliant Mexican painter-sculptor Juan Soriano, the *palacio* added several gigantic bronze **Soriano sculptures.** These new, nature-themed sculptures are blown-up models of some of his best works, including *El Pato* (the Duck) and *Pajaro de Dos Caras* (Bird with Two Faces). *(On the east side of the* zócalo. *Open daily 9am-5pm. Free, but you must trade a piece of ID for a big red* turista *badge at the entrance. Ask local officials and tour guides about tour prices; you should be able to get a guided tour (M-F 10am-4pm) for 60-70 pesos. However, joining a tour that has already begun is free. Museum del Recinto de Homenaje open Th-Tu 9am-5pm. Free.)*

CATEDRAL METROPOLITANA. The third cathedral built in New Spain was the **Catedral Metropolitana,** a mish-mash of architectural styles from three different centuries that somehow turned out beautifully. The area was originally part of the main Aztec temple, but it was quickly replaced by a small cathedral, begun by Cortés in 1524 and completed by the famous bishop Juan de Zumárraga. This small church, in turn, was replaced with a larger cathedral, begun in 1577. For the next 200 years the cathedral was under constant construction, only to be completed in 1813.

The cathedral has no one central altar, but a series of altars and *capillas* (chapels) throughout the interior. Greeting the visitor at the entrance is the **Altar de Perdón** (Altar of Forgiveness), a replica of an altarpiece built by Jerónimo de Balbás between 1731 and 1736 and destroyed by fire in 1967. The cedar interior of the choir gallery, constructed in 1695 by Juan de Rojas, boasts an elegant grille of gold, silver, and bronze, and Juan Correa's murals of dragon-slaying and prophet-hailing cover the sacristy walls. The most magnificent part of the cathedral is perhaps the **Altar de los Reyes** (Altar of the Kings), the high-gilded altar at the far end, constructed between 1718 and 1743. Around the central paintings of the Three Kings are statues of royal saints such as Louis IX of France. Two chapels near the entrance honor Mexico's patron, the Virgin of Guadalupe. Mass takes place almost hourly on weekends; visitors should take extra care to show respect and be silent at these times. Unfortunately, the splendor of the cathedral is today partly compromised by the green support structures, installed to combat ongoing floor damage. Because the huge underground lake below Mexico City has been drained, the city—and the massive, heavy cathedral—is sinking into the ground. What this means for visitors is that the green supports, partially obscuring parts of both the exterior the interior, are here to stay. *(On the north size of the zócalo. ☎ 5518 2043. Information desk open Tu-Su 9:30am-3pm and 4-5:30pm, M 9:30am-4:30pm.)*

▓**TEMPLO MAYOR.** When Cortés defeated the Aztecs in 1521, one of the first things he did was to destroy the Aztec's main center of worship, the *teocalli*. He took stones from the plaza and its main temple (called the Templo Mayor) to build his magnificent cathedral across the street. The temple and surrounding plaza was eventually paved over and almost forgotten until 1978, when workers unearthed it while laying down wires and piping for the Metro. From 1978-1981, the site was extensively excavated, revealing layers of pyramids and artifacts. Today, a catwalk leads you through the outdoor ruins, which include the remnants of several pyramids and colonial structures. The tour makes for an almost surreal escape from the throbbing *zócalo*. Most interesting by far is the Great Pyramid, which houses the remains of a twin temple dedicated to Tlaloc (the god of rain) and Huitzilopochtli (the god of war and patron of the Aztecs). Legend has it that this is very spot at which the Aztecs saw, as Huitzilopochtli predicted, an eagle perched on a cactus eating a snake (see p. 53).

The extraordinary **Museo del Templo Mayor,** now part of the archaeological complex, houses some 7000 artifacts unearthed at the site. The museum is divided into eight rooms that are meant to imitate the layout of the original temple, and the artifacts found in the excavation are accompanied not only by dry museum inscriptions (in Spanish) but also by excerpts from the ancient Aztec texts which describe them (also in Spanish). The highlight of the museum is the flat, round (5m in diameter) sculpture of **Coyolxauhqui,** the goddess of the moon and mother of Huitzilopochtli. *(On the corner of Seminario and República de Guatemala, just east of the cathedral and north of the Palacio Nacional. ☎ 5542 4784. Open Tu-Su 9am-5pm. 30 pesos. Audio guides 30 pesos in Spanish, 40 pesos in English.)*

SUPREMA CORTE DE JUSTICIA. Aside from the spectacle of hand-cuffed foreigners pleading ignorance about the cannabis in their socks, the Supreme Court draws tourists mainly for its murals. The four murals painted by José Clemente Orozco in the 1940s cover the second-floor walls of the court, built in 1929 where the southern half of Moctezuma's royal palace once stood. Filled with roaring tigers, masked evildoers, bolts of hellish flame, and a thuggish axe-wielding Señor Justice, the murals will make you think twice about breaking the law. *(On the corner of Pino Suárez and Corregidora. ☎ 5522 1500. Officially, murals only viewable 9am-noon or by appointment. Call M-F 10am-2pm to schedule a free visit; however, visitors can usually sweet talk their way in any time, provided a big case is not being tried. Bring an ID to leave at the entrance.)*

SOUTH OF THE ZÓCALO

MUSEO DE LA CIUDAD DE MÉXICO. The museum, once one of Cortés's homes, features a random assortment of modern Mexican art and temporary exhibits focusing on the city's colonial history. The spacious courtyard is a good place to rest, and the store has excellent information on the city and the rest of Mexico. *(Pino Suárez 30, at República de El Salvador, 3 blocks south of the zócalo's southeast corner. ☎ 542 00 83. Open Tu-Su 10am-6pm. 10 pesos, students and teachers free; Su free. Free guided tours Sa-Su.)*

MUSEO DE LA CHARRERIA. The wild but small collection of saddles, spurs, and ropes proudly explains in Spanish, English, and French, the development of *charreria* (being-a-cowboy; rodeoing) and its ultimate incarnation as Mexico's national sport. Learn how quintessentially Mexican the cowboy, his clothes, and his sport are as you marvel the artifacts. Oddly enough, the museum is housed in an old Benedictine monastery, **Nuestra Señora de Monserrate,** dating from the 17th century. *(At the corner of Izagaza and Isabel la Católica. Most easily accessible from M: Isabel la Católica, Line 1. Open M-F 10am-7pm. Free.)*

THE ALAMEDA

The Alameda is serviced by 4 Metro stations: **M: Hidalgo,** *Lines 2 and 3, at the intersection of Hidalgo and Paseo de la Reforma, one block west of the park,* **M: Bellas Artes,** *Lines 2 and 8, one block east of the park's northeast corner, between it and Bellas Artes itself,* **M: San Juan de Letrán,** *Line 8, one block south of the Torre Latinoamericana, and* **M: Juárez,** *Line 3, on Balderas one block southwest of the southwest corner of the park.*

The area around the Alameda Central is doubly blessed, filled with must-see sights and easily accessible by public transportation. It's within walking distance of the *centro histórico* and the Monumento a la Revolución, and it has the best crafts market in the city, **La Ciudadela.**

ALAMEDA CENTRAL

Amid the howling sprawl that is downtown Mexico City, the Alameda Central is an oasis of sanity and photosynthesis. The Alameda was originally an Aztec marketplace, then the site at which heretics were burnt under the Inquisition. It was finally turned into a park in 1592 by Don Luis de Velasco II, who intended it to be a place where the city's elite could meander peacefully. Enlarged in 1769 to its current size, the park was repaired after the 1985 earthquake, and in 1997 the sidewalks were restored by the city government. The park takes its name from the rows of shady *alamos* (poplars) that flood it. While the Alameda can feel like an island, it is not impervious to the urban life around it—three major thoroughfares (Avenidas Hidalgo, Juárez, and Lázaro Cárdenas) flank the Alameda, and the park is packed with mimes, young lovers, protestors, vendors, and pick pockets. Since it was opened to the public in this century, Mexico City has fallen in love with the Alameda; even in a city with over-crowding and soaring real estate prices, no one ever considers paving over the park.

At the center of the Alameda's southern side is the **Monumento a Juárez,** a semi-circular marble monument constructed in 1910 to honor the beloved president on the 100th anniversary of Mexican Independence. A somber-faced Benito Juárez, about to be crowned with golden laurels by an angel, sits on a central pedestal among 12 doric columns. On July 19 of each year, a civic ceremony commemorates the anniversary of Juárez's death.

THE MURALISTS. Starting around World War I and continuing into the 1960s, an artistic movement in Mexico flourished and eventually impacted the world. The movement was dominated by three men: **Diego Rivera, José Clemente Orozco,** and **David Alfaro Siqueiros.** Though each had a distinct technique and personality, they shared common aspirations. The three muralists worked during the time of liberation just after the suffocating regime of Porfirio Díaz, and toward the new spirit of nationalism and populism encouraged by the Constitution of 1917. The artists received government commissions to decorate public buildings with themes that glorified the revolution and pre-Hispanic history of Mexico. The principal messages of the murals were easily understood by any Mexican: Rivera, Orozco, and Siqueiros believed that Europeans had strangled the art of Mexico. They returned to *indígena* themes, shunning the elaborate decorations of colonialism and exaltations of the church. With their grand scope of expression, the murals soon became the silent voice of the populace throughout Mexico.

EAST OF THE ALAMEDA CENTRAL

PALACIO DE BELLAS ARTES. This impressive Art Nouveau palace is without a doubt the best thing to come out of Porfirio Díaz's dictatorship (1876-1911). Begun in 1905, construction was halted 1916 when it was noticed that the massive building had started to sink into the city's soft ground. It was begun again in 1919 under Antonio Muñoz, who included the massive dome, and finally completed in 1924. Architecture aside, most tourists come here to see the second and third floors, which are covered with murals by the most celebrated Mexican muralists of the 20th century. The best-known of these is Diego Rivera's mural, on the west wall of the third floor. John D. Rockefeller commissioned Rivera to paint a mural depicting "Man at Crossroads, Looking with Hope and High Vision to the Choosing of a New and Better Future" in New York City's Rockefeller Center. However, Rivera was dismissed from the project when Rockefeller discovered Lenin's portrait in the foreground. The Mexican government allowed Rivera to duplicate the work in this *palacio*, and the result, **El Hombre, Controlador del Universo, 1934,** includes an unflattering portrayal of John D. Rockefeller looking like a mad scientist, his hands on various technological instruments designed to rule the world. The second floor has a permanent collection of less well-known pieces by Rivera, Kahlo, Tamayo, and others, as well as space for temporary exhibits.

On the east wall of the third floor, murals by the leftist José Clemente Orozco depict the supposed tension between human nature and industrialization. In addition to Orozco's work, the *palacio* displays the frescoes of David Alfaro Siqueiros, the 20th-century Mexican muralist, Stalinist, nationalist, and almost-assassin of Leon Trotsky. His **Tormento de Cuauhtémoc** depicts Cortés's attack on the last vestiges of the Aztec nation. On the fourth floor is the **Museo Nacional de Arquitectura** (☎5709 3111), which exhibits early sketches and blueprints of many buildings in the city, including the Teatro Nacional and the *palacio* itself.

The amazing **Ballet Folklórico de México** performs regional dances here and occasionally in the **Teatro Ferrocarrilero** (☎5529 1701), near **M: Revolución,** Line 2. Their exciting and vivacious performances combines *indígena* dancing with the formal aspects of traditional ballet. Attending a Bellas Artes performance is the only way to see the crystal curtain designed by Gerardo Murelli, made of almost one million pieces of multicolored crystal which, when illuminated from behind, represent the Valley of Mexico at twilight. The Bellas Artes **ticket office** sells tickets for these and other performances throughout the city. An **information booth,** up the set of stairs next to the ticket booth, has information on all performances in Mexico City. Travel agencies snatch up a lot of tickets during Christmas, *Semana Santa,* and summer; check first at Bellas Artes, then try along Reforma or in the Zona Rosa. *(Juárez and Eje Central, at the northeast corner of Alameda Central complex; it's hard to miss. Open Tu-Su 10am-6pm. 15 pesos to see the murals and art exhibits on the upper floors. Temporary exhibits on the first floor are generally free. Dance performances W 8:30pm, Su 9:30am and 8:30pm. Tickets 200-330 pesos. Ticket booth open M-Sa 11am-7pm, Su 9am-7pm. Information booth ☎5521 9251, ext. 152 and 159. Open daily 11am-7pm. Some English spoken.)*

MUSEO NACIONAL DE ARTE. Occupying a building built during the Porfiriato to house the Secretary of Communications, the museum was inaugurated in 1982. The architect, Silvio Conti, took particular care with the central staircase; its Baroque handrails were crafted by artists in Florence. The museum contains works from the stylistic and ideological schools of every era in Mexican history. Look for Guerra's **Monumento a José Martí,** a colorful celebration of the young revolutionary's life. The museum has everything from Art Deco to popular portraits of the 19th century; current exhibits are listed downstairs. *(Tacuba 8, a half-block east of the* palacio's *north side. ☎5512 3224. Open Tu-Su 10am-5:30pm. 20 pesos, Su free.)*

TORRE LATINOAMERICANA. Built in 1950, the *Torre* is the second-tallest building in the city at 181m and 44 stories high. The 44th-floor observatory, 2422m above sea level, commands a startling view of the sprawling city on the rare clear day. At night the view from the *Torre* is positively sexy, with city lights sparkling for miles in every direction. The 38th floor holds the gimmicky and depressing **"highest aquarium in the world,"** with uncomfortable-looking snakes, fish, and turtles in small tanks. *(Lázaro Cárdenas and Madero, 1 block east of Alameda Central's southeast corner. Observatory open daily 9:30am-11pm. 35 pesos, children 30 pesos. Aquarium open daily 10am-10pm. 25 pesos, children 22 pesos.)*

TEMPLO DE SAN FRANCISCO. Built in 1525, only four years after the fall of Tenochtitlán, the temple was the first church in the Americas. Soon after it was constructed, Cortés himself came to visit the vast Franciscan complex, which included several churches, a school, and a hospital. In 1838, the church was the site for Emperor Agustín de Iturbide's funeral. Today, after extensive remodeling in 1716, only the temple and the *capilla* (chapel) remain. Two fragments of the original cloisters can be seen at Gante 5, on the east side of the church, and at Lázaro Cárdenas 8, behind a vacant lot. *(Just east of the Torre LatinoAmericana on Madero. Open M-F 9am-1pm and 5-7pm, Sa 9am-1pm.)*

CASA DE LOS AZULEJOS. The *casa*, once called "the Blue Palace," was built in 1730 using *azulejos* (blue and white tiles) from Puebla. To be able to afford even a few of these tiles was a mark of considerable status. An insulted son built this mansion to prove his worth to his father, who never believed he would succeed in life. In 1918, the building was purchsed by an Ohio businessman, Frank Sanborn, the mogul behind the chain **Sanborn's.** An Orozco mural, 1924's Omniscience, is on the staircase wall. Check out the great view of the building from the second-floor balcony. Go through the Sanborn's to view them. *(Across from Templo de San Francisco. Sanborn's ☎ 5512 1331. Both the Casa and Sanborn's open daily 8am-1am.)*

PALACIO ITURBIDE. A great place to duck in for some cool air and cooler architecture, the grand 18th-century *palacio*, best known for having served as the home of Mexico's short-lived first Emperor, Agustín Iturbide, from his coronation in 1821 to his ouster in 1823. The building afterward served for many years as a luxury hotel before it was purchased by Banamex in 1969. There is a gallery on the ground floor with exhibitions that change every three months. *(Madero 17, between Bolívar and Gante, 1½ blocks east of the Torre Latinoamericana, near the Templo de San Francisco. ☎ 5225 0247. Open daily 10am-7pm.)*

WEST OF THE ALAMEDA CENTRAL

■ **MUSEO MURAL DIEGO RIVERA.** Also known as **Museo de la Alameda,** this fascinating building holds Diego Rivera's masterpiece, **Sueño de un Tarde Dominical en la Alameda Central** *(Sunday Afternoon Dream at the Alameda Central)*. Rivera imagines himself as a nine-year-old boy on a fantastic walk through the Alameda, surrounded by the most important figures in Mexican history. The key in front of the mural points out, in English and Spanish, the famous figures woven into the crowd: Frida Kahlo, Antonio de Santa Anna, and Hernán Cortés (portrayed with his hand covered in blood), among others. The centerpiece is José Guadalupe Posada's *La Calavera Catrina*, a smiling skeleton wearing a boa, holding the hand of a chubby young Rivera. Rivera uses the skeleton's "boa," a feathered snake, to represent Quetzacóatl, the plumed serpent god of pre-Hispanic cultures. The museum also has exhibits on Rivera's life and the cultural climate in which he lived. *(Colón and Balderas, facing the small park at the west end of the Alameda. ☎ 5512 0759. Open Tu-Su 10am-6pm. 10 pesos; Su free.)*

CENTRO CULTURAL JOSÉ MARTÍ. The poet José Martí, a leader of the Cuban independence movement in the late 19th century, dreamed of a united and free Latin America, led by Mexico, and repeatedly warned of the dangers of foreign imperialism. This center features a rainbow-colored mural depicting Martí's poetry. A tally sheet in the corner of the mural records Spanish, British, French, and US interventions in Latin America from 1800 to 1969; the grand total is a staggering 784. Temporary exhibits on Cuba share the space. While a white tarp often covers the murals (to avoid clashing with the temporary exhibits), nobody minds

SUNDAY, BLOODY SUNDAY The Rivera masterpiece

Sueño de un Tarde Dominical en la Alameda Central was originally commissioned by the Hotel del Prado in 1946. When the hotel proudly hung the just-finished work in 1948, a national controversy ensued over the figure of Ignacio Ramírez, who is shown holding up a pad of paper that reads, "God does not exist," an excerpt from a speech he gave in 1836. The archbishop of Mexico refused to bless the hotel, and on June 4, at dawn, more than 100 angry students broke in, erased the "does not exist" fragment, and damaged the face of the young Diego Rivera in the center of the mural. After the 1985 earthquake, the mural was moved to the museum, which was constructed solely to showcase the piece. Alongside the mural, the museum displays original clippings from 1948 describing the vandalism.

if you stick your head under and take a look. Movies, concerts, plays and other cultural events take place in the adjoining theater. *(Dr. Mora 2 at Hidalgo, on the Alameda's west end.* ☎ *5521 2115. Open M-F 9am-9pm, Sa 10am-7pm. Free.)*

PINACOTECA VIRREINAL DE SAN DIEGO. This building was constructed as a church between 1591 and 1621, evident by its huge rooms with high, decorated ceilings, stone columns and arches, and wooden floors. The rooms now contain an extensive collection of Baroque and Mannerist paintings almost exclusively religious in nature. Don't miss the almost endless spiral staircase to the left of the entrance. *(Dr. Mora 7, next to Centro Cultural José Martí.* ☎ *5510 2793. Open Tu-Su 9am-5pm. 10 pesos, Su free.)*

NORTH OF THE ALAMEDA CENTRAL

MUSEO FRANZ MAYER. In the small, sunken Plaza de Santa Veracruz, flanked by the beautifully aging facades of the churches of San Juan de Dios and Santa Veracruz, lies one of the loveliest sights in the area. The Museo Franz Mayer, formerly the Hospital de San Juan de Dios, has been expertly restored and now houses the extensive collection of international ceramics, colonial furniture, and religious paintings belonging to Franz Mayer, a German who migrated to Mexico in 1905. The museum, however, focuses primarily on the applied arts: practical art in everyday use, in the home or in the church. Plush red velvet, gleaming display cases, and an extremely professional staff make wandering here a joy. The old cloister of San Juan de Dios is inside the first entrance to the left; its courtyard's upper level holds more exhibits. The courtyard cafe alone, one of the best in the city, is worth the price of admission. *(Hidalgo 45.* ☎ *5518 2265. Open Tu-Su 10am-5pm. Museum 15 pesos, 10 pesos for students with ID; cloister 5 pesos; children under 12 free, Su free. Tours in English Tu-F 10am-2pm. Call ahead for an appointment. 10 pesos.)*

MUSEO NACIONAL DE LA ESTAMPA. The museum houses the National Institute of Fine Arts's graphic arts and engraving collection, tracing the art of printmaking from pre-Hispanic seals to contemporary engravings. Highlights of the museum's rotating collection have included the work of the acclaimed José Guadalupe Posada, Mexico's foremost engraver and printmaker. His woodcuts depict skeletons dancing, singing, and cavorting in ridiculous costumes—a graphic indictment of the Porfiriato's excesses. Catch a nice view of the Alameda from the second floor. *(Hidalgo 39, next to the Museo Franz Mayer, in the pale yellow building.* ☎ *5521 2244 or 5510 4905. Open Tu-Su 10am-6pm. 10 pesos, Su free.)*

NEAR THE MONUMENTO A LA REVOLUCIÓN

To get to the *Monumento a la Revolución*, take *M: Revolución, Line 2.*

The area around the Monumento a la Revolución is home to three fine museums: the Museo Nacional de la Revolución, the Museo del Chopo (the Chopo), and the Museo San Carlos.

MEXICO CITY

MEXICO CITY

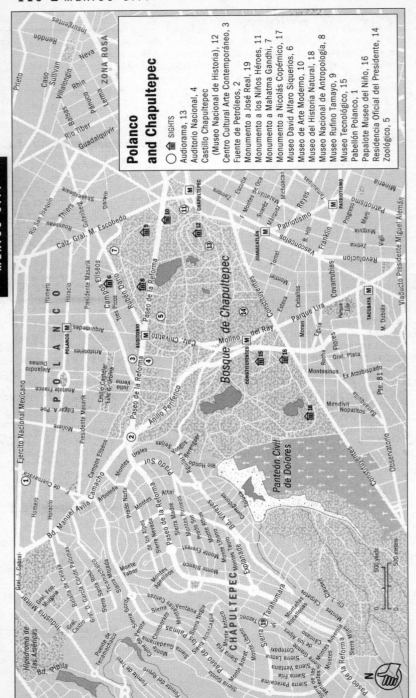

Polanco and Chapultepec

○ 🏛 SIGHTS

Audiorama, 13
Auditorio Nacional, 4
Castillo Chapultepec
(Museo Nacional de Historia), 12
Centro Cultural Arte Contemporáneo, 3
Fuente de Petróleos, 2
Monumento a José Real, 19
Monumento a los Niños Héroes, 11
Monumento a Mahatma Gandhi, 7
Monumento a Nicolás Copérnico, 17
Museo David Alfaro Siqueiros, 6
Museo de Arte Moderno, 10
Museo del Historia Natural, 18
Museo Nacional de Antropología, 8
Museo Rufino Tamayo, 9
Museo Tecnológico, 15
Pabellón Polanco, 1
Papalote Museo del Niño, 16
Residencia Oficial del Presidente, 14
Zoológico, 5

MONUMENTO A LA REVOLUCIÓN/MUSEO NACIONAL DE LA REVOLUCIÓN. In the early 1900s, president Porfirio Díaz planned this site as the seat of Congress, but progress halted as revolutionary fighting paralyzed the city streets; the dome was left only half-completed. It wasn't until the 1930s that the monument and the space below were finally dedicated to the memory of the Revolution. Today, 32 flag poles representing the Mexican states line the pathway to the dome, which now contains the Museo Nacional de la Revolución. The museum features Revolutionary artifacts (cars, clothing, guns, etc.) and a thorough chronology of the Revolution. Temporary exhibits connect contemporary art with political history. Sunday is the only day you can ascend to the top of the monument. *(At the Plaza de la República; the museum is in a park just northeast of the monument. ☎ 5546 2115. Museum open Tu-Sa 9am-5pm, Su 9am-3pm. 5 pesos; Su free. Call ahead to arrange a tour.)*

MUSEO DEL CHOPO. The modern, relatively tourist-free Chopo (as it's commonly called) displays the works of up-and-coming Mexican artists in every medium. Every mid-June to mid-July, for 12 years running, the museum has proudly hosted a show of gay and lesbian photography, sculpture, and painting. The unusual building was built in France and rebuilt at this spot in 1910. *(Dr. Enrique González Martínez 10. Just after Puente de Alvarado turns into San Cosme, turn right on Dr. Enrique González Martínez; it's one block up on the left. Open Tu-Su 10am-7pm. 10 pesos, 5 pesos for students with ID; Tu free. Free guided visits Tu-F 10:30am, noon, 4:30, and 6pm.)*

MUSEO SAN CARLOS. The museum is in the old **Palacio Buenavista,** constructed in 1795 for the Count of Buenavista by his mother. The building served as temporary residence for Santa Anna and later belonged to Emperor Maximilian. Today, it is home to the Museo San Carlos, which will make you feel as though you're in Spain not Mexico. Housing the former collection of the Academy San Carlos, founded by the King of Spain in 1783, its impressive holdings span European art from the 14th to 19th centuries. The museum features excellent work by minor artists, as well as standards by artists such as Rubens and Goya. Temporary exhibits often highlight certain themes in post-Renaissance European art. *(At the corner of Puente de Alvarado and Ramos Arizpe, 3 blocks north of the Monumento a la Revolución. ☎ 5566 8522. Open W-Su 10am-6pm. 20 pesos, students and teachers 10 pesos; Su free.)*

BOSQUE DE CHAPULTEPEC

*To reach the park, get off the Metro at **M: Auditorio,** Line 7, farther west, closer to the zoo, or **M: Chapultepec,** Line 1, farther east, closer to the Niños Héroes monument and most museums. Alternatively, take any pesero on Reforma to Auditorio or Chapultepec.*

Mexico City has to do everything a little bigger and better than everywhere else, and this, the D.F.'s major park and recreational area, is no exception. The Chapultepec area is home not only to the park itself, but to a slew of fabulous museums, including the Museo Nacional de Antropología, the most famous museum in Mexico.

THE PARK. The 1000-acre expanse of green on the western side of the *centro* is the largest and oldest urban park in all the Americas, established in the 15th century when the Aztec emperor Moctezuma I decided to remove a few temples and create a recreational area, with streams and aqueducts. Today, Chapultepec (Grasshopper Hill) is filled with museums, hiking paths, zoos, bikes, amusement parks, castles, balloon vendors, and modern sports facilities. A visitor could easily spend several days in the Bosque. Mexico's most famous museum, the **Museo Nacional de Antropología,** sits among the hills of the park. During the official visitation hours, it is as safe as anywhere in the city. They tend to be a little dirtier and, while full of happy families during the day, should be avoided after nightfall. The best time to visit the Bosque is on Sunday, when families flock to the open-air concerts, and get free admission to the zoo and museums. To explore the entire park, you can rent a bike near the corner of Reforma and Gandhi, across Reforma from the anthropology museum. (30 pesos per hr. Open Tu-Su 5am-4:30pm.) Helpful signs point you toward major sites, but the Bosque's myriad paths wind and curve without warning; pay attention to where you're going. All the museums and sights listed are in Old Chapultepec, the eastern half of the park, which fans out to the west of the *Zona Rosa*. *(The area that is officially the Bosque is open only Tu-Su 5am-5pm. The areas north of Reforma near the Museo Nacional de Antropología are open 24hr.)*

■ **MUSEO NACIONAL DE ANTROPOLOGÍA.** Some journey to Mexico just to consult this magnificent and massive mega-museum, considered by many to be the best of its kind in the world. Housing 4 sq. km of Mexico's most exquisite archaeological and ethnographic treasures in 23 exhibition halls, this museum is the yardstick by which all other Mexican museums are measured. The museum, designed by Pedro Ramírez Vázquez, was built out of volcanic rock, wood, and marble, and opened in 1964. Poems from ancient texts and epics grace the entrances from the main courtyard. In the center of the courtyard, a stout column covered with symbolic carvings supports the tremendous weight of a vast, waterspouts aluminum pavilion, which shields the courtyard from the weather.

It would take days to pay proper homage to the entire museum, though some visitors leave after a few hours, no doubt afflicted with pottery overload. As you enter on the right side of the ground floor, a general introduction to anthropology precedes a series of chronologically arranged galleries moving from the right to the left wings of the building. These trace the histories of many central Mexican groups, from the first migrations to the Americas up to the Spanish Conquest. Among the highlights not to be missed: the **Sala Teotihuacana,** with detailed models of the city of Teotihuacán; the **Sala Toltec,** with huge statues of Quetzalcóatl; the **Sala Golfo de Mexico,** with colossal stone Olmec heads; the **Sala Maya,** where you can descend into a model of the tomb of King Pacal; and the museum's crown jewel, the **Sala Mexica,** with the world-famous **Aztec Calendar Stone (Sun Stone),** featuring Tonatiuh, the Aztec god of the sun, and an enormous statue of Coatlicue ("the one with the skirt of snakes"), goddess of life and death. The museum also has a pricey **cafetería** (open Tu-Su 9am-7pm; entrees 50-90 pesos) and a large **bookshop** that sells English guides to archaeological sites around the country. Across from the museum's entrance, you can see performances by the **voladores,** who, in true Totonac tradition, climb up a wooden mast and slowly swirl to the ground. *(Paseo de la Reforma and Gandhi. Take an "Auditorio" pesero (2 pesos) southwest on Reforma and signal the driver to let you off at the second stop after entering the park. M: Auditorio, Line 7. The museum is just east down Reforma. ☎ 5553 6266. Open Tu-Su 9am-7pm. 30 pesos; Su free. Audio guides in Spanish 45 pesos, in English 50 pesos.)*

MUSEO RUFINO TAMAYO (MUSEO ARTE CONTEMPORÁNEO). The Mexican government built the nine halls of this museum after Rufino Tamayo and his wife, Olga Flores Rivas, donated their international art collection to the Mexican people. The murals of Rufino Tamayo were much criticized in the first half of the century for not being sufficiently nationalistic. Since the museum's opening in 1981, however, his reputation has been restored, though his more abstract style has garnered him less fame than the "Big Three" muralists—Rivera, Orozco, and Siqueiros. The museum houses a large permanent collection of Tamayo's work, as well as works by Willem de Kooning, Botero, and surrealists Joan Miró and Max Ernst. The museum also draws first-rate temporary exhibits, such as the national tribute to Juan Soriano in 2000. *(Just to the east of the Museo Nacional de Antropología, on the corner of Reforma and Gandhi. Take the first right on Gandhi from M: Chapultepec, Line 1. After a 5-minute walk on Gandhi, the museum is to the left down a small, semi-hidden path through the trees. Alternatively, walk due east (straight ahead as you exit) from the entrance of the anthropology museum into the woods; Tamayo is 100m straight ahead. ☎ 5285 6519. Open Tu-Su 10am-6pm. 15 pesos; Su free.)*

■ **MUSEO DE ARTE MODERNO.** This wonderful museum houses a fine collection of paintings by Frida Kahlo, including perhaps her most famous work, the exquisite, gory **Las Dos Fridas.** Works by Siqueiros, José Luis Cuevas, Rivera, Orozco, Angelina Beloff (another of Rivera's lovers), and Remedios Varo are also on display. Temporary exhibits feature up-and-coming Mexican artists. The museum is linked to the **Galería Fernando Camboa,** an outdoor sculpture garden with pieces by

Moore, Giacometti, and others. *(On Reforma and Gandhi, north of the Monumento a los Niños Héroes, on the opposite side of Reforma from the anthropology museum. ☎5553 6233. Open Tu-Su 10am-6pm. 15 pesos; Su free.)*

MUSEO NACIONAL DE HISTORIA. This fascinating museum is in the Castle of Chapultepec, once home of the hapless French emperor Maximilian. The museum exhaustively narrates the history of Mexico since the time of the Conquest. An immense portrait of King Ferdinand and Queen Isabella of Spain greets visitors in the first room. Galleries contain displays on Mexican economic and social structure during the War for Independence, the Porfiriato, and the Revolution. The particularly interesting upper level exhibits Mexican art and dress from the vice royalty through the 20th century. The walls of **Sala 13** are completely covered by Siqueiros's *Del Porfirismo a la Revolución*, a pictoral cheat-sheet for modern Mexican history. Admission to the museum also allows a peek at some of the castle's interior, and access to the most impressive views of Chapultepec and the surrounding area. *(Walk up the hill directly behind the Niños Héroes monument to the castle. Be prepared to open your bag for the guard. ☎5286 9920. Open Tu-Su 9am-5pm. Tickets sold until 4pm. 20 pesos; Su free. Su only 2nd floor open.)*

MUSEO DEL CARACOL (GALERIA DE HISTORIA). The museum's official name is the Museo Galería de la Lucha del Pueblo Mexicano por su Libertad (Museum of the Struggle of the Mexican People for Liberty), but it's more commonly known as Museo del Caracol (Snail Museum) because of its spiral design. The gallery contains of 12 halls dedicated to late Mexican history; the downward spiral begins with Hidalgo's *Grito de Dolores* and ends with the establishment of democracy. The exhibitions consist of amazingly life-like mini-dioramas, documentary videos, paintings, and various historical artifacts. The staircase leads to a beautiful, round, skylit hall that holds a copy of the Constitution of 1917, handwritten by Venustiano Carranza himself. Visitors unfamiliar with the contours of Mexican history may be bewildered by the Spanish-only explanations next to each piece. *(On the southern side of Chapultepec Hill. On the road to the castle, turn right at the sign just before the castle itself. ☎5553 6285. Open Tu-Su 9am-5:30pm. 25 pesos, free for kids under 13 and adults over 60; Su free.)*

MONUMENTO A LOS NIÑOS HÉROES. At the end of the long walkway just inside the park on the east side stand six white pillars capped with monoliths. In 1847, during the Mexican-American War, the US, under the command of general Winfield Scott, invaded Mexico City. The last Mexican stronghold in the capital was the Chapultepec Castle, protected by the military academy cadets. Legend has it that as the invaders closed to within yards, the last five boys and their lieutenant wrapped themselves in Mexican flag and threw themselves from the castle wall refusing to surrender. This monument—and countless streets throughout Mexico—is dedicated to those boy heroes.

TREE OF MOCTEZUMA. The tree has a circumference of 14m and is reputed to have been around since the time of the Aztecs. *(On Av. Gran, east of Gandhi, in the south end of the park.)*

MUSEO SALA DE ARTE PÚBLICO DAVID ÁLFARO SIQUEIROS. Twenty-five days before his death in January 1974, famed muralist, revolutionary soldier, republican, fanatical Stalinist, anti-fascist, and would-be Trotsky assassin David Álfaro Siqueiros donated his house and studio to the people of Mexico. In compliance with his will, the government created this museum. Fifteen thousand murals, lithographs, photographs, drawings, and letters document his fascinating life. *(Tres Picos 29, at Hegel, just outside the park. Walk north from the Museo Nacional de Antropología to Rubén Darío. On the left, Tres Picos forks to the northwest; follow it for 1 block. The museum is on the right. Open Tu-Su 10am-3pm. 10 pesos; Su free. Call to arrange a guided tour.)*

PARQUE ZOOLÓGICO DE CHAPULTEPEC. Although animal lovers might shed a tear or two over some of the humbler habitats, the zoo is surprisingly excellent, mostly shunning the small-cage approach for larger, more amenable tracts of land. Everyone's favorites—those huggable pandas—have survived quite well here.

(Accessible from the entrance on Reforma, east of Calzado Chivatitio. From the M: Auditorio exit, it is in the opposite direction from the National Auditorium. ☎ 5553 6263. Open Tu-Su 9am-4:30pm. Free. Spanish audio guides 25 pesos, maps 3 pesos.)

JARDÍN DE LA TERCERA EDAD. West of the Siqueiros museum, up Reforma past the Auditorio Metro station, is the Jardín de la Tercera Edad, reserved for visitors over age 50. It contains the **Jardín Escultórico,** a sculpture park full of realist and symbolist statues, as well as the **Jardín Botánico,** a botanical garden with a little lake. *(Botanical garden open daily 9am-5pm. Free.)*

LAGO DE CHAPULTEPEC. The big lake in the heart of the action is the Lago de Chapultepec; it has rowboats for rent that fit up to five people. *(Rentals available daily 8am-5pm. 8 pesos per hr.)*

TLATELOLCO

*To get to Tlatelolco, get off at **M: Tlatelolco,** Line 3, and take the González exit. Turn right on González, walk three blocks east until you reach Cárdenas, then turn right and follow it one long block up. The plaza will be on your left.*

Tlatelolco lies north of the *centro*. Archaeological work has shown that the city of Tlatelolco ("Mound of Sand" in Náhuatl) existed long before the great Aztec capital of Tenochtitlán. By 1473, the Tlatelolco king, Moquíhuix, had built his city into a busy trading center coveted by the Aztec ruler, Axayácatl. Tension mounted over territorial and fishing boundaries, and soon Moquíhuix learned that the Aztecs were preparing to attack his city. Even forewarned, Moquíhuix couldn't handle the Aztec war machine, and Tlatelolco was absorbed into the huge empire.

PLAZA DE LAS TRES CULTURAS. Tlatelolco's central square, at the corner of Lázaro Cárdenas and Ricardo Flores Magón, 13 blocks north of the Palacio de Bellas Artes, is marked by the three cultures that have occupied it—Aztec, colonial Spanish, and modern Mexican. Today, the three cultures are represented respectively by ancient ruins, a mammoth church, and the ultra-modern Ministry of Foreign Affairs. A plaque in the southwest corner of the plaza explains: "On August 13, 1521, heroically defended by Cuauhtémoc, Tlatelolco fell to Hernán Cortés. It was neither a triumph nor a defeat, but the birth of the *mestizo* city that is the Mexico of today." That battle marked the last serious armed resistance to the conquest. More than 400 years later, the plaza witnessed another bloody event, for which it is, sadly enough, most famous: the **Tlatelolco Massacre** of October 2, 1968.

PIRÁMIDE DE TLATELOLCO. In the plaza, parts of the Pyramid of Tlatelolco (also known as the **Templo Mayor**) and its ceremonial square remain dutifully well-kept. Enter from the southwest corner, in front of the Iglesia de Santiago, and walk down a steel and concrete path that overlooks the eight building stages of the main pyramid. At the time of the conquest, the base of the pyramid extended from Insurgentes to the Iglesia de Santiago. The pyramid was second in importance only to the great Teocalli, and its summit reached nearly as high as the skyscraper just to the south (the Relaciones Exteriores building). During the Spanish blockade of Tenochtitlán, the Aztecs heaved the freshly sacrificed bodies of Cortés's forces down the temple steps, within sight of the *conquistadores* camped to the west at Tacuba. Nearby is the **Templo Calendárico "M,"** an M-shaped building used

---

THE TLATELOLCO MASSACRE On October 2, 1968, after a silent pro-peace sit-in was held in the Plaza, government troops descended, shooting and killing hundreds of protestors; prisoners were taken and tortured to death. In memory of the victims, a simple sandstone was dedicated in 1993, the 25th anniversary of the incident—before then, the government had repressed all mention of the event, going so far as to remove related newspaper articles from all national archives. In 1998, PRD Congressional members proposed a reopening of the investigation on the army's actions that fateful day.

by the Aztecs to keep time. Scores of skeletons were discovered near its base. A male and female pair that were found facing each other upon excavation have been dubbed "The Lovers of Tlatelolco." *(Open daily 8am-6pm. Free.)*

IGLESIA DE SANTIAGO. On the east side of the plaza is the simple, enormous, fortress-like church erected in 1609 to replace a structure built in 1543. This church was designed to fit in with the surrounding ruins, and with its stonework and solid, plain masonry, it does.

LA VILLA BASÍLICA

*To get to the Villa de Guadalupe (**M: La Villa Basílica,** Line 6), go past the vendor stands, and take a right on Calzada de Guadalupe. A small raised walkway between the two lanes of traffic leads directly to the Basílica.*

Ever since the legend of Juan Diego, Our Lady of Guadalupe has since been the patroness of Mexico, an icon of the nation's religious culture. Diego's famous cloak is now housed in the Basílica de Guadalupe, north of city center.

LA BASÍLICA DE GUADALUPE. Designed by the venerated Pedro Ramírez Vásquez and finished in 1975, the new *basílica* is an immense, aggressively modern structure. Although the flags from different cultures inside of the basilica make it feel more like the United Nations than a church, thousands flock daily to observe the Virgin's miraculous likeness emblazoned in Diego's robe. Visitors, ranging from rural Mexican families to curious tourists, crowd around the central altar and impressive organ to step onto the basilica's moving sidewalk—it allows for easier (and faster) viewing of Diego's holy cloak. On December 12th, the feast day of Our Lady of Guadalupe, pilgrims from throughout the country slowly proceed on their knees up to the altar. Perhaps the most striking feature of the basilica is the set of huge, haunting words written in gold Byzantine script across the top of the edifice: *"¿Aqui no estoy yo que soy tu madre?"* ("Am I not here, I who am your mother?"). *(Open daily 5am-9pm.)*

MUSEO DE LA BASÍLICA DE GUADALUPE. Next to the new basilica is the old basilica, built at the end of the 17th century and remodeled in the 1880s. These days, the old basilica houses the **Museo de la Basílica de Guadalupe.** This gorgeous, lavish museum makes you wonder why they built the new, ungainly basilica. Colonial religious paintings and portraits comprise most of the collection, although they pale in comparison to the emotional collection of *ex votos* in the entryway. A room at the base of the staircase contains a pair of golden *fútbol* shoes offered to the Virgin before the 1994 World Cup by the Mexican star Hugo Sánchez. *(Plaza Hidalgo 1, in the Villa de Guadalupe.* ☎ *5781 6810. Open Tu-Su 10am-6pm. 5pesos.)*

PANTEÓN DE TEPEYAC. Behind the basilica, winding steps lead up the side of a small hill, past lush gardens, crowds of pilgrims, and cascading waterfalls. A small chapel dedicated to the Virgin of Guadalupe, the Panteón del Tepeyac, sits on top

THE DARK VIRGIN Probably the most important figure in Mexican Catholicism is the Virgen de Guadalupe. She first appeared as a vision on a hill to the *indígena* peasant Juan Diego in December 1531. When Juan Diego told the bishop of his vision, the clergyman was doubtful. Juan Diego returned to the hill and had another vision; this time she told him that on the hill he would find, in the middle of the winter, a great variety of roses that he should gather and bring to the bishop as proof. She also instructed him to build her a shrine at that spot. Juan Diego gathered the roses in his cloak, and when he let them fall at the feet of the bishop, an image of the Virgen remained emblazoned on the cloak. The bishop was convinced, and the shrine was built. What is interesting is that the image was of a woman with brown skin, an *indígena*. The Virgen de Guadalupe quickly became a symbol of religious fusion between the *indígenas* and Christians of Mexico. Over the years, depictions of the Virgen have maintained her dark skin and indigenous features, and she is often referred to proudly as La Virgen Morena (The Dark Virgin).

of the hill. The bronze and polished wood interior of the chapel depicts the apparitions witnessed by Juan Diego. Upon entering, visitors can stop in front of a priest to be blessed with holy water. From the steps beside the church, you can absorb a panoramic view of the city framed by the hillsides and distant mountains. Descending the other side of the hill, past the spouting gargoyles, statues of Juan Diego and a group of *indígenas* kneel before a gleaming Virgin doused with the spray from a rushing waterfall. Vendors crowd nearly ever available inch of the basilica's grounds, pushing religious paraphernalia and practical goods.

COYOACÁN

*To reach Coyoacán from downtown, take the Metro to **M: Coyoacán**, Line 3. Taxis cost about 20 pesos.*

The Toltecs founded **Coyoacán** (Place of the Skinny Coyotes, in Náhuatl) between the 10th and 12th centuries. Cortés later established the seat of the colonial government here, and, after the fall of Tlatelolco, tortured Cuauhtémoc here; he hoped the Aztec leader would reveal the hiding place of the legendary Aztec treasure. Although no longer a refuge for the aforementioned "skinny coyotes," it is today a haven for "English-speaking tourists." South of the center, wealthy Coyoacán today is Mexico City's most attractive suburb. Well-maintained and peaceful, it is worth visiting for its museums or simply for a stroll in beautiful **Plaza Hidalgo**, neighboring **Jardín Centenario**, or nearby **Placita de la Conchita**. Coyoacán is centered around the Plaza Hidalgo, which is bounded by the cathedral and the Casa de Cortés. The two parks are split by Calle Carrillo Puerto, which runs north-south just west of the church. Coyoacán's **tourist info** (☎5659 2256, ext. 181) is found in the **Casa de Cortés**, the big red building on the north side of the plaza. The office gives free tours of the area in Spanish on Saturday, every hour 8am-noon.

■ **MUSEO FRIDA KAHLO.** Perhaps Coyoacán's most impressive and moving sight is the Museo Frida Kahlo. Works by Rivera, Orozco, Duchamp, and Klee hang in this restored colonial house, the birthplace and home of surrealist painter Frida Kahlo (1907-54). Kahlo's disturbing work and traumatic life story have gained international fame since her death, and she is today regarded as one of Mexico's greatest artists. A troublemaker as a child, she ran with street gangs. At the age of 18 she was impaled by a post during a trolley accident, breaking her spine, rendering her infertile, and causing innumerable other complications. She never fully recovered, experiencing relapses that confined her to a bed and wheelchair for much of her life. Kahlo married Diego Rivera twice and became a celebrated artist in her own right. Like her womanizing husband, she was notorious for her numerous affairs, both with men and with women, and most famously with Leon Trotsky. Those looking for loads of her work will be disappointed (only a few paintings and early sketches are around), but the museum still has much to offer. Wandering through the house is an emotionally wrenching experience: witness the bed on which Frida suffered, the names "Diego" and "Frida" lovingly scrawled on the kitchen wall, and Diego's painting of his "little girl" Frida hanging next to sultry portraits of various lovers. Read (or have someone translate) the excerpts of her diary and her letters hanging on the walls. They eloquently and intimately describe her childhood dreams, Diego's adultery, and the inspiration for some of her work. The house also hides a gorgeous garden full of flowering lilies and hidden pre-Hispanic artifacts. *(Londres 247. On Allende, five blocks north of Plaza Hidalgo's northeast corner, in the colorful indigo and red building at the northeast corner of the intersection. ☎5554 5999. Open Tu-Su 10am-6pm. 20 pesos.)*

MUSEO CASA DE LEON TROTSKY. After Leon Trotsky was expelled from the USSR by Stalin in 1927, he wandered in exile until Mexico's president Lázaro Cárdenas granted him political asylum at the suggestion of Trotsky's friends, muralist Diego Rivera and painter Frida Kahlo. Trotsky arrived in 1937 with his wife and first lived with Rivera and Kahlo in the "Casa Hazel," now the Museo Frida Kahlo (see above). In 1939, however, Diego became infuriated at the affair Leon was having with his wife Frida, and kicked the Trotskys out of his house. The family relocated to this house, on Churubusco. Though bunny rabbits now nibble peacefully in the gardens, bullet holes riddle the interior walls, relics of an attack on Trotsky by the muralist David Alfaro Siqueiros on May 24, 1940. Intending not to kill Trotsky, only to scare him, Siqueiros wildly sprayed the inside of the house with machine-gun fire and stole many of Trotsky's documents. Fearing further violence, this self-proclaimed "man of the people" living in a posh house in a posh suburb, installed bullet-proof bathroom doors and hired a team of bodyguards. This paranoia wasn't enough; Trotsky was eventually assassinated by a Spanish communist posing as a friend-of-a-friend, who buried an axe in his skull. For more choice details of Trotsky's life, ask Jesús, the English-speaking punk tour guide. *(Río Churubusco 410. From the M: Coyoacán, Line 3, turn right on Universidad, then left onto Churubusco. ☎ 5658 8732. Open Tu-Su 10am-5pm. 10 pesos, students with ID 5 pesos.)*

CASA DE CORTÉS. Originally Cortés's administrative building, the *casa* now houses the municipal government. Inside are murals by local artist Diego Rosales, a student of Diego Rivera's, showing scenes from the Conquest. Dispenses tourist information on all of Coyoacán. *(On the north side of the plaza. ☎ 5659 2256, ext. 181. Open daily 8am-8pm.)*

IGLESIA DE SAN JUAN BAUTISTA. The church, bordered by Plaza Hidalgo on the north and Jardín Centenario on the west, was begun in 1560 and rebuilt between 1798 and 1804. The interior is elaborately decorated with gold and bronze; the roof is decorated with five beautifully painted frescoes, depicting scenes from the New Testament of the bible. *(Open Tu-Sa 5:30am-8:30pm, M 5:30am-7:30pm.)*

CASA COLORADA. Cortés built this house for La Malinche, his Aztec lover. When Cortés's wife arrived from Spain, she stayed here briefly with her husband, but soon disappeared without a trace. It is believed that Cortés murdered his spouse for the love of La Malinche, although he later gave the Aztec woman away as booty to another *conquistador*. The *casa* is now a private residence and cannot be visited. *(Higuera 57. A few blocks southeast of Plaza Hidalgo, facing the Placita de la Conchita and marked by the gardened plaza at the end of Higuera.)*

MUSEO NACIONAL DE LAS CULTURAS POPULARES. Listen to hundreds of tunes, watch videos of dances, and, if you read Spanish, learn an overwhelming amount about indigenous instruments and rhythms from all over the country. Temporary exhibits usually feature specific regions or specific mediums of artistic expression. *(On Hidalgo between Allende and Abasolo, 2 blocks east of Plaza Hidalgo. ☎ 5554 8610. Open Tu-Th 10am-6pm, F-Su 10am-8pm. Free.)*

CONVENTO DE NUESTRA SEÑORA DE LOS ANGELES DE CHURUBUSCO. Built in 1524 over the ruins of a pyramid dedicated to the Aztec war god Huitzilopochtli, the present structure was constructed in 1668. The walls near the main gate are peppered with bullet holes from the US invasion of Mexico in 1917. Inside the ex-convent, the **Museo Nacional de las Intervenciones** commemorates Mexico's valiant defense. The museum's halls cover four eras, from the late 18th century to 1917. A few rooms are dedicated to exhibitions on North American expansionism and cruelty to *indígenas*, US slavery and its significance for Mexico, and European imperialism. *(20 de Agosto and General Anaya. From Coyoacán, walk 4 blocks down Hidalgo and then follow Anaya as it branches left; follow this street 4 blocks. M: General Anaya, Line 2, is only 2 blocks east of the convent along 20 de Agosto. The Gen. Anaya pesero (2 pesos) goes from Plaza Hidalgo to the museum; take the Sto. Domingo back. ☎ 5604 0699. Museum open Tu-Su 9am-6pm. 20 pesos; Su free.)*

MUSEO ANAHUACALLI. Designed by Diego Rivera with Aztec and Maya architectural motifs, the formidable stone building is an exhibit in and of itself. Inside is Rivera's huge collection of pre-Hispanic art. Built atop a hill, Anahuacalli commands an excellent view of the area, including nearby Aztec Stadium. *(On Calle Museo. To reach the museum from Plaza Hidalgo or Churubusco, take a "Huipulco" or "Huayamilpa" pesero going south on División del Nte. and get off at Calle Museo. You might want to ask the driver to point out the stop; it is not immediately visible. Turn right onto Calle Museo and you'll soon be there. ☎ 5617 4310. Open Tu-Su 10am-2pm and 3-6pm. 20 pesos.)*

MEXICO CITY

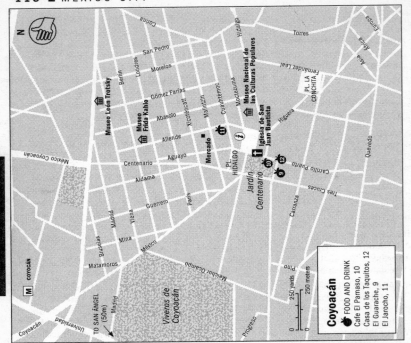

Coyoacán

● FOOD AND DRINK
Cafe El Parnaso, 10
Casa de los Taquitos, 12
El Guarache, 9
El Jarocho, 11

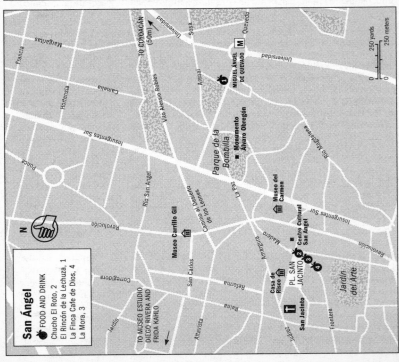

San Ángel

● FOOD AND DRINK
Chucho El Roto, 2
El Rincón de la Lechuza, 1
La Finca Cafe de Dios, 4
La Mora, 3

SAN ANGEL

To reach the San Angel, 10km south of the centro along Insurgentes, take the Metro to M: M.A. Quevedo, Line 3. Head west on Quevedo, away from the big Santo Domingo bakery, for three blocks; when it forks, take a left onto La Paz, and continue along the very green (but sometimes trash-laden) Parque de la Bombilla.

Near Coyoacán is the wealthy community of San Angel. Neither as artsy or bohemian as Coyoacán, San Angel's main appeal is that, quite simply, it's beautiful. Dotted with churches and exquisite colonial homes, this jewel of Mexican suburbia is an ideal place for a stroll.

PARQUE DE LA BOMBILLA. The centerpiece of this park is the **Monumento al General Álvaro Obregón.** Obregón was one of the revolutionaries who united against Victoriano Huerta, the usurper who executed Francisco Madero and seized power in 1913. Because Obregón lost an arm during the Revolution, the statue in the monument shows him thus. A separate statue of the severed limb can be viewed on the lower level of the monument. In 1920, Obregón became the first president of the post-revolutionary era but was ultimately assassinated by a religious fanatic. The inscription on the sunken lower level reads, "I die blessing the Revolution."

IGLESIA DEL CARMEN. Designed and built between 1615 and 1626 by Fray Andrés de San Miguel of the Carmelite order, the church and adjacent ex-convent are decorated with tiles and paintings. An outstanding statue of Christ the Nazarene is in the Capilla del Señor Contreras. *(Open daily 7am-1pm and 5-9pm.)*

MUSEO DEL CARMEN. The Museo del Carmen tells the history of the barefoot Carmelites in the New World, the first order to renounce missionary work. It displays colonial art, crucifixes galore, and portraits of various holy figures, as well as a typical convent room. Note the flat wooden bed and oh-so-comfy log pillow. Most tourists, however, come to see the **mummies,** located in an underground crypt; the grotesque cadavers were originally found in 1916 when the Zapatistas arrived in search of treasure. *(In the converted ex-convent next to the Iglesia del Carmen. At Revolución and Monasterio. ☎5550 4896. Open Tu-Su 10am-5pm. 15 pesos; Su free.)*

CASA DE RISCO. This well-preserved 17th-century house holds an important collection of 14th- through 18th-century European art. The whitewashed inner courtyard has an exquisitely tiled fountain made of pieces of Talavera tile (called *riscos*) and other bits of porcelain from around the world. Also look out for **Crisol de las Razas,** a painted colonial chart that lists racial combinations with names like *lobo* (wolf) and *salto atrás* (a step backward). Not the most politically correct account of racial diversity to say the least. *(Plaza San Jacinto 15, on the north side of the zócalo. ☎5550 9286. Open Tu-Su 10am-5pm. Free.)*

MUSEO CARRILLO GIL. This sleek, skylit building houses the modern art collection of the late Alvar Carillo Gil. The collection includes works by Siqueiros, Orozco, and the young Rivera. The second floor displays Siqueiros's famous **Caín en los Estados Unidos** (*Cain in the United States*, 1947). This work, depicting the lynching of a black man by a faceless crowd of whites, is a powerful cry of protest against US racial violence. The top two floors house more contemporary rotating exhibits. *(Revolución 1608, 3 blocks north on Revolución from the intersection with La Paz, to the right if coming from the Parque de la Bombilla. ☎5550 3983. Open Tu-Su 10am-6pm. 10 pesos, students with ID 6 pesos; Su free.)*

MUSEO ESTUDIO DIEGO RIVERA Y FRIDA KAHLO. This wild and windy studio-turned-museum was the home of Mexican art's royal couple, Diego Rivera and Frida Kahlo from 1934-40. The complex consists of two small houses side by side; Rivera lived in the pink house until his death in 1957, his wife Frida stayed in the blue house until she moved back to her home in Coyoacán in the early 1940s. The museum now houses a small collection of Rivera's work, with photographs and displays on the two artists' lives. On the top floor of the Rivera house, you can see where and how he worked; his leftover paints are even lying around untouched. *(Follow the signs 5 blocks up Altavista, which crosses Revolución. The museum is on the corner of Altavista and Diego Rivera. ☎5550 1518. Open Tu-Su 10am-6pm. 10 pesos; Su free.)*

OTHER SIGHTS. Across the street from the Iglesia del Carmen is the **Centro Cultural,** which borders the lovely **Plaza del Carmen.** Besides hosting changing art exhibits and plays, this building has billboards explaining what's hip and hot in the Mexican art world. (☎5616 1254 or 5616 2097. Open Tu-Sa 10am-8pm, Su 10am-7pm.) One block up Madero, which runs along the left side of the Casa de Cultura as you face the Casa, is the **Plaza de San Jacinto,** at San Francisco and Juárez. Every Saturday, the plaza fills with ritzy shoppers scoping out pricey arts and crafts at the **Bazaar del Sábado** (see p. 128). A gazebo in the center frequently hosts orchestras and big bands, and plastic chairs and peanut vendors span the plaza. One block past the Casa de Risco on Juárez lies the beautiful **Iglesia de San Jacinto,** a 16th-century church with an ancient orange facade, beautifully carved wooden doors, and a peaceful courtyard. (Open daily 8am-8pm.) This neighborhood, the oldest in San Angel, has some jaw-droppingly swank and impressive modern mansions. Come see how the rich live, Mexican style.

CIUDAD UNIVERSITARIA (CU)

*The sheer size of the UNAM makes it difficult to navigate by foot. Luckily, **M: Universidad,** Line 3, lets you off (via Salidas D and E) in front of the free shuttle service. The shuttles are limited and irregular over summer vacation (July 22-Aug. 15), but still available to all campus areas. Taxis, though more expensive, are easy to catch outside the Metro station. Shuttle routes do not always overlap—your best bet to get from one location to the next is usually to ride back to the Metro station and catch a new bus from there. There are three principal routes. The Route #1 shuttle will take you to the green and lively heart of the campus, the Jardín Central, far north of the station. To reach it, walk toward the library (you can't miss it), away from Insurgentes. Maps of the CU are available at the photocopy store across the greenery from the library (20 pesos; open M-F 8am-7pm). Should you have any serious problems, call **university security** (press the button on any security phone throughout campus, or ☎55 on a university phone.)*

The **Universidad Nacional Autónoma de México** (National Autonomous University of Mexico), or **UNAM,** is the largest university in Latin America, with a staggering enrollment of over 100,000. Immediately after the new colonial regime was established, the religious orders that arrived in Mexico built elementary and secondary schools to indoctrinate new converts and to educate young men who had come over from Spain. The first university, the University of Mexico, was established in 1553 in the building at the corner of Moneda and Seminario, just off the *zócalo;* the university that grew out of this University of Mexico is now the UNAM, brought into existence by president Justo Sierra around the turn of the century. The Ciudad Universitaria campus was dedicated in 1952, one of the greatest achievements of the presidency of Miguel Alemán. Designed by famous architects as Félix Candela and Juan O'Gorman, the campus boasts 26km of paved roads, 430,000 square meters of greenery, and four million planted trees—and it's not even residential.

CENTRO CULTURAL UNIVERSITARIO (CCU). Despite its rock-bottom tuition (something like US$130 per semester, though there has been much recent controversy over tuition hikes), the university is able to support an amazingly varied collection of student groups, activities, and social and cultural events. Films, shows, and club meetings abound. *Tiempo Libre* magazine and the leaflets *Cartelera* and *Los Universitarios* provide comprehensive schedules; hundreds of other events are posted on kiosks around campus. Most events of interest to tourists take place in the Centro Cultural Universitario (CCU; not to be confused with CU; Insurgentes Sur 3000.) This large, modern complex houses the **Teatro Juan Ruíz de Alarcón,** the **Foro Sor Juana Inés de la Cruz** (☎5665 6583; ticket booth open Tu-F 10am-2pm and 5-9pm; tickets 50 pesos, students 25 pesos), several other concert halls, the artsy movie theaters **Sala José Revueltas** and **Sala Julio Bracho** (☎5665 2850; tickets 20 pesos, students 10 pesos), and the **Sala Netzahualcóyotl** (☎5622 7111; shows Sa 8pm and Su noon; tickets 50-100 pesos, students 50% off), which regularly hosts big-name concerts and music festivals. *(The CCU is accessible by Line 3 of the UNAM shuttle.)*

ESPACIO ESCULTÓRICO. Just outside the CCU is the impressive Espacio Escultórico, a collection of sculptures by Mathias Goeritz. The metal, cement, and wood scultuptures, made in the early 1980s, rise from a huge lava bed and cave formation. Goeritz strove to revive the architectural traditions of pre-Hispanic ceremonial centers, using modern materials. The Espacio Escultórico should only be visited during the day; its secluded location makes it dangerous after nightfall.

LIBRARY. One of the world's larger mosaics, the work of Juan O'Gorman, wraps around the university library, to the left of the Jardín Central from Insurgentes. The breathtaking, nearly windowless building features eagles and Aztec warriors peering out from the side facing the philosophy department. The esplanade side shows the Spaniards' first encounter with the natives; the opposite side depicts a huge atom with its whirling electrons. Across the *jardín* from the library is the **Museo Universitario de Ciencias y Artes.** Across from the entrance to the Museo de Ciencias is the university's **administrative building,** distinguished by a 3-D Siqueiros mosaic on the south wall showing students studying at desks supported by society. *(Library ☎5622 1613. Open daily 8:30am-7pm. Museo de Ciencias ☎5622 0273. Open Sept.-June M-F 10am-7pm, Sa 10am-6pm. Free.)*

ESTADIO OLÍMPICO. The stadium, built in the 1950s, was somewhat appropriately designed to resemble a volcano with a huge crater—lava coats the ground upon which it is built. The impressive mosaic that covers the stadium was made by the unstoppable Rivera using large colored rocks; it depicts a man and a woman holding two torches, a symbol of the 1968 Olympics which were held in this stadium. Today, the stadium is home to the popular professional *fútbol* team, the **UNAM Pumas;** you'll see their navy blue and gold logo everywhere around campus, in shops, and on students. *(On the opposite side of Insurgentes Sur from the Jardín Centra;. cross via the pedestrian underpass.)*

JARDÍN BOTÁNICO. A beautiful and pleasantly secluded attraction is the Jardín Botánico. With its countless species of cacti, its shady arboretum, and its tropical plants pavilion, the *jardín* offers a look at the Valley of Mexico as it was hundreds of years ago. The trails of red volcanic dust and the helpful map at the entrance ensure you won't get lost. *(Open M-F 9am-4:30pm. Free. Bags must be left at the entrance.)*

CUICUILCO ARCHAEOLOGICAL ZONE. A bit south of the CU is the archaeological zone of Cuicuilco, whose name means "Place of the Many-Colored Jasper." The centerpiece, the **Pyramid of Cuicuilco,** was built between 600 and 200 BC by the some of the earliest settlers of the Valley of Mexico. The area was a ceremonial center with a population of around 20,000, making it the largest central settlement in Mesoamerica before the rise of Teotihuacán in the early Classic Period. Measuring 125m across its base and 20m in height, the pyramid consists of five layers, with an altar to the god of fire at its summit. The area was abandoned near the end of the Pre-Classic Period, when the tiny volcano of **Xitle** erupted around AD 100, leaving eight sq. km covered with several meters of hardened lava. The lava rock around the base has been removed, allowing visitors to walk along it up to the altar. However, very little other restoration has taken place. To an unknowing visitor, the pyramid appears to be little more than a quiet green hill in the middle of an urban area. On a clear day, you can faintly see Xitle to the south and the much larger Popocatépetl to the east. *(On the southeast corner at the intersection of Insurgentes Sur and Anillo Periférico, south of the Ciudad Universitaria. From M: Universidad, Line 3, exit on the side away from the campus, toward the small outdoor market, and take any "Cuicuilco" pesero (2 pesos) to the entrance on the west side of Insurgentes Sur, south of the Periférico. The peseros will let you off on the other side of Insurgentes. Cross the street toward the Cuicuilco shopping plaza, and walk left until you reach the entrance. To return, take any "CU Metro" pesero. ☎5606 9758. Open daily 9am-4pm. Free.)*

XOCHIMILCO

*To reach Xochimilco, get off at **M: Tasqueña**, Line 2, then ride the tren ligero (trolleybus; 1.50 pesos; follow the correspondencia signs) in the Embarcadero direction. For the gardens, get off at the "Xochimilco" stop. For the museum, get off at the "La Noria" stop.*

In Xochimilco (Place of the Flower-Growing; pronounced "so-she-MILK-o"), there are two things to do. The first is what everyone does: cruise the **floating gardens** of Xochimilco in a hand-poled *chalupa*. The second is far less known. Beyond the gardens a gorgeous museum, the **Museo Dolores Olmeda,** houses an impressive Rivera collection and largest Kahlo collection in Mexico.

THE FLOATING GARDENS. The floating gardens of Xochimilco were not for pleasure—they are remnants of the Aztec agricultural system. In fact, this tourist favorite was once an important center of Aztec life. The area had been settled since the pre-Classic times; it was only under the rule of Axayácatl that the city became an Aztec territory. In the Aztec's brilliantly conceived system, *chinampas* (artificial islands) were made by piling soil and mud onto floating rafts. These rafts were held firm by wooden stakes until the crops planted on top eventually sprouted roots, reaching through the base of the canals. They became fertile islands, supporting several crops a year. Although polluted today, the canals still bear the waterborne greenery they did centuries ago.

Multicolored **chalupa** boats crowd the maze of fairly filthy canals, ferrying passengers past a floating market of food, flowers, and music, especially crowded on Sundays. Familes, young people, and couples lounge and listen to the waterborne *mariachis* and *marimba* players, dancing merrily and toasting passers-by, then munch goodies and chug booze from the floating taco stands and bars that tie up pirate-style to the passenger boats. The best way to enjoy the afternoon is to stop at a local store to buy a few beers before the journey, enjoying them as you cruise the pleasure-canal and avoiding the obscene prices asked at many of the floating stands. The key word for almost anything you do in Xochimilco is **bargaining;** it is the only way to get around in this overly popular tourist spot. Be aware that if you come too early, you'll find far fewer boats and much higher prices. For a private boat for two people, expect to pay at least 80 pesos per hour with bargaining; consult the official charts for prices, as boat owners may try to charge eight or 10 times as much. On weekend afternoons, the more the merrier; bigger groups are the most fun and can get the lowest prices. For a group of six or more people, expect to pay at least 12 pesos per person per hour. The standard price for *mariachis* is 40 pesos per song, though you can always just ask your driver to pull up near the musical fun another boat has paid for.

Xochimilco also offers two enormous land-bound **markets,** one with the usual food and household items, the other lusciously filled with live plants and animals. To reach the marketplace from the trolleybus, turn left on any street within three blocks of the station as you walk away from it, then walk until you hit the market, just beyond the Iglesia de San Bernardino de Cera. *(From M: Tasqueña, take the tren ligero to the "Xochimilco" stop. Numerous "Embarcadero" signs and white-shirted boat owners will direct you. Peseros below the station will also take you; ask to be let off at "un embarcadero.")*

■ **MUSEO DOLORES OLMEDA.** As a young woman, the beautiful Dolores Olmeda Patino mingled with Mexico's elite. This museum, once her estate, features the art collection she amassed throughout her life. A fan of Diego Rivera in more than one sense (she was his long-time lover), she is the subject of many of his paintings. These and others bring the number of Rivera paintings in the collection to 144, including a series of 25 sunsets painted by Rivera from Olmeda's Acapulco home in 1956, the year before he died. Perhaps even more impressive, the 25 paintings by Frida Kahlo, much of whose work is abroad or in private collections, make this the best Kahlo collection in all of Mexico. Temporary exhibits support lesser-known but excellent work by current Mexican artists. Those unimpressed by Mexican art will appreciate the museum's gorgeously landscaped grounds; peacocks strut around the green lawns surrounding the mansion and boldly approach visitors. *(From M: Tasqueña, Line 2, take the tren ligero to "La Noria." Av. México 5843. ☎ 5555 1221 or 5555 0891. Open Tu-Su 10am-6pm. 20 pesos; Su free.)*

⏏ ENTERTAINMENT

Do not fear: the monotonous discos that dominate the night in most small towns are a thing of the past. Welcome to Mexico City. The chameleon that is entertainment in the nation's capital can turn any color you choose. Be it the Ballet Folklórico at Bellas Artes, an old Emilio Fernández film at an art cinema, a night of raving in a high-tech club, a bullfight in the Plaza México, or blues in a smoke-filled bar, the city has something for everyone—and more than enough for anyone.

JOIN THE CLUB. Different areas of the city have different specialties, even when it comes to down and dirty partying. Know what you're looking for? Then you should be heading for...

Bump 'n grind discos: Zona Rosa and the *centro* (see p. 123 or p. 124).
Jazz: San Angel and Coyoacán (see p. 126).
Bars: the *centro* (see p. 123).
Merengue and salsa clubs: the *centro* (see p. 123).
Traditional Mexican music: Plaza Garibaldi (seep. 125).
Topless bars and other lewd entertainment: Zona Rosa (see p. 124).

Cover charges range anywhere from 50-200 pesos for men; women are often admitted free or at reduced prices. At many large nightclubs in the *centro* and *Zona Rosa*, men are unofficially required to have a female date for admission. If you're pushy enough, foreign, and appropriately attired, this unwritten rule shouldn't apply to you. A very steep cover charge usually means an open bar; be sure to ask. Places with no cover, on the other hand, often have minimum drink requirements and high prices. Covers magically drop during the week when business is scarce, especially for *norteamericanos*, reputed to have deep pockets and high tolerances. If prices are not listed, be sure to ask before ordering, lest you be charged exorbitant *gringo* prices. Be aware that *bebidas nacionales* (Mexican-made drinks, from Kahlúa to *sangría*) are considerably cheaper than imported ones. In fact, *barra libre* (open bar) often means *barra libre nacional* (open bar including only national drinks).

Women venturing out alone should be aware that they will most likely be approached by men offering drinks, dances, and much more. *Cantinas*, bars with dimly lit interiors, no windows, or swinging doors, are often not safe for unaccompanied women. The most secure area is the *Zona Rosa*, which has the best lighting and most crowded streets.

WE CAN'T WARN YOU ENOUGH. Taxis run all night and are the safest way of getting from bar to disco to breakfast to hotel, but—especially after dark—do not flag a cab on the street. Ask any bartender, bouncer, or waiter to call or give you the number of the local *sitio* taxi company (see **Taxis**, p. 89).

CENTRO HISTÓRICO

A hop, skip, and a jump away from the *zócalo*, a testament to the proud and complex history of the Mexican people, lies a slew of nightclubs, a testament to the good-natured debauchery of those same people. In recent years, many have even picked the *centro* over the *Zona Rosa* as their sin-den of choice. Most clubs here are elegant and upscale (gotta love that valet parking) and have terraces with fully loaded bars and smashing skyline views; you'll end up paying a bit, but it's worth it if you want to party with Mexico's finest. **Metro stops: Zócalo,** Line 2; **Bellas Artes,** Lines 2 and 8; **Allende,** Line 2; and **Isabel la Católica,** Line 1.

🞝 **Opulencia,** Isabel la Católica 26 (☎5512 0417), on the corner of Madero. What's in a name? A heck of a lot. Velvet curtains and a VIP elevator are just the beginning. The enormous dance floor features big bouncers, black lights, video screens, and the best of 80s and contemporary dance music. Totally decadent, totally cool. Cover men 190 pesos, no cover for women; open bar. Open Th-Sa 10pm-late.

■ **Bar Roco,** Filomena Mata 16 (☎5521 3305), at the corner of 5 de Mayo. Angels, stained glass, and portraits cover the walls of this club, so elegant it has a huge chandelier dangling from the high ceiling. The Baroque interior may resemble a cathedral, but the atmosphere is anything but sedate. Cover men 150 pesos, women 60 pesos; open bar. Open Th-Sa 9pm-3am.

■ **La Ópera,** 5 de Mayo 10 (☎5355 3436), just west of Filomeno Mata. A restaurant and bar since 1807, with Baroque ceilings, mirrored walls, a grandfather clock, and dark wooden booths. While it's relatively low-key today, government alliances were made and betrayed between these walls. Grab a whiskey and soda and talk some politics. Drinks 20-32 pesos. Open M-Sa 1pm-midnight, Su 1-6pm.

Salon Bar Aima, Filomena Mata 5 (☎5510 4488), off 5 de Mayo. The small club is packed on weekend nights with salsa and merengue dancers, twisting and twirling to the music of talented live musicians. Try not to be intimidated by the impressive dancing on display—give it a shot. Cover men 50 pesos, women 25 pesos. Beer 25 pesos. Open Th-Sa 8pm-4am.

Oraculo, Motolinia 23 (☎5510 5040). Enter this brand-new 2nd-floor disco and you might think you've descended into the tomb of an Egyptian king (minus the dust, mummified bodies, vengeful curses, etc.). Hieroglyphics cover the domed ceilings, while video screens play pop hits. Cover men 150 pesos, women free. Open F-Sa 10pm-late.

THE ALAMEDA

While bars and discos near the Alameda can't compare to those in the *centro* or the *Zona Rosa*, the prices are at least refreshingly low. Unfortunately, the surrounding neighborhoods can be dangerous, especially late at night. Though Metro stops are abundant, you'll still want to get the phone number of a nearby *sitio* taxi. **Metro stops: Hidalgo,** Line 2; **Bellas Artes,** Lines 2 and 8; **Juárez,** Line 3; and **San Juan de Letran,** Line 8.

Especially noteworthy is the **Hostería del Bohemio,** Hidalgo 107, just west of Reforma. Leave M: Hidalgo, Lines 2 and 3, from the Av. Hidalgo/Calle de Héroes exit and turn left. Situated in the cloister of the ex-convent of San Hipólito, this romantic cafe is saturated with guitar, singing, and poetry in the evenings. Seating is on the outdoor terraces and all four sides of a lush, two-tiered courtyard which at night comes alive with thousands of Christmas lights. The slice-of-a-tree tables are lit by old-fashioned lanterns. You're guaranteed to fall in love here, if not with the attractive, googly-eyed boy or girl next to you, then with the amazing assortment of coffee, cake, and ice cream. (☎5512 8328. Everything on the menu hovers around 18 pesos. No cover. Open daily 5-11pm.)

ZONA ROSA

The *Zona Rosa* has some of the Republic's flashiest discos and highest cover charges—on weekend nights, it can seem like the center of the universe. Club-hopping, however, is becoming more difficult, as many discos are moving over to the high cover charge and open bar system. Sidewalk recruiters will likely try to lure in groups, especially those with high female-to-male ratios; hold out and you might be offered a deal. Dress codes of sorts apply: if you look particularly foreign, it is unlikely that you'll be turned away, but it does happen.

Zona Rosa bars cater to all ages and tastes, from teenyboppers to old-timers. Many feature live music or, at the very least, beamed-in video entertainment. Steer clear of the many strip clubs in the area; even if that's the sort of thing you're looking for, drink prices are astronomical (upward of 50 pesos). A night at the bars in the *Zona* doesn't come cheap, but the high price tags often mean live performances or tasty *botanas* (appetizers). After a wild night, catch a ride home in one of the *peseros* that runs all night long on Reforma or Insurgentes Sur (3 pesos). **Metro stops: Insurgentes,** Line 1; and **Sevilla,** Line 1.

■ **Urano,** Hamburgo 123 (☎5207 9121). At the end of a long metal hallway, a high-ceilinged dance floor features caged dancers (clothed, alas) at one end and on the upper balcony. Let the music move you and hundreds of beautiful, hip young Mexicans. Cover includes open bar. Th 150 men, women free; F 170 men, women 70; Sa 180 men, women 80. Open Th-Sa 9pm-late. Downstairs, **Candela** attracts a considerably calmer crowd to its tropical dance-floor, with *norteña*, salsa, and merengue music. Beers 25 pesos, mixed drinks 30-60 pesos. Cover 60 pesos.

■ **Freedom,** Copenhague 25 (☎5207 8456), at the corner of Hamburgo. Work up an appetite boogying to the latest hits on 3 crowded floors of bars and dancing. The kitchen at this D.F. chain restaurant and bar stays open until 2am, keeping hungry partiers happy throughout the night. *Antojitos* and hamburgers 55-70 pesos, beers 25 pesos, national drinks 25-30 pesos. No cover. Open daily 1pm-2am.

Caramba!, Genova 44 (☎5208 9611), near the corner with Hamburgo, up the spiral staircase. Blasting dance music reverberates off the metal floor and walls of this enormous, lively disco. Cover includes open bar. Cover men 170 pesos; women free until 11pm, after 11pm 70 pesos. Open Th-Sa 9pm-3am.

Rock Stock Bar & Disco, Reforma 261 (☎5533 0907), at Niza. Clubs come and go, but this one is packed year after year. Follow street signs through the darkroom-style doors to a huge open attic room with railings, scaffolding, and metal cages slathered in fluorescent paint. Come early if you want to be part of the late crowd—as the night draws on, swarms outside clamour to be let in. Cheaper and less crowded 3-9pm. Cover 40-60 pesos; after 10pm cover men 150 pesos, women free; women free 3-4pm. Open M-Sa 3pm-late.

El Chato, Londres 117 (☎5511 1758), with a stained-glass awning. The splendid faux old-Euro bar has a smokey rear piano bar with fittingly beat tunes. No glitz and no booming beat, but the older crowd likes it that way. Beer 20 pesos, tequila 25 pesos. Occasional musicians (30 peso cover). Open M-Sa 6pm-1am.

Figa Bar, Londres 142 (☎5514 3168), at Amberes. Chairs are pushed aside to make room for dancing as the night progresses at this new bar. The night starts early, drawing a younger crowd for open soda bar noon-8pm (guys 50 pesos, girls 20 pesos). Soon after they bring out the hard stuff for national open bar (cover men 150 pesos, women 100 pesos). Open daily noon-late.

Melodika, Florencia 52 (☎5208 0198). The 3-part bar is host to everything from rave music to karaoke. Make lots of young local friends as you all huddle together and croon everyone's favorite *rancheros*. Beers 19 pesos. Cover 15 pesos. Open Th-Sa 7pm-late.

Yarda's, Niza 40 (☎5512 2108), is a restaurant by day and a booming disco by night. Catch night fever in the 70s disco atmosphere. Everyone—from youngsters to 40-somethings—keeps this place packed, chugging yard after yard of beer and cocktails. Half-yard beer 50 pesos, quarter-yard cocktail 90 pesos. No cover. Open M-Sa 7-2:30am.

PLAZA GARIBALDI

Plaza Garibaldi has some of Mexico City's gaudiest and most amusing nightlife. By 5pm, both wandering *mariachis* and roving *ranchero* bands begin to play for a negotiable prices. Fifty pesos for a three-song set (10 pesos for solo performers) is a good deal. Of course, a cheap trick is to pick a table close to a rich drunk tourist and leach off the performances he or she pays for. Tourists, locals, prostitutes, musicians, vendors, transvestites, kids—anybody and everybody mingles here, many reeling, dancing, and screaming in the street, enjoying the alcoholic offerings of the plaza. The big nightclubs surrounding the plaza, each with its own *mariachis*, do their best to lure crowds. Though they advertise no cover, per-drink prices are annoyingly high. Your best bet is to find a table at one of the open-air cafes, where you can order cheap beers (11 pesos) or try *pulque*, an alcoholic drink made from the *maguey* cactus. If you're hungry, don't miss the **Mercado de Alimentos San Camilito,** on the northwest corner of the plaza. This indoor market contains tons of small, inexpensive eateries, each clamoring for your business. Look around for the best deals; most will feed you quite well for under 30 pesos.

As in any part of the city, exercise caution while in Plaza Garibaldi. Especially avoid wandering beyond the plaza to the back streets, which are considerably less charming. The best time to visit Garibaldi is in the evening, between 8pm and midnight. The action begins soon after nightfall, so this a great place to kick off a night out on the town.

The plaza is at the intersection of Lázaro Cárdenas (Eje Central) and República de Honduras, north of the Alameda. **Metro stops:** get off at **Bellas Artes,** Lines 2 and 8, and walk three blocks north along Cárdenas; Garibaldi is the plaza on your right. **Garibaldi,** Line 8, plants you three blocks north of the plaza. Exit to your left from the stop and walk south.

COYOACÁN AND SAN ANGEL

While generally very safe sections of town, these two southern suburbs fall just outside many of Mexico City's public transportation axes. The Metro serves both until midnight, after which a taxi is the best option. Most mid- to high-priced restaurants have live jazz at night. Coyoacán and San Angel infamous for their slews of foreigners, getting drunk and wistful to blues and rock. One option is **El Hijo del Cuervo** (☎5658 7824), on the north side of the Jardín Centenario, in Coyoacán. A motley international crew of people-watching, liquor-downing folks come here weekend nights for live rock and Latin music. (Open daily 1pm-2am.) For a pretty sedate evening, simply hang out in Coyoacán's main plaza, sip coffee or cappucino, and soak up the nearby comedians and musicians. **Metro stops: M. A. Quevedo,** Line 3, for San Angel; and **Coyoacán,** Line 3, for Coyoacán.

GAY AND LESBIAN ENTERTAINMENT

Mexico City offers the full range of social and cultural activities for gays and lesbians, and a fledgling and active gay rights movement has made its presence known. Still, general tolerance of public homosexuality is still very low, and although not illegal, public displays of affection by gay and lesbian couples on the street or on the Metro are sure tickets to harassment, especially by the police. Gay men will have a much easier time finding bars and discos, although more and more venues have begun to welcome lesbians. The free pamphlet *Ser Gay* is a great source of information, with listings for gay entertainment, art events, clubs, and bars in the city. Copies are available at all the clubs listed below. For exclusively lesbian activities, contact one of several Mexico City lesbian groups (see p. 94). In June, Mexico's gay pride month, an inordinate number of parties, rallies, art exhibits, marches, and *fiestas* occur throughout the city.

■ **El Antro,** Londres 77 (☎5511 1613), near the intersection with Insurgentes in the *Zona Rosa.* Only men are allowed to enjoy the multiple bars, dance floors, private rooms, video screens, and anything and everything else. Men of all ages come here to check out the acclaimed stripper shows, get down to hard-core disco, and indulge in concerts and live drag shows. Cover 40 pesos; Sa 50 pesos. Open W-Sa 7pm-late, Su 6pm-2am.

■ **Penelope,** Antonio Caso 60 (☎5566 1472), off Insurgentes near the Monumento a la Revolución. Gays, lesbians, straights, bisexuals, drag queens...anybody can have a good time at this techno/house club. One of Mexico's few true mixclubs, the environment is open to any sexual orientation. Surreal live stage shows include Boy George impersonators and go-go dancing midget drag queens. Don't miss the luxurious unisex bathroom, featuring a replica of Michaelangelo's David. Open Th-Sa 11pm-late. Beer 20 pesos. Cover 70 pesos.

■ **Anyway, Exacto, and the Doors,** Monterrey 47 (☎5533 1691), a half-block from Durango in Col. Roma, just south of the *Zona Rosa.* A party in 3 parts. Food and drink at The Doors, dancing and more drinks at the other two. Exacto is the only all-women's disco in the city Th; on the other days it has a high concentration of lesbians. Cover W 35 pesos Th 45 pesos, F-Sa 60 pesos; includes 1 drink. Open daily 9pm-late.

■ **El Celo,** Londres 104 (☎5514 4309), in the *Zona Rosa.* This laid-back bar/club draws one of the city's hippest crowds, with gays and lesbians alike crowding its floors to get down to techno and pop. Su afternoon it becomes a gay-friendly restaurant. Beers 20 pesos. Cover after 11pm 50 pesos; includes 1 drink. Open Th-Sa 9:30pm-late.

Butterfly, Izazaga 9 (☎5761 1861), near M: Salto del Agua, Lines 1 and 8, half a block east of Lázaro Cárdenas, south of the cathedral. Though no signs mark this club, don't be afraid to ask. The big, brash gay nightspot is worth the finding. Video screens and a superb lighting system. Male revue late on weekend nights. Lesbians have begun to frequent as well. Cover F-Sa 35 pesos; includes 2 drinks. Open Tu-Su 9pm-late.

El Almacen, Florencia 37 (☎5207 0727). Mediterranean food and pop dance music. Growing numbers of lesbians are joining the men, who throw back beers on their way to the high-octane gay male club in the basement, El Taller. Open daily 4pm-late.

El Taller, Florencia 37A (☎5533 4984; www.eltaller.com.mx), underground in the *Zona Rosa*. El Almacen bar upstairs. A well-known hangout for blue-collar gay men. Throbbing music, construction-site decorations, and dark, private alcoves create an intense men-only pick-up scene. Private barroom attracts an older crowd. W and Su mostly 20-ish; Sa theme night. Cover Th-Su 40 pesos (includes 1 drink). Open Tu-Su 9pm-late.

La Estación, Hamburgo 234 (☎5207 0727), in the *Zona Rosa*. A brand new all-men leather bar—get your best leather or latex outfit out of the closet and head over to this enormous 2-floor bar. Open daily 4pm-2am.

La Cantina del Vaquero, Algeciras 26 (☎5598 2195), Col. Insurgentes, near Parque Hundido, between M: Mixcoac, Line 7, and M: Zapata, Line 3. The first openly gay *cantina* in Mexico has been a favorite for over 25 years. Working-class gay men still flock to the bar to watch XXX videos, sample the darkroom, or simply grab a beer and chat. Videos screened daily 5-11pm. Cover 35 pesos; includes 2 beers. Open M-Su 5pm-late.

🛍 SHOPPING

While most Mexican cities have one large, central market, Mexico City seems to have one on every corner. Each *colonia* has its own market, and the center of town hosts marketplaces the size of small cities. The markets are all relatively cheap, but vary widely in quality and content. Shopping throughout the *centro* and the Alameda proceeds thematically: there is a wedding dress street, a lighting fixtures street, a lingerie street, a windowpane street, a military surplus street, etc.

 Mercado de La Ciudadela, 2 blocks north of M: Balderas, Lines 1 and 3, off Balderas. An incredible array of *artesanías*, crafts, and traditional clothing at low prices. Its deserved reputation as the biggest and best *artesanía* market in the city makes tourist traffic rampant. Open daily 8am-7pm.

🛍 **San Juan Artesanías,** Plaza El Buen Tono, 4 blocks south of Alameda Central, 2 blocks west of Lázaro Cárdenas. From M: Salto de Agua, Lines 1 and 8, walk 4 blocks up López and make a left on Ayuntamiento. 3 floors of artisanry from all over Mexico. Typical mix of mold-made tourist items and handmade treasures. Prices similar to La Ciudadela, but comparison shopping always helps. Fewer tourists wander around here, which gives you more bargaining power. Open M-Sa 9am-7pm, Su 9am-4pm.

🛍 **La Merced,** Circunvalación at Anaya, east of the *zócalo*. M: Merced, Line 1. Not just a market but a way of life. The largest market in the Americas, it has an unfathomably wide selection of fresh produce from all over the country, and more raw meat than you can handle, all at rock-bottom prices. The nearby **Mercado de Dulces** (candy market) will make you feel like the proverbial kid in a candy store. Between the 2 lies the **Mercado de Flores** (flower market). All 3 markets open daily 8am-7pm.

The Zócalo, along Corregidora, the street between the Palacio Nacional and the Supreme Court, is the unofficial "market," which has been the subject of much controversy through the years. Vendors clog the street with stands, their brightly colored umbrellas stretching as far as the eye can see. The government has long been trying to drive out these non-rent-paying shopkeeps, but to no avail. They persist, with some of the best prices in town on practical goods, clothing, toys, CDs, and electronics. If you don't mind insanely crowded streets, come here for your non-*artesanía* needs. Open daily.

FONART, Patriotismo 691 (☎563 4060), Juárez 89 (☎5521 0171), and Carranza 115 (☎5554 6270) in Coyoacán. A national project to protect and market traditional crafts. *Artesanías* from all over the country: giant tapestries, rugs, silver jewelry, pottery, and colorful embroidery. Regulated prices are not quite as low as the markets, but if you're not in the mood for crowds and haggling, come here and pay only a little more. Open M-Sa 10am-7pm.

La Lagunilla, Comonfort at Rayón, east of the intersection of Lázaro Cárdenas and Reforma. Two large yellow buildings on either side of the street with stands spilling outside. Although now open daily, the market really gets going on Sunday when it turns into a gargantuan flea market, most notable for its antique books. The rest of the week, their specialty is communion and party dresses. Open daily 8am-7pm.

Sonora, Teresa de Mier and Cabañ, 2 blocks south of La Merced. Specializes in witchcraft, medicinal teas and spices, figurines, and ceremonial images. Search no further for lucky cows' feet, shrunken heads, eagle claws, black salt, and powdered skull (for the domination of one's enemies). Beware however; this is a prime spot for pickpockets. Open daily 8am-7pm.

Bazaar del Sabado, Plaza San Jacinto, in the center of San Angel. Spilling onto the plaza, this market tends to be pricey and touristy but is one of the few to which contemporary artists bring their work. One of San Angel's biggest draws. Open Sa 9am-6pm.

Jamaica, Congreso and Morelos (Eje 3 Sur). M: Jamaica, Lines 4 and 9. Immediately as you exit the Metro station, there is a clump of vendor stalls selling cheap eats and some of the juiciest mangos and *piñas* in town. The real pride and joy of the market is the assortment of fragrant and brightly colored flowers, including, of course, the deep-red Jamaica flower, source of the lip-smacking *agua de Jamaica* sold at many stands. Also be sure to check out live animals and exotic birds (all for sale) squawking and screaming in their confining cages. Open M-Sa 8am-6pm.

SPORTS

Whether consumed by their passion for bullfighting, *fútbol* (soccer), *beisbol* (baseball), or horse racing, Mexican fans share an almost religious devotion to *deportes* (sports). If sweaty discos and endless museums have you craving a change of pace, follow the crowds to an athletic event and prepare yourself for a rip-roarin' rowdy good time. *¡Andale!*

▨ **Estadio Azteca,** Calz. de Tlalpan 3465 (☎5617 8080 or 5617 2088). Take a *pesero* or *tren ligero* (trolleybus) from M: Tasqueña, Line 2. Proud home of the *Aguilas de America* (American Eagles), the stadium is the largest in Mexico, regularly packing in 100,000-person crowds for important *fútbol* matches. Keep an eye out for **Mexico-Brazil** matches, and good luck getting tickets. Season runs Oct.-July. Tickets 50-1200 pesos.

▨ **Plaza México,** (☎5563 3959), M: San Antonio, Line 7, on Insurgentes Sur, is Mexico's principal bullring, seating 40,000 fans. July-Nov. professional fights; Nov.-Feb. *novillada* (novice) fights. Tickets run 10-100 pesos, depending on the seat's proximity to the ring and whether it falls in the *sombra* (shade) or *sol* (sun). Next door is the very big and very blue **Estadio Azul,** home of Mexico City's professional *fútbol* team Cruz Azul. Bullfights take place Su 4pm.

El Foro del Sol, in the Ciudad Deportiva (Ticketmaster ☎5325 9000), M: Ciudad Deportiva, Line 9. This "sports city" complex contains volleyball courts, a boxing ring, an ice-skating rink, many soccer fields, and other assorted sports facilities. The *Foro,* at the center of the complex, hosts the home games of Mexico City's two professional baseball teams, the *Diablos Rojos* (Red Devils) and the *Tigres* (Tigers). Sparks fly when the teams face each other; local papers call it the *Guerra Civil* (Civil War). This matchup aside, tickets (10-80 pesos) are easy to come by and can be purchased at the gate.

Hipodromo de las Américas, beyond M: Tacubaya, Lines 1, 7, and 9, houses a horse racetrack and occasionally hosts *jai alai* matches, an extremely fast paced game a bit like raquetball (see **The World's Fastest Game, the World's Strangest Name,** p. 145).

GOOOOOOOOOOOOOOOOOOOOAAAAAAAAAAAAAAAAAAAAAL!
Although *charrería* (horsemanship, rodeo, bullfighting) may be the official national sport of Mexico, *fútbol* (soccer) is by far the most popular. If you want to check out the *fútbol* phenomenon, you're in luck—matches take place year-round. The Winter League runs July-Dec. and the Summer League Jan.-May. In addition, countless minor and amateur *fútbol* leagues play throughout the year. Every fourth June, the World Cup takes Mexico by storm—even gas and water delivery stops as soccer fans throughout the country pack bars and restaurants to watch the games. Whenever Mexico scores a goal, the entire nation shakes in unison as the word "GOAL!" rings from every bar, business, and bus.

Though some may not call it a sport, *lucha libre*, Mexico's version of professional wrestling, has events in the *hipodromo* every F night. Mexico City's main *jai alai* venue, the famous Frontón México, facing the north side of the Monumento a la Revolución, is currently closed due to a strike.

🄳 DAYTRIPS FROM MEXICO CITY

Even those who've fallen in love with Mexico City need some time away (a neccessity in any healthy relationship). Fortunately, its great location makes for easy and painless escape. From small towns to not-so-small towns, from ruins to volcanoes, all of the following places make convenient daytrips.

TEOTIHUACÁN

Direct bus service from Mexico City is available via Autobuses Teotihuacán *(1hr., every 15min. 6am-3pm, 19 pesos), in the Terminal de Autobuses del Norte (☎5781 1812 or 587 0501) at Sala 8. Buy your tickets for the "Pirámides" bus. If you prefer, you can try catching the same buses as they stop outside M: Indios Verdes, though will likely be standing-room only. The last bus back from the pyramids to Mexico City leaves the main entrance at 6pm, Puerta 1. ☎956 0052; from Mexico City ☎01 5956 0052. There are 5 entrances to the site. Buses drop visitors off by Puerta 1, the main entrance. Puerta 5, the easternmost entrance, is by the Pirámide del Sol. Free guided tours for groups of 5 or more can be arranged at the administration building by Puerta 1 (southwest corner). Site open daily 7am-6pm. 30 pesos, free for children under 13; Su free. Free parking.*

Teotihuacán has some of the most enormous ruins in the country, and people still do not know much about them. Nobody is quite sure who the Teotihuacanos were. Perhaps they were the Olmeca-Xicalanca, a Mixtec-speaking group, or, as another theory argues, a Totonac tribe. They were most likely some sort of pre-Toltec or pre-Aztec Náhuatl- or Mixtec-speaking people. Regardless of exact origins, the area was settled in the late pre-Classic period, around 100 BC. Unlike any other city of the time in Mesoamerica, Teotihuacán was meticulously planned. The city was split into quadrants, with the Calle de Los Muertos and a now lost road forming the axes of the city. Teotihuacán spread out over an area of 20 sq. km and controlled the entire valley of Mexico, with evidence of trade and influence extending as far south as the Maya city of Tikal in Guatemala. Because Teotihuacán was such a powerful trade center, it was easily able to attain laborers from nearby subservient cities. It was this labor that was used to construct the magnificent, enormous edifices you see today. The Pirámide del Sol, one of the largest pyramids in the world, was built in the late pre-Classic, while the newer Pirámide de la Luna was built during the Classic. At its heyday (AD 150-250), Teotihuacán accommodated a population of nearly 200,000, making it the sixth largest city in the world.

Sometime around AD 700, Teotihuacán began to fall. While the reasons for its downfall are far from certain, many speculate that the city eventually collapsed under its own weight, having grown so large and crowded that it could no longer produce enough food to keep its inhabitants properly fed. New buildings were built on top of old, possibly due to overcrowding, and evidence of a tremendous

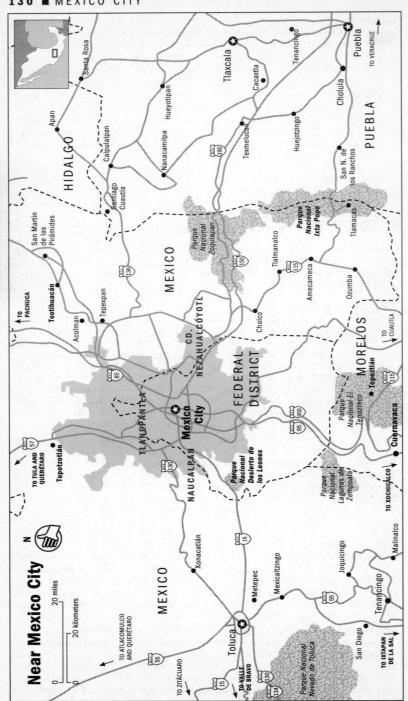

Near Mexico City

N

20 miles

20 kilometers

TO ATLACOMULCO AND QUERÉTARO

TO ZITÁCUARO

TO TULA AND QUERÉTARO

TO VALLE DE BRAVO

TO PACHUCA

TO CUAUTLA

TO XOCHICALCO

TO IXTAPAN DE LA SAL

TO VERACRUZ

HIDALGO

MEXICO

PUEBLA

MORELOS

FEDERAL DISTRICT

Santa Rosa

Tlaxcala

Cacaxtla

Tenanchingo

Puebla

Apan

Calpulapan

Hueyotipan

Texmelucan

Cholula

Nanacamilpa

San N. de los Ranchos

Santiago Cuautla

San Martín de las Pirámides

Tepotzotlán

Teotihuacán

Acolman

Tepexpan

Parque Nacional Zoquiapan

Parque Nacional Ixta Popo

Tlamacas

Tlalmanalco

Huejotzingo

Amecameca

Ozumba

CD. NEZAHUALCÓYOTL

Chalco

Mexico City

TLALNEPANTLA

Tepotzotlán

NAUCALPAN

Parque Nacional Desierto de los Leones

Parque Nacional El Tepozteco

Tepoztlán

Cuernavaca

Parque Nacional Lagunas de Zempoala

Xonacatlán

Metepec

Mexicaltzingo

Joquicingo

Malinalco

Toluca

San Diego

Tenancingo

Parque Nacional Nevado de Toluca

85

57

130

15

55

55

95

950

134

15

130

15

136

150

115

115

190

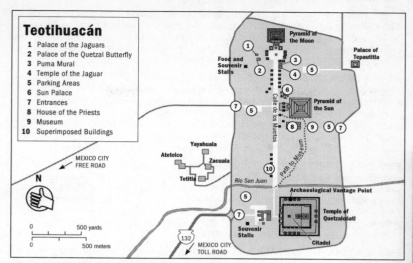

Teotihuacán

1 Palace of the Jaguars
2 Palace of the Quetzal Butterfly
3 Puma Mural
4 Temple of the Jaguar
5 Parking Areas
6 Sun Palace
7 Entrances
8 House of the Priests
9 Museum
10 Superimposed Buildings

MEXICO CITY
FREE ROAD

N

0 ____ 500 yards
0 ____ 500 meters

132 MEXICO CITY
TOLL ROAD

Pyramid of
the Moon

Palace of
Tepautitla

Food and
Souvenir
Stalls

Calle de los Muertos

Pyramid of
the Sun

Path to Museum

Yayahuala

Atetelco
Zacuala

Tetitla

Río San Juan

Archaeological Vantage Point

Temple of
Quetzalcóatl

Souvenir
Stalls

Citadel

fire around AD 800 can be found in layers of blackened stone. By AD 850, few inhabitants remained in the enormous urban complex. When the Aztecs founded Tenochtitlán in the 14th century, Teotihuacán, 50km northeast of their capital, lay abandoned. The Aztecs were so impressed by the size and scope of the buildings that they adopted the areas as ceremonial grounds, believing its huge structures to be built by gods and those buried there to be of some superhuman order. The Aztecs called the area Teotihuacán, meaning "Place Where Men Become Gods." When the Spaniards destroyed Tenochtitlán in the 16th century, they were almost certainly unaware of the pyramid's existence. This fortunate oversight allowed the site to remain astonishingly intact. Extensive excavation began in 1906 under the orders of Porifiro Díaz, in a project meant to emphasize the cultural wealth of the Mexican people and to celebrate 100 years of Mexican independence in 1910.

CALLE DE LOS MUERTOS (STREET OF THE DEAD). The ceremonial center, a 13 sq. km expanse, was built along a 3km stretch now called Calle de los Muertos, so named because the Aztecs believed ancient kings had been buried alongside it. The Teotihuacanos planned their community around the four cardinal points, and this main road runs in a straight north-south line from the Pirámide de la Luna to the Templo de Quetzalcóatl. The southernmost end of the avenue has still not been fully explored. The main structure, the Pirámide del Sol, is on the east side, aligned with the point on the horizon where the sun sets at the summer solstice. An east-west thoroughfare, of equal length and importance, is believed to have bisected the Calle at some point in front of the Ciudadela.

CIUDADELA (CITADEL). At the southern end of the site is the expansive Ciudadela, where priests and government officials once lived. The large plaza was so named because of its resemblance to a military complex, though it is well-documented that it served as royal residences. On the northern end of the Ciudadela lie four small pyramids. The top of the second one is an "Archaeological Vantage Point," which gives a wonderful view of the two pyramids in the near distance.

TEMPLO DE QUETZALCÓATL. At the center of the Ciudadela is the Templo de Quetzalcóatl, dedicated to the plumed serpent god. The pyramid was obstructed by another, later pyramid, subsequently removed to provide access to the older pyramid inside. Lining the main staircase, enormous stone carvings of the serpent Quetzalcóatl regularly pop out from the stone flowers. Along the pyramid's surface, sculptures of Quetzalcóatl alternate with images of the rain god Tlaloc, easily identifiable by his google-eyes and large fangs. The still-visible red paint that originally decorated these sculptures was made by cutting off nopal leaves into which tiny bugs had burrowed, carving out the colorful critters, and smashing them. Also note the shell motifs along the sides of the pyramid; this may be evidence of trade with coastal areas.

MUSEO DE SITIO (SITE MUSEUM). Just southeast of the Pirámide del Sol is the Museo de Sitio. The beautiful design of this museum imitates the forms and colors used by the site's ancient inhabitants. Displays compare the size of the ancient city to various present-day cities, illustrate the architecture and technology of the pyramids, describe the social, religious, and economic organization of the society, and exhibit *indígena* art. All of the pieces in the museum are replicas. The originals are at the Museo Nacional de Antropología in Mexico City (p. 112).

EDIFICIOS SUPERPUESTOS. Continuing north along the Calle de los Muertos, you will cross what was once the San Juan river. On the west side of the street are the remains of two temples, known as the Edificios Superpuestos, that were built in two phases (AD 200-400 and AD 400-750), atop older, partially demolished temples. The older buildings were filled in with rubble to clear way for the construction on top; this had the unintentional effect of preserving the temples, which can now be visited with the aid of metal catwalks.

PIRÁMIDE DEL SOL (PYRAMID OF THE SUN). Farther to the north and east is the Pirámide del Sol, the most massive single structure in the ceremonial area. Second in size only to the pyramid at Cholula, the pyramid's base measures 222m by 225m, and its volume is over one million cubic yards—dimensions comparable to those of Cheops in Egypt. It was built sometime in the late Pre-Classic era, around 100 BC, and completed just before the zenith of Teotihuacano civilization, around AD 150. The inside of the pyramid is filled with rubble and brick, and there is evidence that it was built over the remains of another pyramid, perhaps originally of equal size. In 1971, a natural cave was discovered below the pyramid. Archaeologists now believe that the cave was a sacred site, perhaps the reason the pyramid, and subsequently all of Teotihuacán, was built on this spot. At over 60m in height, the pyramids afford a breathtaking view of the surrounding valley. Smokers and slowpokes: don't quit. A rope railing helps you up the steepest stretch, and the platforms of the multi-tiered pyramid make convenient rest stops. The hard-working vendors never give up, even on the peak of this mammoth pyramid. As soon as you reach the top, weary and awe-struck, be prepared to say, "*No me faltan tortugas de obsidiana, gracias*" (No, I don't need any more obsidian turtles, thank you).

PALACIO DE QUETZALPAPALOTL (PALACE OF THE QUETZAL BUTTERFLY). Between the Pirámide el Sol and the Pirámide de la Luna on the west side of the street is the Palacio de Quetzalpapalotl. This columned structure was the residence of nobles, next to the ceremonial space, far from the residential complexes of the common folk. The inner patio is one of the most beautiful sights of the ancient city; the colored frescoes and bird glyphs, though faded, have survived years of decay and retain much of their intricate detail. On the columns are images of plumed butterflies, which give the *palacio* its name.

PALACIO DE LOS JAGUARES (PALACE OF THE JAGUARS). Behind the palace and through the short maze of an entrance is the Palacio de los Jaguares (Palace of the Jaguars) and the now-subterranean **Palacio de las Conchas Emplumadas** (Palace of the Feathered Seashells). The jaguar palace is entirely restored, complete with fluorescent lights and plastic handrails. Some of the original frescoes remain, adorned with red, green, yellow, and white symbols representing birds, corn, and water. The palace was built over another earlier temple, in which patterns of plumed seashells adorn the walls.

PIRÁMIDE DE LA LUNA (PYRAMID OF THE MOON). At the northern end of the Calle de los Muertos is the stunning **Pirámide de la Luna.** A sculpture of **Chalchiutli-**

cue, a water goddess and important Aztec deity, was found here during excavations. The pyramid was built later than the Pirámide del Sol, most likely during Teotihuacán's zenith around AD 300. Though the hike up this pyramid is a bit steeper and rougher than the walk up the Pirámide del Sol, there are fewer vendors here and the view is even more magnificent.

PALACIO DE TEPANTITLA. If you still have energy, on the northeast side of the Pirámide del Sol near Puerta 4 is the **Palacio de Tepantitla,** which has some of the best-preserved frescoes in Teotihuacán, still showing a full range of colors. You can see priests with elaborate headdresses and representations of Tlaloc. The lower part depicts the Teotihuacano ideal of a butterfly-filled paradise.

DESIERTO DE LOS LEONES

Buses for Desierto de Leones leave from San Angel in front of the Centro Cultural San Angel (see p. 101). Whenever 10 people gather, a bus (1hr., 10 pesos per person) will head off. If people are slow to gather (this is especially likely during the week), you can pay for the empty seats. The last stop is in front of the convent. To return to the city, colectivos to San Angel or M: Tacubaya leave from the entrance approximately every hr., last bus 5pm. Park open daily 6am-5pm. Convent open Tu-Su 10am-5pm. 5 pesos. Guided tours Sa-Su 11am-3pm; around 15 pesos.

Just outside the city, the Desierto de Los Leones (Desert of the Lions) is a breathtaking park, offering solace and clean air among millions of pines. Hundreds of paths wind through the woods, perfect for hiking, picnicking, walking, or jogging; the longest is 30km. At the heart of the park sits the pristine **Convento Santo Desierto,** for which the park is named. There was never a desert here; like all Barefoot Carmelite convents, this one was purposefully placed in a desolate area to facilitate the extreme self-abnegation practiced by its sisters. The woods also probably never held lions; they were home to hundreds of pumas. The convent was originally built between 1606 and 1611. Exactly 100 years later, it was demolished by an earthquake. The re-building was completed in 1723, but between 1780 and 1801, however, the monks abandoned it for another convent in the Nixcongo mountains due to weather conditions. Wander through the immense corridors to catch a glimpse of a bedroom as it was left in 1801. Bring a flashlight or buy a candle (5 pesos) to descend into the basements. It is completely dark underneath the convent; the winding basement passages are not for the claustrophobic.

On Saturdays and Sundays from noon-3pm, the church hosts free (with the entrance fee) **theater,** ranging from passion plays to the more avant-garde work of Federico García Lorca. Shows change weekly. The convent **cafeteria** serves decent food. Another food option is at **Los Leones** restaurant, just outside the convent, which serves delicious *conejo* (rabbit) and *trucha* (trout) specialties (35-55 pesos), homemade *mezcal,* and Mexican traditionals (from 8 pesos).

POPOCATÉPETL AND IXTACCÍHUATL

*From Mexico City's TAPO bus station, several bus lines, including ADO and Cristóbal Colón, go to **Amecameca,** the best jumping-off point for Ixtaccíhuatl. Volcanos has the most frequent service (1½hr., every 30min. 5:30am-10pm, 16 pesos). Taxis in front of Hotel San Carlos on the Amecameca plaza can take you to the La Joya trailhead. Expect to pay at least 300 pesos for a round-trip fare including waiting time while you hike. A one-way trip runs 150 pesos, but no return taxi is guaranteed. If you decide to visit Ixtaccíhuatl via **San Rafael,** catch a pesero from Tlalmanalco (5am-7pm, 5 pesos) and get off in front of La Fábrica, a printing press. From there, another pesero (8 pesos) will take you to the San Rafael trailhead. To return to Mexico City, take a Volcanos bus or any bus labeled Metro San Lázaro (the TAPO station). They stop along the plaza in Amecameca or on the road labeled "Mexico" in Tlalmanalco (every 30min. 6am-8pm). From Cuernavaca, you'll want to take Estrella Roja to **Cuautla** (every 15 min. from 6am-10pm), then walk to the Cristóbal Colón bus station (go right on Ing. Mongoy as you exit the station, walk 1 block and turn left on 5 de Mayo; the station is half a block ahead on your left), and catch a Volcanos bus to **Amecameca** (1hr., every 15min. 5am-7pm, 8 pesos). Buses return to Cuernavaca from Cuautla (1½hr., every 15min. 5am-7pm, 14 pesos).*

MEXICO CITY

Overlooking Morelos and Puebla are two snow-capped volcanoes, Popocatépetl (5452m) and Ixtaccíhuatl (5282m), the second- and third-largest peaks in the country. These mountains are shrouded in Aztec mythology. Legend has it that the warrior Popocatépetl ("Smoking Mountain" in Náhuatl) loved Ixtaccíhuatl ("Sleeping Woman"), the emperor's daughter. Once, when Popocatépetl went off to battle, Ixtaccíhuatl came to believe that he had been killed; she subsequently died of grief. When Popo (as he was known to friends) learned of his lover's death, he built the two great mountains. On the northern one he placed her body (which you can see by looking at Ixtaccíhuatl from afar, with a little imagination), and on the southern one he stood vigil with a torch. Locals pay their respects to the supine, death-pale Ixtaccíhuatl on the mountain's snowy summit. The passage between the two is called *Paso de Cortés* because it is the route the Spanish conqueror took to the valley of Tenochtitlán.

Due to its increasingly volatile status, Popocatépetl has been closed to hikers since 1994; in June 1997, it spat out enough volcanic ash to reach Mexico City. Parts of Ixtaccíhuatl can be explored on easy daytrips, but to reach the peak you'll need to be a seriously seasoned backpacker, or else travel with a tour group. Signs pointing to *Rutas de Evacuación* (escape routes) in all nearby towns are reminders of the omnipresent danger. The Federación Mexicana de Alpinismo, all Mexican officials, and *Let's Go* strongly recommend against making even a daytrip when the **Socorro Alpino** (Alpine Assistance; ☎ 5531 1401) is not nearby. No season is free from rapid weather change; always bring both warm clothes and raingear. By taking all the right precautions, you can have a superb adventure hiking the volcano. The Socorro Alpino is at the **Paraje la Joya trailhead** every weekend to provide guidance. Although Ixtaccíhuatl is most easily reached from San Rafael via Tlalmanalco, a safe hike is well worth the extra pesos it takes to get to La Joya via Amecameca. Arrangements can be made with Socorro Alpino from Mexico City or they can be met at the trailhead on Saturday or Sunday. If you are planning a longer or non-weekend trip, be certain to register with the Socorro Alpino before you go. Should you have an accident or **medical emergency** in the mountains, do your best to reach Danton Valle Negrete, Socorro Alpino's medical director in Mexico City (☎ 5740 6782; beeper 227 7979, code 553 1773).

OTHER DAYTRIPS FROM MEXICO CITY

Cuernavaca: This lovely-colonial-town-turned-chic-upperclass-getaway overflows with expats and language schools. The gaggle of *gringos* and high prices come part and parcel with Cuernavaca's lush greenery, luxurious living, and trendy nightlife. (Morelos; 85km; see p. 335.)

Grutas de Cacahuamilpa: Have you ever wanted to see rock formations shaped like people making out? Of course, we all have. Here, let your imagination run wild through stalagmites and stalactites, some over 85m high. Raucous guides lead you through the underground wonderland. (Guerrero; 130km; see p. 439.)

Ixtapan de la Sal: Despite the nearby Disney-ish waterparks and resorts, Ixtapan couldn't be lovelier or more good-natured if it tried. The Mediterranean-style plaza and church are two of a kind. This is a good place to check out rustic life and take long mid-afternoon *siestas.* (Estado de México; 117km; see p. 330.)

Pachuca: An important silver mining and processing center since the 16th century, Pachuca offers several lovely plazas, extremely friendly inhabitants, and invigorating mountain air. The city exudes a sense of prosperity, and the delightful streets are mostly free of tourists. (Estado de México; 90km; see p. 324.)

Taxco: You've heard about the silver. Have you heard about the cable cars, stunning vistas, and gorgeous church? Taxco is a picturesque pearl of a town way up in the hills. Its pink stone Catedral de Santa Prisca ranks among the loveliest in Mexico. (Guerrero; 180km; see p. 435.)

Tepoztlán: Surrounded by towering cliffs, this cobbled *indígena* village preserves a ancient feel—many still speak Náhuatl here. Bring plenty of spirit (and bottled water and sunscreen) if you plan to scale Tepoztlán's "mother" hill. On Sundays, the small *zócalo* comes alive. (Morelos; 70km; see p. 342.)

Tula: The archaeological site at Tula houses the ruins that were once the capital of the Toltec civilization. Set in a hilly semi-desert terrain, the ruins are famous for the Atlantes, 10m tall stone warrior statues. (Hidalgo; 65km; see p. 327.)

Valle De Bravo: Wealthy *chilangos* go play in the beautiful town of Valle de Bravo, where the lake may be man-made, but the white stucco houses, cobblestone streets, and blossoming bougainvillea are irresistible. Grab a picnic basket and loll around the hills. (Estado de México; 140km; see p. 329.)

Xochicalco: Ceremonial center, fortress, and trading post in one, Xochicalco is the most impressive archaeological site in the state. Among the rolling green hills, only swarms of dragonflies can be heard for miles. Photographers will writhe in ecstasy here. (Morelos; 120km; see p. 340.)

BAJA CALIFORNIA

The peninsula of Baja California, cradled by the warm, tranquil Sea of Cortés on the east and the cold, raging Pacific Ocean on the west, claims one of the most spectacular and diverse landscapes in the world. Sparse expanses of sandy deserts give way to barren mountains jutting into the traditionally azure, cloudless sky at incredible angles. The high-altitude national parks of northern Baja California are home to seemingly out-of-place evergreens and snow during the winter months. And then, of course, there's the bizarrely blue-green water slapping at Baja California's miles of uninhabited shore. This aqua liquid flows past coral reefs, bats around in rocky storybook coves, and laps at the white sandy shores of thousands of miles of paradisiacal beaches lining both coasts. Called "el otro Mexico" (the other Mexico), Baja California is neither here nor there, not at all California, yet nothing like mainland Mexico. Even its history is different—it was permanently settled by the Franciscans and Jesuits in the 1600s. While mainland Mexico has massive Maya and Zapotec temples, Baja has small Jesuit missions. The peninsula's tradition of carefully blending wildness and tranquility, domesticity and simplicity, are emblematized by the Jesuit legacy in sleepy towns like San Ignacio.

Until relatively recently, Baja California was an unknown frontier of sorts; the only way to reach its rugged desert terrain was by plane or boat. With the completion of the Transpeninsular Highway (Rte. 1) in 1973, and the addition of better toll roads and ferry service, Baja California has become a popular vacation spot among Californians, Arizonans, Mexicans, and others. Vacationers range in type from hardy campers setting out to tame the savage deserts of central Baja California to families living in one of Baja California's many RV parks. Large resort hotels and condominium complexes are sprouting like grass to house these human torrents in the south. The heavily Americanized Cabos San Lucas, on the southern tip, now has almost as little integrity and authenticity as Tijuana, the bawdy border wasteland of the **Baja California** state, wedged in the hilly crevices of the peninsula's northern extreme. The honest Mexican city of La Paz, the capital of **Baja California Sur,** is a southern beacon of beauty for resort-weary port-seekers. But it is Baja's southern midsection—from the tranquility of Mulegé to the palm-laden oasis town of San Ignacio to the thousands of undisturbed beaches beneath sheer cliffs—that is most pristine and mysterious. Most of Baja California is still somewhat of an undiscovered country, prime for the hearty budget traveler to explore.

HIGHLIGHTS OF BAJA CALIFORNIA

EXPLORE the secluded and beautiful beaches of **Bahía de La Concepción** (p. 171), 48km of turquoise water, powdery sand, bubbly springs, and abundant marine life.

SLEEP under a million stars in **San Ignacio** (p. 166), a tiny leafy Northern Baja town/oasis with a remarkable **mission** (see p. 194).

HIKE through the amazing **Parque Sierra Nacional San Pedro Mártir** (p. 160), home to mountains, valleys, waterfalls, and Mexico's **National Observatory** (p. 159).

LOSE YOURSELF on the peaceful beaches of **San José del Cabo** (p. 192) by day, and party with reckless abandon in **Cabo San Lucas** (p. 187) by night.

STROLL down the gulf side boardwalk of breezy, beautiful **La Paz** (p. 176), the good-natured capital of Baja Sur, and a favorite Mexican vacation destination.

GETTING AROUND

BY CAR

Driving through Baja California is far from easy. Due to potholes, speeds in excess of 80km/hr. (50 mi./hr.) are a bad idea anywhere in the peninsula; on many roads you will have to go much slower. The livestock on the highways, general lack of guardrails, and uneveness of the roads make night driving impossible. Furthermore, Baja's intense heat pummels cars, and repair service can sometimes be hard to find; it helps if you know some basic mechanics. Still, a car is the only way to get close to the more beautiful and secluded areas of Baja California, and the ride is probably one of the most beautiful in Mexico. Though the proposition might make your mother cringe, driving in Baja is possible if you stay slow, never drive at night, and keep your tank full. If you need roadside assistance, the **Angeles Verdes** (Green Angels) pass along Rte. 1 twice per day. Unleaded gas may be in short supply along this highway, so don't pass a **PEMEX station** without filling up. If you are driving into the peninsula from the US, then consider obtaining a **vehicle permit,** which may be required for driving in parts south of San Felipe on the Sea of Cortés side and Ensenada on the Pacific side. If you will be driving in Baja for more than 72 hours, you only need to get a free permit at the border; to do this, show the vehicle's title and proof of registration. For more information on driving in Mexico see **Getting Around: By Car** p. 31.

BY BUS

If you plan to navigate the peninsula by bus, note that most buses between Ensenada and La Paz are *de paso* (in passing), which means that buses pass through cities, rather than originate and terminate in them. It is therefore impossible to reserve seats in advance. You'll have to leave at inconvenient times, fight to procure a ticket, and then probably stand the whole way. A much better idea is to buy a reserved seat in Tijuana, Ensenada, La Paz, or Los Cabos, and traverse the peninsula in one trip. Getting around by bus, while certainly possible, will test your patience. You will also certainly miss out on out-of-the-way attractions, such as the Mulegé-Loreto beaches (for more info see **Getting Around: By Bus** p. 31). Some swear by hitching—PEMEX stations are thick with rides. *Let's Go* does not recommend hitchhiking; it's unpredictable and potentially hazardous. (For more information on the evils of hitchhiking, see **Getting Around: By Thumb** p. 32.)

BY SEA

Ferry service was instituted in the mid-1960s as a means of supplying Baja California with food and supplies. Passenger vehicles may take up only the ferry space left over by the top-priority commercial vehicles. There are three different ferry routes: **Santa Rosalía to Guaymas** (8hr.), **La Paz to Topolobampo/Los Mochis** (9hr.), and **La Paz to Mazatlán** (17hr.). The La Paz to Topolobampo/Los Mochis route provides direct access to the train from Los Mochis through the **Copper Canyon.** Ferry tickets are generally expensive, even for *turista*-class berths, which are two-person cabins with a sink; bathrooms and showers are down the hall. It's extremely difficult to find tickets for *turista* and *cabina* class, and snagging an *especial* berth is as likely as snow in the Baja California—there are only two such suites on each ferry. This leaves the bottom-of-the-line *salón* ticket, entitling you to a seat in a large room with few communal baths. If, as is likely, you find yourself traveling *salón*-class at night, ditch your seat early on and stake out a spot on the floor or outside on the deck. A small room is available to store your belongings, but once they're secured, there is no way of retrieving them until your arrival. A doctor or nurse is always on board in the (rare) event that someone gets seasick. For those who plan to take their car aboard a ferry, it's a good idea to make reservations a month in advance. For further ferry information, contact a **Sematur** office, listed in the **Practical Information** sections of the cities from which the ferry departs.

BAJA CALIFORNIA

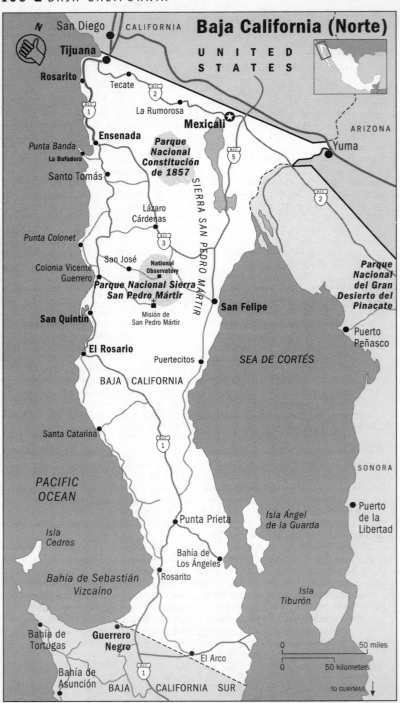

Baja California (Norte)

NORTHERN BAJA CALIFORNIA

TIJUANA   ☎ 6

In the shadow of swollen, sulphur-spewing factories lies the most notorious specimen of the peculiar border subculture: Tijuana (pop. 2 million). By day, swarms of tourists cross the US border to haggle with street vendors, pour gallons of tequila down their throats, and get their picture taken with donkeys painted as zebras. By night, Revolución, the city's wide main drag, becomes a big, bad party with *mariachi* bands and exploding bottle rockets doing little to drown out the thumping dance beats blaring from the packed nightclubs. The city began its upward/downward spiral soon after Santiago Argüello received the title to Rancho Tía Juana in 1829. In the wake of the Mexican-American War, the modest ranch found itself on the new dividing line between American Alta California and Mexican Baja California. Tijuana suddenly became an important frontier town, and the settlement's population began a meteoric rise. The three-ringed, duty-free extravaganza now attracts more than 30 million eager tourists per year, most of them jaunting across the border for a couple of hours to unload wads of cash on everything from *jai alai* gambling to slimy strip shows. In recent years the city has made a conscious effort to clean up its act, nearly successfully eliminating sex shops and prostitution from the center of town. Still, rife with flashy sleaze and border intrigue, it's hard to say whether it's the city's strange charm, its cheap booze, or its sprawling, unapologetic hedonism that attracts tourists to Tijuana like flies.

▟ TRANSPORTATION

GETTING THERE

From San Ysidro: Take the red Mexicoach bus (☎ 685 14 70 or (619) 428 9517 in the US) from its terminal at Border Station Parking next to the Nike factory outlet (every 15min. 9am-9pm, US$1).

From San Diego: Grab a trolly at Kettner and Broadway downtown (25 min., US$20) and ride it all the way to the border. From there you can catch the southbound Mexicoach or walk across the pedestrian footbridge which continues as a walkway over the Río Tijuana and ends at the corner of Calle 1a and Revolución (10min.). Taxis on the Mexican side of the border charge US$5 for the same six blocks.

From Mexicali: If you drive in from Mexicali on Rte. 2, get on to Rte. 2D, the toll road, and follow the *"Aeropuerto"* signs west. The airport road turns into Cuauhtémoc and crosses the river before running into Agua Caliente, and eventually Revolución. Homeward-bound beachgoers on Rte. 1 arrive on 16 de Septiembre, head north until the intersection with Agua Caliente and turn left to reach the *centro*. Those who choose scenic 1D come into town on Calle 2A, which continues east to Revolución.

CROSSING THE BORDER

At the world's largest border crossing, northbound lanes often have backups of more than 150 cars. To minimize the wait, cross during weekday mornings, generally the slowest time. The southbound ride is generally smoother, but weekends can be rough in both directions. If you're crossing into Tijuana for a day or so, it's easier to leave your car in a lot on the US side and join the throngs of people walking across the border. Remember that a **tourist card** (US$20) is needed if you plan to travel farther south than Ensenada or San Felipe. Regardless of which way you are crossing, bring proper ID—ideally a driver's license or passport—and leave your bushels of fruit, truckloads of livestock, stashes of drugs, and extensive armory of weapons behind.

BAJA CALIFORNIA

BAJA CALIFORNIA

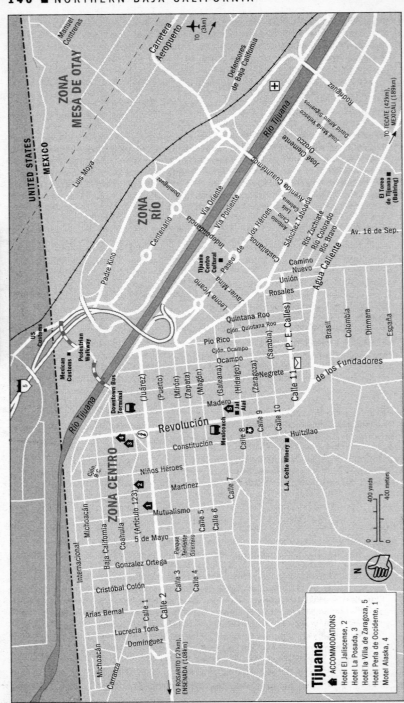

Tijuana

ZONA MESA DE OTAY

UNITED STATES

MEXICO

Manuel Contreras

Carretera Aeropuerto

TO (3km)

Defensores de Baja California

Río Tijuana

José María Velasco

David Alfaro Siqueiros

José Clemente Orozco

Avenida Cuauhtémoc

Rodríguez

TO TECATE (42km), MEXICALI (189km)

El Toreo de Tijuana (Bullring)

Av. 16 de Sep.

Luis Moya

ZONA RÍO

Centenario

Domínguez

Vía Oriente

Vía Poniente

Independencia

Paseo de los Héroes

Castellanos

Antonio Caso

Luis Cabrera

Sánchez Taboada

Río Zuchiate

Río Colorado

Río Bravo

Agua Caliente

Brasil

Colombia

Dinamara

España

Camino Nuevo

Unión

Rosales

Padre Kino

Tijuana Centro Cultural

Leona Vicario

Javier Mina

Quintana Roo

Cjón. Quintana Roo

de los Fundadores

US Customs

Mexican Customs

Pedestrian Walkway

5

Río Tijuana

Downtown Bus Terminal

(Juárez)

(Puerto)

(Mirón)

(Zapata)

(Magón)

(Galeana)

(Hidalgo)

(Zaragoza)

(Sarabia)

(P. E. Calles)

Pío Rico

Cjón. Ocampo

Ocampo

Negrete

Calle 11

Madero

Jai Alai

Mexicacli

Revolución

Constitución

Calle 8

Calle 9

Calle 10

Huitzilao

ZONA CENTRO

Niños Héroes

Martínez

Mutualismo

(Artículo 123)

5 de Mayo

Calle 5

Calle 6

Calle 7

L.A. Cetto Winery

Michoacán

Baja California

Coahuila

Cjón. B.C.

Parque Teniente Guerrero

Gonzalez Ortega

Cristóbal Colón

Arias Bernal

Calle 1

Calle 2

Calle 3

Calle 4

Internacional

Lucrecia Toris

Domínguez

Michoacán

Carranza

TO ROSARITO (27km), ENSENADA (108km)

400 yards

400 meters

N

Tijuana

▲ ACCOMMODATIONS

Hotel El Jaliscense, 2

Hotel La Posada, 3

Hotel la Villa de Zaragoza, 5

Hotel Perla de Occidente, 1

Motel Alaska, 4

By bus: Tijuana has two bus stations. To get to the center of town from the **Central Camionera** (☎621 29 82), the more remote bus station, avoid the cab drivers' high rates (up to 80 pesos to downtown) by exiting the terminal, turning left, walking to the end of the building, and hopping on a local bus marked "Centro" (30min., every 5min. 5am-10pm; 4 pesos), which will let you off on Calle 3 and Constitución, one block west of Revolución. The **downtown station** is more conveniently located, at Calle 1A at Madero, one block east of Revolución.

GETTING AROUND

Traditional **yellow cabs** are used almost exclusively by tourists and charge ridiculous rates; make sure to set a price before getting in. Most **communal cabs** originate on Madero south of Calle 2A and act as small buses, carrying a motley crew of people to points along the specific route painted above the rear tire on the driver's side. Aside from the Central Camionera, colorful station wagons can take you to **Parque Morelos** (5 pesos; orange and grey), **Rosarito** (9 pesos, yellow and white), or **El Toreo** (5 pesos) among other destinations. It's a good idea to take cabs at night in the *centro* and to avoid the area downhill from Calle 1a.

GETTING AWAY

FROM THE CENTRAL CAMIONERA. To get back to the Central Camionera, board a blue-and-white bus labeled "Central Camionera" on Calle 2A between Revolución and Constitución (4 pesos) or jump in a brown-and-white communal cab on Madero between Calles 2 and 3 (5 pesos). Autotransportes de Baja California (☎621 26 68) runs to: **Ensenada** (1½hr., every hr. 6am-9pm; 78 pesos); **La Paz** (24hr., 4 per day 8am-9pm, 725 pesos); **Loreto** (18hr., 4 per day 8am-9pm, 500 pesos); **Mexicali** (3hr., every hr. 6am-9pm, 117 pesos); **San Felipe** (5hr., 3 per day 8:30am-3:30pm, 213 pesos); and **Santa Rosalía** (15hr., 6 per day 8am-9pm, 455 pesos).

FROM THE DOWNTOWN STATION. Elite (☎621 29 49) buses stop at the downtown bus station 30 min. before embarking from the Central Camionera for: **Guadalajara** (36hr., every 30min., 1137 pesos); and **Hermosillo** (12hr., every 30min., 489 pesos). Greyhound (☎688 19 79) also picks up passengers downtown before leaving the *Central* for **Los Angeles** (3hr., every hr. 5am-midnight, US$24), and connecting to other North American cities. **Suburbaja** (☎688 00 82) in the downtown terminal sends buses (every 20min. 5am-9pm) to the neighboring cities of **Rosarito** (9 pesos) and **Tecate** (29 pesos). Mexicoach buses depart from their station on Revolución for **Rosarito** (30min., 5 per day 9am-7pm, US$3) and **San Ysidro**.

▰▱ ORIENTATION AND PRACTICAL INFORMATION

Immediately south of the border, the area surrounding Revolución is known as the **Zona Centro**. East-west *calles*, which are both named and numbered, cross Revolución; perpendicular to the *calles*, *avenidas* run north-south.

TOURIST, FINANCIAL, AND LOCAL SERVICES

Tourist Office: Revolución 711 (☎688 05 55), at Calle 1. Friendly English-speaking staff doles out maps and advice. Open M-Sa 8am-5pm, Su 10am-5pm.

Customs Office: (☎683 13 90) at the border on the Mexican side, after crossing the San Ysidro bridge. Open 24hr.

Consulates: Canada, German Gedovius 10411-101 (☎684 04 61 or 01 800 706 2900 for after hours emergency assistance), in the Zona Río. Open M-F 9am-1pm. **UK,** Salinas 1500 (☎681 73 23 or 686 53 20 for after hours emergency assistance), in Col. Aviación, La Mesa. Open M-F 9am-3pm. **US,** Tapachula Sur 96 (☎681 74 00), in Col. Hipódromo, adjacent to the racetrack southeast of town. In an emergency, call the San Diego office (☎(619) 692 2154) and leave a message and phone number; an officer will respond. Open M-F 8am-4:30pm.

BAJA CALIFORNIA

Currency Exchange: Banks along Constitución exchange money at the same rates. **Banamex** (☎688 00 21), Constitución at Calle 4, usually has a shorter line (open M-F 9am-5pm) than the central/**Bital,** (☎685 00 06), Revolución at Calle 2. Both banks have 24hr. **ATMs.** *Casas de cambio* offer better rates but may charge commission and refuse to exchange traveler's checks.

Supermarket: Calimax (☎688 08 94), Calle 2 at Constitución. Open 24hr.

Car Rental: Bargain Auto Rentals, 3860 Rosecrans St. (☎(619)299-0009), in San Diego, rents to those ages 18-25 and is cheap option if you aren't driving any farther than Ensenada. Before driving into Mexico from the US, get **car insurance** for US$5 per day in San Ysidro. Many drive-through insurance companies have offices just before the border at Sycamore and Primero. **Budget,** Paseo de los Héroes 77 (☎634 33 03; open M-F 8am-7pm, Sa-Su 8am-4pm) and **Hertz,** 16 de Septiembre 213-B (☎686 12 22; open M-F 8am-6:30pm, Sa 8am-4pm), in the Hotel Palacio Azteca, offer similar rates and a wide variety of vehicles.

EMERGENCY AND COMMUNICATIONS

Emergency: ☎060.

Police: (☎638 51 68), Constitución at Calle 8. Special tourist help (☎688 05 55).

Red Cross: (☎621 77 87, emergency 066) Gamboa at Silvestre, across from the Price Club.

Pharmacy: farmacia Vida (☎685 14 61), Calle 3 at Revolución. Open 24hr.

Hospital: Centenario 10851 (☎684 02 37 or 684 09 22), in the *Zona Río.*

Fax: Telecomm (☎684 79 02; fax 684 77 50), to the right of the post office, in the same building. Open M-F 7am-7:30pm, Sa-Su 8am-1pm.

Post Office: (☎684 79 50) on Negrete at Calle 11. Open M-F 8am-5pm.

Postal Code: 22000.

▌ ACCOMMODATIONS

There's no shortage of budget hotels in Tijuana, especially on Calle 1, between Revolución and Mutualismo. Rooms tend to be roachy—ask to see them before paying. The area teems with people during the day, but morphs into something of a red-light district at night, especially between Revolución and Constitución. To return to your hotel, head down Calles 2 or 3, or take a taxi (US$2) from anywhere on Revolución. Exercise caution when walking in this area at night.

Hotel Perla de Occidente, Mutualismo 758 (☎685 13 58), between Calles 1 and 2, 4 blocks from the bedlam of Revolución. Multicolored translucent roofing over the central hallway casts rays of light on the tiled floor. A picture of a chimp smoking a joint hangs two doors down from a mosaic of Jesús. Large, soft beds, roomy bathrooms, and fans on request. Singles 120 pesos; doubles 150 pesos.

Hotel El Jaliscense, Calle 1 7925 (☎685 34 91), between Niños Héroes and Martínez. Small rooms have resilient beds, baths, fans, and phones. If you want to sleep soundly, ask for a room that doesn't face Calle 1. Singles 140 pesos; doubles 160 pesos.

Motel Alaska, Revolución 1950 (☎685 36 81), at Calle 1, in the middle of the madness. Spartan and clean rooms with comfy beds, tiny showers, and not much else—at least you get free parking. Singles 190 pesos; doubles 220 pesos.

Hotel La Posada, Calle 1 8190 (☎685 41 54), at Revolución. Select your room carefully— good ones have fans, comfortable beds, telephones, and bathrooms your mother would approve of. Singles 70 pesos, with bath 130 pesos; doubles with bath 180 pesos.

Hotel La Villa de Zaragoza, Madero 1120 (☎685 18 32), between Calles 7a and 8a. Affordable luxury for those too squemish to handle Tijuana's budget offerings. Spacious rooms come with TVs and lots of good-smelling towels. Laundry, room service, and 24hr. security keep you and your car very safe. Singles and doubles 360 pesos.

FOOD

Bright neon signs and menu-waving waiters welcome tourists—and their dollars—into the over-priced restaurants lining **Revolución.** Claiming to be *"internacional,"* most of these places serve Mexican cuisine with the occasional *hamburgesa;* the ritzier ones will charge up to US$7 for a plate of spaghetti. Better food and a mellower environment can be found on **Constitución,** one block west of the mayhem. Taco stands all over the *centro* hand over several tacos or a *torta* for 10 pesos.

El Pipirín Antojitos, Constitución 878 (☎688 16 02), between Calles 2 and 3. Relax under orange brick arches as you enjoy great food with friendly service. Chicken burritos with rice and beans 28 pesos. Open daily 8:30am-9pm.

Los Panchos Taco Shop (☎685 72 77), Revolución at Calle 3. By day, the orange vinyl booths are packed with locals munching on fresh tortillas. By night, raucous tourists refuel before heading into a neighboring club. Steak tacos US$1. Bean and cheese burritos US$2. Open Su-Th 8am-midnight, F-Sa 8am-2am; in summer Su-Th 8am-midnight, F-Sa 8am-4am.

Hotel Nelson Restaurant (☎685 77 50), Revolución at Calle 1. Good food in a coffee-shop atmosphere. *Gringo* fare (eggs, hotcake, and bacon 26 pesos) or local favorites—try the *huevos con nopales* (eggs with cacti; 25 pesos). Open daily 7am-11pm.

Lonchería Tico-Tico, Madero 688 (☎685 06 16), on the corner of Calle 1. Chatty cooks serve tasty Mexican favorites with generous helpings of friendly advice. Banana milkshake 15 pesos; 4 tacos 25 pesos; liver and onions 23 pesos. Open daily 6am-5pm.

SIGHTS

Photo-ops abound on Revolución, where zebra-striped donkeys and gaudily-costumed cowboys vie for your attention. The multi-tiered dance clubs and curio shops that share the street are often the only sights that Tijuana tourists care to see. Just a few blocks away, however, two of the city's most beautiful and serene attractions provide a welcome respite.

PARQUE TENIENTE GUERRERO. Dedicated in 1924 to the memory of Vicente Guerrero, the beautiful and shady park on Calle 3A and 5 de Mayo is a favorite gathering place for local families and an oasis from the noisy circus of Revolución.

CATEDRAL DE NUESTRA SEÑORA DE GUADALUPE. Originally built in 1902 as a modest adobe chapel, modern expansions and reinforcement have resulted in a huge stone cathedral checkered in adobe orange and grey and crowned with a giant image of the Virgin of Guadalupe. The cathedral's daily mass attracts a diverse congregation of devout locals and curious passersby. Check out the massive, magnificent chandelier. *(At the busy intersection of Calle 2A and Niños Héroes.)*

MUSEO DE CERCA. Home to a motley crew of 81 wax figures, including such strange bedfellows as Eddie Murphy, Gandhi, Gorbachev, and Tía Juana herself. An assortment of American stars share the limelight with Mexican Revolutionary heroes. *(Calle 1A and Madero. ☎688 24 78. Open daily 10am-7pm. 12 pesos.)*

LA CETTO WINERY. Established in 1926 by Italian immigrants, the family-run winery maintains its vineyards in the Valle de Guadalupe, northeast of Ensenada. Visitors are welcome to tour the facilities and sample the products. Avoid removing anything from the storeroom—the staff still remembers the US woman who pulled out the wrong bottle and caused a wine avalanche that destroyed more than 30 cases. *(Cañon Johnson 2108. Follow Constitución south to Calle 10a and turn right. ☎685 30 31. Tours M-F every 30min. 10am-5pm. US$2 including tasting.)*

PARQUE MORELOS. An amazing assortment of exotic birds and picnic tables welcome families to this sprawling state-run park south of the *centro.* Attractions include rides, a miniature golf course, botanical gardens, and an open-air theater.

BAJA CALIFORNIA

(Blvd. de los Insurgentes 26000. Take a green and white local bus (5 pesos) from the corner of Calle 5a and Constitución or any of the orange and grey communal cabs (5 pesos) on Madero south of Calle 2a. ☎625 24 70. Open Tu-Su 9am-5pm. 5 pesos, children 2 pesos.)

🎵 💟 ENTERTAINMENT AND NIGHTLIFE

In the 1920s, Prohibition drove US citizens south of the border to revel in the forbidden nectars of cacti, grapes, and hops. Ever since, Tijuana has embraced its reputation for debauchery, catering to those who come in search of cheap inebriation and good times. Stroll down Revolución after dusk, you'll be bombarded with thumping music, neon lights, and abrasive club promoters hawking "two-for-one" margaritas at the not-exactly-low price of US$5. Inside the throbbing clubs, DJs spin confusing mixes of American pop, reggae, rap, and Latin hits, while beefy security guards frisk suspicious characters and keep out eager US teens who have "forgotten" their IDs. Those who prefer laid-back nights of bar-chat have come to the wrong place; nowhere on Revolución do they know the meaning of quiet.

Eclipse, Revolución at Calle 6a. Brace yourself for this 3-tiered party palace. Miami-esque decor complete with platforms attracts masses of partners eager to toss back some of the cheapest booze in town. Two beers and a shot of tequila US$3. Open M-W 11am-9:30pm, Th-Su 9am-6am.

People's (☎685 45 72), Revolución and Calle 2A. Fluorescent constellations and silver-painted sports equipment decorate the open-air terrace, where revelers guzzle 10 beers for US$18. Open M-W 10am-2am, Th-Su 10am-5am.

Iguanas-Ranas (☎685 14 22), Revolución at Calle 3. Pound beers (US$2.50) in a yellow school bus dangling above Revolución. Clowns welcome you into a world of balloons, *sombreros,* and margarita-drinking reptiles. Lively on weeknights; but packed on weekends with US and Mexican 20-somethings. Open M-Th 10am-2am, F-Su 10am-5am.

Tilly's 5th Avenue (☎685 90 15), at Revolución and Calle 5. Disco balls and flashing lights bounce off mirrored walls in this upscale restaurant/bar, where the dance-happy staff mingles with their customers. Half-price beer (US$1) on W night packs an amazing number onto the tiny dance floor. Open M-Th 10:30am-2am, F-Sa 10:30am-5am.

Caves (☎688 06 09), Revolución and Calle 5. Dinosaurs and prehistoric beasts perch on the rock facade that leads to the dark, airy bar and disco with decorated with stalactites and black lights. Drink 2 beers for US$3.50 with loads of California college students. Open daily 11am-2am.

GAY AND LESBIAN NIGHTLIFE
Clubs catering to gays and lesbians cluster in the southern part of the *centro* around Calle 6A and 7A or down the hill to the north of Calle 1A.

Mike's Disco (☎685 35 34), Revolución south of Calle 6A. A wild bunch, mostly men, gets down on the dance floor, cheering the drag queens who perform every weekend. Straight by day, but gay Th-Tu 10pm-5am.

El Ranchero Bar (☎685 28 00), in front of the fountain in Plaza Santa Cecilia. Rainbow-colored parrots and palm trees decorate the long bar where a mellow mixed crowd drinks 10-peso beers. Open M-W 10am-2am, Th-Su 10am-3am.

Los Equipales, Calle 7A between Revolución and Madero. A transvestite cabaret entertains the mixed clientele in this friendly *discoteca.* Open daily 5pm-2am.

CULTURAL EVENTS
The monumental **Tijuana Centro Cultural,** on Paseo de los Héroes at Mina, houses the **Museo de las Californias,** a series of exhibits exploring the history and culture of Baja California. (☎687 96 50. Open daily 10am-8pm. 20 pesos, children 12 pesos). The Centro Cultural also hosts a variety of other offerings, including a central gallery of temporary art exhibits. The enormous sphere in the plaza contains the **Cine Planetano,** a giant 180° screen which shows OmniMax films dubbed in Spanish.

THE WORLD'S FASTEST GAME, THE WORLD'S STRANGEST NAME

If you think the name *jai alai* (pronounced HIE-lie) doesn't sound like Spanish, you're right. The game and the name are imported from the Basque, a race of people living in the Pyrenees mountains between Spain and France, linguistically distinct and culturally unrelated to either the Spanish or French. In *jai alai*, two to four players take to the three-sided court at once, using slender, otherworldly *cestas* (arm-baskets) to catch and throw an extremely hard ball of rubber and nylon encased in goatskin. The handmade balls fly at speeds up to 300km/hr., earning *jai alai* the Guiness World Record for "World's Fastest Game." The rules are akin to handball or squash, with players rotating on and off the court king-of-the-hill style. The game is so fast that it's quite dangerous—30 professional players were killed between 1900 and 1960, when helmets were introduced. Today, *jai alai* is a popular betting sport not only in Mexico, but many parts of the world, including Chile, the Philippines, and the US state of Florida.

(Open daily 2-9pm. 45 pesos, children 23 pesos.) Another theater shows cycles of foreign films and children's movies. (Sa-Su 10am-8pm. 25 pesos, children's films free.) The **Sala de Ciencia** presents interactive exhibits about health and technology. Performances by visiting dance troupes, musicians, and theater groups, take place in the **Jardín Caracol.** Ask at the information booth in the lobby for details on upcoming shows, and pick up a monthly calendar of events.

Several movie theaters screen first-run films. **Multicinemas Río,** in the Plaza del Río shopping mall across from the Centro Cultural, is closest to the *centro.* (☎684 04 01. Open daily 2pm-midnight, 38 pesos.) Blue and white buses (5 pesos) on Calle 2A at Constitución can take you to the Centro Cultural and the cinema.

SPORTS

Completed in 1947 after 21 years of complications and delays, the grandiose baroque **Frontón Palacio,** on Revolución at Calle 7A hosts daily competitions of **jai alai.** (☎685 16 12. Games take place M-Sa at 8pm. Free.) If you're in town on the right Sunday, you can watch the graceful and savage battle of man versus bull in one of Tijuana's two bullrings. **El Toreo de Tijuana,** southeast of town just off of Agua Caliente, hosts the first round of fights (alternate Su, May-July). To get to El Toreo, catch a bus on Calle 2A west of Revolución. The seaside **Plaza Monumental** hosts the second round (Aug.-Oct.). Mexicoach sends buses (US$4 round-trip) to the Plaza Monumental on fight days. Alternatively, take the blue and white local buses (5 pesos) on Calle 3A at Constitución all the way down Calle 2A. Tickets to both rings go on sale at the gate the Wednesday before a fight (☎685 15 10 or 86 12 19) or at the Mexicoach office (☎685 14 70) on Revolución between Calles 6A and 7A (tickets 95-400 pesos).

SHOPPING

Vendors on Revolución offer "almost free" crafts and curios from all over Mexico. Bargaining is a must, as quoted prices can be more than twice the bottom line. For a good selection of higher-quality *artesanía,* visit the **Bazar de México** on Revolución at Calle 7A. The **Mercado de Artesanía,** on Calle 1A right under the pedestrian footbridge, offers a large assortment of handicrafts, as do the vendors at **Plaza Santa Cecilia** behind the tourist office.

ROSARITO   ☎ 6

Once a little-known playground of the rich and famous, the beach haven of Rosarito (pop. 120,000) has expanded at breakneck speed to accommodate the masses of sun-seekers who have recently discovered its hotels, restaurants, shops, and beaches. Named for the landmark Rosarito Beach Hotel which has hosted celebrities ranging from Latin American presidents to Hollywood stars, Rosarito only

BAJA CALIFORNIA

gained its municipal status in 1995. One of the new municipality's first (and most lucrative) projects was the filming of the highest-grossing film of all time, *Titanic*, in 1996. Today, dollars reign supreme in Rosarito, and on weekends finding a place for your towel amidst the horses and RVs can be quite a struggle.

▐ TRANSPORTATION. To get to Rosarito from **Tijuana,** grab a yellow and white *taxi de ruta* (30min., 9 pesos) from Madero, between Calles 5A and 6A. To return to Tijuana, flag down a *taxi de ruta* along Juárez or at its starting point in front of the Rosarito Beach hotel. To go to **Ensenada,** take a blue-and-white striped "Primo Tapia" taxi from Festival Plaza, north of the Rosarito Beach Hotel, to the toll booth on Rte. 1 (4 pesos). From there, take a bus to Ensenada (every 30min. 6:30am-9:30pm, 30 pesos).

▰▐ ORIENTATION AND PRACTICAL INFORMATION. Rosarito lies 27km to the south of Tijuana. **Rte. 1** runs straight through Rosarito, becoming the city's main drag, **Juárez,** before continuing south. Coming from the toll road, the first Rosarito exit takes you to the north end of Juárez, which, with its non-sequential street numbers, can be befuddling. Virtually all of the businesses in town are on Juárez; most of what is listed below is between the huge and very fluorescent Hotel Festival Plaza and the pink Ortega's Restaurant in Oceana Plaza.

The **tourist office,** toward the north end of Juárez in the Plaza Villa Floresta, offers tons of brochures and a decent map. Some English spoken. (☎612 02 00. Open M-F 8am-5pm, Sa-Su 10am-3pm.) **Banamex,** on Juárez at Ortiz, exchanges currency and checks and has a 24hr. **ATM.** (☎612 15 56. Open M-F 8:30am-4:30pm.) On weekends, go to one of the *casa de cambios* on Juárez, which charge commission. **Supermarket: Calimax,** at Cárdenas and Juárez, just before Quinta del Mar heading south on Juárez. (☎612 15 69. Open 24hr.) **Lavamática Moderna,** on Juárez at Acacias. (Wash and dry 10 pesos. Open M-Sa 8am-8pm, Su 8am-6pm.) **Emergency:** ☎060. **Police:** (☎612 11 10) at Juárez and Acacias. **Red Cross:** (☎132) on Juárez at Ortíz, around the corner from the police. **Farmacia Roma** (☎612 35 00; open 24hr.), **IMSS** (☎612 10 21), and the **post office** (☎612 13 55; open M-F 8am-3pm) are all on Juárez, near Acacias. **Postal code:** 22710.

▐▗ ACCOMMODATIONS AND FOOD. Budget hotels in Rosarito are either inconvenient or cramped, with the exception of the outstanding **Hotel Palmas Quintero,** on Cárdenas near the Hotel Quinta del Mar, three blocks inland from north Juárez. The hotel has a helpful staff and dog, giant rooms with double beds, and clean, private baths. Cool down in the patio under palm trees. (☎612 23 47. Singles US$20; doubles US$40.) **Rosarito Beach Rental Cabins,** on Cárdenas two blocks toward the water, are the cheapest housing in Rosarito. You get what you pay for—and you don't pay much; cabins have bunk beds, toilets, and sinks. The Disney-castle spires make them hard to miss. (☎612 09 76. Key deposit US$5. Erratic reception 8am-2pm and 4-7pm. Singles US$5, with shower US$10; doubles US$8, with shower US$15.)

Serving more than a million lobsters a year, Rosarito's restaurants cater to the financially secure tourist. Loads of smaller, family-owned restaurants, however, also line Juárez and serve tasty pork and fish tacos at negotiable prices. A scrumptious, not-too-pricey seafood awaits at **Vince's Restaurant,** on Juárez between Acacias and Robie, a block past the police station. Enjoy soup, salad, rice, potatoes, tortillas, and an entree. *Filete especial* 60 pesos, calamari 44 pesos, octopus any style 55 pesos. (☎612 12 53. Open daily 8am-10pm.) **La Flor de Michoacán,** Juárez 306, serves tacos filled with choice of meat (7 pesos). Bigger appetites should try the house specialty, *michoacán carnitas* (braised pork, 190 pesos per kg) served with beans, rice, guacamole, tortillas, and fresh salsa. (☎613 02 78. Open daily 9am-10pm.) **Ortega's Restaurant at the Oceana Plaza,** Juárez 200, provides filling morning grub in a gaudy pink building where appetites are often pricked by the US$2 cactus omelette. (☎612 27 91. Open Su-Th 8am-10pm, F-Sa 8am-11pm.)

SEEKING PETIT, DANGEROUS SCORPIO "Scorpions?! But this isn't the jungle," you gasp. Tough break. These nasty little pests (known in Spanish as *alacranes*) frequent Baja, especially around Mulegé and the mid-peninsula. Unless you are allergic to them, you won't encounter a slow, painful death—these aren't the fatal black scorpions found in Asia and Africa. These are beige, desert-and-beach-camouflaged scorpions. The smaller (and lighter-colored) the scorpion, the bigger the bite. The critters like dark, warm, damp places, so shake your shoes and clothing before you put them on. Most scorpion-bite victims experience intense pain for a day or two. Ice packs help alleviate the pain, although locals swear that garlic is the best relief. If you wake up in the middle of the night and a scorpion is crawling up your chest, don't try to flatten or squash it; it will just get angry and sting your hand. Because of their hard protective armor, scorpions are hard to crush. The best thing to do is to give it a hard flick from the side and watch it fly far, far away.

🕹️ 📷 **SIGHTS AND ENTERTAINMENT.** Rosarito draws tourists with fancy resorts, beautiful shores, and rollicking nightlife. Stretching along the coast two blocks west of Juárez, **Rosarito Beach** has soft sand and a gently rolling surf. The **Museo de Historia Wa Kuatay,** on Juárez next to the Rosarito Beach Hotel, showcases the folk art and history of the area. (☎613 06 87. Open W-Su 9am-6pm.) **Fox Studios Baja,** 2km south of Rosarito on the free road, offers a short film and tour of sets and props from the film *Titanic.* (US$5. ☎614 01 10. Open Sa-Su 10am-6pm). Once the sun goes down, throngs cruise Juárez looking for booze and action. To join, follow the striped sidewalk outside Festival Plaza on south Juárez to **ChaChaCha's.** (Beers US$2.75, mixed drinks US$3.75. Open daily 10am-midnight.)

MEXICALI ☎ 6

Capital of Baja California, the sprawling industrial metropolis of Mexicali (pop. 1.2 million) presents a stark contrast to the endless stretches of barren desert surrounding the city. Mexicali straddles both the US and the Mexican mainland in a colorful chaotic maze of liquor stores, auto shops, and Chinese restaurants. Huge industrial plants skirt the southern edges while a constant stream of cars inches across the northern border. Founded in 1903, Mexicali's first citizens came to work as cotton pickers and laborers for the Colorado River Land Company, and many, including thousands of Chinese immigrants, stayed on, creating a unique Chino-Mexican culture that is evident in the architecture, cuisine, and even the dialect of Mexicali. Heavy pollution, dirty streets, and overwhelming crowds deter most tourists, but Mexicali is not all industrial wasteland. Stunning cathedrals, towering monuments, cultural centers, professional sports facilities, and even a forest within the city boundary offer a wide array of options for dallying visitors.

📑 TRANSPORTATION

To get to the **Central de Autobuses** (☎557 24 51) take any bus headed south on Mateos (every 10min., 4 pesos) to the intersection of Mateos and Independencia, two blocks south of the big Plaza de Toros on your right. The station is one block further west on Independencia. To get to the **border** from the bus station, take the local bus marked "Centro," which runs up and down Mateos (every 10min. 5am-11pm, 4 pesos) from outside the bus terminal, just across the footbridge. Ride past the Vicente Guerrero monument and the enormous new mall and get off; the border crossing will be five blocks to the northwest. All buses leaving Mexicali are *de paso,* and prices listed reflect first-class fares. Autotransportes de Baja California (☎557 24 15) goes to: **Ensenada** (14hr., 6 per day, 173 pesos); **Puerto Peñasco** (5hr., 6 per day, 165 pesos); **San Felipe** (2hr., 6 per day, 110 pesos); and **Tijuana** (3hr., every hr., 117 pesos). Elite (☎556 01 10) covers the same routes for slightly higher prices

BAJA CALIFORNIA

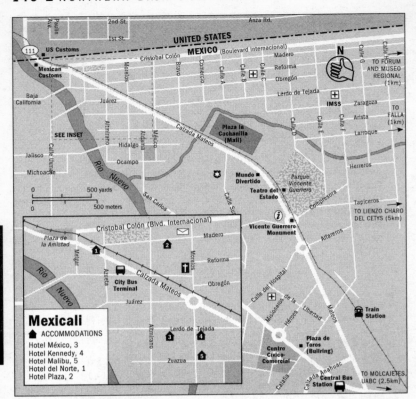

Mexicali

▲ ACCOMMODATIONS
Hotel México, 3
Hotel Kennedy, 4
Hotel Malibu, 5
Hotel del Norte, 1
Hotel Plaza, 2

and goes to: **Chihuahua** (17hr., 10:30am and 2:30pm, 713 pesos); **Ciudad Juárez** (15hr., 4 per day, 588 pesos); and **Nogales** (9hr., 11am, 340 pesos). Golden State (☎553 61 69) can take you to **Los Angeles, CA** (4½hr., 5 per day, US$30) via Coachella, Colton, and Onteria; and **Phoenix, AZ** (6hr., 1 per day, US$40) via Yuma and Tucson. Transportes Nortes de Sonora (☎557 24 10) motors east to **Guaymas** (11hr., every hr., 378 pesos); **Hermosillo** (9hr., every hr., 315 pesos), and **Los Mochis** (17hr., every hr., 560 pesos).

➕🔢 ORIENTATION AND PRACTICAL INFORMATION

Mexicali straddles the US border 189km inland from Tijuana, just south of Calexico and the Imperial Valley. Plagued with zig-zagging, haphazardly numbered streets, Mexicali can be incredibly difficult to navigate. If you drive across the border you'll end up on Mateos, the main boulevard in the *centro*, which heads southeast through **La Chinesca** (Chinatown), past the enormous mall to the civic center, where government and big business coexist with the bulls of the Plaza de Toros. From there continue past the *Central de Autobuses* and the ritzy clubs and restaurants of the **Zona Hotelera** before leaving town, where the road becomes México 2. To add to your confusion, both north-south *calles* and east-west *avenidas* intersect Mateos.

Tourist Office: Comité de Turismo y Convenciones (☎557 23 76; fax 52 58 77), a adobe-colored building on Mateos facing the Vicente Guerrero Monument and park, 3km south of the border. Loads of brochures, huge maps, and knowledgeable English-speaking staff. Open M-F 8am-5pm. For **tourist cards,** visit the Mexican customs office in the immigration office at the border.

Currency Exchange: *Casas de cambio* line Madero, and banks occupy every corner in *La Chinesca.* **Banamex** changes currency and has a 24hr. **ATM.** Open M-F 9am-5pm. As does **Bancomer** (☎553 46 10), closer to the border on Madero at Azueta. Open M-F 8:30am-4pm.

Car Rental: Budget (☎556 08 88 ext. 824), Mateos and Los Héroes in the Holiday Inn Crowne Plaza. Open M-F 8am-6pm, Sa-Su 8am-3pm. **Hertz,** Juárez 1223 (☎568 19 73), opposite the Hotel Araiza Inn. Open M-F 8am-6pm, Sa-Su 8am-3pm. **Optima** (☎568 29 19 or 566 55 91), Argentina and Sierra. 24hr. service.

Luggage Storage: In the **convenience store** in the bus station, to the right after you enter the bus station. 5 pesos per hr. Open 24hr.

Laundromat: Lavamática Josue, Obregón and Morelos. 20 pesos. Open M-Sa 9am-8pm.

Emergency: ☎060.

Police: (☎558 17 00) at Calle Sur and Mateos. English spoken. Open 24hr.

Red Cross: Cárdenas 1492 (☎066), east of Juárez. Open 24hr.

Pharmacy: Farmacia Patty's, México 305 (☎554 14 06), south of Obregón. Open 24hr.

Hospital: IMSS (☎551 51 50), Lerdo at Calle G. English spoken. Otherwise, try the **Hospital General** (☎556 11 23) on Calle del Hospital at Libertad.

Fax: Telecomm (☎552 20 02) next to the post office. Open M-F 8am-6:30pm, Sa 8am-3pm.

Internet Access: Café Internet Mexicali (☎554 12 49), Reforma at Calle D. 25 pesos per 30min., 40 pesos per hr. Open daily 8am-midnight.

Post Office: Madero 491 (☎552 25 08), at Morelos. Open M-F 8:30am-6:30pm, Sa 9am-1pm. **Postal Code:** 21100.

ACCOMMODATIONS

Budget hotels crowd the bar strip on Altamirano between Reforma and Lerdo and line Morelos south of Mateos. Hotels on Madero close to Mateos dig deeper into your wallet but tend to be cleaner and safer for women traveling alone.

Hotel Kennedy, Morelos 415 (☎554 90 62), between Lerdo and Zuazua. Color TVs, A/C, and phones grace the spacious and sparkling rooms. Helpful management and huge baths make it even better. Singles and doubles 200 pesos, with carpeting 220 pesos.

Hotel México, Lerdo 476 (☎554 06 69), at Morelos. Clean, pink rooms with color TV and super-cold A/C overlook a central patio. The office doubles as a grocery store. Free gated parking. Singles 230 pesos; doubles 250 pesos.

Hotel Plaza, Madero 366 (☎552 97 57), between Altamirano and Morelos, provides peace of mind, carpeted floors, and soft cushy beds plus A/C, TVs, phones, and spacious baths a little farther away from all the bustle. Singles and doubles 320 pesos.

Hotel del Norte (☎554 00 24), on Madero at Melgar, faces the pedestrian border crossing and a plethora of *casas de cambio.* Compared to other *frontera* hotels, this bright pink Art Deco building with cheerful carpeted rooms, huge TVs, and attentive staff seems like paradise—for double the price, that is. Singles 360 pesos.

Hotel Málibu, (☎552 80 88), on Morelos at Zuazua. The cheapest acceptable place in town, the Malibu offers A/C, bath, and saggy beds in small (and sometimes windowless) rooms. The clientele, especially those renting *por hora* (by the hour), and tiny cockroaches can be sketchy. Singles 110 pesos; doubles 160 pesos; each additional person 60 pesos.

FOOD

The only city in Mexico where it's easier to find an egg roll than a taco, Mexicali has nearly 200 Chinese restaurants, most of them highly concentrated in the border area known as *La Chinesca.* Restaurants offering lunchtime specialties and veggie combinations line Juárez and Lerdo south of Mateos. For even cheaper fare head to the food court in Plaza la Cachanilla, where huge combination plates of 3-5 entrees cost less than 25 pesos. If soy sauce isn't your thing, you can chow down on hearty *tortas de carne asada* (15 pesos) at any of the sandwich stands on Madero and Reforma west of Mateos.

Restaurant Hollis (☎552 66 96), Morelos and Mateos near Juárez. Tasty dinners from the huge menu of Chinese, Mexican, and American food are served by the owner's friendly young son. Chinese *comida corrida* 37 pesos, whopping sandwiches 20 pesos, filling Mexican breakfast 18 pesos. Open daily 9am-10pm.

Restaurant No. 8, Juárez 150 (☎555 54 35) and Mateos. A favorite among the bar-hopping set, No. 8 stays open all night long, filling growling tummies with massive combinations of soup, egg rolls, and entrees (40 pesos). Open 24hr.

Petunia 2 (☎552 69 51), Madero between Altamirano and Morelos, serves tasty (Mexican!) *comida corrida* (34 pesos) at a friendly, cheerful outdoor counter with bar seating and a private parking lot. Open daily 7am-9pm.

Restaurant Buendía, Altamirano 263 (☎552 69 25). Despite sharing a name with the illustrious family of García Márquez's epic *100 Years of Solitude*, Buendía specializes in Chinese cuisine—but chefs are always happy to whip up some *antojitos*. Heaping plate of beef with broccoli, fried rice, egg roll, and fried chicken 32 pesos, veggie combo 32 pesos. Open daily 7am-9pm.

Tortas El Chavo, Reforma 414 at Altamirano, off Mateos, three blocks from the border. A fast food joint with mirrored walls that reflect its bright green and yellow booths. *Tortas* 15-20 pesos, *tacos de machaca* (tacos filled with strips of beef) 5 pesos. Open daily 8:30am-8pm.

👁 SIGHTS

Mexicali's **Bosque y Zoológico,** on Alvarado between San Marcos and Cárdenas, is in the southwestern part of town. To reach the park area, board a black-and-white bus downtown marked "Calle 3." If you're driving, head south on Azueta over the Río Nuevo. The road becomes Uxmal south of the river; turn left on Independencia, then right on Victoria. Children and adults alike whistle at birds in the aviary, pedal paddleboats on the lake, and admire lions and tigers from the train that circles the park and nature reserve. The grounds contain carousels, bumper cars, a pool, and a **science museum.** (☎555 28 33. Open Tu-Su 9am-5pm. 10 pesos, children 7 pesos.) The city's **Parque Vicente Guerrero,** off Mateos next door to the mall, also entertains the whole family with jungle gyms and clean picnic spots. (☎554 55 63. Open Tu-Sa 8am-10pm.)

The bright orange **Catedral de la Virgen de Guadalupe** on Morelos at Reforma provides a more sedate experience. The cathedral is part of *La Parroquía de Mexicali,* founded in 1918 by Padre Juan Rossi after he discovered that no official church existed and the sacraments were being administered out of a tiny shack. (Open M-Sa 7am-9pm, Su 7am-6pm.) To learn more about Mexicali's past, visit the **Museo Regional,** on Reforma at Calle L. (☎552 57 15. Open M-F 9am-6pm, Sa-Su 9am-4pm. 6 pesos.)

🎵 ENTERTAINMENT

Two very distinct types of entertainment vie for your pesos in Mexicali. In *La Chinesca,* seedy bars, dim pool halls, and strip joints line Altamirano and Morelos south of Mateos, making walking alone at night scary for both male and female travelers. More traditional venues are concentrated in the eastern part of town, closer to the Universidad Autonoma de Baja California (UABC), whose students keep the dance floors shaking late into the night. Closest to the border, **Mandalinos,** Reforma 1070 (☎552 95 44), between Calles B and C, is a classy Italian restaurant by day and a hopping bar by night. **Forum** (☎552 40 91), Reforma and Justo Sierra, is a large and rowdy *discoteca* popular among the younger set. Ten blocks south, **La Falla** (☎568 3 33), on Sierra at Urugua, also spins popular dance tunes. If you prefer your music *en vivo,* head to trendy **Molcayetes** (☎556 07 00) on Montegano south of Independencia. Most clubs get busy about 11pm and keep the music and liquor flowing until 2 or 3am.

Plaza de Toros Calafia (☎ 554 43 73), on Calafia at Independencia hosts regularly scheduled bullfights (Oct.-May Su). To get there, take a blue-and-white "Centro Cívico" bus from the *centro* (10min., 4 pesos). The plaza holds up to 10,000 people (9,999 when the bull has a good day). Wild and crazy rodeos rampage in the winter and spring at **Lienzo Charro del Cetys,** at Cetys and Ordente. Check with the tourist office for schedules.

Mexicali boasts two major theatres and a very active **Casa de la Cultura,** on Madero and Altamirano, just west of the post office. Hundreds of local children and adults gather in the beautiful neo-classic building to study sculpture, drawing, painting, theater, dance, and English. The Casa holds rotating displays of student art and presents plays, concerts, and dance shows in its theater. (☎ 553 40 57. Open M-F 9am-8pm). **UABC,** the university, also presents cultural and theatrical performances in its theatre and has artistic displays in the **Galeria Universitaria** and **Sala de Arte** on campus (☎ 566 42 76 for more information). Major productions are realized in the pink and red **Teatro del Estado** (☎ 54 64 18), on Mateos at the northern end of Parque Vincente Guerrero.

TECATE   ☎ 6

The birthplace of Mexico's unofficial national beer, the peaceful and friendly border town of Tecate (pop. 100,000) prides itself not on the vats of suds produced each day in its brewery, but on the small town camaraderie and the safety of its streets. Free of *burros* and aggressive vendors, Tecate greets visitors with colorful, spontaneous fiestas in its central park, and the smoothest border crossing in Baja California, especially for those headed to Ensenada. Unlike its industrialized neighbors, Tecate's air is refreshingly clean (with just a faint whiff of barley and hops), and even affords glimpses of the twinkling stars above the surrounding hills. A tranquil afternoon spent sipping *cerveza* and tapping your foot to live *mariachi* provides the perfect break from the frenzied streets of Tijuana.

▐ TRANSPORTATION. Catch **buses** one block east of the park on Juárez at Rodríguez. Autotransportes de Baja California (☎ 554 12 21) sends buses to: **Ensenada** (2hr., 6 per day 8am-10pm, 81 pesos); **Mexicali** (2hr., every hr. 6:30am-10pm, 81 pesos); and **Tijuana** (45min., every 20min. 5am-9pm, 29 pesos). Transportes Norte De Sonora (☎ 554 23 43) offers cushy *de paso* buses every hour beginning at 7:30am to: **Guaymas** (13hr., 434 pesos); **Hermosillo** (12hr., 380 pesos); **Mazatlán** (24hr., 812 pesos); **Mexicali** (2hr., 80 pesos); and **Sonoita** (5hr., 210 pesos).

▐▐ ORIENTATION AND PRACTICAL INFORMATION. Tecate lies 42km east of Tijuana on **Rte. 2.** Driving in from either Mexicali or Tijuana you will be on the main street, **Juárez,** which intersects Cárdenas, heading south from the border crossing, at the northwest corner of Parque Hidalgo, the center of social and commercial activity. East-west streets parallel **Av. Mexico,** which runs along the border fence; continuing south, they are Madero, Revolución, Reforma, Juárez, Libertad, and Hidalgo. Streets named for early 20th century presidents run north-south perpendicular to Juárez and the border. Starting from the east, they are Gil, Rodríguez, Rubio, Cárdenas, Elias Calles, Obregón, de la Huerta, Carranza, and Aldrete.

Maps are available at the **tourist office,** Libertad 1305, facing Parque Hidalgo (☎ 554 10 95. Open M-F 8am-5pm, Sa-Su 10am-3pm). **Bancomer,** on the corner of Cárdenas and Juárez, exchanges traveler's checks. (☎ 554 14 50 or 4 13 49. Open M-F 8am-4pm, Sa 10am-2pm.) **Banamex,** Juárez and Obregón, provides the same services. (☎ 554 11 88. Open M-F 8:30am-4pm.) Big, yellow **Calimax,** on Juárez between Carranza and Aldrete, sells groceries and more. (☎ 554 00 39. Open daily 6am-11pm.) **Emergency:** ☎ 060. **Police:** (☎ 554 11 76) at the station on Ortiz Rubio at Juárez. **Red Cross:** Juárez 411 (☎ 554 13 13, emergency 066). Some English spoken. **Pharmacy: farmacia Roma** (☎ 554 18 18), on the corner of Juárez and Aldrete, satisfies your needs 24hr. The **IMSS Centro de Salud** is south of the *centro* on Misión de

Malegé and Santa Rosalía. (☎554 35 90. Open 24hr.) **Fax: Telecomm,** next door to the post office. (☎554 13 75. Open M-F 8am-6pm, Sa 8am-11am.) **Internet: Copyfast,** Ortiz Rubio 40, facing Parque Hidalgo. (☎554 19 10. 50 pesos per hr. Open M-F 8am-8:30pm, Sa 9am-8pm.) **Post office:** Ortiz Rubio 147, two blocks north off Juárez. (☎554 12 45. Open M-F 8am-3pm.) **Postal code:** 21400.

◪◪ **ACCOMMODATIONS AND FOOD.** Many budget accommodations line Madero near the border, while safer and similarly-priced hotels surround busy Parque Hidalgo. Very central **Hotel Tecate,** on Libertad at Cárdenas around the corner from the tourist office, offers simple rooms with private baths and fans. (☎554 11 16. Singles and doubles 180 pesos, with TV 220 pesos.) A short walk away, cheerful English-speaking management welcomes guests at the **Motel Paraíso,** Aldrete 82, just one block north of Juárez. Clean but worn rooms have fans, comfy beds and big baths. (☎554 17 16. Singles 160 pesos; doubles 225 pesos; each additional person 55 pesos.) One of the most trafficked hotels in town, **Hotel Juárez,** Juárez 230, between Ortiz Rubio and Rodríguez, offers small, clean rooms with saggy beds. An open hallway lets in cool breezes and sunlight. (☎554 16 17. Singles 110 pesos, with TV 140 pesos; doubles 140 pesos, with TV 170 pesos.)

Taquerías lining Juárez east of the park serve Tecate's cheapest food, with tacos and burritos starting at 5 pesos. **Restaurant Jardín Tecate,** next to the tourist office on the southern end of Parque Hidalgo, has the best food in town. Enjoy *burritos de machaca* (dry shredded beef) or a huge club sandwich (30 pesos) under the shady trees. (☎554 34 53. Open daily 7am-10pm.) Family-run **La Escondida** hides behind an unmarked door on Libertad between Rubio and Rodríguez. Fill up on huge *comida corridas* (25 pesos) and even bigger combination meals of soup, salad, *antojitos*, guacamole, beans, rice, and a drink (50 pesos). Vegetarians will love the *ensalada de aguacate*—a huge bowl of veggies, olives, and lots of avocado. (30 pesos. ☎554 21 64. Open M-F 8:30am-6pm, Sa-Su 8:30am-5pm.)

◪◪ **SIGHTS AND ENTERTAINMENT.** The biggest building in town, the **Tecate Brewery,** on Hidalgo at Obregón, attracts thousands of beer-loving visitors each year. Opened in 1944, the brewery, officially known as the Cervecería Cuauhtémoc Moctezuma, now pumps out 39 million liters of amber-colored pleasure each month. The **Jardín Cerveza Tecate,** just inside the gate, offers free beer samples to anyone 18 and older. Shady palm trees, big tables, and a bar where everything is free—this may be your vision of heaven. Next to the Jardín, a "soubeernir" shop sells Tecate-emblazoned aprons, clocks, briefcases, and bathing suits, as well as a wide selection of goodies adorned with logos from the company's seven other beers: Bohemia, Carta Blanca, Dos Equis, Indio, Sol, Superior, and the Christmastime-only Noche Buena. (☎554 20 11. *Garden open M-F 10am-5:45pm, Sa-Su 10am-4pm. Groups of 5 or more can arrange free tours by calling ext. 3470.*)

South of Juárez near Parque Hidalgo, several self-proclaimed "ladies clubs" cater to groups of hormonally-charged tourists and local men. More traditional nightlife options are not found in great abundance, but there are a couple of popular places to tip back Tecate's namesake. Locals and visiting *gringos* agree that **Café 68,** on Juárez between Elias Calles and Obregón, is the best place to party on weekends. (Open Th-Su 8pm-2am.) **Ricky's Bar,** at Juárez and Aldrete, attracts a more laid-back crowd.

ENSENADA ☎6

The secret is out—beachless Ensenada (pop. 72,000) is fast becoming a weekend hotspot. The masses of Californians arriving every Friday night have severely *gringo*-ized the town; everyone speaks some English, and store clerks finger their calculators if you hand them pesos. Brightly-dressed vendors wander the main drag, Mateos, and stores of all sizes and shapes populate the streets. Despite weekend congestion, Ensenada is nothing like its brash and raucous cousin, infamous Tijuana; it draws its crowds not with vice but cool sea breezes, warm hospitality, and an assortment of reasonably wholesome diversions.

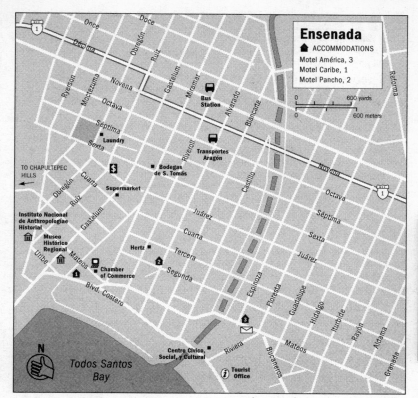

Ensenada

🏠 ACCOMMODATIONS

Motel América, 3
Motel Caribe, 1
Motel Pancho, 2

▐ TRANSPORTATION

GETTING THERE

Ensenada is 108km south of Tijuana on **Rte. 1.** The 1½hr. ride from Tijuana to Ensenada offers a continuous view of the Pacific, and the last 20min. on the Ensenada **cuota** (toll road) are especially breathtaking—if traveling by bus, grab a seat on the right-hand side (cars 16 pesos each). The less scenic **libre** (free road) is a poorly maintained two-lane highway that parallels the *cuota* until La Misión, then cuts inland for the remaining 40km. Drive only during the day—there are no streetlights and many tight curves. Most driving is done in the right lane; the left is for passing only.

GETTING AWAY

Buses: Buses from Tijuana arrive at the **Central de Autobuses,** the main station, at Calle 11 and Riveroll. To get to the *centro*, turn right as you come out of the station, walk south 10 blocks, and you'll be at Mateos (also called Primera), the main tourist drag. Transportes Norte de Sonora (☎ 178 66 80) goes to: **Guaymas** (16hr., 545 pesos) and **Los Mochis** (20hr., 6 per day 7am-9:30pm, 727 pesos). Autotransportes de Baja California (☎ 178 66 80), also at the Central, runs to: **Guerrero Negro** (10hr., 6 per day 10am-11pm, 280 pesos); **La Paz** (22hr., 4 per day 10am-11pm, 655 pesos); **Loreto** (16hr., 4 per day 10am-11pm, 490 pesos); **Mexicali** (4hr., 8 per day 5:30am-8pm, 150-173 pesos); **San Felipe** (4hr., 8am and 6pm, 150 pesos); **Santa Rosalía** (13hr., 7 and 9:30pm, 385 pesos); and **Tijuana** (1½hr., every 30min. 5am-11:30pm, 70-78 pesos). Transportes Aragón (☎ 174 07 17), on Riveroll between Calles 8 and 9, goes to: **Tijuana** (every hr. 5am-9:30pm, 69 pesos). Transportes Brisas (☎ 178 38 88), at Calle 4 771, runs buses to small towns nearby.

✦ 🔲 ORIENTATION AND PRACTICAL INFORMATION

Juárez (Calle 5) runs parallel to **Mateos.** *Calles,* running northwest-southeast, are numbered; *avenidas,* running northeast-southwest are named (except Juárez and Mateos). If you're driving, you'll come into town on Azueta, which later becomes Gastelum. Local *urbano* buses (☎ 178 25 94) leave from Juárez at Calle 6, and from Calle 2 at Macheros (every 8-15min., 5 pesos for most destinations in the city). After sundown, avoid the area near the shore, and use caution while navigating the regions bounded by Miramar, Macheros, Mateos, and Calle 4.

Tourist Office, Costero 540 (☎ 172 30 22; fax 172 30 81), at Azueta. Friendly, English-speaking staff doles out maps and pamphlets in English. Open M-F 9am-7pm, Sa-Su 11am-3pm. The **Chamber of Commerce,** Mateos 693 (☎ 178 23 32, or 174 09 96), 2nd fl., at Macheros, is closer to the center of town. Provides brochures and city maps. Open M-F 8:30am-2pm and 4-6:30pm.

Currency Exchange: Banks cluster along Juárez at Ruíz. **Bancomer** (☎ 178 18 01 or 178 18 03), on Juárez at Ruíz, exchanges dollars and traveler's checks. Open M-F 9am-4pm, Sa 10am-2pm. **ATMs** are everywhere in the bank district.

Supermarket: Supermarket Calimax (☎ 178 33 97), Gastelum at Calle 4. Open daily 6am-10pm.

Laundry: Lavandería Lavadero (☎ 178 27 37), on Obregón between Calles 6 and 7, across from Parque Revolución. Open M-Sa 7am-9pm, Su 8am-4pm.

Luggage storage: in the main station. 7 pesos per 5hr., 0.5 pesos each additional hr.

Car Rental: Hertz (☎ 178 29 82), Calle 2 at Riveroll. Cars 450 pesos per day with unlimited km. Open M-F 8am-6pm, Sa 8-10am.

Emergency: ☎ 060.

Police: (☎ 176 24 21) at Calle 9 at Espinoza.

Red Cross: (☎ 174 45 85) on Clark at Flores. Open 24hr.

Farmacia San Martín: (☎ 178 35 30 or 178 19 21), at Ruíz and Calle 8. Open 24hr.

Hospital General: (☎ 176 78 00 or 176 77 00), on the Transpeninsular Highway at km 111. Open 24hr.

Telephones: Faxes can be sent from **Telecomm** (☎ 177 05 45), on Floresta at Calle 3. Open M-F 8am-6pm, Sa 8-11am.

Internet: Café Internet MaxiComm (☎ 175 70 11), on Juárez between Miramar and Gastelum. 15 pesos per 30min., 20 pesos per hr.

Post office: (☎ 176 10 88), on Mateos and Espinoza. Open M-F 8am-3pm, Sa 8am-noon

Postal code: 22800.

▛ ACCOMMODATIONS

Budget hotels line Mateos between Espinoza and Riveroll and at Miramar. Most are a 15-minute stroll from the beachfront boardwalk and the popular clubs. Although many owners quote prices in US dollars, paying in pesos means saving cash. The beach between Tijuana and Ensenada is lined with RV parks; near Ensenada is **Ramona RV Park,** on km 104 of the Transpeninsular Highway. (☎ 174 60 45. US$10 for full hookup for 2 people; US$2 each additional person.)

Motel Caribe, Mateos 627 (☎ 178 34 81). Great rooms right on the main drag. Free parking for motel guests. More modest rooms across the street. Key deposit US$5. Singles US$15-30; doubles US$35-45; triples US$55. Rates go up on weekends.

Motel Pancho (☎ 178 23 44), on Alvarado at Calle 2, 1 block off Mateos (in line with the giant flagpole), has large rooms with clean baths and tiny showers. Hospitable staff will direct you to neighborhood bars. Singles 120 pesos, doubles 200 pesos.

Motel América (☎ 176 13 33), Mateos at Espinoza. Farther from the action, but rooms have kitchens, fans, and TVs. Singles US$22; doubles US$32.

FOOD

Cheaper restaurants line Juárez and Espinoza, while those on Mateos have jacked-prices. The eateries along the waterfront tend to offer good, cheap, and fresh seafood. There are also fruit, seafood, and taco stands everywhere. If you have a kitchen, the best bargains are at the supermarkets on Gastelum.

Las Brasas (☎ 178 11 85), on the ocean side of Mateos between Ruíz and Gastelum. An exceptional break from the usual sky-high prices of Mateos. Their quarter-chicken is among the best on earth (40 pesos). Take-out available. Open daily noon-8pm.

Cafetería Monique Colonial (☎ 176 40 41), Calle 9 at Espinoza. Friendly atmosphere makes it a local favorite. Over the kitchen, *Galería Infantil* displays the art of local children. Breaded steak, salad, and fries 55 pesos. Open M-Sa 6am-10pm, Su 6am-5pm.

Las Parrillas (☎ 176 17 28), Espinoza at Calle 6. Chefs grill fresh meat cutlets over a flaming pit as onlookers drool. Scarf down burritos (32 pesos) and *súper hamburgesas* with veggies, avocado, and chile (30 pesos). Open daily 6am-10pm.

SIGHTS

A cosmopolitan dream by Baja California Norte standards, Ensenada has a strong selection of museums and other sights from which to choose.

PLAZA CÍVICA. The larger-than-life golden busts of Venustiano Carranza, Miguel Hidalgo, and Benito Juárez stare out on the Plaza Civica. Here you can grab an ice cream cone, strut to the nearby **Ventana al Mar** (Window to the Sea), and marvel at the largest flag in the country.

BODEGAS DE SANTO TOMÁS. The mild, dry climate of northern Baja California's Pacific coast has made it Mexico's prime grape-growing area. Bodegas de Santo Tomás, has made wine since 1888. Today, the *bodegas* distill over 500,000 cases of wine and champagne each year. Tours include free tasting with an assortment of breads and cheeses. (*Miramar 666, at Calle 7. ☎ 178 33 33. Tours daily 11am, 1, and 3pm. Open M-F 8am-5pm. 20 pesos.*)

CENTRO CÍVICO, SOCIAL, Y CULTURAL DE ENSENADA. Once a world-famous casino built in 1930, this center is now a shrine to Ensenada's archaeological and social history. The architecture and gardens alone make a visit worthwhile. (*One block from Costero. ☎ 177 05 94. 5 pesos, children 3 pesos.*)

INSTITUTO NACIONAL DE ANTROPOLOGÍA E HISTORIA. The oldest building in town, the *Instituto* contains artifacts and images of the earliest missionary settlements in Baja California, including several mission church bells. (*Ryerson 99, at Uribe. ☎ 178 25 31. Open M-F 9am-4pm. Free.*)

MUSEO HISTÓRICO REGIONAL. The museum houses artifacts and photographs from all over Baja California. Originally built in 1886 as barracks, it is the oldest public building in the state. The building was converted to a jail in 1914 and served as such until 1986. (*Near the Instituto on Gastelum between Uribe and Mateos. ☎ 178 25 31. Currently closed for renovations; ask the tourist office for information.*)

MUSEO DE CIENCIAS. Housed in an old wooden boat, the museum displays photographs of and information about the endangered species of Baja California. (*Obregón 1463, at Catorce, a 15-min. walk from Mateos. ☎ 178 71 92. Open M-F 9am-5pm, Sa noon-5pm. 15 pesos, children 12 pesos.*)

CHAPULTEPEC HILLS. For a spectacular view of the entire city, climb the Chapultepec Hills. The steep road to the top begins at the foot of Calle 2 (*The hike should take 10-15min.*)

🎵 ENTERTAINMENT

Most of the popular hangouts on Mateos are members of the hybrid restaurant/bar/disco species. Food and drink are served until 8pm or so, when the eateries metamorphose into full-fledged dance club monsters. On weekends, almost every place is packed with tourists. As well-known as Ensenada itself, **Hussong's Cantina**, on Ruíz between Mateos and Calle 2, has been around for 106 years. Hussong's is a prototypical Mexican watering hole: wood-paneled walls full of deer heads and a floor full of sawdust. Gulp down beer (17 pesos) or a margarita (25 pesos) at the long, shiny bar. (☎178 32 10. Open M-F 10am-midnight, Sa-Su 10am-1am.) If you tire of *mariachi* music, cross the street to **Papas and Beer**, a popular and frenetic high-tech music emporium. The younger crowd swigs large margaritas (36 pesos) and spends horse-choking wads of cash. Escape the congestion onto the terrace, where hockey-rink-like plexiglass prevents carousers from cross-checking each other to the street below. (☎174 01 45. Th live music. F ladies' night 8-10pm. Cover US$3-5. Open Su-Th noon-3am, F-Sa 10am-2am.)

If you're looking to stay sober, join the mass of teens whirling to late-80s pop at **Roller Ensenada**, a rink on Mateos at Hidalgo. (☎174 54 34. Open Tu-Su noon-10pm. 20 pesos with skates, 25 pesos including rental.) **Cinema Gemelos**, on Balboa and Mateos, at the south end of town, screens subtitled US hits. (☎176 36 16 or 176 36 13. Shows daily 4-10pm. 20 pesos.)

📷 DAYTRIPS FROM ENSENADA

Ensenada is an excellent base from which to explore Baja California Norte's natural wonders. To reach many of them you'll need wheels, particularly a 4x4 or all-terrain vehicle. Try Hertz in Ensenada, or better yet (if you're driving from California), Bargain Auto Rentals in San Diego (see **Tijuana: Car Rental**, p. 142).

BAHÍA DE TODOS SANTOS

Good sand and a good swim can be found on the beaches along Bahía de Todos Santos, to the west of the city, stretching down to the Punta Banda Peninsula.

PLAYA SAN MIGUEL. To the north, Playa San Miguel, with its rocky coastlines and large waves, is ideal for surfers but not for swimmers. *(Drive north up Calle 10 to the toll gate; turn left at the sign marked "Playa San Miguel." Alternatively, catch a "San Miguel" bus departing Gastelum at Costero (6.50 pesos). Buses back must be flagged down.)*

PLAYA ESTERO. Somewhat more frequented beaches lie 8km south of Ensenada off the Transpeninsular Highway. The nicest beach around is Playa Estero, dominated by the Estero Beach Resort (☎176 62 25). Volleyball courts fill the beach's clean, hard sand, and you can rent water skis, banana boats, or bicycles (US$5 per hr.). Sea lions can be spotted off the coast during low tide. The **Estero Beach Museum**, in the resort, has an impressive display of Mexican folk art. *(Take a right at the "Estero Beach" sign on Rte. 1 heading south. Free parking available in the first lot of the hotel. Alternatively, catch a bus marked "Aeropuerto," "Zorrillo," "Maneadero," or "Chapultepec" from Pl. Cívica. Museum ☎177 55 20. Open W-M 9am-6pm. Free.)*

PLAYA EL FARO. Playa El Faro, 10km south of town, is similarly rife with volleyball courts and *norteamericanos*, but has slightly better sand and allows camping on the beach. Another nearby beach is **Playa Santa María**, where you can rent horses. *(Faro ☎177 46 20. Camp space, parking, and bathroom privileges US$7 per car. Full RV hookup US$12. Rooms for 2 people US$30; for 4 people US$50.)*

PUNTA BANDA

Take a right onto the Transpeninsular Highway off Mateos at the south end of Ensenada, and head past exits for the airport, military base, and Playa Estero. Take a right on Highway 23 after about 20min. at the sign marked "La Bufadora." This road, which splits off Highway 1 north of the town of Maneadero, goes the length of the Punta Banda pen-

insula. To traverse the peninsula by public transport, take a yellow microbús from Ensenada to Maneadero (7 pesos), at the start of the peninsula, and get a connecting "Nativos" bus to La Bufadora (3 pesos). You can ask to get off anywhere along Highway 23, though your trip back is not assured.

Punta Banda, the peninsula at the southern extremely of Bahía de Todos Santos, has good hiking and more solitary beaches than farther north. There are many trails in the mountains around **La Bufadora,** a natural geyser near the tip of the peninsula. Many parts of the peninsula are equally breathtaking, and warrant exploration. The following sights are listed in order from mainland to peninsular tip.

BAJA BEACH. You can swim anywhere along the clean, soft, white sand in front of a quiet scattering of Americans in semi-permanent RV parks. Rolling hills and marshes provide a pleasant backdrop. Horses are often available for rent. The Baja Beach Resort runs a pool of **hot springs** on the left side of Rte. 1, 2km before turning onto the Punta Banda main road. *(By car, bear right at the first fork after turning onto the Punta Banda road and proceed with caution; the road is poorly maintained. Look for "Horses for Rent" and "Aguacaliente" signs.)*

THE TOWN OF PUNTA BANDA. The town of Punta Banda has a roadside **grocery market** and **post office** (open M-F 8am-3pm) on the main road after the turn for Baja Beach. You can camp or park an RV in Punta Banda at **Villarino,** adjacent to the plaza, which has modern bathroom facilities and full hookups. *(☎ 154 20 45; fax 54 20 44. 65 pesos per person; 45 pesos per child. Call for reservations.)*

CERRO DE LA PUNTA. The best spot to enter the hiking trails of Punta Banda is Cerro de la Punta, on the road to La Bufadora near the end of the peninsula. You can hike the mountains for views of the surrounding area or go down the beautiful trails on the ocean. Bring food for cliffside picnics and a bathing suit to refresh your sweaty body in the chilly Pacific. Best of all, the area is essentially undiscovered by tourists. Most of the trails are unmarked footpaths and dirt roads. Be sure to stay on the paths; trail blazing will damage surrounding flora. *(Turn right up a long driveway at the "Cerro de la Punta" sign. You'll see a small clearing and a large house on the cliffs. Parking 10 pesos.)*

LA BUFADORA. La Bufadora is the largest geyser on the Pacific coast. On a good day, the "Blowhole" shoots water 40m into the air out of a water-carved cave. On a bad day, visitors will have to be satisfied with the beautiful view from the Bufadora peak. The area is crowded with visitors, cheesy curio shops, and food vendors. *(Parking US$1 or 8 pesos.)*

PARQUE NACIONAL CONSTITUCIÓN DE 1857

Follow Highway 3 east from Juárez in Ensenada past Ojos Negros. At about km 58, turn left onto the dirt road leading into the park. Follow signs (or, better, ask a guide for help). After about 1¼hr., you will find yourself at Laguna Hanson, a little lake surrounded by basic camping spots.

Hiking farther inland offers completely different terrain, ranging from deep lagoons to cactus forests to ponderosa pine. The rugged mountain range east of Ensenada is the solitary **Sierra de Juárez,** home to the Parque Nacional Constitución de 1857. You'll need an all-terrain vehicle or pick-up truck to make the trek. If you can afford it, find a guide who can show you the correct roads; erosion and brush make it difficult to navigate. **Ecotur** Costero 1094 #14, offers excursions for those without wheels, including a visit to the National Observatory or the San Pedro Martir waterfalls. *(☎/fax 178 37 04; cell ☎ 181 32 04; email ecoturbc@ens.com.mx; www.mexonline.com/ecotur.htm. 3 days. US$125 per person.)* The owner, Francisco Detrell, also leads tours in Ensenada and in other parts of Baja California. Call at least three days in advance.

VALLE DE SAN QUINTÍN ☎ 6

On the lonely mid-Pacific coast of northern Baja, San Quintín Valley (pop. 30,000) is the lifeblood of Baja California agriculture. Driving south from Ensenada on Rte. 1, beginning about km 180, you'll encounter a series of small, bland towns bordered by the ocean on the west and the mountains on the east, with farmland everywhere in between. The valley is composed of numerous ranches and three tiny towns: **San Quintín, Lázaro Cárdenas** (not to be confused with its neighbor Lázaro Cárdenas, only 100km to the northeast), and **El Eje del Papaloto.** The area's biggest draw, the superb fishing off San Quintín Bay, means that foreigners are hard to find on the main strip 5km inland. The valley makes a good rest stop en route to points farther south, or a convenient place to stock up for a camping excursion to the nearby **Parque Nacional Sierra San Pedro Mártir.**

◨▱ TRANSPORTATION AND PRACTICAL INFORMATION. All three towns border Rte. 1, Mexico's Transpeninsular Highway. Small streets off the highway have neither street signs nor common-use names. Addresses are designated by highway location. The beaches are all west of the highway, accessible by small dirt and sand roads. Coming from the north, San Quintín is the first town, Cárdenas (as it is known in the region) is second, and little Eje comes last.

The Valle de San Quintín **tourist office** actually comes before the towns themselves at km 178 in Col. Vicente Guerrero—look for signs. The friendly English-speaking staff provides plenty of information about the valley. (☎ 166 27 28. Open M-F 8am-5pm, Sa-Su 10am-3pm.) To exchange currency or traveler's checks, or for 24hr. **ATMs,** head to **BITAL,** with branches in San Quintín just before the bridge at km 194, and in Lázaro Cárdenas behind the PEMEX station. (Both open M-F 8am-7pm, Sa 8am-2:30pm.) **Emergency:** ☎ 134. **Police:** (☎ 165 20 34) in Cárdenas, by the park. **Farmacia Baja California:** in Cárdenas, Rte. 1 at km 195. (☎ 165 24 38. Open M-F 8am-10pm, Sa-Su 8am-2pm.) **Clínica Santa María:** (☎ 175 22 63 or 175 22 12) in San Quintín, on a dirt road off Rte. 1 at km 190. **LADATELS**: in all three towns, and a **caseta** in Cárdenas. **Internet** cafes dot the Cárdenas strip of Rte. 1. **Network Café** is on the east side of Rte. 1 at km 196 above the BBV bank. (1 peso per min. ☎ 165 39 82. Open M-Sa 9am-7pm, Su 10am-5pm.) **Post office:** a grey building next to the Farmacia Baja California in Cárdenas. (Open M-F 8am-3pm.) **Postal code:** 22930.

▟▞ ACCOMMODATIONS AND FOOD. Sleeping arrangements in the Valle are minimal but comfortable. In San Quintín, **Motel Chavez,** on Rte. 1 at km 194 just before the bridge, offers large, airy rooms, soft beds, and cable TV in the lobby. (☎ 165 20 05; fax 5 38 05. Singles 190 pesos; doubles 255 pesos. Call ahead for reservations.) In Cárdenas, **Motel Romo,** at km 196 on the west side of Rte. 1, has almost-new carpeted rooms, relatively clean bathrooms, and large windows. (☎ 165 28 96. Singles 130 pesos; doubles 160 pesos.) About 4km down a dirt road just south of Cárdenas is **Motel San Carlos.** Follow signs for the Old Mill; be prepared for a bumpy, sandy ride. Near the lapping waves of the old pier on San Quintín Bay, the hotel has carpeted rooms with baths. (Singles US$15; doubles US$22.) It isn't tough to find cheap food in San Quintín. Small *loncherías* along both sides of Rte. 1 serve tacos (7 pesos), while seafood stands serve shrimp or octopus cocktails worth every peso (40-50 pesos). In the A/C-filled **Asadero El Alazán,** in San Quintín at km 190, enjoy a steak (49 pesos) among framed portraits of John Wayne and Clint Eastwood.

◫▟ SIGHTS AND ENTERTAINMENT. San Quintín is best known for the fishing in San Quintín bay. Drive out to the **Molino Viejo** (Old Pier), past the mill machinery of a failed 19th-century English colony, to the Old Mill Hotel (US ☎ (619) 428-2779 or (800) 479-7962; Mexico toll-free ☎ 01 800 025 5141), where you can get a fishing permit and hire a boat for the day. The **Old Mill** itself is a semi-permanent American expat community. To get there, turn west at km 198 on a sand and dirt road and head down about 4km. Signs will point you in the right direction. To see the **salt**

lakes on the edge of the sea, west of Cárdenas, turn left at the corner of the military base in Cárdenas, then travel a dirt and sand road (8.2km). Follow the road carefully to avoid getting stuck. Those armed with four-wheel drive and a surfboard can head to **Surfing Beach,** 19km down a sandy road just south of the military base. Ask the tourist office for a map; the roads are unmarked and difficult to navigate.

Although San Quintín's nightlife is hardly hopping, those in search of spirits can go to **Bar Romo** (☎165 23 96), on Rte. 1 in Cárdenas beside the motel of the same name. *Mariachis* and local singers play until the late hours. In San Quintín, grab a chilly beer (about 18 pesos) or margarita (25 pesos) at the friendly tourist-oriented **Restaurant Bar San Quintín,** on Rte. 1 next to Hotel Chavez. The well-stocked bar and weekend *mariachi music* will help you strum a buzz in no time. (☎165 23 76. Open daily 7:30am-1am.)

PARQUE NACIONAL SIERRA SAN PEDRO MÁRTIR

The road leading to the park is approximately 51km north of San Quintín and runs east of the highway for 100km. The ride to the park is approximately 2½ hours on a poorly maintained dirt road (due to heavy rainfall, the road may be temporarily closed). You can make the trek in a passenger vehicle, but it is highly recommended to go with four-wheel-drive. The road is narrow and the cliffs steep. Watch out for cattle; local vaqueros use the road to herd their cows to greener pastures. In spite of the dangerous curves, the views from the road are unparalleled—the breathtaking canyons and hills tinted yellow and red are spectacular. Trails in the park are not well marked; it is advisable to bring a compass. For some trails authorized guides are mandatory. If you plan on backpacking or spending the night in the park, bring plenty of water.

Although the trippy towns of the Valle de San Quintín appeal mostly to anglers, the nearby Parque Nacional Sierra San Pedro Mártir has enough canyons, peaks, and waterfalls to satisfy the urges of the most zealous land lover. Founded in 1947, the park is situated on a plateau, and because of its elevation, has considerably more rainfall than its lowland desert surroundings. As a result, the park is beautifully shaded by evergreens (pines and junipers abound) and is host to a vast array of wildlife including deer, puma, eagles, not-so-wild cows, and the Nelson rainbow trout (a species endemic to the region). The park's isolated location also makes it one of the least-visited parks in Mexico and a prime destination for backpackers and hikers who wish to be left alone with nature. The park is home to **Picacio del Diablo** (also known as **Cerro de la Encantada** or **La Providencia**), the highest peak in Baja California (3086m above sea level). From its peak on a clear day, you can admire the aquamarine waters of the Sea of Cortés, turn around, and compare them with the waters of the Pacific Ocean. The climb to the peak is said to be one of the most challenging climbs in Mexico. In addition to the peak, the park has three canyons and the splendid **San Pedro Mártir Falls,** an 800m waterfall accessible only with an authorized guide. The park is also home to Mexico's **National Observatory.** Founded in 1967, the observatory is one of the most important in all of Latin America; it houses both reflecting telescopes and a new state-of-the-art infrared telescope. The observatory lies at the end of the road leading into the park (tours Sa 11am-1pm, by appointment).

There are several tent site locations, but none for trailer or car camping. A few trails leading to viewpoints and wilderness campsites are nominally maintained and can be accessed off the park's only road. See a ranger at the entrance to the park for information and help with orientation. Check out the tourist office in San Quintín or contact **Ecotur** (see **Ensenada: Hiking,** p. 152).

EL ROSARIO

Fifty-eight kilometers south of San Quintín on Rte. 1, home to the **last Pemex** for nearly one hundred miles, tiny El Rosario is accustomed to drop-ins. Before hitting the road or on your way back to civilization, indulge in one of **Mama Espinosa's** lobster specialties, two doors down from the Pemex station. Founded in 1930, the family-run business has stuffed thousands of Baja trekkers, and has thirteen signed guest books to prove it. (☎165 87 70. Entrees 40-

220 pesos. Open daily 6am-10pm.) If you've gorged so long you can't move, **Motel El Rosario,** just next door, has basic rooms with comfy beds, fans, and TV. (☎165 88 58. Singles 165 pesos; doubles 198 pesos.) If you want a touristy detour, turn west at the supermarket, bear left at the fork, cross the river, and feast your eyes on the crumbling foundations of the Dominican **Nuestra Senora del Rosario Vinaraco** mission (active AD 1774-1832).

BAHÍA DE LOS ANGELES

Wedged between steep rocky hills to the west and the Sea of Cortés to the east, the Bahía de la Concepción is, quite simply, a beautiful place to watch the sunset. The rich marine life in the surrounding bays is about the only thing that will distract you from afternoons of doing nothing. You'll find no dance clubs or *mariachis* in this little Baja California town; most visitors come to fish or just relax—modern amenities are not yet universal here.

■⚡ **ORIENTATION AND PRACTICAL INFORMATION.** Bahía de los Angeles is very small and easily navigable by foot. The road that leads from the Transpeninsular Highway to the bay becomes the town's main road. None of the streets are named, but everything is right off the main strip. The owner of **Guillermo's,** a market/restaurant/RV park/motel, serves as the official **tourist** liaison. There are no banks; exchange your traveler's checks before you drive into town (oh, you will be driving—there is no bus service). A **public phone** can be found in the office of Hotel Costa Azul on the main road (12 pesos per min.). The **police** are behind the park across from Guillermo's.

⬛⬛ **ACCOMMODATIONS AND FOOD.** Camping is the cheapest way to stay in the Bahía, and the best site is at **Daggett's Campground.** Follow the signs from the main road just before entering town. Right on the beach, each space comes with a small *palapa* and barbecue pit. The campground has bathrooms, hot showers, and a great view. (US$6 per couple; US$2 each additional person.) The owner, **Ruben,** is a great source of information and he also leads fishing and diving tours (half-day US$85). **Hotel las Hamacas** in town off the main road has very clean rooms with concrete floors, A/C, and fans. (Singles 150 pesos; doubles 200 pesos.) Park your RV at **Guillermo's,** off the main road (an unbeatable US$3 per person per night for a full hookup). Because of its isolated location, food in town is not so cheap. Your best bet is to grill up your catch of the day. If the fish just aren't biting, head to the **Restaurante las Hamacas,** in front of the hotel. The simple, trophy-adorned dining room is cooled by fans and ice-cold *cerveza*. Mexican combo 30 pesos. (Open daily 8am-8pm.) **Restaurante Isla** has a great view of the bay from its second floor *palapa*-roofed patio. Silk flowers peeking out of tinfoiled beer bottles grace the tables along with delicious *tacos de pescado* (35 pesos; open 7am-9pm).

⬛⬛ **SIGHTS AND SAND.** Although Bahía de los Angeles is small and relatively undeveloped, it has a rich history. The area was originally inhabited by the **Cochimi,** a group of Native Americans that was prevalent in this area of Baja. More information about the town, its history, and its natural surroundings can be found at the small **Museo de Historia y Cultura,** located directly behind the police office; look for the large white skeleton in front. The well-maintained wooden museum holds detailed exhibits on the Cochimi and local wildlife, fossils, stuffed animal specimens, and a collection of old photographs of the town in its previous incarnations as mining town and fishery. It's well worth the visit. (Open daily in summer 9am-noon and 3-5pm; in winter 9am-noon and 2-4pm. Free, but donations accepted.)

Most visitors to Bahía de los Angeles come to catch fish and many come with their own boats. If you plan to fish, be sure to bring (or borrow) your own supplies—there is no place to pick up fishing supplies in town. Ruben Daggett of Daggett's Campground will take you fishing on his diving boat (half-day US$85). Fill your dive tank or rent your dive gear at the only dive shop in town, **Larry and**

Raquel's, next to Daggett's Campground. They also rent kayaks (US$15 per day). The best beaches lie north of town along **Ensenada la Gringa.** Permanent RVs park along the coast, but you can access the beach via dirt paths off the unpaved road leading to **Punta la Gringa,** the northern lip of the Bahía. The road to la Gringa can be accessed by following signs to Daggett's Campground. Once on the dirt road outlined by white stones, follow it north for about 4km until it ends.

SAN FELIPE ☎6

San Felipe (pop. 25,000) may put on Mexican airs, but it's a tourist-oriented beach town at heart, complete with high prices, sandy volleyball courts, and vendors selling shell sculptures. From December to April, San Felipe's 200 RV parks are packed with migrating *norteamericanos* who have forged a strong expatriate community. Founded as a fishing port in 1916, San Felipe still supports a thriving shrimp fleet. Recently tourism has taken over as the town's greatest source of income. Surrounded by stunning desert valleys and sparkling sand dunes, San Felipe deserves all the attention it gets. The laid back and scenic town offers a stellar selection of seafood and a beautiful stretch of beach teased by the warm, shallow waters of the gulf. This is the perfect place to relax for a day, but beware—before you know it, a day will become a week.

TRANSPORTATION

The bus station is at Mar Caribe. (☎577 15 16. Open daily 5:30am-10:30pm.) To walk downtown (15min.), walk north on Mar Caribe to Manzanillo and turn right toward the water. Walk until you see the Hotel Costa Azul, and you're on Mar del Caribe, one block from the beach. Autotransportes de Baja California go to: **Ensenada** (3½hr., 8am and 4pm, 150 pesos); **Mexicali** (2½hr., 5 per day 6am-8pm, 110 pesos); and **Tijuana** (5 per day 6am-4pm, 227 pesos). All prices listed are for first-class *locales*.

ORIENTATION AND PRACTICAL INFORMATION

San Felipe is 190km south of Mexicali at the end of dip-plagued Rte. 5. The town is also accessible via Rte. 3 from Ensenada, a poorly maintained paved road. Coming from Tijuana, the latter makes for a more pleasant ride, despite sometimes treacherous potholes. Los Arcos (a tall, white double arch) marks the entrance to town. **Chetumal** is the street continuing straight from the arch toward the sea. Hotels, restaurants, and curio shops cluster on **Mar de Cortés,** one block west of the beach. The **malecón,** lined with seafood stands, runs along the beach. Running parallel to the *malecón* and Mar de Cortés, *avenidas* are named for international seas. Starting one block west of Mar de Cortés, *avenidas* **Mar Baltico, Mar de Tazmania, Mar Catabrico, Mar Negro,** and **Mar Blanco** run north-south. Perpendicular to the seas, *calles* named for Mexican port cities run east-west. From north to south they are **Acapulco, Chetumal, Ensenada, Topolobambo, Manzanillo,** and **Isla de los Cedros.**

Tourist Office: Mar de Cortés 300 (☎577 18 65), at Manzanillo. English-speaking staffers cheerfully dispense maps and advice. Open M-F 8am-5pm, Sa-Su 10am-3pm. For a US perspective, direct questions to Linda at the **People's Gallery,** 2 blocks south of the tourist office on Mar de Cortés. Open daily mid-Sept. to mid-June 9am-4pm.

Currency Exchange: Bancomer (☎/fax 577 10 90), Mar de Cortés Norte at Acapulco, is the only bank in town. It exchanges cash and traveler's checks, and has a 24hr. **ATM.** Open M-F 8:30am-4pm, Sa 10am-2pm.

Emergency: ☎134.

Police: (☎577 11 34) on Isla de los Cedros at Mar Negro. Open 24hr.

Red Cross: (☎577 15 44) at Mar Bermejo and Peñasco. English spoken. Open 24hr.

Pharmacy: Farmacia San José, Mazatlán 523 (☎577 13 87). Open 24 hr.

Medical Assistance: Centro de Salud (☎577 15 21), on Mar Bermejo between Chetumal and Ensenada. English spoken. Open 24hr.

Fax: Copicentro (☎577 14 02; fax 577 14 66) on Chetumal. Open daily 8am-9pm.

LADATELS: line Mar de Cortés.

Internet Access: The Net (☎577 16 00), next to the People's Gallery on Mar de Cortes. US$4 per 15min. Open M-Sa 9am-4pm.

Post office: (☎577 13 30) Mar Blanco at Mar de Tazmania. Open M-F 8am-3pm, Sa 9am-1pm. **Postal code:** 21850.

⌐ ACCOMMODATIONS

One of the most expensive cities in one of the most expensive parts of the country, San Felipe offers limited choices for travelers on a budget. Most accommodations line Mar de Cortés and Mar Baltico near the beach, and, as a general rule, the smaller the hotel, the lower the prices. Camping on the federally owned *playas* is, as always, perfectly legal, but tourist officials warn against it. If you must camp, do so within an established RV park. For bargain basement rooms, your best option is to rent a room in a private home; check with the tourist office for an updated list.

Carmelita (☎577 18 31), across from Motel Chapala, rents 4 sparkling rooms with big baths, A/C, mini-refrigerators, and *agua purificada.* 300 pesos per night; 50 pesos per additional person.

Motel El Pescador (☎577 26 48), centrally located on Mar de Cortés at Chetumal, offers spacious, nicely furnished rooms overlooking the beach with A/C, color TV, and private baths. Singles 300 pesos; doubles 350 pesos. Condominiums US$300.

Ruben's (☎577 20 21), toward the end of Golfo de California in Playa Norte, is the best known RV park. Turn left from Chetumal onto Mar de Cortés, take a sharp right onto Guaymas, and turn left onto Golfo de California. Individual beachfront parking spaces are topped with two-story, open-air bungalows that look like *palapa* tree-forts. Each spot easily accommodates carloads of folks with sleeping bags, and RVs can hook up to electricity, hot water, and sewer connections. 2 people in summer US$15, in winter US$12; US$2 per extra person. Office open daily 7am-7pm.

Campo San Felipe, (☎577 10 12), Mar de Cortés, just south of Chetumal, lures campers with a fabulous central beachfront location. A thatched roof shelters each fully loaded trailer spot. Spots US$10-20; US$2 per extra person, children under 6 free; tent space US$10.

◖ FOOD

Mar de Cortés is crammed with restaurants advertising air-conditioned relief, while little *taquerías* line the *malecón*, offering shrimp tacos (10 pesos) and fish or *carne asada* (8 pesos). Locals rave about **Arturo's,** on Mar Baltico just south of Chetumal, where yummy tortilla soup accompanies big Mexican combination plates (*enchiladas,* taco, burrito, rice, and beans 50 pesos). Try the best (and biggest) margaritas in town (25 pesos) to wash it all down. (Open daily 10am-10pm.) Enjoy beef, chicken, or shrimp enchiladas (23 pesos) and a calming view of the sea at **Restaurant El Club,** on the *malecón* at Acapulco. The *camarones al mojo de ajo* (shrimp sauteed in garlic butter; 80 pesos) or the whole fried fish (37 pesos) will make you want to splurge. (☎577 11 75. Open daily 7am-10:30pm.)

◉◖ SIGHTS AND BEACHES

Each year, more than 250,000 people come to San Felipe to swim in the warm, tranquil, and invitingly blue waters in the Sea of Cortés. The beach in town follows the *malecón* and gets very crowded on weekends. South of town, away from the rumbling of shrimping boats and jet skis, clearer water and peaceful beaches provide a better setting for snorkeling. The southern beaches are also a seashell collector's paradise; low tides reveal perfect sand dollars and thousands of colorful shells. Land-lubbers can rent **ATVs** right next to Motel El Pescador (US$20 per hr.; open 8am-6pm) while those who want to get wet choose from the jet skis (US$20 per hr.) and the banana boats (30-50 pesos per 20min.) waiting along the beach.

Take time to visit the **Capilla de la Virgen de Guadalupe,** a shrine to the virgin at the top of a small hill just south of the lighthouse. After a short uphill climb, you'll be rewarded with a spectacular view of San Felipe and the blue bay. The world's largest strand of *cardón* cacti makes its home at the foot of the Sierra San Pedro Martir, 20km southeast of San Felipe. Nicknamed **Valle de los Gigantes,** this hidden valley was the original home of the giant cactus that represented Mexico at the 1992 World's Fair in Seville, Spain. To reach the valley, drive south on Rte. 5 away from town to a small dirt road on the right marked with a sign proclaiming *"Sahuaro, Valle de Los Gigantes,"* and turn right onto the dirt road. The barbed wire fence keeps cows in, and local ranchers don't mind letting visitors in as long as you remember to close the fence behind you. Passenger vehicles with partially deflated tires should be able to navigate the sandy terrain. In the valley, towering *cardón* (many nearly 15m tall), thorny orange-tipped ocotillo, bearded *abuelo* (grandfather), and easily-provoked jumping *cholla* cacti shelter a small community of cows, roadrunners, jackrabbits, coyotes, and other desert dwellers. Local activists are campaigning for designation of the Valle as a national reserve in order to protect the gnarly 200-year-old *cardón*. **Casey Hamlin** in San Felipe offers interpretive tours of the valley, including a side trip to secluded **Shell Beach,** where sand dollars and sparking shells await your discovery. (3½hr, US$5 per person, 4 person minimum.) **Casey's Baja Tours,** on Mar y Sol, a private road two blocks south of Campo San Felipe in town, rents kayaks (US$20 per day) and also offers adventures to nearby waterfalls, hotsprings, and petrified forests. (☎577 14 31. Open daily 8am-8pm.)

♫ ENTERTAINMENT

San Felipe merrily courts hordes of migrant snowbirds and spring break revelers with its picturesque beaches and a variety of venues to get tipsy or blasted. The high-priced, high-profile **Rockodile,** on the *malecón* at Acapulco, attracts a young crowd with a central volleyball court, outdoor terrace, and loud US pop tunes. The mellow daytime crowd gets shoved out on weekend nights by a super-sweaty dance party. Try the obscenely-named electric-blue king-sized beverage (US$4) to begin inducing amnesia. (☎577 12 19. Sa cover US$3. Open daily 11am-3am.) Seasoned veterans nurse drinks at **Bar Miramar,** at the north of the *malecón.* The oldest bar in San Felipe may look like a 60s *cantina,* but the patrons come for friendly company, not debauchery and glitz. Play a round of pool or test your agility in a game of ping pong on the patio overlooking the sea. Beer 15 pesos, margaritas 25 pesos. (☎577 11 92. Open M-Th 10am-2am, F-Su 10am-3am.) **Beach Comber,** on the *malecón* at Chetumal, always has sports on TV and tourists on stools, tranquilly sipping their beers. A well-stocked bar and jukebox make this a quiet, understated place to get trashed. (☎577 21 22. Beer 13 pesos, margaritas 22 pesos, flavored drinks 27-35 pesos. Su karaoke 8pm. Open daily 10am-2am.)

BAJA CALIFORNIA SUR

GUERRERO NEGRO   ☎ 1

Named for a whaling boat, "Black Warrior," that sank in the town's lagoon in 1858, Guerrero Negro (pop. 10,000), though dusty, grey, and industrial, might earn a soft spot in the hearts of heat-weary travelers. There's always a cool breeze here, and even summer nights can be positively chilly. In Guerrero Negro, salt is king. A deep breath of the town's air is enough to send a hypochondriac's blood pressure

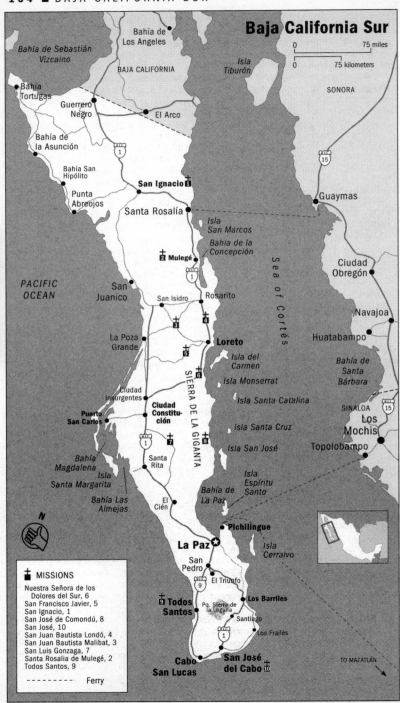

Baja California Sur

0 _____ 75 miles

0 _____ 75 kilometers

BAJA CALIFORNIA

PACIFIC OCEAN

SONORA

SINALOA

Sea of Cortés

Bahía de Sebastián Vizcaíno

Bahía de Los Angeles

Isla Tiburón

Bahía Tortugas

Guerrero Negro

El Arco

Bahía de la Asunción

Bahía San Hipólito

Punta Abreojos

San Ignacio ✝ 1

Santa Rosalía

Guaymas

Isla San Marcos

Bahía de la Concepción

✝ 2 Mulegé

Ciudad Obregón

San Juanico

San Isidro

Rosarito

Navajoa

✝ 3

✝ 4

Huatabampo

La Poza Grande

Loreto

Isla del Carmen

Bahía de Santa Bárbara

✝ 5

Isla Monserrat

✝ 6

Isla Santa Catalina

Ciudad Insurgentes

SIERRA DE LA GIGANTA

Isla Santa Cruz

Los Mochis

Puerto San Carlos

Ciudad Constitu-ción

✝ 7

✝ 8

Isla San José

Topolobampo

Santa Rita

Bahía Magdalena

Isla Santa Margarita

Bahía Las Almejas

El Cién

Isla Espíritu Santo

Bahía de La Paz

N

Pichilingue

Isla Cerralvo

La Paz ✪

San Pedro

El Triunfo

TO MAZATLÁN

9

Los Barriles

✝ Todos Santos

Pq. Sierra de la Laguna

Santiago

Los Frailes

Cabo San Lucas

1

San José del Cabo ✝ 10

✝ MISSIONS

Nuestra Señora de los
  Dolores del Sur, 6
San Francisco Javier, 5
San Ignacio, 1
San José de Comondú, 8
San José, 10
San Juan Bautista Londó, 4
San Juan Bautista Malibat, 3
San Luis Gonzaga, 7
Santa Rosalía de Mulegé, 2
Todos Santos, 9

-------- Ferry

BAJA CALIFORNIA

YOU SAY TOMATO, I SAY CLAMATO Everyone knows that *Mexicanos* prefer to drink their Tecate with a bit of *limón,* and most *turistas* quickly embrace the habit, believing themselves to be sophisticated and knowledgeable of Mexican culture. If you don't know what a clamato is, however, you'll never convince a true local, especially not a sea-side dweller, of your cultural savvy. A bottled blend of *almeja* (clam) and tomato juices, and ubiquitous in *mercado* refrigerators, clamato makes a versatile mixer for vodka, tequila, rum...or Tecate, and often appears on drink lists throughout Baja, California. The next time you find yourself seated in a restaurant watching neighboring groups of men down salty glasses of a peculiar orange mixture at a table littered with bottles of salsa (the more picante the better), order up a clamato and *cerveza,* squeeze in a few *limones* and splash on some salsa to taste.

---

soaring. Its salt plant is now the world's largest, dominating town economy. Although the locals are friendly and the breeze cathartic, during most of the year Guerrero Negro's biggest tourist attraction is its gas station, a beautiful Pemex. From January to March, however, gas takes back seat to whale-watching in the Laguna Ojo de Liebre, better known as Scammon's Lagoon. If you've missed the whales, fill that tank, and burn, baby, burn.

◪ TRANSPORTATION. The **ABC Autotransportes de Baja California** terminal (☎ 157 06 11), on Zapata, is one of the first buildings as you come from the highway. ABC sends buses north (6 per day 6:30am-10pm) to **El Rosario** (6hr., 150 pesos); **Ensenada** (10hr., 280 pesos); **Lázaro Cárdenas** (7hr., 185 pesos); **Punta Prieta** (4hr., 55 pesos); **San Quintín** (8hr., 185 pesos); and **Tijuana** (11hr., 350 pesos); and south to: **La Paz** (11hr., 4 per day 6am-7pm, 375 pesos); **Mulegé** (4hr., 4 per day, 150 pesos); **Santa Rosalía** (3hr., 6 per day, 105 pesos); and points in between. Yellow **minivans** run up and down the Transpeninsular Highway (every 15min. 7am-10pm, 6 pesos).

◪◪ ORIENTATION AND PRACTICAL INFORMATION. Guerrero Negro runs along a 3km strip west of the Transpeninsular Highway. Its two main roads, **Zapata** and **Baja California,** are home to nearly all of the town's industrial and commercial centers. **Banamex,** Baja California in front of the plant, exchanges currency and has **ATMs.** (☎ 157 05 55. Open M-F 9am-3pm.) Travelers continuing south should change currency here, as ATMs and bank services become more sparse. **Police:** (☎ 157 00 22) in the Delegación Municipal, a few hundred meters before the salt plant, on the left. **Internet:** hidden off Zapata at **PC Vision.** Take Sanchez (between Motel San Ignacio and Hotel El Morro) down two blocks, then turn left onto an unnamed street. The Internet cafe will be on your right. (www.pcvision.net.mx. 30 pesos per hr. Open M-Sa 9am-10pm, Su 3-10pm.) **Post office:** Av. Baja California, two blocks past the church and left onto a dirt road just before the basketball courts. (☎ 157 03 44. Open M-F 8am-3pm.) **Postal code:** 23940.

◪◪ ACCOMMODATIONS AND FOOD. The best deal may be the newly-renovated **Motel Las Dunas** on Zapata, below the water tank, a short walk north from the bus station. Immaculate shiny rooms with large showers. The courteous staff helps in every way possible. (☎ 157 00 55. Singles and doubles 185 pesos.)

Cheap food (20-40 pesos) and a daily dose of Mexican talk shows are available at **Cocina Económica Edith** on Tabasco, to the left of Zapata, just before the Pemex station when entering town from the highway. (Open M-Sa 7am-10pm, Su irregular hours.)

◪ SIGHTS. If you're lucky enough to have landed in Guerrero Negro during grey whale season, visit **Eco-Tour Malarrimo,** on Zapata, on the right as you come into town. The friendly staff speaks excellent English. Tours begin in January as soon as 15 whales are sighted in the Laguna, and continue through the end of March. Schedule tours at least one day in advance, and arrive 30 minutes before the tour is scheduled to leave. Be sure you've changed your watch to Mountain Standard

Time—one hour ahead—if coming from the north. (☎157 01 00; fax 157 01 00; www.malarrimo.com. Tours 4hr.; 8 and 11am; US$40, children US$30; price includes a light lunch.) If your Spanish is good and you've got a car, the road to the Laguna is 10km south of Guerrero Negro on Rte. 1—watch for a sign with a whale on it. Follow the sandy bumps 24km until you reach the Laguna. The area is a biosphere reserve and the whales shy and sensitive, so private boats are not allowed while the whales are mating (Dec.-Apr.). Thus, a trained local fisherman is necessary if you want a close look (1½hr.; US$15, children US$10).

SAN IGNACIO ☎1

In the deserts of Baja, San Ignacio (pop. 2000) is a tiny oasis. From a distance, the town appears as a cruel illusion, a mirage of the mind—leafy date palms, flowering bushes, and broad swaths of green appear magically in the middle of the blistering desert. Pinch yourself—you're not dreaming. The area around San Ignacio is blessed with the most plentiful underground freshwater supply in all of Baja California Sur; of late, it's been dammed to form a murky lake, used for swimming and irrigating local orchards. Although it's hot during summer days, San Ignacio earns points for just about everything else. Its intimate atmosphere, nighttime starscapes, and historic mission are just a few reasons so many travelers end up settling here. San Ignacio is also a prime point of departure for cave painting and whale-watching tours.

TRANSPORTATION. Buses pick up and drop off passengers at the sheltered bench across from the PEMEX station, 2km from San Ignacio on the Rte. 1. *De paso* buses head north (2, 5, 6am, 4, 6, and 7pm) to: **Guerrero Negro** (3hr., 78 pesos); **Ensenada** (13hr., 312 pesos); and **Tijuana** (14hr., 372 pesos). Buses head south (8, 10:30am, 6:30, and 9pm) for: **La Paz** (8hr., 278 pesos); **Mulegé** and **Rosarita** (1hr., 43 pesos); and **Loreto** (1hr., 124 pesos), all via **Santa Rosalía.**

ORIENTATION AND PRACTICAL INFORMATION. A winding road canopied by swaying date palms leads south from the Transpeninsular Highway and becomes **Luyando** at the *zócalo*. Within minutes of arrival, you'll know tiny San Ignacio better than your hometown. Life revolves around the tranquil *zócalo*, which is delineated by Luyando and the mission on the north, **Morelos** on the south, **Juárez** on the east, and **Hidalgo** on the west.

There's no official **tourist office,** but for an informative chat visit **Jorge Antonio Fischer,** the owner of the mini-mart next to Restaurant Chalita on Hidalgo. (☎154 01 50 or 4 01 90. Open M-Sa 7am-6pm, Su 7am-1pm.) He also leads whale expeditions and tours to the cave paintings. **Nuevos Almacenes Meza,** on the corner of Juárez and Luyando, facing the *zócalo*, sells general goods. (☎154 01 22. Open M-Sa 8am-noon and 2-7pm, Su 8am-noon.) **Police:** in the Delegación Municipal on Ocampo and Zaragoza. (Open daily 8am-3pm.) **Pharmacy: Boticas Ceseña,** Madero 24A, parallel to and east of Juárez and Hidalgo. (☎154 00 76. Open daily 8am-2pm and 3-11pm. Available 24hr. at ☎154 00 75 in case of emergency.) To reach the **Centro de Salud,** walk down Hidalgo away from the mission and turn right on Cipris, a tiny dirt road; when you reach the auto parts shop, turn right then quickly left, just after the tin-roofed warehouse. Continue straight for two blocks; it's the white building with the white flag on the right side. (Open M-Sa 8am-4pm.) If you have a **medical emergency** after hours, call **Lordes Rouzaud** (☎154 00 81), the local nurse. **LADATEL:** at all four corners of the *zócalo* and in front of Restaurant-Bar Rene's. You can place calls and send **faxes** at a pricier **caseta,** Hidalgo 24. (☎154 02 50. Open M-Sa 8am-1pm and 3-6pm.) **Post office:** in the grey stone building on Juárez next to the *zócalo*. (Open M-F 8am-3pm.) **Postal code:** 23930.

ACCOMMODATIONS. San Ignacio has few hotels, and they don't come cheap. Make reservations or call early if you're going to be in town during *Semana Santa* or the week-long celebration of El Día de San Ignacio (July 30). The family living in **Restaurant Chalita,** Hidalgo 9, rents rooms with fans and black and white TVs. (☎154 00 82. Singles 150 pesos.) **Hotel Posada,** on Ocampo and Independencia, a 3-minute walk down Ciprés from Hidalgo, has remarkably clean rooms with standing fans, private baths, and a family atmosphere. (☎ 154 03 13. Singles and doubles US$20.) **El Padrino RV Park** is 500m from the *zócalo* on the road connecting San Ignacio to the highway. In addition to RV space, it offers four new rooms with private baths and A/C. (☎ 154 00 89. Singles 120 pesos; doubles 200 pesos. Full trailer hookup 100 pesos, without electricity 80 pesos. Motorcycles 36 pesos to park.)

⬛ **FOOD.** There aren't many places to dine in San Ignacio, but not to worry; all of the restaurants are within a stone's throw of the *zócalo*, and serve delectable and affordable cuisine. Seafood receives top billing on most menus. Eat under the starry sky at **Restaurant-Bar Rene's,** just outside the *zócalo*, off Hidalgo. If you'd rather have a roof, head into their round stone-floored thatched hut, complete with ceiling fan and 80s tunes. Wash down the house special, the *calamar empanizado* (breaded squid, 50 pesos), with a beer (10 pesos). Delicious *filete pescado* 50 pesos. (Open daily 7am-10pm.) **Restaurant Chalita,** Hidalgo 9, is housed in an old-fashioned Mexican kitchen. Listen to caged birds sing, and find salvation in a warm garlicky plate of *pescado al mojo de ajo* (40 pesos) or enchiladas (30 pesos). *Chiles rellenos* 35 pesos. (☎ 154 00 82. Open daily 7:30am-10pm.) **Flojo's Restaurant/Bar** is part of El Padrino RV Park and is a 5-minute walk from town. You'll be full for days after eating three chicken burritos, rice, and beans (35 pesos). Breaded Italian meat 55 pesos. (☎ 154 00 89. Open daily 7am-9 or 10pm.)

🎭🎪 **SIGHTS AND FESTIVALS.** The area's main tourist draw is the **painted caves,** 75km away in the Sierra de San Francisco mountains. Five hundred paintings, probably more than 10,000 years old, are contained within a 12 sq. km area. Anthropologists are unsure of who painted these paintings or why. Oscar Fischer of Hotel Posada and his son Dagoberto lead tours to the caves in addition to the impressive **La Pintada** and the minor **El Ratón** caves (☎ 154 03 13 or 154 01 00. US$25-80 per person.). Some adventurous travelers hike between caves on foot (about 8km each way), saving mule costs. All trips must be cleared with the government, so call in advance. Painted caves and whale watching expeditions leaving San Ignacio are also led by the owner of **Flojos Restaurant/Bar** and **El Padrino RV Park** (☎ 154 00 89), and by **Malarrimo** (☎ 157 01 00) of Guerrero Negro (see p. 163).

A colonial colossus towering over wild, leafy vegetation, the **Mission of San Ignacio,** on the north side of the *zócalo*, was founded in 1728 by Jesuit missionary Juan Bautista Luyando. The construction of the mission proved a logistical nightmare; wood had to be hauled from the Guadalupe mission in the Sierras, furniture brought from Mulegé on a scorching four-day mule ride through the unpaved desert, and paintings carried by boat from the mainland. Its walls, over a meter thick, are made from blocks of volcanic rock. The mission is a beautiful achievement—magnificent on the outside, cool on the inside, and heavenly at night when illuminated by spotlights. The newly opened **Mission Museum,** on Luyando, 30m west of the mission, tells the story of the nearby cave paintings, and even has its own huge faux cave painting. (☎ 154 02 22. Open Tu-Sa 8am-3pm. Free.)

For a little fun, hit week-long celebration of **El Día de San Ignacio** (July 30). The town blossoms into a giant *fiesta* with horse races, dances, and fireworks.

SANTA ROSALÍA ☎ 1

Santa Rosalía is not just a transportation hub, but heir to a colorful history. After rich copper ore was discovered here in 1868, a French mining company settled the area, building the town on the sides of the mountain according to rank: the wealthier, higher-ranking officials lived at the top and the poorer classes below. They even brought with them their own church, the Iglesia Santa Bárbara, designed by Gustave Eiffel (of Eiffel Tower fame). Though Santa Rosalía is guarded by heaps of abandoned machinery and railroad cars bristling with rust, the city's tree-lined streets and warm, breezy porches make it a decent stopover. If you're planning to visit, however, keep in mind that the town can get nearly unbearably hot in the summer, and that heavenly Bahía de la Concepción is only a short drive south.

▐ TRANSPORTATION. Most **buses** depart from the ABC station (☎152 01 50), across the street from the ferry office. Buses travel north (6 per day, 3pm-5am) to: **San Ignacio** (1hr., 35 pesos); **Guerrero Negro** (3½hr., 105 pesos); **El Rosario** (9hr., 255 pesos); **San Quintín** (9½hr., 290 pesos); **Ensenada** (13½hr., 385 pesos); **Tijuana** (15hr., 455 pesos); and **Mexicali** (18½hr., 575 pesos). Heading south (6 per day 9:30am-midnight), all buses go to: **Mulegé** (1hr., 35 pesos); **Loreto** (3hr., 95 pesos); **Ciudad Constitución** (4½hr., 170 pesos); and **La Paz** (8hr., 260 pesos).

From Santa Rosalía, you can catch the **ferry** connecting Baja California to **Guaymas** on the mainland (8hr.; Tu and Th 9am; *salón* 140 pesos, *turista* 278 pesos, *cabina* 415 pesos, *especial* 552 pesos). The boat leaves from the blue and green **Sematur** office on Rte. 1, just south of town. Those with cars must purchase tickets in advance and show a tourist card, registration, and proof of their Mexican insurance. (☎152 00 13 or 152 00 14. Cars 1578 pesos; motorcycles 398 pesos. Office open M, W, F, Sa 8am-3pm; Tu, Th 8am-1pm and 3-6pm.) Departure days and times, prices, and office hours are constantly in flux, so be sure to call the office to confirm the schedule. To get from the ferry or bus station to downtown Santa Rosalía, turn right as you leave the ferry compound (left from the bus station) and walk along the water until you come to the old train engine in front of the town's two main streets—the one on the left is Constitución, and the one on the right is Obregón.

▐ PRACTICAL INFORMATION. Banamex, on Obregón and Calle 5, changes traveler's checks and has a 24hr. **ATM.** (☎152 09 84. Open M-F 9am-4pm.) **Farmacia Central,** on Obregón at Plaza, is owned by the English-speaking Dr. Chang Tam (☎152 20 70. Open M-Sa 9am-10pm, Su 9am-1pm). **Centro de Salud:** (☎152 21 80) at Costeau next to the museum. **Red Cross:** on Calle 2 and Carranza, right off Constitución. Nelson Romero speaks English. (☎152 06 40. Open 24hr.) **Internet access** is still becoming widespread in Santa Rosalía. In the interim, visit Calle 8 #41, where Olivia Camul will let you use her private long-distance connection for the cost of the call. She is often out of town; call ahead. (☎152 13 99. 6 pesos per min. Open daily 9am-2pm.) **Post office:** on Constitución, between Calle 2 and Altamirano. (☎152 03 44. Open M-F 8am-3pm.) **Postal code:** 23920.

▐ ACCOMMODATIONS AND FOOD. If you're going to stay in sweltering Santa Rosalía, consider forking over the few extra pesos for A/C. The budget standout is **Hotel Olvera,** Calle Plaza 14, about three blocks from shore on Constitución, just right of the foot bridge. Enjoy spacious bathrooms, large double beds, free lukewarm *agua purificada*, and a breezy porch. (☎152 00 57 or 152 02 67. Singles 130 pesos, with A/C 150 pesos; doubles 180 pesos, with A/C 220 pesos.) **RV Park Las Palmas,** 3.5km south of town, has 32 spots with full hookups, laundry, and a restaurant. (2 people US$10; US$2 per additional person.) Constitución is lined with cheap and good *taquerías* and *comida corrida* joints. Renowned for its French architecture, Santa Rosalía's best-known eatery, **El Boleo Bakery,** on Obregón at Calle 4, has excellent baked goods: fabulous French bread 1.6 pesos, *pan dulce* 1.8 pesos, turnovers 2.6 pesos. (☎152 03 10. Open M-Sa 8am-9pm.)

▐ SIGHTS. The wooden houses, general stores, and saloons in Santa Rosalía recall the town's mining-boom days. Startling specimens of 19th century French architecture include the long and many-windowed **Palacio Municipal,** the **Hotel Francés,** and **El Boleo Bakery,** with pure colors, simple forms, and modern use of glass and steel. The most intriguing is the pre-fabricated, white, cast-iron **Iglesia Santa Bárbara,** at Obregón and Calle 1. Designed by Gustave Eiffel for a mission in Africa, the church was never picked up by the company that had commissioned it. French mining moguls spotted the church at the 1889 Exhibition Universale de Paris and decided Santa Rosalía couldn't do without it. Observers either love it or hate it; the outside panels look like they might have fallen off an industrial washing machine. For a great view of Santa Rosalía, climb the decrepit stone steps just off the beginning of Obregón. The steps lead to the new **Museo Histórico Minero de**

Santa Rosalía. The museum, housed in an old office building of the French miners, exhibits journals, photographs, and mining equipment. (Open M-F 9am-3pm. 10 pesos, children 5 pesos.)

MULEGÉ   ☎ 1

Although many are inclined to keep driving when they reach Mulegé, a small cluster of shops, homes, and restaurants dominated by desert, palm trees, and a winding river, the town has more to offer than meets the eye. Mulegé is one of Baja California's best-kept secrets, bursting with good food and warmhearted people. Best of all, 136km north of Loreto and 300km south of Guerrero Negro, it is the ideal place from which to explore the glistening beaches and storybook-blue sea of **Bahía de la Concepción** (see p. 171). By day, most of the town's visitors—and many of its expats—abandon Mulegé proper and head for the Bahía.

⊏ TRANSPORTATION. The **"Igriega"** bus station is a sheltered blue bench at the turn-off to Mulegé from Rte. 1. All buses are *de paso*, a phrase that might roughly be translated as "arriving late and full." Tickets and bus info are available at the restaurant overlooking the bench. Northbound buses stop daily at 4 and 10:30pm, and head to: **Mexicali** (19½hr., 610 pesos) via **Santa Rosalía** (1hr., 35 pesos), **San Ignacio** (2hr., 85 pesos), **El Rosario** (10hr., 305 pesos), **San Quintín** (10½hr., 340 pesos), **Lázaro Cárdenas** (11hr., 340 pesos), **Ensenada** (14½hr., 435 pesos), **Tijuana** (16hr., 505 pesos), and **Tecate** (17hr., 530 pesos). Southbound buses stop daily at 10, 11:30am, 8:30, and 10pm, and go to: **La Paz** (6hr., 225 pesos) via **Loreto** (2hr., 60 pesos), **Insurgentes** (3hr., 120 pesos), and **Ciudad Constitución** (3½hr., 135 pesos).

▐ ▐ ORIENTATION AND PRACTICAL INFORMATION. Soon after bearing left off the Transpeninsular Highway, the road into Mulegé forks. To the left is **Moctezuma;** to the right is **Martínez.** Both are soon crossed by **Zaragoza.** Take a right onto Zaragoza to get to the *zócalo*, which is one block away. **Madero** heads east from the *zócalo* (away from the highway) and, after following the Mulegé River for about 3km, hits the water of the town beach, **Playa de Mulegé.**

El Candil restaurant serves as the unofficial **tourist office.** There is a helpful photo album/scrap book/self-promotion brochure left downstairs, compiled by Kerry "El Vikingo" Otterstrom. Look for him there after 2:30pm, or ask someone at the restaurant to point out his house. If a red flag is flying or colored lights are ablaze, you can grab a few beers and head on up for a Mulegé history tutorial. The **Hotel Las Casitas,** Madero 50 (☎ 153 00 19), also has tourist info. Ask for Javier; besides leading tours, he has info on beaches, camping, and fishing. You can pick up a sketch **map** of the town from **Cortez Explorers** (☎/fax 153 05 00) on Moctezuma. **Police:** (☎ 153 00 49) in the old Pinatel de Educación building on Martínez, next to the PEMEX station. **Red Cross:** (☎ 153 01 10) on Madero, 20m past the turn-off into town on the Rte. 1. **Farmacia Moderna:** at Madero on the plaza. (☎ 153 00 42. Open daily 8am-1pm and 4-10pm; in the summer open 9am-2pm and 5-11pm.) **Centro de Salud B (ISSTE),** Madero 28. (☎ 153 02 98. open 8am-2:30pm.) **Minisúper Padilla** (☎ 153 01 99; fax 153 01 90), on Zaragoza at Martínez, one block north of plaza, has many **phones** for international calls and now offers **fax** service. **Post office:** in the same building as the police. (☎ 153 02 05. Open M-F 8am-3pm.) **Postal code:** 23900.

▐ ACCOMMODATIONS. Although Mulegé has plenty of cheap rooms, those with sleeping bags will find the best deals on the sand. The most economical hotels crowd the center of town. **Casa de Huéspedes Manuelita,** on Moctezuma, next to Los Equipales, around the corner from Zaragoza, has clean rooms with soft beds, table fans, and private showers. Campers can use bathroom and shower for 15 pesos. (☎ 153 01 75. Singles 80 pesos; doubles 120 pesos; all prices negotiable.) The brand new **Hotel Mulegé** is right near the bus station, on your left heading into town. Live in luxury—all of the big, white-tiled rooms with spotless baths come with TVs and remote controls. Plans for a pool and bar/restaurant are in the works. (☎ 153 00 90. Singles 252 pesos; doubles 280 pesos.) **Orchard RV Park** and **María Isabel RV Park,** both on the Mulegé River, are just south of town and accessible from Rte. 1. (US$16 per night; tents US$5; each additional person US$1.50.)

◘ **FOOD.** For something informal and delicious, **Taquería Doney,** known more commonly as Doney's, is near the bus station, across the street from Hotel Mulegé. Locals cram both indoor tables and outdoor stools, wolfing down delicious tacos (7 pesos). Steak *tortas* 18 pesos. (Open W-M 8am-10pm.) The local hangout **La Almeja** is at the end of Madero near the lighthouse, about 3km from the *centro*. Right on the beach, the restaurant offers a great view and outstanding seafood: filling *sopa de siete mares* (soup of the 7 seas) 75 pesos. (Open daily 8:30am-11pm). Newly renovated **El Candil,** on Zaragoza near Martínez, north of the plaza, serves an enormous Mexican combination platter with rice, beans, *chiles rellenos*, and tacos (60 pesos); excellent fish fillet 35 pesos. (Open daily 7am-10pm.)

🏛 **SIGHTS.** Mulegé's lovely 18th-century **Misión Santa Rosalía de Mulegé** sits on a hill to the west of town. To get there, walk down Zaragoza away from the *zócalo*, go under the bridge, and turn right on the shaded lane with the palms. Not as impressive as the Mission of San Ignacio, the church's massive stone facade is nonetheless imposing and its interior beautiful and quiet. The small hill behind the mission affords a great view of town, river, and palms.

The **Museo Comunitario Mulegé** is housed in the town's old prison, once known as the "prison without doors." To get to the museum, walk down Moctezuma away from the highway until you reach a steep set of stairs on your left. The building was a prison from 1907 to 1975 and, each day, the inmates were allowed to leave their cells to work in town on the condition that they would return at the end of the work day. The exhibit includes artifacts of the indigenous Cohimi people, and displays of local marine life. (Open M-Sa 9am-3pm. 10 pesos.)

Several hundreds of 14,000-year-old Pre-Hispanic cave paintings are located at **La Trinidad** and the **Cuevas de San Borjita.** Salvador Castro of Castro Tours at Hotel Las Casitas leads hiking tours to La Trinidad that include a 200m swim in a narrow canyon to San Borjita. (☎ 153 02 32. US$55 per person.) If you plan to bring a camera you must have a permit issued at the INAH office; Salvador will direct you.

◪ **BEACHES.** Although they are a convenient 3km from the center of town, Mulegé's beaches can't hold a candle to those 18km south in Bahía de la Concepción (see p. 171). **El Faro** is at the end of Madero, which becomes a dirt road long before you reach the beach. Reach the **public beach** by following the Mulegé River to the Sea of Cortés, where it drains. For more isolation, walk to the PEMEX station about 4km south on the highway, continue 20m south, and take the dirt road leading left until you reach a lonely beach with slightly rocky sand. Locals say the area is quite safe, but watch out for jellyfish, especially in June and July.

Mulegé's abundance of sea life makes for good sport-fishing and clamming. Alejandro Bukobek leads tours for both. He can usually be found at the **Hotel Serenidad,** on the Mulegé River. (☎ 153 03 11 or 153 01 11. Fishing US$100 for 3-4 people; kayak trips US$40 per person.) If you want to swim with the fishies, head to **Cortez Explorers,** Moctezuma 75A, just past the entrance to town. This newly opened dive shop is the only one in Mulegé. They rent snorkel and scuba equipment, lead boat excursions into Bahía de la Concepción, and rent mountain bikes (US$15 per day, US$10 per day for 4 days; US$20 per day with snorkel equipment). Make reservations at least one day in advance. (☎/fax 153 05 00. Open M-Sa 10am-1pm and 4-7pm.) The best snorkeling is at nearby **Islas Pitahaya, San Ramón, Liebre, Blanca, Coyote,** and **Guapa.** Ask at the tourist office or dive shop for maps.

BAHÍA DE LA CONCEPCIÓN

Heaven on earth may just be the 48km arc of rocky outcrops, shimmering beaches, and bright-blue sea known as the Bahía de la Concepción. Cactus-studded hills and stark cliffs drop straight down to white sand and translucent waters, creating the most breathtaking beaches in Baja California. Sport-fishers and shell collectors weep for joy at the variety and sheer size of the specimens caught here, and divers fall under the spell of underwater sights. As if this isn't enough, the Bahía is generally blissfully noiseless, with the only serious tourist traffic being during Christmas holidays and *Semana Santa*.

⬚ TRANSPORTATION

To get there from Mulegé (or from anywhere north of Mulegé), check at the bus station for the next *de paso* bus south (10:30, 11am 8:30, and 10pm). Wait to pay the fare until the bus arrives; check with the bus driver to ensure that he will stop at one of the beaches. Don't count on a bus to take you back, however; service to the beaches is infrequent, and bus drivers may not stop along the busy highway. Beach-hoppers might consider renting a car for the day, as access to and from the beaches farther south is limited. Many nomadic travelers hitch (known in Spanglish as *"pedir* ride") from Mulegé to the beaches, catching one of the RVs or produce trucks barreling down the Transpeninsular Highway toward the bay. While *Let's Go* does not recommend hitching, those who do hitch are most successful getting rides right across the island from the bus stop, and telling the driver exactly where they are heading. Hitching back to Mulegé is reputedly even easier, since many people go in that direction.

⬚ BEACHES

Illuminated by millions of stars, the beaches of Bahía are otherworldly after dark. Come at night only if you plan to camp out or are equipped with wheels; it's impossible to hitch back, no buses run, and oncoming cars spell disaster for would-be pedestrians.

PLAYA PUNTA ARENA. Punta Arena is far enough from the road that the roar of the waves drowns out the noise from muffler-less trucks. The waters near the shore are great for **clam fishing,** but beware of the manta rays that lurk under the water's surface. A dozen or so *palapas* line the beach with sand-flush toilets in back. If you walk down the dirt road to Playa Punta Arena, take a left instead of a right at the second fork, and you'll end up at **Playa San Pedro** and **Los Naranjos RV Park,** where payments for your space may be made with freshly caught fish. *(The beach is 16km from Mulegé. From the highway, travel 2km down a rocky dirt road. Bear right at all forks in the road.)*

PLAYA SANTISPAC. During the winter, Santispac is the liveliest beach on the bay, and in the summer, the sands are populated by laid-back sunbathers. Watch out in the water—there are mating sting rays in the spring and manta rays in the summer. In case of a sting, locals recommend treating the affected area with hot, salty water. Such a treatment can be found in the warm, bubbly (though somewhat dirty) **hot springs** on the south end of Playa Santispac. Services on the beach include *posadas*, restaurants, kayak rentals. *(The beach is connected to Playa Punta Arena by a grueling 1km dirt path that winds through the mountains. The beach is most easily accessible by the highway (about 20km south of Mulegé), where it is visible and clearly marked.)*

PLAYA LA POSADA. La Posada, the next accessible beach south of Santispac, looks essentially like a minuscule RV village, complete with its own tennis court. **Eco-Mundo** (☎ 153 04 09), on the south side of the beach, can be reached from the highway a few hundred meters beyond the entrance for La Posada and rents *palapas*, hammocks, kayaks, and snorkeling equipment. It also runs a *palapa*-type restaurant that serves vegetarian food.

PLAYA ESCONDIDA. True to its name, "Hidden Beach," the short, facility-less beach is refreshingly secluded from civilization, affording great views and stunning shoreline reef snorkeling. There is a good snorkeling island about a 30min. swim away. **Playa Los Cocos** is identified by white garbage cans adorned with palm trees. Access to the beaches is free, but use of the facilities is not. A grove of trees and shrubs separates the strip from the highway. At **Playa El Burro,** you can rent a *palapa* next to hordes of RVs. *(At the end of a 500m dirt path winding through the valley between two hills; look for a white sign with black letters at the southern end of Playa Concepción. Palapas rental US$5 per day.)*

PLAYA EL COYOTE. Coyote is perhaps the most populated beach after Santispac. Shelter and camping space can be rented for reasonable, negotiable prices; the better sands and *palapas* are down on the southern end. Down the road 15km is the exquisite (and even less populated) **Playa Resquesón** and its neighbor to the south, **La Perlita,** which also has a few *palapas* (US$4 per night). Park your car and rent a *palapa* (US$4), or just park and enjoy the beach (US$3). While there, check out the natural rock formations on the mountain to the southwest that were outlined by students from the University of Tijuana. A nearly deserted stretch of sand separating Mulegé from Loreto is the last beach before Rte. 1 climbs into the mountains. All of these beaches are marked from the highway.

LORETO ☎ 1

Founded by Jesuit missionaries in 1697, Loreto (pop. 12,000) was the first capital of the Californias and the first in a chain of Jesuit missions along the west coast of Baja California. The Jesuits were no dummies: they sandwiched their capital between the calm blue waters of the Sea of Cortés and golden mountains. It's hard to believe this town would be abandoned for any reason, but after a freakish combination of hurricanes and earthquakes in the 1800s, Loreto stood empty for almost a century. Today, thanks to cobblestone streets, well-tended public gardens, and a tranquil palm-shaded *malecón* (boardwalk), the compact city center is doubtlessly the most beautiful in Baja California Sur.

▮ TRANSPORTATION

Aguila buses stop by **Terminal E,** on Salvatierra two blocks west of Allende near the highway, about 1km from Madero. (☎ 135 07 67. Ticket office open daily 7am-11pm.) To get to the *centro* from the **bus station,** walk down Salvatierra toward the *zócalo* (15min.) or indulge in a taxi (30 pesos). Northbound buses (1am, 3, and 9pm) go to: **San Ignacio** (5hr., 140 pesos) and **Guerrero Negro** (7½hr., 210 pesos); also at 2 and 5pm to **Mulegé** (2½hr., 60 pesos) and **Santa Rosalía** (4hr., 105 pesos). Southbound buses go to: **La Paz** (5hr., 5 per day, 165 pesos).

▤▮ ORIENTATION AND PRACTICAL INFORMATION

Loreto is easy to navigate. Almost everything of interest is on the main road, **Salvatierra,** which connects the Carretera Transpeninsular to the Gulf. Allende, León, and Ayuntamiento run roughly north-south and cross Salvatierra on the way toward the sea. About 1km from the highway and bus station Salvatierra becomes a pedestrian walkway. **Hidalgo** branches off Salvatierra and curves to parallel it to the south. **Juárez** parallels Salvatierra to the north. **Independencia** crosses Salvatierra at Hidalgo, and **Madero** crosses both, closer to the water. The *malecón* outlines the coast, running the width of the city. The *zócalo* is at Salvatierra and Madero, just past the mission and its plaza.

The Palacio Municipal, on Madero, between Salvatierra and Comercio, facing the *zócalo*, holds the helpful **tourist info center.** English spoken. (☎ 135 04 11. Open M-F 8am- 3pm.) The only bank in town, **Bancomer,** on Madero across from the *zócalo*, exchanges dollars and boasts a new 24hr. **ATM.** (☎ 135 03 15 or 135 00 14. Open M-F 9:00-3:30pm.) **Car Rental: Budget** rents cars for US$55 per day. (☎ 135 10 90. Open M-Sa 8am-1pm and 3-6pm, Su 8am-1pm.) **Supermarket: El Pescador,** on Salvatierra and Independencia. (☎ 135 00 60. Open daily 7:30am-10:30pm.) **Red Cross:** on Salvatierra at Deportiva. (☎ 135 11 11; in case of emergency ☎ 135 00 35. Open daily 10am-noon and 3-8pm.) **Pharmacy: Farmacia Flores,** on Salvatierra, between Ayuntamiento and Independencia. (☎ 135 03 21. Open 24hr.) **Hospital: Centro de Salud** on Salvatierra, one block from the bus terminal. (☎ 135 00 39. Open 24hr. for visits, not phone calls.) **Fax: Telecomm,** next to the post office (☎ 135 03 87. Open M-F 8am-2pm, Sa 8-11am.) **Internet access: The Internet C@fé,** on Madero by the *zócalo.* (☎ 135 00 84. 30 pesos per 30min. Open M-F 9am-noon and 4-7pm, Sa 10am-1:30pm.) **Post office:** on Salvatierra and Deportiva, near the bus station, behind the Red Cross. (☎ 135 06 47. Open M-F 8am-3pm.) **Postal code:** 23880.

■ ACCOMMODATIONS

Loreto has good but not great budget accommodations, of which these are four.

Motel Salvatierra (☎ 135 00 21), on Salvatierra, across from the PEMEX and close to the bus station. Small, yellow rooms with loud but mercifully effective A/C. The busy road out front can be noisy in the morning. Singles 200 pesos; doubles 220 pesos.

Motel Davis, on Davis, about four blocks north of the *zócalo* with a hand-painted sign in front. The cheapest rooms in town, if you can tolerate the muddy yard and run-down rooms. Simple, very small rooms with tiny baths and fans. 100 pesos.

Hotel Posada San Martín (☎ 135 07 92), on Juárez one block north of the *zócalo.* Rooms in the new building are immaculate, and better furnished than those in the older building. Singles 150-250 pesos; doubles 200-300 pesos; extra person 50 pesos.

El Moro RV Park, Robles 8 (☎/fax 135 05 42), a couple of blocks inland off Salvatierra. If no one is there, you can park on the honor system and leave your payment under the door. Office open daily 7am-midnight. Trailer US$10; camping US$4 per person.

◖ FOOD

Decent, cheap meals are served on Salvatierra, and a number of restaurants cluster conveniently near the bus terminal, offering good prices.

Café Olé, Madero 14 (☎ 135 04 96), just off the *zócalo* across from Bancomer. Tourists and locals chatter over burritos (36 pesos), fish with fries and *frijoles* (48 pesos), and omelettes with *chilaquiles* (30 pesos). Open M-Sa 7am-10pm, Su 7am-2pm.

Mexico Lindo, on Hidalgo just past the intersection with Salvatierra. The relaxed atmosphere invites laughter, and even the smiling English-speaking waiters will joke with you and let you practice your Spanish. Ample portions and all entrees come with salad. Almost all dishes are 50 pesos, like the mountain of fajita fixin's, or *pollo pipian* (chicken in a sauce of crushed seeds and nuts). Open daily 1:30pm-1am.

Restaurant-Bar La Palapa (☎ 135 11 01), on Hidalgo between Madero and Mateos. A popular spot with enormous portions of excellent food, including free platters of chips, guacamole, and 4 salsas. Massive combination plate 78 pesos. Open M-Sa 1-10pm.

◖ SIGHTS

With shaded benches along the water, Loreto's *malecón* is a popular place for an evening stroll. The **public beach,** a few blocks north of Hidalgo, is coarse and crowded on weekends. Still, the yellow and black fish that swim nearly to shore provide hours of amusement. **Nopoló,** 7km to the south, has better beaches and excellent snorkeling. The Mexican tourist promotion board originally wanted to make this little port a mega-resort like Los Cabos, but lost interest. Now, a couple of lonely hotels tower over white sand beaches and crystal clear water.

BAJA CALIFORNIA

Three desert islands and a few rocky points jut from the water like sentinels guarding the port of Loreto. **Isla Carmen,** the largest island in the Sea of Cortés, has an eerie ghost town and abandoned salt mines—they are all that remain of human presence. Several animal and plant species are unique to the island, including a rattle-less rattlesnake and a type of barrel cactus that can grow to 4m tall and 1½m across. Wide, sandy beaches and herds of sea lions await on nearby **Isla Coronado.**

Las Parras Tours, 16 Madero, take small groups on a boat trip around the island. (☎135 10 10; fax 135 09 00; www.tourbaja.com. 5hr. US$35 per person; min. 2 persons. Las Parras also organizes diving trips (US$70) and land excursions. If you're angling for a fresh seafood meal, rent a fishing boat and a guide.) **Arturo's Sports Fishing Fleet,** on Hidalgo half a block from the beach, offers snorkeling trips to Isla Coronado. (☎135 07 66. 5hr. US$40 per person; min. 2 people.) **Alfredo's** (☎135 01 32), on the *malecón* near the pier, has similar rates. Both rent fishing equipment if you prefer to go it alone (US$5 per day). Sizable red snapper and grouper hide among the large rocks at the end on the left side of the pier.

The **Museo de las Misiones,** one block west of the plaza, is built into the monastic complex reconstructed in the 1940s. Sculptures and paintings accompany displays on Jesuit mission life. English and Spanish panels tell about the history of the area. The museum also provides information on missions throughout Baja. (☎135 04 41. Open Tu-Su 9am-1pm and 1:45-6pm. 22 pesos.) The **Misión de Nuestra Señora de Loreto,** as the plaque above the door proclaims, is the mother of all California missions. The church was consecrated in 1697 as a small tent, made permanent in 1699, and enlarged to its present form by 1752. It mirrors the simple lines and plain walls of early Renaissance churches, with semicircular stone arches in perfect proportion to the height of the whitewashed nave. The earthquakes that prompted abandonment of the town did surprisingly little damage to the church.

CIUDAD CONSTITUCIÓN ☎1

The wide, practically desolate streets of this relatively large transportation hub hold little of interest for the average tourist. Several inexpensive hotels here can prove convenient for visitors to the nearby ports of San Carlos and López Mateos in whale watching season. If you're heading south, the banks here are the last you'll see before La Paz, and they've also got the last gas before El Cien. Autotransportes Águila goes to **Puerto San Carlos** (1hr., 11am and 5:30pm, 35 pesos); **La Paz** (3hr., every hr. 5am-11pm, 105 pesos); **Loreto** (2hr., every hr., 75 pesos); **Tijuana** (20hr., 4 buses noon-midnight, 685 pesos), and points in between. From the bus station on Suárez, walk two blocks to the corner of Olachea, the main street, to the **Farmacia San Martín.** On the door is a list of nearby pharmacies open on any given night. (☎132 14 28. Open daily 8am-10pm.) Turn right down Olachea to reach three nearby **supermarkets.** There's a **Banamex** with a 24hr. **ATM** a few blocks farther on, just before the road to **Puerto San Carlos.** On Olachea two blocks before the bank is the olive-colored **Hotel Conchita.** Rooms vary in size, and are furnished simply and practically, with TV. (Singles 120 pesos, with A/C 150 pesos; doubles 170 pesos, with A/C 200.) Next door, **Super Cocina Lupita** (☎132 36 96) serves cheap breakfasts and lunches, cafeteria-style. On the next corner, at Olachea and Hidalgo, is **Ricos Tacos,** a decent 24-hour taco stand (everything 7 pesos).

 JUST SAY NO At the 11km marker just north of Ciudad Insurgentes, the Mexican military maintains a semi-permanent contraband checkpoint where all automobiles must stop for a search for illegal arms and drugs. The check will go faster if you are not carrying sealed boxes, tied bags, or locked chests (or contraband drugs and weapons). Keep everything available for quick inspection, and they may just wave you through with a cursory glance. Then again, they may thump your automobile ceiling, probe your upholstery, and pick apart the fibers of your floor mats. Buses are not spared this treatment. **Let's Go does not recommend smuggling contraband** (but if you do, find another route north).

WORLDWIDE CALLING MADE EASY

The MCI WorldCom Card, designed specifically to keep you in touch with the people that matter the most to you.

MCI WORLDCOM   WORLDPHONE.

1·800·888·8000

J. L. SMITH

www.wcom.com/worldphone

Please tear off this card and keep it in your wallet as a reference guide for convenient U.S. and worldwide calling with the MCI WorldCom Card.

HOW TO MAKE CALLS USING YOUR MCI WORLDCOM CARD

> **When calling from the U.S., Puerto Rico, the U.S. Virgin Islands or Canada** to virtually anywhere in the world:
1. Dial 1-800-888-8000
2. Enter your card number + PIN, listen for the dial tone
3. Dial the number you are calling :
   Domestic Calls: Area Code + Phone number
   International Calls:
   011+ Country Code + City Code + Phone Number

> **When calling from outside the U.S.,** use WorldPhone from over 125 countries and places worldwide:
1. Dial the WorldPhone toll-free access number of the country you are calling from.
2. Follow the voice instructions or hold for a WorldPhone operator to complete the call.

> **For calls from your hotel:**
1. Obtain an outside line.
2. Follow the instructions above on how to place a call.
   Note: If your hotel blocks the use of your MCI WorldCom Card, you may have to use an alternative location to place your call.

RECEIVING INTERNATIONAL COLLECT CALLS*
Have family and friends call you collect at home using WorldPhone Service and pay the same low rate as if you called them.
1. Provide them with the WorldPhone access number for the country they are calling from (In the U.S., 1-800-888-8000; for international access numbers see reverse side).
2. Have them dial that access number, wait for an operator, and ask to call you collect at your home number.

* For U.S. based customers only.

START USING YOUR MCI WORLDCOM CARD TODAY. MCI WORLDCOM STEPSAVERS℠
Get the same low rate per country as on calls from home, when you:
1. **Receive international collect calls to your home** using WorldPhone access numbers
2. **Make international calls with your MCI WorldCom Card** from the U.S.*
3. **Call back to anywhere in the U.S. from Abroad** using your MCI WorldCom Card and WorldPhone access numbers.

* An additional charge applies to calls from U.S. pay phones.

WorldPhone Overseas Laptop Connection Tips —
Visit our website, www.wcom.com/worldphone, to learn how to access the Internet and email via your laptop when traveling abroad using the MCI WorldCom Card and WorldPhone access numbers.

Travelers Assist® — When you are overseas, get emergency interpretation assistance and local medical, legal, and entertainment referrals. Simply dial the country's toll-free access number.

Planning a Trip?—Call the WorldPhone customer service hotline at 1-800-736-1828 for new and updated country access availability or visit our website:

www.wcom.com/worldphone

MCI WorldCom Worldphone Access Numbers

Easy Worldwide Calling

MCI WORLDCOM.

The MCI WorldCom Card.

The easy way to call when traveling worldwide.

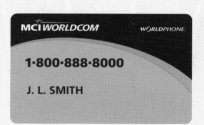

MCI WORLDCOM   *WORLDPHONE*

1·800·888·8000

J. L. SMITH

The MCI WorldCom Card gives you...

- Access to the US and other countries worldwide.
- Customer Service 24 hours a day
- Operators who speak your language
- Great MCI WorldCom rates and no sign-up fees

For more information or to apply for a Card call:

1-800-955-0925

Outside the U.S., call MCI WorldCom collect (reverse charge) at:

1-712-943-6839

COUNTRY — WORLDPHONE TOLL-FREE ACCESS #		COUNTRY — ACCESS #		COUNTRY — ACCESS #		COUNTRY — WORLDPHONE TOLL-FREE ACCESS #	
Argentina (CC)		Ecuador (CC) +	999-170	Korea (CC)		Singapore (CC)	8000-112-112
Using Telefonica	0800-222-6249	El Salvador (CC)	800-1767	To call using KT	00729-14	Slovak Republic (CC)	08000-00112
Using Telecom	0800-555-1002	Finland (CC) ♦	08001-102-80	Using DACOM	00309-12	South Africa (CC)	0800-99-0011
Australia (CC) ♦		France (CC) ♦	0-800-99-0019	Phone Booths +		Spain (CC)	900-99-0014
Using OPTUS	1-800-551-111	French Guiana (CC)	0-800-99-0019	Press red button ,03,then*		St. Lucia +	1-800-888-8000
Using TELSTRA	1-800-881-100	Germany (CC)	0800-888-8000	Military Bases	550-2255	Sweden (CC) ♦	020-795-922
Austria (CC) ♦	0800-200-235	Greece (CC) ♦	00-800-1211	Luxembourg (CC)	8002-0112	Switzerland (CC) ♦	0800-89-0222
Bahamas (CC) +	1-800-888-8000	Guam (CC)	1-800-888-8000	Malaysia (CC) ♦	1-800-80-0012	Taiwan (CC) ♦	0080-13-4567
Belgium (CC) ♦	0800-10012	Guatemala (CC) ♦	99-99-189	Mexico (CC)	01-800-021-8000	Thailand (CC)	001-999-1-2001
Bermuda (CC) +	1-800-888-8000	Haiti +		Monaco (CC) ♦	800-90-019	Turkey (CC) ♦	00-8001-1177
Bolivia (CC) ♦	0-800-2222	Collect Access	193	Netherlands (CC) ♦	0800-022-91-22	United Kingdom (CC)	
Brazil (CC)	000-8012	Collect access in Creole	190	New Zealand (CC)	000-912	Using BT	0800-89-0222
British Virgin Islands +	1-800-888-8000	Honduras +	8000-122	Nicaragua (CC)	166	Using C&W	0500-89-0222
Canada (CC)	1-800-888-8000	Hong Kong (CC)	800-96-1121	Norway (CC) ♦	800-19912	Venezuela (CC) + ♦	800-1114-0
Cayman Islands +	1-800-888-8000	Hungary (CC) ♦	06*-800-01411	Panama	00800-001-0108	Vietnam + ●	1201-1022
Chile (CC)		India (CC)	000-127	Philippines (CC) ♦		**KEY**	
Using CTC	800-207-300	Collect access	000-126	Using PLDT	105-14	**Note:** Automation available from most locations. Countries where automation is not yet available are shown in *Italic*	
Using ENTEL	800-360-180	Ireland (CC)	1-800-55-1001	Filipino speaking operator	105-15		
China ♦	108-12	Israel (CC)	1-800-920-2727	Using Bayantel	1237-14	(CC) Country-to-country calling available.	
Mandarin Speaking Operator	108-17	Italy (CC) ♦	172-1022	Using Bayantel (Filipino)	1237-77	+ Collect calling available.	
Colombia (CC) ♦	980-9-16-0001	Jamaica +		Using ETPI (English)	1066-14	★ Not available from public pay phones.	
Collect Access in Spanish	980-9-16-1111	Collect Access	1-800-888-8000	Poland (CC) ♦	800-111-21-22	♦ Public phones may require deposit of coin or phone card for dial tone.	
Costa Rica ♦	0800-012-2222	From pay phones	#2	Portugal (CC) ♦	800-800-123		
Czech Republic (CC) ♦	00-42-000112	Japan (CC) ♦		Romania (CC) ♦	01-800-1800	● Local service fee in U.S. currency required to complete call.	
Denmark (CC) ♦	8001-0022	Using KDD	00539-121 ▶	Russia (CC) + ♦		▶ Regulation does not permit Intra-Japan Calls.	
Dominica+	1-800-888-8000	Using IDC	0066-55-121	Russian speaking operator		* Wait for second dial tone.	
Dominican Republic (CC) +		Using JT	0044-11-121		747-3320	■ Local surcharge may apply.	
Collect Access	1-800-888-8000			Using Rostelcom	747-3322		
Collect Access in Spanish	1121			Using Sovintel	960-2222	**Hint:** For Puerto Rico and Caribbean Islands not listed above, you can use 1-800-888-8000 as the WorldPhone access number.	
				Saudi Arabia (CC)	1-800-11		

PUERTO SAN CARLOS ☎ 1

Every year at whale watching time, tiny Puerto San Carlos (pop. 4500) undergoes a magical transformation. Beginning in November, hotels dust off their bedposts, tent encampments blossom, and local pilots commandeer every available fishing boat to transport tourists to see the estimated 18,000 grey whales that migrate from the Bering Sea through the Pacific to Bahías Magdalena and Almejas. During peak mating season (mid-Jan. to mid-Mar.), the lovestruck creatures wow crowds with aquatic acrobatics. When they leave in April, the town once again becomes a sleepy village of boarded-up restaurants and vacant sand roads.

■ **TRANSPORTATION.** To get to San Carlos, take a bus from **La Paz** (4hr., 8am and 2:30pm, 125 pesos) or, if coming from the north, transfer at **Ciudad Constitución** (1hr., 11am and 5:30pm, 35 pesos). Don't fret if the bus drops you off in what seems like the middle of nowhere—you're actually in the middle of town. **Autotransportes Águila** buses leave from the small white terminal on La Paz and Morelos and head to: **Constitución** (1hr., 7:30am and 1:45pm, 35 pesos); **La Paz** (4hr., 7:30am and 1:45pm, 125 pesos); and **Cabo San Lucas** (7hr., 1:45pm, 250 pesos).

■■ **ORIENTATION AND PRACTICAL INFORMATION.** In Puerto San Carlos, almost all services are along the main street, **La Paz,** or near the docks on the bay. All streets here are sand, and marked by illegibly bleached street signs. Most streets don't have names. The new, well-marked **tourist office** near the docks is open August through April. If you come during low season, ask the ebullient owner of the **Hotel Alcatraz** for information; her patience and friendliness make up for her limited English. The **post office** is on La Paz near the park in the center. (Open M-F 9am-3pm.) Be forewarned: San Carlos has **no banks, ATMs, casas de cambios, or credit card connections.** Everything here works in cash. The nearest bank is in Ciudad Constitución (see p. 174).

■■ **ACCOMMODATIONS AND FOOD.** Finding budget rooms in San Carlos isn't easy. This town has only 100 simple rooms among its few hotels, and come whale-watching season they are at a premium. The best deal in town is the **Motel Las Brisas.** To get there from the bus station, take a right onto La Paz, then make a right and a quick left on Madero; the hotel will be on your left. Clean, yellow rooms with large fans surround an echoing courtyard. (☎ 136 01 52 or 136 01 59. Singles and doubles 135 pesos.) Off-season discounts up to 50% can get you good rooms at the **Hotel Alcatraz,** on La Paz. (☎ 136 00 17; fax 136 00 86. Singles and doubles 216 pesos, suites with kitchen 360 pesos.) **Nancy's RV park** very near the port (☎ 136 01 95) offers full hookups for 100 pesos. Camping on the barrier islands is free, but they are only accessible by renting a boat and pilot.

Dining in San Carlos is homey—literally. A string of restaurant/living rooms along La Paz and Morelos allow you to meet locals while you enjoy remarkably fresh delicacies from the sea. **El Patio Restaurant-Bar,** in the Hotel Alcatraz on La Paz, welcomes you into a pleasant, open courtyard. Enjoy a fresh fish filet *a mojo de ajo* (70 pesos) or a *bistec ranchero* (50 pesos). (☎ 136 00 17; fax 136 00 86. Open daily 7am-10pm.) **Lonchería La Pasadita,** on La Paz near the post office, is the town favorite for inexpensive meals. Platters of *machaca* (grilled shredded beef with peppers and onions) or *pollo con mole* run 25 pesos. (Open daily 8am-10pm.)

■■ **SIGHTS AND BEACHES.** Both **Bahía Magdalena** and **Bahía Almeja** lie just south of Puerto San Carlos and are home to some of the best whale watching in the world. grey whales migrate south from feeding grounds in Alaska just to visit Baja California every winter. The warm, shallow waters of the Bahía Magdalena make it one of the most important calving areas, and hundreds of whales stop over here in November and December for this purpose. Fertile soon after calving, the whales spend their days from January to March mating in the bay.

Lying at the intersection of temperate and tropical currents, the Bahía Magdalena is rich in both temperate and tropical species of fish, shellfish, and birds, making it a worthwhile visit even in the summer months. The **barrier islands**

HAVING A WHALE OF A TIME! In 1970 the grey whale, long preyed upon by Pacific coast whalers, was thought to be extinct. Today, with a total population of around 18,000, the species has become a poster child for the effectiveness of wildlife preservation laws. Their breeding grounds along the coast of Baja California Sur are among the most important protected coastlines in North America. The entire world population of grey whales gives birth and mates in three sections of Baja California's coast: the lagoons of Ojo de Liebre, the lagoons of San Ignacio, and Bahía Magdalena. The whales are generally friendly, curious, and playful, and some may approach your boat and let you touch them. Watch for the following kinds of behavior:

Sounding: Arching the back above water before beginning a deep dive.

Breaching: A whale will jump out of the water, flip over, and enter the water nose-first. They often slap the water with their flukes (tail) on reentry.

Blowing: As a whale exhales, often it will "spit" water droplets into the air.

Eating: Although whales generally fast during the winter months, they have occasionally been observed eating in the bay late in the season. They will scoop up a large mouthful of sediment from the bottom of the bay and, lying on one side, let the mud and water filter through a series of baleen plates which trap small crustaceans and edible particles.

Dozzing: A whale may noisily slap water with a fins while it lies on its side.

Spyhopping: A whale will pop its head out of the water, fix an enormous eye on whatever strikes its fancy, and stare for minutes on end, like a submarine periscope. They often pivot to survey the area before slipping back into the water

appear to be mostly sand and dunes. However, extensive mangroves, intertidal sand and mud flats, and sea grass beds make these ecosystems as biologically diverse as the bay itself. Two colonies of sea lions call the islands home. The **Center for Coastal Studies** outside of town does research on and studies activity in the bay. The cheapest way to explore the islands is to make an ad-hoc deal with one of the fishermen departing from **Playa la Curva** in front of the PEMEX station. Unless you plan to camp on the islands, make pick-up plans before you embark. The tourist office will help you find a secure boat (licensed and insured), or you can rent one directly through the **Hotel Alcatraz**, a member of the local boating consortium. (US$40 per hr. or US$80 per half day for up to six people.)

Feisty Pacific waves at **Cabo San Lázaro** and **Point Hughes,** both on the western tip of **Isla Magdalena**, will keep even veteran surfers on their toes. A surf encampment here (☎ 136 00 04 for information) operates July through December. Reed huts scattered along the beach offer protection from the oppressive midday sun. Fifteen species of clam and starfish inhabit the waters of these immaculate beaches. An large colony of *lobos marinos* (sea lions) lives near the island's southern tip.

LA PAZ   ☎ 1

John Steinbeck's novel *The Pearl* depicted La Paz as a tiny, unworldly treasure chest. Not long ago it was indeed a precious fishing village, frequently harassed by pirates for the iridescent white spheres concealed in the oysters off its coast. The town's pearl industry was wiped out in the 1940s when the oysters got sick and died, and the tiny capital of Baja California Sur was forced to depend on fish and tourists to pay the rent. Contemporary La Paz (pop. 250,000) is part port, part party-town, and part peaceful paradise. Ten tranquil beaches hug the bathwater-warm **Bahía de La Paz.** The row of nightclubs along the beach may now make La Paz (The Peace) feel sheepish about its name, but pelicans still skip along its lamp-lit water, its fishermen are still friendly, and a merciful breeze still ruffles the hair of couples strolling along its serene boardwalk at sunset.

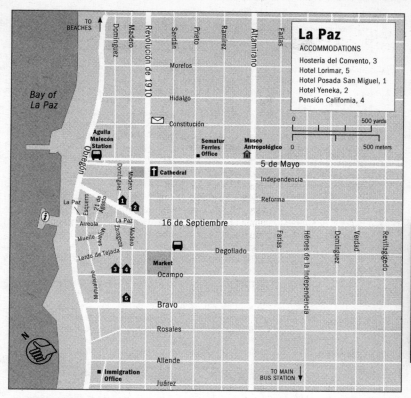

La Paz

ACCOMMODATIONS

Hostería del Convento, 3
Hotel Lorimar, 5
Hotel Posada San Miguel, 1
Hotel Yeneka, 2
Pensión California, 4

BAJA CALIFORNIA

TRANSPORTATION

As the largest city and capital of Baja California Sur, La Paz is the region's main transportation hub. All those going to the ends of the Peninsula will most likely trek through here. In addition, it's possible to reach the Mexican mainland via the ferry connecting La Paz to Mazatlán and Los Mochis.

GETTING AROUND

The **municipal bus system** in La Paz serves the city irregularly (every 15-30min. 6am-10pm, 3 pesos). Flag down buses anywhere, or wait by the stop on Revolución and Degollado, next to the market. From the main bus station, try to convince your driver to drop you in the *centro*. Within the city center, you need not worry about buses; it's easily navigable on foot.

GETTING AWAY

Airport: West of La Paz, easily accessible by taxi (120 pesos). **Hotel Miramar,** on 5 de Mayo, runs shuttles between the airport and any hotel. (☎122 16 07 ext. 35. 120 pesos for up to 7 people.) The airport is served by **Aeroméxico,** at Obregón between Hidalgo and Morelos (☎124 63 53; open M-F 7am-6pm, Sa 7am-3pm) and **Aerocalifornia,** between Ocampo and Bravo (☎124 62 88; open daily 8am-1pm and 4-8pm).

Buses: La Paz has 3 bus stations.

Main station: on Jalisco and Independencia, about 25 blocks southeast of downtown (open for tickets daily 6am-9:30pm). 2 municipal buses, "Central Camionera" and "Urbano," head to the terminal; catch them near the public market at Degollado and Revolución. Taxis 30 pesos. Águila

Autotransportes (☎ 122 30 63, ext. 113) serves points north (9, 10am, noon, 1:30, 6, and 9pm): **Ciudad Constitución** (3hr., 105 pesos), **Loreto** (5hr., 165 pesos), and **Mulegé** (7hr., 225 pesos). The 9am, noon, and 9pm buses continue to **Santa Rosalía** (8hr., 260 pesos); **San Ignacio** (10hr., 295 pesos); **Ensenada** (18hr., 655 pesos). Via Corta buses to **Tijuana** (22hr., 10am, 4, 8, and 10pm, 725 pesos). Nearly direct buses head to **Puerto San Carlos** (4hr., 8am and 2:30pm, 125 pesos) with a stop at **Ciudad Constitución.**

La Paz Autotransportes: (☎ 122 21 57), on Degollado at Prieto, sends buses south. Buses run to: **Todos Santos** (1½hr., 8 per day 6:45am-7:45pm, 33 pesos) continuing to **Cabo San Lucas** (2½hr., 78 pesos).

Águila Malecón: (☎ 122 78 98), on Independencia at Obregón, runs south along the East Cape (8, 10am, noon, 2:30, 4:30, and 6:30pm) to **Los Barriles** (2hr., 55 pesos), **Santiago** (2½hr., 65 pesos), and **San José del Cabo** (3hr., 100 pesos); and to **Cabo San Lucas** (2½hr., 8 per day 9:30-7:30pm, 85 pesos). The same station has buses to nearby beaches: **Playas El Carmancito, El Coromuel, Palmira, Tesoro,** and **Pichilingue** (every hr., 7-15 pesos), and to **Playas Balandras** and **Tecolote** (45min., noon and 2pm, 20 pesos). The last bus back to La Paz leaves Tecolote 5:30pm and Pichilingue 7pm; be sure to confirm schedules with the driver before you get off the bus (it's a long walk).

Ferries: Ferries leave from the suburb of **Pichilingue** to the mainland. **Autotransportes Aguila** buses run between the dock and the downtown terminal on Obregón, between Independencia and 5 de Mayo (M-F 9:30am, every hr. 11:30am-5:30pm, 15 pesos). If you arrive at 9:30am, hurry to catch the bus to the *centro;* otherwise you'll have to wait for two hours. Taxis from the dock to downtown cost 100 pesos. Buy ferry tickets at the **Sematur Company** office, on 5 de Mayo at Prieto. (☎ 125 88 99 or toll-free 01 800 696 96 00. Open daily 8am-4pm, Sa-Su 8am-4pm. Dock office open daily 8am-10pm.) Ferries go to **Mazatlán** (15hr., 3pm, 270-1080 pesos, cars 2700 pesos, motorcycles 550 pesos) and **Topolobampo,** a suburb of Los Mochis (9hr., 10pm, 200-800 pesos, cars 1650 pesos, motorcycles 400 pesos). To get a vehicle on the ferry, you will need proof of Mexican insurance (or a major credit card with the car owner's name on it), car registration showing it is registered to the driver, permission for the importation of a car into Mexico, and a tourist card. Not only that, but **three photocopies** of each. You can get a permit at **Banjército,** at the ferry stop in Pichilingue (☎ 122 11 16. Permits US$16.50. Open daily 9am-2pm), or through **AAA** in the US. Regardless of whether or not you have a car, you will need to obtain a **tourist card (FMT)** if you entered Mexico via Baja California and are bound for the mainland (see p. 178). Clear all of the paperwork before purchasing the ticket; otherwise, Sematur will deny you a spot whether or not you hold reservations.

> **TICKET TO RIDE.** Getting a ferry ticket isn't as easy as it seems—it requires persistence and determination. To secure a ticket, make reservations days in advance. Get to the Sematur office first thing when arriving into town, preferably right after it opens. Get the ticket in hand as soon as possible. During holidays, competition for tickets is fierce. *Clase salón* (third class) class is cheapest, but usually the most in demand. In addition, Semantur has acquired a reputation for raising prices without prior announcement.

⚡ PRACTICAL INFORMATION

TOURIST, FINANCIAL, AND LOCAL SERVICES

Tourist Office: (☎ 122 59 39), Obregón at 16 de Septiembre, in a pavilion on the water. Excellent maps and information. Helpful English-speaking staff. Weekends and evenings staffed by the tourist police. Open M-F 8am-10pm, Sa-Su noon-10pm.

Tourist Police: Fabulous folks easily recognized by their starched white uniforms and big grins. Their job is "protection and orientation," but they will also give recommendations for hiking, beaches, hotels, restaurants, and barbers.

Immigration Office: Servicios Migratorios, Obregón 2140 (☎ 125 34 93; fax 2 04 29), between Juárez and Allende. You must stop here to obtain a tourist card if you entered Mexico via Baja California and are bound for the mainland. Open M-F 9am-6pm. After hours, head to the airport outpost outside of town (☎ 124 63 49). Open daily 7am-11pm.

Currency Exchange: Banks line 16 de Septiembre within a few blocks of the bay. **Bancomer** (☎ 125 42 48), on 16 de Septiembre, half a block from the waterfront, is open for exchange M-F 8:30am-4pm. **BITAL,** (☎ 122 22 89) 5 de Mayo, at Madero, has talking doors. Open for exchange M-F 8am-3pm. Both banks have 24hr. **ATMs.**

American Express: (☎ 122 86 66) 5 de Mayo at Domínguez. Open daily 8am-8pm.

Laundry: at Mutualismo 260 (☎ 123 40 37 or 122 31 12), on Ocampo a block down from Mijares. 20 pesos; full service 36 pesos. Open daily 8am-midnight.

EMERGENCY AND COMMUNICATIONS

Emergency: ☎ 060 or 080.

Police: (☎ 122 13 99) on Colima at México. Open 24hr.

Red Cross: Reforma 1091 (☎ 122 12 22), between Católica and Ortega. Open 24hr.

Pharmacy: Farmacia Bravo (☎ 122 69 33), next to the hospital. Open 24hr. In the *centro,* one of the pharmacies on Plaza Constitución is always open.

Hospital: Salvatierra (☎ 122 14 96 or 122 14 97), on Bravo at Verdad, between Domínguez and the Oncological Institute.

Fax: TELECOM (☎ 125 90 71; fax 125 08 09), upstairs from the post office. Open M-Sa 8am- 7:30pm, Su 8-11:30am.

Internet: Baja Net Café Internet, Madero 430 (☎ 125 93 80), between Hidalgo and Constitución. Cheap coffee (5 pesos) and A/C (0 pesos). 1 peso per minute, 10min. minimum. Open M-Sa 8am-8pm.

Post Office: (☎ 122 03 88 or 125 23 58) on Revolución at Constitución. Open M-F 8am-3pm, Sa 9am-1pm. **Postal Code:** 23000.

◤ ACCOMMODATIONS

Many economical lodgings populate in the downtown area. Most are simple, nonsense rooms for travelers waiting for a ferry.

Hotel Yeneka, Madero 1520 (☎ 125 46 88), between 16 de Septiembre and Independencia. Legendary among backpackers. A Model-T Ford, pet hawk, and stuffed monkey are among the objects suspended from the ceiling. Very firm beds. Laundry, fax, bike rentals, and a restaurant. Singles 178 pesos; doubles 232 pesos; triples 296 pesos.

Pensión California Casa de Huéspedes, Degollado 209 (☎ 122 28 96; fax 123 35 25), at Madero. Windowless small rooms come with concrete furniture and have air vents and effective ceiling fans. Singles 100 pesos; doubles 140 pesos; triples 180 pesos.

Hostería del Convento (☎ 122 35 08), around the corner from the Pensión, same ownership. Almost identical, but somewhat more run-down (and consequently cheaper). Singles 90 pesos; doubles 130 pesos; triples 160 pesos; quads 190 pesos.

Hotel Posada San Miguel, Domínguez 1510 (☎ 125 88 88), off 16 de Septiembre. Photographs, painted tiles, and wrought-iron scrollwork recall La Paz's early days. Too bad the charm hasn't seeped into the spartan rooms. Fans and large, comfortable beds. Singles 110 pesos; doubles 130 pesos; triples 150 pesos; quads 170 pesos.

Hotel Lorimar (☎/fax 125 38 22), on Bravo between Madero and Mutualismo. Half of this family-run hotel has been renovated. The newer rooms are freshly painted, with new baths. Old singles 200 pesos; old doubles 250 pesos. New singles and doubles 360 pesos; new triples 415 pesos. 50 pesos per extra person.

◖ FOOD

On the waterfront you'll find decor, menus, and prices geared toward peso-spewing tourists. Move inland a few blocks and watch the prices plunge, as sit-down restaurants disappear amid the abundant *taquerías.* Seafood meals are generally fresh and the *tacos de pescado* very good (and cheap). Grab fruits, veggies, and fresh fish at the **public market,** Degollado and Revolución. La Paz loves its ice cream and *paletas;* Revolución alone has five **La Michoacana** ice cream shops.

Restaurante El Quinto Sol (☎ 122 16 92), on Domínguez at Independencia. One of the few vegetarian joints in Baja California, the menu includes sausage à la soybean and an assortment of juices. Generous *comida corrida* 50 pesos. Luscious yogurt smoothie 15 pesos. Also serves as a whole-foods store. Open M-Sa 7am-9pm, Su 8am-3pm.

Restaurant Palapa Adriana (☎ 122 83 29), on the beach off Obregón at Constitución. Practically in the water. Red snapper 60 pesos. *Pollo con mole* 40 pesos. Great view, with complimentary sea breeze and lollipop. Open daily 10am-10pm.

Café El Callejón, on de La Paz just off Obregón. Be serenaded by folk musicians as you enjoy the breeze off the sea and munch on traditional Mexican dishes. Generous *antojitos* 21-38 pesos. *Camarones al gusto* 85 pesos. Open Tu-Su 8am-midnight.

El Cortajo, on Revolución off 16 de Septiembre. Portraits of Emiliano Zapata stare down from the walls of what may be the most reasonably priced restaurant in the *centro*. Filling *comida corrida,* including soup and your choice of the day's specials 32 pesos. Big breakfasts 30 pesos. Open Tu-Su 8am-10pm.

🗺 SIGHTS

The **Museo Regional de Antropología e Historia,** at 5 de Mayo and Altamirano, has fascinating exhibits on the Pre-Hispanic history of the southern peninsula. Unfortunately, all the descriptions are entirely in Spanish. An English-speaking guide is sporadically available; ask at the desk. (☎ 122 01 62; fax 125 64 24. Open M-F 8am-6pm, Sa 9am-2pm. Free.) Fans of handicrafts will appreciate the **pottery factory,** Iglesias between Revolución and Serdán, and the **weaver** at Abasolo between Jalisco and Michoacán who works in traditional *hilo de palma* (palm thread). Artisans in both studios will gladly show you around, though their English is limited (both open M-Sa approx. 9am-noon and 4-8pm).

🏖 BEACHES

The beaches of La Paz snuggle into small coves, sandwiched between cactus-studded hills and calm, transparent water. This is prime windsurfing territory. Be careful—lifeguards make appearances only on weekends and at popular beaches.

NEAR PLAYA TECOLOTE. The beachlets scattered along La Paz's *malecón* are not particularly clean and usually crowded with children. The farther outside of town, the better the beaches. The best and most popular is **Playa Tecolote** (Owl Beach), 25km northeast of town. A quiet extension of the Sea of Cortés laps against this gorgeous stretch of gleaming white sand near tall mountains. Though there are no bathrooms, Tecolote is terrific for **camping.** Spots on the east side of the beach, along the road to the more secluded and gorgeous **Playa El Coyote,** come equipped with a stone barbecue pit. The road to El Coyote itself is impassable with a small car. **Actividades Aquatica** (☎ 122 16 07), on Tecolote, organized through Hotel Miramar, rents snorkeling gear (80 pesos per day) and organizes trips to **Isla Espíritu Santo** (300 pesos per person, min. 4 people). The snorkeling off **Playa Balandra,** a cove just south of Tecolote, is excellent. Because facilities are sparse and sporadically open, it is best to rent equipment either in the city or at nearby Pichilingue or Tecolote. *(Take an Autotransportes Águila bus (45min., noon and 2pm, 20 pesos; return bus at 5:30pm only) from the mini-station on Obregón and Independencia.)*

NEAR PLAYA PICHILINGUE. Beaches near Playa Pichilingue are out of walking distance from the city center, though only a short ride away. Take the "Pinchilingue" bus up the coast and decide where you want to get off. From the last stop at the ferry dock, an additional ½km walk leads to **Playa de Pichilingue,** a favorite among teens, who splash in the shallow waters and ride paddleboats (30 pesos per hr.). The view from Pichilingue, however, is corrupted by ferry docks. The first decent beach along the bus route is **Playa El Coromuel,** near La Concha Hotel. **Playa del Tesoro,** a little past Coromuel, is cleaner. Most of the beaches between La Paz and Tecolote have *palapa* shelters and some kind of food and drink available. *(Take the "Pichilingue" bus up the coast (up to 30min., every hr., 7-15 pesos). You'll see the beaches from the bus before you reach them, so if you like what you see, let the driver know.)*

DIVING AND SNORKELING. The fun doesn't stop at the shoreline—magnificent offshore opportunities await snorkelers and certified divers. North of La Paz is **Salvatierra Wreck,** a dive spot where a 91m ferry boat sank in 1976. The wreck is now decked with sponges and sea fans. Also popular is the huge **Cerralvo Island,** east of La Paz, which promises reefs, large fish, and untouched wilderness. **Isla Espíritu Santo** has hidden caves, pristine beaches, good diving reefs, and excellent snorkeling; the shallow reef at **Bahía San Gabriel** here is appropriate for both snorkeling and diving. Due to strong currents, fluctuating weather conditions, and inaccessibility, diving in the La Paz area requires guides. **Baja Diving and Service,** Obregón 1665, between 16 de Septiembre and Callejón La Paz, organizes daily scuba and snorkeling trips to nearby reefs, wrecks, and islands. (☎ 122 18 26; fax 122 86 44. Trips leave at 7:45am. Scuba trips US$77 per day without equipment, US$15 extra for equipment; snorkeling trips US$45 per person per day. Open daily 9am-1pm and 4-8pm.) For excellent snorkeling easily accessible by car, head to **San Juan de la Costa** just past Centenario, 13km north of La Paz on the Transpeninsular. Just past Centenario on the same road is the beachcomber's paradise of **El Comitán,** with sand and mud flats where, particularly after a storm, the tides carry shells, amethyst, and other semiprecious stones.

 NIGHTLIFE

For a small city, La Paz has a lot to offer weekend nightowls. The first sign of nightlife you'll likely see is the garish La Paz-Lapa. Don't let this scare you off. Remember one rule: head for the water. The *malecón* becomes an intense cruise scene, and around midnight the masses crowd into the many waterside clubs. Guys, let her get this one—women are often charged less for drinks.

Las Varitas (☎ 125 20 25), Independencia and Domínguez. A large stage dominates one side of the club, where live bands play, and a young crowd packs multi-level platforms. A dance floor in the middle never seems to have enough room; dancers gradually take over tabletops. Lively and fun, even on weeknights. Open Tu-Su 10pm-3am.

Chaplin's (☎ 122 69 99), Obregón and de León. A very friendly gay/lesbian/straight/ whatever bar, with occasional drag shows. A remarkably mixed crowd mingles on the small dance floor or lounges in comfortable chairs drinking and chatting. W ladies' night, Th salsa and merengue. Cover F-Sa after 11pm, 50 pesos. Open Tu-Su 9pm-3am.

Carlos 'n' Charlie's/La Paz-Lapa (☎ 122 92 90), Obregón and 16 de Septiembre, is the most central and noticeable structure in town. Savor huge margaritas (34 pesos), or go buck-wild at the outdoor booze and rockfest. US and Mexican teens get down to Aerosmith amid giant palm trees. Tu ladies' night before midnight (free drinks and no cover). F open bar before midnight, cover 110 pesos for men, 50 pesos for women. Standard cover 30 pesos. Restaurant open daily; club open Tu and F-Sa 10:30pm-late.

Bling Bling, Arreola 270C (☎ 122 35 26), a block from the water. A lot of glow-in-the-dark trees and monkeys. The vast floor leaves plenty of elbow room to dance to house, disco, and early 80s favorites. Th ladies' night, complete with male dancers 9-11pm. W and Sa open bar 9pm-2am, cover 110 pesos for men and 50 pesos for women. Other nights no cover. Open Tu-Sa 9pm-4am.

Antro (☎ 122 39 21), at Obregón and Ocampo. A new, hi-tech disco with dim interior and TVs above the bar. The boxing-ring dance floor has rails to keep dancers from falling. W cover men 100 pesos, women 50 pesos, includes open bar 9-11pm. F ladies' night. Open M-Sa 9pm-5am.

Paradise Found (☎ 125 73 40), Obregón and Allende. Inexpensive drinks draw crowds for Happy Hour 3-9pm. Quieter later in the evening, though the seashore view and free pool table are decent incentives to stay. Happy Hour beer (8 pesos) and margaritas (11 pesos); prices double past 9pm. Open M-Sa 11am late.

TODOS SANTOS   ☎ 1

Halfway between La Paz and Cabo San Lucas, Todos Santos remains one of the few serene and sophisticated small towns on the southern Baja California coast that is both accessible by bus and so far unmutilated by resort development. John Steinbeck used to hang his hat here, and the town has become known in recent years for the community of English-speaking expats who have fallen in love with the town's rolling cactus hills, killer surf, dusty roads, and laid-back demeanor. This small, highly artistic community makes its presence known. Gourmet shops, classy restaurants, and art galleries now inhabit the brick-chimneyed buildings that are the only remnants of the town's sugarcane-processing past. Developers have had their eye on Todos Santos for several years, but—fortunately for budget travelers—she has resisted. For now, expats and locals seem to coexist in harmony; the result is a hospitable and lively village where contemporary art and a respect for the natural environment reign in harmony.

◤ TRANSPORTATION

The **bus stop** (☎ 145 01 70) is in front of Pilar's taco stand, on the corner of Zaragoza and Colegio Militar. If you have any questions about bus times or anything else, Pilar is an excellent person to talk to. *De paso* buses run north to **La Paz** (1hr., every hr. 7am-8pm, 55 pesos) and south to **Cabo San Lucas** (1hr., every hr. 8am-10pm, 40 pesos) and **San José del Cabo** (1½hr., 56 pesos). The bus may drop you off near Degollado and Militar, where the Transpeninsular Highway turns to head toward Los Cabos from La Paz.

◆◪ ORIENTATION AND PRACTICAL INFORMATION

Todos Santos is built on an expanding grid, with only a few paved roads in the *centro* and services scattered throughout residential and commercial blocks. The two main streets, running parallel and north-south, are **Militar** and, to the west, **Juárez**. Activity centers on the area between **Legaspi**, Militar, **Zaragoza**, and **Topete**; León crosses Legaspi and Centenario at the cathedral and main plaza. If this is confusing, grab the monthly *Calendario de Todos Santos*, which has a small map in the center.

Todos Santos has no tourist office, but the American-owned **El Tecolote Libros**, on Juárez and Hidalgo, sells English-language magazines, maps, and a comprehensive book on the town. (100 pesos. ☎ 145 02 95; fax 145 02 88. Open July-Oct. M-F 9am-5pm, Sa 10am-4pm; Nov.-June daily 9am-5pm.) **BanCrecer**, on the corner of Obregón and Juárez, the only bank in town, exchanges currency and has a 24hr. **ATM.** (Open M-F 9am-1pm.) **Market: Mercado Guluarte,** on Morelos between Militar and Juárez. (☎ 145 00 06. Open M-Sa 7:30am-9pm, Su 7:30am- 2pm.) Get fruit at the small markets on Degollado and Juárez. **Police:** in the Delegación Municipal complex at the plaza. **Pharmacy: Farmacia de Todos Santos,** on Juárez near León. (☎ 146 04 09. Open 24hr; knock at night.) **Hospital:** on Juárez at Degollado. (☎ 145 00 95. Open 24hr.) **Internet Access:** the **Internet Café** across the street from the Message Center. (15 pesos per 10min., 50 pesos per hr. Open M-Sa 9am-5pm.) **Post office:** on Militar at León. (☎ 145 03 30. Open M-F 8am-3pm.) **Postal code:** 23300.

◤ ACCOMMODATIONS AND CAMPING

The best budget options in Todos Santos are undoubtedly the campgrounds. If you have the equipment, Todos Santos has plenty of gorgeous beaches, rolling hills, and pot-smoking, Kerouac-reading, boogie-boarding bodies. There is one inexpensive rooming option, the centrally located **Motel Guluarte**, on Juárez at Morelos.

Clean, cozy rooms have TVs, fans, and refrigerators. The motel also has a pool. (☎ 145 00 06. Singles 150 pesos; doubles 230 pesos.) The five-room **Las Casitas Bed and Breakfast** provides a small space for tents, including bathroom access. (Bungalow rooms singles and doubles US$45-65, including breakfast; camping US$6 for one person, US$10 for two; discount in summer.) The **Way of Nature Bed and Breakfast,** half a mile down the dirt road directly next to Farmacia de Guadalupe, is a cool, breezy, and secluded hotel and campsite. Wake to breakfast, yoga, or tai-chi, head to the beach for body boarding, surfing, or sailing, and end your day with a dip in the pool. The four rooms and shared baths are extremely clean. (☎ 146 57 40. Camping 80-180 pesos; singles 250 pesos; doubles 350 pesos. Breakfast included.)

◖ FOOD

Good budget food isn't hard to find. **Loncherías** line Militar near the bus station, offering tacos for 10-14 pesos. **Pilar's Taco Stand** (☎ 145 03 52), on the corner of Zaragoza and Militar, is not only the town's *de facto* bus station but also a good place to indulge in glorious fish tacos (7 pesos). Because tacos are always tastier on the other side of the street, step across to **The Happy Fish** (tacos also 7 pesos). Locals are understandably addicted to **Barajas Tacos,** an outdoor stand on Degollado and Cuauhtémoc past the PEMEX, with excellent meat tacos (7 pesos; *carnitas* served daily 8am-6pm and *carne asada* 6pm-midnight). The **Caffé Todos Santos,** decorated with local gallery art, serves non-traditional Mexican food with a number of good vegetarian options. Generous *quesadillas* with squash blossoms and mushrooms 60 pesos. Curried *el dorado* (mahi-mahi) in banana leaf 75 pesos. Entrees 50-90 pesos. **Restaurant Santa Monica,** on Degollado and Militar, has been open for 26 years—try their *pescado a la veracruzana* (50 pesos) and you'll know why. Breakfasts 30 pesos. (☎ 145 02 04. Open daily 7am-10pm.)

⊞ ART GALLERIES

Modern art lovers are sure to be wowed by the high quality of galleries in Todos Santos. The town's new pride and joy is the **Todos Santos Gallery,** on Legaspi and Topete, opened in 1995 by artist Michael Cope (☎ 145 05 00. Open June-Sept. M-Sa 11am-4pm; Oct.-May M-Sa 10am-5pm.) The gallery is devoted to artists who reside in Mexico, half of them Mexican and the other half expat. Futuristic bronze and clay sculptures, off-the-wall wall clocks, and ornate mirrors are on parade at the **Santa Fe Art Gallery,** Centario 4, between Hidalgo and Márquez de León. (Open W-M 10am-5pm.) **Casa Franco Gallery,** on Juárez at Morelos, has furniture and bowls from all over Mexico. (☎/fax 145 03 56. Open M-Sa 9am-5pm.) It's worth peeking into the **Charles Stewart Gallery and Studio,** on Obregón at Centenario, which is both Mr. Stewart's home and studio. (☎ 145 02 65. Usually open 10am-4pm.)

◗ BEACHES

If you overdose on art, don't forget that Todos Santos is surrounded by some of the region's most unspoiled beaches. **La Posa,** only 2km from town, is perfect for a romantic stroll. To get there, go up Juárez and turn left on Topete. Follow the road as it winds across the valley past a white building, and...*voilà!* Unfortunately, vicious undercurrents and powerful waves make this beach unequivocally unsuitable for swimming. To reach **Punta Lobos,** the stomping ground of the local sea lion (and human) population, turn left onto Degollado as you walk away from the town center. Roughly six blocks later, the city limits end. Around km 54, turn right and follow the terrible washboard road until you come to the beach. To catch a spectacular view, turn right 1½km south on the highway at the first possible fork in the road. Follow the main dirt path east for 2½km; the path will bear left past an old fish plant and continue up a hill, with steep drop-offs to the seashore. Most other beaches are accessible via the Transpeninsular Highway, south of town. These sights are isolated, and therefore both attractive and potentially hazardous. Bring a friend and plan to return before nightfall.

The only nearby beaches suitable for swimming are **Playa de las Palmas** and **Playa los Cerritos.** Scuffle your feet when you walk in to show stingrays, which mate near the shore in June, that they're not alone. Los Cerritos, a popular family spot and picnic beach, lies approximately 14km south of Todos Santos. Look for a turn-off on the right side of the Transpeninsular Highway. Head south about 3km past the signs for Gypsy's Bed and Breakfast. The current is tamer here than elsewhere, but the waves are just as big, and there's always some sort of party going on. The Todos Santos Surf Shop on the right side of the beach can give the day's conditions and rent surfboards or a boogie board. To reach **Playa de las Palmas,** travel 5km south from town on the highway, and turn right when you see the white Campo Experimental buildings on the left. Travel another 2½km and you'll be bowled over by palm trees; just past these is the beach. The serene and deserted shore is excellent for swimming and body surfing.

A quiet and lovely surfing beach by the highway is **San Pedrito,** 8km south of town. To get there, just turn off at the sign for San Pedrito RV Park. It's easy to find a sunbathing spot on these bohemian beaches, and nobody cares if you bare all. With big waves and swift currents, however, the beach isn't for swimming.

⚡ DAYTRIPS FROM TODOS SANTOS

SIERRA DE LA LAGUNA

To get to the trailhead, drive south out of Todos Santos. After passing the marker for km 53 and climbing a small hill, you will see the turn-off on the left at the top of the hill. Drive down this dirt road through a fenced-off cattle ranch bearing right at the first unmarked major fork in the road. Follow signs for about 40min. until you reach a locked gate and the end of the road. There is a small dirt lot to park your car.

Sierra de la Laguna, the mountain range that fills the foot of Baja, is visible from virtually all beaches around Los Cabos and Todos Santos. Dark rain clouds hovering above the Sierra rarely make their way to the beaches, but are responsible for some of the most exotic flora and fauna in Baja California. The climate of the mountains is completely different from the surrounding coastal areas and can, in the winter, drop below freezing. **La Laguna,** the Sierra's most popular hiking destination, is a meadow of about 4 sq. km perched at an altitude of 1700m amid the jagged peaks of **Picacho la Laguna** and **Cerro las Casitas.** Once a lake, erosion from excessive rainfall destroyed its edges in the late 19th century, transforming La Laguna into a grassy meadow. The climb to the meadow is a grueling eight hours, with steep inclines toward the top. The climb, however, is rewarding—the mountain range is unspoiled and there are many beautiful vistas and rest-stops along the way, one of which (about 3hr. into the hike) offers a view of the entire width of the peninsula. The trail is well-marked with several campsites along the way.

EAST CAPE

LOS BARRILES   Z1

Aficionados insist that windsurfing at the small town of Los Barriles, where brisk breezes can carry you for several kilometers at a run along the inside of the Bahía de Palmas, is the best in Baja California if not in all Mexico. While a number of new, cutely decorated bungalow houses and "for sale" signs around Los Barriles broadcast the resident *gringo* presence, foreign investment and development stops there: tiny Los Barriles is far more quiet and secluded than Los Cabos, and at least for now, giant resort complexes have thankfully stayed away.

⚡ PRACTICAL INFORMATION. From the highway, the *entrada principal* runs into the center of Los Barriles, where a left turn (at the giant EXIT sign) takes you to **Calle 20 Noviembre,** where most services lie. One block past the turn, on the left, is a small complex with the **police, Red Cross,** and **post office.** (☎ 141 01 00. Police and Red Cross open 24hr. Post office open 9am-3pm.) The town **laundromat** is two blocks farther. (Open M-Sa 8am-2pm.) **Supermarkets: Supermercado Chapitos,** on the *entrada* (Open M-Sa 7:30am-10pm, Su 7:30am-7pm) and **Tío Pablo's Tienda,** at 20 de Noviembre and the *entrada.* (Open daily 7:30am-10pm.)

▐▓ ACCOMMODATIONS AND FOOD. Most of the town's accommodations are all-inclusive resorts, but a few camping services exist. **Martín Verdugo's Beach Resort Motel** (☎ 141 00 54), a block before the laundromat, has full RV hookups (US$13) and tent sites (US$11), including *palapa* shelter, baths, and electricity. Martín also has reasonable game fishing packages. **Little Martín** (no relation) has rooms for rent off the *entrada* just past the little mall. Rooms are basic, with washing machines and kitchenettes. Most have A/C. (☎ 141 01 84 or 141 02 06. 200 pesos; reduced rates for longer stays.) Martín's **Rancho Ángel de la Guardia,** 22km away, has rooms for longer stays in the Sierra de la Laguna mountains. Resorts here all have expensive restaurants, but Tío Pablo's bar and grill is more reasonable. **Taquería de Tío Pablo** serves a variety of tacos (6-7 pesos), ice cream (10 pesos), and good hamburgers. (13 pesos. Open daily 11am-10pm.)

◙ SIGHTS. Baja Dive Adventures and **Mr. Bill's Boardsurfing,** both based at Casa Miramar opposite the PEMEX station on the highway, rent equipment and dispense information. The most popular dive spots in the area are around **Cabo Pulmo** and **Los Frailes,** 8km apart and separated by several secluded beaches and coves. Off Cabo Pulmo, eight fingers of a living coral reef—thought to be 25,000 years old and one of only three in North America—are home to hundreds of species of tropical fish, crustaceans, and other crawly critters.

EL TRIUNFO

Gold and silver on the southern tip of the Baja peninsula were discovered as early as the 18th century and first exploited in El Triunfo in 1748. Thanks to the good works of the El Progreso mining company, by the end of the 19th century the town was the largest in the area (pop. around 14,000); it had paved roads, electric lights, the first telephone line in the region (to La Paz), and the first postal service south of La Paz. El Triunfo is today practically a ghost town, with a handful of local artisans working in shell and stone. The only memory of its past is a 1860 towering chimney. While an engineering marvel of its day, the tower is today as abandoned and unused as the town itself.

SANTIAGO

The town of Santiago (pop. 4500) has the only **zoo** in Baja California. The zoo is small, but presents interesting animals and a collection of labeled cacti. (Open daily 6am-6pm. Free, but donations gladly accepted.) To get there, follow the main road and make a left at the far side of the *zócalo.* Follow this road toward Palomar's restaurant until it ends, turn right, and continue down until the Parque Zoológico appears on the right. If you're without a car, hourly Autotransportes Águila buses from La Paz and San José del Cabo will drop you 2km outside Santiago.

The reason many people come to Santiago is for the nearby **hotsprings** in the town of **Chorro.** The tepid sulphur pools await wearied travelers' aching feet, and in the high season, the springs are diverted into more luxurious artificial tubs. To get to the pools, follow the directions to the zoo and continue on the road past the zoo for 7km until you arrive in the town of **Agua Caliente.** Bear right when you encounter the Casa de Salud and follow this road for 5km until it ends at a dam. The sulfur smell indicates you're there. Depending on the level of recent rainfall, you may have to hike up the stream for about 40 minutes to find larger pools; the tranquility and beauty is well worth the effort.

LOS CABOS

The towns of Cabo San Lucas and San José del Cabo comprise the southwestern part of the Los Cabos district (pop. 100,000), which includes most of Baja California's southern coastline. Outside of Tijuana, Los Cabos (the capes) is the most tourist-oriented area in all of Baja. Million-dollar resorts and golf courses infest the otherwise heavenly natural elements of the peninsular tip—spectacular rock formations, surf

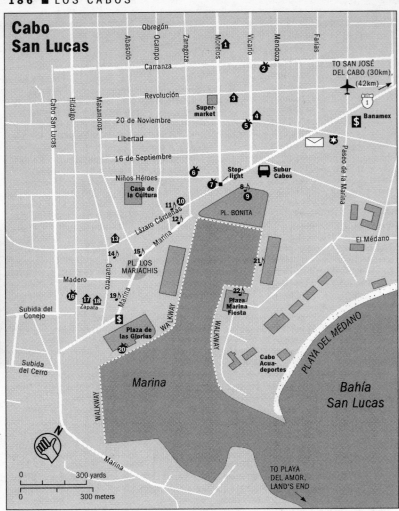

Cabo San Lucas

Cabo San Lucas

ACCOMMODATIONS
Cabo Inn Hotel, 4
Hotel Casa Blanca, 3
Hotel Dos Mares, 17
Hotel El Dorado, 1
Hotel Mar de Cortez, 13
Siesta Suites Hotel, 18

FOOD AND DRINKS
The Crazy Lobster Bar and Grill, 16
El Huarachazo, 2
El Pescador, 6
Mariscos Mocambo, 5
Solomon's Bar and Grill, 20
Stop Light Bar and Grill, 7

♪ **MUSIC AND CLUBS**
Cabo Wabo, 14
Giggling Marlin, 15
Kokomo's, 12
La Concepción, 21
The Rainbow Bar, 22
Rio Grill, 19
Squid Roe, 11
The Wave, 8

● **SERVICES**
American Express, 9
Farmacia Aramburo, 10

that occasionally rivals that of Hawaii, and vast expanses of fine white-sand beaches. Unique underwater sandfalls and rich and varied marine life attract divers and snorkelers. Along the beach leading from San José del Cabo to Cabo San Lucas, luxury hotels form a glittering border between the desert and the ocean. Don't expect wilderness: margarita-guzzling, gift-buying, jet-skiing *norteamericanos* congregate by the thousands in winter to worship Los Cabos' twin deities: Sun and Sea.

CABO SAN LUCAS   ☎1

Cabo San Lucas, known as simply "Cabo," stands at the confluence of the Pacific Ocean and the Sea of Cortés. While whirling eddies have carved unusual shapes out of the rock where they converge, similar undercurrents affect the town itself, as local residents mix with the incoming tides of tourists. Yet while Land's End erodes rapidly, Cabo itself cannot help but grow: its population has doubled to almost 60,000 year-round residents (including some 5,000 expatriates) in the past decade. Suburban colonial haciendas now find themselves in the city center, and the once-tiny marina is a modernized labyrinth of sailboats, million-dollar yachts, glass-bottom tour vessels, and a few decrepit fishing boats. Despite the influx of fast food and neon, Cabo has remained a friendly town highlighted by the fact that every year more and more tourists settle down and become locals themselves. Cabo's tourism means that services in Cabo will run you easily four times what you'd pay on mainland Mexico. Nonetheless, a few days here won't have to break the bank, as it's easy to camp near Cabo, and swimming is free. Even the world-class snorkeling opportunities are not overpriced. So save your money for Cabo's guilty pleasures: fabulous fish tacos, an entertaining and un-self-consciously tacky nightlife, and an endless flow of margaritas beginning at breakfast and lasting until the next day's sunrise.

◰ TRANSPORTATION

Local Subur Cabos buses run along the Los Cabos Corridor to San José del Cabo (30min., every 15min., 15 pesos). ABC Autotransportes and Aguila (☎ 143 04 00) are located out of town to the north, by the Pemex station. To get into town from the ABC/Aguila bus stop, take the local yellow bus (4 pesos) until it hits Blvd. Marina. **Buses** go to **San José del Cabo** (30min., 8 per day every 1-2 hours, 16 pesos); and **La Paz** (3hr., every hr. 6am-7pm, 70 pesos) via **Todos Santos** (1hr., 40 pesos). One *de paso* bus per day leaves at 4:30pm and heads north, stopping at: **La Paz** (3hr., 70 pesos); **Ciudad Constitución** (6hr., 170 pesos); **Loreto** (8½hr., 219 pesos); **Mulegé** (10½hr., 250 pesos); **Santa Rosalía** (11½hr., 315 pesos); **San Ignacio** (12½hr., 340 pesos); **Guerrero Negro** (14½hr., 400 pesos); **San Quintín** (19hr., 554 pesos); **Ensenada** (23hr., 680 pesos); and **Tijuana** (26½hr., 732 pesos).

◈✳◪ ORIENTATION AND PRACTICAL INFORMATION

Restaurants and bars are concentrated on Cárdenas, between Morelos and the western edge of town, and along Blvd. Marina. Plazas are malls or tight conglomerations of shops; their massive concrete structures follow the curve of the marina.

Tourist information: No official tourist office exists, but free, biased information and bad maps are dispensed by time-share hawkers all over the *centro*, from "tourist information" booths. Most car rental agencies have better maps (and often better advice).

Currency Exchange: Many hotels and restaurants actually prefer US dollars, and exchange them at 10 pesos to $1 regardless of the going rate. **BITAL,** in Plaza Bonita (☎ 143 38 88), has a 24hr. **ATM.** Open M-Sa 8am-7pm. Another branch at Plaza de las Glorias has the same hours (and an ATM).

American Express: (☎ 143 57 88) in Plaza Bonita. Open M-F 9am-6pm, Sa 9am-1pm.

Supermarket: Almacenes Grupo Castro, on Morelos and Revolución. Open daily 7am-11pm.

Car Rental: Avis (☎ 143 46 07) at Plaza Los Mariachis, across from Pizza Hut. Tiny Volkswagen with full insurance and unlimited kilometers for US$46 per day. Discounts for multiple days. Open daily 9am-5pm.

Police: (☎ 143 39 77) on Cárdenas, two long blocks north of Morelos.

Ambulance: ☎ 143 40 20.

Pharmacy: Farmacia Aramburo (☎ 143 14 89) on Zaragoza and Cárdenas, at Plaza Aramburo Open 8-11pm. Farther down Cárdenas, across from Hotel Mar de Cortez is a 24hr. pharmacy.

Red Cross: (☎ 143 33 02) at the Delegación Municipal in the outskirts of town toward Todos Santos, 200m from the gas station.

Faxes: Telecomm (☎ 143 19 68; fax 143 02 31) next to the post office. Open M-F 8-7:30pm, Sa 8am-3pm, Su 8am-11am.

Internet access: Francesco's, on the marina at Plaza Bonita, and **Quik** on Blvd. Marina. 25-30 pesos per 15min.

Post office: (☎ 143 00 48) on Cárdenas, next to the police station. Open M-F 9am-4pm, Sa 9am-noon.

Postal code: 23410.

▐ ACCOMMODATIONS

Multi-million-dollar resorts dominate the coast of Cabo San Lucas; as a result, simple, cheap beds are hard to come by. If you decide not to camp out or sleep in San José, you can get by staying in some exceptional mid-range hotels. During the winter high season, make reservations early and be prepared to shell out 25% more pesos than during the slower summer months. Many hotels base rates on US dollars and not pesos (converting 10:1 no matter what the going rate).

Hotel El Dorado (☎ 143 67 37), on Morelos near Carranza. The gigantic tiled rooms are simply furnished, but spotless. A very large swimming pool for grown-ups and a separate little one for the kiddies. Absolutely the best bargain in Cabo. Singles and doubles 275 pesos with TV and fan, 325 pesos with TV and A/C; extra people 50 pesos (up to four). Rates stay the same in high season.

Siesta Suites Hotel (☎ 143 27 73 or (602) 331-1354 in the US; fax 143 64 94; email siesta@cabonet.net.mx), on Zapata near Guerrero. Colorful tiles, bright prints, and painted light fixtures. Most rooms have full kitchens (with utensils) and a separate bedroom off a fully-furnished living/eating area. A/C and satellite TV. Singles US$40; doubles $50. Extra person $10. Rates stay the same in high season.

Hotel Dos Mares (☎ 143 03 30; email hoteldosmares@cabo☎com.mx), on Zapata. Functional yellow rooms come with refrigerator, phone, TV, and A/C. Outdoor swimming pool with slide. Worn and institutional, but one of the better deals around. Singles and doubles 300 pesos, 400 pesos in winter. A few rooms have a fan instead of A/C for 250 pesos, 350 pesos in winter; extra person 50 pesos.

Hotel Mar de Cortez (☎ 143 00 32, or (800) 347-8821 in the US; fax 143 02 32), on Cárdenas, a block from Plaza de los Mariachis. Pseudo-bungalows are clustered pseudo-hacienda-style around a garden, swimming pool, and restaurant. Rooms are decorated pseudo-traditionally, with framed weavings and simple wood furniture. A cheaper version of the giant resorts along the coast, offering in-room physical therapy/massage, A/C, and car, horse, and scuba rentals. Singles and doubles 397 pesos; triples 613 pesos; quads 658 pesos. Rates about 25% higher in fall and winter.

Cabo Inn Hotel (☎/fax 143 08 19; email caboinn@cabo.com.mx), on 20 de Noviembre and Vicario. Run as a brothel for two decades, the old building has two newly-built stories with stained-glass windows overlooking a central courtyard. The upstairs rooms stretch out onto walkways along the courtyard, where small tables and chairs beg you to sit and relax. A tiny pool hides on the sunny roof terrace. Kitchenettes in half of the 20 rooms. All rooms have A/C. Singles or doubles $48. Rates 25% lower July-Aug.

Hotel Casa Blanca (☎ 143 53 60), on Revolución at Morelos. The cheapest place in town. You get what you pay for, and sometimes not even that. Singles and doubles 200-240 pesos. 50 peso towel deposit.

◖ FOOD

You may dream of sitting along the waterfront at a marina-side table and eating a delicious, authentic Mexican meal at authentic Mexican prices. You'll have to keep dreaming. More realistic budget travelers head inland along Morelos or smaller side-streets, or to the abundant *taquerías*.

El Huarachazo, on Carranza near Vicario. No fancy service or fancy atmosphere here, just very good food, cheap. Shockingly large entrees 35-70 pesos. The *combinación mexicana,* a 3-foot platter, is 60 pesos; *enchiladas mole* 35 pesos; *Agua de Jamaica,* all you can drink 8 pesos. Open daily 7am-midnight.

Solomon's Bar and Grill, in Plaza de las Glorias complex, on the marina. What appears to be just another open-air bar in an overpriced resort hides a surprise. Tacos $1 (or 10 pesos), including *de pescado* (fish - whatever is freshest). Will grill up fish you catch for a very small fee. Margaritas 35 pesos. All this, and you can sit in comfortable, covered wicker divans overlooking the marina for no extra charge. Open daily 10am-9:30pm.

The Crazy Lobster Bar and Grill, on Hidalgo near Zapata. Many restaurants advertise inexpensive Mexican breakfasts, but the breakfast here is a bigger bargain than most: *huevos rancheros* or *a la mexicana* US$1; all other breakfast items US$2-3. Lobster is served up in omelettes (US$3) or on a platter (US$10). Open daily 8am-10pm.

Stop Light Bar and Grill (☎ 143 47 40), on Cárdenas at the city's one stoplight. The bright, plaid tablecloths and wooden chairs scream tourist trap, but the food here is both good and reasonable. Traditional *antojitos* and other entrees. *Enchiladas de pollo* 50 pesos; garlic-encrusted mahi-mahi on a bed of salad greens 65 pesos. Open daily 8am-2am.

Mariscos Mocambo (☎ 143 21 22; fax 143 56 50), on Vicario at 20 de Noviembre. No, it's not a bargain eatery, but you won't find better seafood in all Cabo. *Camarones aquachiles* (raw shrimps with *serrano* chile, salsa, and sweet onion) 80 pesos; Mocambo filet (stuffed with shrimp, octopus, and squid) 140 pesos. The restaurant is understandably popular; reserve ahead for large groups. Open daily 11am-11pm.

El Pescador, on Niños Héroes and Zaragoza. This local favorite provides hungry diners with all manner of seafood dishes, from various *sopas* (60 pesos) to large entree platters (90-100 pesos) like luscious imperial shrimp wrapped and cooked in bacon (98 pesos). The service is not elegant, but the food is excellent. Open daily 9am-10pm.

👁 📷 BEACHES

All major daytime activity in Cabo San Lucas involves the pristine waters off the coast. Many head toward the Corridor (see p. 185) linking Cabo San Lucas and San José del Cabo, but there are plenty of beaches right in Cabo. **Playa del Médano,** the best beach for swimming, reaches east from the marina. The waters here are full of parasailers and motorboats full of lobster-red, beer-guzzling vacationers. **Cabo Acuadeportes,** in front of the Hotel Hacienda, rents water equipment (☎ 143 01 17. Open daily 9am-5pm), as does nearby **JT Watersports** (☎ 147 55 43. Snorkeling gear US$10 per day; wave runners US$40 per 30min. Open daily 9am-6pm).

The Arch Rock of Cabo San Lucas, known as **El Arco** or **Land's End,** is only a short boat ride from the marina. Here the light, tranquil Sea of Cortés meets the rough, deep blue Pacific. The rocks around the arch are home to about 40 sea lions who can be seen hanging out or sunning themselves. To get there, walk through the Plaza Las Glorias Hotel or the big Mexican crafts market farther down Blvd. Marina to the docks at the far right of the marina. Eager, English-speaking boat captains will be happy to take you on a glass-bottom boat ride to El Arco and back (45min.; US$8-10; some hotels may offer discounts or free rides).

Boats also stop at **La Playa del Amor** (yes, that's the Beach of Loooove), a good swimming beach near El Arco. You can get out and head back later on a different boat for no additional charge, or 25 pesos if you switch companies. Where there's love there's...the **Playa del Divorcio** (Beach of Divorce). Quiet and beautiful, it is opposite Amor on the Pacific side. Dangerous currents and fierce undertow make swimming there unsafe (how metaphorical). To get there, hop on a yellow bus (4 pesos) or walk on Blvd. Marina and turn right across from the Mexican crafts market (20 min.). Slip out to the beach between massive condo complexes, right after you pass the Terra Sol hotel. The rocky area just before La Playa del Amor is a protected national park, unassuming until you peek underwater. **Snorkeling** is the best way to explore the stony recesses packed with coral, urchins, tropical fish of all

YOU NEVER GIVE ME YOUR MONEY The water's safe—the only sharks lurking around Cabo are the time-share vendors disguised as "tourist officials." If you look like you might be over 28 and possess a major credit card, you will be greeted with a friendly "Can I help you?" or "Hola, amigo!" Take advantage of them while they try to take advantage of you: if you have a free afternoon, they'll happily give you a day's free car rental, take you golfing, or give you a boat ride to El Arco and then let you order anything you want at an expensive restaurant. All you have to do is "listen," ears closed but eyes open, mouth pleasantly grinning, and head nodding. The pitch? You shell out US$15,000 for part ownership at an exclusive time-share resort. A tip: don't admit until after dinner that you're not interested.

sizes and colors, moray eels, stingrays, and octopi. Bring your own gear or rent equipment from a nearby vendor (boat tour and snorkeling package cost around $15). The avid snorkeler will also appreciate **Playa Santa María** and the reef at **Playa del Chileno,** both on the highway between Cabo San Lucas and San José del Cabo.

 NIGHTLIFE

Cabo is a great place to cut loose—for a price, that is. Here, those who play hard pay hard. However, most clubs in Cabo only charge cover on certain nights, or when a particularly good band is playing. Chicas, this town is for you: ladies' nights rotate, so drinks are always free somewhere. **Cárdenas** and **Blvd. Marina** become a huge laser-lit party ground by night, only winding down at 3 or 4am. During the winter high season, the *centro* degenerates into a mass of American and hip Mexican teens smoking Cuban cigars and stumbling drunkenly along the wharf. A number of quieter locales make for mellow hideaways from all the beer-chugging, *La Bamba*-singing, table-pounding. Most nightspots are bars first and foremost, with a small dance floor playing constant pop music.

Rio Grill (☎ 143 13 35), Marina near Guerrero. The nightly drinking circuit begins here during the extra-long happy hour (5-10pm). Snack on mesquite-grilled appetizers before you hit the next stop. Live music F-Su. Open daily 11am-1am; kitchen closes 11pm.

Giggling Marlin (☎ 143 11 82), across Matamoros from Plaza de los Mariachis. A free nightly comedy show (10 or 10:30pm) pulls in crowds to this, the second stop on the standard Cabo tour. Open daily 8am-2am; kitchen closes 11pm.

Cabo Wabo (☎ 143 11 88), on Guerrero. After the show, stumble across the street from the Giggling Marlin for live rock, on the off chance that Sammy Hagar is in town. (He plays at Cabo Wabo five or six times a year.) If you don't see Sammy and don't feel like playing pool or dancing, drown your sorrows in a waborita (40 pesos), the house version of a margarita. Bar open daily 6pm-2am; club open daily 8pm-2am.

Squid Roe (☎ 143 06 55), on Cárdenas at Zaragoza. At first sight of the flying airplane whirling above this carnival calling itself a bar, you will instantly either love it or hate it. Everyone comes here, and most end up reveling in the madhouse pick-up scene, conga lines, vats of tequila, and short-skirted, jello-shot-peddling salesgirls dancing on any and all surfaces. Hookers, pimps, and *tamale* stands await outside if you come out empty handed. Beer 30 pesos; mixed drinks around 40 pesos. Open daily noon-4am.

La Concepción (☎ 143 49 63), on the north end of the marina, next to Hotel Marina Fiesta. Possibly Los Cabos's best-kept secret; the latest in live Mexican reggae and pop. Eye the ceiling's pirate map while you nibble delicious *botanas* or down a shot of one of 105 varieties of tequila (28-500 pesos). Open M-Sa 3pm-2am.

The Wave (☎ 143 87 00), at the stoplight at Plaza Bonita. Space-age decor in the most modern, dance-oriented, and sophisticated of Cabo's clubs. Come to escape the rowdy beer-guzzlers. Salsa and merengue W (the only salsa dancing in Cabo); house and disco Th (ladies' night, US$20 open bar for men until 1am). Cover charge for some bands. Open daily 8pm-4am, low season W-Sa 8pm-4am.

The Rainbow Bar, on the water by the Marina Fiesta hotel. A very mixed crowd frequents Cabo's only gay bar: men and women, locals and tourists all feel at ease. The small, comfortable space has a little room for dancing and an outdoor patio overlooking the quiet end of the marina. Cute bartenders. Open daily 8pm-3am.

Kokomo's (☎ 143 52 52), on Marina, across the street from Squid Roe. Things get pumping at 10:30pm, when this new club starts spouting fog from all corners. The music is "contemporary" (i.e., late 80s Top-40), and there's plenty of room to dance on the mosaic tile floor. Beer 26 pesos; margaritas 26 pesos. Open daily 11am-3am.

🢒 DAYTRIPS FROM LOS CABOS

THE CORRIDOR

Though the easiest way to get to your oasis of choice is to drive there, the "Subur Cabos" buses that run between San José del Cabo and Cabo San Lucas will leave you at any of the listed beaches (8-15 pesos). To get back you'll have to flag down the bus.

The 30km stretch of coast between Cabo San Lucas and San José del Cabo is dotted with many beautiful beaches. Unfortunately, development is creeping over the small strip of land from both sides. The only pristine beaches are those that lie in the middle; you have to maneuver around condos and resorts to access the beaches closer to the two towns. The calmest waters and best areas reserved for swimming are nearest to Cabo. All of the beaches listed below are accessible from the Transpeninsular Highway; many lie at the end of winding, sandy access bars, and all are easily maneuverable in passenger vehicles. Access roads to some are identified by blue and white palm tree signs, the Los Cabos symbol for beach; others are marked a dirt road entrance and little else.

Starting from Cabo San Lucas, the first beach of note is **Playa Barco Varada** (Shipwreck Beach) at km 9. Ideal for scuba diving, this beach is home to a sunken tuna boat that lies just 27m below the water's surface. Look for the access road around the 9km marker. The access road to **Playa Twin Dolphin** is just south of the entrance to the Twin Dolphin Resort. The rough sandy road leads to a small, secluded, rocky beach, unfortunately unsuitable for swimming. **Playa Santa María,** just past Twin Dolphin at km 12, is a small, clear-water beach protected from harsh waves by a slight cove. The snorkeling here is said to be the best in all of Cabo. Rent gear for US$10, or bring your own. Next is **Chileno Bay,** at the 14km marker, a popular swimming spot. Chileno has public baths and showers, as well as a small dock. Kayaks (US$10-15 per hr.) and snorkel gear (US$10 per day) are available for rent from **Cabo Acuadeportes** (open daily 9am-5pm). Santa Maria is the best snorkeling reef in this area. Although no signs point the way to **Playa del Tule,** it's easy enough to find. Just past Hotel Cabo San Lucas (around km 15), there are signs for Punta del Tule. When the road drops to level with the sand and there's a bridge on your left, pull off to the right—you're there. The rocky shore is unsuitable for swimming, however surfers abound. From km 16 to km 20 are *playas* **Canta Mar, Costa Brava, El Zalate, San Carlos,** and **El Mirador,** all of which are currently inaccessible due to heavy construction. **Playa Buenos Aires** comes next, at km 22. It too is under development but is accessible by a crude sand and dirt road. The waves are rough but the beach is long and empty. Under the shadow of Hotel Palmilia, **Playa Punta Palmilia** offers smooth, gentle waves and great swimming. If you get thirsty, you can pop into nearby Restaurant/Bar Pepes. **Playa Acapulquito,** at km 27, is easy to miss. Look for cars parked on the side of the highway just before the Acapulquito Scenic Overlook. Walk down the steep dirt path and slip between the condos; great waves make this a popular beach with surfers. The last beach before San José del Cabo is **Costa Azul,** the best surfing beach in all of Los Cabos. You can rent a board for the day (US$15), or, for virgin surfers, get a lesson for US$25 from **Playa Costa Azul Rentals,** on the beach, around km 28, right across from Zippers, a beachside restaurant. (☎ 147 00 71. Open daily 8:30am-6:30pm.)

SAN JOSÉ DEL CABO ☎1

If Los Cabos were brothers, José would be the one their mother loved more. Unlike his party-animal, bad-boy younger brother Lucas, José would be better-looking, charming, sincere, and polite, yet still a lot of fun. Unfortunately, however, José would suffer from a congenital disease that would make him more humid than his brother, and consequently less popular with tourists. The result: San José del Cabo remains tranquil, collected, and peacefully Mexican, a haven from the Resortville that dominates the rest of the cape, with elegant colonial architecture adding to its simple charm. Religious services with hymns are held in the plaza every Wednesday, and snorkel shops snuggle peacefully with the *loncherías* next door. Budget travelers will find San José del Cabo easier to get along with than expensive Cabo San Lucas, but prices here are still much higher than on mainland Mexico.

◪ TRANSPORTATION

The **Aguila/ABC bus station** (☎ 142 11 00) is on González, two blocks from the highway and a 20min. walk from the *centro*. To get to town, turn left out of the station, and walk 8 to 10min. down González until it hits Morelos. Turn left, walk six blocks and make a right on Zaragoza to get to the *zócalo*. Aguila and ABC Autotransportes travel to: **Cabo San Lucas** (30min., 8 per day every 1-2hr., 16 pesos); **La Paz** (3hr., every hr. 6am-7:30pm, 100 pesos); and **Todos Santos** (2hr., every hr. 6am-7pm, 55 pesos). Modern Subur Cabos buses depart from a stop on the highway 50m uphill from Doblado. To get to the *centro* from the highway stop, walk six blocks down Doblado and head left one block on Morelos. Buses run to **Cabo San Lucas**, stopping near various beaches (every 15 min., 15 pesos).

⚑ PRACTICAL INFORMATION

Tourist Office: (☎ 142 29 60 ext. 150) on Zaragoza and Mijares, in the beige building next to the *zócalo*. Plenty of brochures and advice. Open M-F 8am-3pm.

Bank: Banamex (☎ 142 31 84) on Mijares, two blocks south of the *zócalo*. Bank and **ATM** open M-F 8:30am-4:30pm, Sa 9am-2pm.

Rental Car: Thrifty Rent-A-Car (☎ 142 41 51), on Mijares at Doblado. Rent VW jalopies with insurance and unlimited kilometers for US$35 per day. If you didn't have at least 25 candles on your last birthday cake, they'll turn you away. Open daily 8am-10pm.

Laundry: Cabomatic (☎ 142 29 33), five blocks south of the *zócalo* on Mijares. Wash 11 pesos, dry 11 pesos; full service, 40 pesos. Open M-Sa 7:30am-8pm, Su 9am-5pm; summer open M-Sa 8am-7pm, Su 9am-5pm. The laundromat downhill from the bus station has the same prices; drop off your dirty duds and they will deliver them to your hotel. Open M-Sa 8am-8pm, Su 9am-5pm.

Emergency: ☎ 060.

Police: (☎ 142 03 61), next door to the post office.

Red Cross: (☎ 142 03 16) on Mijares in the same complex as the post office. 24hr. ambulance service.

Hospital: (☎ 142 00 13) on Atunero, in Clamizal neighborhood. **Centro de Salud,** Doblado 39 (☎ 142 02 41).

Pharmacy: Farmacia La Moderna (☎ 142 00 50), on Zaragoza between Degollado and Guerrero. All-night pharmacies rotate; check the list on the door. Open daily 8am-9pm.

Internet Access: on Zaragoza near Morelos. 25 pesos for first 30 minutes, 4 pesos per 5 minutes thereafter. Printing, scanning, and other services.

Post office: (☎ 142 09 11) on Mijares and González, several blocks toward the beach on the right-hand side. Open M-F 8am-4pm, Sa 9am-1pm.

Postal code: 23400.

ACCOMMODATIONS

Thanks to the encroaching mega-resorts of Cabo San Lucas, room prices in the center of San José del Cabo have been increasing. Compared to Cabo San Lucas, however, San José del Cabo is still a virtual heaven for budget accommodations, most of which are on or near Zaragoza.

Hotel Diana (☎ 142 04 90), on Zaragoza near the *centro*. Friendly staff keep the Diana spotlessly clean and pleasant. Bright woven bedspreads add color to the rooms, each with TV and A/C. Singles or doubles 200 pesos; triples 250 pesos.

Hotel Ceci, Zaragoza 22, 1½ blocks up from Mijares. The large, basic rooms have comfortable beds. Singles 130 pesos, with A/C 160 pesos; triples with A/C 180 pesos.

San José Inn (☎ 142 24 64), on Obregón and Guerrero. Worn pink rooms with fans, thick (but old) mattresses, and warm water. Many rooms have open windows on central hallways. Rooms upstairs are quieter and more secure. Singles and doubles 100-120 pesos, with TV 150-180 pesos; key deposit 20-50 pesos.

Hotel Colli (☎ 142 07 25), on Hidalgo. The 12 sizable rooms are a good value. Don't neglect to take advantage of the evening breeze blowing across the large terrace and garden. Singles and doubles 300 pesos; triples and quads 350 pesos.

Hotel Posada Terranova (☎ 142 05 34; fax 142 09 02), on Degollado near Zaragoza. A good option for a mid-range hotel. Rooms are attractively decorated in colored stone, with heavy antique-green doors to block out noise. TV, telephone, A/C, and fresh flowers every morning. Bar and good restaurant in the hotel. Singles or doubles 495 pesos.

Trailer Park Brisa del Mar (☎ 142 39 99), just off the highway to San Lucas where it reaches the coast. Offers communal showers, beach campers, and a TV bar. Beachfront hook-up US$25 (US$5 more in the winter), back row spots US$18.50; tents US$10.

FOOD

Budget restaurants in San José del Cabo are being pushed out by fancy tourist eateries, leaving fewer and fewer options between taco stand and filet mignon. A healthy suspicion of anglophone restaurants will save you money: be wary if the menus are printed in flawless English.

Cafetería Rosy, on Zaragoza and Green. The food is exquisite for the price, and a good bowl of soup comes with your meal. The portions are ample, whether *pescado* in any of a number of styles (60 pesos), a t-bone *a la plancha* (grilled, 60 pesos) or *estofado de mariscos* (seafood stew). Open M-Sa 8am-5pm.

Jazmín (☎ 142 17 60), on Morelos and Zaragoza. This colorful restaurant, where parrots chatter under vine-painted arches, rides the line between tourist and local spot. Professional service complements high-quality food. Breakfasts 28-44 pesos; *especiales* with fish 88 pesos, with meat 66 pesos; entrees from 90 pesos. Open daily 8am-11pm.

Taquería Erika, on Doblado near Highway 1. No place in the *centro* offers light fare as superb or as inexpensive as the tacos, *quesadillas,* baked potatoes, and other *antojitos* served at Erika's. It's well worth the 10min. walk, especially to satisfy an early afternoon or late-night craving. Tacos 8 pesos. Open daily 1pm-5am.

SIGHTS AND BEACHES

A 20 minute walk down Mijares will take you to good, uncrowded local beaches. Hurry—even as you read this, new hotel complexes are springing up. Also, be careful in the water this side of Cabo; undertow makes it potentially hazardous to swim (which doesn't preclude sunbathing and extensive toe-dipping, of course). To get to the best surfing waters, flag down a local bus on Highway 1 (every 15min.) where it meets Doblado, and ask the driver to drop you at **Costa Azul** or **Playa de Palmilla.** Several information booths lie scattered along Mijares. They will be more than happy to "inform" you about the glass-bottom boat tours, fishing

MISSION IMPOSSIBLE. In 1697, Padre Juan María Salvatierra and a group of Jesuit priests landed just north of Loreto, discovered a plentiful water supply, and established the first permanent mission on the peninsula. Mission activities were initiated with the rapid conversion of the Indians, who were promised protection and an education if they agreed to religious schooling. The Indians also provided manual labor for building the missions, which served as offices, bunks, armories, and schools. The Jesuits founded a total of 20 missions in California before they were recalled for political reasons in 1768 and ordered to cede power to the Franciscan sect. Still in existence, these missions can be visited by intrepid travelers with four-wheel-drive. The more isolated of the missions lie along rough dirt roads which are sometimes impossible to drive after heavy winter rains. Ask in nearby towns about accessibility and road conditions. Missions still in service are generally open daily 8am-1pm and 4-8pm. A caretaker invariably lurks nearby to open the church for visitors if it is closed.

San Juan Bautista Londó was founded in 1699 to serve as a visiting station (called *visita*) where the missionary of Loreto could deliver the sacrament to the people of Londó. Now crumbling ruins, the mission was abandoned in 1708 due to a plague. Head to San Juan Londó, 32km north of Loreto on the Transpeninsular.

San Francisco Javier, first established in 1699, the mission was rebuilt 1744-1758 with a cruciform plan, a solid vaulted roof, and cupolas. Just south of Loreto, turn right on the difficult road marked San Javier. Sixteen km farther on a very poor road is the picturesque ruined *visita* **La Presentación,** built in 1769.

San Juan Bautista Malibat is on the delta of the arroyo on the rancho Ligüí, 30km south of Loreto just off the Transpeninsular. Founded in 1705 and permanently abandoned by 1721, only the stone foundations of the mission remain.

Santa Rosalía de Mulegé, in Mulegé, 105km north of Loreto, Santa Rosalía de Mulegé, was founded in 1705. It was completely abandoned in 1828. Later restorations have significantly modified the interior.

San José de Comondú was founded in 1708 and rebuilt in 1750 as a large, three-aisled nave topped by a barrel-vaulted roof. Abandoned in 1827, it was converted into a school before reconstruction in 1972-73. Head north on the Transpeninsular; turn left toward San Isidro about 5km past El Bombador, 140km from Loreto.

Nuestra Señora de los Dolores del Sur was founded in the town of Apaté in 1721 and moved to Todos Santos in 1768. Today, only ruins of the walls remain. From Pepes, a tiny town 27km from El Cien, turn east off the Transpeninsular until El Ciruelo (39km). A difficult, slow road (48km) leads to the mission.

San Ignacio was finished in 1786. The beautiful mission is built on a cruciform plan, with high walls, an attractive bell tower, an ornate facade, and a sturdy cupola.

San José had problems from the start: the first mission was abandoned when founding father Padre Nicolás Tamaral was martyred in the Pericú revolt. Reestablished at its present site in 1740, the mission was repeatedly emptied thanks to malaria epidemics. The present-day church was abandoned following a storm in 1918, but today retains an active parish.

Todos Santos began as a mere *visita* of La Paz in 1723. A gift by Rosa de la Peña allowed the church to elevate its status to an independent mission, founded in 1733, under the name Santa Rosa. An unusual, arcaded brick and stucco clock tower marks the main entrance into the church.

San Luis Gonzaga was established in the Valley of Santo Domingo, 45km southeast of Ciudad Constitución, in 1740, 3 years after its founding as a *visita*. The church is remarkably complete. Two thin bell towers flank a plain facade before a barrel-vaulted nave. On difficult, but passable road, 45km southeast of Ciudad Constitución.

trips, and snorkeling expeditions that they sell, along with condos and time shares. Prices are often not bad, and perhaps even worth the annoying sales pitch. Just outside of town, at km 31 on Highway 1, **Baja Salvaje** (☎/fax 142 53 00; email reservations@bajasalvaje.com; www.bajasalvaje.com), offers high-end sporting equipment rentals, tours, and classes for diving, kayaking, surfing, and rock climbing.

Between trips to the beach San José del Cabo offers little of daytime interest, apart from window-shopping along Mijares. The **Kitsch Galería** has made an art out of the useless; their kitschy cafe also makes a good cappuccino. The **Huichol Gallery,** on Zaragoza and Mijares, features brilliantly colored beadwork and embroidery made by the isolated Huichol peoples. (☎ 142 37 99. Open daily 8am-10pm.)

 NIGHTLIFE

San José del Cabo can't compete with its noisy neighbor, but it's still possible to have a good time here—just kick back, relax, and don't expect conga lines or table dancing. The **Iguana Bar,** under the giant iguana on Mijares, gets large weekend crowds drinking, playing pool, and dancing to pop music. (☎ 142 02 66. Beer 25 pesos, margaritas 30 pesos. Open Tu-Su 6pm-3am.) **Piso #2,** Zaragoza 71, two blocks from the church, is mellower. Red chairs, palm trees, pool tables, and neon lights help you digest your Dos Equis beer (20 pesos) or mixed drink (20 pesos; W open bar). Downstairs, **Piso #1** offers the same prices and a similar atmosphere. (F 9-11pm free, open bar for women; W 9pm-2am men 120 pesos, women free. Open in summer daily 6pm-3am; in winter noon-3am.)

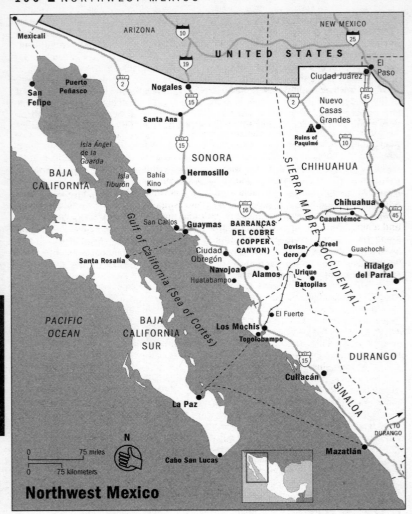

Northwest Mexico

HIGHLIGHTS OF NORTHWEST MEXICO

EXPLORE one of Mexico's best-kept secrets, **Barrancas del Cobre (Copper Canyons;** p. 235), which provide some of the most awe-inspiring vistas in the world—these canyons are four times the size of Arizona's Grand Canyon. Most travelers use the gorgeous town of **Creel** (p. 230) as a base from which to explore.

NAP on the beaches of **Bahía Kino** (p. 208), a pair of tiny laid-back fishing towns.

PRETEND you're an astronaut in **El Pinacate** (p. 202), a four million-acre volcanic preserve and one of the most spectacular biospheres in the world. NASA trained astronauts for the Apollo moon mission here because the terrain is so similar.

BRONZE yourself on the golden shores of the stately beachside resort of **Mazatlán** (p. 243).

NORTHWEST MEXICO

Northwest Mexico is home to raucous border towns, calm fishing villages, vast expanses of desert, and warm water beaches along the alluring Sea of Cortés. For many, the area serves as an introduction to Mexico—full of nights of debauchery, rounds of tequila shots, oversized straw sombreros, and blistering heat. But in the midst of all this madness, many tourists overlook the rows of shantytowns, border-patrol battles, and miles of industrial wasteland that consume a large part of the cities. Things calm down considerably as you venture farther south. The grime and frenetic madness of Ciudad Juárez and Nogales, Mexico's brawny border towns, give way to bustling markets, colonial mansions, iconoclastic museums, and a surreal cactus-studded landscape. In some towns, things slow to a virtual standstill—you can hear the flies buzz and the wind whistle through the desert and you can see *vaqueros* clad in tight jeans swaggering about. You may want to bring along a pair of cowboy boots and a wide-brimmed sombrero of your own—the rugged terrain requires a lot of stamina, and the *noroeste* sun is merciless.

The Sierra Madre Occidental rips through the heart of Northwest Mexico, creating a diverse landscape and natural wonders that are overlooked by speeding tourists, often a little too eager to get to points farther south. To the east of the mountains, the parched desert gives even the larger cities in Chihuahua the feel of dusty frontier; frequent sandstorms enhance the mood. Along the coast, in the states of **Sonora** and **Sinaloa,** a melange of commercial ports, quiet fishing villages, and sprawling beaches overlook the warm waters of the Sea of Cortés. The condominiums, time-shares, and resort hotels that cast their shadows over the light-colored sands mark the presence of US and Canadian expatriates who have discovered the area's elegant beaches. Landlocked **Durango,** traversed by the Sierra Madres, thrives on mining and is known for its Old-West ruggedness. But the most stunning sight in the *noroeste* are the **Barrancas del Cobre (Copper Canyons),** a spectacular series of deep gorges and unusual rock formations in **Chihuahua** brimming with tropical vegetation, all cut through by the Río Urique far below. The caves in the area are home to the reclusive Tarahumara Indians. When it comes to the Northwest, those who look past the border towns and into the region's heartland and coasts will reap the rewards.

SONORA

NOGALES   ☎ 6

Straddled by steep hills covered with brightly colored tin houses and block-long Tecate signs, Nogales (pop. 300,000) welcomes tourists with the typical border town array of curio shops, *burro* photo-ops, and rowdy bars. Most visitors never venture beyond the *primer cuadro*, where outgoing street vendors and daytrippers from Tucson match wits over the price of everything from ice cream to *toro* (bull) skulls. Far above the border bustle on cluttered, candle-lit dirt roads, huge extended families share flimsy walls with workers who have left their own families behind to seek fortune in one of the more than one hundred production centers south of downtown. Competition for dollars and the swelling population have raised crime levels in recent years, but the *primer cuadro* remains a safe and friendly place to sample Sonoran food and practice your *español* before venturing on to points south.

IF YOU PLAN ON GOING FARTHER. If you plan to travel beyond Nogales, obtain a **tourist card** (see **Tourist Cards**, p. 9) at the border and have your passport on hand. It's much simpler to get the card here than farther south. When you cross the border through the arched crossing complex, turn right into the **immigration center,** the first building on the right.

▐ TRANSPORTATION

The **bus terminal** and **train station** are directly across from each other on Carretera Internacional, 4.5km south of town (not to be confused with the border street of the same name). A taxi from the bus station to the center of town will cost an exorbitant 50 pesos; instead cross the street and walk north to the end of the block, where you can catch one of the local white buses (3 pesos) marked "Central Camionera." Downtown Nogales is the last stop. To get back to the bus terminal and train station, wait at the bus stop on López for a "Central Camionera" bus. A large supermarket called *Ley* should be to your right when you reach the correct stop on the corner of Carretera International (the one near the border). There is a second, smaller bus station and a Burger King two blocks before the main station.

At the main station, Elite (☎313 16 03) offers luxurious bus service to: **Guadalajara** (25hr., every hr. 7:30am-6pm, 1002 pesos), with stops in **Los Mochis** (11hr., 341 pesos) and **Mazatlán** (17hr., 698 pesos); **Hermosillo** (3½hr., every hr. 7:30am-11:30pm, 124 pesos); and **Mexico City** (32hr., 6 per day, 1295 pesos). Transportes del Pacífico (☎313 16 06) has buses *de paso* that leave every hour from 8am-8:30pm for: **Guaymas** (5hr., 186 pesos); **Hermosillo** (3hr., 120 pesos); **Puerto Vallarta** (26 hr., 1000 pesos); **Querétaro** (33hr., 1264 pesos); and **Tepic** (22hr., 885 pesos). Transportes Golden State buses (in Nogales, AZ ☎(520) 287-5628) leave for **Tucson** (1½hr., every hr., US$8) from the Greyhound Station half a block from the US side of the border.

✳▐ ORIENTATION AND PRACTICAL INFORMATION

The downtown area is relatively small, making Nogales easy to navigate. If you're crossing the border by foot, you'll be on **Pesqueira**; by car, you'll drive in on López Mateos. From east to west, **Pesqueira, Juárez** (which merges with **López Mateos** several blocks south), **Morelos** (a walkway), **Obregón** (the main tourist drag), **Hidalgo,** and **Ingenieros** run parallel to each other and perpendicular to the border. Internacional runs parallel to the tall picket fence that marks the border. Proceeding south, away from the border, **Campillo, Ochoa, Pierson, Aguirre, Vázquez, Díaz,** and **González** all run parallel.

Tourist Office: (☎312 06 66) next to the immigration center, to your right if you enter from the US. Helpful English-speaking staff. Open 9am-7pm.

Currency Exchange: The *primer cuadro* contains a ridiculous number of **banks,** most of which line López Mateos and Obregón. **Banamex** is at Obregón and Ochoa (☎312 07 80 or 312 55 05). Open M-Th 8:30am-4:30pm, F 8:30am-5:30pm. Also farther south on Obregón at Elías Calles (☎312 12 51 or 312 10 65). Open M-F 8:30am-4:30pm, Sa 9am-3:30pm. Both exchange dollars and traveler's checks and have 24-hour **ATMs.**

Luggage Storage: At the bus terminal. 5 pesos per hr

Emergency: ☎080.

Police: (☎312 01 04 or 312 11 04) at González and Leal. English spoken.

Red Cross: (☎313 58 00) on Elías Calles and Providencia. Open 24hr.

Medical Assistance: Hospital Básico (☎313 06 71, 313 34 65, or 313 34 60), about 3km south of the border on Obregón. English spoken. Open 24 hr.

Fax: Copicentro Xerox (☎312 25 20) at López Mateos and Pierson. Open 8:30am-7pm. Nogales has not yet embraced the Internet; you might be the only one checking your e-mail at **Copy Xpress** (☎312 15 84) on López Mateos, 1 block south of the Hotel Granada. 25 pesos per hr. Open M-Sa 9am-10pm, Su 9am-5pm.

Post Office: Juárez 52 (☎312 12 47). Open M-F 8:30am-2:30pm. Shares a roof with **Telecomm. Postal code:** 84000.

■ ACCOMMODATIONS

Relative to towns farther south in Mexico, rates in Nogales are steep. However, high price does mean high quality. The most economical budget hotels can be found on the block behind the tourist office on Juárez.

Hotel San Carlos, Juárez 22 (☎312 13 46 or 312 14 09; fax 312 15 57), between Internacional and Campillo, features a lobby with comfy chairs and an ice-cold purified water dispenser. Spacious rooms have A/C, color TVs with US cable, great showers, and phones. Reservations recommended. Singles 220 pesos; doubles 290 pesos.

Hotel Regis (☎312 51 81 or 312 55 35), one door down from the San Carlos. Clean rooms with A/C, phone, and TV. Music lovers will appreciate the ceiling speakers—until the *norteño* tunes played over and over drive you to madness. Don't fret: you can turn them off if you like. Reservations required. Singles 250 pesos; doubles 275 pesos.

Hotel Olivia, Obregón 125, (☎312 22 00 or 312 22 87) usually has vacancies. Pristine rooms include A/C, phone, and TV with a few channels. 20 peso key deposit. Singles 270 pesos; doubles 310 pesos.

Hotel Granada (☎312 29 11; fax 312 54 98), Mateos and González. Comfortable beds, big bathrooms, cable TV, and a friendly young staff enchant you, but a good night's sleep can be tough to find between the constant traffic and sirens from the streets. Singles and doubles 300 pesos; triples 330 pesos.

■ FOOD

Nogales is home to oodles of overpriced restaurants that cater to daytrippers from the US. If tourist pricing is driving you crazy, head for the **plaza** on Mateos at Ochoa, where vendors entice your tastebuds with an array of fruits and *tortas*. The best places to get a truly economical meal can be found just a few steps off of Obregón, where local families offer up traditional *antojitos* (5-15 pesos) prepared while you wait at their tiny makeshift counters.

Restaurante Elviras, Obregón 1 (☎312 47 43), has won acclaim from US magazines for its house special, *pescado elvira* (US$12) It is a great place to try *molcojete*, a *sonorense* dish of meat served with a salsa of cheese, tomatoes, chiles, corn, and *pulque* (US$12). Look for Elviras's eclectic interior in the movie *Traffic*. Open daily 9am-11pm.

La Posada Restaurante, Pierson 116 (☎312 04 39), west of Obregón. Chow down on big breakfasts (20-40 pesos) and delicious *carnes* (meats) amidst local families and chirping birds. *Burritos de machaca* (dried beef flavored with onions, tomatoes, and *chile verde*) 12 pesos, *chimichangas* 15 pesos. Open daily 7:30am-10pm.

Café Ajijic, Obregón 182 (☎312 50 74), features live music and a picturesque fountain. The tiled tables, shaded by umbrellas, provide the perfect setting for sipping from the huge selection of espresso drinks (15-22 pesos). Open 8:30am-midnight.

■ ■ SIGHTS AND ENTERTAINMENT

Most of the curio and craft shops line Obregón and Campillo. Merchandise is priced in anticipation of bargaining; confidence and some knowledge of the goods can get you great deals.

Right after lunch, the bars on Obregón open their doors to a mixture of locals and tourists, and by 10pm on a Friday or Saturday night, "packed" becomes an understatement—walking is all but impossible. The huge dance floor and remarkable cleanliness of **Coco Loco,** Obregón 62, draw a young crowd that fights its way to the bar for tequila shots (US$1) and mixed drinks (US$2-3). Before the evening rush you can relax on the balcony with a bucket of 10 beers (US$5), but after dark the DJ-mixed American pop hits will bring you to your dancing feet. F-Sa cover US$5. (☎312 41 05. Open F-Su 1pm-3am.) **Bora Bora,** Obregón 38, between Campillo and Internacional, offers live music nightly after 9pm and one free drink on Sundays. Beer and mixed drinks 10-30 pesos. (Open W-Su noon-3am.) Across the street, giant metal palm trees greet you at the entrance to **Kookaracha's,** Obregón 1, where you can dance the night away and down tequila shots (US$1) or chill with a *cerveza* by the fountain in the "roach's" techno-colored courtyard. (☎312 47 73. Open W, F, Sa 8pm-3am.) At **Catooche Café Bar,** lively salsa and *norteño* tunes sound even better when belted out by tipsy locals during their karaoke nights. F-Sa cover US$5, includes 3 beers. (☎312 31 44. Open T-Sa 1pm-3:30am.)

Not in the mood for tequila? **Cinemas Gemelos,** Obregón 368, between González and Torres, shows second-run American films dubbed or subtitled in Spanish. (☎312 50 02. 38 pesos.) For those looking for a bit of culture, the new **Teatro Auditorio de Nogales,** on Obregón, between Vásquez and González, brings live performances from Mexico City. The box office has showtimes and prices.

PUERTO PEÑASCO   ☎6

Incredible expanses of rocky coastline broken by spotless sandy beaches...and pastel condominiums full of US retirees. This isn't Florida—this is Puerto Peñasco (pop. 4000). Just 105km south of the Arizona border and known to its northern neighbors as "Rocky Point," Puerto Peñasco attracts spring break revelers, vacationing families and aging beach bums by the thousands. Once a launching pad for shrimp boats, the town dried up when overfishing decimated the shrimp population in the Sea of Cortés. Economically widowed, the town now courts investors with a dowry of tax breaks and other incentives. Holiday weekends bring hordes of *gringos* who eagerly purchase heaps of gaudy pottery and plastic sunglasses. Despite the throngs of *gringos*, the magnificent Sea of Cortés and the swaying palms lining nude stretches of pristine beach make for a beautiful if not exactly tranquil, retreat. Budget travelers, however, should beware of the special "tourist pricing." For the better bargain, always ask for prices in pesos instead of in dollars, even if the seller is reluctant.

▐ TRANSPORTATION

Buses depart from Juárez and Calle 24, nine blocks north of Calle 13. To go downtown, turn left as you exit and take an immediate left on Juárez. Continue south and turn right at Calle 13 for budget lodgings and Playa Hermosa or continue to Fremont. Autotransportes de Baja California (☎383 20 19) can take you to: **Ensenada** (10hr., 310 pesos), **Mexicali** (5hr., 165 pesos), **Tecate** (6hr, 238 pesos), **Tijuana** (8hr., 260 pesos), and even **La Paz** (27hr., 999 pesos). All buses are *de paso* and there are only four departures per day. The 1am bus goes as far as Tijuana (via Mexicali and Tecate), the 8am heads to every destination listed above, and the 1pm and 5pm buses head only to Mexicali. For travel within Sonora, Transportes Norte de Sonora (☎383 36 40) can luxuriously transport you to **Guaymas** (9hr., 3 per day, 285 pesos) and **Hermosillo** (7hr., 5 per day, 245 pesos).

◆▐ ORIENTATION AND PRACTICAL INFORMATION

No official *centro* exists. This is a small town, but fear not—it's not nearly as confining as it sounds. Banks and markets cluster around the intersection of **Fremont** and **Juárez,** the main drag, which runs north-south through the entire town, while other services surround Juárez farther north at **Constitución.** Hotels and motels tend to be nearer the beach and concentrate on the *malecón* (at the southern end of Juárez) or just west of Juárez on Calle 13. At its northern end, Juárez runs diagonal to most of the other streets, and at its southern end the ubiquitous boulevard splits into Paseo de los Pescadores, west of the *malecón,* and Campeche, which continues south to the Playa Miramar.

The **tourist office,** a hike out Juárez to the northern outskirts of town, is a tiny green shack where little English is spoken. (☎383 50 10 or 383 61 22. Open M-F 9am-4pm, Sa 9am-1pm.) If you're too lazy to make the trek, stop in at any hotel or shop for one of the many free **tourist guides,** all of which contain decent maps. **Bancomer,** just past Jim Bur Plaza heading south on Juárez, exchanges currency and traveler's checks. (☎383 24 30. Open M-F 8:30am-4pm, Sa 10am-2pm.) **Banamex,** on Juárez, just south of Fremont, provides the same services. (☎383 25 82. Open M-F 8:30am-4:30pm.) Both have 24hr. **ATMs.** Stock up at **Supermarket Jim Bur,** on Juárez in the Jim Bur Plaza. (☎383 25 61. Open M-Sa 8am-9pm, Su 8am-4pm.) **Lavamática Peñasco,** on Constitución across from Hotel Paraíso del Desierto. Wash 12 pesos, dry 15 pesos. (Open M-Sa 8am-7pm.) **Police:** at Fremont and Juárez. Little English spoken. (☎383 26 26. Open 24hr.) **Red Cross,** on Fremont at Chiapas. (☎383 22 66. Open 24hr.) **Farmacia Botica Lux,** Ocampo 146, is two blocks east of Juárez. (☎383 28 81. Open 24hr.) **Hospital Municipal,** Morúa and Juárez. Little English spoken. (☎383 21 10. Open 24hr.) **Fax:** in the same building as the post office. (☎383 27 82. Open M-F 8am-6pm, Sa 9am-noon.) **Infotec,** on Juárez at Ocampo. Look for the white building that says *"Centro de Computación Integral."* (☎383 64 60. 30 pesos per hr. Open M-F 9am-9pm.) **Post office:** on Chiapas, two blocks east of Juárez on Fremont. (☎383 23 50. Open M-F 8am-3pm.) **Postal code:** 83550.

▐▘ ACCOMMODATIONS AND CAMPING

Budget rooms in Puerto Peñasco are a rare commodity these days; small establishments are being torn down to clear space for expensive resorts, condos, and timeshares. The cheapest way to spend the night is to camp in your tent or RV. Trailer parks abound in the south around Playa Miramar. **Playa Miramar RV Park,** at the southern end of Campeche, rents scenic spots year-round with cable TV and full hookup. Washers, dryers, and showers are also available. (☎383 25 87. 1-2 people US$13, each additional person US$2; weekly US$80 with beachfront spaces slightly higher.) Public camping is permitted northwest of the Playa Boruta Resort on sandy beach all the way down to La Choya. Clean and hot showers can be had at **Shoners Perla,** on the Camono a la Choya, two blocks west of Enciras. (US$2. Open daily 8am-8pm.)

The cheapest beds in town surround a small patio and hot tub behind **Margaritaville,** a US-run bar and restaurant on Campeche, one block south of Banamex. Each of the 5 rooms, named for Jimmy Buffet songs, contains two clean and comfortable beds and not much else. Communal baths and showers are in good shape. (☎383 53 44. 1-3 people US$20.) One of the last remaining quasi-budget hotels is the centrally-located **Motel Playa Azul,** Calle 13 and Suárez, about two blocks from Playa Hermosa. It offers nicely furnished rooms with ancient one-channel TVs, generous A/C, and yes, private baths. Bargain with the manager. (☎383 62 96. Singles 250 pesos; doubles 350 pesos.)

▐▘ FOOD

Food vendors line Calle 13 and Juárez offering tree-ripened mangos and grapes, platters of tacos (3 for 25 pesos), and a wide selection of *tortas*. On the beaches and the *malecón*, locals sell budget-priced fresh *mariscos* (seafood) out of trucks, while nearby ritzy waterfront restaurants charge much more for similar concoctions. For traditional Mexican cuisine, head east on Calle 13 and turn left onto Kino to **La Curva,** where locals gather at long tables to down frothy mugs of Tecate while loudly cheering on their favorite *fútbol* teams. The *combinación grande* (45 pesos) includes nachos with cheese, salsa, sour cream, rice, beans, and your choice of entree. (☎383 34 70. Open M-Th 8am-10:30pm, F-Su 8am-11pm.) If you must have an ocean view, **Gamma's,** on Calle 13, in front of Plaza Las Glorias Hotel, specializes in fried fish. Dine at picnic tables under an open air *palapa*, gaze at the sunbathers on Playa Hermosa, and enjoy a tasty breaded filet (40 pesos). Fried shrimp US$3, grilled steak US$3.50. (☎383 56 80. Open daily 8am-11pm.)

SIGHTS AND BEACHES

Puerto Peñasco's long stretches of clean and rarely crowded beaches are blessed with clear, warm waters. Shallow tide pools cradle clams, small fish, and colorful shells. **Sandy Beach** and **Playa Hermosa** are the best choices for swimming; both have curio shops, restaurants, and hotels galore. To reach Sandy Beach, head north on Encinas or Juárez until the intersection with Camino a Bahía Choya. Take a left and follow the souvenirs shops and bars; you should see sights that say "To Sandy Beach." To get to Playa Hermosa, turn right on Calle 13 when heading south on Juárez; the beach is straight ahead five or six blocks down, but you'll have to veer a bit to the right to avoid the impassible wall of hotels. The beaches around **Las Conchas** and **Playa Miramar,** at the southern end of town, are less crowded but also rockier and rougher. To reach Playa Miramar, head south on Juárez, and fork left onto Campeche near the Benito Juárez monument. Continue uphill for three blocks; Playa Miramar will be straight ahead. To reach Playa Las Conchas, head south on Juárez, turn left on Fremont after Bancomber, take a right onto Camino a las Conchas, and follow the rock-slab road for 3km.

Jeff Reeco (☎383 62 09), who lives across the street from Thrifty Ice Cream on Victor Estrella in the old port, rents sea kayaks (single US$35; double US$45 per day) and boogie boards (US$7 per day). Multi-day and group discounts can be negotiated. The only dive shop in town, **Sun n' Fun** can arrange fishing trips (half-day all-inclusive, US$60), whale-watching (3hr., US$30), sunset cruises (2hr., US$25), and guided dives (5hr., US$50). The **Intercultural Center for the Study of Deserts and Oceans** (**CEDO**), at Playa Las Conchas 9km from town (taxi 50 pesos), gives free guided tours of its wet lab and museum—including a 55ft. whale skeleton. (☎382 01 13. Tours Tu 2pm, Sa 4pm. Visitor Center and gift shop open M-Sa 9am-5pm, Su 10am-2pm.) The **Center for Technological Sea Studies (CETMAR)**, 2km before CEDO on the Las Conchas road, operates a small aquarium stocked with local marine species. A large tank in the rear contains a family of sea turtles and another (gigantic foam) turtle guards the entrance. (☎382 00 10. Open M-F 10am-2:30pm, Sa-Su 10am-5pm. 20 pesos, children 10 pesos.)

ENTERTAINMENT

After nightfall, the crows move from the coastline to bar lines for shots of tequila and drafts of Tecate. Calle 13, Campeche, and the *malecón* all play host to ridiculous numbers of bars, pool halls, discotecas, and a peppering of raunchier establishments. Nightspots outnumber clients (except during spring break) and many are forced to close their doors for lack of patrons. The happening **Margaritavilla** holds on to its "most popular" status by offering live music and/or karaoke nightly. US$1 shots and free Cuervo Gold from 11pm-midnight. (Open daily 8am-1am.)

DAYTRIPS FROM PUERTO PEÑASCO

EL PINACATE

Guides are necessary. For information about tours, ask at the tourist office or talk to Peggy Turk Boyer at CEDO (☎382 01 13). If you do decide to go it alone, four-wheel-drive high-clearance vehicles with partially deflated tires are a must, as are tons of water, a shovel, spare tire, compass, and firewood. Camping is permitted, but don't leave anything behind and don't remove any souvenirs. The ideal time to visit is between November and March, when temperatures range from approximately 15 to 32°C, as opposed to summer months, when the daytime temperatures can often exceed 47°C.

Forty-eight kilometers north of Puerto Peñasco on Rte. 8 lies the El Pinacate volcanic preserve, one of the largest and most spectacular biospheres in the world. Created in June 1992 to limit volcanic rock excavation and protect endangered species, El Pinacate encompasses more than 4 million acres and extends from the

Arizona border to the Sea of Cortés. Over 600 craters and 400 cinder cones pockmark the 30,000 year old lava shards and sea of sand that once served as an important source of food for the people of the Tohono O'odham nation for whom this landscape had great significance. Guided by shamans, adolescent men would cross the barren expanse surviving on water retained in natural rock tanks. Weary and tired from the exertion and heat, they were made to run across the beaches, inducing a light-headed semiconsciousness perceived as spiritual nirvana. Upon successful completion of this rite, the men were allowed to marry. Those who passed out failed and were left to die. To this day, members of the Tohono O'odham nation cross the desert on foot from Arizona to bathe in the waters of the Sea of Cortés, which they consider to be sacred and healing.

The preserve's amazing emptiness and endless kilometers of igneous rock are reminiscent of the moon's rough surface; in fact, NASA trained astronauts for the Apollo mission in El Pinacate. Technical climbs and challenging hikes await around every corner, and excellent physical condition plus a whole lot of water are necessary to survive in this strikingly beautiful environment.

CABORCA   ☎ 6

About halfway between Hermosillo and Puerto Peñasco rises the sprawling agricultural city of Caborca (pop. 200,000). Surrounded by desert and pastures of cattle, Caborca lacks both the beautiful beaches of seaside towns and the excitement of more urban areas. Although heavily populated, the city contains few paved roads an a whole bunch of non-functioning *semáforos* (traffic lights). Caborca is virtually void of tourists year-round, and the few who do come often stop only for a quick meal at one of the many *asaderos* before moving on to more glamorous destinations. If you're on your way to the beaches or coming back and need a rest stop, fear not—Caborca has all your needs covered, especially if you've experienced a *gringo* overload or you are salivating for meat.

▐ TRANSPORTATION. From the **Transportes del Pacífico** bus station, on Calle 8 and Av. A, walk to your left as you exit the station and turn left onto (unmarked) Av. B; three more blocks will bring you to Obregón, Caborca's main street. *De Paso* buses leave Transportes del Pacífico (☎372 35 59) every hour for **Guadalajara** (24hr., 974 pesos), **Guaymas** (6hr., 220 pesos), **Hermosillo** (3hr., 148 pesos), **Mexicali** (7½hr., 226 pesos), **Mexico City** (32hr., 1279 pesos), and **Tijuana** (9hr., 357 pesos). The **Transportes Norte de Sonora** bus station is on La Carretera and Calle 8 next to Motel Los Arcos. To get to downtown, cross the street to Motel Los Arcos, walk one block into town, and turn left. A few blocks later you'll find yourself on Obregón with the *centro* on your right. Transportes Norte de Sonora (☎372 12 32) offers almost identical service as Transportes del Pacifico.

▟▛ ORIENTATION AND PRACTICAL INFORMATION. Caborca lies 269km northwest of Hermosillo on Rte. 2. The main drag, **Obregón,** runs east-west, beginning in the east at the carretera (Mex. 2) and becoming Highway 37 heading out of town to the west. Running parallel to Obregón are Calle 1, Calle 2, etc. Bounding the downtown area is Calle 1 to the south and Calle 8 to the north. Perpendicular to the *calles* run the *avenidas*, which are lettered A-Z. Most businesses line Obregón between Av. A, two blocks north of the carretera, and Av. M, 12 blocks to the west. Although the *calles* and *avenidas* intersect nicely at right angles, they can be extremely confusing to navigate as most of the letters and numbers have been replaced by proper street names and there is a frustrating lack of street signs. A few important names to know are Obregón (Calle 5), Juárez (Av. B), 6 de Abril (Av. D), Quiroz y Mora (Av. E), and Sotelo (Av. F).

Bancomer, at Obregón and Av. F, exchanges cash and American Express traveler's checks. It has a 24hr. **ATM.** (☎372 06 16 or 372 06 17. Open M-F 8:30am-3pm.) Stock up on foodstuffs at **Centinela Super,** Calle 8 between Av. B and C. (☎372 18 40. Open M-Sa 7am-10pm, Su 7am-9pm.) **Lavamatic,** Av. E between

NORTHWEST MEXICO

COCO LOCO About twelve miles off Route 1 on the way to San Luis Gonzaga, lives a one-legged man named Coco. Besides being the proprietor of a bar/hotel/restaurant appropriately named "Coco's," he gets his kicks from hauling pathetic *gringos* and their vehicles from the muck of Baja's infamous roads. Constantly the subject of the English Baja newsletter, Coco rescues the inane from the dirt-death-trap running south from Puertocitos to Rte. 1. Besides being a wizard mechanic, Coco is an aspiring short-story writer. If stymied by multiple flat tires, Coco may come to your rescue but retain the story of your vehicular debacle in a 2-inch-thick tome of roadside rescues. Who knows? You, too, may be immortalized in the book-of-big-mistakes if you have too much faith in your SUV.

Calles 6 and 7, offers self or full-service laundry. (Open M-Sa 9am-9pm, Su 9am-3pm.) **Emergency:** ☎080. **Police:** (☎372 08 69.) **Red Cross:** (☎372 16 57 or 372 11 77.) **Farmacia Principal,** at Obregón and Av. M, has the best hours. (☎372 25 79. Open daily 8am-midnight.) **Hospital:** (☎372 08 98), Calle 1 and Av. K. **Fax: Telecomm,** at Av. E, one block north of Obregón. (☎372 03 55. Open M-F 8am-6pm, Sa-Su 9am-noon.) **Internet Access: Sistemas Modernos de Caborca,** Calle 8 between Av. P and Q. (☎372 34 34. 20 pesos per 30min., 25 pesos per hr. Open M-F 9am-1pm and 3-7pm.) **Post Office:** on Av. H between Calle 4 and 5. (☎372 01 16. Open M-F 8am-3pm.) **Postal Code:** 83600.

⊓⊡ ACCOMMODATIONS AND FOOD. If you decide to spend the night in Caborca, you will be in good hands; there are several solid, centrally located hotels. **Motel Jesusita,** Av. B at Calle 4, offers clean rooms with A/C, cable TV, and super high pressure showers. (☎372 13 70. Singles 180 pesos; doubles 230 pesos; triples 280 pesos. Key deposit 50 pesos.) The more central, but shabbier **Hotel La Rivera,** on Av. H between Obregón and Calle 6, has A/C, private baths, and TVs. (☎372 13 90. Singles 180 pesos; doubles 250 pesos.) *Asaderos* line Obregón and Av. E, serving all sorts of delicious carnivorous treats. **Asadero Bífalo,** Obregón and Av. K, is the town's best budget eatery, serving tasty fresh tacos (8 pesos). If you're in the mood to splurge, treat yourself to an *order de carne* (67 pesos), with broiled meat, ribs, veggies, *quesadillas*, beans, tortilla chips, and fresh guacamole. (☎372 27 35. Open daily 10am-midnight.) **Pepe's Burger 3,** Obregón at Calle H, is an all-you-can-eat buffet for 35 pesos. (☎372 63 27. Open M-Sa 10am-5pm.)

⊡⊡ SIGHTS AND ENTERTAINMENT. *Carne asada* aside, Caborca's main attraction is **La Concepción de Nuestra Señora de Caborca,** Av. D, less than 2km south of Obregón. The church, constructed in 1809, served as a defense outpost against invading Americans in 1857. Every year on April 6, the locals commemorate their victory with a *fiesta*.

While the locals claim there is little to do in Caborca at night except sleep, and weekend entertainment consists of heading to Puerto Peñasco, Caborca manages to hold its own thanks to **Dunas Discoteca Bar,** Av. E at the corner of Calle 10, the town's main nighttime hot spot. Dunas offers live music Th-Sa after 11pm. Beer 15 pesos. (☎372 70 00, ext. 173. Cover F-Sa 40 pesos after 11pm. Open Th-Su 9pm-2am.)

HERMOSILLO ☎6

A sprawling metropolitan center of commerce and education, Hermosillo, the capital of the state of Sonora, thrills visitors with imposing government palaces, beautiful murals, huge manicured parks, a glorious cathedral, and an incredible ecological research center and zoo. Not all of Hermosillo (pop. 700,000) is, however, so alluring. The crowded, dusty roads of the *centro* scream with the frenzied activity of urban life, and by sundown, little more than garbage lines the streets. Many visitors breeze through on their way to the

NORTHWEST MEXICO

more glamorous towns and beaches to the south, giving Hermosillo no more than a passing glance. Although parts of the city can be unsavory, those who choose to spend a day or two are in for a pleasant surprise.

⌐ TRANSPORTATION

Airport: (☎261 00 08) 10km west of town on Transversal toward Bahía Kino. To get there, catch one of the small red buses from the bus station (3 pesos) or catch a taxi (70 pesos). Aeromexico (☎218 06 12) goes to: **Guadalajara** (2hr., 2 per day); **Mexico City** (2½hr., 3 per day); **Tijuana** (1hr., 10:45am), and other domestic destinations. Aero California (☎260 25 55) will take you to: **La Paz** (1hr., 2 per day); **Los Angeles** (1½ hr., 1 per day); and **Tucson** (½hr., 2 per day). Call for current schedules and prices.

Buses: 2km east of the city center on Encinas. To get from the station to the center of town, catch a "Centro" bus (every 10min. 5am-10:30pm, 3 pesos). Taxis will cost 45 pesos. To get back to the station form the *centro,* wait for a bus at P. Elías Calles and Matamoros, across from *Óptica Morfín.* All service out of Hermosillo is *de paso;* during holidays and weekends you'll need to lace up your boxing gloves in order to win a seat. Buses leave every hour. Elite (☎213 40 50) will carry you in comfort and style to: **Acapulco** (38hr., 1360 pesos); **Caborca** (4hr., 145 pesos); **Ciudad Juárez** (12hr., 371 pesos); **Guadalajara** (22hr., 855 pesos); **Guaymas** (2 hr., 52 pesos); **Los Mochis** (7hr., 220 pesos); **Mazatlán** (12hr., 551 pesos); **Mexicali** (9hr., 362 pesos); **Mexico City** (32hr., 1234 pesos); **Nogales** (3½hr., 157 pesos); and **Tijuana** (12hr., 489 pesos).

⊁ ⑦ ORIENTATION AND PRACTICAL INFORMATION

Hermosillo lies 271km south of the border on **Mexico 15,** the main highway connecting the western US and central Mexico. Most of the activity in Hermosillo occurs inside the *centro,* the area bordered by **Rosales** on the west, **Juárez** on the east, **Serdán** on the south, and **Encinas** on the north. The interiors of **Jardín Juárez** and **Parque Madero** should be avoided after dark, but the rest of the *centro* is fairly safe. If you get lost in the center, remember that the antenna-capped mountain **Cerro de la Campana** is always to the south.

TOURIST AND FINANCIAL SERVICES

Tourist Office: (☎217 29 64; fax 217 00 60), on the 3rd fl. of the **Centro de Gobierno de Sonora** at Cultura and Comonfort. Walk south on Rosales over the highway, turn right, and walk 1 block west. It is in the second big pink building. Open M-F 8am-5pm.

Banks: Banks line Encinas and Serdán. **Banamex** (☎214 76 15), on Serdán at Matamoros, has a 24hr. **ATM.** Open M-F 8:30am-4:30pm, Sa 9am-3:30pm.

American Express: Hermex Travel (☎217 17 18), on Rosales at Monterrey. Open M-F 8:30am-1pm and 3-6:30pm, Sa 9am-1pm.

LOCAL SERVICES

Supermarket: Ley Centro (☎217 32 94), on Juárez at Morelia. Enormous. Open daily 6:30am-10pm.

Laundry: La Burbuja, on Guerrero and Niños Héroes. Open daily 8am-1pm and 3-7pm.

Car Rental: Budget, Garmendia 46 and Tamaulipas (☎214 30 33 or 214 08 85). Open M-F 8am-6pm, Sa-Su 8am-3pm. **Hertz** (☎212 11 55 or 214 85 03), Rodríguez and Guerrero. Open M-F 8am-6pm, Sa-Su 8am-3pm.

EMERGENCY AND COMMUNICATIONS

Emergency: ☎080.

Police: (☎218 55 64), at Periférico Nte. and Solidaridad. Some English. Open 24hr.

Red Cross: (☎214 00 10), on Encinas at 14 de Abril. Open 24hr. English-speaking staff on hand 9am-5pm.

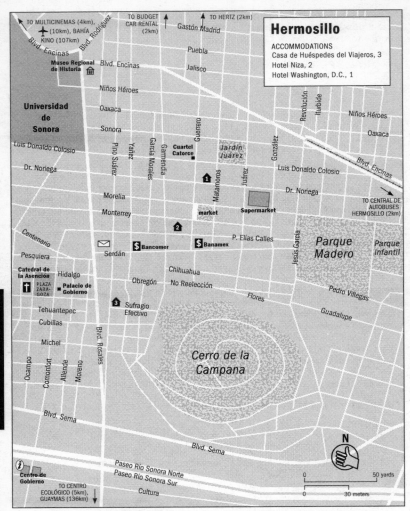

Pharmacy: Farmacia Margarita, Morelia 93 (☎213 15 90), at Guerrero. Open 24hr.

Hospital: (☎213 25 56), on Transversal at Reyes. English spoken. Open 24hr.

Fax: Telecomm (☎217 21 50 or 212 03 56), in the same building as the post office on Rosales side. Open M-F 8am-7pm, Sa 8:30am-4pm, Su 9am-12:30pm.

Internet Access: VirtualCafé Internet, Rosales 97 (☎212 79 00), between Morelia and Monterrey. Open M-Sa 8:30am-10pm, Su noon-8pm. 25 pesos per hr.

Post Office: (☎212 00 11), on P. Elías Calles at Rosales. Open M-F 8am-7pm, Sa-Su 8am-noon. **Postal Code:** 83000.

ACCOMMODATIONS

Though hotels are sprinkled liberally throughout the *centro*, if you won't shell out pesos, you'll likely be left with unsavory lodgings. Cleanliness (and functioning toilets) are a luxury for those on a tight budget.

■ **Hotel Washington, D.C.,** Dr. Noriega 68 Pte. (☎213 11 83), between Matamoros and Guerrero. Owned and managed by the friendly son of two Americans, the D.C. provides clean rooms, central cooling, large private showers, great advice, and a community of young people from across the globe. Communal refrigerator, ironing board, and microwave. Free luggage storage. Singles 145 pesos; each additional person 20 pesos.

Casa de Huéspedes del Viajero, Sufragio Efectivo 90, between Pino Suárez and Yañez. Unbelievably large rooms in an 84-year-old building. Adobe construction and fans keep the rooms cool. Aging outdoor bathroom. Lock your bags, since no one's at the entrance from 7pm-7am. Singles 70 pesos.

Hotel Niza, P. Elías Calles 66 (☎217 20 28 or 217 20 35), between Guerrero and Garmendia. Rooms have A/C and comfortable beds (but uncomfortably dim lights). Private baths are small and not always the cleanest, but Niza's central location makes it a good place for those just looking for a place to sleep. A lobby restaurant serves *comida corrida* (26 pesos). Singles 170 pesos; doubles 200 pesos.

◖ FOOD

Eating in Hermosillo can be an adventure; everything from the typical *sonorense* staple of *carne asada* to authentic Chinese food and veggie burgers can be found within the *centro*. For cheap refueling, head for the taco and *torta* places around Serdán and Guerrero, where *taquitos* and *quesadillas* cost 7-8 pesos and *comida corrida* goes for around 15-20 pesos. If you are feeling braver, the food counters lining the inside of the **Mercado Municipal** on Elías Calles, between Matamoros and Guerrero, cook up tasty and very cheap *antojitos*. Most are sufficiently sanitary, but avoid eating any uncooked vegetables.

■ **Mi Cocina,** Obregón 84 (☎217 55 38), between Suárez and Yañez. Omar opens his *cocina* (kitchen) to budget travelers, serving up a mean two-course home-cooked meal (30 pesos) and making great conversation all the while. Open M-F 7:30am-6pm.

Fonda Chapala (☎212 39 92) on Guerrero between Sonora and Oaxaca. Mexican oldies blare while middle-aged men drown their sorrows in 40oz. bottles of Tecate. Chicken, fish, or meat comes fried to crispy perfection and served with french fries, *frijoles*, tortillas, side salad, and a drink (35-38 pesos). Open M-Sa 8am-10pm, Su 8am-2pm.

Restaurant Jung, Niños Héroes 75 (☎213 28 81), at Encinas. Relax to soothing music and the faint smell of incense as you savor the rejuvenating *comida corrida*, which comes with wheat rolls, soup, freshly-squeezed juice, an entree, veggies, french fries, *queso fresco*, yogurt, and dessert (48 pesos). Whole grain cereals with fruit 20 pesos, Belgian waffles 36 pesos. Open M-Sa 7:30am-8pm, Su 9am-5pm.

Jo Wah, Pino Suárez 180 (☎213 13 99). Enjoy huge portions of authentic Chinese food and chat with the kindly Cantonese owner. *Comida corrida,* including egg rolls, veggies, rice, chop suey, and more (40 pesos). Vegetarians can savor pan-fried tofu and veggie chop suey for 50 pesos. Open daily 2-5pm and 8-11pm.

Restaurant "My Friend" (☎213 10 44), P. Elías Calles at Yañez. A framed photo of a cheeseburger (20 pesos), fries, and a soft drink beckons to homesick *gringos*. Those who prefer Mexican cuisine can enjoy *chimichangas* (15 pesos) or *tacos de cabeza y barbacoa* (barbecued pig snouts; 15 pesos). Open M-Sa 7am-6pm.

◖ ♫ SIGHTS AND ENTERTAINMENT

Look for the cross-capped spires of the adorned pale yellow **Catedral de la Asunción** as you walk south on Rosales. Turn right on Hidalgo and walk two blocks west. (☎212 05 01. Office and gift shop open M-F 8am-7pm, Sa 8am-4pm.) Fugitives from the relentless sun will find refuge under the shady trees of the peaceful and well-kept **Plaza Zaragoza,** which separates the cathedral from the gray-and-white **Palacio de Gobierno.** The *palacio*, from which the state of Sonora is governed, should not be confused with the pink brick **Palacio Municipal** next door, where city government functions are carried out. Both are worth investigating for their architecture. The Palacio de Gobierno contains four historical murals surrounding its tree-laden inner courtyard, where statues immortalize Sonoran patriots and senators.

The **Museo Regional de Historia**, on Rosales at Encinas across from the **University of Sonora**, contains exhibits on pre-Hispanic and colonial history. The building also houses a **university art display.** (Open M-F 9am-1pm and 4-6pm, Sa 9am-1pm. Free.) The **Cuartel Catorce** is a rough structure with walls of brown brick on Guerrero and Colosio. The colonnaded inner courtyard is an oasis; the room in the back of the courtyard was once home to the army's cavalry. (☎ 217 12 41. Open M-F 8am-3pm.)

There is not a great deal of nightlife in Hermosillo. If, however, you're in the mood for a drink, a couple of watering holes can be found on Rosales south of Colosio. Popular with locals are **La Verbena** and **El Grito del Callejón** ("the Cry of the Alley"), both at Obregón and Pino Suárez—La Verbena is to the south and El Grito to the north. Adjacent to La Verbena is **Extasis Night Club**, located in a beautiful colonial building with a neon green glow. Although not exactly dangerous, the area around these bars is less than desirable, and travelers should use caution. If you are staying in the *centro*, conveniently located **Napy's**, Matamoros 109, between Dr. Noriega and Morelia, is a safer bet. After 9pm food service stops and the speakers are pumped to maximum volume as couples hit the dance floor, and friends cheer them on with pitchers of Tecate (50 pesos). F-Sa live salsa. (☎ 213 28 70. Open daily 10am-2am.) Those in need of a bit more levity can head to **Multicinemas**, Encinas 227, a 5-minute bus ride from the center of town. (☎ 214 09 70. Open daily 3-9pm; 38 pesos.)

🄳 DAYTRIPS FROM HERMOSILLO

CENTRO ECOLÓGICO DE SONORA

> To get to the Centro Ecológico, grab a white local "Luis Orci" bus from the corner of Guerrero and Dr. Noriega at the "Ruta 20" stop (20min., 3 pesos). ☎ 250 12 25. Open in summer Tu-Su 8am-6pm; in winter Tu-Su 8am-5pm. 10 pesos.

This is more than just your token neighborhood **zoo**; it is host to an impressive array of animal life, a mini-aquarium (complete with outdoor sea lions), and hundreds of plant species. The Centro Ecológico is also home to ground breaking biological research. A clearly marked walkway dotted with water fountains, shady benches, restrooms, and a wading pool guides visitors through the exhibits and affords a spectacular view of Hermosillo and its surrounding mountains. There is also a *basura* (garbage) exhibit with some crazy cockroaches (although you might not need a zoo to catch a glimpse of these un-elusive critters). The most spectacular feature of the Centro Ecológico, however, is its incredible collection of cacti—over 340 species are labeled and displayed throughout the animal exhibits and just outside the main pavilion. Keep your eyes peeled for the rare and beautiful *cina* and *biznaga*, from which fruit and candy are made, and the *maguey bacanora*, the fanned-out, spiked cactus that is the source of all those tequilas you've been downing. Children delight at the clowns and animated films shown in the air-conditioned movie theater (Sa-Su noon-6pm; free). The enthusiastic and knowledgeable staff happily answers any questions about the *Centro* and its flora and fauna.

BAHÍA KINO   ☎ 6

Bahía Kino, a 20km stretch of glistening sand, brilliant blue water, and radiant sun, is comprised of a pair of beach towns on the beautiful Sea of Cortés. **Kino Viejo**, a dusty, quiet fishing village, lies down the road from **Kino Nuevo**, a 4km-long strip of posh, secluded homes and condos where the satellite dishes and SUVs outnumber the pelicans overhead. Diving, fishing, and sailing entertain the more adventurous traveler, while the soft sandy beaches and gentle waves beckon the more relaxed travelers. As weekend daytrippers from Hermosillo will tell you, Kino provides an ideal destination for an escape from raucous urban desert to *palapa*-shaded tranquility. Soothing breezes, warm waters, and vast expanses of sand make the rickety ride from the city more than worthwhile.

⌐ TRANSPORTATION. Bahía Kino is 107km west of Hermosillo at the end of a dusty two-lane highway. **Buses** in Hermosillo leave from the old blue-and-red-striped **Transportes Norte de Sonora** station on Sonora between Jesús García and González, near the Jardín Juárez (2hr., 10 per day 5:40am-5:30pm, 38 pesos). The bus stops in **Kino Viejo** before going on to **Kino Nuevo.** Look for water on your left and get off where you'd like. Early birds can make it a daytrip—get an early bus from Hermosillo and sleep (if you can) during the ride. Missing the 5:30pm bus back to Hermosillo means spending the night in Kino. To get from one Kino to the other or back to Hermosillo, flag down the bus (every hr., 4 pesos) on Nuevo's main (and only) road, **Mar de Cortés,** or on **Blvd. Kino** in Kino Viejo. If you choose to walk the couple of kilometers between towns, be sure to keep plenty of water and sun protection on hand. Hitching is also a popular mode of transportation in this area.

◪ PRACTICAL INFORMATION. Public bathrooms can be found in Nuevo toward the beginning of the beach directly in front of La Palapa Restaurant. In Kino Viejo, **pleasant potties** are available at the **Centro de Salud** at Tampico and Blvd. Kino; bring your own toilet paper. In any type of **emergency,** your best bet might be to look for the American-run **Club Deportivo,** on the right side of Monaco toward the end of Mar De Cortés, and knock on the door; the friendly expatriate community takes good care of foreign visitors. **Emergency:** ☎ 080. **Police:** at Santa Catalina and Mar de Cortés (☎ 242 00 67) in Viejo or at Blvd. Kino and Cruz (☎ 242 00 32) in Nuevo. **Farmacia San Francisco** at Blvd. Kino and Toplobambo serves the needs of both towns. (☎ 242 02 30. Open daily 9am-1pm and 2pm-9pm.) **Red Cross:** Blvd. Kino and Manzanillo in Kino Viejo, near the post office and police. There is no phone, but it can be contacted via the emergency number. For English-speaking **medical attention,** call Dr. José Luis (☎ 242 03 95). **Long-distance phones** are available at the clothing shop at Blvd. Kino and Tampico in Kino Viejo; **LADATELs** dot Mar de Cortés in Nuevo and can be found across from the *farmacia* in Viejo. **Post Office:** Next to the police in Viejo. (Open M-F 8am-3pm.)

▐▊▐ ACCOMMODATIONS AND FOOD. Safe and comfortable lodgings are plentiful on the beachfront—just find a free *palapa* and set up camp. For those who prefer mattresses to sand, Kino's version of "budget" accommodations awaits at the **Hotel Posada del Mar,** Mar de Cortés at the beginning of Kino Nuevo. Rooms have A/C, baths, and use of the pool. (☎ 242 01 55. Singles 340 pesos; 60 pesos each additional person.) If you've got big wheels you're in luck—more than 10 RV parks offer beachfront hook-ups (about US$15 per day). **Islandia Marina** is right on the beach in Viejo. Take Blvd. Kino and follow the road to the end. It has one of the better locations and also rents cabins complete with four beds, a refrigerator, a kitchen, a bathroom, and two powerful fans. (Quads 350 pesos; 50 pesos per additional person.)

Restaurants in Kino tend to be expensive; for a meal that's as economical as you want it to be, do as the *hermosillanos* do and pack a lunch to enjoy under a beach *palapa.* Otherwise, a decent budget meal can be found in Viejo at the family-run **Dorita,** Blvd. Kino and Sabina Cruz, which is eclectically decorated with "Spice Girls" paraphernalia and paintings of Christ. Plastic-topped tables and kitschy animal-shaped vases crowd this little restaurant known for its moderately-priced breakfasts (25-35 pesos), delicious *carnes asadas* (45 pesos), and all-you-can-drink *agua purificada.* (☎ 242 03 49. Open daily 7am-8pm.) In Nuevo, **Restaurante la Palapa,** toward the beginning of the beach, cooks up some tasty *camarones al mojo de ajo* (shrimp sautéed in garlic butter, 60 pesos) and fresh *pescado* any way you like it (50 pesos). Homesick *gringos* will appreciate the juicy *hamburguesas* (25 pesos). Relax under the *palapa*-covered balcony and watch the sunset. (Open daily 8am-8pm.)

⊡ ◪ SIGHTS AND BEACHES. Kino's **beaches** are peacefully deserted early in the week, but as the weekend approaches, so does the crowd. Fortunately, the masses in Kino are nothing compared to the masses at other beach towns, and it is possible to find an unoccupied and garbage-free *palapa. Gringos* with homes in Kino tend to populate the beaches during the winter, making for some long, lonely stretches of sand during the summer months. In general, the beaches are better in Kino Nuevo. To rent **diving** equipment and/or a guide, call **Carlos Montes** (☎246 0 89 01) or find him at Islandía on weekends. **Fishing** trips can be arranged with **Ernesto Hínojosa** (☎242 03 20). You can also ask one of the local fishermen if you can come along for a ride.

For non-beach entertainment, the **Museo de los Seris,** on Mar de Cortés at Progreso near the end of Kino Nuevo, offers an air-conditioned refuge and teaches you more than you ever thought you'd learn about the Seris, an indigenous fishing tribe. (Open W-Su 9am-4pm. 3 pesos, children 2 pesos.) In Kino Nuevo, 300 yards past the Museo de los Seris, you'll see a giant image of the virgin painted on the face of a hill. The short pilgrimage to her perch affords a breathtaking sea view.

The closest thing to nightlife in Kino can be found a block past Dorita's in Viejo, where locals gather at night to play a few rounds at **Billares Brenda.** (Open daily until 9 or 10pm.)

GUAYMAS ☎ 6

Skirted by steep, rocky hills to the north and the Sea of Cortés to the east, Guaymas (pop. 150,000) is the principal port in Sonora, proud home to an active shrimping fleet, fisheries galore, and delicious restaurants, where you can savor the fresh taste of the most recent catch. Nearby, beachy **San Carlos** wins the prize as destination-of-choice for many *norteamericano* tourists, while the smaller beaches of **Miramar** draw a distinctly Mexican crowd. Guaymas itself is no schmaltzy resort venue, but the port area does offer a view of some of Mexico's most scintillating sunsets (over docked shrimp boats, the sea, and nearby mountains), while its lovely cathedral and picturesque parks provide travelers with comfortable places to relax. The busy streets may call back memories of urban Hermosillo, but the cool sea breeze and the warmth of the people give Guaymas a decided advantage.

◧ TRANSPORTATION

Airport: To reach the airport, catch a bus marked "San José" along Serdán (10min.; 1 per hour, 3 pesos). Aeroméxico (☎222 01 23), Serdán at Calle 16, has flights to: **La Paz** (1½hr., 2:55pm); **Mexico City** (3½hr., 2:55pm); **Phoenix, Arizona** (1½hr., M-W and F-Sa 10:45am); and **Los Angeles** (2hr.; Th, Su; 9:25am). Office open daily 6am-6pm.

Buses: Buses arrive at Calle 14. To get to the main street, Serdán, turn left if you're coming out of the **Transportes del Norte** station and turn right if you're coming out of the **Transportes del Pacífico** or the **Transportes Baldomero Corral** stations. Transportes del Pacifico (☎222 30 19) buses leave every 45min. to: **Guadalajara** (20hr., 790 pesos); **Hermosillo** (1½hr., 30 pesos); **Los Mochis** (5hr., 150 pesos); **Mazatlán** (12hr., 460 pesos); **Mexicali** (12hr., 430 pesos); **Mexico City** (26hr., 1170 pesos); **Nogales** (6hr., 160 pesos); **Puerto Peñasco** (9hr., 209 pesos); **Tepic** (18hr., 640 pesos); and **Tijuana** (13hr., 560 pesos). Transportes Norte de Sonora (☎222 12 71) offers similar service, with buses leaving every hour or two. Across the street, Transportes Baldomero Corral can take you to **Navojoa** (4hr., every hr., 56 pesos).

Ferries: (☎222 23 24). Ferries leave from a small dock on Serdán, about 2km east of the *centro*. To get to the dock, take any local bus headed east on Serdán and ask the driver to let you off at the ferry. A blue and white "Sematur Transboradores" sign will be on your right. Ferries go to **Santa Rosalía** (6hr.; Tu, Th 9am; *salón* 270 pesos, *turista* 540 pesos) and **La Paz** (18hr.; F 3pm; *salón* 680 pesos, *turista* 1360 pesos).

✦ ⧉ ORIENTATION AND PRACTICAL INFORMATION

Guaymas is 407km south of Nogales on **Mexico 15.** The *centro* is the area surrounding Guaymas's colorful main strip, Serdán, beginning at Calle 10 and ending at Calle 29. Running perpendicular to Serdán are Calle 1, Calle 2, Calle 3, etc. If you're walking along Serdán and the numbers of the intersecting streets are increasing, you are headed east toward the waterfront. The waterfront begins at Calle 20, two blocks south of Serdán at Av. 11 (the *malecón*), and Serdán itself continues along the sea after Calle 24. Safety is not a major concern, but women should avoid walking alone more than two blocks south of Serdán after dark. Note that upon leaving the city, northbound vehicles, including buses, are often stopped by narcotics police. Have your identification ready and let them search whatever they want; it's better not to assert the right to privacy when dealing with humorless armed *federales*.

Tourist Office: Located 19km north of the city in San Carlos.

Currency Exchange: Banks are located along Serdán. **Banamex** (☎224 01 23), Serdán at Calle 20, exchanges currency and traveler's checks and has 24hr. **ATMs.** Open M-F 8:30am-4:30pm.

Luggage Storage: Lockers are available at the Transportes Norte de Sonora bus terminal. 12 pesos per first 8hr., 5 pesos each additional hr. Open 24hr.

Car Rental: Hertz, Calzada García López 625 (☎222 10 00 or 222 30 28). Open M-F 8am-6pm, Sa-Su 8am-3pm. **Budget** (☎222 55 55), Serdán and Calle 4. Open M-F 8am-6pm, Sa-Su 8am-3pm.

Market: VH Supermarket (☎224 19 49), on Serdán, between Calles 19 and 20. You can't miss it. Open M-Sa 7am-11:30pm, Su 7am-8:30pm.

Police: (☎224 01 04 or 224 01 05), on Calle 11 at Av. 9, near the Villa School. Some English spoken. Open 24hr.

Red Cross: (☎222 55 55 or 224 08 76), on México 15, about 1½km north of the *centro*. Also has **ambulances.** Open 24hr.

Pharmacy: Farmacia Sonora (☎222 11 00), Serdán at Calle 15. Open 24hr.

Hospital: Hospital Municipal (☎224 21 38), on Calle 12 between Av. 6 and 7. Some English spoken. Open 24hr.

Internet Access: The Web@.com on Serdán just past Calle 14 (☎222 66 40). 15 pesos per hr. Open M-Sa 9am-9pm, Su 2-7pm.

Fax: Telecomm (☎222 02 92), next to post office. Open M-F 8am-7:30pm, Sa-Su 9am-noon.

Post Office: (☎222 07 57), Av. 10 between Calle 19 and 20, next to the pink Luis G. Davila School. Open M-F 8am-7pm, Sa 8am-noon. **Postal Code:** 85400.

ACCOMMODATIONS

Accommodations in Guaymas cluster around **Serdán,** where cheap beds are plentiful but only a handful are comfortable, clean, and convenient. A few *casas de huéspedes* can be found on streets off Serdán.

Casa de Huéspedes Lupita, Calle 15 #125 (☎222 84 09), 2 blocks south of Serdán and across from the castle-like jail. Tidy, small rooms come equipped with fans, and an *agua purificada* dispenser awaits downstairs in the office. Singles 60 pesos, with bath 70 pesos, with A/C 100 pesos; doubles with bath 100 pesos, with A/C 150 pesos.

Hotel Impala, Calle 21 #40 (☎224 09 22), 1 block south of Serdán. Photos of Guaymas's past grace the walls of the pristine rooms with comfy beds, A/C, TV, and *agua purificada* dispensers in every hallway. Singles 180 pesos; doubles 220 pesos; triples 270 pesos.

Motel del Puerto, Yañez 92 (☎224 34 08 or 2 24 91), 2 blocks south of Serdán on Calle 19. Reminiscent of a beachfront motel (without the beach). Rooms have soft beds, satellite TVs, and A/C. Singles 170 pesos; doubles 200 pesos; triples 250 pesos.

Motel Santa Rita, Serdán 590 (☎224 19 19), at Calle 9. Boasts a huge parking lot. Large sparkling rooms with A/C, TV, and phone. Staff is friendly and knowledgeable. Singles 270 pesos; doubles 300 pesos.

FOOD

Seafood is Guaymas's specialty. Local favorites include *ancas de rana* (frog's legs), *cahuna* (turtle steaks), and *ostiones* (oysters) in a garlic and chile sauce. Unfortunately, if you want to sample these local delicacies, you're going to have to pay a fair sum for them. For those on a tighter budget, the **Mercado Municipal,** on Calle 20, one block from Serdán, sells fresh produce, and there are an abundance of *comida corrida* joints on Serdán.

Restaurant Bar La Barca de Guaymas (☎224 30 77), on Calle 9 just north of Serdán. A genuine boat crowns the roof and a huge thatched *palapa* decorates the dining area. Savor *tacos de pescado* (30 pesos) and *ceviche* (12 pesos). Open daily 10am-2am.

Los Barcos (☎222 76 50), on the *malecón* at Calle 22. Huge platters of *chimichangas de camarón* (shrimp), *pescado* (fish), *pulpo* (octopus), and *jaiba* (crab; 50-60 pesos). *Machaca de pescado* (shredded meat flavored with tomato, onion, and *chile verde* combined with seafood, 60 pesos. Open daily 10am-10:30pm.

Las 1000 Tortas, Serdán 188, between Calles 17 and 18. The *torta* rules at this family-run joint (13 pesos each). The friendly owner goes from table to table chatting with customers who munch happily on enchiladas, *gorditas* (27 pesos), and three types of *comida corrida* (33 pesos). Open daily 11am-11pm.

S. E. Pizza Buffet (☎222 24 46), Serdán at Calle 20. Disney images and framed posters of American cars and athletes decorate the walls. Satisfy your appetite with the all-you-can-eat buffet of pizza, spaghetti, and salad (25 pesos). Open daily 11am-11pm.

⬛ SIGHTS AND ENTERTAINMENT

Guaymas's **beaches,** popular with both tourists and locals and accessible via a short bus ride from Serdán, are located to the north in **San Carlos** (see p. 212) and **Miramar** (10 min., 4 pesos). The nicer (but smaller) beaches in Miramar are back along the bus route in front of the fancy villas. The beaches are very safe during the day, but camping is very strongly discouraged as many *borrachos malintentos* (drunk bad people!) spend their evenings on the beaches. One look at the bottle-riddled sand will prove the point.

Most of the scenic places in Guaymas lie on the east side of town near the waterfront. For the best view in town—of the mountains, the port, the city, and the bay—seek out the shady benches of the **Plaza del Pescador,** just off Serdán toward the water, between Calles 24 and 25. While you're in the area, take a stroll across the **Plaza de los Tres Presidentes,** on Calle 23 at Serdán, where three towering bronze statues immortalize early 20th-century presidents, to the grandiose stone **Palacio Municipal,** a classic Colonial-style structure built in 1899. The blue bay waters, the towering green-and-white **Catedral de San Fernando,** and a pretty little park full of swaying palms complete the scene.

Huge signs advertising **travesty shows**—transvestite acts imitating popular Latin singers—are everywhere in Guaymas. **Cyrus,** the club with the concrete wolf façade on Serdán, between Calles 16 and 17, has the most frequent shows. (M, W, Th, and Su. Free and half-price beer 9-11pm.) On the waterfront, **Charles Baby Disco Video,** Serdán between Calle 21 and 22, also has shows. (Th and Su. Beer 12 pesos.) If you're looking for a drink and some dancing without the frills, **Sahuaro Piano Bar** and **Zodiakos,** next to Charles Baby Disco Video, serve beers (10 pesos). Also near the waterfront, on Rodríguez, just behind the easternmost presidential statue (Adolfo de la Huerta), many locals dance the night away at **Gambrinus** or **La Salsa,** while their uncles shoot pool at **The Friends' Club** two doors down.

SAN CARLOS ☎6

Thirty-five years ago, San Carlos (pop. 2500) was just a dusty road in the desert north of Guaymas; now, condos, hotels, and malls are sprouting like wildflowers to accommodate the increasing tourist influx. San Carlos greets visitors with a

I THOUGHT IT WAS A CACTUS... Proud of its beautiful expansive deserts, the US state of Arizona features tall cacti, jagged mountains, and a setting sun on its license plates. Equally rugged and wild, Sonora shares the dry, piercing heat, amazing variety of colorful cacti, and wide open skies of which its neighbor state is so proud. Glance at a *sonorense* license plate and you'll think you're seeing double, but a closer look reveals that the blob of green under the bright orange sun, so grandly emblazoned across so many sheets of metal, is not a plant at all. Proud of their *vaquero* (cowboy) past, the descendants of Pancho Villa's army chose a big green *vaca* (cow) to represent their *norteño*-loving, *sombrero*-wearing, *carne asada*-eating heritage.

lush country club, a five-star hotel (the only one in Sonora), and an artificial shipwreck, the largest and shallowest in the world. With a population that swells to 8000 come winter, when droves of *norteamericano* retirees return to their pastel-colored beachfront homes, San Carlos knows exactly how to pamper its guests.

TRANSPORTATION. White striped buses come from downtown Guaymas and run down the main road to the Marina Real and Plaza Las Glorias, but don't make it all the way to the El Mirador Escénico or Playa Los Algodones. (Approx. every 10min. 6am-11pm; 7 pesos to Guaymas, 3 within San Carlos.)

ORIENTATION AND PRACTICAL INFORMATION. The main (and basically only) road in San Carlos, **Manlio F. Beltrones,** runs east-west. Most of the shops, restaurants, and accommodations lie on Beltrones between Hacienda Tetakawi Hotel and Trailer Park to the east and the small road to Plaza Las Florias to the west. The **tourist office** is in **Hacienda Tours,** on Beltrones just before El Mar Diving Center. (☎ 226 02 02. Open M-F 9am-5pm, Sa 9am-2pm.) **Banamex,** on Beltrones next to the PEMEX station, exchanges dollars and traveler's checks and has a 24hr. **ATM.** (☎ 226 12 40. Open M-F 8:30am-4:30pm.) Buy your groceries at **San Carlos Super Mercado** in front of the church at the end of the road to Plaza Las Glorias. (☎ 226 00 43. Open daily 7am-9pm.) **Lavandería Automática,** next to Piccolo Restaurant, offers full or self-service and hand-washing. (☎ 226 00 13. Open 24hr.) **Emergency:** Call **Rescate,** which is funded entirely by donations from San Carlos residents. (☎ 226 01 01 or 226 01 58. 24hr. medical service and ambulances.) **Police:** (☎ 226 14 00), up the hill on the road to Plaza Las Glorias. **Farmacia Bahía San Carlos,** across the street from Motel Creston. (☎ 226 00 97 or 226 02 42. Open M-Sa 8am-7pm.) **Post office:** (☎ 226 05 06) next to Ana Maria's Beauty Shop. **Café de Internet,** across the street from the San Carlos Bowling Lanes on Beltrones. (☎ 226 13 63. 15 pesos per 15min. Open daily 8am-11pm.)

ACCOMMODATIONS AND FOOD. San Carlos is full of hotels, none of which is priced for the budget traveler. For those wise enough to pack a tent or an RV, **El Mirador RV Park,** on the road to El Mirador Escénico, provides full hookups in RV paradise—scenic views, a glistening pool, abundant free modem access, many table games, plentiful pristine showers, and two new tennis courts. (US$20 per day, US$120 per week.) **Hacienda Tetakawi,** on Beltrones, km 8.5, at the beginning of the main strip, offers full RV hookups and tent spaces. (☎ 226 02 20. RV hookups US$20 per day, US$126 per week; tent space 1-2 people US$10, US$3 each additional person.) **Motel Creston,** across the street from Jax Snax, and an easy walk to the beach, is the cheapest hotel you'll find, with sparkling rooms with two beds, A/C, and bath. The patio faces a clean pool. (☎ 226 00 20. Singles 350 pesos.)

While most restaurants are on the expensive side, a few places here and there cater to the budget traveler. Peso-pinchers can satisfy cravings with *burritos de carne asada* or fresh *almejas* (clams) eaten raw with salsa, *limón,* or chocolate from vendors toward the western end of Beltrones. An eclectic collection of unframed paintings by local artists adorns the walls of **Banana's Restaurant and Bar,** just past El Mar Diving Center. Breakfast includes eggs, toast, and hash browns (US$1). (☎ 226 06 06. Happy Hours 10-11am and 4-5pm. Open daily 7am-1am.)

🔲🔳 SIGHTS AND BEACHES. A colorful array of marine flora and fauna make their homes in the Sea of Cortés, attracting divers eager to catch a glimpse of the underwater brilliance and fishermen eager to catch dinner. Near the town is **San Pedro Nolasco Island,** a popular dive site where sea lions and marine birds coexist in harmony. The state of Sonora recently spent a large sum of money to sink a 120ft. tuna boat and 300ft. passenger liner to create an artificial reef for scuba divers. Dive shops along Beltrones rent scuba gear and sea kayaks and lead guided dives for a pretty penny (US$65 for an 8hr. trip to the island). For those who prefer *terra firma*, **El Mar Diving Center** also rents bikes and leads boat trips. (☎ 226 04 04. US$10 per 8hr. on a cruiser; US$25 for 8hr. on a mountain bike. Open daily in summer 7am-6:30pm, in winter 7:30-5:30pm.) If fishing is your thing, pick up a license (58 pesos per day) at the **Secretaria de Pesca** on Beltrones just before the turn-off to Plaza Las Glorias. (Open 9am-3pm.) It's illegal to fish without one.

If you have access to a car, **El Mirador Escénico,** a vista atop a steep road, affords views of Tetakawi and the secluded coves of **Playa Piedras Pintas.** For swimming or sunbathing, head over to the beaches west of Tetakawi, which are cleaner and more peaceful. **Playa San Francisco,** beginning at the Condominios Pilar and extending to Hotel Fiesta, is rocky. A dirt road near the gate to Costa Del Mar about 8km past the end of the bus route leads to **Playa Los Algodones** (Cotton Beach), so named because the soft sand is often compared to cotton. Taxis can take you on a tour of the area, including El Mirador, Piedras Pintas and Los Algodones (200 pesos per 1½hr.)

ALAMOS   ☎ 6

The sleepy town of Alamos (pop. 8000), in the scenic foothills of the Sierra Madre Occidental, is a rambling collection of handsome colonial *haciendas*. Founded in 1531, Alamos was relatively ignored until silver was discovered in 1683. For nearly a hundred years, Alamos produced more silver than any area in the world, but when the silver veins ran dry at the turn of the century, Alamos shrank to ghost-town proportions. In the last 50 years, however, wealthy Americans and Canadians have taken interest in the town, particularly in the rambling mansions left behind by the silver tycoons. Thanks to their funds, Alamos has returned to its glory days—the refurbished *haciendas* and cobblestone streets give the city a bygone feel unlike any in northwest Mexico.

📲 TRANSPORTATION. To reach Alamos by bus, you must change buses in **Navojoa,** 53km southwest of Alamos. From the Transportes Norte de Sonora and Elite bus stations in Navojoa, stand at the corner of Allende and Ferrocarril, looking down Ferrocarril as you face the bus stations. Walk one block to the Transportes del Pacífico station and turn left (toward the center of town) onto Guerrero. Six blocks along Guerrero (passing the Transportes de Baja California bus station after 3 blocks) is the Los Mayitos bus station at Rincón, where you can catch a bus to **Alamos** (1hr., every hr. 6am-6:30pm, 18 pesos). The return trip from Alamos starts from the bus station at Plaza Alameda (same times and price).

📇🔳 ORIENTATION AND PRACTICAL INFORMATION. You can explore the small and compact town of Alamos on foot. As you come into town on **Madero,** you'll reach a fork in the road at the bronze statue of Benito Juárez; the left branch leads to **Plaza Alameda,** the commercial center (where the bus stops), and the right branch to **Plaza de Armas** in the historic district. A small alley known as the **Callejón del Beso** connects the Plaza de Armas with the market behind the Plaza Alameda. The cathedral south of Plaza de Armas marks the entrance to the **Barrio La Colorada,** where the expats have concentrated their *hacienda*-restoring efforts.

The Alamos **tourist office,** Juárez 6, is under the Hotel Los Portales on the west side of the Plaza de Armas, though it's anyone's guess when the eccentric (and extremely knowledgeable) tour guide will be around. (☎ 428 04 50. Open M-F 9am-2pm and 4-7pm, Sa 9am-2pm.) **Currency exchange: Bancrecer,** on Madero before the

LIKE WATER FOR CHICHARRONES
When in Mexico, there's no escaping the *chicharrones* (pork rinds). In some towns the popular snack has become...an ice cream flavor! On sweltering hot days, vendors push long carts loaded with rows of metal casks and scoop out ice cold salvation in a crazy variety of flavors—*elote* (cornmeal), *cerveza* (beer), *aguacate* (avocado), tequila, and *chicharrones*. Hand a vendor 5 pesos and he'll cram a mammoth portion into a cone or plastic cup. Mexican ice cream is known to harbor more than a few nasty amoebas, so check the cleanliness of the stand before placing spoon in mouth. Once you're confident of your food's safety, tuck a napkin into your shirt front and scarf it down.

fork in the road. (☎428 03 57. Open M-F 8:30am-3pm, Sa 10am-2pm.) A 24hr. **ATM** is next door. **Supermarket: SuperTito's,** at the fork in Maderos, operates as a **pharmacy,** grocery store, and liquor store. (☎428 05 12. Open daily 7:30am-10:30pm.) **Medical Assistance:** farther from the center on Madero is the **Hospital Básico** (☎428 00 25 or 8 00 26), which has ambulance service and free emergency service. **Post office:** in the Palacio Municipal. (Open M-F 8am-3pm.) **Postal code:** 85763.

▐▌ **ACCOMMODATIONS.** Unless you rediscover silver on your way into town, you'll probably have to miss out on the *hacienda* hotels. The **Hotel Enrique,** next to the Hotel Los Portales on Juárez, on the west side of the Plaza de Armas, has rooms with fans and a (very) communal bathroom. Don't be alarmed by the tame wolf that lives on the grounds; the owners say it just wandered down from the hills. (☎428 03 10. Singles 90 pesos; doubles 150 pesos.) **Motel Somar,** Madero 110, near the Plaza Alameda, offers rooms with lukewarm showers and a chance to chat with locals in the lobby. (☎428 01 95. Singles 150 pesos, with A/C 200 pesos; doubles 200 pesos and up.) **Hotel Dolisa,** Madero 72, next to Motel Somar, offers *agua purificada,* A/C, and baths in every room. If there's no one at the desk, be patient. Singles 250 pesos; doubles 280 pesos; 80 pesos each additional person.

▐▌ **FOOD.** Peso-pinchers patronize taco stands, such as **Taquería Blanquita,** in the Me.cado Municipal by Plaza Alameda. (Open daily 7am-10:30pm.) In the market, you can buy delectable fruits and vegetables within walking distance of where they were grown. **Polo's Restaurant,** Zaragoza 4, right off the Plaza de Armas, has friendly ser ice, paintings of local sights, and good food starting at 40 pesos. (☎428 00 03. Open daily 7am-9:30pm.) For a good view of the Plaza de Armas, the distant foothills, and an *hacienda* or two, eat under the arches at **Restaurant Las Palmeras,** Cárdenas 9, northeast of the Plaza de Armas. You're likely to run into US expats and a number of local officials. (☎428 00 65. Breakfasts 20-30 pesos, *antojitos* 20-35. Open daily 7am-10pm.)

▐▌ **SIGHTS.** The best reason to visit Alamos is to get a glimpse of the glory days of the *hacienda.* The manager of the tourist office may be able to suggest a tour or give you one himself. One of the grandest homes in town was constructed in 1720 and refinished in the 19th century, when it became the home of José María Almada, owner of one of the world's richest silver mines. The **Hotel Las Portales** now occupies most of the building, including Don Almada's foyer and courtyard. Other impressive restored homes, many of which are now hotels, can be found around the cathedral, including the Casa de los Tesoros (a former convent), the Hotel La Mansión, the Casa Encantada, and Las Delicias.

The town's cathedral, **La Parroquia de la Purísima Concepción,** was completed in 1786 and occupies a commanding position on the Plaza de Armas. The porcelain plates set into the base of the church tower were donated by upper-class Alamos ladies. The town **jail** and the **Mirador** offer excellent views. To get to the jail, walk along Madero west of the center of town and follow the signs. The **Museo Costumbrista,** the yellow and white building across from Las Palmeras in the Plaza de Armas, has exhibits of Los Alamos' history. (☎428 00 53. Open July-Aug. W-Su 9am-6pm; Sept.-June W-Su 9am-3pm. 10 pesos, 5 pesos for students and children.)

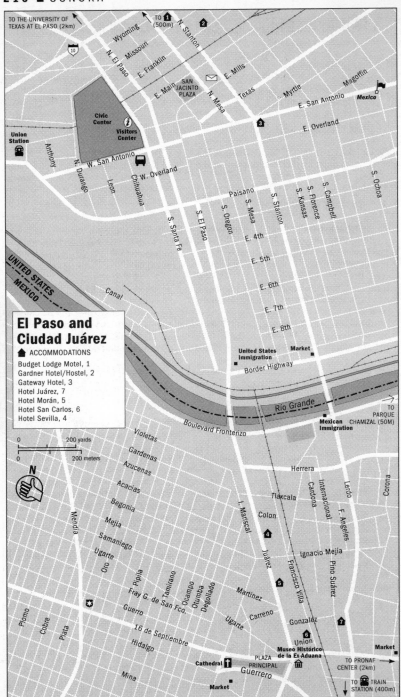

TO THE UNIVERSITY OF
TEXAS AT EL PASO (2km)

TO 1
(500m)

Wyoming

Missouri

N. El Paso

E. Franklin

E. Main

SAN
JACINTO
PLAZA

N. Stanton

N. Mesa

E. Mills

E. Texas

Myrtle

Magoffin

E. San Antonio

Mexico

E. Overland

Civic
Center

Visitors
Center

Union
Station

Anthony

N. Durango

W. San Antonio

Leon

Chihuahua

W. Overland

3

S. El Paso

S. Santa Fe

S. Oregon

S. Mesa

Paisano

S. Stanton

S. Kansas

S. Florence

S. Campbell

S. Ochoa

E. 4th

E. 5th

E. 6th

E. 7th

E. 8th

Canal

UNITED STATES
MEXICO

United States
Immigration

Market

Border Highway

El Paso and
Ciudad Juárez

♠ ACCOMMODATIONS

Budget Lodge Motel, 1
Gardner Hotel/Hostel, 2
Gateway Hotel, 3
Hotel Juárez, 7
Hotel Morán, 5
Hotel San Carlos, 6
Hotel Sevilla, 4

Río Grande

TO
PARQUE
CHAMIZAL (50M)

Boulevard Fronterizo

Mexican
Immigration

0   200 yards
0   200 meters

N

Violetas

Gardenas

Azucenas

Acacias

Begonia

Mejía

Samaniego

Ugarte

Oro

Pipila

Fray G. de San Fco.

Mendia

Plomo

Cobre

Plata

Guerro

16 de Septiembre

Hidalgo

Mina

Tamiano

Ocampo

Otumba

Degollado

I. Mariscal

Colon

Tlaxcala

Cardona

Internacional

Lerdo

F. Angeles

Corona

Herrera

Juárez

4

Francisco Villa

Ignacio Mejía

Pino Suárez

5

Martínez

Carreno

Ugarte

Gonzalez

7

Market

Union

6

**Museo Histórico
de la Ex-Aduana**

PLAZA
PRINCIPAL

Cathedral

Guerrero

Market

TO PRONAF
CENTER (2km)

TO TRAIN
STATION (400m)

CHIHUAHUA

EL PASO, TEXAS ☎915

The largest of the US border towns, El Paso (pop. 700,000) boomed in the 17th century as a stopover on an important east-west wagon route that followed the Rio Grande through "the pass" (*el paso*) between the Rocky Mountains and the Sierra Madre. Today, modern El Paso continues to serve as a passageway, albeit a passageway of a different sort. Sitting amidst rugged mountains and sagebrush, El Paso is now a stopover for travelers crossing between the US and Mexico, and the town's mixture of Mexican and American culture gives those crossing into Mexico a first glimpse of what awaits them. After dark, activity leaves the center of town, migrating either toward the University of Texas at El Paso (UTEP), or south of the border to raucous Ciudad Juárez.

▐ TRANSPORTATION

Airport: Located northeast of the city center. To get to the city, take Sun Metro bus #33. The stop is located on a traffic island outside the air terminal building (50min., every hr. M-F 5:54am-8:59pm, Sa 7:24am-8:59pm, Su 8:12am-7:02pm. US$1). to reach it, take bus #33 from San Jacinto Square (50 min., 5:10am-8:15pm) Get off when the bus arrives at San Jacinto Plaza. When the bus stops running late at night, the only way to get to the city is to take a taxi (approximately US$20-25). To get back to the airport, take the same bus from San Jacinto Square.

Buses: Greyhound, 200 W. San Antonio (☎532-2365 or 800-231-2222), across from the Civic Center between Santa Fe and Chihuahua. Daily service to and from: Dallas (12hr.; 7 per day; US$60), Los Angeles (16hr.; 6 per day; US$45), New York (48hr.; 7 per day; US$99), Phoenix (8-9hr., several per day, US$35), and other US cities. Storage lockers US$2 per hr. Open 24hr.

Public Transportation: Sun Metro (☎533-3333), departing from San Jacinto Plaza, at the corner of Main and Oregon. US$1, students and children US$0.50, seniors and disabled persons US$0.30, transfer US$0.10.

CROSSING THE BORDER. The easiest way to cross the border is to walk. Take the north-south #8 or #10 green trolley operated by Sun Metro to the Santa Fe Bridge, the last stop before the trolley turns around (every 15min.; M-F 6:15am-8:15pm, Sa 7:45am-8:15pm, Su 8:45am-7:15pm, US$0.25). Do not confuse the green trolley with the more expensive Border Jumper Trolley. Two pedestrian and motor roads cross the Rio Grande: **El Paso Ave.,** a crowded one-way street, and **Stanton Ave.,** a parallel road lined with stores and restaurants. Walk to the right side of the Stanton Bridge and pay the US$0.25 fee to cross. Daytrippers, including foreign travelers with multi-entry visas, should be prepared to flash their documents of citizenship. US citizens need proof of citizenship, or a driver's licence. Non-US citizens must have either an I-94 form, a Visa, or a passport. If you are planning to venture more than 22km into Mexico's interior, you need a **tourist card.** Get one at the Mexican immigration office, directly to your right as you enter into Ciudad Juárez.

To enter the United States, cross over the Santa Fe Bridge near the large *"Feliz Viaje"* sign. Be ready to answer questions posed by US border guards and to show a valid visa or proof of citizenship. You must also pay a US$0.30 fee. Once in El Paso, wait at the bus stop on the right-hand sidewalk just across from the bridge. The north-south bus runs from 6:15am-8:15pm, M-F, Sa 7:42am-8:15pm and Su 8:42-7:22pm. Either the #8 or the #10 bus will return you to downtown El Paso. If **driving** into and out of Mexico, note that vehicles are charged US$1.25 each way, and may require a permit.

■✦🛈 ORIENTATION AND PRACTICAL INFORMATION

El Paso is situated in the western corner of the US state of Texas, across the Rio Grande River from its sister city, Ciudad Juárez. El Paso is divided into east and west by **Santa Fe** and into north and south by **San Antonio.** Tourists should be wary of the streets between San Antonio and the border late at night.

Tourist Office: 1 Civic Center Plaza (☎544-0062; www.visitelpaso.com), one of the small round buildings next to the Chamber of Commerce at the intersection of Santa Fe and San Francisco. Maps and brochures available. Open daily 8am-5pm. Also sells **El Paso-Juárez Trolley Co.** tickets for tours across the border. Call to make reservations.

Mexican Consulate: 910 E. San Antonio (☎533-3644), on the corner of Virginia. Dispenses **tourist cards** (see p. 9). Open M-F 9am-4:30pm.

Currency Exchange: Valuta, 307 E. Paisano (☎544-1152), at Mesa St. Conveniently near the border and open 24hr. **Melek,** 306 E. Paisano Dr. (☎532-4283), next to Valuta. All of the banks in the downtown area around San Jacinto Plaza have **ATMs.** Plan ahead—banks usually close by 5pm, and other ATMs are scarce.

Car Rental: Budget (☎532-34-35), locations at 404A N. Mesa and at airport. **Dollar Rent-a-Car** (☎778-5445), Airport Location 6701, Convair Rd. **Enterprise** (☎779-2260), Airport Location 6701, Convair Rd. **Thrifty** (☎881-9089), at airport.

Hospital: Providence Memorial Hospital, 2001 N. Oregon (☎577-6011), at Hague near UTEP. Open 24hr.

Post Office: 219 E. Mills (☎532-2652), between Mesa and Stanton. Open M-F 9am-5pm, Sa 8am-noon. **Postal code:** 79901.

Internet Access: Internet facilities are sparse in El Paso, but if you must check email, **El Paso Community College,** Rio Grande campus, offers Internet access to the public (M-Th 5pm-8:30pm, Sa 9am-3pm, Su 1-4:30pm).

▛ ACCOMMODATIONS

El Paso offers safer, more appealing places to stay than Ciudad Juárez. Apart from the usual hotel chains (La Quinta, Days Inn, etc.) lining **I-10** and some more upper-crust establishments near the airport, several good budget hotels can be found in the center of town near **Main St.** and **San Jacinto Square.**

▧ El Paso International Hostel, 311 E. Franklin (☎532-3661; fax 532-0302, email epihostl@whc.net), between Stanton and Kansas. From the airport, take bus #33 to San Jacinto Park, walk 2 blocks north to Franklin, turn right, and head east 1.5 blocks. Located in the Gardner Hotel, this privately owned hostel takes great pride in meeting the needs of backpackers. Small 4-person dorm rooms and communal bathrooms. Locker rental US$0.75; US$0.50 for four or more days. Linen US$2. Laundry US$1.50 per load. Basement common room with refrigerators, stoves, and couches. Internet access available. Checkout 10am. Beds US$14 with valid US university ID, ISIC, CIEE, or ISTC. US$17.50 without membership.

Gardner Hotel, 311 E. Franklin (☎532-3661; fax 532-0302; email epihostl@whc.net). Comfortable rooms have phones and color TVs, and most have ceiling fans. All amenities at the hostel (see above) are available to hotel guests. Singles US$20, US$30 with private bath; doubles and triples US$32.50, US$45 with bath. Weekly rates available.

Budget Lodge Motel, 1301 N. Mesa (☎533-6821), at California, a 15min. walk from San Jacinto Square up Mesa, six blocks from UTEP. Rooms have A/C, cable TV, and bath. Small cafe serves breakfast and lunch. Outdoor swimming pool open May-Sept. Singles US$29.57; doubles US$34.13. US$4.56 for each additional person.

Gateway Hotel, 104 S. Stanton (☎532-2611; fax 533-8100), at San Antonio. Centrally located, the Gateway offers air-conditioned rooms at reasonable prices. Complimentary breakfast of toast and coffee. Diner serves from 7am-8:30pm. Singles average US$30; doubles average US$35. Group discounts available.

FOOD

El Paso has many small mom-and-pop diners that prepare a wide variety of home-made Mexican and American dishes. Cheap restaurants cluster around Stanton and Texas. As far as local specialties go, the burrito is king, and the array of places that serve 'em up hot is almost dizzying. Unfortunately, many places close early, so your options may be more limited after 6pm on weekdays.

La Malinche, 301 Texas (☎544-8785), at Texas near San Jacinto Square. Authentic Mexican fare in medium to large portions in a brightly colored, cool environment. Breakfasts from US$2.75, steaks US$4.35-7.35, and chili specials US$3.59-5.75. *Menudo* (a local speciality) served Sa and Su. Open M-Sa 7:30-4pm.

Manolo's Café, 122 S. Mesa (☎532-7661), between Overland and San Antonio. *Menudo* (US$2), burritos (US$1), and generous *comida corrida* (US$3.99). Bullfighting and boxing photographs give Manolo's character. Open M-Sa 7am-6pm, Su 7:30-4pm.

La Pachanga (☎544-4454), near the corner of Texas and N. Stanton. This mom-and-pop restaurant serves healthful options, such as *enérgeticas* (fruit salad with granola and honey for US$2.50-3.50), or *aguas frescas* (juices in strawberry, mango, canta-loupe, and papaya flavors). Free delivery in the downtown area. Open M-Sa 8am-5pm.

SIGHTS

The majority of visitors to El Paso are either stopping on the long drive through the US desert or heading south to Ciudad Juárez. For a whirlwind tour of El Paso and its southern neighbor, Ciudad Juárez, hop aboard the **Border Jumper Trolleys,** departing from the tourist office. Historic **San Jacinto Plaza,** in the heart of El Paso, swarms with daily activity and affords an opportunity to sit on a shaded bench or to listen to the Apostolic preachers who occasionally take center stage. Note that the streets surrounding the Plaza will be under construction until approximately the summer of 2001, and buses may or may not be stopping in the Plaza.

For the bargain hunter, many shops can be found along El Paso St., N. Stanton, and San Antonio. To take in a complete picture of the Rio Grande Valley, you will need a car. Head northwest of downtown along Stanton and make a right turn on Rim Road (which becomes Scenic Dr.) to reach **Murchison Park,** at the base of the ridge. The Park offers a commanding vista of El Paso, Ciudad Juárez, and the Sierra Madre mountains.

Museum enthusiasts will coo over the renowned **American Museum** and the **El Paso Museum of Art** (☎541-4040), both near the **Civic Center** on Santa Fe.

ENTERTAINMENT

Many nightlife seekers opt to head across the border to Ciudad Juárez, where a lower drinking age and later hours make for more intense partying—and more danger come nightfall. If you decide to stick to the US side, **The Tap,** 408 E. San Antonio, is under new management, but remains El Paso's nightlife staple. The tap serves authentic Mexican food (burritos US$1.75-3.75) and drinks (Coronas US$2) under its neon lights. Many seats and tables provide for comfortable eating, drinking and con-templation of the Mexican historical paintings on the wall. A jukebox and pool table round out the place. (Bar ☎546-9049; restaurant ☎532-1848; open M-Sa 7am-2am, Sa 12pm-2am.) For something a little racier, try **Club 101,** 500 San Francisco (☎544-101), El Paso's oldest club. Age notwithstanding, this club manages to keep up with the times with its two dance floors and ever-changing party scene (21+; open F-Sa until 2am). **OP,** 301 S. Ochoa (☎533-6055), located on block north of Paisano, is El Paso's premier gay club (open Th and Su 9pm-2am, F-Sa 9pm-4am).

From Apr.-Sept., the **El Paso Diablos** (☎755-2000) are major league fun for minor league prices. To reach the home of the Diablos, **Cohen Stadium,** 9700 Gateway, take Sun Metro bus #42 from San Jacinto Plaza as far north as it goes and walk the rest of the way. Ask the driver for directions. (General admission US$3, box seats US$4.75.) If munching on crackerjacks under the stadium lights isn't outdoorsy enough for you, there's plenty of hiking opportunities outside of town. The tourist office will be happy to provide info on the **Mission Trail** and other hikes. If you're driving and are feeling lucky, check out **Speaking Rock Casino** (☎860-7777). In the fall, the **Border Folk Festival**—complete with *mariachis* and folklore dancers—is not to be missed.

CIUDAD JUÁREZ   ☎1

With a population of almost 2 million, Ciudad Juárez is the largest town on the 3326km border separating the US and Mexico. As part of the *frontera*, Ciudad Juárez is neither Mexican nor American, and is distinct from its mellower sister to the north. The city—including modern-day El Paso—was originally known as El Paso del Norte. It got its modern name in 1860 when President **Benito Juárez** fled to the city to escape the French intervention and seek US aid in the overthrow of Emperor Maximilian (see **History**, p. 61). The city was later occupied by Pancho Villa several times during the Mexican Revolution. Today, Ciudad Juárez is hectic, loud, dirty, and cheap, a mecca for those seeking escape from the more ordered American side. The city's **Cathedral Square** and **Parque Chamizal** maintain Mexican culture in the face of American advance, and are pleasant respites from the sprawling industrial production centers and poor residential areas that form most of the cityscape.

▉ TRANSPORTATION

It's a good idea to grab a map from the **tourist office**. The streets get convoluted outside of Old Juárez, in the area immediately adjoining the Santa Fe and Stanton bridges. You don't want to be caught in the wrong part of town.

GETTING AROUND

Most of Old Juárez can be covered on foot. Street numbers start in the 800s near the two border bridges and descend to zero at **16 de Septiembre,** where **Av. Juárez** (the main street) ends. To reach both the ProNaf and Rio Grande Mall, take public bus "Ruta 8A" (2.80 pesos), which leaves from the intersection of Presidencia and Juárez near the border. Most city buses leave from the intersection of **V. Guererro** and Francisco Villa or thereabouts; ask the driver whether your bus will take you to your destination. **Taxis** are always downtown, but fees are steep. Negotiate before getting in. To get from the bus station to downtown, walk out the left-most door (if you're facing the main station entrance) and up to the street. Don't be satisfied with just any bus that will take you to the *centro;* get on an old converted school bus labeled "Ruta 1A" or "Ruta 6," both of which go to Av. Juárez. Again, ask the driver if he or she is going to Av. Juárez, Ruta 6 can take you to the shantytowns on the outskirts of town if you take it in the wrong direction.

During the day, Juárez is relatively safe for the alert traveler. As darkness increases, however, so does the ratio of alcohol to blood. Be wary of people loitering about late at night, as large numbers of men have a tendency to do. Be careful and avoid places that look at all suspicious. Additionally, be wary of suspicious cab drivers. Don't go out unaccompanied. Women should not walk alone or in dark places; everyone should avoid the area more than 2 blocks west of Av. Juárez at night. The **police station** is on the corner of 16 de Septiembre and Av. Juárez, and there is usually an abundance of police officers patrolling the downtown streets during the day.

GETTING AWAY

Airport: (☎633 07 34), about 17km out on Rte. 45 *(Carretera Panorámica)*. Catch the crowded "Ruta 4" bus and get off at the San Lorenzo Church; then board the "Ruta Aeropuerto" (1.80 pesos). **Aeroméxico** (☎623 23 94 or 623 23 95) flies to Chihuahua, Mexico City, Monterrey, and a few nearby US locations.

Buses: Central Camionera, Blvd. Oscar Flores 4010, (☎613 20 83), north of the ProNaf Center and next to the Río Grande Mall. To get there, take the Chihuahuenses bus from the El Paso terminal to Juárez (US$7), or cram into the "Ruta 1A" (red and white) or "Permisionairos Unidos" (blue) near F. Villa and V. Guererro (3 pesos). Be sure to ask the bus driver whether it is going to the bus station, since not all do. Chihuahuenses (☎629 22 29), Estrella Blanca (☎613 83 02), Omnibus de México (☎610 74 04 or 610 72 97), and others offer service to: **Chihuahua** (7hr.; every 30min.; 193 pesos); **Guadalajara** (24hr.; 10am, 1 and 10pm; 723 pesos); **Hermosillo** (10hr.; 290 pesos); **Mazatlán** (24hr.; 440 pesos); **Mexico City** (26hr.; 6 per day; 851 pesos); **Nogales** (8hr.; 6pm; 250 pesos); and more. Greyhound serves the US, including: **Dallas** (US$75), **El Paso** (50min.; every hr.; US$7); **Los Angeles** (US$45); **San Antonio** (US$79).

🛈 PRACTICAL INFORMATION

TOURIST AND FINANCIAL SERVICES

US Consulate: López Mateos Nte. 924 (☎613 40 48 or 613 40 50), at Hermanos Escobar. From Av. Juárez, turn left on 16 de Septiembre, right on López Mateos, and then walk for 15-20min. Closed Sa-Su. In an emergency, call the El Paso tourist office in the US (☎(915) 544-0062).

Currency Exchange: Banks congregate near the bus station, on Juárez and on 16 de Septiembre. Most are open M-F 9am-3pm. Traveler's checks can be cashed by **Comisiones San Luis** (☎614 20 33), on the corner of 16 de Septiembre and Juárez. Open M-Th 9am-8:30pm, F-Sa 9am-9pm, Su 9am-6pm. Also try **Chequerama** (☎612 35 99), at Unión and Av. Juárez. Open M-Sa 10am-6pm. There are numerous money changers on Juárez, especially the northern section. Rates posted in large numbers allow die-hard cheapskates to find the best rates.

LOCAL SERVICES

Luggage Storage: At the bus station, 3 pesos per hr.

Supermarket: The **Río Grande Mall,** Ruta 8 at Guerrero and López Mateos, sells groceries, clothes, and more. **Soriana Market,** also along Ruta 8, sells groceries. Open Tu-Sa 7am-11pm, Su-M 8am-11pm. For both, catch a bus on Juárez near the border.

Laundry: Lavasolas (☎612 54 61), Tlaxcala and 5 de Mayo. Twelve other locations in town. Washers 8-9 pesos; dryers 9 pesos. Open M-Sa 9am-9pm, Su 8am-5pm.

EMERGENCY AND COMMUNICATIONS

Emergency: ☎060.

Police: (☎615 15 51), Oro and 16 de Septiembre, near Juárez. English spoken. You can also contact the **Federal Highway Police** (☎633 01 95).

Red Cross: (☎616 58 06, 611 43 30 or 611 43 21; fax 616 50 89), in the ProNaf Center next to the OK Corral. English spoken. Open 24hr.

Pharmacy: Pharmacies abound along Juárez, but for late night needs, try **Superfarmacias El Félix** (☎615 30 24 or 615 80 54), at Av. Juárez and Tlaxcala. Open daily 8am-1am.

Hospital: Hospital Latinoamericano, 250 N. López Mateos (☎616 14 67 or 616 14 15; fax 616 13 75), in the ProNaf area. English spoken. Open 24hr. Take "Ruta 8A."

Post Office: Lerdo at Ignacio Peña. Open M-F 8am-5pm, Sa-Su 9am-1pm.

Postal Code: 32000.

Fax: Secrefax (☎615 15 10 or 615 20 49; fax 615 16 11), on Juárez near the Santa Fe Bridge, partially obscured under a white awning. Open 24hr.

Telephones: LADATEL phones are plentiful on Av. Juárez and 16 de Septiembre.

⌐ ACCOMMODATIONS

In Ciudad Juárez, budget hotels meet minimal standards—a place to sleep, maybe a fan, and probably no A/C—and charge some of the highest "budget" rates in Mexico. Moreover, a modest increase in quality, can translate into a significant hike in price. Moderately priced chains can be found along the main strip, **Juárez;** pricier places are located in **ProNaf,** around **López Mateos** and **Américas.**

Hotel Juárez, Lerdo 143 Nte. (☎615 02 98, 615 03 58, or 615 04 18), at 16 de Septiembre. Simple, small rooms, but one of the best deals you'll find downtown. Rooms have A/C and TV, and a diner makes the hotel cozy. Often full so call ahead—up to your day of arrival—to reserve a room. Rates change according to floor. Singles 105-124 pesos; doubles 130-142 pesos; triples 146-168 pesos; quads 145 pesos.

Hotel San Carlos, Juárez 131 Nte. (☎615 04 19). A fair-priced hotel in downtown Juárez, its has all the basic amenities: TV, bathroom, phone, A/C. Rooms are medium-sized, but might vary in quality; ask to see one before deciding. Singles 160 pesos; doubles 225 pesos.

Hotel Morán, Juárez 264 (☎615 08 02 or 615 08 62; fax 612 53 10), near Mr. Fog Bar. Patrons of this hotel don't have to venture far for excitement. Rooms with TV and private bath. All rooms have A/C, though temperature varies from room to room. Easy to find with a large 50s-style "Hotel Moran" sign. Singles 200 pesos; doubles 250 pesos.

Hotel Sevilla (☎612 08 10) in the middle of Juárez on the east side of the street. Offers the lowest prices around. Rooms don't have phones or TVs, but are fine for a cheap night of rest. Singles 80 pesos; doubles 100 pesos. Fifty pesos for each additional person.

FOOD

Eateries in Ciudad Juárez vary from tourist traps to roadside shacks and open pit grills. In general, travelers should avoid the shacks stick to the restaurants on **Av. Juárez** and **Lerdo** or to the **ProNaf Center,** which are tourist-oriented and safe.

Cafetería El Coyote Inválido, Juárez 615 (☎614 27 27), at Colón. Its name means "the crippled coyote," but the place is anything but weak. A bustling, clean, 50s-style diner with heavenly A/C, hamburgers (25 pesos), burritos (from 17 pesos), and an array of Mexican plates (16-32 pesos). Open Su-Th 8am-11pm, F-Sa 24hr.

Hotel Santa Fé Restaurante, Lerdo 675 Nte. (☎615 15 22), at Tlaxcala, in the Hotel Santa Fe. Sample chicken enchiladas or club sandwiches (25 pesos) and wash 'em down with a beer (12 pesos). Open daily 7am-11pm.

Tacos Lucas (☎612 55 31), Av. Juárez and Mejia. This "round-the-clock" open-air restaurant provides ample opportunity to people-watch. Breakfast special includes *chilaquiles*, french fries, beans, steak, two eggs, and salad for 32 pesos. Open 24hr.

Restaurant Morán, Av. Juárez 266 (☎615 08 02), at the bottom of Hotel Morán. Serves hamburgers (20 pesos) for those with north-of-the-border tastes. If you haven't tried it yet, order a hot *taza* of milk with Nescafé. Open for breakfast and closes late.

⚫ SIGHTS

Ciudad Juárez is richer in history and culture than meets the eye. The **Aduana Fronteriza** in the *centro* at the intersection of Juárez and 16 de Septiembre was built in 1889 as a trading outpost. It now houses the **Museo Histórico de Ciudad Juárez,** which chronicles the region's history from the beginning of civilization up to the 20th century. (☎612 47 07; Open Tu-Su 10am-6pm; free.) The **Museo de Arte e Historia,** at the ProNaf Center, exhibits Mexican art of the past and present (☎616 74 14; Open Tu-Su 11am-5pm; admission 8 pesos, students free). Also at the ProNaf Center, the **Centro Artesanal** sells handmade goods, at very high prices; it's in your best interest to haggle. The "Ruta 8" bus will take you there from the *centro* for 3 pesos.

In 1963, the Rio Grande channel was moved, transferring some border land to Mexico. Today, this land is deforested **Parque Chamizal,** down Av. Presidencia east of the Stanton Bridge. The park gives travelers a chance to escape from the clamor and commotion of downtown Ciudad Juárez. You can also see the Mexican flag that is rumored to be as large as an American football field. The **Museo Arqueológico,** Av. Pellicer in Parque Chamizal, houses plastic facsimiles of pre-Hispanic sculptures as well as prehistoric fossils, rocks, and bones (☎611 10 48 or 613 69 83; open Tu-F 11am-8pm, Sa-Su 10am-8pm). The **Misión de Nuestra Señora de**

Guadalupe (☎615 55 02), on 16 de Septiembre and Mariscal, was built in the 1600s, making it the oldest building in the area. It features antique paintings and altars.

🎵 ENTERTAINMENT

Downtown Ciudad Juárez is party central. On weekends, *gringos* swarm the city in a 48-hour quest for fun, fights, and *fiestas*. Every establishment along Av. Juárez that isn't selling booze or pulling teeth is likely to be a club or a bar, and trying to count them all will make you dizzy even before you start drinking. Many establishments are unsavory, however, and even some of the better ones can become dangerous. Safer and more touristy are clubs such as **Chihua Charlie's, Amaryonos,** and **Ayinas** can be found in the **ProNaf area.** At **Mr. Fog Bar,** Av. Juárez Nte. 140 (☎614 29 48), at González, you can enjoy the atmosphere of a "ladies piano bar" (i.e., the bartenders are female). Live music on weekends (beer and liquor 12 pesos). The dance floor is in the back. (Open daily 11am-midnight.) Other clubs, such as **Fred's, Sinaloa,** and the **Manhattan,** are popular among locals.

Ciudad Juárez offers visitors more than just bars and clubs. If you enjoy bullfights or have never seen one, you can find them at the Plaza Monumental de Toros (☎613 16 56), Paseo Triunfo de la República at López Mateos. They usually occur at 5:30pm on Sundays from April to September. Prices go from 70 pesos in the sun to 95 pesos for nice seats in the shade. The **Lienzo Charro** (☎627 05 55), on Charro off República, also hosts bullfights and a *charreada* (rodeo) on Sunday afternoons during the summer. At the western edge of town, **Galgódromo** (also known as the Juárez Racetrack (☎625 53 94) rises from Vincente Guerrero. Dogs run Wednesday through Sunday at 7:30pm and a Sunday matinees at 2:30pm. Also during the summer, there is a traveling carnival that periodically sets up on the soccer fields next to Parque Chamizal.

NUEVO CASAS GRANDES ☎1

Nuevo Casas Grandes belongs to a time when cowboys ruled the land. A quiet town (pop. 80,000) in the expansive Chihuahuan desert, the community arose at the beginning of this century after a group of pioneering families from the old Casas Grandes decided to move to the newly constructed railroad station. Nuevo (New) Casas Grandes is still an agricultural center and a good place to pick up *vaquero* (Mexican cowboy) hat and boots. Travelers use the city as a base for exploring **Casas Grandes** and the ruins of **Paquimé** (pah-kee-MEH)—one of the most important cities in pre-Hispanic northern Mexico—8km to the southwest.

▐ TRANSPORTATION. Nuevo Casas Grandes is most easily reached by bus. To get from the bus stations, on Obregón and 16 de Septiembre, to the center of town, walk one block down 16 de Septiembre to reach **Constitución,** which runs along the railroad tracks. One block further is **Juárez.** Two main streets in town, **5 de Mayo** and **16 de Septiembre,** each run perpendicular to Juárez and Constitución through the heart of the city. The main park, **Plaza Juárez,** is at the intersection of Juárez and 5 de Mayo. **Taxis** loiter near the intersection of 16 de Septiembre and Constitución and on Minerva at Obregón. Everything listed below lies within the nine-block downtown area.

Buses: Estrella Blanca and Omnibus Mexico (☎694 07 80) running to **Chihuahua** (4hr.; 6 per day 2am-midnight; 150 pesos); **Ciudad Juárez** (3½hr.; 12 per day 5am-9pm; 110 pesos); and **Cuauhtémoc** (6½hr.; 3 per day; 115 pesos). Chihuahuenses (☎694 14 75) to **Hermosillo** (8hr.; 6:30pm and midnight; 425 pesos); **Monterrey** (16 hr.; 3 per day; 400 pesos); and **Tijuana** (16hr.; 3 per day; 375 pesos).

▐ PRACTICAL INFORMATION. The tourist office is no longer, but the receptionists at **Motel Piñon** (see below) are experienced in helping travelers. Change money at **Casa de Cambio California,** Constitución 207 (☎694 32 32 or 694 45 45), at 5 de Mayo (open M-F 9am-2pm and 3:30-7pm, Sa 9am-2pm and 3:30-6pm). Banks line 5 de Mayo. **Bancomer,** 16 de Septiembre at Constitución (☎694 61 18), has a 24-

hour **ATM**. **Police** (☎694 09 75) are located on Blanco and Obregón. **Red Cross** (☎694 20 20) on Carranza at Constitución (open 24hr.). **LADATELs** can be found around the central square and Av. Constitucíon. The **post office** (☎694 20 16) is at 16 de Septiembre and Madero (open M-F 8am-6pm, Sa 8am-1pm). **Postal code:** 31700.

◪◱ ACCOMMODATIONS AND FOOD. Nuevo Casas Grandes has plenty of hotels and restaurants. Accommodations cluster on Constitución and Juárez between 5 de Mayo and Jesús Urueta. The **Hotel Juárez**, Obregón 110 (☎694 02 33), is just a block from the bus station. The friendly owner, Mario, speaks flawless English. Rooms are small and lack A/C, but fans are available upon request. Odd bathroom set-up, but, regardless, this is one of the best deals in town. (Singles 70 pesos; doubles 80-90 pesos.) The **Hotel Paquimé**, Juárez 401 (☎694 13 20; fax 694 47 20) a block from the plaza. Walk down 16 de Septiembre away from the bus station and turn right onto Juárez. Slightly pricey, but comfortable rooms have large beds, cable TV, A/C, and carpeting. (Singles 218-273 pesos; doubles 256-329 pesos) You may never leave the **Hotel California**, Constitución 209 (☎694 11 10 or 694 22 14), with its California-style stucco walls and spacious, clean rooms with A/C, tiled bathrooms, TVs, phones, and fans. (Singles 250 pesos; doubles 300 pesos; triples 300 pesos; quads 360 pesos.)

Denni's Restaurant, Juárez 412 (☎694 10 75), is an old West steakhouse that serves hefty breakfasts (28-40 pesos) and speciality steaks (55-145 pesos). Beer (15 pesos), TV and late night hours make it a popular hangout. (Open daily 8am-midnight.) **Dinno's Pizza** (☎694 02 40), Minerva and Constitución, has *jalapeño*, cherry, pineapple, and coconut pizzas (40-70 pesos; open daily 8am-11:30pm). **Restaurante Constantino** (☎694 10 05), at the corner of Juárez and Minerva, has complete meals for 30-40 pesos. Family owned for over 45 years, the service is as good as the food. If you've never tried Mexican hot chocolate, order a *chocolate grande* and you won't be disappointed. (Open daily 7:30am-midnight.)

◪ ENTERTAINMENT. Although there is a small movie theater on Constitucíon and Minerva, the main activity in Nuevo Casas Grandes seems to be drinking one's troubles away. This can be done at the numerous *carta blanca* bars along Constitucíon. ◪ **El Badito Pub** (☎694 10 40) at Juárez and Prado is the most popular hangout in town. Live music on the weekends will make you tap your cowboy boots. Offers an array of American food, including steaks (65 pesos), hamburgers (35 pesos), beers (12 pesos), and hard drinks (20 pesos). Open until 1am M-Th, until 2 F-Sa.

NEAR NUEVO CASAS GRANDES

Surrounding Nuevo Casas Grandes are many points of archaeological interest, including the **Cueva de Olla** (75km southwest), the **Arroyo de los Monos** (35km southeast), and **Mata Ortiz** (40km south). About 254km southeast of Nuevo Casas Grandes is **Madera,** from which the **Cuarenta Casas** site can be reached (54km north). Ask at the tourist office for more info.

THE GUYS WITH MACHINE GUNS

If you are traveling on the roads between Juárez and Nuevo Casas Grandes or between N. Casas Grandes and Chihuahua, your vehicle may be stopped by military officials toting AK-47s. Do not be alarmed! The Mexican Government is currently going to great lengths to stop drug trafficking from Colombia and Guatemala to the United States. Tourists are in no danger, but should be prepared to show a passport and to comply with the soldiers' requests. Specially trained dogs can smell cocaine from the exterior of the vehicle, so searches are usually quick and efficient. The guys with the machine guns are not dangerous, but we must against emphasize that the Mexican government treats drug crimes harshly. Don't carry illegal drugs. Never carry a package for an unknown person, and carry prescriptions for any prescription drugs you may have.

PAQUIMÉ (CASAS GRANDES)

From Nuevo Casas Grandes, take the beige and blue municipal bus at the corner of Constitución and 16 de Septiembre across from the furniture store (10min., 1 per hr., 4 pesos). Get off at the main plaza of Casas Grandes and walk back in the direction the bus just came on Constitución. This road quickly turns into dirt, rounds a bend, and goes straight to Paquimé (a 10min. walk). Almost any taxi driver will take you to the site from Nuevo Casas Grandes and walk around with you for about 70 pesos per hour. ☎ 692 41 46. Ruins open Tu-Su 10am-5pm. Free with purchase of museum ticket. Museum open Tu-Su 10am-5pm. 25 pesos; free Su.

Paquimé (Casas Grandes) 8km southwest of Nuevo Casas Grandes is the most significant site. Its architecture suggests that it grew out of two different cultures; the many-storied *pueblos* resemble those in the southwestern US, while other structures, such as the complex irrigation systems, show the influence of central and southern Mexico. From AD1000-1200, Paquimé was the most important agricultural and trading center in northern Mexico. Its economy largely depended on miners, who mined kaolin, caledonite, selenite, and felstie, and merchants, who dealt in salt, copper, iron, turquoise, mica, and obsidian. Sea shells traded from the Pacific coast were used as currency and in jewelry. The decline of Paquimé began in the 14th century when droughts ravaged the area. No new building of any kind occurred during this period. An attack on the weakened city in 1400 left it burned and nearly leveled.

The museum, displaying artifacts found on the site, explains the history and layout of the ruins. On summer afternoons, the dry and shadeless site can become an inferno, as temperatures approach or exceed 100°F (38°C). Be sure to bring sun protection, a broad-brimmed hat (cheap *sombreros* are available in town), and plenty of water. It might be a good idea to visit during the early morning or late afternoon when the temperatures aren't intolerable.

CHIHUAHUA   ☎ 1

The capital of Mexico's largest state, Chihuahua (pop. 800,000)—whose name in Náhuatl, "Xicuahua," means dry, sandy place—is a historically rich outpost in the northern desert. Founded in 1709, the city has seen its fair share of bloody conflict in its 300-year history; it was here that Miguel Hidalgo's quest for independence from Spain ended with his execution, and here that Pancho Villa established his revolutionary headquarters during the Porfiriato. Revolutionary history aside, modern-day Chihuahua is a tranquil town, with a bustling downtown and beautiful villas in the outskirts. As a major transportation hub for the northwest, Chihuahua attracts a wide array of people, from Mennonites, to backpackers headed for the Barrancas del Cobre, to the *indígena* Tarahumara people who venture into the city on market day to sell crafts.

▐ TRANSPORTATION

Chihuahua serves as an important transportation hub for northern Mexico. From here, it's possible to reach most destinations in the upper half of the country.

Airport: (☎ 420 06 16 or 420 09 18), 14km from town. The "Aeropuerto" bus stops near Niños Héroes and Independencia. **Aerocalifornia** (☎ 437 10 22), **Aeroméxico** (☎ 439 44 39 or 439 44 40), and **Continental** (☎ 420 47 51; fax 435 26 97).

Buses: From the bus station, a municipal bus (3 pesos) will take you to the cathedral; a taxi will cost 40 pesos. Ómnibus de México (☎ 420 15 80 or 420 01 32) sends luxurious buses to: **Aguascalientes** (7 per day, 508 pesos); **Casas Grandes** (6 per day, 152 pesos); **Cuauhtémoc** (7 per day, 54 pesos); **Durango** (7 per day, 311 pesos); **Guadalajara** (3 per day, 633 pesos); **Mexico City** (6 per day, 778 pesos); **Monterrey** (4 per day, 424 pesos); **Torreón** (34 pesos); and **Zacatecas** (441 pesos). Estrella Blanca (☎ 429 02 40) has a slightly older fleet that chugs to nearly all the same locations.

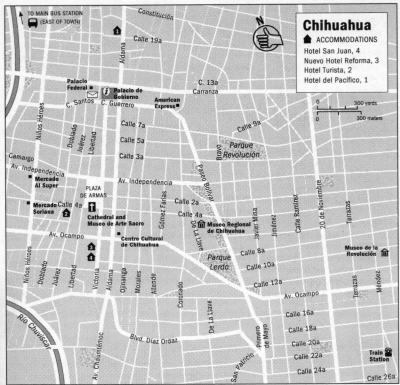

Chihuahua

🛏 ACCOMMODATIONS
Hotel San Juan, 4
Nuevo Hotel Reforma, 3
Hotel Turista, 2
Hotel del Pacífico, 1

Trains: Chihuahua has two major rail stations. The Chihuahua al Pacífico train station, Méndez at Calle 24, is popular with backpackers for its daily trip between Chihuahua and **Los Mochis,** which cuts through the breathtaking **Barrancas del Cobre** (13hr., 7am, 500 pesos). The train stops at various points along the way, including **Creel, Divisadero, Posada Barraces, Bahuichivo, Temoris,** and **El Fuerte.** The station is south of the city center off Ocampo and 2 blocks from 20 de Noviembre. To shorten the 20min. walk to the *centro,* hop on one of the public buses (3 pesos) that run up and down Ocampo to Libertad. A second station, Estación Central de los FFNN, features the night Division del Norte train, with service between **Ciudad Juárez** and **Mexico City.**

◧🛈 ORIENTATION PRACTICAL INFORMATION

Don't let Chihuahua's sheer size intimidate you; while the city is large, most sights are within walking distance of the cathedral. With the exception of Victoria—the hub of Chihuahua's nightlife—the streets in Chihuahua are poorly lit and may be dangerous at night. Don't walk alone.

Tourist Office: (☎410 10 77; fax 416 00 32), on Aldama between Carranza and Guerrero, in the Palacio del Gobierno. Helpful staff and tourist guides. Open daily 9am-7pm.

Currency Exchange: Casas de Cambio cluster along Victoria. **Banorte,** Victoria 104. (☎410 15 93. Open M-F 9am-3pm.) **Hotel San Francisco** (☎416 75 50), across the street, has 24hr. exchange. **ATMs** crowd around the streets near the cathedrals.

Car Rental: Alamo, Borunda #2500 (☎416 50 31 or 416 50 71) before Revolución. **Avis** (airport ☎420 19 19; centro ☎414 19 19 or 426 55 99). **Hertz,** Revolución 514 (☎416 64 73 or 415 78 18; fax 416 99 25), at Santos.

Emergency: ☎060.

Police: Homero 540, across from the Ford plant, at the exit to Ciudad Juárez.

Red Cross: (☎411 22 11 or 411 14 84), Calle 24 and Revolución. Open 24hr.

Pharmacy: Farmacia Hidalgo (☎410 65 08), at Guerrero and Aldama.

Hospital: Hospital General (☎416 00 22 or 415 60 84), Revolución and Colón, in Colonia Centro. **Clínica del Centro,** Ojinaga 816 (☎416 00 22).

Telephones: LADATELs line the *zócalo.*

Internet: Cibernet, Aldama 510. 20 pesos per 30min., 30 pesos per hr., and 20 pesos each additional hr. Open M-Sa 8am-8pm, Su 9am-2pm.

Post Office: (☎437 12 00), on Libertad in the Palacio Federal. Open M-F 8am-7pm, Sa 9am-1pm. **Postal Code:** 31000.

ACCOMMODATIONS

Hotels in Chihuahua are like the city itself—charm smiling through grit. Cheaper hotels lie in the area southwest of the cathedral between Victoria and Juárez.

Hotel San Juan, Victoria 823 (☎410 00 36). Rooms on 3rd fl. have spectacular views, and all rooms have TV and A/C. Perks include a popular bar, small restaurant, and outdoor courtyard. Singles 83-88 pesos; doubles 105-125 pesos; triples 115-140 pesos.

Hotel Turista, Juárez 813 (☎410 04 00), near the cathedral. Lobby sells shampoo, razors, and other necessities. Rooms have A/C. Prices vary by floor. Singles 90 pesos; doubles 115-135 pesos.

Nuevo Hotel Reforma, Victoria 823 (☎410 00 48; fax 416 08 35). Unique architecture and cozy rooms, some of which have balconies over the street. Fans and TV (but questionable plumbing). Singles 83-150 pesos.

Hotel del Pacífico, Aldama 1911 (☎410 59 13), at Calle 21, a few blocks from the Palacio de Gobierno. A/C, fans, and bathrooms in every room. Small restaurant and cafe off the lobby. Singles 120 pesos; doubles 150 pesos; TV 10 pesos extra.

FOOD

Eateries in Chihuahua are seldom geared toward tourists. Good, inexpensive meals can be found in the small *cantinas*, where bands serenade drunken (and often rowdy) men. Women should avoid entering *cantinas* alone.

Las de León, Calle 2a 610 (☎410 74 70), on the corner with Ojinaga. Bring your magic marker—the graffiti-scrawled interior is an artistic free-for-all. Breakfasts from 18 pesos, hamburger, fries, and soda 16 pesos. Open M-Sa 8am-4pm.

Degá Restaurante-Bar, Victoria 409 (☎416 75 50), at Hotel San Francisco south of the *zócalo*. A rare chance at a vegetarian meal. The *plato vegetariano* (49 pesos) includes vegetarian soup, soy steak, and white rice. Real steaks are pricier (73-110 pesos). Open daily 7am-10pm.

Mi Café, Victoria 1000 (☎410 12 38), at Calle 10, across from Hotel San Juan. If you like big portions (and the color orange), then *Mi Café* is ideal. *Milanesa,* a thinly sliced steak, is the speciality (48 pesos). Large breakfasts (38 pesos). Open daily 8am-11pm.

Tortas & Tacos (☎416 40 00), Calle 2 and Ojinaga, across from Las de León. Very cheap hamburgers, fries, and drinks (16 pesos), but portions can be small. *Tortas* 13-18 pesos, tacos 28-30 pesos. Open M-Sa 9:30am-11:30pm, Su 11am-11:30pm.

SIGHTS

■ **MUSEO DE LA REVOLUCIÓN.** Also known as the **Quinta Luz,** this 50-room mansion was the home of Villa's (legal) widow, Luz Corral, who lived here, maintained the museum, and led tours until her death in 1981. Items on display include Villa's personal effects, photographs, and the revolutionary's gun collection. The star of the show is the bullet-ridden Dodge in which the unsuspecting Villa was assassinated. *(Hike 1.5km south on Ocampo, turn left on 20 de Noviembre, and go 2 blocks to Calle 10 and Méndez. Turn right, and the house is 2 blocks down. ☎416 29 58. Open daily 9am-1pm and 3-7pm. 12 pesos.)*

QUINTA GAMEROS CENTRO CULTURAL UNIVERSITARIO (THE MUSEO REGIONAL DE CHIHUAHUA). One of the more stunning mansions in Mexico, this is a prime example of French Art Nouveau. Mining engineer Manuel Gameros, the aristocrat who had it built in 1907-1911, never lived in it—the Revolution drove him to Texas. The house was seized by revolutionaries and at one point served as Pancho Villa's barracks and Venustasio Carranza's home. Upstairs is an impressive collection of modern Mexican art, while the downstairs houses a Japanese doll collection. *(On the corner of Calle 4 and Paseo Bolívar, a 10min. walk from the cathedral. ☎416 66 84. Open Tu-Su 11am-2pm and 4-7pm. 20 pesos, W 10 pesos.)*

PALACIO DE GOBIERNO. This 19th-century palace is a testament to Chihuahuan history. Look for the beautiful Aarón Piña Mora murals, the flames marking the spots of Hidalgo's and Allende's assassinations, and the nude statue of Emiliano Zapata, whose modesty is maintained by a conveniently placed rifle. *(At the center of Chihuahua on Aldama and Victoria.)*

PALACIO FEDERAL. Today the city's post office, the *Palacio* was once the dungeon in which Hidalgo spent the 98 days before his execution. Some of Hidalgo's belongings are on display, including his pistol and crucifix. *(Next to the Palacio de Gobierno, at Juárez and Guerrero. Open Tu-F 10am-1pm and 4-7pm, Sa-Su 10am-1pm.)*

CATHEDRAL. Chihuahua's main cathedral, Nuestra Señora de Regla y San Francisco de Asís, was begun in the 1720s and finished in 1826. The Baroque stone facade depicts the 12 Apostles. The interior was redecorated in 1939 and 1940. *(A few blocks from the Palacio de Gobiero, on the southwest side of the Plaza de Armas on Victoria and Calle 2. Museum open M-F 10am-2pm and 4-6pm.)*

MUSEO DE ARTE SACRO. This museum houses pastoral religious paintings from the 18th century, mingled with photos and portraits from the Pope's most recent visit to Chihuahua. *(In the southeast corner of the cathedral, Libertad and Calle 2. Open M-F 10am-2pm and 4-6pm. 12 pesos.)*

CENTRO CULTURAL DE CHIHUAHUA. The former home of a former governor of Chihuahua, Luis Terrazas, this 1889 mansion houses a small cultural and educational institution. The center has cultural events, artwork, and displays on Paquimé pottery. *(On Aldama and Ocampo. Open Tu-Su 10am-2pm and 4-7pm. Free.)*

🎵 ENTERTAINMENT

Hotspots are scattered across dark Chihuahua, so taking a reputable taxi is the safest option. Check out the three-screen movie theater on Santos and Doblado for a low-key evening. Or head out to the many bars and nightclubs around the city. **La Casa de los Milagros** (☎437 06 93) on Victoria across from Hotel San Juan, has an impressive selection of beers (15-18 pesos) and an elegant and airy patio. Live guitar music on the weekend. Open F-Sa 3pm-2am, Su-W 3pm-midnight.

At night, catch a flick at **Cinépolis** (☎417 52 22), Vallarta at Zaragoza (Shows 3-9:30pm; 20 pesos, first show 15 pesos, W 12 pesos). To get there, hop on a "Cerro de la Cruz" bus in front of the Héroes de la Revolución building, in the *centro* (15min., every 8min. until 9:30pm, 2.8 pesos). If the buses have stopped running, you'll have to take a cab back (20 pesos). **Café Calicanto,** Aldama 411 (☎410 44 52), serves local specialties and a wide selection of coffees and beers. Live Latin American music on the weekends on a beautiful outdoor stage surrounded by citrus trees. (Open Su-Th 4pm-2am, F-Sa 5pm-3am.) **Quinto Sofía,** in front of Lerdo Park, brings out a twenty-something crowd to listen to live Spanish rock. (Beers 12 pesos, cover 15 pesos after 10:30pm.) A somewhat older crowd flocks to **Old Town,** Juárez 3331 (☎410 32 71), between Colón and Calle 39. (Cover F-Sa 30 pesos; open Th 9pm-1am, F-Sa 9pm-2:30am.)

📷 DAYTRIPS FROM CHIHUAHUA

CUAUHTÉMOC

*Cuauhtémoc lies midway between Creel and Chihuahua, a 1½hr. bus ride from each. The easiest way to get to Cuauhtémoc is from Chihuahua via one of the buses leaving the main station. Ómnibus de México (☎420 15 80 or 420 01 32) goes to Cuauhtémoc (7 per day, 54 pesos), as does Estrella Blanca (☎429 02 40; 8 per day, 35 pesos). Public buses run all over the city and stop at the blue bus stop signs—the main stop is on Calle 3 between Allende and Guerrero (3 pesos). To leave town, the Estrella Blanca bus station, Allende at Calle 9, (☎582 10 18), runs buses to: **Casas Grandes** (5hr., 4 per day, 140 pesos); **Chihuahua** (1½hr., every 30min. 8:30am-9:30pm, 35 pesos); **Ciudad Juárez** (9hr., 2 per day, 197 pesos); and **Creel** (3½hr., every hr. 7:30am-7:30pm, 92 pesos).*

As you explore Cuauhtémoc (pop. 131,000), don't look twice if you pass a blond-haired, blue eyed Caucasian in long dress or overalls. The most important agricultural producer in the state of Chihuahua, the city is home to thousands of Mennonites, members of a German pacifist religious group founded in the 16th century. After their expulsion from Europe, thousands of Mennonites settled in the agricultural fields around Cuauhtémoc in the 1921. The hard-working Mennonites have abandoned almost all the conservative tenants of their religion, such as the prohibition of the use of electricity or mechanization, but many still adhere to old dress customs: hats, neatly plastered-down hair, long dresses for women, and overalls and work-shirts for men. The Chihuahuan Mennonites are best known for their **queso menonita** (Mennonite cheese), a mild cheddar-like cheese.

Seeing the Mennonite communities of Cuauhtémoc is difficult unless you have a car. The Mennonites have organized themselves in small, numbered communities of about 20-25 families called **campos.** The *campos* to the north are the easiest to access. On the left of the route, numbers start at one and go up; on the right they start in the mid-20s and count down, and after a certain point, the field numbers switch to the 100s. The Estrella Blanca bus heading to Casas Grandes from the bus station (15 pesos) stops at Campo 6.5. Autobuses Lázaro Cárdenas, from the main bus station, also trips to the various *campos* (10-20 pesos). Taxis will also take you there for a high price. Hitchhikers report success on and off the main route, but drivers are scarce on the dirt roads between colonies.

If you choose to stay in Cuautémoc, budget hotels line Allende and cluster near the *zócalo.* **Hotel Princessa,** Allende 204, one block west of the *zócalo,* has clean rooms with carpeted floors, beautiful furniture, A/C, TVs, and phones. (☎582 25 22. Singles 126 pesos; doubles 134-146 pesos; triples 152-175 pesos.) The most popular night spot and eatery is 📷**Tacos y Salsas,** on Morelos and 16 de Septiembre. Decorated like a hunting lodge with deer heads, beaver pelts, and bull horns, the house specialities are steak (48-50 pesos), and *carne asada* (48 pesos. ☎581 36 66. Open daily noon-midnight.)

HIDALGO DE PARRAL ☎1

Dubbed "The Silver Capital of the World" by King Phillip IV of Spain in 1640, the town of Hidalgo de Parral was founded in 1631 with the discovery of the La Negrita silver mine, now known as La Prieta. The mine, now closed more than 10 years, sits on the hills the above town to which it gave birth. With very little tourist activity, Parral (as it is affectionately known) is one of the most relaxed and cleanest cities in Northwest Mexico. Tranquility aside, the city is known for the 1923 assassination of Pancho Villa, who was gunned down as he traveled through the streets in his 1922 Dodge.

📷 **TRANSPORTATION.** From the bus station, Independencia near the Motel El Camino Real, exit the main doors and go left on Pedro de Sille, which runs into **Independencia.** Turn left and you are on the main strip headed downtown. Ómnibus de México and Estrella Blanca run buses to: **Chihuahua** (4hr., 3 per day, 110 pesos); **Ciudad Juárez** (7hr., 8 per day, 309 pesos); **Mexico City** (20hr., 2 per day, 700 pesos); and **Guadalajara** (1 per day, 530 pesos).

■¶ ORIENTATION AND PRACTICAL INFORMATION. Parral's city center is compact. **Municipal buses** stop at the corner of Mercedes and Gómez downtown. You can always hail a **cab** from downtown or along Independencia. You are never far from the center if you stay near the river. Just after Independencia crosses the river, it runs beside the **cathedral plaza**, where it intersects **Benítez** and **Hernández**, the two other largest streets in town.

There is no tourist office, but you can call ☎522 02 21 for information. **Papelería del Real,** and some other large stationary stores sell city maps. **Currency exchange:** the easiest place is **Banco Serfín** near the cathedral plaza. **Pharmacy:** next to El Camino Market on the corner of Madrazo and Independencia. (☎523 06 63. Open daily 8am-midnight.) **Supermarket: El Camino** (☎523 06 63) on Independencia just outside downtown, next to Hotel Margarita's. **Post office:** on the corner of Rago and Libertad, a few blocks from the cathedral plaza. (Open M-F 8am-3pm.) **Postal code:** 33800.

■◘ ACCOMMODATIONS AND FOOD. The boom days of Parral's mining colony left behind some very stately hotels, few of them in the budget range. The **Hotel Turista,** Independencia 12, is a 15-minute walk down Independencia from the *centro*, where the street curves. Large, spotless rooms come with A/C, TVs, phones, and tiled bathrooms. (☎523 40 70 or 523 40 24. Singles 180 pesos; doubles 210 pesos; triples 240 pesos.) At **Restaurante el Aseradero,** on the left side of Independencia after Primavera heading toward the *centro*, you can watch your food being cooked over a wood fire. Good chicken, beef, and *cabrito* (roasted young goat) for 35-45 pesos. (Open daily 10am-10pm.) The true treasures of Parral, however, are the many family-run **taquerías** that dot the downtown area. Watch the whole city stroll by while downing tacos (10 pesos) and burritos (6 pesos). The homemade salsas will set your mouth on fire. (Most stands open 10am-10pm.)

■◘ SIGHTS AND ENTERTAINMENT. Home to Pancho Villa during the last years of his life, Parral has many museums dedicated to the Mexican hero. Chief among them is the **Museo de General Francisco Villa,** upstairs in the town library. It's only a 10-minute walk, but difficult to find. Turn right on Hernandez, heading away from the cathedral. Outside, a bronze plaque marks the spot where Villa's car was riddled by over 150 bullets. (Open M-F 9am-8pm, Sa 9am-1pm. Free.) Mystery shrouds Villa's grave at the **Panteón Municipal,** on the outskirts of town. According to the government, Villa is interred in Mexico City; Parral residents, on the other hand, believe a government conspiracy moved a decoy body instead of the real body, which still resides in Parral. The interior of the **Catedral de San José,** on the plaza is decorated with ore from local mines and contains the remains Juan Rangel de Viesma, the mine's founder. The **Templo de la Virgen de Fátima,** on a hill by the mine overlooking the city, even has pews made from local ore. The **Palacio Alvarado,** at the corner of Verdad and Riva Palacio, was constructed by Pedro Alvaro, a owner of the Palmilla mine and a man so wealthy he offered to pay off all of Mexico's national debt. The Byzantine-baroque mansion is still home to the remaining living Alvarados. Many of the town's other magnificent buildings, almost all constructed with mining money, are worth a look.

Besides the usual *cantinas*, a good time can be had at **J. Quísseme,** a lounge and dance club on Independencia near the bus station. Things start hopping after 10pm. (Cover 30 pesos. Beer 25 pesos. Open Th-F 8pm-1am, Sa 9pm-2am.) The **Lone Star** club, by the stadium, is another local favorite. (Open W-Sa 9pm-3am.) If you're in town at the right time you can see man fight cow at the city's **bullfights,** two weekends each summer, usually in mid-July and late-August. To get to the stadium follow the noise, a few blocks left of Independencia. Turn left near Pedro de Lille as you are heading out of town.

CREEL ☎1

High amid the stunning peaks and gorges of the Sierra Madres lies the small village of Creel (pop. 7000; elevation 2801m), which welcomes travelers with natural beauty and refreshing air. Cabins dot the hillsides, animals freely roam the streets, and the town's residents are friendly and rugged. The train rumbles through Creel two or three times a day, making it a good base from which to explore the stunning Copper Canyons (see p. 235). While tourism has increased, it hasn't destroyed the 50,000 **Karámuri** (what the Tarahumara call themselves) living in the mountains surrounding Creel. The countryside around Creel is home to a number of other *indígena* groups, including the Pima to the northwest, the Northern Tepehuan to the south, and the Guarojio to the west.

▛ TRANSPORTATION

Creel serves as the starting point for most Copper Canyons explorations. The best way to make the trek is by train, although other options do exist.

Trains: Tarahumara 57 (☎456 00 15), in town on the tracks, diagonally across from the Estrella Blanca bus station. At the train station and facing the tracks, the *zócalo* is down the hill to the left. Trains leave daily for **Chihuahua** (first-class 6hr., 3pm, 387 pesos; second-class 7hr., 4pm, 190 pesos), and **Los Mochis** through the Copper Canyons (first-class 9hr., 11:30am, 463 pesos; second-class 10hr., M, W, F 1pm, 228 pesos). You can get off anywhere along the way and avoid paying full price. Tickets aren't sold in advance, so scramble on quickly when the train pulls up and elbow for a seat (which may be assigned based on your destination). Pay the conductor as he comes around. (See **The Train Through the Canyons,** p. 235.)

Buses: Estrella Blanca (☎456 00 73), in a small white-and-green building diagonally across the tracks from the *zócalo,* sends buses to: **Chihuahua** (5hr., 7 per day, 156 pesos) and **Cuauhtémoc** (3hr., 5 per day, 92 pesos). To travel to **Parral,** take a bus to Guachochi, then transfer to Parral (this will probably require a night's stay in Guachochi). From the Hotel Piños office at Mateos 39, buses (☎456 02 79 or 456 02 30) leave for **Batopilas** (6hr.; Tu, Th, and Sa 7:15am, 200 pesos). From the ticket office (☎456 01 77), on Villa behind the Hotel Posada, buses run from Creel to **San Rafael** (4pm, 60 pesos). See **Tours** (p. p. 233) for additional agencies that run transportation to Batopilas and areas deep in the canyons.

◼▛ ORIENTATION AND PRACTICAL INFORMATION

The railroad tracks function as a rough compass: toward Chihuahua is north and toward Los Mochis is south. The *zócalo* is the best place from which to get your bearings. The main street, **Mateos,** runs parallel to the trains on the opposite side of the *zócalo,* and is the only street near the *zócalo* that extends any distance. Everything you need can be found on or near Mateos. **Caro,** farther south, runs perpendicular to Mateos and up to the tracks. **Villa** runs parallel to the tracks on the opposite side of Mateos. Check the map next to Serfín.

Tourist Information: Artesanías Misión (☎456 00 97), on the north side of the *zócalo.* Not an official tourist office, but the best source of information. Sells maps and Tarahumaran books and crafts. Proceeds are donated to the Tarahumaran Children's hospital fund. English spoken. Open M-Sa 9:30am-1pm and 3-6pm, Su 9:30am-1pm.

Currency Exchange: Banco Serfín, Plaza 201 (☎456 02 50 or 456 00 60), next door to the Misión. Dollars exchanged M-F 9am-1:30pm. Open M-F 9am-3pm. 24hr. **ATM.**

Market: Comercial de Creel, Mateos 55. Open M-Sa 9:30am-7pm.

Bike Rental: Expediciones Umarie, south along the tracks, next to the 2-story cabin. Rents bikes (120 pesos per day, 80 pesos per half-day, 20 pesos per hr.), helmets, and gloves. Also offers a half-day introductory rock climbing course (200 pesos per person, min. 2 people). Bikes can also be rented from **Complejo Turístico Arareco,** Mateos 33 (☎456 01 26), south of the *zócalo,* for 30 pesos per hr. Horses also available.

Emergency: ☎060.

Police: (☎456 04 50), in the Presidencia Seccional, on the south side of the *zócalo.*

Pharmacy: Farmacia Rodríguez, Mateos 43 (☎456 00 52). Open M-Sa 9am-2pm and 3:30-9pm, Su 10am-1pm.

Medical Services: Clínica Santa Teresita, (☎ 456 01 05), on Parroquia at the end of the street, 2 blocks from Mateos. Little English spoken. Open M-F 10am-1pm and 3-5pm, Sa 10am-1pm. Open 24hr. for emergencies.

Fax: Papelería de Todo, Mateos 30. Open daily 9am-8pm.

Telephones: LADATELs in the *zócalo*, on Mateos, and on Villa.

Post Office: (☎ 456 02 58), in the Presidencia Seccional, on the south side of the *zócalo*. Open M-F 9am-3pm. **Postal Code:** 33200.

⚐ ACCOMMODATIONS AND CAMPING

Due to Creel's popularity with Canyon-seeking tourists, a large number of establishments compete for tourist pesos. The result: budget rooms are plentiful and prices may be negotiable during low season. Many budget accommodations are within a couple of blocks of the *zócalo*. For the adventurous type, camping might be the way to go. Campground and lodges abound near **Lago Arareco.**

▨ Margarita's Casa de Huéspedes, Mateos 11 (☎ 456 00 45). Kitty corner with the *zócalo*. An international backpacker's mecca. You'll have no trouble finding it—a young emissary (paid by the hotels so you need not tip) meets almost every train and bus to lead you to the house, where you mingle with Margarita's family, friends, and globe-trotting guests. Dorms and hotel rooms available, as well as canyon tours. Beware the 11:30pm lockout. Rates vary by season. Dorms 60 pesos; singles 200 pesos; doubles 250 pesos. Prices include breakfast and dinner.

Casa de Huéspedes Perez, Flores 257 (☎ 456 00 47). Follow Mateos away from the train station, make a left at the "Café Luli" sign, and cross the bridge. Here you will be more than a hotel guest, you will be part of the family. Luli might make you breakfast herself. Rustic rooms have shared bathrooms; many have wood stoves. Kitchen and laundry facilities available. English tours offered. Singles 60 pesos; doubles 120 pesos.

Departamentos Confortables Casa de Huéspedes (☎ 456 02 15), on Batista off Mateos. On your right, 100m down batista, just after the brick complex. The *casa* with the large name is also a good place for large groups; up to 8 people can stay in the *cabañas,* which come with kitchenette and an outdoor BBQ. Quads 150 pesos.

Hotel Korachi (☎ 456 02 07), on Villa, across the tracks from the train station. A wannabe hunting lodge with rooms and *cabañas. Cabañas* have heaters, rooms do not. Singles 120 pesos; doubles 160 pesos; triples 200 pesos; quads 220 pesos. *Cabaña* doubles 250 pesos; triples 300 pesos; quads 350 pesos.

◖ FOOD

There are several inexpensive restaurants along **Mateos.** While almost everything is cheap, quality varies. Picnicking spots lie on the quiet hillsides, and are reachable by car or hiking.

▨ Cafetería Gaby, Mateos 48, across from the grocery store, serves home-cooked meals. If you're confused by the door, just pull the string. Breakfast 14-23 pesos; lunch and dinner 10-38 pesos. Open daily 7am-10pm.

Restaurante Veronica, Mateos 34. A local favorite. Try the eggs any style (19 pesos) or the *comida corrida* (28 pesos). Open daily 7am-10:30pm.

Restaurante Todo Rico, Mateos 37 (☎ 456 02 05), at Caro. Good food and a friendly atmosphere. *Desayuno* 26-28 pesos, entrees 18-70 pesos, and hamburgers and friends (23 pesos). Open daily 7:30am-11pm.

◉ ♫ SIGHTS AND ENTERTAINMENT

The reason tourists come to Creel is to visit the breathtaking Copper Canyons, which lie south of the town. To explore the beautiful surroundings, you'll need a car, a tour guide, or a brave heart and a strong pair of legs (see **Barrancas del Cobre,**

TOURS

One of the best ways to explore the area around Creel is with a tour. This, of course, will cost a little more than doing it on your own, but it's usually worth it. Most expensive hotels in Creel also offers tours, as do some local residents.

Casa Perez: 6 tours. Good prices.

Casa Margaritas: 5 tours. Reasonable prices with lunch included.

Cabañas Bertis: 10 tours. Various combinations of sights.

KOA Campground: 7 tours. Higher prices but modern transportation.

Compleja Turístico Arenero: Some tours near the *Laguna Arareco*.

Tarahumara Tours: At a booth in the center of the *zócalo*. Competitive prices.

p. 235). Still, the town has some sights closer to home. The **Casa de las Artesanías del Estado de Chihuahua,** on Ferrocarril 17 in the old railroad station across from the *zócalo*, displays local and Tarahumara arts, crafts, and a random assortment of historical relics. Check out the back-room mummy, which may be an ancestor of the Tarahumara. (☎456 00 80. Open Tu-Sa 9am-2pm and 4-6pm, Su 9am-1pm. 5 pesos.) **Laguna Arareco** is 8km down the route toward Cusárare and has a variety of trails perfect for a day hikes. Exploring the countryside with a **bike** is another good option (see **Practical Information,** p. 231).

While most establishments in Creel close before 9pm, a few are open late, and the town is usually full of tourists roaming the streets or people strumming guitars until midnight. At night, **Laylo's Lounge and Bar,** Mateos 25, inside El Caballo Bayo restaurant and hotel, is a local *cantina* with a touch of class. The comfy lounge chairs and nice decor outdo most watering holes. (☎456 01 36. Open daily 3pm-1am.) **Tio Molcas,** Mateos 35, at Caro, also breaks *cantina* stereotypes with its relaxed atmosphere. The place doubles as a restaurant during the day. (Open daily 11am-1am.) One of the most happening places for foreigners is the bar at **Margarita's Plaza Hotel.** Turn left on Caro heading away from the *zócalo*, and then right into the hotel courtyard. Happy Hour lasts 7-10pm and includes a free tequila shot with every beer. (Open daily 6:30-11:30pm.)

DAYTRIPS FROM CREEL

SAN IGNACIO MISSION

Walk south on Mateos until the road forks and stay to the left. The road forks again shortly; take the left path. To enter the Mission and Lake area, you'll need to pay 20 pesos. From this point, the Mission is about 1km straight ahead. There are signs directing you to the other sights.

The mission was constructed in 1744 and is still in use today—services are Sunday at noon in Rarámuri, the native tongue of the Tarahumara. Nearby is the **Valle de los Hongos** (Valley of the Mushrooms), the **Valle de las Ramas** (Frogs), and the **Valle de las Chichis** (Breasts), along with the **Cave of Sebastian.** Don't ask about that last valley. Two-hour tours to the mission and lake are run from Casa Perez.

LAGUNA ARARECO

Walk south on Mateos and bear right when the road forks; follow the path 7km southeast. To reach the lake from the Mission, follow the path up the mountain, jump the fence, and veer to the right through 2 large fields.

Travelers can also hike to the man-made lake, 3km long and eight acres in area. The water here is cold and contains dangerous weeds below the surface. You can rent paddle boats (80 pesos) from the small station next to the lake. Nearby is **Recohuata Hot Springs,** where you can take a break from a long day of hiking in the soothing, warm waters (10 pesos). If you take a tour, it's a 40-minute ride from Creel and a 600m hike down into the canyon (75 pesos). The **Valle de las Monjas** (Valley of the Nuns), 9km away, has fascinating rock formations and makes a great daytrip on horseback.

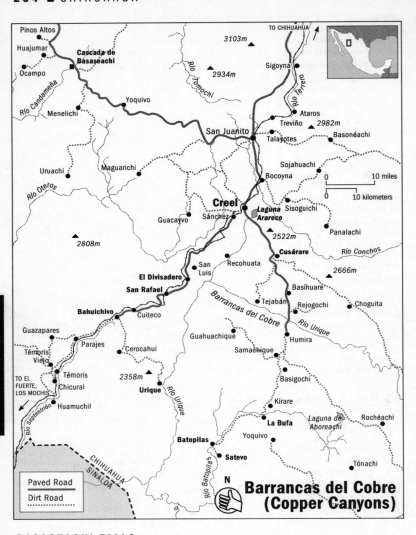

Barrancas del Cobre
(Copper Canyons)

BASASEACHI FALLS

With a car, pick up a map in Creel and enjoy the drive on the newly paved road. Without a car, you can either take a tour or a bus. The latter is cheaper and just as safe. Take an Estrella Blanca bus from either Cuauhtémoc (2 per day, 80 pesos) or Creel (5hr., 3 per day, 91 pesos). The bus from Creel stops at a pair of tiny crossroads called San Pedro. You'll have to change buses there to get to Basaseachi.

With water cascading from a height of 246m, Basaseachi (Rarámuri for "place of the cascade" or "place of the coyotes") is the highest waterfall in Mexico and the fourth highest in North America. Few waterfalls are blessed with such gorgeous surroundings. Tucked into a corner of Canyon Candameña, the falls don't get many visitors. Anyone who makes the trip will be rewarded with scenery from a postcard photographer's wildest dreams. Walk 3km down the paved road that runs through town to the trailhead to see the falls. The path is clearly marked and reaches the top of the falls after about 30 minutes. You won't have much of a view from the top, so hike down the steep path to the natural *ventana* (window), which allows a breathtaking view of the falls and surrounding canyon (45min. each way). Adventurous spirits can trek to the bottom of the falls by following the path. The hike is difficult and takes about another hour from the *ventana*, but you'll be alone at the bottom in a sub-tropical paradise.

Along the way to Basaseachi, you'll pass through some of the most sparsely populated areas of the Sierra Tarahumara. **San Juanito** is the only town along the road with gasoline, reliable phones, and decent restaurants and hotels (most of them near the bus station).

BARRANCAS DEL COBRE

Covering an area four times the size of the United States' Grand Canyon, the Barrancas del Cobre (Copper Canyons), hidden deep within the Sierra Madres, are one of the most spectacular sights in all of Mexico. Comprised of six interlocking canyons in an area known as the Sierra Tarahumara, it hibernates under drifts of snow during the winter months and explodes with blooming plants during the rainy season (July-Sept.). The Copper Canyons, so-named for the minerals in the rock that give the canyon walls a copper color, is transversed on the western side by the tracks of the **Chihuahua-Pacífico Railroad.** Trains making the trip from Chihuahua to Los Mochis career along canyon walls at death-defying angles, plunge into tunnels (99 of them), cross the Continental Divide three times, and soar to a height of 2240m. Perhaps the most amazing feature of the Canyons is that few foreigners, even those familiar with Mexico, have ever heard of them. The immense area of the Canyons makes for a wealth of breathtaking vistas, but with little transportational infrastructure, they are hard to explore. Many travelers stop along the train route at Bahuichivo, and from the there head to the town of Urique, at the bottom of the canyon. Others opt to travel southeast along the dangerous but incredibly scenic road to Batopilas. Those without cars report using kindhearted locals to give them a lift, although *Let's Go* does not recommend hitchhiking. Other options include taking a tour or a really long hike. It almost doesn't matter where one goes—in this beautiful country, adventure awaits everywhere.

THE TRAIN ROUTE

Trains go from Los Mochis to Chihuahua (1st-class 13hr., 6am, 387 pesos; 2nd-class 16hr., 7am, 190 pesos) and from Chihuahua to Los Mochis (1st-class 7am; 2nd-class 8am) through Cuauhtémoc, La Junta, San Juanito, Creel (see p. 230), El Divisadero, Posada Barrancas, San Rafael, Cuiteco, Bahuichivo, Témoris, Loreto, El Fuerte (see p. 238), and Sufragio/San Blas.

Two types of trains make the daily journey between Los Mochis and Chihuahua. The **first-class train** (known as Estrella) is equipped with bathrooms and A/C, and blessed with large, comfortable, tilt-o-matic seats. The **second-class train** (known as Mixto) screeches along the same tracks carrying both passengers and livestock; it's a much slower, sweatier, and less reliable ride. Grab a seat on the **left side** of the train heading toward Los Mochis, and the **right side** if you're on the way to Chihuahua. Note that if you take the second-class Los Mochis-bound train, you'll zoom by some great views in the dark. Since the train only comes through any town twice a day if you get off you'll be there at least 12 hours.

EL DIVISADERO. At El Divisadero Station, the jagged mountain edges overlap to create a maze of gorges at the rim of the Barrancas del Cobre. Eight hours out of Los Mochis and two hours out of Creel, the first-class train stops here for sightseeing (15min.). As you get off, you'll be bombarded by people selling local Tarahumara crafts as well as *gorditas* and burritos (about 8 pesos). If you've got a few pesos to burn, spending a day in Divisadero is well worth it. Three resort hotels near the train station offer tours (about 300 pesos per person) and horseback riding. Several trails of varying difficulty also begin at El Divisadero. The best bet for maps or information is to ask one of the local hotels. For a day hike, trek down to **Las Cuevas** (the caves) and back (about 8hr.). Guides are recommended for the other overnight trips. Aside from an amazing vista of the canyon (perhaps the fullest view of the Barrancas anywhere), Divisadero is also home to **La Piedra Volada,** a large, precariously balanced stone. It is technically possible (though quite difficult) to attempt a full-day hike between Divisadero and **Cusárare,** but an experienced guide is a must. A far more manageable and popular hike (which might force a night's stay at the pricey hotel; camping is not recommended) is down into the canyons—you can go as far as you want. A 4km round trip hike leads to the Tarahumara village of **Bacajipare** (6hr.). The 27km descent to **Río Urique,** at the bottom of the canyon, takes eight hours each way. Guides for hire hang around the hotel; they will take you to Bacajipare, Río Urique, or most anywhere else.

SAN RAFAEL. Eleven kilometers down the tracks from El Divisadero is the dusty village of **San Rafael.** The town sprung up on the hillsides around the saw mill, now outside town, and offers a peek into an older way of life. San Rafael has just a handful of phones and all cooking is still done on wood-burning stoves—running water is a luxury few people have. Because San Rafael is situated in the crook of two intersecting ridges, the views of the Copper Canyons are not that spectacular from the town itself; the high ground around the town offers much better vistas. There is no set path; a compass is advisable.

CUITECO. From San Rafael, continue on to the small town of Cuiteco. Get off the train and marvel at its 300-year-old church; but do it quickly, there is no place to stay in town.

BAHUICHIVO. Bahuichivo, in a forest clearing, is 97km south of Creel. There's not much to see here, but it's a convenient train stop for access to points farther south in the canyon, such as Cerocahui and Urique.

BAHUICHIVO TO URIQUE

The trip from Bahuichivo to Urique is difficult without four-wheel drive. You're better off going with a tour if you're not familiar with the road. The Copper Canyon Railway stops in Bahuichivo, and there's always a posse of vehicles going to Urique waiting at the train station (50-60 pesos). If a man with a brown van offers to take you there for 20 pesos, don't get in.

CEROCAHUI. The mountain village of Cerocahui (pop. 600, elevation 1525m) is 17km southeast of Bahuichivo. The main attraction is the **Jesuit Mission,** founded in 1681 by the priest Juan María de Salvatierra. The gold and silver mines of **Sangre de Cristo,** the **Gallego Mountain** (38km away), the **Misión Churo,** and the **Yeparavo Waterfall** (4km south) are among the possible excursions from Cerocahui. The grocery store at the fork in the road has all the information you need about these excursions. Several locals offer tours for steep prices, but unless you know the way yourself, they are your best bet.

URIQUE. The village of Urique, 154 km from Creel, sits at bottom of the **Barranca de Urique,** the deepest of the six canyons. About halfway to Urique from Cerocahui, the canyon opens up to reveal magnificent cliffs and the village of Urique far below on the canyon floor. The lookout point rivals Divisadero as the best place to take in the Copper Canyons. The limited services available in Urique are all along **Principal,** the main street, parallel to the river. Accommodations are fairly cheap; options include the **campgrounds** on Principal and one or two hotels in town.

CREEL TO BATOPILAS

The best way to get to this end of the Canyon is to hire a guide. If you want to rough it, catch the red-and-white striped converted schoolbus from Creel to Batopilas from in front of the train station ask train station what time it leaves (8hr., 1 per day sometime before 9am, 40 pesos), or a van (6hr.). If you make as far out as Cusárare, getting around is difficult—not having a car limits your options.

Heading south from Creel, a road winds through the more scenic parts of the Copper Canyons. Buses rumble around nail-biting hairpin turns along the edges of steep cliffs that will make your heart pound both from excitement and nervousness. The first 75km section of road is happily paved; the rest, however, is unpaved. If you're averse to walking, you can arrange to navigate it on bikes, horses, or even donkeys.

TARAHUMARA CAVES. On the right side heading south, the still-inhabited Tarahumara caves are within view of the road if you search very hard. On tours, it's possible to go in and visit the homes for a small donation. Beds and other furniture, woodstoves with chimneys, and kerosene lamps adorn many of the dimly-lit caves.

CUSÁRARE. The town of Cusárare, 22km from Creel, features its very own 18th-century Jesuit mission. Check out the mission's Tarahumara interior, with wood floors and indigenous designs. There are no pews—when it is used on Sunday, people sit on the floor. A boardinghouse for children and a small Tarahumara craft museum are nearby, but the most popular attraction is the **Cusárare Falls,** a 3km hike uphill through a pine forest.

BASÍHUARE. Another 20km beyond Cusárare on the road to Batopilas is Basíhuare, an old overnight stop, once frequented by silver carriers en route to Batopilas. Further south the road, now one lane and soon to be dirt, weaves through the narrowing canyon in perhaps its most frightening stretch, offering spectacular vistas as it crawls by the **Cerro de Siete Pisos** (Seven-Floor Hill), so named for the seven distinct layers of earth that lead up along the rocky inner walls of the canyon.

LA BUFA. The seven steps can best be seen from **La Bufa,** 60km from Basíhuare, a scenic lookout with a magnificent view. You can make out the Río Urique far, far below and the yellow wooden bridge that runs across it. If you go left at the fork in the road before La Bufa, you'll come to **Norogachi,** a Tarahumara mission center at the river with beautiful (and often touristed) *Semana Santa* services, and **Guachochi,** a rocky, frontier-like village with both colonial and Tarahumara influences. The right fork will take you to the more impressive town of **Batopilas.** On the way you'll pass over the bridge that spans the Urique; you can get out and walk down through the bushes for a smashing view of the waterfall below. Keep your eyes peeled for **tescalama** trees, which have yellow flowers and grow out of the sheer rock. The last quarter of the ride to Batopilas has plenty of the **piedra cobriza** (copper rock), which gives the canyon its tint.

BATOPILAS. Batopilas (pop. 2000), a small village on the river in the depths of the canyon, is a rough 35km from La Bufa, a thrilling but scary 140km from Creel, and almost 2km below the rest of civilization. A rich silver town founded in 1708, the town's silver supply lasted until the late 1800s. Because of the mine, tiny Batopilas was the second city in all of Mexico (after Mexico City) to receive electricity, though ironically, its availability today is anything but a sure thing. Everything in Batopilas centers around the old stone **plaza,** referred to as the **parque.** Streets do have names, but even the locals don't know them. The main street (which connects Batopilas to Creel) splits off into two, one of which becomes Juárez, the other of which dead ends. As you drive into town, take a left both times the road forks to get to the main *parque.* The magnificent **haciendas** lying in ruins along the river recall of the excesses of the mining days. The brown, castle-like **Hacienda Shepard** belonged to a man from the US. Look for the *tescalama* trees with their mass of yellow roots growing directly from the *hacienda* walls. Guided hikes leave daily for the **Porfirio Díaz mine** and the more interesting **Peñasquito** (both hikes 1hr.), for **Cerro Colorado,** a section of the old Camino Real (12hr.), and for the lost mission of **Satevó** (see below). The best source of information about tours is the **Riverside Lodge,** in town diagonally across from the plaza on the bench side. A restored *hacienda,* the lodge is now an incredibly posh package-tour inn, with a luxuriant piano room, historical photo exhibits, and a great rooftop view. **Artesanías Monse,** on the south side of the plaza next to the Hotel Juanita, sells handicrafts made by nearby Tarahumara, supposedly the least Christianized of any Tarahumara people. You might get a chance to meet the artists, who often hang out in the garden in the back.

SATEVÓ. The most fascinating excursion from Batopilas is to Satevó, a minuscule town with a eerie and beautiful mission. It's a 40-minute drive (you'll need 4WD) or a two-hour walk. In the middle of a valley straddled by the towering canyon rises a lonesome, round mission. No one knows quite why this site was chosen, when it was built (the 15th or 16th century are the best guesses), or how the Taramuhara gathered the materials and energy to build it. To take a peek inside the mission, you'll have to tip the family living next door—they have the key. The inside of the mission is even eerier than the outside, with ancient tombs below and darkness above.

SINALOA

EL FUERTE   ☎6

Founded in 1564 by conquistador Don Francisco de Ibarra, El Fuerte (pop. 30,000) overlooks the Rio Fuerte. In 1824, it became the capital of an area including present-day Sinaloa, Sonora, and part of Arizona. It's now one of the first stops in Sinaloa on the train to Los Mochis, and a good place to prepare for a journey into or out of the canyons (see also **Creel,** p. 230).

▐▞ TRANSPORTATION AND PRACTICAL INFORMATION. From the train station, 7km outside of town, you'll have a hard time getting to El Fuerte without a taxi. In town, **Juárez** is the main street. Walk west from Juárez and turn left onto **5 de Mayo,** which puts you in the *zócalo* in front of the Palacio Municipal. **Trains** leave daily for **Los Mochis** (1st-class 1½hr., 6:30pm; 2nd-class 2hr., 8:30pm), and **Chihuahua** (1st-class 6am, 2nd-class 7am). **Taxis** gather on Juárez to take you to the train station. **Buses** to **Los Mochis** (every 30min., 40 pesos) leave from the corner of Juárez and 16 de Septiembre.

The **tourist office** is inside Palacio Municipal, Room 27. (Supposedly open daily 9am-3pm.) You can get information at the **Hotel Posada,** 5 de Mayo and Hidalgo. **Banamex,** at Juárez and 16 de Septiembre, has a 24hr. **ATM.** (Open M-F 8:30am-2:30pm.) **LADATELs** along Juárez and in the *zócalo.* **Caseta:** at Mariela, Juárez and 16 de Septiembre. (Open M-Sa 8am-1pm and 4-6pm, Su 8am-1pm.) **Post office:** in the Palacio Gobierno in the Playuela. (Open M-F irregularly.) **Postal code:** 81820.

▐▘◌ ACCOMMODATIONS AND FOOD. El Fuerte's budget accomodations cluster along Juárez, while the fancier hotels are near the *zócalo.* **Hotel San José,** Juárez 108 (☎893 08 45), has some of the lowest rates around. Large rooms have cement floors and high ceilings. Don't look up if you have arachnophobia. (Cots without bath 20 pesos; single beds with bath 50 pesos; doubles 80 pesos.) **Hotel Guerrero,** Juárez 210, has rooms with bathrooms, coolers (like A/C but less strong), and comfortable beds. Rates vary by season. (Singles in summer 100 pesos, in winter 150 pesos; doubles 200-250 pesos.) **La Fogata,** Rosales 103, has good food (10-35 pesos) and a semi-outdoor patio connected to Rosa's kitchen. She serves you and her family. There is no menu, but check on the sign at the entrance. **Cocina Economica,** Juárez 57, lives up to its name with *antojitos,* quesadillas, and burritos (5-6 pesos). At **Restaurante El Meson General,** Juárez 202 (☎893 02 06), food is served around an open courtyard, and live music is occasionally played on weekends. They have an interesting menu, and provide a rare chance to try *pulpo* (octopus, 63 pesos) this far north. A wide variety of fish and good drinks (9 pesos).

▨ SIGHTS. El Fuerte has a few pleasant attractions. Follow 5 de Mayo west over the hill to stroll along the **Río Fuerte.** Keep your eyes peeled for native birds such as the Crested Caracara, the Mexican Blue-Rumped Parrotelet, and the Plain-Capped Starthroat. Also keep your eyes on the path ahead of you: it's a frequently used cow path. A beautiful view of the river and city can be found at the hilltop **Hotel Río Vista;** follow 5 de Mayo to the river and walk up the hill.

SOTOL, FROM THE HEART... Since the hearty agave plant is strong enough to survive the harsh desert—it seems only proper to make it into a strong drink. Mexicans in the present-day state of Jalisco believed this, and the drink they made is known far and wide as tequila. Yet the same agave, processed a slightly different way, has also been made into *sotol*, the state drink of Chihuahua, for the last 800 years. In *sotol* production, the heart of the plant is roasted and squeezed, releasing a sweet juice that is collected and naturally fermented. Tequila production mixes the heart with water—the result is a more bitter. After being distilled in copper containers, *sotol* is distilled for a minimum of six months in white oak casks. Today, the number one brand of *sotol* is Hacienda. Go to your local Chihuahuan bar and give it a shot.

LOS MOCHIS ☎ 6

Just 15 minutes from the ocean and linked by ferry to Baja California (departing from Topolobampo to La Paz) and by rail and route to the major cities of Mexico, Los Mochis (pop. 400,000) is a trade and commerce center, and an important stopover for travelers. While not a bastion of Mexican culture, Los Mochis ("Mochis" to locals), founded in 1903, is a good departure point to more exciting destinations, such as the Copper Canyons (see **Barrancas del Cobre**, p. 235).

▐▀ TRANSPORTATION

GETTING AROUND

Municipal buses run throughout the city (2.60 pesos). The main stop is on Zaragoza at Obregón; ask the driver if he goes to your destination. Taxis can be found waiting on the corner of every major intersection, by calling ☎812 02 83.

GETTING AWAY

Buses: Transportes Norte de Sonora (☎812 17 57) and Elite (☎818 49 67) buses run from the modern terminal at the corner of Juárez and Degollado. The cheapest carrier, Transportes Norte de Sonora, goes to: **Guaymas** (5hr., every hr., 145 pesos); **Mazatlán** (5½hr., every hr. 5am-5pm, 195 pesos); **Mexicali** (18hr., 7 and 8:15am, 525 pesos); **Mexico City** (24hr., 6pm, 825 pesos) via **Culiacán** (3hr., 96 pesos); **Tijuana** (22hr., 4, 7, and 8:15pm; 600 pesos) via **Hermosillo** (7hr., 178 pesos); and **Navajoa** (2hr., every 2hr., 80 pesos). Transportes del Pacífico, on Morelos between Leyva and Zaragoza (☎812 03 47 and 812 03 41), sends *de paso* buses south to **Mazatlán** and north through **Guaymas, Hermosillo,** and **Mexicali** to **Tijuana.** Buses to **El Fuerte** and other nearby destinations leave from Zaragoza, between Ordoñez and Cuauhtémoc. Norte de Sinaloa (☎818 03 57) sends rickety green buses every 15min. to **Culiacán** (3½hr., 60 pesos); **Guamuchil** (2hr., 30 pesos); and **Guasave** (1hr., 20 pesos). Bus service to **Topolobampo** (every 20min. 6am on; 8.50 pesos, 6 pesos for students), leaving from a stop on Cuauhtémoc between Prieta and Zaragoza, 1 block north of Obregón.

Ferry: The ferry to **La Paz** leaves from **Topolobampo** daily (10hr., tickets 150 pesos and up). Tickets are sold at 6pm at the **Sematur** office, Rendón 519 or on the ferry (☎862 01 41; fax 886 2 00 35. Open M-F 8am-1pm and 3-7pm, Su 9am-1pm). To get to the office, walk nine blocks from Juárez on Flores, then turn left on Rendón.

Train: The **Chihuahua al Pacífico** train (☎812 08 47) runs between Los Mochis and Chihuahua, passing through the **Copper Canyons.** The first-class train passes through daily (first-class 6am, 463 pesos to Creel, 840 pesos to Chihuahua; second class 7am). **Tickets** are sold on the train or from a travel agency in advance. To get downtown from the train station, take a public bus, leaving down the road about 100m (every 15min., 3 pesos). After dark, your only option will be to take a taxi (60 pesos). During the day, a free bus carries guests to and from the Hotel Santa Anita. No official documentation of guest status is generally required to get on board.

✳️ 🛈 ORIENTATION AND PRACTICAL INFORMATION

The city is laid out in a grid. Downtown, principal avenues parallel to one another are (east to west) Degollado, Zaragoza, Leyva, Guerrero, and Rosales. Perpendicular to these (north to south) are Juan de Batiz, Cárdenas, Morelos, Independencia, Castro, and Ordoñez. The **tourist office**, on Ordoñez and Allende, is next to the Palacio Gobierno in the Unidad Administrativa; go in the entrance off of Ordoñez and turn right. Knowledgeable and helpful staff. (☎815 10 90. Open M-F 9am-3pm.) **Travel agencies: Viajes Conelva,** Leyva 525, at Valdez, inside Hotel El Dorado. (☎815 60 90 or 815 80 90. Open M-Sa 8am-7pm, Su 9am-2pm.) Many travel agencies can be found near the tourist office. **Currency exchange: Bancomer** on Leyva and Juárez (☎812 23 23; open M-F 8:30am-4pm and 3:30-7pm, Sa 9am-1:30pm) has four 24-hour **ATMs.** Additional banks cluster near the intersection of Prieto and Independencia. There is a **market** in the area around Zaragoza, between Castro and Ordoñez. Most stands close around 7pm. **Lavamatic,** Allende 228, is just before Juárez. (Wash 13 pesos, dry 16 pesos. Open M-Sa 7am-7pm, Su 7am-1pm.) **Emergency:** ☎060. **Police:** (☎812 00 33), Degollado at Cuauhtémoc in the Presidencia Municipal. No English spoken. **Red Cross:** Tenochtitlán and Prieto, one block off Castro. (☎815 08 08 or 812 02 92. 24hr. ambulance service.) **Super Farmacia San Jorge,** at Juárez and Degollado. (☎818 18 19. Open 24hr.) **Hospital Fátima,** Jiquilpán Pte. 639 (☎812 33 12). No English spoken. **Medical Assistance: Centro de Salud** (☎812 07 74). **Post office:** Ordoñez 226, two blocks off Castro, between Prieta and Zaragoza. (☎812 08 23. Open M-F 8am-6pm.) **Postal code:** 81200.

🛏️🍴 ACCOMMODATIONS AND FOOD

Budget hotels of variable quality are sprinkled throughout downtown. **Hotel Montecarlo,** Flores 322 Sur, a gracefully aging blue building at the corner of Independencia, comes with large rooms and a quiet, indoor courtyard. Fans, cable TVs, and A/C. (☎812 18 18. Singles 180 pesos; doubles 190-220 pesos; triples 240 pesos.) The **Hotel Lorena** Obregón 186, across from the market, offers rooms furnished with everything but a butler. Huge windows with great views A/C, TV, and phones. (☎812 02 39. Singles 170 pesos; doubles 210 pesos; triples 240 pesos.) **Hotel Hidalgo,** Hidalgo 260 Pte., between Prieta and Zaragoza, has ceiling fans and cool colors that take the heat out of the small rooms. (☎812 34 56 or 815 42 36. Singles 130 pesos, with A/C 140 pesos; doubles 160 pesos; triples 180 pesos.)

The **public market,** along Zaragoza between Castro and Ordoñez, has low prices, high quality, and *taquerías* and *loncherías* that serve cheap, homemade food (stands start to close around 7pm). At **Tortas Moka,** Independencia 216, at Prieto, you can enjoy a *torta* (10-12 pesos) while you people-watch. Call for delivery and have a motorcycle rush your *torta*s hot and fresh. (☎812 39 41 or 812 68 78. Open daily 8am-9pm.) **El Taquito,** on Leyva between Hidalgo and Independencia, is expensive, but it's the price you pay for waiters in red jackets serving *enchiladas suizas* (33 pesos) and cheese-filled shrimp wrapped in bacon (53 pesos). Hamburgers and fries 25 pesos. (☎812 81 19. Open 24hr.) Visit **Video Torta,** Independencia 248, to eat excellent *tortas* (10 pesos) while watching the latest Mexican music videos. Wash it down with a 5-peso pop. (☎815 66 66. Open daily 8:30am-10:30pm.)

👁️ 🎵 SIGHTS AND ENTERTAINMENT

Los Mochis has a few modest amusements. If you can, head to **Topolobampo.** Various agencies on Topolobampo's shore lead tours throughout the day (about 150 pesos), and the town has opportunities for fishing, horseback riding, and dolphin-watching. If you decide to stay in Mochis, visit the extraordinary collection of trees and plants assembled in **Sinaloa Park,** on Rosales and Castro. Walk to the end of Castro and turn left; the entrance is about half a block down on Rosales. The **Museo Regional del Valle del Fuerte,** near the end of Obregón toward the park and Rosales, was the home of an early settler whose guns and personal diary are now housed there. Photographs documenting the growth and development of Northern Mexico are on display. (☎812 46 92. Open Tu-Sa 10am-1pm and 4-7pm, Su 10am-1pm. 5 pesos, free on Su and holidays.) Festivals and musical events are sometimes held at the Plaza Solidaridad and the nearby Plazuela 27 de Septiembre. Adjoining the Plaza Solidaridad is the **Santuario del Sagrado Corazón de Jesús**, Los Mochis's oldest church, which was built after the American founder's Protestant wife donated the land to the people. If you want a little nightlife, head to the **Rodeo Bar,** on Obregón and Constitución, where you can down a few beers and take the mechanical horse for a ride. (F-Sa cover 60 pesos. Open daily 9pm-3am.)

CULIACÁN   ☎6

The capital of Sinaloa, Culiacán (pop. 600,000) is the largest city in the state, and, with its 1533 founding by the hated Nuño de Guzmán, also one of the oldest. While the sprawling, modern city offers tourists little, it is home to the large Universidad Autónoma de Sinaloa, a public university that fuels the town with its youthful energy. Those who find themselves here for a night or two will not leave disappointed; Culiacán offers plenty of nightlife options and, by most estimates, one of the most attractive college populations in the Republic.

⬛ TRANSPORTATION. The **airport,** Aeropuerto Internacional de Bachigualato is approximately 10km to the southeast of downtown (☎760 06 76). Major carriers include AeroCalifornia (☎716 02 50), AeroMexico (☎01 80 00 21 40 00), and Aerolíneas Internacionales (☎712 54 43, 716 03 55, or 01 80 07 16 73 55). The **bus station,** south of downtown on Solano (☎712 48 75), is served by Transportes del Pacífico (☎712 33 36), Estrella del Pacífico (☎715 46 56), Autobuses Azteca de Oro with direct service to **Guadalajara** (425 pesos), Autotransportes TUFESA (☎716 99 99), and the plush Twin Star buses (☎713 74 15) run to **Mexico City** (965 pesos); **Guadalajara** (519 pesos); **Nogales** (446 pesos); as well as most major cities in Sinaloa.

⬛❼ ORIENTATION AND PRACTICAL INFORMATION. The city is concentrated on the south side of the Río Tamazula. The downtown area is roughly delineated by Madero, Granados, the edge of the river along which Niños Héroes runs, and Bravo. **Tourist office:** in the Palacio Gobierno, Insurgentes and Barraza. (Open M-F 8am-3pm and 5-7pm.) 24hr. **ATMs** cluster downtown, especially along Rosales. **Lavandería Automática La Familiar** (☎713 21 81. Open M-Sa 8am-8pm, Su 9am-1pm). **Emergency:** ☎060 or 066. **Police:** ☎761 01 57 or 761 01 58. **Red Cross:** Solano and Paleza (☎752 02 07. 24hr. ambulance.) **Farmacia Red Cross,** 145 Solano. (Open 24hr.) **Hospital Civil de Culiacán,** Obregón and Romero (☎716 46 50). **LADATELs** are scattered throughout downtown. **Internet Access: Net.house,** Juárez 75. (20 pesos per hr. Open M-Sa 9am-8pm, Su 9am-2pm.) **Post office:** 560 Domingo Rubi. (☎712 21 70. Open M-F 8am-1pm, Sa 9am-1pm.) **Postal Code:** 80000.

⬛ ACCOMMODATIONS. Budget hotels in the 200-peso range can be found along Leyva Solano, across from the bus station, and in the west side of downtown, west of Obregón. **Hotel del Valle,** Leyva Solano 180, is across from the bus station. Newly remodeled and with new management. A/C, cable, and phones. (☎713 90 20. Singles 213 pesos; doubles 243 pesos; 30 pesos per additional person.) **Hotel Francis,** Escobedo 135, has clean and carpeted rooms with A/C, cable, safes, sometimes king-sized beds. Laundry, fax, parking, and a restaurant and bar. (☎712 47 50 or 712 47 51. Singles 215 pesos; doubles 240 pesos.) **Hotel Castilla,** Juárez 233, has an indoor courtyard, A/C, TVs, phones, and baths, all in a central location. (☎713 14 38. Singles 195; doubles 220; triples 250; 20 pesos per additional person.)

⬛ FOOD. Good budget restaurants can be found downtown. A sushi trend has recently swept the city. Join the crowd at newly-opened **Sumiko's Sushi,** Rosales 77, the most popular sushi joint in town. Serves sushi (24-39 pesos) and sashimi (37-41 pesos), along with more traditional seafood. (☎730 97 23. Open W-M noon-11pm.) **Ciber Pizzeta,** Rosales 42, in front of the park, north of the cathedral. Pack-

Old Mazatlán

México
Ave. del Mar
16 de Septiembre
Bolívar
Quijano
Zúñiga
Zaragoza
Zaragoza
Morelos
Hidalgo
Estrada
Estrada
Ocampo
Ocampo
Canizales
Leandro Valle
21 de Marzo
Canizales
21 de Marzo
Ángel Flores
Escobedo
PLAZA Constitución
MACHADO
Guerrero
Galeana
Roosevelt
Avenida Miguel Alemán

Ibarra
Arriba
Domínguez
5 de Mayo
Guillermo Nelson
Juan Carrasco
Serdán
Juárez
Canizal
Serdán
Tirso
Niños Héroes
Venus
Osuna
Rojo

Paseo Claussen
Paseo de las 3 Islas
Cerro de Nevería (Ice Box Hill)
High Divers of Mazatlán
Pedregoso
Olas Altas Claussen

N

Mercado

PLAZA REVOLUCIÓN

Isla de los Pájaros
Playa Brujas
Marina Mazatlán
Playa Sábalo
Tiburón
Calz. Camarón Sábalo
Laguna Loaiza
EL CID RESORT
ZONA DORADA
Las Garzas
Lomas de Mazatlán
Bugambilia
Calz. Rafael Buelna
Laguna del Camarón
Insurgentes
del Mar
Universidad
Carretera Internacional
Ferrusquilla
Beltrán
San Lorenzo
Fuente
Baluarte
Pánuco
Benemérito de las Américas
Piaxtla
Gaviotas
Estero del Infiernillo
Estero del Sábalo

Isla de los Lobos
Isla de los Venados
Playa las Gaviotas

Mazatlán
🛏 ACCOMMODATIONS
Hotel Belmar, 6
Hotel Central, 4
Hotel del Centro, 3
Hotel Emperador, 8
Hotel Fiesta and
   Hotel Los Arcos, 7
Hotel La Siesta, 5
Hotel Lerma, 2
Hotel México, 1

N

0   2 miles
0   2 kilometers

Bahía de Puerto Viejo

OLD MAZATLÁN
(See Inset)

Zaragoza
5 de Mayo
16 de Sept.
Juárez
Serdán
G. Nájera
Carrasco
Pesqueira
Calz. Gabriel Leyva Solano
Villa Iturbide
Gemán Eves
A. Flores
Constitución
Potrero del Llano
Miguel Alemán
Canaval
Asalto
Serdán
Emilio Barragán
Playa Norte
Paseo Claussen

Bahía de Olas Altas

Playas del Sur

Canal de Navegación

Isla de la Piedra
Isla de Ocon

Estero del Infiernillo

Mazatlán

age deals (25-35 pesos) include Internet access, food, and drinks. (Open daily 10am-10pm.) **Café Museo,** Rafael Buelna 38, next to the Museo del Arte Sinaloa, is a hip cafe that showcases the art of many renowned Latin American artists. Sample an array of coffees (8-22 pesos) and sandwiches (18-32 pesos) while you stare at the walls. (Open M-F 8am-2pm and 4:30-10pm, Sa 4:30-10pm, and Su 5-10:30pm.) **La Única Pan y Pasteles,** 237 Domingo Rubi, will satisfy even the most discriminating sweet tooth. A variety of sweet breads are available (5 pesos), as well as the drinks (6-10 pesos) to wash them down. (Open M-Sa 7am-11pm.)

◼ SIGHTS. Sights in Culiacán consist of parks and memorials commemorating regional heroes; most cluster in the Parque Municipal Revolución, on Obregón, between Villa and Solano. The **Reloj Conmemorativo Club Rotario** is a familiar landmark for finding the large street, Solano when heading north on Obregón. The park is also home to the **Fuente de la Fertilidad** (Fountain of Fertility)—throw in a couple of pesos and maybe something will happen. **Museo de Arte Sinaloa,** Buelno and Paliza, houses the work of artists such as Diego Rivera, López Saez, and Frida Kahlo in its permanent collection. (☎715 55 41 or 719 99 33. Open Tu-F 10am-3pm and 5-7pm, Sa-Su 10am-5pm. 5 pesos, students and children 3 pesos; Su free.) **Centro Cultural Difocur,** Niños Héroes and Rosales, offers a variety of classes on everything from art to music. Performances held in the sizeable outdoor amphitheater. Check listings at the office. (Open Tu-Su 4-7pm.)

🎵 ENTERTAINMENT AND NIGHTLIFE. Cuilacán's nightlife is fueled by the university across the river from downtown; clubs and bars congregate on Niños Héroes by the waterfront. A popular hangout is **Carlos and Charlie's,** on Niños Héroes. The format is bar and grill, though the crowd on the weekends is often wearing club attire. Live music. (Open M-W 7am-midnight, Th-Sa 7am-1am. Cover varies.) The happening disco **Clips and Beer,** about 50m east on the *malecón*, is mainly a weekend hangout—the college booties here are ready to be shaken not stirred. (☎716 05 77. Open F-Sa 9:30pm-3am and W-Th for special events. Cover 70 pesos.) An up-and-coming club is **The Door,** on the university side of the river.

MAZATLÁN ☎6

Mazatlán (pop. 380,000) means "place of the deer" in Náhuatl. A less appropriate name can hardly be imagined. The only wildlife roaming about today is the *Bronzus norteamericanus,* the animal with the noisy mating call that packs the beaches and clubs in a herdlike manner. Mazatlán was not always like this. In 1531, the city's harbor was chosen as the launching pad for Spanish galleons. Three centuries later, the town weathered both a US blockade (1847) and a French bombardment (1864). In 1859, the city was named the capital of Sinaloa, a distinction rudely snatched away 14 years later. During the Mexican Revolution, Mazatlán became the second city in the world to be shelled from air, a dubious distinction to be sure. Despite its eventful past, Mazatlán offers little of historical or cultural interest to travelers. Far from picky, the *Bronzus norteamericanus* contents itself with the city's great assets—beautiful sunsets, glittering ocean, and wide beaches. The animal is a rarer sight in Mazatlán's downtown, which, with its shady *zócalo,* is more traditionally Mexican. The sage budget traveler will wisely stay and eat in this part of the town, saving the *Zona Dorada* for occasional excursions into the realm of the *Bronzus.* Be careful—they are known to bite.

◼ TRANSPORTATION

GETTING AROUND

Mazatlán's efficient **bus system** makes getting around the city a breeze. At some point, all municipal buses pass the public market on Juárez, three blocks north of the *zócalo* at Ocampo. The most useful bus line is the **"Sábalo-Centro,"** which runs from the downtown market, with stops a few blocks from the *malecón* in Olas Altas and at Playa Sábalo in the *Zona Dorada*. The **"Cerritos-Juárez"** bus continues up to Playa Bruja at Puerta Cerritos. The **"Insurgentes"** route services the bus and train stations, and **"Playa Sur"** goes to the ferry dock and lighthouse (every 15min. 5am-10pm, 3 pesos). For late night disco hopping, you'll have to take a taxi or a *pulmonía* (like a large golf cart). Standard fare between Old Mazatlán and the *Zona Dorada* is 25-30 pesos, depending on the time of night (later is more expensive). Don't be afraid to haggle with the *pulmonía* drivers—there are usually plenty of them to choose from. It will take more than one hour to walk between the two sections. Olas Altas and the *centro* both make convenient home bases. Olas Altas is a 10-minute walk to the *centro* (take a right on Flores from the *malecón*), and is easily accessible by bus.

GETTING AWAY

Airport: Rafael Buelna International Airport (☎982 23 99), 18km south of the city. The "Central Camionera" bus makes the trip to the *centro;* the only way to get back is by taxi (150 pesos). Served by **AeroCalifornia** (☎913 20 42), El Cid Resort; **Aeroméxico**, Sábalo 310A (☎914 11 11 or 01 80 00 21 40 00); **Alaska Airlines** (☎001 80 02 52 75 22; fax 85 27 30); **Mexicana**, B. Domínguez and del Mar (☎/fax 982 28 88).

Buses: Mazatlán's bus station is three blocks away from the *malecón* and about 2km north of Old Mazatlán, between downtown and the *Zona Dorada*. To head downtown from the bus station, catch any of the red buses with "Centro" or "Mercado" written on their windshields, one block west of the bus station and about one block south, to your right along Benemérito de las Américas (3 pesos, 3.50 pesos after 9pm; buses stop running at 10pm). Avoid the "Sabado-coco" bus, as it goes downtown only after making an enormous loop around the city. A cab will make the trip (25 pesos and up). The Estrella Blanca Group sends buses to **Durango** (7hr.; 9:30am, noon, 3pm; 174-212 pesos); **Torreón** (332 pesos), **Monterrey** (536 pesos), **Mexico City** (782 pesos), as well as most major cities in the state of Sinaloa. Transportes de Pacífico services **Culiacán** (2½hr., 140 pesos); **Obregón** (368 pesos); **Tepic** (5hr., every hr., 141 pesos), **Hermosillo** (479 pesos, 4½hr.); **Mexicali** (745 pesos); **Tijuana** (843 pesos); and **Mexico City** (563 pesos). The Tropicales that line the other terminal will take you to nearby locations. The **Transporte Rapido de Sud terminal** is a block away from the station on Benemerito de las Américas.

Ferry: Sematur (☎981 70 20 or 21), at the end of Carnaval, south of Flores and the *centro*. It's a grueling 20min. walk from the *centro* to the ferry docks; the blue "Playa Sur" school bus (3 pesos) makes the trip. Taxis 20-25 pesos. Tickets sold only on the day of departure. Arrive at least 2hr. early to procure a spot, as capacity is very limited. You can buy tickets on the ferry, but you aren't guaranteed a spot, since they let ticketed passengers board first. Ticket office open daily Su-F 8am-3pm, Sa 9am-1pm. One can also purchase tickets in advance at a local travel agency. During the high season (Dec. and July-Aug.), make reservations at least 2 weeks ahead. One ferry every day to **La Paz**, arriving around 8am (17hr.; 3pm; *salón* 270 pesos, *turista* 540 pesos, *cabina* 810 pesos, *especial* 1080 pesos, children 2-11 half-price).

CATCH A PNEUMONIA

The *pulmonía* (pneumonia, which you might get riding in town during the rainy season) is unique to Mazatlán. Resembling large golf carts, these modified Volkswagens rip through town carrying tourists often blasting raucous music. *Pulmonía* drivers either rent their vehicles from the company or purchase them privately. Private owners often "soup up" their vehicles, adding shiny alloy ruins or investing in thundering sound systems. *Pulmonías* cost about 30 pesos for a trip from downtown to the *zona dorar,* while taxis cost about 25 pesos. A good rule of thumb is that taxi fare is about 5 pesos less, but the little extra for the *pulmonía* goes toward working on your tan. Depending on the time of night (and your level of inebriation), the price may climb to 40 or 50 pesos. Taxis may provide air conditioning and shelter from the rain, but *pulmonías* are more fun, so catch a pneumonia and experience this unique Mazatlán oddity.

⚡🔢 ORIENTATION AND PRACTICAL INFORMATION

Mazatlán is divided into Old Mazatlán, home to the *zócalo* and budget hotels and restaurants, and the *Zona Dorada*, home to the *gringo* tourist. The *malecón* (boardwalk) follows the shore and connects the two sides of the town. Since Mazatlán is very spread out, the easiest way to navigate the city is by bus.

TOURIST, FINANCIAL, AND LOCAL SERVICES

Tourist Office: (☎916 51 60 or 916 51 65; fax 916 51 66 or 916 51 67) on Sábalo at Tiburón, in the *Zona Dorada*, on the 4th floor of the pinkish Banrural building past El Cid resort on the "Sábalo-Centro" bus line. Helpful staff doles out helpful maps. Open M-F 9am-5pm; reachable by phone Sa 9am-1pm.

Tourist Police: (☎914 84 44), on Ruíz and Santa Mónica in the *Zona Dorada*.

Consulates: Canada (☎913 73 20), and **US** (☎916 58 89), in Loaiza at Bugambilia in Hotel Playa Mazatlán in the *Zona Dorada*. Both open daily 9am-1pm.

Currency Exchange: *Casas de cambio* are open all day in the northern section of the downtown area, but have poor rates. Stick to banks in the *centro* and the *zócalo*. **Banca Serfín** (☎982 66 66), 21 de Marzo and Nelson, across from the *zócalo*, has a 24hr. **ATM.** Open M-F 8:30am-5pm, Sa 10am-2pm. Most banks open M-F 8:30-11am.

American Express: (☎913 06 00; fax 916 59 08), in the Centro Comercial Plaza Balboa on Sábalo. Open daily 9am-5pm.

Car Rental: Hertz, Sábalo 314 (☎913 60 60, 913 49 55, or ☎985 05 45 airport office; fax 14 25 23). Starting around 300 pesos per day. Must be 21 years old. **Budget,** Camarón Sábolo 402 (☎913 20 00), and **National,** Camarón Sábado 7000 (☎913 60 00). Must be at least 25 years old for both.

Laundry: Lavamatic del Centro, Serdán 2914 (☎981 35 56), on the *malecón*. 35 pesos per 3kg. Open M-Sa 8am-7:30pm.

EMERGENCY AND COMMUNICATIONS

Emergency: ☎060.

Police: (☎983 45 10), on Buelna in Colonia Juárez.

Red Cross: (☎985 14 51), on Zaragoza and Corona.

Pharmacy: Pharmacies congregate in the downtown area. **Farmacia Ibael** (☎982 62 49), on Ángel Flores and Campana. Open daily 8:30am-10:30pm.

Hospital: Sharp Hospital (☎986 56 76), on Kumate and Buelna, near Zaragoza park. English spoken. **Hospital General de Zona #3,** on Mateos (☎984 78 65, emergency ext. 270 and 271).

Fax: in same building as post office.

Internet Access: Cyber Café Mazatlán, Sábalo 204 (☎914 00 08), 20 pesos per 30min., 36 pesos per hr. Open M-Sa 9am-midnight, Su 10am-10pm. Cybercafes also cluster downtown along Flores.

Post Office: (☎981 21 21), on Flores and Juárez, across from the *zócalo*. Open M-F 8am-6pm, Sa 9am-1pm. **Postal Code:** 82000.

▌ ACCOMMODATIONS

High-quality cheap rooms do exist; simply avoid the *Zona Dorada*. Budget hotels cluster in three areas: Old Mazatlán along the two avenues east of the main square (Juárez and Serdán), the area around the bus station, and the pleasant waterfront of Olas Altas, southwest of Old Mazatlán. The cheapest rooms are by the bus station. There is one cheap option near the *Zona Dorada*, a trailer park, **La Posta,** on Buelna. (☎983 53 10. Hook-up 85 pesos.) Check in early during the busy seasons of Christmas and *Semana Santa*.

OLAS ALTAS

Back in the 1950s the focal point of Mazatlán's fledgling resort scene was Olas Altas. Although several restoration projects are underway, the area still feels somewhat deserted. A 10-minute walk from the *centro*, Olas Altas is connected to the rest of Mazatlán by the "Sábalo-Centro" and other bus lines.

■ **Hotel Belmar,** Olas Altas 166 (☎985 11 12 or 985 11 13), at Osuna. A resort of yesteryear, the Belmar glows with marble floors, wood paneling, and colorful arches. Spacious rooms with baths, TVs, and A/C. Match guests ping for pong, take a dip in the pool, or crawl into an antique rocker with a book from their small library. Singles 180 pesos, with ocean view 200 pesos; doubles 220 pesos, with ocean view 240 pesos.

Hotel La Siesta, Olas Altas Sur 11 (☎981 26 40, 981 23 34, or 01 800 71 15 229), at Escobedo. Next door to the Belmar, the Siesta is a newer clone. The beautiful courtyard is connected to the popular Shrimp Bucket Restaurant. Singles 200, with ocean view 280 pesos; doubles 250 pesos, with ocean view 280 pesos.

OLD MAZATLÁN

Downtown is a bit noisy during the day, but the hotels here are farther from the beach and therefore cheaper. Few people remain milling around after dark and streets are poorly lit, but the area is generally considered safe.

Hotel Lerma, Bolívar 622 (☎981 24 36), at Serdán. Central location. Bright colors and ceiling fans make the heat bearable. Great if you don't mind questionable plumbing. Singles 80 pesos; doubles 90 pesos; triples 100 pesos.

Hotel del Centro, Canizales 705 (☎981 26 73), between Serdán and Juárez. Rooms have A/C, TV, and baths. Some come with balconies. Singles 143 pesos; doubles 163 pesos; triples 184 pesos; quads 204 pesos.

Hotel Central, Domínguez 2 Sur (☎982 18 88), at Escobedo. Spotless rooms decorated with funky wood carvings. Phones, TV, A/C, and private bath. Singles 200 pesos; doubles 225 pesos; triples 250 pesos.

Hotel México, Calle México 201 (☎981 38 06), is one of the cheapest joints in town. You don't get what you don't pay for. Mint green interior, fans, private baths, but slight stench. Singles 70 pesos; doubles 120 pesos; triples 180 pesos.

NEAR THE BUS STATION

Hotels here are conveniently located, but bear in mind that since buses never sleep, you might not either. Competitive hotels located a block away along Benemérito de las Américas.

Hotel Los Arcos, Río Panoco 1006 (☎981 06 75), around the block to the left from the main exit of the station. Basic rooms with fans and bath. Singles 80 pesos, with A/C 110 pesos; doubles 100 pesos, with A/C 130 pesos; kitchenette suites 160 pesos.

Hotel Fiesta, Ferrosquila 306, (☎981 78 88), in front of the bus station. Clean rooms have baths, firm mattresses, and purified water. Singles 130 pesos, with TV and A/C 150 pesos; doubles 150 pesos, with TV and A/C 170 pesos.

Hotel Emperador, Río Panoco 1000 (☎982 67 24), next to Hotel Los Arcos. The highrise style hotel has a top-notch cleaning crew, tile floors, and fans. Rooms have A/C and TVs. Singles 150 pesos; doubles 200 pesos. 30 pesos off for not using the A/C.

⌁ FOOD

Restaurant prices escalate as you get closer to the tourist glam of the *Zona Dorada*. The *centro*, however, is just the place for quality meals on a budget. The busy **public market**, between Juárez and Serdán, three blocks north of the *zócalo*, serves the best and cheapest food in the area. If you need a headless pig (or a pig's head), look no further. For something more formal, try one of the *centro's* many inexpensive restaurants or, for the view, an establishment along the *malecón* in Olas Altas. Enjoy your meal with **Pacífico** beer, the pride of Mazatlán.

■ **Restaurante Karica Vegetariano,** Flores 601 (☎981 79 52), at Frías. A fine place for even the non-vegetarian. The enormous *comida corrida* includes salad, soup, a main course, bread, juice, and dessert (40 pesos). A vegetarian bakery sells organic coffees and herbal products. Open daily 8am-4:30pm.

Restaurant la Cocina de Esther, Serdán 1605B (☎982 81 72) at Canizales, tucked back from the street. Esther serves a large selection of entrees and *comida corrida* (24-30 pesos). Open M-Sa 7am-9pm, Su 7am-3pm.

Café Machado, Constitución 515 (☎981 73 31), on the Plazuela Machado. Shady outdoor seating where, depending on the season, you can enjoy 2 for 1 beers (24 pesos). A good selection of *quesadillas* (35-40 pesos), nachos (30-40 pesos), and *antojitos* (10-30 pesos). Open daily 4pm-2am.

Café Pacífico, Constitución 501 (☎981 39 72), across from the Plazuela Machado. This "classic pub" is a relic, with an odd assortment of animal skins, rifles, and stained glass windows. Tuna salad (25 pesos), marlin burritos (50 pesos), or cheese plates (50 pesos). Open daily 9am-2am.

◉ ◗ SIGHTS AND BEACHES

BEACHES. Mazatlán's greatest asset is its 16km of beach, stretching from just north of Olas Altas to well north of the *Zona Dorada.* Just north of Old Mazatlán and along del Mar is **Playa Norte,** a decent stretch of sand if you don't mind small waves and a general lack of activity. As you hone in on the *Zona Dorada,* the beach gets cleaner, the waves larger, and Playa Norte eases into **Playa Las Gaviotas.** Just past Punta Sábalo, in the lee of the islands, is **Playa Sábalo,** whose great waves and golden sand are enjoyed by crowds of *norteamericanos.* "Sábalo-Centro" buses pass all these beaches. As Playa Sábalo recedes to the north, crowds thin rapidly and you can frolic all by yourself. In most places, boogie boards (30 pesos) and sailboats (400 pesos per hr.) are available. Take the "Cerritos-Juárez" bus to the last stop and walk left (if you walk straight ahead you'll end up at a rocky outcropping with restaurants but little sand); you'll soon reach the nearly deserted **Playa Bruja** (Witch Beach), with beautiful sand and 1-2m waves. Camping is permitted, but be cautious after dark, and camp in groups whenever possible.

EL FARO. For a 360° view of Mazatlán, the sea, and the surrounding hills, climb to the top of El Faro, the second-tallest lighthouse in the world. It's located near the ferry to Isla de la Piedra at the end of the "Playa Sur" bus route. The hike (about 30min.) is almost unbearable in the summer; avoid the heat by ascending in the early morning or late evening.

TOWER DIVERS. Mazatlán's tower divers perform acrobatic and dangerous plunges into rocky surf from an 18m high ledge. Dives take place during the day, but be warned that the divers will not perform unless they can pull in a sufficient amount of money beforehand. The best time to watch is 10-11am and 4:30-6:30pm, when guided tour buses arrive and spendthrift tourists fork over their pesos, allowing you—the savvy budget traveler—to see dives for free. The best viewing spots are just south of the towers. The diving platform itself is on Claussen, just south of Zaragoza and north of La Siesta Hotel.

ISLAS VENADOS (DEER ISLAND). For those itching to get away from the beaches, the island is a relatively deserted scrap of land with fine diving; catamaran boats leave from the Agua Sports Center in the El Cid Resort in the *Zona Dorada.* (☎913 33 33, ext. 341. Open daily 10am, noon, and 2pm. 80 pesos round-trip.)

MAZAGUA. Waterpark mania has hit Mazatlán with Mazagua, north of the *Zona Dorada* near Puerta Cerritos. To get there, take a "Cerritos-Juárez" bus (3 pesos). Go bonkers in the wave pool or shoot down slippery slides. (☎988 00 41. Open Mar.-Oct. daily 10am-6pm. 60 pesos, children under 4 free.).

ACUARIO MAZATLÁN. The largest aquarium in Latin America keeps piranhas and other feisty fish (up to 250 breeds in all) in a slew of cloudy tanks. It also hosts performing sea lions and birds. *(Av. de los Deportes 111, off Av. del Mar, 1 block back from the beach; the turn-off is marked with a blue sign.* ☎981 78 15 *or* 981 78 16. *Open daily 9:30am-6:30pm. 40 pesos, children 5-10 20 pesos.)*

TEATRO ANGELA PERALTA. The newly restored and luxurious theater, at Carnaval and Libertad near the Plazuela Machado, hosts an impressive variety of cultural programs. *(Information* ☎982 44 47. *Open daily. 5 pesos.)*

🎵🎬 ENTERTAINMENT AND NIGHTLIFE

Hordes of *norteamericano* high schoolers ditch the prom and hit Mazatlán each year to twist, shout, and drink. More than a dozen discos and bars clamor for *gringo* dollars, with only the occasional Mexican rock tune reminding you that you're not in the US. Most of the hot clubs are in an area known as **Fiesta Land,** in the *Zona Dorada*, a block from Paseo del Mar. Prices vary wildly (especially during high season) and a few hours of open bar can cost up to 200 pesos.

El Caracol (☎913 32 38), in the El Cid Hotel on Camarón Sábado. One of Mazatlán's premier dance clubs, with 4 four levels and insane lights that rise out of the floor. Beer runs 19 pesos, mixed drinks 30 pesos. Cover men 30-125 pesos, women 75 pesos during open bar. Open daily 9pm-4am.

Señor Frog's (☎985 11 10), on Paseo del Mar, several blocks south of Bora-Bora. A chain, but nonetheless a good place to shake that booty. American pop music blasts from a wall of speakers as youngsters wriggle in a wall of flesh. Cover F-Su 45 pesos. During open bar men 150 pesos, women 95 pesos. Open daily 9pm-4am.

Bora-Bora (☎986 49 49), on Paseo del Mar at the southern end of the *Zona Dorada*, next to the beach. Always packed with foreign and local teens clad in neon (or nothing at all). Those so inclined may dance in cages. Clubbers in search of more wholesome activities head to the volleyball court and swimming pool. Order your beer (24 pesos) or mixed drink (30-35 pesos) at the bar, then jump up on top of it (the bar, that is) to bust some serious moves. Cover F-Su 60 pesos. Open daily 9pm-4am.

Joe's Oyster Bar, Louiza 100 (☎983 53 53), next to the Los Sábados Hotel. A good place to put away a few beers before hitting the club scene (2 beers for 20 pesos 5-7pm and 10pm-2am). Oyster usually turns into a dance floor after a while. Cover 25 pesos (includes a beer). Open daily 11am-2am.

Valentino's (☎986 49 49), in the same complex as Bora-Bora. Valentino's attracts a more sophisticated crowd, and dress is slightly more formal. Have a few drinks, then sing some karaoke on the second floor. Beer 24 pesos, mixed drinks 26 pesos. Cover F-Su 40 pesos, open bar 150-240 pesos. Open daily 9pm-4am.

🏖 DAYTIPS FROM MAZATLÁN

ISLA DE LA PIEDRA

Take a green "Independencia" bus (2.6 pesos) from the market at Serdán to the Embarcadero de la Isla de la Piedra. From there, take a boat to the island (5min., every 10min., 7 pesos round-trip; last return 5pm) to the island. Pulmonías (15 pesos) and taxis (10 pesos) take passengers to the beach from the ferry landing. If walking, go straight away from the boat landing and follow the concrete path across the island for about 15min. All the restaurants and stores are in a cluster on the beach.

Just a short boat ride from the mainland, Isla de la Piedra has 10km of glistening sand, crashing waves, and rustling palm trees. Less crowded and shamelessly developed than mainland beaches, the island is an unspoiled haven of sunshine and ocean popular with Mexican families, and, according to some families that live there, "American Hippies." Take a trip on a banana boat (80 pesos), rent snorkeling equipment (120 pesos per hr.), or borrow a body board (30 pesos per hr.).

Aging horses may also be hired (85 pesos per hr.) farther up the beach. If you want to stay longer than a day, **Carmelita's,** a few steps from shore, offers free space for tents, sturdy trees for hammock slinging, and bathrooms and grill. Carmelita also offers clean rooms with electricity, private bathrooms, and kitchenette. (☎987 50 50. Single 200 pesos; doubles 250 pesos.) **Lety's,** adjacent to Carmelita's, offers similar free lodging. It also has spacious rooms with modern bath and desks. (200 pesos for 1-3 people with A/C and TV.) There's nothing nicer than **camping** on a secluded beach, but be careful and don't stray too far from the center.

DURANGO

DURANGO   ☎ 1

State capital and commercial center, Durango (pop. 490,000) is a busy city caught up in the heavy traffic of Mexico's push toward industrialization. The many factories and textile mills lining the way into town contrast with the historic buildings in the town center that contributed to the government's decision to declare Durango a national monument. Hollywood has decided to immortalize the city as well—Durango's outskirts have served as the backdrop for many classic and modern Western films. While it's far from a thriving tourist mecca, the city's collection of colonial architecture and its worthwhile museums offer more than just the John Wayne set a run for its money.

⊏ TRANSPORTATION

Durango's bus station is located on the eastern outskirts of town. To reach the *centro*, catch one of the red buses in front of the station (3 pesos); **taxis** are also available, thankfully with meters to avoid the usual tourist rip-off (about 17 pesos). After dark, a taxi is the only way to travel. Omnibus México goes to **Aguascalientes** (6hr., 9 per day, 214 pesos); **Ciudad Juárez** (18hr., 7 per day, 512 pesos); **Chihuahua** (8hr., 4 per day, 311 pesos); **Mexico City** (11hr., 8 per day, 482 pesos); and **Guadalajara** (10hr., 6 per day, 351 pesos). Chihuahuenses goes to: **Ciudad Juárez** (12hr., 4 per day, 511 pesos); **Chihuahua** (8hr., several per day, 311 pesos); **Parral** (2 per day, 190 pesos); **Torreón** (several per day, 135 pesos); **Zacatecas** (3 per day, 180 pesos); and **Aguascalientes** (3 per day, 214 pesos). Transportes de Durango sends buses to all of the smaller cities within the state of Durango.

⊡⊡ ORIENTATION AND PRACTICAL INFORMATION

The suburbs and outskirts of Durango are full of tractor-trailers and warehouses; to find fun, culture, and amenities, you'll have to head downtown. Most sites of interest lie within a few blocks of the **Plaza de Armas** and the cathedral. **20 de Noviembre** is a major east-west thoroughfare passing in front of the cathedral; **Juárez** runs north-south. Navigating downtown is fairly simple; the streets are in a grid and rarely change names.

Tourist information can be found at the **Dirección de Turismo y Cinematografía,** Florida 100, on the island (or *cuchilla*) at the intersection of 20 de Noviembre and Independencia, through a door around the side of the building, and up the stairs. Staff is very helpful. **Banco Serfín,** Constitución 312 Sur, near the plaza, has great exchange rates, and a 24hr. **ATM.** (☎812 80 33. Open M-F 9am-5pm. Open for exchange 9am-3pm.) **Emergency:** ☎060. **Police:** (☎817 54 06 or 817 55 50) at Felipe Pescador and Independencia. **Hospital General,** on 5 de Febrero and Norman Fuentes. (☎811 91 15. Open 24 hr.) **Fax: Telecomm,** at Felipe Pescada and Zaragoza, about eight blocks from the plaza. (Open M-F 8am-8pm, Sa 9am-4pm.) **Cybercom,** 5 de Febrero 1302. (☎811 37 01. 15 pesos per hr.) **Post office:** at 20 de Noviembre and Roncal, 12 long blocks from the Plaza de Armas. (☎811 41 05. Open M-F 8am-7pm, Sa 9am-1pm.) **Postal code:** 34000.

ACCOMMODATIONS

Inexpensive accommodations can be found near the market, along 5 de Febrero a few blocks west of the Plaza de Armas.

Hotelito La Casa de Huéspedes, Progresso 102 Sur (☎812 31 81), near the market, has clean, basic rooms with TVs and baths. The elderly *dueña* also rents large furnished apartments with kitchens. Singles 60 pesos, with kitchen 100 pesos; doubles 80 pesos, with kitchen 120 pesos.

Hotel Plaza Catedral, Constitución 216 Sur (☎813 26 60), right off 20 de Noviembre and next to the cathedral. The old convent has a dark, mysterious charm. Rooms have phones and cable TV. Singles 170 pesos; doubles 200 pesos; triples 220 pesos.

Hotel Gallo, 5 de Febrero 117 (☎811 52 90), near the market has dirt cheap rooms. Catch a *telenovela* on the lobby TV or admire the many colorful pet birds. Rooms have TVs, with cable for a bit extra. Singles 60 pesos; doubles 80 pesos.

Hotel Reforma, Madero 303 Sur (☎813 16 22, 813 16 23 or 813 16 24; fax 813 19 07), has clean, carpeted rooms. A red refrigerator-looking elevator whisks you up to the rooms, which have baths, color TVs, fans, and interesting wallpaper. Singles 150-230 pesos. 50 pesos each additional person.

FOOD

Inexpensive meals aren't hard to rustle up in Durango. The few blocks of 5 de Febrero before Juárez contain a wide variety of restaurants with everything from cheap fast food to more expensive, family-style dining, to soda fountains.

Café Al Grano, at Negrete and Zaragoza, a few blocks west of the cathedral, somehow manages to cram giant feline masks, a blow-up of a tarot magician, a ceramic clown, a wooden Don Quixote, and countless plants into its small space. Specialties include breakfast plates with fresh squeezed orange juice (20 pesos) along with vegetarian fare such as soy *chorizo* (36 pesos for entire meal). Open M-Sa 8am-8pm.

Café de la Mancha, 20 de Noviembre 807 Pte. (☎811 60 50), at Zaragoza, prepares your meal in front of your eyes. Family members number among the clientele. *Comida corrida* 28 pesos, *gorditas* 5 pesos. Open daily 9am-8pm.

La Terraza, 5 de Febrero 603, across from the Plaza de Armas. A full menu of Mexican and US dishes. Entrees 40 pesos, beer 20 pesos, mixed drinks 26 pesos. Nightly *mariachi* around 11pm. Open M-Th 11am-12:30am, F-Sa 11am-2am, Su 11am-1am.

SIGHTS

The most imposing building in town is the cathedral on the north side of the Plaza de Armas. Construction on the enormous edifice began in 1695, was not completed until the 1770s. The dim interior is filled with marble pillars, carved wood, wrought iron, and gilded pews. Just west of the cathedral, on 20 de Noviembre, stands the white brick **Teatro Ricardo Castro,** which hosts theatrical productions and film screenings and is considered to be one of the highest-quality theaters in northern Mexico. Built around the turn of the century, this elegant, French-styled building is named for the famous Durango musician Ricardo Castro (theater hours vary depending on performance schedule). The huge **Palacio de Gobierno,** on 5 de Febrero between Martínez and Zaragoza, was built by a Spanish mining tycoon, Juan José Zambrano as his residence, and expropriated by the government after Mexico gained independence. Inside, a bronze likeness of Benito Juárez glares amid colorful murals depicting the city's history.

Durango has several excellent museums, including the **Museo de las Culturas Populares,** Juárez 302 at Barreda, which displays ceramics and textiles, and also hosts talks, dances, and other events. (Open Tu-F 9am-6pm, Sa 10am-6pm, Su noon-7pm. 3 pesos.) The **Museo Regional de Durango,** at Serdán and Victoria, known as **El Aguacate** (the Avocado) for its unique shape and texture, houses some paintings by Miguel Cabrera, as well as exhibits on the state's history, indigenous groups, paleontology, and natural resources. (Open Tu-Su 9am-4pm. 1 peso. Su. free.) The **Museo de Arte Contemporanea,** 301 Negrete at Pasteur, hosts well put-together temporary exhibits of local and national artists. (Open Tu-Su 10am-6pm. Free.)

Fans of Western shoot-'em-up-cowboy films should note that over 200 films, including several John Wayne classics, have been filmed in the dusty desert in the outskirts of Durango; some of these **movie sets** have been left standing and are now popular tourist attractions. One of the most impressive sets is at **Chupaderos,** 10km north of Durango. More Westerns have been filmed in the dusty village than anywhere else in Durango. To get there, take a Chihuahuenses bus to Chupaderos (30min., every 25min., 12 pesos), and ask the driver to let you off the route near the sets. With the same bus, you may be able to reach **Villa del Oeste,** a movie set that, in an interesting reversal, was eventually turned into a village. **Los Alamos,** 29km south of Durango, was the set for *Fat Man and Little Boy* (1989), a film about the development of the atomic bomb in Durango, New Mexico. It may be difficult to get to these sets without a car; the tourist office (see above) organizes trips.

♫ ENTERTAINMENT

Come sundown, throw your hands in the air at **La Covacha,** Pino Suárez 500 Pte., at Madero, where locals dance to international and Latin hits. (☎ 812 39 69. Cover 25 pesos. Open Th-Su 9pm-4am.) **Excalibur,** at Mascareñas and Cárdenas, is a mellower hangout, with pool tables and live *mariachi* music on weekends. (Open daily 4pm-late.) **Cinetecha Municipal,** Juárez 217 at Coronado, screens artsy flicks. Several showings daily of classic, foreign, and art films (10 pesos).

On Sundays, head to **Parque Guadiana** to celebrate *Domingo Familiar,* where vendors hawk treats and street performers play to the crowds. For 10 days during the second week of July, Durango commemorates the city's founding with the **Feria Nacional.** Parades, fireworks, auctions, and carnival rides liven things up and reservations are a must. Most of the festivities take place at the **Parque Guardiana,** quite a distance from downtown—you may have to take a taxi (20 pesos).

TORREÓN   ☎ 1

Torreón was founded in 1888, with the completion of international railways running through the area. An important crossroads center for trade and commerce, the settlement flourished. Today, a century after its founding, the modest train stopover has blossomed into a large, modern metropolis, one of the largest cities in northern Mexico. Although the city is relatively untouristed, most visitors traveling across the northern stretch of the country will find themselves near Torreón for a night or two. With wide, clean streets and quality museums, the city merits a closer look.

⌐ TRANSPORTATION

Airport: Torreón's **Aeropuerto Internacional Francisco Sarabia,** is located 2km northeast of downtown. It is serviced by **Aerocalifornia,** Independencia 15 Ote. (☎ 722 18 88), **Aeroméxico,** Independencia 1890 Ote. (☎ 716 36 39, toll-free within Mexico 01 800 021 4000), and **Aeromar** (☎/fax 716 36 39).

Bus Station: The Central de Autobuses de Torreón, Juárez 4700 (☎ 720 31 24), about 4½km east of downtown, is most easily accessible by taxi (22 pesos). Estrella Blanca provides service to: **Ciudad Juárez** (6 per day, 343 pesos); **Guadalajara** (3 per day, 400 pesos); **Matamoros** (4 per day, 325 pesos), **Durango** (9 per day, 135 pesos), **Parral** (1 per day, 157 pesos), **Zacatecas** (every hr., 206 pesos), as well as most other major cities.

✳🛈 ORIENTATION AND PRACTICAL INFORMATION

Torreón, in the state of Coahuila, is defined to the west by the **Río Nazas,** which separates it from Gómez Palacio, next door in the state of Durango. Downtown is situated approximately 2km east of the Río Nazas and 2km southwest of the Francisco Sarabia International Airport. It is bordered by Independencia to the north, Revolución to the south, Muzquiz to the west, and Degollado to the east. It is fairly easy to navigate, as it has the grid formation like most other modern cities. East of downtown is transected by diagonal streets and may require map referencing. The main north-south road is **Colón**, lined with many US fast-food chains.

TOURIST, FINANCIAL, AND LOCAL SERVICES

Tourist Office: Torreón has no tourist office, but the federal government provides tourist info (☎01 800 71 84 220), and has placed several large helpful maps in front of the large Palacio Federal and near the Plaza de Armas.

Currency Exchange: Dolares La Merced (☎716 43 84 and 716 43 91), Matamoros 344 Pte. Open daily 9am-6:30pm. **Dolares** (☎712 98 50), Colón 525 Sur.

American Express: (☎718 36 20), García 95 Sur at Matamoros.

Bank and ATM: Banks with 24hr. ATMs cluster near the Plaza de Armas. The largest bank in town is the **Bancomer,** Juárez and Ortega. With a 24hr. **ATM.** Open M-F 8:30am-4pm

Car Rental: Airways Rent-a-car, Hidalgo 416 Ote. (☎716 15 29, 716 02 79), rents cars from 350 pesos per day. Reservations within Mexico call: ☎01 800 021 0701. There is also an airport location (☎716 09 22). **Hertz** (☎712 66 16, fax 712 67 09) is also located at the airport, and has toll free national (☎01 800 709 5000) and international (☎001 800 654 3030) reservations; **Budget** has locations in the *centro* (☎721 90 91), and airport (☎716 86 02), email budgettr@halcon.laguna.ual.mex); while **Avis** (☎712 16 96) located at the airport may be reached within Mexico toll-free at ☎01 800 2 888 888.

Market: Soriana, located on an entire city block defined by Mina, Hidalgo, Jiménez, and Juárez, is the place to stock up on all your grocery needs. Open daily 8am-10pm.

English Bookstore: Librería Estudiante, Morelos 1030, has a good selection of English reference books. Open M-Sa 9:30am-1:30pm and 3:30-7:30pm.

Laundry: Lavandería Los Angeles (☎713 44 59), Independencia 37 Ote. at Colón. Have a load of laundry washed and dried by the cheery employees (38 pesos).

EMERGENCY AND COMMUNICATIONS

Emergency: ☎060.

Police: Policía Municipal (☎712 13 15), Colón and Revolución.

Red Cross: Cruz Roja (☎713 00 88, 713 01 92), Cuauhtémoc 462.

Pharmacy: Clisson Express (☎716 88 99), Juan Terrazas 632-B at Colón. Open 24hr. **Farmax San José** (☎712 42 44), Allende 300 Pte. Open 24hr.

Hospital: Hospital Los Angeles (☎730 02 02 or 730 03 36), Paseo del Tecnológico 909. Little English spoken. Open 24hr.

Fax: Copias, Juárez 130. Open M-F 9am-8pm, Sa 9am-2pm.

Internet Access: Meganet Internet Café, Juárez and Fuentes. This huge cafe is complete with a snack bar. 18 pesos per hr. Open M-Sa 8am-11pm, Su 10am-10pm.

Post Office: (☎712 02 64), Juárez and Galeana, on the first floor of the Palacio Federal. Open M-F 9am-6pm, Sa 9am-1pm. **MexPost** available next door.

Postal Code: 27000.

■ ACCOMMODATIONS

Budget accommodations can be found scattered throughout the downtown area, but generally cluster along the main east-west streets Morelos and Juárez. More expensive hotels may be found along Paseo La Rosita.

Hotel Princesa, Morelos 1360 (☎712 11 65), has low prices and high popularity. The rooms of this small hotel, equipped with bathrooms and fans, are arranged around an outdoor courtyard. Extremely busy, so reservations are a must. Singles 70 pesos; doubles 100 pesos.

Hotel Galicia (☎716 11 11 or 716 11 19), on Cepeda between Juárez and Morelos, is inexpensive, but you get what you pay for. Rooms have fans, phones, and funky bathrooms. Singles and doubles 125 pesos; triples 140 pesos; quads 155 pesos.

Hotel del Paseo, Morelos 574 (☎716 03 03), has a cafeteria and rooms with phones, TV, and semi-functional A/C. Singles 77 pesos; doubles 212 pesos; 50 pesos each additional person. Checkout 2pm.

🍴 FOOD

The number of good, affordable restaurants in Torreón guarantees that you won't be washing dishes to pay for your meal. Quality meals can be had along Morelos, with more expensive options near the Plaza de Armas and Paseo de la Rosita.

De Granero, Morelos 444 Pte. (☎712 71 44), is the vegetarian restaurant extraordinaire. Veggie burgers (20 pesos), soy *chorizo* burritos (6 pesos), and vegetarian *chichanon gorditas* (4 pesos). The *comida corrida* (25 pesos) and soup of the day (15 pesos) are also vegetarian. Two other locations in town: Estadio and Carranza (☎717 84 41) and Constitución 712 (☎718 76 61). Open daily 8am-9pm.

Restaurant Fu-Hao, Calle Cepede 259 Sur (☎716 55 47). Excellent Cantonese cuisine, as long as you *fu hao* ("pay well" in Chinese). Friendly owner speaks both Spanish and Cantonese. Huge buffet (55 pesos) includes all you can drink soda or one beer. Get your *qian's* (money's) worth by scarfing down as much as possible.

Restaurant La Cope de Leche, Valdes Carrillo 359 Sur (☎716 88 81), gets its name from the 50s-style glasses it uses to serve excellent milkshakes (13.5 pesos). The clean interior is a cozy place to start your day with a large breakfast (35-56 pesos) or a glass of one of the large variety of juices (7.5-13.5 pesos).

👁 SIGHTS

The sights in Torreón revolve around the dozens of parks and museums that dot the downtown area. The centrally located **Plaza de Armas** has many vendors who sell refreshing *paletas* and *aguas frescas* to enjoy under the shade trees of the plaza; in the center of the plaza is a small gift shop. The city's numerous **parks** include the Parque de los Fundadores on Muzquiz and Constitución, the large Alameda Zaragoza, Juárez and Donato Guerra, and the enormous 30-block Bosque Venustiano Carranza, Cuauhtémoc between Juárez and Bravo, which refreshes the heart of the city with its leafy shade. The *bosque* (forest) is also home to the famous **Museo Regional de la Laguna,** Juárez 1300 Ote., covering pre-Hispanic societies from northern and central Mexico (☎713 95 45. Open Tu-Sa 10am-6:30pm. 17 pesos.) The **Museo de la Revolución,** Muzquiz and Constitución (open Tu-Sa 10am-2pm, Su 10am-1pm; free), has displays on Mexican history and Independence. The **Museo del Ferrocarril,** Revolución and Carillo, displays some of the large trains that prompted the growth of Torreón. (☎712 23 12. Open Th-Su 10am-3pm. Free.) Finally, one of the most recognizable sights is the nearby **Cristo de las Noas,** the large statue of Jesus Christ with arms spread over the city. It provides a beautiful view, especially at night. (☎716 22 23 or 712 39 43. 20 pesos.)

🎵🖼 ENTERTAINMENT AND FESTIVALS

Bars and clubs congregate in two locations: downtown, near the Plaza de Armas, and along the Paseo de la Rosita. Across from the plaza, inside the Hotel Palacio Real is **El Greco,** Morelos 1280 Pte., is a "Ladies Bar" that has live music. Check the schedule posted outside for a listing of the live events. (☎716 00 00. Happy hour 7-9pm. Open Tu-Sa 6pm-2am.) For more live music, check out **Jazz Boozz,** Paseo de la Rosita 513A. Gentlemen, don't forget your ties; this is a classy joint. (☎721 22 89. Open daily 9pm-2am.)

Torreón has two main *ferias:* the **Feria del Algodón** (mid-Aug to mid-Sept.) and then Feria Laguna (early to mid-Oct.). The **Gran Reguta del Río Nazas** (early July), is a boat race that involves much fanfare.

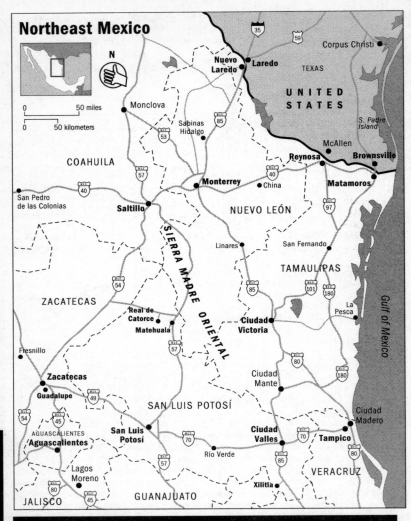

Northeast Mexico

N

0   50 miles

0   50 kilometers

COAHUILA

ZACATECAS

Fresnillo

Zacatecas
Guadalupe

AGUASCALIENTES
Aguascalientes

Lagos
Moreno

JALISCO

San Pedro
de las Colonias

Monclova

Saltillo

Sabinas
Hidalgo

Real de
Catorce
Matehuala

San Luis
Potosí

GUANAJUATO

Nuevo
Laredo

Laredo

TEXAS

UNITED
STATES

Corpus Christi

S. Padre
Island

McAllen

Reynosa

Brownsville

Monterrey

China

Matamoros

NUEVO LEÓN

Linares

San Fernando

TAMAULIPAS

La
Pesca

Ciudad
Victoria

Gulf of Mexico

SAN LUIS POTOSÍ

Ciudad
Mante

Ciudad
Valles

Río Verde

Xilitla

Ciudad
Madero

Tampico

VERACRUZ

SIERRA MADRE ORIENTAL

HIGHLIGHTS OF NORTHEAST MEXICO

MARVEL at the funky architecture and the enormous Gran Plaza of the eclectic, fast-paced **Monterrey** (see p. 267).

RAGE with the best of them in Monterrey's one-of-a-kind **Barrio Antiguo** (see.p. 274) and live it up in the city's thriving **gay scene** (see p. 274).

REWARD yourself with a visit to the lush town of **Xilitla** (see p. 298), which might very well be Eden. Check out **Las Pozas** (see p. 298), a gorgeous expanse of "ruins" built by a kooky Englishman.

GET AWAY from it all at **San Luis Potosí** (see p. 289), dubbed "the city of plazas," one of the most beautiful and tourist-free cities in Mexico.

RELAX in **Real de Catorce** (see p. 296), a tiny ex-mining town high in the Sierra Madres that now specializes in peyote and gorgeous mountain views.

NORTHEAST MEXICO

Dust-swept border towns, former colonial settlements, old mining hotspots, and congested urban centers dot the expansive deserts and occasional rich forests of Northeast Mexico. The lack of tourists—one of the most constant features across the disparate towns and cities of the Northeast—creates a surprising sense of calm among the proud, parched-white missions and wide streets. Eager for the industry and not (yet) inundated with tourists, Northeastern Mexicans welcome the few travelers who do trickle through with boundless hospitality, always open to share the culture of which they are so proud.

This description, though, does not apply to the border towns of **Tamaulipas** and **Nuevo León**. Not for the faint of heart, these towns are replete with money-dropping, booze-guzzling day-trippers, industrious young men and women from all over Mexico and Central America eager for access to a full day's work, and US border police determined to keep them out.

Farther south, however, the *gringo* influence and grubbiness fade. In Monterrey, a metropolis of millions, lovely cathedrals and gorgeous parks peek out of a sea of gray skyscrapers; the city has become chic without catering to tacky tourists and has some of the best nightlife outside of the capital. If it's beach you crave, the *noreste* offers little more than a taste. Fresh, salty Tampico has never been able to draw flocks of tourists: you can swim, tan on the sand, and munch on fresh seafood, but it's far from picturesque.

Perhaps the most wonderful part of the Northeast lies within the state of **San Luis Potosí**. The town of Real de Catorce, a favorite stop for peyote-hungry backpackers, is largely untouched by modernity, with one phone, hundreds of *burros*, and mountain views. Xilitla offers the eco-warrior caves, waterfalls, rivers, wild parrots, semi-tropical rainforests, and ruins an hour or two from congested city centers. The city of San Luis Potosí is a jewel—the capital of the state, it is a playground of regional culture, awesome architecture, and colonial appeal. The state was blessed with a location smack in the middle of Mexico's legendary silver store; as a result, its capital, now a university town, is far more classically colonial, commercial, and cosmopolitan than is customary for the Northeast.

BROWNSVILLE, TEXAS ☎956

The license plates may read "Texas" and the street signs may be in English, but downtown Brownsville (pop. 136,000) may as well be in Mexico. Here, the largely Hispanic population is as likely to greet you in Spanish as in English. Criticized for having little of interest to visitors, Brownsville is working hard, developing rapidly, and offering more to tourists than in recent years. With its mild climate, friendly residents, and laid-back atmosphere, Brownsville serves as a gentle bilingual introduction to life in Mexico.

TRANSPORTATION. Brownsville is too spread-out to explore by foot; the most convenient way to get around is by car. **Local buses** travel long routes throughout Brownsville (6am-7pm; US75¢, seniors US25¢); all buses leave once per hour from **City Hall** on E. Washington between E. 11th and E. 12th (except the "Amigoland" line, which runs every 30min.). Free bus maps and schedules are available at the City Hall station. If staying for more than a day or two, consider getting a 20-ride pass (US$12).

Brownsville and South Padre International Airport, 700 S. Minnesota (☎542-4373), is served by Continental (☎541-2200 or (800) 231-0856), which offers flights to and from **Houston** (8 per day 5:35am-7:30pm, US$100 and up). You can take a **taxis** downtown (US$9-11) or bus #7 (40 min., every 1hr.10min. 6:23am-7:13pm). The **Greyhound** station (☎546-2265), at the corner of 12th and E. Charles, two blocks from the International Bridge, runs buses to: **Dallas** (13hr., 6 per day 5am-10:10pm, US$48); **Houston** (8hr., 10 per day 7am-10:10pm, US$24); **Laredo** (5hr., 11:00am, US$28); and **San Antonio** (7hr., 6 per day 5am-10:10pm, US$35). Many visitors also take the shuttle to **South Padre Island** (30min., 4 per day 7am-5:15pm, US$6).

■🛈 **ORIENTATION AND PRACTICAL INFORMATION.** The area of most interest to visitors is the **Expressway,** which runs through the north part of town. It has the newly-expanded Sunrise Mall (now the largest mall in Texas south of San Antonio) and countless chain restaurants and hotels. The city gets less interesting and more dangerous as one moves southward.

The **Chamber of Commerce,** 1600 E. Elizabeth, has maps and guides that also cover Matamoros. (☎542-4341. Open M-F 8am-5pm.) The **Convention and Visitor's Bureau,** across the street from Sunrise Mall on bus routes #2 and #4, doesn't offer much more information than the Chamber of Commerce, but is more accessible by car. (☎800-626-2639 or 546-3721. Open daily 8:30am-5pm.) You can also check out the **Brownsville City Web Page** (www.brownsville.org) any time. **Casas de cambios** line International; rates are approximately the same or better than at banks. To exchange **traveler's checks** you'll have to use a bank—look for them on Elizabeth and in the lower numbers on the East Side. Exchange rates are similar on either side of the border. **Car rentals** are available at the airport from several national chains including **Hertz** (☎542-7466) and **Budget** (☎546-5119). **Dollar** (☎982-2006) starts at US$32 per day and is the only service renting to those ages 21-25 (US$15 extra). Closer to town, **Mr. B Rent-A-Car** (☎541-6700) starts at US$20 per day. **Police:** 600 E. Jackson (☎548-7000). **Emergency: Brownsville Medical Center,** 1040 W. Jefferson (☎544-1400), at Central. **Post Office:** Elizabeth and E. 10th, is in the brick courthouse building. (Open M-F 7am-7pm.) **ZIP Code:** 78520.

📍 **ACCOMMODATIONS.** The ambiance may be Tex-Mex, but hotel prices in Brownsville are exclusively US. Lodging consists of expensive US chains and a few equally expensive local places. Along the Expressway you can find chains such as **Motel 6** or **Red Roof Inn** (singles start at US$40). Though more expensive, the downtown area is more convenient. For a comfortable and reasonable stay, the **Cameron Motor Hotel,** 912 E. Washington, has rooms with baths, cable TVs, telephones, and A/C. It's a good idea to call ahead. (☎542-3551. Singles US$36; doubles US$42.) If you don't mind the trek, cheaper motels line **Central,** on the Los Ebanos, Jefferson, and Central bus lines. Rooms start at around US$29, but you get what you pay for. The **Hotel Colonial,** 1147 Levee, within sight of the International Bridge on the street parallel to Elizabeth, is a block from the border. Bright rooms come with cable TV, A/C, and enormous beds. A friendly staff awaits you in the quiet, cool lounge. (☎541-9176. Singles US$40; doubles US$46.)

🍽 **FOOD.** Catering primarily to local residents, Brownsville restaurants serve a combination of simple Mexican dishes and hamburgers. Downtown, cafes open and close early, most of them by early evening. For a late snack, **Lucio's Café,** 1041 E. Washington, is a good place to hang out. Meals US$5. (Open Su-Th until 10pm, F-Sa 24hr.) A local institution, **Vermillion Restaurant,** 115 Paredes Line (☎542-9893), in the north part of town, accommodates hungry crowds with tasty Tex-Mex entrees (US$8-15) and what may be the best nachos in town. For the salsa-weary, **Artichoke Deli,** 108 E. Elizabeth, on the #1 bus line, is a 10-minute walk from downtown. Perhaps the closest thing in Brownsville to vegetarian-friendly, the deli has salads and sandwiches (US$5) and the largest selection of beer south of San Antonio (US$3). On the weekends, it turns into one of the most happening places in town with local classic-rock bands drawing in fun-loving crowds. (☎544-7636. Open M-Th 11am-4pm, F 11am-midnight, Sa 11am-1am.)

⊡♫ SIGHTS AND ENTERTAINMENT. Brownsville boasts one of the best zoos for rare and endangered species in the US, as well as several museums honoring the city's role in American history. The **Gladys Porter Zoo,** 500 Ringgold, off E. 6th on the #4 ("Los Ebanos") bus line, is a 31-acre tropical sanctuary where many animals live in open quarters surrounded by only waterways. The collection of over 1500 species includes lowland gorillas, Sumatran orangutans, and white rhinos. (☎546-7187. US$6.50, seniors US$5, children US$3.25. Open daily 9am-7:30pm; tickets sold until 5pm, 6pm during summer weekends.) American history buffs should visit the **Historic Brownsville Museum,** 641 E. Madison, off 6th St., featuring Civil War artifacts and a fully-restored railroad locomotive. (☎548-1313. US$2, children and students US50¢.)

After a hard day of shopping at malls and visiting museums, kick back at the **Artemis Sports Bar and Grille,** 1200 Central, a 5-minute walk from the medical center. The Artemis is hip, clean, and safe, with TVs blaring American sports. Happy hour 11am-7pm. Live music F and Sa. (☎542-2361. Open M-F 11am-2am, Sa-Su noon-2am.)

▨ FESTIVALS. Once a year, Brownsville and Matamoros host **Charro Days,** a twin-city festival of food, dance, and live music, celebrating the relationship between the two towns (last weekend of February). The weekend culminates in an international parade from Brownsville to Matamoros. Nature-lovers flock to Brownsville, located at the southern tip of the Texas Coastal Birding Trail, for its many bird-watching opportunities and bird diversity. The first **Texas Audubon International Bird Festival** took place in July 2000, featuring guided birding tours and ecology workshops. Organizers hope this will become an annual event. (☎US 800-626-2639 for more info.)

TAMAULIPAS

MATAMOROS
☎8.

Though bigger and brasher than its sister city to the north, parts of Matamoros still retain a measure of small-town Mexican appeal. Nevertheless, Matamoros is, for the most part, hectic and alive, with enough stores for even the most exuberant shopper and enough booze and brawls to urge travelers to exercise caution after dark. And, like any self-respecting border town, the streets of Matamoros are packed with young people, most of them American, drinking away to their hearts' content.

CROSSING THE BORDER. To reach Matamoros from Brownsville, walk or drive across the **International Bridge.** Pedestrians pay a budget-busting US35¢ (or 2 pesos) to cross from either side. Cars pay US$1.25. At this point, the **Rio Grande** might not look so big—since much of its water has been diverted for irrigation, it's only a 2min. walk over the bridge. If you're traveling further south than the border zone, pick up your tourist card (US$18) and vehicle permit (US$12). See p. 10 for more information on border crossings.

▣ TRANSPORTATION. From the border crossing, the city extends out in a V-shape following the bend in the Rio Grande. To reach the center of town from the border area, take one of the yellow minibuses labeled "Centro" on the hood (4 pesos). "Central" minibuses go to the bus station, the Central de Autobuses. Take care not to confuse the two. Returning to the border, catch a minibus marked "Puente." These converted school buses (called *peseros*) make continuous stops; just wave your hand at them and they'll stop almost anywhere (local transport info ☎917 88 80). Don't be shy about asking where your stop is—the bus name (e.g. "Centro") might not be indicative of the final stop.

Bus traffic to out-of-town destinations flows through the **Central de Autobuses,** on Canales at Aguilar, off Calle 1. (Open M-Sa.) ADO (☎912 01 81) goes to: **Tampico** (7hr., 5 per day 2:50-11:30pm, 230 pesos); **Tuxpan** (11hr., 4 per day 2:50-11:30pm,

330 pesos); and **Veracruz** (16 hrs., 3 per day 4-10pm, 475 pesos), with numerous stops in between. Noreste (☎913 27 68) services: **Monterrey** (6hr., 18 per day 1:20-11pm, 178 pesos) and **Reynosa** (2hr., 18 per day 6am-10pm, 46 pesos). Transportes del Norte (☎916 65 80) runs to: **Mexico City** (14hr.; *ejecutivo* at 7pm, 633 pesos; 1st-class buses 6 per day, 548 pesos); **Saltillo** (7hr., 6 per day, 211 pesos); and **San Luis Potosí** (10hr., 11 per day, 343 pesos). Omnibus de México (☎913 76 93), sends 18 buses per day to **Reynosa** (49 pesos), **Saltillo** (211 pesos), and **Monterrey** (177 pesos). Travelers to **Reynosa** or **Valle Hermosa** may find it more convenient to depart from the **Noreste station** downtown (☎913 40 50), at the corner of Calle 12 and Abasolo, where it's possible to catch buses coming from the Central de Autobuses en route to their destinations.

🛈 PRACTICAL INFORMATION. The **tourist office** (☎912 36 30), past the turnstile marking entry into Mexico on the right, offers pamphlets about Mexico and lots of friendly advice (in Spanish). Matamoros maps are also available at the Brownsville Chamber of Commerce. **Casas de cambio** dot the *centro*, particularly along Calles 5 and 6. The best exchange rates are in the bus station or at banks such as **Bancrecer** (☎912 34 22), Calle 7 between González and Abasolo, or **Bancomer**, Matamoros and Calle 6, which also exchanges **traveler's checks**. (☎916 30 67. Open M-F 8:30am-4pm, Sa 10am-2pm.) **ATMs** are available at most major banks. **Luggage storage:** at the bus station. 2 pesos per hr., 1 peso each additional hr. **Market:** La Estrella, Abasolo between Calle 10 and Calle 11. **Emergency:** ☎060. **Police:** (☎916 20 21 or 917 22 05) always stationed around International Bridge and the border. **Red Cross:** (☎912 00 44). **Pharmacy: Super Farmacia El Fenix,** Abasolo between Calle 8 and Calle 9. (☎912 29 09. Open daily 8am-10pm.) **Hospital Guadalupe** 72 Calle 6 (☎912 16 55). **Internet Access: Libros y Revistas Proceso** (☎916 23 10) at the corner of Calle 6 and González. You can browse the Internet or the store's wide selection of sexually explicit comic books and magazines. 20 pesos per hr. **Post office:** in the bus station. (Open M-Sa 9am-3:30pm.) **Postal code:** 87370.

🛈 ACCOMMODATIONS. Although prices in Matamoros are reasonable, expect little more than the basics. The market area, where most of the budget accommodations are located, quickly becomes deserted after nightfall—be careful. **Hotel Majestic,** on the pedestrian mall on Abasalo between Calles 8 and 9, offers simple, clean, bright rooms with private bath and fan. (☎913 36 80. Singles 100 pesos, with TV 120 pesos; doubles 150 pesos; each additional person 20 pesos.) **Hotel México,** just a few doors down on the same block, offers rooms of similar quality and price. No TVs. (☎912 08 56. Singles 120 pesos; doubles 160 pesos; each additional person 40 pesos.) Those willing to spend a little more may prefer the relative luxury of **Hotel Roma,** Calle 9 between Bravo and Matamoros. Even singles come with two beds, full cable, private bath, carpeting, and A/C. (☎913 61 76. Singles 355 pesos; doubles 399 pesos.)

🛈 FOOD. The food in Matamoros is often overpriced and border-town bland. There are some good small cafes and taquerías on the streets surrounding the pedestrian mall—just be sure it's clean before chowing down. **Restaurant Frontera,** on Calle 6 between N. Bravo and Matamoros, is filled with locals enjoying the A/C and the optical illusion floor while digging into Mexican specialties for 16-32 pesos. (☎916 71 87. Open daily 7am-10pm.) Slip into an upstairs booth at **Cafetería Deli,** 1307 Calle 7, between Abasolo and Matamoros, to escape the bright sun and to enjoy a range of *antojitos* for 15-25 pesos. (☎913 93 87. Open daily 6am-9pm.) **Las Dos Repúblicas** (☎916 68 94) on Calle 9 between Abasolo and Matamoros, the restaurant where the margarita originated (see **The Original Margaritaville,** p. 259), soothes tourists with its beautiful interior and relaxed atmosphere. Enjoy your drinks (beers US$1.50, mixed drinks US$3) and *antojitos* (US$4) from a cushioned chair, next to a fountain and three-story fresco. The gift shop offers crafts and pottery.

THE ORIGINAL MARGARITAVILLE. When in Mata-
moros, margarita connoisseurs may want to visit **Las Dos Repúblicas,** the cocktail lounge and restaurant that claims to be the birthplace of the famous drink.
According to legend, a lovely young lady from Brownsville, Marguerite Henri,
was a restaurant regular in the 1930s. One day in 1935, the bartender mixed
her that first magical drink and she immediately fell in love. Unfortunately for
the him, it was the drink she was enamored of and, in her honor, the smitten
bartender named the drink the "Marguerita." Whether fact or fiction, the legend makes a good excuse to stop in and order a couple of 18oz. margaritas
from the place where it all began.

■⚑ **SHOPPING AND ENTERTAINMENT. Matamoros** and **Abasolo,** pedestrian
streets between **Calles 6** and **11,** are lined with shops and vendors; Calle 6 has
modern clothing, while crafts abound on Calle 9. Abasolo is known for its
shoes, and every other shop seems to be a *zapatería* (shoe store). Aspiring
cowboys can also find low prices on hats, belt buckles, and leather boots. For
a good mix of tourist kitsch and quality crafts, the old market, **Pasaje Juárez,**
has entrances on both Matamoros and Bravo between Calles 8 and 9. Bright
piñatas and rows of glittering jewelry illuminate the dim interior of **Mercado
Juárez,** the new market on Abasolo between Calles 9 and 10. The aggressive
vendors can get tiresome, but they are more than willing to bargain. Outdoor
markets farther south offer higher quality and lower prices.

For a cultured evening, stop by the **Teatro de la Reforma** (☎912 51 21), on Calle 6
between González and Abasolo. Renovated in 1992, the colonial brick building is
home to everything from classical drama to folkloric Mexican dance. Tickets vary
by event (150 pesos and up, students and seniors half-price). If you're in the mood
to bar-hop, boogie, and booze, think twice. Most reasonably priced **bars** and **discos**
near the border are very unsafe at night. If you insist, **Garcia's** (☎912 39 29),
straight ahead after you cross the International Bridge, on the left side of Obregón,
has everything a border-hopping tourist could want, day or night. Feast on filet
mignon in the classy restaurant (lunch specials US$8, dinner US$11), relax with a
Mexican beer in the bar (beers US$2, mixed drinks US$3-4), or search for bargains
in the gift shop and pharmacy. Live music ranges from *mariachi* to rock.

REYNOSA   ☎8

In Reynosa (pop. 600,000), horse-drawn carts share the streets with 16-wheelers
and pushcarts sell fruit cups outside US 7-11 mini-marts. Just across the border
from McAllen, Texas, Reynosa still manages to exude the atmosphere of a small
border town, despite its increasing size and industrialization. There isn't a lot to do
in this oil town, but with its well-planned center, clean wide streets, shady plaza,
and plenty of shops, Reynosa is a gem by border town standards.

▐ **TRANSPORTATION.** The **bus station** is on Colón in the southwest corner of
town. To reach the *centro,* from the bus station take any "Centro" city bus or turn
left on Colón, walk five blocks, and take a right onto Juárez; the plaza is six blocks
down. ADO (☎922 87 13) goes to: **Tampico** (7hr., 6 per day 4:30-11pm, 233 pesos);
Veracruz (16hr., 6:50 and 8:30pm, 478 pesos); and **Villahermosa** (24hr., 6:50 and
11pm, 653 pesos). Futurama (☎922 14 52) offers *ejecutivo* service to: **Monterrey**
(3hr., 7 and 8pm, 170 pesos); **Mexico City** (15hr., 5:20pm, 730 pesos); and **Guadalajara** (15hr., 7 and 8pm, 693 pesos). Omnibus de México (☎922 33 07) runs to: **Chihuahua** (15hr., 9am and 10:30pm, 460 pesos); **Monterrey** (3hr., 6 per day 4am-7pm,
125 pesos); and **Saltillo** (5hr., 6 per day 4am-7pm, 135 pesos). Noreste (☎922 02 06)
offers the most extensive service including: **Matamoros** (2hr., every 45min., 53
pesos); **Nuevo Laredo** (4hr., every 2hr. 5:15am-9:40pm, 131 pesos); and **San Luis
Potosí** (11½hr., 8 per day 7am-10:45pm, 343 pesos).

⊞⌨ ORIENTATION AND PRACTICAL INFORMATION. Reynosa is 90km from Brownsville and 150km from Monterrey. It can be reached from McAllen by taking 23rd St. 12km south into Hidalgo and then crossing the **International Bridge.** Routes 2 and 40, from Matamoros and Monterrey respectively, lead straight into town. Reynosa is square, with the international bridge border crossing at the northeast corner. The central plaza, **Plaza de Armas,** is bounded by Zaragoza on the north, Hidalgo on the west, Morelos on the south, and Juárez on the east. Minibuses *(peseros)* run in nearly all directions (4 pesos). **Taxis** might overcharge, so bargain before getting in.

Though there is no tourist office, the **Cámara de Comercio,** on the corner of Chapa and Allende, one block north of Zaragoza and one block east of Juárez, has free maps with listings of restaurants, bars, and hotels. (Open M-F 9am-5pm.) **Casas de cambio** are scattered all along Hidalgo and the plaza, but none accept traveler's checks. **Banorte,** on Morelos at Hidalgo (☎ 922 46 90; open M-F 9am-3pm) and **Bancomer,** opposite Banorte on Zaragoza (☎ 922 81 01; open M-F 8:30am-4pm, Sa 10am-2pm), have competitive rates, accept traveler's checks, and offer 24hr **ATMs. Police:** (☎ 922 00 88 or 922 07 90), southwest across Canal Anzaldvas. **Emergency:** ☎ 060. **Red Cross** (☎ 922 13 14). **FAX: Telecomm,** in the building connected to the post office. (☎ 922 01 65. Open M-F 8am-7:30pm, Sa-Su 9am-12:30pm) **Internet: TYM.Com Cyber-café,** corner of Hidalgo and Allende, one block north of the plaza. (☎ 922 43 63. 20 pesos per hr.) **Post office:** on the corner of Díaz and Colón. (☎ 922 01 10. Open M-F 8am-4pm, Sa 9am-1pm.) **Postal code:** 88500.

⌐ ACCOMMODATIONS. Hotels near the plaza are pricey with the cheapest located around south **Díaz** and **Hidalgo.** Though boisterous and congested during the day, this area becomes desolate and a little scary at night. *Cuídate.* (Be careful.) **Hotel Avenida,** Zaragoza 885 Ote., sets its sparkling clean, carpeted rooms around a beautiful leafy patio, complete with chirping birds. With its proximity to the main plaza, A/C-TV combo, and the occasional piece of antique furniture, you can't lose. (☎ 922 05 92. Singles 220 pesos; doubles 270 pesos). A bit farther off the main plaza, **Hotel Rey,** on Díaz between Mendez and Madero, has six floors of cable TV and A/C glory fit for a budget king. (☎ 922 26 32. Singles 240 pesos; doubles 280 pesos.) For lodging close to the town's shopping area, try the **Hotel Riviera,** 615 Mendez. Walking south from the plaza, take a left off the Hidalgo market area. Large, sunny suites come with cable TV and A/C. (☎ 922 13 79. Singles 285 pesos; 40 pesos each additional person.)

⌂⌡ FOOD. Locals know that the outdoor stands and open-air cafeterias near the bus station and the plaza are the places to enjoy delicious, super-cheap fare. If you want to sit down and escape the heat, try the clean, simple **Café Sánchez,** on Morelos off Hidalgo at the southwest corner of the plaza. It pulls in a diverse crowd with fajitas and *enchiladas poblanas.* Very tasty entrees 26-60. (☎ 922 16 65. Open daily 7am-8pm.) **Café Paris,** Hidalgo 815, just past Morelos on the pedestrian mall, is not only beautiful, but it has excellent prices and what may be the best pastries and cakes in town. Breakfast 17 pesos, entrees 20-55 pesos. (☎ 922 55 35. Open daily 7am-10pm.) For affordable dining in an elegant setting, try **Café La Villa,** on the plaza at the corner of Hidalgo and Zaragoza. Sit in the fancy *salon comedor* while you sample a variety of *antojitos* and desserts (30 pesos and up). Breakfast specials 30-40 pesos.

⌧⌦ SIGHTS AND ENTERTAINMENT. In the evening, locals of all ages crowd the main plaza to enjoy street performers and relax after the day's heat. The **Hidalgo Marketplace,** open to pedestrians from the plaza to Colón, is a good spot for people-watching. For an abridged history lesson, check out the beautiful storefront **mural** on the corner of Zaragoza, one block east of Canales, a few blocks south of the border crossing. It was paid for by Bacardi, the rum company, and their billboard forms the last scene of the mural.

Clustered along Ocampo near the border, most nightspots in Reynosa have on-and off-seasons. For a month during US spring break (Mar.-Apr.), the town turns into a miniature Cancún—all the booze, but (alas!) none of the beaches. The off-season (most of the time) is more mellow. Deserted a good chunk of the week, it is only on weekend nights and Wednesday nights that this "Zona Rosa" comes to life with *mariachis* and enthusiastic Texans. Young people head to the **Alaskan Bar and Disco,** on Ocampo between Allende and Zaragosa, a dark, cold discotheque with two levels and an enormous dance floor. Beer US$1, mixed drinks US$1.50. (Open bar F. US$10 cover. W and Sa no cover.)The brand-new **Neptune's Shell Disco** is another option for party-goers, featuring an under-the-sea decor and a young crowd from both sides of the border. It really *is* better down where it's wetter. (F-Sa open bar. Cover US$10 men, US$8 women. Open W, F, and Sa until 2am.) Underage visitors to Reynosa beware—clubs have recently started to enforce the Mexican drinking age of 18, much to the dismay of many high-school visitors. Be sure to bring your ID.

Check out Reynosa's community theater at a free production at **La Casa de la Cultura,** next door to the Cámara de Comercio on Chapa and Allende. The Casa regularly hosts plays, painting exhibits, concerts, and dances; drop in to see the schedule of upcoming events. (☎922 99 89. Open M-F 9am-2pm and 3-7pm.)

LAREDO, TEXAS   ☎956

Founded in 1755 as the only Spanish settlement north of the Rio Grande, Laredo (pop. 190,000) has been ruled by seven different countries in its 250 year long existence. In 1886, the Old West city was the site of the biggest gunfight in US history. Lest this scare you away, Laredo has mellowed considerably, and is now one of the fastest growing cities in the US. The strip malls and interminable suburban sprawl of Laredo are offset by its beautiful central square and surrounding historic districts.

⌐ TRANSPORTATION. El Metro city buses (☎795-2250) run semi-regularly throughout the city (approx. every 30min. 6am-9pm; US75¢, children US25¢, seniors US10¢). Get schedules and catch the buses at the sleek **Laredo Intermodal Transit Center,** on the south side of Jarvis Plaza.

The **airport** (☎795-2000) is on Maher, northeast of town. American Eagle (☎(800)433-7300) serves **Dallas** (2hr., 6 per day). Continental Express (☎(800)523-3273 and 723-3402) covers **Houston** (1½hr., 10 per day). Taesa (☎800-328-2372 and 956-725-1022) goes to **Mexico City** (2hr., M-Tu and Th-F).

The **bus station** (☎723-4325), on San Bernardo and Matamoros, runs Greyhound-affiliated buses to cities throughout the US and sends daily buses to: **Monterrey** (3hr., 4am and 5pm, US$29); **San Luis Potosí** (11hr., 5pm, US$55); and **Querétaro** (13hr., 4am and 5pm, US$79). Note that departures from Nuevo Laredo are cheaper and more frequent.

⊞🔁 ORIENTATION AND PRACTICAL INFORMATION. Laredo's downtown centers around **International Bridge #1,** which runs north and is called **Convent St.** on the US side. Seven blocks north of the border and one block west of Convent is **Jarvis Plaza,** with most newer hotels and nightspots several miles to the north and east. The more modern strip is **San Bernardo,** which originates near the border three blocks east of Convent and stretches north

The **tourist office,** 501 San Agustin, provides colorful, informative, and easy-to-read maps and brochures. (☎(800)361-3360 or 795-2200. Open M-Sa 8:30am-5pm.). Currency can be exchanged at **casas de cambio** found all along Convent and sprinkled throughout downtown. **Laredo National Bank,** 700 San Bernardo, at the corner of Farragut, has both a bubbling fountain and a 24hr. **ATM.** (☎723-1151. Open M-F 9am-4pm, Sa 9am-3pm.) A good **supermarket** is **HEB,** 1002 Farragut, two blocks east of Jarvis Plaza. (☎791-3571. Open daily 7am-10pm.) **Sunshine Laundromat,** 2900 San Bernardo, north of the Chamber of Commerce, with do-it-yourself service (US$1) or same-day full service (US$5-7) available. (☎722-8403. Open daily 8am-10pm.) **Police:** On Farragut next to HEB market. (☎795-2800. Open daily 10am-5pm.) **J&A Pharmacy,** 201 West Del Mar, lies in the northeast of

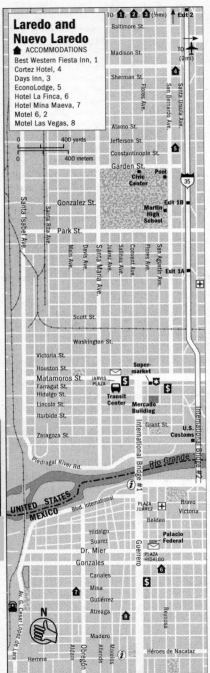

Laredo and Nuevo Laredo

▲ ACCOMMODATIONS

Best Western Fiesta Inn, 1
Cortez Hotel, 4
Days Inn, 3
EconoLodge, 5
Hotel La Finca, 6
Hotel Mina Maeva, 7
Motel 6, 2
Motel Las Vegas, 8

town. (☎717-3839. Open M-F 9am-8pm, Sa 9am-4pm.) **Hospital: Mercy Regional Medical Center,** 1515 Logan (☎718-6222). **Fax: Western Union,** 711 Salinas (☎/fax 722-0850), also on Jarvis. Look for more Western Unions in the bus station and in every HEB supermarket. **Internet Access:** available at the **Laredo Times,** 111 Esperanza (☎729-2500 or 728-2504), off San Dario, accessible by the San Bernardo bus. **Post Office:** at 1300 Matamoros, on Jarvis Plaza. (☎723-3643. Open M-F 8:30am-5pm, Sa 9am-noon.) **Postal code:** 78040.

⌂ ACCOMMODATIONS. Nice hotels in Nuevo Laredo are cheaper than even the most inexpensive Laredo lodgings. Nevertheless, those who value amenities (potable water, carpets, modern furniture) will find an ample selection along the northern stretch of San Bernardo. Expect good deals (by US standards) and cookie-cutter rooms from big names like **Days Inn,** 4820 San Bernardo (☎722-6321); **Best Western Fiesta Inn,** 5240 San Bernardo (☎723-3603); or **Motel 6,** 5310 San Bernardo (☎725-8187). Most of these lodgings are accessible by the #2 El Metro city bus and start at about US$50. Closer to the center, try the **Cortez (Courtesy) Motel,** 3113 San Bernardo, with the entrance a block over on Santa Ursula. With jungle-print bedsheets, dark wood paneling, hanging lamps, and wrought-iron mini-patios, these are perhaps the kitschiest rooms around. (☎727-1001. Singles US$34; doubles US$40.) Another good bargain is **EconoLodge,** 2620 Santa Ursula, at the corner of San Bernardo one block past the Civic Center. The friendly staff and lower prices distinguish this chain hotel from its counterparts farther north. (☎722-6321. Singles US$40; doubles US$50.)

◻ FOOD. Laredo's culinary selection relies heavily on—you guessed it—Tex-Mex cuisine. For the budget-conscious, fast-food joints and *taquerías* line **San Bernardo.** Good food awaits you at **Tacolare,** 1206 San Bernardo, just north of the railroad tracks. The small storefront disguises the large

¡ÁNDALE! *¡Ándale, ándale!* (loosely translated: "Hurry up! Hurry up!") Cartoon fans the world over will recognize this catchphrase, often uttered by Speedy González, the fleet-footed, sombrero-toting Mexican mouse of Warner Brothers fame. Though the stereotype will make Mexicans cringe, Speedy's catchphrase is essential vocabulary for any visitor to Mexico. The word can have a number of meanings, depending on context. There's the standard *¡ándale!* ("hurry the hell up!"), the *¡ándale!* shouted by impatient drivers leaning on their horns ("move it, buddy!"), the more amiable *¡ándale!* exchanged between friends ("I agree"), and the even more congenial *¡ándale!* ("hey, no problem!"). And there's always the "hey, let's go" *ándale.* (*Ándale Mexico: 2001,* perhaps?) The uses are varied and subtle; to command them all is key to speaking true Mexican Spanish.

and inviting restaurant, a local favorite. Most selections are under US$5. (☎727-5115. Open M-Sa 11am-10pm.) **Danny's Restaurant,** 802 Juárez, on Jarvis Plaza near the courthouse, features lunch specials that include Mexican *bistek* (steak) and mushroom burgers (US$4-6). Danny and his staff encourage you to eat three balanced meals a day—to help you, they serve heaping breakfast specials (US$3.50) from 6-11am. (☎724-3185. Open daily 6am-11pm.)

⚅⚆ ENTERTAINMENT AND NIGHTLIFE. The **Civic Center,** entrance on Garden off of San Bernardo, presents the four annual concerts of the **Laredo Philarmonic Orchestra** (☎727-8886). For a dose of the occult, get a consultation, a palm-reading, or a cure at **Yerbería de San Judas,** 711 Salinas (☎725-8336), a witchcraft store selling herbs and religious charms.

Nightlife in Laredo is complicated by the large distances between establishments and the relative scarcity of taxis. Police are cautious and alert, especially at night, frequently arresting people for public drunkenness and drunk driving. That said, the northeastern part of town is home to a good many nightclubs and bars. Saddle up or mosey on down to the new **Round-Up Cowboy Disco Club,** 5924 San Bernardo, for a night of Texas-style fun in an Old West setting. DJs inside spin country-western hits, while outside, patrons try their luck on a rambunctious mechanical bull. (☎726-4347. Open Tu-Sa.)

Laredo is the only US city to properly celebrate **George Washington's birthday** every February. Cut yourself a slice of apple pie and watch the Laredo town princess (dressed as American-icon Pocahontas) lead the parade. Afterwards, you can waltz with Uncle Sam at the Martha Washington Ball.

NUEVO LAREDO
☎8

Nuevo Laredo (pop. 420,000) pulses with commerce. From its small souvenir shops to the enormous trailers passing through with NAFTA-spurred trade, pesos and dollars pour in and out of Nuevo Laredo at such a dizzying pace that many residents are left without any for themselves. The city's cheap liquor, abundant crafts, and many plazas attract lots of afternoon tourists, making Nuevo Laredo a good place to hit for a day or evening, though probably not for an extended vacation.

⌂ TRANSPORTATION. From the **International Bridge #1,** the main pedestrian crossing, **Guerrero** emerges as the main thoroughfare running south. Three plazas along Guerrero, **Plaza Juárez, Plaza Hidalgo,** and **Palacio Federal,** define the downtown. The bus station lies to the far south of town. To get from there to the border, take any blue-and-white or green-and-white bus marked "Puente." To get to the bus station from the border, take the bus marked "Central."

The **airport** (☎714 07 05), is in the extreme southwest of the city, off Rte. 2. Purchase tickets at **Viajes Furesa,** Guerrero 830, to Mexico City or to US destinations leaving via the Laredo airport. (☎712 96 68. Office open M-F 9am-7pm.)

The **bus station,** Refugio Romo 3800, is southwest of the city and quite a trek from the *centro*. Omnibus de México (☎714 06 17) goes to: **Aguascalientes** (8hr., 3 per day, 295 pesos); **León** (12hr., 3 per day, 390 pesos); **Saltillo** (3½hr., 150 pesos); and **Zacatecas** (8hr., 2 per day, 280 pesos). Noreste (☎714 21 00) travels to: **Matamoros** (6hr., 8 per day 7am-midnight, 120 pesos) and **Reynosa** (4hr., 10 per day, 90 pesos). Turistar, Futura, and Transportes del Norte share an information line (☎714 06 70) and a counter, but they maintain separate routes and services. Transportes del Norte runs a bus to **Monterrey** (3hr., every 30min., 120 pesos).

◪ PRACTICAL INFORMATION. The **tourist office,** at the corner of Juárez and Maclovio Herrera, 8 blocks south of Hidalgo Plaza, provides many brochures in both Spanish and English. (☎712 73 97. Open M-F 8am-8pm.) Major banks line Guerrero near Plaza Hidalgo. **Banorte** (open M-F 9am-4pm) and **Serfín** (open M-F 9am-3pm), on the corner of Canales and Guerrero, each have 24hr. **ATMs. Luggage storage** is available at the bus station. 3 pesos per hr. (Open 24hr.) **Supermarket Gigante,** Reforma 4243, is located on the southern extension of Guerrero, *very* far from downtown—take a bus toward the *centro* and get off when you see the enormous pink complex. **Emergency:** ☎7060. **Police:** ☎712 21 46. **Pharmacy: Farmacia Calderón,** on Guerrero west of Plaza Hidalgo. (☎712 55 63. Open 24hr.) **Medical Services: ISSTE** (☎712 34 91), on Victoria and Reynosa to the east of Plaza Juárez, has a limited English-speaking staff. **Post office:** in the back of the Palacio Federal, on the northeast corner of Dr. Mier and Camargo, has **fax** and **telegram** service. (☎712 21 00. Open M-F 8am-6pm, Sa 9am-noon.) **Mexpost** is located on the opposite side of the *palacio*. (☎713 47 17. Open M-F 9am-6pm, Sa 9am-1pm.)

⌂ ACCOMMODATIONS. Hotels of all prices are found within a few blocks of the main plazas. There are good bargains if you're willing to look around. With just six rooms, **Hotel Mina Maeva,** Mina 3521, six blocks west of Guerrero, has better-than-US lodgings at less-than-US prices. Individually decorated rooms have carpet, TV, A/C, telephone, and lush flora. The staff provides superb service and conversation. (☎713 14 73. Singles 336 pesos; doubles 380 pesos. Special rates for students and long-term guests.) **Hotel La Finca,** Reynosa 811, just off González by the southeast corner of Plaza Hidalgo is on a quiet street just a few steps from the *centro*. Spacious, clean rooms rise above a red-tile patio—a good value with A/C, cable TV, and phone. (☎713 14 73. Singles 180 pesos; doubles 230 pesos; each additional person 20 pesos.) **Motel Las Vegas,** Arteaga 3017, 1½ blocks west of Guerrero and four blocks south of Plaza Hidalgo, has cellar-like lodgings featuring A/C, TV, and tidy bathrooms. The smell of extra cash in your pocket may mask the slightly dank odor of some of the rooms. (☎712 20 30. Singles 90 pesos; doubles 124 pesos.)

⊡ FOOD. Pricey tourist border joints aside, most eateries are similar in quality and price, with plenty of tacos, *enchiladas*, and *carne asada* (grilled meat). Fajitas and **cabrito** (roasted goat that tastes similar to lamb) are often sold by the kilogram. Most of the good stuff is right on Guerrero, not far from the plazas. At **Restaurant Principal,** on Guerrero just north of Hidalgo Plaza, you can order chicken or *cabrito* (110 pesos), then watch through glass windows as they roast and cut it. Ambitious meat-loving groups can even devour the whole animal (700 pesos), while standard entrees (40-60 pesos) are available for the less carnivorous. (☎712 13 01. Open daily 9am-1am.) The tiny **Cafetería los Pinos,** on the east side of Plaza Juárez, is a hidden treat for travelers looking for bargain dining close to the border. This family-run place has no menus, but will gladly cook tacos, *carne asadas*, and other traditional Mexican foods at the best prices around. (Entrees 30 pesos and up. Open daily 8am-10pm.)

◉♫ SIGHTS AND ENTERTAINMENT. The largest (and most expensive) *mercados* are concentrated around **Guerrero** near the border. Though they offer an ample selection of sturdy wooden furniture, pottery, and *sombreros*, better prices (and higher-quality goods) can be found farther south. Those in search of cultural titillation can head to the **Teatro de la Ciudad** on Guatemala near Aguirre in the southeast corner of town, accessible via the "Viveros" buses.

Strolling up and down Guerrero can be relaxing in the evening, when the three plazas fill with people gaily chatting and passing time; the fountain on Nacatez and Guerrero is a favorite resting spot. If ambling about is not your style, head to **Señor Frog's**, just blocks south of the border on Belden at the corner of Ocampo. Though beers and tequila shooters are steeply priced (US$2 or 20 pesos), Frog's patrons love the expert bartending and wonderfully campy cartoons papering every inch of this chain restaurant/bar. (No cover. ☎713 30 11.)

TAMPICO ☎1

It's no accident that the northeastern coast of Mexico is not known for its beaches. The waters are filled with oil tankers, not swimmers, and the shores are more suitable for refineries than sunbathers. Though it's somewhat dirty, crowded, and incredibly hot, Tampico (pop. 565,000) is the region's best seaside getaway, a refreshing break for land-locked travelers. The pleasant beach is often uncrowded on weekdays, and Tampico's two main plazas are full of intriguing architecture and much-needed greenery. Founded in the 16th century on the ruins of an Aztec village, the original Tampico was destroyed by booty-hungry pirates in 1623. Two hundred years later, Santa Anna ordered the city re-settled, and it soon grew into one of the most important oil ports in the world. Despite the ominous tankers and loads of litter, Tampico today is trying to carve out a new identity. *Tampiqueños* built the first beach resort in all of Tamaulipas, and their seafood is ridiculously fresh. Tampico may not be terrific yet, but at least it's trying.

■ TRANSPORTATION. The **bus station** is on Zapotal, north of the city. To get to the *centro*, take a taxi (35 pesos), minibus (3.5 pesos), or *colectivo* (5 pesos, with luggage 7 pesos). To return to the bus station, hop in any *colectivo* marked "Perimetral" (3.5 pesos). Omnibus de México (☎2713 43 49) goes to: **Ciudad Valles** (2½hr., 3 per day 7:45am-7:30pm, 83 pesos); **Monterrey** (7hr., 3 per day 7:45am-11:30pm, 269 pesos); **Saltillo** (8½hr., 9 and 11pm, 289 pesos); and **Tuxpan** (3½hr., 5 per day 6am-3:30pm, 100 pesos). ADO (☎213 55 12) goes to: **Matamoros** (7hr., 7 per day, 202 pesos); **Puebla** (10hr., 4 per day, 220 pesos); and **Xalapa** (9hr., 2 per day, 216 pesos). Futura and Frontera (☎213 42 55) go to: **Guadalajara** (12hr., 4 per day, 383 pesos); **Monterrey** (7½hr., 12 per day, 240 pesos); and **Reynosa** (7½hr., 8 per day, 150 pesos). Estrella Blanca, Del Norte, Oriente, and Turistar (☎213 46 55) share travel to **Mexico City** (9-12hr., 8 per day, 226 pesos).

■⑦ ORIENTATION AND PRACTICAL INFORMATION. The town centers around the **Plaza de Armas**, 2 blocks south of which is the **Plaza de la Libertad**. To the north of the Plaza de Armas is Carranza, to the east is Olmos, and to the south Mirón. One block south of Mirón, Madero is the northern border of Plaza de la Libertad. One block east of Olmos, Juárez is the western border of Plaza de la Libertad. Continuing east and parallel to Olmos, you'll find Aduana and López de Lara; to the west and parallel to Olmos, you'll find Colón, 20 de Noviembre, and Sor Juana Ines de la Cruz.

The **tourist office**, 20 de Noviembre 218 Nte., one block west and two blocks north of Plaza de Armas, between Altamira and Obregón, across from an auto parts store, has helpful maps and city guides. (☎212 26 68 or 212 00 07. Open M-F 8am-5pm, Sa 9am-2pm.) **Exchange currency** or traveler's checks at **Central de Divisa**, Juárez 215 Sur. (☎212 90 00. Open M-F 9am-6pm, Sa 9am-1:30pm.) **Bancrecer**, on Díaz Mirón next door to Sixpack, also exchanges traveler's checks and has a 24hr. **ATM.** (☎212 20 32. Open M-F 9am-5pm, Sa 10am-2pm.) **Luggage storage** is available at the bus station. (5 pesos per hr., 35 pesos per day.) **Sixpack**, Díaz Mirón 405 Ote., 3 blocks east of the southeast corner of the Plaza de Armas, is a **supermarket** that sells beer and more. (☎212 24 15. Open daily 8am-10pm.) **Emergency:** ☎060. **Police:** (☎212 10 32 or 212 11 57) on Tamaulipas at Sor Juana de la Cruz. **Red Cross:** has ambulance service. (☎212 13 33. Open 24hr.) **Pharmacy: Benavides**, Carranza 102, in the Plaza de Armas. (☎219 25 25. Open daily 8am-11pm.) **Hospital General de Tampico**, Ejército Nacional 1403 (☎215 22 20 or 213 20 35), near the bus station, has English-speaking doctors. **Fax:**

Telecomm, Madero 311, next to the post office. (☎214 11 21. Open M-F 8am-7pm, Sa 9am-noon.) **LADATELs** are clustered around the corners of the Plaza de Armas. **Internet Access: CNCI,** Obregón 210, off Juárez. (☎219 06 01. 20 pesos per hr. Open M-Sa 7am-9pm, Su 10am-3pm.) **Post office:** Madero 309 Ote., in the yellow building on Plaza de la Libertad (☎212 19 27; open M-F 8am-7pm, Sa 9am-1pm) also has a **Mex-Post** office (☎212 34 81) inside. **Postal code:** 89000.

⌐ ACCOMMODATIONS. Quality budget hotels are relatively rare in Tampico. Those willing to pay 300 pesos or more can get an excellent room in one of the many larger hotels on Madero and Díaz Mirón near the plazas. Walk a few blocks from the main plazas, however, and you can find some much better deals, particularly along Díaz Mirón. **Hotel Posada Don Francisco,** Díaz Mirón 710, furnishes its pretty, pastel pink rooms with carpets, cable TVs, A/C, and phones. (☎219 28 35. Singles 207 pesos, with king-size bed 247 pesos; doubles 293 pesos.) At the Copa, **Hotel Copacabana,** Díaz Mirón 819, you will find good rooms for excellent prices, with A/C, cable TV, and carpeting. Unfortunately, many rooms do not have windows. (☎212 99 58. Singles 90 pesos, with A/C and carpeting 135 pesos; doubles 204 pesos; triples 306 pesos.) **Hotel Buena Vista,** Héroes de Canonero 112, one block from the Plaza de la Libertad, does indeed offer a good view—of docked oil tankers, that is. The cheapest rooms in the downtown area, these small, bare quarters have fans but no hot water. (☎212 29 46. Singles 50 pesos; doubles 80 pesos.)

⌐ FOOD. Seafood is the standard fare in Tampico, where specialties include *jaiba* (blue crab). Yet the city's most well-known dish is *carne asada a la tampiqueña* (a seasoned grilled steak served with guacamole, refried beans, and red enchiladas). Try eating at a seaside stand or at the covered food court, the **Centro Gastronómico de Tampico,** on the Canonero side of the Plaza de la Libertad. As you walk upstairs, you will be accosted by small "restaurant" (read: moving counter top) owners pushing their fresh food and low prices. Have fun—just investigate the kitchen before chowing down. **Naturaleza,** Aduana 107 Nte., one of Tampico's only vegetarian restaurants, offers excellent *tamales, licuados,* and soy burgers (15-25 pesos), as well as vegetarian *comida corrida* (30 pesos). The house specialty *chapati* (20 pesos) is an exotic treat, an Arabian sandwich with soy, mushrooms, cheeses, and spices. (☎212 85 56. Open daily 9am-9pm.) Locals don't mind the wait at **Restaurant Lucy;** on Altamira, half a block past López de Lara, the tiny place is packed for a reason. *Comida corrida* 16 pesos, *antojitos* 10-20 pesos. (Open F-W 11am-11pm.) Serious seafood fans find it worth the extra money to eat at **Salón Palacio,** Aduana 315, in the corner of the Plaza de la Libertad. Carefully prepared regional entrees include plenty of shrimp and crab (50-80 pesos) and *carne asada a la tampiqueña* (80 pesos). Outside, check out the small photo gallery of yesteryear's Tampico, featuring facts about *The Treasure of the Sierra Madre,* the 1947 Humphrey Bogart movie filmed in the city. Live music on weekends. (☎212 43 21. Open Su-Th noon-midnight, F-Sa noon-2am.)

▣ ♫ SIGHTS AND ENTERTAINMENT. For a seaside getaway, **Playa Miramar** is the northeast's best beach, with gentle waves and long stretches of white sand. The beach is accessible by the "Tampico Playa" bus (30min., 3.5 pesos), a shared "Tampico Playa" taxi (3.5 pesos), or a private taxi (15min., 20 pesos). Once there, stake out a spot under a palm-frond umbrella on the beach's 10km of sand.

In the *centro,* nightlife consists of upscale hotel bars or borderline seedy local places. If you really want to party, take a taxi (20 pesos) to ▩**Byblos,** Byblos 1. Byblos spares no expense, with art by Versace and three fountains decorating the black marble bar area. The adjoining club hosts the biggest names in Latin music, and on Saturdays, Byblos's pyramid-shaped disco pulsates with lasers and video screens. (☎217 00 42. Bar open daily 8pm-2am; no cover. Disco open daily 9am-late; cover 70 pesos.) **Papa Cuerva,** Aduana 401, on the Plaza de la Libertad, is the best choice if you don't want to venture far. A tribute to Tampico's seafaring reputation, the bar looks like a pirate ship, sails and all, with octopi and deep-sea divers decorating the walls. Papa's "poop deck" has additional seating and pool tables. (☎219 32 14. W open bar, 50 pesos for women, 80 pesos for men. Th-Sa cover 30 pesos, Sa free for women if accompanied by a man. Beer 25 pesos. Open W-Sa noon-2am, Su-Tu noon-1am.) For more authentic local flavor, head to the intimate **Boys and Girls**, 316 Olmos, for live music, black lights, and beer (15 pesos). Be there late Saturday night for a lively *norteño* show. (Cover 20 pesos. Open W-Su 9pm-late.) To the far northwest of town, a gay atmosphere welcomes you at **Obsession** and **Fiesta;** the taxi ride is 30 pesos.

NUEVO LEÓN

MONTERREY   ☎8

At three million people and growing, Monterrey is the third-largest city in Mexico, and perhaps the most overlooked by foreign tourists. Founded in 1596 by Diego de Monemayor at the foot of Cerro de la Silla (Saddle Mountain), the small trading outpost grew in importance as Monterrey's position between central Mexico and the US made it an ideal place for business and commerce. The city is today home to many of the country's wealthiest businesspeople and known for its shrewd capitalist ambiance. Beautiful parks, chic cafes, sun-drenched plazas, modern art, and cosmopolitan architecture all sit side-by-side. The city's wealth has created a unique blend of the old and the new: across the street from the ancient yellow cathedral, a 30-story modern lighthouse shoots fluorescent blue laser beams into the mountainous night. Monterrey serves as a reminder of where Mexico has been, and of where it wants to go. The city is an eclectic mix of European cobblestone streets, American capitalism, and Mexican spirit.

▐ TRANSPORTATION

GETTING AROUND

Buses: Local buses usually head in only one direction on any given street, except for on Constitución and Juárez (6am-midnight, 3 pesos). Popular routes include stops at the Gran Plaza (#18 or 42), points along Padre Mier and Hidalgo (#15), and along the perimeter of the downtown area (#69). To get from the budget hotel area to the city center, take the #1 Central or #17 Pío X bus, both of which run the lengths of Pino Suárez and Cuauhtémoc. For more detailed route information, ask locals or the English-speaking staff at the tourist office.

Subway: Monterrey's amazing **subway** system, the **Metrorrey,** has all but replaced the large and confusing bus system. Although buses are useful in providing transportation to points far from the *centro* and near the city's periphery, the subway system is new, clean, and efficient—only 7 minutes from the bus station to the Gran Plaza. The system runs on 2 lines. Line 1 (the yellow line) extends from the western station of **San Barnabe** to the **Exposición** station in the east. Line 2 (the green line) runs from the north, at the **Anaya** station, to the Gran Plaza **Zaragoza** stop. Signs will point to which final station the train is headed. Line 2 brings passengers to the downtown *Zona Rosa* and close to the Barrio Antiguo. The **Cuauhtémoc** stop is the crossing point of lines 1 and 2, and is located right next to the bus station and the majority of the city's budget hotels. Buy passes from a machine in quantities of 1 (3.5 pesos), 2 (6.8 pesos), 5 (16 pesos) or 8 (24 pesos). Subway runs daily 6:30am-midnight.

GETTING AWAY

Airport: Far northwest corner of town, off of Rte. 54. **Taxis** charge 80-130 pesos for the 4km trip (20-30min.) to the center. **Aeroméxico** (☎343 55 60) or **Mexicana** (☎340 55 11) require 2-3 day advance reservations, more for weekend flights.

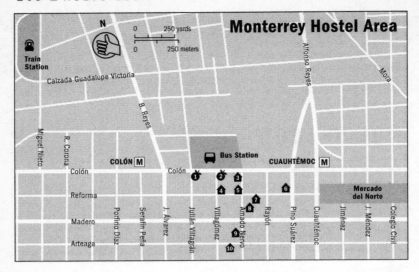

Monterrey Hostel Area

Train Station

Calzada Guadalupe Victoria

B. Reyes

Bus Station

COLÓN M   CUAUHTÉMOC M

Mercado del Norte

Miguel Nieto
R. Corona
Colón
Reforma
Madero
Arteaga

Porfirio Díaz
Serafín Peña
J. Álvarez
Julián Villagrán
Villagómez
Amado Nervo
Rayón
Pino Suárez
Cuauhtémoc
Jiménez
J. Méndez
Colegio Civil

Colón

Central Monterrey

Washington

5 de Mayo

Palacio de Gobierno

Zuazua
Coss

Museo de la Historia Mexicana

V. Guerrero
Galeana
Carranza
Escobedo
15 de Mayo
Ramón
Zaragoza
Parque Hundido
Allende
Teatro de le Ciudad
Matamoros
GRAN PLAZA
Padre Mier
Montemayor

ZONA ROSA
Morelos
Hidalgo

ZARAGOZA

BARRIO ANTIGUO

Fuente del Comercio

Faro del Comercio

Catedral

MARCO

Palacio Municipal

Ocampo

Zaragoza

Montemayor
Mina
Abasolo
Jardón
Prieto
Naranjo

NORTHEAST MEXICO

Monterrey

SEE MONTERREY HOSTEL AREA MAP

Cervezeria
Cuauhtémoc
Moctezuma

Train
Station

Calzada Guadalupe Victoria

Alfonso Reyes

Mora

B. Reyes

COLÓN M

Bus
Station

CUAUHTÉMOC

M

Colón

CUAUHTÉMOC M

Colón

Mercado
del Norte

Reforma

Madero

J. M. Arteaga
C. Salazar
Gral. Treviño
Garza
Tapia
M. M. del Llano
A. Espinosa
Ruperto Martinez

Julián Villagrán
Villagómez
Amado Nervo
Rayón
Pino Suárez
Clauhtémoc
Jiménez
J. Méndez
Colegio Civil
Av. Benito Juárez
V. Guerrero
Galeana
Carranza
Escobedo
Zaragoza
Zuazúa
Dr. J. M. Coss

Diego de Montemayor

M ALAMEDA

Arramberri

Miguel Nieto
R. Corona
Vallarta
Porfirio Díaz
Serafín Peña
J. Álvarez

Alameda

M. Arreola
Washington
5 de Mayo

SEE CENTRAL MONTERREY MAP

Palacio de
Gobierno ■

Museo de la
Historia Mexicana

15 de Mayo

M FUNDADORES

Ramón

Parque
Hundido

Allende

Matamoros
Padre Mier
Hidalgo
Ocampo

ZONA
ROSA

GRAN
PLAZA

Montemayor

Mina

PADRE MIER M

Morelos

ZARAGOZA

Zaragoza

BARRIO
ANTIGUO

TO MERCADO

Av. Constitución

Hidalgo

Faro del
Comercio

M

Catedral

Abasolo

Jardón

Palacio Municipal ■

MARCO

Prieto

Av. Ignacio M. Prieto

16 de Septiembre

0   500 yards
0   500 meters

N

NORTHEAST MEXICO

Monterrey (LEGEND REFERS TO MAPS ON FACING PAGE)

ACCOMMODATIONS
Hotel Amada Nervo, 5
Hotel Casino, 10
Hotel Lozano, 6
Hotel Mundo, 7
Hotel Nuevo León, 8
Hotel Paraíso Reforma, 14
Hotel Posada, 3
Hotel Virreyes, 9

FOOD AND DRINKS
Cafe Paraíso, 20
Casa de Maíz, 21
El Rey de Cabrito, 23
Gigante Supermarket, 2
Restaurant Mi Tierra, 12
Restaurante Fastory, 1
Taquería Las Monjitas, 11

BARS AND CLUBS
Barreiros, 19
Cafe El Infinito, 22
Cafe Iguana, 18
El Reloj, 16
Nueva Luna, 15
Primer Aire, 17

SHOPPING AND SERVICES
Plaza México Shopping
  Center, 13
Benavides Pharmacy, 14

Buses: All buses in and out of the city pass through Monterrey's huge **Central de Autobuses** at Colón and Villagrán. To reach the city center from the bus station, take any bus going south on Pino Suárez, the thoroughfare to the left as you exit the station (#18 lets you off at the central Gran Plaza), or walk two blocks east to the grey subway station at Cuauhtémoc and Colón and take the metro (Line 2; 3.50 pesos) to Padre Mier or Zaragoza. Ómnibus de México (☎374 07 16) departs for: **Aguascalientes** (8hr., 4 per day 12:30-11:35pm, 292 pesos); **Chihuahua** (12hr., 3 per day 5-9:45pm, 429 pesos); **Guadalajara** (12hr., 3 per day 12:30-9:30pm, 418 pesos); **Mexico City** (12hr., 3 per day 7:15-10:30pm, 495 pesos); **Querétaro** (8hr., 9 and 10:30pm, 326 pesos); **Zacatecas** (6hr., 5 per day 11am-11:15pm, 227 pesos); and more. Sendor, Tamaulipas, and Noreste share offices (☎375 00 14) near Sala 5. Noreste heads to **Nuevo Laredo** (3hr., 12 per day, 136 pesos) and **Matehuala** (4hr., every hr., 161 pesos). Frontera (☎375 09 87) rolls to **Saltillo** (1½hr., every 20min., 45 pesos) and **León** (10 hr., 5 per day, 377 pesos). Similar service provided by Estrella Blanca (☎318 37 37), Líneas Americanas, and luxurious Futura and Turistar.

⑦ PRACTICAL INFORMATION

TOURIST AND FINANCIAL SERVICES

Tourist Office: Turinfo, Hidalgo 477 (☎345 08 70 or 345 09 02), just before Escobedo in the *Zona Rosa,* 1 block down from Morelos. Helpful staff, with abundant maps and bilingual brochures. Open Tu-Su 10am-5pm. There are also large **maps** and information booths at various points along Morelos and throughout the *Zona Rosa.*

Consulates: Canada, 1300 Zaragoza (☎344 32 00). Open M-F 9am-5:30pm. **UK,** Priv. Tamazunchale 104 (☎333 75 98). Open M-F 8am-5pm. **US,** Constitución Pte. 411 (☎345 21 20), downtown. Open M-F 8am-1pm for passports and citizens' concerns, 9am-5pm for telephone information. 24hr. guard and emergency service.

Currency Exchange: Banks dot Madero near the budget hotels and flood the *Zona Rosa,* lining Padre Mier in particular. Many refuse to cash traveler's checks and most of those who do charge high service fees (10%). All have 24hr. **ATMs.** Most open M-F 9am-4pm. **Mexdollar Internacional,** 1136 Suárez (☎374 43 11), right by the bus station and the Cuauhtémoc subway stop, offers 24hr. currency and traveler's checks exchange at good rates. **Eurodivisas** (☎340 16 83) in Plaza Mexico on Morelos at Galeana, exchanges traveler's checks at poorer rates but charges no commission. Open M-F 10:30am-8:30pm, Sa 10am-9pm, Su 11am-8pm.

American Express: San Pedro 215 Nte. (☎318 33 04). Catch bus #214 headed for "San Pedro" on Pino Suárez at the stop just past Ocampo. Get off at the stop before Calzada de Valle and cross the street. Open M-F 9am-5pm, Sa 9am-1pm.

LOCAL SERVICES

Luggage storage: At the bus station. 4 pesos per hr. for up to 30 days.

Supermarket: Gigante (☎374 40 24), on Colón across from the bus station. Clothes, groceries, baked goods, and an adjoining **pharmacy.** Open daily 8am-10pm.

Laundry: Laundry services available at most *centro* hotels for about 40 pesos per load.

EMERGENCY AND COMMUNICATIONS

Emergency: ☎060.

Police: (☎345 54 19), on the corner of Carranza and Espinosa or at the 24hr. stand in the middle of Morelos at Paras in the *Zona Rosa.*

Pharmacy: In the bus station, in the Gigante Supermarket on Colón (☎374 40 24), or **Benavides,** on Morelos past Zaragoza (☎345 02 57). Open daily 8am-10pm.

Medical Assistance: Red Cross, Alfonso Reyes 2503 Nte. (☎375 11 77 or 375 12 12), at Henry. Open 24hr. **Cruz Verde** (☎371 50 50 or 371 52 06), at Ciudad Madero and Ciudad Victoria. Open 24hr. English spoken.

Fax: Telecomm, in the bus station next to the post office. Open M-F 8am-7pm, Sa-Su 9am-4pm.

Internet Access: La Tumba Café/Bar, Padre Mier 827 (☎333 88 43), in the Barrio Antiguo. 4 computers. 25 pesos per hr. Open M 11am-9pm, Tu-W 11am-1am, Th-F 11am-3am. **Ships 2000,** Escobedo 819 (☎343 25 68), between Padre Mier and Morelos in the *Zona Rosa.* 14 computers, high speed fiber-optic connection. 20 pesos per 30min., 35 pesos per hr. Scanning, laser printing and CD burning also available. Two-story arcade downstairs features the latest video games. Open daily 10am-10pm.

Telephones: LADATELs in the *Zona Rosa,* metro stops, and most major street corners.

Post Office: (☎342 40 03) on Zaragoza at Washington, inside the Palacio Federal. Open M-F 8am-7pm, Sa 9am-1pm. Also at the 2nd floor of the bus station. Stairs near Sala 5. Open M-F 8am-4pm, Sa 9am-1pm. **Mexpost:** (☎344 94 23) next to the post office inside the Palacio Federal. Open M-F 9am-6pm, Sa 9am-1pm. **Postal Code:** 64000.

▐ ACCOMMODATIONS

Hotels conveniently located near the *Zona Rosa* tend to be of four- or five-star quality, and even three-star accommodations inflate their rates to gouge tourists and business travelers. If you feel like spending 600 pesos, a hotel downtown will reward you with luxury: restaurants, room service, and elegantly decorated lobbies and rooms. But fear not—cheaper accommodations are sprinkled generously in the less glamorous area near the bus station, with easy access to the metro and the city's main points of interest. Just take precautions when walking in this area at night; the streets are less safe after 10pm. Many rooms are full by early afternoon, so act fast. Unless otherwise noted, all hotels listed come with fans.

Hotel Mundo, Reforma 736 (☎374 68 50), just off Nervo. More luxurious than bus station hotels: the A/C works well, the TVs are newer, the floors shine brighter. Singles 200 pesos, with A/C 225 pesos; doubles 250 pesos, with A/C 280 pesos.

Hotel Nuevo Leon, Nervo 1007 (☎354 65 09), 1½ blocks from the Central de Autobuses. Wide, tiled hallways lead you to dim but spacious suites with TV, A/C, and carpet. Many rooms include dressers and tables. Singles 250 pesos; doubles 350 pesos.

Hotel Virreyes (☎374 66 10), on Nervo two blocks from the bus station. The rooms are basic and sterile, but low prices make this an ideal resting place for wallet-conscious travelers. Unfortunately, they also make it nearly impossible to find vacancies. Singles 100 pesos, with A/C 140 pesos; doubles 150 pesos, with A/C 200 pesos.

Hotel Casino, on Arteaga, just off Amado Nervo, with a yellow exterior (☎372 02 19). Despite its name, staying here is no gamble. Guests are guaranteed small, simple rooms in good condition. Singles 180 pesos, with A/C 250 pesos; suites with living room, A/C, and TV 300 pesos.

Hotel Posada, Nervo 1138 (☎372 39 08), across from the bus station. Cross the overhead walkway on Colón. Wonderfully quiet rooms and a staff willing to do its best to combat the steady stream of bugs. The tiny restaurant in the lobby serves breakfast and sandwiches (15-25 pesos). Singles 160 pesos, with A/C 190 pesos; doubles 190 pesos, with A/C 220 pesos.

Hotel Amado Nervo, Nervo 1110 (☎375 46 32), across from the bus station. Somewhat run-down, small rooms come with a TV and a phone. The balconies on the third and fourth floors provide views of the neighborhood and the mountains that surround the city. Singles 145 pesos; doubles 210 pesos, with A/C 290 pesos.

Hotel Paraíso Reforma, on Reforma between Nervo and Villagomez (☎374 67 27). Not quite paradise, but hardly hell either. Small, dark, colorfully decorated rooms. Singles 120 pesos, with A/C and TV 180 pesos.

Hotel Lozano, On Suárez, diagonally across from the Cuauhtémoc metro station. Among the lowest-priced hotels in the area, Lozano is in better shape than some of its sub-100 peso colleagues. The blue plaza will brighten the way to your cramped room and your communal bath. Singles 65 pesos, with private bath 80 pesos; doubles 95 pesos.

FOOD

Roasted meat is king in Monterrey. Don't leave the city without trying *cabrito*, an entire kid roasted over charcoal or wood that has a taste similar to lamb. Make sure to indulge your carnivorous tooth by eating plenty of *bisteks* (steaks), another regional speciality. Other popular dishes include *frijoles a la charra* (beans cooked with pork skin, coriander, tomato, peppers, and onions), and *machacado con huevos* (scrambled eggs mixed with salsa and dried, shredded beef). For dessert, you'll love *piloncillo con nuez*, a hardened brown sugar candy with pecans, and the heavenly *glorias*, candy balls of nuts and goat's milk. Although the *Zona Rosa* is home to some of Monterrey's most expensive shopping (and some of northern Mexico's most expensive hotels), it can't be beat for its selection of food. Catering mainly to hungry businesspeople and shoppers, the service is good, the food succulent, and the prices reasonable. *Buen Provecho.*

Restaurant Mi Tierra, on Morelos across from the Plaza México, gives you the value of the best *taquerías* in an intimate, open-air setting. Tacos, *enchiladas, tostadas* and more (25 pesos). If you can't find a seat, get it to go. Open daily 9am-10pm.

Taquería Las Monjitas, on Morelos and Galeana in the *Zona Rosa*, 2 more on Escobedo and on Galeana. Stained-glass and paintings of angels decorate this open-air restaurant, where you will be served by waitresses dressed as nuns. Heavenly specialty tacos (40-50 pesos) have names like *El Obispo* (the bishop) and *El Pecador* (the sinner).

Casa de Maíz, Abasolo 870B (☎340 43 32), in the *Barrio Antiguo*. Each table at this health-food restaurant is a masterpiece painted by local artists. Savor traditional Mexican dishes made with whole wheat flour, or try vegetarian dishes such as tofu in red sauce (22 pesos). Open Tu-F and Su 1-6pm, Sa 2-10:30pm.

Café Paraíso, on Morelos and Mina. A great place to take a break from sightseeing in the heart of the *Barrio Antiguo*. The huge flavored cappuccinos will reaffirm your caffeine addiction (15 pesos). The hip spot also serves drinks and good French and Mexican cuisine (25-40 pesos). Open daily 9am-midnight.

El Rey de Cabrito, on Constitución and Gonzalitos, behind MARCO, reigns supreme for roasted meat, with plenty of *cabrito* and steak dishes (95-110 pesos). Mounted deer and dueling mountain lions add to the hunting-lodge atmosphere.

Restaurante Fastory, Colón 980 (☎372 32 50), across from the bus station. Whether you're fresh off the bus or just looking for a late-night snack, stop by Fastory for a solid, inexpensive meal. This shiny new cafe serves breakfast specials (30-50 pesos) and international entrees (50-60 pesos).

SIGHTS

Monterrey's architects were kind to tourists. Despite the city's size, most sights are packed into the 40-acre **Gran Plaza** and the nearby **Barrio Antiguo.** A visitor could easily spend the day strolling through the Gran Plaza and admiring the statues, architecture, and greenery, all surrounded by beautiful mountains on the horizon.

GRAN PLAZA. Bounded by Washington on the north, Constitución on the south, Zaragoza on the west, and Dr. Coss on the east, the Grand Plaza is host to a slew of government buildings. Also known as the Macroplaza, it contains the **Palacio Federal,** the **Palacio de Gobierno,** and the **Palacio Municipal.** Just east of the Palacio Federal is the **Plaza 400 Años** (400-Year Plaza), with a man-made river and paddle boats for rent. If the sun is too much for you, try dozing in the cool garden of the **Parque Hundido** (Sunken Park), just south of the Palacio de Gobierno. One of Mexico's most notorious centers for public displays of affection, the *parque* looks like Noah's Ark, with couples napping, nuzzling, and (gasp!) necking. Farther along the Gran Plaza is the **Fuente de La Vida** (Fountain of Life) which douses an immense statue of Neptune and cavorting naked nymphs. Perhaps the most striking construction is the bright orange **Faro del**

LIKE A RHINESTONE COWBOY One cannot visit Monterrey without hearing *norteño*, the signature music of northeast Mexico, absolutely everywhere: at markets, in bars, and on the street. Sung by such popular bands as Intocable, La Mafia, and Los Tigres del Norte, this unique musical genre—the song of the *vaquero*, the Mexican cowboy—is Mexico's answer to American country-western. Groups nearly always consist of five or six men, sporting matching cowboys hats and garish outfits, swaying in unison to *cumbios* (upbeat rhythms good for dancing) or *rancheros* (slightly slower rhythm). The distinguishing characteristic of this music is the accordion; without its trademark polka sound, it just wouldn't be *norteño*. Love it or hate it, after a few days in Monterrey you'll find yourself involuntarily humming the hit songs of the moment...and maybe even swaying along.

Comercio (Commerce Lighthouse), built in 1983 to commemorate the one hundredth anniversary of Monterrey's Chamber of Commerce. Topped with a laser beacon that circles the skies at night, the lighthouse is a testament to the economic ambitions of Monterrey's leaders. The laser begins to pulse after 10pm on weekend nights, when hundreds pack the adjoining *Barrio Antiguo* in search of some late-night fun. Just across Zuazúa from the Faro de Comercio is the resplendent, pale yellow **Catedral de Monterrey.** Constructed in the 17th century, it is the architectural yin to the Faro's yang.

MUSEO DE HISTORIA MEXICANA. This modern, state-of-the-art museum uses movies and interactive computer displays to illuminate thousands of years of Mexican history. The enormous climate display room upstairs includes realistic reproductions of forests, deserts, and jungles, complete with plastic animals and chirping bird sounds. (*Dr. Coss 445 Sur, at the far end of the Plaza 400 Años. ☎ 345 98 98. Open Tu-F 11am-7pm, Sa-Su 11am-8pm. W-F 10 pesos, students with ID 5 pesos; Sa-Su 5 pesos; Tu free.*)

MUSEO DE ARTE CONTEMPORÁNEO (MARCO). Avoid the pedantic placards and focus on some of the best exhibits of Mexico's innovative modern artists, such as Juan Soriano and Enrique Canales. Or, if you prefer, just recline by the enormous decorative pool in the center of the museum and watch the periodic water shows. (*☎ 342 48 20. At the southern end of Dr. Coss across from the Cathedral. Open Tu and Th-Su 10am-6pm, W 10am-8pm. 25 pesos, students and children 15 pesos, W free.*)

TEATRO DE LA CIUDAD. For a calm night away from the city's busy bars and clubs, stop by the Gran Plaza's enormous theater, which regularly hosts plays, operas, and dance performances. Amateur actors occasionally perform outside. (*On the plaza across from the Fuente de la Vida. ☎ 343 89 74. Opens 1hr. before evening performances. Information and tickets available at the office on Zuazúa between Matamoros and Allende, below the theater. Open M-F 9am-7pm. Prices vary with each show.*)

LA CERVECERIA CUAUHTÉMOC MOCTEZUMA. Beer and sports go hand in hand. Perhaps with this in mind, Monterrey's leading beer manufacturer built this complex, which, in addition to a brewery, contains the Mexican Baseball Hall of Fame and Museum. The brewery tours take you through the production of Carta Blanca, Tecate, and Dos Equis beers, and conclude in the Beer Garden, where adults can sample a glass or two under the shade of trees and fermentation tanks. Afterwards, head to the **Salon de la Fama,** a museum which chronicles the birth of baseball in the mid-1800s and its arrival in Mexico shortly thereafter. Interactive exhibits allow kids of all ages to try their luck at batting, pitching, and catching. (*☎ 328 53 55. On Alfonso Reyes, 1½ blocks south of the Anaya metro station on Line 2. Brewery open M-F 9am-5pm, Sa 9am-2pm. Museum open M-F 9am-5pm, Sa-Su 10:30am-6pm. Tours given throughout the day in Spanish and in English. Free.*)

OBISPADO. The former palace of the bishop of Monterrey is now a state museum displaying artifacts from the colonial era. The museum itself may not be worth the half-hour bus ride from the *centro*, but the view and cool breeze compensate. Bring a picnic and enjoy a break from the city on the wandering terraces. (☎346 04 04. *Take bus #1 from Dr. Coss along the Macroplaza. Ask the driver to point out the stop, and hike up to the very top of the hill. Open Tu-Su 10am-5pm. 20 pesos, students and children free; Su free.*)

PLANETARIO ALFA. The large complex (also called the **Centro Cultural Alfa**) houses interactive science exhibits and shows, as well as gardens and halls honoring Mexico's prehispanic cultures with sculpture and art. The centerpiece of the Alfa is its IMAX theater, which provides an intense movie experience on its 79-foot screen. (*Garza Sada 1000, 25min. southwest of the city. Free round-trip transportation available on the hr. from the Alfa stop on the Alameda, at the corner of Villagrán and Álvarez. Open M-F 3-8:30pm, Sa 2-8:30pm, Su noon-8:30pm. 30 pesos, with IMAX ticket 60 pesos.*)

🎵 ENTERTAINMENT

The **Barrio Antiguo** is quiet during the day, but after sundown police cordon it off to cars and the streets come alive with party-goers. The action usually doesn't get started until 10:30pm or so, but note that early birds get in free at many places.

BARS AND CAFES

Nueva Luna, on the corner of Padre Mier and Dr. Coss (☎344 12 17), boasts the best margaritas in town (available in five flavors, 40 pesos) and nightly live music. The 2-for-1 deal on beers (25 pesos) and margaritas (40 pesos) until 9pm makes the relaxed Nueva Luna all the more attractive. Open Su-Th noon-midnight, F-Sa noon-2am.

Barreiros, Padre Mier 1032 (☎301 23 82). The decor of this live-music bar will make you feel like you're relaxing in the *zócalo* of a small Mexican town, surrounded by colonial facades. The loud, live Mexican rock, however, serves as a constant reminder that you've come here to party. Beer 25 pesos, mixed drinks 50-70 pesos. F-Sa cover 30 pesos for men. Women get their first drink free. Open daily 9pm-late.

Primer Aire, Montemayor 839 (☎314 26 07), Monterrey's only jazz and blues bar is a welcome change from the rock music scene. An international crowd comes here for nightly live music. Weekly poetry readings F 11pm. Beer 18 pesos, mixed drinks 30-45 pesos. Cover Th-Sa 25 pesos. Open daily 10am-2am.

Café El Infinito, Jardón 904 Ote. (☎340 36 34). This cafe/bar/used-bookstore/arthouse movie theater promises radical politics and challenging conversation. Sip international wine (starting at 30 pesos a glass) or get a free cup of coffee with the donation of a book. W and Th international art films are shown at 8:30pm. Open M-Th 9am-11pm, F-Sa 9am-1am, Su 4-11pm.

CLUBS

El Reloj, Padre Mier 860 (☎343 42 32). With a young contingent, Reloj always has long lines and reverberating US and Mexican rock. Sa night is the time to see and be seen at this fashionable club. Cover 30 pesos. Open daily 9pm-late.

Café Iguana, Montemayor 927 (☎343 08 22). The young, eclectic crowd fits in with the funky, colorful decor. Big, cushy couches line the stone walls and party-goers revel on the open-air patio. Beer 20 pesos, mixed drinks 25 pesos. Cover on some weekend nights, depending on live music. Open daily 8pm-late.

GAY AND LESBIAN NIGHTLIFE

After its first-ever Pride March in the summer of 1997, Monterrey is quickly becoming one of the most gay- and lesbian-friendly cities in Mexico. Young same-sex couples walk the streets of the *Zona Rosa* and the *Barrio Antiguo*. Although most nightspots cater primarily to men, women are more than welcome. For more listings, ask for a copy of the free gay and lesbian monthly magazine, *Rola Gay*, at either of these bars.

Club Vongole, Pedreras 300 (☎315 72 59), east of *Barrio Antiguo*. The most hip-hop, happening gay and lesbian night spot in town, with over 1000 people W, F, and Sa.

Charao's (☎374 18 72), at the corner of Garza and Zaragoza, 7 blocks north of the Gran Plaza. An exciting, young crowd of men and women stay late every night. Drinks 15 pesos. F-Sa cover 15 pesos for men, no cover for women.

SHOPPING AND FESTIVALS

The **Zona Rosa,** particularly along Morelos, is the city's true commercial center, with a variety of stores and boutiques ranging from mid-priced to expensive. The new **Plaza Mexico** mall, in the center of the Zona Rosa, has the most shopping bang for your buck, with two floors of upscale stores and a food court upstairs. Bargain-hunters may prefer to head to the **Mercado del Norte** (also known as **La Pulga**), the seemingly endless maze of vendor stalls covering Reforma, just south of Colón. The clothing vendors, *taquerías*, and technology stores stretch from Cuauhtémoc all the way to Juárez; enter on Cuauhtémoc, directly across from the metro station. (Open daily 9am-7pm.)

Monterrey celebrates **Mexican Independence Day** in style, with partying and parades September 15 and 16. In late November, the **Festival Del Barrio Antiguo** shuts down the streets around the Old Neighborhood for a week of cultural events, including open-air theater, music festivals, dance, and painting exhibitions.

COAHUILA

SALTILLO
☎8

Only 1½ hours from Monterrey, Saltillo is a treat for the tired traveler. Once you get past the enormous dusty expanse that houses most of the city's 900,000 inhabitants (and several American car companies), the *centro* is surprisingly clean, relaxed, and easily walkable. Early to bed and early to rise, *saltillenses* are proud of their dry climate and pretty spot in the Sierra Madres. Though the limited sights and nightlife do not draw many tourists, excellent budget lodgings, good food, and colorful wool *sarapes* await those who make the trip.

▐ TRANSPORTATION

The **bus station** is about 3km southwest of the city center on Echeverría Sur. To get to the *centro*, exit the terminal, cross the pedestrian overpass, and catch minibus #10 from the small street perpendicular to Echeverría, across the street from the Restaurant Jaslo (20min., 6:30am-11pm, 3 pesos). To get back to the station, catch bus #9 at the corner of Aldama and Hidalgo, a block down the street from the cathedral, in front of the entrance to the furniture store. From the bus station, Frontera runs buses to: **Monterrey** (every 20 min., 45 pesos) and **Matehuala** (3hr., 7 per day 6:15am-11pm, 135 pesos). Ómnibus de México (☎417 03 15) serves **Aguascalientes** (7hr., 10 per day 4am-11pm, 250 pesos) and **Reynosa** (5hr., every hr. noon-9pm, 150 pesos). Transportes del Norte (☎417 09 02) runs to: **Guadalajara** (10hr., 5 per day, 350 pesos); **Mexico City** (10hr., 5 per day 6am-9pm, 447 pesos); **San Luis Potosí** (5hr., 7 per day 6am-11pm, 216 pesos); and **Zacatecas** (5hr., 5 per day 3:30am-9pm, 181 pesos).

◀▶ ❼ ORIENTATION AND PRACTICAL INFORMATION

Located in a valley between the jagged Sierra Madre mountains, Saltillo lies 87km southwest of Monterrey along desolate **Rte. 40.** The *centro's* streets form a slightly distorted grid not quite aligned with the four cardinal directions. The quiet **Plaza de Armas** is home to the cathedral and is bordered by **Juárez** to the south (or right, facing the cathedral) and **Hidalgo** to the east (between the plaza and cathedral). Facing the cathedral, walk one block to the left, then take another left to arrive at **Plaza Acuña**, bordered on its west (far side) by the narrow **Padre Flores**, on the east by **Allende**, on the south by **Victoria**, and on the north by **Aldama**.

Tourist Information: Helpful maps of the city stand outside the bus station and dot the centro. If you want more guidance, go to the tourist office (☎412 51 22) at the corner of Acuña and Coss, 5 long blocks north of Plaza Acuña. Little English is spoken. Open M-F 9am-5pm, Sa 9am-2pm.

Banks: Banamex, at Allende and Ocampo, behind the Palacio de Gobierno. 24hr. **ATM.**

Market: Soriana, on Coss across from the tourist office.

Police: (☎414 45 50) at Treviño and Echeverría Ote.

Emergency: ☎060.

Red Cross: (☎414 33 33), at the corner of Cárdenas and Rayon.

Pharmacy: El Fenix, 360 Juárez (☎412 49 10), across from the Mercado Juárez.

Fax: Telecomm (☎414 25 85), next to the post office. Open M-F 9am-4pm, Sa 9am-4pm, Su 9am-noon.

Internet Access: CNCI, Allende Nte. 744 (☎410 14 44). 2 computers. 20 pesos per hr. Open daily 8am-7pm.

Post office: Victoria 453 (☎414 90 97) after Hotel Urdiñola. Open M-F 9am-4pm, Sa 9am-1pm. **MexPost:** (☎414 18 90) in one corner of the post office. Open M-F 9am-4pm, Sa 9am-2pm.

Postal code: 25000.

⌐ ACCOMMODATIONS

Echeverría, which runs along the bus station, teems with cheap places to rest your head. The *centro* is full of low-to-medium range, clean, comfortable spots. There are also a few more expensive hotels, with accompanying quality.

▨**Hotel Urdiñola,** Victoria 251 (☎414 09 40), behind the Palacio de Gobierno, is exquisite, with a marble staircase, beautiful stained-glass windows, and a friendly courtyard. This elegant retreat is also equipped with fans, cable TV, and phones. The extravagance translates into extravagant prices. Singles 260 pesos; doubles 285 pesos.

Hotel Saade, Aldama Pte. 397 (☎412 91 20 or 412 91 21), a block west of Plaza Acuña, has clean, well-furnished, quiet rooms near the heart of the city. Top-floor rooms offer a panorama of Saltillo and the Sierra. Rooms come in three styles, from *económico* with twin bed and bath, to *ejecutivo* with bed, bath, TV, and phone. Single *económico* 240 pesos; standard 270 pesos; *ejecutivo* 290 pesos.

Hotel Hidalgo, Padre Flores 217 off of Plaza Acuña (☎414 98 53), is a big step down in luxury. Excellent central location and old, simple rooms for the solo traveler. Singles 40 peso, with private bath 60 pesos.

⏣ FOOD

Be sure to sample Saltillo's specialty, *pan de pulque* (bread made with *pulque*, an unrefined cactus drink). Restaurants on Allende and Carranza cater to tourists, while the cafes on the smaller streets near the plazas remain local picks. For upscale dining and adventuresome dishes, head to the cheerful ▨**Restaurant Principal,** Allende Nte. 702, seven blocks north of the Palacio de Gobierno. Their *cabecito* (steamed goat's head, 35 pesos) will leave you with that invigorating after-the-hunt feel, as will a splurge on grilled ram (100 pesos). Squeamish diners, don't worry; traditional *antojitos* (40 pesos) and goat and steak dishes (75-100 pesos) are also served. (☎414 33 84. Open daily 8am-midnight.) **Café and Restaurant Arcasa,** Victoria 263, is a family-run cafe with delicious food and fast breakfasts (19-29 pesos). Three-course *menús del día* (30 pesos) draw in locals. (☎412 64 24. Open daily 7:30am-midnight.) Quality, safe *taquerías* surround Plaza Acuña. **Taquería El Pastor** is a trusted local favorite at the corner of Aldama and Padre Flores. Take a break from *sarape*-shopping with a beef, chicken, or tongue taco (14 pesos).

👁 SIGHTS

Weary travelers rest assured: Saltillo is not sight-intensive. Until recently, the most alluring sight in town has been the **Museo de las Aves,** on Hidalgo three blocks up from the cathedral and one block past Escobedo. The museum is home to hundreds of birds, the large majority of which are dead and stuffed. (☎414 01 68. Open M-Sa 10am-6pm, Su 11am-6pm. 5 pesos.) Saltillo's new pride and joy is the recently opened **Museo del Desierto,** Perez Trevino 3745, at the center of the under-construction **Parque Las Maravillas.** The #6 bus, at the corner of Aldama and Ocampo, takes you there (35min.); ask the driver to point out the stop. The large, state-of-the-art museum includes exhibits on ecology, geology, paleontology, the development of northeastern Mexico under Spanish rule, and, of course, the desert. (☎410 66 33; www.museodeldesierto.net. Open daily 9am-6pm. 20 pesos.)

Perched on a hill overlooking the city, **Plaza México** (or **El Mirador**) offers a smashing view of the whole area and the unconquerable mountains beyond. Follow Miguel Hidalgo uphill, take your first left after the *Museo de las Aves*, continue for another four blocks, turn right onto the winding Gustavo Espinoza, and head to the small pink-painted plaza with benches and old street lamps.

🎵 ENTERTAINMENT

What there is of the city's nightlife lies well beyond downtown, and not much goes on during the week. On weekend nights, however, many head to **Frug's Clubhouse,** Acuña 1212, across from the tourist office, for live music, beer (15 pesos), and billiards. (☎412 77 83. Cover Th 30 pesos for men, F-Sa 40 pesos for everyone. Open M-Sa 4pm-2am.)

The downtown **Centro Cultural (Teatro García Carrillo),** on Aldama in Plaza Acuña, presents regular sculpture and art exhibitions, films, and concerts, all free of charge. Drop by to check the list of weekly events, all held during the day. (Open Tu-Su 10am-2pm and 4-7pm. Theater for children Sa 11am.)

🛍 🎇 SHOPPING AND FESTIVALS

Since the 17th century, Saltillo has enjoyed a long tradition of weaving. The city is known throughout Mexico for its colorful wool *sarapes* (shawls), so much so that the city's *sarape* style is called the "saltillo." While many modern *sarapes* are cheaply manufactured with tourists in mind, be on the lookout for traditional wool *sarapes*. They have softer colors, and are more expensive (350 to 2000 pesos). The best place to shop for a reasonably-priced *sarape* might be the **Mercado Juárez** in the northwest corner of the plaza. You can also try shops that specialize in *sarapes*, such as the **Sarape Factory** on Hidalgo, just before the Museo de las Aves.

Saltillo's streets burst with artistry and cultural pride during the **Feria de Saltillo** in mid-August. This two-week fair, featuring agricultural and art exhibitions, dances, theater, and many, many *sarapes*, dates back to the town's first years of existence in the 16th century.

ZACATECAS

ZACATECAS ☎4

A beautiful colonial city is perhaps the last thing a weary traveler would expect to find rising out of the prickly Central Mexican desert. Yet, almost miraculously, the city of Zacatecas overcomes its arid surroundings, perched between, on, and over the mineral-laden hills that serve as the city's lifeblood. A silver trinket, given to

NORTHEAST MEXICO

Zacatecas

🏠 ACCOMMODATIONS

CREA Youth Hostel, 1
Hotel Colón, 4
Hotel del Parque, 2
Hotel Gami, 6
Hotel María Conchita, 5
Zamora de Zacatecas, 3

early Spanish colonists by an indigenous Cascane in the mid-1500s, triggered the mining frenzy that led to the founding of the town in 1585 and eventually stripped the surrounding hills of 6000 tons of silver. Although the silver mines have since gone dry, Zacatecas managed to survive, and even thrive, without the mine's economic crutch. Under the patronage of the affluent silver barons, the arts flourished, and the rows of grand colonial mansions, beautiful parks, and nationally renowned museums testify to an era of lavish consumption—an era in which, legend goes, the great barons swore they would coat the streets with silver. Today, happy and silver-free are the city's residents, enjoying their busy university town, a trade and tourist center of commerce and tourism. And, of course, they enjoy plenty of Corona beer, home brewed in the state of Zacatecas.

🚌 TRANSPORTATION

Airport: (☎928 03 38), accessible by *combis* (☎922 59 46) departing from the Mexicana office (20min., departs 1¼hr. before flight, 50 pesos). **Mexicana,** Hidalgo 406 (☎922 74 29, 922 32 48). Open M-F 9am-7pm. **Taesa,** Hidalgo 306 (☎922 00 50 or 922 02 12). Open M-F 9am-7pm, Sa 10am-6pm. **Aero California,** Juan de Montoro 203 (☎925 24 00).

Buses: Central de Autobuses (☎922 11 12), Lomas de la Isabélica, at Tránsito Pesado on the outskirts of town. City buses (2 pesos; Ruta 8 to the *centro*) and taxis (20 pesos to the *centro*) wait outside. After dark, a taxi is the only option. To get to the station from the *centro*, take the Ruta 7 or 8 bus on González Ortega, 1 block from Juárez. Omnibuses de Mexico (☎922 54 95) provides the broadest range of service, including: **Mexico City** (8hr., 10 per day, 338 pesos); **Guadalajara** (5hr., 14 per day, 192 pesos); **Ciudad Juárez** (26hr., 13 per day, 642 pesos); **Durango** (6hr., 11 per day, 150 pesos); **Matamoros** (11hr., 7 per day, 386 pesos); **Aguascalientes** (3hr., 3 per day, 66 pesos); and most major Mexican cities. Transportes del Norte (☎922 00 42), Rojos de los Altos (☎922 06 84), Chihuahuenses (☎922 00 42), and Estrella Blanca (☎922 06 84) also service the area.

☷ PRACTICAL INFORMATION

Tourist Office: Hidalgo 403, on the 2nd fl. Helpful staff and useful maps and brochures, many in both Spanish and English. Open daily 8am-8pm. *TIPS,* a Spanish-language weekly, listing cultural events and tourist services, is available during high season at hotels and newsstands.

Currency Exchange: Banca Promex, González Ortega 122 (☎922 93 69 or 922 56 54), has good rates and a 24hr. **ATM.** Open M-F 8:30am-5:30pm, Sa 10am-2pm. The first blocks of González Ortega and Hidalgo away from Juárez are inundated with banks.

Car Rental: Autos Ultimo Modelo, Alcatraces 147 (☎/fax 924 55 09); **Avis,** López Mateos 615 (☎922 30 03); **Alamos** (☎01 800 849 80 01) has an airport location (☎01 57 86 92 14). At **Mazzocco,** Fátima 115 Sierra de Alicia (☎/fax 922 77 02), you can rent anything from a car to a bus. **Budget,** López Mateos 104 (☎922 94 58) rents cars from 450 pesos. Minimum age 25.

Luggage Storage: At the bus station. 1.5 pesos per hr. Open 24hr.

Laundry: Lavamatic Plus, Rosadela 18 at Mexico (☎923 47 06). 40 pesos per load.

Market: Daily along Arroyo de la Plata behind the small bus station, near the Howard Johnson Hotel.

Emergency: ☎060.

Police: Héroes de Chapultepec 1000 (☎922 01 80, 922 05 07, or 922 43 79). No English spoken.

Red Cross: Calzada de la Cruz Roja 100 (☎922 30 05 or 922 33 23), off Héroes de Chapultepec, near the exit to Fresnillo. Some English spoken. Open 24hr.

Pharmacy: Farmacia La Perla de Zacatecas, Hidalgo 131. Open daily 9am-11pm. **Farmacia Isstezac,** Callejón de las Campañas 103 (☎924 37 25, ext. 19), on the right side of the cathedral. Open 24hr. **Farmacia Guadalajara,** across the street from the Howard Johnson next to KFC, on López Mateos, is the most visible pharmacy. Open daily 8am-midnight.

Hospital: Hospital General, García Salinas 707 (☎923 30 04, 923 30 05, or 923 30 06). Open 24hr. **Dr. José Cruz de la Torre González** (☎924 07 03) speaks English.

Fax: Telecomm (☎922 00 60; fax 922 17 96), on Hidalgo at Juárez. Open M-F 8:30am-7pm, Sa-Su 9am-noon.

Internet Access: The **public library,** at the end of Juárez across from Jardín Independencia, provides free service (30min. limit if someone's waiting). Open daily 9am-9pm. If you need more time, try **Computadoras and Accesorias de Zacatecas,** López Velarde 428. 20 pesos per hr. Open M-Sa 9am-2pm and 4-8pm.

Post Office: Allende 111 (☎922 01 96), off Hidalgo. Open M-F 8am-7pm, Sa 9am-1pm.

Postal Code: 98000.

▙ ACCOMMODATIONS

Budget hotels are scarce downtown, and the few cheap hotels may be full on weekends, so it's a good idea to make reservations. Hotels in convenient downtown locations overcompensate for their cheap prices with frequent traffic noise.

Zamora de Zacatecas, Plazuela de Zamora 303 (☎922 12 00), near the Jardín Independencia opposite Juárez. Zamora boasts a central location and unbeatable prices for the area. Clean rooms in bright colors. Singles 70 pesos; doubles 80 pesos.

Hotel María Conchita, López Mateos 401 (☎922 14 94 or 922 14 96), 3 blocks south of the Jardín Independencia. Distinguished architecture with private bathrooms. Rooms have phones and tiny TVs. New 4th and 5th floor rooms have nicer furniture and modern baths. Singles 150 pesos; doubles 138-195 pesos; triples 172 pesos; quads 207-345 pesos.

Hotel del Parque, González Ortega 302 (☎922 04 79), near the aqueduct. Appropriately named—Parque Enrique Estrada is practically the hotel's backyard. Rooms are a bit dark, although the TVs brighten things up. Singles 105 pesos; doubles 120 pesos; triples 150 pesos; quads 170 pesos.

Hotel Gami, López Mateos 309 (☎922 08 05), has simple rooms with desks, TVs, and decent tiles baths, but no fan or A/C. Singles 140 pesos; doubles 250 pesos.

Hotel Colón, López Velarde 508 (☎922 89 25), a good place to crash if everything else is full. Rooms have TV, phone, and bath. If you ask for a room with no TV, you may get a lower price. Singles 197-295 pesos; doubles 224-317 pesos; triples 255-356 pesos; quads 294-403 pesos. 20% discount with ISIC.

CREA Hostel (☎922 02 23, ext. 7), in the Parque La Encantada, southwest of the city. Take the Ruta 8 bus on González Ortega (2 pesos) from Jardín Independencia or the bus station; and get off at the sign for La Encantada (10min.). Walk down Calle 5 Señores for about 15min., turn left on Calle Ancha, and walk uphill until the youth camp. Veer right around the red building; the white hostel is behind the pool to the left. Although near the bus station, it is well removed and not the best option unless you absolutely must have the cheapest room in town. Small, sterile quads and single-sex floors with clean communal bathrooms 50 pesos.

◖ FOOD

Zacatecas has some good deals that won't break the bank. Fantastic restaurants are tucked in between shops along **Hidalgo** near the cathedral. Get that sugar rush with a chunk of *dulce con leche, camote* (a fruit), *coco* (coconut), or *batata* (sweet potato) peddled by vendors throughout the *centro* (5 pesos).

El Pueblito, Hidalgo 403 (☎924 38 18), near Gorditas Doña Julia. Specializing in Zacatecan food in a renovated *hacienda*. Try the *reliquia Zacatecana* (45 pesos). Classy, but a bit pricey. Open daily 1-11pm.

Gorditas Doña Julia, Hidalgo 409 (☎923 79 55), 1 block from the cathedral. Locals devour delicious *gorditas* (5-6 pesos) of all kinds in its colorful interior. If you can't find a table at the restaurant, ask for your *gorditas para llevar* (to go). Open daily 8am-9pm.

Mesón La Mina, Juárez 15 (☎922 27 73), just off the Jardín Independencia. This spacious local favorite features solid Mexican fare like *enchiladas verdes* (38 pesos) and *comida corrida* (42 pesos). Full breakfast menu. Open daily 8am-11pm.

La Terraza (☎922 32 70), in the shopping mall next to the cathedral. A lovely outdoor cafe built on a 2nd floor balcony featuring coffee, ice cream, and fountain drinks. Grab a beer (12-16 pesos) and a burger (15-19 pesos). Open daily 11am-9pm.

◉ SIGHTS

There are enough churches, museums, and lookout points in Zacatecas to keep sightseers busy despite their sore feet. Fortunately for the tender-footed, most sights in the city are grouped in clusters, either near the cathedral or near the mountain housing the mine.

■ **CATHEDRAL.** The pride of Zacatecas, the pink sandstone cathedral, officially called **Nuestra Señora de Asunción,** was begun in 1729, completed in 1752, and consecrated as a cathedral 1862. The magnificent building is undoubtedly one of the most beautiful cathedrals in all of the Americas. The intricate three-story facade is perhaps the best example of the Mexican Baroque and depicts, among a myriad of figures, Christ blessing the Apostles and images of the Eucharist. The northern facade bears a representation of Christ on the cross, and the European Baroque

THE MICHELADA The favorite beer of Zacatecanas is undoubtedly world-famous Corona, *"La cerveza mas fina,"* and the Michelada is one of the most popular ways to enjoy the great brew. This interesting drink is made with 2oz. of tequila (Casa Noble Crystal), the juice of two lemons, a quarter teaspoon of *sal de gusano* (from Oaxaca, toasted agave worms, chili, and salt), and Corona poured over ice. The taste is similar to *tamarindo* (a popular component of Mexican candies) and packs quite a punch, both in terms of the alcohol and the taste. The Michelada may be more of an acquired taste, but locals swear it's the best way to enjoy your Corona.

southern facade pays homage to Nuestra Señora de las Zacatecas. The interior of the cathedral, in contrast to its lavish exterior, is surprisingly plain, although legend has it that it was once as splendid as the outside. The cathedral remains a place of worship, with masses taking place on the weekends. *(Four blocks northeast of Juárez, on Hidalgo. Open daily 7am-1pm and 3-9pm.)*

PALACIO DE GOBIERNO. Next door, the Palacio de Gobierno was built in 1727 as the residence of Joseph de Rivera Bernández, a count. The building distinguishes itself with the mural that surrounds its interior stairwell. Painted in 1970 by Antonio Rodríguez, the work traces the history of Zacatecas from the Pre-Hispanic era until the present. *(Next to the cathedral. Open M-F 9am-8pm.)*

■**MUSEO DE PEDRO CORONEL.** Housed in the former Colegio de San Luis Gonzaga, a Jesuit college established in 1616, the museum is now home to the tomb, sculptures, and paintings of the Zacatecan artist Pedro Coronel. In addition, it has one of the best modern art collections in Latin America, with works by such varied artists as Picasso, Braque, Chagall, Miró, Goya, and Hogarth. *(On the west side of the Plaza, next to the cathedral. ☎922 80 21. Open F-W 10am-5pm. 15 pesos, students and seniors 7.5 pesos, children free.)*

TEMPLO DE SANTO DOMINGO. Built by the Jesuits in 1746, the Temple contains nine impressive Baroque wooden altars and a rare 18th-century German pipe organ. *(Across Hidalgo and up the steep Callejón de Veyna. Open daily 7am-1pm and 5-8pm. Masses held frequently Sa-Su.)*

MUSEO RAFAEL CORONEL. This museum is housed in the dramatic **Ex-Convento de San Francisco,** built by Franciscans in the 17th century and then occupied by the Jesuits until the late 18th century. The building is worth a close look, as is the museum inside, which showcases an impressive collection of masks, figurines, pottery, and puppets donated by Rafael Coronel, brother of Pedro. *(To reach the museum from the cathedral, follow Hidalgo, bearing left at the fountain at the first fork, and right at the second. Open Tu-Th 10am-5pm. 15 pesos, students and seniors 7.5 pesos, children free).*

MINA DE EDÉN. One of the region's most productive silver mines, Mina de Edén was first opened up for mining in 1583. The "Mine of Eden," named to mock the miserable working conditions of its workers, was one of the region's most productive silver mines, but was closed in the 1960s when continual flooding made mineral extraction futile. Today, tour groups trek via *teleférico* (cable cars) and cross rope bridges 500m into the earth's belly to learn more about the mine's haunting myths. *(From where the teleférico drops you, the entrance to the mountain is 100m to the right. Tours begin from this entrance. Otherwise, follow Juárez northwest along the Alameda. Continue along Torreón until it ends, and then turn right and walk one block, veering to the left. From there, a mini-locomotive whisks tourists (tours 1hr. in Spanish) to the mine. ☎922 30 02. Open daily 10am-6pm. 20 pesos, children 10 pesos.)*

ON CERRO DE LA BUFA. Named for its resemblance to a Spanish wineskin, and surrounded by both myth and history, the *cerro* peers down on Zacatecas from the city's highest crag. The **Museo de la Toma de Zacatecas,** adjacent to the Cerro, was built to commemorate Pancho Villa's decisive victory over federal troops in the summer of 1914. The museum displays an array of revolutionary memorabilia, including photographs, displays, a cannon, and small arms. *(☎922 80 66. Open*

Tu-Su 10am-4pm. 10 pesos.) On one side of the museum lies the 18th-century **Capilla del Patrocinio,** whose graceful facade and cloistered courtyards are carved from deep red stone. Nearby shops sell arts, crafts, and loads of geodes. A short, but steep walk up the hill leads to the Moorish **Mausoleo de los Hombres Ilustres de Zacatecas** (Tomb of the Famous Men of Zacatecas), worth the hike if only for the view of the city. There's yet another vista behind the museum, from the castle where the **Meteorological Observatory** is housed. *(The most appealing way to make the trip, if you aren't claustrophobic or afraid of heights, is by the teleférico that runs between the peak of El Grillo and La Bufa (every 10min. 10am-6pm, 20 pesos).* ☎ *922 01 70. To get to the teleférico stop, follow García Rojas northwest up a steep incline to its end. Or, take the lengthy and convoluted Ruta 7 bus from González Ortega. The teleférico doesn't run in rain or high winds.)*

PARQUE ENRIQUE ESTRADA. Southeast of the downtown area, 39 pink stone arches mark the end of Zacatecas's famous colonial aqueduct, **El Cubo.** Beside the aqueduct, **Parque Enrique Estrada** has a little bit of everything—beautiful flowers and green grass alongside barbed wire and numerous dead tree trunks. The park borders the former governor's mansion, now the **Museo de Francisco Goitia,** Enrique Estrada 101. The museum displays regional historical artifacts and gives a good account of Mexican history. *(☎ 922 02 11. Open Tu-Su 10am-5pm. 15 pesos.)*

🎵 ENTERTAINMENT

Zacatecas has several cool nighttime hot-spots. But, if you're feeling a bit more mellow, the **Nova Cinema,** Constituyentes 300 (☎ 922 54 04), and the **Salsa 2000,** on López Mateos opposite the Howard Johnson, reel through the latest in Mexican and American films. Or take advantage of the free performances by the **Banda del Estado** in the Plazuela Goitia, next to the cathedral (Th 6pm, Sa 7pm). As always, be cautious when walking alone at night; streets are lit, but practically deserted.

■ **El Malacate** (☎ 912 13 02), 600m in from the side entrance of the Mina de Edén. You've never experienced a bass beat until you hear it reverberating off the solid stone walls of this former mine shaft. Buy your tickets at the entrance to the shaft, take the train to the dance floor, and enjoy the mellow, slow music and drinks brought to you by waiters in hard hats. Beer 18 pesos, mixed drinks 30 pesos. Cover 50 pesos. Open Th-Su 9pm-2:30am.

El Claustro, Calle Aguascalientes 10 (☎ 044 49 27 05 55 or 044 49 27 02 77), is a two-story converted mansion built for partying. A pool table and foosball are located upstairs if you need a break from dancing. Open F-Sa 9pm-3am.

Cactus, Hidalgo 111 (☎ 922 05 09), at the Juárez intersection. The well-decorated interior is suitable for lounging with a beer (12 pesos), dancing on the faux-cathedral dance floor, or going upstairs to shoot some pool. Happy Hour is 2 for 1 (8 to 10pm). Cover F-Sa 30 pesos. Open M-Sa 9pm-3am.

🎊 FESTIVALS

The yearly cultural highlight is **Zacatecas en la Cultura,** a festival during *Semana Santa,* in which concerts and artistic activities are held in the elegant Teatro Calderón, on Hidalgo near the cathedral, and throughout the city. From September 8-22, the city celebrates the **Feria Nacional de Zacatecas** with musical and theatrical events, bullfights, agricultural and crafts shows, and sporting events.

🔁 DAYTRIPS FROM ZACATECAS

GUADALUPE

Catch a Transportes Guadalupe bus from the bus station or the smaller bus station behind the Howard Johnson on López Mateos (30 min., 3 pesos). It's difficult to discern when Zacatecas ends and Guadalupe begins, so be sure to tell the bus driver you want to get off in Guadalupe's centro. From the bus station in Guadalupe, walk a short distance to your left along Mateos and turn right on Constitución at the monument in the center of the street. The cathedral is a couple of blocks in front of you. Catch a return bus to Zacatecas from the same bus station. (Open daily 10am-4pm. 25 pesos.)

Only 5km away from Zacatecas, the tiny village of Gudalupe is a world apart form the bustling capital. The village, named after the town church, was founded in 1707 as a training site for Franciscan missionaries. The **Ex-Convento de Guadalupe,** located on the main plaza, is known not only for having produced over 3000 missionaries, but also for its famous statue of the **Virgin of Guadalupe,** located above the altar. Next to the cathedral is the **Museo de Guadalupe,** which contains paintings depicting scenes from the life of St. Francis, as well as nearly every known incident in the life of Christ. You can walk away with your very own souvenir poster of *La Virgen del Apocalisis* (Virgin of the Apocalypse) for 65 pesos. Those yearning for some medieval misadventure can walk into the museum courtyard, around to the other side of the stone block, and down the steps into the dank, dark cistern.

JEREZ

Camiones de los Altos buses go to Juárez (1hr., every 30min. 5:15am-10pm, 25 pesos). To get to the centro from the Jerez bus station, turn right on the street directly ahead. It's a good 25-minute walk, so consider taking a cab or a bus (if you can find one).

About an hour's bus ride from Zacatecas lies the rapidly expanding colonial town of Jerez (pop. 12,500). All of the sights are clustered together to the left of the main plaza as you come from the bus station, but, if need be, you can find tourist information at the Edificio de la Torre across from the Iglesia Parroquia. The **Casa-Museo Ramon López Velarde** celebrates the life of the native poet. The **Santuario de Soledad** is a beautiful church dating from the mid-19th century. Also visit the Edificio de la Torre, built by architect Dámaso Muñetón in 1896, the Iglesia Parroquia, and the Teatro Hinojosa, a replica of New York City's Lincoln Center, built in 1878.

LA QUEMADA

Take a Camiones de los Altos bus from the main bus station in Zacatecas (or from a smaller station on López Mateos near the Howard Johnson) to La Quemada (30min., every 30min. 6am-10pm, 20 pesos). Be sure to specify that you want to get off at the ruins, not the city itself. The road to the ruins is on the left of the main route, right after the white, yellow, and blue restaurant with the Corona sign. Walk about 3km along this road to reach the entrance. Site open daily 10am-5pm. 25 pesos. Museum open daily 10am-4pm. 7 pesos. Free Su. To get to Jerez from here, walk back to the main route and hop on a bus heading back to Zacatecas. You'll have to get off in Malpaso and change buses to get to Jerez. Ask the bus driver where to get off to wait for the Jerez bus.

Nearby lie the ruins of La Quemada. The origins and inhabitants of this northernmost Mesoamerican city remain shrouded in mystery. Some postulate that it was the site of the legendary Aztec city Chicomóstoc, Tenotchtitlán precursor and the capital of the region north of the Río San Antonio. Said to have been occupied from about AD 500 to 900, La Quemada has been well-preserved and offers a beautiful view of the surrounding area. There's a museum at the beginning of the site that gives visitors the low-down on its history. The site, with its unique rotund ruins, can be thoroughly viewed in about an hour. If you're brave enough, venture off the trail a bit—it's the only way to reach the part of the ruins on the second hill, which has no official trail.

AGUASCALIENTES

AGUASCALIENTES ☎ 4

The city of Aguascalientes (pop. 520,000), named for the hot springs that once filled the region, was a town that history has passed by. Run your finger down the index of any Mexican history textbook and you'll likely find just one uninspiring entry, which probably would read something like, "The Convention of Aguascalientes was held in Aguascalientes in 1914." Today, Aguascalientes is a city of modern buildings and noisy streets, dotted with Blockbuster Videos, liquor stores, and pizzerias. The city has rallied around what little history it has; to its credit, it has accomplished several feats—its central square, the Plaza de la Patria, is marvelous. Residents claim that the city's annual fair, the *Feria de San Marcos,* it is the biggest, best, and wildest festival in all of Mexico. A large city with small-town ambiance, Aguascalientes is a good place to stay for a day or two.

NORTHEAST MEXICO

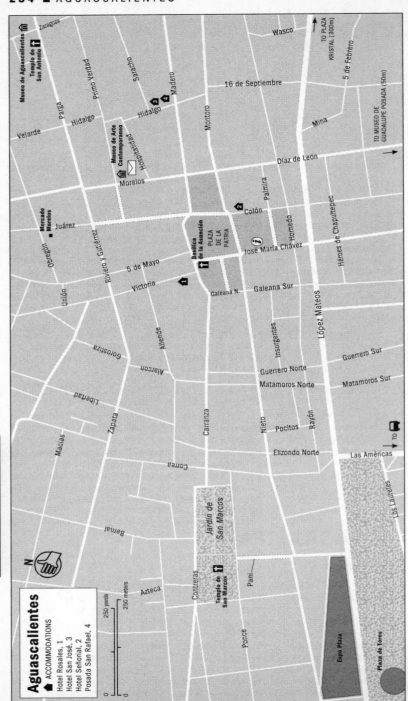

Aguascalientes

▲ ACCOMMODATIONS

Hotel Rosales, 1
Hotel San José, 3
Hotel Señorial, 2
Posada San Rafael, 4

250 yards
250 meters

N

Zaragoza
Museo de Aguascalientes
Templo de San Antonio
Primo Verdad
Saracho
Madero
Wasco
TO PLAZA KRISTAL (300m)
5 de Febrero
16 de Septiembre
Paga
Hidalgo
Hidalgo
Montoro
Mina
Velarde
Museo de Arte Contemporaneo
Hospitalidad
Díaz de León
TO MUSEO DE GUADALUPE POSADA (50m)
Morelos
Palmira
Mercado Morelos
Juárez
Colón
Hornedo
Obregón
Rivero y Gutiérrez
Basílica de la Asunción
PLAZA DE LA PATRIA
José María Chávez
Héroes de Chapultepec
5 de Mayo
Victoria
Galeana N.
Galeana Sur
Unión
López Mateos
Gorostiza
Allende
Insurgentes
Guerrero Sur
Alarcón
Guerrero Norte
Matamoros Norte
Matamoros Sur
Libertad
Carranza
Nieto
Pocitos
Rayón
Zapata
Elizondo Norte
Las Américas
Macías
Correa
TO
Los Laureles
Bernal
Jardín de San Marcos
Azteca
Contreras
Templo de San Marcos
Pani
Ponce
Expo Plaza
Plaza de Toros

⌐ TRANSPORTATION

Buses: The bus station is on Convención Sur and Av. 5a, a few blocks west of José Marí Chávez. Green and white city buses with numbers in the 20s or 30s (3 pesos) run from outside the bus station to the Mercado Morelos, two blocks north of the Plaza de la Patria, the center of town. To get back to the station, take a "Central Camionera" bus or a taxi (20 pesos). Chihuahenses (☎918 27 58) goes to: **Chihuahua** (10hr., 6 per day, 508 pesos); **Ciudad Juárez** (15hr., 6 per day, 703 pesos); **Durango** (7hr., 6 per day, 214 pesos); **Torreón** (6hr., 5 per day, 273 pesos); **Zacatecas** (2½hr., 4 per day, 66 pesos), and other major cities. Futura goes to: **Acapulco** (11hr., several per day, 455 pesos), **Guadalajara** (3hr., every hr. 6am-10pm, 135 pesos); **Mexico City** (6hr., every hr. 6am-10pm, 287 pesos); and other major cities. Ómnibus de México's Mercedes-Benz buses go to **Ciudad Juárez** (15hr., 7 per day, 703 pesos); **Durango** (6hr., 7 per day, 214 pesos); **Guadalajara** (3hr., 8 per day, 135 pesos); and **Mexico City** (6hr., 10 per day, 287 pesos); as well as most major cities. Primera Plus (☎918 26 71), which provides lunch on longer trips, and ETN (☎918 24 29) also go to major cities.

◼◼ ⁊ ORIENTATION AND PRACTICAL INFORMATION

Aguascalientes is 168km west of San Luis Potosí, 128km south of Zacatecas, and 252km northeast of Guadalajara. **Circunvalación** encircles the city, while **López Mateos** cuts through town east to west. From the **Plaza de la Patria,** the center of town, most sights are within walking distance on either **Montoro,** which runs east from the southeast corner of the plaza, or **Carranza,** which begins to the west of the plaza behind the *basílica*. The city takes its *siestas* quite seriously; many sights and businesses close from 2 to 4pm.

Tourist Office: (☎915 11 55 or 916 03 47), off the Plaza de la Patria, in the Palacio de Gobierno. First door on the right on the 1st fl. Decent maps and a plethora of brochures (some in English). Open M-F 8am-7:30pm, Sa-Su 9am-6pm.

Currency Exchange: Moneytron, Montoro 120 (☎915 79 79), 1 block from the *zócalo,* has excellent rates and charges no commission. You can also pawn precious metals. Open M-F 9am-5pm. **Bancomer,** 5 de Mayo 120 (☎915 51 15), 1 block from the plaza, also offers good rates. Open M-F 8:30am-4pm, Sa 10am-1pm.

Emergency: ☎060.

Police: (☎914 20 50), at the corner of Libertad and Gómez Orozco.

Pharmacy: Farmacia Sánchez, Madero 213 (☎915 35 50), 1 block from the plaza. Open 24hr.

Hospital: Hospital Hidalgo, Galeana 465 (☎916 57 77 or 917 29 83). Open 24hr.

Fax: Telecomm (☎916 14 27), Galeana at Nieto. Open M-F 8am-7pm, Sa 9am-1pm, Su 9am-noon. Another office in the bus station. Open M-F 8am-7:30pm, Sa 9am-noon.

Telephones: LADATELs are along the plaza and throughout town; there is a **caseta** (with a good cigar selection) at the Tabaquería Plaza, Colón 102, on the corner of the plaza. Open daily 9am-9pm.

Internet Access: Cybercafé 2000, Allende 105 Internal #1 (☎916 94 15). 25 pesos per hr., students 20 pesos per hr. Open M-Sa 10am-8pm.

Post Office: Hospitalidad 108 (☎915 21 18). Open M-F 8am-3pm, Sa 9am-1pm.

Postal Code: 20000.

▟ ACCOMMODATIONS

Budget accommodations in Aguascalientes can satisfy even the most finicky of travelers, but you have to know where to look. Everything is tucked away on side streets around the plaza. As a general rule, the *centro* is much nicer than the area near the bus station; the hotels are better and the prices are about the same. During the **Feria de San Marcos** (mid-Apr.-early May), reservations are a must.

Hotel Señorial, Colón 104 (☎915 16 30 or 915 14 73), at the corner of Montoro, on the Plaza de la Patria; the location couldn't be better. Nice rooms with cable TV, phones, and a supply of purified water. Singles 140 pesos; doubles 180 pesos; triples 225 pesos; quads 270 pesos.

Posada San Rafael, Hidalgo 205 (☎915 77 61), at Madero, 3 blocks from the plaza. Ceiling fans, cable TV, free parking, and complimentary coffee or tea in the morning. Singles 125 pesos; doubles 140 pesos; triples 160 pesos; quads 200 pesos.

Hotel San José, Hidalgo 207 (☎915 51 30 or 915 14 31), next to Posada San Rafael. Somewhat institutional rooms with TVs, phones, and ceiling fans. Hot water is available in the blue-tiled bathrooms from 6-10am and 7-10:30pm. Ask about the laundry service. Singles 130 pesos; doubles 150 pesos; triples 170 pesos; quads 210 pesos.

Hotel Rosales, Victoria 104 (☎915 21 65), off Madero, right across from the *basílica* and Plaza Patria. Simple, clean rooms, phones, TV, and a nice courtyard, maintained by a nice old couple. Singles 70 pesos; doubles 100 pesos; triples 120 pesos.

🍴 FOOD

You don't have to make bank to get your grub on in Aguas. Check out the San Marcos Plaza, the shopping area north of the Plaza de la Patria, and Madero.

El Zodiaco, Galeana Sur 113 (☎915 31 81). The eye-opening decor combines an open kitchen, orange chairs, formica tables, live canaries, and a painted shrine to the Virgin. Order a sandwich (15 pesos) or a hamburger (15 pesos) from among the many tasty items in this popular local hangout. Open daily 8:30am-10pm.

Gorditas Victoria, Victoria 108 (☎91 8 17 92), next to the Hotel Rosales. The ever-popular restaurant serves up every kind of *gordita* (10.5 pesos) imaginable. Grab your food *para llevar* (to go) and enjoy it in the plaza. Open daily 9am-9pm.

Sanfer Restaurant, Victoria 204 (☎915 45 88). A cozy little place with unbeatable prices. Breakfasts (10-20 pesos), chicken tacos (24 pesos), and *milanesas* (33 pesos). Open daily 8:30am-9:30pm.

La Fogata, Moctezuma 111, across the street from the cathedral, in the Plaza de la Patria. Those with a late-night craving for red meat should make tracks to La Fogata. Savor the mammoth homemade tortillas—the preferred method (as opposed to forks) for eating your steak (28 pesos). Eclectic decor, with a copy of Da Vinci's *Last Supper* hanging next to a shot of a '69 Corvette. Open daily 5:30pm-2am.

👁 SIGHTS

Aguascalientes has a multitude of important historical and cultural landmarks within easy reach of the central district.

PLAZA DE LA PATRIA. The heart and soul of Aguascalientes is the recently remodeled plaza, which is shaded by trees and made inviting by numerous benches. To the north, the Plaza is bordered by the **Palacio de Gobierno,** constructed in the 1660s as a residence for the Marqués de Guadalupe. The interior of the Palacio houses several murals by Oswaldo Barra, a Chilean artist whose mentor was the famed Diego Rivera. To the south of the Plaza is the **Teatro Morelos,** site of the 1914 Convention of Aguascalientes, in which rival factions led by Zapata, Carranza, and Villa grappled over the course of the Mexican Revolution.

BASÍLICA DE LA ASUNCIÓN DE LAS AGUASCALIENTES. The soft greys and rose-colored Solomonic Baroque facade of the 18th-century *basílica* make it the city's most remarkable structure and a center of daily activity. Look for the sculptures of church patrons San Gregorio, San Jerónimo, and San Agustín. The cathedral's interior, restored in the 18th and 19th centuries, is graced with high ceilings, gold trimmings, and ornate icons, along with 17th- and 18th-century paintings by José de Alcíbar, Andrés López, and Miguel Cabrera. *(In the center of the Plaza de la Patria. Open daily approx. 7am-2pm and 4-9pm.)*

MUSEO JOSÉ GUADALUPE POSADA. The museum displays morbidly witty turn-of-the-century political cartoons drawn by Posada, an ardent critic of the Porfiriato who perhaps inspired the scathing social commentary of later Mexican muralists such as Diego Rivera and José Clemente Orozco. The collection includes 220 of his original works and images, the most famous of which is that of La Catrina, a society lady-*calavera* (skull) wearing an outlandish hat. Rivera used her figure in *Sueño de Una Tarde Dominical en la Alameda*, now on display in Mexico City (see **Mexico City: Sights,** p. 106). The museum also displays 100 works by Posada's mentor, Manuel Manilla, and has rotating exhibits of contemporary art. *(On León, next to the Templo del Encino, four blocks south of López Mateos. ☎915 45 56. Open Tu-Su 11am-6pm. 5 pesos, students 2.5 pesos, children free. Free Su.)*

TEMPLO DE SAN ANTONIO. Construction of the church began in 1895 and was completed in 1908 under self-taught architect José Refugio Reyes. The mix of patterns on the interior murals, frescoes, oil paintings, and delicate stained-glass windows matches the eclectic exterior, which is a blend of many styles, including Baroque, Classical, and Oriental. *(On Pedro Parga and Zaragoza. From the plaza, walk 3 blocks down Madero, then 3 blocks left on Zaragoza. ☎915 28 98. Open M-Sa 6:30-10am, 11:30am-12:30pm, and 6-9pm, Su 6:30am-noon and 5:30-9pm.)*

INSTITUTO CULTURAL DE AGUASCALIENTES. Popularly known as the **Casa de la Cultura,** the institute hosts temporary sculpture, painting, and photography exhibits in a beautiful 17th-century *hacienda*. Kiosks in the courtyard are cluttered with listings of cultural events; you can also check the Casa's monthly bulletin. *(Carranza 101 at Galeana. ☎915 34 43 or 916 62 70 for monthly events. Open M-F 10am-2pm and 5-9pm, Sa-Su 10am-2pm and 5-8pm. Free.)*

CENTRO CULTURAL LOS ARQUITOS. Serving as a public bathroom from 1821 until 1973, the building became a beautiful cultural center in 1994 after a magnificent restoration process. It now houses a bookshop, a video room that shows children's movies (F 5pm), and a small museum. *(On the Alameda at Héroes de Nacozari. ☎917 00 23. Open M-F 9am-1pm and 3-8pm, Sa 9am-1pm and 3-6pm, Su 9am-1pm.)*

MUSEO DE AGUASCALIENTES. Built in the 1900s, this museum was designed by José Refugio Reyes, who also designed the Temple de San Antonio. The bright orange museum showcases local and national art, highlighting the works of Aguascalientes native Saturnino Herrán. A strange collection of classical busts is tucked away in a corner of the building. *(On Parga and Zaragoza, across from Templo de San Antonio. Open Tu-Su 11am-6pm. 5 pesos, students and seniors 2.5 pesos; Su free.)*

JARDÍN DE SAN MARCOS. The area around the *jardín* was originally an Indian pueblo, but around 1600, *indígenas* erected the Templo Evangelista San Marcos on the site. The small church still has services today and is the center of a crowded pedestrian thoroughfare popular with Mexican families in the evenings. The adjacent arcade is lined with bars and vendors and remains active late into the night. During the waning weeks of April, the *jardín* plays host to the **Feria de San Marcos.** *(The jardín is a 5- to 10-minute walk on Carranza from the Plaza de la Patria. Church open daily 7am-2pm and 4-9pm.)*

OTHER SIGHTS. Clustering around the *centro* are other museums worth a look. The **Museo de Arte Contemporaneo,** at the corner of Morelos and Verdad, houses a collection of contemporary art. *(☎916 79 53. Open Tu-Su 10am-6pm. 5 pesos, students and teachers 2.5 pesos.)* The **Museo Regional de Historia,** Carranza 118, occupies yet another building designed by Refugio Reyes. The collection explores the area's history, from Pre-Hispanic to Revolutionary. *(Usually open daily 10am-2pm and 5-10:30pm.)*

🎵 ENTERTAINMENT

Aguascalientes is not a beacon of wild nightlife, but the intrepid partier can find a good time. By city ordinance, *discotecas* in Aguascalientes are not allowed in the *centro histórico* around the Plaza de la Patria and can only open their doors Thursday to Saturday. Bars, on the other hand, are open every night of the week; **Pani,** between Ponce and Nieto, draws tourists and locals alike. Buses stop running around 10pm, making taxis the best way to get around.

San Luis Potosí

ACCOMMODATIONS	FOOD AND DRINK	BARS AND CLUBS	SERVICES
Hotel Plaza, 7	"Chalita" Supermarket, 3	El Mito, 5	Farmacia Mexicana, 8
Hotel Filher, 10	Restaurant Cafeteria, 6	La María, 12	
Hotel Alameda, 4	Tokio, 11	Delirio Azul, 13	
Hotel Progreso, 9	Yu Ne Nisa, 1	La Terapia, 2	

Those not into the club scene may be able to find mellower diversions. Be part of Mexican *beisbol* by cheering on the hometown **Rieleros** (www.rieleros.com.mx). To get to the stadium, catch a #12, 24, or 25 bus heading east on López Mateos. Snag a bleacher seat in the sun (9 pesos) and compete with local kids in chasing down home run balls. (Games Apr.-Sept.)

Disco El Cabús (☎ 913 04 32), Zacatecas at Colosia in the Hotel Las Trojes. Shake your caboose amid the usual flashing lights and bass-heavy dance beats. Don't wear shorts, though—you may be apprehended by the fashion police. Cover Th-F 40 pesos, Sa 50 pesos. Open Th-Sa 9pm-3am.

Jubilee, Laureles 602-101 (☎ 917 05 07 or 918 04 94). The place to go if you value drinking over dancing. Drinks are about half as much as at other *discotecas,* and the lounging areas are more happening than the dance floor. Live music Th-Sa until 3am. Cover 30 pesos for men, women free. W no cover.

Merendero San Marcos, Arturo Pani 144. This bar and grill is one of the most happening places in town. Beer (16 pesos), tequila (30 pesos), and heart-felt live *mariachi* music are served to a mix of tourists and locals. Open daily 1pm-2am.

❀ FESTIVALS

During the ◧**Feria de San Marcos** (mid-Apr. to early May), one of Mexico's largest celebrations, everything from cockfights to milking contests takes place in the Jardín de San Marcos. To reach the Expo Plaza, filled with shops and restaurants, walk two blocks to the left down the pedestrian route as you face the *templo* in the *jardín*. The expansive plaza has everything: a 10-screen movie theater, upscale dining and accommodations, great shopping, cheap snacks, and a rose garden. The festival of the patron saint of Aguascalientes, **La Romería de la Asunción** (Aug. 1-15), takes place with dances, processions, and fireworks. The **Festival de las Calaveras** (last week in October and the first week in November) is another occasion for the city to cut loose and celebrate.

NORTHEAST MEXICO

SAN LUIS POTOSÍ

SAN LUIS POTOSÍ ☎4

With spacious plazas, plenty of pedestrian walkways, and cathedrals dotting the landscape like overgrown trees, San Luis Potosí (pop. 830,000) is a crash course in good urban planning. Founded in 1592, after Franciscan missionaries began to convert local Guachichil and Tlaxcaltec tribes and discovered silver and gold, San Luis Potosí has twice served as the capital of Mexico. The tranquility of the city belies a tumultuous history—it was here in 1910 that Francisco Madero was incarcerated and wrote his dramatic *"Plan de San Luis Potosí,"* proclaiming the beginning of the Revolutionary War. Today, the residents of San Luis set the city apart with their eager and friendly embrace of the few tourists who arrive. As lanterns glow in the cathedrals and fountains at dusk, bands, magicians, and soap-bubble blowers gather in the town plazas to entertain assembled crowds of young and old. On a warm evening, it's hard to ignore the feeling that San Luis Potosí is the quiet capital of some magical world.

▐ TRANSPORTATION

San Luis Potosí is at the center of a triangle formed by Mexico's three largest cities—Monterrey, Guadalajara, and Mexico City. Five main routes (**Rtes. 57, 85, 70, 49,** and **80**) snake their way into the city. Once in the city, the streets have a nasty habit of changing names as they pass through the main plazas, so keep that in mind (and a map in hand).

Airport: (☎822 00 95) 25min. north of the city. Tickets can be purchased at **2001 Viajes**, Obregón 604 (☎812 29 53). Open M-F 9am-2pm and 4-8pm, Sa 9:30am-2pm. **Aerocalifornia** (☎811 80 50) has flights to Mexico City beginning at 480 pesos. **Aero-Literal** (☎818 73 71) has flights to Monterrey starting at 1450 pesos. **Mexicana** (☎813 33 99) flies to various destinations.

Buses: To get downtown from the **Central de Transportes Terrestres,** catch an "Alameda" or "Centro" bus (5:30am-10:30pm, 2 pesos) and hop off at Parque Alameda, the first big stretch of green. Continue walking in the direction the bus was going, up Othón, past the Plaza del Carmen, until the city's center, the Plaza de Armas (also called Jardín Hidalgo). A taxi costs 20 pesos. When going to the *Central* from the *centro*, ask the driver for the *Central nueva* in order not to confuse it with the old *Central*, which has been shut down. The driver will let you off at the back side of the station. Del Norte (☎816 55 43) goes to **Chihuahua** (14hr., 10 per day, 372 pesos). Estrella Blanca (☎816 54 77) sends buses to: **Aguascalientes** (3hr., 7 per day, 102 pesos); **Monterrey** (7hr., every hr., 254 pesos); **Ciudad Valles** (4 hr., 10 per day, 158 pesos); **Guadalajara** (6 hr., 5 per day, 190 pesos); and **Zacatecas** (3hr., every hr., 72 pesos). Omnibus de México (☎816 81 61) goes to: **Mexico City** (6 hr., 9 per day 12:45am-10:30am, 221 pesos); **Reynosa** (9hr., 2pm and 8pm, 343 pesos); **Saltillo** (5hr., 2 per day, 192 pesos); and **Tampico** (7hr., 3 per day, 171 pesos). Oriente serves **Tampico** (7hr., 7 per day, 172 pesos). Transportes Tamaulipas and Noreste (☎816 69 64) jointly serve: **Matehuala** (2hr., 14 per day, 91 pesos); **Monterrey** (6hr., 12 per day, 268 pesos); and **Matamoros** (10 hr., 2 per day, 343 pesos).

▐ PRACTICAL INFORMATION

TOURIST, FINANCIAL, AND LOCAL SERVICES

Tourist Office: Visitors to San Luis have the luxury of two excellent offices. The **Turismo Municipal** (☎812 27 70) is on the 1st floor of the Palacio Municipal, at the northeast corner of Plaza de Armas. Friendly, English-speaking staff and excellent information. Open M-F 8am-7pm, Sa-Su 10am-2pm. The **state tourist office,** Obregón 520 (☎812 99 06 or 12 23 57), is 1 block west of the Plaza de los Fundadores. Information on attractions in the rest of the state. Open M-Sa 8am-8pm.

Consulate: US, Mariel 103 (☎812 15 28). Take the "Morales" bus. Open M-F 8:30am-1:30pm, and sometimes available in the afternoons. In case of an emergency, the police and the tourist office have consulate employees' home numbers.

Currency Exchange: Casas de Cambio can be found along Morelos, north of Plaza de Armas. **San Luis Divisas** (☎812 66 06), at the corner of Morelos and Bocanegra, usually accepts traveler's checks. Open M-Sa 9am-8pm. Many banks lie near the Plaza de Armas and are open M-F 9am-3pm. **Banamex,** at Allende and Obregón, 1 block east of Plaza de Armas, has a 24hr. **ATM** and exchanges traveler's checks with no commission.

American Express: Grandes Viajes, Carranza 1077 (☎811 11 27), will help you out with lost or stolen checks or cards and will sell checks. They do not cash American Express traveler's checks. Open M-F 9am-2pm and 4-6pm.

Luggage Storage: At the Central de Transportes Terrestres. 4 pesos per hr., 40 pesos per day. Open 24hr.

Supermarket: Chalita, on the corner of Bravo and Escobedo, three blocks north of the Plaza de Armas. Open daily 9am-9pm.

Laundry: Lavandería La Gotita, on 5 de Mayo and Hernandez. 20 pesos for a medium load. Open M-Sa 10am-8pm.

Car Rental: Hertz, Obregón 670 (☎812 95 00). 280 pesos per day plus insurance and mileage. Must be 25. Open M-F 9am-2pm and 4-8pm, Sa 9am-2pm.

EMERGENCY AND COMMUNICATIONS

Emergency: ☎060 or 072.

Police: (☎812 54 76 or 812 25 82) can always be found in the Palacio Municipal.

Red Cross: (☎815 36 35 or 820 39 02), on Juárez at Díaz Gutiérrez.

Pharmacy: Farmacia Mexicana, Othón 180 (☎812 38 80), next to the cathedral. Open 24hr.

Hospital: Hospital Central, Carranza 2395 (☎813 03 43 or 817 01 64), 20 blocks west of the *centro*. Some English spoken. Open 24hr.

Fax: Computel, Carranza 360 (☎812 01 89; fax 812 01 86), opposite Hotel Panorama. Open M-Sa 7:30am-9pm.

Telephones: LADATELs are scattered throughout the plazas.

Internet Access: Fox Cyber Café, Iturbide 335, off of Plaza del Carmen. 12 pesos per hr. Open M-Sa 10am-10pm.

Post Office: Morelos 235 (☎812 27 40), 1 block east and 3 blocks north of the Plaza de Armas. Open M-F 8am-3pm, Sa 9am-1pm. Contains a **MexPost.** Open M-F 9am-3pm, Sa 9am-1pm. **Postal Code:** 78000.

▟ ACCOMMODATIONS

Some good, cheap accommodations are located near the bus station, but they fill up quickly. Hotels closer to the *centro* tend to be a little past their prime, but offer luxuries such as large rooms, plaza views, and low prices. Alternatively, you can spring for a more expensive room in the middle of the *centro* and get a real treat.

▧ **Hotel Filher,** Universidad 335 (☎812 15 62 or 812 15 63), at the corner of Zaragoza, 3 blocks south of the Plaza de Armas. Everything a traveler could want: bright, tidy rooms with beautiful wooden furniture, purified water, TVs, phones, fans, and big baths. Singles 225 pesos, with balcony 271 pesos; doubles 260 pesos, with balcony 320 pesos.

Hotel Plaza, Jardín Hidalgo 22 (☎812 46 31), on the south side of the Plaza de Armas. This hotel, the city's first, has seen better days, but the clean rooms have a certain charm. Central location. Ask for a room facing the plaza or with a balcony. Singles 150 pesos; doubles 170 pesos; each additional person 10 pesos.

Hotel Progreso, Aldama 415 (☎812 03 66), off Guerrero, near the Plaza de San Francisco. Another older hotel in the *centro*. Small rooms with TV and fans. Squint your eyes and you can imagine its former beauty. Singles 135 pesos, with TV 165 pesos; doubles 145 pesos, with TV 175 pesos; triples 165 pesos, with TV 185 pesos.

Hotel Alameda, Callejón La Perla 3 (☎818 06 06), next to the Pemex gas station on the northwest corner of the Alameda, is the cheapest option in San Luis Potosí. Rooms are small, dark, and in minor disrepair, but the plumbing is new, the water is hot, and the manager is accommodating. Singles 80 pesos; doubles 90 pesos.

Motel Potosino, Carretera Mexico, km 426 (☎818 25 56), on the left after you exit the bus station. A good choice if you're unable to get into the more scenic downtown. Spacious, carpeted rooms with TV and phone. Singles 180 pesos; doubles 240-360 pesos.

◖ FOOD

Many of the restaurants in the *centro* offer bland or mediocre dishes and poor service. The farther you stray, the better your chances are of stumbling upon a gem. Regional favorites such as *tacos potosinos* and *enchiladas potosinas* (both stuffed with cheese and vegetables then fried) are served at nearly all local restaurants. *Nopalitos* are tender, absolutely delicious pieces of cactus with the spine removed and cooked in a salty green sauce of garlic, onion, and tomato. The most popular dessert is the *chongos coronados*, curdled milk in sweet maple water.

■ **La Güera,** Tata Nacho 799 (☎811 87 28), on the left as you approach the Parque Tangamanga, on the block before the entrance. This traditionally decorated treasure offers some of the best meals in all of Northeast Mexico. Specializes in breakfast (35 pesos, 8:30am until noon) and *comida corrida* (45 pesos, 1-6pm). From the pickled *nopalito* garnish to the homemade *mole*, everything here is excellent. Open Tu-Su 8:30am-6pm.

Restaurant Cafetería (☎812 29 57), with the orange doors on Madero, just west of the Plaza de Armas. It may not look like much, but at one of its three tiny tables, you can get a lip-smacking breakfast, lunch, or dinner (*tortas* and *gorditas* 15-25 pesos, meals 20-60 pesos), and rare and scrumptious desserts (10-15 pesos). Open M-F 8am-9pm.

Tokio, Zaragosa 305 (☎814 61 89). Only the jade-colored decor fits the quasi-Japanese name. Tokio serves tasty Mexican dishes in a cool, modern atmosphere. *Comida corrida* (30 pesos) starts at 1:30pm. Open daily 7:30am-11pm.

Yu Ne Nisa, Arista 360 (☎814 36 31). A Yucateco celebration of vegetarianism on the cheap, serving veggie burgers (20 pesos), *quesadillas* (15 pesos), and *comida corrida* (30 pesos). Luscious *licuados* are freshly squeezed behind the counter. Has a large variety of juices, yogurt concoctions, and wheat breads. Open M-Sa 9:30am-8:30pm.

◖ SIGHTS

As the former center of the state's booming silver and gold trade, prosperous San Luis Potosí had the money and the stature to build some of the country's finest buildings, cathedrals, and plazas. The sheer number of beautiful things to see can be almost intimidating; fortunately, the great majority have historical markers in both English and Spanish and are within easy walking distance of each other. When exploring churches, it is discourteous to interrupt mass.

PLAZA DE ARMAS. Called the "City of Plazas," San Luis Potosí has four main town squares. The most central of these is the Plaza de Armas, filled with trees and lounging *potosinos*. At the beginning of the 17th century, residents watched bullfights from the balconies of the surrounding buildings. Since 1848, a red sandstone gazebo bearing the names of famous Mexican musicians has graced the plaza, which hosts local bands. (*Concerts Th and Sa evenings.*)

PALACIO DE GOBIERNO. The west side of the Plaza de Armas is marked by the Neoclassical facade of the Palacio de Gobierno, constructed in 1798. Briefly serving as the capital of the country and the seat of the presidency in 1863, the structure was renovated in 1950 and continues to serve as San Luis Potosí's administrative center. The building has interesting rooms on the second floor filled with murals, statues, plaques, and legends. *(Open M-F 9am-2:30pm. Free.)*

CATEDRAL SANTA IGLESIA. Opposite the Palacio de Gobierno stands the cathedral, with two bell towers that play a different melody every 15 minutes. The cathedral was completed in 1710, and when San Luis Potosí became a diocese in 1855, the building was "upgraded." Miners donated gold and silver to glorify the interior, and marble statues of the apostles (copies of those at the Basilica of San Juan de Letrán in Rome) were placed in the niches between the Solomonic columns of the Baroque facade. *(Open daily 8am-7pm.)*

JARDÍN DE SAN FRANCISCO. San Luis Potosí has at least one garden for each of its seven districts. This one, on the Plaza de San Francisco, is distinguished by its bronze fountain, cobblestone streets, and red sandstone buildings. Book stalls line the east side, while artisan sellers extend down the west side.

IGLESIA DE SAN FRANCISCO. Construction began on the Iglesia de San Francisco, on the west side of the garden by the same name, in the 1860s. Less ornate than its counterparts, the orange stucco facade displays a Baroque interior beautifully accentuated by the flickering votives. *(Open daily 6:30am-1:30pm and 4:30-9pm.)*

MUSEO REGIONAL POTOSINO. The museum occupies the grounds of a former Franciscan convent. The first floor contains artifacts from all of Mexico, including a collection of Pre-Hispanic Huasteca relics. The marvelous **Baroque Capilla a la Virgen de Aranzazu** is on display on the second floor. According to legend, a local 18th-century shepherd found the altar's wooden image of the Virgin Mary in a prickly thicket. The name *aranzazu* means "from within the thorns." *(On Independencia near the corner of Galeana, behind the Iglesia de San Francisco. ☎812 51 85. Open Tu-Su 10am-7pm. 10 pesos, free on Su.)*

PLAZA DEL CARMEN. The bright, lively Plaza del Carmen, two blocks east of the Plaza de Armas, hosts Sunday festivals. The most active of the plazas, street performers, vendor stands, and a young crowd mill around here well past nightfall.

TEMPLO DEL CARMEN. This serene church was constructed from 1749-1764 and is regarded by many *potosinos* to be the most beautiful religious building in the city. It features hanging chandeliers, golden altars, and a huge mural of the Crucifixion. During the Mexican Revolution, the government used the convent to jail local rebels. Once released, these leaders went on to lead the revolt of San Luis Potosí. *(In the northeast corner of the Plaza del Carmen. Open daily 7am-1:30pm and 4-9pm.)*

EL TEATRO DE LA PAZ. This theater is one of the four most famous and acoustically well-constructed in Mexico—many performers don't even need microphones. The *salón* holds a collection of modern art, the foyer is filled with sculptures and murals, and the theater hosts everything from international dance festivals to "Sesame Street Live." The best news? Prices are cheap. *(Behind the Templo del Carmen. ☎812 26 98. Pick up a schedule at the tourist office or look for posters outside the theater. 40 pesos and up.)*

MUSEO NACIONAL DE LA MÁSCARA. The museum displays hundreds of ancient and modern masks from all of Mexico, from devils to dancing cows. Nearly every mask has ceremonial origins, and many were used in elaborate dances. Be sure to check out all of the oversized *mojigangas* in the hall—these enormous, eccentric representations are taken out of the museum and paraded around the streets during seasonal festivals. *(Villerías 2, in the Plaza de Carmen across from the Teatro de la Paz. ☎812 30 25. Open Tu-F 10am-2pm and 5-7pm, Sa-Su 10am-2pm. 3 pesos.)*

PARQUE TANGAMANGA. With lakes for paddle-boating and fishing, a baseball field, electric cars, and bike paths, this *parque* is an ideal place to take a blanket and a picnic and spend the day lounging. The tree- and lawn-filled park is huge, but you can rent a bike and explore it all. *(Catch a Route #10 "Perimetral" bus on Constitución across from the Alameda (20 min., 2.20 pesos). Get off at the Monumento a la Revolución, a* *statue of soldiers firing rifles, in the middle of a rotary. Facing the soldiers' backs, take a left and go three blocks. Open Tu-Su 9am-6pm. Bike rental 20 pesos per hr.)*

MUSEO DE LAS CULTURAS POPULARES. Parque Tangamanga houses this museum of indigenous crafts and rare photo exhibitions of indigenous communities and ceremonies. *(☎812 29 76. Open Tu-Su 10am-4pm. 2 pesos.)*

NIGHTLIFE

In the past, downtown San Luis Potosí offered little in terms of nightlife, making it difficult to party without venturing to the outskirts of town. In the past couple of years, however, the *centro* has become the *centro* of the town's nightlife scene, with new establishments popping up just off of the main plazas. In the middle of everything, the brand-new **El Mito**, on the Plaza de Armas, is *the* place to be on a weekend nights. An exclusive young crowd packs the dance floor and the adjoining balcony as DJs spin the latest Latin dance and pop. (☎814 41 57. Cover F-Sa 50 pesos. Open W-Sa 9pm-2:30am.) The club **La Terapia**, Arista 425, attracts a crowd of 30-somethings who still know how to get down. **La María**, at the corner of Escobedo and Guerrero, pumps electronica in a small former home near the Plaza del Carmen. Check out the 5m-deep well in the middle of the dance floor, a vestige of the city's past. Fortunately, a grate keeps tipsy patrons from stumbling in. (☎812 36 44. Cover F-Sa men 25 pesos, women 15 pesos. Open Th-Sa 9pm-2am.) Also close to the *centro* are **Staff**, Carranza 423, where a young, gay-friendly crowd grooves to Latin and dance music (☎814 30 74; cover 25 pesos; open F-Su), and **Delirio Azul,** on Ocampo and Independencia behind the Templo de San Francisco, a bar specializing in salsa music and dance.

SHOPPING

Much of San Luis Potosí's charm emerges from the city's quiet plazas and fountains, usually devoid of frantic shoppers and crowded stores. But, have no fear, hard-core shopper—one does not have to stray far to find good shopping. Shops line Morelos north of the Plaza de Armas, and the expansive **Alameda Juan Sarabia,** three blocks east of from the Plaza de Armas along Othón, has artisans and trinket-vendors as well as game operators along the western side. It's best to avoid this area at night. The best shopping can be found along Hidalgo, which is called Zaragoza south of the Plaza. The pedestrian street has blocks and blocks of bargains, coffee shops, and *heladerías* (ice cream stands).

FESTIVALS

The last two weeks of August mark the **Fiesta Nacional Potosina,** often called FaNaPo. With concerts, bullfights, fireworks, and a parade, a splendid time is guaranteed for all. The festival pales in comparison to the city's celebration of **Semana Santa** the week before Easter. The powerful culmination of this festival is the **Procesión del Silencio** on the evening of Good Friday. This silent procession involves 25 *cofradías* (local groups), who bear life-like statues portraying the events leading to Christ's death. Each group dresses in a hooded costume, with different colors for each *cofradía* as a sign of repentance for their sins.

MATEHUALA   ☎4

Although Matehuala (pop. 100,000) derives its name from a Náhuatl phrase meaning "don't come," the town is anything but unfriendly. The few tourists who do trickle in are often adventure-seeking backpackers en route to Real de Catorce. They are usually surprised to find this town, once a base for Spanish silver and gold mining, so relaxing and open—well worth a stay.

TRANSPORTATION

Matehuala is 261km from Saltillo and 191km from San Luis Potosí. The **Central de Autobuses** is located on Calle 5 de Mayo, just south of the city and near the large, red *Arco de Bienvenida*. Across the street from the station, a *pesera* labeled "Centro" will take you to the downtown area (2 pesos)—ask the driver to let you off near the cathedral. Easier still, get off at Hidalgo, next to the Chalita market. **Taxis** charge 20 pesos for the trip. The bus station provides consolidated service of Transportes del Norte, Frontera, Estrella Blanca, and El Águila to: **Mexico City** (7hr., 9 per day, 332 pesos); **Monterrey** (4hr., every hr., 161 pesos); **Nuevo Laredo** (7hr., 10 per day, 297 pesos); **Querétaro** (6hr., 3 per day, 198 pesos); **Saltillo** (3hr., every hr., 138 pesos); and **San Luis Potosí** (2hr., every hr., 91 pesos). Noreste (☎882 09 97) serves **Monterrey** (4hr., every hr., 161 pesos) and **Reynosa** (7hr., 8 per day, 248 pesos). Tamaulipas (☎882 27 77) goes to **Real de Catorce** (5 per day, 31 pesos) and **San Luis Potosí** (2 hr., 18 per day, 91 pesos).

ORIENTATION AND PRACTICAL INFORMATION

Constantly forking or changing names, the streets of Matehuala are confusing, but so short and close together that you'll never be lost for long. **Hidalgo** runs north-south through most of the city; **Juárez** runs parallel to the west. Most points of interest lie somewhere on or not far from **Hidalgo** and **Morelos**.

Tourist information: Cámara de Comercio (☎882 01 10), Morelos 427, one block east of Hidalgo. Helpful staff. These friendly people will even let you use their computer for **Internet access.** 15 pesos per hr. Open M-F 9am-1:30pm and 4-7:30pm. **Maps** are for sale (15-20 pesos) at the blue **Papelería Corias,** Morelos 512, across the street and a half block from the *Cámara de Comercio.* Open daily 9am-8:30pm.

Currency Exchange: Casas de cambio dot the *centro,* all offering good rates. **Bital,** 111 Reyes (☎882 48 18), exchanges cash and traveler's checks and has a 24hr. **ATM.** Open M-Sa 8am-7pm.

Markets: Chalita, on Hidalgo 2 blocks from the cathedral, sells groceries and clothing. Open daily 8am-8pm. The **indoor market** next to the Templo de la Inmaculada Concepción sells crafts and produce. Open daily 9am-6pm.

Laundry: Lavandería Acuario (☎882 70 88), Betancourt and Madero, offers self-service wash and dry of 5kg per 40 pesos. Open daily 8:30am-2pm and 4-8pm.

Emergency: ☎060.

Police station: (☎882 06 47), next to the bus station.

Red Cross: (☎882 07 26), at Ignacio y Ramírez and Betancourt, about 8 blocks east of the fork from Morelos.

Pharmacy: Farmacia del Centro, Morelos 623 (☎882 05 92). Open daily 9am-midnight.

Hospital: Hospital General (☎882 04 45), on Hidalgo a few blocks north of the *centro.* Little to no English spoken. Open 24hr.

Fax: Telecomm, 5 de Febrero at Juárez (☎882 00 08), a few blocks east of the *centro.* Also houses a **Western Union** office. Open M-F 9am-7pm.

Telephones: LADATELs are not as common in Matehuala as in other cities but can be found in the *centro.*

Post office: (☎882 00 71), at Valle and Negrete. Walk up Constitución, turn right on Independencia one block before the Iglesia Santo Niño, turn right again on Negrete, and it's on your left at the corner. Open M-F 8am-3pm, Sa 9am-1pm.

Postal code: 78700.

ACCOMMODATIONS

Budget accommodations populate the *centro*. Starting at around 50 pesos, the *casas de huéspedes* on Bocanegra are the cheapest options, but, by spending slightly more, you can get considerably nicer rooms.

 Hotel y Casino Del Valle, Morelos 612 (☎882 37 70), right off the Plaza de Armas. Comfort and fun for reasonable prices. Hyperactive ceiling fans, *agua purificada*, TVs in the rooms, and an attached dance hall make this hotel as swank as a Las Vegas casino. 180 pesos per person; each additional person 20 pesos. Maximum 4 per room.

Hotel del Parque (☎882 55 10), on the corner of Rayon and Bocanegra. Luxury digs close to the *centro* and next to Parque Vincente Guerrero. Large rooms with cable TV. Singles 320 pesos; doubles 360 pesos.

Hotel Matehuala, Bustamante 134 (☎882 06 80), just north of the Plaza de Armas. A huge (and empty) tiled courtyard is monastic in a good way. Though the rooms are dark as confessional booths, the 15 ft. ceilings with wooden rafters, the white walls, and the rust-colored bureaus are decidedly appealing. Ask for a room with a balcony and windows to the outside. Singles 150 pesos; doubles 170 pesos.

Hotel Blanca Estela, Morelos 406 (☎882 23 00), next to the video store. Fans cool small, clean, colorful rooms with TVs. Beautiful wooden furnishings give a classy feel to the rooms in this narrow hotel. Check in early; this may well be the most crowded place in town. Singles 130 pesos; doubles 150 pesos.

 ## FOOD

The few restaurants in Matehuala are family-owned cafeterias with good food at low prices. **Restaurant Fontella,** Morelos 618, between hotels Casino and Matehuala, serves some of the best food in town with charcoal-roasted specialties (27-34 pesos). The *comida corrida* (23 pesos) comes with copious servings. (☎882 02 93. Open daily 7:30am-4am.) **Restaurant Video Bar House Rock,** on Hidalgo directly across from the *templo*, has simple fare upstairs in a cool, family-style restaurant (*comida corrida* 28 pesos.) Downstairs, the hippest 20-30 year-olds hang out in the video bar where antique decorations mix with modern music. (☎882 20 08. Restaurant open daily 9am-10pm; bar open W-Sa 7pm-1am.) **La Cava,** Callejón del Arte 1, between Hidalgo and Morelos a half block in front of Hotel Matehuala, is a pleasant escape from the merciless sun. The sleek dining room serves a mix of Mexican, French, and American cuisine (33-50 pesos). Cocktails here are especially smooth. (☎882 28 88. Open daily 1:30-10:30pm.)

SIGHTS

Standing solemnly at the center of Matehuala between Juárez and Hidalgo is the nearly completed **Templo de la Inmaculada Concepción,** a copy of Saint Joseph's cathedral in Lyon, France. Construction began in 1905, and although poor funding has slowed progress, more than three generations of Matehualans are proud of their all-but-finished cathedral. In front of the main cathedral is the **Plaza Juárez,** now permanently occupied by vendor stalls and makeshift cafes. Sprawling onto adjoining streets, the bazaar is collectively known as **Mercado Arista,** selling leather and ceramic goods and slews of cheap plastic trinkets. The **Alameda,** a few blocks south of the main plaza, offers shade and jungle-like lushness.

Two other large parks stand at the northeast and southeast corners of downtown. Approximately three blocks east of Hidalgo, between Bocanegra and Altamirano, is the soothing **Parque Vicente Guerrero** (also called the **Parque del Pueblo**). The more lively **Parque Álvaro Obregón** is just south of Insurgentes. With basketball courts and benches aplenty, Álvaro Obregón draws families in the early evening.

REAL DE CATORCE   ☎ 4

Once a thriving mining town with 30,000 inhabitants, Real de Catorce now looms mysteriously on the side of a mountain, a veritable ghost town with barely 1500 residents. Once one of the largest silver producers in the country, the early 20th century brought on flooding, destruction, and desertion, leaving behind the empty mine shafts and carts that give Real de Catorce its eerie feel. Today, backpackers and travelers trek to see this town's *burro*-trodden paths and brick ruins and to pay respects to the town's patron saint, Saint Francis. Huichol Indians make springtime pilgrimages to Real de Catorce to gather peyote, which they consider sacred. Its history and natural beauty is on display in a new Brad Pitt and Julia Roberts movie, tentatively called "The Mexican," scheduled for release in 2001. The cobblestone streets and carts of holy candles make Real de Catorce a Mexican miracle—the town that time left behind.

▐ TRANSPORTATION

To get to Real de Catorce, you must go through Matehuala. From Matehuala's cathedral, walk one block up Hidalgo, take a left onto Guerrero, and walk down two blocks to Mendez. Buses leave from the station at the corner of Guerrero and Mendez. The bus also stops at the Matehuala Central de Autobuses. Autobuses Tamaulipas (☎ 882 08 40) runs buses from **Matehuala** to Real de Catorce (1½hr.; F-M 6, 8, 10am, noon, 2, 6pm; Tu-Th 8am, noon, 2pm; in Oct. every 20min.; return buses depart 15min. earlier; 31 pesos). Purchase tickets before leaving Matehuala or from the driver (31 pesos). Passengers should always check with the bus driver about the schedules and arrive early if possible.

The ride to "Real de 14" is guaranteed to whiten the knuckles of the timid traveler; the bus rambles along a winding path chiseled into the mountain, and riders change to a lower bus for the tunnel at the end of the ride. This trip seems like an amusement park ride and is the true beginning to the Real de Catorce experience.

✴▌ ORIENTATION AND PRACTICAL INFORMATION

The town's main path is **Lanzagorta,** which runs from the bus stop past the famed cathedral and a few hotels and restaurants to a town square. Constitución runs parallel to Lanzagorta up the hill, through the **Plaza Principal.**

Self-appointed guides offering **tourist information** can be found as you get off the bus or in the back streets of the city. Official brochures are available in the **Matehuala Chamber of Commerce. Police:** at the **Presidencia Municipal,** just by the Plaza Principal. (Open 24hr.) **Telephone:** on a side street running perpendicular to Constitución, next to the Presidencia Municipal. (☎ 882 37 33. Available M-Sa 9:15am-3pm 5-8pm, Su 10am-3pm.) **Post office:** on Constitución to the right of the Presidencia Municipal as you are facing it, on the right side of the street. (Open M-F 9am-1pm and 3-6pm.) **Postal Code:** 78550.

▐◖ ACCOMMODATIONS AND FOOD

For so tiny a town, Real de Catorce has a number of good budget accommodations. Look for the *casas de huéspedes* on the streets off of Lanzagorta. Most of the hotels are beautiful and, if not equipped with amenities such as TV, A/C, and phone, are at least richly decorated. For lower price without lower quality, try ▨ **Hotel San Francisco,** on Terán right off Constitución. The family-run hotel has only a few rooms, but it is clean and comfortable. (60 pesos, with bath 90 pesos.) A more luxurious option is **El Mesón de la Abundancia,** Langazorta 11. The oldest edifice in town, it used to be the town treasury in the 1880s. Furniture is made by hand, blankets are woven out of fine wool, and rooms are adorned with private terraces and sitting rooms. (Singles 150 pesos; doubles 380 pesos; triples and quads 500 pesos. Singles price not available on weekends.) At the adjoining restaurant/bar, the menu includes vegetarian options along with Mexican and Italian entrees (47 pesos). **Hotel Providencia,** Lanzagorta 29, offers a few bare-bones rooms (singles 100 pesos; doubles 200 pesos) and a few more expensive and modern rooms with bathtubs and impressive views (singles 250; doubles 300). The restaurant downstairs serves *comida corrida* with homemade tortillas (25 pesos).

Interestingly, Real has good Italian food, thanks to the number of Italians who settled here. The dim, intimate **Restaurant El Real,** off of Lanzagorta, proves that Mexico really can do Italian, with pizzas and pasta dishes (50-90 pesos). Many restaurants are open only during tourist season (June-Oct.).

🔭 SIGHTS

Lanzagorta runs past most major sights. The **Templo de la Purísima Concepción** is down the road on the right; go up the white walkway to reach the entrance. The altar still retains its original stucco and a painting of the Virgin of Guadalupe, and houses a life-like image of St. Francis, whose miracles have created a devoted following. The rectangular blocks of wood on the floor are doors to subterranean tombs. The side room is filled with letters to St. Francis—they give thanks for everything from miraculous cures to visa waivers. Across from the cathedral is the **Casa de Moneda,** formerly a mint, whose third floor houses a small photography exhibit of Real de Catorce. (Open daily noon-2pm. Free.) A steep climb to the right of the cathedral brings you to **Plaza Principal,** once the thriving center of the town. Today only a crumbling fountain remains.

Much of the action in Real revolves around the gazebo at the **Jardín Hidalgo,** beyond the cathedral between Lanzagorta and Constitución. *Norteño* and *mariachi* bands occasionally play there. The right immediately after the *jardín* takes you to Zaragoza, which leads to several attractions. On Xicotencatl off Zaragoza, the terraced steps of the **Palenque de Gallos** (cock-fight ring) replicate the layout of a classical Athenian theater. At the top of Zaragoza stands the white **Capilla de Guadalupe** (also called the **Panteón**), which overlooks a cemetery full of the graves of local priests. At the high end of Constitución lies **El Mirador,** an area full of ruined miners' homes that offers a vista of the city. The surrounding cliff, known as **El Voladero,** grants breathtaking views of mountains and valleys, dry riverbeds, and herds of cows on distant hilltops. To reach it, walk downhill on Constitución.

For a 🐴**horseback tour** of the region, walk from the bus stop down Lanzagorta until you reach the Plaza Hidalgo. To the left across Lanzagorta is a stable that rents out horses (40 pesos per hr.). Try a two-hour trip to the **Ciudad de las Fantasmas** ("Ghost City"), an abandoned mining town nearby, or a descent into the desert valley. If you're feeling really adventurous, you can even make a two-day trip to a nearby ranch. The guides expect a tip of 50 to 70 pesos; try to arrange a fixed price before the trip to avoid a hassle.

🌼 FESTIVALS

October 4 is the feast day of St. Francis of Asisi, Real de Catorce's beloved patron saint. From the end of September through October, the normally quiet town explodes with activity as visitors come from all over Mexico to pray at the cathedral. This **Feria de San Francisco** packs the streets with people for daily and nightly *fiestas* outside of the cathedral. Local hotels will double their rates, but buses run in and out of town every 20 minutes, ensuring everyone can enjoy the festivities.

CIUDAD VALLES ☎ 1

Ciudad Valles (pop. 350,000) is a major crossroads between the northeast and central Mexico, and provides the easiest access to the state's Huastecan region, including Xilitla. Commonly known as Valles, the hot and dirty city lacks the charm and culture of San Luis Potosí. The city has little trace of the rich Huastecan culture surrounding the area and it feels more like Industrytown, Anywhere.

The **Central de Autobuses** lies on the outskirts of town, on Luis Venegas. To get into town, exit the station and take any "Mercado" bus (3 pesos); this will take you to the station for municipal buses. Tickets for **taxis** are available from the **ServiBus** stand in the middle of the station (15 pesos to the *centro*).

From the station, Oriente (☎382 39 02) serves: **Ciudad Victoria** (4hr., 20 per day, 110 pesos); **Guadalajara** (10hr., 5 per day, 290 pesos); **Matamoros** (8hr., 8 per day, 259 pesos); and **Monterrey** (7½hr., 10 per day, 264 pesos). Vencedor goes to: **San Luis Potosí** (5hr., every hour, 150 pesos); **Tampico** (2½hr., every hr., 83 pesos); and **Xilitla** (1½hr., every hour 4am-7pm, 35 pesos).

Banorte, on the corner of Hidalgo and Carranza, has a 24-hour **ATM. Red Cross:** (☎382 00 56). **Police:** (☎382 21 85 or 382 27 38). **Post office:** Juárez 520. (☎382 01 04. Open M-F 8am-3pm, Sa 9am-1pm.) **Postal code:** 79000.

If you have the misfortune of finding yourself stuck in Valles for a night, the area around the bus station has several good, inexpensive hotels. **Hotel San Carlos,** Venegas 140, across the street from the bus station, offers bright, clean rooms with TV and much-needed A/C. (Singles 120 pesos; doubles 140 pesos.) For an easy meal, **Restaurant Don Felix,** also across from the station, serves *comida corrida* for 20 pesos and cheap *antojitos* (open daily 7:30am-11:30pm).

XILITLA ☎1

A serpentine road winds through the rocky *huasteca* highlands to the tiny, lush hamlet of Xilitla (pop. 10,000), 1½ hours from and 1000m above Ciudad Valles. The town encompasses dozens of sidewalk stores and a tiny market. Xilitla's main attraction, however, is its incredible beauty: the town rises to a picturesque central plaza with a phenomenal view. The area has over 150 caves, including **El Sótano de las Golondrinas,** a spelunker's dream with a cave floor 450m deep, covering approximately six acres. Xilitla's most notable attraction is the beautiful and bizarre "ruins," known locally as **Las Pozas,** built by English millionaire Edward James. Dozens of waterfalls, wild orchid sanctuaries, rare animals, horseback trails, and rivers ripe for rafting are all accessible from Xilitla.

TRANSPORTATION AND PRACTICAL INFORMATION. The bus station sits on the hillside just below town. To get to the **Plaza Central,** officially named **Jardín Hidalgo,** go up the stairs to the right of the bus station and turn right on Zaragoza. Vencedor runs to: **Ciudad Valles** (1½hr., every hr. 5:30am-7:30pm, 35 pesos); **San Luis Potosí** (6½hr.; 5am, 12:30 and 1:30pm; 164 pesos); and **Tampico** (4½hr., 7 per day, 113 pesos).

Helpful brochures, including maps of the town and Las Pozas, are available at the bus station and nearly every store in town (25 pesos). Another valuable resource is www.junglegossip.com, the website of El Castillo, a lovely resort down the hill from Xilitla's main plaza. Exchange currency or traveler's checks at the **Centro de Cambio,** on the right-hand side of Zaragoza as you go toward the plaza. (☎365 02 81. Open daily 8am-8pm.) **Banorte,** on the Zaragoza side of the plaza, also exchanges currency and checks and has a 24hr. **ATM.** (☎365 00 29. Open M-F 9am-2:30pm.) **Police:** on the plaza, in the Palacio Municipal (☎365 00 85). **Emergency:** call the police station—Xilitla has neither a hospital nor a Red Cross. **Pharmacy: Farmacia San Agustín,** on Hidalgo, at the northwest corner of the Plaza Principal. (☎365 01 25. Open daily 8:30am-9pm.) No **LADATELs,** but there is a long-distance public phone in the Hotel Ziyaquetzas, on the Zaragosa side of the plaza. **Post office:** in the back of the Palacio on Zaragoza on the south side of the plaza, on the 2nd floor. (Open M-F 9am-3pm.) **Postal code:** 79902.

ACCOMMODATIONS AND FOOD. In mid-summer and during *Semana Santa*, Xilitla's few but wonderful hotels fill up fast and require reservations. Along Jardín Hidalgo, **Hotel Ziyaquetzas** offers clean rooms with fans and astounding views. (☎365 00 81. Singles 110 pesos; doubles 150 pesos.) Nature-lovers will be happy to spend the extra pesos to sleep near the forest in **Las Pozas.** Rooms are as wild and varied as you can imagine. (☎365 02 03. Doubles 200 pesos; quads 450 pesos.) Las Pozas also has a small **restaurant** where you can eat accompanied by the rushing noise of the waterfall. (25-50 pesos. Open daily 9am-5pm.) In town, tiny restaurants line Escobedo just past the plaza, offering meals at rock-bottom prices. (20-30 pesos. Open from about 7am until no one is left on the streets.)

🌐 **SIGHTS. Las Pozas** (the pools), formally called the **Enchanted Garden of Edward James,** are Xilitla's main attraction. Head downhill on Ocampo; continue as it veers right and turns into a path after the northwest corner of the plaza. This path lets you out onto the main road at a white bridge. Cross the bridge and take your first left, following the upward dirt path until you get to a gravel road; make a left and walk on for about 2km. The walk is about 30-45 minutes long. Las Pozas will be on your right. Those with sore feet can take a *combi* (5 pesos) from the top of the stairs near the bus station to the white bridge, or find a taxi to take you right to the gate (60 pesos). The son of a wealthy nobleman, James was an old-fashioned English eccentric. An aspiring artist and friend of Salvador Dalí, his early experiments in poetry and art were largely unsuccessful. In the early 1950s, James visited Xilitla and, enchanted by its natural beauty, he decided to build his home as a living surrealist monument. The result is a universe of concrete, steel, and stone in wild colors and even wilder shapes. The melange of bridges, arches, and artistic relics recalls *Alice in Wonderland*, with winding staircases that lead nowhere, a library without books, and other touches of madness. James channeled the waterfall running through Las Pozas's 36 structures into nine pools. They're wonderful for swimming—bring your bathing suit. (Open daily 9am-8pm. 15 pesos.)

If a day of exploring Las Pozas hasn't left you exhausted, the nearby **Cueva del Salitre** (Parrot Cave) makes a good early evening excursion. To reach the cave, head down Ocampo, take a left at Morelos, and follow the road to its end. There, take a left and walk past the Pemex station. A few hundred meters later, you will come to a mechanic's shop. The cave is a 5-minute walk down the hill behind the shop; you may want to ask the people working there if they can find you a guide (about a 10 peso tip is expected). Each night at dusk, over two hundred green and yellow "parrots" gather outside this cave, squawking loudly and creating an impressive spectacle. These beautiful birds are not, in fact, parrots; they are green parakeets. To all but the most discriminating bird-watcher, however, the misnomer is convincing. The gaping cave itself is worth seeing.

In town, Xilitla's historical draw is the quietly greying **Templo de San Agustín,** on the west side of the plaza. Built between 1550 and 1557, the ex-convent is the oldest colonial building in the state. Though the exterior could use a good whitewashing, the interior is beautifully preserved, where a large, quiet courtyard is surrounded by altars and childrens' creations.

For the commercially inclined, shops selling fruit, shoes, crafts, and trinkets line either side of the plaza on Zaragoza and Escobedo. Each August 28th, the plaza comes alive for the **Feast Day of San Agustín,** with fireworks and regional dances.

CIUDAD VICTORIA
☎ 1

Ciudad Victoria (pop. 230,000) may be the sleepiest state capital in Mexico. On the edge of the Sierra Gorda, Victoria makes an ideal stopover near the US border. The city also serves as a good starting point for exploring nature. Among the sights a short ride from the city are the **Cañón del Novillo,** a glorious spot for hiking and camping, and the **Boca de San Juan Capitán,** a stream of unmatched beauty. Ardent naturalists or those simply looking for escape may want to visit the **Reserva de la Biosfera El Cielo,** approximately 100km from the city. Though nondescript, Ciudad Victoria offers a relaxed, welcoming environment for the weary traveler.

▐ **TRANSPORTATION.** From the **Central de Autobuses,** a "Boulevard" minibus can take you to the *centro* (3 pesos). From there, walk two blocks up Calle 8 or 9 to Plaza Hidalgo, the home of most of Ciudad Victoria's attractions. A taxi will cost about 30 pesos. From the station, Transpaís (☎316 77 99) runs to: **Matamoros** (4hr., every hr., 149 pesos); **Reynosa** (4hr., every hr., 152 pesos); **Ciudad Valles** (4hr., every hr., 110 pesos); and **Tampico** (3½hr., every hr, 113 pesos). Transporte del Norte (☎316 01 38) runs to **San Luis Potosí** (10hr., every hr., 166 pesos) and **Monterrey** (4hr., 7 per day 9:15am-10:45pm, 144 pesos).

🔲🔃 ORIENTATION AND PRACTICAL INFORMATION. The **tourist office**, Calle 8 #1287, between Anaya and Ramírez, seven long blocks past the cathedral, will be happy to tell you everything you need to know about Victoria and the state of Tamaulipas. (☎314 05 21. Open M-F 9am-9pm.) Exchange currency or traveler's checks at **Ban-Crecer** (☎312 75 88) on Hidalgo in the main plaza, with a 24 hour **ATM. Luggage storage** is available at the bus station. (3.50 pesos per hr. Open daily 7am-10:30pm.) **Market: Tienda ISSSTE,** on Calle 13 between Matamoros and Guerrero. (Open daily 9am-8pm.) **Laundry: Lavandería Virues,** Matamoros 939, between Calles 8 and 9. (10 pesos medium load; 30 pesos to dry. Open M-Sa 9am-8pm.) **Emergency:** ☎060. **Police:** (☎312 01 95 or 312 42 43). **Red Cross:** (☎316 20 77). **Hospital General Libramiento Fidel:** 1845 Velázquez Ote. 1845 (☎316 21 97 or 316 22 57). **Pharmacy: Benavides,** on the corner of Hidalgo and Calle 9. (Open 24hr.) Plaza Hidalgo has **LADATELs** every couple of inches. **Tel.Net Cyber Café,** Calle 8 between Hidalgo and Juárez, off of the Plaza Hidalgo, also provides **fax** service. (☎315 39 26. 5 computers, 18 pesos per hr. Open daily 8am-11pm.) **Post Office:** on Calle 8 between Morelos and Matamoros, in the Palacio Municipal. (☎312 12 85. Open M-F 8am-7pm, Sa 8am-noon.) **Postal Code:** 87000.

🔲🔃 ACCOMMODATIONS AND FOOD. While expensive luxury hotels surround Plaza Hidalgo, quality budget lodging can be found a few steps away, hiding in the nearby streets. **Hotel de Escandon,** Calle 8 143, just off the plaza, provides comfortable rooms with TV and phones, in addition to three square meals a day. The rooms face a small courtyard, protected from the brutal sun by a sky-blue dome. (☎312 90 04. Singles 135-195 pesos; doubles 165-295 pesos. 30 pesos extra for A/C.) Also close to the *centro,* the **Posada Don Diego,** Juárez 814 (☎312 12 79), on the street behind the Hotel Sierra Gorda, embellishes its tiny rooms with muscular ceiling fans and TVs. The hotel centers around a sunny, vibrant courtyard.

If you get an urge to lose the backpack and don the bow tie, try some of the fancy restaurants in the hotels around the *centro*. On the other end of the spectrum, streetside vendors line the shopping area on Hidalgo by Calle 7 until about 6pm. For a filling *comida corrida* (30 pesos), **Café Canton,** Colón 114, just south of the plaza, soothes the palate and helps you beat the empty-wallet blues. Entrees, from *antojitos* to hamburgers, 20-40 pesos. (☎312 21 77. Open daily 6am-10pm.) The **Restaurant Carolina,** next to the Posada Don Diego, has better prices. Breakfasts 20 pesos, entrees 15-35 pesos, *comida corrida* 25 pesos. (Open daily 6am-10pm.)

🔲🔃 SIGHTS AND ENTERTAINMENT. As the state capital, Ciudad Victoria's **Palacio de Gobierno,** on the corner of Hidalgo and Calle 17, is appropriately grandiose and harbors large, impressive murals. The **mercados** north of Hidalgo between Calle 6 and 7 offer everything from crafts to goat liver. For those craving knowledge, the **Museo de Antropología e Historia,** on the north side of Plaza Hidalgo, is allegedly open M-F 9am-7pm, but often closes unexpectedly. The collection displays indigenous art and artifacts, historical photographs, and assorted fossils.

Victoria provides relatively easy access to **El Cielo Reserva de la Biosfera,** the state's most impressive nature reserve. Often referred to as simply "La Reserva," it covers over 300,000 acres of lush vegetation, mountains, and wildlife. The area is home to hundreds of species of birds, reptiles, and mammals. To reach the reserve by bus, go to the Transpais booth at the bus station and ask for a ticket to la "griega" (the "Y") of Gómez Farias. You'll get on a bus to Ciudad Mante, but make sure to have the driver let you off at the "Y," about two hours from Victoria (112km). After disembarking from the bus, wait for a blue minibus that takes you to downtown Gómez Farias (every hr., 5 pesos). There, register at the **caseta de vigilancia** in order to enter the reserve. In town, accommodations and further information are available. Take a 7km hike or rent the services of a 4WD taxi (up to 1000 pesos per day). If you are interested, contact Ciudad Victoria's office of **Dirección General de Recursos Naturales y Medio Ambiente** (☎312 60 18), on Calle 13 between Guerrero and Bravo. These friendly people can help the ecotourist plan the perfect adventure.

If you come to Ciudad Victoria in the second week of October, be sure not to miss the **Ciudad Victoria Expo,** featuring music, dancing, and artisanry from the area.

CENTRAL MEXICO

The states of **Guanajuato** and **Querétaro** form a vast, bowl-shaped plateau of fertile soil, rolling farms, and verdant hillsides, all home to some of Mexico's most exquisite colonial cities. Since the 16th century, their silver-rich underground has brought the region prosperity and shaped its history. In the 18th century, the city of Guanajuato supplied most of Mexico's minting silver, later becoming the commercial and banking center of this thriving region. Today, the area is home to a growing expatriate population in and around San Miguel de Allende, one of the most lively and culturally charged cities in Mexico. Nearby **Hidalgo,** one of the most mountainous states in Mexico and home to the pine-laden edge of the Sierra Madre Oriental, also lived on silver for much of its colonial history and is best known for its archaeological sites, including Tula.

After beginning in Veracruz in 1919, Cortés moved his way inland, making his mark on **Puebla** and **Tlaxcala,** where many local tribes joined the entourage. A glimpse into one of the region's 16th-century temples, where images from *indígena* mythology mingle with Catholic icons, indicates the pervasiveness of elements from indigenous cultures, despite attempts at complete subjugation.

Contrary to popular belief, the **Estado de México** has more to offer than the insanely populated Mexico City. In the area outside the *Distrito Federal's* smog cloud, green plains creep up snowy volcanoes and swollen towns expand against their natural barriers. The state is speckled with stellar archaeological sites, solemn convents, and vestiges of the colonial era.

After Emperor Maximilian built his summer home in Cuernavaca, thousands of Mexicans followed him, making **Morelos** a prime vacation spot. Mexicans and foreigners alike flock to Morelos to take advantage of Cuernavaca's "eternal spring," Xochicalco's beautifully desolate ruins, and Tepoztlán's striking landscape. Unlike the overpopulated capital, parts of Morelos remain undeveloped, with plentiful tree-covered vistas and unspoiled streams.

HIGHLIGHTS OF CENTRAL MEXICO

COME for a year and stay for a month in **Guanajuato** (see p. 303) and **San Miguel de Allende** (see p. 309), two of Mexico's most perfect and picturesque colonial towns. They've got everything from cobblestone streets to mountain views to huge international student populations. Guanajuato is especially notable during its yearly festival in October, **El Cervantino** (see p. 309).

CLIMB the **great pyramid of Cholula** (see p. 363), one of the largest in the world, rivaling those at Giza, Egypt.

SALSA with thousands of language-school students in **Cuernavaca** (see p. 335), a lively, posh city with an impressive array of **nightclubs** (see p. 349).

CHECK OUT the **massive statues of warriors** (**the Atlantes;** see p. 328) at the archaeological site of **Tula** (see p. 327), once the capital of the Toltec Empire.

STUFF your face with delicious **mole dishes** and **sweets** (p. 351) in the modern metropolis of **Puebla** (see p. 351).

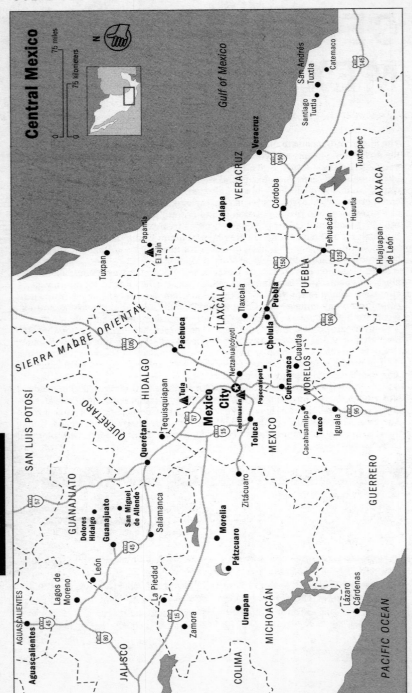

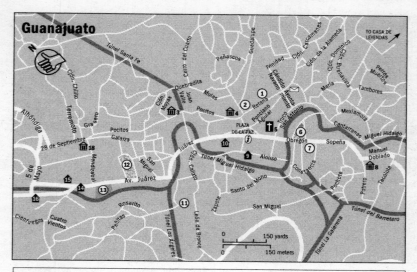

Guanajuato

⌂ ACCOMMODATIONS

Casa Kloster, 9
Hotel La Condesa, 10
Hotel Posada del Carmen, 15
Hotel Posada San Francisco, 14
Posada Hidalgo, 16

🛈 🏛 ◯ SIGHTS

Basílica de Nuestra Señora
de Guanajuato, 5
Callejón del Beso, 11
Jardín de la Reforma, 12
Jardín Unión, 6
Mercado Hidalgo, 13

Museo de la Alhóndiga
de Granaditas, 18
Museo del Pueblo de Guanajuato, 4
Museo Iconográfico del Quijote, 8
Museo y Casa de Diego Rivera, 3
Teatro Juárez, 7
Templo de la Compañía, 1
Universidad de Guanajuato, 2

GUANAJUATO

GUANAJUATO
☎ 4

The contours of Guanajuato's history—the peaks of economic recession and the pits of horrific repression—were mapped out in 1558, when massive veins of silver were discovered in the era. Over the next 200 years, the city would become one of Mexico's wealthiest, supplying much of the world's silver. Wealth without liberty, however, meant little to the *guanajuatense* men and women; after getting fat under Spanish rule, Guanajuato bit the hand that had fed it. It was during Hildago's stop here in 1810, that the wealthy and poor united, helping Hildago overrun the Spanish stronghold at Alhóndiga de Granaditas. Though the electrifying spirit of the War for Independence is long gone, Guanajuato is livelier than ever. The city's serpentine slate streets overflow with monuments honoring the silver barons and revolutionary luminaries, while *callejones* (stone alleyways) sneak through Spanish archways and courtyards and lead to the city's myriad museums, theaters, and cathedrals. University students and musicians promote an animated and light-hearted lifestyle, and the city continues to enjoy its status as a favorite destination among national and foreign tourists.

⌐ TRANSPORTATION

GETTING AROUND

Guanajuato's **bus station** is 3km west of town; from there, the "El Centro" bus takes you to the heart of the city, while the "Mercado" bus takes you to the market. Buses cross the city running westward above ground and eastward underground (every 5 min., daily 6am-10:30pm, 2 pesos). The bus system is easy to follow, but make sure to request a stop from the driver because they shout out locations rapidly and incoherently. Taxis within the city cost about 15 pesos. Taxis from the *centro* to the airport cost about 180 pesos.

GETTING AWAY

Buses: Central de Autobuses, 3km west of town. To get to the *centro*, take an "El Centro" bus; the "Mercado" bus will take you to the market. To get back to the station, take the "Central de Autobuses" bus from Plaza de la Paz. A taxi will make either trip for 30 pesos. Futura (☎733 13 44) goes to: **Acapulco** (1 per day, 450 pesos); **Durango** (3 per day, 278 pesos); **Mexico City** (5hr., 4 per day, 195 pesos); **Monterrey** (4hr., 5 per day, 369 pesos); **Nuevo Laredo** (3 per day, 505 pesos); **Reynosa** (1 per day, 428 pesos); **Tampico** (1 per day, 278 pesos); and **Tijuana** (1 per day, 976 pesos). Ómnibus de México (☎733 26 07) goes to: **Colima** (3 per day, 376 pesos); **Guadalajara** (4hr., 6 per day, 230 pesos); **Manzanillo** (3 per day, 435 pesos); and **Mexico City** (5hr., 9 per day, 262 pesos). ETN sends buses through Guadalajara to: **Colima** (3 per day, 376 pesos) and **Puerto Vallarta** (8 per day, 570 pesos). Flecha Blanca (☎733 13 33) also services Guanajuato, with free lunch on its longer trips.

■↗ ORIENTATION AND PRACTICAL INFORMATION

Guanajuato lies 380km northwest of Mexico City. The city's tangled maze of streets and *callejones* can leave even the best spatial navigator walking around in circles. The **Plaza de la Paz,** the **basílica,** and the **Jardín Unión** mark the center of town. **Juárez** climbs eastward past the *mercado* and Plaza de la Paz. Just past the *basílica*, the street becomes **Luis Obregón;** past Teatro Juárez, it turns into **Sopeña.** Most sights are accessible along this strip. Beneath the city run badass subterranean roads, more conducive to driving than to pedestrian traffic.

Tourist Office: Coordinación de Turismo, Plaza de la Paz 14 (☎732 15 74; fax 732 42 51; email turismo@quijote.ugto.mx.), on your right as you head up Juárez from the market to the *basílica*. Open M-W 9am-7pm, Th-F 9am-8pm, Sa 10am-4pm, Su 10am-2pm.

Currency Exchange: Banks line Juárez and Plaza de la Paz. **BITAL,** Plaza de la Paz 59 (☎732 00 18). Open for exchange M-Sa 8am-7pm. **Banco Bilbao Vizcaya,** Plaza de la Paz 69 (☎732 94 78 or 732 94 79). Open for exchange M-F 9am-5pm.

Laundry: Lavandería Automática, Manuel Doblado 28 (☎732 67 18). Self- and full-service. 38 pesos per wash and dry (full service). Open M-Sa 9am-8pm.

Emergency: ☎060.

Police: Alhóndiga 10 (☎732 02 66 or 732 27 17), close to Juárez. Open 24hr.

Red Cross: Juárez 131 (☎732 04 87), 2 blocks beyond the *mercado*. Some English spoken. Open for emergencies 24hr.

Pharmacy: San Francisco de Asís, Ponciano Aguilar 15 (☎732 89 16), just off the Plaza de la Paz. Open daily 7am-10:30pm.

Hospital: Clínica Hospital de Especialidades (☎732 23 05 or 732 13 38), Plaza de la Paz. English spoken. Open 24hr.

Fax: Sopeña 1 (☎732 69 91), to your left facing Teatro Juárez. Open M-F 8am-7pm, Sa-Su 9am-noon. Also in **Computel.**

Telephones: LADATELs are around Plaza de la Paz and throughout the city. **Lonchería y Caseta de Larga Distancia Pípila,** Constancia 9 (☎ 732 00 75), behind the Templo de San Diego, has additional telephone access. Open M-Sa 10am-9pm, Su 11am-3pm.

Internet Access: Redes Internet Guanajuato, Alonso 70 (☎ 732 06 11; email root@redes.int.com.mx). 15 pesos per 30min., 25 pesos per hr. Open M-F 9am-8pm, Sa 9am-2pm. The **Picasso's Café** building (see Food), Juárez 5, has connections.

Post Office: Ayuntamiento 25 (☎ 732 03 85), across from the Templo de la Compañía. Follow Truco, the street running behind the basilica, for 1 block and turn left. Open M-F 8am-7pm, Sa 9am-1pm.

Postal Code: 36000.

ACCOMMODATIONS

The neighborhood around the *basílica* is home to some inexpensive hotels, often occupied by young people from every corner of the globe. More economic lodgings cluster near the *mercado*. Those visiting Guanajuato on weekends and during the *Festival Cervantino* in October should make hotel reservations in advance and expect prices to rise dramatically. The tourist office keeps a list of families who rent out rooms during the festival.

Casa Kloster, Alonso 32 (☎ 732 00 88). Clean, airy dormitory rooms overlook an open courtyard filled with flowers and birds. Sparkling communal bathrooms. Most guests are friendly international students. Extremely helpful management. Reservations recommended. 80-90 pesos per person.

Posada Hidalgo, Juárez 220 (☎ 732 31 45), 1 block past the *mercado*. Livable rooms have faux wood paneling and very small bathrooms. The restaurant inside serves breakfast and lunch specials (all-you-can-eat 35 pesos). Singles 100 pesos; doubles 170 pesos triples 225 pesos.

Hotel La Condesa, Plaza de la Paz 60 (☎ 732 14 62). Neon signs and suits of armor brighten up the spooky (but fun) lobby. Rooms are old but clean, with bathrooms and bottled water. Expect noise from the *discoteca* downstairs. Students can sometimes get a discount. Singles 100 pesos; doubles 120-180 pesos; triples 300 pesos.

Hotel Posada San Francisco, Juárez 178 (☎ 732 24 67 or 732 20 84), the big green hotel next to the market. Clean, brightly colored bedrooms with shiny, white bathrooms and an antechamber for entertaining guests. Rooms have bottled water and TV. Beware of noise from the street. Singles 170 pesos; doubles 220 pesos.

Hotel Posada del Carmen, Juárez 111-A (☎ 732 93 30) near the market. Offers budget travelers from all over the world a place to lay their weary heads. Rooms have TVs and private baths. Singles 100 pesos, doubles 200 pesos.

FOOD

Inexpensive restaurants eagerly await you in Guanajuato's plazas and near the *basílica*. Prices near the **Jardín Unión** rise proportionally with the *gringos*-per-square-inch ratio. Several open-air food bargains exist at the Mercado Gavira, to the left of the Mercado Hildalgo.

Truco No. 7, Truco 7 (☎ 732 83 74), the first left beyond the *basílica* heading toward the *jardín*. Artsy, funky, dark, and popular with local and foreign students and families. Fruit salad (15 pesos), sandwiches (10 pesos), espresso (7 pesos), cappuccino (12 pesos), and *antojitos* and *comida corrida* (20-40 pesos). Open daily 8:30am-11:30pm.

Panaderia Purisima, Juaréz 138 (☎ 732 01 14), on the right side of the street heading to Plaza de la Paz, 1 block past the *mercado*. Follow the wafting scents of fresh baked rolls, *galletas* (cookies), and pastries (1-3 pesos each). A cheap and delicious way to fulfill morning and afternoon cravings. Open daily 6am-10pm.

Carnitas Sam, Juárez 6 (☎ 732 03 55), is the competing olfactory temptation in this part of town. The smell of *carnitas* (cut and marinated pork) draws customers late into the night. Open M-Sa 8:30am-3am, Su 8:30am-6pm.

Picasso's Cafe, Juárez 5B (☎ 732 38 25), houses dozens of replications of Pablo Picasso's works painted by the owner, who has also constructed all the furniture and created 20 different cappuccinos (15 pesos), from flavors like strawberry to *jamaica,* to *tamarindo. Torta*s (8 pesos), sandwiches (9 pesos), and a stocked bar may keep you here late into the night. Open daily 10am-10pm.

El Retiro, Sopeña 12 (☎ 732 06 22), across from Teatro Juárez. Escape from the *jardín* to join families savoring breakfast (20-30 pesos), Mexican specialties (20-40 pesos), or the *menú del día* (30 pesos). Finish your meal with a beer (20 pesos) or a drink (20-50 pesos) from the bar. Vegetarian selections available. Open daily 8am-11pm.

La Loca Rana, Pozitos 32 (☎ 732 13 25), across the street from Diego Rivera's house. Catch a *fútbol* game while filling up on the tasty 3-course *menú del día* (20 pesos). Breakfast 15-22 pesos. Open M-F 8am-midnight, Sa 8am-5pm.

▨ SIGHTS

Guanajuato has a slew of attractions, ranging from the historically fascinating to the mind-numbingly grotesque. Most sights are located in the *centro;* the rest are accessible via bus (2-3 pesos).

JARDÍN UNIÓN. One block east of the *basílica,* the triangular *jardín* is the town's social center, boasting enough shops, cafes, and guitar-strumming locals to satisfy any tourist. During the afternoons and evenings, crowds gather to relax on the benches under the shade of the surrounding trees or listen to the state band perform (Tu, Th, and Su 7pm).

▨ MUSEO ICONOGRÁFICO DEL QUIJOTE. One of the best museums in Guanajuato is housed in a gorgeous example of 18th-century Spanish architecture. Ten large galleries contain over 600 works of art inspired by Cervantes's anti-hero Don Quijote, including paintings, sculptures, stained-glass windows, clocks, and chess pieces created by artists such as Dalí, Picasso, Daumier, Ocampo, and Coronel. *(Manuel Doblado 1. East of the Jardín Unión following Sopeña. ☎ 732 33 76 or 732 67 21; www.guanajuato.gob.mx/mquijote. Open daily 10am-2:30pm. Free.)*

TEATRO JUÁREZ. Constructed from 1873 and completed in 1903 for dictator Porfirio Díaz, the theater has an unabashedly ornate Doric-Roman facade—columns, lampposts, statues, bronze lions and eight staring muses. In addition to housing government offices, the Teatro still hosts plays, operas, ballets, classical music concerts, and the main events of the Festival Cervantino. *(☎ 732 01 83. Faces the corner of Jardín Unión. Open Tu-Su 9am-1:45pm and 5-7:45pm, except on days of performances. 10 pesos, students 5 pesos; performance tickets 30-50 pesos.)*

BASÍLICA DE NUESTRA SEÑORA DE GUANAJUATO. This elegant 17th-century Baroque structure took 25 years to construct. Dozens of candelabra illuminate the Doric interior, including fine ornamental frescoes and paintings of the Madonna by Miguel Cabrera. The wooden image of the city's protectress, Nuestra Señora de Guanajuato, rests on a pure silver base and is believed to be the oldest piece of Christian art in Mexico, a gift of King Phillip II of Spain. *(On the Plaza de la Paz. Basílica open daily 8am-9pm.)*

TEMPLO DE LA COMPAÑÍA. Constructed from 1747-65, this Jesuit temple and college was eventually shut down in 1785; just two years later, the Jesuits were expelled from Spanish America altogether. In 1828, the building served as the location for the Colegio del Estado, which gave birth to the city's modern university. The building's ornate stone exterior remains striking, with four of the original five Churrigueresque facades still intact. Life-like statues of the *Virgen* and the apostles as well as gruesome representations of Christ surround the interior. The art collection includes a 17th-century painting of San Ignacio de Loyola and an 18th-century representation of both San Francisco de Asis. At the end of the exhibit is a spooky *relicario*, a wooden shelf enveloped in gold leaf and holding a collection of human bones. (*Next to the university and one block north of the* basílica. ☎ *732 18 27. Open daily 7am-9pm. 5 peso donation requested.*)

■ **MUSEO DE LAS MOMIAS.** The high mineral content of Guanajuato's soil naturally mummified the 122 corpses now on display in the museum. Cautiously tread through catacombs like the *Salón de Culto a la Muerte*, and view morbid holograms, a mummified fetus, and torture weapons of the colonial era. Gag at the purplish, inflated body of a drowning victim; a woman buried alive, frozen in her attempt to scratch her way out of the coffin; two fashionable Frenchmen; a man who died by hanging; and another who was stabbed. The museum's oldest mummy has been around for 135 years, while its youngest has been on display for less than 15 years. The mummies are the most popular sight in Guanajuato, drawing a larger crowd than the less gory museums downtown. At the exit, vendors offer disgusted visitors 5 peso candy figurines of the more memorable mummies, some wearing little *sombreros*. (*Next to the city cemetery west of town. To get to the museum, catch a "Las Momias" bus (2 pesos) in front of the* basílica *or the market. To catch the bus back, go up the hill to your right as you exit the museum and follow it as it goes downhill. At the bottom of the hill, take a left and walk to the end of the street.* ☎ *732 06 39. Open daily 9am-6pm. 20 pesos. 14 pesos for students and seniors.*)

MUSEO DE LA ALHÓNDIGA DE GRANADITAS. Constructed between 1797 and 1809 to guard the city's grain supply, this neo-classical building witnessed the victory of Mexican hero "El Pípila," who massacred over 300 Spaniards holed up here on September 28, 1810. After Hidalgo's rebellion was squelched, the angry Spanish displayed the severed heads of the executed leaders—Hildalgo, Allende, Aldama, and Jiménez—from the corners of the building. Today, the Alhóndiga is an ethnographic, archaeological, and historical museum. Captivating murals overwhelming the ceiling and sides of the stairwells are often mistaken for those of José Clemente Orozco or Diego Rivera; the true painter, José Chávez Morado, was a contemporary of both artists. (*At the west end of Pozitos on the corner of Calle Mendizabal. Open Tu-Sa 10am-1:30pm and 4-5:30pm, Su 10am-2:30pm.* ☎ *732 11 12. 20 pesos; free for students, seniors, and children under 13; Su free.*)

MUSEO Y CASA DE DIEGO RIVERA. The museum chronicles the life of Guanajuato's most famous native son, born in 1886 in this house. Visitors can admire furniture from his childhood home and then move upstairs to study works arranged chronologically and representatively of his different artistic periods. Don't miss the outstanding watercolor illustrations for the *Popol Vuh* (the sacred book of the Maya), which imitate Maya iconography, as well as Rivera's preliminary sketch for a section of the mural commissioned in 1933 by New York's Rockefeller Center, which was later destroyed. The museum also holds several photos of Rivera and his wife of 22 years, fellow artist Frida Kahlo. (*Positos 47.* ☎ *732 01 97. Open Tu-Sa 10am-7:30pm, Su 10am-2:30pm. 8 pesos.*)

MUSEO DEL PUEBLO DE GUANAJUATO. This 18th-century colonial mansion houses a permanent collection of 18th- and 19th- century works by Mexican artists and rotating exhibits of work by contemporary Mexican artists. (*Positos 7.* ☎ *732 29 90. Open Tu-Su 10am-6:30pm. 8 pesos.*)

MONUMENTO AL PÍPILA. Looking down on the *jardín* from the nearby hill is the Monumento al Pípila, commemorating the miner who torched the Alhóndiga's front door, opening the way to a riotous massacre of the Spanish. The titanic Pípila looks most impressive at night, when he is illuminated by spotlights. While the view of Pípila from the base is striking, the monument itself affords a magnificent vista of the city and the surrounding mountains. Pay a couple pesos to climb the narrow staircase inside the monument to a small platform behind the back of the infamous miner. For a panoramic view of the city while descending the hill, follow the steeper path down the west side which ends near the *Tunel de los Angeles*. If you're planning to walk up at night, take a friend. *(To reach the statue, follow Sopeña to the east and take the steep but manageable Callejón del Calvario to your right (5min.), or hop on "Pípila" bus from Plaza de la Paz (every 20min. 6am-10pm, 2 pesos). Open daily 8am-8pm.)*

CALLEJÓN DEL BESO. The most famous alley in the city, the "Alley of the Kiss" is so narrow that a person can literally lean out of one balcony to kiss someone on a balcony across the alley. According to local lore, a Spanish aristocrat living on one side of the Callejón became so upset upon discovering his forbidden daughter kissing her forbidden lover across the alleyway, that he flew into a rage and stabbed her to death. Sometimes there are frogs here. *(From Juárez, walk south along the Plaza de los Angeles and turn left into the alley.)*

MERCADO HIDALGO. Constructed in 1910 in honor of the 100th anniversary of the struggle for national independence, the *mercado's* sells everything from meat to small, hand-crafted woolen dolls; most of the fun is haggling over the price. The market is also home to some of the best and cheapest meals and candies in town. *(Another block farther down Juárez from the Callejón del Beso. Most stalls open daily 11am-9pm.)*

CASA DE LEYENDAS. The museum aims to convey and preserve Guanajuatense legends, with dioramas and moving figures retelling many of the city's tragic and humorous myths. Cringe as you watch the father of the famous lover from *Callejón del Beso* violently stab his daughter, then enter an elevator and "descend" into a mine filled with snakes, skeletons, and miners' unrealized dreams. *(Catch a "La Presa" bus (2.5 pesos) in the Subterránea or across from the basílica and ask the driver to let you off at the Escuela Normal. From the Escuela, walk up the unmarked street to your left for 2 blocks. Veer left at the fork; the museum will be in front of you at Súbida del Molino and Panorámica. ☎731 01 92. Displays and guides in Spanish. Open Th-Tu 10am-2pm and 4-7pm. 25 pesos.)*

EX-HACIENDA DE SAN GABRIEL DE BARRERA. Seventeen glorious gardens, covering about three acres, are perhaps the most beautiful of Guanajuato's many natural attractions. Cobbled paths, well-groomed flora, and whistling birds create the perfect atmosphere for a dreamy stroll. The ex-hacienda itself, a 16th-century structure, borders the gardens; its rooms contain 16th-century furniture, silverware, and paintings. *(Catch a "Noria Alta/Marfil" bus across from the mercado (every 15min. 7am-9pm, 2.5 pesos), and tell the driver you're headed to San Gabriel de la Barrera. ☎732 06 19. Open daily 9am-6pm. Closed from Christmas to New Years. 10 pesos.)*

MONUMENTO A CRISTO REY. The mountain, called the **Cerro del Cubilete,** 2850m above sea level and 20km from Guanajuato, is considered the geographical center of Mexico. The dark, bronze statue of Jesus that towers over it is 16m tall and weighs more than 80 tons. Although the statue is striking, you may end up spending more time observing the surrounding landscape; long stretches of blue hills are visible from the summit. *(Take the "Cristo Rey" bus (1hr., 7 per day 6am-4pm, 10 pesos) from the bus station.)*

♪ **ENTERTAINMENT**

The large numbers of international visitors to Guanajuato make for interesting nightlife. Many bars and clubs, often featuring live music, are concentrated near the Jardín Unión and the Plaza de la Paz.

Damas de las Camelias es Él, Sopeña 32. A sophisticated crowd of local professionals and thirtysomething tourists groove to late-night Latin rhythms, while downing *cerveza* (15 pesos) and mixed drinks (30 pesos). A wide selection of flamenco, jazz, salsa, Cuban, Peruvian, and Portuguese music. No cover. Open daily 8pm-4am.

Café Dada, Baratillo 16. Follow Truco until it meets Nuevo, then head down Nuevo until you reach Baratillo, a small avenue extending upwards to the left. A casual hangout where you can play chess or chat over espresso (5 pesos) or cappuccino (6 pesos) while enjoying the work of local artists. Open daily 8:30am-11pm.

Guanajuato Grill, Alonso 4 (☎ 732 02 87 or 732 02 84), 1 block behind the Jardín Unión. Scantily clad men and women shimmy on the many dance floors while students flock around the center bar. The booming bass shakes the block. Beer 10 pesos. Open bar Tu and Th 9-10pm. Cover 50 pesos and up. Open Tu and Th-Sa 9:30pm-3:30am.

El Capitolio, (☎ 732 08 10) Plaza de la Paz, next door to Hotel La Condesa. Similar to the Grill (techno, dance, etc.) but with more tables and seating. Don't show up in sneakers and shorts or the bouncer will turn nasty. Beer 12 pesos, mixed drinks 30 pesos. Occasional cover. Open Tu-Sa 9pm-3am.

❊ CULTURAL EVENTS AND FESTIVALS

Theater, dance, and music performances abound; check the tourist office for information or consult posters around town. On Thursday and Sunday nights in the Jardín Unión, the state band performs at about 7pm. *Callejonadas* (sing-alongs with the minstrels down Guanajuato's winding alleys) are organized on Friday and Saturday nights at 8:30pm and depart from the Teatro Juárez. Student groups present films almost every day of the week. Call the **Teatro Principal,** Hidalgo 18 (☎ 732 15 26; 20 pesos, students and seniors 10 pesos) or the **Teatro Cervantes,** on Plaza Cervantes (☎ 732 11 69; 15 pesos, students and seniors 13 pesos).

Guanajuato explodes for two weeks in October during the **Festival Internacional Cervantino.** The city invites repertory groups from all over the world to make merry with the *estudiantinas* (strolling student minstrels). Festivities take place mostly at local theaters, but also at museums and churches. Tickets are sold by TicketMaster a month in advance and sell rapidly. The **Office of the Festival Internacional Cervantino** (☎ 732 11 69; fax 732 67 75) provides more information. Guanajuato also celebrates the **Feria de San Juan** (June 24), at the Presa de la Olla, with dancing, cultural events, fireworks, and sports. Shorter celebrations occur on **Día de la Cueva** (July 31), when residents walk to a cave's entrance to honor San Ignacio de Loyola, first patron saint of Guanajuato and founder of the *Compañía de Jesús*.

SAN MIGUEL DE ALLENDE ☎ 4

Founded by the Franciscan friar Juan de San Miguel in 1542, San Miguel (pop. 80,000) has been dually shaped by its reign as a bustling commercial center in the 18th century and by its pivotal role in the struggle for Mexican independence. Every Mexican schoolchild can recite the story from memory: on September 16, 1810, when Hidalgo, the priest of nearby Dolores, led his rebel army into the city, the town rallied in opposition to Spanish rule under the leadership of the patriot Ignacio Allende. In 1826, the infant republic recognized Allende's role in the drive for independence by adding his name to San Miguel's. These days, San Miguel de Allende is overrun by North American expats rather than revolutionaries. The city is bloated with Reuben sandwiches, Haagen Daäz ice cream, and yuppies looking to painlessly inject their children with some Spanish skills. Still, although surrounded by US culture, Mexican life marches on. The lively mercado refuses to yield to the air-conditioned malls, and the city's shady plazas, colonial churches, and quiet green gardens could be those of Any Pueblo, Mexico. San Miguel has tamed its rebellious reputation in favor of artistry and academics. Perhaps it is precisely because Mexican culture has not been suppressed that the expatriate invasion has not been met with the same hostility shown toward the Spanish.

CENTRAL MEXICO

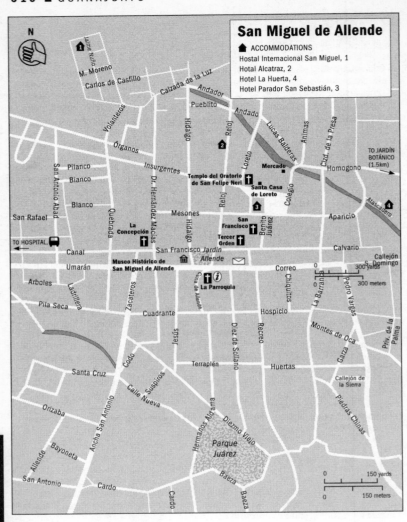

San Miguel de Allende

⌂ ACCOMMODATIONS

Hostal Internacional San Miguel, 1
Hotal Alcatraz, 2
Hotel La Huerta, 4
Hotel Parador San Sebastián, 3

▊ TRANSPORTATION

Buses: To get from the bus station to the center (known as the Jardín Allende or Plaza de Allende), take a "Centro" bus to the corner of Colegio and Mesones, near the statue of Allende on horseback (every 15min. 7am-10pm, 2.5 pesos). Walk 2 blocks down Mesones, then left 1 block on Reloj to the Plaza Allende. Alternatively, take a taxi (20 pesos). Flecha Amarilla (☎152 73 23 or 01 800 849 90 01) goes to: **Aguascalientes** (3¼hr., 2 per day, 100 pesos); **Dolores Hidalgo** (every 15min. 5:15am-9:15pm, 18 pesos); **Guanajuato** (8 per day 6:45am-5:00pm, 45 pesos); **Querétaro** (every 40min., 30 pesos); **San Luis Potosí** (4 hr., 7 per day, 92 pesos); and **San Felipe** (14 per day, 39 pesos). Service is also provided by Ómnibus de México (☎152 32 18) and Primera Plus (☎152 32 18).

✦ 🔃 ORIENTATION AND PRACTICAL INFORMATION

San Miguel is 94km southeast of Guanajuato and 428km northwest of Mexico City. Most attractions are within walking distance of the town center, the **Jardín Allende (or Plaza Allende)**, and the streets form a near-grid. **San Francisco, Reloj, Correo, and Hidalgo** border the *jardín*. East-west streets that run south of the *jardín* change their names every few blocks. The always-visible, towering *basílica* (cathedral) in the Jardín Allende can orient even the most frustrated of travelers.

TOURIST AND FINANCIAL SERVICES

Tourist Office: Delegación Regional de Turismo (☎/fax 152 65 65), on Pl. de Allende, to your left as you face the Parroquia. Knowledgeable staff distributes maps. Also sells posters and the useful guidebook *The Insider's Guide to San Miguel de Allende* (150 pesos). Open M-F 10am-7pm, Sa 10am-3pm, Su 10am-2pm. During high season, groups gather in front of the church in the jardín for **tours** of the city (1½hr., 25 pesos per person). Departure times vary; call the tourist office for more information. The public library gives guided **home and garden bus tours** in English, although some say these are more of a real estate pitch. Arrive 30min. prior to departure (2hr., Su noon, US$15).

Consulates: US, Macías 72 interior 6 (☎ 152 23 57, after hours emergencies ☎ 152 00 68 or 152 06 53; fax 152 15 88), across the street from Bellas Artes. Open M-F 9am-1pm or by appointment. For other countries, or to extend visas or visitors' permits, contact the **Delegación Regional de Servicios Migratorios,** Plaza Real del Conde Shopping Center, 2nd fl. (☎ 152 25 42 or 152 28 35). Catch the "Gigante" bus from Colegio and Mesons or from Juárez. Documents may be dropped off 9am-12:30pm and picked up 1:30-3pm. Processing takes at least 1 day. Open M-F 9am-3pm.

Currency Exchange: Deal, Correo 15, San Francisco 4, and Juárez 27 (☎ 152 29 32, 152 17 06, or 152 34 22), has great rates. Open M-F 9am-5:30pm, Sa 9am-2pm. **Helados Holanda,** Juárez 1 (☎ 152 05 67), at San Francisco, not only serves tasty ice cream but doubles as a *casa de cambio* with excellent rates. Open M-F 10:30am-3:30pm, Sa-Su 11am-2pm. **Banamex,** on the west side of the *jardín*, has 24hr. **ATMs,** as does **Bancomer,** at Juárez 11.

American Express: Hidalgo 1 (☎ 152 18 56 or 152 16 95; fax 152 04 99). Full financial and travel services. Open M-F 9am-2pm and 4-6:30pm, Sa 10am-2pm.

LOCAL SERVICES

English Bookstore: El Colibrí, Sollano 30 (☎ 152 07 51), near Cuadrante. Paperback fiction and art supplies, some in French and German. Open M-Sa 10am-2pm and 4-6pm. **Lagundi,** Umarán 17 (☎ 152 08 30), at Macíashas. A large selection of magazines and books in English and in other languages. Open M-Sa 10am-2pm and 4-8pm, Su 11am-3pm.

Library: Insurgentes 25 (☎ 152 02 93), between Reloj and Hidalgo. Art-filled courtyard serves as a gathering place for expats and students. Wide selection in both English and Spanish. Old paperbacks (6-8 pesos), postcards, and posters sold. Open M-F 10am-2pm and 4-7pm, Sa 10am-2pm. The building is also home to **Café Santa Ana,** which serves breakfast and lunch (20-30 pesos). Open M-F 9am-6pm, Sa 9am-2pm.

Supermarket: Bonanza, Mesones 43A (☎ 152 12 60), has a good selection of Mexican and American groceries. Open M-Sa 8am-3pm and 4-8pm, Su 8am-5pm. **Gigante** is even bigger. Take the "Gigante" bus (2.5 pesos).

Laundry: Lavandería El Reloj, Reloj 34 (☎ 152 38 43), between Mesones and Insurgentes. Wash and dry 35 pesos per 4kg. Open M-F 8am-8pm, Sa 8am-6pm.

EMERGENCY AND COMMUNICATIONS

Emergency: (☎ 152 09 11). Direct contact with Red Cross, fire department, police. A few dispatchers speak English.

Red Cross: (☎ 152 16 16) 1km on the Carretera Celaya. 24hr. emergency service.

Pharmacy: Botica Agundis, Canal 26 (☎ 152 11 98), at Macías. Helpful staff. Open daily 9am-11pm. Call police to find out which pharmacy is on call 24hr.

Hospital: Hospital de la Fe San Miguel (☎ 152 22 33, 152 00 22, or 152 23 20; 24hr. emergency line 152 25 45; fax 152 29 00), Libramiento Rte. 43 to Dolores Hidalgo, near the bus station. English spoken. In case of emergency, you may also call Hospital Civil (☎ 152 09 11).

Fax: Telecomm, Correo 16-B (☎ 152 32 15; fax 152 00 81), next to the post office. Open M-F 9am-5pm, Sa-Su 9am-noon.

Telephones: LADATELs are scattered throughout town. **La Esquinita,** Correo at Recreo (☎ 152 36 21 or 152 39 39). 5 pesos for international collect calls. Open M-Sa 10am-2:30pm and 5-9pm, Su 10am-2:30pm. **El Toro Caseta,** Macías 58A (☎ 152 11 00). 4 pesos. Open M-Sa 8am-8pm, Su 8am-2pm.

Internet Access: Cybercafé Punto.com, Zacatecas 3, has one of the best rates in town. 15 pesos per hr. Open M-Sa 10am-9pm, Su 10am-4pm. Access is also available at the International Youth Hostel (see **Accommodations**).

Post Office: Correo 16 (☎ 152 00 89), 1 block east of the *jardín.* **MexPost** available. Open M-F 8am-7pm, Sa 9am-1pm.

Postal Code: 37700.

▛ ACCOMMODATIONS

As is the case in many hot spots on the *gringo* trail, budget accommodations can be hard to find in San Miguel, particularly during the winter, *Semana Santa,* and the month of September, when the city throws a month-long *fiesta* in honor of Independence Day and the city's founding. Reservations (if possible) are strongly recommended during these times.

▨ **Hostal Internacional San Miguel,** Jaime Nuno 28 (☎ 152 31 75). From the corner of Quebrada and Organos take Volanteros until it reaches Calzada de Luz. Turn left, walk one block, and turn right onto Jaime Nuno; the red hostel is 3½ blocks on the left. Students and backpackers engage in afternoon discussions around the courtyard. Kitchen use, clean communal bathrooms, laundry machines, Internet access (15 pesos per hr.), and book swap. No lockout, but lights out at 11pm. Reservations not accepted. Key deposit 50 pesos. Quick morning chores required. Includes breakfast. 70 pesos per person, with ISIC card 50 pesos.

Hostal Alcatraz, Relox 54 (☎ 152 85 43; alcatrazhostal@yahoo.com), another popular hostel, with a hotel feel. Dormitories house males and females separately, though everyone mingles in the TV room and kitchen. Internet access (30 pesos per hr.). No curfew. Office open 9am-9pm. 80 pesos per person, with ISIC or HI card 70 pesos.

Hotel Parador San Sebastián, Mesones 7 (☎ 152 70 84), about 6 blocks from the *jardín;* take Relox away from the *jardín* and turn right onto Mesones. The hotel is on the left. Friendly and family-owned. Pleasant rooms with tiled baths, some with kitchennetts. Common sitting room off the courtyard is filled with books and has a TV. Spacious singles 117 pesos; doubles 117 pesos and up.

Hotel La Huerta, Callejon de Atascarero 9 (☎ 154 44 65). Walk up Mesones, 3 blocks past Colegio; when you see a stream to your left, turn right onto Atascadero. Follow the stone path about 1 block uphill—the hotel is the large blue building on your left. Just outside the main avenues of town, the hotel has rooms with great views of the town, *agua purificada,* and large baths. Students can sometimes get discounts. Singles and doubles 200 pesos, 50 pesos each additional person. With TV add 50 pesos.

FOOD

The sweet aroma of international cuisine wafts through the cobbled streets of San Miguel, and restaurants and cafes sit at almost every corner. Unfortunately, their prices can be as *norteamericano* as their clientele. The occasional splurge is sometimes worth it at the restaurants around the *jardín* that offer sunny, flower-filled courtyards. For a good value, try **Calle Insurgentes** and the streets around the *mercado* on **Colegio**.

La Villa de Pancho, Quebrada 12 (☎ 152 12 47). From the corner of Hidalgo and Insurgentes, follow Insurgentes 3 blocks down to the west until it meets Quebrada. Follow Quebrada for half a block to your left. Welcome to the kitchen of Cristina, the bubbly owner, who is very popular among backpackers. *Comida corrida* 25-40 pesos, breakfast 18 pesos, and *cerveza* 10 pesos. Open daily 9am-9pm. A **Casa de Huespedes** is on the 2nd floor with 3 spacious rooms connected by a communal bathroom. 70 pesos per person.

La Piñata, (☎ 152 20 60), on the corner of Jesús and Umarán, 1 block from the *jardín*. The vegetarian-friendly restaurant serves devourable food at prices that won't devour your wallet. Join the mellow mix of artists, students, backpackers, and Mexican families feasting upon *tostadas* (4 pesos), *tacos de guisado* (3 pesos), and sandwiches (10-15 pesos). Open W-M 9am-8pm.

El Capri, Hidalgo 10 (☎ 152 05 26). The key word here is late. The only place open after all the clubs close offers out-of-this-world *pozole* (22 pesos), *tortas* (10 pesos), and *taquitos* (20 pesos). Open daily 1pm-7am.

Los Burritos, Mesones 69-A (☎ 152 32 22), between Hidalgo and Reloj. Watch while cooks prepare tasty and economical *comida rápida*. *Burritacos* or *burriquesos* under 10 pesos. For the ravenous traveler, the *burrito maxi* (10 pesos) really makes a meal. Open M-Sa 10:30am-6pm.

El Tomato, Mesones 62B (☎ 152 03 25). This all-natural, all-organic restaurant prepares fruit juices (16 pesos) and scrumptious salads (30 pesos) in a very clean and modern atmosphere. The 3-course vegetarian meal of the day (50 pesos) is a break from typical taco fare. Open M-Sa noon-9pm.

The Bagel Cafe, 19 Correo, across from the post office, serves excellent sandwiches, freshly baked bagels, and sourdough bread (about 40 pesos). Homemade cookies and soups are excellent, and the level of cleanliness is well above normal Mexican standards. Open M-Sa 8:30am-3pm.

SIGHTS

The cheapest and most effective way to experience San Miguel is on your own two feet. Nearly all of the many sites of interest lie within walking distance of the *jardín*, and San Miguel's cobbled streets are fairly easy to navigate.

LA PARROQUIA. The neo-Gothic facade and tower were designed in 1890 by *indígena* mason Zeferino Gutiérrez, who is said to have learned the style from postcards of French cathedrals. The church is one of the most distinctive churches in central México. The pointed arches and flute-like towers attract eyes upward and inside, the ceilings are graced by glittering chandeliers and gold trim catching the sunlight from the tower windows. At the front is a tremendous gold-leaf altar. The basement contains the tomb of former president Anastasio Bustamante. (*Next to the jardín.* ☎ *152 41 97 or 152 05 44. Open daily 5:30am-9:30pm. Mass M-F 6am, noon, and 7pm; Sa 6 and 11am; all day Su.*)

MUSEO HISTÓRICO DE SAN MIGUEL DE ALLENDE. This home and birthplace of Ignacio Allende has a respectable collection of ancient ceramics, pre-classical artifacts, exhibits on the history of the region, and, of course, a tribute to the man himself. *(Cuna de Allende 1 at Umarán, is just across the street from La Parroquia. ☎ 152 24 99. Open Tu-Su 10am-4pm. Free.)*

TEMPLO DEL ORATORIO DE SAN FELIPE NERI. Founded in 1712 and rebuilt many times, the church is an amalgamation of styles; its interior is mainly Neoclassical but its engraved Baroque facade shows distinct *indígena* influences. On the west side of the church, the towers and the dome belong to the *Santa Casa de Loreto*, a reproduction of the building of the same name in Italy; enter on the right side of the altar in San Felipe Neri. The floors and the lower wall are covered with glazed tiles from faraway China, Spain, and Puebla. *(At the corner of Insurgentes and Loreto, 2 blocks east of the library. ☎ 152 05 21. Open daily 6:30am-1pm and 6:30-8:30pm. Santa Casa open M-Su 8am-2pm.)*

IGLESIA DE LA CONCEPCIÓN. An enormous church, construction began in 1755 and was not finished until the high altar was completed in 1891. The church is graced by the representation of the Immaculate Conception on its two-story dome, and the ornate gold altar features a likeness of the *Virgen* in blue metallic robes. *(At the corner of Canal and Macías, one block west of the jardín. ☎ 152 01 48. Open daily 7:30am-7pm. Mass M-F 7:30am and 7pm; Su 9:30, 11:30am, and 7pm.)*

BELLAS ARTES. Housed in an 18th-century former convent, this cultural center and art school has a concert hall and galleries with rotating exhibits. The stunning murals echo the impressive talent of the students and enliven the walls surrounding the peaceful, perfectly manicured courtyard, where many students can be seen painting or drawing. Look for *campesina* L. R. Santos lassoing a dreaded purple *chupacabras* (a monster that sucks the blood of goats). The school offers classes in ceramics, dance, art, guitar, and more, (a few are even in English). European and US films are occasionally screened. *(Macías 75, next door to the Iglesia de la Concepción. ☎ 152 49 46. Open M-Sa 9am-8pm, Su 10am-2pm.)*

OTHER SITES NEAR THE CENTRO. The **Instituto de Allende,** Ancha de San Antonio 20, a walk up Zacateros from Iglesia de la Concepción, houses several galleries with exhibits by local artists and offers art, Spanish, and social studies classes. (☎ 152 01 90. Open M-F 8am-6pm, Sa 9am-1pm.) Every Tuesday, vendors from all around San Miguel converge upon the **Tianguis del Martes** (Tuesday market) near the municipal stadium to sell their wares (Tu 7am-4pm). Clothing, groceries, old doorknobs, and assorted odds and ends await the adventurous shopper. To get there, take a "Gigante" bus from Calle Juárez (1.8 pesos) or a taxi (15 pesos). Reverberating with the calls of tropical birds, **Parque Juárez** is a large, lush garden just south of the *centro*. From the *jardín*, head down Luna de Allende until it meets Cuadrante. Follow Cuadrante for one short block to your left, and take your first right on Hermanos Aldama.

OTHER SITES AWAY FROM THE CENTRO. Jardín Botánico Cante, Mesones 71, the spectacular home of a dazzling array of cacti and succulents, is not to be missed. About 1,300 species grow along the *jardín's* 8km of walking paths. Walk past the Mercado Ignacio Ramirez, then turn right at Homobono, and continue on a steep uphill incline until it flattens (10min.). Continue straight (20min.), following the signs; the *jardín* will be to the left. Or, take a taxi (12 pesos) from Jardín Allende. (☎ 152 29 90. Open daily sunrise-sunset. 8 pesos, children 5 pesos. Proceeds benefit Cantes, a nonprofit conservation group.)

Catch a breathtaking view of San Miguel and the surrounding mountains by visiting the **mirador** above the city. To get there from the *jardín*, walk two blocks up Correo to Recreo. Take a right and walk about 10 minutes. One block past the Plaza de Toros, take a left and walk uphill three blocks until the street ends at the main road, with a sign that says *"Salida a Querétaro."* The mirador is a few minutes to your right. Or, take the "Gigante" bus from Colegio and Mesones or Juárez and ask to be let off at the *mirador* (2 pesos).

Hot springs fans will find their paradise at **La Gruta,** just outside San Miguel (10min., 8 pesos). Catch the Dolores Hidalgo bus and ask to be let off at a hotel near a billboard that says "La Gruta." Walk in the direction of the billboard and take a left on the dirt road directly ahead. To reach the springs, veer to your left. When returning to San Miguel, wait on the side of the route for one of the numerous buses to stop. (Open daily 8am-5pm. 50 pesos.) **Centro de Crecimiento,** organizes trips to San Miguel's surroundings and the profits benefit children in need of health care. (Zamora Ríos 6. ☎ 152 03 18. Sa 10:30am. 150 pesos.)

🎵🍸 ENTERTAINMENT AND NIGHTLIFE

Did you think all these students came here just to learn? There are as many clubs as churches in San Miguel, and the music pumps through the city's veins daily. The magazine *Atención,* available every Monday in the tourist office and in local newsstands, is the best source of information on upcoming concerts, theatrical productions, and lectures by both locals and foreigners. **Bellas Artes** and the **Instituto Allende** also have bulletin boards crammed with posters advertising art exhibits, openings, and other events. Tourists permeate the nightlife scene, which centers around drinking and dancing, where you may be charged over 20 pesos for a single beer. Expect cover charges at clubs to skyrocket during *fiestas,* especially *Semana Santa.*

BARS

🍸 **La Cucaracha,** Zacatecas 22A (☎ 152 01 96), the former hangout of Jack Kerouac, Bob Dylan, and Alan Ginsburg remains a mecca for artists, writers, and the like. G*ringos* and Mexicans are everywhere, but the only *cucaracha* in sight is the large decoration on the wall. Have a beer (9 pesos) or a mixed drink (about 17 pesos) as you listen to US, British, or Mexican tunes on the jukebox. Open daily 9pm-3am.

Char Rock, Correo 7, 2nd fl. (☎ 152 73 73), right off the *jardín.* The best part about this relaxed and casual place is not the cheap drinks from the well-stocked bar, but the fabulous view from the top floor terrace. Happy Hour. Live music every night after 8pm. No cover. Open daily 6:30pm-2am.

Agave Azul, Mesones 80 (☎ 152 51 51), By the time evening rolls around, live jazz, Reggae, or Latin music will be playing in this bar/restaurant. During Happy Hour (5-8pm), which precedes the daily music fest, drinks are 15 pesos.

CLUBS

Mama Mía, Humarán 8 (☎ 152 20 63), just off the *jardín,* is a favorite destination of foreigners and friendly (especially *gringita*-friendly) locals. Restaurant, bar, and *discoteca* in one, this enormous building is divided into several smaller establishments. **Mama Mía Bar,** to your right as you enter, attracts a twenty-something crowd and features jazz, soul, and rock music M-W, salsa Th-Su. Open daily 8pm-3am. **Leonardo's,** across the entryway, scores points for its big-screen TV. Techno music blares as college-age customers crowd the bar. Open M-W 7pm-2am, Th-Sa 7pm-3am. Directly in front of the entrance is a rather pricey **restaurant** appealing mainly to tourists and hosting nightly *música folklórica* (traditional music performances). Open M-W 8am-midnight, Th-F 8am-1am. The **terrace** upstairs often pulsates with the beat of live and loud rock performances F-Sa. When there is no live music, a young crowd enjoys the view of the city and makes conversation over a couple of beers (22 pesos). Open F-Sa 9pm-2am.

Pancho and Lefty's, Mesones 99 (☎ 152 19 58), provides hours of entertainment for students craving a pounding beat and a big drink from the well-stocked bar. Loud rock and cover bands or DJs spinning techno, disco, and Mexican pop songs thrill the young and tightly packed crowd every night. W 2-for-1 beers. Sa cover 30-50 pesos. Open W and F-Sa 8pm-3am.

El Ring, Hidalgo 25 (☎ 152 19 98), features standard *discoteca* fare and a lively and very young Mexican crowd. Latin and US dance hits will keep even the weariest club-hopper bouncing until the wee hours. Drinks 25-80 pesos. Cover W-Th 20 pesos, F 40 pesos, Sa 60 pesos. Open W 8pm-3am, Th-Sa 10pm-4:30am, Su 5:30-10:30pm, nightly in July.

100 Angeles, Mesones 97 (☎ 152 59 37), next door to Panchos, is a private club that caters to a primarily gay and lesbian clientele. Disco balls illuminate the otherwise dark dance floor as the all-ages crowd gets down to tunes from the 70s and 90s. Cover F 30 pesos, Sa 50 pesos with one drink. Open F-Sa 10pm-4am.

▓ FESTIVALS

San Miguel is reputed to have more *fiestas* than any other town in Mexico, with a celebration of some sort taking place nearly every weekend. Nearly all of September is a party as San Miguel celebrates its independence and founding. On the third Saturday in September, the city emulates Spanish tradition and hosts **San Miguelada,** a running of the bulls in the *jardín*. The impressive **International Chamber Music Festival** is held in August at Bellas Artes, Macías 75 (☎/fax 152 02 89). Ticket packages start at 1000 pesos and go on sale at the end of February. Other festivals include the **Jazz Festival** in November and **El Día de San Antonio** and **El Festival de Locos** on June 13. San Miguel celebrates the birthday of **Ignacio Allende** (January 21) with parades and fireworks. Hotels tend to fill up during festivals, so tourists should plan accordingly.

DOLORES HIDALGO   ☎ 4

"Mexicanos, viva México!"
——Miguel Hidalgo, "Grito de Dolores"

Nearly 200 years later, Miguel Hidalgo's rousing words still echo through Mexico's dusty "Cradle of Independence." A good daytrip from San Miguel, the small town of Dolores Hidalgo (pop. 40,000) has little more to offer than hot, dirty streets, a thriving ceramics industry (the town is known for its colorful *talavera*, a painted ceramic), and an amazing story. On Sunday, September 16, 1810, Miguel Hidalgo y Costilla, the town's priest, learned that the independence conspiracy that he had led had been discovered by the Spanish. Deciding to take immediate action, Hildago woke the entire town at 5am by tolling the parish church bell. The town's residents tumbled out of bed and gathered at the church, where, on that morning, Hidalgo delivered a electrifying speech proclaiming Mexico's independence—the *Grito de Dolores*. Then, calling his flock to arms, Hidalgo rallied an army to march on to Mexico City. With the brazen move, Hidalgo not only signed his own death warrant (he was executed a year later), but he single-handedly began the movement that led to Mexican independence. Today, Hidalgo is one of Mexico's most admired heroes, second only to Benito Juárez in the number of statues, streets, and plazas commemorating his heroism.

▐ TRANSPORTATION. To get downtown from the Flecha Amarilla bus station, walk straight out the door and walk left on Hidalgo. Three blocks down the street are the Jardín, the tourist office, Plaza Principal, and the Parroquia. Flecha Amarilla (☎ 182 06 39) goes to: **Guanajuato** (1½hr., every 20min. 5:20am-9pm, 28 pesos); **San Miguel de Allende** (40min., every 30min. 5:10am-8:50pm); **Mexico City** (5hr., every 40min. 5am-7pm, 140 pesos); **Querétaro** (every 40min. 5am-7pm, 46 pesos), and many other destinations. To get to the Plaza Principal from the Herradura de Plata bus station, go out the door on your left as you face Yucatán. Go down Chiapas, which turns into Tabasco, take a left on Hidalgo, and follow it into the plaza. Herradura de Plata (☎ 182 29 37) goes to many of the same destinations.

🛈 PRACTICAL INFORMATION. Streets change names as they cross the plaza, and the town's points of interest all lie within a few blocks of the center. The **tourist office,** in the Presidencia Municipal, is the large yellow building on the left side of the Plaza Principal as you face the Parroquia. (☎/fax 182 11 64. Open daily 10am-8pm.) **Centro Cambiar Paisano,** Plaza Principal 22, has good exchange rates (☎ 182 46 55; open M-Sa 9am-6pm) and the **Bancomer,** on Dolores Hidalgo, has **ATM** access (M-F 8:30am-5:30pm). **Hospital General,** Hidalgo 12 (☎ 182 00 13). Some English spoken. **Pharmacy: Botica de San Vincente,** Potosí and Zacatecas. (Open daily 9am-10pm.) **Cybercafé Punto Com,** Zacatecas 3. (15 pesos per hr. Open M-Sa 10am-9pm, Su 10am-4pm.) **Post office:** Puebla 22 at Jalisco, one block from the Plaza Principal. (☎ 182 08 07. Open M-F 9am-3pm, Sa 9am-1pm.) **Postal code:** 37800.

🍴 ACCOMMODATIONS AND FOOD. Quality budget rooms are rather scarce in Dolores Hidalgo. Prices rise and vacancies fall dramatically during *Semana Santa* in March and April, and between September 8 and 17 when Dolores is overrun by Independence Day celebrants. Reservations are advised during all peak seasons. One of the cheapest hotels in town is the **Hotel Hostal de Insurgente,** Calz. de los Héroes 13. (☎ 182 24 97. Singles 190; doubles 210 pesos.) For the same price, **Hotel Candillo,** Querétaro 8, will put you up in its simple, but tidy rooms. (☎ 182 01 98. Singles 190 pesos; doubles 200 pesos.) If you must have your cable TV, **Hotel Posada Hidalgo,** Hidalgo 15, can give it to you, but for slightly more. (☎ 182 04 77. Singles 219 pesos; doubles 244 pesos.)

Around the *jardín,* most restaurants are reasonably priced, and those that aren't betray themselves by their touristy clienteles. **Torticlán,** Plaza Principal 28, on the west end of the plaza, serves inexpensive and tasty food in a cafeteria-style setting. Join families and fellow tourists as you munch on *tortas* (8 pesos) with juice (5 pesos) or beer (7 pesos). Soyburgers (15 pesos) mean vegetarians can have their fill too. (☎ 182 26 76. Open daily 9am-5:30pm.) **La Moderna,** Potosí 51 (☎ 182 04 61), offers economical *tortas* (9 pesos), *hamburguesas* (12 pesos) and orders of three burritos (12 pesos) in a homey environment. Ask about the rooms for rent if the hotels are full.

📷 SIGHTS. Most of Dolores's sights lie within four blocks of the bus station, and revolve around the beautiful **Parroquia de Nuestra Señora de los Dolores,** where the *Grito de Dolores* was sounded. Constructed between 1712 and 1778, the church is by far the most striking building in town. The lavish interior features a main altar surrounded by columns beautifully ornamented with gold leaf, and two side altars—one Churrigueresque and the other Ultrabaroque. Dress appropriately— no shorts or tight dresses are allowed. Unfortunately, what would have been the star of the show, the original bell, is now positioned atop Mexico City's Palacio de Gobierno. (Open daily 9am-2pm and 4-8pm.)

On the west side of the plaza is the **Casa de Visitas,** built in 1786 to house Spanish officials. The building hosts the Mexican president when he reissues the *Grito* during his last year in office. In the center of the plaza is a huge bronze statue of Hidalgo, the man who made Dolores Hidalgo *la cuna de la independencia nacional* (the cradle of national independence).

Museo de la Independencia, Zacatecas 6, lies less than one block northwest of the Parroquia. Gory technicolor paintings detail the material and spiritual conquest of Spanish rule and the fight for independence. Relive Hidalgo's *Grito* in an eerie life-sized diorama with wooden statues of an inspired Hidalgo and anxious Mexicans. The museum also includes Mexican *artesanía* and a shrine to Dolores Hidalgo's favorite musical son, *mariachi* legend José Alfredo Jiménez. (Open F-W 9am-5pm. 5 pesos; Su. free.)

CENTRAL MEXICO

Querétaro

🛏 ACCOMMODATIONS

Hotel de Márques, 2
Hotel Hidalgo, 8
Hotel R.J., 1
Posada Colonial, 12
Posada La Academia, 10
Villa Juvenil Youth Hostel, 14

⭘🚺🏛 SIGHTS

Academia de Bellas Artes, 11
Casa de la Corregidora, 6
Convento de la Santa Cruz, 13
Ex–Convento de San Francisco, 7
Museo de Arte, 9
Museo de la Ciudad, 3
Santuario de Nuestra Señora
   de Guadalupe, 5
Teatro de la República, 4

Hidalgo's home from 1804 until 1810, the **Museo Casa Hidalgo,** at Morelos and Hidalgo, one block from the Plaza Principal, is less than thrilling. The collection contains contemporary religious paraphernalia, documents, and artwork relating to the independence movement. It was here, however, that Hidalgo made his decision to strike at once for independence. (☎ 182 01 71. Open Tu-Sa 10am-5:45pm, Su 10am-5pm. 14 pesos; free Su.)

Seasonal activities include the **Fiestas de Septiembre,** a traditional Mexican *fiesta* commemorating Independence Day; the **Purísima Concepción** (Nov. 28-Dec. 8), a fair that includes massive *artesanía* sales and pyrotechnic displays; and the **Expo Artesanales** (Mar./Apr., July, Sept., and Dec.) where the best of Dolores Hidalgo's *talavera, alfarería* (pottery), and handcrafted furniture are displayed and sold in the Centro Expositor.

QUERÉTARO

QUERÉTARO   ☎ 4

Between Mexico City and Guadalajara on the busiest stretch of road in the Republic, Querétaro (pop. 870,000) has been the site of some of the most decisive moments in Mexican history. A prosperous agricultural and industrial center, the whining grain elevators, monstrous warehouses, and truckloads of squealing pigs on the outskirts of town assault the senses. Inside the commercial ring, the city is a colonial wonder, with lantern-lit squares and an 18th-century aqueduct of graceful arches. In Querétaro's heart, students and entrepreneurs mill on centuries-old brick streets and *andadores* (pedestrian walkways). Though often overlooked by foreign travelers, the city is a popular destination for Mexican tourists.

Querétaro's central role in modern Mexican history began with the death of Emperor Maximilian. Abandoned by Louis Napoleon and captured by Juárez's troops, it was here that he climbed the *Cerro de las Campañas* (Hill of the Bells) and uttered his famous words: "Mexicans, I am going to die for a just cause: the liberty and independence of Mexico." The country was plagued by violence until victorious Carranza drafted the new constitution here 50 years later. Though Mexico relinquished a great deal of land and power in this city (the Treaty of Guadalupe Hidalgo was signed here) the many museums and monuments nevertheless attest Querétaro's pride in its history.

◤ TRANSPORTATION

GETTING AROUND
Querétaro lies between Mexico City and Guadalajara on **Rte. 57.** The modern **bus station** (☎229 00 61) is on the south side of town, not within walking distance of the *centro*. It is accessible via the "Ruta 25" bus on Allende and Zaragoza; "Ruta 8" on Ocampo and Constituyentes; "Ruta 19" at the corner of Madero and Guerrero; and "Ruta 72" on Universidad—all are labeled "Central" (every 5-10min. 6am-10:30pm, 3.5 pesos). To catch a bus to the *centro* (3.5 pesos), walk towards the highway, veering to the right, toward the sign that says "Paradero de Micros." Taxis to most destinations are 22 pesos—tickets are sold inside the station and handed to the driver.

GETTING AWAY
First-class bus service: in *Accesos* 1 and 2. ETN (☎229 00 19) sends plush buses to: **San Luís Potosí** (2½hr., 1pm, 150 pesos); **San Miguel de Allende** (1¼hr., 4:15 and 7:45pm, 50 pesos); and **Guadalajara** (4½hr., 7 per day6am-12:30am, 265 pesos). Primera Plus (☎211 40 01) sends buses to: **Mexico City** (2¾hr., every 20min., 128 pesos) and **Guadalajara** (5hr., 8 per day noon-12:45am, 207 pesos). Omnibus de Mexico (☎220 00 29) sends buses to: **Aguascalientes** (4½hr., 2:15am and 1:15pm, 160 pesos); **Zacatecas** (5hr., 11pm and 12:45am, 222 pesos); and **Acapulco** (8hr., midnight, 340 pesos). Servicios Coordinados (☎211 40 01) sends buses to **Guanajuato** (2½hr., 8 and 11:30am, noon, and 5pm; 80 pesos) and **Morelia** (3½hr., about every 2hr. 3:30am-10:55pm, 88 pesos).

Second-class bus service: in *Accesos* 3 and 4. Estrella Blanca (☎229 02 02) has service to: **Pachuca** (4½hr., about every hr. 5:15am-8:15pm, 89 pesos). Oriente (☎229 00 22) sends buses to: **Matamoros** (13hr., every hr. 5pm-10pm, 438 pesos); **Monterrey** (9½hr., every hr. 3-10pm, 375 pesos); and **Salamanca** (9½hr., every hr. 6am-7pm, 43 pesos). Flecha Amarilla (☎211 40 01) sends buses to: **Manzanillo** (12hr., 7am and 7pm, 314 pesos); **San Luís Potosí** (3hr., every hr. 6am-10pm, 94 pesos); and **Mexico City** (2¾hr., every 10min., 107 pesos). Flecha Roja (☎229 00 01) goes to **Toluca** (3hr., about every 40min. 2:30am-5:30pm, 78 pesos). Herradura de Plata (☎229 02 45) goes to **San Miguel de Allende** (1¼hr., every 40min. 6am-10pm, 30 pesos) and **Toluca** (3¼hr., every 40min. 2am-8pm, 78 pesos).

◪ PRACTICAL INFORMATION

Tourist Office: Pasteur Nte. 4 (☎238 50 00; email turismo@queretaro.com.mx). From the Jardín Zenea, take 5 de Mayo to the end of the Plaza de Armas. Maps and events schedules available. City tours in English or Spanish depart at 9, 10, 11am, 4, 5, and 6pm (1hr., 15 pesos). Helpful staff speaks English. Open daily 8am-2pm and 4-7pm.

Currency Exchange: Banks can be found all over the *centro*. **Banamex** (☎ 211 90 04), on the corner of Juárez and 16 de Septiembre on Jardín Zenea, has a 24hr. **ATM.** Open M-F 9am-5pm, Sa 10am-2pm; currency exchange M-F 9am-3pm, Sa 10am-2pm. **Casa de Cambio,** Corregidora Sur 108 (☎ 212 80 86), 2 long blocks south of Jardín Zenea, just past Reforma. Open M-F 9am-5pm, Sa 9am-2pm.

Laundry: Speed Wash, Montes Nte. 42 (☎ 214 14 45) Go 4 blocks west of the *jardín* down Hidalgo, then turn left. 12 pesos per kg, 3kg minimum. Dry cleaning available. Open M-F 9am-8pm, Sa 9am-3pm.

Luggage Storage: In bus station Accesos 3 and 4. 3 pesos per hr. Open 6:30am-midnight.

Supermarket: Comercial Mexicana, Zaragoza Pte. 150 (☎ 216 33 57), 7½ blocks west on Corregidora. Take any westbound "Zaragoza" *micro* or walk 20min. Open M-Sa 8am-10pm, Su 8am-9pm.

Mercado: Mercado Hidalgo, on Montes between Hidalgo and Morelos. Small, but offers fresh produce and meat. Open daily 7am-5pm.

Emergency: ☎ 066. **LOCATEL** finds lost people (☎ 214 33 11).

Police: Pie de la Cuesta 112 (☎ 220 83 83), in Colonia Desarrollo San Pablo. No English spoken. **Angeles Verdes** (☎ 213 84 24) rescues stranded motorists.

Red Cross: (☎ 229 05 45), at Balaustradas and Circuito Estadio, near the bus station. **Ambulances** (☎ 229 05 05). Both available 24hr. No English spoken.

Pharmacy: Súper Farmacia Querétaro, Constituyentes Pte. 17 (☎ 212 44 23), 4 blocks south of the *jardín*. Open 24hr.

Hospital: Sanatorio Alcocer Poza, Reforma 23 (☎ 214 19 20), near Corregidora. Open 24hr. A little English spoken.

Fax: Telecomm, Allende Nte. 4 (☎ 212 07 02; fax 214 39 48), 1 block west of the *jardín*. **Telegrams** and **Western Union.** Open M-F 8am-7:30pm, Sa-Su 9am-1pm.

Telephones: LADATELs abound. There is a long-distance **caseta,** 5 de Mayo 33 (☎ 224 19 67), half a block from the *jardín*. Open M-F 9am-6pm, Sa 9am-2pm. Collect calls 10 pesos. Also offers fax services.

Internet: CNCI, Juárez Nte. 82 (☎ 214 45 84), 3 blocks north of the *jardín*. 20 pesos per hr. Open M-F 7am-9pm, Sa 9am-7pm.

Post Office: Arteaga Pte. 5 (☎ 212 01 12), between Juárez and Allende, 2 blocks south of the *jardín*. Open M-F 8am-7pm, Sa 9am-1pm.

Postal Code: 76000.

◤ ACCOMMODATIONS

There are a handful of colorful places to lay your head near Querétaro's *jardín*. The cheapest accommodations, though, are a hike from the *centro*. You may want to call ahead on summer weekends, since Querétaro is a favorite for weekend warriors from Mexico City.

◪ Hotel Hidalgo, Madero Pte. 11 (☎ 212 81 02), half a block from the *jardín*. A huge arch-filled courtyard leads to comfortable rooms with small bathrooms and cable TV. Parking available. The attached restaurant serves tasty, inexpensive food. Singles 125 pesos; doubles 145 pesos; triples 160 pesos; quads 180 pesos.

Hotel del Márques, Juárez Nte. 104 (☎ 212 04 14 or 212 05 54), 4 blocks north of the *jardín*. An enormous stained-glass depiction of Querétaro's aqueduct welcomes guests. *Agua purificada* in the lobby and from dispensers on each floor. Carpeted rooms have cable TV, telephones, and sparkling clean tiled bathrooms. Check-out 1pm. Singles 120 pesos; doubles 145 pesos; triples 165 pesos; quads 185 pesos.

Villa Juvenil Youth Hostel (☎223 31 42), on Ejército Republicano. From the *jardín*, walk 1 block south on Corregidora, then go left on Independencia for 8 blocks. Veer right onto Ejército Republicano, just past the Convento de Santa Cruz. Follow the stone wall on the right until you reach the sports and recreation complex. Hostel is inside next to the swimming pool. While a bit remote, it's a bargain—large groups of athletes fill the rooms quickly so be sure to call ahead. No drinking or smoking. Reception 7am-10pm; call if arriving later, and notify management if you plan to stay out late. Single-sex dorms with 8 bunks per room. 30 pesos per person; 20-peso linen deposit.

Posada Colonial, Juárez 9 (☎212 02 39), just two blocks south of the *jardín*. 10 newly remodeled rooms, 5 with shared bathroom. Reception 24hr. Prices vary with bathroom and TV, but are approximately 50-70 pesos for 1 to 2 people.

Posada La Academia, Suárez 3 (☎224 27 29), 1 block southwest of the *jardín*. Although rooms are a little dingy, they are for the most part clean and all have private baths and TVs. Great location for the price. Singles 65 pesos; doubles 75 pesos, with 2 beds 125 pesos; 25 pesos per extra person.

Hotel R.J., Invierno 21 (☎212 04 88). Walk 5 long blocks north of the *jardín* to Universidad, cross the bridge onto Invierno and continue half a block; RJ is on the left. Not the lap of luxury, but reasonably clean and easy on the wallet. All rooms have private bathrooms. Singles and doubles 70 pesos; triples 115 pesos; quads 130 pesos.

⊓ FOOD

Inexpensive restaurants face Jardín Zenea; pricier *loncherías* and outdoor cafes rim the nearby Plaza Corregidora. Taco, *torta*, and other fast-food stands line 5 de Mayo and Juárez. Many restaurants stop serving their *menú del día* at 5 or 6pm.

La Mariposa, Peralta 7 (☎212 11 66), one block north of the *jardín*. This cafeteria and *pastelería* has been a local favorite for 57 years and counting. Enjoy *enchiladas verdes* (with green salsa; 32 pesos), fresh fruit juice (7.5 or 15 pesos), or tasty *tamales* (12 pesos). Get a bite to go, or eat in the spacious dining area. Open daily 8am-9:30pm.

Café del Fondo, Suárez 9 (☎212 09 05), between Juárez and Allende. Good food and great prices make this local hangout an enticing budget stop. The cafe boasts one of the largest coffee grinders you'll ever see, constantly churning out strong, exotic coffee drinks (around 18 pesos). Chess played throughout the day. *Quesadillas* 10.5 pesos, sandwiches 7.5 pesos, breakfast specials 14.5-17 pesos. Open daily 7am-10pm.

Restaurante de la Rosa, Juárez Nte. 24 (☎212 87 84), at Peralta, across from the Teatro Republicano. Mexican cuisine seasoned to perfection. Red wooden chairs, plaid tablecloth, and brick floors complement *enchiladas queretanas* (25 pesos) and the 4-course *menú del día* (24 pesos). Open M-Sa 9am-7pm, Su 9am-1pm.

Ibis Natura Vegetariana, Juárez Nte. 47 (☎214 22 12), half a block north of the *jardín*. Social staff sells vitamins and supplements to rescue your meat-weary metabolism. Lip-smacking veggie cheeseburgers 10 pesos, hearty *menú del día* 25 pesos. A glass of freshly-made fruit or vegetable juice 8-9 pesos. Open daily 8am-9:30pm.

La Parroquia, Juárez Sur 31A (☎212 94 07), 2½ blocks south of Jardín Zenea on the left. Business men and families come here for the good food at cheap prices. In this diner-like setting you will find filling breakfast combos (20-25 pesos), creamy *enchiladas suizas* (19.5 pesos) and spicy *chilaquiles* (22 pesos). Open M-Sa 9am-6pm.

◉ SIGHTS

Querétaro has more to see and to do than most colonial towns. For those tired of historical museums and Churrigueresque churches, Querétaro offers plazas, parks and walkways perfect for a post-meal, pre-siesta stroll.

CONVENTO DE LA SANTA CRUZ. Built on the spot where the Spaniards defeated the Chichimeca Indians, this convent was an integral part of the evangelistic movement in Mexico and lower California. Nearly everything inside Santa Cruz (founded in 1683) is original—the clay pipes and rain-catching system date from the city's aqueduct days. On the second floor is the cell where Maximilian spent his last moments; it has been left exactly as it was on the day of his execution. In one courtyard, trees grow thorns in the shape of crosses. A type of mimosa, they are known simply as the **Arbol de la Cruz** (Tree of the Cross). It is said that these are the only trees of their kind in the world; attempts to plant seedlings elsewhere have failed. (☎ 212 03 35. *South of Jardín Zenea, follow Corregidora to Independencia; you'll reach the convent after 5 blocks. Open Tu-Sa 9am-2pm and 4-6pm, Su and holidays 9am-4:30pm. Free, but a small donation is requested. Monks still inhabit the convent, so access to courtyard only with 20min. guided tours, in Spanish or English.)*

CERRO DE LAS CAMPAÑAS (HILL OF THE BELLS). Named for the peculiar sound its rocks make when they collide, this hill is where Emperor Maximilian first established his military headquarters and later surrendered his sword to General Escobedo in 1867. To the left of the *Cerro* and up a low hill, Maximilian's family built a small **chapel** over the ground where the emperor and two of his generals were shot. Flowering trees and quiet paths lead the way to an impressive panoramic view of Querétaro. Up the stairs to the left of the chapel stands a large stone sculpture of Benito Juárez, the man responsible for Maximilian's execution. Within the park you can also find the **Museo del Sitio (siege) de Querétaro**. *(Walk a few blocks north of the jardín on Corregidora and turn left onto Escobedo. Proceed until Escobedo ends at Tecnológico (30min. walk), or catch the "Ruta R" bus on Allende anywhere south of Morelos. Entrance in front of the statue of Maximilian. ☎ 215 20 75. Open daily 6am-6pm. 1 peso.)*

MUSEO REGIONAL. In the **Ex-Convento de San Francisco,** this impressively modern museum brings visitors through the highlights of Mexican history, with numerous *indígena* artifacts and colonial pieces, such as the table upon which the 1848 Treaty of Guadalupe was signed. The second floor is devoted to colonial-era religious paintings, and artifacts of Querétaro's military and political history. Probably the best museum in Querétaro. *(At Corregidora and Madero, on the east side of the jardín. ☎ 212 20 31. Open Tu-Su 10am-6pm. 25 pesos; seniors, national students and teachers with ID, and children under 12 free; free Su.)*

TEATRO DE LA REPÚBLICA. Newly remodeled, the *teatro* has borne witness to many historic events: in 1867, the final decision on Emperor Maximilian's fate; in 1917, the drafting of the constitution in the **Sala de Constituyentes** upstairs; and in 1929, the founding of the Partido Nacional de la Revolución (PNR), the precursor to today's Partido Revolucionario Institucional (PRI). The theater looks like a European opera house, with four levels of red velvet seating. Look for a copy of *Tesoro Turistico* in the lobby to learn about upcoming events. *(☎ 212 03 39. At Peralta and Juárez, 1 block up from the jardín. Open Tu-Su 10am-3pm and 5-8pm. Free.)*

MUSEO DE ARTE DE QUERÉTARO. Housed in a rebuilt 18th-century Augustinian monastery with a beautiful courtyard. An exhibition on local architecture supplements the bounty of Baroque paintings. European canvasses, 19th- and 20th-century Mexican art, and Cristóbal de Villa Pando's 19th-century depictions of the 12 apostles round out the formidable collection. *(Allende Sur 14, between Madero and Pino Suárez, 2 blocks south of the jardín. ☎ 212 23 57. Open Tu-Su 10am-6pm. 12 pesos; national students and teachers with ID, seniors, and children under 12 free. Tu free.)*

SANTUARIO DE NUESTRA SEÑORA DE GUADALUPE. This church's two white towers and central dome rise above their surroundings. The stained-glass windows toward the top let in dim light, and delicate chandeliers are suspended against a backdrop of pillars and frescoes. The image of *La Guadalupana* is by Miguel Cabrera. (☎ *212 07 32. 1 block north of the Casa de la Corregidora, at Pasteur and 16 de Septiembre. Open daily 7am-9pm. Mass M-F at 8, 10am, and 8pm. Sa-Su also at 2 and 7pm.*)

LA ALAMEDA HIDALGO. Built in 1790, the Alameda is a huge park perfect for a morning jog, romantic rendezvous, or afternoon stroll. The many trees provide ample shade for picnics, and there is a duck pond and a skating rink. (*Three blocks south on Corregidora from the* jardín. *Th-Tu 6am-7pm. No skate rental.*)

MUSEO DE LA CIUDAD. Contains a well-organized display of religious art and an ever-changing exhibit of contemporary art. (*Guerrero 27, near Hidalgo.* ☎ *212 47 02. Open Tu-Su 11am-7pm. 5 pesos, free for national students and teachers with ID, seniors, children under 12; Su free.*)

OTHER SIGHTS. Querétaro's **Acueducto** stretches along de los Arcos, west of the *centro*. This distinctive structure, with its 74 arches of pink sandstone, was constructed in 1735 as a gift to perpetually parched Querétaro from the Marqués de Villas del Águila. A *mirador* overlooking all 1280m of the aqueduct is on Republicano, about three blocks past the Convento de la Santa Cruz. Up 5 de Mayo to the east of the *jardín* is the **Plaza de la Independencia (Plaza de Armas)**, a monument to the aforementioned Marqués. Faithful stone dogs surround his statue, drooling respectfully into a fountain. The plaza is bordered by old square-rimmed trees, colorful cafes, shaded benches, and beautiful colonial buildings, including the **Casa de la Corregidora**, home of Doña Josefa Ortíz de Domínguez, heroine of the Independence movement. The **Andador Libertad**, two blocks from the *jardín*, connects the Plaza de la Independencia and Corregidora. It is host to a slew of mellow vendors and *artesanía* shops. (*Open Th-M approx. 10am-9pm.*)

PEEL IT, SLICE IT, SUCK IT, DICE IT

Mangoes may be one of Mexico's more delicious offerings, but the fruit is often avoided by foreigners who can't figure out how to eat them. Both the red-and-green *paraiso* mango and the smaller yellow *manil*, have a thick skin and a disc-shaped pit, and sloppily gush juice at any provocation. One of the easiest ways to spot a tourist is by the orange pulp slathering his shirt, hands, and face after an unsuccessful attempt. For the uninitiated, a brief tutorial:

The Easy Way: Pluck an end with your fingernail or fork, peel it like a banana, and suck away. Of the three methods, this is most likely to make a mess. Mexicans sometimes buy their mangoes on a stick and suck them like ice cream cones, which reduces spillage.

The Slice/Scrape Method: Cut the fruit into strips however possible and use your teeth to scrape the pulp from the skin. Probably the most efficient.

The Fun Way: Cut along both sides of the pit, leaving yourself with two bowl-shaped pieces and a pit with some fruit around the edges. Take your two bowl-shaped pieces and cut down into the fruit, creating a grid in the pulp. Turn the skin inside out and...diced mango! Afterwards, nibble around the pit.

 ENTERTAINMENT

Local entertainment, like almost everything else in Querétaro, revolves around the *Jardín Zenea*. Open-air brass-band concerts are given in the gazebo Sunday evenings 6-8pm, and myriad jugglers, *mariachis*, and magicians perform there now and again. Balloons are sold here in bunches big enough to lift the scrawny. **Jardín de los Platitos,** where Juárez meets Universidad north of the *zócalo*, dances to *mariachi* music. Things heat up around 11pm on Fridays and Saturdays.

The *Cartelera de Eventos*, published monthly by the tourist office, is an excellent source of information about cultural events, concerts, performances, and festivals. The **Academia de Bellas Artes,** Juárez Sur at Independencia, has information on what the students of the Universidad Autónoma de Querétaro have in store for the public. You might catch a ballet recital, piano concert, theatrical event, or folk dance presentation. (☎212 05 70. Performances usually begin at 5pm.) Ready for the millennium, **Querétaro 2000,** on Quintana, is a huge stretch of parks and facilities, including a pool, football field, basketball court, amusement park, library, open-air theater, and camping area. (To get there, take a "Ruta 15" from Ocampo or "Ruta B" from Allende. ☎220 68 14. Open daily 6am-8pm.)

◩ NIGHTLIFE

Querétaro is home to a slew of night clubs popular with locals and visiting twenty-somethings from Mexico City. Leave your flip-flops, jeans, and T-shirts at home.

Quadros, 5 de Mayo 16 (☎212 63 86). Look for the blinking light on the walkway to the left of the Ex-Convento de San Francisco. Local artwork decorates this spacious but intimate cafe/bar. Each night at 8pm musicians start hour-long sets of anything from blues to *trova*. F and Sa, would-be Selenas compete for drinks and prizes during amateur hour (around 10pm). Drinks, appetizers, and a small menu served. Beer 17 pesos. (Cover F and Sa 25 pesos, but depends on musician. Open Tu-Su 7pm-2am.)

Vazzo, Juárez 30 (☎214 30 33), on the west side of Pl. de la Constitución. This new club is the hip place to be for the local young crowd. Candlelight and a huge balcony make this place slightly calmer than the other clubs in Querétaro. Though there is no dance floor, many dance between the tables to English and Spanish pop music. Beer 17 pesos, drinks 28-35 pesos. Open Th-Sa 9pm-3am. Cover 30 pesos.

Jota B Jota Club and Bar, Quintana 109 (☎213 43 07), a 20-peso cab ride from the *centro*. Patrons hit the dance floor to booming rhythms and a merciless strobe light. For a more relaxed environment, the bar next door has pool tables (free for customers). Sip a *fuerte* margarita prepared with purified ice (35 pesos) while gazing at vintage coke signs and the ornately carved bar. Live music starts at midnight. Open W-Sa 8pm-3am. Bar cover F-Sa 10 pesos. Disco cover F-Sa 20 pesos.

Van Gog, Pasteur Sur 285 (☎212 65 75), a 15-peso cab ride from the *centro*. Vincent Van Gogh with no "H" in sight. The dance floor isn't huge, but that just gives you more of an excuse to get on the tables and speakers. Cover Th and F 30-50 pesos, Sa 50 pesos. Open Th-Sa 9pm-3am.

✿ FESTIVALS

The annual **Feria de Querétaro** usually takes place during the second week of December. The **Feria de Santa Anna,** complete with bulls running through the congested streets, takes place every July 26. The whole town dances during the **Celebración de la Santa Cruz de los Milagros** and the **Fiestas Patrias,** which take place during the second or third week of September. Other festivals include the **Feria International del Queso y del Vino** in May or July, the festival commemorating the founding of the city on July 25, and, of course, **Semana Santa** in March and April.

HIDALGO

PACHUCA ☎7

An easy hour's trip from Mexico City, Pachuca (pop. 220,000), Hidalgo's capital city, appears on the tourist map like a breath of fresh mountain air. The town, crowded but untouristed, draws its delectable flavor from the combination of original Spanish settlers and from English miners, who arrived in hordes in the 19th century. From Pachuca, visitors can explore the breathtaking mountains nearby or stay within the crowded city for a good lesson in silver mining processing.

TRANSPORTATION. Pachuca is approximately 90km northeast of Mexico city on **Rte. 85.** The bus station is a fair distance from downtown. Frequent *combis* run from the station to the Plaza de la Constitución (6am-10pm, 2.5 pesos). To get from there to the *zócalo* (Plaza de la Independencia), make a left on Hidalgo and a right on Ocampo. From the bus station, ADO (☎713 29 10) goes to: Mexico City's **Cién Metros** (1¼hr., every 15min. 24hr., 37 pesos); **Poza Rica** (4½hr.; 8:20am, noon, 3, 8:45pm; 77 pesos); and **Tuxpan** (6hr., 8:45pm, 100 pesos). Flecha Roja (☎713 24 71) goes to: **Mexico City** (1¼hr., every 10min. 4am-10:30pm, 33 pesos). Estrella Blanca (☎713 27 47) goes to: **Mexico City Airport** (2hr., every hr. 4:15am-6:15pm, 60 pesos) and **Querétaro** (4½hr., every hr. 5:15am-6:15pm, 89 pesos).

ORIENTATION AND PRACTICAL INFORMATION. Finding one's way can be difficult in Pachuca, as many streets curve and change names. Be prepared to ask for directions. Pachuca's *zócalo* is **Plaza de la Independencia,** bordered by **Matamoros** on the east and **Allende** on the west. **Guerrero** is parallel to Allende, one block farther to the west. Matamoros and Allende converge a few blocks south at **Plaza Juárez.** Plaza Juárez has two parts: an open cement space with a huge statue of the man himself and a small park. **Av. Juárez** juts from the statue's base, while **Revolución** extends from the park.

Pachuca's **tourist office** is at the bottom of the clock tower in the *zócalo*. The friendly staff speaks English and offers road maps to surrounding sights. (☎715 14 11. Open M-F 9am-3pm, Sa-Su 10am-6pm.) **Bancomer,** on Allende at the west side of the *zócalo*, has a 24hr. **ATM.** (☎718 00 22. Open M-F 8:30am-4:30pm, Sa 10am-2pm. Open for exchange M-F 8:30am-3pm.) **Mercado Juárez** lies on the north side of Plaza de la Constitución. **Emergency:** ☎060. **Police:** (☎711 18 80) in Plaza Juárez. **Red Cross** (☎714 17 20) provides 24hr. ambulance service. **Farmacia Similares**, Revolución 702, seven blocks south of Plaza Juárez. (☎714 43 61. Open 24hr.) **Medical Assistance: IMSS** (☎713 78 33), off Maderos, is a bit far from downtown. **LADATELs** can be found in all of the plazas. **Internet Access: Compu Renta**, Revolución 303, a block past the rotary on the left side of the street. 20 pesos per hr. (☎714 56 54 Open M-F 10am-9pm, Sa 10am-6pm.) **Post office:** Juárez at Iglesias, two blocks south of Plaza Juárez. (☎713 25 92. Open M-F 8am-5pm.) **Postal code:** 42070.

ACCOMMODATIONS AND FOOD. Pachuca has great budget lodging. Fewer than two blocks south of the *zócalo* is **Hotel Noriega,** Matamoros 305. Spacious rooms with tiled floors and wooden furniture include clean private baths; some have TVs. (☎715 15 55. Singles 120 pesos; doubles 155 pesos; triples 175 pesos; quads 190 pesos. TV 10 pesos extra.) A few blocks farther south is **Hotel Hidalgo,** Matamoros 503. Carpeted rooms have clean private baths and bottled water. (☎715 17 35. Singles 140 pesos; doubles 160 pesos; triples 200 pesos; quads 280 pesos. Cable TV 20 pesos extra.) For those really pinching their pesos, try **Hotel Grenfell,** Allende 116, across from the clock tower. The location is great, but the plumbing less so. Rooms are not for the faint of heart. (☎715 05 15. Singles 60 pesos, with bath 90 pesos; doubles 70 pesos, with bath 100 pesos; triples 80 pesos, with bath 120 pesos.)

In the 19th century there was an influx of Cornish miners to the Pachuca area. Their two lasting legacies are *fútbol* and *pastes* (pastry shells full of meat, potatoes, and onions, and a dash of *chile* to keep it all tasting Mexican). The filling snacks are sold all over town (3 pesos), stuffed with anything from beans to tuna. Try **Pastes Kikos,** across from Plaza Juárez in the *portal* facing the statue's back. (*Pastes* 3.5 pesos.) **Lisú Vegetariano,** Revolución 401, four blocks south of Plaza Juárez, is *the* place to go for delicious food in Pachuca.

The hearty *menú del día* (25 pesos) is a full-course vegetarian feast. You're likely to find entrees such as veggie pizza with avocados, peppers, and jalapeños, or eggplant lasagna. All fruits and vegetables are disinfected. The owner is a *Let's Go* aficionado. (☎714 78 73. Open M-Sa 9am-6pm.) **La Luz Roja,** at the corner of Guerrero, in the *portal* next to Plaza Juárez facing the statue's left shoulder, is a bit cramped, but that's because it's so popular. Try the delicious *pozole* or *morelianos* (15 pesos each; open M-Sa 8am-9pm.)

🎦 **SIGHTS.** The *zócalo* is dominated by the impressive **Reloj Monumental,** built in England by the manufacturers of Big Ben in celebration of 100 years of Mexican independence. This huge clock tower is an example of the French architecture that was popular during the Porfirio Díaz regime. Female statues represent Independence, Liberation, Constitution, and Reform. Funded by local mining companies, the clock was fashioned out of white stone brought from nearby Tezoantla de Mineral del Monte. To reach the **Archivo Histórico** and **Museo de Minería,** Mina 110, walk one block past the *zócalo* on Matamoros and take your first left onto Mina (the street across from the Bital). Follow it for 1½ blocks. A former mining company office, it holds an impressive collection of rocks, minerals, mining tools, and heavy machinery. (☎715 09 76. Open Tu-Su 10am-2pm and 3-6pm. 6 pesos. Video in English and Spanish at 11am, noon, 1, 4, and 5pm.)

The **Centro Cultural Hidalgo** is in the **Ex-Convento de San Francisco.** To get there from the *zócalo*, take Matamoros south of the square for one block, turn left on Mina, take it for two blocks, and turn right on Hidalgo (not to be confused with Viaducto Hidalgo). After three blocks you'll be in front of the *centro*. The cultural center contains the **Museo Nacional de la Fotografía,** an impressive survey of the technological history of photography. The museum holds a fascinating collection of Mexican photographs, one showing Pancho Villa and Emiliano Zapata as they marched into Mexico City in 1914. (☎714 36 53. Open Tu-Su 10am-6pm. Free.) Adjoining the cultural center is the **Church of San Francisco.** One block past the Ex-Convento is **Parque Hidalgo,** a favorite hangout for local teens.

NEAR PACHUCA: MINERAL DEL CHICO

Combis *run to Mineral el Chico (40min., every 30min. 7:30am-7:30pm, 6.5 pesos). They leave from Galeana; follow Guerrero north of the zócalo and make a left on Galeana, then head uphill about 2 blocks. The stop is in front of Bazarcito, a blue shop.*

Forty minutes of breathtaking scenery separate Pachuca from the tiny town of Mineral del Chico (pop. 500). Nestled in the **Parque Nacional el Chico,** the town has only a couple of restaurants, a small church, and a few houses. The numerous hikes and striking views of nearby rock formations make it a great escape from urban congestion. Follow the road that runs uphill to the right from the *combi* stop to reach the spectacular vista point, **Peña del Cuervo** (6km). If the trek is too long for your tastes, ask the *combi* driver; he may agree to take you there. Walking past the church and heading downhill to the left will take you through some old silver mines. This trail leads to the rock formation dubbed **Tres Monjas** (3km) because of its resemblance to nuns bowed in prayer. Locals are very friendly and will happily suggest other trails to explore.

NEAR PACHUCA: REAL DEL MONTE

Catch a colectivo *in front of the Iglesia de la Asunción, on the corner of Carranza and Villigran, near the east side of Plaza de la Constitución (4 pesos).*

Real del Monte's streets used to reverberate with the sounds of nearby mines. Now, it's just a colorful, idyllic little town 9km north of Pachuca. Its cobbled streets are lined with pleasant but slightly expensive shops. **Mina Acosta,** on Guerrero north of the Plaza Principal (20min.), is a relic of Real's mining history. This mine passed through the hands of Spanish, English, Mexican, and US owners before finally coming under government control. The building on your left as you enter housed mine managers. The obsidian shards that line the tops of the walls surrounding the mine kept silver-robbers out. (Open M-F 9am-3pm.)

Real del Monte also offers good hiking and climbing opportunities. *Combis* depart from La Madre in front of the Deportivo de la Ciudad, also known as the Escuela Primaria, for **Peñas Cargadas** (every hr. 6am-5pm; 5 pesos), a massive rock formation 3km away. You can also hike there, mostly uphill, by following the signs. At the site, *cargada mayor*, on your left, stands 100m. To its right is *cargada menor*, a mere 80m. Next to *menor* stands *el pilón* (70m tall), and on the far right, *cerrote* (30m). Many hiking paths weave through *Peñas Cargadas*. Only very experienced rock climbers should attempt to scale the rocks (crosses at the bottom mark the spots where several have met their deaths). Interested climbers should contact **Lucio Ramírez** (Club Alpino, Lerdo de Tejada 4, Mineral del Monte, Hidalgo 42130) or stop by the **Club Alpino** headquarters in the Deportivo de la Ciudad. (Climbing excursions Su 7am. Open Su 7am-7:30pm.)

TULA ☎ 7

Travelers come to Tula (pop. 90,000) for one reason and one reason alone: to see the ruins that made her famous. The archaeological site of Tula, is, without a doubt, one of the most historically significant in all of Mesoamerica. Ruins aside, the city of Tula is unexciting at best, with little to distinguish it from any other Mexican town. Daytrippers from Mexico City (80km) and Pachuca (75km) are lured here by glossy National Geographic photos and the myth of Quetzalcóatl, but usually leave quickly when the day and the ruin-stomping is done.

▐▀ ▐▌ TRANSPORTATION AND PRACTICAL INFORMATION

From Mexico City to Tula, take an AVM (☎ 737 96 91) bus from the Central de Autobu_es del Norte, *Sala 8* (2nd-class 2hr., every 15min. 5am-10:30pm, 30 pesos; first-class 1½hr., every 40min. 7am-9pm, 36 pesos). Once in Tula, to get to the *zócalo* from the **bus station** (☎ 732 02 25), turn right down Xicoténcatl, left on Ocampo, left on Zaragoza, and right on Hidalgo. Confused? Just head toward the cathedral, visible from most points in the city. From the bus station, AVM (☎ 732 01 18) sends buses to **Mexico City** (2nd-class 2hr., every 20min. 6am-8pm, 30 pesos; 1st-class 1½hr., every 40min. 6am-8pm, 36 pesos) and **Pachuca** (2hr., every hr. 5:30am-6:30pm, 30 pesos). Flecha Amarilla (☎ 732 02 25) has 2nd-class service to: **Guanajuato** (5hr., 10:20am, 140 pesos); **Morelia** (6hr., 8am, 143 pesos); and **Querétaro** (2½hr., 4am-7:30pm, 58 pesos).

Banamex, at Valle and Juárez, exchanges currency and traveler's checks and has a 24hr. **ATM.** (☎ 732 37 72. Open M-F 9am-5pm, Sa 10am-2pm.) **Farmacia Central,** is on the corner of Hidalgo and Zaragoza. (☎ 732 01 04. Open daily 8am-10pm.) **Market:** behind the cathedral. (Open daily 6am-8pm.) **Police:** (☎ 733 20 49) are at 5 de Mayo 408. **Red Cross:** ☎ 732 00 18 or 732 12 50. **LADATELs** are near the bus station and on Zaragoza and Hidalgo. **Internet Access: Ditesa,** Hidalgo 12, half a block from the *zócalo*. (☎ 732 00 51. 20 pesos per hr. Open M-Sa 9am-8pm.)

▐▘▐ ACCOMMODATIONS AND FOOD

Budget rooms don't come easy in Tula. The best deal in town is the **Auto Hotel Cuéllar,** 5 de Mayo 23. Cute rooms with phone, cable TV, carpet, and slightly worn baths surround a quiet courtyard full of flowering plants and singing birds. Your car will have a place to sleep, too. (☎ 732 04 42. Singles 130 pesos; doubles 150 pesos.) Some of the best, cheapest food in town is cooked right in front of your eyes in the market behind the cathedral. *Comida corrida* 15 pesos. Also try the *roticerías* found all over the *centro* that offer rice, beans, tortillas, and an entire roast chicken (42 pesos). **Restaurante Casa Blanca,** Hidalgo 114, serves a tasty five-course *comida corrida* (42 pesos) in a bright, traditional setting. (☎732 22 74. Open M-Sa 8am-8:45pm, Su 8am-7pm.)

▓ THE ARCHAEOLOGICAL SITE OF TULA

Taxis will take you from the sitio stand on Zaragoza at Hidalgo in Tula. (☎732 05 65. 20 pesos.) Once at the site, taxis aren't available, but frequent peseros will return you to the bus station or centro (3 pesos). You can also walk (30min.). From the bus station, turn right on Ocampo and follow signs to the archaeological zone. Open daily 9am-5pm. 25 pesos; Su free. Museum free. Visit during the week when the site is less crowded.

Tula's importance in pre-Hispanic Mexico cannot be overstated. Settled and occupied by various small nomadic tribes during the pre-Classic and Classic Periods, control of the city is thought to have been concentrated in the hands of the powerful Teotihuacán. In the late Classic Period, however, the area was abandoned and then resettled by a different group—the Tolteca-Chichimeca (more commonly, the Toltec). By the early Post-Classic Period (AD 900-1000), the Toltec capital entered a period known as the Tollán phase, marked by great construction and expansion. New pyramids were constructed, the city was carefully realigned, and the population peaked at around 40,000. Archaeologists believe the Toltec trade network was incredibly extensive. A close resemblance in architecture between Tula and the Post-Classic Maya center at Chichén Itzá (see p. 601) has led archaeologists to hypothesize on some sort of relationship between the two, perhaps through trade or conquest. (Archaeologists are unsure of who influenced whom.) The Toltecs, whose name means "builders" in Náhuatl, relied on irrigation, and modeled their architecture after the style of Teotihuacán. During the 200-year-long Toltec heyday, the once-peaceful kingdom turned violent and vicious. When crop failures and droughts weakened the capital in 1165, neighboring Chichimecas sacked the city, burning temples and destroying much of what the Toltecs had built. The devastated city was further ruined when the Aztecs subsequently occupied and looted it. Today, among the Toltec remains is evidence of the Aztec's temporary stay—bits of Aztec ceramics and pottery are scattered about. Unfortunately, the ruins as they stand provide little testament to the Toltec's power—only 17 sq. km of the ruins have been excavated and many buildings have eroded due to poor rock quality, poor maintenance, and the destructive practices of the original excavators. Of course, it didn't help that the city had already been sacked twice.

JUEGO DE PELOTA #1 (BALLCOURT #1). From the entrance area, a 600m dirt path zigzags past cacti through two sets of vendor stalls before arriving at the main plaza. (The vendors sell mostly junk, but on rare occasion you can find delicate reproductions at low prices.) The first structure to your right (north) as you reach the main plaza is Ballcourt #1, just north of the large Edificio de los Atlantes. This court, nearly 70m long, once held a depiction of a ball player in ritual dress, now located in the Museo Nacional de Antropología in Mexico City (see p. 112).

EDIFICIO DE LOS ATLANTES (PYRAMID B). To the left (south) is the monumental Edificio de los Atlantes, Tula's signature edifice. In front of the pyramid stand three rows of 14 columns, which, presumably, supported some sort of walkway leading to the pyramid. Close inspection of these statues (each a whopping 9.6m tall) at the top of the pyramid reveals traces of red pigment. These statues of warriors originally supported a temple and altar dedicated to Quetzalcóatl. The sides of the pyramid were decorated with reliefs of jaguars, coyotes, eagles, and feathered serpents, each symbolizing different classes of warriors; some of these reliefs are visible today.

CORTÉS AS GOD Tula's history contains one of the most told stories of the Spanish conquest. Though accounts diverge, the most widely accepted version is this: Ce Técpatl Mixcóatl, the leader of a Tolteca-Chichimeca tribe, was assassinated by rival factions. His son, Ce Acatl Topiltzin, born in the year 1 Reed (AD 947) avenged his father, then led his people to establish the new capital of Tollán (later known as Tula). The benevolent and beloved Ce Acatl Topiltzin identified himself with and worshipped Quetzalcóatl, the peaceful, feathered-serpent god and sponsor of the arts. After many years, a rival faction favoring Quetzalcóatl's rivals, worshippers of the war god Tezcatlipoca, tricked Ce Acatl into neglecting his religious duties (or, by other accounts, into sleeping with his mother). Horribly disgraced, Ce Acatl left Tula in self-imposed exile and boarded a raft of serpents, promising to return in the year 1 Reed. Hundreds of years after Ce Acatl's departure, the *conquistador* Hernán Cortés by chance landed on Mexico's shores in the year 1 Reed. The rest, as they say, is history.

EL COATEPANTLI (THE WALL OF SNAKES). Along the pyramid's northern side, and currently covered by a tin roof, is El Coatepantli. This wall, which depicts jaguars and serpents in procession, so impressed the Aztecs that they built copies of it around the plazas of their own cities. Reliefs of serpents feasting on humans adorn the adjacent wall.

PALACIO QUEMADO (BURNT PALACE). Immediately west of the Edificio de los Atlantes is the Palacio Quemado, so named because it was originally believed to have been burned during Tula's sacking by the Chichimecas. Whether this actually happened is unclear. Regardless, the building is believed to have been an administrative center. A *chac-mool* (a reclining version of the rain god Tlaloc) was originally found in the central patio; the figure now reclines near the Edificio de los Atlantes, under the awning.

TEMPLO PRINCIPAL (PYRAMID C). Like many other indigenous cultures, the Toltecs built their largest building, the Templo (or Edificio) Principal, on the eastern boundary of the plaza facing the sunrise. The object of deliberate destruction by the Chichimecas and others following Tula's abandonment at the end of the 12th century, the Templo Principal now pales in comparison to the Edificio de los Atlantes. Not fully excavated and still overgrown with weeds, the Templo Principal cannot be climbed from the front—one must scramble up a steep path in its southeast corner. The temple was once most likely adorned with the massive sculptural slab found nearby, covered with images of Quetzalcóatl in his manifestation as Tlahuizcaltec Uhtli, "the morning star."

OTHER SIGHTS. Adjoining **Ballcourt #2** on the interior of the plaza is **El Tzompantli,** a small platform built by the Aztecs. Tzompantli means "place of skulls;" the platform was used to display the victims of sacrifice. Ballcourt #2 is smaller than Ballcourt #1, and associated more with the sacrificial uses of the game.

ESTADO DE MÉXICO

VALLE DE BRAVO   ☎ 7

Everything about this 16th-century town is perfect, from the mountain views at the end of every cobblestone street to the luscious fruit sold in the market by traditionally-clad *indígenas*. Even the stray dogs look well-fed. Wealthy Mexico City residents keep vacation homes on the edges of Valle, and though new business has made it wealthy, it still has a cozy, traditional feel. This is not accidental; in 1972 Valle was declared a "typical town," and, among other restrictions, construction on new buildings was strictly curtailed. You don't come to Valle to "do" anything, but rather to wander and marvel at the beauty of it all.

▛ TRANSPORTATION. From the **Central de Autobuses Poniente** in Mexico City, Autobuses Mexico-Toluca-Zinacantepey sends buses to Valle de Bravo (3hr., every 20min., 46 pesos). Almost all are second-class, but, mercifully, they're rarely full. From the bus station in Valle de Bravo, to get to the *centro* turn right as you exit, walk downhill one block, and make a right on Zaragoza. Follow it two blocks until you see the Centro Comercial Isseymym, and turn left. You will see the church at the end of the street. The **market** is one block before the church on the right. To the right of the church, as you face the *zócalo*, is the **Plaza Independencia.** Valle's bus station services **Mexico City** (3hr., 2 per hr. 1:20am-5:30pm, 61 pesos) and **Toluca** (2hr., every 20min. 6am-6pm, 34 pesos).

▟ PRACTICAL INFORMATION. Bital, Bocanegra 205, has a 24hr. **ATM** and exchanges currency and traveler's checks. (☎262 44 04. Open M-Sa 8am-7pm.) **Emergency:** ☎060. **Police:** Díaz 200. (☎262 01 26. Open 24hr.) **Red Cross:** on the corner of Jiménez and de la Cuenca. Some English spoken. (☎262 03 91. Open 24hr.) **Farmacia Paty,** on the right of the plaza, facing the church. (☎262 01 62. Open daily 8am-9pm.) **Fax: Telecomm,** 16 de Septiembre 415B, near the bus station. (☎262 01 71. Open M-F 9am-3pm, Sa 9am-1pm.) **LADATELs** are easy to find in the plaza. **Internet Access: Internet Toluca,** Pagaza 327. Walk down Pagaza four blocks. (☎262 05 26. 30 pesos per hr. Open daily 10am-8pm.) **Post office:** Pagaza 200. (☎262 03 73. Open M-F 9am-4pm, Sa 9am-1pm.) **Postal Code:** 51200.

▛▟ ACCOMMODATIONS AND FOOD. Hotel Mary, Plaza Independencia 1, offers prime location and affordable prices. Clean, simple, and comfortable rooms have a smattering of mismatched decorations. Try to get one with a plaza view. (☎262 42 61. Singles 150 pesos; doubles 200 pesos; cable TV 20 pesos extra.) Another alternative is **Posada Familiar,** 16 de Septiembre 417, down the street from the bus station. Look for a sign on the left that says "Hotel Interior." The hotel is not luxurious, but it has a pleasant courtyard and clean rooms and baths. (☎262 12 22. Singles 120 pesos; doubles 130 pesos; triples 160 pesos.)

If you're hungry for something small, cheap, and quick, try any of the holes-in-the-wall between the bus station and the *centro*. For something a little nicer, duck into **La Parilla,** Bocanegra 104. The bright and tiny restaurant serves mouth-watering food in a homey atmosphere. *Comida corrida* and dessert 40 pesos. (Open daily 9am-8:30pm.) If you want to throw back a beer (or five) with the locals, check out **Restaurant Bar Los Torres,** across from the Centro Vocacional Isseymym, *en route* from the bus station to the *centro*. Patrons are friendly, and have been known to bust out guitars and start singing. Breakfasts 20-28 pesos, *comida corrida* 30 pesos. (☎262 27 24. Open daily 8am-8pm.)

IXTAPAN DE LA SAL ☎7

Most people go to Ixtapan de la Sal (pop. 40,000) for three reasons: the US$200-per-day resorts, the upscale spas, and the water park. There is one reason why *you* should go: everything else. Only a quarter of a mile separates Ixtapan's *centro* from the slew of ritzy resorts and spas that have made this town famous, but in Ixtapan proper, horses and *burros* still amble down the streets while people arrange flower offerings for the Virgin Mary. Ixtapan welcomes its visitors with a gorgeous and refreshingly simple rust-and-whitewash cathedral and quiet, clean streets where the smell of home-cooked meals wafts from the doorways. Come quickly before resorts swallow the town itself, but once you're here, rest easy—life is slow, and good.

▛ TRANSPORTATION. The bus station is actually in Tonatico, a small town just to the south of Ixtapan. From the front of the bus station, take an Ixtapan *combi* (2 pesos). From the Tonatico bus station, **Tres Estrellas de Centro** (☎141 10 05) sends 2nd-class buses to: **Mexico City** (2hr., every hr. 6am-7pm, 57.5

pesos); **Taxco** (1hr., every 40min. 6:10am-7:35pm, 31.5 pesos); and **Toluca** (1hr., every 20min. 6am-8pm, 30 pesos). Flecha Roja (☎141 10 05) sends 2nd-class buses to: **Acapulco** (6hr., 10:50am, 1:20, 5:20pm, 140 pesos) via **Taxco** (1¼hr., 27 pesos), and **Cuernavaca** (3hr., 7 per day 8am-6pm, 34 pesos).

■*7* **ORIENTATION AND PRACTICAL INFORMATION.** The main street in Ixtapan is **Juárez**, which ends 500m ahead in the spa, water park, and resorts. Running parallel to Juárez, to the right if you're looking toward the resorts, is **Allende**. Some of the main streets perpendicular to Juárez, listed in order from the south end of town to the resorts, are 20 de Noviembre, Independencia, 16 de Septiembre, Aldama, and Constitución.

There is no tourist office, but an **information booth** can be found at the end of Juárez, on the north side of the market in front of the resorts. **Banco Santander,** Allende Sur 20, exchanges currency. (☎143 07 77. Open M-F 9am-4pm.) **Farmacia El Fénix,** Plaza de Mártires 1, on the *zócalo.* (Open M-F 8am-10pm, Sa-Su 9am-3pm and 5-9pm.) **Luggage storage:** in the bus station. (3.5 pesos per day. Open daily 7am-8pm.) **Police:** (☎143 02 44. Available 24hr.) **Red Cross:** on the route before the sports complex. (☎143 19 39. 24hr. emergency service.) **Fax: Computel,** Juárez 7. (☎143 25 37. Open daily 7am-9pm.) **LADATELs** can be found up and down Allende and Juárez, and around the *zócalo.* **Internet: Inter Coffee,** 16 de Septiembre 208. 20 pesos per hr. (☎143 02 42. M-Sa 9am-7:30pm, Su 9am-noon.) **Post Office:** on 16 de Septiembre, two blocks from the cathedral. (☎143 02 23. Open M-F 9am-4pm, Sa 9am-1pm.) **Postal code:** 51900.

■*❖* **ACCOMMODATIONS AND FOOD.** If you stay away from the obscenely priced resorts and spas, some real deals can be found in Ixtapa. ☒**Hotel María Isabel,** Kiss 11, is the best place in town. To get there, face the resorts on Juárez, turn right on 20 de Noviembre, take the first right onto Matamoros, and then take the first left. The hotel is in the middle of the block on the right and has impeccable rooms and baths, cable TVs with remotes, and a sun deck on the top floor. (☎143 01 02. 80 pesos per person; 140 pesos per person with 3 meals.) **Casa de Huéspedes Sofia,** 20 de Noviembre 4, is off Juárez, down about one block on 20 de Noviembre. Pink walls, cable TVs, fluffy floral bedspreads, and large baths with purple fixtures. (☎143 18 51. 70 pesos per person.) The pleasant **Casa de Huéspedes Francis,** Obregón 6, near the cathedral, has a large, fern-filled lobby and a friendly dog. Rooms have the basics. (☎143 04 03. 60 pesos per person.)

Ixtapan has great budget restaurants. **La Puga,** off the *zócalo* on Guerrero, is a favorite local hangout. Tacos 6 pesos, *tostadas* 7 pesos. (☎143 38 10. Open Th-Tu 6-11:30pm.) **Pepe's Pizza and Pasta,** on the corner of Juárez and Aldama, is a Mexican-style pizzeria. Pizzas start at 19 pesos, pastas at 14 pesos. Vegetarian options available. (☎143 11 15. Open daily July-Aug. 9am-10pm; Sept.-June noon-10:30pm.) For the do-it-yourself traveler, ☒**Panificadora Ixtapan,** Obregón 101, near Allende, offers delicious freshly baked bread (0.8 pesos per loaf). Or spring for the most expensive thing in the bakery—a cream-filled *barkillo* pastry (3 pesos; ☎143 06 54; open daily 7am-9:30pm).

■ **SIGHTS.** Most people come to Ixtapan to enjoy the massive water park/ spa/thermal springs complex appropriately named **Ixtapan,** at the end of Juárez. (☎143 22 00. Open daily 7am-7pm. Water park open M-F 11am-5pm, Sa-Su 10am-5:30pm. 90 pesos, children 40 pesos.) For a less expensive dip in soothing thermal springs, check out the **balneario** in town at the corner of Allende and 20 de Noviembre. Splurge on a massage (60 pesos per 25min.) or mud mask. (☎143 06 00. Open daily 7am-6pm. 10 pesos, children 7 pesos.) To get to the **Plaza de los Mártires,** make a right off Juárez (facing the water park) onto Independencia and continue straight three or four blocks. The plaza is surprisingly modern and clean, with a new obelisk-like monument dedicated to the martyrs of the Revolution. Adjoining the plaza is the **Santuario de la Asun-**

ción de María, an astonishing white church with burgundy and rust trim. Inlaid mosaic benches surround the garden, while gold ornamentation, stained-glass windows, and murals adorn the interior. Adjoining is the **Capilla del Santísima y del Perdón,** in which a glass case holds a silver Christ. (Open daily 6am-8pm.)

TOLUCA   ☎ 7

Toluca ("Those who bow their heads") was a thriving pre-Hispanic center until the time of the conquest. In the 15th century, the city was claimed by Hernán Cortés for his descendants. It was officially declared a city in 1799, and the capital of the Estado de México in 1846. Since then, however, the city has struggled. Industry has rapidly expanded, traffic congestion and pollution have become serious problems, and the not-so-invisible hand of American capitalism has replaced its simple colonial beauty with a host of billboards. Still, Toluca—a mere hour away from the country's capital—offers beautifully preserved colonial architecture, elegant cathedrals, and rich museums that make it a worthwhile escape from Mexico City.

▐ TRANSPORTATION

The **bus terminal** is tucked between Paseo Tollocan and Felipe Berriozabal, southeast of the *centro*. Buses run to the *centro* from the terminal, and return trips can be caught on Juárez north of Independencia on any bus marked "Terminal" (3 pesos). Taxis make the jaunt for 20-30 pesos. Flecha Roja serves **Mexico City** (3½hr., every 5min. 4:40am-8:30pm, 26 pesos) and **Querétaro** (3½hr., every 20min. 4:40am-7:20pm, 72 pesos). Naucalpan goes to Mexico City's Metro stop **Torero** (1½hr, every 7 min. 5am-9pm, 28 pesos). Herradura de Plata (☎217 00 24) heads for **Morelia** (4hr., every 45 min. 6:15am-7pm, 75 pesos) and other destinations. Tres Estrellas serves: **Cuernavaca** (2½hr., every 30min. 5am-7:45pm, 35.5 pesos); **Ixtapan** (1hr.10 min., every 20min. 3am-8:15pm, 30 pesos); and **Taxco** (2½hr., every 40min. 6:20am-8:20pm, 61 pesos).

◀▮ ORIENTATION AND PRACTICAL INFORMATION

Toluca is connected to Mexico City by the **Paseo Tollocan.** The *zócalo*, cathedral, and the *portales*, constitute the *centro* and are bounded by Hidalgo on the south, Lerdo de Tejada on the north, Juárez on the east, and Bravo on the west. Independencia runs parallel to Hidalgo one block to the north and forms the south side of the *zócalo*. Morelos runs parallel to Hidalgo one block to the south. A word of warning: the address numbers on Hidalgo increase in either direction from the center of the *portales*.

Tourist Office: Urawa 100, #110 (☎212 60 48 or 01 800 849 13 33), at Paseo Tollocan, 6 blocks northeast of the bus station in the large yellow municipal government building behind Wal-Mart. Accessible by taking any bus marked "Wal-Mart." Open M-F 9am-6pm.

Currency Exchange: Bancomer (☎214 37 00), on the corner of Juárez and Hidalgo, with a 24hr. **ATM.** Open M-F 8:30am-5:30pm, Sa 10am-2pm.

Luggage Storage: In the bus terminal, on the far left if facing arriving buses. 5 pesos per hr. Open daily 7am-9pm.

Markets: Mercado 16 de Septiembre, Manuel Gómez Pedraza between Ignacio Rayón and Sor Juana Inés de la Cruz, 2 blocks north of the Cosmovitral. Open M-Sa 8am-7:30pm, Su 8am-6:30pm. **Mercado Juárez,** behind the bus station on Fabela. Friday, when people pour in from the countryside, is the best day. Open daily 8am-6:30pm. Artisans sell crafts in the square west of the Cosmovitral. Usually open daily 9am-7pm.

Supermarket: Gigante (☎215 94 00), on the corner of Juárez and Instituto Literario. Open daily 8:30am-10pm.

Emergency: ☎060 or call **LOCATEL** (☎213 31 83).

Police: Morelos 1300 (☎214 93 52).

Red Cross: (☎217 25 40) Jesús Carranza, southwest of the *centro*, 1 block south of Paseo Tollocan and one block west of Paseo Colón. Open 24hr.

Pharmacy: Farmacia Regis, Morelos 510 (☎213 28 80), 1 block south of Hidalgo on the corner of Aldama. Open M-F 9am-10pm, Sa-Su 9am-9pm; if closed, knock.

Medical care: IMSS, Paseo Tollocan 620 (☎217 07 33), 5 blocks from the bus station. Some English spoken.

Internet Access: Punto Imagen (☎215 95 38), on the corner of Hidalgo and Aldama, across from the *portales*. Stationery store, bookstore, and Internet cafe all in one. 30 pesos per hr. Open daily 8:30am-8:30pm.

Fax: Telecomm (☎217 07 74), in the bus station. Open M-F 9am-3pm, Sa-Su 9am-1pm.

Post office: Hidalgo 300 (☎214 90 68), 2 blocks east of Juárez. Open M-F 8am-4pm, Sa 9am-1pm.

Postal code: 50141.

▌ ACCOMMODATIONS

Modest accommodations surround the *centro*, a good escape form the noise and filth near the bus station. Although the hotels aren't particularly exciting, most are close to the action and, for the most part, clean and friendly.

Hotel La Hacienda, Hidalgo 508 (☎214 36 34), between Ascension and Ocampo. Comfortable rooms with clean, private bathrooms and TVs. The tastefully decorated, well-lit lobby makes up for the slightly musty smell in the rooms. Singles 150 pesos; doubles 150-250 pesos.

Hotel Maya, Hidalgo 413 (☎214 48 00), a few blocks west of the *centro*, is small and homey. Quirky homespun quilts, clean communal bathrooms, and a flower-laden courtyard. Singles 35 pesos; doubles 60-150 pesos.

Hotel Alpez, Ascencio 200 (☎214 86 19), 2 blocks north of Hidalgo and west of the *zócalo,* across the street from the Museo de la Acuarela. Although the rooms surround a parking garage, Alpez has a quiet atmosphere. The pink walls and flowered bedspreads give the rooms a cheerful feel. Private bathrooms are clean but small. Singles 85 pesos, with TV 100 pesos; doubles 85-150 pesos.

Hotel Azteca, Hidalgo 400, at the corner of Suárez, east of the *zócalo*. The hotel looks like a small, converted *hacienda* with an open courtyard where guests can gather to watch TV. The rooms are simple but comfortable, and the communal bathrooms are kept spic-and-span. Bring your own towel. Singles 60 pesos; doubles 60-150 pesos.

◖ FOOD

Restaurants and cheap stalls clutter the storefronts of the *portales*. *Chorizo* (spicy sausage), a local specialty, is served with everything—from *queso fundido* (melted cheese) to *tortas*. Traditional candies including *palanquetas* (peanut brittle), candied fruits, and *dulces de leche* (milk sweets) are also popular. The various *panaderías* that dot Hidalgo serve delicious sweet breads that make good breakfasts or snacks.

▨ **Café Dalí,** 108A Villada, less than a block south of the *portales*. This cozy cafe is a great place to hang out and relax with either coffee (6-15 pesos) or beer (12 pesos). Pie, tortas, donuts, and *cuernitos* (8-18 pesos) are at hand to satisfy any late-night cravings. A neon jukebox supplies all the latest music. Open Tu-Su 9am-midnight.

Restaurant Lambian't, 231 Hidalgo (☎ 215 33 93), right across the street from the *portales*. Serves simple but cheap cuisine, consisting of a *menú del día* (22 pesos), various *tortas* and sandwiches (12-20 pesos), and regional entrees (20-45 pesos). Vegetarian options available. Open daily 9am-9pm.

Taquería Las Brisas del Sur, Morelos 104, 1 block south of Hidalgo, between Juárez and Aldama. This carnivore's paradise specializes in *carnes al carbon* (24-28 pesos). The mouth-watering smell wafting onto the sidewalk will tempt you in. Tacos 12-16 pesos. Open daily 1pm-midnight.

■ SIGHTS

Toluca is not at a loss for culture. The city's museums are wonderful places to explore, allowing you to enjoy anything from stained glass to currency. All of Toluca's museums are organized and maintained by the **Centro Cultural Mexiquense** which has outdone itself in presenting the artifacts in easily digestible forms.

COMOVITRAL AND JARDÍN BOTÁNICO. Housed one block east of the northeast corner of the *zócalo* in a building dating back to the turn of the century, the Cosmovitral occupies 3000 square meters and is made of half a million pieces of stained glass. Designed by the muralist Leopoldo Flores, the glass masterpiece depicts the timeless struggle between universal opposites: good vs. evil, light vs. dark. The mural's beauty is enhanced by the many plants and pools of the garden. A small plaque and friendship lantern commemorate Toluca's sister city, Saitama, in Japan. (☎ 214 67 85. Open daily 9am-6pm. 10 pesos, children 5 pesos.)

THE CENTRO CULTURAL MEXIQUENSE. This complex outside of town houses three separate museums. The **Museo de Culturas Populares** is a beautifully restored *hacienda* with a large collection of Mexican folk art crafts, including an impressive Metepec Tree of Life, a large tree-like figure composed of clay figurines. The **Museo de Antropología e Historia** offers a large collection of assorted Mexican artifacts and exhibits. Don't miss the hair-raising collection of preserved animals, including a pig with two snouts. The **Museo de Arte Moderno's** collection of modern art includes paintings by Diego Rivera and Rufino Tamayo. (8km out of town and accessible by "C. Cultural" buses running along Lerdo de Tejada (30min., 3.5 pesos). All museums open Tu-Su 10am-6pm. 5 pesos each, all 3 museums for 10 pesos, free W and Su; purchase tickets at the kiosk in the parking lot.)

MUSEO JOSE MARIA VELASCO AND MUSEO FELIPE S. GUTIÉRREZ. Hidalgo 400 and Bravo 303, on the northwest corner of the *zócalo*. Housed in adjoining restored colonial buildings, these museums hold the permanent collections of Velasco and Gutiérrez, two important 19th-century Mexican naturalists. The museums also hosts visiting collections. (☎ 213 28 14 and 213 26 47 respectively. Both open Tu-Sa 10am-6pm, Su 10am-4pm. Free.)

MUSEO DE LA ACUARELA. Also housed in a restored colonial home, La Acuarela offers impressive watercolor paintings from contemporary Mexican painters like **Vicente Mendiola** and **Ignacio Barrios.** Their beautiful landscapes and lounging nudes dazzle the eye. (Located on Pedro Asencio 13, two blocks west of the portales. ☎ 214 73 04. Tu-Sa 10am-6pm, Su 10am-4pm. Free.)

MUSEO NUMISMATICA. If you love money, this museum is for you. Filled with bills and coins, the museum houses currency from different times and countries. (☎ 213 29 27. Hidalgo 506, a few blocks west of the portales. Tu-Su 10am-6pm. Free.)

Here's your ticket to freedom, baby!

NAME YOUR OWN PRICE!

**Wherever you want to go...
priceline.com can get you there for less.**

- Save up to 40% or more off the lowest published airfares every day!

- Major airlines serving virtually every corner of the globe.

- Special fares to Europe!

If you haven't already tried priceline.com, you're missing out on the best way to save. **Visit us online today at www.priceline.com.**

priceline.com℠
Name Your Own Price℠

MORELOS

CUERNAVACA ☎7

Whether you're ambling around Jardín Juárez, fruit drink in hand, or moving your hips to a salsa beat in one of the city's hot clubs, Cuernavaca (pop. 317,000) will have you on your feet. Known as the "City of Eternal Spring" for its temperature, the city was first populated by the Tlahuica, an Aztec tribe who called it "Cuauhnahuac" (Place on the Outskirts of the Grove). Mexico's *criollo* elite transformed the city into their private summer camp, and the original name was corrupted into the Spanish quasi-homonym Cuernavaca. As word spread about the City of Eternal Spring, Cuernavaca became a magnet for famous visitors like Hernán Cortés, Gabriel García Marquez, Muhammad Ali, and the Shah of Iran; magnificent *haciendas* with vined fences began to radiate from the *zócalo*. The trend continues; fleeing the hassles of Mexico's larger cities, wealthy Mexicans have descended upon Cuernavaca in droves. This surge has been accompanied by equal, if not greater, swarms of foreign students and expatriates, with innumerable foreign-language schools pulling them in by the class-load. A victim of its own good graces, the city has become more noisy and industrialized. Still, there's a reason people can't stay away— bars and clubs throb, scores of fine restaurants pepper the streets, and a lively foreign scene has emerged. The city is hip, young, international, and full of art, culture, and Spanish language instruction.

▐ TRANSPORTATION

GETTING AROUND
Taxis will go almost anywhere in the city for 20 pesos. After dark cabs charge 20-25% more. Make sure you only take **Radio Taxis** (☎322 12 00, 322 06 41, or 317 37 66). They are the safest, and you'll be less likely to be swindled. In any case, set prices before hopping in. Frequent local buses (3.5 pesos) called **rutas** run up and down Morelos; the final destination of the bus is painted on the windshield.

GETTING AWAY
Buses: The **Estrella Blanca** station, Morelos 503 (☎312 81 90), is 4 long blocks north of Jardín Borda. To get to the *centro* from the bus station, take a right at the exit and head south on Morelos. Turn left onto Rayón or Hidalgo. Flecha Roja goes to: **Acapulco** (4hr., every 2hr. 8am-midnight, 150 pesos); **Guadalajara** (9hr., every hr. 6:15am-10pm, 335 pesos); **Mexico City** (1¼hr., every hr. 7am-7pm, 40 pesos); and **Taxco** (1¾hr., every hr. 7am-10:35pm, 37 pesos). Tres Estrellas serves **Toluca** (2½hr., every 30min. 5am-7:45pm, 35 pesos). Those arriving via **Estrella de Oro** should cross the street and flag down any northbound minibus on Morelos (3.5 pesos)—they all run past the center of town. Estrella de Oro goes first class to **Acapulco** (4hr., 8 per day 7:15am-10:30pm, 167 pesos). Pullmande Morelos goes to **Mexico City** (1¼hr., every 15 min. 6am-9:30pm, 42 pesos). Estrella Roja goes to: **Matamoros** (3hr., every hr. 5am-8pm, 41 pesos) and **Puebla** (3½hr., every hr. 5am-8pm, 70 pesos).

▐▟ ORIENTATION AND PRACTICAL INFORMATION

Route 95 from Mexico City intersects many of Cuernavaca's main avenues. To get to the city center, exit onto **Domingo Díaz** or **Emiliano Zapata,** which splits into the northbound **José María Morelos** and the southbound **Obregón.** Cuernavaca is not an easy city to navigate—expect irregularities, random turns, and sudden name changes, especially near the plaza. Even and odd numbers usually stay on different sides of the street but, because of two different number-

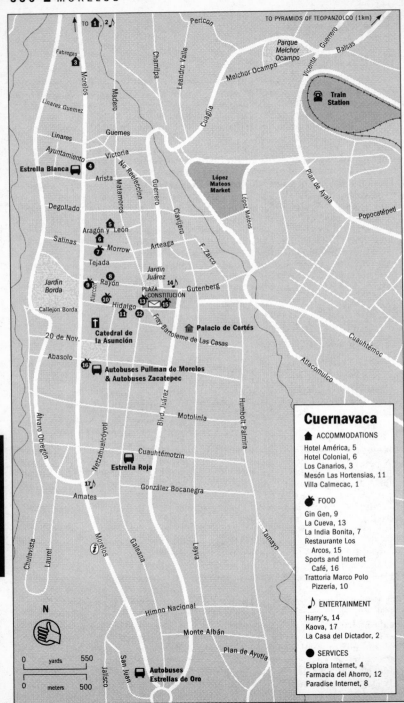

Cuernavaca

🏠 ACCOMMODATIONS

Hotel América, 5
Hotel Colonial, 6
Los Canarios, 3
Mesón Las Hortensias, 11
Villa Calmecac, 1

🍎 FOOD

Gin Gen, 9
La Cueva, 13
La India Bonita, 7
Restaurante Los
   Arcos, 15
Sports and Internet
   Café, 16
Trattoria Marco Polo
   Pizzería, 10

♪ ENTERTAINMENT

Harry's, 14
Kaova, 17
La Casa del Dictador, 2

● SERVICES

Explora Internet, 4
Farmacia del Ahorro, 12
Paradise Internet, 8

ing systems, buildings opposite each other may have addresses several hundred numbers apart. As if this isn't headache enough, by some strange governmental decree, the official address system has changed. On Morelos and nearby streets, it's not uncommon to see two addresses on each building. "400/antes 17" means that the old address was 17 and the new "official" one is 400.

Tourist Offices: State Office, Morelos Sur 187 (☎314 38 72, 314 39 20, or 312 67 47), a 15min. walk south from Hidalgo and Morelos. Look for a yellow wall on the right side of the street. Helpful staff. Information on language schools. Open M-F 8am-5pm.

Currency Exchange: Banca Serfín (☎317 05 06), on the corner of Galeana and No Reelección, has a 24hr. **ATM.** Open for exchange M-F 9am-3pm, Sa 10am-2pm. *Casas de cambio* can be found all along Morrow.

American Express: Marín Agencia de Viajes Gutenberg 3, #13 (☎314 22 66), in Las Plazas shopping mall on the *zócalo*. Open M-F 9am-2pm and 4-6pm, Sa 10am-1pm.

Luggage Storage: At the Estrella Blanca bus terminal. 2-6 pesos per hr., depending on the size of the bag. Open 24hr.

Market: Mercado López Mateos. Head east on Degollado, up the pedestrian bridge, and past the vendor stands. Open daily 9am-8pm.

Supermarket: Superama Morelos 249 (☎314 01 19) at Morelos, behind Helados Holanda, south of the Estrella Blanca bus station. Open daily 7am-11pm.

Laundry: La Burbuja, Morelos 393 (☎387 33 17). Head straight up Morelos, less than a block north of Hotel Canarios. 20 pesos per 3kg. Open daily 8am-7pm.

Emergency: ☎08 or 060.

Police: Policía Judicial, Zapata 802 (☎317 17 79).

Red Cross: (☎315 05 51 or 315 35 55), on Ixtaccíhuatl at Río Amatzmac. Open M-F 8am-5pm, but there is someone always handling the phones.

Pharmacy: Farmacia del Ahorro, Hidalgo 7 at Galeana. Open daily 7am-11pm.

Medical Assistance: IMSS (☎315 50 00) on Plan de Ayala. **Hospital General C.P.R.** (☎311 22 10), on the corner of Díaz and Gómez Ascarrate. Some English spoken.

Fax: Telecomm, Plaza de la Constitución 3 (☎314 31 81; fax 318 00 77), to the right of the post office. M-F 8am-7:30pm, Sa 9am-4:30pm, Su 9am-12:30pm.

Internet Access: Explora, Morelos 266A (☎318 55 28), just north of the bus station on the right. 12 pesos per hr. Open M-Sa 8am-9pm, Su 10am-4pm. **Paradise,** Rayón 20 #6 (☎312 94 88), towards the *zócalo* on the 2nd floor. Sip sodas as you check your email. 20 pesos per hr. Open M-F 9am-8pm, Sa 9am-3pm.

Post Office: Plaza de la Constitución 3 (☎312 43 79), on the southwest corner of the *zócalo*. Open M-F 9am-3pm, Sa 9am-1pm. **Postal Code:** 62001.

ACCOMMODATIONS

Hotels in Cuernavaca are chronically overpriced. The cloud has a silver lining, though—even the most meager of accommodations is often outfitted with a swimming pool or a courtyard. There are some less glamorous (but cheap) *casas de huespedes* on Aragón y León between Matamoros and Morelos. Numerous hotels are located within a short walking distance of Cuernavaca's center.

Villa Calmecac, Zacatecas 114 (☎313 21 46; www.turismoalternativo.org). From the *centro*, hop on a Ruta 3 or 12 bus (3.5 pesos) and head north up Morelos/Zapata. Get off just past the statue of Zapata and continue past it, taking your first left on Zacatecas. It's worth the trip. Billing itself as an "ecotourist hostel," the hotel offers opportunities to visit the great outdoors (daytrips 450 pesos). A vegetable garden, an art gallery, and a high-tech recycling system make it an earth-lover's dream. Clean communal baths. Breakfast included. 10% discount with HI or ISIC. Reception open 8am-8pm; call before arrival. Dorms 150 pesos; doubles 250 pesos.

Hotel Colonial, Aragón y León 19 (☎318 64 14), uphill between Matamoros and Morelos. Despite the low quality of nearby hotels, this one is a gem. Orange colonial home with a central courtyard and hospitable staff. Front door closes at 11pm but a bell summons the person at the desk. Singles 150 pesos; doubles 180 pesos.

Los Canarios, Morelos 369 (☎313 00 00), 5 long blocks north of the *centro* (not to be confused with the restaurant "El Canario" a few doors before). Colorful rooms with bathrooms, 2 swimming pools, and a restaurant. The friendly staff is helpful and prompt. Singles 100 pesos, with TV 160 pesos; doubles 190 pesos, with TV 250 pesos; triples 230 pesos, with TV 300 pesos.

Mesón Las Hortensias, Hidalgo 13 (☎318 52 65), right near the Cathedral, across the street from the plaza. A tad expensive, but, oh, the location! Clean, green rooms with TVs and baths. Hurry—the rooms go fast. Singles 170 pesos; doubles 215 pesos.

Hotel América, Aragón y León 14 (☎318 61 27) between Morelos and Matamoros. A rose-tiled courtyard livens up this otherwise inconspicuous hotel. Situated just a few blocks from the *centro*, América's great location, well-kept rooms, and private bathrooms make it appealing to any connoisseur of convenience. Singles 113 pesos, with TV 143 pesos; doubles 154 pesos, with TV 194 pesos.

FOOD

Cuernavaca has plenty of budget eateries. Galeana and Juárez, along with some smaller side streets, offer less expensive fare. In the market, *comida corrida* costs about 13-15 pesos. Along Guerrero, north of the plaza, street vendors sell mangoes, *piñas* (pineapples), and *elotes* (corn on the cob).

■ **Trattoria Marco Polo Pizzería,** Hidalgo 30 (☎312 34 84), on the 2nd floor. The Marco Polo's hanging geraniums, candlelit tables, and the sweet music put Italy in the heart of Mexico. Pizzas smothered in thick cheese come in 4 sizes (starting at 25 pesos). Reservations accepted. Open M-Th 1:30-10:30pm, F-Sa 1:30pm-midnight, Su 1:30-10pm.

Restaurante Los Arcos, Jardín de Los Héroes 4 (☎312 15 10), on the south side of the *zócalo*. Flanked by plants and a bubbling fountain, the restaurant's outdoor tables are ideal for watching the day slip by. The restaurant doubles as a evening watering hole; kick back some beers and dance the night away. *Comida corrida* 50 pesos, breakfast 35-45 pesos, *antojitos* 20-30 pesos. Open daily 8am-midnight.

Sports and Internet Café, Morelos Sur 178 (☎314 10 47), on the corner of Abasolo across the street from a supermarket. An upscale cafe without the upscale prices. Internet access available (25 pesos per hr.). Exceptional coffees (7-22 pesos) and baguette sandwiches (26 pesos). *Platillos fuertes* (35-45 pesos) feature *chilaquiles* and *enchiladas*. Breakfast 10-28 pesos. Vegetarian options available. Open M-Sa 8am-10pm.

THESE AIN'T NO SUNDAY FUNNIES

As you are waiting for the bus, you notice that the teenage boys standing next to you are completely absorbed in the pocket-sized comic books in their hands. Your curiosity wins out and you take a closer look and see pictures of scantily clad couples doing things you thought couldn't be done by two-dimensional characters. Surprised, but amused, you shrug it off (after all, boys will be boys). Suddenly you spot an elderly woman reading the very same comic. Don't worry, you haven't entered the twilight zone. These little comics (called *revistas*) are all the rage in Mexico. Each book graphically weaves tales of romance, passion, and lust, leaving little to the imagination. You'll find someone selling them and someone reading them on virtually every street corner and at every bus stop in Mexico. Although they may seem a little strange at first glance, the comics are harmless and often even amusing. Check one out—if nothing else, they're bound to teach you some new slang.

Gin Gen, Rayón 13 (☎318 60 46), 2 blocks east of the *zócalo* at the corner of Alarcón. Fans, lanterns, and pictures of Chinese pop stars adorn the walls. From 1-5pm, the filling *guisados del día* (soup, rice, 2 entrees, and dessert) are available for only 43 pesos. Great tofu and vegetarian options (20-30 pesos). Gin Gen also boasts a small bakery. Open M-Th 8am-9pm, F-Sa 8am-midnight, Su 8am-6pm.

La India Bonita, Morrow 15 (☎318 69 67 or 312 50 21), less than a block east of Morelos. Once the private home of Ambassador Dwight Morrow, La India features regional cuisine in an outdoor, canopied courtyard. Although on the pricey side, the frugal traveler can find regional delights like *pozole* and *albondigas* (45 pesos). Open T-Th 8am-10pm, F-Sa 9am-11pm, Su 9am-6pm.

La Cueva, Galeana 4 (☎312 40 02), across the street from the south side of the *zócalo*. A wide range of food—from seafood to sandwiches to soup. Its friendly service and well-stocked (yet inconspicuous) bar make it a hangout for local youth, who pour in around 9pm. The *comida corrida* (25 pesos) offers large portions. Open daily 9am-11pm.

◉ SIGHTS

Cuernavaca's popularity has little to do with its scintillating sights, but there is a lot to see in the City of Eternal Spring besides the city's sunglasses-clad elite sipping iced tea and speaking newly acquired Spanish or English.

PLAZA DE LA CONSTITUCIÓN AND JARDÍN JUÁREZ. Extending east from the Palacio de Gobierno is the **Plaza de la Constitución,** the heart and soul of the city. Food vendors, *mariachis*, and shoe shiners tempt passersby. A kiosk designed by Gustave Eiffel and commissioned by Cuernavaca's Viennese community stands in the **Jardín Juárez,** at the northwest corner of the Plaza de la Constitución. A mediocre (but merry) local band belts out polkas, classical music, and Mexican folk music (Th and Su 6pm). The kiosk also houses a number of juice stands.

MUSEO CUAUHNAHUAC (PALACIO DE CORTÉS). The Palacio de Cortés stands as a reminder of the city's grim history. The *conquistador* Hernán Cortés set Cuernavaca on fire in 1521, and then built this two-story fortress atop the remains of a ruined pyramid. Cortés occasionally lived at this castle up until his return to Spain in 1540; his widow continued to live there until her death. The building functioned as a prison during the 18th century, and then was turned into the city's Palacio de Gobierno during the dictatorship of Porfirio Díaz. A grant from the former British ambassador to Mexico (none other than pilot Charles Lindbergh's father-in-law) transformed the Palacio de Cortés into the Museo Cuauhnahuac. The first floor features exhibits on pre-Hispanic cultures, including a collection of indigenous depictions of the conquest. A Diego Rivera mural decorates the western balcony of the second floor. *(Southeast corner of the Plaza de la Constitución, east of Juárez. ☎312 81 71. Open Tu-Su 9am-6pm. 20 pesos; Su free.)*

CATEDRAL DE LA ASUNCIÓN. Begun in 1525 and completed by the 1550s—mainly through the labor of indigenous craftsmen—this former Franciscan convent is one of the oldest churches in the Americas. Age notwithstanding, it was only 20 years ago that the removal of aisle altars revealed **Japanese frescoes** depicting the persecution and martyrdom of Christian missionaries in Sokori, Japan. Historians speculate that these startling frescoes were painted in the early 17th century by a converted Japanese artist who settled in Cuernavaca. Two smaller chapels flank the main entrance. To the right is the 17th-century **Capilla de la Tercera Orden;** to the left is the late 19th-century **Capilla del Carmen.** *(Three blocks down Hidalgo from the zócalo, at Morelos. Open daily 7am-2pm and 4-7pm. Masses daily at 11am.)*

JARDÍN BORDA. In 1783, the priest Manuel de la Borda built this garden of magnificent pools and fountains as an annex to the house of his father, the wealthy silver tycoon José de la Borda. In 1864, Emperor Maximilian and his wife Charlotte established a summer residence here. Today, the Jardín Borda is in a state of faded splendor. Modern amenities include an art collection near the entrance, a small theater, a cafe, and a museum near the emperor's old summer home. **Rowboats** are also available on the small duck pond. *(The park's stone entrance is on Morelos, across from the cathedral. ☎312 92 37. Open Tu-Su 10am-5:30pm. 10 pesos; Su free. Rowboats 10 pesos per 15min., 15 pesos per 30min., 20 pesos per hr.)*

PYRAMIDS OF TEOPANZOLCO. Strangely deserted and unkempt, the small archaeological site of Teopanzolco consists of three pyramids, two of which exist only as foundations. The two central pyramids were meant to resemble the twin temples of Tláloc and Huitzilopochtli in Tenochtitlán. The first stairway leads to a ledge, at the bottom of which a second stairway, belonging to the second pyramid, begins. A partial staircase suggests that the third pyramid was unfinished when Cortés arrived. *(To get to the site from the marketplace or along Morelos, take a taxi (12 pesos) or the ruta #10 at the corner of Degollado and No Reelección (3.5 pesos) and ask the driver to let you off at the pirámide. Open daily 9am-6pm. 17 pesos; Su free.)*

🎵 ENTERTAINMENT

Cuernavaca's popularity as a vacation spot fuels its glitzy nightlife. **Discos** are typically open from 9 or 10pm to 5am on Friday and Saturday. The more popular discos lie beyond walking distance from the *zócalo* in the different *colonias*, and are best reached by *rutas* or taxis after 9pm. (Note that most *rutas* stop running around 10:30pm.) All the spots listed are familiar to cab drivers. Only Kaova is within walking distance of the *zócalo*.

- ☒ **Zúmbale,** Chapultepec 51 (☎322 53 43 or 322 53 44), next to Ta'izz. This 4-story salsa club is unbelievable—an indoor waterfall, live music, and some of the best Latin dancing around (salsa, rumba, merengue). Watch practiced pelvises grind, but don't be discouraged—the friendly atmosphere (and bar) invites foreigners of all ages to give it a go. Beer 20 pesos. Open bar Th 9-10pm. Th no cover. F-Sa cover 100 pesos men, women free. Open Th 9pm-4:30am, F-Sa 9pm-5am.

- ☒ **La Casa del Dictador,** Jacarandas 4 (☎317 31 86), a few blocks south of the Zapata statue, on the corner of Zapata in Col. Buenavista. Raging music welcomes a strictly gay clientele (mostly men). Beer 20 pesos. Cover 30 pesos. Open F-Sa 10:30-late.

- **Barbazul,** Prado 10 (☎313 19 76). This club would make even Bluebeard shake his "booty." A staple of Cuernavacan nightlife, popular with the early-20s, hard-hitting techno crowd. Drinks 20 pesos and up. Sa cover 100 pesos for men, women free. Open W and F-Sa 10pm-late.

- **Kaova,** Av. Morelos Sur 241 (☎318 43 80), 3 blocks south of the cathedral. Starts off mellow and turns into a full-fledged dance party later. Senior citizens and college students alike hit the small dance floor as waiters clad in bowties and suspenders scurry about. Beer 20 pesos; domestic drinks 30 pesos. F-Sa cover 50 peso; bar tab up to 50 pesos on F only. W 10-11pm beer 2 for 1. Open W-Sa 9pm-late.

- **Harry's,** Gutenberg 5 (☎312 76 69) at Guerrero, southeast corner of Jardín Juárez. Harry's caters to the local 20-something crowd, and, even though it doesn't have a dance floor, friendly waiters invite you to get up and boogy on the tables. The place starts to swing after 10:30 when the fashion-conscious clientele arrives—fashionable late, of course. F open bar. Cover 120 for men, women 30 pesos. Open Tu and Th-Sa.

🎭 DAYTRIPS FROM CUERNAVACA

XOCHICALCO

From Cuernavaca, Pullman de Morelos buses will go to the Crucero de Xochicalco (16 pesos). Either take a taxi to the site (25 pesos) or attempt the 4km uphill climb yourself (1hr). Bring a hat, sunblock, and some water. Returning home is easier; small buses pass by the site every hour en route to Cuernavaca (7 pesos, last bus

6pm). Buses may run a little late. Site open daily 9am-6pm. Observatory open daily 11am-5pm. 25 pesos; free Su. Guides gives tours in Spanish and English starting in the museum as soon as a group has assembled.

Little is known about Xochicalco (zoh-chee-CAL-co, "place of the house of flowers" in Náhuatl), an archaeological site perched atop a steep plateau. More of a religious and trading center than a city, Xochicalco was first settled during the early Classic Period, around the time neighboring Teotihuacán was reaching its zenith; it was not until the demise of the Teotihuacanecos around AD 700-900 that Xochicalco truly began to flourish. Xochicalco was an important trading and cultural center and maintained important diplomatic and trading relations with the Maya, Zapotec, and Toltec civilizations, traces of which are visible in the architecture of the site. Indeed, among the several construction projects initiated in AD 700 is a ball court almost identical to those built by the Classic Maya. Its presence has led archaeologists to speculate that Xochicalco might have been a Maya outpost. Others believes that Xochicalco was the mythical city of **Tamoanchan,** the place where Maya, Zapotec and Toltec sages met every 52 years to synchronize calendars and renew the cult of Quetzalcóatl. Xochicalco fell around AD 1200, probably due to internal insurrection.

Before entering the ruins, visit the **Museo del Sitio de Xochicalco,** to the right of the entrance. Comprehensive exhibits, invaluable brochures (5 pesos), and the ticket office make the museum a necessary stop. From there, a rocky path leads to the ruins, which are best explored in a circular manner. Start at the elevated plaza to the left of the first patch of greenery. On the right side of the first plain is the **Pirámide de las Estelas (Structure A),** which forms the northern boundary of the **Plaza Central.** Because of the convergence of roads, this area was most likely a trading center. Twin pyramids on the east and the west sides of the plaza, **Structure C** and **Structure D,** were used in the worship of the sun. One is oriented toward sunrise, the other toward sunset. At the center of the plaza is a carved obelisk that bears two glyphs relating to the god Quetzalcóatl. It is believed that priests plotted the sun's trajectory over the pyramids by tracing the obelisk's shadow.

The southwest corner of this plaza offers a good view of the **Juego de Pelota** (ballcourt) below. Many archaeologists believe that this ballcourt was one of the earliest built in Mesoamerica; ballcourts as far south as Honduras show signs of a heavy Xochicalco influence. After heading up the hill to the central plaza, make your way to the base of the **Gran Pirámide (Structure E),** atop which rest the remains of an even more ancient structure. To the left is the stairway/portico section, used to protect the city in case of invasion. Past the portico and up two sets of impressive stairways rebuilt in 1994, find the **Plaza Ceremonial,** which served as the ceremonial center of the city. The top of the Pirámide de las Estelas is accessible from here, enclosing a huge pit in the center that was the burial site for high priests and a place for ritual offerings. In the center of the plaza is the renowned **Pirámide de la Serpiente Emplumada** (Pyramid of the Plumed Serpent). Haphazardly reconstructed in 1910, it bears carved reliefs of Quetzalcóatl.

At the rear end of the plaza is the tremendous **Montículo 2,** the highest area of the site and supposedly the spot where the rulers of Xochicalco lived. The east side was intended for daily activities, while the west end was exclusively ceremonial. Down the slope to the west is the **Hall of the Polichrome Altar,** where a colored altar rests beneath a reconstruction of Toltec roofing. Farther down is a cistern, a sauna used for pre-ballgame initiation rites, and **Teotlachtli,** the northern ballcourt. Two massive rings of rock are attached in the middle—most ballcourts in Mesoamerica have only one ring. Teams competed for the privilege of being sacrificed atop the Pyramid of Quetzalcóatl, a true honor and a sign of good sportsmanship. Nearby remain the foundations of the **Calmecac,** the palace in which Toltec and Aztec priests underwent training and initiation.

To the west along a weed-ridden path, around the back of the base of Montículo 2, is the entrance to the underground **Observatorio**. On summer solstices, Aztec sages and stargazers adjusted their calendar by peering through a shaft in the ceiling to trace the path of the sun. It is said that you can see the aura of a person who stands in the middle of the shaft of light.

MALINALCO

Getting to Malinalco is simple but time-consuming. Estrella Blanca buses go to Chalma from Cuernavaca. (2hr.; W-M 7:15am and 9:15am, Tu 9:15am; 35.5 pesos). The only return trip is at 2pm. Once you've arrived at Chalma and marveled at the scenery, hail a taxi to Malinalco (20min., 30-35 pesos for taxi especial, 6 pesos if shared) or take a ruta that says "Malinalco" (45min., 3 pesos). To get to the ruins from the zócalo, follow the blue pyramid signs along Guerrero and go straight. Take a left on Milgar, a right at the next blue arrow, and another right at the blue sign that appears to lead visitors into someone's driveway. Site open Tu-Su 9am-6pm. 16 pesos; Su free. Malinalco's helpful tourist office is in a red building located on one corner or the zócalo. (☎017 147 0111. Open M-F, 9am-3pm, Sa 9am-1pm.)

Malinalco (pop. 20,000) is a peaceful town with one huge attraction—one of the best-preserved Aztec temples in the country. The **Templo de la Iniciación** (Temple of the Initiation) was cut whole from the rock of a nearby mountain, and, along with pyramids in India, Jordan, and Egypt, is one of only four monolithic pyramids in the world. Every year on March 21, hundreds of people pour into Malinalco to witness the temple's dazzling spring equinox wonder—a ray of light shines through the doorway and reveals the image of an eagle on the floor. Modern architects still marvel at this feat of design. The ruins at Malinalco were the sacred ground for the rituals that officially transformed an Aztec youth into a tiger or eagle warrior. On the open circular stone platform—the first structure on the right as you enter—prisoners were bound to a pole with only their arms left free and made to wrestle the recently initiated warriors. If the prisoner won consecutive bouts with two *águila* and two *tigre* warriors, he was matched against a left-hander. If the prisoner defeated the lefty, he was granted freedom. Defeat, on the other hand, had more unpleasant consequences: the small rectangular basin in front of the entry way to the pyramid was used to hold the prisoner's blood after his ritual sacrifice. Behind the pyramid, the bodies of the sacrificed were burned to ashes on the oval bed of rock. Inside the pyramid, all of the statues, rooms, and facades were originally painted a brilliant crimson. To the right of the pyramid stand the remains of a *temascal*, the ancient predecessor to the sauna.

TEPOZTLÁN   ☎7

Only 22km northeast of Cuernavaca, Tepoztlán is a small town where many locals still speak Náhuatl. The cobbled streets and well-preserved *haciendas* are surrounded by towering cliffs that make Tepoztlán somewhat impenetrable—it can only be entered from the south on Rte. 95D. Its natural beauty has attracted a great many expatriates to the surrounding area making prices steep—forget budget anything! The town's impressive museum and pyramid, however, make it a good daytrip from Cuernavaca or Mexico City (75km).

■ **TRANSPORTATION.** The *centro*, consisting of the *zócalo*, several government buildings, and the church, is bound by **5 de Mayo** on the west and **La Conchita** on the east. **Revolución** lies to the south while **Zaragoza** lies to the north. 5 de Mayo turns into **Tepozteco,** which leads straight to the pyramid. To reach Tepoztlán from Cuernavaca, take **Ometochtli** buses (1hr., every 15min. 5:45am-10pm, 8 pesos) or **Tepoztlán Directo** buses (30min., every 30min. 6am-10pm, 12 pesos) from the east side of

Mercado López Mateos. If you arrive at the Ometochtli depot, follow the main road; it will curve and become 5 de Mayo.

⚏⚏ ACCOMMODATIONS AND FOOD. Tepoztlán is a good daytrip, but if you find yourself unable to leave, your best bet is to stay at **Casa Iccemanyan,** Calle de Olvido 26. Though on the expensive side, this beautiful hacienda offers several bungalows, a pool, and a common kitchen. Meals are served by welcoming family members who are willing to pick up guests at nearby airports if they call beforehand. (☎395 08 99; fax 395 21 59. Singles 200 pesos; doubles 320 pesos. Group rates available.) You'll have no problem finding a place to eat but don't expect to stay within a strict budget. Many international, vegetarian-friendly restaurants line 5 de Mayo and Revolución. One of the more reasonable restaurants is **Mesón de Convento,** Revolución 6 (☎395 29 00), right across from the *zócalo*, where you can find traditional Mexican food (40-60 pesos). Their most popular dish is *barbacoa*, shredded cow cheek and tongue, served in tacos with lots of salsa (35 pesos). If you're unwilling to indulge, head for the market.

⚏⚏ SIGHTS AND FESTIVALS. Tepoztlán's main draw is the **Pirámide del Tepozteco,** on the northern ridge of the cliffs 3km from the valley. Some say the 10m tall pyramid was a Tlahuica observatory and defense post (it is inscribed with barely discernible Tlahuica glyphs), while others swear it served as an Aztec sacrificial temple. To reach the pyramid, follow 5 de Mayo north out of town (passing the *zócalo* on your right) until the road ends. If you intend to make the steep, hour-long climb, equip yourself with appropriate footwear, water, and spirit. If you can't make it all the way up, don't worry—there are numerous vistas to reward you along the way. (Open daily 10am-4pm. 20 pesos; Su free.)

The **Museo de Arte Prehispánico** (more commonly known as the **Museo Carlos Pellicer**), at the rear of Capilla Asunción, holds a collection donated to the city by the renowned poet Carlos Pellicer. The impressive holdings include masks, pottery pieces, and clay figures. (☎395 10 98. Open Tu-Su 10am-6pm. 4 pesos.)

Celebrations take place every September 8 in honor of **Tepozécatl,** also known as Quetzalcóatl, who was thought to have been born in this magical valley over 1200 years ago. *Chinelos*—colorfully attired folk dancers—invite visitors to join in their traditional dance, *el salto*, while musicians play age-old tunes.

TLAXCALA

TLAXCALA ☎2

There is no better place to sit in all of Mexico than the colonial city of Tlaxcala (pop. 100,000), whose *talavera* architecture fills the small valley just beyond the last sagging remains of Poblano sprawl. Tlaxcala was not always so tranquil. During the 16th century, the Tlaxcalans, in an attempt to save their culture from the advancing Aztec empire, made a pact with Cortés. Tlaxcala sent 6000 of its own warriors to raid and plunder the city of Cholula, and it helped Cortés force the final fall of Tenochtítlan in 1521. In return, Tlaxcala was given special Spanish protection as well as the title of *"muy noble y muy leal"* (very noble and very loyal) in 1563. Today few traces of Tlaxcala's mercenary history are visible, and its all-pervasive calm draws refugees from Mexico City and Puebla on weekends. Tlaxcala may be peaceful, but it's hardly a dead end. The best place to begin to explore a state full of now-deserted convents, untouristed *indígena* communities and well-preserved ruins, Tlaxcala's museums, art galleries, and cultural center make accessible an unpackaged portion of Mexico's heartland.

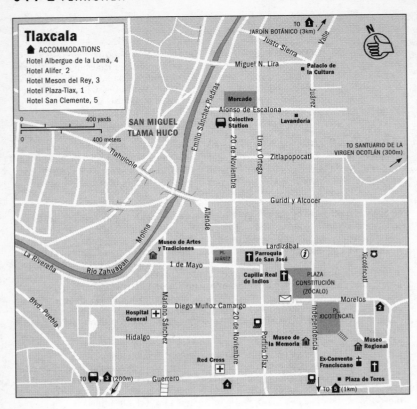

Tlaxcala

🏠 ACCOMMODATIONS

Hotel Albergue de la Loma, 4
Hotel Alifer, 2
Hotel Meson del Rey, 3
Hotel Plaza-Tlax, 1
Hotel San Clemente, 5

TRANSPORTATION

GETTING AROUND

Tlaxcala is approximately 85km east of Mexico City. It is most easily accessed by **Mexico 150.** Don't be fooled by the large number of *colectivos* leaving from the market; Tlaxcala is a very walkable city. Distances are manageable, and it's always cheaper and sometimes more direct to chug up the hills yourself than to ride in the VW vans, whose 1600cc engines can't handle the steep grades, forcing drivers to take longer, more roundabout routes. Just remember the mantra: "I think I can. I think I can." Most services can be found in and around **Plaza de la Constitución** (the *zócalo*) and **Plaza Xicoténcatl,** diagonally adjacent to it. **Revolución** is the city's main commercial strip. To get from the *zócalo* to Revolución, catch a "Santa Ana" *colectivo* at 20 de Noviembre, three blocks from the *zócalo*, behind San José (3 pesos). It's a 40min. walk if you're pinching pesos and want to enjoy the air.

GETTING AWAY

To get to the *centro* from the **bus station,** the Central Camionera, exit through the glass doors to a swarm of idling *colectivos*. Those facing the right go to the downtown area, the market, and the hotel district on the northern edge of the city (3 pesos). To return to the bus station, take a "Central" *colectivo* from the market at 20 de Noviembre and Alonso y Escalona, or flag one down behind

San José at 20 de Noviembre and 1 de Mayo. Autotransportes Tlaxcala (☎462 00 87) runs to **Mexico City** (1.5hr., every 20min. 6am-9pm, 61 pesos) and **Veracruz,** stopping in **Xalapa** (Veracruz 5.5hr., Xalapa 3.5hr., 10:30am and 3:30pm, 110 and 72 pesos respectively). Autotransportes México-Texcoco has similar service to **Mexico City** (1½hr., 7:40pm and 9pm, 61 pesos) and **San Lorenzo** (2½hr., 5:30am and 7:30pm, 28 pesos). Flecha Azul, under the PTC sign (☎462 33 92), serves **Puebla** (45min., every 10min. 5:30am-9:30pm, 11pesos).

🛈 PRACTICAL INFORMATION

TOURIST, LOCAL, AND FINANCIAL SERVICES

▩ Tourist Office: Juárez 18 (☎462 00 27). At the beautiful turn-of-the-century building at Juárez and Lardizábal. The office sponsors cheap and comprehensive tours of Tlaxcala and the surrounding area every Saturday and Cacaxtla and Xochitécatl every Sunday. The comprehensive tours leave at 10:15am from the Hotel Posada San Francisco on the south side of the *zócalo* (15 pesos). A gold mine of information, pamphlets, videos, and fancy computer presentations from a friendly, and sometimes English-speaking, staff. Open M-F 9am-7pm, Sa-Su 10am-6pm.

Currency Exchange: Banamex, Plaza Xicoténcatl 8 (☎462 20 55 or 462 25 36), and **Bancrecer,** Hidalgo 10 (☎462 67 41), under the *portales* have 24hr. **ATMs.** There are also several banks on Juárez past the tourist office. The **Centro de Cambio Tlaxcala,** Guerrero 3 (☎462 00 85), at the corner of Independencia, exchanges cash, money orders, and traveler's checks. Open M-F 9am-4pm.

Supermarket: Practical goods can be found at **Gigante,** the city's behemoth supermarket, Valle 66 (☎462 58 46), in the shopping center on the corner of Vera. Open daily 8am-9pm.

Markets: The entire street of **Alonso Escalona** west of Lira y Ortega teems with market activity. Open M-Sa 8am-8pm, Su 8am-5pm. On weekends, vendors sell *artesanía* in **Plaza Xicoténcatl.**

Laundry: Lavandería de Autoservicio Acuario, Alonso Escalona 13A (☎462 62 92). Full-service 11 pesos per kg.; self-service 8 pesos per 10min.; 1 hr. service available. Open M-Sa 8:30am-7:30pm.

Car Rental: Budget, Juárez 45 (☎466 19 73).

EMERGENCY AND COMMUNICATIONS

Emergency: call police station or hospital directly.

Police: (☎462 07 35 or 462 10 79) on Lardizábal, 1 block past the tourist office, at the corner with Xicoténcatl. Open 24hr. No English spoken.

Red Cross: Allende Nte. 48 (☎462 09 20). Go 2 blocks behind San José to Allende, turn left and continue 1½ blocks past Camargo. 24hr. walk-in emergency service. No English spoken.

Pharmacy: Farmacía Bethanía, Valle 17A (☎462 11 55). Take Juárez from the *zócalo* until it turns into Valle; the pharmacy is on the right just before the stadium appears on the left. Open 24hr. **Unión de Farmacías de Descuento,** Juárez 14A (☎462 34 30), between Lardizábal and Guridi y Alcocer. Open daily 9am-9pm.

Hospital: Hospital General, Jardín de la Corregidora 1 (☎462 00 30 or 462 35 55), 5 blocks from the *zócalo* on Camargo, past the post office. No English spoken. Open 24hr. **IMSS** (☎462 34 00), Valle, across the street from the stadium, right after the Nestlé factory. Take Juárez from the *zócalo* until it turns into Valle. Open 24hr.

Fax: Telecomm, Díaz 6 (☎462 00 47), behind the post office. Open M-F 8am-6:30pm, Sa-Su 9am-noon.

Telephones: LADATELs under the arches in the *zócalo,* near the Parroquia de San José.

Internet Access: Internet Café, Independencia 21 (☎462 44 64), south of the Plaza Xicoténcatl. Fast connection and two floors of computers. 20 pesos per hr. Open M-F

9am-8pm, Sa 10am-8pm. **Mic@fe.com,** Díaz 7 (☎466 21 62), on the second floor, has fewer computers and a slower connection. 20 pesos per hr. Open 10am-9:30pm.

Post Office: Plaza de la Constitución 20 (☎462 00 04), on the corner of Camargo. Open M-F 9am-4pm, Sa 9am-1pm. **Postal Code:** 90000.

ACCOMMODATIONS

While dirt cheap accommodations aren't exactly plentiful in Tlaxcala, those willing to pay 150 pesos for a single and 200 pesos for a double will be able to stay close to the *zócalo* in very comfortable rooms. Be sure to make reservations on the weekends and holidays, as low-cost hotels in the good locations fill up quickly.

Hotel Alifer, Morelos 11 (☎462 56 78; email alifer@tlax.net.mx). A pastel-colored hotel conveniently located on Morelos, a 2min. uphill climb east of Plaza Xicoténcatl. The modern rooms are a tad expensive, but feature wall-to-wall carpeting, cable TV, phone, and bath. The only drawback? The bells of the neighboring *Ex-Convento* start ringing at 6am. Rooms go fast at this hotel, so if you plan on arriving late, call ahead. Singles 150 pesos; doubles 160-220 pesos.

Hotel Albergue de la Loma, Guerrero 58 (☎462 04 24). Rustic wood stairs lead up a hill to the white-washed building with wide balconies and picture windows. The views of San José, Ocotlán and the surrounding valley are spectacular. With two to three beds each, spacious rooms are perfect for family stays. All rooms have TVs and private bathrooms. The downstairs restaurant serves inexpensive food daily 8am-10pm. Singles 150 pesos; doubles 190 pesos; triples 220 pesos.

Hotel Meson del Rey, Calle 3 #1009 (☎462 90 55), across the intersection to the left when one exits the bus station doors. Its proximity to public transportation is counterbalanced by an unglamorous locale. Clean, upholstered rooms with TV, phone, and private bath. Singles 95 pesos; doubles 175 pesos.

Hotel San Clemente, Independencia 58 (☎462 19 89). Follow Independencia south past Plaza Xicoténcatl for about 10min. The bright yellow hotel is on the left 4min. after Independencia starts to curve. In the same price range but farther afield than its competitors, San Clemente makes up for the trek with a fountain, a courtyard, and tiled baths. TVs and phones. Singles 150 pesos; doubles 200 pesos.

Hotel Plaza-Tlax, Revolución 6 (☎462 78 52). From the *zócalo*, put on your walking shoes and head north on Juárez. Follow the road as it changes to Valle; the hotel will be on your left soon after Valle changes to Revolución. Though slightly cheaper than the hotels near the *zócalo*, Plaza-Tlax's bargain-value decreases with each of the many steps you'll have to take to get there. The clean rooms have cable TV, and a garden has playground equipment. Singles 140 pesos; doubles 180 pesos.

FOOD

Tlaxcalteca specialties include *pollo en xoma* (chicken stuffed with fruits and other meats), *barbacoa en mixiote* (meat cooked in *maguey* leaves), and *pulque* (an unrefined alcoholic drink made from the *maguey* cactus). You can either drink *pulque* straight, eat it with your chicken, or try *pulque verde*, a drink made with honey water, *yerba buena* (spearmint), and lemon juice. With all these culinary *tours de force*, it's hard to go wrong when picking a place to eat. For delicious midday meals, duck into one of the small family-run restaurants on **Juárez** between **Zitlalpopocatl** and **Alonso de Escalona**, where *comida corrida* is usually 25 pesos or less. Around the *zócalo*, 40-50 pesos will buy you a very quality meal, often served by intimidatingly classy waiters.

■ **Restaurante Sharon,** Guerrero 14 (☎462 20 18), between Independencia and Díaz. This friendly, family-owned establishment offers all the quality of the *zócalo* at more reasonable prices. Take your pick of 8 different *quesos fundidos* (32 pesos), or make a meal out of 3 tacos (26 pesos). Meat dishes come with vegetable salad and refried beans (34-37 pesos). Open Su-F 2-9pm.

El Quinto Sol, Juárez 12 (☎466 18 97), just north of the tourist office. With the highest quality fruits and veggies in Tlaxcala, this vegetarian joint serves generous portions for low prices. Sprinkled with grains and smothered with fruit, their yogurt will leave your taste buds begging for more. Breakfasts include coffee, juice, yogurt, eggs, and fresh bread (20-22 pesos). Specialty cure-all juices 11-14 pesos. Open M-Sa 8am-7pm.

Los Portales Restaurant-Bar, Juárez 11 (☎462 54 19), on the *zócalo* under the arches. Los Portales can afford to be a bit pricier than its *zócalo* competition. Good *antojitos* start at 25 pesos, but beware: most beef dishes are 60 pesos or more, while chicken ranges from 45 to 50 pesos. Open Su-Th 7am-11pm, F-Sa 24hr.

Restaurant Tirol, Independencia 7A (☎462 37 54), along Plaza Xicoténcatl. Impeccable service and fancy table settings help to atone for the somewhat pricey menu. This colorful restaurant caters to weekday business luncheons and hip evening and weekend clientele. For authentic local food, try the *sopa Tlaxcalteca* (25 pesos). *Comida corrida* from 30 pesos. Open M-Sa 7:30am-midnight, Su 9am-6pm.

👁 SIGHTS

Most of Tlaxcala's attractions center around peaceful streets off the **Plaza de la Constitución,** but easy-to-find *colectivos* make the trek to farther sights manageable. Visitors should make sure to see **Cacaxtla** and **Xicoténcatl,** two well-preserved archaeological sites nearby. The tourist office provides cheap, well-structured tours of both Tlaxcala city and the archaeological sites.

PLAZA DE LA CONSTITUCIÓN. The Plaza de la Constitución is the heart of Tlaxcala. Keep an eye out for the octagonal fountain of Santa Cruz in the center by the bandstand. Built in Europe during the 14th century, it was given to the city by King Phillip IV in 1646—no small token considering the distance those stones were hauled—to symbolize Spanish gratitude towards *La Ciudad Leal* (The Loyal City) and its instrumental role in Mexico's colonization.

CAPILLA REAL DE INDIOS (PALACIO DE JUSTICIA). On the plaza's west side, the Capilla Real is an important symbol of Tlaxcala's Spanish alliance. Dedicated in 1528 to Charles V and financed by the four Tlaxcalteca chieftains who formed the pact with Cortés, the chapel was termed *real*, or "royal," both for its dedication, and because Tlaxcalan nobility worship there. Today, the Capilla Real no longer operates as a chapel, but as Tlaxcala's head court. *(Open M-F 8am-8pm. Free.)*

PALACIO DE GOBIERNO. Tlaxcala's unique history can be followed in the immense murals by Desiderio Hernández Xochitiotzin covering the interior walls of the 16th-century palace. After 30 years of labor on the murals, Xochitiotzin is at present researching Tlaxcala's Reform and Revolutionary history in order to continue his work. Read about them yourself using the coded number system. On the right side of the building are the elaborate upper chambers of the old royal houses, where visiting 17th century viceroys stayed while in the city. *(Open daily 8am-8pm. Free. Guides hang out within the palace, offering to explain the murals for 50 pesos in Spanish, 100 pesos in English.)*

PLAZA XICOTÉNCATL. Southeast of the *zócalo* is Plaza Xicoténcatl, dedicated to the young Tlaxcalan lord **Xicoténcatl Axayacatzin.** As one of the few Tlaxcalans who tried to defeat Cortés, Xicoténcatl is a hero today, and his statue commands a center spot in the Plaza. Normally a tranquil area, the plaza livens up on weekends as a carousel and small artisan market occupy the grounds.

EX-CONVENTO FRANCISCANO DE LA ASUNCIÓN. Built sometime between 1537 and 1540, the ex-convent was one of the first four Franciscan convents in the Americas. The thick, wooden door of the cathedral opens into a beautifully romanesque nave and a ceiling of intricate Muslim-influenced *(mudéjar)* woodwork. The main altar contains, among other artifacts, *la conquistadora*, the canvas of the Virgin that Cortés is said to have kept between his armor and his breast. In the first of four chapels is a corn paste sculpture dating back to the 16th century. The side chapel closest to the altar, **La Capilla de la Tercer Orden,** contains the basin used to baptize the four Tlaxcalteca lords at the time of the alliance. *(On the southeast side of Plaza Xicoténcatl; a 400-year-old cobblestone way leads about 200m up to the ex-convent. Open M-F 6am-2pm and 4-8pm, Sa 6am-7:30pm, Su 6am-8:30pm.)*

MUSEO REGIONAL DE TLAXCALA. The small museum presents artifacts from nearby archaeological zones, examples of colonial art, and a library with works on Tlaxcalan history. Take a peek through the fence across from the ex-convent to discover one of Tlaxcala's pride and joys, the **Plaza de Toros.** Named after the famous *torero* Jorge "El Ranchero" Aguilar, the plaza has been in use since 1788 and comes to life during the last week of October and first week of November, when Tlaxcala celebrates its annual fair. *(Next door to the ex-convent, on the side closest to the entrance. ☎ 462 02 62. Open Tu-Su 10am-5pm. 20 pesos.)*

MUSEO DE LA MEMORIA. The museum occupies a 16th-century building that once housed the sisterhood of Santa Cruz of Jerusalem; still visible on the building is a Franciscan shield of the five crosses. Five rooms guide visitors through Tlaxcalan history from 1521 to the end of the 18th century. New interactive computer programs and videos located throughout help explain the various exhibits. Highlights include the enormous diorama of the *Ex-Convento Franciscano* as it appeared during colonial times, and the room of the *Virgen de Ocotlán,* where thunderous holy music plays while visitors examine paintings and read about the legend of the virgin. *(Independencia 3, across from the Plaza Xicoténcatl. ☎ 466 07 92. Open Tu-Su 10am-5pm. 10 pesos, students with ID 5 pesos.)*

PARROQUIA DE SAN JOSÉ. Its immense yellow bulk visible from afar, the old parish church was originally built atop a hermitage dating from 1526. At its entrance stand two stone fonts of holy water, on the sides of which people often perch to relax for a moment before continuing on they way. The *talavera* tile and brick now covering the exterior of the church were laid over the original mortar facade in the 17th and 18th centuries. *(Northwest of the zócalo. Open daily 6am-8pm.)*

MUSEO DE ARTES Y TRADICIONES POPULARES DE TLAXCALA. The museum features seven exhibition halls in which artisans demonstrate their crafts. Presentations include a tour of a traditional indigenous kitchen, an explanation of textile production, and a discourse on how *pulque* is made—including a taste of the fiery drink. *(Mariano Sánchez 1, on the corner of Lardizábal. A short walk west on Lardizábal from the Parroquia. ☎ 462 23 37. Open Tu-Su 10am-6pm. 6 pesos, students 4 pesos.)*

SANTUARIO DE NUESTRA SEÑORA DE OCOTLÁN. While San José is Tlaxcala's main place of worship, Ocotlán has greater religious, symbolic, and historical significance and is a prime example of the Churrinqueresque style. A Tlaxcala-style Virgin of Guadalupe, Nuestra Señora de Ocotlán appeared in 1541 to an ailing Indian named Juan Diego Bernardino, curing him and ordering him to build the church. The modern-day *santuario* holds the 16th-century wooden image of the Virgin, which is carried through the city streets every year on the first Monday of May. In the interior, golden conch shells top the pilasters, and another giant shell frames the end of the nave. The star of the show, however, is the *camarín,* the small octagonal room off to the side where the Virgin is "dressed" for important festivals. *(Take an "Ocotlán" colectivo from the market (3 pesos). Tell the driver your destination; he or she will tell you where to go. To return, take a colectivo from the street to your left when facing the church. To walk there, head one block past the tourist office on Juárez, and hang a right on Guridi y Alcocer. When the road forks, follow it up the hill to the left. The road climbs to a small Capilla del Pocito de Agua Santa, where it becomes a cobblestone street with a staircase alongside; the stairs lead directly to the church.)*

JARDÍN BOTÁNICO TIZATLÁN. For indigenous beauty without tourist packaging, this garden delivers Mexican plants in an otherworldly setting. No bikes, balls, radios, or beer are allowed in this pastoral paradise. The rocky paths meander across a creek to reveal a hidden greenhouse. *(To get there, take a colectivo from the market labeled "Camino Real," and tell the driver where you want to get off. To walk, follow Juárez past the tourist office until it turns into Valle and finally Revolución From the hotel district on Revolución, turn left at Camino Real before the brick bridge passes over the road. ☎ 462 65 46. Open daily 9am-3pm and 6-8pm. Free.)*

THE RUINS OF TIZATLÁN. Located about 4km outside of Tlaxcala, these tiny ruins compose all that is left of one of Tlaxcala's four *señoríos* (warrior city-states). Although the ruins themselves are unimpressive, the view from the site compensates. A plaque points to the three locations in the surrounding hills where the other three *señoríos* once stood. In front of the site is the golden-domed **Templo de San Estéban.** For an additional 11 pesos, visitors can view the original 16th-century *capilla* of the church. *(To reach the ruins, take a 3-peso colectivo from the corner of Sanchez and 1 de Mayo labeled "Tizatlán." Tell your driver where you want to go, and he or she will drop you off in front of a small, yellow building. Walk left on the stone path, following it up several flights of stairs; the ruins are at the top behind the Templo de San Estéban. Open Tu-Su 10am-5pm. 12 pesos, students with ID 5 pesos. Su free.)*

🎭 ENTERTAINMENT

On weeknights in Tlaxcala, lights are out by 10:30pm. Weekends, on the other hand, are wild. Discos scattered throughout the city and a cluster of bars opposite the north side of Plaza Xicoténcatl keep it hopping. Many of the restaurants and bars under the *portales* feature live music, and a swarm of hip sophisticates invade the outdoor seating, coolly sipping their flavored coffees.

BARS AND CLUBS

In Tlaxcala, many of the bars have the dual functions as discos on weekends—hence the term "disco-bar." Early in the evening, patrons sit calmly at their tables. Around 11:30pm, some sort of universal twitch sinks in, and the crowd surges to its feet, grinding and undulating in sweaty, drunken bliss.

El Ajua, Interior Centro Expositor (☎462 67 18), in the *Recinto Ferial*. Although it's a 20-peso cab ride away, a regular 20- to 30-year old crowd make this the most popular disco-bar in town. Frequented mostly by rich young folk, Ajua has both live music and DJs, a boogying staff, and a raucous good time. Cover 25 pesos. Restaurant open daily noon-9pm; bar open F-Sa 9pm-5am.

La Revolución Discotheque, Portal Hidalgo 9 (☎462 60 52), under the *portales*. Dirty dancing a bit closer to home. Young clubbers get down to a variety of music, including pop, techno, reggae, and salsa. Live rock F-Sa. Cover 20 pesos. Open Tu-Su 5pm-5am.

Royal Adler's Disco, Revolución 4 (☎462 15 77), at the Hotel Jeroc. Ritzy hotel patrons drift to the disco for high-class clubbing. Pay for the cab ride over, the 30-peso cover, and the pricey drinks and you too can be part of this elite set. Open F-Sa 10pm-3am.

THE CHILL SCENE

Café La Fuente, Guerrero 29 (☎462 97 22), at the corner of 20 de Noviembre. If the bar scene along the *zócalo* is too social, this cafe offers the opposite: couples sip typical coffeehouse fare and share tiny private balconies. The candlelight flickers, the live music plays, and the strongly spiked *cafés* work their magic (8-19 pesos). Live music F-Sa starting at 9pm. Open daily 10am-2am.

Cinema Tlaxcala, on the south side of the *zócalo* across the street from the post office. Shows first-run American movies (20 pesos).

🎊 FESTIVALS

For information on *haute-couture* in Tlaxcala, head to the city's Cultural Center, **Palacio de la Cultura,** Juárez 62, 4 blocks from the *zócalo* at the corner of Justo Sierra. You can find monthly schedules and announcements of theater productions, dances, and art expositions. The *Palacio* also stages concerts, exhibits, and performances all over town and in its own courtyard. **Teatro Universitario** and **Teatro Xicoténcatl** host most of the events. (☎ 462 36 23 or 462 52 29. Open M-F 9am-8m.)

Tlaxcala's state fair, **Feria de Tlaxcala,** is held from October 16 to November 15. During the month-long *feria*, exhibitions of *artesanía* and *ganaderos* (livestock) dot the town, while Tlaxcalans from across the state participate in cultural and sporting events. If you have a taste for religious events, stop by Tlaxcala on the first Monday of May to see the sacred pine image of the **Virgin of Ocotlán** paraded through the streets. If that doesn't suit your schedule, visit the Church of Christ the Good Neighbor (to the right of the ex-convent) on July 1 for the celebration of the **Día de la Purísima Sangre de Cristo** (Day of the Purest Blood of Christ).

⚅ DAYTRIPS FROM TLAXCALA

CACAXTLA

From Tlaxcala, take a bus marked "Nativitas" or "San Miguel del Milagros" from 20 de Noviembre next to the market or behind San José. Tell the driver where you want to go, and he or she will drop you off at the main entrance (40 min., 6 pesos). If you happen to be dropped in San Miguel del Milagros, walk up the windy road, following the signs.

One of the best-preserved and best-presented archaeological sites in the country is the hilltop ruin of Cacaxtla (kah-KASH-tla), 19km southwest of Tlaxcala. The Olmecas-Xicalancas, who once dominated the southwest corner of Tlaxcala state and most of the Puebla Valley, built and expanded the city during the Classic Period, around AD600 and 750. Cacaxtla was abandoned by 1000, and its inhabitants were finally driven from the area by Toltec-Chichimec invaders in 1168. Excavation began at Cacaxtla in 1975, and the area is now reconstructed as the ceremonial center it once was, now complete with restaurant and gift shop.

The small museum on the right after the entrance contains artifacts and bones collected from the site. From the museum, a dirt path leads toward the ruins. To prevent erosion, the ruins are covered by the world's second largest archaeological roof. Once upstairs, visitors move clockwise around ceremonial courtyards, temples, tombs, and palatial remains. The remains of many small rooms within the palace are thought to have been priests' quarters. Several features distinguish this site from others. One is a latticework window, **La Celosia,** on the west side, opposite the entrance. The free-standing window is the only one of its kind—made by surrounding a latticework of twigs and branches with mud and stucco. Cacaxtla's other attraction is the series of murals scattered about the site, considered to be among the best-preserved pre-Hispanic paintings in Mesoamerica. The largest, the **Battle Mural,** depicts a historical-mythological battle of two armies, one dressed in jaguar skins defeating another dressed in eagle feathers. The original mineral-based colors have been preserved and show a distinct Maya influence. Archaeologists do not know precisely why this influence exists, but speculate that it is perhaps due to a trading network between the Maya and the Olmec-Xicalancas.

XOCHITÉNCATL

Public transportation between Cacaxtla and Xochiténcatl is difficult to find. From Cacaxtla, turn towards the rear of the site and follow the path 4km to Xochiténcatl—you can see the path from the latticework window exhibit. To return to Tlaxcala, walk 1km down the base of the hill to the town of San Miguel Xochitecatitla. The town is nearest to the pyramid, on the left when facing away from Cacaxtla. From there, take a colectivo marked "Tlaxcala." Open Tu-Su 10am-4:30pm. 17 pesos, students with ID free. Su free.

The civilization at Xochiténcatl (so-chee-TEN-cahtl) predates Cacaxtla by several hundred years, and its ruins are located on a hill just opposite Cacaxtla. Before they were conquered in AD300 by the Olmec-Xicalancas, the inhabitants of Xochiténcatl constructed the temple to honor Xochiqueteali, the goddess of fertility. For this reason, archaeologists think, many of the artifacts at the site are figures of women or babies, which were sacrificed with some regularity at the site. There are four pyramids, the largest of which, **The Pyramid of Flowers,** is actually a pyramid on top of a pyramid. The columns on top are thought to have been constructed to bring great fertility to all women who passed through them. To the left of the pyramid is the **Pyramid of the Snake.** The basin on top of the pyramid caught water and served as a mirror in which to observe the stars. Behind the Pyramid of the Snake is a small, flat pyramid, the **Basement of the Volcanoes.** At the far left of the site is the **Spiral Pyramid.** Dedicated to the wind god Ehecatl, it is the only such spiral pyramid known to exist. The site offers a spectacular view of nearby volcanoes **Popocatépetel, Ixtaccihuatl,** and **La Malinche (Malintzin).** On your way to the site, peek into the small museum near the entrance and view some of the many artifacts found atop the Pyramid of Flowers.

HUAMANTLA

From Tlaxcala, take a ATA bus from the station to Huamantla (every 10 min., 10 pesos). A large statue of a bull marks the entrance into town. Ask to be let off near Parque Juárez. To return, continue past Museo Taurino to Absolo and hang a right. Buses marked "Tlaxcala" return to the city from the corner of Absalo and Bravo Nte.

Though most visitors come to Huamantla, 45km east of Tlaxcala, for its renowned bull-runnings, other sights attract plenty of daytrippers from the capital city. Sights are centered around the *zócalo,* **Parque Juárez.** Northeast of the *zócalo,* the **Museo Taurino,** Allende Nte. 200, commemorates Huamantla's famous bullfighting history. Posters, bullfighting attire, and photographs dating from the early 1900s are displayed. Before leaving the museum, peek through the fence in the hallway to the left of the courtyard for a glimpse of Huamantla's famous bull ring. (Open M-F 9am-3pm and 5-7pm; Sa-Su 9:30am-2pm. Free.) Not all in Huamantla is bull-related. The **Museo Nacional del Títere,** Parque Juárez 15, on the west side of the *zócalo,* along De La Reforma. In the year 1835, Huamantla became famous for its *títeres* (puppets) when Rosete Aranada, a *títere* company located in the city, began putting on shows involving more than 5000 puppets. Today, the museum contains the third largest collection of the original Rosete Aranada puppets in Mexico. The friendly staff offers guided tours, included in the cost of admission. (☎472 10 33. 10 pesos, students with ID 5 pesos. Open T-Sa 10am-2pm and 4-6pm, Su 10am-3pm.) From the museum, walk to the yellow church, the **Parroquia de San Luís,** Parque Juárez 3, located half a block to the left. Constructed in 1641, the parish church's plain exterior belies a respectable collection of artifacts within. The baptismal chapel to the right of the entrance contains a wood carving of the Christ of Bristo, the creation of which is thought to have been a miracle. (☎472 03 10. Open daily 7am-8pm.) Located on the east of the *zócalo* opposite the museum and parroquia, the **Templo y Convento Franciscano** contains. Intricate paintings of angels decorate the ceiling. (Open daily 9am-7pm.)

Huamantla fills with visitors, carpets of flowers and sawdust, and newly-free bulls in a spectacular early August festival. It all begins on ⬛**La Noche que Nadie Duerme** (The Night No One Sleeps), August 14, when flower and sawdust designs are crafted over 2km of the city streets, and the image of the Virgin is paraded down the carpeted path. Later in the week, on August 19th, the streets close for the traditional Huamantlada, the running of the bulls.

PUEBLA

PUEBLA ☎2

Puebla (pop. 2 million) was a great social experiment—Renaissance meets ruffian, Enlightenment meets real world. Conceived by a group of humanist Spaniards, Puebla was to be a crossroads of faith and education, with libraries, schools, and

CENTRAL MEXICO

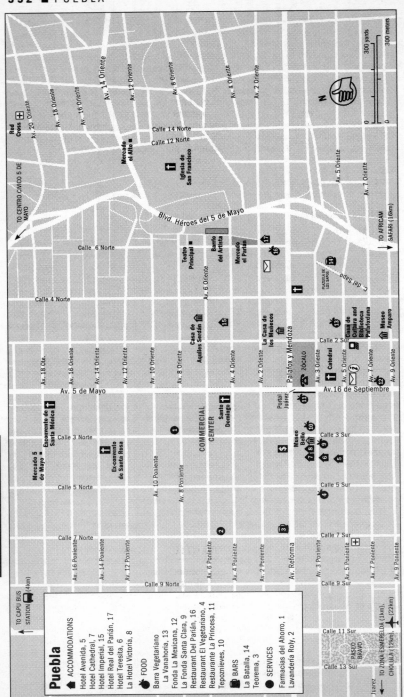

Av. 20 Oriente
Av. 18 Oriente
Av. 16 Oriente
Av. 14 Oriente
Av. 12 Oriente
Av. 8 Oriente
Av. 4 Oriente
Av. 2 Oriente
Av. 5 Oriente
Av. 7 Oriente

Red Cross ✚

TO CENTRO CÍVICO 5 DE MAYO

Calle 14 Norte
Calle 12 Norte

Mercado el Alto ■

Iglesia de San Francisco

Blvd. Héroes del 5 de Mayo

TO AFRICAM SAFARI (16km)

Calle 6 Norte

Teatro Principal ■
Barrio del Artista ■
Mercado el Parián

C. del Sapo
PLAZUELA DE LOS SAPOS

Calle 4 Norte

Casa de Aquiles Serdán 🏛

La Casa de los Muñecos 🏛

Casa de Cultura and Biblioteca Palafoxiana

Museo Amparo 🏛

Av. 18 Ote.
Av. 16 Oriente
Av. 14 Oriente
Av. 12 Oriente
Av. 10 Oriente
Av. 8 Oriente
Av. 6 Oriente
Av. 4 Oriente
Av. 2 Oriente

Palafox y Mendoza
Calle 2 Sur
Calle 3 Sur

Catedral

Av. 5 de Mayo
Av. 16 de Septiembre

ZÓCALO

Portal Juárez

Exconvento de Santa Mónica ■

Mercado 5 de Mayo ■

COMMERCIAL CENTER

Santo Domingo

Ex-convento de Santa Rosa

Calle 3 Norte
Calle 5 Norte
Calle 7 Norte

Av. 10 Poniente
Av. 8 Poniente

Museo Bello

Calle 3 Sur
Calle 5 Sur

Calle 9 Norte

Av. 16 Poniente
Av. 14 Poniente
Av. 12 Poniente

Av. 6 Poniente
Av. 4 Poniente
Av. 2 Poniente

Av. Reforma

Av. 3 Poniente
Av. 5 Poniente
Av. 7 Poniente
Av. 9 Poniente

Calle 7 Sur
Calle 9 Sur

TO CAPU BUS STATION (4km)

Calle 11 Sur
Calle 13 Sur

PASEO BRAVO

Juárez

TO ZONA ESMERELDA (1km), CHOLULA (12km), (22km)

300 yards
300 meters

N

Puebla

▲ ACCOMMODATIONS
Hotel Avenida, 5
Hotel Cathedral, 7
Hotel Imperial, 15
Hotel Real del Parián, 17
Hotel Teresita, 6
La Hotel Victoria, 8

● FOOD
Barra Vegetariano
La Vanahoria, 13
Fonda La Mexicana, 12
La Fonda Santa Clara, 9
Restaurant Del Parián, 16
Restaurant El Vegetariano, 4
Restaurante La Princesa, 11
Tepoznieves, 10

▮ BARS
La Batalla, 14
Teorema, 3

● SERVICES
Farmacias del Ahorro, 1
Lavandería Roly, 2

administrative buildings designed to civilize and Christianize. Surprisingly enough, Puebla was completed as planned, and to this day is a mix of 17th- and 18th-century European art and ideals and colorful Mexican energy. Built on solid, empty ground (as opposed to the lake beds and Mesoamerican ruins that some other cities lie on), Puebla's streets are said to have been laid by angels who flew down and streaked ribbons across the land, forming the grid that makes the city so simple to navigate. Angels notwithstanding, the city has been shaped by pious visitors. Franciscans built hospitals, libraries, and orphanages for illegitimate children, while nuns from a variety of orders set up cloisters and kitchens, where they invented some of Mexico's most famous dishes and the sugar-candy sweets which the city is known for. Today, Puebla is one of the largest and most important cities in the country. Despite its size, it elegantly blends gilded churches with trendy clothing stores, while in the shady *zócalo*, teen hipsters and older locals relax together.

TRANSPORTATION

GETTING AROUND

Most sights and accommodations are located within walking distance of the *zócalo*. If traveling farther in an independent **taxi**, set a price before getting in and don't be shy about haggling. Municipal **buses** and **micros** (also known as *combis*), white Volkswagen vans that operate like buses, cost 3 pesos. Anything labeled "Centro" will take you close to the *zócalo*.

GETTING AWAY

Airport: There is an **airport** (☎232 00 32) in nearby Huejotzingo, 22km northwest of Puebla on Rte. 150. Regional airline **Aeromat** flies to Monterrey and Guadalajara; **Aerocalifornia** flies to Tijuana and Guadalajara.

Bus: CAPU (Central de Autobuses Puebla; ☎249 72 11), at Norte and Tlaxcala, is one of the largest bus stations in the country. To get to the *zócalo* from the station, exit the station to the street and flag a "Centro" bus. To get back to the bus station, take a bus labeled "CAPU" on Calle 9 or on Héroes de 5 de Mayo. Official yellow **taxis** labeled *taxis controlados* will make the trip for 24 pesos. From the station, ADO (☎225 90 01) goes to: **Cancún** (20hr., 11:45am, 668 pesos); **Mérida** (16½hr., every 20min., 68 pesos); **Mexico City** (2½hr., every 20min., 68 pesos); **Oaxaca** (4½hr., 7 per day, 165 pesos); **Veracruz** (3½hr., 7 per day, 133 pesos); and **Xalapa** (3hr., 7 per day 6:45am-9:15pm, 76 pesos). Cristóbal Colón (☎225 90 07) goes to: **Huatulco** (12hr., 7:30 and 9:55 pm, 324 pesos); **Puerto Escondido** (14hr., 7:30pm, 326 pesos); **Tehuantepec** (12hr., 9:50pm, 294 pesos); and other resort cities. Estrella Roja (☎249 70 99) goes to: **Mexico City** (every 20min. 5am-2am, 63 pesos). Estrella Blanca (located under sign for Futuro; ☎249 74 33) goes to: **Acapulco** (7hr., 5 per day, 300 pesos); **Chilpancingo** (6hr., 10:30am and 2:30pm, 221 pesos); and **Taxco** (5hr., 8am, 109 pesos). Flecha Azul (under PTC; ☎249 76 40) goes to: **Tlaxcala** (50min., every 10min. 6am-10pm, 11 pesos). Smaller buses also serve the CAPU station.

ORIENTATION AND PRACTICAL INFORMATION

Puebla, capital of the state of Puebla, is connected through an extensive route network to **Mexico City** (120km northwest along Rte. 150), **Oaxaca** (Rte. 190, 125, or 131), **Tlaxcala** (Rte. 119), **Veracruz** (Rte. 150), and countless other cities. Street names change as they pass the *zócalo*. Numerical addresses follow a rigid pattern. They correspond to the number of the lowest cross-street. For example, Av. 4 Ote. 237 would be bounded by Calle 2 Nte. and Calle 4 Nte. One block farther down, between Calles 4 Nte. and 6 Nte., addresses are in the 400s. Note that there are two major streets in Puebla celebrating the date of Mexico's victory over the French: **Av. 5 de Mayo** and **Blvd. Héroes 5 de Mayo**. Take care not to confuse them.

TOURIST AND FINANCIAL SERVICES

Tourist Office: The **State Office,** Av. 5 Ote. 3 (☎246 12 85 or 246 20 44), has free maps and pamphlets. Fairly helpful staff. Open M-Sa 9am-8:30pm, Su 9am-2pm. **Tourist booth** at the CAPU bus station. Open daily 9am-5pm.

Currency Exchange: Banks line Reforma and 16 de Septiembre around the *centro*. Most have 24hr. **ATMs. Bital,** Reforma 316 (☎246 30 50), changes money. Open M-F 8am-7pm, Sa 8am-5pm. **Casas de cambio** offer slightly better rates and cluster in the *Zona Esmeralda* along Juárez, far from the *zócalo*. Try **Casa de Cambio Puebla,** Juárez 316A (☎248 01 99). Open M-F 9am-6pm, Sa 9am-1pm.

American Express: Díaz Ordaz 6A Sur 2914, #301 (☎237 55 51), in the Plaza Dorada. Cashes and replaces AmEx checks. Holds client mail for 10 days. Open M-F 9am-6pm.

LOCAL SERVICES

Luggage Storage: Lockers at the bus station. 2 pesos per bag per hour. Open 24 hr.

Markets: Puebla's squawking **Mercado 5 de Mayo,** on Av. 18 Ote. between Calles 3 and 5 Nte., spills into 5 de Mayo and adjoining streets, selling everything from fresh veggies to raw meat. Prices fall as you go north. Open daily 7am-7pm. For your processed and packaged needs, try **Ultramarinos el Puerto de Veracruz,** Av. 2 Ote. 402 (☎232 90 52). Open daily 8am-9:30pm.

Laundry: Lavandería Roly, Calle 7 Nte. 404 (☎232 93 07). 36 pesos for 3kg self-service. Open M-Sa 8am-9pm, Su 8am-3pm.

Car Rental: The many car rental companies in Puebla include **Hertz** (☎/fax 232 31 99); **Avis** (☎249 61 99; fax 231 79 38); and **EconoRent** (☎236 96 95; fax 234 54 26).

EMERGENCY AND COMMUNICATIONS

Emergency: ☎060. Also try **Policía Auxiliar** (☎232 31 54 or 242 25 87). Open 24hr.

Police: Dirección de Policía, 16 Sur 1419 (☎232 22 23 or 232 22 22).

Red Cross: Av. 20 Ote. and Calle 10 Nte. (☎235 80 40, 235 86 31, or 234 00 00). 24hr. ambulance service. Some English spoken.

Pharmacies: Farmacías del Ahorro (☎231 33 83), in Plaza San Pedro. Open 24hr. Also located at Av. 8 Pte. 116. Open daily 7am-1pm.

Hospital: Hospital UPAEP, Av. 5 Pte. 715 at Calle 39 Sur (☎232 32 21 or 246 69 99). **Hospital Universitario** (☎246 64 64), Calle 13 Sur at Av. 10 Pte., 10 blocks south and 7 blocks west of the *zócalo*. 24hr. emergency service. Some English spoken.

Fax: Telecomm, 16 de Septiembre 504 (☎232 77 19), just south of the post office. Western Union, telegrams, fax. Open M-F 8am-6pm, Sa-Su 9am-noon.

Telephones: LADATELs are easy to find around the *zócalo*.

Internet Access: Internet Cyber-Byte, Calle 2 Sur 505B, has lots of computers, fast connections, and cool drinks. 20 pesos per hr. Open M-Sa 10am-9pm. **Cyber-Café,** Calle 2 Sur 907C (☎232 42 42), two blocks farther south. Computer screens embedded in rustic wooden tables. Reasonably quick connections. 20 pesos per hr. Coffee 8 pesos. Open M-Sa 9am-9pm, Su 11am-4pm.

Post Office: (☎242 64 4816) 16 de Septiembre at Av. 5 Ote., 1 block south of the *zócalo*, just around the corner from the state tourist office. Open M-F 8am-6pm, Sa 9am-1pm. **Administración 1,** Av. 2 Ote. 411 2nd fl.(☎242 11 36). Open M-F 8am-4pm. The branches have separate *Listas de Correos,* so be sure to know where your mail waits.

Postal Code: 72000 or 72001.

ACCOMMODATIONS

Puebla is well stocked with budget hotels with most of them within a five or six block radius of the *zócalo*. When walking around the *zócalo*, be on the lookout for large, red "H" signs jutting from tightly-packed buildings. These signs, friends of the weary traveler, indicate that a hotel—most often a cheap one—is near.

Hotel Imperial, Av. 4 Ote. 212 (☎/fax 242 49 80). On the expensive side, but oh, the amenities! Telephone and TV in all rooms, internet access, a mini-golf course, a workout area, purified water, a laundry service, a pool table, and a Hershey's Kiss on your pillow. Breakfast in the downstairs cafe (7:30-10:30am) and *cena del patrón*—snacks and drinks (8-9:30pm)—are included. A **30% discount** for proud *Let's Go* readers makes the Imperial's luxury more affordable. Singles 240 pesos; doubles 345 pesos.

Hotel Cathedral, Av. 3 Pte. 310 (☎232 23 60). The 19th-century building has warm high ceilings, hardwood floors, balconies, planted courtyards, and a spectacular roof. Cold communal showers, though. Singles 85 pesos; doubles 120 pesos. Second location, at Av. 3 Pte. 724, has private bathrooms (15 pesos more).

Hotel Real del Parián, Av. 2 Ote. 601 (☎246 19 68), two blocks from the *zócalo*, across the street from the *mercado*, upstairs from some of Puebla's best bargain restaurants. All rooms have private baths and some have balconies. Drinking water, laundry facilities, and accommodating staff add to its appeal. Singles 100 pesos; doubles 115 pesos; triples 190 pesos.

La Hotel Victoria, Av. 3 Pte. 306 (☎232 89 92). Brave the suspended concrete walkways connecting upper-level rooms to take advantage of a convenient location, accommodating staff, and affordable prices. Though the decor is somewhat lacking, rooms and bathrooms are tidy and spacious. Singles 85 pesos; doubles 130 pesos.

Hotel Teresita, Av. 3 Pte. 309 (☎232 70 72). Although cramped, quarters are comfortable for their modernity. Cable TV in all rooms. Social guests gather in the downstairs lobby to meet their neighbors. Singles 140 pesos; doubles 230 pesos.

Hotel Avenida, Av. 5 Pte 336 (☎232 21 04), is arguably the cheapest hotel in Puebla, and it shows. Discolored toilets lack seats. Bedrooms have soft, sagging mattresses and lumpy pillows. Hot water available only 7-10am and 7-10pm. Still, the price and location make Hotel Avenida an option for the (hard-core) budget traveler. Singles 50 pesos, with bath 80 pesos; doubles 90 pesos, with bath 120 pesos.

FOOD

Puebla is most famous for its *mole poblano*, a dark chocolate chile sauce that can be found slathered on chicken, rice, and just about everything else. *Mole poblano* just might be the national dish of Mexico, but don't leave Puebla without tasting other regional specialities. Try *mole pipian*, containing pumpkin seeds and chiles, and *mole adobo*, a spicier blend with cumin powder. Leaving *mole* behind, try *chiles en nogada*, green peppers stuffed with beef and fruit fillings and smothered in white walnut sauce. The patriotic green, red, and white recipe was devised by the nuns of Santa Monica as a birthday present for Mexican Emperor Augustín de Iturbide when he visited the city in 1821 and is eaten throughout August—Iturbide's birth month. Puebla's famous cooking nuns are perhaps best known for their *dulces* (sweets). Sample their centuries-old recipes and creative genius in the *dulcerías* along **Av. 6 Ote.,** just east of 5 de Mayo, which are filled with delicate, colorful candies, some of which are named after the convents of their origin.

Puebla is also home to a plethora of taco stands, many of them on **Calle 5 Nte.** between Avs. 10 and 12 Pte., on **Av. 5 de Mayo** at Av. 14 Ote., and at the **Mercado El Alto,** on the far side of La Iglesia de San Francisco. In addition to the taco-stand staples of *tortas* and tacos, these cheap joins feature *cemitas*, sandwiches made with a special long-lasting bread. In colonial times, Puebla exported the sandwiches to Veracruz, where they were subsequently consumed on trans-Atlantic ships. While Puebla has a number of fine restaurants, visit these stands for a more authentic (and cheaper) sampling of *poblano* cuisine.

■ **Fonda La Mexicana,** 16 de Septiembre 707 (☎232 67 47), 3 blocks south of the *zócalo*. On the wall hangs the first-place certificate that says it all: the best *chiles en nogada* in the state of Puebla. Locals will agree—no place ranks higher for authentic *poblano* cuisine. Although prices are a little steep (*mole* dishes 50-60 pesos), you can order the *menu económico diario* (soup, a main dish, and dessert or coffee, 30 pesos). Speedy, no-frills service is a plus. Open daily 10am-8pm.

■ **Barra Vegetariano La Zanahoria,** Av. 5 Ote. 206 (☎232 48 13). A high ceiling, bubbling fountain, and winding cast-iron stairs give this veggie hangout the most agreeable ambience around. The real attraction, however, is the food: trendy but inexpensive. Order dishes from the menu or go with the plate of the day, which includes five different vegetarian dishes and a fruit beverage (30 pesos; Su buffet 45 pesos). Top it all off with a fruit-flavored *licuado* made from milk or soy (9 pesos). Open M-Su 7:30am-8:30pm.

Restaurante La Princesa, Portal Juárez 101 (☎232 1195), under the *portales* on the west side of the *zócalo*. Mingle with locals as you enjoy *platillos mexicanos* (4-30 pesos, with meat 54-65 pesos). A convenient location, casual atmosphere, and friendly staff add to its appeal. Open daily 8am-11pm.

Restaurant El Vegetariano, Av. 3 Pte. 525 (☎246 54 62). While the Vege's cafeteria-style 1950s decor may make you think you've come to the wrong place, stay cool—the *chorizo* and *jamón* (sausage and ham) on this menu are made of spiced soy. Fruit drinks (9-15 pesos) and gigantic salads (24 pesos). Their *energética* (26 pesos), tropical fruits topped with yogurt and granola, will make you wish for a franchise in your neighborhood. Open daily 7:30am-9pm.

La Fonda Santa Clara, Av. 3 Pte. 307 (☎242 26 59). Good for regional cuisine and hard-to-find seasonal dishes, though somewhat expensive and touristy (*mole poblano* 70 pesos). Nice touches include *talavera* and waitresses in traditional dress.

🔎 SIGHTS

Historic Puebla is a sightseer's paradise. Perhaps this is why bus loads of Mexican students and North Americans from nearby language schools file into the *zócalo* every weekend, cameras and maps in hand. Most sights are clustered around the *zócalo*, but some are located a few minutes away in the **Centro Cívico 5 de Mayo.**

SIGHTS NEAR THE ZÓCALO

The 1999 Puebla earthquake damaged several of the major sights near the *zócalo*. Most damaged sights are scheduled to reopen by the summer of 2001.

CATEDRAL BASÍLICA DE PUEBLA. Visible from all directions, the massive cathedral is the obvious starting point for any tour of the city. Constructed between 1575 and 1649 by an indigenous labor force working under Spanish direction, the building is Baroque in style, enlivened by its *talavera* domes. No less impressive is its interior, with ornate, inlaid choir stalls behind the free-standing octagonal Altar of the Kings, and a statue of the Virgin, known as *la conquistadora* because she arrived with the first Spaniards. *(Guided tours start at 30 pesos. Open daily 6:30am-8pm.)*

■ **MUSEO AMPARO.** Three blocks south of the *zócalo*, the Museo Amparo contains a history and modern art collection, decorated with suspended glass flowers and butterflies and with the occasional burly guard. The history exhibit guides you through the artistic trends of dozens of Mesoamerican civilizations. A colonial era reconstruction shows the building as it once looked. Headphones provide visitors with more information on the exhibits; explanations come in five languages. *(Calle 2 Sur 708. ☎246 46 46. Open M-Su 10am-6pm. 16 pesos, students 8 pesos; M free. Guided tour Su at noon. Headphones 10 pesos with 10 peso deposit.)*

CASA DE LOS MUÑECOS. The 1999 earthquake badly damaged the *casa*, and it is expected to be closed until summer 2001. If it's open, the museum, one of Puebla's most entertaining buildings, is worth a visit. This "House of the Dolls" is decorated on the outside with *talavera* renditions of the labors of Hercules. Some say the sculptures on the outside are the architect's rivals, while others say they are meant to be the city aldermen who protested when the *casa* was built higher than the municipal palace was. Inside, the **University Museum** displays exhibits on regional history and portraits of over 200 martyrs. *(Calle 2 Nte. 4 at the zócalo's northeast corner. ☎ 246 28 99. Open Tu-Su 10am-5pm. 11 pesos, with student ID 5 pesos; W free.)*

MUSEO BELLO Y GONZÁLEZ. The Museo Bello, like the Casa de los Muñecos, was badly damaged in the 1999 earthquake. Because the stairs and part of the second floor caved in, the museum is expected to be closed until the summer of 2001. The museum displays the art collection of late textile magnate José Luis Bello. The collection includes ivory, iron, porcelain, earthenware, and *talavera* artifacts from various places and periods. Guided tours are offered in Spanish and English, but English tours can be indecipherable. *(Av. 3 Pte. 302 at Calle 3 Sur, 1 block west of the southeast corner of the zócalo. ☎ 232 94 75. Open Tu-Su 10am-4:30pm. 10 pesos, students with ID 5 pesos; Tu free.)*

IGLESIA DE SANTO DOMINGO. Puebla's first great religious foundation, this extravagant, gilded church is one of the most important examples of Spanish and international Baroque. The building was constructed between 1571 and 1611 by Dominican rural converts. Statues of saints and angels adorn the altar, but the church's real attraction is the **Capilla del Rosario,** a chapel laden with enough 22-karat gold to make the King of Spain jealous. Masks depicting an Indian, a *conquistador* in armor, and a *mestizo* hang above three doors on the side of the chapel. On the ceiling, three statues represent Faith, Hope, and Charity. The 12 pillars represent the 12 apostles; the six on the upper level are each made from a single onyx stone. Since there was no room for a real choir, designers painted a chorus of angels with guitars and woodwinds on the wall over the door. *(Between Av. 4 and 6 Pte. on 16 de Septiembre. Open daily 10am-2pm and 4-8pm.)*

■**CASA DE AQUILES SERDÁN.** Originally the home of Aquiles Serdán, printer, patriot, and martyr in the 1910 Revolution, the house is today the **Museo Regional de la Revolución Mexicana.** Hundreds of bullet holes, both inside and out, bear witness to Serdán's assassination. The museum also includes photos of Serdán and other revolutionary faces and names. One room is dedicated to Carmen Serdán and other female revolutionaries. *(Av. 6 Ote. 206. ☎ 242 10 76. Open Tu-Su 10am-4:30pm. 20 pesos, children 10 pesos.)*

■**EX-CONVENTO DE SANTA MÓNICA.** When Benito Juárez's Reform Laws went into effect in 1857, they not only weakened the power of the Church, but forced the nuns at the *convento* into hiding. The convent operated in secrecy for 77 years before it was accidentally rediscovered. Today, the *ex-convento* serves as a museum of curious and sporadically-labeled religious art, much of which was produced by the nuns themselves. Particularly eerie is a life-sized re-enactment of the Last Supper, in which plaster apostles in real robes sit around a colonial dinner table. Even more unnerving is the nun's crypt, where those who died during the period of hiding were quietly plastered into the walls. Also open to visitors is the beautiful kitchen (doubling as a laboratory) where the nuns first made *chiles en nogada*. *(Av 18 Pte. 103. Open Tu-Su 9am-6pm. 12 pesos; Su free.)*

IGLESIA DE SAN FRANCISCO. Across Blvd. Héroes de 5 de Mayo from El Parián, Puebla's oldest neighborhood contains the city's oldest church, San Francisco. Built by the Franciscans between 1535 and 1585, it features an incredible *talavera* and orange-red tile facade that contrasts sharply with the extremely ominous bell tower. On your way out, look for the nuns selling delectable *dulces típicos* in the surrounding plaza. *(Av. 14 Ote. and Blvd. Héroes del 5 de Mayo. Open 24 hr.)*

CASA DE LA CULTURA. Starting point for exploring cultural events in the city, the *casa* houses the **Biblioteca Palafoxiana,** an impressive 43,000 volume library. The museum began with Juan de Palafoxiana's 6000-book collection, which he donated to the city in 1646. His original library includes an illuminated copy of the Nuremberg Chronicle from 1493. Although it, too, sustained extensive damage in the 1999 earthquake, the library is expected to reopen by January 2001. *(Av. 5 Ote. 5.* ☎ *246 13 01. Open Tu-Su 10am-5pm. 10 pesos, students with ID 5 pesos.)*

CENTRO CÍVICO AND OTHER SIGHTS

With the exception of Africam Safari, the following sights are located in the **Centro Cívico 5 de Mayo.** A short trip from the *centro,* the Centro Cívico was the location of the May 5, 1862 **Battle of Puebla,** in which general Ignacio Zaragoza defeated the French in their advance toward Mexico City. The former battleground is now a large, unkempt park, where austere patriotic signs compete for attention with frolicking young lovers. *(To get to the Centro Cívico, Catch a #72 bus or #8 colectivo (both 3 pesos) on Blvd. Héroes de 5 de Mayo, three blocks east of the zócalo. Get off when you see a large, multi-armed cement monument to Zaragoza that sits on an empty glorieta. Facing away from the monument, cross the street and walk uphill toward the park.)*

MUSEO DE LA NO INTERVENCIÓN. This oddly-named museum houses artifacts, paintings, and documents dealing with the Battle of Puebla and the actions of general Zaragoza. The museum also features a panoramic recreation of the battlefield as it might have looked in 1862. Downstairs are more exhibits on French rule in Mexico. *(From the Zaragoza monument, walk past a now defunct information center. A large concrete Mexican flag marks a fork in the road. To the right is the Fuerte de Loreto, which now houses the museum. Open Tu-Su 10am-4:30pm. 25 pesos; Su free.)*

MUSEO DE HISTORIA NATURAL. This museum teems with fossils, live snakes, and well-behaved school kids. Life-sized (but out of date) dinosaur models hold court the foyer, while a spectacular butterfly collection lights up the left exhibition wing. The museum also boasts the largest collection of stuffed deer heads you'll ever see under one roof. *(Take the road to the left of the Museo de la No Intervención.* ☎ *235 34 19. Open Tu-Su 10am-5pm. 11 pesos, children 5 pesos; Tu free.)*

PLANETARIUM. Next to the Museo de Historia Natural, the planetarium—in the shape of a giant, glittering silver pyramid—features the typical slew of space exhibits and an **Omnimax** theater. Across from the museum is the **Recinto Ferial,** an exposition center and fairground. *(Next to the Museo de Historia Natural.* ☎ *235 20 99. Open daily 10am-5pm. 11 pesos, children 5 pesos; Tu free. Including Omnimax 23 pesos. Shows play approx. every hr. noon-5pm.)*

PARQUE RAFAELA PADILLA DE ZARAGOZA. This large park has a playground, benches, and trails descending to a theater. The Administration building at the entrance shows nature videos. Nature immersion is complete save for the piped-in radio shows and oversized animal statues. *(Open Tu-Su 10am-4pm. Videos 1 peso.)*

FUERTE DE GUADALUPE. This fort, "an altar to the patriotism of the heroes of the Fifth of May," offers stunning views of Puebla and the surrounding mountains. *(At the tip of the loop, about a 10min. walk from the rest of the museums.)*

CENTRAL MEXICO

THE GOOD KIND OF INFESTATION Where have all the Beetles gone? They're all in Mexico—1.1 million of them. More than one in every eight passenger vehicles in Mexico is a classic VW Beetle, and Puebla is the last place on Earth to manufacture them. The VW factory on the outskirts of town employs more than 16,000 workers and churns out 1,000 cars each day. Many of these are the chic, New Beetle (US$20,000), but almost all are shipped north. Mexican drivers still overwhelmingly prefer the classic model (US$6,700), affectionately known as "Vochos." Souped-up Beetles often sport chrome fenders, oversize tires, and mini steering wheels, and many of Mexico City's 35,000 Beetle taxis are meticulously customized.

COOKING NUNS! In 17th century Puebla, nuns of the Santa Rosa order lived lives of extreme devotion. They slept without cover on beds of wooden slats, wore crowns of thorns to ward off bad thoughts, and installed 4ft. doors throughout their convent so that they would have to bow their heads in prayer each time they entered a room. Self-denying to a fault, the one area in which the nuns didn't skimp was food. Sor Andrea de la Asunción is said to have concocted the first ever *mole poblano* inside the convent. As the story goes, her sisters gathered around her as she rolled four different types of chiles together, commenting on her skill in grinding the peppers. *"¡Que bien muele!"* ("how well she grinds") became *"¡que bien mole!"* and thus the famous regional specialty earned its name. To balance the spicy peppers, the sisters added chocolate, sugar, and eventually 21 other ingredients before they were satisfied with the final product. Today, the nuns' culinary expertise is celebrated during the month of June by the *Festival del Mole Poblano.* At the festival, chefs submit samples of their own family recipes, hoping to win the civic honor of best *mole* in town. The cooking nun phenomenon seems to have been widespread in Puebla; nuns of Santa Rosa, Santa Monica, and other orders are credited with the invention of Puebla's unique *dulces, chiles en nogada,* and nearly all of the city's other specialties.

MUSEO REGIONAL DE ANTROPOLOGÍA. The museum features clothing, artifacts, and information about the historic state of Puebla. *(On your right as you leave the fort. Open Tu-Su 10am-5pm. 25 pesos; Su free.)*

AFRICAM SAFARI. A longer trip takes you to Africam Safari, an ecological zoo dedicated to conservation and recreation. The park holds over 3000 live animals, representing approximately 250 species. Geographically organized, the park has theme areas spanning Asia, America, and Antarctica. What sets the Africam Safari apart from your average zoo is that the animals roam freely. Visitors drive through the park, stopping at designated locations to take photos and mingle with the quadrupedal residents. *(16km southeast of Puebla, the easiest way to get to Africam Safari is by bus. Estrella Roja offers packages that include roundtrip fare from CAPU and park admission (every 45min. 10:45am-2:45pm; 82 pesos, children 75 pesos, 30 pesos without admission). If driving, head to the south of the city and then go east, following the signs to Valsequillo. Africam ☎235 88 29 or 235 87 18. Open daily 10am-5pm. 60 pesos, children 55 pesos.)*

🎵 ENTERTAINMENT

Bars and theaters pile up in the *zócalo,* while a young, more local crowd packs the numerous bars in **Plazuela de los Sapos,** creating a loud and social weekend scene. Further from the *zócalo,* between Calles 21 and 29 Sur on Juárez, is the **Zona Esmeralda,** lined with even more bars and discos. If you're prepared to spring for a cab, however, you may as well continue on to the clubs and bars on the **Recta Cholula,** the highway connecting Puebla and Cholula. The true center of the area's thriving nightlife, the *Recta* is jam-packed with college and language school students every night, all night. Since buses stop running early, it's best to take a taxi. Ask to be let off by the clubs near UDLA (Universidad de las Américas).

Teorema, Reforma 540 (☎242 10 14), 3 blocks west of the *zócalo.* A bookstore/café by day, Teorema is a trendy alternative to the bar scene by night. After 9pm, a young, diverse clientele crowds in to hear nightly live music, chat with friends, and drink *café con licor* (starting at 25 pesos) in this literary lair. Cover M-Th 11 pesos, F-Sa 20 pesos, Su 15 pesos. Open 9:30am-2:30pm and 4:30pm-2am; music starts at 9:30pm.

La Batalla, Calle 6 Sur 504A (☎246 35 65), in Plazuela de los Sapos. Spiffy young socialites mingle under low lights and a pounding beat. Beer from 13 pesos; drinks 22 pesos. Cover Tu-Th and Sa 20 pesos, F 30 pesos, Su 10 pesos. Open Tu-Su noon-3am.

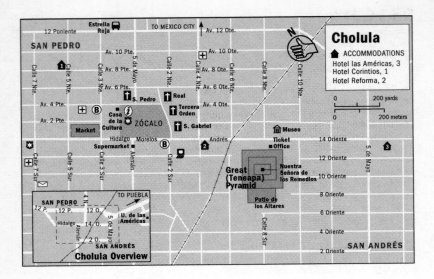

Cholula

🔺 **ACCOMMODATIONS**
Hotel las Américas, 3
Hotel Corintios, 1
Hotel Reforma, 2

Cholula Overview

 SHOPPING

With embroidered textiles, clay ornaments, woven palms, and 450-year tradition of *talavera*, Puebla offers numerous and diverse shopping opportunities. At **Mercado El Parián**, with entrances on both Av. 2 Ote. and 4 Ote. at Calle 6 Nte., tourists gather to buy hand-painted *talavera* ceramics and tiles, as well as leather purses, beads, and other trinkets. For less expensive *talavera* purchases, head to **Av. 18 Pte.**, west of Av. 5 de Mayo. North of El Parián, at Calle 8 Nte. 410, is the **Barrio del Artista,** where *poblano* artists paint and sell their works in the street. Sundays from 10am-6pm, the **Plazuela de los Sapos,** south of the *zócalo* on Calle del Sapo, fills with antique bazaars selling bronze figures, old coins, and *talavera*. To learn more about *poblano* crafts, head to the **Ex-Convento Santa Rosa,** where the admission fee includes a guided tour through the Museo de Las Artesanías.

 FESTIVALS

The **Casa de la Cultura,** Av. 5 Ote. 5, is the place to go for information about Puebla's cultural events. Pick up a monthly calendar and check the board on the right as you walk in from the street for the latest schedules. (Folk dances Sa and Su. Movies Th-Su. ☎246 13 01. Open 24hr.) Also be sure to check the schedule posted inside the **Teatro Principal,** which lists weekly performances. The developing program at **Centro Cultural Santa Rosa** (☎232 92 40), located in the **Ex-Convento de Santa Rosa,** includes performances of popular and traditional music, experimental theater, and indigenous productions.

In addition to June's *mole* cook-off and August's *festival de chiles en nogada,* the city of Puebla celebrates several secular events throughout the year. The end of April kicks off a month-long *fiesta* celebrating May. Each day the streets fill with various types of expositions. Special events include *corridas de toros* and cock fights. In the **Festival Palafoxiana,** Juan de Palafox is remembered for his religious influence and the generous donation of his namesake library to the city. The celebration runs F-Su, from the last Friday in September until November 19, and features dances, concerts, theater performances, and art.

CHOLULA

☎2

Founded over 2500 years ago, the quiet and religious Cholula (pop. 95,000) was inhabited by several pre-Hispanic cultures. Olmecs, Zapotecs, Toltecs, and Aztecs all ruled over the city and each left their mark by adding another tier or temple to the city's Great Pyramid. When Cortés arrived in 1520, he uncovered an alliance between the Cholutecos and the Aztecs; enraged, he proceeded to slaughter 6000 Cholutecos in what is now known as the **Cholula Massacre.** To further punish the city, Cortés vowed to erect 365 churches—one for every day of the year—on top of the city's native temples. While he never quite reached his goal, the 37 churches in Cholula today (128 total in the municipality) have ensured the city's continued role as a sacred place of pilgrimage, both for the faithful and for the curious. An easy daytrip from Puebla or Mexico City, Cholula draws urban escapists with its churches, balmy weather, and lively *portales.* Pray in one of churches built by Cortés before hitting the Recta Cholula for a night on the town with students from the nearby **Universidad de las Américas (UDLA).** Just don't expect to get much sleep—bells from the 37 church towers start ringing early on Sunday morning.

█ TRANSPORTATION

GETTING AROUND

Colectivos to Puebla and destination within Cholula can be flagged down at a variety of locations in the city center, including the corner of **Av. 4 Pte.** and **Calle 3 Nte.,** as well as at **Morelos** and **Calle 2 Sur** (30 min. to Puebla's CAPU, 4 pesos). After the *colectivos* stop running at 10pm, you'll have to negotiate a price with a local taxi (40 pesos or more). *Sitios,* readily available throughout the city, can always be found at the southeast corner of the *zócalo.*

GETTING AWAY

To get to the *zócalo* from the Estrella Roja bus station, Av. 12 Pte. 108 (☎247 19 20), between 5 de Mayo and Calle 3 Nte., walk east to the intersection of Av. 12 Pte. and 5 de Mayo and turn right on 5 de Mayo. Walk four blocks downhill toward the large yellow church of San Pedro. Estrella Roja runs buses to: **Mexico City** via Puebla (2½hr., 2 per hr. 4:25am-8pm, 39 pesos) and **Puebla** (30 min., 2 per hr. 4:25am-9pm, 4-5 pesos). For more destinations, head to Puebla's CAPU (see p. 353).

█ █ ORIENTATION AND PRACTICAL INFORMATION

Cholula is on Rte. 150, 122km east of Mexico City and 8km west of Puebla. The municipality of Cholula encompasses two small towns—**San Pedro Cholula** and **San Andrés Cholula.** The *zócalo,* tourist office, and most restaurants are located in San Pedro. San Andrés, on the other hand, is mostly residential and encompasses everything to the east of the Great Pyramid. The walk between the two can be lonely at night; taxis travel the distance for 20 pesos.

TOURIST AND LOCAL SERVICES

Tourist Office: Av. 4 Pte. 103 (☎247 31 16). From the *zócalo,* walk north past the *portales* and turn left at the library. The tourist office is second on the left. The helpful staff offers pamphlets, advice, and a nearly-illegible free map. Open M-Su 10am-6:30pm.

Currency Exchange: Casa de Cambio Azteca, Calle 2 Sur 104 (☎247 21 90). Open M-F 9am-7pm, Sa 9am-2pm. Banks on Morelos at the *zócalo* have more limited hours but offer comparable rates and have **ATMs. Bancomer,** Morelos 10, on the south side of the *zócalo,* is open M-F 9am-5:30pm.

Market: Cosme del Razo, with entrances on Calles 3 and 5 Nte., between Hidalgo and Av. 4 Pte., also in the *zócalo*. On W and Su, the already crowded market swells with even more merchants.

Supermarket: For pre-packaged food and toiletries, try **Tienda Sindical de Consumo Crom,** Alemán 116, a small supermarket near the corner of Av. 3 Ote.

Laundry: Lavandería Aquiahuac, on Av. 14 Ote. 2D, 4 blocks east of the pyramid, just after 5 de Mayo. 7 pesos per kg. Open M-F 9am-8pm, Sa 9am-6pm. Close to the *zócalo*, **Lav-Ale Lavandería Automática** (☎247 70 89), on Av. 6 Ote. 2 at the corner of 5 de Mayo, charges a hefty 24 pesos per kg. Open M-Sa 9am-7pm.

EMERGENCY AND COMMUNICATIONS

Emergency: ☎060.

Police: At the Presidencia Municipal, Portal Guerrero 1 (☎247 05 62), in the arcade under the arches. The station is at Hidalgo and Calle 7 Sur. Little English spoken.

Red Cross: Calle 7 Sur 301 (☎247 85 01), on the corner of Av. 3 Pte., a bit of a hike from the *centro*. Walk-in service. Open 24hr. No English spoken.

Pharmacy: Droguería Medina, Hidalgo 502 (☎247 16 44), on the corner of Calle 5 Nte. Open 24hr. **Farmacía San Juan Bautista,** Calle 3 Nte. 405 (☎247 34 45), on the corner of Av. 6 Pte. Open 24hr.

Hospital: Clínica de IMSS (☎247 53 14), at Calle 4 Nte. and Av. 10 Ote. Open 24hr. **Hospital San Gabriel,** Av. 4 Pte. 503 (☎247 00 14), 2 blocks west of the *zócalo*. No English spoken.

Fax: Telecomm, Portal Guerrero 9 (☎247 01 30). Telegrams, fax, Western Union. Open M-F 8am-7:30pm, Sa-Su 9am-noon. **Papelería Toño,** Morelos 8 (☎/fax 247 11 49), on the south side of the *zócalo*. Open daily 8am-8pm.

Telephones: LADATELs, line Morelos and Hidalgo on the south side of the *zócalo*.

Internet: Café Internet La Gioconda, Av. 3 Ote. 203 at Calle 2 Sur (☎247 77 01). Relatively quick connection is a bargain at 10 pesos per hr. Open M-Sa 10am-8:30pm, Su 10am-4pm. **Café Internet La Tienda,** Portal Guerrero 11 (☎247 41 98), on the west side of the *zócalo*. Fast connection, 20 pesos per hr. Open M-Sa 10am-8pm.

Post Office: 7 Sur 505, just past Av. 5 Pte. Open M-F 8am-4pm.

Postal Code: 72760.

█ ACCOMMODATIONS

Near the *zócalo* and the pyramid, budget hotels are scarce. While several moderately-priced hotels are located just north of Cholula on **Carretera Federal México-Puebla,** visitors willing to make the trek should consider staying just 30 minutes away in Puebla, where they will hit the hotel jackpot.

Hotel Reforma, Calle 4 Sur 101 (☎247 01 49), near Morelos. A short stumble from the *portales*. Private baths, knowledgeable staff, and a chipper cactus garden compensate for street noise and somewhat flimsy doors. Duck into the connected **Bar Reforma** to examine wall murals and photographs of all 128 churches in and around Cholula. Ring to enter after 10:30pm. Singles 80 pesos; doubles 130 pesos.

Corintios, Calle 5 Nte. 801 (☎247 94 40; fax 247 05 64), a slightly longer walk from the *zócalo*. Spacious, aesthetically simple rooms feature white walls, dark woodwork and private baths. Prices lower for 3-day and week-long stays. Night-owls beware—you can ring to enter after the front door locks at 10:30pm, but the staff will only stay awake to let you in until 11:30pm. Singles 100 pesos; doubles 150 pesos.

Hotel Las Américas, Av. 14 Ote. 6 (☎247 09 91). From the *zócalo*, take Morelos and walk past the pyramid approximately 4 blocks. The hotel is on the right after 5 de Mayo. The bright flowers and uncut grass surrounding the empty courtyard swimming pool do little to disguise the hotel's 70s architecture. Dark rooms have TVs and phones; curtainless private bathrooms are one giant shower. Visitors should be wary of walking the long, desolate path past the pyramid at night. Singles 90 pesos; doubles 120 pesos.

🍴 FOOD

Influenced in part by Puebla's culinary traditions, most of Cholula's restaurants feature several variations of *mole poblano*. For a good variety of cheap local food, wander through the **Cosme del Razo** market and the food stands in the *zócalo*. Many of Cholula's most affordable establishments are located on **Hidalgo,** perpendicular to the *portales*. Toward the bus station, family-owned *torta* shops and market stands offer even better prices, but eating in the *zócalo* is a great way to meet locals, and the *charla* (chat) is worth the few extra pesos.

Los Tulipanes, Portal Guerrero 13 (☎247 17 07), on the west side of the *zócalo*. Locals and visitors alike relax in the shade beneath *portales* as they consume a sampling of Cholula's best *comida típica*. The moderately-priced menu features breakfast (starting at 18 pesos), *antojitos* (15-25 pesos), *comida corrida* (33 pesos; Su 38 pesos), and meat and fish entrees (27-50 pesos). Open daily 8am-9pm.

Güeros, Hidalgo 101 (☎247 21 88). A crowd of local families and couples populate the modern, spacious eating area, while the bar functions as an informal meeting place for solo diners. Though the food is of the Tex-Mex variety, Güeros does offer some regional specialties at good prices. Tacos start at 5 pesos, sandwiches and *tortas* 12-26 pesos, and main dishes 25-30 pesos. Open daily 8am-2am.

El Pecas Parrilla, Alemán 512A (☎247 16 18), at the corner of 7 Pte., offers all the quality service, savory meat dishes, and colorful ambience of tourist restaurants at slightly lower prices. Tacos 6 pesos; tender *Arracheras* complete with excellent guacamole 45 pesos. Open daily 2pm-2am.

Chialingo, Av. 7 Pte. 113 (☎247 28 31), half a block west of Alemán. With its verdant, secluded courtyard and subtle *vaquero* (cowboy) motif, Chialingo is a first-class haven from Cholula's sometimes overwhelming activity. Patrons dress well and pay handsomely for their high-brow tastes. The atmosphere, though, is worth every peso. Meat 49-65 pesos, chicken 45 pesos, seafood 49-125 pesos. Open daily 1-9pm.

👁 SIGHTS

Cholula's chief attractions are also its most visible: the **Great Pyramid** looms over the town's center, while the brightly-colored towers of Cholula's 37 churches jut above the cityscape. The June 1999 earthquake that devastated so many of Puebla's sights left its mark in Cholula as well: many churches sustained extensive interior and exterior damage. Fortunately, the combined efforts of the government, churches, and community have enabled the reconstruction of many of the churches, and restoration on all of Cholula's most well-known cathedrals are scheduled for completion by early 2001.

THE GREAT PYRAMID AND ENVIRONS

TENEAPA PYRAMID. When Cortés destroyed the Toltec temple atop the misshapen hill that dominates Cholula, he was unaware that the hump of earth was actually a giant pyramid, built centuries before. When archaeologists tunneled into the "hill" in the twentieth century, they discovered three other pyramids built one on top of the other, indicating successive enlargement of a smaller original pyramid. Archaeologists believe that the original pyramid, dating from roughly 200BC, may have been built by the Olmecs or a related group. When the Toltec-Chichimec groups settled in Cholula in the 12th century, they named the pyramid Tlachiaualtepetl, or "man-made hill," and are believed to have practiced human sacrifice atop it. Sophisticated drainage systems have kept the structure, by volume the largest pyramid in the world, intact. Today, the tunnels and some excavations on

CENTRAL MEXICO

the south and west sides of the pyramid are open to visitors. A joint conservation-excavation program is currently under development, with plans to resume excavation of the pyramid in 2005. (*Entrance is on Morelos, across from the railroad. Ruins and tunnels open daily 9am-6pm. 20-25 pesos. Su free.*)

MUSEO AL SITIO. Before entering the Indiana-Jones-style tunnels at the pyramid's base, visit the museum across the street from the ticket booth. Centered around a helpful diorama of the pyramid (guaranteed to convince skeptics that it is not, in fact, a hill), the museum features artifacts from the area. A reproduction of "Los Bebedores," one of the site's famous frescoes and one of the largest murals in pre-Hispanic Mesoamerica, graces the spooky back room. The curators are friendly and helpful. (*Open daily 9am-6pm. Free with tickets to the pyramid.*)

TUNNELS AND PATIOS. To get to the open-air excavations on the side of the pyramid opposite the entrance, most visitors walk through the labyrinthine archaeological tunnels that riddle the pyramid's base. Deeper, darker, slightly scary side tunnels can be explored with a guide or by yourself. Look for a particularly stunning section of one of the interior pyramid's main staircases, which has been excavated from bottom to top. The underground adventure ends at the south side of the pyramid in the **Patio de los Altares,** a mostly unexcavated grassy area dotted with pyramid chunks in various states of renovation. English language pamphlets can be purchased at the bookstore near the end of the outdoor excavations, though the bare essentials can be gleaned from the explanatory markers. Guides help greatly. (*Guide 40 pesos; 50 pesos in English.*)

SANTUARIO DE NUESTRA SEÑORA DE LOS REMEDIOS. No ticket is required to reach the Santuario, a church built atop the pyramid in 1594, but the trek up is more taxing than a Stairmaster workout. When the Spanish built the sanctuary, they dedicated it to La Virgen de los Remedios as a safeguard against the gods from whose ruined temple the sanctuary walls had been constructed. After collapsing in a 1864 earthquake, the structure was re-built using much of the original material. Nature seems to repeat herself, for once again Cholulans are repairing the small, flower-filled sanctuary after the 1999 earthquake. Fortunately, the virgin figure, set in her fabergé jewelry box, remained unharmed, and celebrations in her honor continue each June and September. On a clear day, the snow-capped volcanoes **Popocatépetl** and **Ixtaccíhuatl** are visible from the church site, as well as the rest of Cholula and its many churches. (*From the patio, follow the path as it takes you back to the railroad tracks. Make an immediate right where the fence ends and begin climbing. Free.*)

CHURCHES OF THE ZÓCALO

If you don't have the energy to hike to every single one of Cholula's 37 churches, don't despair: four of the most spectacular border the *zócalo* itself.

CONVENTO FRANCISCANO DE SAN GABRIEL. When the 16th century Franciscans used Indian labor to construct San Gabriel on top of the Templo de Quetzalcoátl, they hoped to use the church for a great conversion. The altar in today's chapel was built in 1897, utilizing a neoclassical style designed to emphasize the mass of the already weighty church. Despite San Gabriel's imposing size, the Franciscans found it too small for their epic conversion campaign, and in 1575 began work on the Capilla Real, two doors down. (*On the south side of the zócalo.*)

CAPILLA REAL. Possibly the most striking of the city's churches, the 49-domed structure was finished in the early 17th century, filling its role as the long-awaited auditorium where thousands of Indians could hear mass at once. The wall behind the splendid altar is covered with three famous paintings depicting the story of the Virgin of Guadalupe. The Capilla Real lacks the ornate gold filigree of the surrounding churches; its simplicity is defined by the ever-changing panorama of whitewashed arches, soaring domes, and uniquely decorated side-chapels. (*The northernmost church on the east side of the zócalo.*)

CAPILLA DE LA TERCERA ORDEN. Lavish gold ornamentation and seven large 18th and 19th century paintings decorate the interior, while the church's three small domes balance Capilla Real's vastness. *(Behind San Gabriel and Capilla Real.)*

PARROQUIA DE SAN PEDRO. As a 17th-century construction, San Pedro displays an architectural style unique to its age: Baroque meets Renaissance in ornate fashion. 18th-century paintings adorn the walls, including one of Diego de Borgraf's most powerful depictions of Christ. *(In the northwest corner of the zócalo.)*

ON THE OUTSKIRTS OF CHOLULA

SANTA MARÍA TONANTZINTLA. Almost as famous as Cholula itself are several churches in the surrounding villages, particularly the church of Santa María Tonantzinla. Built in the 10th century on top of a pre-Hispanic temple, the church's bright saffron facade hides a startling interior, in which over 450 stucco faces stare out from the walls and ceiling. Saints, musicians, and chiefs congregate with animals and flowers in an explosion of iconography, the handiwork of the same indigenous artisan who executed the plans of European artists in Puebla's Capilla del Rosario (see p. 357). *(To get to Tonantzintla, take a colectivo marked "Chipilo" at Ave. 6 Ote. and 5 de Mayo (3 pesos). Get off when you see a yellow church on your left; Tonantzintla is a short walk down the pedestrian-only street to your right.)*

SAN FRANCISCO ACATAPEC. A 15-minute walk away (or an even shorter 3-peso bus ride) lies the town and church of San Francisco Acatapec. Built in 1588, the facade of the church is almost as ornate as Tonantzintla's walls. Entirely covered in brilliant *talavera* tile set into an overgrown graveyard, this is perhaps the most exquisite application the famous tiles yet found. *(To go directly from Cholula to Actapec, simply ride a few km further on the same "Chipilo" bus that you would take for Tonantzintla.)*

UNIVERSIDAD DE LAS AMÉRICAS. The elite, private university UDLA (pronounced OOHD-lah), is a perfect example of the universality of university culture. The verdant, bench-filled campus is a respite from the city's dusty mayhem. Students, locals, and visitors find cheap diversion watching UDLA's *beisbol* and *fútbol* teams take on neighboring colleges during the fall and spring semesters. **Cafetería Santa Catarina** serves the Mexican version of institutionalized food. Souvenirs are available in the nearby social center kiosk. *(Take an eastbound colectivo anywhere on Av. 14 Ote. (30 pesos). Cafeteria open M-F 7am-9:30pm, Sa-Su 7:30am-8pm.)*

🎦 NIGHTLIFE

Whether you're in the mood for socializing in bars around the *zócalo*, or for clubbing in the wild and costly Recta Cholula, a night out in the city is first-rate.

BARS

Bars in Cholula center around the lively *zócalo* and Av. 14 Ote., west of Hotel Las Américas in San Andrés. The bars in San Andrés serve local, slightly older clientele, but those in the *centro* cater to a more diverse, younger crowd. **Bar-Restaurant Enamorada,** Portal Guerrero 1, under the *portales*, feeds and inebriates a social, varied crowd. While patrons visit Enamorada earlier in the day for its affordable *comida típica*, the young crowd flocking to its doors around 10:30pm come for the live music, which lasts until midnight. (Beers 13 pesos, mixed drinks 30 pesos, and *café con licor* 28 pesos. ☎247 02 92 or 247 70 22. Open Th-Su 8am-3am.) **Café Tal,** Porral Guerrero 5, also under the *portales*, provides coffee lovers with a cheap, relaxing place to caffeinate. Take your coffee with a kick of *licor* to start the night off right. (Coffees start at 7 pesos. Open M-Su 9am-2am.)

CLUBS

Undoubtedly, the **Recta Cholula** is *the* place to be. The highway between Puebla and Cholula is littered with warehouse-sized *discotecas* fueled by the youthful energy of both cities. Bars and discos in this area frequently re-invent themselves in an attempt to get an edge on the market, but you'll find the same student-filled scene regardless of the packaging. Those looking for a wild night of clubbing should dress well and fill their wallets with cash; this is no place for amateurs. To get to the Recta, take a Puebla-bound bus from Av. 14 Ote. past UDLA. Buses stop running around 10pm, so the return trip is best made in a taxi—a pricey finish to a pricey evening. ⊠**Roka,** Recta Cholula 1411, is the top choice of the UDLA crowd. (Cover F and Sa 40 pesos; Th 40 pesos for women, 90 pesos for men, with open bar. No reservations required. ☎247 94 62. Open Th-Sa 10:30pm-late.)

GAY AND LESBIAN NIGHTLIFE

In Cholula, the young, mostly gay and bisexual clientele of **Keops,** on the corner of Av. 14 Ote. and 5 de Mayo, keeps it jamming to a techno beat. Don't miss *Travesty,* the midnight drag show. (Cover 40 pesos. Open F-Sa 9pm-5am.)

FESTIVALS

A deeply religious town, Cholula celebrates religious festivals with great flair. Two different celebrations honor the Virgen de Remedios. Since 1640, Cholula has celebrated the **Bajada de la Virgen** for two weeks in June, when the Virgin comes down from her celestial sanctuary to visit the city and surrounding towns. Cholulans carry the figurine through the streets by motorcycle every morning at 7am during the week of the festival. In the evenings, locals revel under the elaborate gateways of flowers, seeds, and glitter decorating the Virgin's route. An even bigger festival takes place from the first day in September to the 8th, the Virgin's *Día Santa.* Celebrations for *Carnival, Semana Santa,* and Christmas are also big events, when Cholula fills with visitors from Puebla, Mexico City, and surrounding villages.

CENTRAL PACIFIC COAST

Stretching from the quiet fishing hamlets near San Blas to the busy port of Manzanillo, the central Pacific coast is lined with kilometer after kilometer of smooth sand. Hot but comfortably dry, the weather is beautiful and the sun rarely fails to illuminate the azure skies. Priding itself on diversity, the central Pacific states range from the fertile jungle lands of Nayarit, to vibrant Jalisco, to the sleepy beachtowns of Colima.

A state of varied terrain, **Nayarit** is marked by volcanic highlands, tropical jungles, and a network of lakes and rivers. This verdant region grows the lion's share of the nation's marijuana, and is home to the oldest native group in Mexico, the Huichol. Even in the state's larger cities, it is not uncommon to see Huichol people in their colorful dress. Men typically wear light-colored pants and light, wide shirts belted at the waist, all brilliantly embroidered with religious figures and eye-catching designs. Women's clothing consists of a similarly colorful embroidered blouses and long skirts. Peyote may be carried in colorfully woven knit or stitched bags worn across the shoulders.

South of Nayarit lies **Jalisco,** the most touristed state along the central Pacific coast. Much of the world's perception of Mexican pop culture could be stamped *"Hecho en Jalisco"* (Made in Jalisco). The *jarabe tapatío* (hat dance), *mariachis, charreria* (cowboy culture), and tequila all originated in this state. For much of its history, however, the province remained isolated from the rest of the Republic, possessing neither silver nor gold, jewels nor fertile land. It wasn't until the 1920s, when railroad tracks extended to Guadalajara, that this Sierran town (elevation 1552m) grew into a metropolis; today, it is Mexico's second-largest city.

Tiny **Colima** has spectacular beaches and pleasant mountain towns where tourists can escape the resort scene and breathe cool, crisp air. The state is also home to the city of Colima, a sparkling, untouristed gem, and Manzanillo, the workhorse of Mexico's Pacific coast. This port has not paused once in 700 years of commerce to wipe its sweaty brow, and only recently has it attempted to polish its image for the benefit of visitors.

HIGHLIGHTS OF THE CENTRAL PACIFIC COAST

EXPERIENCE Guadalajara (see p. 373), Mexico's second-largest city; it's clean and green, and comes complete with great **museums** (see p. 378) and exciting **nightlife** (see p. 380).

BE A TOURIST in **Puerto Vallarta** (see p. 387), no longer the quiet, secluded paradise of the 1960s. The thriving tourist industry is due to its glitzy nightlife, luxury hotels, and shop-crowded streets. There is also a booming **gay scene** (see p. 381). The **best beaches,** however, lie south of the city (see p. 392).

SNEAK AWAY from it all in the **Bahía de Navidad** (see p. 394), which isn't hyper developed—yet. Swim, surf, and sunbathe on your choice of beautiful beaches. Both **Bahía de Navidad** and **Melaque** (see p. 394), located on the bay, offer budget accommodations and gorgeous beaches.

BE DAZZLED by **Cuyutlán** (see p. 402): solitude, black-sand beaches, and a wondrous lagoon.

TIRED of "authenticity"? Travel to **Tequila** (see p. 385), the touristy and fun birthplace of your favorite liquor.

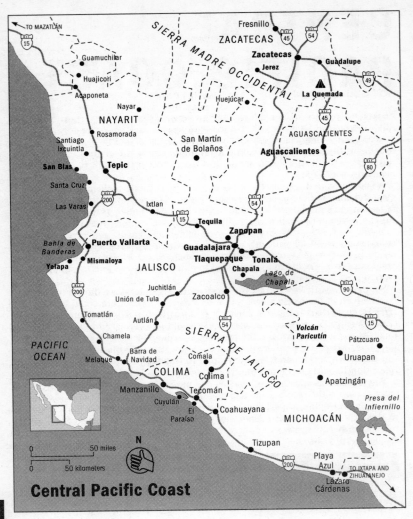

Central Pacific Coast

NAYARIT

SAN BLAS   ☎ 3

San Blas (pop. 19,000) is a small, dusty fishing village that feeds off its ecological wealth: huge beaches and over 300 species of birds. Though there is not much to see or do in the town itself, the nearby jungles attract North American expats, birdwatchers, and tourists en route to Puerto Vallarta, while the smooth sand beaches and long waves make San Blas a mecca for surfers. Bring plenty of bug repellent; ravenous mosquitoes are everywhere.

☰ TRANSPORTATION. The **bus station** is on the *zócalo*, but has limited departure schedules; check early for departure times. Estrella Blanca (☎285 00 43) goes to: **Guadalajara** (6hr., 7am, 161 pesos); **Puerto Vallarta** (3hr., 7 and 10am, 94 pesos); and **Tepic** (1¾hr., every hr. 6am-7pm, 36 pesos). Transporte Noreste y Nayarit sends its rickety fleet to **Villa Hidalgo** (every hr. 9am-4pm, 12 pesos); **Santiago** (9am, 11am, 1pm; 24 pesos); **El Llano** (every hr. 8am-5pm, 8 pesos); and other local destinations.

◪☷ ORIENTATION AND PRACTICAL INFORMATION. San Blas is 69km northeast of Tepic by Rte. 15 and 54. **Juárez,** the town's main drag, runs parallel to the bus station on the south side of the *zócalo*. **Batallón** runs perpendicular to Juárez from the *zócalo*'s center and leads to the closest beach, **Playa Borrego.**

The **tourist office,** on Mercado, one street west of Juárez, provides maps and information about trips to La Tovara and hikes to some of Nayarit's waterfalls. (☎285 03 81. Open daily 9am-1pm and 6-8pm.) **Banamex,** on Juárez east of the *zócalo*, changes money and has a 24hr. **ATM.** (☎285 00 30. Open M-F 8am-2pm.) **Police:** on Sinaloa opposite the bus station, through the last door in the Palacio Municipal as you walk away from the *zócalo*. (☎285 00 28. Open 24hr.) **Farmacia Económica,** at Batallón 49. (☎/fax 285 01 11. Open daily 8:30am-2pm and 4:30-9pm.) **Centro de Salud,** on Batallón and Campeche, five blocks south of the *zócalo*. No English spoken. (☎285 02 32. Open 24hr.) Also, **Clínica IMSS,** at Batallón and Guerrero. (☎285 02 27. Open daily 7am-6pm; at other times, enter on Canalizo.) **Phones:** Make long-distance calls from the **caseta** at Juárez 4; there is also a **fax** service. (Open daily 8am-10pm.) **Post office:** at Sonora and Echeverría, one block north and one block east of the northeast corner of the *zócalo*. (☎285 02 95. Open M-F 8am-2pm, Sa 8am-noon.) **Postal code:** 63740.

▛▟ ACCOMMODATIONS AND FOOD. Finding a place to sleep in San Blas isn't difficult during the low season, but autumn storms bring mile-long waves and plenty of bed-seeking surfers. During September, October, *Semana Santa,* and Christmas, make reservations and expect higher prices. The blood-sucking mosquitoes near the water make camping difficult; rooms inland are the best choice. **El Bucanero,** Juárez 75, is reminiscent of a creaky pirate ship. Large, dim rooms have high ceilings and clean baths. There is a swimming pool, and a huge, fading crocodile scares guests in the lobby. Fans make things comfy, but the adjoining disco is a little noisy on the weekends. (☎285 01 01. Singles 150 pesos; doubles 200 pesos; triples 300 pesos.) To reach **Bungalows Portolá,** Paredes 118, at Yucatán, turn right out of the bus station, go past the *zócalo*, then turn right again on Paredes. The hotel is three blocks down on the right. Clean, furnished bungalows house up to four people and come with fans, baths, and kitchens. Owner offers laundry service, rents bicycles, and trades English books. (☎285 03 86. Singles 100 pesos, high season 170 pesos; bungalows 200 pesos.)

La Isla, on Mercado and Paredes, nearly lives up to its name—every surface, crack, and crevice of "the island" is covered with shells. (Shrimp 65 pesos, fried fish 40-50 pesos.) (☎285 04 07. Open Tu-Su 2-9pm.) **La Familia,** Batallón 18, is a family joint, right down to the conversation-starting, wall-mounted shark's teeth, old drums, sea bottles, and provocative cow statue. Try some of the excellent fried fish (42 pesos) and salads (25 pesos and up) while wondering how La Familia got its framed Mike Tyson boxing glove. (☎285 02 58. Open daily 8am-10pm.)

◪ BEACHES. San Blas, known for its perfectly symmetric waves and safe, sandy bottom, has churned out many a surfing champ. To rent surfing equipment or take lessons, **La Tumba de Yako,** Batallón 219 (☎285 04 62), about six blocks from the *zócalo*, is run by Juan García, a.k.a. "Juan Bananas." As president of San Blas's surfing club and technical director of Mexico's surf team, he has more than enough experience to help. San Blas' main attraction is the smooth water, packed sand, and long waves of **Playa Las Islitas.** During the stormy months of September and October, surfers flock to San Blas in hopes of catching the famous, yearly mile-long wave that carries them from Las Islitas all the way to **Playa Matanchén.** To reach Las Islitas, you can take a bus from the station (every hr. 6am-5pm, returning 7:30am-4pm; 6 pesos) or from the corner of Sinaloa and Paredes in front of the green-trimmed building (15min., 4 per day 8:30am-2:30pm, 6 pesos). The latter bus continues to other beaches, passing Las Islitas on its way back to town about an hour later. A taxi to Las Islitas costs 60 pesos. The first few stretches of sand that greet you are lovely, but more seclusion and prettier coves await farther along. At the southern end of Batallón, **Playa Borrego,** a grey sand beach easily accessible and offers a relaxing, though somewhat bland, view of the coast. Borrego's mosquitoes feast on those who dare to venture there around sunrise or sunset. Quiet and pretty **Playa del Rey,** off the coast of Borrego, has somewhat stronger currents. A *lancha* will take you there from the pier at the west end of Juárez (approx. 7am-4pm; round-trip about 5 pesos).

🔆 **SIGHTS.** Locals hype the springs of **La Tovara**—not the beaches—as San Blas's main attraction. The winding jungle boat ride to La Tovara springs can be expensive, but seeing a live crocodile just might make it worthwhile. Guides navigate the shallow, swampy waters, pointing out rare birds and the stilted huts left over from the set of the film *Cabeza de Vaca*. Trips can be arranged through the tourist office or directly with a boat owner; they're found at the small wharf area on Juárez's eastern end (1½-2½hr.; daily 7am-4pm; 200-300 pesos, depending on the tour). It's best to journey to La Tovara early in the morning, when the water is still calm and the birds undisturbed by the *lanchas*.

The short hike to the top of **La Contaduría,** the hill near town, affords a beautiful view of the city and coast. The splintering stone fortress that protected the city stands impressively above while an 18th-century church is farther downhill. To get there, head east on Juárez as if leaving town. Just before the bridge and the sign that reads "Cape Victoria 7," turn right onto the dirt road behind the houses and restaurants. Veer right off that road onto a stone path that winds uphill.

🎭 **ENTERTAINMENT.** Except for bands of youths crowded in the *zócalo* on weekends, the nights in San Blas are about as tranquil as the days. **Mike's CantaBar,** rarely gets wild or crazy. Dance music rolls, and Mike performs vintage rock in what looks like an antique airport lounge. (☎285 04 32. Beer 5 pesos, mixed drinks 36 pesos. Live music Th-Su starting around 10pm. No cover. Open daily 8pm-midnight.) If you are in the mood for something more upbeat and raucous, join the teen and pre-teen population of San Blas at **Disco Voga,** Juárez 75, next to Hotel El Bucanero. Writhe along with the standard *discoteca* fare. (☎285 01 01. Beer 12 pesos. Cover up to 30 pesos. Open F-Su 9pm-2am.)

NEAR SAN BLAS: EL CUSTODIO DE LAS TORTUGAS

Transportes Norte de Sonora gets you there from Puerto Vallarta (2hr., noon and 2:30pm, 55 pesos) or San Blas (1½hr., 6 per day 6am-2pm, 18 pesos). Ask the bus driver to let you off at Platanitos, then walk down the road and up the hill on your right. ☎292 29 54.

El Custodio de las Tortugas (The Guardian of the Turtles) is an eco-resort in the tiny village of **Platanitos,** between San Blas and Puerto Vallarta. The villa, run by owners Min and Mona, is perched on a precipice and overlooks 20km of virgin beach and the longest stretch of turtle camp in Nayarit. Between July and August, the Mexican government and several ecological organizations collect turtle eggs, protecting them from thieves and predators. Two elegant three-bedroom villas and one two-bedroom villa have TVs, A/C, and huge breezy terraces for whale watching and sunset-worshipping. The gorgeous pool perched on the overlook offers a respite from the salty water. Rooms at the resort are far too expensive for budget travelers, but those who volunteer in the turtle camp receive cheap lodging. Don't miss going into town to try the local specialty, *pescado sarandeado* (mesquite grilled fish; which usually goes for 80 pesos per kg).

TEPIC
☎ 3

The steam-belching sugar refinery visible as you exit Tepic bus station provides an appropriate introduction to this hard working city. Once called *Tepique* (the Place Between the Hills) by its pre-Hispanic inhabitants, Tepic became a center for trade and commerce under the Spanish in the 16th and 17th centuries. Now housing the Nayarit state government, this city of around half a million people is still an important crossroads. However, there is not yet much of interest to tourists here. Some shady parks and a few museums will satisfy those who come through Tepic to connect to another city, a use which brings most tourists here in the first place.

⬛ TRANSPORTATION. Buses leave Tepic from the newer long-distance station, east of the *centro* following the Insurgentes route. To get to the *centro*, cross the street and catch one of the yellow buses (6am-10pm, 3 pesos). Taxis charge around 15 pesos for the trip. To get back to the new station, take a "Central" or "Mololoa Llanitos" bus from the corner of México Sur and Hidalgo. Estrella Blanca (☎213 13 28) goes to: **Aguascalientes** (6hr., 4:30 and 7:45pm, 287 pesos); **Monterrey** (15hr., 4:30pm, 495 pesos); and **Zacatecas** (10hr., 4:30 and 7:45pm, 298 pesos). Norte de Sonora (☎213 23 15) goes to: **Culiacán** (6hr., every hr., 220 pesos); **Guadalajara** (3hr., 10 per day 5:30am-5pm, 147 pesos); **Mazatlán** (5hr., 9:30am, 126 pesos); **San Blas** (1½hr., every hr. 5am-7pm, 36 pesos); **Santiago** (1½hr., every 45min. 5:30am-8pm, 41 pesos); and **Tuxpan** (1½hr., every hr. 6:15am-8:15pm, 32 pesos). Transportes del Pacífico (☎213 23 20) goes to: **Mexico City** (10hr., every hr. 3pm-7am, 408 pesos) and **Tijuana** (29hr., every hr., 982 pesos); and second-class service to **Puerto Vallarta** (3½hr., 19 per day 1:30am-10pm, 110 pesos). A **smaller station,** three blocks north of the plaza on Victoria, serves local destinations.

⬛⬛ ORIENTATION AND PRACTICAL INFORMATION. Tepic, 170km north of Puerto Vallarta, 230km northwest of Guadalajara, and 280km south of Mazatlán, has a strategic location. The main drag, **Av. Mexico,** runs north-south six blocks west of the bus station. Addresses on this street change from Nte. to Sur about four blocks north of **Insurgentes,** which is the largest east-west street. The yellow minivan *combis* (6am-midnight, 3 pesos) run back and forth daily along México and Insurgentes. At its northern terminus, the many-fountained **Plaza Principal** (officially called the Centro Histórico) is dominated by the cathedral on one end and the **Palacio Municipal** on the other. Six blocks to the south, **Plaza Constituyente** is usually shockingly desolate. Most tourist services lie on or near Av. México.
  Dirección de Turismo Municipal, Puebla at the corner of Nervo, one block from the cathedral, hands out maps and brochures. (☎216 56 61 or 212 80 36. Open daily 8am-8pm.) **Casas de cambio** (most open M-Sa 9am-2pm and 4-7pm) clutter Mexico Nte. **Bancomer,** Mexico Nte. 123 (open M-F 8:30am-5:30pm, Sa 10am-2pm), and **Bancapromex,** Mexico Nte. 103 (open M-F 8:30am-5:30pm), both a few blocks south of the plaza, have **ATMs. Luggage storage:** in the new bus station (1.5 pesos per hr.). **Police station:** Tecnológica Ote. 3200 (☎211 58 51), accessible by cab only (10 pesos). **Farmacia CMQ:** Insurgentes at Mexico. (Open 24hr.) **Hospital General:** on Paseo de la Loma next to La Loma Park. From the bus station, take a left as you leave the building and another left on Av. México. After three blocks, take the right-hand fork at the rotary; the hospital is two blocks down on the left. Taxis from the *centro* cost 15 pesos. (☎213 79 37. Open 24hr.) **Fax: Telecomm,** Mexico Nte. 50, about one block from the cathedral. (☎212 96 55. Open M-F 8am-7pm, Sa-Su 8am-4pm.) **Internet Access:** at **Cafetería La Parroquia,** Nervo 18. 20 pesos per hr. **Post office:** at Durango Nte. 33, between Allende and Morelos. (☎212 01 30. Open M-F 8am-7pm, Sa 8am-noon.) **Postal code:** 63000.

▉⬛ ACCOMMODATIONS AND FOOD. Besides the large four-star behemoths that seem to cover entire city blocks, Tepic has smaller, affordable hotels that hide in their shadows. Hotels in the *centro* are closer to Tepic's few sights, but those near the bus station are more convenient for those just stopping through. **Hotel Las**

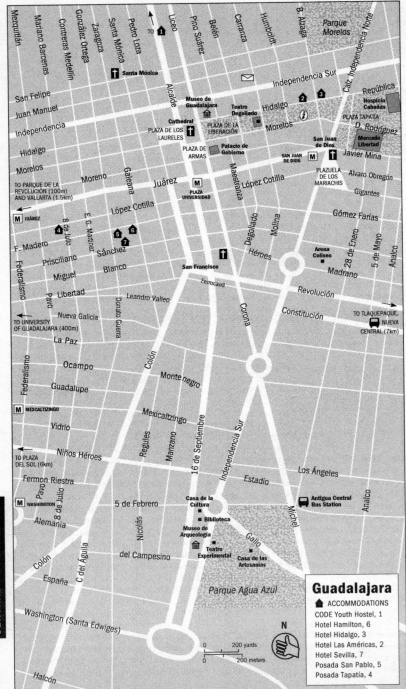

Guadalajara

⌂ ACCOMMODATIONS

CODE Youth Hostel, 1
Hotel Hamilton, 6
Hotel Hidalgo, 3
Hotel Las Américas, 2
Hotel Sevilla, 7
Posada San Pablo, 5
Posada Tapatía, 4

Americas, Puebla 317, at Zaragoza, has clean rooms with TVs, fans, tiled baths, wooden furniture, and sunny patchwork quilts. (☎216 32 85. Singles 80 pesos; doubles 100 pesos.) **Hotel Librian,** Nervo Pte. 163, is a slight upgrade with "sanitized" baths, fan, TV, and bottled water. (Singles 145 pesos; doubles 170 pesos; triples 200 pesos; 20 pesos per additional person.) For a touch of class, try **Hotel Ibarra,** Durango Nte. 297, complete with room service (7am-10pm), laundry and dry cleaning, cable TVs, fans, and phones. Clean tile rooms have sterilized bathrooms. (☎212 36 34. Singles 155 pesos; doubles 170 pesos.)

Mangos and *guanábanas* (soursops) make their way to the stalls at the **mercado,** on Mérida and Zaragoza, four blocks south and three blocks east of the Museo Regional. For something better than market-stand fare, head to **Restaurant Vegetariano Quetzalcóatl,** León Nte. 224, at Lerdo, four blocks west of Plaza Principal. Good vegetarian food in a leafy courtyard, decorated with indigenous artwork and vibrant tablecloths. Sample the *comida corrida* (30 pesos), or stuff yourself with the breakfast buffet (served Tu-Sa, 40 pesos; ☎212 99 66. Open M-Sa 8:30am-6pm). **Cafetería La Parroquia,** upstairs at Nervo 18, offers excellent sandwiches (ham, chicken, or cheese 8 pesos), *tostadas* (8 pesos), and a variety of coffee drinks. Cappuccino 12 pesos, *café americano* 7 pesos. (Open M-Sa 8am-9:30pm.)

🔲 **SIGHTS.** In front of the Plaza Principal is the **Catedral de la Purísima Concepción de María,** a church marked by twin 40m towers. The motley **Museo Regional de Antropología e Historia,** Mexico Nte. 91, south of the plaza at Zapata, houses a small collection of Toltec and Aztec bones, pottery, and artifacts, as well as a stuffed 6m-long crocodile and a collection of religious works from the 16th to 19th centuries. (☎212 19 00. Open M-F 9am-6pm, Sa 9am-3pm. Free.) The **Museo Casa de los Cuatro Pueblos,** Hidalgo Ote. 60, displays the colorful artwork, embroidery, and beadwork of Nayarit's four major indigenous groups: the Coras, Huichols, Náhuatls, and Tepehuanos. (☎212 17 05. Open M-F 9am-2pm and 4-7pm, Sa 9am-2pm. Free.) Also south of the plaza, at Mexico and Abasolo, is the **state capitol,** a gracefully domed structure dating from the 1870s. At Mexico's southern end, turn west (uphill) on Insurgentes to get to **La Loma,** a huge park. If in service, a miniature train will take you through the park's many playgrounds (3 pesos).

JALISCO

GUADALAJARA
☎3

More Mexican than Mexico itself, the city of Guadalajara (pop. 8 million) is the crossroads of the Republic. The capital of the state of Jalisco and the second-largest city in the country, Guadalajara is where north meets south, colonial meets modern, and traditional meets cutting-edge. The city has spawned many of Mexico's most marketable icons: bittersweet *mariachi* music, the *jarabe tapatío* (Mexican hat dance), and tequila. Founded in 1532 by Nuño de Guzmán, the most brutal of the *conquistadores*, the city was born in bloodbath; most of the region's *indígenas* were killed, and very few pre-Hispanic traditions survived. In the years following, the city served as the capital of Mexico and a key battle ground in the Revolution. Today, Guadalajara has parks galore, a bounty of fine museums, four large plazas, and stately colonial architecture. Its markets overflow with Jalisco crafts, and local painters, thespians, dancers (including the renowned *Ballet Folklórico*), and street performers continue the city's fine artistic traditions. Meanwhile, the Universidad de Guadalajara, the second oldest in Mexico, keeps Guadalajara young and shades it with a measure of intellectual sophistication. Though not built specifically for tourists, Guadalajara nevertheless fulfills their hopes entirely. One can understand why—the city's *tapatío* (as the city's residents call themselves) heritage epitomizes all that was, is, and will be Mexican.

◨ TRANSPORTATION

GETTING AROUND

Local Buses: Though usually crowded, always noisy, and sometimes uncomfortable, **minibuses** and **regular buses** (3 pesos) and big blue **TUR** buses (5-7 pesos, depending on destination) are an excellent way to get around. Be sure to check what letter (A, B, C, or D) your bus is—in general, A and B have almost the same route along the main thoroughfares (with the same numbers), and the C and D buses have very different routes into the residential neighborhoods. Buses **#60** and **#62** run the length of Calzada Independencia, from the train station past the zoo and Plaza de Toros. The wired **"Par Vial"** bus runs west on Calzada Independencia, then Hidalgo, before turning onto Vallarta, just short of Mateos. Coming back eastward, it cruises Hidalgo 3 blocks north of Juárez. Bus **#258** from San Felipe, 3 blocks north of Hidalgo, runs from near the Plaza Tapatía down Mateos to the Plaza del Sol, nightclub central. Bus **#52** and **#54** are direct links to downtown along 16 de Septiembre from locations north and south of the city. Bus **#24A** runs the length of Mateos, from Zapopan to beyond the Plaza del Sol, in both directions. TUR bus **#707A** circles from the *centro* on Juárez west to Mateos, down to Otero at the Plaza del Sol, up to Niños Héroes, and north on 16 de Septiembre and Corona to the start of the route. The big red **Cardenal** bus runs west on Madero to Chapultepec along the Zona Rosa, the upscale shopping district west of the *centro*. The **aqua** TUR bus and bus **#45** return east on Cotilla. Bus **#51** runs up and down La Paz. Buses run 6:30am-10pm; TUR buses run slightly later.

Subway: (☎853 75 70). The 2 subway lines run smoothly (every 5-10min. 6am-10pm, 3 pesos) and are a great alternative to the bus system if you're tired of breathing exhaust. A very good map is posted in the stations. **Line 1** runs from the northern boundary of the city, Periférico Nte., more or less along Federalismo to Periférico Sur. There is a stop at Federalismo and Juárez. **Line 2** runs from Juárez and Alcalde/16 de Septiembre, conveniently passing Mina, to Patria in the east. The limited coverage of the 2 lines makes the subway more practical than the bus for only a handful of destinations.

GETTING AWAY

Airport: Aeropuerto Internacional Miguel Hidalgo (☎688 51 20 or 688 51 27), 17km south of town on the road to Chapala. *Combis* (☎688 59 25 or 812 43 08) run 24hr. and will pick you up from your hotel (40min., 80 pesos). A yellow-and-white "Aeropuerto" bus passes through the *centro* on Independencia at Los Arcos (every hr. 5:45am-8:45pm, 10 pesos) and makes the trip back from outside "Sala Nacional." Get off at 16 de Septiembre and Constituyentes. Some cabs are metered, and some are not; when making a trip to the airport, negotiate for a price around 80 pesos. This can be done even if the cab has a meter (on the meter, a trip to the airport runs 120 pesos). Served by **AeroCalifornia** (☎616 25 25), **Aeroméxico** (☎669 02 02), **American** (☎616 40 90), **Continental** (☎647 42 51), **Delta** (☎630 35 30 or 01 800 902 21 00), **Mexicana** (☎678 76 76), **Taesa** (☎679 09 00), and **United** (☎616 94 89 or ☎/fax 616 79 93).

Buses: The station, **Nueva Central Camionera**, is in nearby Tlaquepaque. Fixed-fare buses and taxis (30-60 pesos, depending on time of day) head downtown frequently, as do "Centro" buses (3 pesos). From downtown, catch a #275, 275A, or "Nueva Central" bus on Revolución or 16 de Septiembre, across from the cathedral. In a taxi, be sure to specify the *new* bus station. Unless you're partial to a particular bus line, you can pretty much get where you're going from any of the 7 terminals. Only partial listings provided; call for more info. **Terminal 1:** Primera Plus and Flecha Amarilla (☎600 02 70); **Terminal 3:** Transportes del Pacífico (☎600 08 54), which provides first and second class service for peso-pinchers; **Terminal 4:** Transportes de Sonora (☎679 04 63); **Terminal 5:** Línea Azul (☎679 04 43); **Terminal 6:** Ómnibus de México (☎600 02 91 or 600 04 69) provides some of the most comprehensive service to: **Aguascalientes** (every hr. 6:30am-midnight, 135 pesos); **Ciudad Guzmán** (9 per day, 70 pesos); **Ciudad Juárez** (24hr., 10 per day, 828 pesos) via **Chihuahua** (633 pesos); **Durango** (7 per day, 351 pesos); **La Piedad** (5 per day,

88 pesos); **Matamoros** (7 per day, 542 pesos); **Mexico City** (every 2hr. 7am-midnight, 305 pesos); **Monterrey** (7 per day, 418 pesos); **Querétaro** (3 per day, 192 pesos); **Reymosa** (7 per day, 519 pesos); **Tampico** (3 per day, 381 pesos); **Tepic** (every 30min., 151 pesos); **Torreón** (8 per day, 400 pesos); **Tuxpan** (6 per day, 86 pesos); and **Zacatecas** (every hr. 5:30am-12:15am, 192 pesos). **Terminal 7:** Estrella Blanca (☎679 04 04) is the parent company of numerous smaller lines, including Rojo de los Altos and Transportes del Norte. This is the biggest terminal and it serves almost every major city in the Republic for competitive prices.

✴🔃 ORIENTATION AND PRACTICAL INFORMATION

The heart of the city is the *centro histórico* around **Plaza Tapatía** and **Plaza de la Liberación**. Guadalajara is divided into quadrants along the major streets **Calzada Independencia Norte/Calzada Independencia Sur** and **Hidalgo/República** (known as República to the east of Calzada Independencia, Hidalgo to the west). Streets change names at the borders of these quadrants. Note that in addition to Calzada Independencia, Guadalajara has a Calle Independencia, crossing the city east-west just north of the *centro*. The poorer *colonias* (suburbs) of Guadalajara can be dangerous any time of day; check with the tourist office before blazing new trails. Throughout Guadalajara, it is wise to keep to lit streets and take taxis after 10pm. Solo women travelers may wish to avoid Calzada Independencia after hours; the street attracts raucous, drunken men and supports a thriving prostitution trade all hours of the day and night. Neighborhoods tend to be significantly worse east of Calzada Independencia than west of it.

TOURIST AND FINANCIAL SERVICES

Tourist Office: State Office, Morelos 102 (☎613 03 06, or toll-free in Mexico ☎01 800 363 22 00; http://vista.jalisco.gob.mx or www.jaliscotour.com), in Plaza Tapatía. Friendly staff with helpful maps. Pick up *Guadalajara Weekly* (a free tourist paper) or *Mexico Living and Travel Update.* Open M-F 9am-7:30pm, Sa-Su 9am-1pm. Another office in the Palacio de Gobierno. Open daily 9:30am-3pm and 4-7:30pm.

Consulates: Australia, Cotilla 2030 (☎615 74 18; fax 818 33 90), between Vega and Bara. Open M-F 8am-1:30pm and 3-6pm. **Canada,** Local 30 (☎615 62 70 or emergency 01 800 706 29 00; fax 615 86 65), at Hotel Fiesta Americana, on the Minerva traffic circle. Catch a "Par Vial" bus. Open M-F 8:30am-5pm. **UK,** Parra 2339 (☎616 06 29; fax 615 01 97). Open M-F 9am-3pm and 5-8pm. **US,** Progreso 175 (☎825 27 00 or 825 29 98; fax 826 65 49). Open M-F 8am-4:30pm. The **Oficina de la Asociación Consular,** at the UK consulate, can provide listings for other consulates.

Currency Exchange: The block of Cotilla between Degollado and Molina is a *mercado* with only one product: money. Rates don't vary much. **Bancapromex** is on Corona at Juárez. Open M-F 8:30am-5:30pm, Sa 10am-2pm.

LOCAL SERVICES

English Bookstores: Sandi Bookstore, Tepeyac 718 (☎121 08 63), near the corner of Rosas in Colonia Chapalita. Take bus #50 from Garibaldi or the green "Plus" bus from Juárez. New books and newspapers. Open M-F 9:30am-2:30pm and 3:30-7pm, Sa 9:30am-2pm. The **Hyatt,** at Mateos and México, has day-old *New York Times.*

Cultural Information: Dirección de Educación y Cultura, 5 de Febrero and Analco (☎669 13 80 ext. 1487). **Instituto Cultural Cabañas,** Cabañas 8 (☎617 43 22), in Plaza Tapatía. Open M-F 9am-3pm and 6-9pm. Blue and yellow *Ayuntamiento* stands in the major plazas also field cultural and tourist queries. Open daily 8am-8pm.

Market: Mercado Libertad, Calle Independencia, next to the plaza. This enormous market has an entire wing dedicated to family-run restaurants. Open daily 8am-8pm.

Supermarket: Gigante, Juárez 573 (☎613 86 38) between Martínez and 8 de Julio. Has just about everything. Open M-Sa 8am-9:45pm, Su 8am-9pm.

Laundry: Lavandería Canadá, Patria 1123 (☎628 74 34), at Tepeyac. Open M-Sa 8am-8pm.

Car Rental: Dollar, Euro Rent-A-Car (☎673 84 07, 673 54 08), **Auto-Rent** (☎825 15 15), and **Vega's Rent-A-Car** (☎613 19 20 or 658 03 16) are all budget options.

EMERGENCY AND COMMUNICATIONS

Emergency: ☎060.

Police: Calzada Independencia Nte. 840 (☎617 60 60, ext. 126 and 143), just before the Olympic fountain.

Red Cross: (☎613 15 50 or 614 27 07), at Manuel and San Felipe, on the 1st fl., behind Parque Morelos. Some English spoken. Open 24hr.

Pharmacy: Farmacia Guadalajara, Mina 221 (☎617 85 55), at Cabañas. Open 24hr.

Hospitals: México Americano (☎641 31 41 or 641 44 58), at Colones and América. English spoken. **Green Cross Hospital** (☎614 52 52 or 643 71 90), at Barcenas and Veracruz. English spoken.

Fax: Palacio Federal (☎614 26 64; fax 613 99 15), at Alcalde and Álvarez. Open M-F 8am-6pm, Sa 9am-noon.

Internet Access: Café Internet, Madero 413, a few blocks from the *centro.* You can also grab a bite to eat. 20 pesos per hr. Open M-Sa 9am-7pm. Internet access providers cluster near the intersection of Juárez and Calzada Independencia.

Post Office: (☎614 74 25), on Carranza between Manuel and Calle Independencia. Open M-F 8am-6:30pm, Sa 9am-1pm. **Postal Code:** 44100.

▟ ACCOMMODATIONS

Guadalajara is full of cheap places to stay, with budget hotels most common in the *centro histórico*, and east of downtown along Mina. *Posadas* are an intriguing option—the small, family-run establishments, often in beautiful homes, usually have large, well-furnished rooms and good security. Some have curfews, and in general are less private than a typical hotel. Regardless of where you stay, call ahead; many places fill up early in the day.

THE CENTRO

The widest variety, best location, and safest spots are in the *centro histórico.*

Hotel Las Américas, Hidalgo 76 (☎613 96 22, 614 16 41, or 614 16 04), at Humboldt. Comfortably carpeted with TVs, phones, and fans. Good location and prices. Singles 130 pesos; doubles 145 pesos; triples 190 pesos.

Posada Tapatía, Cotilla 619 (☎614 91 46). A beautiful mansion with peachy walls, fuchsia sofas and spreads, and a courtyard with a collection of books. Clean rooms have fans and private baths. Singles 150 pesos; doubles 190 pesos; triples 240 pesos.

Hotel Sevilla, Sánchez 413 (☎614 91 72 or 614 93 54), between Ocampo and Guerra. Old but clean. Rooms have TVs, phones, fans, and baths, and are graced by landscape photos. Singles 140 pesos; doubles 290 pesos.

Hotel Hamilton, Madero 381 (☎614 67 26). The tiled rooms have baths and TVs. Discounts for extended stays. Singles 70 pesos; doubles 90 pesos; TV 20 pesos extra.

CODE Youth Hostel, Prolongación Alcalde 1360 (☎624 65 15). Take bus #52 or #54. The CODE is just past the traffic circle, across from the Foro de Arte y Cultura in a blue, fence-encircled sports complex. Clean, single-sex rooms hold 20 bunks each. Bedding, pillows, and lockers provided; bring your own lock. Reception M-F 8am-2pm and 4-9pm, Sa-Su 9am-3pm and 5-9pm. Curfew 10pm. Closed during *Semana Santa* and Christmas. 50 pesos per person.

Hotel Hidalgo, Hidalgo 14 (☎613 50 67), has the cheapest rooms in town if you can survive without fans, A/C, TVs, or private baths. Extremely busy, but no reservations are accepted. Singles 35 pesos; doubles with bath 70 pesos.

EAST ON MINA

Hotels in this area are close to the Mercado Libertad, the Hospico Cabañas, and the Plaza de los Mariachis. Some of the surrounding areas require extra caution at night. If everything else is full or if you just want to be closer to Plaza de los Mariachis, these hotels are basic, modern, and clean.

Hotel México 70, Mina 230 (☎617 99 78), at Cabañas. White tile floors, red bedspreads, aqua tile bathrooms, and very dark hallways. Singles 100 pesos; doubles 110 pesos; triples 130 pesos; TV 20 pesos extra.

Hotel Imperio, Mina 180 (☎617 50 42). Large rooms have TVs and baths. Dark red and gold overtones scream love-naysium. Singles 100 pesos; doubles 110 pesos.

Hotel San Jorge, Mina 284 (☎617 79 97), has the same owner as México 70, and, consequently, very dark hallways. Simple rooms have baths and desks for writing letters home, though there is little to write home about. Singles 90 pesos; doubles 120 pesos.

Hotel Ana Ísabel, Mina 164 (☎617 79 20 or 617 48 59), at Cabañas. Small, somewhat dark rooms with ceiling fans and TVs overlook a green courtyard. Singles 135 pesos; doubles 170 pesos.

ZONA ROSA

Hotels in the Zona Rosa, the ritziest area of Guadalajara, are predictably pricey. If you have pesos to burn, classy lodgings are everywhere. One fairly economical option is **Hotel La Paz,** La Paz 1091, between Guerra and 8 de Julio, reachable via bus #51 or #321. Smart blue rooms have lovely faux marble countertops and phones. (☎613 30 07. Singles 120 pesos; doubles 160 pesos; triples 185 pesos.)

◪ FOOD

Guadalajara has plenty of budget eateries as well as many expensive, upscale restaurants serving international cuisine. *Birria* is the hearty local specialty of stewed meat (usually pork) in tomato broth, thickened with cornmeal and spiced with garlic, onions, and chiles. The city is also famous for its *taquerías* and varied taco ingredients. After your meal, quench your thirst with an Estrella beer, brewed *clara dorada* (golden clear) right in Guadalajara.

THE CENTRO

Ice cream and fast food are everywhere, and *panaderías* (bakeries) cluster southwest of the Plaza, primarily on the blocks enclosed by Pavo, Sánchez, Galeana, and Juárez. A feast for both tastebuds and eyes is the **Mercado Libertad,** Calle Independencia, next to the plaza. You can find anything here, from *birria* to fried chicken to live animals, all at prices that will leave you with plenty of pesos for shopping (huge meals average 26 pesos).

Restaurante Vegetariano, Hidalgo 112 (☎614 54 47), to the left of the black-painted window. A wide array of vegetarian foods, including salads (10.5 pesos), sandwiches (5.5 pesos), and *quesadillas* (5 pesos). Open M-Sa 9am-7pm, Su 9am-5pm.

El Farol, Moreno 466 (☎613 03 49), at Galeana, 2nd fl. *Comida típica* at rock-bottom prices. The friendly owner makes a mean *chile relleno*. Complementary *buñuelos*, a fried dough dessert doused with syrup. Entrees 20-40 pesos, tacos 5 pesos, beer 12-16 pesos. Open daily 10am-8pm.

Restaurant Acuarius, Sánchez 416 (☎613 62 77), across from Hotel Sevilla. The age of Restaurant Acuarius dawned in 1974, and it has been raising the cosmic consciousness of Guadalajaran vegetarians ever since. The restaurant has a natural foods store. Vegetarian *comida corrida* 40 pesos; juice 9 pesos. Open M-Sa 10am-6pm.

Café Madrid, Juárez 264 (614 96 04), at Corona. An American 1950s diner. Waiters sport white jackets and bowties, and serve continental breakfast (23 pesos), *enchiladas* (28 pesos), and divine cappuccino (13.5 pesos) to patrons seated beneath the enormous Alfredo Santos mural. Open daily 7:30am-10pm.

Restaurant Villa Madrid, Cotilla 553 (☎ 613 42 50). Both veggie and traditional fare in a clean, somewhat institutional environment. The real bargain is the lunch special; choice of sandwich with every vegetable imaginable 17.5 pesos. Burritos 30 pesos, salads 42 pesos. Open M-F 12:30-9pm, Sa 12:30-8pm.

Taco Cabaña, at Moreno and Maestranza near the Palacio de Gobierno by the Plaza Tapatía. Celebrate the cheap beer (two for 17 pesos) and tacos (3 pesos) with the *mariachi*-filled jukebox and panel of TVs tuned to *fútbol*. After the game, down one of the many varieties of tequila (13-22 pesos). Open daily 10am-9pm.

ZONA ROSA

Most of the places listed below are near the intersection of Vallarta and Chapultepec, on the "Par Vial" and bus Rte. #321. It's worth the trip—the extra pesos buy excellent food and even a measure of elegance.

■ **Restaurant Samurai,** Vidrio 1929 (☎ 826 35 54), a quarter-block north and to the right of the Niños Héroes monument on Chapultepec. Authentic Japanese-Mexican cuisine with goldfish pond, rock garden, and hummingbirds. Many vegetarian options. Japanese *comida corrida* with rice, soup, and main course 26 pesos. Samurai *especial* of teriyaki steak, fish, and shrimp 64 pesos. Open M-Sa 12:30-10pm, Su 12:30-7pm.

Naló Café, Sierra 2046 (☎ 615 27 15), just off Chapultepec Nte. Outside seating under a big umbrella. Delicious breakfast and lunch specials 25-35 pesos. Menu changes daily, but friendly servers and relaxing atmosphere don't. *Fettucine alfredo* 35 pesos, salads 17 pesos, carrot cake 15 pesos. Open daily 8am-9pm.

Café Don Luis, Chapultepec 215 (☎ 625 65 99), at La Paz, has a large coffee and drink selection with a few desserts such as cheesecake (16 pesos). The *Beso de Angel* (Angel's Kiss; 23 pesos) is more than just a peck on the cheek; it's a rum, kahlua, and eggnog make-out session. Open daily 8:30am-3pm and 5pm-midnight.

👁 SIGHTS

On cool evenings, Guadalajara fills with families out for a stroll. The sheer number of monuments testifies to the city's rich history and culture. Guadalajara's plazas are clean, crowded, and full of *mariachis*, and statues commemorate all the favorites, from the Niños Héroes to Benito Juárez. Don't limit your exploration to the *centro* alone—the efficient bus and subway systems make getting anywhere easy.

THE CENTRO

PLAZA DE LA LIBERACIÓN. Plaza de la Liberación is one of downtown Guadalajara's four plazas. Always abuzz with activity, the Plaza is the center of historic Guadalajara. Horse-drawn carriages sit near the Museo Regional across from the cathedral, waiting to whisk you around the city (45 min., 120 pesos). The spacious plaza, with its bubbling fountain and large Mexican flag, is surrounded by the cathedral, Museo Regional, Palacio de Gobierno, and Teatro Degollado. Military personnel ceremonially retire the colors at daily 7pm. An enormous sculpture depicts Hidalgo breaking the chains of servitude, in commemoration of his 1810 decree abolishing the slave trade, which was signed in the Palacio de Gobierno.

PALACIO DE GOBIERNO. On the plaza's south side, the palace, built in 1751, the headquarters of the Hildago government from 1810-11. The building later served as base for the Juárez administration in 1858. Today, the Palacio is graced by several José Clemente Orozco murals. Climb to the roof for a great view. (*Open M-F 9am-8pm. Guided tours available in English.*)

CATHEDRAL METROPOLITANA. Facing the Teatro Degollado across Plaza de la Liberación, the church was begun in 1561 and completed 60 years later. After a 1848 earthquake destroyed its original towers, ambitious architects replaced them with much taller ones. Fernando VII of Spain donated the cathedral's 11 richly ornamented altars in appreciation of Guadalajara's aid during the Napoleonic Wars. One of the altars is dedicated to Our Lady of the Roses; it is this altar that gave Guadalajara its nickname, "City of Roses." Inside the sacristy is the *Assumption of the Virgin*, painted by 17th-century painter Bartolomé Murillo. The towers, known as the *cornucopías*, can be climbed with the permission of the cathedral's administrators, holed up in the side of the building facing the Teatro Degollado. Descend underneath the altar (take the steps on the right-hand side) where the remains of three cardinals and two bishops keep good company. The 60m jaunt to the tower tops affords the best view in town. *(Open daily 7:30am-7:30pm. Visit after Su after 3pm so as not to interrupt Mass.)*

MUSEO REGIONAL DE GUADALAJARA. This popular museum, housed in the old San José seminary, chronicles the history of western Mexico beginning with the Big Bang. Collections of colonial and modern art are displayed here as well. Artsy and educational movie screenings, plays, and lectures take place in the museum's auditorium—inquire within or at the tourist office. *(Liceo 60 at Hidalgo, on the north side of the Plaza de la Liberación. ☎ 614 99 57 or 614 52 64. Open Tu-Sa 9am-5:45pm, Su 9am-1pm. 25 pesos; seniors and children under 12 free. Su free.)*

TEATRO DEGOLLADO. Attend the *ballet folklórico* to get a good look at the breathtaking Teatro Degollado, named for former governor Santos Degollado. Built in 1856, the neoclassical structure has gold arches, a sculpted allegory of the seven muses, and Gerardo Suárez's interpretation of Dante's *Paradiso* on the ceiling. In addition to ballet, the theater plays host to the Guadalajara Philharmonic and amateur acts. *(On the Plaza de la Liberación's east end. ☎ 614 47 73. Ballet Folklórico performed by the University of Guadalajara Su 10am. Open Tu-Sa 10am-1pm for non-ticket holders. Tickets available at the theater box office.)*

PLAZUELA DE LOS MARIACHIS. Immediately after sitting down in this crowded plaza, roving *mariachis* will pounce on you, using every trick in their bag to separate you from your pesos. Prices for songs are completely variable, around 20-35 pesos. The *mariachis* continue playing long into the night, but you probably don't want to be around to hear them—the Plazuela becomes a stage for roving unsavories, who may try other ways to get you to part with your pesos. *(On the south side of San Juan de Dios, the church with the funky blue neon cross on Independencia at Mina.)*

HOSPICIO CABAÑAS. Also known as the Casa de Cultura Cabañas, the building was constructed in 1801 to house an orphanage. In two hundred years, it has served as an art school and military barracks as well. The building's chapel was built in the 1840s and is now decorated with murals by José Clemente Orozco. The most striking of these, painted in the late 1930s, is *El Hombre de Fuego* (the Man of Fire), on the dome. Mirrors are free for those who don't want to strain their necks. The Hospicio also hosts photography and sculpture exhibits. *(At Hospicio and Cabañas, 3 blocks east of Independencia. Open Tu-Sa 10am-6pm, Su 10am-3pm. 8 pesos; with student ID 4 pesos, children under 12 free; Su free. 10 pesos for camera rights—no flash.)*

PARQUE AGUA AZUL. If you're sick of the congested city streets, take a stroll in the green, 168,000 square meter park, with tropical bird aviaries, an orchid greenhouse, a butterfly house, and a sports complex. *(South of the centro on Calzada Independencia; take bus #60 or #62 heading south. Open Tu-Su 10am-8:30pm. 6 pesos, children 4 pesos.)*

ZONA ROSA

Cultural activity in the city's wealthier area focuses on the **Plaza del Arte**, on Chapultepec, one block south from Niños Héroes.

GALERÍA DE ARTE MODERNO. National artists bare their souls on a rotating basis in the plaza's gallery, though the artwork displayed can be variable in quality. It's worth it to stop in if you're in the area. *(On Mariano Ote. and España. ☎ 616 32 66. Open Tu-F 10am-7pm, Sa-Su 10am-2pm. Free.)*

TEATRO JAIME TORRES BODET. The theater hosts everything: book expositions, concerts, theatrical productions, stand-up comedy, and performance art. *(In the Plaza del Arte. ☎ 615 12 69. Open M-F 9am-8pm, depending on performance times.)*

NORTH OF THE CENTRO

For the sights below, take Ruta #60 or #62 north on Calzada Independencia.

ZOOLÓGICO GUADALAJARA. To visit more than 2000 furry and feathered friends, head to the Zoológico Guadalajara, which features an especially impressive collection of 360 species of tropical birds. At the far end of the zoo is a spectacular view of the Barranca de Huentitán, a deep ravine. *(Continue north on Calzada Independencia past the Plaza de Toros. It's a 1½ km. walk to the entrance of the zoo from the bus stop on Independencia. ☎ 674 44 88 or 674 43 60. Open W-Su 10am-7pm. 25 pesos, children 15 pesos.)*

CENTRO DE CIENCIA Y TECNOLOGÍA. The center houses a planetarium, exhibits on astronomy and geology, and a sculpted plant garden. *(A 20min. walk from the zoo. Open Tu-Su 9am-7pm. ☎ 674 41 06 or 674 39 78. Museum 4 pesos, planetarium 6 pesos.)*

♫ 🎭 ENTERTAINMENT AND NIGHTLIFE

Guadalajara is known for its cultural sophistication and dizzying variety of entertainment options. To keep abreast of Guadalajara's goings-on—from avant-garde film festivals to bullfights—check the listings in *The Guadalajara Weekly*, *Vuelo Libre* (a monthly calendar of events), and the kiosks and bulletin boards in places like the Hospicio Cabañas. Be prepared to take a taxi after buses stop running (10pm), and, as always, use caution when walking at night or alone.

BARS

If you're not big on the club scene, fear not. The city offers an impressive array of bars—from the traditional *cantina* to commercial US imports. Live entertainment in these hotspots ranges from techno to *mariachi*.

La Maestranza, Maestranza 179 (☎ 613 20 85), at Cortilla, in the *centro*. If you think you've seen bullfighting posters and regalia before, wait until you swing open these old saloon doors. The food (enchiladas 28 pesos) and beer (12 pesos) are good too. Live trio daily 3-5pm. Open daily 10am-3am.

Copenhagen, upstairs at Castellanos 120-2 (☎ 825 28 03), between Juárez and Cortilla. A jazz haven. Live music M-Sa 9pm-12:30am. Open M-Sa 2pm-1am, Su 1-7pm.

Bananas Café, Chapultepec 330 (☎ 615 41 91), at Tejada. Step up to a bar and order a Metallica, Rolling Stones, or Doors. The walls are decked in US and British pop stars. Crazy mixed drinks 15-20 pesos. Open daily noon-midnight.

La Cripta, Tepeyac 4038 (☎ 647 62 07), at Niño Obrero. Cool locals, mostly university types, down beers (16 pesos) and bop to alternative tunes. The small dance floor fills after midnight. Cover 30-60 pesos. Open daily 8pm-3am.

CLUBS

Elegantly dressed partygoers line up to get into the classy joints along **Vallarta,** accessible by taxi from the centro (40 pesos), while more classic discos with complex track lighting and elevated dance floors surround **Plaza del Sol,** accessible by taxi (60 pesos). In general, Guadalajara discos are fancy; most won't let you in without leather shoes. Dress to the nines and shake that booty.

Pixie, Vallarta 2503 (☎ 658 10 80 or 658 70 23), near Los Arcos. The young and happening put on a little pixie dust and float into Never-Neverland at this new disco. The DJ plays heavy techno and electronica sprinkled with pop tunes as writhing dancers hit the high-tech and dance floor. Cover 40-80 pesos. Open W and F-Sa 10pm-3am.

La Marcha, Vallarta 2648 (☎ 615 89 99), at Los Arcos, has fancy art, fountains, and pretension. Pulse to electronic beats in this converted two-story 19th century mansion and dress to impress. Cover men 120 pesos, women 80 pesos. Open W-Sa 10pm-4am.

Lado B, Vallarta 2451 (☎616 20 96), at Queredo at Los Arcos. Creepy murals with images of the sphinx and phoenix hover over the metal and wire furniture. The dance floor is packed until 3am, and some stay later. Cover men 150 pesos, women 80 pesos. Open bar. Open W and F-Sa 9pm-4am.

Danny Rock, Otero 1989 (☎121 13 63), by the Plaza de Sol. A brand new place appealing to an older, 30+ crowd. Plenty of tables to sit and listen to 60s and contemporary music. Cover men 60 pesos, women 50 pesos. Open W-Su 9pm-3am.

GAY AND LESBIAN NIGHTLIFE

There is more gay nightlife here than anywhere in Mexico, outside of Mexico City. Most is along Chapultepec, in the upscale *Zona Rosa*, and at the Plaza de los Mariachis. The popular drag shows are attended by those of all orientations.

Sahara, Otero 3445 (☎621 88 40), 2 blocks from Pasaje in the Plaza del Sol. The latest in lights, glitz, and racy drag shows. Consistently packs a full house. Cover 35 pesos. Drag shows 10:30pm and 1:30am. Open W-Su 9pm-4am.

Caudillós, Sánchez 407 (☎613 54 45), near Hotel Cervantes, about 3 blocks from the *centro*. The small bar and disco draws loyal regulars who enjoy the 2-for-1 brew (18 pesos), spirited dance floor, and occasional live "sensual performances." Cover 20 pesos. Music starts at 8:30pm. Open Th-Su 3pm-3am.

Mascara's, Maestranza 238 (☎614 81 03), at Madero. A popular gay bar with 2-for-1 beers (18 pesos). Don your favorite mask (optional) and step into the fun. Packed on the weekends. Open daily 9am-midnight.

SPORTS

Bullfights take place almost every Sunday October through March in the **Plaza de Toros,** on Nuevo Progreso at the northern end of Independencia (take Ruta #60 or #62 north). Tickets can be purchased at the Plaza de Toros. (☎637 99 82 or 651 85 06. Tickets 40-250 pesos. Open M-Sa 10am-2pm and 4-6pm.)

Even by Mexican standards, *fútbol* is huge in Guadalajara. The **Chivas,** the local professional team, are perennial contenders for the national championship, and you will notice many fans wearing their red, white, and blue jersey around town. Matches are held September through May in **Jalisco Stadium** at Calzada Independencia Norte, in front of the Plaza de Toros (☎637 05 63 or 637 02 99; open daily 8am-4pm) and in **Estadio 3 de Marzo,** at the Universidad Autónoma. Ticket office at Colomos Pte. 2339. (☎641 50 51 or 641 50 73; open M-Sa 8am-5pm).

CULTURAL EVENTS

The **Ballet Folklórico** dazzles the world with precise rhythmic dance, intricate garb, and amusing stage antics. There are two troupes in Guadalajara: one affiliated with the University of Guadalajara and the other with the state of Jalisco. The former, reputedly better, performs in the **Teatro Degollado.** Tickets can be purchased on the day of the performance or one day in advance. (☎614 47 73. Performances every Su 10am. Box office open daily 10am-1pm and 4-7pm. Tickets 50-150 pesos.) The **Ballet Folklórico de Cabañas,** the state troupe, performs in the Hospicio Cabañas. (Every W 8:30pm. Tickets 60 pesos.) If you arrive before 8pm, you can take a tour of some of the murals of the Hospicio. The Hospicio also shows Mexican film premieres. (Shows daily noon, 3:50, 6:50, and 9pm. 20 pesos.) The **Instituto Cultural Cabañas** presents live music on an open-air stage in the Hospicio Cabañas at least once a week. For schedules, drop by the ticket counter or look for their flyers with the Cabañas insignia (a building with a dome and pillars) for schedules.

University facilities, scattered throughout the city, have created a supply of high culture for low budgets. The **Departamento de Bellas Artes,** García 720, coordinates activities at a large number of stages, auditoriums, and movie screens throughout the city. The best source of information on cultural events is the blackboard in the lobby that lists each day's attractions. (Open M-Sa 9am-5pm.)

For both modern and cultural art films, head to the **Cinematógrafo,** Vallarta 1102, just west of the university. A different film is presented each week. (☎825 05 14. Showings at 6, 8, and 10pm. 35 pesos.) Guadalajara has dozens of other cinemas (about 30 pesos); check the newspapers for listings.

Although they close earlier than bars, cafes are still happening nighttime spots. **Café La Paloma,** López Cortilla 1855, at Cervantes, is a *rendez-vous* point for the hip university crowd. Local artwork spanks the imagination, while the body enjoys dishes and desserts. *Café de olla* 16 pesos, chocolate cheesecake 22 pesos. (☎630 00 91. Open M-Sa 8:30am-11pm, Su 9am-10pm.)

 SHOPPING

The cavernous **Mercado Libertad,** at Mina and Independencia, is touted as the largest covered market in the Americas. Though its size may be exaggerated, there are still oodles of sandals, *sarapes*, jewelry, guitars, dried iguanas, and other witchcraft supplies filling tier after tier of booths. Don't be afraid to bargain. (Open daily 6am-8pm.) The Sunday market **El Baratillo,** on Mina approximately 15 blocks east of Mercado Libertad, is even more tempting. From Mercado Libertad, walk two blocks north to Hidalgo and catch bus #40 heading east or a "Par Vial" bus on Morelos. If you thought the Mercado Libertad was huge, you should see this big daddy, which sometimes sprawls over 30 or 40 blocks. Vendors sell everything imaginable, from *tamales* to houses. (Open all day Su.)

For shopping in a more controlled environment, try the **Casa de las Artesanías de Jalisco,** on Gallo, the street bisecting Parque Agua Azul. High quality pottery, jewelry, clocks, hammocks, china, blankets, chessboards, shirts, and purses have been carted over from Tlaquepaque and Tonalá. Convenient, but prices here can be up to 50% higher than in surrounding villages. (☎619 46 64. Open M-F 10am-6pm, Sa 10am-5pm, Su 10am-3pm.)

❊ FESTIVALS

Finding a bench in the Plaza de Armas, across from the Palacio de Gobierno, can be a tricky task—several nights a week, the **Jalisco State Band** draws crowds of locals. (Performances Tu, Th, Su 6:30pm, but seat-seekers should arrive before 6pm. Free). The **Plaza de los Fundadores,** behind the Teatro Degollado, serves as a stage every afternoon and evening for clown-mimes. Watch and give tips, but, unless you like being the butt of jokes, keep out of the mime's eye. Every October, Guadalajara explodes with the traditional **Fiestas de Octubre,** a surreal, month-long bacchanal of parades, dancing, bullfights, fireworks, food, and fun. Each day of the month is dedicated to a different one of Mexico's 29 states and two territories.

 DAYTRIPS FROM GUADALAJARA

TLAQUEPAQUE

Take the local #275 or 275A bus or the "Tlaquepaque" TUR bus (10 pesos, 30min.) from 16 de Septiembre on the southbound side. For the main markets, get off at Independencia by the Pollo-Chicken joint on the left; if the driver turns left off Niños Héroes, you've gone too far. To get back to Guadalajara, hop back on a #275 or TUR bus at the corner of Niños Héroes and Constitución, 2 blocks north of Independencia.

The "village" of Tlaquepaque is little more than the strip along Independencia and Juárez, where upscale shops set in old colonial mansions sell silver, leather, ceramics, and other *artisanía*. Though geared toward tourists, Tlaquepaque has the best quality and prices in the Guadalajara area (other than Tonalá). Tlaquepaque was made for shopping, so bring a wad of cash (not all places accept credit cards) and a big bag to bring home loot. The **Museo Regional de las Cerámicas y los Artes Populares de Jalisco,** Independencia 237, at Alfareros, set in a beautiful 19th-century residence, sells an interesting collection of regional crafts. (☎635 54 04. Open Tu-Su 10am-6pm.) Another fun, if touristy, spot is **La Rosa de Cristal,** Independencia 232, at Alfareros, where artisans blow glass by hand and sell their work at inflated prices. (☎639 71 80. Glass-blowing M-F 10:30am-1pm, Sa 10:30am-noon. Open M-Sa 10am-6pm, Su 10am-2pm.) Just off its main square is the *mercado*, where goods are cheaper and of lesser quality than in the shops. There is a small

tourist information booth on Independencia at the Parque Hidalgo (☎635 57 56). Fancy, expensive restaurants dot Independencia, offering menus in English, outside seating, and delicious food. More affordable meals can be had near the *mercado*. Forget about accommodations: come to Tlaquepaque by the day, but spend your nights in far more economical Guadalajara.

ZAPOPAN

Catch the local #275A bus northbound on 16 de Septiembre (40min., 3 pesos). Ask the driver when to get off; Zapopan is fairly non-descript. Last bus back 10pm.

Northwest of Guadalajara, the town of Zapopan is famous for the **Basílica de la Virgen de Zapopan,** at Hidalgo and Morelos, a giant 18th-century edifice erected after a peasant's vision of the Virgin. The walls of the church are hung with many decades' worth of *ex votos*, small paintings on sheet metal that commemorate the Virgin's curing powers. The small image of the Virgin was made from corn stalks by *indígenas* in the 16th century. During the early fall, the figure of Our Lady of Zapopan is frequently moved from church to church throughout Jalisco—each move is occasion for serious partying. One of the most major transfers occurs on the **Día de la Raza** (Oct. 12, the day Columbus landed in America), when the figure makes her way from Guadalajara's cathedral to Zapopan in a large procession. Pope John Paul II visited the *basílica* in 1979, and a statue of the pontiff holding hands with a beaming village boy now stands in the courtyard in front of the church. The **Sala de Arte Huichal,** on one side of the cathedral, displays indigenous art and handicrafts. (Open daily 9am-2pm, 4-7pm.) Both the *basílica* and *sala* are situated around the **Plaza de las Américas,** whose 28 lances represent the nations of the Americas. The market adjacent to the fountain and tree-rich plaza is the best place to grab a cheap taco or roasted chicken.

TONALÁ

Local bus #275 or TUR bus #706, which run southbound along 16 de Septiembre, are the best ways to reach Tonalá (30min., 2 pesos). Get off at the intersection of Av. Tonalá and Tonaltecas. The rows of pottery stores let you know you've arrived. Tonaltecas is a main drag; bear right to reach the plaza.

A shopper's paradise, Tonalá is a less accessible, mercifully less touristed version of Tlaquepaque. It is most fun on market days (Th and Su), when activity centers around the **Plaza Principal** and spills west on Tonaltecas. Merchants, vendors, and restaurant owners sit with their feet up and let tourists inspect their ornate metal or glassware. Women weave multicolored rugs and sew dolls, while patient ceramics merchants paint their pieces with personalized messages for their buyers. Here, the soft sell rules; merchants will take time to talk with you, and you won't feel obliged to buy anything. Tonalá specializes in inexpensive, decorated ceramics, and high quality, low-priced silver and glass dishes.

When you get tired of shopping, walk north of the city up the **Cerro de la Reina** for an astonishing view of Guadalajara from 2500m. The **tourist office,** Zapata 275A (☎683 60 47 or 683 17 40; open M-F 9am-3pm), one block off the plaza, will be able to direct you to other worthwhile sights, such as the **Museo Nacional de la Cerámica,** where you can see how the vase you bought was made.

CHAPALA   ☎3

Forty kilometers from Guadalajara lies the **Lago de Chapala,** Mexico's second-largest lake. Although industrial waste has made swimming here a bad idea, a visit to the nearby town of Chapala still provides a great respite from the city. Home to a peaceful mix of Mexican tourists, *norteamericano* retirees, and artists, Chapala is tucked between the lake's serene northern shore and the surrounding mist-cloaked mountains. The town is named after the Tecuexe Indian chief Capalac, who founded the village in 1510. Its history and physical beauty have inspired artists for centuries; D.H. Lawrence lived here in the 20s and 30s, and it was here that he began writing *The Plumed Serpent*. Chapala is a bit less developed than neighboring, plusher **Ajijic** (see p. 384), but neither escape the tourist feel entirely.

TRANSPORTATION. From the old bus station in Guadalajara, take a Guadalajara-Chapala bus (45min., every 30 min. 6am-9pm, 25 pesos). Guadalajara's new bus station also has service to Chapala (1¼hr., every hr. 7:45am-5:45pm, 16 pesos). From Ajijic, hop on any bus to get here; all roads lead through Chapala (20min., every 20min., 3.50 pesos). In Chapala, the main entrance of the **bus station** lies on Madero and Martínez. Turn left on Madero as you walk out of the station to reach the lake. Guadalajara-Chapala buses back to Guadalajara leave the station on roughly the same schedule as they come in.

■■ ORIENTATION AND PRACTICAL INFORMATION. The lake is Chapala's southern and eastern boundary. **Hidalgo** (known as **Morelos** east of Madero) runs west to Ajijic from two blocks north of the lake. **Banamex**, Madero 222, has an **ATM.** (☎765 22 71 or 765 39 18. Open M-F 9am-4pm.) The **mercado de artesanías** is on the waterfront and extends four blocks east of Madero's end, on Corona.

■■ ACCOMMODATIONS AND FOOD. If you plan on spending the night in Chapala, the **Hotel Nido**, Madero 202, which once played host to dictator Díaz's weekend soirées, has comfortable rooms with cable TV, a pretty courtyard, and a pool. Parking available. (☎765 21 16. Singles 200 pesos; doubles 250 pesos.) The hotel also has a somewhat pricey restaurant. A much cheaper option is the conveniently located **Hotel Cardilejas**, Cotilla 363, with a red and white sign, one block off Madero near the bus station. Rooms are small but cozy, and the rooftop patio has a lake view. (☎765 22 79. Singles 120 pesos; doubles 160 pesos; triples 240 pesos.) For dining, follow Madero or walk along the waterfront to **Restaurant Superior,** Madero 415, which has a full bar. Steaks 35 pesos, hamburgers 16 pesos, breakfasts 14 pesos. (☎765 21 80. Open W-M 8am-10pm, Tu 8am-5pm.) More standard fare, including the fish specialty (30 pesos), is served at **Chabela's Fonda**, Rosa 62, at the far right corner of the plaza. (☎765 43 80. Open daily 8am-6pm.)

■ SIGHTS. For a spectacular view of Chapala, Ajijic, and the surrounding countryside, walk up the stone stairway that winds up the hills from Madero, about four blocks from the lake. Reeds thriving in the lake's now-polluted waters have caused the lake to shrink, but the beautiful walkways bordering the old water line are still perfect for a stroll. You can walk or take a bus (suggested donation 10 pesos) from the edge of town to the waterfront, but there isn't much to see there.

AJIJIC   ☎3

Hugging the shores of Lake Chapala and commanding a beautiful view of the surrounding mountains, the village of Ajijic is unfortunately tourist-central, full of fat *gringos* and the vendors who love them. For this reason, it may be best to enjoy the Ajijic's landscape and the provincial architecture of adobe facades and tile roofs by day, opting to stay the night (and spend your money) in Guadalajara or less-touristed Chapala.

TRANSPORTATION. From the old bus station in Guadalajara, take a Guadalajara-Chapala **bus** (45min., every 30min. 6am-9:40pm, 20 pesos); ask to be dropped off at Ajijic. Buses back to Chapala or Guadalajara can be caught along the route (45min., every hr. 6am-8pm, 20 pesos). From Chapala, take the bus to Ajijic via San Antonio from the bus station on Madero and Martínez (20min., every 15min. 6am-8pm, 3.50 pesos). In Ajijic, buses to Chapala or Guadalajara can be flagged down on the Carretera Chapala.

■■ ORIENTATION AND PRACTICAL INFORMATION. The only paved street in Ajijic is the **Carretera Chapala,** which divides the town into north and south. The town's north-south strip is **Colón.** The **plaza** is towards the lake, and can be accessed via Colón. While Ajijic lacks an official tourist office, longtime resident **Beverly Hunt,** owner of **Laguna Axixic Realty,** Carretera 24 (☎766 11 74; fax 766 11 88), provides maps, brochures, English newsletters, and a friendly cup of coffee. **Bancapromex,** Parroquia 2, has a 24hr. **ATM.** (☎766 05 46 or 766 04 18. Open M-F 9am-5pm, Sa 9am-1pm.) **Farmacia Jessica,** Parroquia 18, is on the plaza. English spoken. (☎766 11 91. Open daily 9am-9pm.) **Post office:** Colón 23, at Constitución (☎766 18 88. Open M-F 8am-3pm, Sa 9am-1pm.)

▐▗▐ ACCOMMODATIONS, FOOD, AND ENTERTAINMENT. The prices of most accommodations in Ajijic are out of reach of the budget-conscious. **Las Casitas,** Carretera Chapala Pte. 10, is one of the best options, with red tile floors, a little kitchen, and a cozy living room with fold-out couch and chimney. (☎766 11 45. Bungalows for 2 people 220 pesos.) At the **Posada Las Calandrías,** Carretera Chapala Pte. 8, there is a flower-filled garden, barbecue space, and a great view of the *laguna* from the terraces. (☎766 10 52. Small bungalow with 2 single beds 350 pesos; large bungalow with 4 single beds also available.) Both establishments have pools. It's difficult to find a good place to eat in Ajijic; tourist traps like **El Serape** on the Carretera Chapala have high prices and US-style food. On weekends, live Latin rhythms spice up the old **Posada Ajijic,** 16 de Septiembre 2, on the *laguna* at Colón. (Live music F-Sa 9pm-2am. Cover 20-50 pesos.)

TEQUILA   ☎3

Surrounded by gentle mountains and prickly, blue-green *agave* plants stretching as far as the eye can see, Tequila has been dedicated solely to the production and sale of its namesake liquor since the 17th century. The town is home to 16 tequila distilleries, and nearly every business in town is linked to the alcohol in some way. Tourism sustains a slew of t-shirt and souvenir shops, as well as numerous liquor stores in the *centro* and along the route just outside of town. Although touristy (surprise!), the town is lots of fun and makes a great daytrip from Guadalajara.

▐ TRANSPORTATION. Buses to Tequila leave from Guadalajara's Antigua Central (2hr., about every 15min. 5:40am-9:15pm, 27 pesos) and return on the same schedule. From the **bus station,** continue on the same road into town, turn right, then take your first left at the cathedral to reach the main plaza.

TEQUILA TIME! The best tequila, as the tour guides will tell you, bears a label boasting its content: 100% *agave*. Around 1600 varieties of this cactus exist in Mexico but only the blue *agave* is used to make tequila. Plants take eight to 12 years to mature, at which point their huge, dense centers (called *piñas*—pineapples—for their appearance) weigh 35-45kg. Once harvested, each plant provides around 5L of tequila. Not bad for a cactus. From the field, the *piñas* are taken to the factory where they are cooked for 36 hours in enormous traditional ovens, or for 12 hours in the modern and speedy autoclave. A slightly different cooking process will yield *sotol,* the famous Chihuahuan alcohol (see **Sotol from the Heart,** p. 239). You can take a taste of a cooked *piña* on the factory tour—it's similar to a sweet potato. *Piñas* are then chopped and mixed with water, and the stringy pulp that's strained off is used for rugs, animal food, and stuffing furniture. The remaining mixture is poured into huge tubs where it ferments, attracting bees, flies, ants, and other bugs that inevitably join this not-so-appetizing concoction. Only 10% of this mixture will actually become tequila. Be thankful for modern yeast fermentation—in the old days fermentation options included naked, sweaty workers sitting in the vats, or throwing in a piece of animal dung wrapped in cloth. The tequila then goes through two distillations to remove the methanol and lower the alcohol content. In the factory, you can take a sip of tequila after its first distillation, with an alcohol content as high as 80%. Afterwards it is aged in white oak barrels; the longer, the smoother. This whole process can only happen here: it's against the law to produce tequila anywhere but Jalisco and a few surrounding areas.

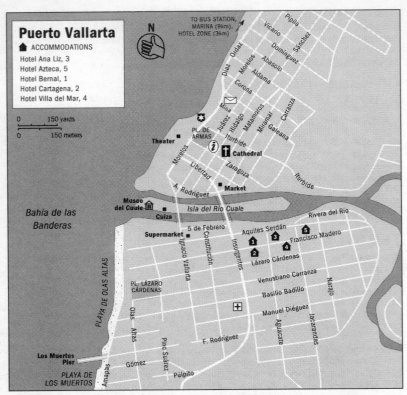

Puerto Vallarta

⌂ ACCOMMODATIONS

Hotel Ana Liz, 3
Hotel Azteca, 5
Hotel Bernal, 1
Hotel Cartagena, 2
Hotel Villa del Mar, 4

🔟🔢 ORIENTATION AND PRACTICAL INFORMATION. The town is organized around the **Plaza Principal;** all roads lead to and from it. The distilleries are all within easy walking distance of downtown. The José Cuervo and Sauza plants, the two biggest distilleries, are next door to each other two blocks north of the plaza. Tequila's **tourist office** is on the plaza across from the Presidencia Municipal. The staff will arrange tours of the distilleries and museum. (Open daily 10am-5pm.) Also in the plaza, a slew of guides stand ready to take you on factory tours. (Most tours 10am-4pm.) **Banamex,** at Gorjón and Juárez, has an **ATM.** (Open M-F 9am-4pm, Sa 9am-1pm.) The **police** are on the plaza at Cuervo 33, by the tourist office.

🍴 FOOD. There isn't a great selection of restaurants in Tequila. One option is **Restaurant Bar El Sauzal,** Juárez 45, between Gorjón and Cuervo, home to a garish mural and many locals. Steak 45 pesos, *quesadillas* 6 pesos, beer 12 pesos. (Open daily 10am-1am.) Budget hunters will appreciate the **Aricola,** Gorjón 20, where a roasted half-chicken costs 30 pesos. (Open daily 7:30am-4pm.) Rock to MTV videos and chicken burgers (with fries and soda, 24 pesos) at **Pizzas Danny,** Rojas 16, or try a two-topping small pizza (37 pesos), enough for two. (☎742 01 49. Open daily 11am-10pm.)

🍸 DRINK. There's not much to do here other than drink or take a **tequila factory tour.** But hey, why else did you come to a town called Tequila? The tourist office will take you on a tour pretty much whenever you show up (daily 10am-5pm; about 30 pesos), while the **Sauza** and **José Cuervo tours** kick off at the respective plants every hour (daily 9am-5pm; 25 pesos). To really see a factory in action, try to get there as early in the morning as possible and also avoid the *siesta* (2-4pm). For the price of a few shots, you'll learn more than you ever wanted to know about *agave* (the plant from which tequila is distilled), the distillation and aging processes, and the history of the famous liquor. The private tours end in the factories' very own bars, where the first three shots of tequila are free; subsequent doses will run you 10-30 pesos. The **Museo de Tequila,** Coran 34, offers another lesson in tequila history, as well as a gift shop. (☎742 24 10. Open Tu-Sa 10am-5pm. 10 pesos, children and students 5 pesos.) The **Museo Familia Sauza,** Rojas 22, also has tours. (approx. every 30min. Open M-F 10am-1:30pm, Sa-Su 10am-4:30pm. Donation suggested.) Those who can spare the pesos will find good deals here on hard-to-find varieties and tequila-related knick-knacks for the folks back home.

▩ **FESTIVALS.** For 15 days, beginning with a huge parade on the last Saturday of November, Tequila celebrates its **Feria Nacional del Tequila.** Each of the town's factories has its own day on which it holds rodeos, concerts, cockfights, fireworks, and other festivities. And of course, there are always plenty of drinks to go around.

PUERTO VALLARTA   ☎3

In 1956, tabloid headlines had the world fantasizing about Puerto Vallarta (pop. 150,000). The torrid affair that took place here between Richard Burton and Elizabeth Taylor on the set of *Night of the Iguana* painted the city, at that time a remote and mysterious *pueblo* with neither highways nor phone lines, as the world headquarters of sensuality. Forty years later, Vallarta has become a world-class resort town rife with showy mansions, groomed beaches, and upscale clubs and restaurants—a pleasure-dome designed for those living out their own long-held Vallarta fantasies. What is more, Vallarta, unlike Acapulco and Cancún, has yet to fully decay in tourist sleaze. Sometimes more Mediterranean than Mexican, Puerto Vallarta is a resort town just hitting its stride.

▐ TRANSPORTATION

GETTING AROUND

Taxis charge about 20 pesos to the *centro* and about 60 pesos to go from the *centro* to the Marina Vallarta or to the airport in the north. **Buses** enter the city on Av. México, which becomes Díaz Ordaz. All *combis* and any municipal bus operating south of the Sheraton or labeled "Centro" pass the main plaza. Buses and *combis* labeled "Hoteles" pass the hotel strip. For the most part, buses stop only at the clearly marked *parada* signs and at the covered benches. Most buses and *combis* pass along Insurgentes between Madero and Cárdenas at some point on their route. (Buses and *combis* operate daily 6am-10pm. 3 pesos.)

GETTING AWAY

Airport: 8km north of town. To get downtown from the airport, take a "Centro" or "Olas Altas" bus or a taxi. To back from town, catch a "Novia Alta," "Marfil," or "Aeropuerto" bus on Cárdenas, Insurgentes, or Juárez. Served by **Aeroméxico** (toll-free ☎01 800 36 202), **Alaska** (☎221 13 50 or toll-free ☎95 800 426 0333), **American** (☎221 17 99 or toll-free ☎01 800 904 6000), **Continental** (☎221 10 25), **Mexicana** (☎224 89 00), and **Taesa** (☎221 15 31 or toll-free ☎01 800 904 6300).

Buses: The modern, mammoth, A/C bus station is north of the *centro*, just beyond the airport. To get downtown, take a "Centro" or "Olas Altas" bus or taxi. To get to the bus station from downtown, take an "Ixtapa" bus (3 pesos) northbound at the Plaza. Elite, Futura, and Norte de Sonora of the Estrella Blanca group (☎221 08 48 or 1 08 50) offer service to most major destinations. Transportes del Pacífico (☎221 08 69) has second-class buses to **Guayabitos** (every 30min., 50 pesos), and first-class buses to **Guadalajara** (6hr., every hr., 246 pesos) and **Tijuana** (38hr., 985 pesos). Flecha Amarilla (toll-free ☎01 800 849 9001) goes to **Guadalajara** (6hr., approx. every 2hr., 268 pesos) and other major destinations. ETN (☎221 05 50) goes to: **Mexico City** (13hr., 6:45am and 7pm, 775 pesos); and **Querétaro** (12hr., 8:30pm, 605 pesos). Norte de Sonora is the only direct service to **San Blas** (4hr., 12:15 and 2:30pm, 95 pesos).

■✴⃣ ORIENTATION AND PRACTICAL INFORMATION

Running roughly east-west, the river **Río Cuale** bisects Puerto Vallarta before hitting the ocean. **Rte. 200** from Manzanillo runs into town south of the river, becoming **Insurgentes**. The ritzy waterfront between Plaza Mayor and 31 de Octubre, called the *malecón*, contains overpriced restaurants, hotels, clubs, and tacky shirt shops. North of the Malecón, Morelos becomes Perú and before joining the coastal route. North along the route lie the **airport**, the **marina**, and the **bus station**. The south end of town has virtually all the cheap hotels, best beaches, budget restaurants, and dance clubs.

Tourist Office: (☎222 02 4 or 223 25 00, ext. 230 or 231), in the Presidencia Municipal, on the north side of the Plaza Mayor (enter on Juárez), and at Ascencio 1712 (☎223 07 44 or 223 08 44; ☎/fax 222 02 43); the street is also known as Las Palmas. Free maps, brochures, and *Passport*, a publication that lists discounts at bars and restaurants (only with American Express card). English spoken. Open M-F 9am-5pm.

Consulates: Canada (☎222 53 98; fax 222 35 17; open M-F 9am-5pm) and **US** (☎222 00 69; fax 3 00 74; open M-F 10am-2pm) are both at Zaragoza 160 in the Vallarta Plaza, on the Plaza Mayor above "Subway."

Currency Exchange: Banamex (☎226 61 10), at Juárez and Zaragoza, in front of the Presidencia Municipal. Open M-F 9am-5pm, Sa 9am-2pm. **Bancrecer,** Olas Altas 246 (☎223 04 84), between Carranca and Badillo. Open M-F 9am-5pm, Sa 9am-1pm. Both banks have **ATMs.** *Casas de cambio* are everywhere, especially near the *malecón.* Their rates are lower than the banks; better deals are generally found away from the beach. Usually open daily 9am-7pm.

American Express: Morelos 660 (☎223 29 55; fax 223 29 26), at Abasolo. Open M-F 9am-5pm, Sa 9am-1pm.

Laundry: Laundry Aguamatic, Constitución 275 (☎222 59 78), between Cárdenas and Carranza. 21 pesos per 3kg. Open M-Sa 9am-8pm.

Bookstore: Señor Book Café, Olas Altas 490 (☎222 03 24), at Gómez. Book exchange. Also serves coffee and cold drinks (13-20 pesos). Open daily 7am-11pm. **Una Página en el Sol,** Olas Alta 339 at Diéguez. English-language books 10-70 pesos. Banana splits 30 pesos. Open daily 7:30am-midnight.

Supermarket: Gutiérrez Rico (☎222 02 22), at Constitución and Serdán. Open daily 7am-11pm. **La Ley,** Peru and Panama, is even bigger. Open 24hr.

Car Rental: Almost all rental companies have offices on Ascencio, the hotel strip. Prices are high. **National,** Ascencio km 1.5 (☎221 12 26 at the airport), has the lowest rates. VW with tax, insurance, and 200km US$50 per day. **Thrifty,** Ascencio km 5.5 (☎224 07 76 or 224 92 80). VWs with tax, insurance, and unlimited km US$60 per day.

Emergency: ☎060.

Police: (☎222 01 06) on Iturbide at Morelos. Some English spoken. On call 24hr.

Red Cross: (☎222 15 33) on Río de la Plata at Río Balsas. English spoken. Open 24hr.

Pharmacy: Farmacia CMQ, Badillo 365 (☎222 13 30, 222 29 41, or 222 35 92), at Insurgentes. Other locations. All open 24hr.

Hospital: CMQ Hospital, Badillo 365 (☎223 19 19), at Insurgentes. Some English spoken. Open 24hr. Up the hill is **Hospital Medasist,** Diéguez 360 (☎223 04 44), at Aguacate. Some English spoken. Open 24hr.

Internet Access: Cafe.com, Olas Altas 250 (☎/fax 222 00 92), at Rodríguez. Chic cafe and small bar, plush sofas, and fax and copy service. Internet use 15 pesos per 30min, 25 pesos per hr. **The Net House,** Vallarta 232 (☎222 69 53), at Cárdenas. 25 pesos per hr., with student ID 20 pesos per hr. Open 24hr. **Eclipse,** Juárez 208 (☎224 49 50), by Plaza de Armas. 15 pesos per 15min., 45 pesos per hr.

Post Office: Mina 188 (☎222 18 88), left off Juárez past the Plaza Mayor. Open M-F 8am-4:30pm, Sa 9am-1pm. **Postal Code:** 48300.

⌐ ACCOMMODATIONS AND CAMPING

The best budget hotels in Puerto Vallarta are south of Río Cuale, on or near Madero. Though relatively cheap for Vallarta, almost all cost at least 100 pesos per night. Prices vary with season: June is the least expensive, December the most. Reservations November through January should be made two months in advance; even in July they should be made a few days ahead of time. Officially, Vallarta frowns on shiftless beach bums, but it is said that most travelers who choose to camp encounter few problems. Some beachfront clubs have night guards who may keep an eye on those who request their permission before bedding down—a tip is appropriate. Many people sleep on the sand behind the Hotel Los Arcos or the Castle Pelícanos, or on the open space between the J. Newcombe tennis courts and the Sheraton. Exercise caution when selecting any camping site.

Hotel Azteca, Madero 473 (☎222 27 50), between Jacarandas and Naranjo. Clean and simple rooms at a great price. Long-term *huéspedes* create a friendly atmosphere. Fans and *agua purificada*. Long-distance phone for patrons. Towel deposit 40 pesos. Singles 130 pesos; doubles 160 pesos; small suites with kitchen 250-300 pesos.

Hotel Villa del Mar, Madero 440 (☎222 07 85), 2 blocks east of Insurgentes. Brick detailing, wooden doors, and lanterns give the well-scrubbed rooms a rustic feel. Rooftop terrace has a fabulous view of the *centro*. Try for a room with a balcony. Towel deposit 50 pesos. Singles 150 pesos; doubles 190 pesos; triples 230 pesos.

Hotel Ana Liz, Madero 429 (☎222 17 57), at Jacarandas, has basic, small, dim rooms with tiny bathrooms. Tasteful landscape photos do their best to brighten the place. Singles 130 pesos; doubles 160 pesos; triples 190 pesos.

Hotel Bernal, Madero 423 (☎222 36 05), has an inviting covered courtyard with clean but old rooms, fan, and purified water. Singles 130 pesos; doubles 160 pesos.

Hotel Cartegena, Madero 428 (☎222 69 14). New tile floors and complimentary coffee (if you're nice to the desk attendant). Clean rooms have fans and homey colors. Purified water in the hallway. Towel deposit 40 pesos. Singles 130 pesos; doubles 160 pesos.

⌐ FOOD

Puerto Vallarta's *malecón* specializes in tourist-oriented, North American cuisine, but some excellent, decently-priced restaurants can be found elsewhere on the north side. Near the beach on the south side, many upscale restaurants exist especially for *gringos*, particularly on the blocks enclosed by Badillo, Olas Altas, Cárdenas, and Constitución. Cheaper down-home eateries cluster along Madero, in the *mercado* (open M-Sa 9am-8pm) on the north side, where Insurgentes crosses Río Cuale, and along Mexico to the north. Taco and *quesadilla* stands thrive south of the river.

▨ A Page in the Sun, Una Pagina en El Sol, Morelos 950 (☎222 36 08), is a combination cafe, vegetarian restaurant, used English bookstore, and cybercafe. Books (5-70 pesos) go well with the coffee (7-9 pesos) and veggie sandwiches (25 pesos). Another location, Olas Altas 399, in front of Hotel los Arcos. Open M-Sa 7am-11pm.

▨ La Casa de los Hot Cakes, Badillo 289 (☎222 62 72), at Constitución. Stupendously good breakfasts. Indulge in the specialty pancake or waffle platters (22-30 pesos) or delectable cheese blintzes (36 pesos). Scrambled egg whites (22 pesos) and traditional Mexican breakfast foods, such as *chilaquiles* (25 pesos). Open daily 8am-2pm.

KUA-TLAI, Madero 441 (☎223 28 07), means "eat-drink" in Náhuatl, and that's exactly what you'll do. *Huevos* (*rancheros* or *con chorizo;* 16 pesos) are the specialty with tortas (cubanas, de pierna, or de panelo; 11-15 pesos) a close second. Orange, grapefruit, carrot, and beet juices 7-9 pesos. Banana, strawberry, and apple licuados 9 pesos. Open daily 7am-3pm.

Restaurant Buffet Vegetariano, Iturbide 270 (☎222 30 73), at Hidalgo, a few blocks inland from Plaza Mayor and up the steep steps of Iturbide. 100% vegetarian cuisine, with strong Indian influence. Buffet includes beans, rice, and soy patties (40 pesos). Open M-Sa noon-7pm.

Café de Olla, Badillo 168 (☎223 16 26), 1 block from the beach. A tourist joint with attentive waiters, reasonable prices, and exceptional food. *Mariachis* weave between tables to serenade vacationers. Beautiful burgers 40 pesos, *chiles rellenos* 38 pesos. Open M and W-Su 10am-11pm.

👁 🌊 SIGHTS AND BEACHES

Although the veneer of tourism detracts somewhat from Puerto Vallarta's natural beauty, the panorama of the city's 40km coastline and surrounding palm-tree-covered mountains is still enchanting. Water sport enthusiasts will have a happy stay in Vallarta—aquatic activities are extremely popular, especially during the morning hours. This is your chance to go **parasailing** (US$30, price negotiable). **Wave runners** (doubles 250 pesos per 30min.), **banana boat** rides (100 pesos per person), **kayaks** (120 pesos per hr.), and **waterskis** (about US$60) are also there for the taking. **Chico's Dive Shop,** 772 Díaz Ordaz, offers scuba diving courses and certification classes. (☎222 18 98 or 222 18 97; www.chicos-diveshop.com. 1hr., US$18. US$290 for certification classes. Tell them Jeremy from *Let's Go* sent you and get a 15% discount. Open daily 8am-10pm.) Equestrian fanatics can take to the hills on **horseback;** rentals are available near Daiquiri Dick's on Olas Altas, at Carranza (horses 90-100 pesos per hr.; open daily around 7am-5:30pm).

Some of the least crowded and most gorgeous beaches stretch south of town on the road to Mismaloya (see p. 392) and north into Nayarit (see p. 368). The most popular within the Puerto Vallarta city limits is **Playa de los Muertos** (Beach of the Dead), a strip in front of the south side's costliest hotels. It begins at its south end at a rocky cliff spotted with small white homes, and stretches north to the small dock that separates it from the **Playa de Olas Altas** (High Waves Beach). To get there, walk all the way west on Cárdenas and then south along Playa de Olas Altas, which continues to the Río Cuale then becomes the rocky *malecón*. Near the southern end of Playa de los Muertos is a small section of the beach known as **Las Sillas Azules** (the blue chairs), one of Mexico's only gay (male) beaches.

Isla Río Cuale lies between and underneath two bridges spanning the ponderous **Río Cuale.** A cool pathway runs the length of the verdant island, full of small stores selling postcards, jewelry, and souvenirs. The **Museo del Cuale,** at the seaward end of the island, houses interesting displays on Mesoamerican culture and regional history. (Open Tu-Sa 10am-7pm, Su 10am-2pm. Free.) During the day the walk along Río Cuale is pleasant, but at night it can be dangerous. The river can be reached from the north via Zaragoza. Stairs, beginning behind the Church of Guadalupe, lead up the mini-mountain amid bougainvillea and hibiscus into the wealthy Zaragoza neighborhood known locally as Gringo Gulch. The prominent bridge spanning the apex of the street once connected Elizabeth Taylor's humble pad with Richard Burton's.

🎵 NIGHTLIFE

After dark Puerto Vallarta offers something for everyone, whether it's a cocktail in the moonlight or a shimmy on the dance floor. The *malecón* swarms with hundreds of tanned young Mexicans and Americans batting eyelashes at each other. Vallarta has sprouted a thriving **gay scene,** and boasts several clubs catering exclusively to gay men and, occasionally, to gay women. Most of the action takes place along **Díaz Ordaz** on the northern waterfront. Nightlife transportation is greatly aided by the "Marina Vallarta" bus, which goes to the marina, and the "Pitillal" bus, which takes you just past the hotel strip. After 11pm, you'll be stuck with taxis (60 pesos to the *centro*).

BARS AND CLUBS

Discos are aimed at those who don't mind dropping 50-70 pesos or more for cover and 20-50 pesos for a drink. Most worth visiting until 11pm or midnight; the time before then is better spent tossing back drinks in cheap bars. For the clubs with covers, save a small fortune by obtaining free passes (which may not be honored during peak tourist season) from the condo-hawkers lurking on the *malecón* (you don't need to buy a condo, just to pretend you might).

Carlos O'Brian's Bar & Grill & Clothesline (☎ 222 14 44), Díaz Ordaz at Pípila. The only things hanging out to dry are the totally trashed high-school students. Teens bounce between here, **Kahlúa** (☎ 222 24 86), a few blocks south on the waterfront, and the **Zoo,** Díaz Ordaz 638 (☎ 222 49 45), next door. It's the biggest party in town—block-long lines wrap around the building all night. A taxi stand out front aids you in the long stumble home. Open daily 9am-4am.

Collage (☎ 221 08 61 or 62), next to Marina Vallarta, is big enough to house all of Vallarta. Bowling, pool tables, video games, a sushi bar (with 100% cholera-free fish from abroad), a sports bar in back, temporary tattoo parlors, an Internet cafe, bars, and a high-tech dance floor. Cover 60 pesos after 9pm. Cover 150 pesos for men, 90 pesos for women. No cover M; Th. open bar. Open daily 11am-6am.

J & B (☎ 224 46 16), Ascencio km 2.5 toward the hotel zone. An older crowd dances to live salsa, merengue, and the occasional Michael Jackson tune. The raised dance floor makes it impossible to be shy. Those determined not to dance can play pool instead. Cover 60 pesos. Open daily 10pm-4am.

Club Roxy, Ignacio Vallarta 217, between Madero and Carranza. An international clientele jams to live reggae, blues, and rock. Santana and Marley covers are skillfully sung to a crowd of all ages. Beer 18 pesos. No cover. Open M-Sa 8am-3:30am.

Cuiza (☎ 222 56 46), on Isla Río Cuale, at the foot of the *puente nuevo.* Doesn't get any mellower than this: find a table on the shady patio, order a margarita (20-60 pesos), and listen to the jazz as Mexican professionals and older vacationers bob their heads. Live music daily 8pm-1am. Open daily 9am-1am.

GAY NIGHTLIFE

A **gay cruise,** departing daily at noon from the Los Muertos pier, takes partners Noah's ark-style to a private beach (around US$50; includes drinks, snorkeling, and table dancing). Tickets are available from travel agents or time-share hawkers; for more info, ask at Paco Paco (below), or see www.pacopaco.com.

■ **Paco Paco,** Ignacio Vallarta 278, at Cárdenas. Vallarta's hottest gay disco, with great music, lots of floor space, mirrors, strobe lights, and aquariums, has a rooftop bar for a relaxing view of the sunset before kicking off the night. The friendly owner is a fountain of information on Vallarta's gay scene. It's also home to Paco's Ranch, around the corner on Carranza, a "man's bar" that hosts different theme nights and strip shows at midnight. Cover Th-Su; men 40 pesos, women 70 pesos. Open daily noon-6am.

Porque No, Morelos 101 (☎ 222 63 92), on the Plaza Río next to the Vallarta Bridge. Art Deco coffee and video bar (with pool tables) sits above the vibrations of a rocking basement. Wall-to-wall dancing. Almost exclusively gay men. Happy Hour with noon-8pm. Open daily noon-4am.

Los Balcones, Juárez 182 (☎ 222 46 71), at Libertad. International gay crowd practices looking languid on the balconies. Scantily dressed patrons sizzle on the neon-lit dance floor. Starts hopping 11:30pm. F mixed drinks half-price; M beer 15 pesos. Cover F-Sa 20-30 pesos. Open daily 9pm-4am.

⚡ DAYTRIPS FROM PUERTO VALLARTA

The **Bahía de Banderas** (Bay of Flags), the bay that Puerto Vallarta calls home, owes its name to a blunder: when Nuño Beltrán de Guzmán sailed here in 1532, he mistook the colorful headdresses of the thousands of natives awaiting him for flags. Today, the Bay offers miles of beautiful and often untouristed beaches. Using Puerto Vallarta as a base, it is possible to get to all points around the Bay.

SOUTHERN COAST

Buses run to Mismaloya from the corner of Constitución and Badillo in Puerto Vallarta (every 10min. 6:20am-10:30pm, 3 pesos; returning on the same schedule). Taxis to Mismaloya cost 80 pesos. Buses labeled "Tuito" run to Chico's Paradise from the corner of Carranza and Aguacate (every 30min. 5am-9pm, 10 pesos). Taxis Acuáticos are the cheapest way to get to the boats-only beaches. They leave from the Muelle de los Muertos and stop at Las Ánimas, Quimixto, and Yelapa (45min.; departs at 11am, returns at 4pm; 90 pesos). If you prefer something more organized, cruises to points south of Vallarta leave the marina (9am, returning 4pm; US$25 and up). Information can be found in the tourist office, at any large hotel, or at the marina.

Vallarta's most popular beaches lie a few kilometers south of the city itself. The first few you'll come across are monopolized by resorts and condos, and access to them is usually only through the hotels.

LOS ARCOS. Farther down the coast lies Los Arcos, a group of pretty rock islands hollowed out in some spots by pounding waves. The coast lacks sand but serves as a platform from which to start the 150m swim to the islands. Bring a mask or goggles or risk missing the tropical fish that flit through the underwater reefscape. Mind your step—the coral is sharp enough to draw blood; use caution and swim with a friend. *(Take the bus to Mismaloya and ask the driver to stop at Hotel de los Arcos.)*

MISMALOYA. The beautiful crescent beach of Mismaloya lies just around the bend to the south. Best known as the site of *Night of the Iguana* and Arnold Schwarzenegger's *cinéma vérité* classic, *Predator*, Mismaloya has recently been encircled by large hotels. It is only slightly less crowded than the beaches in town.

BOCA DE TOMATLÁN. Farther down, the road veers away from the coast just beyond the Boca de Tomatlán, a narrow cove with only a small but relatively untouristed beach. The last place to see on the southern road is **Chico's Paradise,** 5km inland from the Boca de Tomatlán. Wash down the view of the nearby **Tomatlán Falls** with a drink at Chico's huge, airy *palapas.*

LAS ÁNIMAS AND QUIMIXTO. Farther south lie the beaches of Las Ánimas and Quimixto, which are only accessible from the ocean. The twin beaches have long stretches of unoccupied sand backed by small villages and a few *palapas.* Quimixto also has a small waterfall. *(The trip can be made by foot (1hr.) or by rented mule (30min.). Scuba tours also come from downtown Vallarta and Mismaloya to these beaches.)*

YELAPA. A destination of a popular boat ride and highly touted by locals, Yelapa a bit of a fake. Supposedly a secluded peasant fishing village, its seemingly simple *palapa* huts were designed by a North American architect whose definition of "rustic" apparently included interior plumbing and hot water. Many of these *palapas* are occupied for only part of the year, and short- and long-term rentals can be arranged easily for varying (and sometimes surprisingly) low prices. The beach fills with vendors and parasailers during the day, but the town, a 15-minute walk from the beach, remains tranquil, with waterfalls and nude bathing upstream and poetry readings downstream. Don't miss the secluded swimming hole at the top of the stream that runs through town. Follow the path along the stream uphill; just before the restaurant, duck under the water pipes to the right of the trail and head up the track. About 15m before it rejoins the stream, an inconspicuous trail leads to the left to a deep pool overlooking the bay.

NORTHERN COAST

From Puerto Vallarta, flag down a Camiones del Pacífico "Punta de Mita" second-class bus on Cárdenas, Insurgentes, Juárez, or Ascencio (every 20min. 9:15am-5pm; to Piedra Blanca (40min., 15 pesos); to Destiladeras (1hr., 17 pesos); to Punta de Mita (1¼hr. plus a 4km walk, 20 pesos).

The northern edge of the bay has some of the prettiest and least-exploited beaches on Mexico's central Pacific coast. **Nuevo Vallarta,** the largest and southernmost of nine small towns on the north bay, is 150km south of Tepic and 20km north of

Puerto Vallarta. Protected by a sandy cove, **Playa Piedra Blanca** has wonderfully calm waters. Farther north along the bay is **Playa las Destiladeras,** named for the water that trickles through the rocky cliff. Although the sandy bottom is colored with occasional rocks, the rougher waves make this strip of beach perfect for body-surfers and boogie boarders. **Punta de Mita,** the northernmost point along the bay, is a lagoon sheltered by two rock islets. It is marked by the **Corral de Riscos,** a living reef. Freshwater showers in Destiladeras make the bus ride home more comfortable. Bring a bag lunch to avoid inflated prices at the beachside *palapas*.

BAHÍA DE CHAMELA

The tranquil and secluded Bahía de Chamela, 60km northwest of Melaque, marks the northern point of Jalisco's "Ecological Tourism Corridor." A chain of small rocky islands breaks the horizon, and 11km of golden-brown sand, dotted with gnarled driftwood and the occasional *palapa*, beckon to the beachcomber. The largest village in Chamela is **Perula,** which lacks most services beyond a few hotels and seafood *palapas*, but keeps its visitors content with a charming beach. Though Chamela receives its share of tourism, especially in December and April, the Midas touch has yet to spoil the natural beauty and seclusion of the bay. This, however, presents other problems: lone travelers (particularly women) and small groups should be wary of deserted beaches, especially during the low seasons.

⬛ TRANSPORTATION. Second-class buses from **Puerto Vallarta** to **Manzanillo** (3½hr., 40 pesos) pass through Perula; buses going from **Melaque** or **Barra de Navidad** to **Puerto Vallarta** (1½hr., 29 pesos) or **Manzanillo** (3hr., 53 pesos) also pass through Perula. Always tell the bus driver where you're going in advance so you don't miss the stop. To get to Playa Perula, get off by the big white "Playa Dorada" sign and walk 30 minutes down a winding dirt road—don't be surprised if friendly locals offer you a ride. To get to Playa Chamela, get off farther south at "El Súper," marked by the colorful figure directing passersby to the Villa Polinesia. Walk 15 minutes down the country road until you hit the beach. Perula is a 30-minute walk along the shore. Hotels in Perula will pick you up or send a taxi. To get back, catch a Primera Plus bus from the Primera Plus station. They head to: **Guadalajara** (3hr.; 8, 10:30am, and 4pm; 60 pesos); **Manzanillo** (2½-5hr., every hr. 7:30am-10:30pm, 50-65 pesos) via **Melaque** (1½hr., 27-35 pesos); and **Puerto Vallarta** (every hr., 7:30am-10:30pm, 65 pesos).

◪ PRACTICAL INFORMATION. There is one **LADATEL** phone outside the Primera Plus Station; your best bet for placing a long-distance call is cajoling one of the hotel or restaurant owners into letting you call collect.

▛▟ ACCOMMODATIONS AND FOOD. The **Hotel Punta Perula,** on the corner of Juárez and Tiburón, two blocks from the beach, features a massive courtyard laden with trees and overhanging hammocks, eclipsing the comfortable, floral rooms. (☎285 50 20. Low-season singles 125 pesos; doubles 200 pesos; high season 175 pesos, 250 pesos.) In Perula, **Tejamar Restaurante y Cuartos,** on Independencia, one block south of Hotel Punta Perula and less than a block from the beach, is a small, family-run taco restaurant and *posada*. Its basic rooms have ceiling fans and open onto a small courtyard. Friendly owners are eager to accommodate guests with bargain meals, trips to the nearby islands, and weekly discounts. (☎285 53 61. Singles and doubles with shared bath 120 pesos, with private bath 150 pesos.) Feast on the catch of the day as you relax under palm frond umbrellas at **Mariscos La Sirena,** one of several *palapas* along the shore. La Sirena serves shrimp and fish (50 pesos) and a cold beer is 10 pesos well-spent. (☎285 51 14. Open daily 7am-8pm, or until the last person leaves.)

◪ BEACHES. Punta de Perula, the bay's northernmost point, shelters **Playa Perula,** making it perfect for swimming. A 30-minute walk down the coast along virgin beach will bring you to the **Villa Polinesia Motel and Campsite,** marking **Playa Cha-**

THE TIMES THEY ARE A-CAMBIANDO On July 2, 2000, Mexico elected Vicente Fox of the National Action Party (PAN) to the presidency, marking the end of a 70-year rule by Mexico's leading party, the Institutional Revolutionary Party (PRI). The monumental 2000 elections are considered to be the first truly democratic elections in Mexico, despite the many domestic and international efforts to ensure electoral integrity in the past 15 years. Ironically, it was Ernesto Zedillo, Mexico's outgoing president, whose progressive reforms ultimately made possible the recent change of power and the defeat of his own party. Political affiliations aside, all Mexicans anxiously await the prospect of change President Fox represents.

mela. Here and farther south, the rougher waves invite body-surfing and boogie-boarding—watch out for the frequent and powerful undertow. Continuing south will bring you to **Playa Rosada** and even more secluded beaches. Occasional *palapas* refresh the parched and weary body-surfer, and *lanchas* from Playa Perula transport Robinson Crusoes to the nearby islands (round-trip about 250 pesos).

BAHÍA DE NAVIDAD   ☎3

Along with Guadalajara and Puerto Vallarta, Bahía de Navidad forms Jalisco's "Tourist Triangle." However, power is not shared equally within the triumvirate. With the exception of December and *Semana Santa*, few tourists are spotted on the placid shores of Bahía de Navidad. The *bahía*, a sheltered cove of talcum sand and shimmering water, is home to the towns of **Melaque** and **Barra de Navidad.** It is a wonder more vacationers don't come here year-round—the water is clear and gentle, the beach long and empty, and the whole bay enclosed by scenic, rocky cliffs. During high season, however, the beach between the towns is transformed into a river of bronzed bodies, and hotels in both towns overflow with tourists. Restaurants, hotels, and clubs are beginning to invade. A Xanadu-esque hotel at the end of the bay opened in early 1997, and a 300-boat marina under construction threatens to overwhelm the bay with hordes of yachting foreigners.

Although Barra and Melaque lie only 5km from each other, they are worlds apart. Barra is pretty, but has few places to eat and sleep, and with a powerful undertow, its steep beach is better for surfing or boogie-boarding than swimming. Conversely, Melaque treats visitors to gentle, choppy waves and an abundance of accommodations; however, it is hot, dusty, and full of bikini shops.

Melaque and Barra de Navidad are 55km northwest of Manzanillo on Rte. 200 and 240km southwest of Guadalajara on Rte. 54. Melaque is the northernmost of the two. They're well-connected by **municipal buses** that shuttle between the two towns (20min., every 15min. 6am-8:30pm, 3 pesos). Of course, the 40-minute walk along the beach is the hard-core budget option. Don't walk after sunset; some dangerous encounters have been reported. **Taxis** cost 35 pesos.

MELAQUE   ☎3

In the placid town of Melaque visitors amble through the *zócalo*, splash in the waves, and nibble on fresh fish while watching the sunset from a beachside restaurant. There's not much to do in beautiful Melaque, which suits the place just fine.

▐ TRANSPORTATION. Melaque's **bus station** (☎355 50 03) is on **Farías**, the parallel-to-the-beach main drag. From the bus station, turn left on Farías and walk two blocks to reach **Mateos.** Another left turn takes you to the plaza, a few blocks inland. Mateos and **Hidalgo** are the main cross-streets toward the ocean.

Autocamiones Cihuatlán (☎355 50 03) sends **buses** to: **Guadalajara** (6½hr., 14 per day, about every 2hr. 4am-12:30am, 178 pesos); **Manzanillo** (1½hr., about every hr. 3am-11:30pm, 30 pesos); **Chamela** (1½hr., every 30min. 6am-11:30pm, 30 pesos); and first class to **Puerto Vallarta** (5hr., 9:30am and 1:30pm, 122 pesos). Across the street, Primera Plus, Farías 34 (☎355 61 10), has first-class service to: **Guadalajara**

(5hr.; 8am, 3:15, 5:15 and 6:15pm; 178 pesos); **Manzanillo** (1½hr.; 5, 11:45am, 2:15, and 7:15pm; 36 pesos); and **Puerto Vallarta** (4hr., 1:45 and 4pm, 122 pesos); second-class to **Guadalajara** (6½hr., 6 per day 5:30am-10:30pm, 149 pesos); **Manzanillo** (1½hr., 6 per day 2am-10:20pm, 30 pesos); and **Chamela** (1½hr., 11am, 30 pesos).

▇ PRACTICAL INFORMATION. Banamex, on Farías, right from the bus station, has a 24hr. **ATM.** (☎355 52 77 or 355 53 52. Open M-F 9am-3pm.) Change money at **Casa de Cambio,** Farías 27A, inside the commercial center across from the bus station. (☎355 53 43. Open M-Sa 9am-2pm and 4-7pm, Su 9am-2pm.) **Police:** Upstairs at Mateos 52 (☎355 50 80), north of the plaza. **Red Cross:** (☎355 23 00) 15km away in Cihuatlán, accessible by buses that leave from the plaza (every 15min. 6am-8pm, 6 pesos) or by taxi (60 pesos). **Súper farmacia Plaza,** Mateos 48, on the south side of the plaza. (☎355 51 67. Open daily 8:30am-10pm). **Clínica de Urgencias,** Carranza 22, two blocks from the bus station. (☎355 61 44. Open M-F 8am-3pm, Sa 8am-noon.) The **public telephones** by the bus station can be used for long-distance collect calls. **LADATELs** can be found on both Farías and Mateos. **Casetas:** next to the bus station is **Yimmi's,** Farías 34 (☎355 63 10; fax 355 54 52. Open M-Sa 8:30am-9pm, Su 8:30am-noon. **Internet Access: Ciber@net,** in the commercial center, Farías 27A. (☎355 55 19. Open M-F 9:30am-2pm and 4-7:30pm, Sa 9:30am-2pm. 45 pesos per hr.) **Post office:** Orozco 56 (☎355 52 30), near the corner of Corona, one block from the pool hall with the brown fence. **Postal code:** 48980.

▛▜ ACCOMMODATIONS AND FOOD. Melaque boasts a crop of snazzy hotels, but few could be considered budget. Expect rates to rise, of course, during high season. Camping is feasible in Melaque if you arrange to stay next to one of the beachside restaurants; expect to pay a small fee. **Hotel Emanuel,** Bugambilias 89, is half a block from the beach. Spacious rooms and bungalows have floral decor and clean, white-tile bathrooms. Turn right on Farías from the bus station and walk 5 long blocks, turning left after the large blue-green house. Look for the "Abarrotes Emanuel" sign. (☎355 61 07. Singles 80 pesos; doubles 160 pesos, 300 during high season.) **Casa de Huéspedes San Juán,** Farías 24, is on the first block on the right leaving the bus station, across from the bank. Rooms are a bit old and worn, but they're the best deal in town. Kitchen units in some rooms, and a large, sunny courtyard. (☎355 52 70. 1-3 people 150 pesos; quads 200 pesos). You can also try the slightly more expensive **Bungalows Los Arcos,** Farías 2. Take a right at the bus station and walk to the end of the street; it's on the right. If you can ignore the musty smell, rooms are clean with powerful ceiling fans. Private bathrooms have hot water. (☎335 55 18. 1-3 people 200 pesos; quads 230 pesos.)

During the summer, restaurants ship in shrimp from the north, but come high season, local fishing boats catch everything served in Melaque. Cheaper, more authentic Mexican places are near the central plaza. Cheaper still are the sidewalk food stands that materialize after sunset and the unnamed, dirt-floored eateries in the *mercado*. Locals hail **Restaurant Ayala** as the place to go. Turn left on the street before Mateos and walk a block; it's on the left. Tasty fish (25 pesos) and burgers with fries (10-12 pesos) are served in an open-air environment. The *tortas* (10-15 pesos) are delicious. (☎355 66 80. Open daily 7am-5pm.) On the *zócalo* sits **Cafetería Siete Estrellas.** It's not much, but this small joint offers terrific food at incredibly low prices. Try the filling *comida corrida* (18 pesos) or hot *tortas* (10-15 pesos), house favorites. (☎355 64 21. Open daily 7am-midnight.) A happening place to grab dinner is **Caxcan Restaurant,** on the corner of the *zócalo* above the pharmacy as you enter from Mateos. The bar hands out cheap two-for-one drinks to wash back the fishies. (Open daily 6pm-1am.)

▛▜ BEACHES AND ENTERTAINMENT. The main attraction in Melaque is, of course, the beach. Waves get smaller and the beach more crowded toward the western end of Melaque's sandy strip. Rent **jet-skis** at the Restaurant Moyo, on the far west end of the beach. (☎537 11 04. 200 pesos per 30min., 2-person maximum. Available daily 10am-7pm.) Be prepared to get wet if you go for a spin in a **banana**

boat (25 pesos); rivers regularly dump unsuspecting riders into the ocean. Nightlife in Melaque concentrates on the beach until 9:30 or 10pm, when people swim and stroll along the sand enjoying the remnants of the glorious sunset. The after-hours oasis of Melaque's under-30 tourist crowd is **Disco Tanga,** at the end of Farías to the right of the bus station. Multicolored walls and stairs lined by strip lights create a game show effect. (☎355 54 72 or 355 54 75. Cover 20-30 pesos. Open daily in high season; F-Sa off-season 9pm-2am.) For something more mellow and smoky, twirl cues with the middle-aged men at **Billiard San Patricio,** Melaque's pool hall, on Orozco and Juárez, up the street from the post office, three blocks from the *zócalo.* (Pool and *carambola* 10 pesos per hr., dominoes 4 pesos per hr.; open daily 10am-11pm.) This is the type of place women might want to avoid. In general, don't get your partying hopes up during the low season; nightlife just about dies for those months of the year.

BARRA DE NAVIDAD   ☎ 3

Of the two cities, Barra is smaller and has less crowded beaches (due to the strong undertow) than its sister Melaque. However, its shaded streets, numerous sidewalk eateries and popular seaside bars give it a vitality lacking in Melaque. The saltwater *laguna* at the end of town makes a great place to swim, play volleyball, or sunbathe. Like Melaque, Barra doesn't offer much in the way of sights, museums, or the high-tech entertainment, but who could ask for more?

▐ TRANSPORTATION. Veracruz, the main street, runs toward the southeast, angling off at its end. There it meets **Legazpi,** another main street, which runs north-south, hugging the beach. The **bus stop** is at Veracruz 226, on the corner of Nayarit. Turn left on Veracruz from the bus station to get to the *centro.* Primera Plus/Costa Alegre, Veracruz 269 (☎355 61 11), at Filipinas, has first-class service to: **Guadalajara** (5hr.; 10am, noon, 2, 4pm, and 2am; 179 pesos) and **Manzanillo** (1hr.; 12:15, 4:15, 6:15 and 8:15pm; 36 pesos). Second-class buses go to **Guadalajara** (6½hr., 8 buses 7:30am-10:30pm, 150 pesos); **Manzanillo** (1½hr., about every hr. 7:45am-10pm, 30 pesos) and **Chamela** (2hr., 8 per day 7am-9:30pm, 35 pesos).

▐ PRACTICAL INFORMATION. The **Tourist office,** at Jalisco 67, offers brochures and illegible maps. (☎355 51 00. open M-F 9am-5pm.) The friendly Texans at **Crazy Cactus** (☎355 60 99), next to the church on Jalisco, between Legazpi and Veracruz, can help with insider's advice. The **travel agency,** Veracruz 204A, sells tickets for ETN buses departing from Manzanillo. (☎355 56 65 or 335 56 66; fax 355 56 67. Open M-Sa 10am-2pm and 4-7pm.) Barra has no bank, but a **casa de cambio,** Veracruz 212C, exchanges money at high rates without commission (☎355 61 77. Open M-Sa 9am-2pm and 4-7pm, Su 9am-2pm.) **Emergency:** ☎060. **Police:** Veracruz 179 (☎355 53 99). **Centro de Salud:** (☎355 62 20), on Puerto de la Navidad down Veracruz, just out of town. Take a right after signs for El Márquez, just before Veracruz becomes a route; it is the second building on the right, with the red-and-white gate. No *casetas,* but **LADATEL** calling cards can be used at the phones that

---

TELENOVELA, ANYONE? Every evening, grown men and women across Mexico can be found glued to their TV sets, clutching boxes of tissues, oblivious to the outside world. Why? They are watching *telenovelas,* the strange hybrid of soap opera and mini-series that monopolizes Mexico's airwaves from afternoon to late night. Each *telenovela* lasts between six months and a year and contains enough gooey love stories, heart-wrenching tragedies, and finger-gnawing cliff-hangers to put other series to shame. Characters and story lines are added and removed according to ratings; as a result, each show's plot is, in part, guided by audience response. The protagonist of a poorly watched show might suddenly get hit by a truck, and his younger, sexier brother called upon to assume the leading role. Having celebrated its 40th birthday in 1998, the *telenovela* looks like it's here to stay.

line the main streets. **Internet Access: Mango Bay** Jalisco 70, is also an English book exchange. (☎355 59 96. Open M-F 10am-3pm and 5-7pm, Sa 10am-7pm. 1 peso per min.) **Post Office:** Nueva España 87. **Postal code:** 48987.

╓ ACCOMMODATIONS. Budget accommodations in Barra are available only to the keen-eyed traveler. Reasonable rooms are sometimes available in private residences—ask around and look for signs in restaurants. All prices are subject to high season hikes. **Hotel Caribe,** Sonora 15, has decent pastel rooms with fans and fluorescent-lit desks. The large lobby is enlivened by socializing elderly ladies. (☎355 59 52. Singles 125 pesos; doubles 175 pesos; triples 190 pesos; 40 pesos extra for TV.) **Mama Laya,** Veracruz 69, is the best deal in town. Turn left at the bus station and walk all the way down the road. Rooms are spacious but a little dark, with striped bedspreads. Communal bathrooms are adequate and have hot water. (Singles 100 pesos; doubles 140 pesos.) It's no longer possible to camp in Barra de Navidad; try Melaque instead.

For delicious, inexpensive Mexican food in a pleasant atmosphere, try **Restaurant Paty,** Jalisco 52 at Veracruz. Red tablecloths are even brighter in the outdoor sunshine. (Grilled chicken 30 pesos, enchiladas 18 pesos. Open daily 8am-11pm.) **Tucan,** Legazpi 154, at Yucatán, offers great food with an ocean view. Turn left on Legazpi and walk all the way down. (Breakfast runs 15-20 pesos; burgers and fries 25 pesos. Open daily 9am-10pm.) **Tacos Pitufos** (Smurf Tacos), Veracruz 130, is right outside of the bus station. Tacos (4-5 pesos) are enjoyed in a cool A/C environment. (☎355 57 08. Open daily 5pm-2am.)

▣ ▣ SIGHTS AND ENTERTAINMENT. Crazy Cactus, at the corner of Jalisco and Veracruz, is closed during the summer months but rents equipment during the rest of the year. (☎355 60 99. Snorkeling equipment and boogie-boards 50 pesos per half-day, 80 pesos per day; surfboards 70 pesos per half-day, 120 pesos per day; bikes 100 pesos per day.) Serious fishers will want to call **Z Pesca,** Tampico 71, for a day-long deep-sea fishing expedition. (☎355 64 64. 1400 pesos per day for up to 4 people. Open daily 9am-9pm, low season 9am-7pm.)

The short trip across the lagoon to the village of **Colimilla** is pleasant; a *lancha* will deposit up to 10 passengers at the far end of the lagoon or amid Colimilla's palms, pigs, cows, and open-air restaurants (100 pesos). Deserted **Playa de los Cocos,** 1km away, has larger breakers than those in Barra. If you don't want to swim back, remember to set a time to be picked up. Another option is to tour the **lagoon** behind Barra (up to 8 people 80 pesos) or take a fully equipped *lancha* (up to 4 people 150 pesos per hr.) for tuna or marlin **fishing.** Operators have formed a cooperative, so prices are fixed. Their office and docks lie at the end of Veracruz. (Office open daily 7am-7pm.) Bibliophiles should not miss **Beer Bob's Book Exchange,** Mazatlán 61, a few blocks to the right as you face the Posada Pacífico. It's purely a book exchange—no cash involved. They have quite a collection. In the back room sit Bob and company, watching TV, playing cards, or engaging in "some serious beer-drinking." (Usually open M-F 1-4pm.)

Everyone out past midnight parties at **El Galeón Disco,** Morelos 24, in Hotel Sand's. Sit on cushioned horseshoe-shaped benches and drink the night away. (☎355 50 18. Beer 15 pesos, mixed drinks 25 pesos. Cover 20 pesos. Open daily 9pm-3am, F-Sa during low season.) Those who prefer singing to dancing may want to mellow out at the **Terraza Bar Jardín,** Jalisco 70, a **karaoke** bar above Mango Bay. Somebody will sing "New York, New York" all night if you won't. (☎355 61 35. Beer 15 pesos. Open daily 6pm-2am.) If you just want to concentrate your efforts on drinking, make your way to **Piper Lovers,** Legazpi 138A, where drinks are cheap and pool and ping-pong are free for customers. (☎355 64 34. Beer 15-20 pesos, mixed drinks start at 25 pesos. Open M-Th noon-midnight, F-Sa noon-2am.) If you tire of Lovers, the many two-for-one happy hours along Legazpi make the giddy trip toward inebriation that much cheaper. **Sunset,** on Legazpi across from the church. Play pool while watching the waves nuzzle the coast. (20-peso deposit, 10 pesos all night. Happy hour 2-10pm. Open daily 2pm-2am.)

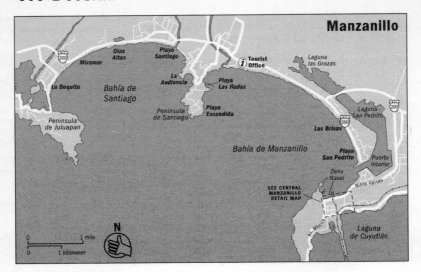

COLIMA

MANZANILLO ☎ 3

Residents of Colima state proudly point to Manzanillo (pop. 124,000) as the brightest hope for its economic future. With its golden stands and green waters, the city is known as the emerald of the Pacific and is touted as the sailfish capital of the world for its famous fishing tournaments. Nevertheless, those shrewd resort builders have one strike against them—Manzanillo is the workhorse port of Mexico's Pacific coast, attracting ships from as far away as Russia, and conventional wisdom holds that a working port can never become a truly world-class resort. Indeed, Manzanillo's best beaches lie west of the dynamic, sweaty *centro*, beyond a huge stretch of barges and cranes. Those seeking only sand and surf would do better to retreat to a secluded village such as Cuyutlán, but for those excited by beautiful, immensely popular beaches—and a real city—Manzanillo delivers.

▐ TRANSPORTATION

White and blue "Miramar" and "Centro" buses run back and forth between the *centro* and the resort strip at the west of town (about 30min., every 15min. 5am-11pm; prices vary).

Airport: (☎333 25 25), Playa de Oro, on the route between Barra de Navidad and Manzanillo. Airlines include: **Aerocalifornia** (☎334 14 14) and **Mexicana** (☎333 23 23). The travel service **Viajes Vamos a...**, Carrillo Puerto 259 (☎332 17 11), 1 block west of Av. México and 3 blocks south of the *zócalo*, can facilitate ticket purchase. Open M-F 9am-2pm and 4-7pm, Sa 9am-2pm. **Taxis** (☎333 19 99) from the airport to the *zócalo* cost 230 pesos.

Buses: station on Hidalgo, southeast of *Jardín Obregón* in the *centro*. You can take a taxi (10-12 pesos) or bus (3 pesos) to the *centro*. Autobuses de Occidente/La Linea/Autobuses de Jalisco (☎332 01 23) has first-class service to: **Guadalajara** (4¼hr., every hr. 6:30am-9:30pm, 158 pesos); **Colima** (1¼hr., every hr. 1am-11:30pm, 40 pesos); and **Morelia** (8hr., 10:45pm, 230 pesos). Second-class service to: **Uruapan** (9hr., 8:30pm, 175 pesos); and **Mexico City** (14hr., 5 per day 2:45am-7:30pm, 410 pesos) via **Morelia** (10hr., 192 pesos) and **Colima** (2hr., 34 pesos). Autocamiones Cihuatlán (☎332 05 15) provides first-class service to: **Guadalajara** (6½hr., 6 per day 8:45am-

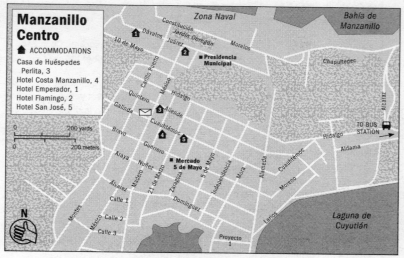

Manzanillo Centro

🏠 ACCOMMODATIONS

Casa de Huéspedes
Perlita, 3
Hotel Costa Manzanillo, 4
Hotel Emperador, 1
Hotel Flamingo, 2
Hotel San José, 5

Zona Naval

Bahía de Manzanillo

Laguna de Cuyutlán

11:45pm, 158 pesos) and second-class service to: **Guadalajara** (8hr., every hr. 2:30am-9pm, 140 pesos) and **Puerto Vallarta** (7hr., approx. every 2hr. 4:30am-10pm, 133 pesos) via **Melaque/Barra de Navidad** (1½hr., 37 pesos). Autotransportes Sur de Jalisco (☎332 10 03) goes to: **Lázaro Cárdenas** (6½hr., 6 per day 3:15am-10pm, 125 pesos) and **Colima** (2hr., every hr. 2am-7pm, 34 pesos). **Primera Plus/Costa Alegre** (☎332 02 10) goes to: **Puerto Vallarta** (6hr.; 1:30am, 6:30, 9:30pm; 133 pesos); **Melaque/Barra de Navidad** (1½hr.; 1, 4, 5:30pm; 30 pesos); **Zamora** (7hr.; 4:20, 7:15, 10:15am, 3:45, 6:15pm; 144 pesos); and **Querétaro** (12hr.; 7:15am, 3:45, 6:15pm; 314 pesos). Elite/Futura/Estrella Blanca (☎332 04 32) provides cushy service to: **Acapulco** (12hr., 6am, 360 pesos); **Mexico City** (12hr.; 7:30 and 9pm, 450 pesos); **Zihuatanejo** (9hr., 6am, 219 pesos); and **Tijuana** (36hr., 4 and 9pm, 1200 pesos) via **Hermosillo** (25hr., 1013 pesos), **Mazatlán** (12hr.; 4, 7:30, 9pm; 426 pesos), and **Tepic** (7hr.; 4, 7:30, 9pm; 258 pesos).

🛈 PRACTICAL INFORMATION

Tourist Office: Costera Miguel de la Madrid 1033 (☎333 22 64 or 333 22 77; fax 333 14 26; email sectur@bay.net.mx), 2 blocks past Fiesta Mexicana. Catch a "Miramar" bus (4 pesos) and tell the driver where you're headed. Provides great maps. Open M-F 9am-3pm and 5-7:30pm, Sa 9am-3pm. Helpful **tourist police** (☎332 10 02) in the Palacio Municipal on the *zócalo* distribute maps and brochures. **Information booths** in front of the *palacio*, around town, and along the beaches. Open daily 7:30am-7:30pm.

Currency Exchange: Bital, Av. México 99 (☎332 09 50 or 332 08 09), at 10 de Mayo, has better rates and longer hours than most. Open M-Sa 8am-7pm. 24hr. **ATM.**

Market: Mercado 5 de Mayo, on 5 de Mayo at Guerrero, 5 blocks down Av. México and 4 blocks left on Guerrero. Open daily 7am-7pm.

Supermarket: (☎333 13 75) Comercial Mexicana, Costera de la Madrid km 11.5. Take a "Miramar" bus from the *zócalo (4 pesos)*. Open Su-Th 8am-10pm, F-Sa 8am-11pm.

Laundry: Lavi-Matic, Calle 1 #1 (☎332 08 44), about 8 blocks down Av. México, across the small plaza, to the left. Wash and dry 10 pesos per kg., 3kg minimum. Open daily 9am-7pm.

Emergency: ☎060.

Police: (☎332 10 02 or 332 10 04) on Juárez in the Palacio Municipal, facing the Jardín.

Red Cross: (☎336 57 70) on Barotes. Open 24hr. No English spoken.

Pharmacy: Farmacia Guadalajara, Av. México 301 (☎332 29 22), at Galindo, 4 blocks from the *zócalo*. Open daily 24hr.

Hospital: (☎332 00 29) in Colonia San Pedrito, Sector 7. English spoken. Open 24hr.

Fax: Telecomm (☎332 30 30), in the Palacio Municipal, to the left of the stairs as you enter. Open M-F 8am-6pm, Sa-Su 9am-12:30pm.

Internet Access: Internet La Luna, Av. México 69 (☎332 48 03), half a block from the *zócalo*. 25 pesos per hr.; students 20 pesos per hr. Open daily 9am-9pm.

Post Office: Galindo 30 (☎332 00 22), 4 blocks down Av. México from the *zócalo*, on the right. Open M-F 9am-6pm, Sa 9am-1pm. **Postal Code: 28200.**

■ ACCOMMODATIONS

Manzanillo's budget accommodations tend to be basic and plain, but you won't care if you're on the beach the whole time. In general, the *zócalo* area is safer than the bus station. **Camping** on Playa Miramar is generally only feasible during *Semana Santa* and in December, when bathroom facilities are available and security is heightened.

Hotel Emperador, Dávalos 69 (☎332 23 74), 1 block west of the plaza. Small rooms with rustic wooden furniture are hot, but fans help cool things off. Cold-water baths are cramped but clean. Singles 80 pesos; doubles 100 pesos; triples 140 pesos.

Hotel Flamingo, Madero 72 (☎332 10 37), 1 block south of the *zócalo*. Rooms with stucco walls and wooden furniture; fans and large windows keep it cool. *Agua purificada* available. Singles 80.5 pesos; doubles 103.5 pesos; triples 126.5 pesos.

Hotel Costa Manzanillo, Madero 333 (☎332 27 40), 4 blocks down Av. México, left on Galindo and right on Madero. The courtyard plants and bright bedspreads make the hotel cheery. Medium-sized rooms with clean baths. Singles 130 pesos, 20 pesos each additional person.

Hotel San José, Cuauhtémoc 138 (☎332 51 05), 4 blocks down Av. México, take a right at Galindo which becomes Cuauhtémoc. Though there's a high chance you'll get a room with no windows, rooms and baths are clean and the beds are firm. Singles 120 pesos; doubles 200 pesos.

■ FOOD

Since tourists mostly stake their claims closer to the beach, food at the market and in downtown is simple and cheap. During the many festivities enlivening the *zócalo*, food vendors pop up at every corner offering homemade goodies.

Restaurant Emperador, Dávalos 69 (☎332 23 74), below the Hotel Emperador. The blank walls, white tablecloths, and fluorescent lights aren't as pleasing to the eye as the food is to the palate. Gargantuan *comida corrida* (25 pesos), delicious *enchiladas* (13 pesos) and filling hot cakes (10 pesos). Open daily 8am-11pm.

Restaurant Del Río, Av. México 330 (☎332 25 25). A small, inexpensive place that will fill you up in no time with *comida corrida* (24 pesos) or Mexican specialties (12-17 pesos). Try a barbecued taco (3 pesos) and wash it down with a chilly beer (10 pesos) or a *licuado* (8 pesos). Open M-Sa 8:30am-8pm.

Restaurante Chantilly, Madero 60 (☎332 01 94), at Juárez on the plaza. Crowds of professionals, families, and stragglers off the *zócalo* feast on good staples in a diner-like setting. Enchiladas 24 pesos, *licuados* 14 pesos. Open Su-F 7:30am-10:30pm.

Pisa Pizza, Av. México 60 (☎332 04 15), at Juárez on the *zócalo*, above the arcade. Serving incredibly cheesy pizzas (starting at 25 pesos) and greasy hamburgers (10-15 pesos), this place is popular with the high school crowd. Open windows provide a great view of the *zócalo* and passersby. Open daily 8:30am-11pm.

BEACHES

Manzanillo's beaches stretch from west to east along two bays, **Bahía de Manzanillo** and **Bahía de Santiago,** formed by the Santiago and Juluapan Peninsulas. The Bahía de Manzanillo has more expensive hotels and cleaner, golden sand. Unfortunately, its beach slopes steeply, creating a strong and sometimes dangerous undertow. The beaches at Bahía Santiago are better protected and ideal for swimming, water sports, and sun worshipping.

PLAYA LAS BRISAS. The beach most accessible from the *centro* is Playa Las Brisas, on Bahía Manzanillo. It has a few secluded spots, but is for the most part crowded with luxurious hotels and bungalows. *(From downtown, take a taxi (25 pesos), the "Las Brisas" bus (4 pesos), or catch the "Miramar" bus and ask to be let off at the crucero (crossroads). Go left for more populated beaches or stake out a private spot nearer the junction.)*

OLAS ALTAS. Along the rest of the bay, west of Peninsula Santiago, lie cleaner water and excellent beaches. Beyond **Olas Altas,** a beach popular with experienced (largely US) surfers and infamous for its powerful waves and dangerous undertow, is **Miramar Beach.** *(Get off where the footbridge crosses the route. This is the most crowded section of the beach, but boasts top-notch beachfront restaurants from which you can rent bodyboards and surfboards for 20 pesos per hr.)*

PLAYA LA BOQUITA. The calmer waters of the *palapa*-lined **Playa la Boquita,** the westernmost point on the Juluapan Peninsula, make it a popular spot for children and water-sport enthusiasts. **Club Eureka** (☎336 57 02) is the last *palapa* on the shore. Be sure to make reservations for snorkeling excursions (2hr., 10am, 200 pesos), scuba diving excursions (2hr., 10am, 500 pesos), and deep sea fishing (7am or 8am, 350 pesos per hr.). If you're not much of a deep-sea enthusiast, try taking a horse for a sandy jaunt, available for rent near Club Eureka (150 pesos per hr.), or renting a banana boat for 30 pesos. *(Take a "Miramar" bus to Club Santiago (40min., 4 pesos). Walk through the white gate along the cobblestone street which becomes a dirt road; you'll hit the road after 25min. Taxis 15 pesos.)*

PLAYA AUDIENCIA. Also reveling in tranquility is **Playa Audiencia,** a small but magnificent cove with calm waters, light brown sand, a few small boats, and a gorgeous, rocky vista. *(Take a "Las Hadas" bus (4 pesos) from Niños Héroes or anywhere on Miramar Rte. to the Sierra Radison, then follow the path to the beach. The bus back offers a spectacular view of the peninsula.)*

NIGHTLIFE

Manzanillo doesn't sleep when the sun sets, and trendy, tourist-oriented clubs along the resort strip are open all hours, playing the latest music. "Miramar" buses run along the strip until around 9pm, and taxis back to the *centro* cost 30-50 pesos.

Colima Bay Café (☎333 11 50 or 333 18 30), Costera de la Madrid 5.5km, on the beach side. *The* place to be on a Saturday night. Two bars, a sizable dance floor, and a terrace overlooking the Pacific. Beer 21 pesos, national drinks 30-47 pesos. No cover, but 80 peso min. for drinks. Open M-Th 5pm-2am, F-Sa 5pm-4am.

Vog and Bar Félix (☎333 19 95 or 334 14 44), Costera de la Madrid 9.2km, on the beach side. Vog lets you get your groove on, while Bar Félix will have you throwing back beers and shooting pool. Trendy 20-somethings gallivant between the two. Beer 15 pesos, national drinks 25-30 pesos. Vog open F-Sa 11pm-7am, high season W-Sa. Bar Félix open W-M 7pm-2am.

Tropigala, Costera de la Madrid near Santiago Beach (☎333 24 74 or 75). After frolicking in the sun, throngs head to Tropigala to get down to live tropical music. The mixed-age crowd dances up an appetite, only to gorge on the all-you-can eat buffet (included in cover). Beer 22 pesos, national drinks 30-40 pesos. Open W-Su 9pm-4am.

CUYUTLÁN   ☎ 3

With its lush vegetation, black-sand beach, and mysterious lagoon, quiet Cuyutlán (pop. 1650) offers the traveler a few days of solitude. In the low season, darkened buildings and silent streets give the place a ghost-town feel; the huge golden head of Benito Juárez amidst the palm trees of Cuyutlán's *zócalo* is often the only face visible. Summer weekends are slightly busier, but it is only during the high tourist season (Dec. and *Semana Santa*) that Cuyutlán truly comes alive.

⊑ TRANSPORTATION. Cuyutlán is about an hour's ride down the coast from Manzanillo, off Mexico 200. The only way to get to Cuyutlán is through **Armería,** on the highway about 15km inland. From Manzanillo, take a "Colima" bus (45min., every 15min. 5am-10:30pm, 19 pesos) from the entrance of the station and ask to be let off at Armería. To reach the Terminal Sub-Urbana in Armería, get off at the blue "Paraíso" sign and follow the street to the left. Buses to Cuyutlán leave from here (20min., every 30min. 6:45am-7:30pm, 5 pesos). Buses return to Armería on the same schedule and pick up near the *zócalo*.

▰▱ ORIENTATION AND PRACTICAL INFORMATION. The road from Armería parallels the coast and becomes **Yavaros** as it enters town. It intersects **Hidalgo,** which runs by the east border of the *zócalo;* a left at this intersection takes you to the beach. **Veracruz,** Cuyutlán's other mighty boulevard, runs parallel to Yavaros, one block off the beach. Most of Cuyutlán's municipal services are within one block of the *zócalo*. **Currency Exchange:** the English-speaking owners of the **Hotel Fenix** will change money if they have the cash. **Police:** (☎326 40 14) 2 blocks from the *zócalo* on Hidalgo. The friendly officers also provide what little tourist information is available in town. **LADATELs** are located around the *zócalo* and the intersection of Hidalgo and Veracruz.

▰▱ ACCOMMODATIONS AND FOOD. Hotels are well-maintained, affordable and comfortable. During high season (mainly December and *Semana Santa*), rates skyrocket to 200 pesos per person; meals are included to help justify the price. Make reservations a month in advance during this time. The rooms at **Hotel Fenix,** Hidalgo 201, at Veracruz, may be taller than they are wide, but on the second story, they open to a breezy balcony with hammocks. The friendly, English-speaking owners run a popular bar that serves as the town watering hole. (☎326 40 82. 80-100 pesos per person). **Hotel Morelos,** Hidalgo 185, at Veracruz, has spacious rooms with clean baths and wooden furniture. Tiled floors, festive colors, a restaurant, a small pool, and all the artificial flowers in Cuyutlán give the place pizazz. (☎326 40 13. 180 per person including 3 meals, 80 pesos per person without meals.) Unofficial camping sites lie 200m from Cuyutlán's hotels. Some travelers string hammocks among the *palapas* near the hotels. For 5 pesos, campers and daytrippers can use the toilets and showers at Hotel Fenix. For 15 pesos, they can use the pool at Hotel Morelos. Almost all of the food in Cuyutlán is served up in **hotel restaurants;** seafood (40-70 pesos) is the obvious specialty.

▰▱ SIGHTS AND FESTIVALS. Aside from its gorgeous beach, Cuyutlán's biggest claim to fame is the **green wave,** a phenomenon that occurs regularly April through June. Quirky currents and phosphorescent marine life combine to produce 10m swells that glow an unearthly green. The town itself reaches high tide during the **Festival de la Virgen de Guadalupe,** the first 12 days of December when twice a day—at 6am and 6pm—men, women, and children clad in traditional dress walk 5km to the town's blue church. The celebrations peak on the twelfth day, when *mariachis* accompany the procession, and the marchers sing tributes to the Virgin. Cuyutlán's **Tortugario,** 3.5km east of town along Veracruz, is a combination wildlife preserve and zoo. Taxis will take you there for 40 pesos. Home to turtles, iguanas, and crocodiles, the Tortugario also has saltwater pools for (human) swimming. (Open daily 8:30am-5:30pm. 10 pesos, children 5 pesos.)

PARAÍSO
☎ 3

Paraíso outclasses its unsightly sister city, nearby **Armería**, but not by much. The city has good, black-sand beaches for swimming, but the lack of amenities and city beautification projects make it a less desirable getaway than Cuyutlán. Nevertheless, Paraíso is popular among Mexicans for daytrips and weekend vacations; during the high seasons (Dec. and Apr.) and on Sundays, the beachfront has a true family atmosphere and the town's single dirt road is crammed with buses and cars.

⌨ TRANSPORTATION. A well-paved road connects Armería and Paraíso, cutting through 7km of banana and coconut plantations before ending at the lava-black sands surrounding Paraíso's few hotels and beachfront restaurants. Follow the directions to Cuyutlán, but instead take a "Paraíso" bus (15min., every 30min. 6:45am-7:30pm, 5 pesos) from Armería's Terminal Sub-Urbano. Buses return on the same schedule, and honk as they leave town.

◨◪ ORIENTATION AND PRACTICAL INFORMATION. Besides the main road from Armería, Paraíso's other street is the dirt **Juventud** (also called **Adán y Eva**), which runs along the back of the beachfront restaurants. Long-distance **phone calls** can be made from **Abarrotes Valdovinos,** next to the bus stop. (☎322 00 25. Open daily 7am-10pm.) The **police station** (☎322 09 90) is 2 blocks up from Juventud on the main road. Basic medical attention can be found at the **Centro de Salud,** next to the police station.

▛▟ ACCOMMODATIONS AND FOOD. The first building on the beach to your left is **Hotel Equipales,** where you'll find no-frills rooms with a view of the shore. The cramped bathrooms leave much to be desired, especially since there is no hot water. (Singles and doubles 120 pesos; triples 150 pesos.) Farther to the left lies **Hotel Paraíso,** a cut above Equipales, but pricier. Spacious beachfront rooms have ceiling fans and cold showers. A jungle-theme mural adds a splash of color to the popular pool. (☎322 10 32. Singles 180 pesos, with hot water 250 pesos; 30 pesos each extra person.) At the opposite end of the strip lies **Posada Valencia,** where the beds are waist-high and the rooms are clean. Bright bedspreads make up for dark bathrooms. (Singles 80 pesos; doubles 120 pesos.) Paraíso's extensive beach makes a soft pillow for campers, and the Hotel Paraíso provides showers (5 pesos) and free access to bathrooms. Hotel Equipales also offers bathroom (1 peso) and shower access (5 pesos). Some *enramada* (beachside restaurant) owners may let you hang your hammock under their thatched roofs. During the high season, rooms may be available in **private houses;** ask in stores.

Restaurants run the slim gamut from rustic *enramadas* to cement-floored *comedores,* with freshly caught seafood dominating menus. **Restaurant Paraíso,** in the Hotel Paraíso, at the east end of Juventud, is more popular than the hotel pool. Uniformed waiters provide snappy service, and string quartets and *mariachis* sometimes appear in the afternoon. (Breakfast 18-28 pesos, tasty shrimp dishes 65 pesos. Open daily 8am-6pm.) The restaurant at **Hotel Equipales** also offers a pleasant atmosphere and reasonable prices.

COLIMA
☎ 3

With 160,000 residents, the capital of the state of Colima maintains a measure of small-town benevolence and informality. The streets and parks are magnificently groomed and the civic-minded inhabitants remarkably friendly in this, the first Spanish town in western Mexico. On Sundays, slews of stores close shop as families attend mass, walk in the park, or sit and listen to *mariachi* bands in the gazebo of the Plaza Principal. In the shadows of El Volcán de Fuego and El Nevado, Colima has experienced its fair share of natural disasters—many of its colonial buildings have, over the years, succumbed to the volcanoes. But, despite the looming giants, under-touristed Colima is blessed with cool mountain air, a string of museums, beautiful plazas and the Universidad de Colima, making it a beautiful place to stop on the way to or from the coast.

Colima

▲ ACCOMMODATIONS

Casa de Huespedes
Miramas, 3
Hospedajes del Rey, 4
Hotel Colonial, 1
Hotel La Merced, 2

N

0   200 yards
0   200 meters

Hospital Civil ✚

San Fernando

TO BUS TERMINAL
(1km)

Julio García

Farías

Valle

Gallardo

Sandoval

Museo
Universitario
de Artes
Populares

27 de Septiembre

Los Regalado

TO MUSEO DE LAS CULTURAS
DE OCCIDENTE, CASA DE LA
CULTURA (400m)

Corregidora

de los Pinos

Madre Selva

Paseo de la Rivera

Constitución

Barreda

Matamoros

Medina

Emilio Carranza

Herrera

Aldama

✚

Obregón

Sedán

Galindo

Corregidora

Allende

✝

Núñez

Domínguez

Cadenas

Álvarez

Guerrero

5 de Mayo

Nigromante

Venustiano Carranza

Constitución

Zaragoza

Torres
Quintero

Madero

✉

Jiménez

16 de
Septiembre

PLAZA
PRINCIPAL
(Jardín
Libertad)

Jardín
Quintero

Hidalgo

Jardín
Núñez

Teatro
Hidalgo ■

Museo
de Historia

Palacio
de Gobierno

$ ⓘ

2

3

Xicoténcatl

Cuauhtémoc

Independencia

Morelos

Juárez

Revolución

Rey Colimán

4

1

Bravo

Gómez

Degollado

de la Vega

TERMINAL SUBURBANA
(500m)

Abasolo

Galeana

Victoria

J. Jardín
J. Carranza
Juárez

Mirón

Parque
Regional

Reforma

Medellín

B. Juárez

Duck

Zoo

Pond

J. Torres

Javier Mina

Brizuela

✚
Centro de Salud

⌐ TRANSPORTATION

Airport: Aeropuerto Nacional Miguel de la Madrid (☎314 41 60 or 314 98 17), 2hr. from Colima. Served by **Aerocalifornia** (☎314 48 50) and **Aeroméxico** (☎313 80 57).

Bus: The main bus station is on the northeast side of town, about 2km from the *centro*. To get there, pick up a "Bital" or "Ruta 5" on Bravo, or "Ruta 4" on Zaragoza (every 5min. 6am-8:30pm, 2.5 pesos). From the station, Autobuses de Occidente (☎314 82 79) goes to: **Uruapan** (8hr., 8am and 10pm, 160 pesos) and **Mexico City** (12hr.; 5, 8am, 2, 10pm; 375 pesos) via **Zamora** (6hr., 103 pesos) and **Morelia** (8hr., 157 pesos). Autotransportes Sur de Jalisco (☎312 03 16) has 2nd-class service to **Manzanillo** (1½hr.; 6, 6:35, 7, 7:35, 11:45am; 34 pesos) via **Armería** (1hr., 19 pesos). Elite (☎312 84 99) sends 1st-class buses to **Mexico City** (10hr., 9:30 and 11pm, 414 pesos); **Hermosillo** (28hr., 5pm, 939 pesos) via **Mazatlán** (12hr., 418 pesos); and **Tijuana** (37hr., 5pm, 1200 pesos) via **Tepic** (6hr., 268 pesos). ETN (☎314 10 60) sends plush buses to the **Guadalajara airport** (2½hr., 3 and 9:30am, 155 pesos); **Guadalajara** (3hr., 8 per day 3am-7:30pm, 155 pesos); and **Morelia** (6hr., 11:45pm, 250 pesos). **Omnibus de México** (☎312 16 30) sends 1st-class buses to: **Aguascalientes** (6hr., 3:10pm, 256 pesos); **Mexico City** (10hr.; 7:45, 8:30, 10pm; 414 pesos); and **Monterrey** (15hr., 6:50pm, 524 pesos). Primera Plus/Flecha Amarilla (☎314 80 67) sends 1st-class buses to: **Aguascalientes** (5½hr., 4pm, 268 pesos); **Guadalajara** (3hr., about every hr. 5:15am-7:30pm, 118 pesos); **Manzanillo** (1¼hr., about every hr. 2am-11:40pm, 40 pesos); and **Mexico City** (10hr., 9 and 11:30pm, 430 pesos). Second-class service to **Querétaro** (8hr.; 9:30am, 12:30, 3:30, 10:30pm; 280 pesos). Another bus station, **Terminal Suburbana,** is southwest of the *centro*.

⌐ PRACTICAL INFORMATION

Tourist Office: Hidalgo 96 (☎312 43 60; fax 312 83 60; email turiscol@palmera.colimanet.com), on the corner of Hidalgo and Ocampo, between Plaza Principal and Jardín Núñez. Helpful staff, pamphlets, and maps. Open M-F 8:30am-8:30pm, Sa 10am-2pm.

Currency Exchange: Banamex, Hidalgo 90 (☎312 02 85), 1 block east of Plaza Principal, has a 24hr. **ATM.** Open M-F 9am-5pm. **Majapara Casa de Cambio,** Morelos 200 (☎314 89 98; fax 314 89 66), on the corner of Juárez at Jardín Núñez, has slightly better rates. Open M-F 9am-2pm and 4:30-7pm, Sa 9am-2pm.

Luggage Storage: At the bus station. 0.5 pesos per hr. Open M-Th 6am-10pm, F-Su 24hr. Restaurant can assist after hours.

Laundry: Lavandería Automática Amana, Domínguez 147, behind Hospedajes del Rey. 9 pesos per kg, 3kg minimum. Open daily 8am-9pm.

Emergency: ☎060.

Police: (☎312 09 67 or 312 25 66) Juárez at 20 de Noviembre.

Red Cross: (☎313 87 87) Aldama at Obregón. No English spoken. Open 24hr.

Pharmacy: Sangre de Cristo (☎314 74 74), Obregón 16 at Madero, 1 block northwest of Jardín Núñez. Some English spoken. Open 24hr.

Medical Assistance: Hospital Civil (☎312 02 27), San Fernando at Zandoval. **Centro de Salud** (☎312 00 64 or 312 32 38), Juárez at 20 de Noviembre.

Fax: Telecomm, Madero 243 (☎312 60 64), in the same building as the post office. Open M-F 8am-7:30pm, Sa 9am-noon.

Telephones: LADATELs abound in the plazas. Long-distance **caseta,** Revolución 99 (☎313 83 70 fax 312 71 14), at Morelos on the southeast corner of Jardín Núñez. Open daily 8am-10pm.

Internet Access: Colegio Nacional de Capacitación Intensiva, Hidalgo 83 (☎312 01 50), off the southeast corner of Jardín Quintero. 20 pesos per hr. Open M-F 7am-9pm, Sa 9am-2pm. **CiberCafé,** Sevilla del Rio 80, on the second floor of Plaza Country Mall, next to the movie theater. Follow Sandoval past Fernando and turn left on Sevilla del Rio. 25 pesos per hr., 20 pesos for students with ID. Open daily 9am-10pm.

Post Office: Madero 247 (☎312 00 33), on the northeast corner of the Jardín Núñez. Open M-F 9am-5pm, Sa 8am-2pm. **Postal Code:** 28001.

ACCOMMODATIONS

Cheap lodging may be found near the Jardín Núñez, while higher-priced hotels cluster by the university. Rooms are generally well-kept and come with TVs.

Hotel Colonial, Medellín 142F (☎313 08 77), between Morelos and Bravo, 2 blocks south of Jardín Quintero. Friendly staff. Rooms have fans, wicker chairs, wrought-iron beds, and spotless baths. Singles 90-120 pesos; doubles 100-140 pesos.

Hotel La Merced, Juárez 82 (☎312 69 69 or 314 27 34), on the west side of Jardín Nuñez. This comfortable hotel in the middle of everything offers immaculate, decent-sized rooms with fans and wooden furniture. Its private parking lot makes it popular with families passing through town. Singles 120 pesos; doubles 150 pesos.

Hospedajes del Rey, Rey Colimán 125 (☎313 36 83), half a block from the southeast corner of Jardín Núñez. "Fit for a king" couldn't describe it better: enormous, plush rooms have fans, cable TVs, tiled floors, and wall-to-wall windows. You could eat off the bathroom floors. Singles 180 pesos; doubles 200 pesos; triples 270 pesos.

Casa de Huéspedes Miramar, Morelos 265 (☎312 34 67), off the southeast corner of Jardín Núñez. A friendly family-run *posada* with breezy but decaying rooms. The bathrooms could use a good scrub. Singles 50 pesos, with bath 60 pesos; doubles 60 pesos, with bath 70 pesos.

FOOD

Because of the town's lack of tourism, restaurant fare in Colima consists of inexpensive and authentic Mexican meals with traditional favorites like *pozole blanco* and *sopitos*. A few pricey joints adjoin Plaza Principal, but a jaunt down the smaller side streets will lead to budget meals aplenty.

Samadhi, Medina 125 (☎313 24 98), 2½ blocks north of Jardín Núñez. Walk up Juárez; Samadhi is next to the red and white church. Delicious vegetarian cuisine served in a leafy courtyard. The service is a little slow, but the food is worth it. Breakfast buffet 27.5 pesos, soy burger and fries 20 pesos. Open F-W 8am-10pm, Th 8am-5pm.

Comedor Familiar El Trébol, 16 de Septiembre 59 (☎312 29 00), at Degollado on the Plaza Principal. A popular and cheap family spot. Modest *comida corrida* 18 pesos, breakfast 10-18 pesos. Open Su-F 8am-11pm.

Los Naranjos, Barreda 34 (☎312 00 29), almost a block north of Madero, northeast of Jardín Quintero. A classy but comfortable restaurant. Magazine-perusing baby-boomers sip coffee over bright orange tablecloths. Breakfast 9-29 pesos, *pollo a la mexicana* 27 pesos, *antojitos* 9-26 pesos. Open daily 8am-11:30pm.

Cenaduría Selecta de Morelos, Morelos 292 (☎312 93 32), at Domínguez, 1 block off the southeast corner of Jardín Núñez. Delicious and cheap. Both *pozole* (pork stew) and *enchiladas dulces* (sweet enchiladas) come with a mountain of diced onions and fiery sauce (14 pesos). Open Tu-F 5-11pm, Sa-Su 1-11pm.

SIGHTS

While most visitors come to Colima primarily to explore the natural wonders nearby, the sage traveler will take advantage of Colima's quiet, untouristed Plaza Principal and discover the quality sights the city itself has to offer.

PLAZA PRINCIPAL. The gazebo and fountains of the plaza (officially the **Jardín Libertad**) is bordered on the north side by the **Palacio de Gobierno,** which contains historical murals within. The double arcade around the plaza contains the **Museo Regional de Historia de Colima,** the city's newest museum and home to a respectable collection of pre-Hispanic ceramics and a creepy replica of a western Mesoamerican burial site. In the same courtyard is an eclectic art gallery. *(Portal Morelos 1 at 16 de Septiembre and Reforma, on the south side of the Plaza. Museum ☎312 92 28. Open Tu-Sa 9am-6pm, Su 5-8pm; Su free.)*

SANTA IGLESIA CATHEDRAL. The Spanish first built a church on this spot in 1527, but an earthquake destroyed the original wood-and-palm structure, and a fire destroyed its replacement. Undeterred, the Spanish built the current church, whose neoclassical interior sparkles with gilt paint, chandeliers, polished marble, and statues. A statue of San Felipe de Jesús, the city's patron saint, resides in the pulpit designed by Othón Bustos. *(Adjoining Colima's Palacio de Gobierno on the east side of the Plaza. ☎312 02 00. Open daily 6am-2pm and 4:30-8:30pm.)*

TEATRO HIDALGO. Completed in 1883, yet unmarred by the passage of time, the theater's four tiers of side-seating almost touch the high ceiling, and its swooping red curtains lend the stage 19th-century ambience. Inquire at the tourist office for performance schedules. *(1 block down Degollado, to your right as you face the Cathedral.)*

MUSEO UNIVERSITARIO DE ARTES POPULARES. This museum has collections of stunning traditional dresses and masks, figurines recovered from nearby tombs, and descriptions of the pre-Aztec western coast. A gift shop sells handmade reproductions of local ceramics. *(At Barreda and Gallardo. Catch the #7 bus (2.50 pesos) on Barreda between Zaragoza and Guerrero, or walk 15min. north on 16 de Septiembre from the Plaza. ☎312 68 69. Open Tu-Sa 10am-2pm and 5-8pm, Su 10am-1pm. 10 pesos, children 5 pesos, students free; Su free.)*

PARQUE REGIONAL METROPOLITANO. This park offers afternoon strolls along a man-made duck pond, home to 2 large, brazen pelicans. A miniature **zoo** houses monkeys, crocodiles, and lions in disturbingly small cages. *(On Degollado, 4 blocks south of the Plaza. ☎314 16 76. Zoo open daily 7am-7pm. 1.50 pesos. Pool and waterslide open Tu-Su 10:30am-4:30pm. 6 pesos, children 4.50 pesos. Waterslide and boat rides 7.50 pesos per hr., children 5 pesos.)*

MUSEO DE LAS CULTURAS DE OCCIDENTE. The museum features the playful and captivating Colima ceramic figures, rarely seen outside the state, and provides an excellent Spanish narrative of the artifacts' significance to indigenous culture. The **Casa de la Cultura,** at the same site, is the best source of information on cultural events in Colima. *(Galván at Ejército Nacional, an easy ride from the centro. Take the yellow "Ruta #3 Sur" bus (2.5 pesos) on Colimán at Jardín Núñez, or a taxi (7 pesos). ☎313 06 08. Museum open Tu-Su 9am-6:30pm. 15 pesos. Casa de la Cultura open daily 8:30am-9pm.)*

PINOCATECA UNIVERSITARIA. The center displays the artwork of students and local painters, and provides performance spaces for theater, music and poetry readings. For a schedule of events, call the office. *(Guerrero 35 at Barreda. ☎312 22 28. Open Tu-Sa 10am-2pm and 5-8pm, Su 10am-1pm.)*

◪ NIGHTLIFE

Erupting volcanoes aren't the only things shaking in Colima. Hot nightclubs pull in locals and students with cheap beer and fast music. For something more relaxing, Colima offers 2 movie theaters, both along Tecnológico/Sevilla del Río. Plaza Country (☎312 01 73) and Plaza Diamante (☎311 32 13, next to Soriana) show contemporary, usually US-made movies (22 pesos).

 Argenta, Sevilla del Río 615 (☎313 80 12), a 15-peso cab from the *centro*. The place to be if you know you're cool and you can dance. Huge TV screen, lofty balcony, alternative crowd, and good ambience. W-Th no cover, 2 for 1 beers until midnight. F-Sa cover 30 pesos for men, free for women. Open W-Sa 10pm-3am.

La Velisaria, Domínguez 479 (☎312 86 88), a 10-peso cab from the Plaza. Although there is no dance floor to speak of, the young crowd has no qualms about dancing between the tables. With the music blaring, don't expect to have meaningful conversation. Cover W 30 pesos women, 100 pesos men; F 30 pesos women, 80 pesos men; Sa 25 pesos women, 50 pesos men; open bar W and Sa. Open W-Sa 10pm-3am.

Danza, Colón 113 (☎312 08 14). Colima's only gay night club is actually in the next town over, Villa de Álvarez, a 20- or 25-peso cab ride from the Plaza. Though on the small side, the pool table, Madonna posters, and great dance music will have you entertained. Transvestite shows F-Sa 2am. Cover F-Sa 25 pesos. Open Th-Su 9pm-4am.

Aha, Béjar 903 (☎313 77 08), in the southeast end of town, a 15-peso cab from the *centro*. For those not easily frightened. The smoke-filled, dark club has glowing eyes greeting you at the entrance. The loud music will have you vibrating on the spacious dance floor. Th open bar until 1am; cover 80 pesos men, 30 pesos after 1am; women 30 pesos after 1am; F no cover; Sa cover 30 pesos. Open Th-Sa 6pm-3am.

Dalí, the Casa de la Cultura's cafe. Melancholy tunes pierce the air and wrench the heart, as prints from the surrealist master himself drip from the walls under dim, smoky lights. Food isn't exactly cheap, but it's worth it just to drink beer while a *tocador* wails from the cafe's small platform, a guitar cradled in his arms (9-11pm). *Muy romántico.* Beer 10-12 pesos, national drinks 20 pesos and up. Open daily 5:30pm-midnight.

■ DAYTRIPS FROM COLIMA

If you want to commune with nature, feel the heat of the nearby volcanoes, or relax by serene lakes and quiet towns, Colima serves as an ideal base. This is where the wild things are.

VOLCANOES

To get to El Fuego, take a Guadalajara-bound bus from the new bus station to the town of **Atenquique,** *57km away. From here, a 27km dirt road runs to the summit. The trip is only recommended for 4x4 vehicles, though logging trucks make trips to spots near the summit. You can get to El Nevado by car or bus. Autobuses Sur de Jalisco (☎312 03 16) runs from Colima to* **Guzmán,** *83km away (1hr., approx. every hr. 4:20am-8:30pm, 43 pesos). Buses from Guzmán limp up to Joya, from which you can make your epic summit assault.*

In Náhuatl, Colima means "place where the old god is dominant." The old god is **El Volcán de Fuego** (3960m), 25km from Colima City. Puffs of white smoke continuously billow from the volcano, and lava was visible in 1994, when El Fuego reasserted its status as an active volcano. (Fear not—the tourist office assures visitors that the volcano is not a threat to the city.) The nearby and slightly taller **El Nevado de Colima** (4335m) earned its name from the blanket of snow draping it in the winter. The park is open sporadically; if you're planning a trip to the top, call the Dirección de Pública for information. (☎312 02 01. Open 24hr.) You can also call the police (☎312 18 01). The ascent should not be attempted solo, or by those without sufficent hiking experience. It's especially dangerous during the rainy season.

LAGOONS

Take the "Ruta 2" bus (2.50 pesos) in Colima to the Terminal Suburbano, where green buses destined for San Antonio, La Becerrera, or Zapotitlán make the bumpy ride to La Becerrera (1½hr.; 7am, 1:20, 2:40, and 5pm; 10 pesos). From the La Becerrera bus stop, follow the wooden sign that says "La María" (a 15min. hike). Buses back leave from the same crossroads (8am, 3, 4:30pm).

The waters and banks of **Laguna Carrizalillo** teem with life. Birds keep a constant twitter in the trees, while lizards and frogs leap underfoot, making the beautiful spot 27km north of Colima a peaceful retreat from the city. Larger, closer to the volcanoes, and more visited is **Laguna La María,** whose green waters and dense plant life attract flocks of ornithologists in search of tiny yellow Singing Henkins. Fishing equipment is available for rent (25-30 pesos per hr.).

THE HILLS ARE ALIVE In your travels, you have probably marveled at intricate bead work designs on carved bowls and masks. The masters behind the artwork are the Huichol Indians, considered Mexico's oldest indigenous group. More than 15,000 Huichol still live in rural mountain regions, entering towns to sell their work. The **Comunidad Cultural Huichol** in San Blas is a non-profit organization that provides a non-exploitative forum for the Huichol artists as an attempt to perpetuate the market for their products. For the best prices, buy works straight from the artist stands themselves, not from expensive stores.

COMALA

Green buses head to Comala from Colima's Terminal Suburbano (45min., every 15min. 6am-10:30pm, 3.50 pesos). Taxis charge 30 pesos.

South of the lagoons and just 9km north of Colima is the picturesque town of Comala, known as "El Pueblo Blanco de America" (The White Town of America) for the original white facade of its buildings. The town's lovely *zócalo* is full of white benches, fountains, and orange trees and is bordered by cobblestone streets and lively restaurants serving *ponche* (warm rum-and-fruit-punch), one of the region's traditional drinks. The city's main claim to fame, however, is its colony of indigenous artisans who craft wooden furniture and bamboo baskets. The **Cooperativa Artesenal Pueblo Blanco,** a small *tianguis* (market), stands just outside Comala's *centro*, 200m past the restaurants on Progreso, a 20min. walk from the *zócalo*. (☎315-5600. Open M-Sa 8am-4pm.)You can also find *artesanía* at the southeast corner of the *zócalo*.

To the east of the *zócalo* lies the **Iglesia San Miguel del Espíritu Santo** with its beautiful, sky-blue vaulted ceiling and dozens of pigeons. On the other side of the *zócalo* are the city offices, with a four-wall **mural** commemorating Comala's 130 years and celebrating the "richness of its soil." Unfortunately, the birds who now control the church have graciously added their own artistic expression to the mural. For more information, contact Jorge Eduardo Torres, Director of Education, Culture, and Tourism, in the building south of the *zócalo*, next to Los Portales restaurant. (☎315-5547. Available M-F 8:30am-2:30pm and 5-8pm, Sa 8:30am-2:30pm.)

Ask a taxi driver to take you to Colima's famous *magnético*—a segment of road where cars can have their engines turned off but still appear to run uphill. Optical illusion or freak of science, it's buckets o' fun.

SOUTHERN PACIFIC COAST

Because many of the region's indigenous Purépecha lived by rod and net, the Aztecs called the lands surrounding Lake Pátzcuaro **Michoacán** (Country of Fishermen). The distinctive Purépecha language (a variant of which is still spoken) and the terraced agricultural plots have convinced scholars that the Purépecha were not originally indigenous, but in fact immigrants from what is today Peru. Purépecha rule lasted from around AD 800, when they first settled Michoacán, to 1522, when the Spanish arrived. Michoacán's red, fertile soil, abundant rain, and mild weather make for bountiful crops, and agriculture swells the state's coffers. The gorgeous beaches and forested mountain ranges serve as prime attractions for wildlife enthusiasts and tourists.

The state of **Guerrero** has been blessed with good fortune. During the colonial period, the rich mining town of Taxco kept the state and most of New Spain swimming in silver. More recently, the state's riches have come from the rugged shores of the Pacific coast. In the 1950s, Acapulco became the darling of the international resort scene, and, almost four decades later, wallflower Ixtapa and even quieter Zihuatanejo are beginning to fill their older sister's role.

Oaxaca has been fractured into a crazy quilt by the rugged heights of the Sierra Madre del Sur. Despite its intimidating terrain, the land has inspired a violent possessiveness in the many people—Zapotecs, Mixtecs, Aztecs, and Spaniards—who have fought and died for the region. More than 200 indigenous tribes have occupied the valley over the past two millennia. Over one million *oaxaqueños* still speak an *indígena* language as a mother tongue, and more than 20% of the state's population speaks no Spanish whatsoever. This language barrier, and the cultural gap that it symbolizes and exacerbates, has long caused tensions between the Spanish-speaking Oaxacan government and its indigenous population.

HIGHLIGHTS OF THE SOUTHERN PACIFIC COAST

CHILL in **Puerto Escondido** (see p. 483) and nearby **Zipolite** (see p. 479), which draw legions of backpackers ready to sun, surf, and smoke on the beach.

EXPLORE the site of **Monte Albán** (see p. 470), the home to the most important Pre-Hispanic ruins in the region and some of the best preserved in Mexico.

SIP hot chocolate in Oaxaca (see p. 453), one of the most attractive cities in the country. Its international student population, temperate weather, and gorgeous location drive foreign and national visitors wild.

SAVE UP for **Taxco** (see p. 435), which not only offers silver, but narrow streets, dazzling mountain views, and the beautiful **Catedral de Santa Prisca** (see p. 438).

SUNBATHE in the beautiful **Barra de Potosí** (see p. 446) and other beaches along the northern **Guerrero coast** (see **Costa Grande** p. 446), or even at aging, ultra-corny **Acapulco** (see p. 447).

GET TO KNOW the inseparable combo of **Ixtapa** (see p. 441) and **Zihuatanejo** (see p. 441) and marvel at the size of the western hemisphere's largest Club Med.

HIDE OUT in the gorgeous beaches of the stormy **Michoacán coast** (see p. 433), which boast powerful waves, privacy, and rugged terrain.

BROWSE through the amazing variety of regional handicrafts in the quiet mountain jewel of **Pátzcuaro** (see p. 418) and the **nearby area** (see p. 422).

MICHOACÁN DE OCAMPO

URUAPAN   ☎ 4

Surrounded by red soil, rolling hills, and rows upon rows of avocado trees, Uruapan (ur-AH-pan; pop. 300,000) sits on a checkerboard of farmland wrested from
the surrounding jungle and mountains. Mountain air and plenty of rain keep the
city lush and green year-round. Farmers and their families come to Uruapan to sell
their produce and buy wristwatches and modern contrivances. While Uruapan is
developing into an important center of commerce, the surrounding countryside
remains a naturalist's dream. Tourists come to Uruapan in droves to explore the
nearby waterfall, national park, and **Paricutín Volcano.**

▐ TRANSPORTATION

Uruapan lies 120km west of Morelia and 320km southeast of Guadalajara. To
reach the *centro* from the **bus station** on Juárez in the northeast corner of town,
hail a **taxi** (18 pesos) or hop aboard a "Centro" bus—later in the day, you may have
to wait at the bus stop on the street in front of the bus station (6am-9pm; 3 pesos).
Primera Plus/Flecha Amarilla (☎ 524 39 82) sends first-class buses to **Guadalajara**
(4½hr., 6 buses 12:30am-10:45pm, 146 pesos); **Morelia** (1½hr., 8 buses 6:45am-mid-
night, 70 pesos); **Querétaro** (5hr.; 1, 2:15, 9:45pm, midnight; 175 pesos); **San Luis
Potosí** (8hr., 9am and midnight, 287 pesos); and **Zamora** (2hr., 5 per day 12:30am-
11:45pm, 60 pesos). Second-class service to **Aguascalientes** (10hr., 7:30am, 210
pesos); **Guadalajara** (4½hr., 7am and 3:15pm, 106 pesos); **Mexico City** (7hr.; 5:45,
7:20am, 6:45, 7:10pm; 190 pesos); **Morelia** (1¾hr., 6 per day 5:10am-6:45pm, 57
pesos); **Pátzcuaro** (1hr., 6 per day 5am-6:45pm, 28 pesos); **Querétaro** (5hr., 7:10pm,
144 pesos); **San Luis Potosí** (7½hr., 5:10 and 9:30am, 231 pesos); and **Zamora** (2hr.,
about every hr. 6am-3:15pm, 43 pesos). La Linea (☎ 523 18 71) sends first-class
buses to **Guadalajara** (3½hr., 7 per day 1am-midnight, 132 pesos) and second-class
to **Guadalajara** (5-6hr., 6 per day about every 2hr. 6:30am-2:45pm, 116 pesos). Elite
(☎ 523 44 67) sends first-class buses to: **Mazatlán** (12hr., 6:30 and 8:30pm, 430
pesos); **Monterrey** (15hr., 7pm, 1562 pesos); and **Zihuatanejo** (8hr., 12:30am, 196
pesos). Ruta Paraíso/Galeana (☎ 523 02 82) sends second-class buses to: **Pátzcuaro**
(1hr., every 15min. 4am-midnight, 28 pesos); **Los Reyes** (2hr., every hr., 6am-8pm,
28 pesos); and **San Juan Nuevo** (40min., every 10min. 6am-8:30pm, 5 pesos).

▐ PRACTICAL INFORMATION

Tourist Office: Subdirección de Turismo Municipal, E. Carranza 44 (☎ 524 30 91), in
the Casa de Turismo about 3 blocks from the *zócalo.* The friendly folks here provide
good maps. Open daily 9am-7pm. If you arrive in Uruapan on a weekend, you can go to
the **information booth** in the bus station for the same maps (Sa-Su 9:30am-6pm).

Currency Exchange: Bancomer, Carranza 7 (☎ 524 14 60), offers good exchange rates
and a 24hr. **ATM.** Open M-F 8:30am-5:30pm, Sa 10am-2pm. A block south of the
zócalo on Cupatitzio, many banks have competitive exchange rates and ATMs.

Luggage Storage: At the bus station; 5 pesos per bag per day. Open daily 7am-11pm.

Laundry: Autoservicio de Lavandería, Carranza 47 (☎ 520 99 38), at García, 4 blocks
west of the *zócalo.* Wash and dry 3kg per 30 pesos. Open M-Sa 9am-2pm and 4-8pm.

Emergency: ☎ 060.

Police: (☎ 523 27 33), at Eucaliptos and Naranjo. Some English spoken.

Medical Services: Hospital Civil, San Miguel 6 (☎ 523 36 17), 7 blocks west of the
northern edge of the *zócalo.* The **Red Cross,** Del Lago 1 (☎ 524 15 88), is one block
from the hospital. No English spoken. Both open 24hr.

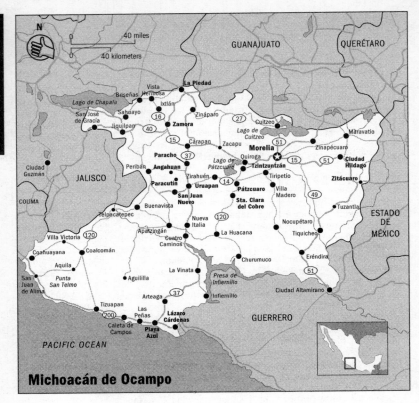

Michoacán de Ocampo

Pharmacy: Farmacia Guadalajara, Carranza 3 (☎524 27 11). Also a mini supermarket. Open 24hr.

Internet Access: Logicentro, Juárez 57 (☎524 94 94 or 524 77 40). 20 pesos per hr. Open M-Sa 9am-9pm.

Post Office: Reforma 13 (☎523 56 30), 3 blocks south of the *zócalo* on Cupatitzio and one block left. Open M-F 8am-3pm, Sa 9am-1pm. **Postal Code:** 60000.

Telephones: LADATELs line the plaza. Otherwise, make long-distance phone calls or fax from **Computel,** Ocampo 3 (☎527 17 11), on the plaza. Open daily 7am-10pm.

ACCOMMODATIONS

The place to stay in Uruapan is on or near the *zócalo*, where the ritzy and affordable coexist. Straying too far could be hazardous to your health: Uruapan's cheaper hotels, oozing east of the *zócalo*, tend to be filthy, sleazy, and infested.

■ **Hotel del Parque,** Independencia 124 (☎524 38 45), 5½ blocks from the plaza and half a block from the beautiful Parque Nacional. Far and away the best place in Uruapan. Large rooms surround an airy patio. Squeaky clean bathrooms are popular with backpackers—the sitting room with cable TV in the courtyard is a great place to meet them. Singles 80 pesos, doubles 120 pesos, triples 140 pesos.

Uruapan

▲ ACCOMMODATIONS

Hotel del Parque, 1
Hotel Los Tres Caballos, 3
Hotel Moderno, 4
Hotel Oseguera, 5
Hotel Villa de Flores, 2

Hotel Moderno, Degollado 4 (☎524 02 12), next door to the Hotel Oseguera on the eastern side of the *zócalo*. A semi-shabby place, but peach-colored rooms with dark wood furniture are OK. Birds, both live and stuffed, keep watch over the lobby TV. Get used to the jingle of the electric pony ride at the front door. Singles 50 pesos, doubles 100 pesos.

Hotel Los Tres Caballeros, Constitución 50 (☎524 71 70). Go north up Degollado (the eastern border of the *zócalo* to the right of the church), then plunge into the depths of the market for about 2 blocks; the hotel is on the right before you emerge at 16 de Septiembre. Red tile floors and stone stairways lend subtle charm. Rooms are very clean, but the tiny bathrooms might cramp your style and your legs. Singles 60 pesos, doubles 100 pesos, triples 130 pesos.

Hotel Oseguera, Degollado 2 (☎523 98 56), on the eastern side of the *zócalo*. The floors and walls are painted every shade of pastel green, but this does little to enliven the dreary rooms. Bathrooms are miniscule and could use a good wash, but there's hot water and some rooms have balconies. Singles 60 pesos, doubles 120 pesos.

Hotel Villa de Flores, Carranza 15 (☎524 28 00), less than 2 blocks west of the *zócalo*. It ain't the Hilton, but probably the best bet for a reasonably priced upscale hotel. Flores lives up to its name with a beautiful flower-dappled courtyard with glowing pink walls. Singles 225 pesos, doubles 295 pesos, triples 325 pesos.

FOOD

Eating near the *zócalo* is a good bet. The bountiful farmland surrounding Uruapan means delicious avocado, tomato, and mango dishes are available in town for next to nothing. Coffee is a local specialty, and most places serve it strong and hot.

Mercado de Antojitos, between Constitución and V. Carranza, on the north side of the *zócalo* (look for the sign to the left of the church). An outdoor square where dozens of eager restaurateurs vie for your taste buds with unique house specialties for about 18-25 pesos; even cheaper prices can be found in some of the small restaurants near the *mercado.* Open daily 9am-9pm; some stands open a little earlier.

Comedor Vegeteriano, Morelos 14 at Aldama, 1 block south of Carranza and about 3 blocks east of the *zócalo.* A variety of *licuados,* including concoctions for stomach problems and colds (7-10 pesos); soy *milanesa tortas* (13 pesos). Open M-Sa 9am-6pm, Su 1-6pm.

Café Tradicional de Uruapan, E. Carranza 5B, (☎523 56 80), west of the *zócalo.* Follow your nose to the Tradicional, where locals sip their *café* so slowly they might lose a race with a second-class Mexican train. Dining here is like sitting inside a cigar box—the cafe's entire surface area is covered in richly stained wood. Enjoy a sandwich (18-27 pesos) along with a wide variety of coffee (8-23 pesos) and ice cream drinks (26 pesos); breakfast 21-42 pesos. Open daily 8:30am-10pm.

Jugos California, Independencia 9, just off the *zócalo.* Get your health food kicks under artificial palms while imbibing *licuados* (15-18 pesos), *tortas* (11-18 pesos), fruit, yogurt, and breakfast specials. Open daily 7am-10pm.

ENTERTAINMENT AND NIGHTLIFE

Most of the dazzling sights of Uruapan are outside the city. However, if you're anxious to see what this city itself has to offer, be sure to visit the **Parque Nacional Barranca del Cupatitzio.** A stunning bit of jungle right on the edge of town, the park brims with waterfalls, dense vegetation, and shaded cobblestone walkways. A fish farm inside the park allows you to fish (40 pesos per hr.). The park is on San Miguel, at the western end of Independencia. (☎524 01 97. Open daily 8am-6pm. 6 pesos, children 3-10 years and adults over 70 years 4 pesos.) Though it may be tempting to get lost in the jungle, the art exhibits, occasional movie screenings, and archaeological and historical museum at the **Casa de Cultura,** Ortiz 1, off the north side of the *zócalo,* are quite worthwhile. (Open daily 10am-8pm.)

Much of the after-hours scene is set in cafes. **Café Sol y Luna,** Independencia 15A, about two blocks west of the *zócalo,* is a great place to hang out with a drink and the locals while listening to live music. Email your friends in the adjacent internet room. (☎524 06 29. Live music F-Sa night. Internet 25 pesos per hr. Coffee 9-17 pesos, beer 15 pesos. Open daily 10am-11pm.) The main *discotecas* in Uruapan, **La Scala** and **Euforias,** both at Puertas de Capitzio 12 in Colonia Huerta del Cupatitzio, are just outside of town on the road to Tzaráracua, a 20-peso cab ride from the *centro.* A young, local crowd dances to US Top 40 and Mexican dance tunes at La Scala. (☎524 26 09. Cover 20 pesos Tu-F; 40 pesos Sa-Su. Open Tu-Su 6pm-3am.) A more sophisticated crowd parties at the more upscale Euforias. (☎524 26 32. Cover 40 pesos after 10pm for women, men 100 pesos all night. Th and Su open bar. Open Th-Su 9pm-3am.)

DAYTRIPS FROM URUAPAN

Uruapan is a convenient place from which to explore the interior of Michoacán. The diverse landscape is home to everything from ill-tempered volcanoes to picture-perfect waterfalls. If you're tired of appreciating natural things, check out the immensely revered image of Christ in **San Juan Nuevo** that was rescued by the whole village after a volcano. In nearby **Paracho,** a world-famous guitar competition rages for two weeks in August.

PARICUTÍN VOLCANO

From the bus station, take a Ruta Paraíso/Galeana bus to Angahuán, headed for Los Reyes (☎ 523 02 82. 30min, every hr. 6am-8pm, 10 pesos). From your stop, you have a 3km walk to the Centro Turístico on the other side of the village. Go straight down the main road, go right at the market and left at the sign that points for the Centro Turístico. To return, wait for buses on the other side of the stop (on the half hr.; last bus 8:30pm.)

A visit to the still-active Paricutín Volcano makes a great daytrip from Uruapan. In 1943 the volcano began erupting, and by the time it quit spewing lava eight years later, there was little dust left to settle—the land had been coated in a thick layer of porous lava. Entire towns had been consumed and a 700m mountain had sprung up. The lava covered the entire village of San Juan, save part of the church, which now sticks out of a field of cold, black stone. At the Angahuán **Centro Turístico** (☎ 452 0 87 86, open daily 9am-7pm), you can rent horses (180 pesos). Plan to get an early start to avoid the frequent afternoon thunderstorms, and bring warm clothing just in case. The trip is long but worth the time (4.5 km to the church and 13km to the volcano). If you decide to tackle the volcano on your own, take care and ask directions first—trails are very poorly marked. The Centro Turistico has a small museum (8 pesos) and restaurant. Cabins are available for rent from the tourist center (1-6 people 400 pesos; bunks 70 pesos).

SAN JUAN NUEVO PARANGARICUTIRO

From Urupan, take a Ruta Paraíso/Galeana bus to San Juan Nuevo (40min., every 10min. 6am-8:30pm, 5 pesos). To get back, wait for the same bus on the corner of Cárdenas and Iturbe 2 blocks up from the cathedral.

Ten kilometers west of Uruapan is San Juan Nuevo, founded after the destruction of the old village by the Paricutín Volcano in 1943. Many devotees come to the village for one reason—to see the **Lord of Miracles,** an image of Christ dating back to the late 16th century. When the volcano erupted, San Juan's 2000 inhabitants abandoned the village and began a three-day, 33km pilgrimage carrying their beloved icon. A beautiful rose brick sanctuary with pastel tiles was eventually built to house the image. The interior's white walls and vaulted ceilings are adorned with gold leaf, delicate stained-glass windows, and sparkling chandeliers. Not quite as refined is the gaudy blue neon sign above the statue that reads "*Sí de los Milagros, en ti confío*" ("Lord of Miracles, I trust in you." Open daily 6am-8pm; mass held on Su about every hr. 6:30am-1:30p and, 5-7pm.) The **museum,** Av. 20 de Noviembre, a block past the cathedral down the street to the left, has photos of the eruption as well as before-and-after shots of the village. (Open M-F 10am-6:30pm, Sa-Su 9am-6:30pm. Free.)

San Juan has little to offer besides its church and icon. The best dining option in San Juan is not to dine in San Juan, but a **mercado** in front of the cathedral does offer *artesanía* at good prices. If you're stranded in here, the **Hotel Victoria,** Cárdenas 26, across from the cathedral, will take you in. Clean, large rooms with TV, some with a cathedral view. (☎ 594 00 10. Singles 120 pesos, doubles 180 pesos.)

TZARÁRACUA AND TZARARECUITA

"Zapata-Tzaráracua" buses leave from the south side of Urupan's zócalo (every hr. 7am-5pm, 4 pesos). During the week, the schedule is unpredictable; Su is a bit more reliable. Meet the return bus in the parking lot. Taxis 40 pesos.

The waterfalls at **Tzaráracua** (sah-RA-ra-kwa), 10km from Uruapan, cascade 20m into small pools, surrounded by lush vegetation. The first waterfall, Tzaráracua, is about 1km from the parking lot. Walk down the steps to the right or ride a horse, if you have one, down the rocky path to the left (40 pesos). At the main waterfall look but don't swim—there's a dangerous undercurrent. Walk over the water on the bridge or ask a worker to take you in a suspended boxcar. (Open daily 9am-6pm. 4 pesos, parking 5 pesos, 2 pesos for cable car.)

Tzararecuita, a waterfall with two smaller pools perfect for swimming, is another 1.5km beyond the larger pool. It's okay to swim buck naked if you heart demands. The aid of a guide is necessary to find the falls since there are many confusing trails. Most children will ask 40-60 pesos, but you can probably find something cheaper. Though it's not recommended, to attempt it alone, walk up the hill on the left at Tzarácua and continue down the other side of the river.

LOS CHORROS DE VARRAL

From the Uruapan station, take a Ruta Paraíso/Galeana (☎523 02 82) bus to Los Reyes (2hr., every hr. 6am-8pm, 28 pesos). Once in Los Reyes, head for the centro and grab a "Los Pallilos" combi (1hr., every 2hr. 7am-7pm, 8 pesos) on Bravo near the temple.

Los Chorros de Varral is an area of beautiful waterfalls and pristine vegetation— unfortunately it's more than three hours from Uruapan. From where the *combi* stops, it's 4km and 1000 steps down to a series of three waterfalls; make sure to tell the driver where you want to get off.

PARACHO

Hop on a Flecha Amarilla (☎524 39 82) bus bound for Zamora via Paracho (45min., every hr. 6am-3:15pm, 10 pesos).

Thirty kilometers north of Uruapan, **Paracho** gives aspiring *guitarristas* a chance to strum their hearts out and unleash the *mariachi* within. Carefully crafted six-strings pack just about every store, and fantastic bargains are available for all varieties of guitar. For two weeks in August, the town holds an internationally renowned **guitar festival.** Musicians and craftspeople partake in a musical dervish of classical concerts, fireworks, dancing, and strumming competitions. A smaller, one-day music fest occurs on October 22, in honor of Santa Ursula.

The main street in town is **20 de Noviembre,** which runs by the plaza and the market and is the site of the bus stop. The **Casa de Arte y Cultura,** on the corner of the plaza, has displays on (who could have guessed it?) guitars. (Supposedly open daily 10am-8pm.)

ZAMORA ☎3

Founded in 1574, Zamora is affectionately known as the *Cuna de Hombres Ilustres* (Cradle of Illustrious Men). Its list includes figures such as Manuel Martinez de Navarrete and Nobel Peace Price winner Alfonso García Robles. It was surely with the help of these illustrious men that the valley of Zamora become the leading producer of potatoes in all of Mexico. Besides potatoes, Zamora yields strawberries and manufactures many famous varieties of *dulces* (candy)—especially *chongos.* While not exactly bursting at the seams with tourist offerings, Zamora is a quiet, pleasant place to pass a day and is a convenient stop between Guadalajara (176km) and Morelia (152km).

▐ TRANSPORTATION. The **bus station** is on Juárez, at the edge of town. To get there from the *centro,* take a "Central" bus (3 pesos) from Colón and Hidalgo or take a taxi (13 pesos). Autobuses de Occidente and La Linea (☎515 11 19) go to: **Guadalajara** (3hr., 5:20am-10:10pm, 70 pesos); **Uruapan** (2½hr., approx. every hr. 5:30am-6pm, 43 pesos); **Colima** (5hr., 7 per day 1:45am-11:30pm, 103 pesos); **Lázaro Cárdenas** (7hr., 6:10pm and 9:30pm, 184 pesos); and **Mexico City** (9hr., approx. every hr. 2:30am-11pm, 207 pesos) via **Morelia** (3hr., 55 pesos) and **Toluca** (7hr., 157 pesos). Elite (☎515 13 24) and Flecha Amarilla (☎515 12 37) serve more destinations, but are more expensive.

⛭⛭ ORIENTATION AND PRACTICAL INFORMATION. Almost everything needed can be found in or around the *centro*, bordered by **Nervo** to the north, **Guerrero** to the south, **Morelos** to the west, and **Allende** to the east. **Hidalgo** curves to the north behind the cathedral, intersected by **Ocampo** running east-west 1 block north of the *centro* up **Morelos.** If you turn right on Ocampo and walk up the street for 4-5 blocks, you'll run into **5 de Mayo** running north-south.

The **tourist office,** Morelos Sur 76, a few blocks from the *centro*, provides good maps and information. (☎512 40 15. Open daily 9am-3pm and 5-8pm.) **Bancomer,** Morelos 250, in the *centro*, has a 24hr. **ATM.** (☎512 26 00. Open M-F 8:30am-5:30pm, Sa 10am-2pm; currency exchange open M-F 8:30am-3:30pm.) **Emergency:** ☎060. **Police:** ☎512 00 22. **Red Cross:** ☎512 05 34. **Farmacia Guadalajara,** in the plaza. (☎515 70 55. Open daily 24hr.) **Hospital: Hospital Civil** (☎512 12 02). **Internet access:** Oficom 2000, Hidalgo 99, at Colón. Behind the cathedral. Turn left on Hidalgo and walk 4 blocks. (☎512 17 13. 5 pesos per hr.) **Post Office:** Hidalgo 112 in the Palacio Federal. (Open M-F 8am-4pm.)

⛭⛭ ACCOMMODATIONS AND FOOD. Though not lacking in budget accommodations, the hourly traffic of couples coming in and out of many of Zamora's cheaper hotels may inspire you to look elsewhere. Try the family-oriented **Hotel Nacional,** Corregidora 106, just off the *centro*, with its cramped, clean, comfortable rooms and even cleaner baths. A nice balcony juts off the 4th floor, and TVs blare in every room. (☎512 42 24. Singles 120 pesos; doubles 140 pesos; triples 170 pesos.) Zamora has a large number of small restaurants and stands with delicious food and even more delicious prices. Restaurants close around 6 or 7pm; candy shops are open until about 9pm. **Centro Comercial (Mercado) Morelos,** just off the *centro* across from the cathedral is the place to go for local sweets. **La Pantera Rosa** (The Pink Panther), Hidalgo Sur 234, offers *carnes asadas en su jugo* (grilled beef with beans and tortillas, 26-30 pesos) and *quesadillas* for 15 pesos. (☎512 18 66. Open daily 10:30am-10pm.)

NEAR ZAMORA: ZARAGOZA ARCHAEOLOGICAL ZONE

From Zamora, take the bus to La Piedad (1hr.). Once in La Piedad, catch the "Zaragoza" bus from Cárdenas near the Jardín Principal (30min., every hr. 6:20am-6:20pm, 5.5 pesos; last return 7pm). It will drop you a short walk from the archaeological zone. Site open M-F 10am-5pm. Free.

To explore Zaragoza, it's almost imperative to have a guide of some sort, even if it is boys from nearby villages. Guides will point out many etchings and carvings in boulders, several small coves, and a shrine to the Virgin of Guadalupe. There is no trail to speak of, and scaling the mountainside can be treacherous, but the vista is spectacular. Before departing, try to find Fernando Tejera in the **Museo Zaragoza,** next to the Presidencia Municipal in the *Jardín* of La Piedad. He may be willing to show you around the site, and at the very least will point you in the right direction.

NEAR ZAMORA: LAGO CAMECUARO

Catch a "Camecuaro" bus from the station in Zamora (15 min., every 30min. 6:30am-9pm, 6 pesos; last return 8:30pm) and tell the driver you want to go to the lake and not the village. The road to the lake is to your right after you pass a cemetery on your left; it's about a 1km walk from there to the lake. Open daily 8am-7pm. 5 pesos.

Peaceful little Lake Camecuaro is a haven for outdoor recreation. The lake offers rowboats (50 pesos per hr.), shady picnic tables, grill pits, volleyball courts, and soccer fields, as well as a few restaurants. Swimming is permitted, but the water is murky. Camecuaro has unfortunately large goose and mosquito populations. Bring your insect repellent.

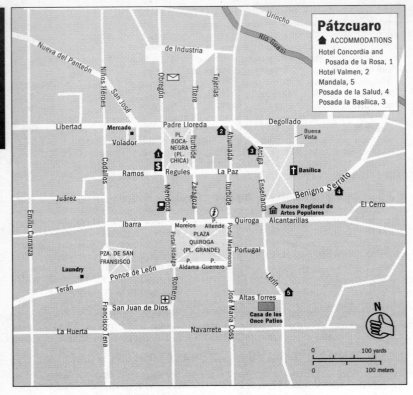

Pátzcuaro

🏠 ACCOMMODATIONS

Hotel Concordia and
    Posada de la Rosa, 1
Hotel Valmen, 2
Mandala, 5
Posada de la Salud, 4
Posada la Basílica, 3

NEAR ZAMORA: GEYSER DE IXTLAN

*Board an "Ixtlan" bus from the Zamora station (45min., every 30min. 7am-8pm, 12
pesos) and tell the bus driver you want to get off at the geyser. The stop is just before the
village of Ixtlan, on the right hand side, next to a Coca-Cola billboard. ☎551 60 46 or 551
63 37. Open daily 9am-6pm. 10 pesos, children 5 pesos.*

Near the village of Ixtlan lies an impressive geyser that erupts sporadically, creating a fountain shooting up to 60m in the air. Unfortunately, the geyser doesn't
erupt on a predictable schedule, so you may have to make do with the surrounding
warm-water pools, which provide a relaxing swim.

PÁTZCUARO   ☎4

Michoacán's earthy jewel, Pátzcuaro (pop. 70,000), is slowly becoming a travelers' favorite. Set high in the mountains, the city is surrounded by rolling hills
and forests kept lush by daily afternoon showers, extending to the shores of
the expansive and polluted Lake Pátzcuaro. The compact and busy center is
nearly as spectacular as the surrounding landscape—tolling cathedral bells
resonate through cobblestone streets and white stucco colonial-style buildings. However, Pátzcuaro isn't the safest town at night, especially for women.
Hotels and what there are of clubs tend to close their doors around 11pm.

    Pátzcuaro's biggest selling point is its crafts. To increase economic develop-
ment in the 1530s, the Spanish Bishop Vasco de Quiroga encouraged residents
of each Purépecha village around the lake to specialize in a different craft.
Today Pátzcuaro's plazas overflow with stacks of handmade woolen sweaters,
meticulously carved wooden toys, and decorative masks.

▐ TRANSPORTATION

Pátzcuaro lies 56km southwest of Morelia and 62km northeast of Uruapan. To reach the *centro* from the **bus station,** off Circunvalación, 8 blocks south of the *centro*, catch a *combi* (7am-9:30pm, 3 pesos) or city bus (6:30am-10pm, 3 pesos) from the lot to the right while leaving the station. **Taxis** cost 15 pesos.

Autobuses de Occidente (☎342 12 43) sends a first-class bus to **Guadalajara** (5hr., 12:15pm, 160 pesos) and a second-class bus to **Morelia** (1hr., every 15min. 7am-8pm, 22 pesos). Ruta Paraíso/Galeana (☎342 08 08) sends second-class buses to surrounding towns, plus **Lázaro Cárdenas** (7hr., every hr. 6am-9pm, 148 pesos); **Morelia** (1¼hr., every 10min. 6am-9pm, 22 pesos); and **Uruapan** (1¼hr., every 10 min. 6am-9pm, 28 pesos). Herradura de Plata (☎342 10 45) sends a first-class bus to **Mexico City** (5hr.; every hr. 7:15am-3:15pm, 11:50pm, and 12:30am; 195 pesos). Primera Plus/Flecha Amarilla (☎342 09 60) send first-class buses to: **Guadalajara** (5hr., 9:30am and 11:30pm, 126 pesos); **Mexico City** (5hr.; 6:45am, 8, and 11:30pm; 170 pesos); and **Morelia** (1hr., 11:45am, 30 pesos); and second-class buses to: **Morelia** (1hr., 11:45am, 30 pesos); **Querétaro** (5hr., 11:30pm, 118 pesos); and **San Luis Potosí** (7hr., 10:30am, 207 pesos). Parhikuni sends a first-class bus to **Morelia** (50min., 8 per day 9am-7pm, 26 pesos).

✦ ℹ ORIENTATION AND PRACTICAL INFORMATION

Pátzcuaro centers around two principal plazas, the **Plaza Quiroga** and the **Plaza Bocanegra.** Each of these is also, rather confusingly, called by a nickname. The Plaza Quiroga is commonly known as **Plaza Grande,** while Plaza Bocanegra often goes by **Plaza Chica.** Don't make the mistake of thinking there are four plazas.

Tourist Office: Delegación Regional de Turismo, Plaza Quiroga 50A (☎342 12 14), on the northern side of Pl. Grande. Staff speaks some English and hands out good maps. Open M-F 9am-3pm and 4-7pm, Sa 9am-2pm and 4-7pm, Su 9am-2pm.

Currency Exchange: Banks with competitive exchange rates can be found in both Pl. Grande and Pl. Chica. Try **Banamex,** Portal Juárez 32 (☎342 15 50), on the west side of Pl. Chica, with a 24hr. **ATM.** Open M-F 9am-5pm, Sa 10am-2pm. Open for exchange M-F 9am-2pm.

Luggage Storage: At bus station. 4-10 pesos per day, by size. Open 7am-10pm.

Mini-supermarket: Merzapack, Mendoza 24 (☎342 52 55), between the Pl. Chica and Pl. Grande, closer to Pl. Chica. Open daily 7am-10pm.

Emergency: Protección Civil (☎342 02 09). On call 24hr. Ambulance, some English.

Police: (☎342 00 04), on Ibarra and Tangara, 4 blocks from Pl. Quiroga. Some English.

Pharmacy: Farmacia Popular (☎342 32 42), Ibarra at Codallos, 1 block west of Pl. Grande. Open 24hr.

Hospital: Hospital Civil, Romero 10 (☎342 02 85), next to San Juan de Díos church. No English spoken.

Telephone/Fax: Computel, (☎342 27 56), on Lloreda next to the Teatro. Offers fax and long distance services, plus it has a **caseta.** Open daily 6am-midnight.

Internet: Meg@Net, Mendoza 8 (☎342 33 33), between Pl. Chica and Pl. Grande, closer to Pl. Grande. 20 pesos per hr. Open daily 9:30am-9pm.

Post Office: Obregón 13 (☎342 01 28), half a block north of Pl. Chica. Open M-F 8am-3pm, Sa 9am-1pm. **Postal Code:** 61600.

▌ ACCOMMODATIONS

Budget hotels are spread all over the place. Those in the **Plaza Bocanegra** usually have clean and comfy rooms. If you're lucky, you can score a balcony on the plaza and a private bathroom. Be advised many hotels have curfews.

Mandala, Lerín 14 (☎ 342 41 76), just past the Casa de los Once Patios. Not the cheapest place in town, but definitely one of the nicest. Beautiful rooms with very clean bathrooms in a friendly environment. The cheapest rooms are downstairs with shared bathrooms: singles 130 pesos, doubles 220 pesos, triples 300 pesos.

Posada de la Salud, Serrato 9 (☎ 342 00 58), 3 blocks east of the plazas and half a block past the *basílica* on the right. A courtyard draped in tropical flowers, surrounded by clean chambers with bathrooms. If you get sick, they have an all-night medicine store. A real family place. Singles 150 pesos; 50 pesos per additional person.

Posada de la Rosa, Portal Juárez 29, 2nd fl. (☎ 342 08 11), on the west side of Pl. Chica. Red-tiled rooms have a lone lightbulb, tiled floors, and comfortable beds. Communal bathrooms are rough but have hot water and running toilets. Curfew 11pm. Singles 60 pesos; doubles 70 pesos, with bath 150 pesos.

Hotel Valmen, Lloreda 34 (☎ 342 11 61), 1 block east of Pl. Chica. Vibrant Aztec tile fills the lime-green courtyards, and some of the well-lit rooms have balconies. Doors locked 10pm sharp. Popular with international travelers. 70 pesos per person.

Hotel Concordia, Portal Juárez 31 (☎ 342 00 03), on the west side of Pl. Chica. The cheapest rooms are spacious and clean, but do not have private baths. Cheery bright walls and floors, but communal bathrooms consist of non-running toilets and a vat of water used for a sink. To take a shower, ask at the desk and they will lend you a key to another room. Singles 80 pesos, doubles 170 pesos, triples 240 pesos.

FOOD

Economical restaurants surround **Plaza Chica** and the accompanying market, while fancier joints cluster in and around the hotels on Plaza Grande. *Pescado blanco* (whitefish), *charales* (small fish eaten fried and whole), and *caldo de pescado* (a fish soup) are the specialties of the region—head near the lake for prices half those in the city itself. Within the city you can find *sopa tarasca*, a creamy tortilla soup, for decent prices.

■ **Restaurant Yunuhen,** Portal Juárez 24 (☎ 342 50 34), on the west side of Pl. Chica. This tiny gem, adorned with fascinating murals depicting local history and culture, serves a filling *comida corrida* (30 pesos). Open daily 8am-8pm.

Hamburguesas El Viejo Sam, Mendoza 8 (☎ 342 36 55), right behind Meg@Net, between the two main plazas. Tasty burgers (8-14 pesos) cooked to order. Try the *sopa tarasca* (15 pesos) or *tortas* (16 pesos). Open daily 10am-10pm.

Restaurant Posada la Basílica, Arciga 6 (☎ 342 11 08). If facing the *basílica,* to the left on the corner. A petal-strewn courtyard leads to an elegant, tiled room with colorful tablecloths and windows overlooking the town and lakes. Expect high prices for good food. *Pollo en mole* 48 pesos; breakfast 14-35 pesos. Open daily 8am-5pm.

Mandala (see **Accommodations**), has vegetarian food good enough to convert even the most blood-hungry of meat lovers. Huge *menú del día* with soup and dessert (40 pesos), and homemade wheat spaghetti (42 pesos). Open W-M 8:30am-9:30pm.

Restaurant Los Escudos, Portal Hidalgo 74 (☎ 342 01 38), on the west side of Pl. Grande, inside the Hotel Los Escudos. The ambience is set by bow tied waiters and attractive wood furniture. *Sopa tarasca* 20 pesos and *comida corrida* 35 pesos. See the *danza de los viejitos,* a dance ridiculing the Spanish (Sa 8:30pm). Live organ music daily 3-5pm and 7-10pm. Open daily 7:30am-10pm.

SIGHTS

The following sights are within earshot of the *basílica,* but some of the most notable are a short trip from downtown (see **Near Pátzcuaro,** p. 422).

BASÍLICA DE NUESTRA SEÑORA DE LA SALUD. When the Bishop Vasco de Quiroga came to Pátzcuaro, he initiated social change and bold architectural projects. Quiroga conceived the pink-and-gold Basílica, at Lerín and Serrato, as a colossal structure with five naves arranged like the fingers of an extended hand. Each finger represents one of Michoacán's cultures and races; the hand's palm is the central altar representing the Catholic religion. Today, an enormous glass booth with gilded Corinthian columns protects the potentially edible *Virgen de la Salud.* When Quiroga asked Tarascan artisans to design an image of the Virgin in 1546, they complied by shaping her out of *tatzingue* paste, made of corn cobs and orchid honey, a typical 16th-century statue material. *(Open daily 7am-7:30pm; mass Su every hr. 7am-1pm, 7, and 8pm.)*

PLAZAS. Statues of Pátzcuaro's two most honored citizens stand in the town's principal plazas. The ceremonious, banner-bearing Vasco de Quiroga inhabits **Plaza Quiroga** (Pl. Grande), a vast and green space. The massive, bare-breasted Gertrudis Bocanegra looks out from the center of **Plaza Bocanegra** (Pl. Chica). A martyr for Mexican independence, Bocanegra was executed by a Spanish squadron in the Plaza Quiroga in October, 1817. Locals claim that bullet holes still mark the ash tree to which she was tied, whose stump is in the southwest corner of Pl. Grande.

MUSEO REGIONAL DE ARTES POPULARES. Housed within old fort-like walls and sporting a flower-filled courtyard, the museum displays regional pottery, copperware, and textiles, and an arresting collection of *maque* and lacquer ceramics. (☎ 342 10 29. *Enseñanza 20, at Alcanterillas, one block south of the basílica. Open Tu-Sa 9am-7pm, Su 9am-2:30pm. 25 pesos, free for national students and teachers with ID; Su free.)*

TEATRO CALTZONTZÍN. Once part of an Augustine convent, this building on the Pl. Chica became a theater in 1936. A prophecy was uttered at the theater's ground breaking: one Holy Thursday, it will crumble as punishment for the sin of projecting movies in a sacred place. Recently, the proprietors got scared—in the last few years the theater has stopped showing movies. You can still take in a dramatic or musical performance. Look for posters or ask at the adjacent library.

BIBLIOTECA GERTRUDIS BOCANEGRA. Next to the theater, the library contains a mural by Juan O'Gorman, illustrating the history of Purépecha civilization from pre-Hispanic times to the 1910 Revolution. *(☎ 342 54 41. Open M-Sa 9am-8pm.)*

SHOPPING

Pátzcuaro's unique handcrafts—hairy Tócuaro masks, elegant Sierra dinnerware, and thick wool textiles—are sold in Plaza Chica's **market** and in the small shops along the passage next to Biblioteca Gertrudis Bocanegra. Bargaining is easier in the market or when you buy more than one item. Don't expect much of a discount on the stunningly handsome wool articles. The thick sweaters, brilliantly colored *saltillos* and *ruanas* (stylized ponchos), rainbow-colored *sarapes,* and dark *rebosos* are some of Pátzcuaro's specialties. For many of the same items at much cheaper prices, you may want to make the trek to some of Pátzcuaro's surrounding villages. (Most shops are open daily 8am-8pm.)

Some higher quality and expensive items can be found at **La Casa de los Once Patios,** so named for the 18th-century building's 11 patios, on Lerín near Navarrete. Originally a convent, the complex now houses craft shops and a mural depicting Vasco de Quiroga's accomplishments. The *casa* sells cotton textiles, wooden and copper crafts, and superb musical instruments such as flutes and student, concert, and classical guitars (250-8000 pesos). Don't miss the dance performances that occur sporadically in the main courtyard, usually on weekends. (Open daily 10am-8pm; some shops close in the afternoon.)

♫ ENTERTAINMENT

Although Pátzcuaro isn't the most happening of towns, it does offer great places to hang out with friends or by yourself. The motto of **Kilómetro X,** Urincho 17 (☎ 342 13 35), 2 blocks west of Pl. Chica on Lloreda, left on Ahumada then right in front of the gas station, is you don't have to buy anything to enjoy the ambiance. This cozy cafe, delicatessen, and (often English) book exchange also screens free *avant garde* movies two days a month.

Unless there's an outdoor festival in one of the plazas, nightlife is confined mainly to restaurants and a few bars. At **Charanda's N,** Plaza Vasco de Quiroga 61B, the local chess club meets M-F 6-9pm amid wood carvings and potted plants, and live music stirs things up on weekends. (☎342 19 46. Cover F-Sa 9-11:30pm 15 pesos. Open M-Th 9am-10:30pm, F-Su 9am-midnight.) Off-beat **El Viejo Gaucho,** Iturbe 10, a colorful Argentine bar and restaurant with art exhibits, features live music every night, from rock and blues to *cumbias* and salsa. Candlelight and communal tables make this place cozy and romantic. (☎342 03 68. Cover 15 pesos. Music starts at 9pm. Open W-Su 6pm-midnight.)

Outside of town lies **El Estribo,** a lookout point near the top of a hill 4km from town. The walk takes about an hour, but you are rewarded with a magnificent view of the Lago de Pátzcuaro. The pilgrimage is only recommended on Saturday and Sunday mornings when other families are making the climb. Otherwise, the hill should be avoided since incidents of foul-play have been reported.

🎊 FESTIVALS

Pátzcuaro parties year-round, but its biggest celebration is without a doubt the spectacular **Noche de Muertos** (Oct. 31-Nov. 2). Tourists from around the globe flock to Pátzcuaro to watch candle-lit fishing boats proceed to the tiny island of Janitzio. There, families and neighbors keep a two-night vigil in the graveyard, feasting at the graves of their loved ones. The first night commemorates lost children; the second remembers deceased adults. Soon after Christmas celebrations come to a close, the town is electrified by **Pastorelas,** religious dances performed on January 6th to commemorate the Adoration of the Magi, and on January 17th to honor St. Anthony of Abad, the patron saint of animals. On both occasions, citizens dress their domestic animals in bizarre costumes, ribbons, and floral crowns. A few months later, Pátzcuaro's *Semana Santa*, the week before Easter, attracts devotees from all over the Republic. On Holy Thursday, all the churches in town are visited, and on the night of Good Friday, the **Procesión de Imágenes de Cristo** is held, during which images of a crucified Christ are carried around town. The faithful flock from all over the state on Saturday for Pátzcuaro's **Procesión del Silencio,** celebrated elsewhere the day before. On this day, a crowd marches around town mourning Jesus's death in silence. If you aren't around for the bigger festivals and parties, don't fret—most weekends at least see bands playing in the plazas.

🔳 DAYTRIPS FROM PÁTZCUARO

The area around Pátzcuaro is blessed with some of the most diverse landscape in all of Mexico. Surrounding villages sell beautiful handicrafts, usually at cheaper prices than the cities.

JANITZIO

In Pátzcuaro, hop a "Lago" combi or bus (3 pesos) at the corner of Portal Regules and Portal Juárez, at Pl. Chica. At the docks, buy a ferry ticket at the Muelle General (40min., ferries leave every 15min. or when full 8am-7:30pm, 24 pesos round-trip; 28 pesos round-trip to the smaller, less-developed islands of Yunuen and Pacanda). Janitzio does not accommodate the stranded, so make sure you catch the last boat at 5:30pm.

The tiny island of Janitzio, inhabited exclusively by Purépecha *indígenas* who still speak their native language, subsists on its tourist trade. The boat ride to Janitzio provides a peek at local fisherman, who use butterfly nets more for show rather than actual fishing. The town's steep main street is lined with stores selling wool goods and hand-carved wooden chess sets and masks. Among the shops, the bulk of which are quite pricey, restaurants offer meals of fresh whitefish (45-50 pesos) and *charales*, crispy sardine-like fish (20-25 pesos), as well as *jarro locos*, a strange concoction with fruit juices, wine, and red seasonings. Janitzio is known for the enormous **statue of Morelos** that towers over the island. Inside the statue, a mural traces the principal events in Morelos's life and struggle for independence. Endless steps lead you to a fantastic lookout point, right around the height of Morelos' sleeve. There are really only two directions in Janitzio—up and down. Keep walking up and you'll reach the statue. For information, go to the **tourist booth** as you get off the docks in front of the shops (☎431 3 61 52. Open daily 8am-7pm).

TZINTZUNTZÁN

Tzintzuntzán is perched on the northeastern edge of the Lago de Pátzcuaro, 15km from Pátzcuaro, on the road to Quiroga and Morelia. Second-class Ruta Paraíso/Galeana buses (☎342 08 08) leave the Pátzcuaro bus station for Tzintzuntzán (30min., every 15min. 5:45am-8pm, 5 pesos) en route to Quiroga. Buses back, same schedule, stopping near the ferry dock to Janitzio.

The most exciting thing about Tzintzuntzán (seen-soon-SAHN; "Place of the Hummingbirds") may be saying the name—it is believed to be an imitation of the sound of the many **hummingbirds** that flit through the sky here in the spring. Tzintzuntzán was the last great city of the Purépecha empire. Before his death in the middle of the 15th century, the Purépecha lord Tariácuri divided his empire among his son and two nephews. When the empire was reunited years later, Tzintzuntzán was made the capital. Today, its claims to fame are the delicate, multicolored **ceramics** for sale along Principal. Also of interest is the atrium and 16th-century Franciscan **convent** (open W-M 9am-4pm), across from the bus stop. The olive shrubs that now cover the extensive, tree-filled atrium were planted under Vasco de Quiroga's instruction over 450 years ago. If you need guidance, head for the **tourist office,** conveniently next to the bus stop. (Open Th-Tu 10am-2pm and 4-6pm.)

Yácatas, the ruins of several pre-Hispanic temples, sits on a hill just outside the city. Walk up the street in front of the market and convent all the way around the hill until you reach the small museum/ticket booth (15min.). The bases of the structures, all that remain today, are standard rectangular pyramids—the missing parts, however, were what made them unique. Each was originally crowned with an unusual elliptical pyramid constructed of shingles and volcanic rock. At the edge of the hill overlooking the lake is a sacrificial block from which victims were hurled; the bones of thousands are said to lie at the base. Another structure was used to stockpile enemy heads. The small museum at the entrance includes some Mesoamerican pottery, jewelry, and a narrative of Purépecha history. (Open daily 9am-6pm. 22 pesos, children under 13, and free for national students and teachers with ID. Su free.)

SANTA CLARA DEL COBRE

From Pátzcuaro, take a Ruta Paraíso/Galeana bus to Santa Clara (20min., every 30min. 5:30am-8pm, 5 pesos; last return 7:30pm).

Santa Clara, 16km south of Pátzcuaro, shines when it comes to crafting *cobre* (copper). Long ago rich copper mines filled the area. They were hidden from the Spanish during the Conquest, and have still not been found again. However, the townspeople's passion for copper work remains unrivaled. When electricity was brought to the town, blackouts occurred when the artisans hammered the wires into pots and pans. Nearly every store in town sells highly individualized and decorative copper plates, pans, bowls, and bells. Prices here are only slightly better than elsewhere in Mexico, but Santa Clara is unbeatable for quality and variety. For a quick look at some highly imaginative pieces, step into the **Museo del Cobre,** near the plaza. Santa Clara celebrates the **Feria del Cobre** in early August.

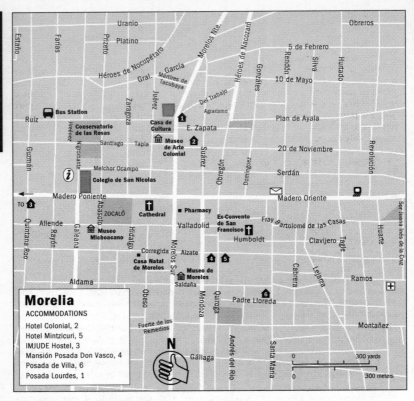

Uranio · Obreros · Estaño · Farías · Prieto · Platino · Morelos Nte. · Héroes de Nacozari · 5 de Febrero · Rendón · Silva · Hurtado · Héroes de Nocupétaro · Gral. · García · Mártires de Tacubaya · Juárez · 10 de Mayo · Gonzáles · Ruiz · 🚌 Bus Station · Zaragoza · Del Trabajo · Agrarismo · Casa de Cultura · E. Zapata · Plan de Ayala · Conservatorio de las Rosas · 🏛 Museo de Arte Colonial · Santiago · Tapla · Suárez · 20 de Noviembre · Revolución · Guzmán · Jiménez · Negromante · Melchor Ocampo · Obregón · Domínguez · Serdán · ⓘ · Colegio de San Nicolas · Madero Poniente · ✉ Madero Oriente · Sor Juana Inés de la Cruz · TO 🔼 3 · Abasolo · ZOCALÓ · 🏛 Cathedral · ■ Pharmacy · Ex-Convento de San Francisco · Fray Bartolomé de las Casas · Huarte · Allende · Rayón · Galeana · Hidalgo · Valladolid · Humboldt · Clavijero · Tagle · Quintana Roo · 🏛 Museo Michoacano · Morelos Sur · Corregida · Alzate · 🔼 4 🔼 5 · Cabrera · Lejara · Ramos · Casa Natal de Morelos · 🏛 Museo de Morelos · Aldama · Obeso · Saldaña · Quiroga · 🔼 6 Padre Lloreda · ✚ · Mendoza · Montañez · Fuerte de los Remedios · **N** ☞ · Gállaga · Andrés del Río · Santa María · Saldaña · 0 ──── 300 yards · 0 ──── 300 meters

Morelia

ACCOMMODATIONS

Hotel Colonial, 2
Hotel Mintzicuri, 5
IMJUDE Hostel, 3
Mansión Posada Don Vasco, 4
Posada de Villa, 6
Posada Lourdes, 1

LAGO DE ZIRAHUÉN

From Pátzcuaro, take an Occidente (☎342 12 43) bus to Lago de Zirahuén (45min.; 7:15, 9:30, and 11:50am, 1, 2, 4, and 5pm; 6 pesos; last return 5:30pm). Taxis from Pátzcuaro run about 50 pesos.

The Lago de Zirahuén ("where smoke rose") is a fun trip for those who like the pace of life slow—very slow. You could pull a Rip van Winkle and probably not miss a thing here. Smaller than Lake Pátzcuaro and much cleaner, Zirahuén is bordered by green farmland and gentle sloping hills. Camping here is quite safe; hike one of the ridges that border the lake and set up in any of the spots overlooking the water. Make sure to bring a tarp and wet-weather gear. If the land is privately owned (usually fenced off), you may have to pay a few pesos—ask before you pitch your tent. A choice spot is the sizable piece of lakefront on the west end of town (left, as you face the lake). The strip, about 15m wide, is covered in grass cut short by grazing horses. The *cabañas*, to the right along the dirt road bordering the lake (5min.), allow campers to use their bathrooms (1 peso). Be forewarned; heavy rains mid-June to early October can turn your camping soggy.

After roughing it in the great outdoors, head to the *lancha* dock for a smooth ride around the lake (1hr.; "yacht" 35 pesos, *lancha* 20 pesos), then sit down at one of the informal lakefront restaurants (tortillas, rice, salad, and fresh fish 25 pesos). Although there is no formal canoe rental, you can ask around and a local fisherman might rent you his canoe (50-100 pesos), depending on how long you want to use it. Many of the restaurants will pack a meal to go if you decide to take a picnic, but be sure to establish the price beforehand.

MORELIA ☎4

The state capital Morelia (pop. 575,000) is at the center of a proud tradition of Michoacán culture and history. Museums, art exhibits, theater, dance productions, and concerts create a vibrant cultural scene, fueled by the city's sizeable student population. But this isn't the only thing growing; the city has of late been caught in a whirl of development. Sophisticated department stores and US fast food joints press in from the outskirts of town, while in the *centro* vendors sell traditional textiles and wooden crafts alongside bootleg cassettes, sweat socks, and spare blender parts. Nearby stand incongruous rose-colored stone arcades and grand, white-washed houses, relics of Morelia's colonial magnificence. With eclectic art and a lively downtown, Morelia is one of the most vital cities in Mexico.

▐ TRANSPORTATION

GETTING AROUND
Morelia lies some 230km west of Mexico City on **Rte. 15.** Buses and *combis* provide transportation within the city (daily 6am-10pm, 3 pesos). Most routes can be picked up on **Nigromante** and **Galeana,** one block west of the *zócalo*, and on **Allende,** south of the *zócalo*. **Taxis** cluster in front of the bus station.

GETTING AWAY
Airport: Aeropuerto Francisco J. Múgica (☎313 67 80), on the Carretera Morelia-Cinapécuaro at km 27. There is no longer bus service to the airport; a taxi costs 100-150 pesos. **Aeromar** (☎313 68 86). **Aeroméxico** (☎313 01 40 or 313 42 08). **Mexicana** (☎312 47 25).

Buses: The **Central** station (☎313 55 89), on Ruíz at Farías. Getting downtown from the bus station, is a 10min. walk, a short taxi ride (12 pesos), or a quick bus ride (3 pesos) on any *combi* that says "Centro." Walk to the left (east) as you exit the station, take the first right onto Farías, walk three blocks, then take a left on Madero—the *zócalo* is three blocks ahead.

Autobuses de Occidente (☎312 06 00) send 2nd-class buses to: **Guadalajara** (6hr., 8 per day 2:10am-4:40pm, 132 pesos); **Manzanillo** (8hr.; 1:30, 6:55am, 3:15, 8, and 11pm; 247 pesos); and **Mexico City** (6hr., about every 30min. 24hr., 140 pesos) via **Zitácuaro** (3hr., 64 pesos). ETN (☎313 64 40) sends executive-class buses to: **Manzanillo** (7½hr., 10:30pm, 300 pesos) and **Mexico City** (4hr., every hr. 2am-midnight, 220 pesos).

Primera Plus/Flecha Amarilla (☎313 55 89) sends first-class buses to: **Aguascalientes** (5½hr., 6 per day 2:30am-5:05pm, 195 pesos); **Querétaro** (4hr., about every 2hr. 12:15am-11:30pm, 98 pesos); and **San Luís Potosí** (6hr., 7 per day 12:15am-11:30pm, 210 pesos). 2nd-class buses go to: **Aguascalientes** (6hr., 8:50am and 4pm, 146 pesos); **Colima** (8½hr., 7:40am and noon, 157 pesos); and **Guanajuato** (4hr., 6:50am and 12:50pm, 88 pesos).

Ruta Paraíso/Galeana (☎312 55 05) sends 2nd-class buses to: **Lázaro Cárdenas** (8½hr., every hr. 2:30am-7:30pm, 177 pesos); **Pátzcuaro** (1hr., every 10min. 5am-9pm, 22 pesos); and **Uruapan** (2hr., every 20min. 4am-9pm, 57 pesos).

Parhikuni (☎313 24 44) sends first-class buses to: **Lázaro Cárdenas** (7½hr., 8 per day 8:20am-1:30am, 215 pesos); **Pátzcuaro** (45min., 8 per day 7:30am-5:30pm, 26 pesos); and **Uruapan** (1½hr., every 20min. 6am-9pm, 65 pesos).

Herradura de Plata (☎312 29 88) sends first-class buses to **Mexico City** (4hr., about every 30min., 175 pesos).

Autobuses Mexico Toluca Zinacantepec (☎312 73 40) sends second-class buses to: **Toluca** (4½hr., every 40min. 6am-6pm, 112 pesos) via **Zitácuaro** (3hr., 64 pesos) and **Hidalgo** (2hr., 46 pesos). Transportes Fronteras (☎312 29 89) sends executive class buses to **Nuevo Laredo** (16hr., 5pm, 805 pesos) and **Tijuana** (38hr.; 1:15, 9:20, 11:45pm; 1248 pesos).

▐ PRACTICAL INFORMATION

Tourist Office: State Tourist Office, Nigromante 79 (☎312 80 82), at Madero Pte., 2 blocks west of the *zócalo* in the castle-like building on the right. Staff distributes maps and a monthly list of cultural events. Walking tours of the city (50 pesos) leave M-Sa noon and 4:30pm, Su noon. Open M-Sa 9am-7pm, Su 9am-2pm.

Currency Exchange: Banks cluster on Madero near the cathedral. **Bancomer,** Madero Ote. 21 (☎312 29 90), has a 24hr. **ATM.** Open M-F 8:30am-5:30pm, Sa 10am-2pm. **Banamex,** Madero Ote. 63 (☎322 03 38), also has a 24hr. **ATM.** Open M-F 9am-5pm.

Laundry: Lavandería Cuautla, Cuautla 152 (☎312 48 06), south of Madero. 8 pesos per kg, 3kg minimum. Open M-F 9am-2pm and 4-8pm, Sa 9:30am-1:30pm.

Emergency: ☎060.

Police: (☎312 00 73 or 312 22 22), on 20 de Noviembre, 1 block northwest of the Fuente de las Tarascas, at the end of the aqueduct. No English spoken. Open 24hr.

Red Cross: Ventura 27 (☎314 51 51 or 314 50 25), next to Parque Cuauhtémoc. Some English spoken. Open 24hr.

Pharmacy: Farmacia Guadalajara, Maderos Sur. 117 (☎312 13 60), near the cathedral. Also a mini-supermarket. Open 24hr.

Hospital: Hospital Civil (☎312 01 02), on the corner of Ramos and Huarte. No English spoken. Open 24hr.

Fax: Computel, Portal Galeana 157 (☎/fax 313 62 56), across from the cathedral. Has a **caseta.** Open daily 7am-10pm. Also **Telecomm,** Madero Ote. 371 (☎312 03 45), in the Palacio Federal next to the post office. Open M-F 8am-7:30pm, Sa-Su 9am-noon.

Internet Access: Morelia is crawling with Internet cafes, especially near the *centro*. **ShareWeb Cyber Café,** Madero Ote. 573C. 15 pesos per hr. Open M-Sa 10am-10pm, Su 2-10pm. **Telecomm** (see above). 25 pesos per hr. Available M-F 8am-2pm.

Post Office: Madero Ote. 369 (☎312 05 17), in the Palacio Federal, 5 blocks east of the cathedral. Open M-F 8am-5pm, Sa 9am-1pm. **Postal Code:** 58000.

▌ ACCOMMODATIONS

Unfortunately, budget hotels with vacancies are about as rare as jackrabbits in Morelia. Your best bet is the IMJUDE hostel.

■ **IMJUDE Villa Juvenil Youth Hostel,** Chiapas 180 (☎312 03 56 or 313 03 24), at Oaxaca, 20min. from the *zócalo*. Walk west on Madero Pte., turn left on Cuautla, walk 6 blocks, then turn right on Oaxaca and continue 4 blocks to Chiapas. Alternatively, take an *amarilla* (yellow stripe) *combi* from the *centro*. IMJUDE is a very happening place, part hostel, part community center. Exceptionally well-maintained 4-person single-sex dormitories, bathrooms, and red-tiled lobby. Sports facilities and pool can be used with permission. Linen deposit 50 pesos. Open daily 7am-11pm; call ahead if you are arriving after 11pm. 48 pesos per person; 15 pesos per meal.

Mansión Posada Don Vasco, Vasco de Quiroga 232 (☎312 14 34), 2 blocks east and 1½ blocks south of the cathedral. Spacious rooms have cable TV, phones, wood furniture, carpeting, and purified water. Singles 161 pesos, doubles 184 pesos, triples 207 pesos, quads 230 pesos. Fully-loaded smaller rooms off the courtyard 100 pesos.

Hotel Mintzicuri, Vasco de Quiroga 227 (☎312 06 64). Wrought-iron railings overflowing with flowers enclose sparkling clean, cozy, wood-paneled rooms equipped with phones and cable TV. Very popular with Mexican tourist families—come early or call ahead. Singles 161 pesos, doubles 184 pesos, triples 207 pesos, quads 230 pesos.

Hotel Colonial, 20 de Noviembre 15 (☎312 18 97), at Morelos Nte. Welcoming courtyard glows deep yellow. Rooms have high ceilings, large windows, private baths, and *agua purificada;* some even have balconies. Friendly staff. Singles 100 pesos, with TV 150 pesos; doubles 130 pesos, with TV 170 pesos; triples with TV 240 pesos.

Posada de Villa, Lloreda 166 (☎312 69 95), 3 blocks south of the Museo de las Artesanías. Gigantic rooms have great views and tasteful decor. Try to get a room at the rear of the hotel—the street can be loud. Single 125 pesos, 25 pesos each extra person.

Posada Lourdes, Morelos Nte. 340, at del Trabajo near the Casa de Cultura. Not incredibly attractive from the outside, but rooms are pleasant, clean, and most importantly, cheap. Purified water available in the pleasant courtyard. Singles 45 pesos, with bath 75 pesos; doubles 75 pesos, with bath 95 pesos.

◖ FOOD

Budget hotel rooms may be scarce, but it's a breeze to find good, cheap food in Morelia. Almost every thoroughfare has at least one family-run restaurant that dishes out delicious, inexpensive *comida corrida* (usually around 20 pesos) in the afternoon. The best deals (though not necessarily best quality) cluster around the bus station. Restaurants on the *zócalo* are pricier but tend to stay open later.

▧ Trico, Valladolid 8 (☎313 42 32), at Madero Sur just east of the cathedral, 2nd fl. This restaurant is elegant but economical, populated by businessmen in suits and families in jeans. Vegetarian options available. Offers huge breakfasts (36-40 pesos), baguette sandwiches (18-25 pesos), and regional specialties. Open daily 7am-9pm.

Super Cocina la Rosa, Tapía 270 (☎313 08 52), at Prieto next to the Conservatorio. This family-run restaurant draws patrons in droves—go at an off time to guarantee a seat. Great food (and lots of it). *Huevos al gusto* 15 pesos, *comida corrida* 30 pesos. Open daily 8:30am-4:30pm.

Alborada, Lejarza 36 (☎313 01 71), right off Madero near the Palacio Federal. A bakery in front and a kitchen in back. Tons of food, for less money than most *comida corridas.* Veggie burgers 10 pesos, *energéticos* (yogurt, fruit and honey) 12 pesos, *licuados* (smoothies) 7 pesos. Open M-Sa 8am-4:30pm; bakery open M-Sa 8am-9pm.

La Flor de Calabaza, Hidalgo 75, south of the *zócalo.* Set in a huge inner courtyard with a non-working fountain, this restaurant offers a mammoth *comida corrida* (24 pesos.) The service is friendly and the food delicious. Open daily 9am-5pm.

El Tragadero, Hidalgo 63 (☎313 00 92). This open-front restaurant, packed with artificial flowers and old pictures of Morelia, provides a great view of the marketplace. Very filling *comida corrida* 30 pesos, *milanesa* and fries 39 pesos, *tortas* 11-13 pesos. Open M-Sa 7:30am-10:30pm, Su 7:30am-8pm.

◉ SIGHTS

Packed with museums and cultural centers spanning all aspects of Michoacán's heritage, Morelia is a history buff's dream come true. Many of Morelia's famous buildings are ornamented in a style peculiar to the city—imitation Baroque.

CASA DE CULTURA. A gathering place for artists, musicians, and backpackers, the *casa* houses a bookstore, art gallery, theater, palatial inner courtyard, and lovely cafe. Offers dance, voice, theater, guitar, piano, and sculpture classes, and hosts book signings, art festivals, and literature workshops. A great place to find out about Morelia's cultural events. The on-premises **Museo de la Máscara** exhibits a small collection of masks from all over the Republic. *(Morelos Nte. 485, 4 blocks north of Madero. Museum ☎312 41 51. Casa de Cultura ☎313 12 15 or 313 13 20. Center and museum open M-F 9am-3pm and 5-9pm, Sa-Su and holidays 10am-6pm. Free. Classes for 3 months, 150 pesos.)*

BOSQUE CUAUHTÉMOC. More a park than an actual forest, the *bosque* lets you lose yourself among trees and fountains. For the young at heart, there is a **mini amusement park** with bumper cars and a train. The **Museo de Historia Natural,** situated in the southeast corner of the *bosque,* is a tiny museum offering live and dead fish, dissected animals, an extensive collection of butterflies, and the skeleton of a woolly mammoth. On the eastern side of the *bosque* is the **Museo de Arte Contemporaneo,** which displays rotating contemporary art. *(To get to the bosque, take a "Ruta Rojo" combi from behind the cathedral on Allende. Amusement park open daily noon-8pm. Free.*

Museo de History, Puente 23. ☎ *312 00 44. Open daily 10am-6pm. Free. Museo de Arte, Acueducto 18.* ☎ *312 54 04. Open Tu-Su 10am-2pm and 4-8pm. Free.)*

PARQUE ZOOLÓGICO BENITO JUÁREZ. One of the larger and more pleasant zoos in Mexico, the parque zoológico keeps most of its animals in natural settings rather than tiny cages. *(Take a maroon combi south on Nigromante or pink "Santa María" combi in front of tourist office (both 3 pesos), or walk south on Nigromante until it becomes Juárez (3km). Entrance on the south side of zoo.* ☎ *314 04 88. Open M-F 10am-5pm, Sa-Su 10am-5:30pm. 10 pesos, children 5 pesos.)*

MUSEO DE MORELOS. Originally bought by José María Morelos, the parish priest who led the Independence movement after Hidalgo's death, this 19th century building now houses a museum displaying religious vestments, military ornaments and uniforms, and other mementos of the fight for independence. *(323 Morelos Sur, 1 block east and 2 blocks south of the cathedral.* ☎ *313 85 06. Open daily 9am-7pm. 17 pesos, Children under 13 and seniors free. Su free.)*

CASA NATAL DE MORELOS. More of a civic building than a museum, the "Birthplace of Morelos" holds glass cases which preserve Morelos's wartime cartography, communiqués, and letters. Also notable is the shady courtyard and the murals by Alfredo Zalce. *(113 Corregidora, at Obeso, 1 block south of the cathedral.* ☎ *312 27 93. Open M-F 9am-8pm, Sa-Su 9am-7pm. Free.)*

MUSEO MICHOACANO. This museum houses exhibits on the ecology, archaeology, anthropology, history, and art of Michoacán. The most notable object on display is a huge, anonymous painting completed in 1738, called The Procession of the Nuns from a University to Their New Convent. *(Allende 305, 1 block west of the zócalo at Abasolo.* ☎ *312 04 07. Open Tu-Sa 9am-7pm, Su 9am-2pm. 25 pesos; children under 14, seniors, and Su free.)*

CATHEDRAL. Overlooking the *zócalo*, the massive cathedral has a stunning interior graced by vaulted ceilings, chandeliers, tapestries, stained-glass windows, and a stunning dark wood pipe organ. The church's oldest treasure is the *Señor de la Sacristía*, an image of Christ sculpted by *indígenas* out of dry corn cobs and orchid nectar. Phillip II of Spain donated a gold crown to top off the masterpiece. *(Open daily 5:30am-8:30pm. Masses held Su, ever hr. 6am-noon and 6-8pm.)*

CASA DE LAS ARTESANÍAS. This *casa*, occupying part of the **Ex-Convento de San Francisco**, is a huge crafts museum and retail store, selling colorful macramé *huipiles*, straw airplanes, pottery, carved wood furniture, and guitars. However, better prices await in nearby Pátzcuaro. *(*☎ *312 12 48. Humboldt at Fray Bartolome de las Casas, 3 blocks east of the zócalo. Open M-Sa 10am-3pm and 5-8pm, Su 10am-4:30pm. Free.)*

CONSERVATORIO DE LAS ROSAS. Built in the 18th century to protect and educate widows and poor or orphaned Spanish girls, the building, with its beautiful rose-filled courtyard, is now home to Morelia's premiere music school, the oldest in the Americas. There are no summer concerts; check with the conservatory or tourist office for performance schedules the rest of the year. *(Tapía 334, two blocks north of the tourist office.* ☎ *312 14 69. Open M-F 8am-8pm, Sa 8am-2pm.)*

OTHER SIGHTS. At the eastern end of Madero is the statue of **Las Tarascas**, probably the most recognizable landmark in Morelia. The statue shows three indigenous women making an offering to the heavens. Nearby is **El Acueducto**, built in the 18th century to meet the city's growing water needs. Though no longer functional, it is a magnificent sight at night. Av. Acueducto runs right along it, to the university. Also nearby is the lookout **Santa María** (ask the tourist office for specific directions). Across from the cathedral is the **Palacio Gobierno**, Madero 63. Inside, murals by Alfredo Zalce depict the history of Morelia The **Museo de Arte Colonial** is three blocks north at Juárez 240 *(Palacio Gobierno open M-F 8am-10pm, Sa-Su 8am-9pm. Museo de Arte* ☎ *313 92 60. Open M-F 10am-2pm and 5-8pm, Sa-Su 10am-2pm and 4:30-7pm.)*

🎵🎭 ENTERTAINMENT AND NIGHTLIFE

Everything you've heard is true—Morelia overflows with culture. Listings of all sorts can be found at the Casa de Cultura and at the tourist office.

Bright lights, music, and high theater draw crowds to **Teatro Morelos** (☎314 62 02), on Camelina at Ventura Pte., and to **Teatro Ocampo** (☎312 37 34), on the corner of Ocampo and Prieto. **Corral de la Comedia,** Ocampo 239 (☎312 00 01), at Prieto one block north of Madero, is a theater/cafe that presents comedies written and performed by local artists (Th-Sa 8:30pm; Su 7:30pm; 60 pesos). **La Casona del Teatro,** Serdán 35 (☎317 33 53), at Morelos one block north of Madero, hosts comic dramas in Spanish (shows generally Th-Sa 9pm; Su 11am and 7:30pm; 30 pesos). The theater/cafe is popular with students and bohemians who play chess and drink coffee (8 pesos) until show time (cafe open M-Sa 10am-6pm, later when there are shows). The **Conservatorio de las Rosas** (see **Sights** above) holds concerts during all but the summer; visit for calendars. The **Casa Natal de Morelos** (see **Sights**) shows family movies and holds cultural events (events F 8pm; films Tu-W 5 and 7pm; films 5 pesos). **Multicinema Morelia** (☎312 12 88), on Tapía at Jiménez, next to the conservatory, shows Hollywood's latest. (Open daily 1:30-10:30pm; 20 pesos before 6pm, 25 pesos after; Spanish subtitles).

The **Planetario** (☎314 24 65), on Ventura Pte. at Ticateme, in the Centro de Convenciones, has both standard fare and kid's shows (Tu-Sa 7pm, Su 6:30pm; 16 pesos; kids shows Th and Sa 5pm). Take the "Ruta Rojo #3" *combi* from Allende/Valladolid, and watch for the convention center on the right.

If you prefer scantily clad bodies to heavenly ones, writhe with the student hordes of Morelia's nightclub scene. Most clubs are a 15- to 20-peso cab ride away. Twenty-somethings bounce to the latest Spanish and English pop tunes at **XO Club,** Campestre 100. (Open bar F. Cover men 100 pesos, women 50 pesos; Sa everyone 50 pesos. Open W-Sa 10pm-3am.) For real multi-level, block-rocking club madness, head to either **Akbal** and **Belam** (cab drivers know the way). The jungle motif suits the party animals as they tear apart the dance floor and throw back the drinks. Partners dance on the bar, the tables, and every square inch of the terraced floor. (Beer 9 pesos; domestic drinks 15 pesos. Cover 30-40 pesos. Open W-Su 9am-3pm.) Clubs here have short half-lives, so ask around for the latest.

CIUDAD HIDALGO ☎1

Not exactly a tourist hot spot, Hidalgo is notable for several nearby attractions. The **Laguna Larga** and the spas of **Los Azufres** are great places to enjoy Michoacán's natural beauty.

📋 TRANSPORTATION AND PRACTICAL INFORMATION. Ciudad Hidalgo is a two-hour bus ride from Morelia. The **bus station,** Morelos Pte. 9 (☎154 09 60), is on the main east-west street The *centro* is a block north of the bus station between Hidalgo and Cuauhtémoc, which run north-south. La Linea/Via 2000 buses depart the station to: **Mexico City** (4hr., every 15min. 9am-7pm, 93 pesos) via **Toluca** (3hr., 64 pesos); **Morelia** (2hr., every 15min. 6am-7pm, 46 pesos); and **Guadalajara** (8½hr., 5 and 11:30pm, 168 pesos). **Tourist office:** in the Palacio Municipal in the *centro*. (☎154 11 79. Open M-F 9am-3pm and 5-7pm.)

🍴 ACCOMMODATIONS AND FOOD. Your best bet in Ciudad Hidalgo is the **Hotel Central,** Abasolo 12 (☎154 00 55). From in front of the Palacio Gobierno in the *centro*, turn right for one block then left on Abasolo for 1½ blocks. The large clean rooms have TV and phone. (Singles 110 pesos; doubles 130 pesos; triples 160 pesos; quads 190 pesos.) A less attractive, less expensive option is the **Hotel San Carlos,** Cuauhtémoc Sur 22 (☎154 56 47), near the bus station. (Singles 50 pesos, with TV 80 pesos; doubles 60 pesos, with TV 90; triples 90 pesos, with TV 120 pesos; quads 120 pesos, with TV 150 pesos.) Hidalgo is not the place for fine dining. Food vendors can be found around the *zócalo* and the *mercado*. If you're wary of these, try **Güero's Pizza**, Hidalgo 8 (☎154 57 66), near the *centro*. Sesame seed crust pizza (9 pesos) whole pizzas with 3-4 toppings (from 54 pesos).

◪ OUTDOOR ACTIVITIES. Los Azufres, 23km northwest of Morelia, is perfect for a nice, relaxing bath (20 pesos). Nearby, the **Laguna Largas** are a series of manmade lakes or *presos*, perfect for hiking, fishing, or camping. Buses to Los Azufres and Laguna Larga leave daily from the parking lot at Hidalgo 40 (about 1 hr., 7am and 2pm, 15 pesos, return bus 6pm). Stop by the helpful **tourist office** for more detailed information on these sites.

ZITÁCUARO   ☎ 7

Zitácuaro would be a much larger city had it not been destroyed three times during the 19th century—once during the War for Independence (1812), another time by Santa Anna's troops (1855), and finally during the French Intervention (1865). It is the city's long tradition of defiance and survival that led Benito Juárez to ordain it the Ciudad de la Independencia (the City of Independence). Today, Zitácuaro is a small city (pop. 200,000) with safe streets, large markets, and a population that rises with the sun. Tucked into the eastern edge of the Sierra Madres Occidentales, the city seems to have mountains looming at the end of every street. Outdoors-enthusiasts will discover endless opportunities for camping and hiking in the immediate area, but city-folk may not find much in Zitácuaro to suit them. Despite the growing population and increasingly urban economy, Zitácuaro's cultural traditions have remained as immutable as the mountains.

▐ TRANSPORTATION. Zitácuaro is about 165km west of Mexico City on **Rte. 15.** The **bus station** is at Pueblita Nte. 17 (☎153 72 65), at the end of Cuauhtémoc Nte., two blocks north of Hidalgo and six blocks east of Revolución Nte. Tickets for taxis to the *centro* are sold at the booth inside (15 pesos). "Centro" *combis* are outside the station (6am-9pm, 3 pesos). Occidental (☎153 08 66) goes to: **Guadalajara** (8hr., approx. every 2hr. 1:20am-1:10pm, 179 pesos); **Manzanillo** (2hr.; 3:50am, noon, 4:40, 7:50, 10:25pm; 264 pesos); **Mexico City** (3hr., every 30min. 24hr., 75 pesos). Flecha Amarilla (☎153 14 88) sends second-class buses to: **Morelia** (3hr., every hr. 6am-11:30pm, 64 pesos); **Toluca** (2hr., every hr. 2am-7pm, 46 pesos); and **Uruapan** (5hr., 5pm, 118 pesos). Transportes Frontera (☎153 71 73) sends second-class buses to: **Acapulco** (12hr., 5am and 11:30pm, 273 pesos); **Nuevo Laredo** (20hr., 12:40am, 631 pesos); and **San Luis Potosí** (9hr., 12:40 and 2:40pm, 138 pesos) via **Querétaro** (6hr., 232 pesos).

▐▐ ORIENTATION AND PRACTICAL INFORMATION. The **Plaza Principal** is the center of the city, and consists of the Plaza Cívica de Benito Juárez, the Plaza Municipal, and the Mercado Juárez. The Plaza Municipal is bordered by **Tejada** (south), **García** (west), **5 de Mayo** (east) and **Ocampo** (north). **Hidalgo** runs parallel to Ocampo on the other side of the market. The main avenue in Zitácuaro, **Revolución**, is one block east of 5 de Mayo. North-south streets end in either "Nte." or "Sur," depending on whether they are north or south of Hidalgo.

The **tourist office**, Carretera Zitácuaro km 4, is far from the *centro*, but the staff provides helpful maps and brochures. To get there, take an orange *combi* heading south on Revolución and tell the driver where to let you off. No English spoken. (☎153 06 75. Open M-F 9am-3pm and 5-7pm, Sa 9am-2pm.) **Banamex**, Tejada 30, will exchange currency and has a 24hr. **ATM.** (☎153 04 07. Open M-F 9am-5pm, Sa 9am-2pm.) **Luggage storage:** in the bus station. (2.5 pesos per 6hr., 1 peso each additional hr., 4.5 pesos per night. Open daily 6am-10pm.) **Emergency:** ☎060. **Police:** at the north end of the Plaza Municipal. (☎153 11 37 or 153 11 47. 24hr. service.) **Red Cross:** Prieto 11 (☎153 11 05). Many pharmacies surround the plaza, including the **Farmacia Guadalajara**, 5 de Mayo Sur 12A. (☎153 86 33. Open 24hr.) **Hospital: Sanito-**

rio Memorial, Valle Nte. 10 (☎ 153 11 08), one block east of Revolución Nte. between Ocampo and Tejada. **Internet: Evonet,** Revolución Sur 8, next to Hotel América. (☎ 153 64 54. 15 pesos per hr. Open M-Sa 9am-9pm, Su 9am-3pm.) **Post office:** Valle Sur 2, down the street from Sanitorio Memorial. (☎ 151 38 73. Open M-F 8am-3pm, Sa 9am-1pm.) **Postal code:** 61500.

▉◻ ACCOMMODATIONS AND FOOD. Illuminated signs all over Revolución and the plaza area advertise conveniently located (and sometimes inconveniently priced) hotels and *posadas.* The pesos pay off at the **Hotel Michoacán,** 5 de Mayo Sur 26. Pricey, but right off the plaza, this peach colored hotel receives guests with scented rooms, TVs, bottled water, and comfortable beds. (☎ 153 00 08. Singles 100 pesos, doubles 150 pesos.) Another option is **Hotel América,** Revolución Sur 8. Offers parking, private baths, and TVs. Rooms are clean with hardwood floors. (☎ 153 11 16. Singles 90 pesos, 40 pesos per extra person.)

The best eating options in Zitácuaro are on-the-go: fresh market fruits and vegetables, hot *quesadillas,* and ice cream stands. A few sit-down restaurants can be found on Revolución. Converse with the friendly waitstaff at the inexpensive **Café Chips,** Hidalgo Ote. 22, east of Revolución past Hotel Conquistador. Savory *tortas* 6-8 pesos. (☎ 153 11 95. Open Tu-Su 9am-9pm.) **Restaurant Cordegali,** Revolución Sur 101, sells traditional Mexican food served hot with spicy salsa. *Comida corrida* 25 pesos. (Open M-Sa 8am-8pm.)

▣ SIGHTS. Afternoons in Zitácuaro swirl and fade in the **Plaza Cívica de Benito Juárez,** where vendors gather, uniformed school kids play *fútbol,* and older people escape the sun on one of the few shaded benches. The **Palacio Municipal,** watching over the north end of the plaza, holds a stunning mural that tells Zitácuaro's history, from its settling by the Mazahuas, through independence, to the modern day. The small **Jardín de la Constitución,** on Ojeda Sur, three blocks west of the plaza, provides flowers, fountains, and shady seats for starry-eyed couples.

From Zitácuaro's **Cerrito de la Independencia** one can see not only the city itself, but the miles of lush valleys, forested hills, and spectacular distant blue peaks beyond. To reach the lookout, follow Tejada as it crosses Revolución Sur until it reaches Altamiano, then turn right and follow the paved path climbing through the woods. (Open daily 6am-7pm.) You can also take an orange *combi* south on Revolución to Cañonaso and walk the four blocks uphill. Ten kilometers south of town on the Huetamo Rte., **Presa del Bosque** also provides spectacular views of the countryside. The dirt road to the right of the main road leads to a lake where adventurous souls can swim, camp, fish, and hike. To get there, go to the Tuzuntla taxi stop on Morelos Sur, just south of Zaragoza Pte. (5 pesos each way). To return, flag down one of the numerous taxis passing by.

HOLDING COURT Eastern Michoacán is home not only to vast coniferous forests and rolling hills peppered with small farming communities, but, during the months of November and December, to over 20 million monarch butterflies. Each year in October, monarchs from all over the US and Canada begin their journeys in unison, flying at a regal 20km/hr., and gather just north of Zitácuaro. Some scientists say the mass migration instinct is a relic of the ice ages, when southward travel was necessary for reproduction, while others insist that even now monarch reproduction is impossible in all but the warmest of climates. Whatever reason, the sight is stupendous. The butterflies cover trees so that they are writhing orange masses, with not so much as a patch of bark visible. To visit the annual convergence, take a green bus labeled "Angangueo" from the station in Zitácuaro to El Rosario, the sanctuary.

LÁZARO CÁRDENAS   ☎7

Named after the *michoacano* president whose ardent socialist measures included nationalizing oil in 1938, the hot, noisy city of Lázaro Cárdenas (pop. 150,000) is Mexico's most important Pacific port. The city's size, services, and location make it a convenient departure point or pit stop on an exploration of Michoacán's rugged and beautiful 260km coast. Cárdenas itself is a filthy pit: get in and get out.

⌂ TRANSPORTATION. Lázaro Cárdenas lies 382km southwest of Morelia and 122km northwest of Ixtapa. The town's principal thoroughfare is **Av. Lázaro Cárdenas.** The main *zócalo*, **Plaza de la Reforma,** is three blocks east of the *avenida's* intersection with Prieto. *Combis* and buses run up and down Av. Lázaro Cárdenas and whisk passengers to nearby beaches.

The **airport** (☎532 19 20), named after Lázaro himself, hosts carriers **Transporte Aeromar** (☎537 10 84), and **Aerolínea Cuahonte** (☎532 36 35 and 532 00 04). **Buses** run out of independent stations on or close to the main drag. Autotransportes Cuauhtémoc and Estrella Blanca, Villa 65 (☎532 11 71), four blocks west of Corregidora, send buses to: **Acapulco** (6hr., about every 2hr. 4:45am-midnight, 138 pesos); **Tijuana** (48hr., 12:30pm and 2:30pm, 1301 pesos) via **Mazatlán** (20hr., 592 pesos), and points along the way. Estrella Blanca also provides second-class service to: **Zihuatanejo** (2hr., about every hr. 2:30am-9pm, 45 pesos) and **Acapulco** (6hr., every 2hrs. 4:15am-9pm, 138 pesos). Autotransportes Galeana, Lázaro Cárdenas 1810 (☎532 02 62), provides service to: **Manzanillo** (6hr.; 4:30, 5:30, 10, 11:30am; 125 pesos); **Morelia** (8hr., 14 per day 2am-10pm, 177 pesos) via **Pátzcuaro** (7hr., 148 pesos); and **Uruapan** (6hr., 120 pesos). Estrella de Oro, Corregidora 318 (☎532-0275) travels to: **Mexico City** (13½hr., 9pm, 346 pesos); **Acapulco** (6hr.; 6:30, 7am and 3pm; 124 pesos); via **Zihuatanejo** (2hr., 39 pesos). La Linea, Lázaro Cárdenas 171 (☎537 18 50) runs to: **Manzanillo** (7hr., 2:30 and 5:30pm, 125 pesos); **Colima** (5hr., 10:30am and 8:45pm, 150 pesos); **Guadalajara** (9hr.; 10:30am, 8:45 and 9:15pm; 280 pesos); and **Mexico City** (12hr.; 3:30, 6:10, 7:50, and 11:45pm; 320 pesos). **Luggage storage** in the Estrella Blanca bus station, 2-6 pesos per bag per hr.

⛿ PRACTICAL INFORMATION. Get the maps and info you need for attacking the coast from the **Delegación Regional de Turismo,** Bravo 475, one block east of Av. Lázaro Cárdenas and two blocks north of Corregidora, in the big white Hotel Casa Blanca. (☎/fax 532 15 47. Open M-F 9am-3pm and 5-7pm, Sa 10am-1pm.) **Banamex,** Lázaro Cárdenas 1646, exchanges currency and has an **ATM,** (☎532 20 20. Open M-F 8:30am-4:30pm, Sa 10am-2pm), as does **BITAL,** Lázaro Cárdenas 1940. (☎532 26 33. Open M-Sa 8am-7pm, Sa 9am-2:30pm.) **Red Cross:** Aldama 327. (☎532 05 75; open 24hr.) **Police:** (☎532 18 55), Palacio Municipal, on Av. Lázaro Cárdenas at Av. Río Balsas. **Farmacia Paris,** Lázaro Cárdenas 2002. (☎532-1435; some English spoken; open 24hr.) **Hospital General** (☎532 08 21 5 or 532 05 97), on Av. Lázaro Cárdenas. Long-distance international **phone calls** can be made and **faxes** sent from **Caseta Goretti,** Corregidora 79. (☎537 31 55. Open daily 7am-1am.) **Internet: Sin Límite,** Cárdenas 1745, at the corner of Corregidora. (☎532 14 80. Open daily 9am-9pm, 25 pesos per hr., 15 pesos per 30min.) **Post office:** Bravo 1307. (☎532-0047. Open M-F 8am-3pm, Sa 9am-1pm.) **Postal Code:** 60950.

▟▛ ACCOMMODATIONS AND FOOD. The rent-by-the-hour atmosphere of most budget accommodations in town will make you happy to arrive at reputable **Hotel Reyna Pio,** Corregidora 78, at Av. Lázaro Cárdenas. Clean rooms boast A/C, telephone, mustard-yellow furniture, and TVs. (☎532-0620. Singles 120 pesos; doubles 150 pesos.) Fill your stomach at **El Chile Verde,** Madero 66. Hot chili peppers dance happily on the walls while waiters serve spicy *enchiladas verdes* (21 pesos) and *comida corrida* (20 pesos) in this casual, open-air cafe. (☎532-1085. Open daily 7am-10pm.) The slightly pricier but A/C-filled **El Paraíso,** Lázaro Cárdenas 1862 (☎532-3233), near the Galeana bus station, offers traditional fare amid orange, green, and yellow decor straight out of the 70s. The *sopa de tortilla* (15 pesos) and fish (50 pesos) are both worth a try.

MICHOACÁN COAST

Michoacán's temperamental, wildly beautiful coastline offers solace and tranquility one moment, and ripping, turbulent surf the next. Hills are pushed against each other; rocks are defaced by crashing white waves spraying into blue skies. Lush tropical vegetation lends a loving touch of green to the state's 260km of virgin beaches. Rte. 200, the solitary coastal route, twists up, down, and around Michoacán's angry terrain. Michoacán's coast is dangerous, and should be treated with cautious respect. Powerful waves make the beaches better suited for surfing than splashing around, and the currents are strong even in designated swimming areas. There are no lifeguards, so use extreme caution. Rte. 200 tends to be deserted and dangerous at night; *Let's Go* does not recommend traveling on it after dark.

PLAYA AZUL ☎ 7

Playa Azul (pop. 5000), a small town bordering the Pacific 26km west of Lázaro Cárdenas, is renowned for a long stretch of soft, golden sand and majestic rose-colored sunsets. Here, the sea is a temptress: for surfing and boogie-boarding, the strong undercurrent makes swimming treacherous. Crowded with Mexican tourists during December and *Semana Santa*, the beach is much more quiet during the rest of the year. Far from being a polished tourist town, Playa Azul is typically *michoacano:* unmarked dirt roads lined with thatched-roof houses and open-air markets are the main thoroughfares, while chickens and tanned locals in bathing suits walk the streets. The village is so small that street names are seldom used (or known) by locals.

TRANSPORTATION AND PRACTICAL INFORMATION. The *malecón* runs parallel to the beach; it is called **Serdán** to the west of the plaza and **Zapata** to the east. The other streets bordering the plaza are **Montes de Oca** to the west, and **Filomena Mata** to the east. Av. Lázaro Cárdenas runs into Playa Azul, runs perpendicular to the beach, and intersects with Carranza, Madero, and Independencia, the three main streets parallel to the beach. From Lázaro Cárdenas, take a "Playa Azul" *combi* straight to the beach (45min., every 2min. 5am-9pm, 10 pesos).

Playa Azul has no bank or *casa de cambio*, but does offer most other services. **Market: Flores Magón**, two blocks east of the plaza. (Open daily 8am-5pm.) **Police:** (☎ 532 18 55 or 532 20 30), across from the PEMEX station. **Farmacia Eva Carmen:** Av. Lázaro Cárdenas at Madero. (Open daily 8am-9:30pm.) **Centro de Salud:** next door to the post office. (Open 24hr.) For **long-distance calls,** visit the town's **caseta,** on Independencia (☎ 536 01 22; open M-Sa 8am-9pm, Su 8am-1pm), or simply use one of the **LADATELs** that can be found on the *malecón.* **Post office:** on Madero at Montes de Oca, just behind Hotel María Teresa. (☎ 536-0109. Open M-F 8am-3pm.)

ACCOMMODATIONS AND FOOD. Bucolic Playa Azul offers several adequate budget hotels. Reservations are recommended in August, December, and during *Semana Santa.* **Hotel Costa de Oro,** on Madero, 3 blocks from Lázaro Cárdenas, is the best deal in town. An elegantly scalloped bannister leads to clean, comfortable rooms with funky tile floors, fans, and mismatched bedspreads. Bathrooms are clean and have hot water. (Doubles 100 pesos; triples 150 pesos; quads 200 pesos). **Bungalows de la Curva,** on Madero at Lázaro Cárdenas, is a good deal for groups. Bungalows have kitchenettes and basic furniture. A swimming pool is surrounded by a patio with tables for pool-side relaxing or dining. (☎ 536 00 68. Singles 100 pesos; small bungalow 200 pesos; large bungalow 400 pesos.)

Palapa restaurants are so close to the shore that the waves will tickle your toes, but the hammocks swinging between tables remain high and dry. The bubbly owners of **Coco's Pizza** will make you feel right at home and the *camarones al diablo* (shrimp with chile, 48 pesos) are a spicy taste of heaven. (Open daily 8am-6pm low season, 8am-9pm high season.) Inland, **Restaurante**

Familiar Martita, on Magón at Madero, is a cozy family-run restaurant that serves just about everything. With one of the only TVs in town, it's a prime local hangout when *telenovelas* are on. (☎ 536 01 11. *Comida corrida* 30 pesos; breakfast combos 25-30 pesos. Open daily 7am-11pm.)

PLAYA AZUL TO CALETA DE CAMPOS

Beautiful beaches cover the 43km stretch of coastline from Playa Azul to Caleta de Campos. **Las Peñas,** 13km west of Playa Azul, is a beach better appreciated from the shore: it's terribly turbulent but great for surfing. **El Bejuco,** only 2km farther west, has a sandy cove with tamer waves and fewer rocks. Another 12km west, you'll find **Chuquiapan,** a long sandy beach with reasonable waves and a shore studded with tall green palms. **La Soledad,** enclosed by rocky formations 4km farther west, is more secluded and cozy, lying at the base of a hill covered with dense vegetation. Its grey sands are strewn with rocks and driftwood and, typical of Michoacán's Pacific coast, rough waters make for dangerous swimming. **Mexcalhuacán,** 2km west, offers a fantastic view from a bluff overlooking a rocky coast. **Caleta de Campos** comes 7km later. **Nexpa,** a sandy beach with powerful waves, is a surfer's heaven 5km west of Caleta. *Palapa* restaurants, known as *enramadas*, line most of the beaches. **Buses** running from Lázaro Cárdenas to Caleta de Campos leave from Galeana bus station and pass by each of the beaches, listed above, except Nexpa (every 20min. 6:20am-8:10pm). The beaches are a short walk from the route (5-10min.). To return to Playa Azul or Lázaro Cárdenas, simply wave down a bus going in the opposite direction (last return at 7:40pm). To get to Nexpa, take a white *combi* from the bus depot at the beginning of Principal in Caleta de Campos (10min., every 40min., 7am-7pm).

CALETA DE CAMPOS   ☎ 7

A tiny fishing village 47km west of Playa Azul, Caleta de Campos has a pleasant beach but little else for the fun-loving traveler. The entire town is laid out along its one main street; blink and you'll miss it. A dirt path climbs along the hills, offering a spectacular view of the coast. Because the water is somewhat sheltered, the surf is calmer than at Playa Azul, and the rolling waves make for good boogie-boarding and body surfing. For most of the year, Caleta's two hotels are empty, but they fill up during *Semana Santa* and Christmas.

▐ TRANSPORTATION. From Lázaro Cárdenas, **Rutas de Transportación Colectiva** (☎ 532 02 62) buses run from the Galeana bus station to **Caleta** (1½hr., every 20 min. 6:20am-8:10pm, 27 pesos). To return to Lázaro Cárdenas from Caleta, pick up a bus at the stop near the end of Principal (5:30am-7:40pm). From Playa Azul, get on any bus leaving town, across from the PEMEX gas station (5min., every 10min., 3 pesos). Get off at **Acalpican,** a marked city just a few km north of Playa Azul (be sure to tell the driver where you want to go in advance) and catch a bus labeled "Caleta" at the intersection (every 30min. 5:45am-8:45pm, 23 pesos).

▐ PRACTICAL INFORMATION. Caleta de Campos has one paved main street, Melchor Ocampo, locally known as **Principal.** The **police, post office** (open M-F 8am-3pm), and **bus stop** are all on Principal. **Casetas** (☎ 531 50 06) on the right side of the far end of Principal, as you face away from the church. **LADATELs** along Principal. **Farmacia Morelia,** on Principal, will sometimes change dollars, and is a pharmacy to boot. (☎ 531-5052. Open daily 7am-9pm.) **Centro de Salud:** turn right on the side street before Principal turns left and walk three blocks. (Open 24hr.)

▐▐ ACCOMMODATIONS AND FOOD. Caleta has only two hotels, both of which are nice and affordable. The **Hotel Los Arcos,** next to the church as Principal turns left, has very clean rooms with golden doors, tiled floors and bathrooms and fans. Arch-shaped windows provide a spectacular view of the coast. (☎ 531 50 38.

Singles 120 pesos; doubles 150 pesos, with A/C 200 pesos.) It's always Christmas at the **Hotel Yuritzi,** off Principal after the church to the left. Yuritzi has spiffy rooms with fans, TV, and red and green bedspreads. (Doubles with fan 170 pesos, with A/C and TV 300 pesos). To get to the beach from the hotels, walk to the end of Principal. Pass the church and the Lonchería Bahía on your right, and follow the dirt road as it bends to the right; the beach lies at the bottom of the hill (10min. walk).

Across the street from Hotel Yuritzi is one of Caleta's only restaurants, **Lonchería Bahía.** The laid-back cafe serves hamburgers (16-25 pesos), *tortas* (11-13 pesos), and fruit drinks (11-13 pesos; open daily 9am-10pm.) Also popular is **Enramada Omar,** the third *palapa* restaurant on the sandy cove. It serves shrimp any style (40-50 pesos) and other seafood specialties. (Open daily 7am-9pm.)

GUERRERO

TAXCO ☎ 7

White buildings capped with red roofs, windy cobblestone streets, and sparkling *platerías* (silver shops) make the old mining town of Taxco (pop. 150,000) an antique gem set into the mountains. Cobblestone alleys coil around colonial churches, and streets are so narrow that people have to flatten themselves along walls to let a lone Volkswagen Bug pass. Beneath all the swarming confusion and old-fashioned beauty are the veins of silver which shaped Taxco's history. When silver was discovered here in 1524, Taxco became the continent's first mining town with riches enough to lure craftsmen and fortune seekers from all over the world. The town's fortune ebbed with the supply of silver and it was not until the 1930s, when the tourist industry took hold, that the town exploded with *platerías*. Today, Taxco is aflutter with tourists buzzing through the labyrinthine alleys, drawn like bees to the sweet honey of countless jewelry shops.

▐ TRANSPORTATION

Taxco has two main bus stations, the **Estrella de Oro** and **Flecha Roja** stations. To get to the *zócalo* from the **Estrella de Oro station,** Kennedy 126 (☎ 622 06 48), cross the street and walk up the steep hill known as Pilita. When you reach the Plazuela San Juan, with a small fountain, veer left and you will come out facing Santa Prisca in the *zócalo*. A "Zócalo" *combi* will make the trip (2.5 pesos), as will a taxi (10 pesos to almost anywhere in the city). Estrella de Oro has first-class service to: **Acapulco** (4hr., 5 per day 7:10am-6:10pm, 120 pesos); **Cuernavaca** (1½hr., 4 per day 9:15am-6:15pm, 38 pesos); and **Mexico City** (2½hr., 5 per day 7am-6pm, 78 pesos).

To reach the *zócalo* from the **Flecha Roja station,** Plateros 104 (☎ 622 01 31), turn right out of the station on to Plateros and turn left on Juan Ruíz de Alarcón. Turn left on Agustín de Tolsa to get to the *zócalo*. **Flecha Roja** goes to: **Acapulco** (4½hr. 4 per day 12:10pm-6pm, 120 pesos); **Cuernavaca** (1½hr., every hr. 6am-10pm, 37 pesos); and **Toluca** (3hr.; 1am, 11:40pm and 2pm; 62 pesos).

✶▐ ORIENTATION AND PRACTICAL INFORMATION

Taxco lies 185km southwest of Mexico City in the state of Guerrero. A hillside position makes its steep winding streets unavoidable. Due to its relatively small size, however, most streets eventually lead uphill to the *zócalo*, **Plaza Borda,** and the town's centerpiece, the **Catedral de Santa Prisca.**

Tourist Office: Subsecretaría de Fomento Turístico (☎ 622 22 74), at the entrance to town. "Los Arcos" *combis* end their route in front of the office, located on the second fl. Open daily 8am-8pm. Free tourist information at the Flecha Roja station; most hotels on the Plaza Borda offer maps.

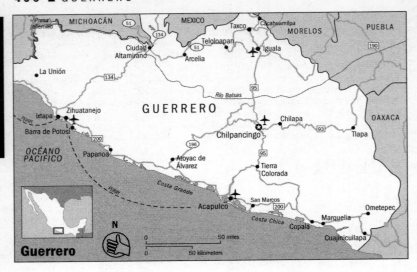

Guerrero

Currency Exchange: Citibank, on the *zócalo*, has an **ATM.** Open M-F 9am-4pm. **Banco Santander Mexicano,** Cuauhtémoc 4 (☎622 35 35 or 622 32 70), off the *zócalo*, changes money until 4:30pm. Open M-F 9am-5pm, Sa 10am-2pm.

Market: Mercado Tetitlán can be entered on the street to the right of Santa Prisca or off of Hidalgo. Sells everything from meat to jewelry. Open daily 8:30am-8pm.

Police: (☎622 00 07). Some English spoken. Open 24hr.

Emergency: Procuraduría del Turista (☎622 22 74 or 622 66 16). Open M-F 9am-7pm.

Red Cross: (☎622 32 32), on Plateros, next door to the tourist information *caseta*. No English spoken. Open daily 9am-2pm and 5-7pm. 24hr. **ambulance service.**

Pharmacy: farmacia Guadalupana, Hidalgo 8 (☎622 03 95) near Plaza San Juan. Open daily 8:30am-10pm.

Hospital: IMSS (☎622 35 10), on Plateros. 24hr. emergency service.

Fax: Alarcón 1 (☎622 48 85; fax 622 00 01), on the *zócalo*. Open M-F 9am-3pm, Sa 9am-noon.

Telephones: LADATELs found around the main plazas. farmacia Guadalupana has a long-distance **caseta.** Open daily 8:30am-10pm.

Internet Access: XNet, Delicias 4 (☎622 17 21), inside Bora Bora Pizza. 30 pesos per hr. 30% discount for students and teachers. Open daily 10:30am-11pm.

Post Office: Plateros 382 (☎622 05 01), near the Estrella de Oro station. Open M-F 9am-3pm.

Postal Code: 40200.

■ ACCOMMODATIONS

Although a good night's sleep does not come cheaply in Taxco, almost any accommodation you choose will provide a well-kept room with a classy courtyard, scenic balcony, or even a refreshing swimming pool. Make advance reservations if arriving during local holidays and in March, April, or November.

Casa de Huéspedes Arellano, Pajaritos 23 (☎622 02 15). From the zócalo, walk down the street to the right of the cathedral and descend the first stairs to the right; the hotel is 3 levels down through the vendors' stands. Potted plants liven up the entrance of the

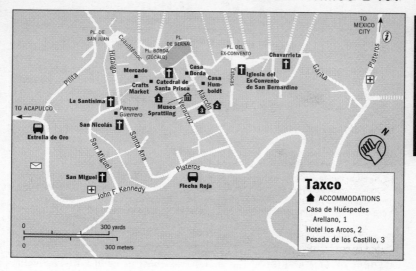

Taxco
▲ ACCOMMODATIONS
Casa de Huéspedes
Arellano, 1
Hotel los Arcos, 2
Posada de los Castillo, 3

casa, built by the owner's father. Three terraces on which to sunbathe, hang laundry, and chat with backpackers. Communal baths. Clean dorm rooms house up to 6 people. Dorms 80 pesos; individual rooms 150 pesos.

Hotel Los Arcos, Alarcón 4 (☎622 28 36), follow Agostín de Tolsa from the north end of the *zócalo* and then turn right on the first street. From its cool shaded courtyard to its expansive rooftop terrace, the hotel is begging to be explored. Carved wooden furniture in rooms and wrought iron bars on windows create a medieval atmosphere. Private bathrooms are clean but small. Singles 200 pesos; doubles 250 pesos.

Posada de Los Castillo, Alarcón 7 (☎622 13 96), across the street from Hotel Los Arcos. All the furniture, from the doors to the headboards, is painted in reassuring earth tones. Even more reassuring are the firm beds with fluffy pillows. Small but scenic terrace on the fifth floor. Singles 165 pesos; doubles 215 pesos; triples 305 pesos.

Hotel Agua Escondida, Guillermo Spratling 4 (☎622 11 66), on the Plaza Borda. Upscale and quite expensive, guests of this stunning hotel wake up to pink sandstone, flowers, and breakfast. Lounge, ping-pong, swimming pool, and video arcade make the hotel worth every peso. Singles 199; doubles 250.

Casa Grande, Plaza de San Juan 7 (☎622 09 69), on the *zócalo,* with entrance to the left of the building up the street. In the middle of what little nightlife Taxco has to offer. Don't expect to get to sleep until after 1am, when the adjacent bar turns out its lights. Rooms are clean, but small and dark. Communal baths are cramped but adequate. Singles 100 pesos, with bath 120 pesos; doubles 180 pesos, with bath 200 pesos.

🍴 FOOD

Taquerías and *torterías* are virtually extinct around Plaza Borda, but increase in number as you descend into the swarming market areas. Eating out in Taxco can be quite enjoyable—numerous restaurants have balconies with lovely views of the populated streets. Watch the sunset slip by while you sip *sangría* or *mezcal.*

🍴 Sasha's, Alarcon 1, down the street from Hotel Los Arcos. This vegetarian-friendly cafe serves delicious pastas (32-34 pesos) and pizzas (25-35 pesos). Though the open windows don't offer much of a view, the fun music and quiet street below make Sasha's the ideal hang out. Open M-Th 8am-midnight, F-Su 8am-3am.

Sotavento, Juárez 2, down the hill from the Iglesia del Ex-Convento toward the *zócalo.* A bit more upscale, Sotavento offers delicious food at reasonable prices, serving its chic clientele everything from pastas (30 pesos) to traditional dishes (26-32 pesos). Also provides Internet service for 15 pesos per hour. Open daily 1pm-midnight.

La Concha Nostra, Plaza de San Juan 7 (☎622 79 44), 2nd fl. of the Hotel Casa Grande. A youthful hangout, with live music on Saturday nights. While you're waiting for your *quesadillas* (20 pesos), lasagna (32 pesos), or pizza (starting at 19 pesos), watch the angsty language students blow smoke rings and scribble tormented poetry in their notebooks. Open daily 7:45am-1am.

Pizzas Bora Bora, Delicias 4 (☎622 17 21), on the unmarked street that slopes up to the right from Cuauhtémoc, just off the *zócalo.* Fishing nets and basket lamps dangle from the wooden ceiling. Dimly lit with low tables and stools. Pizzas start at 30 pesos, spaghetti at 25 pesos. Open daily 1:30pm-midnight.

La Hamburguesa, Plaza de San Juan 5 (☎622 09 41), the next plaza over from the *zócalo,* down the street of Casa Grande. Lives up to its name by offering satisfying burgers starting at 10 pesos, with fries 17 pesos. More traditional fare is also served (12-30 pesos). Popular with US language school students. Open daily 8am-midnight.

⬛ SIGHTS

CATEDRAL DE SANTA PRISCA. The church was constructed in 1751-1758 with funds donated by silver tycoon José de la Borda. The beautiful Baroque facade is made of faded rose stone and decorated with inverted Corinthian columns. Inside are paintings done by the indigenous artist Miguel Cabrerra, whose racy subjects include a pregnant Virgin Mary and the circumcision of Baby Jesus. *(Open daily 8am-8pm, mass still held every hour on Su between 6am and 2pm.)*

CASA BORDA. To the left of the church is the 18th-century home of silver tycoon José de la Borda; enter through the bookstore on the *zócalo.* The house has been turned into the **Instituto Guerrerense de Cultura.** In addition to a library, a dance studio, and several exhibition galleries, the center organizes book readings and concerts. Ask for a schedule. *(☎622 66 17. Open Tu-Sa 10:30am-8pm, Su 10:30am-4pm.)*

CASA HUMBOLDT. The late 18th-century colonial home has unusual bas-reliefs in Moorish *mudéjar* style and served as a rest stop for explorer Alexander Von Humboldt for just one night in 1803. The restored house now holds the collection of the **Museo de Arte Virreinal,** which contains exhibits on 18th-century Catholic rituals and dress. *(Alarcón 12, down the street past the Hotel Los Arcos. ☎622 55 01. Open Tu-Sa 10am-5pm, Su 9am-3pm. 15 pesos, students with ID 5 pesos.)*

EX-CONVENTO DE SAN BERNANDINO. Built in 1592 as a Franciscan monastery and destroyed by a fire two centuries later, the *ex-convento* was reconstructed in Neoclassical style in 1823. The struggle for independence from the Spanish officially ended when the Plan de Iguala was signed within these walls in 1821. A school now convenes under its roof. *(In the Plaza del Convento. Follow Juárez past the city offices. Open daily 8am-1pm and 2-6:30pm. Free.)*

MUSEO GUILLERMO SPRATLING. Named after American silversmith William Spratling, who helped jump-start the silver industry with his successful shop in the 1930s, this museum houses his collection of prehistoric indigenous artifacts. *(Delgado 1. Follow the downhill road to the left of the cathedral; the museum is on the left. Open M-Sa 10am-5pm, Su 9am-3pm. 15 pesos.)*

VIEWS OF TAXCO. The vistas of the city and surrounding hills from the hilly streets are superb. One of the more striking views is at the **Church of Guadalupe.** From the *zócalo,* take Ojeda, to the right of Cuauhtémoc, to Guadalupe, and veer right until you reach the plaza in front of the church. For a more sweeping view, you can take a **cable car** to Hotel Monte Taxco. *(Take a "Los Arcos" combi to the white arches at the city's entrance (2 pesos). Before passing through the arches, turn left up a hill, and* *bear left into the parking lot.* ☎ 622 14 68. *Runs daily 7:40am-7pm. Round-trip 26 pesos, children 14 pesos, hotel guests free.)*

 NIGHTLIFE

As the silver shops shut their doors and vendors pack their wares, people head to the **Plaza Borda** in front of the illuminated cathedral. Those with enough energy to dance after hiking Taxco's hills will get their chance on weekends. **Windows,** in the Hotel Monte Taxco, has the area's hottest dancing. Accessible only by cable car or taxi, this bar/dance club offers an unparalleled view combined with a party atmosphere. (☎ 622 13 00. Cover 50 pesos. Open F-Su 10pm-late.) For a more relaxed evening, make your way to **La Concha Nostra** in Hotel Casa Grande, Plaza de San Juan 7, for beer (15 pesos) and great conversation. (Open daily 8am-1am)

 SHOPPING

Taxco is like one giant shop. More than 300 *platerías* cater to the zombied tourists drawn to Taxco by its silver sheen. If you're dipping uncomfortably deep into your pockets, browse the shops that sell *artesanías* as well as silver. You can also stop by **Mercado Tetitlán.** Enter behind the cathedral or from one of the alleyways off Hidalgo. Here, produce stands are interspersed with standard *platerías.* (Open daily 8:30am-8pm.) The **Mercado de Plata,** just behind the Flecha Roja station, is where locals buy their silver and where silversmiths from the countryside often sell their wares at cheaper prices. (Open Sa 10am-6pm.)

 FESTIVALS

Taxco's crowded streets somehow manage to accommodate the tsunami of tourists that descend on the town during its two major festivals: the **Feria Nacional de la Plata,** a national contest during the first week of November designed to encourage silver artisanship, and the more popular **Semana Santa** festivities. On Good Friday, hooded *penitentes* carry logs made out of cactus trunks on their shoulders, or subject themselves to flagellation to cleanse them of their sins. During the annual **Día del Jumil,** on the first Monday of November, Taxco residents make a pilgrimage to the *Huizteco* hill, where they collect insects known as *jumil* to eat. The 1.5cm-long brown bugs contain more protein per gram than beef, and only appear during this time of year. In December, the **Church of Guadalupe,** from which you can see all of Taxco, comes alive with celebrations in honor of the Virgin.

 DAYTRIPS FROM TAXCO

▧ **GRUTAS DE CACAHUAMILPA.** Some of the most beautiful natural wonders in Taxco lie underground in an extensive network of *grutas* (caves). According to lore, the **Grutas de Cacahuamilpa** were once a hideaway for runaway Indians.

ALL THAT GLITTERS IS NOT...SILVER Although unscrupulous sellers and cheating craftspeople occasionally pass off *alpaca* (fool's silver) or *plateados* (silver-plated metals) to unsuspecting tourists, buying silver in Taxco is usually a sure thing. Many proprietors speak English and accept US currency, but if you stick with Spanish and talk in pesos while bargaining, you lower the risk of being charged tourist prices. While it's fun to ogle glamorous and expensive silver in the shops around the Plaza Borda, the silver gets less expensive and the employees more amenable to bargaining the farther you go from the *centro.* Bargain at stores with silver workshops by faking out the clerk and heading straight for the artisan. Remember that only the official ".925" stamp on the object's side guarantees that your shiny new charm is indeed silver; inspect merchandise carefully before purchasing anything.

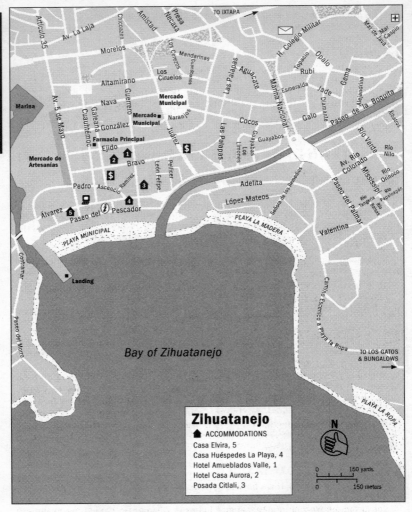

Bay of Zihuatanejo

Zihuatanejo

🏠 ACCOMMODATIONS

Casa Elvira, 5
Casa Huéspedes La Playa, 4
Hotel Amueblados Valle, 1
Hotel Casa Aurora, 2
Posada Citlali, 3

0   150 yards
0   150 meters

Twenty huge *salones* (halls) are filled with stalactites, stalagmites, and rock formations in curious shapes, sizes, and colors. The columns and ceilings—some as high as 85m—are the work of the subterranean stream which developed into the **Río San Jerónimo.** The guide will point out funny rock shapes complete with fabricated anecdotes. (*"Grutas" combis make the trip from Taxco's Flecha Roja station, dropping off and picking up passengers at the gruta parking lot (every hr., 13 pesos). Taxis cost 80-100 pesos. Flecha Roja buses make the trip (30min., every hr. 6:30am-3:30am, 16 pesos), but will drop you off a short jaunt away. To get to the gruta parking lot, take a right, then another right after the curve. Open daily 10am-5pm. 30 pesos, children 20 pesos. Tours leave from the visitors center (2hr., every hr.). You can only enter the caves with a tour guide.*)

LAS GRANADAS. Twenty-six kilometers from Taxco, the ecological reserve of Las Granadas is little more than a hike in the woods. This 5km rock trail curls around mountain tops and dips into the valley, bringing hikers to a stunning natural waterfall. The path is both hilly and sunny, so wear comfortable walking shoes and sunblock. *(To get to there, grab a combi heading to Acuitlapan (40min., every 25min. 7am-8pm, 13 pesos). Once there, follow the one road into the tiny town. As you enter the main square of town, look to the far end where the path starts as a dirt road. No set hours. Free.)*

IXCATEOPAN. Forty-two kilometers from Taxco, the town of Ixcateopan is known for both its beauty and its history. The marble and stone streets supply the former, while the **Museo de la Resistencia Indígena** provides information on the latter. (Open daily 9am-5pm. Free). What are said to be the remains of Cuauhtémoc, the last Aztec emperor, are kept in a display case in the **Templo de Santa María de la Asunción.** *(To get to Ixcateopan, take the "Ixcateopan" combi (1¼hr., every 30min. 6am-9pm, 13 pesos), leaving Taxco in front of Seguro Social on J.F. Kennedy.)*

ZIHUATANEJO AND IXTAPA ☎ 7

Before resort engineers got their hands on Ixtapa (eeks-TAH-pa), it was a wild landscape filled with coconut palms, rocky cliffs, and mangrove swamps. Not until the 1970s, when development began on "the place of the white sands," did both Ixtapa and its counterpart, Zihuatanejo (see-wah-tah-NEH-ho), find themselves on the tourist map. Separated by 6km of land and three centuries of development, the towns' combined population of about 80,000 thrives almost exclusively on the tourist trade. Ixtapa has been meticulously constructed by Mexican pleasure engineers to cater to moneyed foreigners. Expect few budget restaurants and fewer budget accommodations. Meanwhile Zihuatanejo, just a 15-minute bus ride away, hasn't shaken the net of its fishing town past. Here, budget hotels are just a few steps from the glittering beach. The night-and-day difference between Ixtapa and Zihuatanejo makes a trip here two vacations in one. If you stay in Zihuatanejo and play in Ixtapa, these twins will supply tourist-town glitz with fishing-village prices.

▐▀ TRANSPORTATION

GETTING AROUND

Ixtapa's main road, **Blvd. Ixtapa,** lies past a phalanx of waterfront luxury hotels on the left and overpriced stores to the right. **Buses** shuttling between the two cities leave Zihuatanejo from the intersection of Juárez and Morelos, across from the yellow Elektra store; they leave Ixtapa from various stops on Blvd. Ixtapa (15-25min., every 15min. 6am-10pm, 4 pesos). **Taxis** scuttle between the two towns (30 pesos by day, 40 pesos by night). Taxis in Zihuatanejo can always be found on Juárez, in front of the market.

GETTING AWAY

Airport: (☎554 20 70) 15km outside of town. Taxis go from the airport to Zihuatanejo (125 pesos) and Ixtapa (160 pesos). *Combis* go from the left side of the airport parking lot to the intersection of Morelos and Juárez in Zihuatanejo (daily 6am-11pm, 4.5 pesos). You can catch *combis* to the airport from the intersection of González and Juárez in Zihuatanejo. They are marked with a picture of a plane (daily 6:30am-10:30pm, 4.5 pesos). Served by **Aeroméxico** (☎554 22 37 or 554 26 34), **America West** (☎554 86 34), **Continental** (☎554 25 49 or 554 42 17), and **Mexicana** (☎554 22 27). Branch offices in Zihuatanejo: **Aeroméxico,** 5 de Mayo 34 (☎554 20 18), at Álvarez, 1 block from the water. Open daily 9am-2pm, 4-6pm. **Mexicana** (☎554 22 08 or 554 22 09), Guerrero at Bravo. Open daily 9am-6pm.

Buses: arrive in Zihuatanejo at the **Estrella Blanca** and **Estrella de Oro** stations, side-by-side on the outskirts of the *centro. Combis* (3.5 pesos), to the left as you leave the station, or taxis (15 pesos) bring you to the center of town. To reach the bus station from the *centro*, hop on a *combi* labeled "Coacoyul" (7am-8:30pm, 3.5 pesos) across from the market on Juárez. Estrella de Oro (☎554 21 75) sends buses to: **Acapulco** (4½hr., every hr. 7am-5pm, 65 pesos); **Cuernavaca** (8hr., 8pm and 11pm, 251 pesos); **Mexico City** (9hr.; 6:40am, 9, 10 and 11pm; 295 pesos); and **Papanoa**

(1½hr., every hr. 7am-5pm, 26 pesos). Estrella Blanca (☎554 34 77) goes to: **Acapulco** (4hr., every hr. 7am-9:35pm, 95 pesos); **Lázaro Cárdenas** (2hr., every hr. 1am-11:30pm, 45 pesos) and **Puerto Escondido** (12hr., 7:30pm, 260 pesos).

🛈 PRACTICAL INFORMATION

TOURIST, FINANCIAL, AND LOCAL SERVICES

Tourist Office: SEFOTUR (☎553 19 67), on Blvd. Ixtapa, in Ixtapa across from Hotel Presidente, offers a comprehensive *Guía Turística Urbana* to beaches and services. Some English spoken. Open M-F 8am-9pm, Sa 8am-3pm. For complaints or emergencies call the **Agencia de Ministerio Publico en Atención al Turista** (☎554 19 67) in Ixtapa, or **Profeco** (☎554 52 36) in Zihuatanejo.

Currency Exchange: Bancomer (☎554 74 93), in Zihuatanejo on the corner of Juárez and Bravo. Open M-F 8:30am-5:30pm, Sa 10am-2pm. Also has a 24hr. **ATM. Money Exchange,** Galeana 6 (☎554 28 00), has worse rates but no commission. From the beach, walk a block on Cuauhtémoc, take a right on Ascencio and make the first left onto Galeana. Offers **fax** and **long-distance** service as well. Open daily 8am-9pm.

Bookstore: Byblos, Galeana 2 (☎554 38 11), in Zihuatanejo, has English magazines, paperback novels, and the handy *Owen's English Language Guide to Ixtapa and Zihuatanejo* (written by a member of Cousteau's team). Open M-Sa 9am-9pm.

Market: The **mercado municipal** in Zihuatanejo on Juárez, 4 blocks from the water, sells fresh produce and has several small eateries. Open daily 7am-8pm. The **Mercado de Artesanías** in Zihuatanejo offers jewelry and souvenirs. Open daily 9am-8:30pm.

Supermarket: Scrupples (☎553 15 14), Blvd. Ixtapa in Ixtapa, in the plaza to the right of the tourist office. Open daily 8am-11pm.

Laundry: Súper Clean, González 82 (☎554 23 47), in Zihuatanejo at Galeana. 12 pesos per kg., 36 peso minimum. Same day delivery. Open M-Sa 8am-8pm.

Luggage Storage: Estrella Blanca station in Zihuatanejo. Open 24hr. 2 pesos per hr.

Car Rental: Hertz, Bravo 13 (☎554 22 55; fax 554 30 50), in Zihuatanejo, rents small VWs for 670 pesos per day including insurance and unlimited mileage. Open daily 8am-6pm. Hertz (☎554-2590) also has an office in the airport.

EMERGENCY AND COMMUNICATIONS

Police: (☎554 20 40), in Zihuatanejo in the Palacio Municipal in front of Playa Principal.

Red Cross: (☎554 20 09), on Huertas as you leave Zihuatanejo. 24hr. emergency and ambulance service. No English spoken.

Pharmacy: Farmacia Principal (☎554 42 17), Cuauhtémoc at Ejido in Zihuatanejo, 3 blocks from the water. English spoken. Open M-Sa 9am-9pm.

Medical Services: Centro de Salud (☎554 20 88), Boquita at Palmar, in Zihuatanejo. Open M-F 8am-8pm, Sa 8am-3pm.

Emergency: ☎060

Internet Access: Net World 2000, Álvarez 34 (☎554 29 56), in Zihuatanejo across from Casa Elvira. 30 pesos per hour, half off between 2 and 5pm. M-Sa 9am-10pm. Ixtapa: **Xtapa Connexión,** (☎553 22 53), Ixtapa Plaza on the walkway to the left of Señor Frog's. 85 pesos per hour, 20 pesos to check email. 10:30am-10pm.

Post Office: (☎554 21 92), off Palmar in Zihuatanejo. From Juárez, turn right on Morelos. At the Pollo Feliz, take a right and walk down 2 blocks. Open M-F 8am-3pm, Sa 9am-1pm. **Postal Code:** 40880.

▐ ACCOMMODATIONS

Zihuatanejo has plenty of budget accommodations within a few blocks of the Playa Municipal. Prices rise substantially during the high season (Dec.-Apr.), as does the number of gringos per square foot. If you visit during an off time, with a large group, or plan to stay several days, you will have excellent leverage for negotiating a discount. The tourist office discourages unofficial camping, partly for safety reasons, but if you insist on pitching a tent, **Playa Quieta,** near Club Med in Ixtapa, is the most sensible place. All of the following listings are in Zihuatanejo.

Casa Elvira, Álvarez 8 (☎554 20 61), 1 block from the Playa Municipal, was the first guest house in Zihuatanejo, and remains a bargain. Rooms are cozy and extremely clean, if a bit small, and have private cold-water bathrooms. The courtyard is filled with plants, birds, and gregarious family members; step out back and you're on the beach. With strong ceiling fans cooling the rooms, it doesn't get more comfortable than this. Singles 80 pesos; doubles 100 pesos. Prices often negotiable.

Hotel Casa Aurora, Bravo 27 (☎554 30 46), between Guerrero and Galeana. This budget mainstay has a friendly staff, neat, good-sized rooms, and 70s bedspreads. Bathrooms are clean and have hot water. 100 pesos per person, 150 pesos with A/C. Beachside bungalow with kitchen and no A/C holds 3 people for 300 pesos.

Casa de Huéspedes La Playa, Álvarez 6 (☎554 22 47), at Guerrero. The best thing about this place is the location. The waves of the Pacific will lull you to sleep, as will the soothing light of the moon shining on the sea. Basic and clean, with fans and no hot water. There are no fixed prices, but rooms with 2 beds usually cost 200 pesos.

Posada Citlali, Guerrero 3 (☎554 20 43), near Álvarez. On the expensive side, but quite charming. Vines dangle lazily in the central courtyard; wooden rockers on the terrace encourage you to do the same. All rooms have overhead fans. Singles 200 pesos; doubles 250 pesos; triples 300 pesos.

Hotel Amueblados Valle, Guerrero 14 (☎554 20 84), between Ejido and Bravo. 8 fully-equipped apartments give guests a large kitchen/eating area, ceiling fans, balconies, and daily towel service. Rooms are spacious and packed with amenities. One person 300 pesos, 2 people 350 pesos, 3 people 400 pesos. Prices rise during high season.

◖ FOOD

Like the neighboring hotels, restaurants in Ixtapa are pricey. However, they are spotless and offer an array of authentic-tasting international cuisine. Your meal may be more reasonably priced (50-70 pesos) if you eat at a cafe before they switch to the main menu (around 2pm). Restaurants in Zihuatanejo serve freshly caught fish from the bay at consistent budget prices. All of the following listings are in Zihuatanejo.

Los Abánicos, (☎55420 20) on the corner of Ascencio and Galeana. Though this open-air restaurant may look like every other in Zihuatanejo, it's not. The food here is delicious and cheap—try their more than satisfying *comida corrida* (25 pesos), which comes with a choice of 3 rotating entrees, rice or soup, tortillas, and *agua fresca*. great *ceviche* 35 pesos. Open M-Sa 8am-6pm.

La Carreta, Bravo 9 (☎554 55 58), less than a block west of Juárez. This local eatery, though not far from the beach, is far enough that many tourists don't find it. With a diverse menu of scrumptious home-cooked meals, Carreta will please even the most discerning palate. Try their breakfasts (15-20 pesos) or *comida corrida* (20 pesos). Open W-M 8am-midnight.

Los Braseros, Ejido 64 (☎55487 36), between Galeana and Guerrero. This exuberant open-air eatery specializes in heavenly stir-fried combinations of meat, veggies, and cheese (42 pesos), with a sprinkling of veggie options. Large portions are served with hot tortillas by an attentive staff. Open daily 8am-1am.

La Sirena Gorda (The Fat Mermaid), Paseo del Pescador 20A (☎55426 87), next to the pier. Start your morning off with a stack of hotcakes (30-34 pesos), and when the sun goes down you can dine on seafood tacos (30-35 pesos). Paintings of fat and jocular mermaids decorate the interior. Open Th-Tu 9am-11pm.

◨ ◙ BEACHES AND SIGHTS

Neither Zihuatanejo's self-conscious charm nor Ixtapa's resorts could eclipse the area's natural beauty. In Zihuatanejo, four patches of sand make excellent beaches. They are, clockwise from the municipal pier: Playa Principal, Playa La Madera, Playa la Ropa, and Playa Las Gatas. The latter two are the two best beaches in Zihuatanejo. Ixtapa overlooks the unbroken stretch of Playa del Palmar on the Bahía del Palmar, but the prettiest beaches lie beyond Laguna de Ixtapa: Playa Quieta, Playa Linda, and, at the bay's west edge, Isla Ixtapa.

ZIHUATANEJO

PLAYA PRINCIPAL. Playa Principal is downtown Zihuatanejo's beach, in front of the Paseo del Pescador. This beach is more suited to seashell collectors and fishing boats than to swimmers. The attractions here are the basketball court, the pier, and the fish being unloaded onto the dock.

PLAYA MADERA. About 200m long, Playa Madera (Wood Beach) got its name from its role as a loading site for local hardwood export. The fine sand and gentle waves show no trace of its lumberyard past, but offer a great place to bodysurf or play in the waves. A number of restaurants and bungalows have sprung up along the shore. *(To get there, follow the cement pathway at the end of Playa Principal.)*

PLAYA LA ROPA. Protected from the rough Pacific by the shape of the bay, Playa La Ropa's crescent of sumptuous white, often-uncrowded sand attracts tourists from the hotels on the surrounding cliffs. *(Taxis are the easiest way to reach La Ropa (20 pesos). You can also make the 4km trip by foot: follow Paseo de la Boquita along the canal over the bridge and turn left, passing Playa Madera. The road curves to the right and passes Hotel Casa que Canta; follow the stone road to the left down to the beach.)*

PLAYA LAS GATAS. According to local lore, Purepecha king Calzontzin ordered the construction of the stone wall in Playa Las Gatas as protection from the sharks while he bathed. Since then, coral and marine life have overtaken the stone barricade. Just as colorful but not nearly as pleasant, lawn chairs and umbrellas, available from local restaurants (30 pesos), have taken over the beach. The calm, transparent waters welcome snorkelers (equipment rental 40 pesos per day) and kayakers (single-person kayaks 100 pesos per hr., 300 pesos per day). Escape the shops and restaurants by taking the path (2km) behind the last restaurant to the **Garrobo Lighthouse,** which offers a panoramic view. Since it's well hidden, ask any of the waiters for specific directions to the lighthouse. *(To reach Las Gatas, take a lancha from the pier in downtown Zihuatanejo (10min.; every 15min. 9am-4pm, last boat returns 5pm; round-trip 30 pesos). It is possible to walk over the rocks to Las Gatas from La Ropa, but not easy. Alternatively, you may walk on the road that brought you to La Ropa for another 45min., keeping to the left as it splits.)*

IXTAPA

PLAYA DE PALMER. Well guarded from Blvd. Ixtapa by a line of posh hotels, Playa de Palmer is an active, spacious, and beautiful beach. Walk a few km on the soft yellow sand or stop by a massage hut and have your worries released by a Shiatsu master (200 pesos per hr.). Without the protection of a bay, the beach is pummeled by sizeable waves, attracting para-sailers, scuba divers, and jet skiers. Along the sand next to the swimming pools, people jog, play volleyball, and play soccer. *(The beach can be reached by public access paths at either end, near the Sheraton Hotel, or near Carlos 'n' Charlie's. Otherwise, clutch your Let's Go confidently, wear your swimsuit proudly, and cut right through the fancy hotel lobbies.)*

PLAYA QUIETA AND PLAYA LINDA. About 6km northwest of downtown lie Playas Quieta and Linda. This stretch of rocky sand may not be fun to walk on, but the calmer waves are great for swimming. One or two nearby restaurants rent horses for 150 pesos per hr. *(From Ixtapa, follow the Blvd. Ixtapa northwest beyond most of the hotels, and turn right at the sign for Playa Linda. From Zihuatanejo, it is more convenient to use the access road from Rte. 200; go past the exit for Ixtapa in the direction of Puerto Vallarta and take the next left, marked Playa Linda. The road skirts Laguna de Ixtapa and hits the beach farther northwest. Taxis from Ixtapa 50 pesos, from Zihuatanejo 75 pesos. A "Playa Linda" bus (5 pesos) begins in Zihuatanejo and passes through Ixtapa on its way to Playas Quieta and Linda. Buses come every 15min. or so to return to Ixtapa (4 pesos) or Zihuatanejo (5 pesos). You can also walk along the road for about 4km on the bicycle path.)*

ISLA IXTAPA. Some claim that of all the area's beaches, the most picturesque are those on **Isla Ixtapa,** about 2km off-shore from Playa Quieta. The island is a must for snorkeling enthusiasts. The main beach is **Playa Cuachalalate,** frequented by fishermen and waterskiers. **Playa Varadero** is a small beach with calm waters and *palapa* restaurants. On the ocean side of the island, **Playa Coral** is the least-visited of the three. It has no services and poor swimming, but the coral makes for excellent scuba diving. *(To get there, take a boat from the pier at Zihuatanejo (1hr.; boats leave at noon, return at 5pm; 60 pesos round-trip). A cheaper alternative is to take a microbus from Zihuatanejo (3 pesos) or Ixtapa (2.50 pesos) to the pier at Playa Linda and catch a* lancha *(every 15min. 9am-5pm, round-trip 30 pesos.)*

⬛ NIGHTLIFE

Although the beaches in both towns promise spectacular days of sun, sand, and waves, the only place to go for rip-roarin' nightlife is Ixtapa. **Blvd. Ixtapa,** like most resort strips, is littered with fancy clubs and relaxed bars that rock with the beat of young people having a great time. If you're looking for a relaxing night away from all the tourists, Zihuatanejo may hit the spot.

IXTAPA

Christine, (☎553 04 56), in front of Hotel Krystal. Ixtapa's premiere club. With stadium-like seats around the dance floor, hanging vines, and a light show, it is as artificially beautiful as Ixtapa itself. Beer 29 pesos, and *bebidas nacionales* 38-45 pesos. No cover M; Tu, W and Su cover 230 pesos, open bar; Th ladies night, 100 pesos for men; F-Sa cover 100 pesos.

Carlos 'n' Charlie's (☎55300 85 and 55320 41), at the end of the public access path next to the Posada Real hotel that leads to the end of Playa Palmar. Like all Carlos 'n' Charlie's, it attracts a lot of parched party-goers to its bar and specializes in beachfront dancing. There's a swimming pool that you're welcome to take a dip in if you so desire. Beer and national drinks start at 30 pesos. No cover. Open daily 8pm-3am.

Señor Frog's (☎553 22 82), may be a restaurant until midnight, but when the clock strikes twelve, there's no pumpkin to be seen—simply, drunk Americans climbing on tables to begin the ball. Spiral fans whirring at top speed and beers (30 pesos) keep the party cool. National drinks 30-42 pesos. No cover. Open daily 6pm-2am.

ZIHUATANEJO

D'Latino (☎554 22 30), on the corner of Bravo and Guerrero. This spicy Latin dance club features salsa and reggae, with occasional live music. Short skirted dancers get down under the black lights while others sip drinks (30-45 pesos) from the fully stacked bar. M-Th free; F-Su cover 40 pesos. Open daily 10pm-6am.

Ventaneando, Bravo 23 (☎55453 90), across from D'Latino. This dark, smoky bar boasts that its waitresses are the most beautiful in town. Listen to cheesy Mexican ballads while watching even cheesier early 90s music videos on the TVs. Things start picking up after midnight when amateur singers strut their stuff. Beer 18 pesos, national drinks 30 pesos. Open daily 7pm-4am.

Canta Bar Splash, Guerrero between Ejido and González. Sip a beer (20 pesos) or a mixed drink (25-30 pesos) as you croon at this karaoke bar. Open daily 7pm-3:30am.

COSTA GRANDE

The Guerrero coast north of Acapulco is often called the Costa Grande to distinguish it from its smaller counterpart, Costa Chica, to the south. Though the stretch from Acapulco to Zihuatanejo/Ixtapa has few inviting beaches, **Barra de Potosí**, 20km southeast of Zihuatanejo, and **Papanoa**, 60km farther along Rte. 200, are hidden treasures ideal for wasting the day in the waves.

BARRA DE POTOSÍ   ☎7

For the traveler whose head is spinning from ruins, cathedrals, and kitsch, there is no better tonic than a spell on the seemingly infinite stretch of sand known as **Playa Barra de Potosí.** This small town, consisting of a shallow lagoon, a forest of palm trees, and waterfront huts, appears caught in perpetual *siesta*. Water babies can take a dip in the lagoon or stroll over to the beach. Don't be deceived by the crashing waves. Once you get a little past the breaking point, the water is peaceful and crystal clear. Eat until you're full, walk on the beach, snooze on a hammock in the shade; there is no rush here, and the surrounding beauty has no limit.

Those still unskilled in the art of beachside hammock-napping can indulge themselves at **Hotel Barra de Potosí,** a small-scale resort hotel and recent addition to this virginal beach. From the *enramadas* (open-air seaside restaurants), walk away from the lagoon—you can't miss the large white building with blue balconies. Not all rooms have the same amenities, but all have access to the beachside swimming pool and restaurant. (☎554-8290 or 554-8191. Quads with ocean view 350 pesos, with kitchen 450 pesos; doubles 250 pesos.)

There are 10 or so *enramadas*, which serve simple seafood dishes at reasonable prices. While you enjoy the home-cooked food you are more than welcome to relax in one of the many hammocks that swing in the shaded restaurants. In keeping with the casual spirit, restaurants do not have set menus. Rather, they ask you what type of seafood you'd like to eat (expect to spend 40-50 pesos per person). **Enramada Bacanora,** the third restaurant from the right facing the water, offers a very friendly atmosphere and the cheapest prices. (Open daily 7am-6pm.)

If you insist on exerting yourself while in Barra de Potosí (something the locals may not understand), the only option is to hike up the dirt road to the lighthouse atop **Cerro Guamiule** (2000m), the peak near the restaurants that guards the southern entrance to the bay. After a 30-minute walk, you will be rewarded with a view of the bay and its 20km of beaches. However, beware of the creepy, crawly critters on this path. After gaping, walk north along the shore of **Playa Potosí,** the southernmost beach on the bay, to the aptly named **Playa Blanca** ("white beach," 3km). You will pass **Playa Coacoyul** (8km), **Playa Riscaliyo** (19km), and pebbly **Playa Manzanillo** (24km) before reaching another lighthouse (26km) that overlooks the northern edge of the bay. All beaches are free of tourists in the summer months, but fill with hundreds of domestic visitors during Christmas.

⬛ TRANSPORTATION. From Zihuatanejo, "Petatlán" buses leave for Potosí from a station on Las Palmas, around the corner from Restaurante La Jaiba on Juárez (30min., every 15min. 6am-9pm, 6 pesos). Ask to be let off at **Achotes,** an unmarked intersection. A pick-up truck will be waiting (or arriving soon) on the side road to collect passengers for the bumpy trip to the *enramadas* (30min., 7 pesos). Trucks return to the intersection from the same spot (every 30min. until 6pm). The bus to Zihuatanejo leaves from the other side of the route.

PAPANOA   ☎7

Much like Barra de Potosí, **Papanoa** is a tiny, delectable town with lolling waves. Pigs and roosters scuttle along a road that ends in waterfront *enramadas*. **Cayaquitos,** 2km from town, is a bit more accessible (and therefore more crowded) than **Playa Vicente Guerrero,** 5km from town. And while there's a scarcity of eateries on Cayaquitos, there are numerous restaurants in Vicente Guerrero to fill your belly with the day's fresh catch. (Fish 40-50 pesos. Open 7am-6pm.)

Hmm, call home or eat lunch?
With  you can do both. ^{SM}

Nathan Lane for YOU℠.

No doubt, traveling on a budget is tough. So tear out this wallet guide and keep it with you during your travels. With YOU, calling home from overseas is affordable and easy.

If the wallet guide is missing, call collect 913-624-5336 or visit www.youcallhome.com for YOU country numbers.

Dialing instructions:
Need help with access numbers while overseas? Call collect, 913-624-5336.

Dial the access number for the country you're in.
Dial 04 or follow the English prompts.
Enter your credit card information to place your call.

Country	Access Number	Country	Access Number	Country	Access Number
Australia ⌄	1-800-551-110	Israel ⌄	1-800-949-4102	Spain ⌄	900-99-0013
Bahamas ✚	1-800-389-2111	Italy ✚ ⌄	172-1877	Switzerland ⌄	0800-899-777
Brazil ⌄	000-8016	Japan ✚ ⌄	00539-131	Taiwan ⌄	0080-14-0877
China ✚ ▲ ⌄	108-13	Mexico ∪ ⌄	001-800-877-8000	United Kingdom ⌄	0800-890-877
France ⌄	0800-99-0087	Netherlands ✚ ⌄	0800-022-9119		
Germany ✚ ⌄	0800-888-0013	New Zealand ▲ ⌄	000-999		
Hong Kong ⌄	800-96-1877	Philippines ⊤ ⌄	105-16		
India ⌄	000-137	Singapore ⌄	8000-177-177		
Ireland ⌄	1-800-552-001	South Korea ✚ ⌄	00729-16		

YOU ℠
Service provided by Sprint

⌄ Call answered by automated Voice Response Unit.   ✚ Public phones may require coin or card.
▲ May not be available from all payphones.   ∪ Use phones marked with "LADATEL" and no coin or card is required.
⊤ If talk button is available, push it before talking.

Pack the Wallet Guide

and save 25% or more* on calls home to the U.S.

It's lightweight and carries heavy savings of 25% or more* over AT&T USA Direct and MCI WorldPhone rates. So take this YOU wallet guide and carry it wherever you go.

To save with YOU:

- Dial the access number of the country you're in (see reverse)
- Dial 04 or follow the English voice prompts
- Enter your credit card info for easy billing

Service provided by Sprint

▛ TRANSPORTATION. Buses from Acapulco to Zihuatanejo (2½hr., 34 pesos) and back (1½hr., 16 pesos) drop passengers off in Papanoa. In Papanoa, white pick-up trucks carry passengers to and from the beach (until 6pm, 5 pesos). Taxis run to **Cayaqutos** (10 pesos) and to **Vicente Guerrero** (20 pesos). If you plan to leave the beach later than 6pm, arrange for a taxi to pick you up ahead of time.

ACAPULCO   ☎ 7

Once upon a time, Acapulco (pop. 2 million) was the stunningly beautiful playground of the rich and famous. Hollywood legends celebrated their silver-screen successes by dancing the Mexican nights away in its chic clubs, and the privileged few spent their honeymoons lounging on its attractive shores. But time passes and fairy tales fade; today, Acapulco is a mere shadow of the beautiful, relaxing retreat it once was. The city now consists of the crowded beach flanked by tightly-packed 14-story hotels, and the slum that starts behind them continues up the hill. This grimmer Acapulco was born when the wealthy stopped vacationing here, and the hotel job market could no longer keep pace with the waves of immigrants drawn seaward by the prospect of plentiful pesos. Everyone in Acapulco is still driven by money, though now by the need to earn it rather than to spend it. Persistent cabbies and peddlers of everything from bubble gum to "free information" run at tourists like eager bulls. Though the high-rise hotels crowding the waterfront have lost the flush of youth, a roster full of festivals and beautification projects promise a revamped Acapulco. Perhaps it's best to visit the city at night, when darkness shrouds the grime and street lamps evoke Acapulco's fairy tale past.

▛ TRANSPORTATION

Airport: Rte. 200, 26km south of the city. Taxis make the run to the airport for 75 pesos; shared taxis (☎462 10 95) can do it for 45 pesos. Served by **Aerocaribe** (☎486 76 45), **Aerolines Internacionales** (☎486 56 30), **Aeroméxico** (☎485 16 25), **American** (☎466 92 32), **Continental** (☎466 90 63), **Delta** (☎484 14 28), and **Mexicana** (☎486 75 85).

Buses: Taxco has two bus stations. To get from the **Estrella de Oro station** (☎485 87 05), on Cuauhtémoc at Massiu, to the *zócalo* (40min.), cross the street and flag down any bus heading southwest or labeled "Zócalo" (3 pesos). A taxi between the *zócalo* and either bus station costs 30-40 pesos. Estrella de Oro sends buses to: **Cuernavaca** (4hr., every hr. 6am-8pm, 184 pesos); **Mexico City** (4hr., every hr. 7am-2am, 220 pesos); **Taxco** (3½hr., every 2hr. 7am-6:40pm, 120 pesos); and **Zihuatanejo** (4hr., every hr. 4:50am-4:50pm, 90 pesos). A "Zócalo" bus will also get you to the center from the **Estrella Blanca station** (☎469 20 28), Cuauhtémoc behind Parque Papagayo. Estrella Blanca sends buses to: **Cuernavaca** (4hr., 2:20pm and 5pm, 197 pesos); **Mexico City** (5hr., every hr. 12:30am-11:30pm, 220 pesos); and **Puebla** (7hr., 4:30pm, 357 pesos).

▛▟ ORIENTATION AND PRACTICAL INFORMATION

Acapulco Bay lies 400km south of Mexico City and 239km southeast of Ixtapa and Zihuatanejo. Rte. 200 feeds into **La Costera** (Costera Miguel Alemán), the main drag that crosses all of Acapulco. **Acapulco Dorado,** full of restaurants, malls, and hotels, stretches from **Parque Papagayo** to the naval base. The ultra-chic resorts are found on **Acapulco Diamante,** farther east. Budget accommodations and restaurants lie between the *zócalo* and **La Quebrada,** the famous cliff-diving spot. "Hornos" or "CICI" buses run from Caleta along the Costera to the naval base (3 pesos). "Cine Río-La Base" buses go from the *zócalo* to the base down Cuauhtémoc.

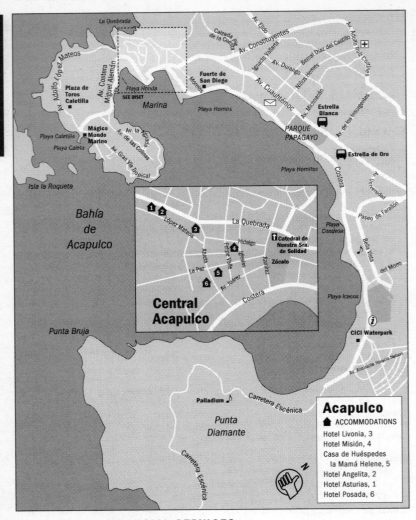

Acapulco

🛏 **ACCOMMODATIONS**

Hotel Livonia, 3
Hotel Misión, 4
Casa de Huéspedes
    la Mamá Helene, 5
Hotel Angelita, 2
Hotel Asturias, 1
Hotel Posada, 6

TOURIST AND FINANCIAL SERVICES

Tourist Offices: SEFOTUR, Costera 4455, in the Centro Cultural de Acapulco, a little west of the CICI water park across the street. Helpful staff will happily overload you with brochures and maps. Open daily 9am-11pm. In an emergency, contact the **Procuraduría del Turista** (☎484 45 83 or 484 44 16), in the same office.

Consulates: Canada (☎484 13 05), Costera at Juan Pérez, in the Continental Hotel. Open M-F 9am-1pm and 2-5pm. **UK** (☎484 66 05), in the Hotel Las Brisas. Open M-F 1-3pm and 4-8pm. **US,** Costera 121 #14 (☎469 05 56), in the Continental Plaza Hotel. Open M-F 10am-2pm.

Currency Exchange: Banks on Costera have good rates. All open M-F 9am-4pm. **Casas de cambio** line the north side of Costera and are often open until 8pm.

American Express: Costera 1628 (☎469 11 00; fax 469 11 88), on the bottom floor of the Gran Plaza shopping center. Open M-Sa 10am-7pm.

LOCAL SERVICES

Car Rental: Hertz, Costera 137 (☎485 68 89), across from Universidad Americana. Small VW with insurance 520 pesos per day. Open daily 8am-7pm.

Markets: Constituyentes at Hurtado. Open daily 6am-6pm.

Supermarket: Supermarket Comercial Mexicana, just east of the tourist office and 4 blocks east of the *zócalo.* Open daily 8am-11pm.

Laundry: Super Lavandería, José Maria Iglesias 9 (☎480 01 46), 1 block from the cathedral. 38 pesos per 4kg. Open M-Sa 8:30am-8:30pm.

EMERGENCY AND COMMUNICATIONS

Emergency: ☎060.

Police: LOCATEL (☎481 11 00). **Tourist Police** (☎485 04 90) wander the *zócalo.* Office open daily 9am-1am

Red Cross: (☎485 41 01), on Cortínez, north of the *zócalo.* Take a "Hospital" bus. 24hr. emergency service. Some English spoken. **Sociedad de Asistencia Médica Turística** (☎485 58 00 or 485 59 59) has doctors 24hr. English spoken.

Pharmacy: ISSTE Farmacias, Quebrada 1 (☎482 34 77), directly behind the cathedral on the *zócalo.* Open daily 8am-8pm.

Hospital: IMSS, Ruiz Cortínez 128 (☎486 36 20), north of the *zócalo* along Madero. Take a "Hospital" bus. 24hr. emergency service. No English spoken.

Internet: Cetec, Hidalgo 2 (☎480 03 50), by the cathedral. 20 pesos per hour. Open 24hr.

Telephones: LADATELs line the Costera. **Caseta Carranza,** Carranza 9, 2 blocks from the *zócalo* also has **fax.** Open daily 8am-10pm.

Post Office: Urdareta 1 (☎483 53 63), in front of Sears. Open M-Sa 9am-3pm.

Postal Code: 39300.

▐ ACCOMMODATIONS

Camping on Acapulco's beaches is relatively unsafe. Fortunately, budget accommodations are easier to find here than anywhere else on Mexico's Pacific coast. Though a far cry from the posh hotels you mind conjures up when you think Acapulco, cheap, no-frills hotels are easily found near the *zócalo.* Rates double during *Semana Santa,* and it's a good idea to make reservations.

▨ **Hotel Asturias,** Quebrada 45 (☎483 65 48), on the street behind the *zócalo,* up the hill to the left. The powerful ceiling fans, firm mattresses and clean private baths provide an oasis from the frenzied city. A well-tended courtyard and pool set the stage for drinking, relaxation and conversation. Singles 140 pesos, each additional person 90 pesos.

▨ **Casa de Huéspedes Mama Hélène,** Juárez 12 (☎482 23 96), at Valle. Owner presides over a posse of ping-pong-playing, coffee-drinking, chain-smoking backpackers. Rooms are simple and comfortable. No hot water. Singles 70 pesos; doubles 120 pesos.

Hotel Misión, Felipe Valle 12 (☎482 36 43), at La Paz, 2 blocks left of the *zócalo* as you face the church. Guests chatting over a courtyard breakfast (25-50 pesos) and lazy cats napping on the stairway give Misión a homey feel. Rooms have fans and baths; some have desks and sofas. Singles 150 pesos; 50 peso discount for students.

Hotel Angelita, Quebrada 37 (☎483 57 34), up the street behind the cathedral, two doors down from Hotel Asturias. Spacious rooms, clean private baths, and fans compensate for lack of courtyard and scenic view. Singles 100 pesos; doubles 150 pesos.

Hotel Posada, Azueta 8 (☎483 19 30). No consistent hot water, but the firm beds and pleasant hospitality welcome the sun-weary. Flowered curtains brighten up the locker-room-esque hallways. Singles 80 pesos; doubles 100 pesos.

FOOD

Acapulco's international restaurants cater to tourists' palates and wallets, and the chic restaurants between Playa Condesa and the naval base are meant for travelers who don't fret about money. However, interspersed along Costera are many local eateries ready to satisfy any craving without the high prices.

Mariscos Nacho's, Azueta 7 (☎482 28 91), at Juárez, 1 block west of the *zócalo*. An open-air *marisquería* serving everything from octopus (38 pesos) to *camarones al mojo de ajo* (garlic shrimp; 60 pesos). Bustles with sunburned families straggling in from the beach and party-kids dolled up for a night on the town. Open daily 8am-10pm.

100% Natural, Costera 248 (☎485 13 12 ext. 100), at the corner of Vizcaíno, west of the tourist office. Other branches line the Costera. A health food restaurant serving sandwiches (36-42 pesos), fruit salads (18-24 pesos), and *licuados* (20-24 pesos). Vegetarian options include soy burgers (28-38 pesos). Open daily 8am-midnight.

Jovito's, Costera 116 (☎484 84 33), across from Fiesta Americana. Indistinguishable from the rest of the restaurants lining Acapulco's main strip, Jovito's offer fresh seafood and satisfying Mexican favorites. Try the *tacos de mariscos* (44.5 pesos) or the vegetarian tacos (25 pesos). Open M-Th 2pm-midnight, F-Su 2pm-1am.

El Fogón (☎484 36 07), Costera and Yañez, across from the Continental Plaza Hotel. Offers tacos (37 pesos), sandwiches (20-40 pesos), and satisfying breakfast combos (18-50 pesos). Try the *chilaquiles* (45 pesos). Open 24hr.

La Flor de Acapulco, Costera 711 (☎484 87 18), west of the Kentucky Fried Chicken. The flowered tile and big screen TV make La Flor a refuge from the sand and sun. The menu doesn't differ much from other restaurants, but the prices are slightly cheaper and the *milanesa* is delicious (45 pesos). Open daily 8am-midnight.

SIGHTS AND BEACHES

If you're in Acapulco, chances are you seek two things: beaches and booze. Have no fear, intrepid traveler—Acapulco delivers. Keep in mind that you won't be the only one seeking these pleasures; the beaches here are hardly quiet or virginal. Vendors will harass you incessantly, and you will have to fight back the crowds for a stretch of sand. Those in the mood for unadulterated people-watching will be satisfied. Just don't be surprised if people watch you too.

PENÍNSULA DE LAS PLAYAS. At the westernmost tip of Acapulco Bay, on the seaward side of the peninsula, lie **Playas Caleta** and **Caletilla.** If you don't mind sharing the sea with small fishing boats, swimming is good in the calm water, though the hundreds of frolicking families make it hard find empty beachside turf. A narrow causeway separating the two beaches leads to the island occupied by **Mágico Mundo Marino,** a water park with slides, pools, and a small zoo. (☎483 12 15. Open daily 9am-7pm. 30 pesos, children 15 pesos.) You can also take boats to **La Roqueta,** a little island with a zoo across the bay. (Boats leave in front of Mágico Mundo (25 pesos). Zoo open daily W-M 10am-5pm. 3 pesos.)

FROM HOTEL LAS HAMACAS TO PARQUE PAPAGAYO. The stretch of sand along the **Costera,** away from Old Acapulco, is blessed with fewer high-rises and smaller crowds than other beaches. **Playas Tamarindo, Hornos,** and **Hornitos,** between Las Hamacas Hotel and the Radisson, are called the "afternoon beaches" because the fishermen haul in their midday catches here. The waves are moderate, and the sand is ideal for beach sports. Still, you can't escape urban Acapulco—only a thin line of palm trees blocks the traffic on Costera.

Those who need a break from the relentless sun should head to **Parque Papagayo,** sprawling from Costera to Cuauhtémoc. Entering on Costera by the Gigante supermarket, you'll find a roller skating rink and shaded paths for bikers and walkers; an artificial lake in the center surrounds an aviary. Children will find a wading pool, exotic birds, and a zillion spots for playing hide-and-seek. (☎485 24 90. Park open daily 7am-8pm; rink open daily 4pm-midnight. 13 pesos; skate rental 5-10 pesos.)

FROM LA DIANA TO THE NAVAL BASE. A trip to **Playa Condesa,** at the center of the bay, is worth the 2km-plus trek from the *zócalo,* although there are strong waves and a rapidly dropping sea floor, making the swimming conditions less than ideal. The poor swimming conditions don't bother the throngs of sun worshippers who lounge under their blue umbrellas and catwalk down the beach in their minimal-clothing fashion shows. Farther down, between the golf course and naval base, is **Playa Icacos.** As you move toward the base, the waves become gentler.

The **CICI,** a fun water park, lets you hurl yourself head-first down winding water slides, then watch trained dolphins perform. *(Costera at Colón. Follow Costera until you see the orange walls painted with large green waves; otherwise take a "CICI" or "Base" bus.* ☎ *484 19 70. Open daily 10am-6pm. 50 pesos. Dolphin shows M-F 2pm, Sa-Su 1pm and 4pm.)*

PUERTO MARQUÉS. Lacking the prepackaged polish of the strip, the beach town of **Puerto Marqués** encompasses a ribbon of sand lined with restaurants. The bus ride is the real attraction; views from the top of the hill are magnificent. As the bus rambles along, the Bahía de Puerto Marqués and the pounding surf of **Playa Revolcadero** come into view. Catch a "Bonville" bus to get to quieter and less crowded **Playa Bonville.** *(Buses depart across from Comercial Mexicana at Playa Hornitos, on the beach side of the street (45min., approx. every 30min. 5:30am-9pm, 3 pesos) to Puerto Marqués.)*

🎵 🎦 ENTERTAINMENT AND NIGHTLIFE

In Acapulco, every night is Saturday night. Luring young party-seekers from the capital, the town transforms at night into one continuous strip of partying with the best clubs clustering on the beach side near the CICI. Most clubs thump from 11pm to dawn, and charge over 100 pesos for cover, which usually includes open bar. It's always easier and cheaper for women to get in, and many clubs offer no cover (and open bar) to women on weeknights.

CLUBS AND BARS

🏆 Palladium (☎ 446 54 86), on the Carretera Escénica Las Brisas. Accessible only by taxi (30-40 pesos). The space-age structure is on a cliff with a fabulous view of downtown. The club reverberates with pop music and the dancing begins at midnight when the light descends from the ceiling. Cover 250 pesos for men, 190 pesos for women, Tu and Th women free until 12:30am. Open bar. Open daily 10:30pm-5am.

Andrómedas (☎ 484 88 15), Costera, 2 blocks east of Planet Hollywood and the Hard Rock Cafe, is more accessible. A torch-lit path leads to the castle-like club where scantily-clad women and men disco dance. Cover 250 pesos for men, 200 pesos for women; M, W, F, Su before 12:30am 50 pesos for women. Open bar. Open daily 10pm-6am.

Barbarroja, Costera 107A (☎ 484 59 32), two blocks west of Carlos 'N Charlie's, on the beach side. An open deck has a great view of Acapulco bay. Pirate-clad waiters serve up buckets of beer (40 pesos for 2 beers), and dance music rages as you enjoy the beautiful Acapulco night. Open daily 10pm-5am.

Baby 'O, Costera 22 (☎ 484 74 74). Slightly less frenetic and more sophisticated than its rambunctious neighbors. No cover M-Th; F-Su cover 100 pesos for men, 50 pesos for women. Drinks 35 pesos. Open daily 10:30pm-late.

Nina's, Costera 2909 (☎ 484 24 00), on the beach side near CICI. A more mature clientele grooves to live tropical music. Cover 190 pesos. Open bar. Open daily 10pm-5am.

GAY AND LESBIAN NIGHTLIFE

Picante, Privada Piedra Picuda 16 (☎ 484 23 42), behind Carlos 'n' Charlie's. A spicy gay club with young, lithe, and predominantly male clientele enjoying late-night racy entertainment. No cover; 2-drink min. Beer 25 pesos. Open daily 10pm-4am.

Relax, Lomas del Mar 4 (☎ 484 04 21), one block east of Carlos 'n' Charlie's. Mixed, but mostly male dominated. Above average bar and fine service make this place more chill than most. Su-Th no cover, F-Sa cover 50 pesos. Transvestite shows F-Sa 3am.

CLIFF DIVERS OF ACAPULCO Hurling oneself half-naked off jagged cliffs is not a coming of age ritual in Acapulco, but a serious occupation for trained professionals. It is also one of Acapulco's biggest attractions. At La Quebrada cliffs around the north side of the bay, *clavadistas* perform daily shows, diving 25 to 35 meters off a cliff and slipping effortlessly into the frothing surf. Although most spectators congregate at the bottom level, the view is better from the area to the immediate right of the ticket booth. To get to La Quebrada, follow López Mateos, the road on your left side when facing the cathedral's entrance. The walk takes about 15 minutes and ends at the top of a very steep hill. As if the dives weren't enough of a show, all the divers pray rather theatrically (who can blame them?) at a small shrine before the plunge. It's all part of the everyday business of challenging death and impressing the tourists. Shows at 7:30, 8:30, 9:30, and 10:30pm, 15 pesos.

Demas, Picuda 17 (☎484 13 70), next to Picante's. Table dancers and neon lights aside, Demas gives you a peek into the seedier side of Acapulco's gay nightlife. Drinks 30 pesos and up. Cover 50 pesos. Open daily 10pm-5am. Transvestite shows F-Sa.

OTHER ENTERTAINMENT

Those too tired for yet another night clubbing will find milder forms of entertainment at **Plaza Bahía,** a large shopping mall on Costera, past La Gran Plaza on the beach side. Speed around a tiny race course at **Go-Karts,** on the third floor. (☎486 71 47. 20-25 pesos per 5min. Open daily 10am-11pm.) **Bowl** away on the fourth floor. (☎485 09 70. 18-28 pesos per hr.; shoes 5-9 pesos. Open daily 2pm-1:30am.) There is also a **movie theater** on the second floor. (☎486 42 55. Tickets 25-30 pesos.)

▓ SPORTS AND FESTIVALS

Corridas take place at the **Plaza de Toros Caletilla,** 200m west of Playa Caletela near the abandoned yellow *jai alai* auditoriums. (☎483 95 61. Dec.-Apr. Su 5pm.) Tickets are sold at the Centro Kennedy box office (☎485 85 40) near Costera at Saavedra, or at the Plaza after 4:30pm on the day of the fight.

The Acapulco tourist office organizes a variety of festivals designed to lighten tourists' wallets. **Festival Acapulco** in May is a celebration of music; the self-explanatory **Black Film Festival** takes places during the first week of June. In December, men and women from around the globe journey to Acapulco to test their cliff diving skills during the **Torneo Internacional de Clavados en La Quebrada.**

▓ DAYTRIPS FROM ACAPULCO

PIE DE LA CUESTA

Buses leave from Costera, across the street from Woolworth's next to the zócalo. Buses marked "Pie de la Cuesta Playa" stop on the road along the beach; those labeled "Pie de la Cuesta Centro" stop on a parallel street in a marketplace (40min., 3 pesos). From there, turn left down a dirt road; you should see the ocean in the distance. At the end of the road, turn right toward the base. Buses shuttle between the base and the centro (3 pesos). A combi will take you as far as La Barra, the spot where the lagoon water flows into the ocean (3.5 pesos). To return to Acapulco, go back to the market and hail a bus in the opposite direction.

A single-lane route runs through Acapulco's hills to Pie de la Cuesta—a small town known for its truly magnificent sunsets—ending at the narrow road that separates the Pacific from the placid waters of **Laguna de Coyuca.** At Playa Pie de la Cuesta, pleasure-seekers can choose between salt and fresh water. Since the Pacific's rough waves preclude swimming, many head to the lagoon instead, the site of the area's best waterskiing. **Sunset,** a ski club near the air base, offers **ski rental.** (☎460 06 53 or 460 06 54. 350 pesos per hr.) Unfortunately, rest and relaxation are all too often interrupted by aggressive *lancha* agents offering tours of the lagoon (about

Oaxaca State

30 pesos per person in a *colectivo* boat). If you need a place to stay, **Villa Nirvana,** a blue-and-white building a few blocks from the bus stop, carves out its own utopia with a restaurant, swimming pool, and rooms with fans and private baths. (☎460 16 31. 150 pesos per person.) Beyond the pharmacy toward the base is **Acapulco Trailer Park,** with campgrounds, trailer hook-up sites, bathrooms, and a pet raccoon named Charlie. (☎460 00 10. 50 pesos per night, prices negotiable.)

OAXACA

OAXACA   ☎9

Perched on a giant plateau that gracefully interrupts the Sierra Madre del Sur's descent into the Oaxaca valley, the city of Oaxaca de Juárez (wa-HAH-ka dey WA-rez; pop. 300,000) is a true beauty. The city's surname was added in honor of native son Benito Juárez, a Oaxacan Zapotec and Mexico's only *indígena* president. Oaxaca was also the birthplace of the much less-loved dictator Porfirio Díaz, who received nothing save a lone street name to commemorate his iron reign. As the center of the Zapotec and Mixtec civilizations that once occupied the valley, Oaxaca is rich with ruins and indigenous culture. Native presence is strong in the city and surrounding villages, and, at times, tensions run high between *indígenas* and the Spanish-speaking elite. Lined with sprawling jacaranda trees and outdoor cafes serving rich Oaxacan hot chocolate, the city's *zócalo* resembles a miniature Mexico: *indígenas*, merchants, and professionals jostle elbows while restless stu-

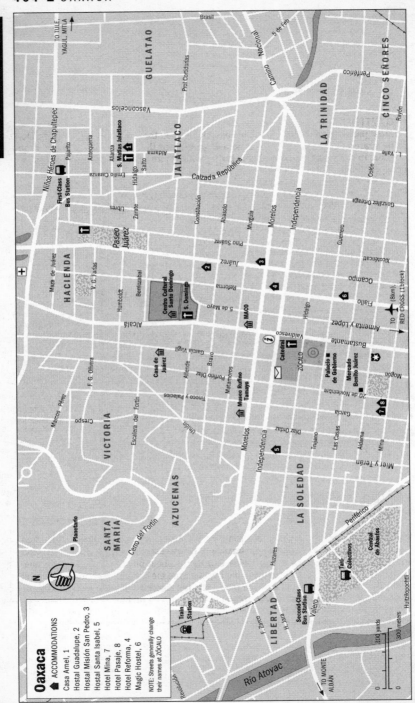

Oaxaca

▲ ACCOMMODATIONS

Casa Arnel, 1
Hostal Guadalupe, 2
Hostal Misión San Pedro, 3
Hostal Santa Isabel, 5
Hotel Mina, 7
Hotel Pasaje, 8
Hotel Reforma, 4
Magic Hostel, 6

NOTE: Streets generally change
their names at ZÓCALO.

dents tear around on expensive motorbikes or agitate for labor reform. With the help of its famous museums and outstanding archaeological sites, Oaxaca has recently become a tourist destination as well. One-month stays at language schools often expand to whole summers or longer as visitors become smitten with Oaxaca's superb food, culture, highland setting, and sheer beauty.

▛ TRANSPORTATION

GETTING AROUND

Most parts of the city are easily accessible by foot. **Local buses** cost 2.5 pesos. Don't be scared by the bus system—just ask around for the correct line. Service is sporadic in the evenings, but reliable **taxis** go anywhere in the city (20-25 pesos).

GETTING AWAY

Airport: Aeropuerto Juárez (☎511 50 40), on Rte. 175, 8km south of the city. You can hire a private **taxi** from the airport, but it is cheaper and just as easy to share one of the **Transportes Aeropuerto** vans with other travelers. Buy a ticket at the airport exit (to the *centro* 17 pesos). For the same price, a van will take you from your hotel to the airport. Arrangements should be made a day in advance by phone, or at the office several doors down from the post office on Plaza Alameda. (☎514 43 50. Open M-Sa 9am-2pm and 5-8pm.) Airlines served by the airport include: **AeroCaribe,** Fiallo 102 (☎516 02 29 or 511 52 47); **Aeroméxico,** Hidalgo 503 (☎516 10 66, or 511 50 44); **Mexicana,** Independencia 102 (☎516 84 14 or 511 52 29), at Fiallo.

Buses: Oaxaca is served by two bus stations. The **first-class bus station,** Niños Héroes de Chapultepec 1036 (☎513 33 50), is 11 blocks north of the *centro*. To get to the *centro,* exit, cross the street, and take a westbound "Centro" *urbano* (2.5 pesos); a taxi will cost 20 pesos. ADO (☎515 17 03) runs to: **Mexico City** (6hr., 15 per day, 221 pesos); **Puebla** (4½hr., 7 per day, 165 pesos); **Tuxtepec** (6½ hr.; 3, 9:30, 11:30pm; 159 pesos); and **Veracruz** (8 hr., 8:30am and 8:30pm, 218 pesos). Cristóbal Colón runs to: **Puerto Escondido** (12hr.; 9:30am and midnight, 145 pesos); **Bahías de Huatulco** (8hr.; 9:30am, 10:40pm, midnight; 143 pesos); **San Cristóbal de las Casas** (12hr., 7:30 and 9pm, 221 pesos); **Tehuantepec** (4hr., 14 per day, 92 pesos); and **Tuxtla Gutiérrez** (10hr., 9 and 10:15pm, 197 pesos). Tickets for ADO and Cristóbal Colón also available at 20 de Noviembre #204. The **second-class bus station** houses regional bus lines and is 7 blocks southwest of the *zócalo,* just past the Central de Abastos market. To get to the *centro,* take a "Centro" *urbano* in front of the main terminal. If you want to walk, exit left out of the terminal, cross busy Periférico, and follow the street as it turns into Trujano. After seven blocks, Trujano reaches the *zócalo.* A taxi will cost 20 pesos. Because the station is almost always packed, it's a good idea to buy tickets early. (Open daily 7am-2pm and 4-8pm.) Estrella del Valle (☎514 57 00 or 516 54 29) runs to **Puerto Escondido** (8hr., 13 per day 4am-10:15pm, 80 pesos).

EXCEPTIONS TO THE RULE. Under most circumstances it's better (not to mention safer) to take a first-class bus than a second-class bus. An exception to the rule is the ride from **Oaxaca** to **Puerto Escondido.** First-class buses tend to take a route through Salina Cruz that is about 5hr. longer than the second-class bus route, which goes directly. Measure the increased efficiency and lower costs against the increased (albeit shorter) discomfort.

✳▛ ORIENTATION AND PRACTICAL INFORMATION

Oaxaca de Juárez rests in the Oaxaca Valley, between the towering Sierra Madre del Sur and the Puebla-Oaxaca range, 523km southeast of Mexico City. Principal access to Oaxaca from the north and east is via **Rte. 190.** The city's ground zero is the *zócalo,* comprised of the square and the two-block long Plaza Alameda de

León, just north of the square. Branching north from the *zócalo* is Valdierso, which becomes the **Alcalá**, a hog-heaven of *casas de cambio*, expensive local crafts, and museums. Many of Oaxaca's streets change names as they pass the *zócalo*. It is also common for two or more streets to share the same name. It is wise to specify neighborhood as well as street when directing cabbies.

TOURIST AND FINANCIAL SERVICES

Tourist Offices: SEDETUR, Independencia 607 (☎516 01 23; email info@oaxaca.gob.mx; http://oaxaca.gob.mx/sedetur), across the street from the cathedral. Maps, brochures, and a *cabaña* in one of the *pueblos* outside of the city. Open daily 8am-8pm. **CEPROTUR,** also at Independencia 607 (☎514 21 55; fax 516 09 84), handles grittier problems such as robbery. Open daily 9am-8pm. **Info Booth** at the airport. Also check the *Oaxaca Times* (www.oaxacatimes.com), a free monthly English newspaper available at SEDETUR.

Consulates: In an emergency, CEPROTUR (see above) will obtain consular assistance. **Canada,** Suárez 700 (☎513 37 77). Open M-F 11am-2pm. **US,** Alcalá 201 #204 (☎514 30 54), at Morelos, hidden under an arched doorway. Open M-F 9am-3pm.

Currency Exchange: Banamex, Valdivieso 116, on the east side of the cathedral, changes currency and has 24hr. **ATMs.** Open M-F 11am-6pm, Su 10am-2pm. **Inverlat,** at the corner of Independencia and Alcalá, offers similar rates and 24hr. **ATMs.** Open M-F 9am-5pm. **Internacional de Divisas** (☎516 33 99), next to the *zócalo* on Alcalá, changes currency M-Sa 8:30am-8pm, Su 9am-5pm. **Money Exchange,** half a block north of the *zócalo* at Alcalá 100. Open daily 8am-8pm.

American Express: Valdivieso 2 (☎516 65 22 or 516 27 00), at Hidalgo across from the *zócalo*. Houses a **travel agency** that sells plane tickets and first-class bus tickets. Financial services open M-F 9am-2pm and 4-6pm; travel agency open M-F 9am-8pm.

LOCAL SERVICES

Bookstores: Librería Granen Porrua, Alcalá 104 (☎516 99 01), is well-known for its collection of art and architecture books; a small number of the books are in English. The cafe in back serves *comida corrida* (35 pesos). Open daily 10am-9pm. **Librería Universitaria,** on Hidalgo between Armenta y López and Valdivieso, has a small collection of trashy English paperbacks (10 pesos). Open M-Sa 9:30am-2pm and 4:30-8pm.

Libraries: Biblioteca Circulante, Alcalá 305. A haven for displaced US tourists. Everything from the *New Yorker* to *Sports Illustrated*. Open M-F 10am-1pm and 4-7pm, Sa 10am-1pm. The **Instituto de Artes Gráficos de Oaxaca,** Alcalá 507 (☎516 69 80), across from Santo Domingo, has a library with works in various languages, as well as a museum of changing art exhibits. Open daily 9:30am-9pm; museum open W-M 9:30am-8pm. Free.

Cultural Centers: Centro Cultural Ricardo Flores Magon, Alcalá 302 (☎514 03 95), at Independencia, hosts plays, dance performances, concerts, and gallery openings (daily during peak season). Monthly listings can be found on the *Programación Cultural* on the wall. **Casa de la Cultura,** Ortega 403 (☎516 24 83), at Colón, hosts theater productions, concerts, summer music and art classes, and art exhibits. Open M-F 9am-6pm, Sa 9am-3pm and 4-6:30pm. **Instituto Oaxaqueño de las Culturas** (☎516 34 34), at the corner of Madera and Tecnológica, has similar programming. To get there, take a westbound "Sta. Rosa" *urbano* from the corner of Independencia and Tinoco y Palacios (2.5 pesos). Listings in the monthly *Guía Cultura,* free at SEDETUR.

Markets: Oaxaca's **Central de Abastos** is the ultimate shopping experience. Walk 8 blocks west from the *zócalo* on Trujano. Open daily 8am-8pm; Sa is the biggest day. **Mercado Benito Juárez,** at the corner of 20 de Noviembre and Aldama, 2 blocks from the *zócalo*, sells crafts, produce, flowers, and clothing. Its annex, **Mercado 20 de Noviembre,** on the next block, has lots of food. Both open daily 6am-9pm. **Mercado de Artesanías,** at the corner of García and Zaragoza, offers artisan wares. Prices and quality are often better in nearby villages where the crafts originate. Open daily 8am-8pm.

Luggage Storage: At the first-class bus station. 5 pesos per day.

Laundromats: Súper Lavandería Hidalgo, García 200 (☎514 11 81), 2 blocks west of the *zócalo*. Open M-Sa 8am-8pm. **Clin Lavandería,** 20 de Noviembre 605B (☎516 23 42). Open M-Sa 9am-8pm. Both charge 40 pesos per 3.5kg of clothes.

Car Rental: Budget, 5 de Mayo 315 (☎516 44 45). Also at the airport (☎511 52 52). VWs 500 pesos per day, less off-season. Open daily 8am-1pm and 4-7pm. **Hertz,** Labastida 115 (☎516 24 34), between 5 de Mayo and Alcalá in Posada Margarita, charges 580 pesos for a VW sedan. Open M-Sa 8am-7pm.

EMERGENCY AND COMMUNICATIONS

Emergency: ☎060.

Police: Aldama 108 (☎516 27 26), south of the *zócalo*, between Cabrera and Bustamante. Little English spoken. Open 24hr.

Red Cross: Armenta y López 700 (☎516 48 03), between Pardo and Burgoa. Some English spoken. 24hr. ambulance service.

Pharmacy: Farmacias del Ahorro, Niños Héroes de Chapultepec 1102, next to ADO. Open 24hr. Also Hidalgo 603, at 20 de Noviembre. Open daily 7am-11pm.

Hospitals: IMSS, Chapultepec 621 (☎515 20 33 or 515 28 31), at Reforma. No English spoken. 24hr. ambulance service. **Hospital Civil,** Díaz 400 (☎515 13 00), 1.5km north of town. No English spoken. Open 24hr. **Hospital Reforma,** Reforma 613 (☎516 09 89), at Humboldt. English spoken. Open 24hr.

Fax: Telecomm (☎516 49 02), Independencia at 20 de Noviembre, around the corner from the post office. Open M-F 8am-7:30pm, Sa 9am-4pm, Su 9am-noon.

Telephones: LADATELs are everywhere, with an especially large concentration in front of the post office in the *zócalo*. *Casetas* available at **Computel,** Independencia 601 (☎514 80 84), across from the Telecomm office. Open daily 7am-10pm.

Internet Access: Café Internet, on Valdivieso at Independencia, 2nd fl., has a central location and speedy connection. 15 pesos per hr. Open M-Sa 8am-11pm, Su 11am-10pm. For ambience, try **Internet Axis,** 5 de Mayo 412-3 (☎514 80 24), near La Iglesia Santo Domingo. Helpful staff and caffeine from **Café Gecko** (in the same building) make it worth 18 pesos per hr. Open daily 8:30am-8pm. **Café Red,** Vigil 512 (☎514 94 03). 15 pesos per hr. Open M-Sa 10am-9pm, Su 11am-3pm.

Post Office: (☎516 26 61), in the Plaza Alameda de León. Open M-F 8am-7pm, Sa 9am-1pm.

Postal Code: 68000.

▌ ACCOMMODATIONS AND CAMPING

As Oaxaca attracts more visitors, many old budget standbys have transformed into upscale tourist-traps. Bargains still await the penny-pinching soul, however, especially in the busy blocks south of the *zócalo*, within easy walking distance of the second-class bus station and most major sights and services. The city's numerous youth hostels are its best bargains; most are cheap, clean, and full of international travelers. Reservations are a must on *fiesta* weekends, especially during the *Guelaguetza* in July, *Semana Santa* in late March and early April, and during the celebration of *El Día de Los Muertos* in early November.

For longer stays in the city, reasonably priced rooms are available for rent. Check the tourist office and *Oaxaca Times* for listings. **Departmentos del Cuento,** Quintana Roo 107, off Berriozabal past La Iglesia Santo Domingo, rents six one- or two-person rooms with kitchen and bath. (☎614 22 88. 2000-2300 pesos per month, utilities included.)

NORTHEAST OF EL CENTRO/JALATLACO

Cobblestone streets 20min. northeast of the *zócalo* lend Jalatlaco, which has the best bargain hotels in the city, a quiet feel. In the evenings, nearby **Parque Juárez** fills with *ballet folklórico* dancers and residents out for their nightly stroll.

■ **Casa Arnel,** Aldama 404 (☎ 515 28 56; email casa.arnel@spersaoaxaca.com.mex), at Hidalgo, across from the Iglesia San Matias Jalatlaco. Arnel's courtyard jungle has enough mystique to inspire the next García-Márquez novel, and the hotel's more practical amenities make it an excellent choice: bar, Internet (20 pesos per hr.), a travel agency, spotless rooms, and friendly, helpful staff. Entertainment provided by the social breakfasts (7:30-9:45am) and the talking parrots in the courtyard. Tours of the surrounding areas leave from the hotel. Do-it-yourself and full laundry service. Singles 90 pesos, with bath 240 pesos; doubles 180 pesos, with bath 240 pesos.

Hostal Guadalupe (HI), Juárez 409 (☎ 516 63 65), between Abasolo and Constitución. Ideally situated between the buzz of the *zócalo* and the peace of Jalatlaco, Guadalupe may well be Oaxaca's best bargain. Luxuriate in the communal bath's clean, white splendor and rest easy in single-sex dorm-style rooms. TV, courtyard seating, kitchen access, and new laundry facilities make the place a steal. 40 pesos, with HI card 35 pesos; private bedroom 100 pesos.

NORTH OF THE ZÓCALO/EL CENTRO

Old colonial buildings make lovely museums and even lovelier hotels. This part of town not only offers the best architecture, but also the best location for those longing to stay close to Oaxaca's artifacts and galleries.

Hotel Reforma, Reforma 102 (☎ 516 09 39), between Independencia and Morelos, 3 blocks past the left side of the cathedral. Kick back in rustic, hand-carved wood furniture, and soak up the view of the city. Rooms are usually full; reservations are recommended. Singles 130 pesos; doubles 180 pesos; triples 250 pesos; quads 400 pesos.

Hostal Misión San Pedro, Juárez 200 (☎ 516 46 26), on the corner of Morelos. Though San Pedro lacks the ambience and services of many of the other hostels in town, bathrooms and dorm-style bedrooms are clean, bright, and extremely cheap. 35 pesos per night; singles 110 pesos; doubles 130 pesos.

SOUTH OF THE ZÓCALO

This area is thick with budget hotels—four or five often share the same block, particularly along **Díaz Ordaz** and **Mina.** Many hotels face noisy streets; ask for a room in the back or on an upper level.

■ **Magic Hostel,** Fiallo 305 (☎ 516 76 67), between Guerrero and Colón, is the hottest backpacker hangout in town. The jungle-style, upper-level eating area, inexpensive vegetarian meal options (25 pesos), hip international staff, and fun, laid-back ambience quickly trump the inconvenience of the sometimes messy bathrooms and 11pm lights-out policy. Services include Internet (20 pesos per hr.), laundry (10 pesos), and kitchen. Travelers are welcome any time of the day or night; if beds are full, you can sleep on a couch. 50 pesos per person; private doubles 120 pesos.

Hotel Mina, Mina 304 (☎ 516 49 66), at 20 Noviembre, is one of the cheapest options for those who prefer a private room. Plain rooms have sturdy beds. Communal baths are tidy and convenient. Singles 100 pesos; doubles 120 pesos; triples 170 pesos.

Hostal Santa Isabel, Mier y Terán 103 (☎ 514 28 65), between Independencia and Hidalgo. Some of the cheapest beds in town. Standard dorm-style rooms and serviceable bathrooms are supplemented by a kitchen, a bar, Internet access (20 pesos per hr.), and camaraderie. Beds 40 pesos per person; private doubles 100 pesos.

Hotel Pasaje, Mina 302 (☎ 516 42 13), 3 blocks south of the *zócalo*. Well-scrubbed, tiled rooms open onto a plant-filled courtyard. Bathrooms are large and clean. Rooms near the street are noisy, but you can smell chocolate from nearby sweet shops. Singles 140 pesos; doubles 170 pesos; triples 230 pesos.

▐ FOOD

Fast food may be a last-ditch option in most parts, but in typical Oaxacan fashion, even the cheapest and fastest roadside snacks are something of an art.

Exotic, delicious, and scandalously inexpensive meals are everywhere. Some of the best and most intriguing regional fare can be found in various stages of preparation at the **markets,** while more finished dishes can be procured from the amazing line of taco stands on **Guerrero,** just southeast of the *zócalo.*

Oaxaca has seven versions of *mole* (a rich sauce of chiles, chocolate, and over 28 other ingredients). Many restaurants also serve *tlayudas* (large, crisp tortillas topped with just about everything). If you're feeling adventurous, try *botanas oaxaqueñas*—plates full of regional goodies including chile, *quesillo* (boiled string cheese), *chorizo* (spicy sausage), guacamole, and *chapulines* (tiny, cooked grasshoppers doused with chile; they're good, seriously). Another specialty is the *tamale,* now found in all parts of the Republic. Made of ground corn wrapped in banana leaves then baked or boiled, *tamales* are stuffed with beans, chicken, or beef. And there's no better way to wrap up a feast of *comida oaxaqueña* than with a large swig of *mezcal,* (the potent, cactus-based liquor only manufactured in Oaxaca Valley).

Restorán Café Alex, Díaz Ordaz 218 (☎514 07 15). Extensive menu running the gamut of Mexican cuisine. Garden seating available. Breakfasts (starting at 25 pesos), *comida corrida* (36 pesos), and vegetarian dishes (starting at 19 pesos) are, in a word, amazing. Open M-Sa 7am-9pm, Su 7am-noon.

La Casa de la Abuela, Hidalgo 616, 2nd fl. (☎516 35 44), at the corner of the *zócalo* and Plaza Alameda. The authentic Oaxacan dishes are an excellent way to get one's culinary bearings. Savor delicious renditions of Oaxaca's famous *sopa de guias* (squash flower soup; 22.5 pesos) and *chapulines* (45 pesos) while marveling at the restaurant's postcard-perfect views of the cathedral and *zócalo.* Finish with a cup of *té de poelo* (a regional herbal brew; 9.5 pesos) or *café de olla* (a spiced coffee; 9.5 pesos). Unfortunately you'll pay for the privilege. Entrees 55 to 60 pesos. Open daily 1-9pm.

Restaurant Morelos, Morelos 1003 (☎516 05 58). Start your day off right with a high-quality breakfast at what is possibly the cheapest place in the city. A friendly staff serves full breakfast plates (14 pesos) to the flocks of earlybirds gossiping around its tables. *Antojitos* and *tostadas* 10 pesos. Open daily 7am-6pm.

Antojitos Regionales Los Olmos, Morelos 403, at Crespo. For those still unaccustomed to Oaxaca's big breakfast and diminutive dinner lifestyle, Antojitos is the right place. When other restaurants close their doors for the night, Antojitos is just beginning to fill up. Whatever they whip up, it's likely to be cheap—the *patitas en vinagre* is the most expensive item on the menu (12 pesos). *Tomate de mole, quesadillas,* and *tortas* 8 pesos. Open daily 7pm-midnight.

La Primavera (☎516 25 95), at the corner of the *zócalo* and Plaza Alameda. Decent food, and the lowest prices in the *zócalo* area. Huge *tlayudas* 30 pesos, *tamales* 19 pesos. Open daily 7am-11pm.

Las Quince Letras, Abasolo 300, (☎514 37 69). The *comida corrida* is not cheap, but 50 pesos will buy soup, salad, a main dish, and coffee or dessert. Delicious breakfasts start at 20 pesos. For dinner, try the *sopa oaxaqueña* (28 pesos), a powerful Oaxacan super-stew. Open daily 8am-9pm.

Mariscos Los Jorges, Suárez 806 (☎513 43 08), across the street from Parque Juárez, toward the north end of the park. After their huge, bargain breakfasts (20 pesos; 8am-1pm), Los Jorges serves delicious Veracruz-style seafood baked in the restaurant's old *indígena* oven, excellent both on its own (you can ask to see the fresh fish cuts before ordering) or wrapped up in tacos (39 pesos). Open daily 8am-6:30pm.

Flor de Loto, Morelos 509 (☎514 39 44). Though fluorescent lighting and quiet clientele leave this restaurant low on ambience, vegetarians in this blood-thirsty town can find a haven here. "Regional" (i.e., meaty) food also served. Veggie soups 15 pesos, *enchiladas de soya* 30 pesos, mushroom tacos 30 pesos. Open daily 8am-10pm.

EAT THE WORM! As the *mezcal* capital of the world, Oaxaca is justifiably proud of itself. Production of *mezcal,* the potent liquor made from the maguey plant and usually containing a *gusano de maguey* (maguey worm), started soon after the Spanish arrived and has been going strong ever since. During the yearly **Fiesta Nacional del Mezcal,** July 17-24 10am-9pm, Oaxacans and foreigners alike gather in Parque Juárez to drink themselves numb. Countless vendors crowd the park, and everyone stumbles from booth to booth, giddy with unlimited free shots. Try *mezcal* with the traditional worm at the bottom, but don't miss exotic *mezcal* variations, flavored with nut, blackberry, coconut, chicken breast, and strawberry, among other things. *Mezcal*-filled chocolates are a hit as well. If you've exceeded your taste-test tolerance, take a seat and enjoy the festival's live music, traditional dances, firework show, giant paper parade, and the crowning of the *Mezcal* Queen.

CAFES AND CHOCOLATE

About the only *oaxaqueño* fare more adored than the *chapulines* is the city's famous chocolate. Made from home-grown *cacoa* beans, the aroma wafts from shops clustered on the corner of **Mina** and **20 de Noviembre.** Follow your nose to see the chocolate-making process in action and grab lots of free samples. If you don't make it to the area, don't worry—nearly every restaurant in the city serves steaming mugs of *chocolate caliente* (hot chocolate). Also keep an eye out for *calle de olla,* a sweet, spicy coffee, and *tejate,* a cold, corn-based drink. While most chocolate shops and restaurants serve all the hot drinks you could want, those who want a true cafe experience, complete with the trendy student crowd, should head to **5 de Mayo** on the corner of **Reforma** and **Abasolo.**

Chocolate Mayordomo, (☎516 16 19), at the corner of Mina and 20 de Noviembre, with a second shop across the street. The undisputed king of Oaxaca's sweets market, Mayordomo churns out the chocolate while onlookers drool and gobble free samples. Buy some solid chocolate for the road (20 pesos per 500 grams), or sit with a cup of the city's cheapest hot chocolate (small 5 pesos). Open daily 7am-9pm.

Café Gecko, 5 de Mayo 412-3 (☎514 80 24), half a block south of Iglesia de Santo Domingo. With a vine-covered courtyard, breakfasts (20 pesos), convenient Internet access (18 pesos per hr.), and the ever-present *chocolate caliente* (14 pesos), Café Gecko draws museum-hoppers in need of a caffeine boost. Open daily 8:30am-8pm.

Coffee Beans Cafe and Bar, 5 de Mayo 205. Typical coffeehouse fare is supplemented by drinks from the over-priced bar; be prepared to pay for the admittedly great ambience (*café americano* 12 pesos). Open daily 8am-midnight.

SIGHTS

Oaxaca's museums, churches, and historical sights are seamlessly integrated into the city's daily life. Museum corridors are well trodden by tourists and locals alike, and most of the city's old buildings lead a double life, both preserving the past and serving the state's active, creative citizens. Many museums, cultural centers, and art stores are located on **Alcalá.** On the east side of the cathedral, a cobbled pedestrian street, the **Andador,** leads to Alcalá.

CATEDRAL DE OAXACA. Originally constructed in 1535 and reconstructed in 1702-33 after earthquake damage, the cathedral dates from a time when the Mexican church and state were one. The building is governmental and imposing, with the structural focus provided by the ornate bishop's seat. The facade is Baroque-style bas relief. The interior contains 14 side chapels. These days it is almost more of a place of congregation than of sanctuary—the patio outside the church acts as a stage for pageants and *payasos* (clowns) on weekend evenings. *(In the northeast corner of the zócalo. Open daily 7am-9pm.)*

PALACIO DE GOBIERNO. One of the most pleasant *palacios* in the country, Oaxaca's Palacio de Gobierno was constructed in the mid-19th century. Contemporary art expositions decorate the open-roofed *palacio.* At the top of the stairs, a mural by Arturo García Bustos acts as a pictorial pop-quiz on state history. The narrative culminates with Benito Juárez's oft-repeated phrase *"El respeto al derecho ajeno es la paz"* ("Respect for the rights of others is peace") above him and his wife Margarita Masa. *(On the south side of the zócalo. Open 24hr.)*

⬛ CENTRO CULTURAL SANTO DOMINGO. The ex-convent next door to the Iglesia de Santo Domingo was converted into the prestigious **Museo de las Culturas de Oaxaca,** and after a year-long renovation in 1994, the 16th-century building is in better condition than ever. The stellar museum houses a large collection of Mixtec and Zapotec pieces, but the prime attraction is the treasure extracted from Tomb 7 in Monte Albán; the old, silver, turquoise, bone, and obsidian jewelry and artifacts constitute one of the best assortments of Zapotec material ever found. The *Centro* also houses the new **Jardín Etnobotánico** and the 17th-century **Fray Francisco de Burgoa** library collection. *(☎516 29 91. Open Tu-Su 10am-8pm. 25 pesos; Su free.)*

IGLESIA DE SANTO DOMINGO. Higher and mightier than the *catedral*, Santo Domingo is the city's spiritual center and its tallest building. One of the best examples of Mexican Baroque, the church was begun in 1570, but was not finished and consecrated until 1611. Since then, Santo Domingo has functioned as a place of worship, a museum, and even as military barracks for both sides of the Reform Wars and the Revolution. The interior is spectacular, with waves of gilded stucco covering the ceiling and walls. Built in 1959 by Oaxacan artists and workers, the massive gilded altar is one of the most elaborate (and expensive) of its kind and a treat even for even the most jaded, seen-every-church tourists. The **Capilla de la Virgen del Rosario,** to the right as you walk in, was built in 1724 with funds given by Dionisio Levanto. It features relatively new altar works, some of them inaugurated as late as the 1960s. *(3 blocks past MACO, on the Andador Turístico. Open daily 7am-1pm and 4-8pm. Capilla open daily 7am-1pm and 4-7pm.)*

MUSEO DE ARTE CONTEMPORÁNEO DE OAXACA (MACO). This colonial building is known as the Casa de Cortés, although historians insist that it was not, in fact, Cortés's estate. Nevertheless, the 18th century upper-class home is an example of vice-regal architecture, a style used by *conquistadores* and their heirs. The 15-room museum features three-month rotating exhibitions and in the past has showcased *oaxaqueños* Rufino Tamayo, Francisco Toledo, and Rodolfo Morales. *(Alcalá 202, a block down Andador Turístico on the right. ☎514 71 10. Open W-M 10:30am-8pm. 10 pesos; free Su.)*

CASA DE BENITO JUÁREZ. Once home to Mexico's most beloved president, who lived here for ten years during his childhood (1818-1828), the house actually belonged to Juárez's benefactor, Antonio Salanuevo. With living room, bedrooms, kitchen, as well, and a "bookbinding/weaving shop," the house is reconstructed in 19th-century, upper-class *oaxaqueña* style. *(Vigil 609, 1 block west of Alcalá. ☎516 18 60. Open Tu-Sa 10am-7pm, Su 10am-5pm. 22 pesos; free Su.)*

MUSEO DE ARTE PREHISPÁNICO DE MÉXICO RUFINO TAMAYO. The museum shows off this Oaxacan artist's personal collection of pre-Hispanic objects. The figurines, ceramics, and masks that Tamayo collected are meant to be appreciated as works of art rather than artifacts, resulting in a hybrid art gallery and archaeological museum. *(Morelos 503, between Díaz Ordaz and Tinoco y Palacios. ☎516 47 50. Open M and W-Sa 10am-2pm and 4-7pm, Su 10am-3pm. 14 pesos.)*

BASÍLICA DE LA SOLEDAD. A minor but absorbing attraction is the funky museum of religious art located next to the 17th century church. The museum houses an astonishing array of objects—from model ships to shell-and-pasta figurines—sent from around the world as gifts to the Virgin, who is said to have appeared here in 1620. *(Independencia 107, 4 blocks behind the post office. ☎516 50 76. Open daily 10am-2pm and 4-6pm. 2 pesos.)*

SOUTHERN PACIFIC COAST

TEATRO MACEDONIO ALCALÁ. One of the most beautiful buildings in Oaxaca, the theater, constructed in the 1900s, exemplifies the style fostered by dictator Porfirio Díaz, who had a taste for French art and intellectual formulas. Currently closed for renovations, the museum is expected to reopen by summer 2001. (*5 de Mayo at Independencia, 2 blocks behind the cathedral. ☎516 33 87. Weekly shows 6 or 8pm. 20 pesos.*)

OTHER SIGHTS. For a beautiful view of the city and surrounding hills, head to the **Cerro de Fortín** (The Hill with the Beautiful View). The *Escalera de Fortín* begins on Crespo, leading past the Guelaguetza amphitheater to the **Plantearium Nundehui.** The stairs are a favorite destination for fitness fiends—prepare to be passed by joggers loping effortlessly uphill. (Planetarium ☎514 75 00. Open Th-Su 10am-1pm and 5-8pm. 10 pesos.) Also worth a visit is the **Centro Fotográfico Álvarez Bravo,** Murguía 302, between Reforma and Juárez. It displays rotating photography exhibits. (☎516 28 80. Open W-M 9:30am-6pm. Free.)

🎵🎭 ENTERTAINMENT AND NIGHTLIFE

On warm summer nights it's impossible to walk around Oaxaca without running into entertainment. Street performers sing on the Alcalá, dancers sway in the Parque Juárez, art galleries astound north of the *zócalo*, and cinemas screen films—both artsy and profane—everywhere. Some of the cheapest entertainment can be found in the *zócalo*, where people-watching can be as exciting as watching *telenovelas*. Watch the city's children toss strange, oblong-shaped balloons, or join the tableau yourself—sound track provided by the *marimba* bands that hammer away under the *portal* (M, W, F-Sa after 7pm). When the streets quiet down around 10 or 11pm, Oaxaca's huge student population congregates in bars and discos that keep rocking until morning. For those made geriatric by the previous night's activity, catch a recent flick in English with Spanish subtitles at **Ariel 2000** (☎516 52 41), at the corner of Juárez and Berriozabal. **Sala Versailles,** Ocampo 105 (☎516 23 35), three blocks east of the *zócalo*, hosts live shows as well as movies. At the **Teatro Macedonio Alcalá** (☎516 33 87; see p. 462), weekly shows cost 20 pesos. Much of the city's nightlife can be reached on foot, but, for those who choose to travel in style, taxis go to most destinations (20 pesos).

BARS

The city's many bars provide a place for travelers and locals alike to mingle, socialize, drink, and make merry. Clustered on the **Alcalá** and two blocks west near **Díaz** and **Allende,** most are within safe walking distance of the *zócalo*.

La Costumbre, Alcalá 501, opposite the entrance to Santo Domingo. A little too tight for dancing, trips to La Costumbre usually come either before or after an expedition to the discos at the north of town. A good place to find fellow bar hoppers. Beer 15 pesos, cocktails 27 pesos. Open M-Sa 8pm-2:30am.

La Divina, Gurion 104, across from the south side of Santo Domingo, continues to be popular among the city's student bourgeoisie. Trippy ceramic artwork and plentiful nooks for conversation are lubricated by the beers from the crowded bar (15 pesos). No cover. Open Tu-Su 9pm-1:30am.

Café Bar del Borgo, Alcalá 303, a bit closer to the *zócalo*, del Borgo has a chill coffeehouse atmosphere, with couples and groups sipping cappuccino (13 pesos) and beer (12 pesos) around small, intimate tables. Open daily 9am-11pm.

Café-Bar La Resistencia, Díaz 503 (☎514 95 84), at Allende. Yet another bar jampacked with an international crowd. Beer 15 pesos. No cover. Open M-Sa 8pm-2am.

La Catrina, around the corner at Bravo and Palacios, has a slightly more national crowd, although many international travelers come here as well. Murals featuring huge skeletons decorate the walls. Beers 12 pesos. No cover. Open daily 5pm-2am.

CLUBS

Crowded with energetic students in tight black pants, Oaxaca's clubs are the perfect opportunity for foreign students to blend in. After all, no one will be able to hear your rotten Spanish as you writhe in the mass of sweaty, gyrating humans. Several hard-core discos cluster near the first-class bus station on **Díaz Ordaz** at **Niños Héroes de Chapultepec,** 11 blocks north of the *zócalo.* A taxi is the best way to reach these clubs (20 pesos).

La Candela, Allende 211 (☎514 20 10), 2 blocks from Santo Domingo. Whether you are a beginner or an expert, the live salsa band will keep you moving all night long. A diverse crowd comes for the intimate atmosphere, great dancing, and moderately-priced restaurant fare. Cover 25-35 pesos depending on the band. Live music Tu-Sa from 10pm. Open daily 2pm-1:30am.

NRG, Díaz 102-B (☎515 04 77), down 1 block from Héroes de Chapultepec, is, quite simply, a great place to dance. Spanish music W, pop mix other nights. Beer 15 pesos. No cover W; cover Th 30 pesos men, women free; cover F-Sa 40 pesos. Open W-Sa 9pm-3am.

Zelantro, Díaz 208 at Matamoros, 2 blocks west of the Alcalá. Though the uncategorizable Zelantro offers just about everything—billiards, ping pong, a cushioned room for lounging, and a quieter downstairs bar—its soul is in its rooftop dance floor. An eclectic mix of ska, reggae, salsa, and rap works international 20-somethings into a groove. Beer 12 pesos, *mezcal* 10 pesos. Bar open daily 9pm-2am; club open Th-Sa 9pm-2am. Cover F-Sa 20 pesos.

GAY AND LESBIAN NIGHTLIFE

In typical *machisimo* fashion, Oaxaca's gay and lesbian nightlife is a well-kept secret. The city's one gay club is, however, popular, well-managed, and safe.

502, at Díaz 502, across from La Resistencia. As the city's only gay and lesbian nightclub, 502 can afford to be selective. The club is private; ring the bell outside the door and they'll decide whether you're fit to enter. No drugs, heavy drinking, or transvestism allowed. Cover 35 pesos. Open F-Sa 11pm-5am.

❀ FESTIVALS

On the two Mondays following July 16, known as **Los Lunes del Cerro** (Hill Mondays), representatives from all seven regions of Oaxaca state converge on the Cerro del Fortín for the festival of **Guelaguetza.** "Guelaguetza" refers to the Zapotec custom of reciprocal gift-giving, and at the end of the day's traditional dances, performers throw goods typical from their regions into the outstretched arms of the crowd. In between the gatherings are festive food and handicraft exhibits, art shows, and concerts. (Front-section seats 150-300 pesos, back-section seats free, but you must come very early to get a seat. Call tourist office for reservations.)

Oaxaca's exquisitely beautiful **Día de los Muertos** (Nov. 1-2) celebrations have become a huge tourist draw in recent years. Most travel agencies offer expeditions to the candlelit, marigold-filled village graveyards. Shops fill with molded sugar *calaveras* (skulls) and dancing skeletons, while altars to memorialize the deceased are erected throughout the city. Because these celebrations occur for very personal reasons, locals might not appreciate being photographed as they remember their deceased.

On December 23, Oaxacans celebrate the unique **Noche de los Rábanos** (Night of the Radishes). The small tuber is so honored for its frequent use in Oaxacan cuisine and its extremely carvable form. Masterpieces of historic or biblical themes made entirely in radish fill the *zócalo,* where they are judged. Hundreds of people admire the creations and eat sweet *buñuelos,* tortillas with honey. Upon finishing the treat, make a wish and throw the ceramic plate on the ground; if the plate smashes into pieces, your wish will come true.

SPORTS

Most likely due to the high student population, Oaxacans exercise a bit more than the average Mexican. To get your morning run without being turned into road-kill, head to **Campo de Venustiano Carranza,** several blocks east of Iglesia Santo Matias on Alianza. This public complex has a track, gym, pool, and several stadiums. Here you can also catch fierce *fútbol* games between the Chapulines, the local college team, and their rivals. The Guerreros, Oaxaca's professional baseball team, play just northwest of the complex at the **Estadio Eduardo Vásconcelos,** on the corner of Vásconcelos and Niños Héroes de Chapultepec.

◪ DAYTRIPS FROM OAXACA

The villages surrounding Oaxaca are known for their artisanship and their Zapotec and Mixtec ruins. As stores and museums of folk art took interest in the imaginative handicrafts made in these villages, many residents left farming to devote themselves full-time to craft production. Villages often specialize in particular products: **Arrazola** and **San Martín Tilcajate** make wooden animals, **San Bartolo Coyotepec** black clay pottery, **Atzompa** green clay pottery, **Ocotlán** natural clay pottery, **Teotitlán del Valle** wool *sarapes*, and **Villa Díaz Ordaz** and **Santo Tomás Jalietza** textiles and weavings. Likewise, many villages hold *mercados* on specific days to attract visitors: Miahuatlán (Monday), Atzompa (Tuesday), San Pablo Etla (Wednesday), Zaachila (Thursday), Ocotlán (Friday), and Tlacolula (Sunday).

The "Tourist Yu'u" program operated by SEDETUR (☎516 01 23; open daily 9am-2pm) rents out guest houses in Abasolo, Papalutla, Teotitlán del Valle, Benito Juárez, Tlacolula, Quialana, Tlapazola, Santa Ana del Valle, and Hierve el Agua. Accommodations include five beds, a kitchen, and clean bedding; proceeds benefit the community. (70 pesos per person; 25 peso discount for students in some villages; camping in the garden 25-30 pesos.) Additionally, you can try one of the *paseos culturales*, which introduce visitors to the traditional medicinal, agricultural, and artistic practices of the 13 villages in the area.

All the villages can be reached by the taxi *colectivos* that leave the Central de Abastos (1hr., 6-10 pesos depending on distance). At the intersection of Periférico and Las Casas is an Inverlat bank. *Colectivos* depart from north of the bank from the road within the market. Destinations are labeled on taxi windows and on signs along the road. Buses are easy to find on the Mitla route (Rte. 190), but may be more difficult to locate on other routes. Some companies offer bike tours to outlying towns; contact the tourist office for more information.

OAXACA TO MITLA (RTE. 190)

All following destinations are accessible via a Mitla-bound bus, leaving the second-class station in Oaxaca (1hr., every 10min. 8am-8pm, 10 pesos). Most people visit these sites as daytrips, but the tourist office in Oaxaca can arrange for overnight stays in Teotitlán del Valle, Tlacolula, or Hierve el Agua (see p. 466).

SANTA MARÍA EL TULE. This friendly little town (pop. 7000), just 14km outside Oaxaca, houses one of Mexico's great roadside attractions: the **Tule Tree.** The 2000-year-old, 42m sabino tree has an astounding circumference of 58m—the largest girth of any tree on earth. Ask the bus driver to drop you off at El Tule; then ask for *el árbol* (the tree). Don't be deceived into thinking the first tree you see is the big one—it's just the 1000-year-old baby. There is a fee (2 pesos) to approach the fence closest the tree, but the glory of this botanical behemoth can be appreciated from within a 100m radius. In fact, farther may be better, as pictures taken too close will look like nothing more than a big piece of bark.

DAINZÚ. The Dainzú ruins, 22km from Oaxaca, just off the road branching to Macuilxochitl, date from the first Pre-Classic phase at Monte Albán. A series of magnificently carved figures at the base of the tallest pyramid represent ballplayers in poses similar to Monte Albán's "dancers" (see p. 468). Two humans and two jaguars, gods of the sport, supervise the contest. Up the hill from the pyramid, another game scene is hewn in the living rock. Bring your walking shoes; the ruins are 2km from the main road. *(Open daily 8am-6pm. 17 pesos.)*

SAN JERÓNIMO TLACOCHAHUAYA. The walls of the **Iglesia de San Jerónimo** in nearby San Jerónimo Tlacochahuaya (pop. 5300), 23km from Oaxaca, illustrate Zapotec decorative techniques applied to Catholic motifs. It was built at the end of the 16th century by Dominicans seeking to escape worldly temptation. *(Open daily 7am-2pm and 4-6pm.)*

TEOTITLÁN DEL VALLE. Twenty-eight kilometers from Oaxaca, Teotitlán is the oldest community in the state, settled about 2000 years ago. The source of many beautiful woolen *sarapes* and rugs, Teotitlán is home to 200-300 families who earn their livelihood by spinning and weaving. Many allow tourists to visit their workshops. Unfortunately, Teotitlán is not as accessible as many of the other stops on the road; it's 4km from where the bus drops you off. *Taxi colectivos* run sporadically from the main road to town, and a few workshops are scattered within walking distance of the main road.

TLACOLULA DE MATAMOROS. Tlacolula (pop. 12,700), 33km from Oaxaca, is one of the largest towns in the area, and shows the slightly gritty underside of this rural region. It hosts a lively market (Su 6am-2pm, but officially Su 6am-7pm), which features the speciality *mezcal*. Slightly more interesting than the town itself are the small Zapotec ruins of **Lambityeco,** several kilometers before the town itself. Occupied AD 600-1000 while the Zapotecs were abandoning Monte Albán, the village reached its peak from AD 700-775. The ruins consist of one main pyramid and several houses. Some murals remain visible. *(Open daily 8am-6pm, 17 pesos; Su free.)*

■ **YAGUL.** Thirty-six kilometers from Oaxaca, Yagul was a Zapotec city inhabited primarily from 700 BC-AD 1521, though there is evidence of human presence as early as 3000 BC. Less archaeologically impressive than Mitla, the rarely-visited Yagul is decidedly more aesthetically striking. A gorgeous 1.5km jaunt through cornfields and up a hill preps the visitor for the wide green view of a mountain-ringed valley that awaits at the top. If you go on a weekday, you'll be able to act out your long-held fantasies of Zapotec kingship with lizards as your only audience. The more famous buildings and tombs are in the **Acrópolis,** the area closest the parking lot, 2km north of the road. If you bring some friends you can start a pick-up game in the restored ball court, the largest of its kind in the Oaxaca Valley. The **Court of the Triple Tomb** is to the left of the ball court. Carved with an image that resembles a jaguar, the tomb is divided in three sections, with stone faces covering the largest section. Beyond the ball court rises the **Council Hall;** behind that is the **Palace of the Six Patios,** believed to have been home to the city's ruler. Heading back to the parking lot, take the left-hand trail that climbs uphill to the rocky out-cropping to catch a spectacular view of the cactus-covered hills. Look for the small stone bridge, behind the tomb on your right as you climb the hill. Continuing up the rocky path you will be rewarded with even more spectacular views and, ultimately, **bathtubs.** The two sink-looking bins on the right-hand side of the moun-taintop supposedly served as Zapotec bathtubs. There is a picturesque *palapa*-style restaurant before the hill on the way to the ruins, which serves inexpensive regional specialties. *(Site open daily 8am-5pm. 22 pesos; Su free.)*

MITLA

The second-class "Mitla" bus stops right in front of a sign (1¼hr., 10 pesos); follow the sign's arrow to the left onto the town's main drag. Following the green signs, continue on the road for 20min. until you reach the church in front of the ruins. Site open daily 8am-5pm. 22 pesos; Su free.

Tucked into a dusty Zapotec-speaking village, the archaeological site of Mitla, 44km east of Oaxaca, is smaller and less popular with tourists than the immense Monte Albán. Although Mitla began as a small village around 1000 BC, the Zapo-tecs only came to occupy it when the Mixtecs forced them out of Monte Albán. It was later appropriated by the Mixtecs and became the largest and most important of late Mixtec cities. The site has a bloody history: until the 16th century, it was a place of worship for the gods of the underworld and witnessed both animal and human sacrifice. When the Spaniards arrived in the valley, Mitla was the only ceremonial center of the Mesoamerican Classic period still in use. Interestingly, the Catholic archbishop of Oaxaca built his home to echo the horizontal lines of the Zapotec priest's residence in Mitla, thus paying architectural tribute to an ancient indigenous religion virtually exterminated by Catholicism.

Walking to the ruins from the town's main road you will first come upon the **Grupo del Arroyo,** a rather unimpressive construction dating from AD 1100. Continuing on the main road, the ticket booth is in the yellow building on the far side of the red-domed church; it contains a few artifacts and several dioramas of the site. To the left of it and behind the church are the three patios known as the **North Group** or **Catholic Establishment.** One of them has been almost completely buried by the church. The central patio is on the other side of the church; here, and in the surrounding rooms, you can see pieces of Mixtec paintings, supposedly telling Mixtec history, done in red on stone. The more impressive ruins are across the road in the **Grupo de las Columnas (Group of the Columns).** Intricate geometric designs decorate both the exterior and interior. Beyond the entrance are two patios joined at one corner. In the first one, the **Hall of the Columns,** the tombs of the pyramids form a cross; for years, Spaniards thought this proved that the Mixtecs somehow knew the story of Jesus. On the second patio behind and to the right of the first, two tombs are open to visitors. The eastern-most tomb has large stones covered with mosaic patterns. The roof of the northern-most tomb rests on a single huge column known as the **Column of Life.** Pilgrims travel here each year to embrace the column. In exchange for the hug, the column supposedly tells them how much longer they have to live. The two other groups, **Grupo del Sur (South Group)** and **Grupo de Adobe,** are farther from the site, southeast and across the river from the main ruins. Use the diagrams at the site to find these two ruins if you wish to see them, though neither is well-preserved.

HIERVE EL AGUA

The site is 13km east of Mitla and 57km east of Oaxaca. Buses from Oaxaca take at least 2hr. From Mitla, take a camioneta from the terminal (45min., every hr. 8am-6pm, 15 pesos). Ask if the camioneta is headed to Agua Dulce, as they are unmarked. Open daily 8am-6pm. 10 pesos.

Hierve el Agua (The Water Boils), takes its name from two springs of carbonated water that look like they are boiling. The waters are actually not hot, and make for refreshing baths. The high concentration of mineral salts in the water resulted in the strange petrification of several waterfalls, or, more properly, rockfalls. A path to the top of the largest rock form offers an impressive view. Be careful when climbing, as rocks are often wet and slippery. The site includes three pools for bathing—two of sulfur water closest the petrified waterfall, and one of *agua dulce* on the left-hand side of the path.

ARRAZOLA, CUILAPÁN, ZAACHILA, AND AZTOMPA (RTE. 131)

Arrazola, Cuilapán, and Zaachila can all be reached by taking a taxi colectivo from Oaxaca's Central de Abastos. It's easy to hop from one town to the next; go back to Rte. 131 and flag down another colectivo. Though close to the other three, Aztompa does not lie on Rte. 131. From Oaxaca, it can be reached via a separate colectivo (40min., 8 pesos).

ARRAZOLA. This small, hilly village is the hometown of Manuel Jiménez, one of Mexico's most famous artisans. Jiménez is the creator of **alebrijes,** brightly colored figurines of demons and zoo animals. While success has made his pieces unaffordable to most (small pieces go for US$170), his workshop is worth visiting. To get there, walk up Arrazola's main road, passing the plaza and turning left at the first intersection. Continue past the end of the pavement, following as it turns right. The home is the only major structure on the right hand side, opposite a corn field. A glimpse of the Jiménez family's kinetic cedar wood sculptures and the possibility of a conversation with the man himself make the substantial trek from Rte. 131 worth the effort. Nearly all the households in town make figurines to supplement their incomes. Pick your way through yards full of goats and chickens to the workshops, or simply follow one of the 10-year-old guides; the owners will happily show you their wares and haggle for a fair price. A medium-sized iguana *alebrije* will cost about 120 pesos. *(20min. from Oaxaca on Rte. 131.)*

CUILAPÁN DE GUERRERO. Cuilapán (pop. 11,000) has an isolated and hauntingly lovely 17th-century **Dominican monastery.** The highlight of the site—aside from the breathtaking vistas—is the cell that was once occupied by the Revolutionary hero Vicente Guerrero in 1831 before his death by firing squad on the patio outside. Today, all that remains is a portrait of him in his cell and a monument where he fell. Built as a retreat for Spanish monks wishing to exile themselves as far as possible from civilization, the upper floor now cloisters archaeologists laboring to reconstruct the region's history in the monk's old stone cells. *(25min. from Oaxaca on Rte. 131. Open daily 10am-6pm. 17 pesos.)*

ZAACHILA. Zaachila (pop. 15,000), the stronghold of the Zapotecs before they fell to the Spanish in 1521, hosts a fascinating market each Thursday. Spend your pesos on preserved bananas and squealing pigs. A yellow and orange cathedral dominates the center of town. To the right and behind the church, a street heads uphill to a partially uncovered archaeological site. Until 1962, locals prohibited excavations to prevent the intrusion of outsiders. Exploration since has been limited, but two Mixtec tombs with well-preserved jewelry have been uncovered. The town's gold, turquoise, jade, and bone artifacts (as well as the tourist dollars they would have attracted) have been spirited away to the national museum in Mexico City. The eerie tombs—the only decorated ones in Oaxaca—are worth a visit. Wide-eyed owls (messengers of the Zapotec underworld) stare from the damp stone walls, while portrayals of the Gods of Death await in the dimmer recess of the tomb. *(30min. from Oaxaca on Rte. 131. Open daily 9am-6pm. 17 pesos; Su free.)*

AZTOMPA. Atzompa (pop. 11,000) is where that magnificent blend of clay and sprouts, the **Chia Pet®,** was born. Natural, green-glazed pottery, the town's specialty, can be found here at better prices than in Oaxaca. The **Casa de Artesanías** is a publicly funded forum that brings together the work of the town's artisans. While selection is good at the Casa, bargaining is easier with the artisans themselves. *(Though close to the other villages, Aztompa does not lie on Rte. 131. Take a taxi colectivo marked "Aztompa" (40min., 8 pesos) from the Central de Abastos.)*

SAN BARTOLO COYOTEPEC AND THE ROAD SOUTH (RTE. 175)

For all three towns, take an "Ocotlán" taxi colectivo from the market (San Bartolo 15min., Santo Tomás 20min., Ocotlán 40min.; all three towns 10 pesos by colectivo).

SAN BARTOLO COYOTEPEC. San Bartolo, 12km south of Oaxaca, is the only place in Mexico that creates the ink-black pottery that populates souvenir shops throughout the state. The dark color comes from the local mud. Though the town had been making the pottery for centuries, it wasn't until 1953, when the diminutive Doña Rosa accidentally discovered that it could be polished, that it became an art form. Doña Rosa kept the polishing technique a family secret for 12 years, then gave it to the town, which has been supported by the craft ever since. In the market, on the right side of Rte. 175, villagers sell jet-black vases, luminaires, figurines, you name it. Many substantial pieces go for under 20 pesos. The polished pottery will only hold water for 20min. or so before soaking it up—don't buy anything you plan to drink out of. Doña Rosa's son carries on the family tradition and gives demonstrations in the Nieto workshop, several blocks up the town's main street, Juárez, on the left side of Rte. 175. *(Market open daily 10:30am-8pm. Nieto workshop open daily 8:30am-7:30pm.)*

SANTO TOMÁS JALIETZA. Four kilometers farther south and slightly left of the main road, Santo Tomás's artisans specialize in weaving on back-strap looms. The town has a handsome 17th-century church dedicated to its patron saint.

OCOTLÁN DE MORELOS. Above the valley in the foothills of the Sierra Madre del Sur, 33km south of the Oaxaca, Ocotlán offers a fairy-tale powder blue church and a huge Friday *mercado* (10am-8pm), specializing in *sarapes*. It's less tourist-oriented than other towns, so visitors willing to be the market's sole and very conspicuous buyer will be rewarded with authentic prices for authentic goods. Afterwards, take a ride on one of the town's unusual, bicycle-powered buggies.

■ MONTE ALBÁN

Autobuses Turisticos buses to Monte Albán leave the Hotel Rivera del Angel, Mina 518 (☎516 53 27), between Mier y Terán and Díaz Ordaz, several blocks southwest of the zócalo (30min; every 30min. 8:30am-4pm; later buses leave little time at site). Round trip ticket with fixed return 2hr. after arrival 16 pesos; 7-8 pesos extra to come back later. Site open daily 8am-6pm. 30 pesos, 30 pesos more with video camera. Free Su and holidays. Unless you're an expert on pre-Hispanic civilizations (or the type that likes her ruins unexplained) a good guide to Monte Albán can really make the visit. Though many travel agencies can set you up with hassle-free transportation and excellent guides, it is usually cheaper to transport yourself and find a guide once you reach the mountain. English language guides charge 150-300 pesos for a 1½hr. tour, depending on the size and negotiating skills of your group.

High above Oaxaca de Juárez, Monte Albán, the ancient mecca of the Zapotec "cloud people," now watches over the surrounding mountains in utter stillness. Visitors to Oaxaca should not leave without seeing the ruins, some of the most important and spectacular in Mexico. The history of Monte Albán can be divided into five parts, spanning the years from 500 BC until the Spanish conquest in the 16th century. First constructed around 700 BC, Monte Albán did not grow until **Periods I** and **II**, when Maya and Zapotec cultures intermingled. The Zapotecs adopted the Maya *juego de pelota* (ball game) and steep pyramid structure, while the Maya appropriated the Zapotec calendar and writing system. The city did not truly flourish until **Period III** during the Classic Period (AD 300-750), when it shared the spotlight with Teotihuacán and Tikal as a major cultural and ceremonial center of Mesoamerica. This was the greatest Zapotec capital—the people cultivated maize, built complex drainage systems for water, and engaged in extensive exchange networks, especially with Teotihuacán (see p. 129). Almost all of the extant buildings and tombs, as well as several urns and murals of *colanijes* (richly adorned priests) date from this period. Burial arrangements of varying size and richness show the social divisions of the period: priests, clerks, and laborers lived and died apart. As Monte Albán grew, daily life was carefully constructed to harmonize with supernatural elements: architecture adhered to the orientation of the four cardinal points and the proportions of the 260-day sacred calendar; residences were organized in families of five to 10 people in four-sided houses with open central courtyards. To emphasize the congruence between household and cosmos, families buried their ancestors beneath their houses to symbolize their transmigration to the underworld below. Excavations of burials in Monte Albán have yielded not only dazzling artifacts, but also valuable information on social stratification.

For reasons that remain unknown, Monte Albán began to fade around AD 750. Construction ceased, and control of the Zapotec empire shifted from Monte Albán to other cities such as Zaachila, Yagul, and later, Mitla. Explanations for the abandonment include drought, over-exploitation of resources, and unrest. As with other Zapotec strongholds during the subsequent **Periods IV** and **V,** the Mixtecs took over. The Mixtecs used Monte Albán as a fortress and a sacred metropolis, reclaiming the tombs left by the Zapotecs. When Alfonso

Caso discovered **Tomb 7** in 1932; the treasure found within more than quadrupled the number of previously identified gold Mixtec objects. The treasures from Tomb 7 are now on display at the Museo de las Culturas de Oaxaca (see **Oaxaca: Sights,** p. 461).

BALLCOURT. After passing through the ticketing station just beyond the museum, walk left up the inclined path leading diagonally toward the ruins. Before reaching the Main Plaza, you will see the remains of several small buildings on your left and the ballcourt in front of you. The sides of the court, which now look like bleachers, were once covered by stucco and plaster, and served as bouncing boards for the ball toward the goal. In contrast to the Aztecs' more gory use of the game to determine sacrificial victims, the Zapotecs used it to solve all kinds of conflicts and as a means of predicting future events.

MAIN PLAZA. Passing the ballcourt on your left, you will enter the huge Main Plaza, with the mountain-like **North Platform** on the right, and smaller structures lined up on your left. The Main Plaza is flat, remarkable when one considers that the mountain from which is was cut was originally peaked. On your left, look for **The Palace.** Under like other pre-Hispanic ruins, the structures at Monte Albán were civic and residential as well as religious; this pyramid served as a the home of one of Monte Albán's important dignitaries. On top of the pyramid, several main rooms center around a patio.

SOUTH PLATFORM. Citty-corner from the palace and forming the Plaza's south end is the South Platform, one of the site's highest structures. If you climb only one pyramid in Monte Albán it should be this one: the top affords a commanding view of the ruins, valley, and mountains beyond. On both sides of the staircase on the plaza level are stelae carved with priests and tigers. One stela is believed to depict a former Monte Albán king.

BUILDING OF DANCERS. Walking left of the platform to the plaza's west side, you will first come across **System M** and the Building of Dancers, bordered on either side by identical pyramids that were once crowned by one-room temples. The haunting reliefs on the center building are known as "dancers," though they more likely depict chieftans conquered by Monte Albán. The over 400 figures date from the 5th century BC and are nearly identical to contemporary Olmec sculptures on the Gulf Coast. Many of the figures show evidence of genital mutilation.

BUILDINGS G, H, I, AND J. Crossing back to the center of the platform, the first structure you hit is Building J, formed in the shape of an arrowhead and containing a labyrinth of tunnels and passageways. Unlike any other ancient edifice in Mexico, it is asymmetrical and built at a 45° angle to nearby structures. Its broad, carved slabs suggest that the building is one of the oldest on the site, dating from 100 BC to AD 200. Many of the glyphs depict an upside-down head below a stylized hill. Archeologists speculate that these images represent conquests, the head indicating the tribe defeated and the glyph identifying the region conquered. The next group of buildings moving north, dominating the center of the plaza are buildings G, H, and I—likely compromising the principal altar of Monte Albán.

THE NORTH PLATFORM. Finish off the Main Plaza by visiting the North Platform near the entrance, a structure almost as large as the plaza itself. The complex Platform contains the **Sunken Patio** as well as the site's highest altar, which you can climb for yet another *buena vista*.

TOMBS AND MUSEUM. Continue straight on the path, exiting the site to **Tomb 104.** Duck underground, look above the entrance, and gaze at the urn, which is covered with interwoven images of the maize and rain gods. On your way out of the site, be sure to stop by the museum, which gives a chronological survey of Monte Albán's history and displays sculpted stones from the site's earlier periods. Although the collection is still impressive, some of the more spectacular artifacts

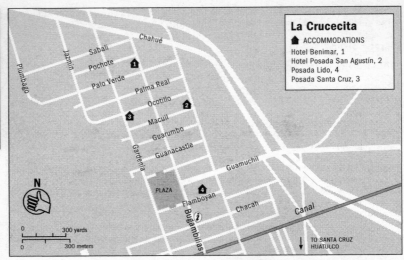

La Crucecita

🏠 ACCOMMODATIONS

Hotel Benimar, 1
Hotel Posada San Agustín, 2
Posada Lido, 4
Posada Santa Cruz, 3

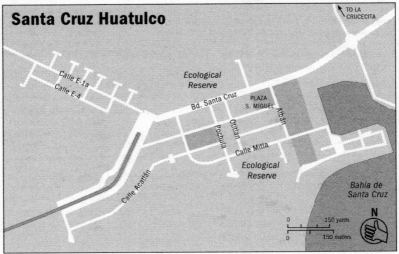

Santa Cruz Huatulco

have unfortunately been hauled off to museums in Oaxaca and Mexico City. Near the parking lot is the entrance to **Tomb 7,** where the spectacular cache of Mixtec ornaments mentioned above was found.

BAHÍAS DE HUATULCO   ☎ 9

With wide, palm-lined streets, shimmering electric lights, and sprawling, high-priced resorts, Bahías de Huatulco, a string of towns and beaches on the Oaxacan coast, is a paradise for those who like their vacations planned, packaged, and posh. If everything looks new here, that's because it is: Mexican government officials began building Huatulco (as it's usually called) from the bottom up in 1986. The recent economic recession has set back government plans;

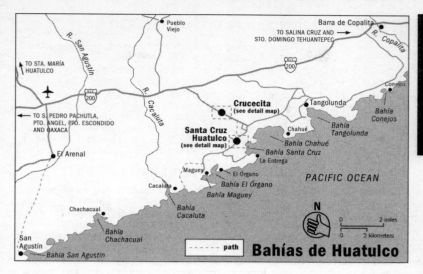

Bahías de Huatulco

many buildings in Huatulco sit in mid-construction. Still, the city has the feel of a seaside country club. The *zócalo* and supposedly-authentic downtown smack of freshly poured concrete and professional landscaping. Visitors are primarily moneyed Mexicans who spend lavishly come vacation time. The situation would seem dismal for the budget traveler in Huatulco, yet remarkably it is not. Those content to sit on the sand and bask may find themselves alone on shore, watching as yachts of *ricos* pass on their expensive, all-day tours of the coast. In contrast with the hyped-up expat beach towns further north, budget travelers will live a tourist-free existence here, sharing meals with the hotel staff in the barrio northwest of the *zócalo*, and sunning all day in solitude. One must be resourceful, however, as finding cheap transportation to and from Huatulco's 36 beaches is a challenge.

▐ TRANSPORTATION

Airport: The airport (☎581 90 07), 19km from the town of Santa Cruz, is served by **Aerocaribe** (☎587 12 20) and **Mexicana** (☎587 02 43). To get to the airport, take a taxi (25min., 100 pesos) or a "Sta. Maria" microbus from the corner of Guamuchil and Carrizal in Santa Cruz (8 pesos). Ask to be let off at the airport. You will need to walk approximately 500m to the right of where the driver lets you off.

Buses: The Cristóbal Colón bus station (☎587 02 61) is at the corner of Gardenia and Ocotillo in the town of La Crucecita. To get to the *zócalo,* exit left and walk four blocks down Gardenia. Cristóbal Colón goes to: **Mexico City** (12½hr., 3 and 6pm, 382 pesos); **Oaxaca** (8hr., 3pm, 143 pesos); **Puebla** (11hr., 3 and 6pm, 324 pesos); **Puerto Escondido** (2hr.; 3:30, 5, 8am, 5:30pm; 42 pesos); **San Cristóbal** (10hr., 10:45am and 11:30pm, 197 pesos); and **Tuxtla Gutiérrez** (9hr., 10:45am and 11:30pm, 166 pesos). Estrella Blanca (☎587 01 03), farther down Gardenia at Palma Real, sends buses to: **Acapulco** (9hr.; first-class 5, 9am, 9pm, 207 pesos; second-class 6:25, 7:25am, 12:25pm, 154 pesos); **Mexico City** (13½hr., 6pm, 374 pesos); and **Puerto Escondido** (2hr., 5pm, 46 pesos). Estrella del Valle (☎587 01 93), on Jazmín at Sabali, sends buses to: **Oaxaca** (8hr., 10:15pm, 97 pesos). The best way to get to **Pochutla**, gateway to Puerto Ángel, Zipolite, and Puerto Escondido, is a Transportes Rápidos de Pochutla microbus; they leave from Carrizal after it curves into an east-west road on the north end of town (1hr., every 15min. 6am-8:30pm, 10 pesos).

✦🔒 ORIENTATION AND PRACTICAL INFORMATION

Huatulco and its *bahías* (bays) consist of 35km of beach and cove on the southern Oaxacan coast between the Coyula and Copalita rivers, about 295km south of Oaxaca de Juárez. The most practical place to stay is **La Crucecita,** in the middle of a string of nine bays, which are, from east to west: Conejos, Tangolunda, Chahué, Santa Cruz, El Órgano, Maguey, Cacaluta, Chachacual, and San Agustín. La Crucecita houses the bus stations and what little there is of the budget accommodations. **Santa Cruz,** the bay closest to La Crucecita, is the least attractive of the lot, but offers the best access to the airport. Hotels and an *artesanía* market clutter its main road, Blvd. Santa Cruz. Tangolunda Bay is known as the **Zona Hotelera;** it houses seven resorts, including the Western Hemisphere's largest Club Med.

TOURIST, FINANCIAL, AND LOCAL INFORMATION

Tourist Office: SEDETUR (☎581 01 76 or 581 01 77), inconveniently across from the commercial center in Tangolunda on Juárez; cross to the left side of Juárez at the Argentina Restaurant. Open M-F 8am-3pm, Sa 9am-1pm. Help is more accessible at the **Módulo de Información,** in the *zócalo* toward the east side. Helpful maps and advice. Be sure to check the **official taxi tariffs,** posted on the side of the Módulo; many tourists pay more than they should. Open M-F 9am-2pm and 4-7pm during peak seasons.

Currency Exchange: Casa de Cambio Condig, Guamuchil 210 (☎587 13 09), cashes traveler's checks. Open M-Sa 9am-7pm. Three doors down is a 24hr. Bital **ATM. Bancrecer,** Bugambilia 1104, at the corner of Macuil in La Crucecita, exchanges currency and has a 24hr. **ATM.** Open M-F 9am-5pm, Sa 10am-2pm. Large hotels exchange money at slightly less favorable rates.

Market: 3 de Mayo, on Guamacho off the *zócalo*, has trinkets, produce, and meat. Open daily 7am-8pm.

Laundry: Lavandería Estrella, on Flamboyan at the corner of Carrizal, offers same-day service. 24 pesos per 3kg. Open M-Sa 8am-9pm.

Car Rental: Budget, Ocotillo 404 (☎587 00 10), 1 block from the first-class bus station. VW sedans 480 pesos per day. Also at the airport (☎581 90 00). Open daily 8am-8pm.

Bike Rental: The owner of Restaurant Bar La Tropicana rents out serviceable bikes. 15 pesos per hr., 75 pesos per day.

EMERGENCY AND COMMUNICATIONS

Police: At Blvd. Chahué 100 (☎587 02 10), in the peach government building, 200m south of the intersection of Guamuchil and Chahué. No English spoken.

Emergency: ☎060.

Red Cross: Blvd. Chahué 110 (☎587 11 88), next door to the post office and police. Little English spoken. 24hr. ambulance service.

Pharmacy: Farmacia La Clínica (☎587 05 91), at Gardenia and Sabali, 4 blocks to the right when exiting the bus station. Open 24hr. Closer to the *zócalo* is **Farmacia del Carmen** (☎587 20 12), on Guamuchil at Carrizal. Open daily 8am-10pm.

Hospital: IMSS (☎587 02 64), on Blvd. Chahué past the government building. 24hr. ambulance service. No English spoken. **Centro de Salud,** Carrizal 202 (☎587 14 21) at the corner of Guamuchil. 24hr. emergency service. No English spoken.

Fax: Telecomm (☎587 08 94; fax 587 08 85), next to the post office. Open M-F 8am-7pm, Sa-Su 9am-2:30pm.

Internet Access: Internet access is hard to find in La Crucecita. **Informática MARE,** Guanacaste 203 (☎587 08 41), across from the market, on the 2nd fl., has quick connections. 30 pesos per hr. Open M-F 10am-9pm, Sa 10am-4pm.

Post Office: Blvd. Chahué 100 (☎587 05 51), in the peach government building. Open M-F 8am-7pm, Sa 9am-1pm.

Postal Code: 70989.

◤ ACCOMMODATIONS AND CAMPING

Camping is one way to escape Huatulco's high-priced hotel scene, but it's allowed only on Chahué, Cacaluta, and Conejos bays. Even in these locations, camping is a risky affair; there is little security, and Cacaluta and Conejos have in the past been sites of confrontation between police and illegal Central American immigrants. Under no circumstances should you attempt to camp on Santa Cruz or Tangolunda; hotel security will not be kind. If camping isn't your thing, prepare yourself for slim pickings. All affordable hotels are in La Crucecita, and even those tend be overpriced. Some families rent out rooms, and those willing to search around and negotiate will be rewarded for the effort. Rates rise uniformly by 25-50% during the high season (July-Aug.); listings below are low-high season ranges.

Hotel Posada San Agustín (☎587 03 68), on Macuil at Carrizal. From the bus station walk 1 block to the left, turn left on Macuil, and walk for 2 blocks to the blue and white hotel. Spotlessly clean and bright and run by a young family, San Agustín has fans, balconies, and an upbeat, homey air. Singles 100-130 pesos; doubles 150-250 pesos.

Posada Santa Cruz (☎587 00 41) on Gardenia, near the Cristóbal Colón station. With TV, fans, double beds, and large, clean rooms, Santa Cruz is probably La Crucecita's best bargain—if you can get one of its 5 rooms, that is. Some rooms have balconies. Singles and doubles 120 pesos, with TV 150 pesos; quads 200 pesos; super-suite (with TV and A/C) 300 pesos.

Posada Lido, Flamboyan 209 (☎587 08 10), ½ block east of the *zócalo*. Five very clean, eclectically assembled rooms, with double beds, fans, and TV. The family that shares the building keeps things fun and clamorous. Communal baths. Singles 100 pesos; doubles 200 pesos, with private bath 300 pesos.

Hotel Benimar, Bugambilias 1404 (☎587 04 47), at Pochote, 3 blocks to the right from the station on Gardenia, and then another block right on Pochote. Dusky interior harbors fans and full baths. The neighborhood congregates in the lobby to watch TV. Singles and doubles 160-200 pesos; triples 200-300 pesos; quads 250-350 pesos.

◔ FOOD

In Huatulco, pricey tourist restaurants venture into the realms of Italian pasta and poorly rendered sushi, while restaurants near the *zócalo* charge handsomely for Mexican dishes that would cost a mere pittance outside town. The best bargains in Huatulco are tacos and barbecued chicken. Uniformly cheap and available around the clock, tacos are best procured on **Carrizal,** north of the *zócalo*. The taco's affordable colleague, the *pollo asado,* can be found in the restaurants clustering north of the *zócalo* on **Bugambilimas.**

El Pollo Imperial (☎587 04 98), on Carrizal, just north of Macuil. El Pollo's popular and surprisingly *sabroso* barbecued chicken comes with generous portions of beans and pasta salad (¼ chicken, 18 pesos, entire chicken 56 pesos). Proper table etiquette requires diners to hold the chicken with a tortilla in their left hand while prying the meat with a fork in their right. It's much easier to use your fingers. Open daily 9am-8pm.

La Crucecita (☎587 09 06), 1 block past the *zócalo* at Bugambilias and Chacah. Upgrade from the plastic tables of the taco shops to the breezy, plant-rich courtyard of La Crucecita, which manages pleasant dining without exorbitant prices. Huge *tlayudas* 30 pesos, *tortas* and sandwiches 20 pesos. Open daily 7am-10pm.

Restaurant Bar La Tropicana (☎587 06 61), Guanacastle at Gardenia, across from Hotel Flamboyant. So-so food comes second to location, popularity, and 24hr. openness. Fish filet 35 pesos. *Antojitos* (20 pesos) are the best bet.

🅰 BEACHES

As might be expected in a town meticulously designed to rake in tourist dollars, Huatulco's nine bays and 36 beaches, spread across 35km, pose a transportation challenge. It's hard to get off the beaten track without handing over precious pesos for a taxi or *lancha*. Fortunately, three of the bays (albeit those with the big hotels nearby—Santa Cruz, Chahué, and Tangolunda) are accessible by the blue-and-white *microbúses* that leave from the intersection of Guamuchil and Carrizal, one block east of the *zócalo* (5-10min., every 20min. 6am-6pm, 2 pesos). *Taxi colectivos* leave from the same junction (4 pesos to Tangolunda, 3 pesos to Santa Cruz). If you plan to take a tour, the tourist bureau recommends going through an official agency in town rather than one of the numerous "guides" vending their services in the street; many tourists have been ripped off in the past. The Módulo de Información next to the Cristóbal Colón station is not official; only the *módulo* in the *zócalo* offers solid advice. If you plan on indulging in water sports, consider the cheaper option of going through the company itself rather than dealing with a travel agency. **Hurricane Divers,** at Bahía Chahué, offers reliable diving expertise. (☎587 11 07. Open daily 9am-7pm.) **Piraguas** (☎587 13 33), in La Crucecita, takes white water rafting trips down nearby Río Capolita.

BAHÍA CHAHUÉ. Closest to La Crucecita is Bahía Chahué, which remains relatively unpopulated save for the beachside camp of Hotel Castillo. The economic recession left the cranes at Chahué in midair, leaving hotels half-finished and causing most tourists to find their delights elsewhere. Though the weedy construction zone before the beach is ugly, the beach itself offers a fine stretch of sand perfect for quiet sunbathing. The water, while rough, is generally safe for swimming. *(Take either the Tangolunda or Santa Cruz bus or taxi colectivo and ask to be let off at Chahué. Alternatively, walk 2 blocks east on Guamuchil to Blvd. Chahué and take a right, then walk 10min. until it comes to a T-intersection. The left branch leads to Tangolunda, the right to Santa Cruz. Walk left 1 block and then turn right; the sand is 5min. down the road.)*

BAHÍA SANTA CRUZ. Instead of stopping at Bahía Chahué, most choose to continue on to Bahía Santa Cruz, which harbors *lanchas*, a profusion of *palapa* restaurants, and a huge, overpriced commercial district. Of its two beaches, **Playa Santa Cruz** and **Playa La Entrega,** Entrega is the better, offering good snorkeling, swimming, a smaller chance of colliding with a banana boat. Equipment can be rented at Entrega (40 pesos per day). Playa Santa Cruz, just past the *lanchas* at the entrance to town, is easier to reach, but is smaller and tends to be crowded. **Restaurant Ve el Mar,** on the side of the beach nearest the *lanchas*, is known for having the best seafood in the area. Fish and shrimp cocktails start at 45 pesos. At high tide, waiters carrying towering plates of *mariscos* are forced to leap onto chairs to avoid drenching their white patent shoes. (☎587 03 64. Open daily 8am-10pm.) Equipment can be rented past the *lanchas*. *(A taxi (36 pesos) or a lancha (100 pesos per 10 people.) will take you from La Crucecita to Playa Entrega. To get to Bahía Santa Cruz, continue farther down the right branch of Blvd. Chahué, a 10min. walk or 5min. ride past Bahía Chahué.)*

BAHÍA MAGUEY. Also 2km from Playa Santa Cruz and less crowded then Entrega, Bahía Maguey is the other hot spot for snorkeling and swimming. From Maguey, a rough footpath leads to **Bahía El Órgano.** *(Taxis (45 pesos) and lanchas (300 pesos per 10 people) will take you to Bahía Maguey.)*

BAHÍA TANGOLUNDA. Another cheaply accessible beach, Tangolunda, in the town of Tangolunda, is home to the *Zona Hotelera* and the Bahía's swankest resorts. You can swim at the public beach on the eastern side, where, unfortunately, a long line of hotel *palapas* litter the beach. The surf is often rough and the beach is quite steep. *(To get there, take the blue-and-white microbuses from Guamuchil and Carrizal and ask to be let off the bus at the public beach entrance; alternately; walk to the right from the hotels when facing the sea.)*

OTHER BAHÍAS. If you don't mind splurging on transportation, **La India, San Agustín,** and **Cacaluta** are best for snorkeling and diving. Cacaluta is also known for its lush plant life and breezes. San Agustín, and Tangolunda are more crowded, while Cacaluta, La India, Conejos, and El Órgano are your best shots at solitude. The only other beaches accessible by land are **La Bocana, Bahía Cacaluta** (four-wheelers only), and **Bahía San Agustín;** taxis charge hefty rates to travel this far. Another option is renting a bike or car for the day (see **Practical Information** p. 471). *Lanchas* operating out of the **Cooperativa Tangolunda** in Santa Cruz will take you to other beaches (prices vary by beach and size of boat, but they are guaranteed to be high, over 400 pesos). If you go in the morning you may be able to find people to share the ride, and during the off-season you can bargain for much lower rates. The *cooperativa* also offers the most economical all-day tour of the bays, stopping at Maguey and San Augustín, where you can snorkel with an English-speaking guide and get lunch. (☎587 00 81. 9:45am and 11am high season; 11am low season. 150-170 pesos. Call a day in advance. Open daily 8am-6pm.)

🎵 ENTERTAINMENT

Huatulco's tendency to attract vacationing families makes for fairly low-key nightlife. Folks swing to live bands playing in the *zócalo* every evening except for Tuesday, and ride around on the automobile train which makes tireless loops around La Crucecita. For the younger set, a bar or two in town and several discos across the way in Santa Cruz keep things exciting enough. Buses stop running to Santa Cruz at 6pm, so a taxi from La Crucecita (13 pesos) will be necessary both ways.

LA CRUCECITA

Restaurant Bar la Crema (☎587 07 02) at Guanacaste and Gardenia, on the 2nd fl. overlooking the *zócalo*. The best ambience in Crucecita. Funky decor and good tunes make the place seem like an import from Puerto Escondido. The bar has a billiard table, and people occasionally dance. Open daily 7pm-3am.

Café Internet Choco Latte (☎587 01 65), across from Crema, in the bottom floor of Hotel Misión Los Arcos. A quieter crowd sips the *café americano* (10 pesos). Stay away from the specialty flavored drinks (25-30 pesos) and the Internet access (a whopping peso per min.). Open daily 7am-11:30pm.

SANTA CRUZ

El Dexkite (☎587 09 71), in Santa Cruz to the left past the *lancha* docks. Torches light a strip of private beach, while partiers dance in the sand and consume the economical drinks. 25 pesos for ½L of beer, and 40 pesos for 1L. The action starts at midnight. Cover 50 pesos. Open daily 10:30pm-5am during high season.

Magic Circus (☎587 00 17), past the public beach entrance, down Mitla to where it curves, offers a standard disco experience. Open bar W. Cover 60 pesos. Open nightly 10pm-5am during high season.

Magic Tropics, its *latino* twin, closer to the public beach entrance on Mitla, plays only Spanish beats. Cover 40 pesos. Open daily 10pm-5am during high season.

POCHUTLA ☎9

Pochutla serves as the gateway to Puerto Ángel and Zipolite; if you're traveling by bus, you'll have to pass through this dusty transportation hub. The lack of services in both beach towns makes Pochutla a good place to stock up on money and pharmaceuticals, but doesn't offer much else for the traveler.

📧 TRANSPORTATION. *Taxi colectivos* headed to **Puerto Escondido** (50 pesos), **Puerto Ángel** (10 pesos), **Zipolite** (15 pesos), and beyond leave from the downhill part of town, across from the Estrella del Valle bus station. Microbuses also run

A NIGHT ON THE PUEBLA. You've spent endless hours conjugating verbs and rolling your "r"s, but you still don't fit in. What you need is something that no seventh grade Spanish teacher could (or would) teach—a brief review of all the slang necessary for a night out on the town. Luckily, *Let's Go* has compiled a list of the basics. Incorporate these into your vocab, and perhaps you'll lose your *gabacho* (gringo) status. The night begins when you meet your friends and greet them, *"¿Qué onda?"* (What's up?). You guys head out *al antro* (to the disco). At the disco, grab a *chupe* (drink) or a *chela* (beer) and comment on how *chido* or *padre* (cool) the place is. *Fresas* (snobs) prefer the phrase *de pelos* (cool, but don't use this). Of course, keep your eyes peeled for *papasitos* (studs) and women that are *buenísima* (very fine). Perhaps you'll flirt a bit, *ligar* (hook-up), and—if you are *cachondo* (horny)—maybe you'll *fajar* (to make out/get down) with a fellow discotechie. The next day be sure to review the events of the previous night with your friends, exclaiming *"¡Qué peda la de ayer!"* (I was so wasted yesterday!).

this route, though they leave less frequently (2.5 pesos to Puerto Ángel). The most efficient way to travel between coast towns is by *camioneta* (every 20min. 6am-7pm, 2.5 pesos to Puerto Ángel, 5 pesos to Zipolite or Mazunte). To get to places farther away, Cristóbal Colón (☎584 02 74) on the left side of Cárdenas as you enter the city, sends buses to: **Bahías de Huatulco** (1hr., 4 per day 9:45am-9pm, 17 pesos); **Mexico City** (15hr., 7:15pm, 383 pesos); **Oaxaca** (12hr., 7:45 and 10:15pm, 144 pesos); **Puerto Escondido** (1½hr.; 6:20, 10:30am, noon; 26 pesos); and **Tehuantepec** (4½hr., 9:45am and 7:15pm, 77 pesos). It is fastest to get to **Oaxaca** with Estrella del Valle (7hr., several per day, 85 pesos).

■ ■ **ORIENTATION AND PRACTICAL INFORMATION.** Most banks, services, and shops—as well as the town's two bus stations—are on **Cárdenas,** the main street. The stations and cheaper hotels are downhill from the bus station, closer to the freeway entrance, while banks and supermarkets are farther uphill, where the road curves right. The *zócalo,* church, and main outdoor market can all be reached by following Cárdenas uphill, then turning right on Juárez.

Inverlat, just after Juárez branches off Cárdenas to the right, uphill from the bus stations, has a 24hr. **ATM.** (Open for exchange M-F 9am-5pm.) **Banamex,** in the *zócalo,* has a 24hr. **ATM** as well. **Mercado 15 de Octubre,** 25m uphill from Cristóbal Colón on the right, sells mainly produce. (Open daily 6am-9pm.) **Police:** in the Palacio Municipal, in the *zócalo* to the left of the church. No English spoken. (☎584 01 59. Open 24hr.) **Pharmacy:** Just before Juárez on Cárdenas, **Farmacias de Más Ahorro** is open 24hr. **Hospital General,** also known as **SSA,** between Pochutla and Puerto Ángel. No English spoken. (☎584 02 16. 24hr. ambulance service.) **Internet:** on the right side of Cárdenas, across from Estrella Blanca. Also has long-distance **casetas** and **fax.** (0.8 pesos per min. Open daily 9am-9pm.) **Post office:** make a right on Juárez toward the church and the *zócalo;* it's to the left of the church, behind the Palacio Municipal. (Open M-F 8am-3pm.) **Postal code:** 70900.

■ ■ **ACCOMMODATIONS AND FOOD. Hotel El Patio,** on the left side of Cárdenas, up from the Estrella Blanca station, is a good place to crash if the wait for your bus is a long one. Though the showers are cold, the rooms are clean and well-maintained. (Singles 80 pesos; doubles 80-100 pesos.) Excellent seafood can be found to the right on Juárez, one block before the *zócalo,* at the **Restaurant y Marisquería Los Angeles.** *Antojitos* 15 pesos, *mariscos* 40-55 pesos. (☎584 00 46. Open daily 9am-9pm.)

PUERTO ÁNGEL ☎9

Tucked between the more glamorous towns of Huatulco and Puerto Escondido, Puerto Ángel is a haven for urban escapists. It is home to a moderately sized naval base, a few restaurants and hotels, and a scenic cove. Popular with Europeans, the town even has an international flair. Unfortunately, Puerto Ángel—and Zipolite further down the coast—bore the brunt of Hurricane Pauline in 1997. Since then, the town has struggled to rebuild; construction continues on many streets, trash lines once picturesque pathways, and the dog population seems on the verge of taking over. Still, Puerto Ángel's beaches remain pristine and underpopulated. They merit a visit, especially for those fleeing the commercialism of Huatulco or the beach-bum atmosphere of Puerto Escondido.

TRANSPORTATION. Puerto Ángel is 240km south of Oaxaca de Juárez and 68km east of Puerto Escondido. All transportation in or out of Puerto Ángel passes the **sitio stand** on Uribe, at the beginning of town. Puerto Ángel is second in line in the great **camioneta** loop linking Pochutla, Zipolite, and Mazunte (every 20min., 6am-7pm, 2.5-7.5 pesos depending on which way you're going). **Taxis** link Puerto Ángel to: **Pochutla** (15min., 50 pesos, 10 pesos shared) and **Zipolite** (25min., 30 pesos, 15 pesos shared). They can be flagged down anywhere along Uribe or Principal. A microbus goes to: **Pochutla** (every 30min. 6am-8pm, 2.5 pesos), returns to town, and leaves again for **Zipolite** (2.5 pesos) and **Mazunte** (2.5 pesos).

ORIENTATION AND PRACTICAL INFORMATION. The *carretera* that connects Pochutla to Zipolite becomes Puerto Ángel's main drag as it runs through town; it is re-named **Principal** as it descends the hillside from Pochutla, then re-christened **Uribe** once it curves 90 degrees to the right and hits downtown. The *sitio* stand and all the town's hotels lie directly on or close to this main road. Shortly after Uribe curves right, **Playa Prinicipal,** the "fishing and everything else" beach, skirts the road on the left. The only significant side street, **Vasconcelos,** branches to the right off Uribe soon after the turn. Playa Principal and **Playa Panteón,** the town's lounging beach, are linked by a footpath. Panteón can also be reached via a footpath entrance near the footbridge on Uribe, or by the paved side-streets branching left off Uribe as the street begins uphill.

Services in Puerto Ángel are minimal; most must be begged, borrowed, or imported from nearby Pochutla. **Tourist information,** mostly in the form of advice, can be found at the turquoise **Gobierno del Estado,** on the right side of Vasconcelos just before it starts to curve. (Open M-Sa 8am-11pm, Su 10am-3pm.) For a map, try the **Agencia Municipal,** next to the post office at the 90-degree turn. (Open daily 9am-2pm and 5-8pm.) There is **no bank** in Puerto Ángel; several upscale hotels change money at exorbitant rates. A **market** 25m to the right on the side street after Vasconcelos offers little more than produce. (Open daily 6am-7pm.) **Supermarket: Super Puerto,** in the turquoise and white building on the right as Uribe starts to climb. (Open daily 8am-9pm.) **Police:** can be reached through the Agencia Municipal. (☎584 31 30. Open daily 9am-2pm and 5-8pm.) **Farmacia Villa Florencia,** attached to the hotel of the same name, on Uribe shortly past the turnoff for Vasconcelos. (☎584 30 44. Open daily 8:30am-9pm.) **Hospital General (SSA),** between Puerto Ángel and Pochutla, No English spoken. (☎584 02 16. Open 24hr.) **Centro de Salud,** at the top of Vasconcelos to the left on a dirt path, offers limited services. (Open 24hr.) **Telecomm,** next to the post office. (Open M-F 9am-3pm.) **Gel@net,** at Vasconcelos 3, just after Hotel Soraya, also has a long distance **caseta.** (Internet 35 pesos per hr. Open daily 8am-10pm.) The town lacks **LADATELs;** there are several other casetas farther up on Uribe. **Post office:** at the 90-degree turn. (Open M-F 8:30am-3pm.) **Postal code:** 70902.

ACCOMMODATIONS. Staying in Puerto Ángel, one can upgrade from a hammock or *cabaña* without bending the budget. Though prices rise during June and August, the city is filled with options year-round. Most hotels are on or right off

Uribe. **Hotel Capy,** on the left as Uribe climbs uphill, at the street leading to Playa Panteón, offers clean, well-maintained rooms, private baths, and an amiable staff. Its impressive view of the cove is best appreciated while enjoying a moderately-priced meal in the quality balcony restaurant. Fish fillet 35 pesos. (Singles 90 pesos; doubles 130-148 pesos; triples 150 pesos.) **El Peñasquito,** on the left after the turn-off for Playa Panteón, on the side street leading to the beach, offers a clean and safe bungalow with hammocks. The view of the coast is better here than you'll find in any hotel. (35 pesos per night.) For an upgrade, try the secluded, environmentally-conscious **La Buena Vista,** off Uribe before it starts climbing—watch for the sign. The adjoining restaurant may be worth a visit even if you're not staying here. Vegetarian *tamales* 35 pesos, fish 45 pesos. (☎584 31 04. Doubles 280 pesos; cabins 380 pesos.) Farther up and out, **Cabañas Coco Loco** has great views, a kitchen, huge rooms with king-sized beds, and good prices. Look for signs on the right side of Uribe, past the exit for Hotel Capy. (Doubles 100 pesos; triples 120 pesos.)

📷 **FOOD.** Much of the fish that fries in Zipolite first saw land in Puerto Ángel. Shellfish, octopus, lobster—if it's from the sea, it's on your plate, cheap and fresh. On the main beach, **Restaurant Marisol** keeps prices low (25-30 pesos), and serves breakfast for under 10 pesos in an informal atmosphere. (Open daily 7am-9pm.) By the basketball court between Playa Principal and Uribe, **Restaurant Maca** has cookbook-worthy seafood that compensates for its less-than-ideal view. Prices aren't the cheapest, but the freshness of the fish and tastiness of the dressings are hard to pass up. Fish fillet 35-40 pesos, seafood soup 50 pesos. (Open daily 8am-11pm.) **Beto's Restaurant Bar,** on Uribe across from Hotel Capy. Excellent fish fillets 27 pesos. (☎584 30 11. Open daily 4pm-midnight.)

📷 **BEACHES.** Though Puerto Ángel's cove is small and a little crowded, its beaches still have sparkling water and clean, white sand. **Playa Principal,** off Uribe, is closest to the docks and the fishing boats. Though slightly grimier for the boats, it offers a little more breathing room than **Playa Panteón.** The two beaches, connected by a stone walkway, encircle a harbor with excellent snorkeling. On Playa Panteon, **Azul Profundo** rents quality snorkeling gear and leads snorkeling and scuba tours. (☎584 31 09. Snorkeling tours 100 pesos, scuba tours 350-600 pesos.)

Sand-wise, the best move is a little bit east to **Playa Estacahuite** (pronounced "a stack o' Wheaty"). Over the headland from Puerto Ángel's bay, Estacahuite's three little beaches (the third is to the right of the path) are pristine. Although they can be reached by *lancha* from Puerto Ángel (100-150 pesos) or taxi (starting at 60 pesos round trip), the walk is pleasant and easy (30min.). From Playa Principal, turn right on Uribe and walk uphill toward Pochutla. The dirt road to Estacahuite branches to the right as the road curves uphill, just past the telephone pole numbered E0034. Follow the road as it climbs and curves left around a hill and finally plunges steeply to the beach. The only place to stay in the area are the hammocks on the second beach (20 pesos per night). They are owned by Felipa Ramírez Cabieras, who also rents snorkel gear with flippers (20 pesos per hr.) and will make you food if you get hungry. The owners of the first *palapa* on the left will do the same. Snorkeling is good and the beach is a beauty, but be careful—emergency services are far away. Farther down the coast is **Playa Boquilla,** the only other beach accessible by land. The sand is smooth and the waves small—perfect for swimming and sunbathing. Unfortunately, the beach is difficult to reach without taxi or *lancha*. It's 4km on the road to Pochutla, then another 3km along a dirt road to the right (marked by a "Playa Boquilla" sign). Either take a *camioneta* (2.5 pesos) to the sign and walk, or take a snorkeling trip and remain at the beach, arranging to be picked up when the tour returns (100 pesos). Keep in mind that, like in Playa Estacahuite, services are nonexistent in Playa Boquilla.

ZIPOLITE ☎ 9

Zipolite's reputation precedes it. Joints are rolled on the beach, at the dinner table, on hotel counters—you name it—while backpacks from around the world lean against countless *cabaña* doors. The town is a prime stop on the Euro-trail, and locals smile wistfully as foreigners parade nude up and down its beaches. When Hurricane Pauline hit Zipolite in 1997, government aid was slow to come, a fact attributed by some to resentment of the town's unrestrained tourist trade. Zipolite has indeed had problems with drug-related crime, and visitors here are wise to exercise their common sense. Since the hurricane, the town has rebuilt and regained all its scantily-clad glory. Both in and out of the waves, visitors here still find the perfect ways to chill.

⊑ TRANSPORTATION. Just 4km west of Puerto Ángel and close to Pochutla, Zipolite is easily accessible by any vehicle rumbling down the poorly-paved coastal road. *Microbúses* run between Zipolite and Puerto Ángel (supposedly every 30min. 6am-8pm, 2.5 pesos), but *camionetas* (pick-up truck *colectivos*; 2.5 pesos), *taxi colectivos* (10 pesos), and *taxi especiales* (30 pesos) seem to pass more frequently. From Pochutla, *taxi colectivos* are 15 pesos during the day. At night the ride will probably have to be made by a private taxi (25min., 70 pesos). In general, transport is in sync with the beach—plentiful, and easy.

▚🗹 ORIENTATION AND PRACTICAL INFORMATION. Zipolite consists of one 2km-long stretch of beach. Look for the beach sign pointing toward the waves; to get to the major hotels, get off at the dirt road at the west end of the beach. While there is no **currency exchange** in Zipolite, most hotels/*cabañas* accept dollars and some of the bigger ones accept travelers checks. **Police:** (☎584 01 76) on a bluff just beyond the beach's east side. Officers patrol frequently. The nearest hospital, **General Hospital,** is between Puerto Ángel and Pochutla. No English spoken. (☎584 02 16. Open 24hr.) **Farmacia Zipolite,** on the road across from the police station at the east edge of town, has limited medical supplies and houses a small general store. (Open daily 7am-11pm.) Supplies are cheaper in Pochutla. **Caseta Oceana,** on the dirt road in back of La Choza and Tao, has **casetas, fax,** and **Internet.** (☎584 31 51. Internet 50 pesos per hr. Open daily 7am-10pm.)

🗝 ACCOMMODATIONS. Lounge around long enough and someone will eventually ask you if you want a *cabaña* for the night. Every *palapa* on the beach has a village of huts out back, most with relatively clean shared baths. (Cheapest *cabañas* 80 pesos per night, hammocks 25 pesos.) Whichever you choose, be sure to put valuables in a safe box, a service offered by most *palapas*. Most of the nicer, more secure *cabaña*s and rooms are on the west side of the beach. At **Posada Brisa Marina,** a relatively new blue and white establishment on the west side of the beach, night guards and a *caja de seguridad* ensure a safe stay. Pleasant enough cement rooms are clean and have wood furnishings and fans. (☎584 31 93. Singles 60 pesos, with bath 100 pesos; doubles 80 pesos, with a *vista* 200 pesos.) For a more private experience, try **Lo Cósmico,** at the far west end of the beach, with rustic, Swiss-Family-Robinson-esque cabins perched on a hill overlooking the sea. Communal baths. (Single with terrace 70 pesos; doubles 90-150 pesos; 25 pesos per additional person.) **La Choza,** a short walk east of the Brisa, rents hammocks. The elevated hammock rooms with night guards and security box are the safest you'll find on the beach. Also rents rooms. (☎584 31 90. Hammocks 30 pesos; rooms 100 pesos, with private bath 150 pesos.) **Tao,** next to the Brisa, has clean, safe, slightly pricier *cabaña*s with communal baths. (Singles 100-150 pesos; doubles 220 pesos.)

SOUTHERN PACIFIC COAST

⚲ FOOD. Zipolite is all about eating, drinking, and sleeping in the sun. Seafood and pasta restaurants are everywhere, and the hordes of health-conscious tree-huggers ensure that vegetarian dishes are easy to find. Most of the best restaurants are at the west end of the beach. **San Cristóbal** is a breakfast (starting at 15 pesos) and lunch hot spot. The menu is seafood-based. Fish fillets 35 pesos. (☎584 31 91. Open daily 7am-11pm.) Your best bet for Italian is **El Alquimista Restaurant and Pub,** just past San Cristóbal. Spaghetti 20 pesos, pizza 35 pesos. (☎584 31 70. Open daily 5pm-1am.) **El Eclipse** also offers a very good Italian menu (spaghetti 30-45 pesos); the famed dish here, however, is the 45-pesos fillet of fish in white wine. (Open daily 8am-10pm.) **3 de Diciembre,** on the main road about two blocks east of the Brisa Marina, serves stellar vegetarian meals (35 pesos). Also popular is their extensive *pay* (pie) menu (11 pesos per slice), ranging from all-natural fruit pies to the decadent *pay de chocolate.* (Open W-Su 7pm-2am.)

⚲ BEACHES AND WARNINGS. Besides the sea, the only sights in Zipolite are naked sunbathers. You can also watch waves coming in from two directions, creating a series of channels that suck unsuspecting, naked swimmers out to sea. Although ferocious, these channels are not very wide. If you find yourself being pulled from shore, do not panic and do not attempt to swim directly toward the beach; rather, calmly swim parallel to the beach until you're clear of the seaward current. Also watch for red and yellow warning flags on the beach that mark especially dangerous areas. Many people have drowned at Zipolite, and warnings should be taken seriously. If you do swim, stay in areas that are highly populated, and stay close to the shore. Zipolite is unfortunately plagued by theft, so keep an eye on your valuables when you step in (naked) for a dip. Better yet, leave them locked somewhere. A final warning: scorpions are common in Zipolite. Give your boots a good shake before plunging your foot in.

WEST FROM ZIPOLITE

The road leading west of Zipolite to Pochutla passes several other beaches, all of which are less crowded and more friendly to swimming than Zipolite's killer surf. Two such beaches are **San Agustinillo** and **Mazunte,** perfect stretches of sand growing in popularity with international backpackers. The road also passes three very worthwhile ecotourism projects, **El Mariposario,** the **Museo de la Tortuga,** and the **Cooperativa Ventanillo,** all dedicated to the preservation of native species. The following sites, listed from east to west, are all accessible via a Pochutla-bound *camioneta* from Zipolite (every 20min. 6am-7pm, 2.5 pesos). They are also accessible via any Zipolite-bound *camioneta* from Pochutla.

EL MARIPOSARIO. An easy walk or short *camioneta* ride on the road to Mazunte leads to the Mariposario, the closest of the three conservation-education centers. The netted sanctuary pays a much overdue tribute to the butterflies that flutter through Mexican forests like confetti. Frogs and iguanas are also on display. The preserve covers three hectares of land, and the butterflies get special attention from the guides, one of whom speaks English. The tour (20min.) includes a visit to the sanctuary. *(Open Tu-Sa 9am-4pm. 15 pesos.)*

PLAYA ARAGÓN. The waves break father from shore at Playa Aragón, next on the route to Pochutla, making the swimming far better than at Zipolite. No *palapas* crowd the shore of this beach, so take care—you'll most likely be swimming alone. *(Accessible via the main road, or by a footpath from the west side of the Zipolite beach.)*

SAN AGUSTINILLO. Four kilometers from Zipolite, the small town of San Agustinillo perches on the beach of the same name. A very European scene awaits under the *palapas.* Although it is developing rapidly, San Agustinillo remains cleaner, less colonized, and less-hyped than Zipolite. The two coves that form the harbor have a fairly manageable surf (stay away from the rocks) which can be harnessed with body boards, fins, or surfboards rented from **Mexico Lindo** (30-50 pesos per hr.). Many beginners like to start here before braving the bigger waves at Zipolite. Mexico Lindo also rents some of the best rooms on the beach; the new, clean rooms have fans, private baths, and double beds. (Singles and doubles 100 pesos.) The restaurant serves a mean fish fillet (45 pesos; open Tu-Su 8am-10pm). Most *palapas* will offer you a hammock under the stars (around 10 pesos per night). For a more secure location, you'll have to pay a bit more. **Palapa Olas Altas** has a safe sleeping area (20 pesos per night).

MUSEO DE LA TORTUGA (NATIONAL MEXICAN TURTLE CENTER).

Another bumpy kilometer down the road to Pochutla lies **Mazunte,** a one-horse town with surprising attractions. The first thing you'll see when entering town is the Museo La Tortuga on your left. Though the number of people looking out for the health of the Oaxacan coast is still dangerously small, interest is growing. An anchor in the movement, the museum draws large tour buses to Mazunte to view its specialized aquarium, which contains seven sea turtle species, seven river species, and three land species. The museum also serves as a research center, seeking new ways to protect the species. *(Open M-Sa 10am-4:30pm, Su 10am-2:30pm. 20 pesos, 10 pesos for children 6-12.)*

PLAYA MAZUNTE.

Just a few blocks past the turtle center lies the short dirt path leading to Playa Mazunte, friendlier than Zipolite, but not quite so calm as San Agustinillo. "Mazunte" is the magic word rolling off everyone's tongue, accompanied by such phrases as "*so* chill" and "an unspoiled Zipolite." Many claim they had set aside a day for the beach, but that it stretched to two, then three, then a week, then five weeks. Time takes on a different meaning here, possibly because most of the backpackers hanging out here are high. Despite its popularity, Mazunte is not yet overpopulated, and good lodgings can be had cheaply.

The nicest accommodations on the beach are the beautiful wooden **Cabañas Ziga,** perched on the hill overlooking the beach. Private bathrooms and fans ensure a comfortable stay. (Singles 80 pesos; double 120 pesos. 20 pesos more in high season.) Ziga's also has a restaurant that fries up fish fillets (35 pesos; open Tu-Su 8:30am-10pm). Although the rooms rented out at **Carlos Einstein's** aren't quite as posh, they're cheap, and you're not going to meet such a character elsewhere on the coast. The owner looks like (surprise) a Mexican Einstein, but specializes in the science of herbal healing and *brujería* (witchcraft) instead of physics. If nothing else, make a visit to try the vegetarian spaghetti (35 pesos), which Carlos brews up Tu-Su 8am-10pm. (Rooms 50 pesos per person, hammocks 25 pesos.) **Palapa El Mazunte** allows camping under its roof and also rents hammocks. Its *cabañas* have communal bathrooms. At the restaurant, breakfast starts at 15 pesos. (Restaurant open 9am-10pm. Hammocks 30 pesos; singles 80 pesos; doubles 100-200 pesos.) Many nearby *palapas* will allow tents under their awnings (20 pesos or less per person).

LA VENTANILLA.

Playa Ventanilla, one and a half kilometers past Mazunte, has waves frightful enough to make the most hard-core surfer shudder. The reason to make the trip is not the beach but the **Cooperativa Ventanilla.** The *cooperativa* houses a small colony of families dedicated to preserving the wetland wildlife system at the mouth of the Tonameca River. The group runs amazing *lancha* tours (1hr., 30 pesos) that pass through the mangrove swamps. Guides point out crocodiles and birds, and explain Oaxaca's part in complex migration systems. *(A 700m walk down the dirt path marked by the "La Ventanilla" sign. Open daily 6am-7pm.)*

Puerto Escondido

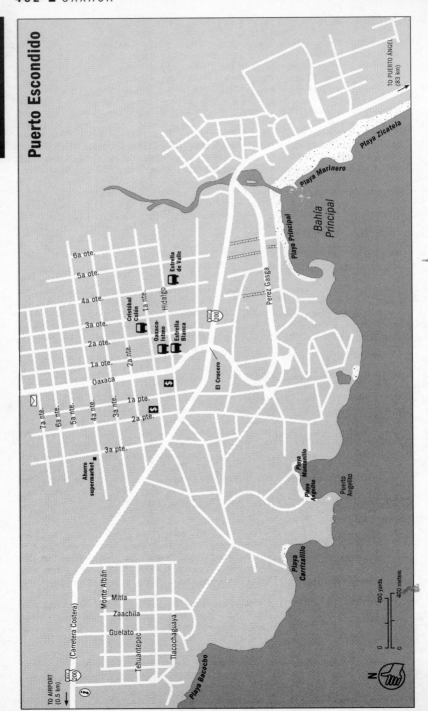

TO PUERTO ÁNGEL (83 km)

Playa Zicatela

Playa Marinero

Playa Principal

Bahía Principal

6a ote.

5a ote.

4a ote.

3a ote.

2a ote.

1a ote.

Estrella de Valle

Cristóbal Colón

1a nte.

Hidalgo

Oaxaca-Istmo

Estrella Blanca

2a nte.

Perez Gasga

El Crucero

Oaxaca

1a pte.

7a nte.

6a nte.

5a nte.

4a nte.

3a nte.

2a pte.

3a pte.

Ahorro supermarket ■

Playa Manzanillo

Playa Angelito

Puerto Angelito

Playa Carrizalillo

Monte Albán

Mitla

Zaachila

Guelato

Tehuantepec

Tlacochaguaya

Playa Bacocho

(Carretera Costera)

TO AIRPORT (0.5 km)

400 yards

400 meters

N

PUERTO ESCONDIDO

Even with row upon row of trinket stores and shores teeming with people and *palapas*, Puerto Escondido (pop. 45,000) remains a standby of Mexican beachside pilgrimages. New arrivals may wonder what the fuss is about, but a few days of basking with Puerto Escondido's incredibly diverse populous tends to send all doubts to sea. And then there's Zicatela. Visible across the cove from town, locals say that it's the third most important surfing beach in the world. Whatever the ranking, one needs no engineering degree to see that the waves here come close to being perfect. Wave-watching is a pastime that transfixes the international crowd of men, women, surfers, kooks, and hipsters, who swing in hammocks, nurse drinks, or simply gaze on as the masterful surfers ride. If Puerto Escondido's beaches have been sullied by the dark side of tourism, the waves of Zicatela and the vibrant community they attract are its redemption.

▐ TRANSPORTATION

Airport: (☎582 04 92) is best reached by taxi (20 pesos). **AeroCaribe** (☎582 20 23) flies to Mexico City, Oaxaca, and Bahías de Huatulco.

Buses: All of the bus stations are scattered uptown, just past the *crucero*. To get to the beaches and hotels, simply walk downhill. The parking lot of Estrella Blanca (☎582 00 86) can be seen across the freeway at the curve of Oaxaca. Buses go to: **Acapulco** (7hr.; *ordinario* every hr. 5am-3pm, 120 pesos; semi-direct 4 per day 4-11:30am, 161 pesos); **Bahías de Huatulco** via **Pochutla** (1½hr., 4 per day 7:30am-7:45pm, 46 pesos); and **Mexico City** (12hr.; 7:30, 8, 9pm; 328-365 pesos). Oaxaca-Istmo (☎582 03 92) on Hidalgo just behind the Estrella Blanca station, goes to **Oaxaca** (6½hr., 5 per day 7:45am-10:15pm, 80 pesos) and **Salina Cruz** (6am and 2pm, 75 pesos). On Hidalgo 2 blocks to the right of Oaxaca is Estrella de Valle (☎582 00 50), with the best service to **Oaxaca** (6½ hr., 11 per day 7:30am-10:30pm, 80-85 pesos). Cristóbal Colón, 1 Nte. 207 (☎582 10 73) sends buses to: **Bahías de Huatulco** (2hr., 6 per day 8:45am-9:30pm, 42 pesos); **San Cristóbal de las Casas** (12hr., 8:45am and 9:30pm, 239 pesos); and **Tuxtla Gutiérrez** (10hr., 8:45am and 9:30pm, 208 pesos). Cristóbal Colón also travels first-class to Oaxaca, but by a route that takes 5hr. longer than second-class service. *Micros* to **Pochutla** leave from the *crucero* (1hr., every 30min., 12 pesos).

▐▌ ORIENTATION AND PRACTICAL INFORMATION

Built on a hillside 294km south of Oaxaca on **Rte. 175,** Puerto Escondido is bisected by **Rte. 200,** also known as Carretera Costera, which divides uphill from downhill. The main tourist corridor, known as the **Adoquín, Las Cadenas,** or **Gasga** at different sections, loops down from the Rte. 200, scoops the main beach, and reconnects again at the **crucero,** the intersection of everything in Puerto Escondido. Going east from the *crucero* will take you to Zicatela. Locals may insist Puerto Escondido is safe, but recent assaults on tourists show it can at times be dangerous. The tourist office recommends playing it safe by staying in groups and avoiding isolated beaches, even during daylight hours. **Taxis** can be found by the tourist information booth and along the Carretera Costera; they are the safest way of getting around after nightfall (15 pesos).

▓ **Tourist Office: Módulo de Información Turística** (main office ☎582 01 75), is an amazingly helpful booth at the beginning of the pedestrian walkway, down Gasga from the *crucero*. Staffed by the dedicated and connected Georgina Machorro. Advice in your language or something close to it. Open M-F 9am-2pm and 4-6pm, Sa 10am-1pm.

Currency Exchange: Banamex (☎582 06 26), on Gasga as it curves up from the tourist corridor, exchanges traveler's checks and has an **ATM.** Open M-F 9am-3pm. **Money Exchange** (☎582 05 92), on the Adoquín across from Farmacia Cortés, has bad rates

YOUR CABBY, YOUR FRIEND. So they've nearly turned you into road kill more times than you care to remember, and you're sure you've paid their "special" tourist rates more often than not. On August 12, however, forget your bitter memories and join in celebrating the Día del Taxista, the country-wide taxi holiday. The day begins with a special 8am mass and blessing of the cabs, guaranteeing their safe travels for the next year. Radiator grills are then strung with flowers as the cabs pass proudly through the city streets—hopefully a little more slowly than usual. Later in the day, cabbies celebrate amongst themselves, and you'll have a hard time finding a driver on the street. If you do manage to flag one down, be prepared to thank the driver profusely and offer a hefty *propina*—it is, after all, the day of the cabbie.

but convenient hours. Open M-Sa 9am-10pm, Su 9am-5pm. Good rates and **ATM** machines are available at **Bancrecer,** on Hidalgo between Oaxaca and 1 Pte. Open M-F 9am-5pm, Sa 10am-2pm. **Bital** (☎582 18 24), 1 Nte. at 3 Pte., also has convenient hours and **ATMs.** Open M-Sa 8am-7pm.

Markets: Mercado Benito Juárez, 8 Nte. at 3 Pte. Typical goods in an organized setting. Open daily 5am-8pm, but most lively W and Sa.

Supermarket: Ahorrara (☎582 11 28) at 3 Pte. and 4 Nte. Open M-Sa 8am-9pm, Su 8am-4pm.

Laundry: Lavamática del Centro, Gasga 405, uphill from the pedestrian walkway on the right. 12 pesos per kg. Open M-Sa 8am-8pm, Su 8am-5pm.

Library: IFOPE Library (email ifope@yahoo.com), in Rinconada by Monte de Piedad. 900 books in English, French, German, and Spanish. Open W and Sa 10am-2pm.

Luggage Storage: None at the bus stations, but the nearby Hotel Mayflower will guard luggage. 6 pesos per day.

Car Rental: Budget (☎582 03 12), Juárez on the corner of Monte Albán.

Emergency: In an extreme emergency, contact Sheila Clarke (☎582 02 76) or Minnie Dahlberg (☎582 03 67), who head **Friends of Puerto Escondido International,** a neighborhood watchdog group of area expats. They will get you in contact with your embassy, the police, or medical help.

Police: (☎582 04 98), on the bottom floor of the Agencia Municipal, on 3 Pte. at the corner of Hidalgo. No English spoken. Open 24hr.

Red Cross: (☎582 05 50), 7 Nte. between Oaxaca and 1 Pte. No English spoken. 24hr. ambulance service.

Pharmacy: Farmacia La Moderna 1 (☎582 06 98 or 582 27 80), at Gasga 203 as it curves down from the *crucero.* Open 24hr.

Medical Assistance: IMSS (☎582 01 42), Av. 2 Pte. and 7 Nte. Open 24hr. **Centro de Salud,** Gasga 409 (☎582 23 60), is a small, minimal-expense medical clinic. No English spoken. Open 24hr. for emergencies.

Fax: Telecomm (☎582 09 57), next door to the post office. Open M-F 8am-7:30pm, Sa 9am-noon.

Internet: Though not as conveniently located as those on the tourist corridor, **Multimedia P@,** Oaxaca 102 (☎582 06 79), at the corner of 2 Nte., offers the cheapest rates in town. 30 pesos per hr. Open M-Sa 10am-9pm. **Coffeenet2,** on the Adonquín, nearly across from the tourist booth, has free coffee and fast connections. 40 pesos per hr. Open daily 9am-10pm. Another location is up from the Adonquín, at Gasga 406.

Post Office: (☎582 09 59), 7 Nte. 701 at Oaxaca, a 20min. walk uphill from the *crucero.* Open M-F 8am-4pm, Sa 9am-1pm. **Postal Code:** 71980.

ACCOMMODATIONS

Puerto Escondido's beaches are not safe for camping, but many hotels cater to budget travelers, particularly during the low season. Reservations are an absolute must during *Semana Santa*, Christmas, July, and August. The least expensive places are the rented rooms, trailer parks, and *cabañas* across the street from Zicatela. Unfortunately, not all the cheapest *cabañas* are secure—take care when choosing. To get away from city, try **Trailer Park Villa Relax** on the Carretera Costera. Use of pool and tennis courts comes with the price. (☎ 582 08 19. 60 pesos per night; parking fee.) All prices below reflect high season rates; expect rooms to be 30-50% cheaper during low season.

IN TOWN

Budget accommodations are best found by walking up Gasga from the Adoquín toward the *crucero*. Guests tend to be young Europeans coming from or going to San Cristóbal de las Casas. As you climb, keep an eye out for the "Se Rentan Cuartos Economicos" sign, which pops up near the bus stations.

▨ **Hotel Mayflower** (☎ 582 03 67), on Libertad. From the bus station, cross the *crucero* and go left down a steep hill. The road ends, but stairs descend on the right to the entrance. Clean, tiled rooms with private baths and balconies, many with *vistas*, surround a common area with hammocks and shelves of books. The closest thing to a youth hostel in town, the hotel also has clean dorm rooms. An international crowd plays pool at the bar on the upstairs terrace, and the friendly, multilingual owner provides valuable information. Dorm beds 60 pesos; singles 160 pesos; doubles 200-240; 30 pesos per additional person.

▨ **Cabañas Estación B** (☎ 582 22 51). From the *crucero*, follow Gasga down as it winds left and look for a sign on the right, soon after Banamex. Although their *cabañas* are on the shores of a gutter rather than the blue Pacific, Estación remains true to the original *cabaña* spirit. Each comes with mosquito netting, a hammock, and the use of the clean communal baths. Cool people lounge in the central *palapa*, enjoying the complimentary breakfast. Cabañas 60 pesos; hammock 20 pesos; camping 20 pesos.

Los Dos Costas, Gasga 302 (☎ 582 0159), in the curve just down from the *crucero*. The best bargain in town, if you want a private room and a sand-less front porch. Rooms are slightly run-down, but have private baths and are surprisingly clean. Singles 50 pesos; doubles 80 pesos; triples 120 pesos.

ON ZICATELA

The prices are higher, but this is unquestionably *the* place to stay for surfing action. Despite its location (15min. by foot from tourist corridor), the many restaurants, bars, and *cabañas* on **Calle del Morro**, which runs in front of the beach, make Zicatela a self-sufficient neighborhood. The cheapest *cabañas* (around 15 pesos) might not be secure; lock your valuables if possible. Most safe *cabañas* have taken advantage of the tourist horde, and their rates are now higher than those at many budget hotels. During high season, make reservations several weeks in advance. Other than the first, *cabañas* below are listed east to west on Calle del Morro.

▨ **Hotel Buena Vista** (☎ 582 14 74; email buenavista101@hotmail.com), on Calle de Morros, is, with its spectacular view of the beach, good for people who have a hard time pulling themselves away from the surf. Some of the rooms come with kitchen, and all have clean private baths. Be sure to call several weeks in advance. Doubles 100-300 pesos; 50 pesos each additional person.

Cabo Blanco, some of the cheapest *cabañas* on the strip. Clean, pleasant rooms with portable fans. Singles 60 pesos; doubles 100 pesos.

Las Olas, a bargain for all its amenities. Rooms have small kitchens, fans, personal security boxes, and private baths. Singles 120 pesos; doubles 140 pesos.

Bungalows Zicatela (☎582 07 98), a laid back atmosphere, pool, and high-class bungalows. Singles 140 pesos; doubles 300 pesos. Farther along the strip it has pricey but very nice *cabañas*. Singles and doubles 250 pesos.

Hotel Acuario (☎582 10 27). Though on the expensive side, this place is a perennial favorite with the surfers. Spend the extra pesos to frolic in the pool and support the hotel's conservation efforts—they've installed a special water purifier that cleans and reuses all hotel wastewater. Doubles 250 pesos.

Buena Onda, possibly the best deal on Zicatela. A 20min. walk farther down the beach (or an easy 2-peso *mini* ride). The new *cabañas* sit right on the water. A great place for beginning surfers to practice, but the water is not safe for swimming. 60 pesos.

🍴 FOOD

With all the water, it doesn't take much thinking to pinpoint the regional cuisine. Seafood is as abundant as surfers, and even in the tourist sectors can be had complete with trimmings for a mere 20 pesos. There are other flavors in here as well. When expats don't open hotels in Puerto Escondido, they open restaurants—Italian food takes up a good portion of Gasga. Swim wear leads to a health-conscious crowd, so vegetarian fare is abundant, especially along Zicatela.

El Cafecito (☎582 0516). After the surf, El Cafecito may well be Puerto Escondido's greatest phenomenon. Across the street from Zicatela's best bakers, the outdoor tables are always full of European backpackers, beach babes, studly surfers, and hammock vendors. The menu makes everyone happy, with vegetarian-friendly Mexican cuisine (30 pesos), homemade *pan integral* (6 pesos), and amazing fruit-granola salads for the string bikini set (15 pesos). Open daily 6am-10pm.

Herman's Best, just past the east end of the tourist corridor. Herman may not know how to cook too many things, but if you've got a hankering for grilled fish, this is the place. Savory, garlic-encrusted whole fish comes complete with rice, salad, and tortillas (20 pesos). Chat with the big man himself about his fish-flipping prowess and impressive collection of family photos. Open daily 2-10pm.

La Gota de Vida, on Zicatela, in front of Hotel Acuario. This veggie haven keeps prices low and veggies fresh. A selection from the huge vegetable fruit salad menu (10-25 pesos) can be enjoyed on its own or with another entree. Vegetarian enchiladas (19 pesos), sandwiches (starting at 14 pesos), and homemade yogurt (12 pesos) keep customers coming back, despite the somewhat slow service. Open daily 8am-10:30pm.

Restaurante Vitamina T, on the east end of the Adoquín. Start your day properly with a *vitamina*-packed breakfast. Conveniently located and cheap, the Vitamina serves fullblown breakfasts (20 pesos) and fruit salads (10-15 pesos). The *tortas* are some of the best in town (8 pesos). Open daily 7am-1am.

👁 SIGHTS AND BEACHES

Beach, beach, and more beach—and each with its own allure. Snorkeling equipment may be rented from **Puerto Angelito** (30 pesos per hr.) or **Aventura Submarina,** on the Adoquín across from the tourist booth. (☎582 23 53. 70 pesos per day.) Aventura Submarina also leads diving trips (550 pesos). At most beaches, umbrellas can be rented from nearby restaurants (35 pesos per day); it probably makes more sense to buy a few over-priced drinks and use them for free. The following beaches are all established and considered relatively safe. Still, you should stick to a group, and not visit them at night unless at a restaurant. Adventurers exploring secluded beaches must exercise caution.

PLAYA PRINCIPAL. The main beach of Puerto Escondido, Principal is just beyond the stores and restaurants that line the Adoquín. It can get awfully crowded and full of *lanchas*, *palapas*, and cavorting families.

PLAYA MARINERO. Continuing east along the shore, you'll pass a small *laguna* on your left. Immediately after is Marinero, slightly less crowded than Principal and good for swimming and sunbathing.

PLAYA ZICATELA. Stepping over the rocks will take you to Zicatela, the third best surfing beach in the world (supposedly). Those dudes bobbing up and down in the water waiting to ride the next killer wave all have several years of experience. Watching them is exhilarating, but don't even think about trying to partake of their fun—you risk a fate worse than wiping out. The best times for surf-watching are at around 7:30am and 6:30pm, though times vary depending on the tide.

PLAYAS MANZANILLO AND ANGELITO. On the other side of Playa Principal are these beaches, which have clear, calm water—perfect for snorkeling and swimming. Both tend to be quite crowded in the early afternoon, with Manzanillo being the quieter of the two. *Lanchas* from Playa Principal (15 pesos) or taxis (15 pesos) will take you there. Walking (20min.), go west on Gasga to the Banamex and take a left; continue, heading left toward the ocean when the road turns to dirt. You will come to a fork in the dirt path; the left path leads to Manzanillo, the right leads to Angelito. The two beaches are separated by an easily-crossed rock barrier.

PLAYA CARRIZALILLO. Even farther west is Carrizalillo, your best bet for a pleasant, uncrowded day at the beach. The water is calm, and you can easily while away the afternoon swimming or snorkeling. To get there, take a taxi (15 pesos). Because the waters between Angelito and Carrizalillo are very rough, taking a *lancha* may be a bad idea. To walk, continue straight on the dirt road instead of turning left for Angelito and Manzanillo until you come to the Rotary Club basketball courts. Make a left and keep walking downhill.

PLAYA BACOCHO. Past Carrizalillo the waves again turn wild and dangerous—do not attempt to swim here. Sunsets on the beach are amazing, and if you feel the need to get out of the salt for a day, the beach club **Coco's** offers the use of its pool and facilities (70 pesos, one meal included). Bacocho is best reached by taxi (20 pesos).

◪ NIGHTLIFE

When the sun goes down, sun worshippers become bar crawlers, making their way to the Adoquín, Puerto Escondido's nightlife hot spot. Conveniently, all the best places are clustered together on the strip, eliminating the need for a taxi, or making for one easy ride if you're coming from Zicatela (15 pesos).

BARS

In the early evening, every restaurant and bar has a Happy Hour, which oddly enough lasts three or four hours (usually 8pm-midnight). Hint: two-for-one drinks are the reason why everyone's so happy. Head to the tourist corridor for the ideal bar-hopping setting. **The Barfly,** in the middle of the strip, is the most popular bar in town. Squeeze your way to the bar, where you can slam back drinks at good prices. Beer 15 pesos, cocktails 30 pesos. (Open daily 8pm-2am.) **The Wipeout Bar,** just past Barfly on the right, has a similar atmosphere, a slightly tamer crowd, and an open-air second level. (Open daily 8pm-3am.) Farther down the strip, **La Terraza** and **Moctezuma's Revenge** have quieter settings. Moctezuma's small tables are perfect for couples looking for a private corner. (☎582 19 17. Both open daily during high season 8pm-2am.) Just past the strip, **Banana's** has a sports bar setting, with TV and pool. (☎582 00 05. Open daily 7:30am-12:30am. Pool 30 pesos per hr.)

CLUBS

After a day of surfing and sun, most are too wiped out to dance, leaving the disco scene a little weaker than one might expect. **El Tubo,** directly behind the Wipeout Bar on the Playa Principal, plays reggae, salsa, and rock. A popular after-bar destination, the crowd that gathers here spills onto the beach by the end of the night. (Open daily 10pm-4am.) **Discoteque Bacocho,** in the Bacocho residential district, is the only full-fledged dance club. You'll have to shower and throw something nice over that thong bikini. Taxis whisk you there for 35 pesos. (☎582 21 37. Cover 30 pesos. Open F-Su 10pm-5am.)

ISTHMUS OF TEHUANTEPEC

East of Oaxaca, the North American continent narrows to a slender strip of land 215km wide, known as the Isthmus of Tehuantepec (TEY-wan-teh-PECK) or just the *istmo*. Wedged between the Yucatán Peninsula and the highlands of south-central Mexico, the region is home to a thriving Zapotec culture. Its three main cities—**Tehuantepec, Juchitán,** and **Salina Cruz**—serve mainly as stopover points for tourists to switch buses and refuel. Those who choose to stay for a day or so, however, may find themselves pleasantly ensnared in a living local history. Because Zapotec society is primarily matriarchal, women in the isthmus take a far more active role in society than most Mexican women. Their openness is evident in the warm welcome they give travelers.

TEHUANTEPEC ☎9

Tehuantepec (pop. 60,000) is the oldest and most historically significant of the three principal cities. Founded by Zapotec emperor Cosijoeza, the town contains some of the first Catholic churches ever constructed by *indígenas*, including the Templo y Ex-Convento de Santo Domingo, a Dominican church dating to 1544.

TRANSPORTATION. To get to town from the Cristóbal Colón/ADO bus station, 1.5km north of the *centro*, make an immediate left as you exit the station. This street becomes Héroes, veers to the right, and eventually dead-ends. Turn right and walk a few more blocks; make a left on Hidalgo and follow it to the *zócalo*. Taxis 15 pesos. From the station, Cristóbal Colón (☎715 01 08) travels to: **Huatulco** (3hr., 6am and 1:30pm, 51 pesos), **Mexico City** (11hr., 6:30 and 8:30pm, 409 pesos); **Oaxaca** (4hr., 2am and 1:30pm, 109 pesos); **Tuxtla Gutiérrez** (6½hr.; 12:30am, 2, 10pm; 108 pesos) and more. Buses also go to: **Juchitán** (30min., every hr., 8 pesos); and **Salina Cruz** (30min., 5 per day 5-8pm, 10 pesos). The fastest, cheapest way to travel to neighboring Juchitán and Salina Cruz is to walk west of the plaza for two blocks on 5 de Mayo to the *carretera*. Southbound buses to Salina Cruz stop frequently (7 pesos), as do northbound buses to Juchitán (8 pesos).

ORIENTATION AND PRACTICAL INFORMATION. Most of Tehuantepec's action centers around the *zócalo*, which is bounded on the north by 22 de Mayo, the east by Juárez, the south by 5 de Mayo, and the west by Romero. Hidalgo runs north-south and begins on the north side of the plaza between the parallel streets of Romero and Juárez. **Tourist information** is available at the Casa de la Cultura. **Serfín,** on the north side of the *zócalo*, has a 24hr. **ATM,** as does **Bital,** on Romero next to Hotel Oasis. **Farmacia El Pastillero** is just south of the plaza at Juárez 13. (Open daily 8am-10pm.) **LADATELs** are in the plaza. **Post office:** on the north side of the *zócalo*. (Open M-F 8am-3pm.) **Postal Code:** 70760.

ACCOMMODATIONS AND FOOD. Travelers to Tehuantepec should head straight to **Hotel Oasis,** a block south of the plaza on Romero. Rooms are clean, sunny, and breezy, with fans, large beds, and firm mattresses. (☎715 00 08. Singles 85 pesos; doubles 85-100 pesos.) The real reason to go to the hotel, however, is the knowledgeable staff. Sra. Julin Contreras, mother of the owner and former tourist advisor in the Casa de la Cultura, can tell you all about the history of the area, while Victor Velásquez, who usually arrives at the hotel at 9pm, serves as a guide to the nearby ruins of Guiengola. The hotel also contains the **Restaurant El Almendro,** one of the nicer eating establishments (breakfasts 10-30 pesos). **Hotel Posada Donaji,** Juárez 10, two blocks south of the *zócalo,* offers impeccable and slightly higher quality rooms with TVs and fans. (☎715 00 64. Singles 95 pesos; doubles 125 pesos.) For budget meals, your best bets are the restaurants in the upper level of the market, **Mercado de Jesús Carranza,** on the plaza's west side. (Open daily 5am-8pm.) A quieter option is Café Colonial, two blocks south of the plaza at Romero 66, with colorful tablecloths and pictures of traditional Tehuantepec dress on the wall. Filling *antojitos* 32 pesos. (☎715 01 15. Open daily 8am-10pm.)

🔲 **SIGHTS.** Tehuantepec's most notable sight is also the best place to find tourist information; the morning library staff at the **Casa de la Cultura** will be happy to fill you in. (☎715 01 14. Open M-F 9am-2pm and 5-8pm, Sa 9am-2pm.) The *casa* is housed in the **Ex-convento Rey Cosijopi,** a 16th-century Dominican building named after the Zapotec leader who ordered its construction, and now holds a small wax museum (featuring such greats as Porfirio Díaz), a library, and diverse workshops and exhibits. A 10-minute walk south of the *zócalo* on Juárez will bring you to **San Blas,** where the you can best see Tehuantepec as it once was. Here, as in Juchitán's *mercado,* you can observe traditional dress and customs.

▦ **FESTIVALS.** Tehuantepec's many *fiestas* are celebrated with traditional food and dress, parades of flower-decked floats, band performances, fireworks, and the election of the *Reina de la Vela* (Queen of the Festival). The most important festivals are the *Vela Sandunga* (the last week of May); the *Vela Tehuantepec* (Dec. 26); the *Vela Guiexoba,* in honor of the flowers' return (the last two weeks of May); the festival of the Patron Saint of the Barrio de Santa María Reoloteca (Aug. 15-18); and the *Fiesta de Laborío* (Aug. 31-Sept. 11).

NEAR TEHUANTEPEC: GUIENGOLA

From the carretera 2 blocks west of the zócalo in Tehuantepec take a southbound "Jalapa" bus. Tell the driver to let you off at the third bridge, Puente de las Tejas (25min., every hr. 6am-5pm, 5 pesos). From the bridge, start down the dirt road to the right, marked by an archaeological zone sign. Walk 3½km (approx. 45min.) to a road branching to the left, again labeled; this marks the beginning of the mountain. Alternatively, you can take a taxi from Tehuantepec to this point (50 pesos). Take the left road and walk until you reach a platform with a view (1½hr.). At the far end of the platform, two paths branch; take the rougher one on the left. After another 30min., the path splits again; go right another 15min. to the ruins. "Jalapa" buses return from the bridge (every hr. until 5pm). "Oaxaca" buses run later and get you back as well.

Approximately 15km southwest of Tehuantepec, the Zapotec ruins of Guiengola are a little-visited, little-known wonder. The ruins lie a steep and rocky 3.5km up the Monte de Guiengola. The trip to the top takes anywhere from 1½hr. (if you're lucky, in great shape, and manage to get a ride the first 3½km to the base) to 2¾hr. (if you hike the whole 7km and take your time). Regardless of your walking prowess, start the day early (take the 6am or 7am bus), bring at least 3L of water, bug repellent, sunscreen, a hat, long pants, and a flashlight if you plan to see the nearby caves. The trip is best made in July, when full foliage makes the heat more tolerable. Though guides are not necessary to reach the top, they are recommended, especially for groups of two or fewer. Guides will point out several poisonous plants to avoid, and help you steer clear of rattlesnakes.

The main ruins of the Zapotec ceremonial center consist of two pyramids, the ceremonial plaza, a ballcourt, and the Palacio de Rey. Typical of Zapotec construction, all face southwest. Guiengola reached its peak at same time as Monte Albán (see p. 468), during the Classic period (AD 300-750), and was later the stronghold of Rey Cosijosa, who successfully repelled the Aztecs from the mountain around 1480. Relics of the battle can be seen on the way up the trail; at one point the path is lined by massive stones that once served as a checkpoint for soldiers.

Directly on your left as you enter the site is a 25m long **ballcourt.** Unlike the Aztec ball games, which determined sacrificial victims, the slightly more mellow Zapotecs played ball games primarily for sport. On the right of the path, just after the ballcourt, is the **larger of the two pyramids,** rising 9m. The pyramid was constructed in three sections and at one point had 35 stairs in the middle section, though these are now mostly eroded away. In front of the pyramid is the **ceremonial plaza.** The **second, smaller pyramid** sits to the left, opposite the larger one. Continuing straight on the path, you arrive at a rocky area, from which another path branches off to several nearby unexplored caves with impressive salt formations and plenty of bats. Caving opportunities exist for experienced spelunkers only. Don't attempt to reach the caves without a guide; the path is hard to pick out. The same goes for exploring the caves themselves. Backtrack on the main path 50m to a small path on the left, which leads to the **Palacio del Rey Cosijoesa.** The palace consists of 64 rooms, including the quarters of the king, located at a *mirador* (lookout) so that he could keep watch over his kingdom. Other points of interest include the king's portly bathtub and a dark and ancient storage cellar. Keep track of your route if you intend to explore to the palace without a guide; no clear paths exist among the ruins themselves.

JUCHITÁN ☎9

If grandmothers ruled the world, it would probably look like Juchitán. Ordinary days tend to be colorful, when the town's huge market fills with old women wearing traditional dress—a loose fitting, embroidered shirt and a long, full floral skirt. Juchitán's traditional crafts are meant to be worn, and the aesthetic is an overwhelmingly important part of town life. Flower vendors get the stalls of honor right on the main street of the *zócalo*, and ribbon stores predominate.

TRANSPORTATION. To get to town from the first-class bus station, follow **Prolongación 16 de Septiembre** to the right. It soon splits into **5 de Septiembre** and **16 de Septiembre,** which run parallel and eventually form the west and east sides of the *zócalo*, respectively. **Gómez** is the street to the north of the *zócalo*, **Juárez** is to the south. *Taxi colectivos* leave frequently from the left side of the bus station exit and run to the *centro* (3 pesos). **Local buses** connect Juchitán with the isthmus towns of **Tehuantepec** (30min., 8 pesos) and **Salina Cruz** (1hr., 15 pesos). Cristóbal Colón (☎711 25 65) sends buses to: **Mexico City** (11½hr.; 8:30, 9:20, 9:30pm; 341 pesos); **Oaxaca** (4½hr., 8 per day, 102 pesos); and other destinations.

PRACTICAL INFORMATION. The **tourist office** is upstairs in the Palacio Municipal. **Rosalinda,** a knowledgeable staff member, speaks some English. (☎711 24 32. Open M-F 9am-2pm and 6-8pm.) **Banamex,** 5 de Septiembre 12 on the *zócalo*, exchanges currency and has several 24hr. **ATMs.** (Open M-F 9am-5pm.) **Farmacia Central,** Gómez and 16 de Septiembre. (☎711 15 52. Open daily 8:30am-9pm.) **Police:** in the Palacio Municipal. No English spoken. (☎711 12 35. Open 24hr.) **Post office:** Gómez and 16 de Septiembre. (Open M-F 8am-7pm.) **Postal code:** 70000.

ACCOMMODATIONS AND FOOD. While Juchitán doesn't have the budget hotel market of Tehuantepec, there are several reasonable options. **Hotel Modelo,** 2 de Abril 21, half a block from the market, offers large, spare rooms and cold showers. Bathrooms could be cleaner. (☎711 24 51. Singles 70 pesos; doubles 80 pesos.) Only stay at **Hotel Don Alex,** 16 de Septiembre 48, if you plan to get A/C and TV—rooms without amenities are not worth the price. (☎711 10 64. Singles 130 pesos, with A/C and TV 200 pesos; doubles 130 pesos, with A/C and TV 250 pesos.)

Juchitán is perhaps the best of the three principal *istmo* towns in which to sample regional cuisine. Unusual food prevails: iguana, deer, armadillo, and rabbit are plentiful and easy to catch, and often turn up stuffed into various tortillas, *tamales*, and tacos. The tame of heart can stick to *topotes*, an interesting variant on the *tostada*, with a frisbee-like airy corn patty as a base. While the town's **market** is a must-eat, ▨**Los Chapulines,** 5 de Septiembre at Morelos, five blocks north of the *zócalo*, offers regional cuisine at regional (low) prices. The head-clearing A/C will help you think rationally before ordering the house specialty, which is, not surprisingly, *chapulines* (grasshoppers; 35 pesos). If insects aren't your style, go for one of the meat entrees (30-40 pesos), which come with salad, rice, refried beans, bread, and tortillas. (☎712 01 96. Open daily 7am-11:30pm.)

🔲 **SIGHTS.** It could take a while to see **Mercado 5 de Septiembre,** which takes up the entire block east of the *zócalo*. Vendors love a good-natured haggle and any gossip you can bring to town. Inquire about spices and buy lots of flowers. Then try on some of the festival clothing sold on the second floor of the market building; these skirts and blouses are made of velvet and ornately embroidered with flowers to represent women's powerful connection with nature. (Open daily 5am-9pm.)

At the corner of Domínguez and Colón, Juchitán's **Casa de Cultura** is filled with art and music workshops and home to a wonderful collection of regional archaeological artifacts. To get there, walk south on 5 de Septiembre from the *zócalo* toward the Banco Serfín sign. Turn right at Serfín and pass Parque Chariz on the left; the *casa* is on the right. (Open daily 10am-3pm and 5-8pm.) Next door, the church of **San Vincente Ferraro** is worth a peek. Constructed in 1528, the church has been remodeled many times but retains an ancient air. Most of the simple, whitewashed architecture dates from the 17th century.

NEAR JUCHITÁN: EL OJO DE AGUA

Across from the first-class station in Juchitán, second-class buses leave often for Ixtepec (30min., 6 pesos). Tell the driver to drop you in Ixtepec near the buses that go to Tlacotepec, which are right around the corner from the return buses to Juchitán. Tlacotepec buses drop off and pick up at the balneario (25min., every hr., 6 pesos). Balneario open 24hr. Free.

Approximately one hour northwest of Juchitán by bus, El Ojo de Agua, a bubbling *balneario* (natural spring) is perhaps the best way to beat the oppressive *istmo* heat. Cement walls have been erected at the source, directing the spring's flow through several large pools connected by makeshift waterfalls. The allure of the *balneario* is its authentic natural setting: in contrast to most crusted-tile Mexican spas, small fish swim near the sand and rock bottom of the pools, and tree trunks jut from the sides. Though trash detracts from the scene, the water itself remains clean, clear, and cool, constantly replenished by the spring. Until the bathers, the water is safe to drink.

WATCH FOR FALLING POTS Next time you're walking down a sidewalk, check out the amorous couple walking in front of you. More than likely, the woman will be walking on the inner part of the sidewalk and the man closer to the street. *Hombres* gallantly profess that they walk nearer the street to ensure that they, and not their *mujeres*, will be splashed by passing cars hitting puddles. However, a second, far less chivalrous theory exists...Many of the buildings in Mexico have balconies from which hang huge, heavy flowerpots, or *potes*. If one of the pots were to fall, it would land smack on the inner part of the sidewalk—where the women walk. In their more honest moments, some men confess that they walk nearer the street to avoid falling pots, not to protect their womenfolk from errant droplets of dirty street water. Gallant *caballeros* or sneaky, self-serving wretches...¿quién sabe?

SALINA CRUZ

Salina Cruz does not have much to offer the tourist aside from oil refineries, but its central location makes it a common stop for buses. Cristóbal Colón (☎714 14 41) runs buses to: **Huatulco** (3hr., 6 per day 12:30am-4pm, 53 pesos); **Mexico City** (11½hr.; 7:30, 8:20, 9:15pm; 357 pesos); **Oaxaca** (5hr., 5 per day, 99 pesos), and elsewhere. The **Cristóbal Colón station** is a 30-minute hike from the *zócalo*. Spare yourself the trouble: turn right and walk until you hit the main street, then catch a blue *microbus* (2.5 pesos); taxis 10 pesos. Estrella Blanca sends second-class buses to **Acapulco** and all stops in between, including **Bahías de Huatulco** and **Puerto Escondido** (4 per day 6:15am-11pm). From Cristóbal Colón, walk right on the main street three blocks, then take another right. The **Estrella Blanca station** is half a block down on the right. To get from the second-class **Istmo stop** to Cristóbal Colón, walk left past the buses to the first cross street and take a left. Walk approximately five blocks and hang a right; the station is near the corner on the left.

VERACRUZ

The state of **Veracruz** is one of the hottest, poorest, and most diverse in the Republic. Stretching 300km along the Gulf of Mexico, Veracruz encompasses breathtaking beaches, burgeoning cities, and vast spaces filled only by roaming cattle and lush vegetation. Although many local residents make their livings from tobacco and coffee cultivating and small-scale cattle ranching, the state's main income comes from oil and fishing, and and the state is known as the country's foremost producer of oil and petroleum. But the state that works hard also parties hard: *veracruzanos*, also known as *jarochos*, are renowned for their delightful sense of humor, their wonderful seafood and coffee, and their Afro-Caribbean inspired music that relies heavily on the *marimba*. The Afro-Caribbean influence dates back to the days when the city of Veracruz was the main slave trading port for the country—it pervades not only the state's music but also its cuisine and ethnic makeup. Today, the state of Veracruz, especially the volcanic hills of La Sierra de los Tuxtlas, remains relatively untouristed; those who come are pleasantly surprised. *Marimba* rhythms and Caribbean colors flow through the steamy port city of Veracruz day and night, and the beautiful mountain city of Xalapa overflows with art and culture.

HIGHLIGHTS OF VERACRUZ

DANCE the night away to the sounds of *marimba,* and spend your days checking out the **Castillo de San Juan de Ulúa** (see p. 511) in **Veracruz** (see p. 507), the state capital, a sweaty and alluring port city.

UNEARTH the treasures of the **Museo de Antropología** (see p. 498) in the temperate, green, beautiful city of **Xalapa** (see p. 493), a cultural center.

STRIKE a pose at the unearthly **Cascada de Texolo** (see p. 500); several movies have been filmed there. Check out these scenic falls and find out why.

DITCH the beach resorts in favor of the beautiful **Gulf coast** (see p. 524) south of Veracruz.

EXPLORE Papantla (see p. 504), not only a clean and friendly town, but a bastion of Totonac culture—it's the best base from which to explore **El Tajín** (see p. 506), the most impressive ruins in the state.

XALAPA   ☏ 2

Not the kind of city willing to stand by and let Veracruz—its bigger, more glam counterpart to the southeast—bowl it over, Xalapa (hah-LAH-pah) has muscled its way into the state's hot and steamy limelight. A self-declared cultural center, Xalapa has a lot to back up its claim, including an excellent orchestra, burgeoning university, and one of the top archaeological museums in the Americas. Xalapa is rich in history as well as culture. The city was conquered by the Aztecs in 1460, and remained part of the empire until Cortés came through in 1519, claiming the land for Spain. Though citizens spell their town's name (Náhuatl for "spring in the sand") with an "x," they struggle against the more commonly used Hispanic "j" spelling. The name game says it all—this is a city that thrives on debate. Even the cuisine is built upon contradictions: Xalapa is both the birthplace of the Xalapeño (jalapeño) pepper and the fertile soil for some of the most mellow coffee in the country. Though the center bursts with commerce, work and money are almost always second to coffee-time, when talkative groups of friends fill the tables to overcapacity. With such a blend of contrasts, culture, conversation and *café*, Xalapa's attractions are as varied and topsy-turvy as its many rolling hills.

Veracruz State

TRANSPORTATION

The **train station** is at the extreme northeast edge of the city, a 40min. walk or 14-peso taxi ride from the *centro*. To get from the **bus station** to the *centro*, catch buses marked "Centro" or "Terminal" (3 pesos); a taxi will cost 16 pesos. There are two bus stations. **CAXA**, in a state-of-the-art building at 20 de Noviembre 571, east of the city center, is the station for service to distant cities. The station has long-distance phones, telegraph and luggage service, shopping, and restaurants. The **Terminal Excelsior** is a roundabout where you can catch buses to small neighboring towns. Make sure to clarify which bus station you want to go to.

From CAXA, ADO (☎ 812 25 25) travels first-class to: **Catemaco** (5hr., 8 per day, 108 pesos); **Mexico City** (5hr., 21 per day 1am-midnight, 132 pesos); **Papantla** (4hr., 8 per day 103 pesos); **Puebla** (3hr., 9 per day, 72 pesos); **San Andrés Tuxtla** (3hr., 12 per day, 104 pesos); **Santiago Tuxtla** (3hr., 10:15am, 2:05pm, 7:15pm, 11:30pm, 98 pesos); **Tuxtepec** (5hr., 6am and 3:35pm, 107 pesos); and **Veracruz** (2hr., 46 per day 5am-11pm, 45 pesos). Slightly slower, 10-peso cheaper second-class service to almost identical destinations is provided by **Autobuses Unidos (AU).**

◄▌🔢 ORIENTATION AND PRACTICAL INFORMATION

Located at the midpoint of the state, Xalapa is 104km northwest of Veracruz on **Rte. 140** and 302km directly east of Mexico City. Xalapa, like many other hill towns, can be quite confusing. The downtown area is centered around the **cathe-**

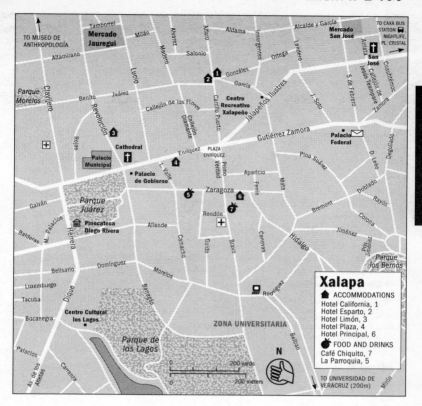

Xalapa

🏠 ACCOMMODATIONS
Hotel California, 1
Hotel Esparto, 2
Hotel Limón, 3
Hotel Plaza, 4
Hotel Principal, 6

🍎 FOOD AND DRINKS
Café Chiquito, 7
La Parroquia, 5

dral and **Palacio de Gobierno. Enríquez,** which runs along **Parque Juárez,** separates the two. Streets that branch from Enríquez toward the park and the Palacio de Gobierno run downhill; streets that split from Enríquez on the cathedral side run uphill to the market and main commercial district.

TOURIST, FINANCIAL, AND LOCAL SERVICES

Tourist Office: (☎ 812 85 00), a kiosk at the far left of the bus station as you enter the terminal is the best source of information. Open daily 4-8pm.

Currency Exchange: Banks with **ATMs** line Enríquez and the surrounding streets. Most will change money, but better rates can be found at **Centro Cambio Jalapa** (☎ 818 68 60; open M-Sa 9am-2pm and 4-6:30pm) or **Casa de Cambio Orisatal,** both further down the road on Zamora. Open M-Sa 9am-3pm and 4-7pm, Su 10am-1pm.

American Express: Carrillo 24 (☎ 817 41 14; fax 819 95 48), 3 blocks from Parque Juárez, off Enríquez. Cashier open M-F 9am-1:30pm and 4-7pm, Sa 9am-1pm. **Viajes Xalapa,** a full-service **travel agency,** with English language assistance, shares the office. Open M-Sa 9am-8pm.

Markets: Mercado Jauregui, 2 blocks behind the cathedral, sells fresh produce. The surrounding stands sell everything from jewelry to electronic equipment. Open M-Sa 7am-9pm, Su 7am-5pm. **Mercado San José,** just northwest of La Iglesia de San José, off Zárate. A 24hr. wonder of fruits and vegetables.

Supermarket: Chedraui is a **supermarket** and **pharmacy** on the corner of Lucio and Róa Bárcenas. Open daily 8am-9pm.

Laundry: Lavandería Express Salmones, Morelos 13 (☎818 52 15), between Guido and Camacho, downhill from Enríquez. 3kg for 17 pesos; 21 pesos express service. Open M-F 8:30am-8:30pm, Sa 10am-6pm.

Luggage Storage: The bus station has luggage storage. 30 pesos for 24 hrs.

Bookstores: Several excellent bookstores are located at the intersection of Xalapeños Ilustres and Mata just past the Centro Recreativo. Some, such as **Gandi Colorines,** sell English-language books and magazines.

Cultural Centers: Centro Recreativo Xalapa at Xalapeños Ilustres 31, at the intersection with Mata and Insurgentes, has art galleries, posts cultural information, and gives classes on everything from salsa to political cartooning. Open M-Sa 10am-2pm and 4-8pm, Su 11am-5pm.

Car Rental: Alamo, 20 de Noviembre Ote. 522 (☎817 43 13). Exit to the right of the bus station; walk down the stairs and through the small walk-through shopping center. On the opposite side of the street. Open M-Sa 9am-2pm and 4-8pm.

EMERGENCY AND COMMUNICATIONS

Emergency: ☎060.

Police: (☎818 18 10 or 818 99 86), sprinkled throughout the city; station at the Cuartel San José, with offices at the intersection of Arteaga and Aldama.

Red Cross: Clavijero 13 (☎817 34 31 for emergencies or 817 81 58 for administration), a block uphill from Parque Juárez. 24hr. ambulance service. No English spoken.

Pharmacy: Farmacia Reforma, Enríquez 41 (☎817 22 20). Open 24hr.

Hospitals: Hospital Civil, Pedro Rendón 1 (☎818 44 00), at Bravo. 24hr. emergency care. No English spoken. **IMSS,** Lomas del Estadio (☎818 55 55). No English spoken.

Fax: Telecomm, Zamora 70 (☎816 21 67), just before the Palacio Federal. Open M-F 8am-7:30pm, Sa 9am-5pm, Su 9am-1pm.

Telephones: LADATELs line Enríquez; several are in front of the Palacio de Gobierno.

Internet Access: PC Manía, Rodríguez B. 29 (☎841 09 00), ½ block east of the intersection of Morelos and Bravo, in the Zona Universitaria. Fast connections and prices low enough to attract even the most thrifty college student. 10 pesos per hr. Open M-Sa 9am-10pm, Su 10am-8pm. **Intercys** (☎818 52 31), out the lower doors of the bus station to the right of the taxi stand. With very few, very slow computers, its only advantage is location. 15 pesos per hr., students with ID 10 pesos. Open daily 9am-2pm and 4-8pm.

Post Office: (☎817 20 21), at Zamora and Diego Leño in the Palacio Federal. Open M-F 8am-4pm, Sa 9am-1pm. **Postal Code:** 91001.

▌ ACCOMMODATIONS

For the penny-pinching traveler, Xalapa is a gold mine. The city is full of comfortable, inexpensive, and convenient lodging, much of it on **Revolución,** close to the *centro*, the market, and the parks. For 100-150 pesos (average budget prices in most towns) you splurge on a more upscale establishment.

▧ **Hotel California,** Gonzáles Ortega 1, on the north side of a small park, where Juárez intersects with Carrillo Puerto. Not the most lovely place in Xalapa, but it compensates with low prices. Rooms are spartan, white, and extremely clean. Singles 45 pesos, with private bath 55 pesos; doubles 80 pesos.

Hotel Plaza, Enríquez 4 (☎817 33 10; fax 818 27 14). Central location. If you get a room facing Enríquez, you won't forget it—expect noise around the clock. Rooms are nice, especially on the 2nd floor. All rooms have color TVs and a near-constant *marimba* sound track that drifts up through the shady lobby from the street below. Singles 90 pesos; doubles 120 pesos; triples 150 pesos.

Hotel Principal, Zaragoza 28 (☎817 64 00), about 2½ blocks from the Palacio de Gobierno along Zaragoza. Principal is pleasant, bright, and full of toned-down 70s swellness.

Most of the rooms have TVs, and all have phones. Friendly staff will help you with whatever you need. Singles 110-130 pesos; doubles 140-160 pesos; triples 170 pesos.

Hotel Limón, Revolución 8 (☎817 22 04; fax 817 93 16), just past the cathedral. As long as you're willing to deal with the crotchety staff, Hotel Limón is a steal. Brightly-covered tiles give the lobby and hallways a cheerful glow. Rooms are tidy and all have color TV. Singles 80 pesos; doubles 120 pesos; triples 150 pesos.

Esparto, Juárez 6 (17 24 55), 1 block up from Enríquez to the right of the cathedral. A bit pricier but stuffed with amenities—TVs, phones, fans, tables, and a reasonably priced restaurant (breakfasts for under 15 pesos; open daily 7am-11pm). Singles 120 pesos; doubles 140-165 pesos.

◖◗ FOOD AND CAFES

Xalapeño food is cheap, plentiful, and always accompanied by *lechero* (*café con leche*—almost a meal in itself). Along with Xalapa's specialty *cafés*, visitors should be sure to sample several regional foods: pickled chiles, jalapeño peppers, *picaditas* (flat corn cakes with mashed beans and cheese), and *garnachas* (bean-filled, fried corn cakes). Also, don't miss the *pambozo*, a sandwich-type food served on round bread and stuffed with beans, tomato, lettuce, and other goodies.

RESTAURANTS

In Xalapa, you'll be able to eat at the nicer places in the *centro* without doing much financial damage. Cheap *taquerías* and enchilada stands are located 1 block north of Mercado Jauregi. The sides of the streets are lined with 5-10 peso hand-patted tortilla wonders.

Restaurante La Sopa, Callejón del Diamante 3A (☎817 80 69), 2 blocks from the park along Enríquez. Hip waiters cater to a hip crowd in this joint, located on—you guessed it—an ultra-hip walkway. Whitewashed arches and red tablecloths. Try the amazing *chiles rellenos* (5 pesos) or enchiladas (15 pesos) while tossing back your obligatory coffee. Music and dancing on Th night, *Veracruzano Huasteco* trio F night, and harp music Sa night. Open M-Sa 1-6pm and 7:30-11:30pm.

La Hacienda, Xalapeños Ilustres 66 (☎817 80 92), one block past the *Centro Recreativo*. For high class dining budget-style, head to La Hacienda, where you'll enjoy a 20 peso meal to soft music and a gurgling fountain. Prompt service, rustic wooden decorations, and an immense, colorful wall mural. Choice of soup, bread, rice or pasta, main dish, dessert and juice (20 pesos). Eat your meal early in the day; the restaurant closes by dinner time. Open daily 8:30am-4pm.

T-Grill, Xalapeños Ilustres 1 (☎824 57 78). The engine behind this taco emporium is the 2 women who pat fresh tortillas endlessly. Chat with them about carpal-tunnel syndrome while gorging on the fruits of their labor. 5 "traditional" tacos filled with *cabeza* (head) and other semi-unsavory animal bits (12 pesos). Open daily 11am-2:30am.

Restaurant Rosalia, Abosolo 2 (☎817 56 38), one block past the north end of the market. The funny wooden booths and great food of this 50-year-old market-side institution attract tired vendors who slake their thirst on cold drinks. Super enchiladas (7 pesos for 4); *mole poblano* (10 pesos). Top it off with *café con leche* (3 pesos). Open M-Sa 9am-9pm, Su 9am-2pm.

CAFES

Leading up from Enríquez, **Carillo Puerto** is lined with small, pleasant *cafés*. The homey feel of Café Moretto, on Carrillo Puerto off Plaza Enríquez, makes the 5-peso cup taste even better. Just down the street on Primo Verdad, Café Colón makes its money selling its famous bagged beans, but free "samplers" of hot *Café Americano* are worth a taste. At night, sip to music at Café Cali, on Callejón del Diamante, and at La Parroquia—both stay open into the wee hours and are good places to flirt. Cafes are the inroad to Xalapeño life for foreigners; it's easy to get to know people at the coffeehouses.

Café de la Parroquia, Zaragoza 18 (☎817 74 01), 1 block downhill from Enríquez. The Parroquia is a 70s dream, with tinkling elevator music wafting through the tan, smoky, "recessed lighting" interior. Heavily-lapelled patrons fill the tables with debate, discussion, and plenty of head-wagging gossip. The ambience is topped off by the justifiably wonderful coffee (9 pesos), famous *lechero* (12 pesos), succulent pastries, and *antojitos* (25-32 pesos). Open 7:30am-11pm.

Café Chiquito, Bravo 3 (☎812 11 22), 2½ blocks south of Enríquez. When not engaged in lovers' quarrels, the 18-30 year-old set mobs Chiquito's tables, practicing for the Parroquia-style Big League. Webs of soap opera intrigue and deceit. A second location is on Zamora, across from the Palacio Federal. Open daily 8am-11:30pm.

◪ SIGHTS

▨ MUSEO DE ANTROPOLOGÍA. This museum is the finest museum in the country after Mexico City's Museo Nacional de Antropología (see p. 112). But while the Mexico City museum covers pre-Hispanic history from all of Mesoamerica, Xalapa's museum focuses exclusively on the state of Veracruz. Start your visit at the front, with the museum's 10 Olmec heads, the most imposing of the 3000 artifacts, and work your way through the rectangular main gallery in chronological order. The museum is best viewed with the knowledgeable University of Veracruz students who lead tours through the museum. The bookstore in the lobby sells anthropology books. *(To get there, catch a yellow "Tesorería" bus on Enríquez (3 pesos), take a taxi (12 pesos), or walk on Enríquez/Camacho away from the cathedral. Make a left on Av. Xalapa and continue on for several blocks until you see the museum on your left (45min.). ☎815 09 20 or 815 07 08. Open daily 9am-5pm. 15 pesos, students 8 pesos. Camera 10 pesos, video camera 40 pesos. Free tours in Spanish given daily at 11:30am (1½ hr.). English tours can be arranged at any time for 100 pesos.)*

PARQUE ECOLÓGICO MACUITÉPETL. If Xalapa is a difficult city to navigate, it's probably because every street ends in a park. The biggest, most beautiful park is the Parque Ecológico Macuitépetl, where, with a little trekking, you can enjoy the flora and fauna native to the hills around the city. A brick path meanders past lip-locked lovers to the summit of an extinct volcano 186m above the city, where a spiral tower looks out over city and mountains. *(Take a "Mercado-Corona" colectivo (3 pesos) from Revolución and Altamirano, or hail a taxi (25 pesos). Open daily 6am-6pm.)*

UNIVERSITY OF VERACRUZ. The large, man-made "lakes" of **Paseo de los Lagos** lap against the university's hillsides below Enríquez. Not exactly an architectural gem, UV has lots of institutional box-style buildings painted in comely shades of blue and green. Still, pine trees, Internet access, and a path that winds around the lake make it worth a visit. Join the student runners and walkers who use the path, or pop into one of the art galleries for information on workshops and exhibitions.

PARQUE JUÁREZ. This park serves as Xalapa's surrogate *zócalo.* Its benches are usually filled with people catching the breeze and taking in the superb vista. Two staircases in the park's platform lead down to the **Agora de la Ciudad,** a currently under-construction cultural center that should be completely remodeled by January 2001. The center harbors a small cafe, several galleries, and a screening room where film festivals take place. *(Open Tu-Su 8am-9:15pm.)*

PINOCATECA DIEGO RIVERA. The city's artistic jewel is the Pinocateca, a small museum that houses many of Rivera's more experimental canvasses—Impressionism, collage, Cubism, travel sketches, and a good dose of horse-human bestiality. *(Herrera 5, just below Parque Juárez. ☎818 18 19. Open Tu-Su 10am-6pm. Free.)*

CALLEJÓNES. Xalapa takes pride in its older cobblestone alleys, nearly all of which are associated with gory love stories. **Callejón del Diamante,** off Enríquez, is named after a diamond which could tell when a lover was unfaithful. Legend has it that a Spaniard gave the diamond to his Mexican wife, who then played hanky-panky with a local while he was away. The darkened diamond alerted the Spaniard who, enraged, slaughtered his wife. Off Enrique C. Rebsamen is **Callejón de la Calavera,** named for the legend of a wife who decapitated her cheating, drunken husband. On the **Callejón de Jesús te Ampare,** the lovers in question were killed by a widower who went mad with jealousy upon seeing the happy couple. *"Jesús te ampare"* (Jesus protect you) was the only thing the girl managed to say to her lover before their demise. Sanctuary from the carnage can be found next door at the 18th century **Iglesia de San José.**

LOS MADRES CAPUCHINAS. If you're in the mood to satisfy your sweet tooth while getting a dose of religion, head to the convent of the *Adoratrices Perpétuas,* whose nuns have been making candy for the past 50 years. The easiest way to get there is to take a cab (12 pesos). At the store, pick up trinkets and *dulces de Jamoncillo;* good-sized boxes of candy in the shape of fruits, vegetables, and birds cost 20-40 pesos. *(20 de Noviembre Ote. 150. ☎817 37 51. Open M-F 9am-6pm.)*

ENTERTAINMENT

Xalapa, in typical college-town fashion, has two varieties of nightlife: the cultural (theater, classical music, *ballet folklórico*) and the bawdy (drinking, dancing, sex). After attending a high-culture performance, bicker about the symbolic use of color in one of the city's cafes, most of which are full until about 11:30pm. A little later, the city's disco fever rages on **Camacho** and near the bus station on **20 de Noviembre.** Late night jaunts require a taxi (16 pesos), but it's a small price to pay for wild, sweaty fun.

CLUBS AND BARS

Discoteque La Estación, 20 Noviembre 571 (☎817 31 55), just below the first-class bus station. Worth the cover and the trip from the *centro,* La Estación must be reached through a dark, private road that runs through the chirping, whirring Xalapeño jungle. The Station pulsates with the almost 2000 bodies it takes to fill the exquisite wooden dance floor. An upper floor with balconies has live rock music, but manages to be a bit more mellow. The clientele is young, but anyone willing to get down will fit in. Casual dress. Cover 30 pesos, free 9-10:30pm. Open W-Sa 9pm-4am.

La Roka (☎812 19 19), right across 20 de Noviembre from the bus station, on Calzada del Tajar 2. Patrons are young, casually-dressed, and move to the beat of pop/rock. On F and Sa, *Grupo Salsa Picante* plays live salsa, complete with *sombreros* and traditional dress. Cover 30 pesos. Open Th-Sa 10:30pm-3am.

Bistro Café del Herrero, Camacho 8 (☎817 02 68), hosts a mature, bar-like scene with jam-packed passageways more conducive to pressing than dancing. Lighted aquariums house iguanas, who sway to the beat of Tex-Mex rock. They get a break on Su and M, with live guitar music. Open daily 4pm-4am.

XCAPE, 20 de Noviembre 641 (☎812 50 75), 4 long blocks down 20 de Noviembre to the right of the station. A more sedentary scene, with well-dressed patrons clustered around Lilliputian-sized tables listening to live rock provided by a 3-band rotation. Cover 30 pesos. Open Th-Su 9pm-3am.

✹ FESTIVALS

For information on cultural events, visitors should check entertainment listings in the local newspapers or head down to the **Centro Recreativo** (☎817 31 10) to find out what's happening at the **Teatro del Estado.** A 10min. walk up Enríquez and Camacho from Parque Juárez, the *teatro,* at the corner of Ignacio de la Llave, is the home of the **Orquesta Sinfónica de Xalapa,** which performs there weekly and at other locations throughout the city. Other performances by university students and professionals keep the stage lights warm all week long. The **Centro Cultural Los Lagos** (☎812 12 99), 4 blocks off of Camacho on Dique, also hosts concerts.

> **XALAPA'S ROLLING HILLS** If you think you've tired of trekking up and down the hilly streets of Xalapa, just imagine the frustration of those in charge of constructing its stadium. In 1925, builders couldn't find ground level and dry enough on which work. The solution? Drain a lake! By pumping all the water out of one of the city's lakes, they not only ensured that the stadium's base would be on level ground (the bottom of the lake), but also used the steep sides of the lake to their advantage, constructing the stands against the natural grade of the land. Today, *Estadio Xalapeño* remains the only one of its kind, and visitors can only shake their heads in wonder at the designers' ingenuity.

Xalapa celebrates its culture in the **Festival de Junio Musical** (late May-June). During the festival, the symphony hosts concerts, and performers stage theater productions and recitals throughout the city. Xalapa also celebrates the month-long **Feria Internacional de Xalapa,** which features a variety of cultural, artesanal, and sporting events (April or May).

⚑ DAYTRIPS FROM XALAPA

▨ XICO'S CASCADA DE TEXOLO

To get to Xico from Xalapa, take the "Terminal" bus from the stop in front of the 3 Hermanos shoe store on Enríquez, and get off at the Excelsior bus roundabout (about 8min., 3 pesos). From Excelsior, take a "Xico" bus (45min., 7.5 pesos). When you see a blue "Entrada de la Ciudad" sign on the right side of the road, alert the driver and exit the bus. From the main street, climb straight up the hill in front of you (a white building is to the left of the rocky path). After a 4min. walk, you will reach the wide, stone-paved road at the top; turn left. Continue walking on the street, which will change into a rocky stone road. The road forks at two points along the way—take the right fork both times. Taxis sometimes make the trip to the falls, but the ride is neither smooth nor quick.

In the town of Xico (HEE-koh), 19km outside of Xalapa, there are almost as many mules on the road as automobiles. Besides pastoral bliss, Xico has one huge selling-point—the dramatic waterfalls of **Texolo,** just 3km from town. The thundering *cascada* and dense vegetation make this an ideal daytrip from Xalapa.

If it looks like it's out of a movie, that's because it is. Several US movies were filmed here, including *Romancing the Stone* and *Clear and Present Danger.* Somewhat less glamorously, car and deodorant commercials have also been filmed at the falls. In any case, Hollywood has left no trace of its presence, and few tourists frequent the site. The only sign of civilization is the conveniently placed **Restaurant El Mirador** (entrees average 30 pesos; open daily 9am-7pm). The best viewing area is located just beyond the restaurant. Head left before the footbridge crossing the gorge, and go down the cement steps with the orange railings. Take a right at the fork. The vista at the base of the falls is like something out of a fantasy book. The rocks are often slippery and deserted, so exercise caution and wear appropriate footwear. Also note that the walk to the falls is a long and lonely one: try not to go by yourself and don't hike to the falls at night. The insects are silent but ferocious—bring bug repellent.

TUXPAN (TUXPAM)   ☎ 7

Yes, the name of this town is weird. The Toltecs first established it as "Tochpan" in 1400. The town became part of the Spanish Colony in 1552 and was called "Tuxpan" for years thereafter. In 1955, the name was officially and somewhat inexplicably changed to "Tuxpam de Rodríguez Cano." Today, the town goes by "Tuxpan" slightly more often than "Tuxpam," but will answer to either.

The first thing you notice when you step into Tuxpan (pop. 120,000) is a funky smell—something like seafood, sweat, and sulfur. As you approach the heart of the town, however, the odors fade and the town's charm shines through. Just beyond the fresh seafood markets, couples amble along the Río Tuxpan, while the humidity in the mellow plaza makes for lovely, lethargic lounging. Much like their Olmec, Huastec, and Toltec predecessors, boys stand on the shore flinging fishing nets into the water, and fruit vendors traverse the streets near the riverfront selling bananas and mangoes by the bag. Tuxpan makes for beautiful, low-key living.

F TRANSPORTATION. Tuxpan, 347km northwest of Veracruz, spreads along the northern bank of Río Tuxpan. Each bus line has its own station; to get to the town center from any one, first walk to the river. From the Estrella Blanca station, walk toward and past the bridge—from the other stations, walk away from the bridge for just a few blocks. ADO, Rodríguez 1 (☎834 01 02), close to the bridge, three blocks east of Parque Cano down Reyes Heroles, goes to: **Mexico City** (5hr., 13 per day, 139 pesos); **Papantla** (1½hr., 7 per day, 29 pesos); **Poza Rica** (1hr., every 30min., 24 pesos); **Tampico** (3½hr., every hr., 100 pesos); **Veracruz** (5hr., 13 per day, 130 pesos); and **Xalapa** (5hr., 5 per day, 131 pesos). Estrella Blanca, Turistar, and Futura, at Cuauhtémoc 18 (☎834 20 40), two blocks past the bridge and two blocks inland, goes first-class to: **Matamoros** (12hr., 7 and 9:30pm, 315 pesos); **Mexico City** (6hr., 7 per day, 140 pesos); and **Monterrey** (12hr., 9pm, 326 pesos) and second-class to most nearby destinations. Omnibus, Independencia 30 (☎834 11 47), under the bridge, goes to: **Guadalajara** (15hr., 5 and 9:15pm, 445 pesos); **Mexico City** (6hr., 7 per day, 138 pesos); and **Querétaro** (10hr., 3 per day 5-9pm, 222 pesos).

■↗ ORIENTATION AND PRACTICAL INFORMATION. Blvd. Reyes Heroles (often referred to simply as the Boulevard) is Tuxpan's main thoroughfare, running along the river. One block north lies Juárez, followed by Morelos. Activity centers around two foliated plazas. **Parque Rodríguez Cano** is on the waterfront, just south of the busiest part of town, and **Parque Reforma,** the town's *centro*, is between Juárez and Morelos a few blocks west of Parque Rodríguez Cano. The bridge lies on the east edge of town, and streets perpendicular to the bridge and parallel to the water run roughly east-west.

The **tourist office,** Juárez 20, on the 1st floor of the Palacio Municipal in Parque Rodríguez Cano, has lots of maps and brochures on Tuxpan and the state of Veracruz. Enter on the Juárez side across from Hotel Florida. (☎834 01 77. Open M-Sa 10am-5pm, Su 10am-2pm.) **Serfín,** on Juárez between the two parks exchanges traveler's checks and has a 24hr. **ATM.** (☎834 09 25. Open M-F 9am-3pm.)

Lavandería Mejico, Reyes Heroles 57, three blocks west of the *centro*, will wash, dry, and iron your clothes in two hours. (☎834 27 08. 12 pesos per kg. Open M-Sa 8am-8pm.) **Supermarket: Super Alan,** Ortega 11, entrance on Santander, off Morelos between the two plazas. (Open daily 8am-9pm.) **Red Cross:** Galeana 40 (☎834 01 58), 8 blocks west of the *centro* along the river, then 4 blocks up Galeana, at the mini-bridge. English spoken. **Emergency:** ☎060. **Police:** Galeana 38, next to the Red Cross, west of the *centro*. (☎834 02 52. Open 24hr.) **Pharmacy: Benavides,** Rodríguez 9, at the bridge-side of the market one block in from the river. (☎834 12 41. Open daily 7am-10pm.) **FAX: Telecomm,** Ortega 20, 2 blocks off of Morelos. (☎834 01 67. Open M-F 8am-7:30pm, Sa 9am-5pm, Su 9am-noon.) **LADATELs** scattered around the 2 main plazas. **Internet: Sesico,** Juárez 52 (☎834 45 05), in the corner of Parque Reforma. (12 pesos per hr. Open M-Sa 9am-8:30pm, Su 10am-3pm). **Post office:** Mina 16, with a **MexPost** inside. From the Parque Reforma, follow Morelos toward the bridge, and take the first left onto Mina. (☎834 00 88. Open M-F 8am-6pm, Sa 8am-2pm.) **Postal code:** 92800.

Γ ACCOMMODATIONS. Budget accommodations in Tuxpan cluster around the two central parks, ensuring reasonable safety into the evening. **Hotel Parroquia,** Escuela Militar 4, to the left of the cathedral on Parque Rodríguez Cano, offers rooms with spacious baths, some with TVs, fans, and balconies, all at rock-bottom prices. No electrical outlets in rooms. (☎834 16 30. Singles 106 pesos; doubles 126 pesos.) **Hotel El Huasteco,** Morelos 41, is half a block east from the northeast corner of Parque Reforma. Claustrophobes may do well to skip the small, windowless rooms, but the low prices, freezing A/C, and good location make comfortable enough for a night's stay. (☎834 18 59. Singles 94 pesos; doubles 120 pesos; triples 155 pesos.) Those in search of luxury at low rates should head for **Hotel Plaza,** Juárez 39. Smack between Tuxpan's two main plazas, the large rooms come with beautiful wooden furniture, phones, TVs, and A/C. (☎834 07 38 or 834 08 38. Singles 255 pesos; doubles 305 pesos.)

🗹 **FOOD.** Along the Boulevard, especially close to the bridge, food vendors grill the cheapest tacos and *gorditas* in town, while the downtown has no shortage of small restaurants and *taquerías*. On a hot, humid evening in Parque Reforma, there's nothing more refreshing than a *licuado* made with the freshest seasonal fruits (10-12 pesos). If you're looking for regional flavor, try *bocoles*, a rich pork dish in a corn tortilla. They come in two varieties: *blancos* (the standard variety) and *negros* (with black beans and chile). Balancing traditional Mexican decor with modernity, **El Mejicano,** Morelos 49, at the corner of Parque Reforma, serves the best in regional cuisine. *Pescado a la mexicana* 45 pesos, *bocoles* 20 pesos. Breakfast buffet 25 pesos, lunch and dinner buffet 35 pesos. (☎834 89 04. Open daily 6am-midnight.) The atmosphere is a little upscale at **Restaurante El Quixote** (☎834 77 00), on Juárez across from the Parque Rodríguez Cano. The international menu includes seafood (65-70 pesos), filet mignon (75 pesos), and chicken cordon bleu (50 pesos). **Restaurant Don Carlos,** Escuela Amerigo Militar 12, near the Hotel Parroquia, is small but very clean. The resident family will whip up delicious regional seafood and meat right before your eyes (10-30 pesos). *Comida corrida* is a hard-to-believe 16 pesos. (☎834 20 97. Open daily 7am-11pm.)

🗹🗂 **SIGHTS AND BEACHES.** *Tuxpeños* are justly proud of their river's beauty and scenic shores. Palm trees line the boardwalk, and under the bridge, piles of pineapples, bananas, shrimp, and fish can be had for a next to nothing. A huge open-air market flows out of the indoor market on Rodríguez.

Those interested in Mexico's somewhat intimate relationship with Castro should visit **La Casa de la Amistad Mexico-Cuba,** across the river via a blue ferry (1 peso). Photos of a strapping, beardless Castro line the walls, taken during his stay in Tuxpan while exiled from Cuba in the late 1950s. From the ferry, walk two blocks from the river, then turn right on Obregón and follow it to its end; the museum is on your left. (Open daily 8am-7pm. Free.)

Twelve kilometers from the city center, Tuxpan's **Playa Azul** can be crowded with families and slightly dirty, but the fine sand stretches far enough for you to stake a claim somewhere under the wild coconut palms. Accessible by the "Playa" bus (30min.; every 15min. 6am-10pm, last bus returns 8pm; 5 pesos).

🗹 **NIGHTLIFE.** There are a number of bars in Tuxpan's *centro*, but the town has problems with brawls and rowdy night owls; clubs and bars have short lifespans. The best and safest nightlife in town can be found after the crowds in the Parque Reforma thin out, a few blocks down the river at **Los Girasoles,** Reyes Heroles at Hernandez, a few blocks from Parque Reforma, away from the bridge. Neon sunflowers illuminate the cheerful paintings and diverse patrons of this new restaurant/bar. Saturday nights, live rock draws the town's biggest crowds. (☎834 03 92. Open Su-Th 10am-midnight, F-Sa 10am-late. Cover Sa 40 pesos.) **Mantarraya,** Reyes Heroles, one block past the bridge, is the perfect place to break it down with a mixed-age crowd. Not-quite-current pop and techno hits. One Saturday a month, the club features "go-go dancers" (essentially, strippers who don't get naked) of both the *chica* and *chavo* variety (girls and guys). (☎834 00 51. Cover 20-40 pesos, including 2 drinks. Open Th-Sa 8:30pm-3am.)

🎊 **FESTIVALS.** Every Sunday evening, townspeople crowd the two parks for **Domingos Familiares** (Family Sundays). Young children play with oversized balloons while their parents and siblings watch local singers and dancers perform in Parque Rodríguez Cano. Makeshift stands sell food and display the work of local schoolchildren. In Parque Reforma, older couples prove that romance never dies as they dance to Latin classics. On a grander scale, August 15 marks the beginning of the **Feria Exposición,** a week-long display of town spirit. Traditional dance and song, cockfights, and open-air theater productions are everywhere. On December 7, Tuxpan celebrates the **El Día del Nino Perdido** (Day of the Missing Child). This holiday remembers the oft-overlooked Gospel story of the day Mary and Joseph lost the child Jesus when returning from the temple. In the evening, hundreds of local children light candles and walk the streets with colorful homemade "cars" made of cardboard, to help Mary and Joseph find their missing son.

POZA RICA   ☎ 7

Unlike much of Veracruz, Poza Rica is known more for its industry than its history, culture, or beauty. One of the most important oil towns in the country, it serves as a busy transportation hub for the northern part of the state, particularly nearby Papantla. Poza Rica also provides easy access to the ruins of **El Tajín.**

▐ TRANSPORTATION. From the two adjoining bus stations in the northwest corner of town, the *centro* is accessible by "Centro" or "Juárez" minibuses (10-15min., 3 pesos). One station is served exclusively by ADO, while the other has several lines with less extensive service. ADO goes to: **Brownsville** (6 per day, 426 pesos); **Mexico City** (5 hr., every hr., 116 pesos); **Papantla** (30min., every hr., 9 pesos); **Tampico** (5 hr., every 30min., 124 pesos); **Tuxpan** (45min., every 30min., 24 pesos); **Veracruz** (4 hr., 20 per day, 107 pesos); **Villahermosa** (10 per day, 337 pesos); **Xalapa** (4 hr., 12 per day, 111 pesos). The station next door contains Estrella Blanca, which goes to: **Mexico City** (5hr., every 30min., 118 pesos) and **Tampico** (5 hr., every hr., 122 pesos). Transportes Papantla goes to **Papantla** (40min., every 30min., 10 pesos) and smaller regional destinations. Omnibus to Mexico goes to **Tuxpan** (45min., every hr., 24 pesos) and **Guadalajara** (10 hr., 3 per day 6:15pm-10:15pm, 406 pesos).

▐ PRACTICAL INFORMATION. There is a small **tourist office** in the ADO station with city and state information and maps (15 pesos; open M-Sa 9am-8pm). **Bank: Bital,** in the Soriana Plaza next to the bus stations, exchanges traveler's checks and has a 24hr. **ATM.** (☎822 18 77. Open M-Sa 8am-7pm.) **Supermarket: Soriana,** the enormous center of an ultra-modern shopping plaza, to the right as you exit the bus stations. (Open daily 8am-10pm.) **Emergency:** ☎060. **Red Cross:** ☎822 01 01. **Police:** ☎822 04 07. **Pharmacy:** in either bus station. Open 24hr. **FAX: Telecomm,** next to the post office. (Open M-F 8am-7:30pm, Sa 9am-5pm, Su 9am-noon.) **Post Office:** Calle 16 Ote., across from Parque Juárez, accessible by the minibus to the *centro*. **Mex-Post** inside. (☎823 01 02. Open M-F 8am-4pm, Sa 9am-1pm.) **Postal code:** 93261.

▐▐ ACCOMMODATIONS AND FOOD. Should you decide to spend a night in town, several mid-priced to expensive hotels are available in the *centro*, along **Cortínez.** Near the stations, a dirt-cheap option is the **Hotel Farolito,** to the left as you exit either station. The friendly staff makes the stay in the somewhat run-down rooms more pleasant. (☎823 24 25. Singles 70 pesos, with A/C and TV 92 pesos; doubles 85 pesos, with A/C and TV 110 pesos; triples 140 pesos.) While they may not be the most authentic of Mexican restaurants, there are several good, sterile chain restaurants in the Soriana shopping plaza to the right of the bus stations. Options include **Dona Torta's,** with great gorditas (5-10 pesos) inside Soriana, and **Super Cream,** a trusted national chain. (Open daily 7am-11pm.)

▐ SIGHTS. The archaeological site of **El Tajín** (see p. 506) is just 20 minutes from Poza Rica, halfway to Papantla. To get there from the bus station, first take the minibus to the *centro*, asking the driver to let you off at the **Monumento a la Madre,** on the corner of Cortínez and Cárdenas. From there, hop on any bus that says "Papantla" or "Chote" (6.50 pesos); it'll drop you right at the entrance.

PAPANTLA ☎ 7

Papantla (pop. 81,293) is almost picture-perfect. Crawling over the green foothills of the Sierra Madre Oriental, the city looks out on the magnificent plains of Veracruz. The city is one of the few remaining centers of Totonac culture, just 12km north of the ruins of **El Tajín,** one of the Tonotac's largest cities during the Classic Period. Conquered by the Aztecs in 1450, the Totonacs soon got revenge upon their enemies by joining Cortés in his march to Tenochtitlán. After the conquest, the Spanish discovered the city's delicious vanilla, long cultivated in the area, and introduced it to the world, giving the city the name "Vanilla Town." Today, Papantla reflects its indigenous heritage, as bare-foot white-clad indígenas mingle with tattooed teens in the town zócalo. Perhaps the most enduring image of the city's indigenous history is in the flight of the *voladores,* a thrilling acrobatic ceremony that, once laden with religious meaning, is performed on weekends for delighted tourists.

🖪 TRANSPORTATION. Papantla lies 250km northwest of Veracruz and 21km southeast of Poza Rica along **Rte. 180.** From the **ADO bus station,** Juárez 207 (☎842 02 18), to the *centro,* turn left on Juárez and veer left at the fork. The walk is steep but not long. Taxis (8.50 pesos) pass frequently along Juárez. If arriving at the second-class bus station, 20 de Noviembre 200, commonly called **Transportes Papantla,** turn left outside the station and ascend 20 de Noviembre three blocks, to the northwest corner of the plaza. ADO goes to: **Mexico City** (5hr., 9 per day 9:40am-12:45am, 119 pesos); **Tuxpan** (1½hr., 7 per day, 28 pesos); **Veracruz** (4hr., 7 per day, 97 pesos); and **Xalapa** (4hr., 8 per day, 74 pesos). Call ahead—buses are often booked before they arrive in Papantla. The second-class terminal sends buses to the nearby transportation hub of **Poza Rica** (40min., every 20min. 4am-10pm, 10 pesos). Pay after boarding.

🖪🔳 ORIENTATION AND PRACTICAL INFORMATION. Downtown activity centers around **Parque Téllez,** the central plaza. The white-washed cathedral on Nuñez y Domínguez rises on the plaza's southern side, while **Enríquez** borders it on the north. The **tourist office** has recently moved into the Palacio Municipal, Reforma 100, on the main plaza. The entrance to the office is on the side of the building, around the block to the right if you're facing the Palacio. The knowledgeable staff sells a comprehensive guide to Veracruz (40 pesos) and provides free maps. (☎842 00 26, ext. 714. Open M-F 9am-3pm and 6-9pm.) A slew of banks on the northern side of the plaza, including **Banamex,** Enríquez 102, have 24hr. **ATMs.** (☎842 00 01. Open M-F 9am-5pm, Sa 9:30am-2pm; open for exchange M-F 9am-2pm.) **Supermarket: General de Muebles de Papantla,** Azueta 200, half a block from the main plaza. (☎842 00 23. Open M-Sa 8:30am-8:30pm, Su 10am-2pm and 4-8pm.) **Emergency:** ☎060. **Police:** in the Palacio Municipal. (☎842 00 75. Open 24hr.) **Red Cross:** on Escobedo off Juárez. Some English spoken. (☎842 01 26. Open 24hr.) **Pharmacy: El Fenix,** Enríquez 103E, at the northern end of the plaza. (☎842 06 36. Open daily 8am-11pm.) **Hospitals: IMSS,** 20 de Noviembre at Lázaro Cárdenas. From the ADO station, take a right and walk two blocks to Cárdenas, then turn left; IMSS is half a block up on your right. (☎842 01 94. Open 24hr.) **Clínica del Centro Medico,** on 16 de Septiembre just down from the tourist office. Little English spoken. (☎842 00 82. Open 24hr.) **FAX: Telecomm,** on Olivo, off of 20 de Noviembre near the Hotel Totanacapán. (Open M-F 8am-7pm, Sa 9am-5pm, Su 9am-noon.) **LADATELS** stand along Enríquez in the main plaza. **Internet: Estación Web,** Juárez 201, downhill from the plaza. (☎842 15 48. 10 pesos per hr. Open daily 9am-11pm.) **Post office:** Azueta 198, 2nd fl., with **MexPost;** unmarked from the outside—head to the supermarket building General de Muebles. (☎842 00 73. Open M-F 9am-4pm.) **Postal code:** 93400.

█ ACCOMMODATIONS. Few lodgings are available in tiny Papantla. A lovely, economical option is **Hotel Totanacapán,** 20 de Noviembre at Olivo, 4 blocks from the plaza. Here, hallway murals, crazy colors, funky re-tiling jobs, and large windows make things unintentionally retro-cool. TVs, phones, and the most affordable A/C around. (☎842 12 24 or 842 12 18. Singles 165 pesos; doubles 190 pesos; triples 220 pesos.) A step up in ritz, **Hotel Tajín,** Núñez y Domínguez 104, half a block to the left from the plaza as you face the cathedral, has a replica of a carved El Tajín stone wall in its lobby. Perched on a hill above the city, the balconies open to panoramic views. Bottled water, cable TVs, and phones are perks. Guided horseback tours available with a week's advance notice. (☎842 01 21. Singles 240 pesos, with A/C 320 pesos; doubles 330 pesos, with A/C 430 pesos; each additional person 60 pesos. Horse tours US$30 per hr.) If these rates make you uneasy, head to **Hotel Pulido,** Enríquez 205, two blocks to the left of the main plaza if you're facing the cathedral. Older rooms aren't much to look at, but come with fans. (☎842 00 36. Singles 120 pesos; doubles 170 pesos; each additional person 30 pesos.)

█ FOOD. Papantla's tourist-oriented downtown restaurants serve regional goodies: usually beef and pork, with a smattering of seafood. Specialties include *molotes*, the Mexican version of a dumpling, with spiced meat wrapped in a boiled corn shell. **Restaurant Plaza Pardo,** on the corner of Enríquez and Juárez, serves out-of-this-world food. Watch wise locals stuff their faces full of soft, delicious *tamales* (7 pesos) and *molotes* (19 pesos), or heavier meat dishes (10-50 pesos). There's also a balcony that catches a cool breeze and a superb view of the town: an ideal place to watch the *voladores* dance their way to earth. (☎ 842 00 59. Open daily 7:30am-11:30pm.) Large, tacky murals enliven **Sorrento,** Enríquez 105, next to Restaurant Plaza Pardo, a popular breakfast hangout with delectable early-morning *menús económicos* (8-18 pesos). The *comida corrida* is a deal, though it doesn't include dessert (18 pesos). *Antojitos* 15 pesos. (☎842 00 67. Open daily 7am-11pm.)

█ █ SIGHTS AND ENTERTAINMENT. Papantla's biggest attractions are the relics of its Totonac heritage. South of the plaza is the **Catedral Señora de la Asunción,** remarkable not so much for its interior, but for the stone mural carved into its northern wall, which measures 50m long and 5m high. Called the **Homenaje a la Cultura Totonaca,** the mural was created by Teodoro Cano to honor local Totonac heroes and focuses on a relief of El Tajín's Pirámide de los Nichos, depicting the discovery of corn, as well as eager Totonac ballplayers vying for the right of ritualistic death and deification. The cathedral's spacious courtyard, the **Plaza de los Voladores,** commands a view of the city and is the site at which *voladores* (see **Fly Guys,** below) acrobatically entreat the rain god Tlaloc to water the year's crops (Su afternoon and evening). Papantla's latest effort to enshrine its *voladores* is the **Monumento al Volador,** a gigantic flute-wielding *indígena* statue erected atop a hill in 1988 and visible from all over town. To get to the monument, from which you can see all of Papantla, walk up Reforma, the road that passes the entrance to the cathedral; the road winds uphill (5-10min.). There are no benches and little shade at the monument, but a small shop has drinks for the thirsty sightseer.

█ SHOPPING. The town's two markets are situated next to the *zócalo*. **Mercado Juárez,** at Reforma and 16 de Septiembre off the southwest corner of the *zócalo*, specializes in fresh fruits and vegetables and freshly-butchered meats. **Mercado Hidalgo,** on 20 de Noviembre off the *zócalo*'s northwest corner, has fun *artesanía*, clothing, and souvenirs. This is the best place to pick up some of Papantla's world-renowned **vanilla**—nearly every stand offers high-quality vanilla extract (20-100 pesos) and yummy vanilla liqueur (100 pesos per bottle). If you can't afford to get your own, shopkeepers are more than happy to give out small samples—hit every stand and you might get a buzz.

FLY GUYS The performance begins with five elaborately costumed men climbing a stationary pole to a platform at least 28m above the ground. Having consumed courage-enhancing fluids, the *voladores* (literally "fliers") begin by saluting the four cardinal points in a traditional dance around the pole: the sun, the wind, the moon, and the earth. Four of the hardy five then wind ropes around the pole, tie them to their waists, and start to "fly"—hanging from the ropes, spinning through the air, and slowly descending to earth. The fifth man plays a flute and dances on the pole's pinhead. Originally, each of the fliers corresponded to one of the four cardinal directions; positions assumed during descent were related to requests for specific weather conditions. Now, however, the ritual is commercial: instead of performing once every 52 years, the *voladores* fly as often as tourists hand over pesos. You can watch the ceremony in Papantla during the festival of Corpus Christi in early June, at El Tajín whenever a crowd gathers, or in New York or Denmark when the *voladores* go on tour.

■ **FESTIVALS.** In early June, the 10-day **Festival of Corpus Christi** celebrates both the indigenous and Christian traditions of Papantla. Most of the action takes place at a fair just outside of town, with artistic expositions, fireworks, traditional dances, and cockfights. To get to the festival from the *centro*, flag a taxi (15 pesos) or take any *pesero* (3 pesos) from 16 de Septiembre behind the cathedral and ask for the *feria*. In town, the *voladores* perform as often as three times a day, morning, afternoon, and evening. Once every 52 years, at the turning of the Totonac century, the festival takes on larger proportions.

NEAR PAPANTLA: EL TAJÍN

El Tajín is accessible from Papantla via the white and blue peseros that stop at the corner of 16 de Septiembre and Reforma, next to the cathedral's courtyard (20min., every 15min. 5am-8pm, 6.50 pesos). Hop on a "Poza Rica" bus (it may also say "Chote" and "Tajín") and check with the driver to make sure it stops at El Tajín. Your bus will first pass through the tiny town of El Chote, then stop at the entrance to El Tajín, marked by a stone mural. To return to Papantla, catch a "Papantla" bus just outside the museum (last bus leaves at 5pm, 6.50 pesos). Ruins open daily 8am-7pm. 30 pesos, children under 13 and adults over 60 free. Free Su. For more information, check out www.Tajin2000.com.

The impressive ruins of El Tajín only hint at the thriving Totonac civilization that once spread across modern-day northern Veracruz in the Classic Period. Though the ruins were "discovered" by the Spanish in 1785 (natives of the area had always known of its existence), it was not until 1939 that restoration work began. The area was probably settled around AD 100 by Huastec peoples, whose structures were subsequently razed by the Totonacs, who began seriously constructing the area early in the Classic Period (AD300-400). The Totonac people are so named as a Spanish derivative of the Náhuatl *Tutu Nacu*, which means "three hearts" and refers to the three major city centers of Totonac culture, of which El Tajín is one. In the native language, "Tajín" means "thunder," "lightning," or "hurricane," and so it is believed that the Totonacs dedicated this city to the god of rain. In the mid-Classic Period, AD 600-900, El Tajín was a Totonac capital, perhaps subservient only to Teotihuacán in the Valley of Mexico, and traces of Teotihuacán architecture are visible at El Tajín. For reasons still unclear, however, the area declined early in the Post-Classic Period, around AD 1200. Most archaeologists now believe that the city was conquered and burned by invading nomadic tribes such as the Chichimecs. The Totonacs who remained in the area were brought under the control of the Aztecs in the late 15th century.

MUSEUM AND ENTRANCE AREA. Next to the entrance stands a large pole, the apparatus of the *voladores* (performances June-Aug. every hr., Sept.-May weekends only). The daring acrobats typically request a 10-peso donation. A tiny but useful brochure and map (6 pesos) about El Tajín in English or Spanish can be purchased at the store adjoining the **information desk.** There is also a small **restau-**

rant at the entrance that serves a seafood *comida corrida* (35 pesos). As you enter the ruins, you will pass the **Museo de Sitio,** a museum featuring original mural fragments and a morbidly fascinating display of sand and ancient skeletons, some with cracked skulls and visible bone injuries. From the museum, a straight path leads to the ruins, which are not labeled or explained in any way. Your best sources of information are the guidebooks or the guided tours (15 pesos).

PLAZA DE ARROYO. The Plaza, the central rectangular plaza formed by four tiered pyramids, lies just to the left of the gravel road. Each pyramid points toward the northeast at a 20° angle, a feature common in all of the site's early buildings.

JUEGO DE PELOTA SUR (SOUTH BALLCOURT). Just past the pyramids, two identical, low-lying, slanted constructions to the left of the main path form a central grass ballcourt in which the famous one-on-one ball game was played. Every 52 years, a contest was held between the most valiant ballplayers. The winner earned the honor of being decapitated, sacrificed, and deified, putting the World Cup to shame. Approximately 17 such courts grace the ruins of Tajín. This ballcourt is famous for its carved stone walls depicting the ball games in action.

THE CENTRAL ZONE. Across from the plaza stands an elevated central altar surrounded by two climbable temples. Just left of the altar is a split-level temple that displays a statue of Tajín. This area, known as the Central Zone, is notable for the diverse styles and functions of its buildings.

LA PIRÁMIDE DE LOS NICHOS. To the northwest stands this pyramid, El Tajín's most recognizable structure, with seven levels and a total of 365 niches corresponding to the days of the year. Each niche was once painted crimson and blue. The Totonacs kept time in 52-year epochs, during which a single flame was kept continuously burning. At the end of each epoch, the carefully nurtured flame was used to ritually torch many of the settlement's buildings. Each new epoch of rebuilding and regeneration was inaugurated by the lighting of a new flame. Ritual ceremonies are now held annually at the pyramid during the vernal equinox; farmers place seeds in the pyramid's niches and later retrieve them for planting.

TAJÍN CHICO. Farther north atop a hill is **Tajín Chico,** accessible by a series of large stepping stones and an easy-to-ascend staircase to the west. While Tajín was a public religious and social center, archaeologists hypothesize that Tajín Chico was where the ruling class and political elite lived. One of the less-excavated areas, it is rimmed by "no access" signs where more structures may be hidden. East of Tajín Chico, down the hill and around the curve in the gravel road is the **Great Xicalcoliuhqui,** a recreational and religious area still being unearthed.

VERACRUZ ☎2

The oldest port city in the Americas, Veracruz (pop. 327,500) possesses the untranslatable qualities of *sabor*, for its rich and alluring flavor, and *ambiente*, for its unique and sensual atmosphere. Amid a slew of new construction projects, the sounds of *marimba* music—distinctive for its wooden xylophone sound—and *bamba* beats fill the warm Gulf nights as tourists and residents alike sip the city's delicious *café con leche* and fall sway by nighttime to a seductive beat. Since Cortés landed in La Rica Villa de la Vera Cruz in 1519, Veracruz has been Mexico's port to the outside world, although the city moved twice before settling in its current location in 1589. Pirates long frequented the steamy coastal mecca, and Veracruz has seen more than its share of plunderings and invasions by armies under the command of men like Francis Drake, Napoleon III, and Woodrow Wilson. Today, Veracruz's streets continue to fill with sailors—and tourists—from around the world. The steamy city sprawls along the Gulf coast, merging gracefully with **Boca del Río,** the prosperous site of the best beaches, chic discos, and expensive hotels. A hot, humid urban sprawl dripping with sweat into the night, the twin cities are a wonder to behold.

VERACRUZ

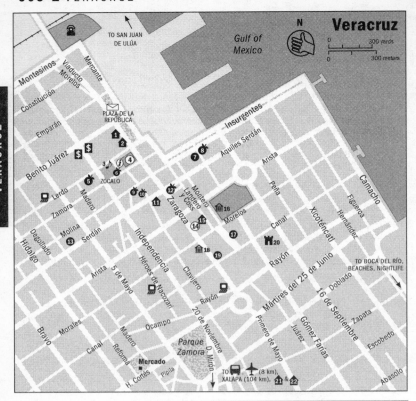

TO SAN JUAN
DE ULÚA

Gulf of
Mexico

N

Veracruz

0 ————— 300 yards
0 ————— 300 meters

Montesinos
Viaducto
Mercante
Morelos
Constitución
Emparán
Benito Juárez
Lerdo
Zamora
Madero
Molina
Serdán
Degollado
Hidalgo
Arista
5 de Mayo
Héroes de Nacozari
Independencia
Clavijero
Rayón
20 de Noviembre
Ocampo
Madero
Reforma
Canal
Bravo
Morales
H. Cortés
Pígila
D. Mirón
**Parque
Zamora**
■ **Mercado**

PLAZA DE LA
REPÚBLICA
ZÓCALO
Montero
Landero
y Cos
Zaragoza
Morelos
Canal
Peña
Arista
Insurgentes
Aquiles Serdán
Arista
Camacho
Figueroa
Hernández
Xicoténcatl
Rayón
Mártires del 25 de Junio
Primero de Mayo
Gómez Farías
Juárez
Doblado
16 de Septiembre
Zapata
Escobedo
Abasolo

TO BOCA DEL RÍO,
BEACHES, NIGHTLIFE

TO [bus] [plane] (8 km),
XALAPA (104 km), **21 & 22**

Veracruz

🏠 **ACCOMMODATIONS**

Casa de Huespedes
  La Tabasqueña, 1
Hotel Amparo, 11
Hotel Central, 21
Hotel México, 2
Hotel Rosa Mar, 22
Hotel Santillana, 15

🍎 🎵 FOOD, DRINKS, AND NIGHTLIFE

Cochinito de Oro, 12
El Alba Supermarket, 5
El Portal del Ángel, 6
Gran Café de la Parroquia, 8
La Gaviota, 10
Mariscos Tano, 9
Regis, 3

● 🛈 🏛 ○ SIGHTS AND SERVICES

Baluarte de Santiago, 20
Casa de la Cultura, 17
Casa de Salvador Díaz Mirón, 14
Farmacia del Ahorro, 7
Instituto Veracruzano de Cultura (IVEC), 19
Lavandería Ultra Clean, 13
Museo de la Ciudad, 18
Museo Histórico Naval, 16
Palacio Municipal, 4

FOUR TIMES HEROIC Ravaged by pirates and disease, Veracruz seemed ill-fated from its founding. After Mexico won its independence from Spain, the Spanish continued to attack the port city for 26 months—from September of 1823 to November of 1825. In 1838, during the Pastry War, Veracruz again had to withstand foreign invasion, this time from the French, who occupied the city and demanded repayment for damages suffered after the War of Independence. Santa Ana, heroic general of the recent war with America, lost his leg trying to defend Fort San Juan de Ulúa. American troops first occupied the city in 1847, when General Winfield Scott led an attack that resulted in the loss of the city and the deaths of over 1000 Mexicans in one week. In 1914, American marines again took the city, halting a shipment of arms to Mexican dictator Victoriano Huerta. For these four disastrous military encounters, Veracruz has christened itself *Cuatro Veces Heróica*. And heroic it is; after so many defeats, it's a wonder the city still stands.

▐ TRANSPORTATION

Airport: (☎934 37 74) 8km south of downtown Veracruz on Rte. 150. **Aeroméxico** (☎935 01 42) and **Mexicana** (☎932 22 42).

Buses: From Parque Zamora, Mirón connects the *centro* to the **Central de Autobuses Veracruz (CAVE),** Mirón 1698, which houses all of the city's major bus lines. To get to the *centro* from the bus station, get on a "Díaz Mirón" bus headed north to Parque Zamora (3 pesos). Some buses run all the way to the *zócalo,* and others stop at the park, 7 blocks south on Independencia. To return to the bus station, take a southbound "Díaz Mirón" bus from anywhere along 5 de Mayo. ADO (☎937 57 88) goes to: **Cancún** (21hr., 10:35pm, 530 pesos); **Catemaco** (3hr., 7 per day, 64 pesos); **Mexico City** (5½hr., 16 per day, 189 pesos); and **Xalapa** (1¾hr., 50 per day 2:30am-11:30pm, 45 pesos). Cristóbal Colón (☎937 57 88) goes to **Oaxaca** (6½hr., 11pm, 253 pesos) and **Tuxtla Gutiérrez** (12hr., 4pm and 8:15pm, 236 pesos). Cuenca (☎935 04 03) sends 2nd-class buses to **Oaxaca** (6hr., 8pm, 131 pesos) and **Tuxtepec** (3hr., every hr. 5am-8pm, 58 pesos). AU (☎937 57 32), one block behind ADO station on the right side, offers 2nd-class service to: **Córdoba** (1½hr., 16 per day 6am-12:30am, 49 pesos); **Mexico City** (6hr., 16 per day 1am-12am, 158 pesos); **Orizaba** (2½hr., 16 per day 6am-12:30am, 58 pesos); **Puebla** (4½hr.; 2, 8, 10:15am, and 12:30pm; 120 pesos); and **Xalapa** (1¾hr., 16 per day 6am-12:30am, 95pesos).

Train: (☎932 33 38 or 932 29 94), at Mercante and Montesinos, north of the post office.

▐▐ ORIENTATION AND PRACTICAL INFORMATION

Sprawling along the coast in a series of docks, harbors, and boardwalks, Veracruz is located on the southwest corner of the Gulf of Mexico, 104km south of Xalapa and 424km west of Mexico City. Along the south coast, Veracruz merges with the glam suburb **Boca del Río.** Home to the best discos, restaurants, and coastlines, it is easily reached by the "Boca del Rio" buses which leave from **Zaragoza,** one block toward the bay from the *zócalo* (3 pesos). Buses are less frequent at night; taxis are a safer choice.

Tourist Office: (☎939 88 17) on the right side of the Palacio Municipal, facing the *zócalo.* Open daily 9am-9pm.

Currency Exchange: A slew of banks and *casas de cambio* on the corner of Juárez and Independencia, 1 block north of the *zócalo.* **Banamex,** open M-F 8:30am-5pm, Sa 9am-2pm, and **Bital,** open M-Sa 8am-7pm, both have **24hr. ATM's.**

American Express: Camacho 221 (☎931 46 36), inside Viajes Olymar, across from Villa del Mar beach. Take the "Villa del Mar" bus. Open M-F 9am-8pm, Sa 9am-noon.

Markets: Mercado Hidalgo, on the corner of Cortés and Madero, 1 block from Parque Zamora away from the Gulf, sells fruit, vegetables, *piñatas,* etc. Open daily 8am-8pm.

Supermarket: El Alba, Lerdo 270 (☎932 24 24), between Independencia and 5 de Mayo. Open M-Sa 9am-2:30pm and 5-9pm.

Laundry: Lavandería Ultra-Clean, Serdán 789, between Madero and 5 de Mayo. Same day service. 7 pesos per kg. Open M-Sa 9:30am-7:30pm.

Luggage Storage: At the bus station. 5 pesos per hr.

Bicycle Rental: at the corner of Camacho and Bolívar, along Villa del Mar beach. 25-30 pesos per hr.

Emergency: ☎060.

Police: (☎938 06 64 or 938 06 93), at Colonial Palieno.

Red Cross: (☎937 55 00) on Mirón between Orizaba and Abascal, 1 block south of the Central de Autobuses. No English spoken. Open 24hr. with **ambulance.**

Pharmacy: Farmacía del Ahorro, on Díaz Mirón, in front of the Social Security building. Open 24hr. Also on the *malecón* at Gómez Farías 2, (☎937 35 25).

Hospital: IMSS, Mirón 61. No English spoken. (☎932 19 20. 24hr. emergency service.)
Sanitario Español, 16 de Septiembre 955, has a good reputation for treating foreigners. No English spoken. (☎932 00 21. 24hr. emergency service.)

Fax: Telecomm (☎932 25 08), on Plaza de la República, left of the post office. Open M-F 8am-7pm, Sa 9am-5pm, Su 9am-noon.

Telephones: LADATELs on the *zócalo* and in front of the Palacio Municipal.

Internet Access: Netchatboys, Lerdo 369, between Madero and 5 de Mayo. 8 pesos per 30min., 15 pesos per hr., students with ID 12 pesos per hr. Open M-F 9am-9pm, Sa-Su noon-8pm. **La Casa de la Abuela,** Callejón Héroe de Nacozari 201, between Morales and Canal, serves great cappuccino as well. 12 pesos per hr. Open M-Sa 5-10pm. **Webcafé,** Rayon 579A, is an easy step from Parque Zamora. 18 pesos per hr., students with ID 15 pesos per hr. Open M-Sa 10am-10pm.

Post Office: Marina Mercante 213 (☎932 20 38), at the Plaza de la República. Open M-F 8am-4pm, Sa 9am-1pm. **Postal Code:** 91700.

▼ ACCOMMODATIONS

Veracruz has three peak seasons: *Carnaval* (the week before Ash Wednesday), *Semana Santa* (the week before Easter), and summer (July and August). The city is saturated with hotels, but many fill up well in advance and most raise their rates during these times; expect to pay 20-100 pesos more for your room. The luxury of a room with A/C, much needed in this steamy city, ups the price even more.

NEAR THE CENTRO
Budget hotels cluster on Serdán, two blocks over from the *zócalo*. Several others are on Morelos, just north of the *zócalo*. Both streets, full of revelers all night every night, are fun, loud, and relatively safe.

Hotel Amparo, Serdán 482 (☎932 27 38), half a block west of Zaragoza. If there are backpackers in Veracruz, they're probably here. Clean, inexpensive rooms and close to the harbor. Singles 85 pesos; doubles 100 pesos.

Hotel México, Morelos 343 (☎932 43 60), across the street from the Aduanos building. Superb location. Bright rooms have fans and TVs, although bathrooms could be cleaner. Singles 150 pesos, doubles 200 pesos.

Casa de Huespedes La Tabasqueña, Morelos 325. Poorly ventilated rooms are somewhat clean, and the fans fend off the mildewy smell and keep things relatively cool. Expect chipped tiles, poor decorations, and a cheap sleep. Singles 70 pesos; doubles 120 pesos; triples 150 pesos.

Hotel Santillana, Landero y Coss 208 (☎932 31 16), at Dehesa. Rooms with fans, TVs, phones, and carpeting surround a purple-green courtyard, which emanates a garish charm. Singles 120 pesos; doubles 150 pesos; 80 pesos more in summer.

NEAR THE BUS STATION
Convenience comes at a price near the bus station. Most hotels are on La Fragna, behind the ADO station.

Hotel Latino, La Fragua 280 (☎937 65 99). Exit left from the ADO station and walk 1½ blocks. The best bet for a stay near the station. Bare-bulbed rooms don't exactly exude high class, but they are well-cleaned by an attentive staff and have fans and TVs. Singles 130 pesos, with A/C 180; doubles 150-180 pesos, with A/C 180-250.

Hotel Rosa Mar, La Fragua 1100 (☎937 07 47), behind the ADO station. Rosa valiantly tries to remain clean, wholesome, and convenient. Cramped rooms have TV and fans. Singles 160 pesos, with A/C 190 pesos; doubles 210 pesos, with A/C 240 pesos.

Hotel Central, Díaz Mirón 1612 (☎932 22 22), to right of ADO. A modern-looking hotel with a faux-marble lobby and dim hallways. Large rooms have TV, phone, and bath. Singles 195 pesos, with A/C 250 pesos; doubles 245 pesos, with A/C 325 pesos.

FOOD

If the seafood coming off the docks, mixed with the aroma of grinding coffee comprises 80% of Veracruz's famous *sabor*, the other fraction surely resides in the little restaurants surrounding the fish markets on **Landero** and **Coss**. Eccentrically decorated, these are the places to dig into the mountains of fish, shrimp, octopus, and crab hauled out of the Gulf on a daily basis. For a cheaper, slightly more frantic experience, try **Mercado Hidalgo,** where seafood stands sell fish and shrimp dishes for around 30 pesos. Restaurants under the *portales* in the *zócalo* offer quality, seasonal dishes and a *marimba* beat—for a price. Wherever you choose to take your meal, don't miss out on the distinctive *veracruzano* fare. Steer clear of raw fish and the risk of contracting cholera. Instead, order *huachinango a la veracruzana* (red snapper decked out in olives, capers, onions, and olive oil). Other regional specialties include *filete relleno* (fish fillet stuffed with *mariscos*), *arroz a la tumbada* (rice in a sauce that includes—of course—shellfish), and *jaiba* (a large local crab).

▨ **Gran Café de la Parroquia,** Farías 34 (☎932 35 84), on the *malecón*. A Veracruz tradition, the entire town seems to gather here, and every president since 1810 has sipped the famous *lechero* (coffee with milk, 13 pesos). Sit back and enjoy yourself while you eavesdrop and people watch. Entrees 14-70 pesos. Open daily 6am-1am.

▨ **El Cochinito de Oro,** Zaragoza 190 (☎932 36 77), on the corner of Serdán. Cheap, excellent seafood explains El Cochinito's 50-year popularity with locals. Memorabilia scattered over the interior entertain you as you wait. *Fillete de pescado* and fish or shrimp stews average 35 pesos. Open daily 7am-5pm.

Mariscos Tano, Molina 20 (☎931 50 50), 1 block south of the *zócalo*. A good place for anyone with limited Spanish proficiency. The menu entrees are listed in English, and just about everything listed is stuffed and hanging from the ceiling. The *mariscos* (shellfish) are good, and the photo-history of *Carnaval* on the back wall is museum quality. The singing staff adds to the the laid-back atmosphere. Open daily 9am-10pm.

La Gaviota, Callejón de Trigueros 21 (☎932 39 50), half a block from the intersection of Zaragoza and Serdán. The quiet, simple ambience and regional specialties are reminiscent of the *zócalo's* quality at more affordable prices. *Filete a la veracruzano* 48 pesos, *antojitos* 12-22 pesos. Open 24hr.

El Portal del Ángel, Zamora 138 (☎903 22 28), in the *zócalo*, under the *portales*. With delicious *filete relleno*, classy waiters, and an ideal social location, El Portal offers the ultimate in dining, *veracruzano* style. The experience doesn't come cheap, however; fish fillets are about the cheapest items on the menu (45 pesos), while specialty dishes such as *huachinango* and *camarones* are pricier (70 pesos). Open daily noon-11pm.

SIGHTS

When it wasn't being blasted by bullets or mobbed by mosquitos, Veracruz had to contend with the fierce north wind called *nortes*—both its curse and the reason the city rose to such importance as a center for Transatlantic trade. Most of the city's sites relate to one of its many military encounters, and young naval officers staff the museums, ready to offer official information. Note that one of the city's premier sights, the **Museo de la Revolución,** featuring displays on the life of Venustiano Carranza, former president of the Republic, is undergoing renovations and will reopen at a later date.

▨ **CASTILLO DE SAN JUAN DE ULÚA.** The fortress, Veracruz's most important historic site, rests on a fingertip of land jutting into the harbor. Using coral chunks as bricks, construction of the fortress began sometime after Cortés's arrival under the order of Charles V. It was intended as part of the system of fortifications built to protect Spanish treasure from Caribbean pirates. After 1825, however, the building was used as a high-security jail for big name political prisoners such as presidents Benito Juárez and Porfirio Díaz. The famous *politicos* aside, San Juan's best-known prisoner was the folk hero **Chucho el Roto,** a Robin Hood-like figure who stole from the rich and gave to the poor. El Roto's legend has grown to mythic proportions, as he was believed to have escaped from San Juan not once, but thrice. *(Take a "San Juan de Ulúa" bus (3 pesos) in front of the Aduana building in the Plaza de la República. Buses come infrequently and stop running at 5pm. Taxis charge around 40 pesos. ☎ 938 51 51. Open Tu-Su 9am-5pm. 20 pesos, Su free. Guided tours 10 pesos in Spanish, 15 in English; they are well worth the money.)*

■ **MUSEO HISTÓRICO NAVAL.** The museum, located on the grounds of Veracruz's Naval School, is a sailor's air-conditioned dream. Gallery after gallery of model ships, entertaining dioramas on man's seafaring history, and displays on Veracruz's naval successes and shortcomings make for an enjoyable navigation of Mexico's rich maritime history. *(Walk 3 blocks down Independencia and turn left on Arista for 2 blocks; the Naval School is on your right, occupying the entire block bordered by 16 de Septiembre, Arista, Montero, and Morales. ☎ 931 40 78. Open Tu-Su 9am-5pm. Free.)*

BALUARTE DE SANTIAGO. Built in 1526, the Baluarte is today the sole remnant of the stone wall that once encircled a good part of the city, protecting the city's inhabitants from pirates. The wall, along with the other eight *baluartes* (small forts), was torn down in the late 19th century. The museum inside displays a small and none-too-impressive collection of pre-Hispanic gold ornaments called *Las Joyas del Pescador,* so named because of their rescue from the ocean by a lucky octopus fisherman. Around the back of the fort, a small spiral staircase leads to a nice tower view. *(On Canal between 16 de Septiembre and Farías, 1 block down from the Naval School. ☎ 931 10 59. Open Tu-Su 10am-4:30pm. 25 pesos, Su free.)*

MUSEO DE LA CIUDAD. Completely renovated in summer 2000, this vamped-up museum features paintings, models, and dioramas depicting the history of the city from pre-Hispanic times to the present. Television clips and guides help you as you go. In the back stairwell, a stained-glass window depicts the legend of Talinmasca, an orphan whose transgressions brought thunder, lighting, and the fierce autumn *nortes* to the area. *(Zaragoza 397. Down Canal away from the water, and right on Zaragoza. ☎ 931 84 10. Open Tu-Su 10am-6:30pm. Free.)*

CASA DE SALVADOR DÍAZ MIRÓN. The famous *veracruzano* poet Díaz Mirón lived here for the last seven years of his life (1921-1928), and people say that they have heard his ghost pacing in the house's upper chambers. Today it serves as a literary center for Veracruz. Recently renovated, the foyer holds temporary art exhibitions. Upstairs, a small museum replicates what the house looked like while occupied by Mirón. *(On Zaragoza 332, between Morelos and Arista. ☎ 989 88 60, ext. 146. Open M-Sa 10am-8pm. Free.)*

ACUARIO DE VERACRUZ. A popular family beachside attraction, the aquarium features fish, sharks, and turtles native to the Gulf. *(In the Centro Comercial Plaza Acuario, a shopping mall on the left when facing the ocean at Villa del Mar. Catch a "Villa del Mar" bus on Zaragoza (3 pesos). ☎ 931 10 20. Open daily 10am-8pm. 20 pesos, children 10 pesos.)*

◢ BEACHES

The general rule for beaches in Veracruz is that the farther from the city, the nicer the beach, although it's practically impossible to escape the oil barges and tugboats in the distance. **Playa Villa del Mar** is a pleasant hour-long walk from the *zócalo* along the waterfront on the *malecón* (Camacho); it is also accessible via one of the frequent "Villa del Mar" or "Boca del Río" buses (3 pesos) that stop on Zaragoza behind the tourist office. Few people swim at Villa del Mar—restaurants have set up camp along the boardwalk, and their beachside presence makes frolicking in the sand almost impossible. Still, the restaurant huts and bars create a lively atmosphere; at night, the Villa del Mar area is even more festive. Farther on

Camacho away from downtown Veracruz is a peaceful stretch of sand called **Costa de Oro,** between the orange-pinkish hotels Fiesta Americana and Torremar.

The best beach in the Veracruz area (although that's not saying much) is **Playa Mocambo,** in the neighboring city of **Boca del Río.** Take a "Boca del Río" bus from Zaragoza and Serdán and get off at the mall, Plaza de Las Americas (30min.). The beach is on the other side of Hotel Torremar. Veer left to head for the beach or go straight into the **Balneario Mocambo,** which has a clean, Olympic-sized public pool surrounded by artificial palm trees, changing rooms, and a poolside bar-restaurant. (☎931 02 88. Open daily 10am-6pm. 20 pesos, children 15 pesos.) Those whose beach experience is defined by attitude rather than turquoise water will find plenty of laid-back lounging in the residential area down the coast from the hotel. The sand is peaceful, and the neighborhood barbecues doubling as street restaurants are a great place to meet locals and negotiate cheap, informal lodging. Though the area is very friendly, there is petty crime; keep an eye on your bag. The bus back to town can be caught at the nearby open-air market (on the side of the road back to town) or at the top of Balneario Mocambo's driveway.

🎵🎭 ENTERTAINMENT AND NIGHTLIFE

In the evening, the hymns of the cathedral spilling out into the *zócalo* yield to the sexy rhythms of *marimbas.* Vendors spread their wares on the paths, and the bars and restaurants fill with merry drinkers and *mariachi* bands. On weekend nights, some of the world's hottest senior citizens strut their stuff on the civic dance floor. Apart from this spontaneous merrimaking in the *zócalo,* most action takes place along **Camacho,** the sea-side road connecting Veracruz and Boca del Río. Just before the purple high-rise landmark Hotel Lois, **Ruiz Cortínes** branches off Camacho—a good place to get off the bus.

BARS

Regis (☎931 41 91), one of a string of bars on the northeast side of the *zócalo.* If you can stand the hawkers, the jam-packed outdoor social scene continues all night. Beer 12 pesos. Open daily 10am-2am.

Café Andrade (☎932 82 24), on Camacho at the corner of Callejón and 12 de Octubre, across the street from the Plaza Acuario and Playa Villa del Mar. Beautiful people of all ages flock to the cool outdoor patio and enjoy coffee (8 pesos). The cafe sells beans from nearby Coatepec. Open daily 8am-midnight.

Master Club Billar, Camacho 4 (☎937 67 48), is one of the friendliest, safest pool-houses you've ever seen, with TV, music, bar, A/C, and tables for dominoes or cards. Pool 30 pesos per hr. Open daily 4pm-2am.

Carlos 'n' Charlie's, Camacho 26 (☎922 29 10), has been bestowed on Veracruz by Señor Frog's, the tourist-ridden joint that just keeps on giving. The restaurant regularly fills to the point of immobility—but that's okay. Everyone sits, drinks, and sings along merrily with the salsa music. Open Su-Th 9am-midnight, F-Sa 9am-2am.

CLUBS

Zoo (☎921 79 35), at Camacho on the corner of Medica Militar. A notch above all in style and popularity, the monolithic stone zoo provides a place for trend-setters to blow air kisses, scrutinize each other's *haute couture,* and dance all night. Cover 40 pesos. Open F-Sa 10pm-5am.

El Palacio de la Salsa, Calle 12 33, four blocks down Camacho from the Cortínes intersection, one block right on Medico Militar and another block left on Calle 12. Cover 20 pesos. Open Th-Sa 10pm-6am.

CULTURAL EVENTS

On any given night, *marimba* bands perform in the *zócalo,* while *mariachi* musicians hover nearby, ready to break into song at the sight of pesos. If you seek more structured entertainment, the **Instituto Veracruzano de Cultura (IVEC)** holds weekly

IF IT'S GOOD ENOUGH FOR IKE... A guy can't claim he really knows Veracruz until he's worn the traditional white shirt called a *guayabera*. The name comes from the word *guayaba,* Spanish for "guava." Cuban guava collectors got tired of shimmying up and down the tree countless times, so they designed a shirt with four pockets to expedite the task. From Cuba, the *guayabera* shirt passed to Panama and then to Mexico, where Carlos Cab Arrazate added the thin pleats that form vertical stripes connecting the pockets. His grandson continues the family business, **Guayaberas Finas,** Zaragoza 233 (☎931 84 27), between Arista and Serdán, in Veracruz city. Everyone who's anyone has bought one of their high-quality, hot-weather shirts—check out US president Dwight D. Eisenhower's note of appreciation on the store's wall. Fashion tip: shirts are not meant to be tucked in. (*Open M-F 9:30am-8pm, Sa 9:30am-7pm, Su 10am-4pm.*)

music, dance, and folklore performances in addition to movies, expositions, and art shows. Pick up a monthly schedule at IVEC or at the **Casa de la Cultura,** at the corner of Canal and Zaragoza. (☎931 43 96. Open M-F 9am-8pm, Sa-Su 9am-6pm.)

❀ FESTIVALS

Every December 31, from midnight to dawn, *veracruzano* families dress in their Sunday best and fill Camacho, looking east to the Gulf of Mexico to witness the first sunrise of the year. With that auspicious start, a year of celebrations begins. The climax comes early, in late February or early March, just before Ash Wednesday, when **Carnaval** invades the *zócalo* with nine days of festivities. The tourist office has programs of the events.

⌘ DAYTRIPS FROM VERACRUZ

ZEMPOALA

*From the 2nd-class bus station on La Fragua behind the ADO station, Autobuses TRV sends buses to **Cardel** (45min., 13 pesos). Exit out the right side of the station and walk right 2 blocks; the Zempoala bus pick-up is on the cross street at the T-intersection. From there, take a bus to **Zempoala** (15min., 5 pesos). Ask the driver to let you out at the ruins, at the intersection of Ruíz and Troncoso Norte. To get back, stand across the street from where you were dropped off and hail a passing "Cardel" bus (5 pesos). From Cardel, catch a bus to Veracruz (45min; every 10min. midnight-8pm, every 15min. 8-10pm; 10 pesos). Site open daily 9am-4:30pm. 15 pesos, Su free.*

The ruins at **Zempoala** (sometimes spelled **Cempoala**), some of the most impressive in the state, lie 40km north of Veracruz off Rte. 180. Zempoala was one of the largest southern Totonac cities and part of a federation that covered much of Veracruz. At its height, in the 14th and 15th centuries, the city may have had as many as 120,000 inhabitants and is thought by many to have been the Totonac Post-Classic sucessor to El Tajín (see p. 506). In 1458, however, the Aztecs conquered the Zempoala and forced the Totonacs to join the Aztec federation. When Cortés arrived in 1519, the humbled city had only about 30,000 residents and was eager to assist any enemy of the Aztecs, lending Cortés soldiers and supplies.

The site now consists of stone structures surrounding a grassy field next to present-day Zempoala. A museum left of the entrance displays a small collection of pottery and figurines unearthed here. The structure closest to the entrance is the **Temple of Death.** Continuing to the left, you will see three **pyramids.** The pyramid on the left is dedicated to Tlaloc (god of rain), the one on the right to the moon, and the one in the center, decorated with circular stone receptacles for the hearts of people sacrificed in religious offerings, to the sun. To the right is the **Templo Mayor,** the largest building on the site. When Cortés arrived, the Spaniards erected an altar to the Virgin on top of the temple, forcing Catholicism on the Totonacs. In front of the Templo Mayor is the **throne** where the king sat to observe the sacrifices. The throne also faces the temple known as **Las Chimeneas.** Moving toward the entrance of the site, you will see a fenced-in structure. For the Totonacs, this piece played a central role in the "New Five Ceremony," a five-day fast that took place every 52 years when a "century" of the ritual calendar ended. Every spring Equinox, people still come to the circle to expel negative energy and absorb positive energy.

LA ANTIGUA

Catch a second-class TRV bus from the Central, around the back of the ADO station (9.5 pesos). Tell your driver you want to get off at La Antigua and keep an eye out for your stop, marked by a tollbooth and a small sign. Cross the road and head up the dirt street on the other side which becomes the town's main drag. To return, walk back down the road and climb on the first form of public transportation headed to Veracruz. Buses pass frequently from dawn to 9pm. You can also catch a bus from the TRV station in town, but this involves more waiting than it's worth.

When Cortés landed on the coast of Mexico in 1519, he and his army moved north, settling in this town, the first Spanish town in Mexico. Cortés named the town Villa Rica de la Vera Cruz, but when the city was reestablished in 1599 in its present location 28km away, the old town came to be known as just that—La Antigua. Dotted with overgrown ruins from centuries past, a walk through the town is rather like entering a time warp, where buildings seem to range in age from the 10th to the 21st century.

Unlabeled streets and the jungle's tendency to interrupt all things orderly make finding the town's 10th-century buildings something of a scavenger hunt. Crossing the street and taking the perpendicular road branching left of the main road, you'll come to the **Parroquia de Cristo del Buen Viaje,** which dates from the mid-17th century; the interior contains two 16th-century baptismal fonts carved by early indigenous converts. Passing the *zócalo* and continuing down the street, the famous **Casa de Cortés,** where the *conquistador* supposedly lived for a time, is back from the road on the left. The canon was brought over from Spain by the man himself. Farther down the street, the monster tree that divides the road holds legendary status as the site where Cortés first donned his arms for his fateful 1519 expedition. Built in 1523, the **Edificio del Cabildo** was the first office of the Spanish government in Mexico. The most beautiful of the buildings is the **Emerito del Rosario.** Finished in 1524, the building features stations of the cross rendered in Talvera tile. To find these buildings, it's often best to ask locals to point the way.

After watching chickens scuttle in and out of the old buildings, the best thing to do in La Antigua is to take a *lancha* ride around the area. After experiencing the novelty of the long **suspension bridge** that spans the Río Antigua, head down toward the deserted beaches at the river's mouth, an hour downstream by *lancha* (30 pesos, 120 for a *lancha especial*). Though fishermen and impenetrable vegetation comprise most of the view, the cooling ride is worth the money.

CÓRDOBA ☎ 2

At just an hour and a half away from Veracruz, friendly and bustling Córdoba (pop. 200,000) feels like a rare breeze off the Gulf in comparison to the sultry and overwhelming state capital. When the Spanish founded Córdoba in 1618, they intended the city to serve as a defensive stronghold against anticipated slave rebellions at nearby sugarcane plantations. By 1821, the city had established itself instead as a place of compromise—in Córdoba's Casa Zevallos, the Treaty of Córdoba was signed, establishing Mexico's independence from Spain. Córdoba's residents seem to have a knack for bargaining and making deals; today the city is a key regional distribution center for fruit, coffee, and tobacco. In Mercado Revolución and in the city's chaotic streets, Córdobans bargain and trade, continuing the tradition of compliant cheerfulness that served them so well in the past.

VERACRUZ

TRANSPORTATION. All buses travel to **Cordinados Córdoba** (☎727 04 68), 3km from the *zócalo* along Av. 4. To get to the *zócalo*, **Plaza de Armas,** from the bus station, exit out of the right of the station and take a right-bound bus marked "Centro" from the bus stand. ADO has first-class service to: **Mexico City** (4½hr., 24 per day, 144 pesos); **Oaxaca** (6hr., 12:10am and 8:50am, 166 pesos); **Orizaba** (40 min., 19 per day, 10 pesos); **Palenque** (8½hr., 8:35pm, 295 pesos); **Puebla** (3hr., 14 per day, 88 pesos); **Tulum** (17½hr., 5:30pm, 542 pesos); **Tuxtepec** (3hr., 4:10pm, 60 pesos); **Tuxtla Gutiérrez** (11hr., 9:50pm and 10:25pm, 308 pesos); **Veracruz** (1½hr., 22 per day, 53 pesos); **Villahermosa** (5½hr., 5 per day, 232 pesos); and **Xalapa** (3hr., 10 per day, 65 pesos). Cristóbal Colón has similar first-class service to Mexico City, Oaxaca, Puebla, and Veracruz. Several other lines offer second-class service, including AU, which has slightly slower, 10-peso cheaper service to most ADO destinations.

ORIENTATION AND PRACTICAL INFORMATION. Córdoba is 125km southwest of Veracruz, along Rte. 150. The city is easy to navigate; numbered *avenidas* run northwest to southeast, with numbered *calles* crossing them at right angles. The *zócalo* is at the center, bounded by Calles 1 and 5 and Av. 1 and 3.

The **tourist office** (☎712 11 40) is under the *portales* in the Palacio Municipal, on the northwest side of the *zócalo*. **Casa de Cambio Puebla,** 117 Calle 2, between Av. 1 and 3, changes currency, as do many of the banks on the streets around the *zócalo*. **Iverlat,** on the corner of Av. 1 and Calle 3, and **Bital,** at Av. 1 and Calle 2, have 24hr. **ATMs** as well. **Lavandería Automatica Santa Maria,** at Av. 7 (☎712 67 58), provides **laundry** service. The **market** is bounded by Calles 7 and 9 and Av. 6 and 8. (Open daily 7am-10pm.) The bus station provides **luggage storage** (3 pesos per hr.) **Emergency:** ☎060. **Police:** (☎712 67 20 or 712 1027), in the Palacio Municipal. **Red Cross:** (☎712 03 00 or 712 00 90), at 710 Calle 9, between Av. 7 and 9. **Farmacías de Dios,** is at 510 Av. 1, between Calles 5 and 7. (☎712 00 64. Open 24hr.) **Hospital:** IMSS (☎714 38 00), on Av. 11 between Calles 1 and 2. **LADATELs:** located under the *portales* in the *zócalo*. **Internet Access: Cibermania Café-Internet,** 303 Av. 2 (☎712 88 35), between Calles 3 and 5, has an average connection. 10 pesos per hr. **Post Office:** at 303 Av. 3, one block southwest of the *zócalo*. (☎712 00 69. Open M-F 8am-4pm, Sa 9am-1pm.) **Postal Code:** 94500.

ACCOMMODATIONS AND FOOD. Córdoba's numerous cheap restaurants and budget hotels, located on Av. 2 between Calles 9 and 11, make it ideal for a one-night stopover. **Iberiam,** 919 Av. 2, is the best bargain; luxurious rooms feature TVs, phones, fans, reclining chairs, dark wood furnishings, and windows with a view of the courtyard garden. Lovers beware: sound travels through adjacent showers. (☎712 13 49. Singles 90 pesos; doubles 100 pesos.) For a cheap, no-frills stay, **Hotel Trescado** offers small, fairly clean rooms. (☎712 23 74. Singles 50 pesos, with TV 60 pesos; doubles 60 pesos, with TV 70 pesos.) If you can get past the ugly grey color at the **Hotel Regis,** at Av. 2, it's a fairly good deal. A slightly more pleasant peach tone brightens the walls of the rooms. (☎712 19 10. Singles 75 pesos; doubles 100 pesos.)

At **Casa de La Abuela** (☎712 06 06), on Calle 1 between Av. 2 and 4, meals are as well-prepared and cheap as they were two generations ago. Check out the family pictures on the wall as you munch on tacos (4 pesos), *antojitos* (6-17 pesos), and meat dishes (22-33 pesos). For *comida corrida* (15 pesos), try **Las Delicias** (☎714 86 51), on Av. 2 between Calles 5 and 7, where *antojitos* start at an all-time low of 2 pesos. **Restaurant Virreynal,** (☎712 23 77), part of the swanky hotel at the corner of Av. 1 and Calle 5, offers a classy, pricier experience. The austere decor enhances the flavor of the fish fillets (46 pesos) and meat entrees.

SIGHTS. Dominating the *zócalo*'s southeast side is the **Parroquia de la Inmaculada Concepción.** Constructed in 1621, the design of the church combines both Baroque and Neoclassical styles. Now the city's primary place of worship, the *parroquia* is distinctive not only for its mango-colored exterior, but also for its infamous bells, which can be heard for miles around. Located less obtrusely under the *portales* on the *zócalo*'s northeast side is the **Casa Zevallos**. For a meal with history, check out the restaurant inside the *casa*. Or try to slip past the watchdog at the entrance to see the plaque in the courtyard that commemorates the site where Juan O'Donojú, viceroy of Spain, and Augustín Iturbide, conservative rebel leader, agreed on the terms of Mexico's independence on August 24, 1821. To learn a bit more about the history of the town, cut across the *zócalo* and walk half a block down Calle 3 to #303, the site of the **Museo de la Ciudad de Córdoba.** Inside the 17th-century building are archaeological finds and historical documents.

ORIZABA ☎2

Huddled in a valley at the foot of Mexico's highest peak, the **Pico de Orizaba** (5747m), Orizaba (pop. 175,000) valiantly struggles to be seen from under the dormant volcano's shadow. Previously a center of sugarcane distribution, Orizaba is today an industrial city, manufacturing beer, cement, and cotton. The city's emphasis on labor has caused problems with the government. In 1906 President Porfirio Díaz ordered an unfavorable settlement to a worker's strike, causing Orizaba workers to riot in the streets. Their audacity resulted in their deaths, but also served to undermine the Porfiriato. Though far more tranquil today, Orizaba retains the working-class and industrial feel that it has possessed in times past.

■ TRANSPORTATION. The city's two bus services, ADO and AU, operate out of two different stations. To get to the *zócalo* from the **ADO station** (☎724 27 23), at Av. 6 Ote. 577, between Calles 11 and 13 Sur, exit left out of the station and walk to 3 Sur; cross the road and walk 3 blocks to the *zócalo*. ADO offers first-class service to: **Cancún** (19hr., 8:10pm, 597 pesos); **Córdoba** (40min., 28 per day, 10 pesos); **Mexico City** (4hr., 23 per day, 135 pesos); **Oaxaca** (6hr., 16 per day, 79 pesos); **Veracruz** (2hr., 22 per day, 62 pesos); and **Villahermosa** (7hr., 4 per day, 249 pesos). From the second-class **AU station** (☎725 19 79), at 8 Pte. 425 between Calles 5 and 7 Nte., exit left out of the station and over the bridge; take the first right and walk toward the yellow church towers of San Miguel. AU offers similar second-class service to Mexico City, Córdoba, Oaxaca, Puebla, Veracruz, and Villahermosa. To reach Orizaba from Córdoba, either take a bus from the station or hop on a westbound bus marked either "Orizaba" or "Autopista" (98 pesos) from the corner of Av. 11 and Calle 13; the bus will drop you along Av. 6 Ote. in Orizaba.

■▐ ORIENTATION AND PRACTICAL INFORMATION. Orizaba lies 16km west of Córdoba and just 25km northwest of Mexico's tallest mountain, **Pico de Orizaba.** Most points of interest are near **Parque Castillo,** bounded by Madero on the west, Colón on the south, 3 Sur on the east, and 3 Ote. on the north. Av. 6 Ote., 3 blocks south of the *zócalo*, is the main thoroughfare.

The **tourist office** is located in the Palacio Municipal, 2 blocks west of the *zócalo* at the intersection of Colón and Calle 7 Nte. Several banks south of the *zócalo* provide both **currency exchange** and 24 hr. **ATMs,** including **Banamex,** on the corner of Av. 2 Ote. and Madero, and **Serfín,** directly across from it. **Laundromat: Super Lavandería Orizaba,** at the corner of Calle 11 Sur and Av. 4 Ote. **Mercado Melchor Ocampo,** between Av. 5 and 7 Ote. and Madero and Calle 3 Sur, sells fruits, vegetables, meat, and clothing. **Luggage storage** is available at the ADO station (5 pesos per 3hr.). **Emergency:** ☎060. **Police:** (☎724 38 84), at the corner of Circunvalación Nte. and 5 Ote. **Red Cross:** at Colón Ote. 253, between Calles 5 and 7 Sur. (☎725 22 50 or 725 47 67. 24hr. ambulance service.) **Farmacías Covadonga** is at the corner of Calle 5 Sur and Av. 4 Ote. (☎725 74 33. Open 24hr.) **Hospital: IMSS,** at Gardenias. (☎726 30 69 or 725 85 51. 24hr. emergency care.) **LADATELs** are on the northwest side of the *zócalo*, just past the *parroquia.* **Internet Access: MultiComp,** Av. 4 Ote. 782. 8 pesos per hr. (☎724 52 72. Open daily 9am-10pm.) **Post office:** Av. 2 Ote. 282 (☎725 03 30), at the corner of Sur 7. **Postal Code:** 94300.

▚▛ ACCOMMODATIONS AND FOOD. Orizaba has several budget hotels, all centrally located. **Hotel San Cristóbal,** Calle 4 Nte. 243, between Av. 5 and 7 Ote., has simple, pleasant rooms with arched doorways and plenty of light. (☎725 11 40. Singles 60 pesos, with TV 90 pesos; doubles 85 pesos, with TV 115 pesos.) With its jungle-like courtyard and friendly, family-run service, **Hotel Arenas,** Calle 2 Nte. 169, between Av. 3 and 5 Ote., runs a close second to San Cristóbal. Rooms have TVs, colorful bedspreads, and ugly but clean bathrooms. (☎725 23 61. Singles 90 pesos; doubles 130-140 pesos.)

Although pricier than many, the *menú del día* at **La Hogaza,** Calle 4 Nte. between Av. 3 Ote. and Colón, includes specialty rabbit and fish dishes (35 pesos). The peach-colored walls and the fresh wildflowers on the tables make for a bright experience. (☎726 05 29. Open daily 8am-7:30pm.) For a fast, cheap meal, **Antojitos Mexicanos,** Calle 2 Nte. 174., offers—you guessed it—*antojitos. Taquitos de pollo* (3 pesos), *tortas* (6 pesos), and full-fledged meals of eggs, ham, tortillas, and refried beans (12 pesos) are among the specialties. (☎723 47 24. Open daily 8am-11pm.) **La Pergola,** with entrances on both Av. 4 and 6 Ote. at 7 Sur, offers large, reasonably priced portions. *Quesos fundidos* are 25 pesos, while meat entrees range from 25-50 pesos. (☎725 84 11. Open daily 7am-10pm.)

▨ SIGHTS. The ▨**Museo de Arte del Estado,** Av. 4 Ote. between Calles 25 and 27, is well worth a visit, although it is a bit of a trek from the *zócalo.* If you prefer riding to walking, take an eastbound bus from Av. 6 Ote. The museum is located in a 1776 colonial building that resembles a large, pink church; the entrance is in the back. Rooms inside hold works by Diego Rivera and contemporary *veracruzano* artists. Most other sites are closer to the *zócalo.* The **Parroquia de San Miguel** dominates the *zócalo's* northern side. 18th-century architecture meets 21st-century technology: TVs showing sermons are nestled among ornate gold furnishings. Just northwest of the *zócalo* is the grey-hued **former Palacio Municipal.** Prior to being the forner Palacio, the building was the Belgian pavilion at the 19th-century Paris International Exhibition. Today, it houses a small art gallery.

▟ DAYTRIPS FROM ORIZABA

CASCADA DE LA TROMPA DEL ELEFANTE

Catch an Estrella Roja bus from the corner of Av. 3 Ote. and 2 Nte. and tell the driver where you want to go (20min.). He should let you off on Calle Isabel la Católica; follow the street as it turns into a dirt road and curves left around a small blue church. Following signs for the Hotel Fiesta Cascada, continue on the road over the autopista and then around a curve to the right. To return, retrace your steps to the street and walk to the second street intersection, where buses pick up and return to the centro.

The Casada de la Trompa del Elefante offers scenic refuge from the city's busy streets. Upon arriving at the *cascada,* descend the city's famous **500 Escalones,** keeping an eye out for the waterfall, which will come into view on your right. Right around the 250th stair, the path becomes crumbling and slick in places, so continue with care. At the bottom of the stairs, the path splits; the left fork follows the rushing river for several kilometers, while the right fork crosses the river and continues past a power station up into the mountains. Soon after the station is a small swimming hole; bring your suit to cool off after your hike.

LOS TUXTLAS

Nestled in the moist foothills of southern Veracruz, the area known as Los Tuxtlas remains calm and relatively free of tourists. The area's three main towns—San Andrés Tuxtla, Santiago Tuxtla, and Catemaco—have distinct personalities. With quality cheap accommodations and transportation options, the fairly large town of **San Andrés** makes a good base from which to explore the foothills. The more touristed **Catemaco** is known for its *brujería* (witchcraft) and for its beautiful lagoon. With the Olmec site of Tres Zapotes 30 minutes away, **Santiago Tuxtla,** the smallest of the three, is primarily an archaeological draw.

SAN ANDRÉS TUXTLA   ☎ 2

Though San Andres Tuxtla doesn't have any particularly glaring attractions, this sensible town (pop. 125,000) is a great place to relax. Lodged between the lush lakeside resorts of Catemaco and the Olmec artifacts of Santiago, San Andrés is the relatively untouristed anchor that keeps the Sierra de los Tuxtlas peacefully down to earth. The town serves as a center for the tobacco and cattle industries, and offers a cache of budget hotels, an entertaining *zócalo* and some nearby natural attractions. As the transportation hub of the region, San Andrés serves as a good base from which to stage repeated daytrips.

TRANSPORTATION. Both the first and second class bus stations are on **Juárez,** which branches off of Rte. 180. To get to the center from either station, exit left out of the station and follow Juárez as it descends a steep hill, crosses a small stream, and gradually ascends to meet the cathedral at the north corner of the *zócalo.* The walk takes 15 minutes; taxis costs 9 pesos. Autotransportes Los Tuxtlas (☎942 14 62), based in the second-class station, sends **buses** to: **Catemaco** (20min., every 10min. 4:30am-6pm, 3 pesos); **Santiago Tuxtla** (20min., every 10min. 2:45am-6pm, 5 pesos); and **Veracruz** (3½hr., every 15min. 4:30am-6pm, 48.5 pesos). ADO (☎942 08 71), at the first-class station, serves: **Mexico City** (7½hr., 9:45pm, 10:30pm, and 11:10pm, 248 pesos); **Veracruz** (2½hr., 22 per day 12:20am-9:25pm, 59 pesos); and **Villahermosa** (5hr., 11 per day, 123 pesos). AU (☎942 09 84) goes to **Puebla** (6hr., 9:50pm, 172 pesos); **Veracruz** (2½hr., noon and 9:50pm, 53 pesos); and **Xalapa** (4hr., 9:50pm, 92 pesos). Cuenca covers **Tuxtepec** (3hr., 12 per day, 63 pesos).

ORIENTATION AND PRACTICAL INFORMATION. San Andrés is located midway between Catemaco and Santiago. Right before reaching the cathedral, Juárez passes by the **Palacio Municipal** on the right and intersects **Constitución** to the left and **Madero** to the right, in front of the Palacio Municipal.

Exchange money at **Bancomer,** half a block south of the *zócalo* on Madero (open M-F 9am-5pm, Sa 9am-1pm), or **Serfín,** at Carranza as it curves to intersect 16 de Septiembre. (☎942 11 00. Open M-F 9am-3pm, Sa 10am-2pm.) Both have 24-hour **ATMs. Mercado 5 de Febrero,** spills onto the streets several blocks from the *zócalo.* To get there, walk on Madero, turn right on Carranza and walk uphill. (Open daily 6am-10pm; food stands close at 6pm.) **Laundry: Lava Maac,** Hernández 75, at the intersection with Revolución. 8 pesos per kg. (☎942 09 26. Open M-Sa 8am-8pm.) **Police:** on Madero, in the Palacio Municipal. No English spoken. (☎942 02 35. Open 24hr.) **Red Cross:** Boca Negra 25, north of the *zócalo.* No English spoken. (☎942 05 00. Open 24hr.) **Farmacía Garysa,** Madero 3, in the "Canada" building left of the Palacio Municipal. (☎/fax 942 44 34. Open 24hr.) **Hospital Civil,** at the edge of town. (☎942 04 47. 24hr. ambulance service.) **LADATELs** are in the Palacio Municipal and across the street from the Hotel de los Pérez. **SAT Internet** is at the corner of Suárez and Argudín. (☎942 38 05. 15 pesos per hr. Open daily 9:30am-10:30pm.) **Internepolis,** three blocks down Suárez, is cheaper. (☎942 41 60. 10 pesos per hr. Open daily 8am-2am.) **Post office:** at La Fragua and 20 de Noviembre, one block from the *zócalo.* (☎942 01 89. Open M-F 8am-3pm.) **Postal code:** 95701.

ⅢⅢ ACCOMMODATIONS AND FOOD. San Andrés has great budget accommodations. Two of the best bargains are within spitting distance of each other on Suárez. To get there, walk left from the cathedral and turn right at the orange supermarket, continuing uphill past the movie theater. Many who stay at the cheap **Hotel Colonial,** Suárez 7, never want to leave. With mountain view balconies, ceiling fans, a comfortable lobby, and an upstairs *sala* perfect for hanging out, the only drawback might be the insects sharing your room. (☎942 05 52. Singles 40 pesos; doubles 80 pesos.) **Hotel Figueroa,** Suárez 10, across the street, has portable fans, slightly nicer rooms, no insects, and higher prices. (☎942 02 57. Singles 80 pesos; doubles 100 pesos; with TV 40 pesos more.) Those living in the A/C fast lane may upgrade to **Hotel Isabel,** at Madero 13, to the left of the Hotel Parque next to the *zócalo*. The large rooms include TV, but bathrooms could be cleaner. (☎942 16 17. Singles 140 pesos, with A/C 170 pesos; doubles 180 pesos, with A/C 210 pesos.)

Several sidewalk cafes on the *zócalo* serve breakfast and coffee and allow a pleasant view of small-town life. Famous for elegant cakes and pies, **Winni's Restaurant,** south of the *zócalo*, across from Hotel Isabel on Madero, also serves good food (*antojitos* 6-22 pesos) to the congregation of locals that gather to chat and smoke at its outdoor tables. (☎942 01 10. Open daily 8am-midnight.) Right next door, **La Surianita** cooks dirt-cheap, filling meals. *Antojitos* and egg dishes 10 pesos, meat entrees 25 pesos. (☎942 44 42. Open daily 8am-10:30pm.) The older and more affluent **Restaurant del Parque,** on the ground floor of the Hotel Parque on the *zócalo*, is slightly more expensive (*antojitos* 20 pesos) with a classier atmosphere and good coffee. (☎942 01 98. Open daily 7:30am-midnight.) Cheap, filling *comida corrida* (15 pesos) awaits at **El Pequeño Archie,** right on Suárez across from the movie theater. The non-stop stream of *telenovelas* is a good balm for the lonely traveler, as are the 15-peso *antojitos*. (☎942 47 96. Open M-Sa 8am-8pm.)

ⓈⅢ SIGHTS AND ENTERTAINMENT. Even non-smokers will be impressed by the **Fábrica Tabacos San Andrés** (☎942 12 00), where Santa Clara cigars are made. From the *zócalo*, walk up Juárez to the ADO terminal and right around the corner; continue about 200m down the street past the entrance to the bus parking lot. The management welcomes visitors, and, if you're polite, someone from the amiable staff will walk you through the entire process. The store near the entrance sells the final product. Bottom of the line cigars are affordable (105 pesos and up), but a box (25) of their finest *puros* goes for much more (1000 pesos). Note that customs regulations may limit the number of cigars you can take back into your country.

The sheer number of video rental stores says it all: San Andrés is not a town that parties until dawn. Most of the action centers in the *zócalo*, where folks gather to meet, gossip, see, and be seen. **Café de la Catedral,** to the right of the Singer store on the north side of the *zócalo*, used to be a coffee shop but now functions as the town's most popular bar, filling around 11pm and emptying only when daylight falls. **Cinemas San Andrés,** on Pino Suárez across from El Pequeño Archie, shows American movies. (☎942 42 50. 15 pesos.)

SANTIAGO TUXTLA   ☎ 2

Of the three Los Tuxtla cities, Santiago (pop. 50,000) has the least to offer visitors in terms of sights and recreational activities. Its main attraction is its close connection to the Olmec ceremonial center of Tres Zapotes.

Ⅲ TRANSPORTATION. The ADO bus station, like everything else in Santiago, is just a few blocks from the *zócalo*. To reach the town center, walk downhill from Rte. 180 where the bus drops you. ADO (☎947 04 38) sends buses to: **Mexico City** (7hr., 30 per day, 242 pesos); and **Xalapa** (4½hr., 5 per day, 98 pesos). Autotransportes Los Tuxtlas buses leave from next to the ADO station for: **Catemaco**

(40min., every 10min. 4:30am-7pm, 10 pesos); and **San Andrés** (20min., every 10min. 4:30am-7pm, 5 pesos). To get to other surrounding towns, take the taxi *colectivos* that leave a block from the *zócalo* on the side of the market.

⚑ PRACTICAL INFORMATION. Inverlat, on the corner of the Palacio Municipal, has a 24hr. **ATM.** The **Mercado Municipal Morelos** begins on the *zócalo* and continues one block downhill. (Open daily 5am-7pm.) **Police:** downstairs in the Palacio Municipal. (☎947 00 92. Open 24hr.) **Red Cross:** the nearest is in San Andrés; 24hr. ambulance service (☎942 05 00). **Super Farmacía Roma:** 5 de Mayo just off the *zócalo.* (☎947 09 99. Open daily M-Sa 8:30am-9pm, Su 8:30am-3pm.) **Clínica Doctores Castellanos,** across from the Hotel Castellanos. (☎947 02 60. Open daily 8am to 8pm.) **Ladatels** are located across from Hotel Castellanos and in front of Palacio Municipal. **Post office:** on the right side of the yellow building across the *zócalo* from the Palacio Municipal. (Open M-F 9am-4pm.) **Postal code:** 95830.

▥▨ ACCOMMODATIONS AND FOOD. Built in the early 80s in a feeble government attempt to get Santiago's tourist industry ticking, **Hotel Castellanos,** at the far corner of the *zócalo* on the corner of 5 de Mayo and Comonfort, is not only a place to stay but is Santiago's most interesting attraction. The rooms fit together like slices of a pie; each offers A/C, phone, color TV, and a balcony. (☎947 03 00. Singles 207 pesos; doubles 230 pesos.) Grub in Santiago is cheap, and sometimes is just that—grub. During the rainy season, small, winged insects seek refuge inside the *zócalo's* streetlamps. In the morning, the bugs are captured, de-winged, and sauteed with salsa to make the region's favorite taco filling. This and more normal food abound in the *mercado.*

▣▧ SIGHTS AND SEASONAL EVENTS. The largest Olmec head ever discovered (45 tons) sits complacently at the far end of Santiago's *zócalo,* shaded from the sun by a large cupola. The **Cobata head,** named for the place of its discovery, is distinctive not only for its size but also because its eyes are closed. The **Museo Regional Tuxteco,** to the left of the head, displays an Olmec head discovered at Tres Zapotes and other Olmec and Totonac artifacts from around the region. (☎947 01 96. Open M-Sa 9am-6pm. 22 pesos, Su free.) Celebrations for the **fair** in honor of Santiago's namesake patron saint take place July 20-29 and include a choreographed fight between Christians and Moors and a *torneo de cintas* with men dressed in medieval gear riding horses.

NEAR SANTIAGO: TRES ZAPOTES

Exit right from the Museo Regional Tuxteco in Santiago, and take a right on Zaragoza. Walk two blocks to a T-intersection and cross the footbridge across the street to Morelos. From there, take a taxi colectivo to Tres Zapotes (30min., 12 pesos). Upon exiting, turn left and walk to the T-intersection. Take another left and walk to the first cross-street. Turn left and walk around the chain-link fence until you see the entrance on your right. Buses marked "Tres Zapotes" also pass through this stop, and, while cheaper, they are also slower (8 pesos). Open daily 9am-6pm. 17 pesos, Su free.

Half an hour's ride from Santiago through small tobacco-growing towns is the site of Tres Zapotes. Along with San Lorenzo and La Venta, Tres Zapotes was a chief Olmec ceremonial center, peaking between 300 BC and AD 300, though evidence indicates that the area may have been occupied as early as 900 BC. Though the site itself remains largely unexcavated, artifacts can be seen in the town's small museum. Most impressive is the museum's large Olmec stone head. The first of the dozen or so Olmec heads ever found, it was discovered in 1862 by a *campesino* who first thought it was an overturned cooking pot. To the left of the head is **Stela C,** which, together with its more famous upper half (now at the Museo Nacional de Antropología in Mexico City; see **Mexico City: Sights,** p. 112), bears the oldest written date in the Americas—31 BC— inscribed in late Olmec, or Spi-Olmec, glyphs similar to those later used by the

Maya. The date is depicted as a bar (representing "5") and two dots, totaling seven on the Olmec calendar. **Stela A** lies in the trancept to the left. Decorations on the stela include an Olmec face, a man holding an axe, and a serpent coiling in upon itself. **Stela D,** to the right of the head depicts four people whose relative heights symbolize their power and importance.

NEAR SANTIAGO: CASCADA DEL SALTO DE EYIPANTLA

To get there, take a micro labeled "El Salto" from the west side of the market (30min., 3.5 pesos). The micro drops off and picks up at the entrance to the falls; last bus back leaves at 8:15pm. 5 pesos.

Although a bit touristy, with market stands and eating areas, the beautiful *cascada* is impressive for its girth and force. At 40m across and 50m high, the Salto soaks viewers who stand at the end of the path, which is close enough to the falls to nearly be a part of them. And it's a good thing—after huffing down 262 stairs to see the falls, most visitors are by that time ready for a heavy misting.

CATEMACO   ☎2

In most parts of the world, Catemaco (pop. 51,000) would be covered with rangers, regulations, and well-marked trails. In Mexico, the only people to disturb your pastoral reverie are the *lanchistas* who stumble over each other for the opportunity to ferry you around the **Laguna Catemaco,** a tranquil lagoon surrounded by rolling hills and crowned with vivid green foliage. Exciting transportation options continue on land, where locals and visitors alike hang out of the back of grungy pick-up trucks (called *piratas*), which travel at breakneck speed over bumpy country roads toward the ocean. Fairly quiet in the off-season, Catemaco picks up during *Semana Santa* and the week of the town's patron saint, Saint Carmen, when hotels fill with *gringos* and urbanites from Mexico City who come to enjoy the regional food and the town's much-hyped *brujería* (witchcraft).

▙ TRANSPORTATION. Catemaco lies along **Rte. 180** and is a frequent bus stop. From the **Autotransportes Los Tuxtlas,** the 2nd class stop, turn right and follow the curve of the road, past the "Bienvenidos a Catemaco" arches. Follow a straight path for 10-15 minutes until you arrive at the spires of the *basílica.* Autotransportes Los Tuxtlas goes to: **San Andrés** (20min., every 20min. 2am-7pm, 3 pesos), as well as other regional destinations. The **ADO** (1st class) station is on the *malecón,* along the waterfront. To get there from the church, take a right onto the street and follow it for several blocks until you reach Hotel Julita and then take a right. ADO (☎943 08 42) goes to: **Mexico City** (9hr., 10pm, 252 pesos); **Puebla** (6hr., 10pm, 196 pesos); **Veracruz** (3hr., 6 per day 5:30am-5pm, 64 pesos); and **Xalapa** (3hr., 4 per day 6:15am-5pm, 108 pesos). AU (☎943 07 77) goes to: **Mexico City** (9hr.; 11:30am and 9pm, 226 pesos) and **Veracruz** (20min., 11:30am and 9:15pm, 57 pesos).

▉█ ORIENTATION AND PRACTICAL INFORMATION. Streets are poorly marked, but the *basílica* on the *zócalo* is usually visible. Using the *basílica* as a reference point, **Carranza** is the street to the left that runs past the Palacio Municipal. Straight ahead, the road becomes **Aldama.** One block downhill to the right is **Playa** and then the **malecón,** which follows the curve of the beach.

The **tourist office,** in the Palacio, offers maps of *pirata* routes, brochures, and helpful, although somewhat limited advice. (☎943 00 16. Open M-F 9am-3pm.) **Currency exchange: Bancomer,** across Aldama from the *basílica,* also has 24hr. ATMs (☎943 03 17. Open M-F 9am-1:30pm.) **Market:** on Madero before the *zócalo.* (Open daily 6am-7pm.) **Police:** (☎943 00 55) are in the Palacio Municipal on the *zócalo.* No English spoken. **Farmacía Nuestra Señora del Carmen,** at the corner of Carranza and Boettinger. (☎943 00 91. Open daily 7am-9pm.) **Centro de Salud,** on Carranza, in a white building with a blue roof, three blocks up from the *zócalo* on the left. Some English spoken. (☎943 02 47. Open 24hr.) **LADATELs** line the Palacio; long-distance **casetas** are on the right-hand side of the entrance to the Palacio. **Internet: PC Center,** Calle Matamoros 3, in a white and blue building five blocks up from the *zócalo* on the right. (☎943 01 70; www.gorsa.net.mx. Open M-Sa 9am-9pm.) **Post office:** on Aldama, 2 blocks past the *basílica* on the right. **Postal code:** 95870.

ACCOMMODATIONS AND FOOD. Most hotels cluster around the *zócalo* and the waterfront. During Christmas, *Semana Santa*, and most of July, hotels fill up quickly, and prices usually rise 20-30 pesos. Unfortunately, due to crime, it is not advisable to camp on the beaches. The **Hotel Julita,** Playa 10, one block downhill from the *zócalo*, is a good deal, blessed with a kindly owner, an unbeatable location, and large rooms with fans. (☎943 00 08. Singles 60 pesos; doubles 120 pesos.) **Hotel Acuario,** at Boettinger and Carranza, across from the Palacio, provides large, relatively clean rooms with 70s curtains; some have balconies. (☎943 04 18. Singles 85 pesos; doubles 145 pesos.)

Lake views differ more than menu choices in Catemaco's waterfront restaurants. The fish *mojarra* and *topote* are endemic to the lagoon, as are *tegogolos*, the famous Catemaco sea snails. *Mojarra* is prepared in a variety of ways, while the bite-sized *topote* is fried up whole and often heaped with *tamales*. Amazing *mojarra* can be had at **Los Sauces,** a modestly priced restaurant on the *malecón* at Rayon, three blocks east of Carranza. The restaurant also offers *topotes* (15 pesos), and a nice lakeside view. (☎943 05 48. Open daily 8am-8:30pm.) **El Pescador,** on the *malecón* at Bravo, offers similar flavors, fares, and views. *Mojarra* 40-50 pesos; *topotes* 12 pesos. (☎943 07 05. Open daily 9am-8:30pm.) If something classier is in order, head to **La Casona del Recuerdo,** across the *zócalo* on Aldama. A haven from the lurking *lanchistas*, the terrace overlooks a peaceful wooded garden. The *tegogolos* (25 pesos) are safe to try. (☎943 08 22. Open daily 8am-8pm.)

SIGHTS. The rocky beaches of **Laguna Catemaco** don't resemble Cancún, but a dip in the lake can be a refreshing break from the hot Veracruz sun. The water immediately in front of town is not safe for swimming, but a hiking path runs along the edge of the lake—walk down from the *zócalo* to the waterfront and turn left. The trail will guide you 1.5km to **Playa Expagoya** and then another half km to the more secluded and sandy **Playa Hermosa,** the first swimmable beach on the trail. The path is not safe at night. It's also possible to swim off a *lancha* in the deeper and sometimes clearer waters in the middle of the lake.

One of the best ways to see Catemaco's sights is to take one of the *lancha* tours, which depart from the shore of the lagoon down the hill from the *zócalo* (standard tour 250 pesos per boat, 40 pesos per person on a *lancha colectiva*). Of the several small islands that dot the surface of the 9km-wide lake, **Isla de los Changos** is the most popular for *lancha* tours. A group of wild, red-cheeked *changos* (mandrills, a kind of baboon) was brought from Thailand for a scientific experiment by the University of Veracruz in 1979; the scientists wanted to see if the animals could survive in their new environment. Lo and behold, 21 years later the *changos* are alive, well-fed, and posing for snapshots. En route to the island, you'll pass a cave-shrine that stands on the spot where Juan Catemaco, a local fisherman, had a vision of the Virgin Mary over a century ago. The town is named for him, and his statue, poised elegantly at the tip of the lagoon, overlooks the calm waters. Negotiate with the *lanchistas* for longer trips, including an exploration of the rivers that feed the lake or a trip to the tropical forests of the nearby national park.

ENTERTAINMENT AND FESTIVALS. Catemaco's **bars** and **discos** are the best in the Tuxtlas, although nightlife only really heats up during the high tourist seasons. Many bars and clubs shut down or operate irregularly in the off-season. The road along the beach dominates nightlife in Catemaco. Four blocks from the Hotel Julita and one block away from the water on Madero is **Jahac 45,** a video bar and disco that sometimes sponsors concerts by locals bands and remains open faithfully during the off-season. (☎943 08 50. Cover 25 pesos. Open Sa-Su 10pm-4am.) To experience the witching hour, head to **7 Brujas,** another video-bar on the *malecón* near the corner of Playa. (☎943 01 57. Open Tu-Su 8am-3am.) **Chanequa's** (☎943 00 42 or 943 00 01), a video-bar in the Hotel Playa Azul, caters to the chic hotel crowd. Walking there at night is dangerous; a taxi will take you for 25 pesos. Catemaco's major secular celebration, **Day of the Fisherman,** occurs on May 30th, when a procession of manually-powered *lanchas* parade across the lagoon and locals compete in a fishing tournament. The town also celebrates the day of its patron saint, **Saint Carmen,** on July 16.

NEAR CATEMACO: THE GULF COAST

Public transportation is limited to Transportes Rurales's pick-up trucks, called piratas *by locals. Piratas depart from the eastern edge of town. To get there from the zócalo, cross Carranza, keeping the Palacio Municipal on your left, and walk six blocks, turning right onto Lerdo. From there, walk five more blocks until you pass the last restaurant. Turn left and walk until the intersection of a paved road. A taxi will take you for 10 pesos. Just outside of town the road forks into two main routes. One heads north to Montepío on the Gulf Coast and the other goes east to Coyame on the opposite side of Lake Catemaco. Piratas are scheduled to depart for both routes (every 50min. 6am-7pm), but they only leave when enough passengers have gathered.*

Some say the only reason to go to Catemaco is for its proximity to secluded beaches on the Gulf Coast. Here you will find hiking, fishing, posh spas, rare wildlife, and, of course, mile upon mile of gorgeous beach.

CATEMACO TO MONTEPÍO. On the way to Montepío is **Sontecomapán** (18km from Catemaco), a small town beside a saltwater lake that empties into the Gulf. *Lanchas* are available for excursions on the lake and down the coast (250 pesos per boat; 40 pesos per person on a *colectivo*). Just to the left of the *lanchas* is the **Pozo de los Enanos** (Pond of the Midgets), a fresh pond so clear that an optical illusion makes you appear half your size when you look into it. The next stop is **La Barra,** a fishing community where Laguna Sontecomapán empties into the Gulf. Take a *lancha* or *pirata* 8km beyond Sontecomapán until the road forks. Your *pirata* will normally follow the left fork; negotiate with the driver to take the right fork or hop off and hike the 5-6km to La Barra yourself. If you want to reach Playa Jicacal and Playa Escondida, you will have to ask the *lancha* driver to let you off and then walk 30min. to the stony, empty **Playa Jicacal.** The pink *cabañas* of **Hotel Icacos,** near the entrance to the beach, contain two large beds, a fan, and little else. (☎942 05 56. *Cabaña* singles 120 pesos; doubles 150 pesos.) Instead of turning right to Playa Jicacal, you can walk uphill 10 minutes to the left to **Playa Escondida** and the simple, white **Hotel Playa Escondida.** (☎942 30 61 in San Andrés. Singles and doubles 200 pesos.) This beach offers the safest camping in the area; access is available through the hotel (25 pesos). Access to the beach for non-guests 10 pesos. Visitors who want a secluded beach without the walk through the jungle can have the *pirata* drop them off at the next stop, **Balzapote.** Farther down the road is a **biological research station** operated by the University of Veracruz. The young scientists can show you the surrounding wildlife. The *pirata* route ends on a bluff overlooking the beach of **Montepío,** also home to a small fishing town (2hr. from Catemaco). Susana Valencia Contreraz, the proprietor of **Loncheria Susi** offers rooms come with private bath. (Singles 40 pesos; doubles 80 pesos.) More expensive and more luxurious is the new **Hotel Posada San José,** on the bank of the small river leading to the beach. (☎942 10 10 or 942 20 20 in San Andrés. Singles 200 pesos; doubles 240 pesos.) Beaches aside, the big attraction in Montepío is the **cascadas** up from the beach. The best way to reach the falls is with a guide; you can find one at the driveway to Posada San José. Most people go by horse, taking the guided trip to the **Cascadas de Revolución,** inland and midway down the beach (80 pesos). Excursions to the other *cascadas* can be arranged, or you can rent the horse and try to find them yourself (30 pesos per hr., 40 pesos with guide).

CATEMACO TO COYAME. Alternatively, *piratas* head to Coyame (13km east of Catemaco), the underground springs that give birth to the soft drink "Coyame." Seven km toward Coyame is the **Proyecto Ecológico Educacional Nanciyaga**, or simply **Nanciyaga** (☎943 01 99; 3 pesos in *pirata*). From the road, turn right and walk in front of the "Nanciyaga" sign on a dirt path that leads toward the shore of the lake. *Lanchas* (40 pesos) or taxis (25 pesos) will also take you to Nanciyaga. To return to Catemaco, walk back to the road, cross the street, and flag down any *pirata* headed back to town; note that they usually only pass about once per hour. The "ecological educational park" is more like a spa than anything else. Guests stay overnight in candle-lit bungalows and enjoy the Olmec *temascal* sweat lodge, the full-body mud baths, the open-air concerts, and the boat tours of the lake (250 pesos). **Playa Hermosa** is another 8km down the beach from Montepío. Up a dirt road from the beach and past some buildings, is the **Cascada Cocoliso.** Turn right after the beer stand and follow the road to its conclusion. If you're too tired to walk back and no *colectivos* seem to be leaving from the docks, you can hire a private *lancha* (120 pesos). The Coyame area makes for good hikes, although no tourist facilities exist. A good route begins from the town of **Tebanca**, near Coyame. By following cattle paths and the educated guesses of ranchers, you can explore the **Cerro los Cumbres Bastonal,** a 4½hr. hike. During the summer, however, the paths are often covered in water. If you start early, you can climb the Bastonal and return in time to catch the last *pirata* back to Catemaco at 7pm.

ACAYUCAN ☎9

At the junction of Highway 180 (which runs between Veracruz and Villahermosa) and Highway 185 (which crosses the Isthmus of Tehuantepec), lies Acayucan (pop. 100,000), a major transportation hub for the southern part of the state. Although the city contains no noteworthy sites, its location, bus terminal, and budget hotel and food options make it a key stopover point.

⊏ TRANSPORTATION. Acayucan's bus terminal (☎245 11 42), on Acuña in Barrio Tamarindo, is on the eastern edge of the city. To get to the *zócalo*, exit right out of the station and walk straight to the town's main street, Hidalgo. Either turn left and walk straight for 10min. to reach the *centro*, or catch a westbound "Centro" *colectivo* (3 pesos). ADO goes to: **Mexico City** (7hr., 9 per day, 290 pesos); **Oaxaca** (4.5hr., 12:50am, 2pm, and 11:50pm, 162 pesos); **Palenque** (6hr., 4 per day, 233 pesos); **San Andrés Tuxtla** (2hr., 8 per day, 34 pesos); **San Cristóbal de las Casas** (10hr., 3am, 213 pesos); **Veracruz** (3½hr., 19 per day, 108 pesos); **Villahermosa** (4hr., 15 per day, 90 pesos); and **Xalapa** (6hr., 7 per day, 149 pesos). Cristóbal Colón and AU offer similar service. Sur provides second-class service to many regional destinations. *Urbanos* line up on the street outside of the terminal; they travel to regional destinations.

⑦ PRACTICAL INFORMATION. Bital and Serfín, side-by-side on the corner of Victoria and Zaragoza on the plaza's south side, provide **currency exchange** and have 24hr. **ATMs.** (Open M-Sa 8am-5pm.) **Emergency:** ☎060. **Police:** (☎245 10 78), station outside of the city. **Red Cross:** south of the *zócalo* on Ocampo Sur 4, between Victoria and Negrete. Some English spoken. (☎245 00 28. 24hr. ambulance service.) **Internet Acayucan** (☎245 12 70), a block north of the *zócalo*, off Pipla at Guerrero Pte. 24. Open daily 9am-9pm. **Post office:** a block north on Moctezuma, then left on Guerrero. (☎245 00 88. Open M-Sa 8am-4pm.) **Postal Code:** 96001.

⌐⊡ ACCOMMODATIONS AND FOOD. Budget hotels and restaurants center around the *zócalo*. **Hotel Ancira,** Bravo 2, just south off Victoria on the *zócalo*, has large, clean rooms with fans. (☎245 00 48. Rooms 75-130 pesos.) More upscale is

Hotel Jesymar, Moctezuma 206, 1 block north of the *zócalo*. Rooms have TVs, fans, and phones; ask for one with new bathrooms fixtures (☎245 02 61. 120-150 pesos.) For quick and inexpensive *tortas* (13 pesos) and tacos (2.5 pesos), try **Obélix** (☎245 01 41), along the *zócalo* on Victoria.

NEAR ACAYUCAN: SAN LORENZO TENOCHTITLÁN

From the mercado in Acayucan, go to the line of regional buses and ask for one going to "Texistepec" (sometimes labeled just "Texi") which will bring you to the town's bus depot (30min., 6.5 pesos). From Texistepec, catch a blue "Villa Alta" urbano, which drops off in both Tenochtitlán (45min., 10 pesos) and Zona Azuzul (1¼hr., 17 pesos). Buses leave at 8am, 10am, 2pm, 3pm, and 5pm; last bus from Zona Azuzul back to Texistepec leaves at approximately 5:15pm. Taxis can be taken to the two sites (70 pesos and 120 pesos); if enough can be rounded up to go colectivo, fares are 14 and 21 pesos, respectively.

A pilgrimage best reserved for archaeology buffs, reaching the Olmec remains of San Lorenzo is a labor of love. San Lorenzo Tenochtitlán is the collective name given to the three Olmec sites of San Lorenzo, Tenochtitlán, and Zona Azuzul. Of these three centers, San Lorenzo is thought to have been the largest and oldest, flourishing between 1200 and 900BC. Among the Olmec artifacts unearthed here are the earliest known ball player figurines, as well as various other figurines of serpentine and jadeite. Though many of the artifacts found in the initial 1947 excavations have been relocated to museums elsewhere, finds from excavations in 1994 have remained in the area and strengthened the local collection. Today, the largest collection is in **Tenochtitlán,** where an assortment of artifacts are displayed under a protective shelter near the town's main dirt road. The collection includes a giant Olmec stone head, the only one of the 10 heads found at the three sites to remain in the area. (Open daily. Free.)

About 5km farther down the main dirt road lies the microscopic town of San Lorenzo. Several kilometers from the town are the actual ruins of **San Lorenzo,** but little remains to be seen of the site. Approximately 3km past San Lorenzo is the third original Olmec ceremonial center, **Zona Azuzul.** Two small shelters atop the hill house the modest but remarkably well-preserved collection. The first hut holds four stone statues, two depicting kneeling human forms and two depicting jaguar forms. The second hut has larger jaguar figure. These make evident the pre-Hispanic obsession with the jaguar, which began with the Olmecs but later spread to the other civilizations. (Site open daily 8am-6pm. Free except for a good tip for the site's caretaker.)

TABASCO AND CHIAPAS

Tabasco, Chiapas' neighbor to the north, is often overlooked in favor of its more glamorous neighbors. But while Tabasco lacks the party attitude of Veracruz, the turquoise beaches of the Yucatán Peninsula, and the *indígena* tradition of Chiapas, the state has plenty to offer its visitors. Dotted with lakes and swamps, criss-crossed by rivers, and swathed in dense jungle, Tabasco (which means "Damp Earth") possesses natural beauty. Beaches, most of them untouristed, line its northern side, and the southern and eastern sides team with parks and nature sanctuaries. Once in the heartland of Olmec territory, Tabasco also offers a precious glimpse into its mother culture. The ruins of La Venta have been made incredibly accessible; visitors must only travel to **Parque-Museo La Venta** to experience the artifacts as they were in their original environment. Its capital, the city of Villahermosa, rises from the center of the steamy jungle, struggling to retain its colonial identity in the midst of a modern growth spurt. While the city deserves attention for its sights and natural beauty, happy (and dry) is the well-prepared tourist: the weather behaves like clockwork–be prepared for the showers every afternoon during the rainy season (June-Sept.).

For centuries, **Chiapas** has been known for its environmental diversity—its cloud-enveloped heights provide a stark contrast to the dense, lowland rainforest. Cortés must have had the Sierra de Chiapas in mind when he crumpled a piece of parchment and dropped it on a table to demonstrate what Mexico looked like. One of Mexico's most beautiful cities, San Cristóbal de las Casas, known for its cobblestone streets and surrounding *indígena* villages, rests high amid these peaks. Throughout the state, you will hear diverse Mayan dialects and find markets and other public places filled with *indígenas*. Indeed, the state is part of the Maya heartland; the Lacandón Rainforest shields the remote ruins of Bonampak and Yaxchilán and is still home to the Lacandón Maya, whose isolation has kept them from both the Spanish and the tourist invasions. Chiapas's *indígenas* remain fiercely traditional—in many communities, schools teach in the local dialect as well as in Spanish, and regional dress is almost always maintained. The EZLN rebellion of 1994 succeeded in drawing the world's attention to the central Mexican government's lack of attention to the needs and rights of the highland region's poor indigenous villages.

HIGHLIGHTS OF TABASCO AND CHIAPAS

GULP the thin air of the mountaintop city **San Cristóbal de las Casas** (see p. 545). The reason many people come to Mexico, it is inevitably a good visit.

SKIP the town of **Palenque** (see p. 555) and head straight to the startling **jungle ruins** (see p. 559), set amidst a dense backdrop of beautiful falls, foliage, and wildlife.

TIPTOE through the indigenous villages near **San Cristóbal** (see p. 545), especially the community of **San Juan Chamula** (see p. 551) and its famous **church**, host to a fascinating syncretic religious ritual involving **burping.**

TREK through the jungle to the neighboring archaeological sites of **Yaxchilán** (see p. 560) and **Bonampak** (see p. 562)–they house some of the most well-preserved Maya ruins in the country.

DROOL in amazement at the spectacular way to view Olmec artifacts in **Villahermosa's Parque-Museo La Venta** (see p. 532).

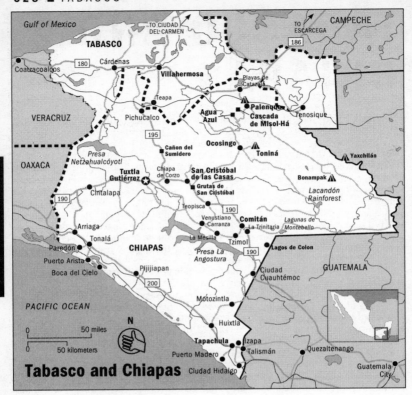

Tabasco and Chiapas

TABASCO

VILLAHERMOSA ☎ 9

Contrary to its name, Villahermosa (pop. 1.6 million) is neither a *villa* (small village), nor is it *hermosa* (beautiful). The capital of the state of Tabasco is actually a sprawling metropolis whose recent growth has been driven by rich oil discoveries and a strategic location along the Río Grijalva, one of the few navigable rivers in the Republic. Founded in 1519 as Santa María de la Victoria by Hernán Cortés, the city was an agricultural center of minor importance accessible only by river. In the past 50 years, oil-spurred growth has given the ailing city a shot in the arm, transforming Villahermosa from boondocks to boomtown and creating a dense urban forest of satellite antennae, luxury hotels, and apartment complexes. It is Villahermosa's proximity to the Palenque ruins and its position as a crossroads between Chiapas and the Yucatán that make it a common stopover for travelers. The city also offers museums and sights that make longer stays worthwhile.

◨ TRANSPORTATION

Airport: (☎356 01 56), on the Villahermosa-Macupana Highway, 14km from downtown. Taxis shuttle between the airport and the *centro* (40 pesos *especial*, 15 pesos *colectivo*). Most major airlines have offices in Tabasco 2000, including: **Aeroméxico,** Cámara 511, Locale 2 (☎01 800 021 40 00); **Aviacsa,** Via 3, #120 Locale 10 (☎316 57 33); **Aerocaribe,** Via 3, #120 Locale 9 (☎316 50 47); **Mexicana,** Via 3, #120 Locale 5-6D (☎316 31 32).

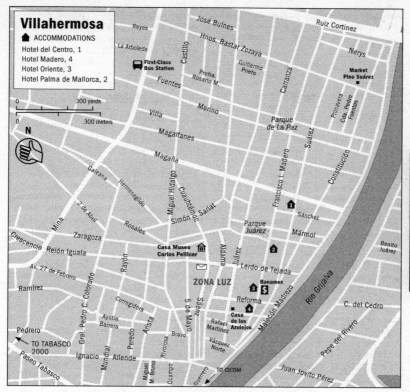

Villahermosa

🏠 ACCOMMODATIONS
Hotel del Centro, 1
Hotel Madero, 4
Hotel Oriente, 3
Hotel Palma de Mallorca, 2

Buses: The 1st-class terminal is on Mina at Merino. To reach downtown from the **1st-class ADO station,** walk 2½ blocks to your right on Mina to Méndez. From there, take a *combi* labeled "Pqe. Juárez" and get off a few minutes later at **Parque Juárez.** Most hotels are south of the park on either **Madero** or the parallel **Constitución.** Walking from the station to Parque Juárez takes 15-20min. Upon exiting the terminal, head right down Mina for eight blocks, then turn left onto 27 de Febrero. Eight more blocks take you to the intersection with Madero. ADO (☎312 89 00) runs to: **Acayucan** (4hr., 17 per day 1am-10:30pm, 90 pesos); **Campeche** (5hr., 12 per day, 169 pesos); **Orizaba** (7hr., 4 per day, 249 pesos); **San Cristóbal de Las Casas** (6hr., 7:35am, 124 pesos); **Cancún** (11hr., 8 per day, 348 pesos); **Jalapa** (9hr., 5 per day, 239 pesos); **Mexico City** (11hr., 20 per day, 376 pesos); **Oaxaca** (11hr.; 6, 7:55, and 9:25pm; 276 pesos); **Palenque** (2hr., 11 per day 3am-7:40pm, 56 pesos); **Puebla** (8hr., 4 per day, 320 pesos); **San Andrés Tuxtla** (4hr., 9 per day, 123 pesos); and **Veracruz** (7hr., 16 per day, 182 pesos). Also serving the station are Cristóbal Colón, TRT, and Sur; Servicios Altos offers buses to **Tuxtla Gutiérrez** (6½hr., 6 per day, 100 pesos). To get downtown from the **2nd-class bus terminal,** located on Ruiz Cortines (☎312 10 91) 2 blocks left of Mina, cross Grijalva on the pedestrian bridge to the left of the station exit, then jump on a bus labeled "Indeco Centro" (3.5 pesos) and disembark at Parque Juárez on Madero. To make the walk from the station (25min.), cross the bridge and continue south on Mina for three blocks until you reach the ADO station (see above). A cab ride to the center of town costs 12 pesos. This terminal offers service to many regional destinations.

⚡🛈 ORIENTATION AND PRACTICAL INFORMATION

Villahermosa is 20km from the border with Chiapas and 298km west of Escárcega. The spine of the downtown area is **27 de Febrero**. The **Zona Luz**, the city's pedestrian-only downtown area, is bordered by 5 de Mayo, Zaragoza, Madero, and 27 de Febrero. Paseo Tabasco runs north-south and connects the Tabasco 2000 complex to the *centro*, intersecting 27 de Febrero in front of the cathedral. *Saetas* (public buses) and *combis* (each 3.5 pesos) run from 6am to 10:30pm.

TOURIST AND FINANCIAL SERVICES

Tourist Office: In **Tabasco 2000**, de los Ríos 113 (☎316 36 33 or 316 28 89), diagonally behind the Palacio Municipal. Their glossy brochures come at a price. Open M-F 9am-3pm and 6-9pm, Sa 9am-1pm. Booths are located at the entrances of **Parque Museo la Venta** (open daily 8am-4pm), the **ADO station** (open daily 7am-11pm, though someone is not always at the booth), and the **airport**.

Currency Exchange: Banks are plentiful in the *Zona Luz* and along Paseo Tabasco. **Banamex,** on Madero at Reforma, has 24hr. **ATMs.** Open for exchange M-F 9am-5pm, Sa 9:30am-2pm. **BITAL** has three 24hr. **ATMs** at the corner of Lerdo and Juárez. Open M-Sa 8am-5pm.

American Express: Paseo Zabarco 715 (☎315 39 99 or 315 39 88), in the office of Turismo Creativo. Open M-F 9am-6pm.

Radio Taxi: (☎315 82 33 or 315 23 39). On call 24hr.

Car Rental: Budget, Zaragoza 301 (☎312 26 00 or 312 06 76). **Renta de Autos Tabasco,** Paseo Tabasco 600 (☎315 48 30), next to the cathedral. The lowest prices in town for the over-25 set. Open M-Sa 8am-6pm, Su 8am-3pm.

LOCAL SERVICES

Luggage Storage: At the bus station. 2 pesos per hr. Open daily 7am-10pm.

Market: Pino Suárez, encompassed by Pino Suárez, Constitución, Hermanos Zozaya, and Grijalva, in the northeast corner of town. Open daily 4am-8pm.

Supermarket: Maz (☎312 10 06), on Madero at Zaragoza. Open daily 7am-9:30pm.

Laundry: Lavandería Top Klean, Madero 303, next door to Hotel Madero. 15 pesos per kg. Open M-Sa 8am-8pm, Su 8am-2pm.

EMERGENCY AND COMMUNICATIONS

Emergency: ☎060.

Police: Aldama 101 (☎315 26 33 or 315 26 30), in the *Zona Luz*. Open 24hr. The main office is at 16 de Septiembre at Periférico (☎315 25 17). No English. Open 24hr.

Red Cross: (☎315 56 00), on Sandino in Col. 1 de Mayo. Take a taxi. Some English. 24hr. ambulance service.

Pharmacy: Farmacias del Ahorro, Méndez 1405, (☎314 06 03), after Pages Llergo. Open 24hr. Also in the *Zona Luz* near the corner of Reforma and Aldama, across from the Howard Johnson. Open daily 7am-10pm.

Hospital: IMSS, Sandino 102 (☎315 20 15 or 315 26 91). No English spoken.

Fax: Telecomm, Lerdo 601 (☎314 24 94), at Sáenz around the corner from the post office. Open M-F 8am-7:30pm, Sa 9am-5pm, Su 9am-1pm.

Internet Access: Several providers cluster around the intersection of Zaragoza and Aldama. **Hardware-Net,** at Aldama 627-B (☎312 27 55), has fast computers. 12 pesos per hr. Open daily 9am-9pm. **Multiservicios Computacional,** at Aldama 621 (☎312 21 66), has an average connection. 10 pesos per hr. Open daily 8:30am-9pm. Computers are only slightly faster at **Compucel,** Zaragoza 608 (☎314 58 58). 12 pesos per hr. Open M-Sa 9am-10pm.

Post Office: Sáenz 131, at Lerdo. Open M-F 8am-3pm, Sa 9am-1pm.

Postal Code: 86000.

ACCOMMODATIONS

In Villahermosa, cheap means convenient. The closer the hotel is to the *Zona Luz*, the more inexpensive it tends to be. The secret is out, though, so if you plan to take advantage of the low prices during the high season, it's best to call ahead, especially if you plan on arriving late in the day. Try the two located side by side on Lerdo for some of the lowest prices in the *zona*. Hotels on Madero are slightly nicer and are also beginning to charge higher rates.

Hotel Oriente, Madero 425 (☎312 01 21). Couch potatoes will appreciate the TVs and the easy access to VIPS across the street. Rooms are quiet, clean, and have sturdy fans. Singles 90 pesos, with TV 100 pesos; doubles 150 pesos, with TV 180 pesos.

Hotel Palma de Mallorca, Madero 510 (☎312 01 44 or 312 01 45), near the intersection of Zaragoza and Madero. Crank up the chiller—you'll notice the difference. Singles 77 pesos, with mighty A/C 133 pesos; doubles 102 pesos, with A/C 153 pesos.

Hotel del Centro, Suárez 209 (☎312 59 61), between Sánchez and Méndez. In the lobby, weary travelers relax and enjoy card games with the young, sociable staff. Rooms are clean and have TVs and fans. Singles 100 pesos; doubles 125 pesos.

Hotel Madero, Madero 301 (☎312 05 16), near 27 de Febrero. Central location, but try to get a room not on the street. All rooms are clean and have fans and TVs, but vary in quality; shop around. Singles 150 pesos; doubles 180 pesos; triples 200 pesos.

FOOD

Villahermosa, like the rest of Tabasco, specializes in *mariscos* (seafood) and various swamp creatures. A typical *tabasqueño* dish—not for the faint of heart—is tortoise sautéed in green sauce and blood and then mixed with pickled armadillo. Another favorite is *pejelagarto* (lizardfish), a fish with the head of a lizard and the body of a fish, and *mojarra* (a local fish), flavored with ingredients like *chipilín*, *chaya* leaves, and *amashito* chile. To drink, try *pozol*, a traditional beverage made from ground cornmeal, cocoa, and water. If someone offers you *venado* (venison) be aware that wetland deer are rare, and the process of catching them is very destructive. Unfortunately, although *taquerías* litter the downtown area, most restaurants specializing in seafood are either far away or expensive. The best places to find regional foods just might be the roadside restaurants and *palapas* along tourist routes such as the Teapa Comalcalco.

Cocktelería Rock and Roll, Reforma 307 (☎312 05 93), across from the Hotel Miraflores, serves seafood and local specialties. The jukebox and swarm of customers make for a swinging, rowdy atmosphere. Seafood 48 pesos; popular *sopa de mariscos* 60 pesos. Open daily 9am-11pm.

Restaurant Los Tulipanes (☎312 92 17 or 312 92 09), in the CICOM complex, specializes in *comida tabasqueña*. Enjoy fresh seafood on the banks of the Río Grijalva in this sophisticated, local favorite. Unfortunately, it's a tad expensive; seafood dishes start at 70 pesos. Open M-Sa 8am-11pm, Su 1pm-7pm.

Café Bar Impala, Madero 421 (☎312 04 93). A cluttered hole in the wall with superb *tamalitos de chipilín, panuchos* (fried tortilla shells stuffed with meat and beans), and tacos (a mere 4 pesos). Open daily M-Sa 9am-8pm.

Café la Cabaña, Juárez 303 (☎312 50 06) near 27 de Febrero. A gathering place for the town's elders. Whether you get your coffee to go or sit down to bicker at an outdoor table, the superb brew is sure to jump-start your neurons. Don't miss the frappuccino (15 pesos) or the cappuccino (13 pesos). Open daily M-Sa 7am-10pm, Su 9am-9pm.

La Flor de Tabasco, Madero 604 (☎312 48 97), your one-stop fruit shop. If you can squeeze your way into this popular breakfast joint, take your fruit platter (14 pesos) or *licuado de fruta* (13 pesos) to go—you can eat your meal more restfully across the street in Parque Juárez. Open daily 7am-9pm.

SIGHTS

For a city unconcerned with tourism, Villahermosa has a surprising number of fine museums, many of which are within walking distance of the *Zona Luz*. The downtown area is comprised of a series of pedestrian streets lined with specialty *tiendas*, *licuado* stands, gurgling fountains, shaded benches, and more hair salons than should be legal.

PARQUE-MUSEO LA VENTA. Located just south of Tabasco 2000, Parque Museo La Venta features 33 Olmec sculptures lifted from their original locations in La Venta, Tabasco and western Veracruz and re-planted in Villahermosa by Carlos Pellicer Cámara. From the small museum at the entrance, enter the outdoor jungle-setting that reveals the impressive Olmec artifacts on a well-marked 1km path. The tropical setting is completed by wild animals in the park's **zoo**. *(Take a "Petrolera" bus (3.5 pesos) from Parque Juárez to the intersection of Pages Llergo and Ruiz Cortínez. Walk northeast on Ruiz for 10min. until you reach the entrance. Alternatively, take a "Tabasco 2000," "Carrisal," or "Palacio" bus to the intersection of Tabasco and Ruiz Cortínez, and then cut through Parque Canabal to the entrance. Taxis 12 pesos. From the Tabasco 2000 complex, follow Paseo Tabasco to the intersection of Ruiz Cortínez; a 10-15min. walk.* ☎ *314 16 52. Open daily 8am-5pm. 15 pesos. Free Spanish tours leave from the park entrance, while tours in other languages can be arranged with independent guides who lurk beyond the gates (50 pesos for 30min.).)*

PARQUE TOMÁS GARRIDO CANABAL. Surrounding the museum is this large park, complete with a large lagoon, landscaped alcoves, hidden benches and fountains, and several large, concrete sculptures. While the *mirador* claims to offer a panoramic view of Villahermosa, all you get in reward for your 40-meter climb is a good look at a few treetops and the lagoon below. *(Main entrance is the corner of Tabasco and Grijalva.)*

MUSEO DE HISTORIA DE TABASCO. The small museum displays artifacts and pictures dealing with the history of the state and, while fascinating, the real show-stealer is the house itself. Known as the **Casa de los Azulejos** (House of the Tiles), the famous blue edifice was built between 1889 and 1915 by a wealthy merchant and is decorated with Italian and Spanish baroque tiles; a different style adorns each room. Eleven classical sculptures sit atop the roof; the seated female figures are said to be members of the merchant's family. Also note the Egyptian tiles decorating the ledge on the outside walls. *(At the corner of Juárez and 27 de Febrero in the Zona Luz. Open Tu-Sa 9am-8pm, Su 10am-5pm. 5 pesos.)*

CASA MUSEO CARLOS PELLICER. If you're wondering about the man whose name plasters every wall in town, head to this small museum, which focuses on the preservation of the poet and philanthropist's personal belongings (i.e., his nightshirt) displayed with the furniture and decorations belonging to his typical, well-to-do 19th-century *tabesqueño* family. *(Sáenz 203.* ☎ *312 01 57. Open Tu-Su 10am-7pm, Su 10am-4pm. Free.)*

CICOM. Carlos Pellicer's name graces yet another museum—the **Museo Regional de Antropología Carlos Pellicer Cámara,** the main attraction at Villahermosa's Center for the Investigation of Olmec and Maya Cultures (CICOM). The museum collection showcases Olmec and Mayan artifacts, with a scant selection of artifacts from other cultures. Most of the items and pictures on display are from the nearby archaeological sites of La Venta and Comalcalco. The center also houses a public library, an art school, a theater, and traveling exhibits. *(From the Zona Luz, the museum is a 15min. walk south along the Río Grijalva. The #1 and "CICOM" buses pass often.* ☎ *312 63 44. Open Tu-Su 9am-6pm. Free.)*

TABASCO 2000. Northwest on Paseo Tabasco, away from the city center and Río Grijalva, the complex features futuristically bland buildings and pedestrian-unfriendly streets that are light years away from the cozy, car-free walkways of the *Zona Luz*. The long strip of stucco and concrete buildings includes the city's **Pala-**

cio Municipal, a convention center, several fountains, a shopping mall, and a **planetarium** with **OmniMax** shows dubbed in Spanish. *(Take the "Tabasco 2000" or "Palacio" bus from Parque Juárez and get off by the Liverpool store, right smack in the middle of the complex. ☎316 36 41. Shows Tu-F 6 and 7pm; Sa-Su 5, 6, and 7pm. 20pesos.)*

YUMKÁ. Just 16km from the hustle and bustle of Villahermosa, animals run free throughout the 101-hectare park, which mimics the three *tabasqueño* ecosystems: jungle, savannah, and wetlands. Visitors view the animals in their natural habitats, traveling throughout the park in trolleys, boats, and by foot. *(To get there, take a combi marked "Ranchería Dos Montes" from the market on Suárez (4 pesos). Tell the driver where you want to get off. A taxi especial (80 pesos) is the quickest way to get there. Open daily 9am-5pm. 20 pesos, children 10 pesos.)*

🎵📺 ENTERTAINMENT AND NIGHTLIFE

Those itching to hit the discos and nightclubs should head to the *Zona Hotelera* in and around Tabasco 2000. Here, Villahermosa's young and sophisticated get down to a hot mix of salsa, tropical music, and visual stimuli. Taxi drivers are well-acquainted with disco hot spots, and their vehicles are the only efficient means of reaching them.

CLUBS

Disco Dasha (☎316 21 74 or 316 62 85), in front of the Galerías Tabasco 2000 behind the government buildings. *The* place to go for dancing on weekends. F-Sa "crazy" (open) bar. Cover Th 50 pesos, for men 40 pesos for women; F-Sa 140 pesos for men, 90 pesos for women. Open Th-Sa 10:30pm-3am.

Ku Rock House, Sandino 548 (☎315 94 31 or 315 94 33), in Colonia Primero de Mayo. The same rocking, sweaty, pounding atmosphere, but at a more manageable price. Cover W-Th 40 pesos, F-Sa 50 pesos. Open W-Sa 9pm-3am.

BARS

Liquid o Solid Sports Bar, in the *Zona Hotelera,* right next to the Hyatt. Food served in the "solid" portion of the bar, while drinks in the "liquid" video-bar. Blue-ish lighting and a lively, social atmosphere prevail. Solid bar open daily 8am-2am; liquid bar open daily 9pm-2am.

Flambouyant (☎315 12 34), a sophisticated, elegant bar and club in the lobby of the five-star Hyatt Hotel featuring rotating bands playing every night. Be prepared to pay to mingle with the elite, though; beer starts at 28 pesos. Open daily 9pm-2am.

CULTURAL EVENTS

Villahermosa presents numerous cultural options. The **Instituto de Cultura Tabasco** (☎312 91 66 or 312 74 97), on Magallanes in the Edificio Portal del Agua, publishes a monthly calendar of musical, theatrical, and other cultural events; look for it in museums and major hotels. The cafe in the back of **Galería El Jaguar Despertado,** Sáenz 117, near Reforma in the *Zona Luz,* sometimes features live classical music or jazz. Even without the tunes, though, fountains, original Mexican art, and the gallery upstairs attract an interesting mix of intellectuals and romantics. A weekly program of cultural events is posted outside the door; performances are usually at 8pm. (☎314 12 44. Open M-Sa 9am-9pm, Su 3pm-8pm.) Across the street, **Galería de Arte Tabasco,** Sáenz 122, features a slew of contemporary *tabasqueño* artwork, much of it for sale. (Open M-F 9am-9pm, Sa 10am-2pm.)

🎆 FESTIVALS

For over 100 years, representatives from the 17 municipalities of the state of Tabasco and onlookers from across the country have gathered in Villahermosa for the *Feria del Estado* during the second half of April. At the fair, representatives exhibit livestock and crafts; other events include parades, dance contests, sporting events, and theater. Among the most important of the fair's events is the crowning of the "Most Beautiful Flower in Tabasco," a traditional beauty contest.

🎏 DAYTRIPS FROM VILLAHERMOSA

As the largest city in the mostly rural and undeveloped state of Tabasco, Villahermosa serves as a base for staging dozens of daytrips into the state's upper coastal areas and southern jungle.

COMALCALCO

The ruins of Comalcalco are 3km outside of the large and chaotic city of the same name, 52km northwest of Villahermosa. Though Comalcalco has a historic church and several budget hotels, it's better to skip the city altogether and make the visit directly from Villahermosa. Taxi-colectivos to Comalcalco leave frequently from Calle Alberto Reyes at Mina on the other side of Chedraui's from the first-class bus station (1hr., 25 pesos). The taxi stops at the edge of Comalcalco's market, facing the zócalo. From there, take a taxi especial (20 pesos). Getting back from the site is easier, especially toward closing time when the bus makes stops at the main gate (3.5 pesos). Site open daily 10am-5pm. 25 pesos, Su free. Guides are available in English, Spanish, and Italian, 150 pesos for 1½hr.

Unpublicized and under-touristed, the Maya ruins of Comalcalco are surprisingly spectacular. Uniquely constructed from mounded earth sealed under a cement-like adobe shell, the city, on the western frontier of Mayan territory, was built during the Classic Period (100 BC-AD 800). Because the Tabasco Maya, known as Chontals, lacked stone to construct their temples, they used baked clay, making Comalcalco the oldest brick city in all of the Americas. Before baking the bricks, the Maya pressed designs into many of them, recording daily events and practices; some of the designs are believed to be architectural drafts for future construction. Before viewing the buildings, stop at the **museum**, directly in front of the ticket office. With fragments of stucco facades found at the site, as well as jewelry, codices, urns, and jade objects, the display illustrates the nuances of Maya culture.

To see the buildings themselves, follow the main road left from the museum entrance into the main plaza. With 10 levels, the 25m **pyramid** to the left of the entrance to the site is Comalcalco's best-known landmark. Under an awning on the building's north face, carvings of a giant winged toad and several humans are all that remain of the decorations that once covered the entire surface of the structure. Beyond the pyramid to the right, a road leads up to the **Gran Acropolis,** an 80m complex of temples and private residences believed to have housed the city's elite. If you look closely at the dilapidated walls, you'll be able to see the insides of Comalcalco's brickwork and oyster-shell mortar. Among the ruins is the precarious-looking **Palacio,** of which the center support for two vaults remains. The acropolis also contains what is thought to be a bathtub and cooling system, the necessity of which becomes more obvious after the trek through the jungle. Walk back down through the acropolis, keeping an eye out for the sculptural remnants that have been preserved in protected corners of the structures. Some especially interesting reliefs can be found on the east side in the small **Tomb of the Nine Men of Night;** the figures are believed to represent the nine gods of the Maya pantheon.

TEAPA AND LAS GRUTAS COCONÁ

To get to Teapa, take a taxi colectivo from the corner of Madero and Sánchez, past Parque Juárez (1hr., 30 pesos). Second-class buses travel between the two cities each hour, but take much longer to arrive. To return to Villahermosa, take on the of the red taxi colectivos that gather on Teapa's main drag. Combis for the grutas leave from Bastar on the right-hand side of the church in Teapa (every 30min., 3 pesos). Taxis charge 15 pesos. Caves open daily 9am-4pm. 15 pesos, children 7 pesos. Guides cost about 20 pesos.

Located 52km south of Villahermosa amid countless farms and ranches, Teapa provides a pleasant base from which to explore the nearby natural attractions. Several 18th-century churches in the town, including the Franciscan Temple of

Santiago Apostol and Jesuit Temple of Tecomajica, are also worth a visit. The real reason for traveling to Teapa, however, are **Las Grutas Coconá,** located just 2km outside of the city. Discovered in the late 1800s by two adventurous brothers hunting in the woods, the caves (or *grutas*) contain a lighted path that winds for 500m into the hillside, passing impressive caverns and underground lagoons along the way. Guides offer their services at the entrance; though they are unnecessary, they do point out formations that resemble other objects (the Virgin Mary, the head of a moose, etc.). The explanations are interesting, but your time may be better spent strolling through the *grutas* on your own. For some real spelunking, negotiate with the guides to take you to the unexplored *gruta* about 200m away. Tours of this *gruta* last anywhere from 1½ to three hours and are a bad idea for anyone claustrophobic or afraid of the dark. Try to pay less than 35 pesos for the tour.

EL AZUFRE

Take a combi from Teapa's market; tell the driver where you want to go (5 pesos). Taxis cost 40 pesos. Returning is more difficult: climb the hill from the spa to the main road, and flag down a taxi or bus. Open daily 6am-7pm. 10 pesos, 5 pesos for children.

Another 15-minute *combi* ride from Teapa is El Azufre, a spa with two large sulfur *albercas*. Although the pools could be better maintained, visitors claim the water has therapeutic qualities. Also available at the site are bathroom facilities, *palapas*, and a hotel. (150 pesos per room; camping is free.)

TAPIJULAPA AND PARQUE NATURAL DE LA VILLA LUZ

Two buses serve the town, leaving every hour from Tacotalpa. To get to Tacotalpa, catch one of the taxi-colectivos (1hr., 25 pesos) from the opposite side of the Chedraui's next to the ADO station. Second-class buses leave for Tacotalpa every 30min. (PSI; 1½hr., 5:30am-9pm, 23 pesos), Colectivos stop on Tacotalpa's main drag. Half a block farther down on the same street, red and white buses leave for Tapijulapa every hour (40min., 5am-6pm, 5 pesos). Buses drop off at Tapijulapa's plaza. To reach the lancha dock, head straight 2 blocks past the plaza to the end of the street, turn right and head 1 block downhill. Return buses to Tacotalpa leave from the plaza (every hr., last one at 6pm). Buses and tax-colectivos returning to Villahermosa from Tacotalpa stop running around 8pm.

Traveling to Tapijulapa, 90km south of Villahermosa, is like entering another world. The bus ride to the town crosses into the state's highest mountains, where the humidity lets up and time slows down. While its main attraction is its proximity to the waterfalls, spas, and caves of **Parque Natural de la Villa Luz,** the village itself should not be overlooked. Known for their traditional sardine festival and woodworking, Tapijulapa's friendly residents make the stay a pleasant one, and young guides are eager to show you around the town.

The **Parque Natural de la Villa Luz,** 3km away from Tapijulapa, is best reached by *lancha* (15 pesos roundtrip). Upon exiting the *lancha*, climb the stairs in front of you to enter the park. Follow the cow path through a pasture until you come to a fence; the gate on the far left is open. Taking the left fork will take you to the abandoned home of the illustrious former Tabasco governor Tomás Garrido Canabal, whose name is plastered all over Villahermosa. Continuing along the path for 10min., you will arrive at the top of the *cascadas*. It is safe to bathe in the waist-high, sulfur-rich water, although you may want to wait until you reach the spas at the end, where you'll have much surer footing.

The right fork will take you to yet another fork in the road. Take the right fork to reach **La Cueva de Las Sardinas Ciegas.** The cave's odd name comes from the sardines that, having adapted to their dark environment, are all blind. Every year on the Sunday before Easter, residents of Tapijulapa gather at the cave for the *Pesca de la Sardina*. While dancing to the music of the *tamborileros*, celebrants toss powdered narcotic plants into the water, which stun the fish and cause them to float to the top of the water for easy harvesting. The left fork leads to the spas—an area with several pools, all filled with the therapeutic sulfur water (free). Make sure to bring your bathing suit. Follow the water a little farther to see its bubbling source. To return to the *lancha* dock, retrace your steps; the walk will take around

25min. The entire trek takes approximately 2hr. Tip your guide at least 20-25 pesos. Plans are pending to install complete camping facilities at the site; construction should be completed by January 2001.

OXOLOTÁN

From the plaza in Tapijulapa, walk straight through the building opposite the plaza and climb the large flight of stairs on the opposite side of the street. Be sure to check out the view from the small courtyard at the top; the 17th-century Santiago Apostol church on the right side of the courtyard is also worth a visit. Walk straight through the courtyard and downhill for one block to the main road; the green and white striped Oxolotán bus picks up here every hr. (40min., 5 pesos). Upon exiting the bus in Oxolotán, with your back to the station, turn right and walk two blocks; the church is to your left on the cross street and the museum entrance is on the church's opposite side. Return buses to Tacotalpa leave every 1-1½hr., 5:30am-5pm. Museum open daily 9am-5pm. Free.

A bit farther down the road from Tapijulapa is Oxolotán (pop. 2000), a tiny, sleepy town in the middle of nowhere, albeit an exquisitely beautiful nowhere. The town's **Ex-convento de Santo Domingo** is a good excuse to visit, but the real reasons for going are the bus ride into the mountains and the amenity-free restfulness of the town. In 1550, when the Dominicans finally got around to evangelizing Tabasco, Oxolotán was an important trade center because of its position as the last navigable point on the Río Grijalva. When the ex-convento was finally finished in 1578, though, the town's importance had flagged, and the Dominicans relocated to Tacotalpa, leaving Oxolotán with a grand (and empty) parish church. The church has been in use for the last 400 years, and recent renovations have made the cloister a polished museum. The undecorated stone walls and strikingly quiet courtyards have a tranquility that permeates the town, whose old *zócalo* is formed by the ex-convento's ex-patio.

RESERVA DE LA BIOSFERA PATANOS DE CENTLA

Though Tabasco's eco-tourism industry has been slow and cumbersome in its attempts to take flight, the state's predominant feature (after its oil reserves) is its natural beauty. If you're willing negotiate a bit, it's possible to see the amazing jungle on a very limited budget. One of the best places to do this is the Reserva de la Biosfera, a preserve encompassing 302,000 hectares of the wetlands formed by the huge river systems that wind their way into the state. Set aside by the government in 1992, the land is home to 50,000 people, most of whom live in small fishing villages along the river systems deep inside the preserve. In addition to the Centla's waterfalls, swamps, rivers, and the incredible variety of animals that inhabit them, the preserve is fascinating as a point of conflict between ecological interests and the economic interests of the indigenous peoples who live there. Small turtles sell for 100 pesos in the open market, and the rare venison goes for even more, giving residents a good reason to hunt many of the protected animals. The hunting of these animals is the bane of the people who work at the preserve's station at **Tres Brazos.** By contacting the director of the program, Juan Carlos Romero (☎310 14 31), Paseo de la Sierra 613 in the Colonial Reforma, it is possible to get permission to stay at the Tres Brazos station, paying no more than the cost of gas and minimal fees for food in the cheery little restaurant. The station has two clean, separate dorms for men and women, and a satellite TV that entertains the attendants who keep the place open 24 hours. When sending requests, explain that you'd like to stay at the station and see the *patanos* (wetlands) by *lancha*. Don't forget to drop the key word: *ecoturismo*. Once you have permission, the office will arrange transportation to the station just south of **Frontera** on the Río Orijalva, about 1½ hours northeast of Villahermosa. Exploring the reserve will take some initiative, but the *lanchistas* and locals will help you out, and the *crocodilos* will ensure an exciting time.

AGUA SELVA ECOTOURISM PROJECT

Reaching the Project is a challenge. Buses to **Herradura** *leave from the second-class terminal in Villahermosa (4 per day, 43 pesos). Stop first in Huimanguillo (each 30min., 22 pesos) for a tour; Gorge Pagole del Valle (☎ 375 00 02 or 375 06 28), of the Hotel del Carmen at Morelos 39, will guide you (100 pesos per day). From Herradura, pick-up trucks (pasajeras) leave for Malpasito daily at approximately 9am, noon, and 3pm (20min., 5 pesos). They return to Herradura from the town's main street at around 11:30am and 2pm. An unofficial taxi to Malpasito from Herradura costs 40 pesos. Pasajeras leave from Herradura to Francisco J. Mújica daily from 2-3pm (20 pesos). The only transportation returning to Herradura leaves at 4am the next morning. No transportation exists between the Francisco J. Mújica and Malpasito, although it may be possible to rent a bike (ask Catalina Martínez).*

Yet another option for city-weary adventurers is Agua Selva, a region encompassing 15,000 hectares of land bordering Chiapas and Veracruz. Located 142km southwest of Villahermosa, the project aims to draw visitors to its two main attractions: water and the jungle. With over 100 waterfalls, small mountains ranging up to 1000m, thick vegetation, and abundant wildlife (including armadillos, jaguars, and a wide variety of birds), the natural attractions necessary for the project's success are certainly there. Unfortunately, the human resources behind the project have so far been insufficient to maintain the project's infrastructure. Nonetheless, Agua Selva's natural beauty compensates for the hassle involved in reaching it, and many individuals within the communities, eager for the project's success, can help you upon your arrival.

MALPASITO. The nearest and most accessible village is Malpasito, the site of several not-to-be-missed attractions. Upon arriving to the town, ask to be dropped off at the home of **Catalina Martínez** (everyone knows everyone), who manages the flow of tourism into Agua Selva and is available for questions at any time. She can provide you with information about Malpasito and also arrange a **guide** for you (Delfino Santos comes highly recommended). Guides are necessary and cost 50 pesos for a full day. The **Albergue Ecológico** is a rustic two-room lodging with beds and pillows for up to 13 people (35 pesos per person). Bath includes two toilets, a sink, and a bucket for bathing. Alternatively, **Guillermo Pérez Cajija** rents out a two-room *palapa* which houses up to eight people (20 pesos). Baths include showers, but you have to provide your own hammock. The *Señora* of the house prepares meals for 15-50 pesos, depending on the dish.

A short 1km hike from a path just uphill from the *albergue* leads to the **Zoque Ruins of Malpasito,** Post-Classic Maya ruins. Little is known about the Zoque Maya other than that they offered little resistance to the Spanish. Upon entering the site, immediately begin looking for the **petroglyphs,** sketches of animals, birds, humans, and geometric shapes in the rock. They are the site's most predominant feature, and over 60 have been found so far. As you continue along the path, you will come to a **ball court,** complete with what appears to have been a sort of locker room. On the plaza past the ball court, stairs lead to a second, smaller plaza, which offers a breathtaking view of the surrounding mountains. Ask your guide to lead you to the waterfall on the trail beyond the ruins, which has a pool at its base that is safe for swimming. From here, several other trails lead farther into the mountains, where you can check out the rock formations of *La Pava* and *La Copa*.

FRANCISCO J. MÚJICA. The other village with accommodations and some organized tourist resources with Agua Selva is Francisco J. Mújica, located approximately 20km west of the transportation hub Herradura. **Antonio Domínguez** manages an *albergue* nearly identical to that in Malpasito (35 pesos per person). Sr. Domínguez can help you find a trustworthy guide with whom to view the surrounding area. The Cascada Velo de Novia (Bridal Veil Falls) is just an hour's hike away from the village; beyond it is a steep canyon which you can descend (carefully and with the aid of the guide's rope) to a ledge that leads beneath the falls. The caves in the surrounding area contain petroglyphs as well, which the guide can point out to you. If you can arrange an escort to the village of Carlos A. Madrazo, 4km beyond Francisco J. Mújica, **Raimundo Cruz,** a guide within the village, can lead you to several other noteworthy sites, including Cascada de Aguaima, another 4km from Madrazo. At this thundering *cascada*, two rivers converge to form the Río Pedregal.

Tuxtla Gutiérrez

🏠 ACCOMMODATIONS

Hotel Avenida, 3
Hotel Del Pasaje, 6
Hotel Don Candido, 7
Villas Deportivas Juvenil, 5

🍴 FOOD

La Antigua Fogata, 4
Restaurante Imperial, 1
Restaurante Vegetariano Nah-Yaxal, 2

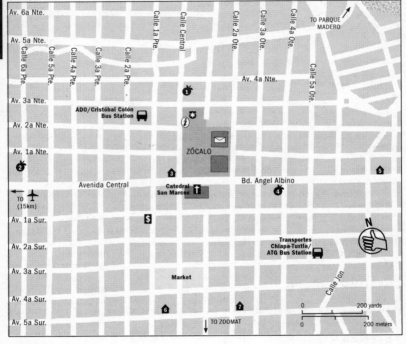

PARAÍSO

Second-class buses run from Villahermosa to the second-class terminal in Paraíso; the ride is long, bumpy, and hot (2¼hr., every hr., 16 pesos). Alternatively, take a quicker taxi-colectivo from the far side of Chedraui's (1¼hr., 28 pesos). Colectivos stop on 2 de Abril near Paraíso's zócalo. To reach the second-class station from the zócalo, walk 2½ blocks away from Juárez, the main street, to Buenos Aires. The station is 9 blocks to the left.

At only 71km away from Villahermosa, Paraíso and its beaches offer one of the best ways to conquer the heat—if just for a day or two. The town is home to numerous seafood restaurants and native oysters are sold both cooked and raw (be careful!) on the streets. Other fresh seafood delicacies include crab, *mojarra*, and shrimp. The town also has several budget hotels, although your best option may be to sleep in a hammock on one of the beaches: many have facilities and *palapas* for hammock-hanging, and although the sand may not glitter as brightly as along the Caribbean, beaches are clean, uncrowded, and safe.

Public beaches lie to the east and west of the city. The beaches northwest of the city, including **Varadero, El Paraíso, Pal Mar,** and **Paraíso y Mar** can easily be reached by the "Playa" *combi* that leaves from the second-class bus station (20min., every hr., 5 pesos). All lie around 500m right of the main road and have *palapas* in which visitors can hang their hammocks free of charge. Varadero and El Paraíso are by far the nicest of the four; both have restaurants, and El Paraíso has hotels and a pool (10 pesos, 5 pesos for children).

Alternatively, an eastbound bus to Chiltepec leaves every half hour from the second-class bus station. The first stop along the route is **Puerto Ceiba** (15min., 3.5 pesos), a small fishing village on the edge of Laguna Mecoacán, a 51,000 hectare oyster breeding ground. Local fishermen happily give *lancha* tours of the lagoon; just ask at any of the docks along the way. Across the bridge from Puerto Ceiba is **El Bellote,** another small fishing town located between the lagoon and the Río Seco. Although the town itself offers few attractions, it does have several affordable, high-quality restaurants. Near the end of the route to Chiltepec and 27km east of El Paraíso is the town of Playa Bruja; just east is the beach itself, which has a restaurant and *palapas* (50min., 8 pesos).

CHIAPAS

TUXTLA GUTIÉRREZ ☎ 9

An energetic young city, Tuxtla Gutiérrez (pop. 466,495) is the capital of Chiapas and the focal point of commerce and transportation for most of southern Mexico. The "Tuxtla" comes from Náhuatl *tuchtlan,* meaning "place where rabbits abound," while the "Gutiérrez" originates with Miguel Gutiérrez, a progressive *chiapaneco* governor who, rather than succumb to imperialist right-wing forces, wrapped himself in the Mexican flag and dramatically leapt to his death from a church spire. In some ways, the city has adopted his indomitable spirit: rather than bow to the pressures of industrialization, Tuxtla has flourished as a result of its vibrant citizens, active *zócalo,* and one of the most colorful zoos in Latin America.

▐ TRANSPORTATION

GETTING AROUND

Combis (VW van *colectivos*) run frequently throughout the city, heading east and west on Av. Central, north on Calle Central, south on Calle 1 Pte. Sur, and south on Calle 1 Sur Ote. (6am-10pm, 2.5 pesos).

GETTING AWAY

Airport: Aeropuerto Francisco Sarabia (☎615 05 37) is 15km southwest of town. Taxis 20 pesos. **Aerocaribe,** Av. Central Pte. 206 (☎612 00 20, or at airport ☎612 17 72). **Aviacsa,** Av. Central Pte. 1144 (☎612 80 81, or at the airport ☎612 33 55).

Buses: To get to the *zócalo* from the **ADO/Cristóbal Colón bus station,** 2 Nte. Pte. 268, walk left on 2 Nte. Pte. (away from the buses) for 2 blocks. The *zócalo* is to your right along Calle Central. Cristóbal Colón (☎612 51 22) goes to: **Cancún** (18hr., 12:30pm, 414 pesos); **Mexico City** (15hr.; 2:30, 5:35, 9:30pm; 440 pesos); **Oaxaca** (10hr., 11:30am and 7:15pm, 197 pesos); **Palenque** (6hr., 6 per day 6am-11:30pm, 98 pesos); **Puebla** (13hr., 3 per day, 387 pesos); **Puerto Escondido** (11hr., 9:45am and 8:15pm, 208 pesos); **San Cristóbal de las Casas** (2hr., 5 per day 5:30am-1:30pm, 32 pesos); **Tehuantepec** (6½hr., 5 per day, 108 pesos); **Tapachula** (6hr., 14 per day 6am-midnight, 146 pesos); **Teapa** (6hr., 11:15am, 85 pesos); **Veracruz** (12hr., 9:30pm, 260 pesos); and **Villahermosa** (7hr.; 11:15am, 3, 11:30pm; 110 pesos). **Autotransportes Tuxtla Gutiérrez bus station,** Av. 3 Sur 712, sits in a cul-de-sac at Av. 3 Sur and Calle 7 Ote. To get to the *zócalo,* exit right out of the station and make another right into the alley that doubles as a market. Make the first left onto Av. 2 Sur and continue west to Calle Central—the *zócalo* is two blocks to the right. Autotransportes Tuxtla Gutiérrez (☎612 03 22 and 612 02 88) has less frequent, slower buses at cheaper fares to similar destinations. Travelers from **Chiapa de Corzo** disembark at the small station at the corner of Calle 2 Ote. and Av. 2 Sur. To get to the *zócalo*, exit the station and walk right two blocks to Av. Central; the *zócalo* is two blocks to the left.

Local Transport: One of the cheapest ways to get to **San Cristóbal** is via Transporte Colosio, which sends *combis* from Av. 3 Sur between Calles 2 and 3 Ote., and Av. 2 Sur between Calles 3 and 4 Ote. (every 10min. 3am-9pm, 25 pesos). To reach **Chiapa de Corzo,** hop on a Transportes Chiapa-Tuxtla *microbús* at the station at Av. 2 Sur and Calle 2 Ote. (25min., every 10min., 5.5 pesos) or grab one leaving town on Blvd. Corzo.

✳🛈 ORIENTATION AND PRACTICAL INFORMATION

The city lies 85km west of San Cristóbal and 293km south of Villahermosa. *Avenidas* run east-west and *calles* north-south. The central axis of the city, upon which the *zócalo* rests, is formed by **Av. Central** and **Calle Central**. Streets are numbered according to their distance from and geographical relation to the central axis. For example, Calle 2 Oriente Sur lies south of Av. Central and two blocks east of Calle Central.

TOURIST AND FINANCIAL SERVICES

Tourist Office: Dirección Municipal de Turismo (☎612 55 11, ext. 214), 2 Nte. Ote. at Calle Central, tucked into the northwest corner of the *zócalo*. Useful city maps and information. Open M-F 8am-9pm, Sa 8am-8pm.

Currency Exchange: Bital, on Calle Central, between Av. Central and Av. 1 Nte., across from the *zócalo*, has 24hr. **ATMs.** Open for exchange M-Sa 8am-7pm. **Bancrecer,** on the corner of Av. Central and Calle 1 Pte., also changes currency and has 24hr. **ATMs.**

LOCAL SERVICES

Laundry: Lavandería Automática Burbuja, Av. 1 Nte. 413A (☎611 05 95), at Calle 3 Pte. 33 pesos per 3kg. Open M-Sa 8:30am-8pm.

Markets: Tuxtla's crazy **Mercado Díaz Orden,** on Calle Central between Av. 3 and 4 Sur, has food and trinket stands. Open daily 6am-6pm. **Mercado Andador San Roque** has the best straw hats in town, oodles of wicker, and several cheap eateries. Open daily 8am-8pm.

Supermarket: Chedraui's, Blvd. Corzo, on the left just past the military base. Take an eastbound "Rutal" *combi* from a block west of the *zócalo* on Av. Central.

Car Rental: Hertz, Blvd. Domínguez 1195 (☎615 53 48), in Hotel Camino Real. VW Sedan 520 pesos per day. Open daily 7am-9pm. **Budget Rent-A-Car,** Blvd. Domínguez 2510 (☎615 13 82). VW Sedan 557 pesos per day. Open daily 8am-7pm.

EMERGENCY AND COMMUNICATIONS

Emergency: ☎060, or call **Policía de Seguridad Pública** (☎612 05 30 or 613 78 05).

Luggage Storage: The trustworthy owner of **Jugos Minoslava,** across from the Cristóbal Colón terminal, guards luggage. 3 pesos per day.

Police: (☎612 11 06), in the Palacio Municipal, north of the *zócalo*. Go left upon entering the building. No English spoken. Open 24hr.

Red Cross: 5 Nte. Pte. 1480 (☎612 95 14), on the west side of town. Little English spoken. 24hr. ambulance service.

Pharmacy: Regina Farmacias, Calle Central 247 (☎612 14 66), at the corner of Av. Central. Open 24hr.

Hospital: Sanatorio Rojas, 2 Av. Sur Pte. 1487 (☎612 54 14 or 612 54 66). English spoken. 24hr. emergency service.

Fax: Telcomm (☎613 65 47; fax 612 42 96), on Av. 1 Nte. at 2 Ote., next to the post office. Open M-F 8am-6pm, Sa 9am-5pm.

Telephones: LADATELs cluster in the plaza and pepper the surrounding streets.

Internet Access: Internet cafes cluster on Calle Central past Av. 4 Nte., and around the intersection of Av. 2 Nte. and Calle 4 Pte. **Ciber Café,** at Calle Central Nte. 402 (☎614 63 36), has fast connections, lots of computers, and free coffee. 15 pesos per hr. Open M-Sa 9am-9pm. **Cybercafé Net-Cropper,** 2 Nte. 427 (☎613 88 58), between 3 and 4 Pte., has an average-speed connection. 15 pesos per hr. Open daily 9am-9pm.

Post Office: (☎612 04 16), on Av. 1 Nte. at 2 Ote., on the northeast corner of the *zócalo* in the corridor to the right of the Palacio Municipal. Open M-F 9am-5pm, Sa 9am-1pm. **Postal Code:** 29000.

ACCOMMODATIONS

Budget accommodations are as they should be: affordable, decent, and convenient. The best bargains can be found near the *mercado* around Av. 5 Sur, where cheap hotels cater to vendors from the surrounding countryside. If you want to avoid the mayhem of the market, head north to Av. Central Pte., where rooms are only slightly more expensive. Unfortunately, bathing in these budget hotels may be a lukewarm experience at best.

Villas Deportivas Juvenil, Blvd. Corzo 1800 (☎612 12 01), next to the yellow footbridge over the road. From 1 block west of the plaza on Av. Central, catch an eastbound *combi* and ask the driver to let you off at INDEJECH. Immaculate, single-sex 4-person rooms have comfortable bunks, fans, and spotless hall baths. A favorite of international travelers; join the gang for a pick-up game on the basketball courts or soccer fields. Breakfast, lunch, and dinner 15 pesos each. 30 pesos per person.

Hotel Del Pasaje, Av. 5 Sur Pte. 140 (☎612 15 50 or 612 15 52), ½ block west of Calle Central. The undisputed king of the budget hotel market. Near the *mercado,* the rooms are quiet, clean, and comfortable. Singles 65 pesos, with A/C 99 pesos; doubles 85 pesos, with A/C 130 pesos.

Hotel Don Candido, Av. 5 Sur Ote. 142 (☎612 66 06), half a block east of Calle Central, is pricier, but has colorful decor and a sunny courtyard of potted plants. The prime location minimizes the constant noise problematic in cheaper hotels. Clean rooms with fans and color TVs. Singles 95 pesos; doubles 110 pesos.

Hotel Avenida, Av. Central 244 (☎612 08 07), between 1 and 2 Pte., is all about location. The fragrant whiff of coffee lingers by the door. With spacious, clean rooms, it's worth the price. Singles 100 pesos; doubles 150 pesos.

Hotel Velmar, Av. 3 Nte. Ote. 143 (☎612 32 26), at Calle Central. Travelers stay here for the price and the cleanliness, but overlook the wobbly furniture and tacky paint job. Modest bathers beware: frosted bathroom windows facing the courtyard are too clear for comfort. Singles 60 pesos, with TV 80 pesos; doubles 80 pesos, with TV 100 pesos.

FOOD

Culinary miracles don't happen in Tuxtla, but the city is speckled with inexpensive eateries. *Carnes,* Chiapas-style, come prepared in *pepitas de calabaza* (squash seeds) or *hierba santa.* Other regional favorites include *pozol* and *tazcalate,* (two beverages with corn and cocoa base). *Tamales* in Tuxtla come with every filling imaginable and can often be had for a mere 5 pesos. For the gastronomically adventurous, *nucús,* edible ants, are plentiful at the beginning of the rainy season and turn up in everything from guacamole to taco fillings. Those preferring to stick to vegetables rather than ants should feel right at home—there's been a recent upsurge of local interest in natural and vegetarian foods.

Las Pichanchas, Av. Central 837 (☎612 53 51), between Calles 8 and 9 Ote. Sway to live *marimba* music or watch the *ballet folklórico* (9-10pm) as you indulge in some of the finest regional cuisine in all of Chiapas. Classy waiters, traditional decorations, and an upscale courtyard belie reasonable prices for *carne salada con pepita de calabaza* (40 pesos), *tamales* (16 pesos), and *tazcalate* (9 pesos). Open daily noon-midnight.

Restaurante Vegetariano Nah-Yaxal, Calle 6 Pte. 124 (☎ 613 96 48), half a block north of Av. Central. A leader in Tuxtla's vegetarian movement, Nah has colonized several storefronts around the *centro*. Full-blown vegetarian *comida corrida* (36 pesos). The biggest hit is in the joint around the corner from the pilot store, where frozen yogurt can be mixed with almost every fruit and grain imaginable (11 pesos). Other location Av. Central Ote. 649. Open M-Sa 7am-10pm, Su 3-10pm.

Restaurante Imperial, Calle Central Nte. 263 (☎ 612 06 48), 1 block north of the *zócalo*. Excellent *comida corrida* (24 pesos), *antojitos* (19 pesos), and breakfasts (8-18 pesos) are the secret to the imperialism. Open daily 8am-8pm.

La Antigua Fogata, Calle 4 Ote. Sur 115, just off Av. Central. The restaurant may look like a tin-roofed shack, but they have 25 years of experience behind their chicken *al carbón*. The quarter-chicken is quite a find (26 pesos). Open daily 7:30am-midnight.

◉ SIGHTS

MIGUEL ÁLVAREZ DEL TORO (ZOOMAT). The shady forest foliage of this zoo offers a refreshing change from Tuxtla's gritty urban landscape. Renowned throughout Latin America, the zoo houses over 1200 animals native to Chiapas, including the quetzal and tapir, two species that cannot be found in any other zoo. Some animals roam freely in the park's natural setting. *(From Calle 1 Ote. between Av. 6 and 7 Sur take the "Cerro Hueco" or "Zoológico" bus (every 30min., 2.5 pesos). Open Tu-Su 8:30am-5:30pm. Free.)*

CONVIVENCIA INFANTIL. Conveniently grouping together many of Tuxtla's attractions, the Convivencia's focal point is the large and modern **Teatro de la Ciudad Emilio Rabasa.** Films by Latin American directors and performances of *ballet folklórico* dominate the schedule (most events start 7-8pm Th-Sa). A children's amusement park, on the pleasant *paseo* to the right of the theater, features pony rides and a mini-train. (Open Tu-Su 9am-8pm.) Toward the far end of the amusement park is the open-air **Teatro Bonampak,** where free folk dance performances are held (Su 5-8pm). Next to the theater is a light aircraft, usually crawling with eight-year-old fighter-pilots-in-training. To the west is a broad concourse, lined with fountains and bronze busts of famous Mexicans. Down the walkway on the right is the **Museo Regional de Chiapas,** which displays regional archaeological finds as well as Olmec and Maya artifacts. (Open Tu-Su 9am-4pm. 25 pesos; Su free.) Farther down the concourse, at the **Jardín Botánico Dr. Faustino Miranda,** one can amble under towering *ceibas* (silk-cotton trees) and admire colorful Chiapanecan flora. (Open Tu-Su 9am-6pm.) Head directly across the garden to the **Museo Botánico** to learn a little more about the plant life you've just seen. (Open M-F 9am-3pm, Sa 9am-1pm.) *(The Convivencia Infantil begins in the northeast part of town at the intersection of 11 Ote. and 5 Nte. Walk, or take a "KM. 4-Granjas-5 de Mayo" combi (2.5 pesos) from Calle 4 Ote. between Av. 4 and 5 Sur.)*

THE ZÓCALO. Back in the *centro*, the *zócalo* is a happening hang-out, especially when live music is playing (Su 8-9pm). Check out **Catedral San Marcos** and the plaque on its north side commemorating Pope John Paul II's 1990 visit.

PARQUE DE MARIMBA. West of the *zócalo* at Av. Central and Calle 8 Pte., the park fills with people when live *marimba* plays (6-9pm). Coffee shops and small cafes abound. Stop at **Cafetería Nubliselva,** Av. 1 Nte. between Calles 7 and 8 Pte., for some of the best cappuccinos around (13.5 pesos; open daily 5-10pm).

▶ DAYTRIPS FROM TUXTLA GUTIÉRREZ

SIMOJOVEL

From Tuxtla Gutiérrez, buses to Simojovel leave from **Transporte Pichucalco** *at the corner of Calle 4 Ote. and 5 Sur (4:30, 10am, 1:30, 3:45, 5:30pm). It is also possible to get there by minis, town-hopping all the way. A faster option than both is to take a taxi-colec-*

Call the USA

"feel free to call"

1-800-COLLECT

When in Ireland
Dial: 1-800-COLLECT (265 5328)

When in N. Ireland, UK & Europe
Dial: 00-800-COLLECT USA (265 5328 872)

Member of
Dublin Tourism

Australia	0011	800 265 5328 872
Finland	990	800 265 5328 872
Hong Kong	001	800 265 5328 872
Israel	014	800 265 5328 872
Japan	0061	800 265 5328 872
New Zealand	0011	800 265 5328 872

tivo from Tuxtla (50 pesos) that leaves only in the morning from the same corner as the bus. Catch return buses at the station (3½hr.; 4:45, 5:30, 8:30am, 2, 5:30pm; 30 pesos). To return to Tuxtla, it may be easier to take a combi or pasajera from 20 de Noviembre and Allende to Bochil, a town on the route to Tuxtla (1¼hr., approx. every 20min., 20 pesos). From there, buses leave frequently for Tuxtla (2hr.; every half hr. 5am-6pm, 8 and 10pm; 19 pesos). Bochil is notable for being inhabited by Tzotzil Maya.

Simojovel sits above some of the best amber mines in the world, and everybody in town seems to have a foot in the business. When foreigners visit the town, they are instantly mobbed by people carrying baskets of toilet paper and calling out *ambar* and *insectos*. Give them the chance and they will carefully unwrap the toilet paper cocoons to reveal shining chunks of the 30-40 thousand-year-old tree sap, most of which entomb unlucky prehistoric insects. While the uninitiated are sure to be given the *gringo* price, it will still be far lower than what you'd pay elsewhere. You may want to head first to one of the three official stores in town. The most expensive is **Bazar Choj-Choj,** on 26 de Abril just right of the far side of the *zócalo*. Going here will help you get an idea of what you're aiming to beat on the street. (☎615 01 21. Open M-Sa 8am-8pm.) If you feel uncomfortable bargaining, several residencies in town serve as unofficial stores, with well-made jewelry and cheaper prices than at the bazaars. **Irma Yesenia Suárez Ramos,** Allende 41 (☎615 00 81), three blocks past the *zócalo* on the right, sells an impressive collection of finely-cut, reasonably-priced pieces. If you can find a *lupa* (a magnifying glass) and some good sunlight, you'll be able to see a menagerie of bugs—from little *moscas* (flies) to transparent *mariposas* (butterflies) whose wings have lost their color in the chemical process that turns the sap to amber. The entrance to the mines themselves is over two hours away, and the visit probably isn't worth the time and hassle necessary to arrange transportation.

CHIAPA DE CORZO ☎9

Fifteen kilometers and 25 minutes from Tuxtla, the two cities enjoy a symbiotic relationship: Chiapa de Corzo (pop. 120,000) serves as Tuxtla's main attraction, and Tuxtla takes care of Chiapa's dirty work, allowing the city to remain quaint and scenic. Graced by an unusual 16th-century fountain and church, the town's greatest blessing is its proximity to the **Cañón del Sumidero,** carved by the Río Grijalva's decent from the highlands. Once unnavigable, the dam built at the edge of the canyon has made it accessible to *lanchas,* which leave from Chiapa's dock and zip through the canyon's lush, 1km-high walls. Although usually a daytrip from Tuxtla, Chiapa is an ideal place to spend a night or two.

☰ TRANSPORTATION. Chiapa de Corzo overlooks the Río Grijalva, 15km east of Tuxtla and 68km west of San Cristóbal de las Casas. Buses from Tuxtla drop you off in the *zócalo*. **Transportes Chiapa-Tuxtla** microbuses back to Tuxtla stop on 21 de Octubre opposite the police station (25min., every 10min., 5.5 pesos). **Boats** leave for **El Sumidero** from the riverbank two blocks southwest of the *zócalo*, on 5 de Febrero. Because Chiapa is the last stop on Rte. 190 before the mountains, most buses and *combis* headed north from Tuxtla pick up passengers along the way. It's sometimes easier to sit at the edge of the highway in Chiapa and wait for buses to stop than it is to hunt them down in Tuxtla.

◼◪ ORIENTATION AND PRACTICAL INFORMATION. Most sights are located around **Plaza Ángel Albino Corzo,** the town's *zócalo*. The plaza is bounded on the north by 21 de Octubre (the Tuxtla-San Cristóbal Highway), on the east by La Mexicanidad, on the south by Grajales, and on the west by 5 de Febrero. Contact the **tourist office** in **Tuxtla** for tourist information on Chiapa. **Bancomer,** on the east side of the *zócalo*, has a 24hr. **ATM.** (☎686 03 20. Open M-F 8:30am-4pm.) **Police station:** in the Palacio Municipal, on the northeast side of the *zócalo*. (☎686 02 26. Open 24hr.) **Farmacia Esperanza,** on 21 de Octubre, one block east of the *zócalo*. (☎686 04 54. Open daily M-Sa 7am-11pm, Su 7am-2pm.) **Post office:** on the north side of the plaza in the "Transito" building. (Open M-F 8am-3pm.) **Postal code:** 29160.

▐▌ ACCOMMODATIONS AND FOOD. If you're deciding between a daytrip or a longer stay in Chiapa, the **Hotel Los Angeles,** Grajales 2, at La Mexicanidad, on the southeast corner of the *zócalo*, makes a good case for staying the night with its high ceilinged rooms, some of which have balconies. The restaurant in the pleasant courtyard serves *comida corrida* for 30 pesos. (☎ 686 00 48. Singles 100 pesos; doubles 120 pesos; triples 140 pesos; quads 160 pesos.) Since you've probably come to Chiapa to see the river, you may as well head to the waterfront for midrange, filling meals. **Restaurant Comitán,** to the left as you hit the dock, offers a breakfast special (25 pesos), occasional live *marimba* performances, and a partly-obscured view of the river. (Open daily 8am-7pm.) At the corner of the *zócalo* at Madero, **Restaurante Los Corredores** looks much more expensive than it is. A great place for seafood and regional dishes, the restaurant has a beautiful courtyard and a cool, colorful interior. Breakfasts 25 pesos, regional cuisine like *chiles rellenos de pollo* 40 pesos, fish fillets with all the fixings 45-50 pesos. Cheaper food can be found at the market to the left of the church. (Open daily 6am-5pm.)

◙ SIGHTS. *Chiapañecos* are so proud of their immense **Cañon del Sumidero,** the landmark that adorns the state seal. A *lancha* journey begins with humble views of cornfields, but shortly after the Belisario Domínguez bridge, the hills jump to form near-vertical cliffs that rise over 1200m above the water. When the Spanish defeated the Chiapa Indians in 1528, the Chiapa threw themselves from these cliffs rather than submit to capture and slavery. Now protected as a natural park, the steep walls are home to troupes of monkeys, hummingbirds, and falcons, while the murky waters harbor crocodiles and turtles. Along the meandering river lie several caves and the park's most famous waterfall, the **Árbol de Navidad.** The spectacular *cascada* dashes over a series of vegetation-covered, scalloped rock formations before disintegrating into the fine mist that envelops passing boats. El Sumidero's northernmost extremity is marked by the 200m-high hydroelectric dam **Netzahualcóyotl,** which, along with three other dams on the Río Grijalva, provides 25% of Mexico's electricity. *Lanchas* leave as soon as they're full from Chiapa's dock at the end of 5 de Febrero, two blocks from the southwest corner of the *zócalo* (2hr., 8am-5pm, 60 pesos per person). Boats can also be taken up the canyon from **Cahuaré,** where the highway to Tuxtla Gutiérrez crosses the river near the Cahuaré Island Resort. The trip down the river is best made during the month of August, at the height of the rainy season, when waterfalls are fuller and less trash floats on the river.

Back in Chiapa de Corzo, the *zócalo* contains two interesting colonial structures: a small **clock tower** and a **fountain** shaped like the crown of Queen Isabella of Spain. Often called **La Pila,** this famous Moorish fountain taps underground waterways 5km long and provided the town with fresh drinking water during a 1562 epidemic. Inside the fountain, tile plaques tell the story of Chiapa's colonial history. The red-and-white 16th-century **Catedral de Santo Domingo** sits one block south of the *zócalo* near Río Grijalva. The most famous of the four bells dangling in its tower, Teresa de Jesús, is named after a mystical Spanish saint. (Open daily 6am-2pm and 4-6:30pm.) Alongside the cathedral on La Mexicanidad, a 16th-century ex-convent houses the **Museo de la Laca,** which displays examples of Mexican lacquer work, a handicraft practiced only in Chiapa de Corzo and four other Mexican cities. (Open Tu-Su 10am-6pm. Free.) You can join one of the ongoing lacquering lessons during the summer months (check posted schedules in the museum).

▓ FESTIVALS. During Chiapa's **Feria de San Sebastián** (Jan. 6-23), *los parachicos,* men in heavy costumes and stifling masks, dance from dawn to dusk. The fair's grand finale is a mock **Combate Naval** between the *"españoles"* and *"indios."* More a beauty pageant than a battle, the event features fireworks to simulate cannons, decorated boats, and costumed sailors.

SAN CRISTÓBAL DE LAS CASAS ☎ 9

If San Cristóbal de las Casas (pop. 200,000) isn't on your list of must-see spots, you're looking at the wrong list. Founded in 1528, the city is named for its now-desanctified patron saint, Saint Christopher, and Bartolomé de Las Casas, a crusader for indigenous rights. While much of the city's powerful *indígena* population has adopted Western lifestyles, many still dress in clothing whose patterns haven't altered in centuries. High in the pine-filled cloud forests of the Valley of Jovel, San Cristóbal outdoes virtually every other town in the Republic with its unsullied colonial garden courtyards, red-tile roofs, and narrow streets. Top this combination off with a panorama of lush green mountains, enshrouded by spectacular cloud formations, and you'll see why so many tourists and backpackers come here.

> **❗ INSURRECTION.** On January 1, 1994, *indígena* Zapatista insurgents caught all of Mexico by surprise by taking hold of parts of San Cristóbal. The situation is currently stable; tourists visiting the city and neighboring villages should not encounter any difficult situations so long as they always carry their visa and passport. People who come here with political or human rights agendas, however, could very well face deportation.

▐ TRANSPORTATION

First- and second-class bus stations are scattered along the Pan-American Highway near Insurgentes. The **Cristóbal Colón station** is on Insurgentes. To get downtown, take a right (north) on Insurgentes and walk seven blocks to the *zócalo*. Cristóbal Colón (☎678 02 91) sends buses to: **Campeche** (10hr., 11am, 266 pesos); **Cancún** (17hr., 2:30pm, 380 pesos); **Comitán** (1½hr., 10am, 32 pesos); **Mexico City** (18hr., 3:30pm and 6pm, 455 pesos); **Oaxaca** (12hr., 5 and 10pm, 228 pesos); **Palenque** (15hr.; 1:15, 7:30am, and 2:30pm; 80 pesos); **Playa del Carmen** (11am, 362 pesos); **Tapachula** (7, 9am, noon, and 5pm; 110 pesos); **Tulum** (13hr., 2:30pm, 342 pesos); **Tuxtla Gutiérrez** (2hr.; 7:45, 11:30am, 2:30, and 9:15pm; 32 pesos); and **Veracruz** (7:30pm, 290 pesos). Altos is your best bet for **Mérida** (9:30am, 270 pesos); **Villahermosa** (11:30am and 4pm, 120 pesos); and **Ocosingo** (2, 9:30, and 11:30am; 110 pesos). From the other bus stations, walk east on any cross-street and turn left on Insurgentes. Since San Cristóbal is a popular destination for tourists, most of whom travel by bus, bus reservations are a good idea.

▟ PRACTICAL INFORMATION

TOURIST AND FINANCIAL SERVICES

Tourist Office: State office **Sedatur** (☎678 65 70), on Hidalgo, half a block south of the *zócalo*. Open M-Sa 9am-9pm, Su 9am-2pm. **City office** (☎678 06 65) at the northwest end of the Palacio Municipal. Open M-Sa 8am-8pm, Su 9am-8pm.

Currency Exchange: Bancomer, Plaza 31 de Marzo 10 (☎678 13 51), on the south side of the *zócalo*. 24hr. **ATM.** Open M-F 8:30am-5:30pm, Sa 10am-2pm.

Car Rental: Budget, Mazariegos 39 (☎678 31 00), 3 blocks west of the *zócalo*. Also at travel agencies throughout town. Open M-Sa 8am-2pm and 4-8pm, Su 8-11am.

▨ Bike Rental: Los Pinguinos, 5 de Mayo #10-B (☎678 02 02; email pinguinos@hotmail.com), between 5 de Febrero and Victoria. 55 pesos per 5 hr., 70 pesos per day. Tours available. Open M-Sa 10am-2:30pm and 4-7:30pm, Su 10am-2:30pm. Tours leave at 8:15am. 2 person minimum and 1-day advance reservations necessary.

LOCAL SERVICES

English Bookstore: La Pared, Hidalgo 2 (☎678 63 67), half a block south of the *zócalo*, buys and sells new and used books. Open M-Sa 10am-2pm and 4-8pm. **La Casa de la Luna Creciente,** Real de Guadalupe 118, between Guerrero and Isabel la Católica, also shows feminist films. Open M-Su 9am-2pm and 4-8pm.

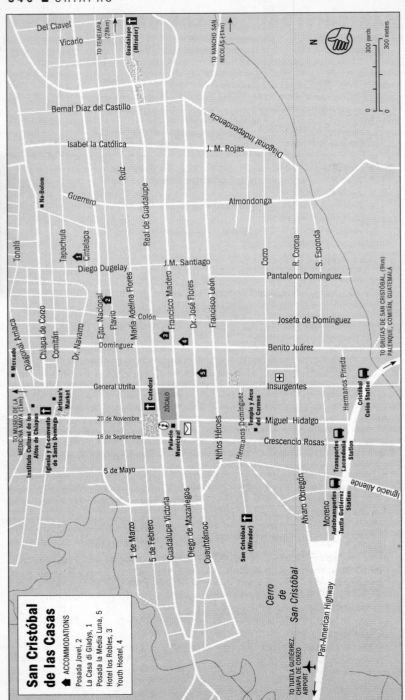

San Cristóbal de las Casas

▲ ACCOMMODATIONS

Posada Jovel, 2
La Casa di Gladys, 1
Posada la Media Luna, 5
Hotel los Robles, 3
Youth Hostel, 4

Markets: The *mercado* between Utrilla and Domínguez, 7 blocks north of the *zócalo*. Best selection on Sa. Open daily 6am-2pm. A huge **artisan's market** forms around the Santo Domingo Church, 5 blocks north of the *zócalo* on Utrilla. Open daily 8am-5pm.

Supermarket: Su Super (☎678 30 21), on Insurgentes across from the Iglesia de San Francisco. Open daily 9am-9pm.

Laundry: Lavomart, Real de Guadalupe 70A, 3½ blocks east of the *zócalo*. 30 pesos per 1-5kg, 60 pesos per 5-8kg; dryer 6 pesos. Open daily 8:15am-8pm.

EMERGENCY AND COMMUNICATIONS

Emergency: ☎060.

Police: (☎678 05 54) in Palacio Municipal, on the west side of the *zócalo*. No English.

Red Cross: Allende 57 (☎678 07 72), 3 blocks south of the Pan-American Highway. No English spoken. 24hr. emergency service.

Pharmacy: Farmacia Regina (☎678 75 35), Mazariegos at Rosas. Open 24hr.

Hospital: Hospital General, Insurgentes 24 (☎678 07 70), 4 blocks south of the *zócalo* across from Santa Lucía in Parque Fray Bartolomé. Open 24hr.

Fax: Mazariegos 29 (☎678 42 71), 2½ blocks from the *zócalo*. Open M-F 8am-6pm, Sa 9am-noon.

Telephones: LADATELs can be found in many hotel lobbies and on the *zócalo*.

Internet Access: Tapanco Cybercafé (☎678 10 14), 1 de Marzo at 20 de Noviembre. 15 pesos per hr. Open daily 8am-11pm. **El Puente,** Real de Guadalupe 55 (☎678 41 57), 2½ blocks east of the *zócalo*. 15 pesos per hr. Open daily 8am-11pm.

Post Office: (☎678 07 65) on Cuauhtémoc at Rosas, 1 block southwest of the *zócalo*. Open M-F 9am-5pm, Sa 9am-1pm. **MexPost** in the same office. Open M-F 8am-2pm.

Postal Code: 29200.

ACCOMMODATIONS

The influx of backpackers has created demand for cheap hotels and hostels, and San Cristóbal has responded with a plentiful supply, most conveniently near the *centro*. Camping is available only outside of town (see below). Due to altitude, the temperature often drops below 10°C (50°F), making blankets indispensable.

La Casa di Gladys, Cintelapa 6 (☎678 57 75) in El Barrio del Cerrillo, 7 blocks northeast of the *zócalo*. The halls are lined with hammocks and cozy alcoves, perfect for doing nothing. Beds 35-45 pesos; rooms with private baths 100 pesos.

Youth Hostel, Juárez 2 (☎678 76 55), between Madero and Flores. The name says it all. Very cheap, clean rooms with spotless communal bathrooms and a TV in the common area. Beds 25 pesos, with private bath 35 pesos.

Posada Jovel, Paniagua 28 (☎678 17 34), 2½ blocks east and 2 blocks north of the *zócalo*. Small rooms with colorful *sarape* bedspreads, multi-level terraces offering city views, and cozy reading areas. Singles 70 pesos, with bath 100 pesos; doubles 80 pesos, with bath 120 pesos; triples 90 pesos, with bath 150 pesos.

Hotel Los Robles, Madero 30 (☎678 00 54), 2 blocks from the *zócalo*. Rooms come with private bath, and tiles cover all floors as far as the eye can see. Singles 80 pesos; doubles 120 pesos; triples 150 pesos. Discounts for larger groups.

Posada La Media Luna, Dr. José Flores 1 (☎678 88 14), between Insurgentes and Juárez. Rooms decorated with pastels. Common baths. A 600 movie video library keeps guests occupied. Breakfast included. Singles 100 pesos; doubles 150 pesos.

Rancho San Nicolás, Dobilla 47 (☎678 00 57), on the extension of León, 1km east of town. A taxi is your best bet (12 pesos). If no one is around, ring the bell of the *hacienda* across the road. Rooms, camping, and a trailer park. Horse rental 160 pesos per day. During high season (mid-July to Aug. and Dec.-Feb.), call in advance. Camping 30 pesos per person; rooms 40 pesos per person. Vehicles 20 pesos extra.

⌐⌐ FOOD AND CAFES

Restaurants in San Cristóbal cater to the international scene, so authentic regional cuisine is sometimes hard to come by. Don't let this discourage you—there is still plenty of great, inexpensive food in the city, and vegetarian restaurants are as plentiful as *churro* stands. Try the *sopa de pan* (bread soup) and grainy wheat breads from the Barrio San Ramón, and end your meal with an exquisite *cerveza dulce*, or a cup of Mexico's best coffee.

El Gato Gordo, Madero 28 (☎678 04 99), between Domínguez and Colón, is ideal for budget-style face-stuffing. The *menú del día* (17 pesos) comes with enough food to feed a small family. Open W-M 8:30am-11pm.

Restaurante Madre Tierra, Insurgentes 19 (☎678 42 97), opposite the Iglesia de San Francisco, 2½ blocks south of the *zócalo*. Choose a cozy corner and dig into the *menú viajero* (30 pesos). Open daily 8am-10pm.

Restaurant Flamingo's, Madero 14, half a block east of the *zócalo*. Specializing in regional, national, and international cuisine, the best bet is the *menú del día* (26 pesos). The two painted flamingoes go unexplained. Open daily 11am-11pm.

La Salsa Verde, 20 de Noviembre 7 (☎678 72 80), 1 block north of the *zócalo*. It's hard to miss this taco diner with its red and green sign, red lamps, green tablecloths, and pine-covered floor. Tacos 5 pesos. Open daily 8am-midnight.

Restaurante París México, Madero 20 (☎678 06 95), half a block east of the *zócalo*. French and Mexican culinary hybrids take center stage. Extensive *menú del día* comes with a margarita and goes for 32 pesos. Open daily 6am-11pm.

Centro Cultural El Puente, Real de Guadalupe 55 (☎678 37 23), 2½ blocks from the *zócalo*. This cafe/language-school/cinema mixes local art and jazz with distinct leftist flavors. Vegetarians can feast on the cheese, tomato, and avocado omelette (26 pesos) and sandwiches (20 pesos). Open daily 8am-9pm.

Cafetería del Centro, Real de Guadalupe 15B (☎678 63 68), 1 block east of the *zócalo*. *Comida corrida* (soup, entree, rice, bread, desert, and coffee) and breakfasts (22 pesos) fill the tables of this friendly restaurant. Open daily 7am-9:30pm.

CAFES

Café Museo, María Flores 10 (☎678 78 76), between Utrilla and Domínguez. A coffee museum, garden, and pastry shop. Live music, usually F-Sa 8-10pm. Organic coffee 8-15 pesos. Proceeds help indigenous coffee producers. Open daily 10am-10pm.

La Selva Café, Rosas 9 (☎678 72 43), at Cuauhtémoc. A jungle patio and diagrams on coffee production entice sippers and pastry enthusiasts alike. Organic coffee and tea 8-20 pesos; tiramisu, cheesecake, and ice-cream 5-24 pesos. Proceeds help indigenous coffee producers. Open daily 9am-11pm.

👁 SIGHTS

NA-BOLOM. San Cristóbal's most famous attraction is Na-Bolom (House of the Jaguar), a private house that turns into a museum twice daily. Guided tours lead you through the estate of Frans and Trudy Blom, who worked among the dwindling *indígena* communities of the **Lacandón Rainforest** on the Guatemalan border. Each year volunteers from all over the world carry out the projects the Bloms began, and conduct tours of Bloms' library and neoclassical *hacienda*. The library's manuscripts focus on Maya culture, rainforest ecology, and the plight of Indian refugees. The small chapel (the building was originally intended as a seminary) serves as a gallery of colonial *chiapaneco* religious art. Other rooms are devoted to archaeological finds from the nearby site of **Moxviquil** (mosh-UEE-queel), religious artifacts from the Lacandón Rainforest, and the works of artists in residence. If the museum is not enough for you, stay as a dinner guest at the

Bloms' original table, set for 33. If you're still not satisfied, stay as a house guest in one of the 15 rooms furnished by Frans and decorated by Trudy, with a fireplace, mini-library, antique bath, and original black and white photos. *(Guerrero 33. In the northeast section of the city at the end of Chiapa de Corzo. ☎ 678 14 18; fax 678 55 86. Guided tours at 11:30am and 4:30pm, followed by a 15min. film. 25 pesos. Shop open daily 9am-1pm and 3-7pm; library open M-Sa 11am-2pm. Dinner daily 7pm; 75 pesos; make reservations the morning or day prior to your visit. Rooms 375 pesos per person; discounts for longer stays. Those interested in volunteering should contact the main office (or email nabolom@sclc.ecosur.mx) at least 2 months prior to arrival.)*

MUSEUM OF MAYA MEDICINE. Also called the **Centro de Desarrollo de la Medicina Maya (CEDEMM),** this museum features simulated Maya healing rituals, strong-smelling Maya herbs, and hypnotic shaman prayers. If you have an iron stomach, ask to see the video on Maya midwifery. Medicine men are on hand to advise you on any problems you might be having. *(Blanco 10, 1km north of the market. ☎/fax 678 54 38. Open M-F 9am-6pm, Sa-Su 10am-5pm. 15 pesos.)*

ZÓCALO. Since its construction by the Spanish in the 16th century, San Cristóbal's *zócalo,* known as the **Plaza 31 de Marzo,** has been the physical and spiritual center of town. The **Palacio Municipal,** on the west side of the plaza, was begun in 1885, burned to the ground in 1863, and, when completed, was only a quarter of the planned size. The yellow **Catedral de San Cristóbal** is on the north side of the plaza. Inside, the cathedral features a splendid wooden pulpit and chirping birds in the rafters. *(Cathedral open daily 7am-7pm.)*

IGLESIA Y EX-CONVENTO DE SANTO DOMINGO. North on Utrilla beyond the Iglesia de la Caridad, is the Iglesia y Ex-Convento de Santo Domingo, whose grounds make up the artisan market. The most beautiful church in San Cristóbal, it was built by the Dominicans in 1551 and rebuilt and enlarged to its present size in the 17th century. The elaborate stone facade houses an inner sanctuary, delicately covered in gold leaf and dozens of portraits, most of then anonymously painted in the 18th century. *(Open daily 7am-8pm.)*

CENTRO CULTURAL DE LOS ALTOS DE CHIAPAS. Located in the Ex-Convento, the Centro Cultural houses an excellent multimedia exhibit on the history of San Cristóbal and Chiapas, with colonial artifacts, photographs, and *chiapaneo* textiles. *(Open Tu-Su 10am-5pm. 20 pesos; Su free. Tours in Spanish.)*

LOOKOUT POINTS. San Cristóbal is overlooked by two hilltop churches. **El Templo del Cerrito San Cristóbal,** on the west side of town, is accessible by a set of stairs at the intersection of Allende and Domínguez. **El Templo de Guadalupe,** its eastern counterpart, can be reached by walking west on Real de Guadalupe. Both areas are considered slightly unsafe—go during the day or with friends.

🎭🎵 NIGHTLIFE AND ENTERTAINMENT

A walk down the glitzy drags of Madero or Guadalupe will take you past hordes of foreign travelers and euro-bohemians. Don't be too jaded—hip locals infuse some reality into the scene. Both energetic discoers and fans of the mellow, kick back approach will be pleased by a night on this town. For those with aching feet, technophobia, or a lack of attire, US movies are screened at **Cinemas Santa Clara** (☎ 678 23 45), on 16 de Septiembre between Escuadrón and 28 de Agosto, and **Cinema El Puente,** Real de Guadalupe 55 (☎ 678 37 23), three blocks from the *zócalo,* inside El Centro Cultural El Puente.

BARS

🍸 **La Margarita,** Real de Guadalupe 34A (☎ 678 09 57), 1½ blocks off the *zócalo,* hosts a scorching flamenco, rumba, and salsa quartet. Free "Tequila Boom-Boom." Music daily 9:30pm-midnight.

La Galería, Hidalgo 3 (☎678 15 47), half a block south of the *zócalo*. The cavernous interior is filled with live music and circles of friends engaged in intimate conversations. Cocktails 20 pesos. Live music 9pm-2am. Open nightly until 2am.

Cocodrilo (☎678 08 71), on the south side of the *zócalo*, cues the band at 10pm every night. Grab a pint from the bar and enjoy.

CLUBS

Not to be outdone by the Yucatán, San Cristóbal has its own Ruta Maya—here, the temples are smoke-filled discos, and virginity is the only sacrifice.

Blue Bar, Rosas 2, one block west of the *zócalo*. The guards pat down all the men before letting them into this den of sinful pleasures. Nightly live music gives way to thumping dance beats. Two-for-one beers until 11pm. Open daily 9pm-6am.

Las Velas, Madero 14 (☎678 04 17), half a block east of the *zócalo*. The candles light the way to the bar and the stage, where the band, after descending the spiral staircase, jams from 11pm onwards. Two-for-one beers 9-11pm. Cover 10 pesos.

A-DOVE, Hidalgo 2 (☎678 66 66), on the southwest corner of the *zócalo*. Nightly techno until the wee hours. For a breather, step out onto the balconies overlooking the plaza.

SPORTS

Saddle up, *vaquero!* San Cristóbal's prized recreational activity is horseback riding. Horseback rides to San Juan Chamula leave from **La Casa de Gladys** (☎678 57 75; daily at 9:30am). **Rancho San Nicolás** also offers horse rentals. (☎678 00 57. 160 pesos per day.) If you happen to be in the vicinity of Las Grutas de San Cristóbal, **Ranch Nuevo,** across from the entrance to the caves, also rents horses. (50 pesos per hr., 100 pesos with guide.)

SHOPPING

San Cristóbal is a financial crossroads for the indigenous peoples of Los Altos de Chiapas. The daily morning market overflows with fruit, veggies, and an assortment of cheap goods. For souvenirs and jewelry, look to the market around **Iglesia de Santo Domingo.** Try coming on Sunday, when *indígenas* from nearby villages turn out in droves, or go to the villages themselves (see **Near San Cristóbal** p. 551). **Utrilla** and **Real de Guadalupe,** the two streets radiating from the northeastern corner of the *zócalo*, are dotted with colorful shops that sell *típico* attire and amber. (Market open daily 7am-5pm or until the afternoon rain.) Tucked into the Ex-Convento is **Sna Jolobil,** which means "House of Weaving" in Tzeltal. It is a cooperative of 800 weavers from Tzotzil and Tzeltal villages in the *chiapaneco* highlands whose objective is to preserve and revitalize ancestral weaving techniques. While many of the top-quality *huipiles* will cost more than your plane ticket home, Sna Jolobil is a good place to window-shop the area's traditional garments. (☎/fax 678 26 46. Open M-Sa 9am-2pm and 4-6pm.)

FESTIVALS

Three blocks south of the *zócalo* on Hidalgo is the Centro Cultural El Carmen, where university students stage dances. (☎678 23 49. Every Th.) Mid-July brings the month-long **Feria de Ambar** to the Centro Cultural, and artisans from all over Chiapas flock to San Cristóbal to sell amber. A true treasure of San Cristóbal is its bi-annual film festival, held in the Teatro Zebadúa (☎678 36 37), two blocks north of the *zócalo* on 20 de Noviembre. In San Cristóbal and the nearby villages, hardly a week goes by without some kind of religious festival. On Easter Sunday, Semana Santa gives way to the week-long **Feria de la Primavera y de la Paz.** Before the riotous revelry gets under way, a local beauty is selected to preside over the festivities, which include concerts, dances, bullfights, cockfights, and baseball games. Hotel rooms must be reserved several months in advance. The **Fiesta de San Cristóbal,** the city's desanctified saint is vigorously celebrated July 18-25 with religious ceremonies, concerts, and a truly staggering number of fireworks. Among the weirder traditions of the *fiesta*, a procession of cars, trucks, and *combis* from all over Chiapas proceed slowly up the road to Cerro San Cristóbal. At the top, the driver opens the hood and door on the driver's side so that the engine and controls can be sprinkled with holy water by a Catholic priest, a blessing to avoid accidents on the perilous mountain roads for yet another year.

⊠ DAYTRIPS FROM SAN CRISTÓBAL DE LAS CASAS

A host of indigenous villages lie within easy reach of San Cristóbal, each with its own unique history and traditions. Sunday morning is the best time to visit the markets of nearby villages, but, because service is always routed through San Cristóbal, visiting more than one village in a single morning is almost impossible. *Combis* leave from various stands in the vicinity of the market. Destination signs are only occasionally accurate; always ask drivers where they're going.

Visiting on your own may give you more freedom, but a guide will provide you with more information and let you in on secrets you'd otherwise miss. The highly-regarded and knowledgeable **Mercedes Hernández Gómez** leads tours. Look for her and her huge golf umbrella at the *zócalo* (5hr., daily at 9am; 100 pesos for Chamula and Zinacantán tours). **Raul and Alex** have a wealth of information on everything from regional customs to the Zapatista uprising. Look for their blue *combis* daily at 9:30am on the cathedral side of the *zócalo* (☎678 37 41; 85 pesos for Chamula and Zinacantán tours). For a tour of San Nicolás, Chamula, and Zinacantán, join **Pepe Santiago** at Na-Bolom. Pepe is a native of nearby Tenejapa, and part of his profits are given to volunteer programs at Na-Bolom (daily at 10am; 100 pesos).

 NO PICTURES, PLEASE. The Maya of the villages surrounding San Cristóbal de las Casas practice a unique fusion of Catholicism and native religion. In this system of faith, it is commonly believed that when a person is photographed, a piece of his spirit is captured. While in these villages, **do not take photographs under any circumstances.**

SAN JUAN CHAMULA

Combis to Chamula leave San Cristóbal on Cárdenas, 1 block west and 1 block north of the market (15min., every 15min. 6am-4pm, 6 pesos). To reach Chamula by car, drive west from the zócalo on Victoria and bear right after crossing the small bridge on Diagonal Ramón Larraínzar. At the fork, go right; Chamula is at the end of the 4km road.

The community of San Juan Chamula, "the place of adobe houses" in Tzotzil, (80,000 inhabitants) is the largest and most touristed village near San Cristóbal. Ten kilometers northwest of San Cristóbal, the town is comprised of 98 *parajes* (clusters of 15-20 families). It is known for its colors (black and blue), its carnival, and its shamanic-Catholic church. Chamulans expelled their last Catholic priest in 1867 and are famous for their resistance to Mexico's religious and secular authority. Villagers have far greater faith in the powers of the local shamans than in the regional Catholic church—the Catholic bishop, residing in Tuxtla Gutiérrez, is allowed into the church but once a month to preform baptisms. Similarly, the government medical clinic is only used if shamanic methods have failed. Before entering the **church** (open daily 5am-7pm), which also functions as a hospital, you must obtain a permit (5 pesos) from the tourist office in the *zócalo*. At the front of the church is a sculpture of St. John the Baptist, who, after the Sun, is the second most powerful figure in the Chamulan religion. Jesus Christ resides in a coffin, since he is believed never to have been resurrected. Chamulans take their religion seriously, and if a resident is found to have lost faith in the Chamulan church, he or she is promptly expelled from the village. The village has a shrine for each saint, which occupies the residence of the current *cargo* holder *(or mayordomo)*, responsible for that saint—just look for the leaf arches outside signaling the house's holy function. Homes and chapels are generally not open to the public—join an organized tour for a peek into private Chamulan life.

The best time to visit Chamula is one week before Ash Wednesday, during **Carnaval,** which draws approximately 70,000 *indígenas* and 500 tourists per day. The festivities have their origins in the ancient Maya ritual concerning the five "lost" days, or *wayeb*, at the end of a 360-day *tun* cycle. In addition to Chamula's *carnaval* and the assumption of the *cargo* (Dec. 30-31), the *fiesta* of **San Juan Bautista** (June 22-24) is a major celebration. Also popular are the *fiestas* of **San Sebastián** (Jan. 19-21), **San Mateo** (Sept. 21-22), and the **Virgen de Fátima** (Aug. 28).

SAN LORENZO ZINACANTÁN

Combis to Zinacantán (6 pesos) leave San Cristóbal from the lot near the market (daily 6am-8pm). If driving, follow Victoria west from the zócalo and turn right after crossing the bridge on Diagonal Ramón Larraínzar. At the fork, turn left.

Eight km from Chamula lies the smaller, colorful community of Zinacantán (pop. 38,000). Comprised of a ceremonial center and outlying hamlets, village women wear ribbons on each braid, and men flaunt dazzlingly red *chuj.* Of late, the village's flower industry has flourished, and Zinacantán has actually started international exploration of its flowers. The many structures with the plastic roots that you will see dotting the hillsides are, in fact, greenhouses. Somewhat exceptional for a *chiapaneco* village is the fact that Zinacantán has accepted the Catholic clergy. The village's handsome, white-washed **church** dates back to the 16th century and, along with the small white convent, it is used for both Catholic and pre-Conquest forms of worship (5 peso entrance fee in addition to a small donation in the *limosna* box). Ever-present native religion is attested to by the animal sculptures lining the interior. The Catholic priest, independent of the village church, merely busies himself with confirmations, baptisms, and wedding ceremonies. Zinacantán's major festival is the **Fiesta de San Lorenzo** (Aug. 18-21). Others include the **Fiesta de San Sebastián** (Jan. 19-22) and **Semana Santa.**

SAN ANDRÉS LARRAÍNZAR

Combis leave San Cristóbal from the small lot on the right side of the road after you cross the bridge north of the market on Utrilla (50min., 5am-4pm, 12 pesos). It's best to return before 2pm—soon after the market shuts down and the combis stop running. By car, take the road northwest from to Chamula and continue past the village. On a curve some 10km later, a sign reading "S.A. Larraínzar" points left to a road climbing the steep side of the valley; the village lies approximately 6km beyond the fork.

The site of the Zapatista negotiations in 1995 and 1996, San Andrés Larraínzar lies 26km northwest of San Cristóbal. Because there are no convenient tours to the village, its 5000 citizens are better disposed to visitors. The village colors are red, black, and white, appearing on most clothing and market items. Mexicans refer to the village as Larraínzar, but local Tzotziles prefer San Andrés. Since many of the villagers are reluctant to carry their produce all the way to San Cristóbal, San Andrés's **market** (open F-Su until 1pm) is better stocked than the ones at Chamula or Zinacantán. For a panoramic view of the valleys and patches of cornfields surrounding the city, walk up the hill from the main church to La Iglesia de Guadalupe. **Carnaval** is the seasonal highlight of this town.

CHENALHÓ

Combis for Chenalhó leave San Cristóbal from an alley off the right side of Utrilla, 1 block before the bridge as you walk north from the market (45min., 6am-4pm, 13 pesos). If you choose to drive, continue on the road past Chamula for about 20km.

Foreigners are rare entities at Chenalhó (pop. 10,000), which seems more remote from San Cristóbal than 32km would suggest. Typical dress for men varies from white or black ponchos worn over pants and bound with heavy belts to short, light, white tunics. Women who have not adopted more current fashions dress uniformly in dark blue skirts and white *tocas* (shawls) embroidered with bright orange flowers. The **market** spreads into the plaza in front of the church on Sunday and sells mostly foodstuffs, including *chiche*, a potent drink made from fermented cane. Villagers enthusiastically wave visitors into **San Pedro,** the church in the town's center, which serves as both a secular and a religious meeting place. Chenalhó residents celebrate **Carnaval** and **La Fiesta de San Pedro** (late June).

HUÍTEPEC ECOLOGICAL RESERVE

The reserve lies just off the road to Chamula, 3½km from San Cristóbal, and can be reached by any combi headed in that direction; ask the driver to let you off at the "Reserva Huítepec" (10min., every 15min., 6 pesos). To get back, walk 500m down the hill toward San Cristóbal and you will come across a combi stop (2.5 pesos). Open Tu-Su 9am-4pm. 10 pesos. Guided tours of groups of 10 or more 150 pesos.

The Huítepec Ecological Reserve, on the east face of the **Huítepec Volcano**, offers the chance to explore an evergreen cloud forest ecosystem. Two trails wind around the park, home to over 100 species of birds and more than 300 species of plant. Those with medicinal properties or religious importance are marked with small signs. The shorter of the two trails makes for a self-led, invigorating 2km hike, rising to a height of 2390m. The longer 8km hike is headed by a guide.

ROMERILLO AND TENEJAPA

Combis and taxis to Romerillo and Tenejapa leave from San Cristóbal, on Utrilla 1 block west and 1 block north of the market (15-20 pesos).

El Cementerio de Romerillo, on the way to Tenejapa (pop. 5000), sits atop Los Altos de Chiapas with 32 tall blue and green wooden crosses. This indigenous cemetery comes alive during the **Día de los Muertos** (Nov. 2). The plank on each mound of dirt is a piece of a relative's bed or door, and beaten shoes are scattered around for the spirits' use. Tenejapa, 28km from San Cristóbal, is surrounded by mountains, canyons and corn fields. Crosses representing the tree of life stand at crossroads, near adobe homes, and in front of **La Iglesia de San Ildefonso.** The women's *huipiles* are replete with pre-Hispanic symbols such as the sun, earth, frogs, flowers, and butterflies. The men wear a black poncho tied at the waist with a belt, red and white trousers, dark boots, and a purse diagonally across the chest. Religious and community leaders carry a staff of power and a long rosary necklace. Tenejapa's *mercados* (Th and Su mornings), the **Fiesta de San Alonzo** (Jan. 21), and the **Fiesta de Santiago** (July 23) attract crowds from near and far.

AMATENANGO DEL VALLE

Walk 2 blocks east of the bus station on the Pan-American highway, and a small bus terminal will be on your right. Take a bus to Teopisca (10 pesos) and from there transfer to a bus headed for Amatenango del Valle (3 pesos).

Amatenango del Valle, known for its fine pottery, is 37km southeast of San Cristóbal toward Comitán. Women are the sole creators of hand-molded pitchers, vases, pots, and jars. Each piece is baked with firewood, following pre-Hispanic techniques. **La Casa de Juliana** is the most visited cooperative pottery house, with an original *temascal* or *baño de vapor* (steam bath). Look for Juliana's sculpture in San Cristóbal, one block east of the Cristóbal Colón bus station.

GRUTAS DE SAN CRISTÓBAL

Take the bus to Teopisca (see above) and ask to be let off at the grutas (6 pesos). To return, hop on any westbound combi. From the highway, a 5min. walk through the park brings you to the entrance. Open daily 9am-4:30pm. 10 pesos.

From the small entrance at the base of a steep wooded hillside, a tall, narrow fissure, incorporating a chain of countless caves, leads almost 3km into the heart of the rock. A modern concrete walkway, at times 10m above the cave floor, penetrates some 750m into the caverns. The dimly lit caves harbor a spectacular array of stalactites and columns. For a little post-cave recreation, try horseback riding, offered by the fellows from Rancho Nuevo, across from the entrance to the caves.

OCOSINGO ☎9

More rural than its busy *zócalo* first lets on, tourist-free Ocosingo (pop. 27,000) straddles the head of a valley in central Chiapas. As the nearest large settlement to the Lacandón rainforest—the fringes of which harbor the majority of Zapatista rebels—the strategic importance of Ocosingo's location is as obvious as the many

(Mexican military) personnel who walk its streets. Ocosingo's residents still bear painful memories of the January 1994 uprising, when a shootout in the market between the army and Zapatista-allied locals claimed dozens of lives. Despite the military backdrop, dusty streets, and ramshackle buildings, Ocosingo is a relatively safe and quiet base from which to explore the nearby ruins of **Toniná.** Perhaps most importantly, the city is also the home of *quesillo*, huge balls of cheese which are sold from windows and doorways city-wide.

⌐ TRANSPORTATION

Ocosingo lies 72km northeast of San Cristóbal de las Casas and 119km south of Palenque. To get to the *zócalo* from the **Cristóbal Colón bus station** or the **Autotransportes Tuxtla station,** walk uphill two blocks and take a left at the "centro" sign. The *zócalo* is three blocks downhill. Autotransportes Tuxtla Gutiérrez (☎673 01 39), on the highway, sends buses to **Villahermosa** (8 per day, 85 pesos); **Palenque** (8 per day, 45 pesos); **Tuxtla Gutiérrez** (10 per day, 50 pesos); **San Cristóbal** (10 per day, 28 pesos); **Chetumal** (3pm, 170 pesos); **Tulum** (3pm, 235 pesos); **Playa del Carmen** (3pm, 245 pesos); **Cancún** (3pm, 300 pesos); **Campeche** (9pm, 170 pesos); and **Mérida** (9pm, 225 pesos). Cristóbal Colón (☎673 04 31), right next door, goes to **México City** (7pm, 427 pesos) and **Puebla** (7pm, 342 pesos).

✦🔛 ORIENTATION AND PRACTICAL INFORMATION

Ocosingo is laid out in the customary compass grid, with **avenidas** running east-west and **calles** running north-south. Street numbers increase in all directions from **Av. Central** and **Calle Central.** From the *zócalo*, cardinal directions are marked by the Hotel Central to the north, the Iglesia de San Jacinto to the east, and the Palacio Municipal to the west. **Banamex,** on the northwest corner of the *zócalo*, does not change currency, but will give cash advances on major credit cards. 24hr. **ATM.** (☎673 00 34. Open M-F 9am-2pm.) **Market:** 4 blocks downhill east on 2 Av. Sur. **Luggage storage:** available at the Cristóbal Colón station (5 pesos per day). **Police:** (☎673 05 07), in the Palacio Municipal on the west side of the *zócalo*. **Pharmacy: Cruz Blanc,** Av. 2 Sur and Calle 1 Ote., one block south of the church. (☎673 02 33. Open daily 7am-10pm.) **Centro de Salud,** Av. Central 16, just west of the *zócalo*. No English spoken. (Open 24hr.) **Telecomm,** on Av. Central, 2 blocks west of the *zócalo*. (Open M-F 9am-3pm, Sa 9am-1pm.) **Post office:** Av. 2 Sur #12 between Calle Central and Calle 1 Ote. 12, one block south of the *zócalo*. (Open M-F 8am-3pm, Sa 9am-1pm.) **Postal code:** 29950.

▌▐ ACCOMMODATIONS AND FOOD

Ocosingo has a broad range of accommodations, with a couple spots offering luxurious amenities for decent prices. **Hotel Bodas de Plata,** Av. 1 Sur at Calle 1 Pte., off the southwest corner of the *zócalo*, is a true budget hotel, with fans, private baths, and a distinctive odor. (☎673 00 16. Singles 70 pesos; doubles 80 pesos triples 100 pesos; quads 120 pesos.) **Hotel Central,** Central 5, on the north side of the *zócalo*, is an oasis of clean, well-ventilated rooms with comfortable beds and spacious baths. Bottled water and cable TV. (☎673 00 24. Singles 120 pesos; doubles 160 pesos; triples 180 pesos.) **Hotel Nakum,** Calle Central Nte. 19, a half-block north of Hotel Central, is newly renovated with firm beds, phones, TVs, and spanking new bathrooms. (☎673 02 80. Singles 150 pesos; doubles 180 pesos; triples 200 pesos.)

Restaurant La Montura, Central 5, in the Hotel Central on the north side of the *zócalo*, is overpriced, but the outdoor tables are the most pleasant in town. Entrees 40-45 pesos, *tortas* with beans and avocado 18 pesos. (☎673 05 50. Open daily 7am-11pm.) **El Buen Taquito,** on Central on the north side of the *zócalo*, is everything a budget taco joint should be. Blaring TV, plastic tables and chairs. Tacos 2.5 pesos, sodas 5 pesos. (Open daily 6:30pm-midnight.)

DAYTRIPS FROM OCOSINGO

TONINÁ RUINS

The ruins are 15km east of Ocosingo and easily accessible by "Toniná" combis, which leave from the market (20min., every 30min., 10 pesos) and drop you at the newly-dedicated museum. Ruins are 500m farther down the road. Open daily 9am-4pm. 25 pesos; free Su. Because the ruins have no explanations, a guide can be very helpful (about 100 pesos for a group of 5).

The Toniná complex, (15 acres of ruins) was a religious and administrative center that flourished during the Classic Period (AD 300-1000), with most construction taking places around AD 700. The city was abandoned in the 13th century for unknown reasons, and many statues have lost pieces to decay and neglect. At the turn of the century, the governor of Ocosingo took stones from the site to build roads; because of this, the pyramids can never be fully restored.

The entrance path leads across the river east of the ruins and up a small gully, emerging at the **juego de pelota** (main ballcourt), with remains of stone rings and five ground markers. Beyond the ballcourt is the sacrificial altar, situated on the first artificially terraced level of the site, the **Temple of War.** The ruins of a smaller ballcourt lie near the steps of the **acropolis.** The seven tiers corresponded to the city's social strata. The first tier contains the **Palace of the Underworld,** with a few representations of Ik (god of the wind) decorating its facade and inner walls. It is believed that if you travel through the corridors of the labyrinth without man-made light you will gain power from the gods of the underworld. Past the fourth tier, the level of governors' bedrooms gives way to the impressive fifth tier's **El Mural de las Cuatro Eras** (The Mural of the Four Eras), on the far right. At the center of this same level is a royal grave where archaeologists discovered a stone sarcophagus, holding a king's body and two unidentified corpses. To the left of the grave is a shrine to Chac, the Maya rain god. **The Altar de Monstruo de la Tierra** is on the right-hand side of the sixth level. The seventh level of the pyramid, Toniná's religious focal point, supports four large pyramids. **The Temple of Agriculture,** on the far right of the terrace is decorated with roof combs. To the left is the **Temple of the Prisoners.** Despite the name, which comes from the reliefs of prisoners at the base, archaeologists believe that this mound once housed the king and the royal family. Behind it is the symmetrical **Pyramid of Finances** and, on the right, the higher **Pyramid of War,** which served as an observatory.

PALENQUE ☎9

In all of Mesoamerica, three sites are world-renowned for their reflection of the beauty, power, and glory of the Maya Classic period. Honduras has Copán, Guatemala has Tikal, and Mexico has Palenque. These impressive ruins straddle a magnificent 300m high natural palisade (*palenque*) in the foothills of the Altos de Chiapas. Dense jungle reaches to the bases of Palenque's breathtaking pyramids, and the sounds of birds, monkeys, and crushing waterfalls echo off the walls of the grand palace, temples, and numerous courtyards. The town of Palenque (pop. 63,000) is not nearly as picturesque, but nevertheless is an important crossroads for travelers arriving from all directions to visit the ruins, sample the waters of the famous cascades of Agua Azul and Misol-Ha, make forays into the heart of the Lacandón jungle, and begin excursions to Maya sites in Guatemala.

☐ TRANSPORTATION

All bus stations are five to eight blocks west of the *parque* on Juárez. To get to the *parque* from the stations, walk uphill (east) on Juárez. ADO (☎345 13 44) runs first-class buses to: **Campeche** (6hr., 8am and 9pm, 138 pesos); **Can-**

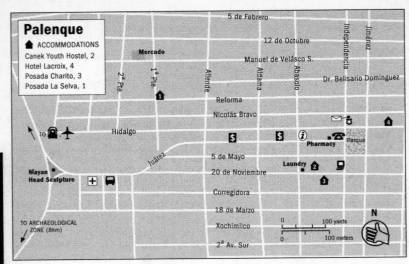

Palenque

ACCOMMODATIONS
Canek Youth Hostel, 2
Hotel Lacroix, 4
Posada Charito, 3
Posada La Selva, 1

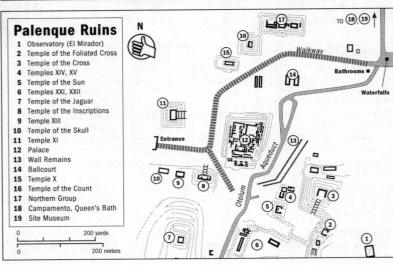

Palenque Ruins

1 Observatory (El Mirador)
2 Temple of the Foliated Cross
3 Temple of the Cross
4 Temples XIV, XV
5 Temple of the Sun
6 Temples XXI, XXII
7 Temple of the Jaguar
8 Temple of the Inscriptions
9 Temple XIII
10 Temple of the Skull
11 Temple XI
12 Palace
13 Wall Remains
14 Ballcourt
15 Temple X
16 Temple of the Count
17 Northern Group
18 Campamento, Queen's Bath
19 Site Museum

cún (12hr., 8pm, 317 pesos); **Chetumal** (7½hr., 8pm, 180 pesos); **Mérida** (8hr., 8am and 9pm, 208 pesos); **Mexico City** (12hr., 6 and 8pm, 431 pesos); **Oaxaca** (13hr., 5:30pm, 330 pesos); **Playa del Carmen** (11hr., 8pm, 294 pesos); **Puebla** (10½hr., 7pm, 380 pesos); **San Cristóbal** (4hr., 10am, 68 pesos); and **Villahermosa** (2hr., 9 per day, 65 pesos). Altos makes the run to **Tuxtla Gutiérrez** (100 pesos) and **Ocosingo** (45 pesos) at 9:30am. **Taxis:** (☎345 01 12) are 40 pesos to the ruins, 15 pesos within town.

ORIENTATION AND PRACTICAL INFORMATION

Palenque is in the northeast corner of Chiapas, 274km from Tuxtla Gutiérrez. Streets running east-west are *avenidas*, and those running north-south are *calles*.

Tourist Office: In the **Casa de las Artesanías,** at the corner of Juárez and Abasolo. Helpful staff speaks some English. Open M-Sa 9am-9pm, Su 9am-1pm.

Currency Exchange: Bancomer, Juárez 40 (☎345 01 98), 2 blocks west of the *parque* with a 24hr. **ATM.** Open for exchange M-F 9am-3:30pm. **Banamex,** Juárez 62 (☎345 04 90). Open M-F 9am-2pm. Also has a 24hr. **ATM.**

Luggage storage: At the Autobuses de Tuxtla Gutiérrez station, half a block toward town from the ADO station. 2 pesos per hr.

Laundry: Lavandería, 20 de Noviembre, west of the Canek Youth Hostel. 20 pesos per 1-2kg, 9 pesos each additional kg. Open M-Sa 8am-2pm and 5-8:30pm, Su 8am-1pm.

Police: (☎345 18 44), on Independencia, in the Palacio Municipal. Open 24hr.

Pharmacy: Farmacia Central (☎345 03 93), Juárez near Independencia. Open daily 7:30am-10:30pm.

Medical Assistance: Centro de Salud y Hospital General (☎345 07 33), on Juárez near the main bus station, at the west end of town. No English spoken. Open 24hr.

Fax: (☎345 18 89) next to the tourist office on Juárez. Open daily 7am-9pm.

Internet Access: Cibernet (☎345 17 10), Independencia between 5 de Mayo and 20 de Noviembre. 20 pesos per 30min., 30 pesos hr. Open daily 9am-9pm.

Telephones: LADATELs are everywhere. **Caseta California,** Juárez 4 (☎345 12 12), is just off the *parque.* Open daily 7am-11pm.

Post Office: Independencia at Bravo, north of the *parque.* Open M-F 9am-4pm, Sa 9am-1pm. **Postal Code:** 29960.

▌ ACCOMMODATIONS AND CAMPING

Slowly but surely, prices are making their way upwards in Palenque. Never fear, some excellent deals are still to be had, especially along the highway to the ruins.

ON THE WAY TO RUINS

▨ **El Panchan,** 5km from town, 1½km from the ruin entrance. This family-run backpacker's oasis is divided into four sections, each with its own accommodations. Three have restaurants, one of which is vegetarian. Bag storage 5 pesos. Camping and hammock space 15 pesos. Cabañas 50 pesos, some with private bath.

Mayabell Trailer Park and Camping (☎348 42 71), 6km from town and 500m from the ruins. Accessible by *combi* (30 pesos). Pitch a tent, string a hammock, or put down a sleeping bag (20 pesos per person). They also have trailer (30 pesos) and car space (20 pesos). The few rooms have fans and private baths. Singles 115 pesos; doubles 125 pesos; triples 150 pesos; 20 pesos per additional person; 100 pesos deposit.

IN TOWN

Canek Youth Hostel 20 de Noviembre 43 (☎345 01 50), is an average hostel with large rooms, decent bathrooms, mountain views, and fans in each room. Dorm beds 40 pesos. Singles with private bath 100 pesos; doubles 100 pesos; triples 150 pesos.

Posada Charito, 20 de Noviembre 15 (☎345 01 21), between Independencia and Abasolo, half a block west of the *parque,* has a friendly, familial atmosphere with large rooms and private baths. Singles 80 pesos; doubles 120 pesos; triples 150 pesos; 80 pesos per additional person. Prices lower during low season.

Posada la Selva, Reforma 69 (☎345 06 41), between Allende and Calle 1a Pte., 5 blocks northwest of the *parque. Agua purificada* in the hallway. Green and white rooms with sparkling private baths, and if you're lucky, a view of the jungle. In-house agency organizes tours. Singles and doubles 120 pesos; triples 140 pesos.

Hotel Lacroix, Hidalgo 10 (☎345 00 14), just off the *parque* and next to Na Chan Kan Travel Agency and Restaurant. A large, gaudy Maya mural with Spanish poetry leads the way to cozy, cool, blue rooms with blue baths. No hot water. Singles 150 pesos; doubles 180 pesos; triples 210 pesos. Prices drop 30 pesos in low season.

TABASCO & CHIAPAS

FOOD

Travelers have about as much chance of finding a cheap restaurant in Palenque as of uncovering an ancient Maya ruin. For cheap produce, try the **market** on Suárez, about seven blocks northwest of the *parque*. The travel agency on the corner of Hidalgo and Jiménez doubles as a bargain food joint. There is also a surprisingly good restaurant at the ruins.

Restaurante Las Tinajas, 20 de Noviembre 41, at Abasolo. Popularity has nudged up prices, but the quality local dishes and large servings keep the tourists coming back for breakfast, lunch, and dinner. Breakfast specials 22 pesos. Open daily 7am-11pm.

Restaurante Maya (☎345 00 42), Independencia and Hidalgo, at the northwest corner of the *zócalo*. Known as the "most ancient restaurant in Palenque," it should stick around for years to come. *Antojitos* 30 pesos. Open daily 7am-11pm.

Restaurant Maya Palenque (☎345 07 81), 20 de Noviembre 38, between Restaurant Las Tinajas and Posada Charito, serves healthful yogurt and fruit platters (18 pesos), salads (15-25 pesos), and local dishes (25-40 pesos). Open daily 7am-11pm.

THE ARCHAEOLOGICAL SITE OF PALENQUE

*The ruins are 8km west of town, most easily accessible by combis (6am-6pm, 10 pesos) which depart from Hidalgo on Allende. There are two entrances to the ruins; one is 50m from the site museum, 2km before the other. Take this entrance if walking from Mayabell or Panchan. Visiting the ruins at night is prohibited and extremely unsafe. Do not take shortcuts to the back entrance from the campgrounds or the road—the dense jungle will isolate you from any other tourists who may be nearby. **Site** open daily 8am-4:45pm. **Museum** 2km before the main entrance open daily 9am-3:45pm. **Crypt** open daily 10am-4pm. 30 pesos, Su free. Guided tours available at main entrance (1-7 people 338 pesos; 8-14 people 423 pesos; 15-25 people 507 pesos).*

Palenque got its start as a small farming village in 100 BC, but grew steadily in the Pre-Classic Period. By around AD 600 Palenque had begun to flourish, in the next two hundred years it saw the zenith of its power. Palenque owes much of its success to the club-footed king **Pacal** (Pak-AL) who inherited the throne from his mother **Zac-Kuk** in AD 615 at the age of 12 and was believed by his subjects to have been semi-divine. According to inscriptions made at the time of his death, Pacal lived into his fifth *katun* (20-year period) and was succeeded in AD 683 by his elderly son **Chan-Bahlum.** Chan-Bahlum celebrated his ascension by building a great pyramid-crypt (Temple of the Inscriptions) for his father. It was during the rule of these two kings that most construction at Palenque took place. Soon after Chan-Bahlum's death in AD 702 Palenque slipped into oblivion, perhaps due to siege at the hands of the rival Totonacs or another Maya city. The city was abandoned around AD 800, and when Cortés arrived in the 16th century, he marched past the city without noting its existence. Today, though impressive, the ruins of Palenque merely hint at the city's former majesty. Only a small fraction of the structures have been excavated from the jungle; new discoveries are ongoing.

TEMPLO DE LAS INSCRIPCIONES (TEMPLE OF THE INSCRIPTIONS). On entering the site, note the tomb of Alberto Ruz, one of Mexico's most famous archaeologists, so devoted to Palenque that he insisted on being buried there. To the right is the Temple of the Inscriptions, with 69 steps representing King Pacal's 69 years of reign. Named for its magnificent tablets, the temple was the burial place of King Pacal and the first substantial burial place unearthed in the Americas. After the disappointing discovery of six unimpressive skeletons, Ruz bore into the interior crypt, removing more than 400 tons of rubble by hand to reach the chamber. There he discovered the perfectly preserved, elaborately carved sarcophagus of the king. The figure in the lower center of the tablet is Pacal himself, shown descending into the underworld with the *ceiba* tree directly over him. Visitors must scramble the long way down slippery stone steps in a steep and stuffy tunnel to view the royal crypt. A hollow duct, which allowed Pacal's spirit to exit the underworld and communicate with Palenque's priests, is on the right after the staircase.

TEMPLO DEL JAGUAR (TEMPLE OF THE JAGUAR). A trail leads up the mountainside to the east of the Temple of the Inscriptions. About 100m along this trail, on the right, is the Temple of the Jaguar. Descend the pitch-black stairwell inside the structure and you'll come upon an ancient well. There, a few faint traces of paint are slowly surrendering to the green slime of the jungle.

EL PALACIO (THE PALACE). Back in the main center, across from the Temple of the Inscriptions, is the trapezoidal Palace complex, consisting of labyrinthian patios and rooms. The palace was most likely used for residential purposes, with royalty occupying the spacious quarters on the north side, and maids and guards occupying the cramped quarters on the south side. The tower, an unusual Maya construction, may have been used for astronomical observation or for watching the winter solstice strike the Temple of the Inscriptions. Carvings throughout the complex laud the royals and priests who inhabited the palace, where the T-shaped ducts cooled the air and doubled as representations of Ik, the god of the breezes. Visitors can clamber down the staircase from the top of the platform to explore the extensive, dimly-lit network of underground passageways with complete remnants of king-size beds and a kitchenette. It is said that the royal family was big-boned and hefty due to their carnivorous feasts. Check out the left leg in one of the outdoor patios. An exclusively female steam bath and latrine has also been excavated, and eight large sculptures of tortured prisoners will keep you staring.

PLAZA DEL SOL (PLAZA OF THE SUN). The path between the palace and the Temple of Inscriptions fords the recently reconstructed aqueduct before leading to the Sun Plaza, another landscaped platform comprised of the **Temple of the Sun,** the **Temple of the Cross,** the **Temple of the Foliated Cross,** and the smaller **Temples XIV** and **XV.** The Temple of the Cross was named for a stucco relief of a cross discovered inside, which inspired a flurry of hopeful religious theories among the *conquistadores.* For the Maya, the cross represents the *ceiba* tree with a snake as its horizontal branch and a bird perched atop it. The outer layer of stucco has worn away, but the inner sanctum protects a large, sculpted tablet and reliefs on either side of the doors. About to be swallowed again by the jungle, the Temple of the Foliated Cross lies across the plaza from the Temple of the Sun. The inner sanctum contains a carved tablet with tints of red fresco. To the south of the Sun Plaza, through the wall of trees, several unreconstructed temples surround the uncleared **Plaza Maudslay,** such as the newly discovered **Temples XVII, XX, XXI,** and **XXII.** Downhill from Temple XIV and past the palace lie the vestiges of a **ballcourt.**

GRUPO NORTE (NORTH GROUP). Across the path from the ballcourt is the **Templo del Conde (Temple of the Count),** named after the kooky archaeologist Frederick Waldeck, who lived here for three years in the 1830s. The four other temples that share the platform with the Temple of the Count comprise the North Group.

QUEEN'S BATH AND MONTIEPA. After crossing the bridge, waterfall enthusiasts may shower and splash in the **Queen's Bath** (so named for its exclusively female clientele). A second set of falls, **Cascada Montiepa,** is hidden in the jungle 600m down the road from the ruins. At the right-hand bend, follow the path into the woods. Unfortunately, overgrown banks and shallow water make swimming impractical. Palenque is full of small paths leading to unrestored ruins and cascades; bring bug spray and a buddy if you intend to explore on your own.

🔁 DAYTRIPS FROM PALENQUE

CASCADAS DE AGUA AZUL AND MISOL-HA

The most painless way to visit Agua Azul and Misol-Ha is by joining a Transportes Misol-Ha tour (80 pesos round-trip). Transports leave daily from the Palenque station in front of Bancomer (9am and noon) and proceed to Agua Azul after a 30min. photo-op at Misol-Ha. Passengers are dropped off by the falls for 3hr. Few buses pass after 4pm, so you should leave by early afternoon. Combis from the bus station in Palenque also go to Misol-Ha (20 pesos) and Agua Azul (30 pesos); wait for a combi to show up to take you back. Agua Azul open daily 8am-5pm. 5 pesos, 20 pesos per carload. Misol-Ha open 24hr. 5 pesos, 25 pesos per carload.

Both of these large *cascadas* (waterfalls) have seduced tourists of late, and for good reason. **Agua Azul,** 58km south of Palenque, is a breathtaking spectacle. The Río Yax-Há jumps down 500 individual falls, slipping in and out of rapids, whirlpools, and calm spots. Currents are extremely dangerous, however, so swimming is only advisable in a few places. *Comedores* and gift shops cluster within a 20 minute walk of the entrance, and **camping** is available 10 minutes upstream from the entrance. (Tents 15 pesos; hammocks 20 pesos; beds 50 pesos.) Instead of having numerous small falls, **Misol-Ha,** 20km south of Palenque, has one giant one—30m tall. At its base is a pool for swimming. Bring a flashlight if you want to explore the underground cave behind the falls. There is only one **restaurant** nearby (open daily 8am-6pm).

YAXCHILÁN

Rising from the banks of the Usumacinta River deep within the Lacandón jungle is the archaeological treasure of Yaxchilán, and, 8km away, its sister site, **Bonampak.** Covering eight square kilometers and extending across the river into Guatemala, only a fourth of Yaxchilán has been fully excavated. Already the vast number of stelae and hieroglyphics have revealed a rich history. The political trouble of the mid-90s postponed plans for a museum and development of the site, so a journey to Yaxchilán is still like the archaeological expeditions of old. This ancient city is so remote, its carvings so clear, and the enveloping jungle so wild that families of toucans, spiders, and howler monkeys are more frequent visitors than humans.

■ PRACTICAL INFORMATION

The nearest town to Yaxchilán, **Frontera Corozal,** is 197km southeast of Palenque. The site is a *lancha* cruise (40min.) down on the Río Usumacinta, and the strong currents make it a longer trip back (1hr.). The road between Palenque and Corozal is a smooth ride, and constant patrolling by Mexican security has made it safer of late. The safest and cheapest way to reach Yaxchilán, however, is through a travel agency that is insured and familiar with Mexican security. Prices with Palenque travel agencies range from 450 pesos for one-day trips to 650 pesos for two days, and usually include meals, boat fare, lodging, transportation, and a visit to Bonampak. If you want to venture off on your own, **Transportes Chancalan** runs *combis* to Frontera Corozal (2½hr., every 2hr. 6am-4pm during the high season, 80 pesos). Beware, however, that you will most likely face roadblocks, pay many tolls, and have to shell out a hefty sum for a *lancha.* No matter how you choose to get to Yaxchilán, be sure to bring your passport and visa to deal with various army roadblocks. Also, make sure to get any errands done before leaving—the nearest services of any kind are in Palenque.

■ ACCOMMODATIONS

The handful of residents near the site entrance have so recently begun to offer **camping** space that prices have not yet been set. The new, self-proclaimed **Centro Ecoturístico Escudo Jaguar** in Frontera Corozal offers colorful *cabanas* with firm beds and fans. It also offers camping and a *palapa* with 15 hammock spaces and common bathroom. The Escudo runs *lancha* trips to the site. Arrangements are made at the hotel. (☎345 03 56. Singles and doubles 250 pesos; triples and quads 350 pesos; hammock and tent space 40 pesos. Tours 695 pesos for 1-6 people, 1000 pesos for 7-10 people.)

SIGHTS

THE ARCHAEOLOGICAL SITE OF YAXCHILÁN
Open daily 8:45am-4:45pm. 30 pesos, Su free.

Yaxchilán ("Green Rocks") is famous for its thousands of glyphs, telling an almost complete history of the city. It had its humble beginnings around 350 BC as a fishing and farming village along the Usumacinta. Yaxchilán's emblem glyph began to appear at other places such as El Cayo, Piedras Negras, and Bonampak after AD 526, suggesting that it played a role at those sites and may have been a regional capital. Years of bloody conquest and expansion during the reign of **Shield-Jaguar** (AD 726-742) made Yaxchilán one of the most important cities of the late Classic Maya. Shield-Jaguar's son, **Bird-Jaguar,** took the throne in AD 752, and, when the validity of his rule was questioned, reinforced his legitimacy undertaking the greatest construction projects Yaxchilán had ever seen. It was during these years that Yaxchilán rose to the peak of its power through royal intermarriages and alliances with neighboring regions. Evidence of trade and iconographic exchange with cities as far as Teotihuacán can also be found in this period. By AD 900, lesser nobles were flouting whatever ruling authority was left and began constructing their houses in the midst of old royal ceremonial centers. Along with many other Maya cities of this time, Yaxchilán was depopulated and eventually abandoned.

Visitors enter Yaxchilán through the **Labyrinth,** underground passageways symbolizing the underworld that have not yet been fully explored. Bring a flashlight to see the original stucco work. The end of the labyrinth opens into the vast **Grand Plaza.** Running west to east, the 500m long and 60m wide plaza was the monumental heart of the city, lined by temples and palaces on both sides. The first significant structure on the north side of the plaza, across from the Labyrinth, is **Building 16.** Three doorways are all that remain of the building, each with carved lintels. The middle one depicts a scene with Bird-Jaguar holding a ceremonial bar dated AD 743. Further down the Grand Plaza is the **ballcourt,** built for two players during Shield-Jaguar's rule. Between Building 16 and the ballcourt on the south side of the plaza stands a 350 year-old *ceiba* tree of life.

Continuing east past the ballcourt, visitors arrive at **Stela 1,** dating from AD 782 and showing the king and his wife undergoing a ritual self-sacrifice. Still on the north of the plaza, past Stela 1, stands **Building 6,** also called the **Temple of Chac,** with original stucco still retaining some of its colors. A few meters past the Temple on the left lie remains of the hieroglyphic steps leading to the ancient bridge, connecting Yaxchilán to Guatemala. Yaxchilán's most elaborate and important carving—**Stela 11,** to the east of Building 6, is engraved on four of its six sides and depicts the transfer of power from Shield-Jaguar to Bird-Jaguar. The monolith was originally found towering in front of Building 40. It was dropped here after numerous efforts to send it to the Museo Nacional de Antropología in Mexico City failed. Across from Stela 11 on the south side of the plaza, past some circular altars and another stela dedicated to Bird-Jaguar, is **Building 20.** Next door to the west is **Building 21,** with original stucco on its superior facade and an engraved lintel depicting the birth of Bird-Jaguar. Inside the building is a stela dating from AD 743 showing one of Shield-Jaguar's wives, **Lady Ik-Skul,** sacrificing her tongue. Along the back wall are stucco reliefs that retain some original red, blue, and green colors.

Some minor buildings line the rest of the south side of the plaza. Before them is a long, steep slope with lintels describing the rise of power of Shield-Jaguar and his first wife, **Lady Fist-Fish,** that climbs past **Buildings 25** and **26** on the left, reaching the immense **Building 33** at the top. The best-preserved of Yaxchilán's buildings, it was ordered to be constructed by Bird-Jaguar IV, and is called the **House of Music.** Legend has it that as storms blow in from the north over Guatemala, the wind creates music was it passes over the building's openings. Inside sits the decapitated statue of Bird-Jaguar himself. No one knows how, when, or why his head came to rest in the next room, but when archaeologists attempted to replace

THE REAL PEOPLE Travelers visiting the ruins of Yaxchilán or Bonampak may have the fortune to meet a member of an indigenous group. The Lacandón Maya, or **Winik** (Real People) as they call themselves, have succeeded for centuries longer than any other Maya people in maintaining their traditional religious practices and beliefs. While the rest fused indigenous religion with Christianity within the first two centuries of Spanish colonialism, the Lacandón refused to accept any facets of Christianity until the 1950s. At that time, the town of Lacanha Chan Sayab converted to Protestantism; in the 1970s, their neighbors in Mansabak converted to Seventh Day Adventism. Today, the Lacandón in the town of Nahá still continue to live entirely outside Christianity. Only a few hundred people still identify themselves as Lacandón (largely defined by speaking Lacandón Mayan); the settlement near Crucero Bonampak known as **San Javier** is home to a number of Lacandóns.

it, they were stopped by the Lacandón Maya, who believe that at the moment the head is rejoined the end of the world will begin. The trail behind Building 33 leads to the opposite side of the grand acropolis composed of **Buildings 39, 40,** and **41.** To reach Building 41, cut through the small plaza. The unimpeded 360° view of the Mexican jungle and Guatemalan highland is well worth the 10-minute hike. If you've got some energy left, take the detour up the mountain to the left to the **small acropolis.** This group is composed of 13 buildings perched about 75m above the grand plaza. The ruins themselves are not particularly striking, but a glimpse of the river below can be caught through the trees.

BONAMPAK

Transportes Chancalan runs combis from Palenque at 5 de Mayo between Allende and Juárez (45 pesos). They stop in San Javier, a 5km walk from Lacunjá, where you can catch a cab for the remaining 3km. Colectivos are not protected by Mexican security, making assaults easier and more frequent. Open daily 8am-5pm. 20 pesos, Su free.

Since their discovery in 1946, the murals of Bonampak ("Painted Walls"), 8km from Yaxchilán, have single-handedly changed scholars' conceptions of Maya civilization. The city was probably subordinate to Yaxchilán, and reached its peak late in the Classic Period, around AD 600-800. Bonampak has fewer engraved glyphs than Yaxchilán. Subsequently, its history is less detailed. The real reason to visit Bonampak is to see the spectacular murals, which, to be sure, have aged after 12 centuries and an ill-advised kerosene dousing by a restoration team. Yet these one-of-a-kind *al fresco* paintings still leave visitors gaping.

Much of what is known about Bonampak pertains to a ruler known as **Chaan Muan II,** who is depicted on the 6m-high **Stela 1,** the first major sight in the **Great Plaza.** Aligned with the central floor of the House of Paintings, the uppermost portion is in total disrepair. Enough remains to present the figure of the king holding spear and shield (dated AD 787). Two other important stelae are situated close to the plaza on the wide steps: **Stela 2,** on the left, depicts Chaan Muan II with two women performing a ritual self-sacrifice. **Stela 3,** on the right, features a richly attired Chaan Muan II standing over a prisoner. The prisoner's beard is a rarity in Maya art, which seldom portrayed facial hair. Stela 2 depicts Chaan Muan II and his mother initiating an alliance with his wife from Yaxchilán.

The **Temple of Paintings,** or **Building 1,** is a three-room building just above and to the right of the Great Plaza. Over the three doorways, from left to right, are lintels of Knotted-Eye Jaguar (an ancestor of Chaan Muan II), Shield-Jaguar II of Yaxchilán, and Chaan Muan II, all about to execute a prisoner. The two-headed serpent bar is a staff of rulership. Inside, the murals of the three rooms combine to form a narrative that reads from left to right. In Chamber 1, the murals depict a procession and the ascendence of an heir to the throne on the right side of the room. Note the musicians and lobster-costumed figure to the lower left. Chamber 2 shows a fierce battle in a forest—over the doorway is a display of tortured prisoners pleading for mercy from the jaguar-skin-robed royalty of Bonampak. The third chamber is a portrait of a victory celebration with dancers and musicians, as well as of the royal family undergoing self-sacrificial rituals. Behind and above the Temple of Paintings are a set of buildings numbered four to eight from right to left. Climb behind Building 4 to get a look at roofless Building 10.

COMITÁN ☎ 9

Eighty-four kilometers southeast of San Cristóbal, Comitán (pop. 110,000) is the last major town on the Pan-American Highway before the Guatemalan border (85km away). Known in Mayan as Balún Canan (Nine Stars), Comitán has recently undergone rapid growth. However, it still offers easy access to some of Chiapas' finest natural wonders, all at a good price. The city doesn't draw the crowds San Cristóbal does, and that can be a good thing. A visit to the *centro* will reward you with steep, cobblestoned streets and the occasional hill-top church.

▐ TRANSPORTATION

The **Cristóbal Colón bus station** (☎632 09 80), is at Domínguez 43. To reach the *zócalo*, cross the highway and turn left. After 200m, take the first right onto Calle 4 Pte. Sur. Walk five blocks to Central Benito Juárez, turn left and then walk three blocks north past the post office to the *zócalo*. **Taxis** (☎632 56 30) cost 15 pesos from bus station to *zócalo*, and can be found in either place. Cristóbal Colón goes to: **Tuxtla Gutiérrez** (3hr., 9 per day, 55 pesos) via **San Cristóbal** (1½hr., 28 pesos); **Tapachula** (6 per day, 82 pesos) via **Ciudad Cuauhtémoc** (29 pesos); **Palenque** (4:30pm, 78 pesos) via **Ocosingo** (36 pesos); **Puerto Escondido** (6:15am, 271 pesos); **Cancún** (1:05pm, 394 pesos); **Puebla** (4 per day, 390 pesos) and **Mexico City** (5 per day, 435 pesos).

> **WHY, CERTAINLY, MAN WITH THE BIG GUN.** Traveling through Chiapas, you will most definitely be stopped frequently for customs, immigration, and military inspections. If you get singled out, don't take offense—it's probably because you seem out of place. Comply with everything asked of you, and **always carry your passport and visa.** Unless you're, say, running arms for the Zapatistas, you should have no troubles.

◤◣▐ ORIENTATION AND PRACTICAL INFORMATION

Domínguez (aka The Pan-American Highway) runs north-south, passing the town to the west. Street numbers increase in all four directions away from the *zócalo*, and are named according to the quadrant in which they fall. **Avenidas** run north-south and **calles** east-west. If an address reads Av. 5 Pte. Sur between Calles 2 and 3 Sur Pte., your destination is 5 blocks west and 2½ blocks south of the northwest corner of the *zócalo*, which is the intersection of Calle Central (also called Juárez) and Central.

Tourist offices: The municipal tourist office, **Codetur,** is on the second floor of the Palacio Municipal on the northern side of the *zócalo*. They will proudly give you the new tourist brochure they have just started publishing. (☎632 62 13 or 632 19 31, ext. 39. Open M-F 9am-2pm and 5-7pm.) Another **tourist office,** Plaza Central #6, next to Palacio Municipal, overflows with brochures, maps, and a friendly staff. (☎632 40 47. Open M-F 8am-3pm.) Guatemalan visas can be obtained from the **Guatemalan Consulate,** Av. 1 Sur Pte. #26, at Av. 2 Sur Pte., marked by a blue and white flag. (☎632 04 91. Open M-F 9am-5pm.) Depending on your country of origin, obtaining a visa will take 10-30 days (US$25). **Bancomer,** on the southeast corner of the *zócalo*, has a 24hr. **ATM.** (Open M-F 8:30am-5:30pm, Sa 10am-2pm.) **Market:** on Calle Central, just before Av. 2 Ote., one block east of the *zócalo*. (Open daily dawn-dusk.) **Supermarket: Supermás,** on Calle 2 Sur Pte. between Domínguez Sur and Av. 1 Pte. Sur. (☎632 17 27. Open daily 8am-8:30pm.) **Police:** (☎632 00 25) in the Palacio Municipal. No English spoken. **Red Cross:** (☎632 18 89) on Calle 5 Nte. Pte., 3½ blocks west of the highway. **Farmacia Regina,** Calle 1 Sur Ote. 1, on the south side of the *zócalo.* (☎632 11 96. Open daily 24hr.) **Medical Assistance: Centro Médico de Comitán,** on Av. 1 Pte. Sur between Calles 2 and 3 Pte. Sur. No English spoken. (☎632 00 67. 24hr. service.) **Telecomm,** Domínguez Sur 47, 1½ blocks south of the *zócalo.* (Open daily 8am-7pm.) **Café Internet,** Morales 12, to the right of the Palacio Municipal. (20 pesos per hr. Open M-F 9am-2pm and 4-8pm, Sa 9am-2pm.) **Post office:** Av. 3 Pte. Norte 5, between Calle Central and Calle 1 Nte. Pte. (Open M-F 8am-3pm, Sa 9am-1pm.) **Postal Code:** 30000.

ACCOMMODATIONS

The three commandments of budget accommodation in Comitán are thus: thou shalt have a central courtyard, thou shalt be near the *zócalo,* and thou shalt spend little. **Hospedaje San Francisco,** Av. 1 Ote. Nte. #13, 1 block from the *zócalo* on the corner of Calle 1 Ote. Nte., has a *hacienda*-style courtyard with overflowing plants. Comfortable beds and private baths. (☎632 01 94. Singles 50 pesos; doubles 100 pesos; triples 150 pesos.) In **Hospedaje Montebello,** Calle 1 Nte. Pte. 10, just east of Av. 1 Pte. Nte., pale yellow rooms open to a concrete courtyard. (☎632 35 72. 40 pesos per person, with private bath 50 pesos.) **Hospedaje Primavera,** Calle Central 2, has shoebox rooms with shared bathrooms. (☎632 20 41. Singles 50 pesos; doubles 60 pesos; triples 120 pesos.) **Hospedaje Río Escondido,** 1 Av Pte. Sur 7, between Calle Central and Calle 1 Sur Pte., offers a colorful tile courtyard and matchbox rooms. (☎632 01 73. Singles 20 pesos; doubles 40 pesos.)

FOOD

Finding a cheap meal in Comitán is easy as *flan.* For meals on the go, several taco stands line the road in front of the market. If instead you want some home-cooked *chiapaneco* cuisine, such as *butifara* (pork served cold), grab a seat and take the time to enjoy your meal. For elegant dining at bargain prices, try **Alis,** Calle Central #21 between Av. 1 Pte. Nte., and Av. Pte. 2 Nte. Gaze at Diego Rivera paintings and the wooden beam ceiling while you enjoy the three-course *menú del día* (35 pesos) or *huevos chiapanecos* (25 pesos), scrambled eggs with strips of tortillas and onions. (☎632 12 62. Open daily 8:30am-6pm.) Tacos are big at **Taco-Miteco,** Central Nte. 5, near the Palacio Municipal. (3 tacos 13.5 pesos. Open daily 7am-11pm.) For an artsy time, hang out in Comitán's hotspot, **Café Quiptic,** housed in the Casa de Cultura. Drink tasty coffee (7-20 pesos) or take home a kilo (70-100 pesos). All proceeds aid **La Sociedad Campesino Magisterial de la Selva,** a grassroots organization for farm workers. (Open daily 8am-11pm.)

SIGHTS

If you harbor a secret penchant for 19th-century medical instruments, pop into the **Casa Museo Dr. Belisario Domínguez,** Domínguez Sur 35, where you can learn more about the man after whom everything in Comitán is named. (Open M-Sa 10am-6:45pm, Su 9am-12:45pm. 5 pesos.) In the mood for something more modern? Head to the **Museo de Arte Hermila Domínguez de Castellanos,** Domínguez Sur 51, 1½ blocks south of the *zócalo.* Behind the colonial facade looms a Guggenheim-esque structure housing paintings, sculptures, and photography. (Open Tu-Sa 10am-6pm, Su 10am-1pm. 2 pesos.) Go old-school at the **Museo Arqueológico de Comitán,** Calle 1 Sur Ote. and Av. 2 Ote Sur, in the Centro Cultural Rosario Castellanos, where you'll find prehistoric artifacts, information on the site of Chinkultic, and flattened Maya skulls. (Open Tu-Su 10am-5pm.)

COMITÁN BLOODY MURDER
Everything seems normal enough. Yet ask around discreetly; a good majority of Comitán residents will be able to direct you to the **Calle de Llorona** (Street of The Weeping One). Many are soundly convinced that, late at night, you can still hear the shrill cries of a mother who slaughtered her children in a fit of rage. Other odd tales circle about: several of the city's richest inhabitants came into their wealth not by traditional means (like timber and ranching) but by unearthing **buried gold** on their property. And that door that just closed behind you? Well it could have been the wind, or it might have been the mischievous spirit of a **huérfano** (orphan children who perished before baptism), often blamed for minor mishaps by locals. From spirit-children to buried treasure to restless, murderous ghosts, Comitán is a city where old stories have yet to bow to the modern age.

⁂ DAYTRIPS FROM COMITÁN

PARQUE NACIONAL LAGUNAS DE MONTEBELLO
From Comitán, the blue combis leave from Av. 2 Pte. Sur 23 between Calles 2 and 3 Sur Pte. for either Bosque Azul or Tziscao (1hr., 5:30am-4:30pm, 15 pesos). The combis swing by the Cristóbal Colón bus station for those who want to head straight to the lakes.

A hop, skip, and a 58km *combi* ride from Comitán lie the pine-covered hills of the Parque Nacional Lagunas de Montebello, where 59 lagoons and lakes await exploration. Unfortunately, only 16 have trails from the main road, and some are notorious for bandit attacks. Be sure to inquire at the Comitán tourist office before undertaking any hikes off the beaten path. Women traveling alone should consider traveling in *combis* to and from the different lakes. The main destination for visitors is the **Lago Bosque Azul,** which has a few facilities, a restaurant (the Bosque Azul, open 7am-10pm), and free camping. You will doubtlessly be bombarded by kids offering to lead you to **Las Grutas,** a cave with an underground lake. Behind the restaurant, you can rent horses and paddle boats.

Similar services can be found on the shores of **Lago Tziscao.** The *combi* will drop you off at the road into town; follow this road until just prior to where it changes to dirt. Take a right over the hill, where the road will curve to the left, and continue along the shore for 500m to the **Hotel Tziscao,** with baths and showers available for all. A large dining and socializing lobby plays *ranchero* music or your own tapes. (☎633 13 03. Home-cooked meals 30 pesos. Restaurant open 6am-10pm. Campground 10 pesos per person; outdoor cabins 40 pesos per person; hostel-type rooms 30 pesos per person.) Two nearby accommodations provide easy access to the *lagos* and the Maya site of **Chinkultic.** A few km west of the entrance to the park at the access road to Chinkultic, **Doña María's** and **El Pino Feliz** offer *cabañas* at very reasonable prices.

LA CASCADA EL CHIFLÓN
To get to Chiflón, take a combi to El Puente de San Vincente en La Mesilla (not La Mesilla in Guatemala) from the La Angostura bus station on the highway between Calles 1 and 2 Sur Pte. (45min., every 20min. 5am-5pm, 16 pesos). From the bridge, follow the dirt road 500m before coming to a barbed-wire fence. Cross it (somehow) and continue along the road. The path becomes a narrow trail, skirting the banks of the river upstream to the falls (40min.). The trail is not marked but is fairly well-trod; if lost, follow the river downstream and you will soon spot the trail.

Named for their whistling sound, this series of waterfalls 45km west of Comitán on the Tzimol-Tuxtla road are an impressive 120m high. Your hiking efforts will be rewarded when you set foot on the highest and nearest mount to the waterfall. **El Restaurante** serves fresh fish from the lake, and cooks meat from the ranch for 20 pesos; beer and *botanas* (appetizers) are 10 pesos. (Open daily 8am-9pm.)

LAGOS DE COLÓN

Catch a lake-bound combi from the Transportes Mariscal station, adjacent to the La Angostura station between Calles 1 and 2 Sur Pte. on the Pan-American highway (every 20min. 6am-4pm, 20 pesos).

The warm, crystal-clear waters of the Lagos de Colón contrast with the cool, mineral-colored waters of the Montebello lakes. These 44 lakes lie in a valley 70km southeast of Comitán and are connected by rushing streams, producing waterfalls. To reach the mouth of the waterfalls follow the path, starting 100m before the lakes, into the woods for 15-20min. Lagos de Colón also houses a turtle pond near its entrance. Unfortunately, they must swim amidst soda bottles and beer cans. A Maya ruin, **Lagartero**, stands 2km from Lagos de Colón.

CHINKULTIC

The "Montebello" combis drop you off at the access road; from there, it's a 2km walk uphill to the entrance. Walk or bike there (local restaurant owners rent bikes for 20 pesos). Site open daily 9am-4pm. 23 pesos.

The ruins of Chinkultic lie 32km from the Pan-American Highway, on the way to Lagunas Montebello. The ruins date from the late Classic Period, and the city probably reached its peak in the 1st or 2nd century AD, making it one of the last western Maya settlements. Follow the *sacbé* road, traverse the jungle, cross the stone bridge, and climb the wooden steps to reach Chinkultic's 7th century pyramid. Chirping birds, lily pads, a cool breeze, and the ripples of **Lago Tepancuapan** are but a few of Chikultic's virtues. Back toward the entrance, on the left, is a quadrangle for religious sacrifices. Immediately before exiting, stelae of victorious warriors and ball players guard the ballcourt. There is also a *cenote* here.

TENAM PUENTE

Combis leave the station at Av. 1 Pte. Sur between Calles 2 and 3 Sur Pte. and drop you at the ruins (every hr. 6am-6pm, 9 pesos). Site open daily 9am-4pm. Free.

This white stone city, whose name means "fortification" in Náhuatl, commands two square kilometers of Comitán's valley. This commercial and religious acropolis, with a T-shaped ballcourt, burial palaces, *cruz de la madera* (wooden cross), and tiered pyramid, reached its apogee during the Classic Period.

TAPACHULA ☎ 9

Tapachula (pop. 300,000), the southernmost major city of Chiapas, is alive with sidewalk swapmeets, cheap food diners, and *marimba* music echoing through the hazy afternoon and into the night. The gold and green *zócalo* provides a haven from Tapachula's loud and dirty daily life, and welcomes hundreds of Guatemalan immigrants who sit alongside *chiapanecos*, reading newspapers or socializing. For tourists, Tapachula is primarily a point of entry into Guatemala.

🖹 TRANSPORTATION. The **airport** is on the road to Puerto Madero, about 17km south of town. It's served by **Aeroméxico**, 2 Av. Nte. 6 (☎626 20 50) and **Aviacsa** (☎626 03 72). Tapachula's **first-class bus station** (☎626 28 91) is located northwest of the *zócalo* at 17 Calle Ote. and 3 Av. Nte. To get to the *zócalo*, take an left upon exiting onto 17 Av. Ote, walk 1½ blocks and take a left on Av. Central, and walk south six blocks. Take a right on 5 Av. Pte and continue three blocks west; you will arrive at the plaza's northeast corner. A *centro*-bound *combi* can be caught across the street from the bus station (2.5 pesos). **Altos de Chiapas** goes to **San Cristóbal de las Casas** (110 pesos), **Comitán** (82 pesos), and **Palenque** (205 pesos; buses leave at 7:30am, 11:05am, 2:30pm, 5:35pm, 8pm, and 10:30pm). Altos also goes to **Chetumal** (373 pesos) and **Cancún** (492 pesos; 7:30am). **Cristóbal Colón** goes to **Tuxtla Gutiérrez** (13 per day, 146 pesos); **Veracruz** (10pm, 330 pesos); **Oaxaca** (5:45pm, 249 pesos); **Puerto Escondido** (10:45pm, 260 pesos); **Mexico City** (7 per day, 489 pesos); **Puebla**

(1:30pm, 4:30pm, and 9:20pm, 433 pesos); and **Tonalá** (9 per day, 82 pesos). **Tika** runs buses to **Guatemala City** (7am, 150 pesos).

 ORIENTATION AND PRACTICAL INFORMATION. Tapachula is 18km from Talismán at the Guatemalan border on Rte. 200 and 303km west of Guatemala City. *Avenidas* run north-south, and *calles* run east-west. *Calles* north of **Calle Central** are odd-numbered, while those south are even-numbered. Similarly, *avenidas* east of **Av. Central** are odd-numbered, while those west of it have even numbers. Tapachula's *zócalo* is at **3 Calle Pte.** between **6** and **8 Av. Nte.**, northwest of the intersection between Av. and Calle Central. Each street is divided by the axes centered at this intersection into Norte and Sur or Oriente and Poniente.

The **tourist office** is in the Antiguo Palacio Municipal, south of the Iglesia de San Agustín, on the west side of the *zócalo*. (☎ 626 14 85, ext. 140. Open M-F 8am-8pm, Sa 8am-2pm.) **Bank: Inverlat**, on the east side of the *zócalo* at Calle 5, has a 24hr. **ATM.** Open M-F 9am-5pm. **Market: Mercado Sebastián Escobar,** 10 Av. Nte. between 5 and 3 Calles Pte., sells produce and baked goods. **Police:** on 8 Av. Nte. and 3 Calle Pte., in the Palacio Municipal. No English spoken. (☎ 625 28 51. Open 24hr.) **Pharmacy: Farmacia 24 Horas,** 8 Av. Nte. 25 (☎ 628 64 48), at 7 Calle Pte. Free delivery 7am-11pm. **Hospital:** on the highway to the airport. (☎ 628 10 70. Open 24hr.) **Internet Access: Ciber Pacheco 1,** at Calle Pte. 16, between 2 and 4 Av. Nte. 20 pesos per hr. (Open daily 9am-10pm.) **Post office:** at 1 Calle Ote. 32, between 7 and 9 Av. Nte. (☎ 626 24 92. Open M-F 8:30am-2:30pm, Sa 9am-1pm.) **Postal code:** 30700.

ACCOMMODATIONS AND FOOD. Due to the influx of Guatemalans, budget accommodations are a dime a dozen in Tapachula, especially near the market. Unfortunately, many hotel rooms are as noisy and dirty as the rest of the city. **Hotel Cervantino,** 1 Calle Ote. #6 between Av. Central and 1 Av. Nte, has clean and colorful rooms with private baths surrounding a pleasant atrium. (☎ 626 16 58. Singles 90 pesos, with TV 120 pesos; doubles 130 pesos, with TV 160 pesos.) **Hotel La Amistad,** 7 Calle Pte. 34, between Av. 10 and 12 Nte, has a verdant courtyard and peachy rooms with clean private baths. (☎ 626 22 93. Singles 75 pesos; doubles 100 pesos; triples 140 pesos; quads 185 pesos; quints 220 pesos.)

A variety of aromas exude from the streets of Tapachula due to its rich ethnic mix of German and Chinese immigrants from World War II, and lots of cheap taco and pastry stands crowd the streets nearest the *zócalo*, offering 4-8 peso tacos and *tortas*. Also try the **San Juan food market** on 17 Calle Pte., north of the *centro* (open daily 6am-5pm). A string of restaurants line the southern edge of the *zócalo*, most specializing in typical Mexican fare.

CROSSING THE BORDER. The Maya may have known no borders, but you are not so lucky. However, new policies have made crossing the border easier. Citizens of the US, Canada, and European Union countries don't need a visa and can enter Guatemala for up to five months. Citizens from other countries will need a **visa,** which can be obtained from the Guatemalan consulate in town. If you plan on staying longer than five months, check in with a Guatemalan consulate; otherwise, you might have to pay an additional fee when you leave. By far, the easiest and safest way to cross into Guatemala is to take a direct bus from Tapachula or Talismán to Guatemala City. If you choose to brave the crossing on foot, **Unión y Progreso** buses leave from Calle 5 Pte., half a block west of Av. 12 Nte., for Talismán (30min., every 15min., 5.5 pesos). Tapachula buses drop passengers at the entrance to the Mexican emigration office. Present your **passport** and visa at the office, and follow the crowd across the bridge, where you'll need to pay a toll (approx. 65 pesos). Proceed to a small building on the left to have your passport stamped. A **taxi** from the *zócalo* to Talismán costs 60 pesos. This route has recently been plagued by assaults. Exercise caution.

GUATEMALA

The Classic Maya knew no borders, and spent at least as much time in Guatemala as in Mexico. Sites in the Petén rainforests of Guatemala make fine day and weekend trips from Mexico. Of particular note are the spectacular Maya ruins of Tikal, which, along with Palenque (see p. 555) and Copán (Honduras), was one of the three major Maya capitals of the Classic Period. If your excursion into Guatemala should whet your appetite for more, pick up *Let's Go: Central America 2001*, an absolutely scrumptious guide to Guatemala and the rest of Central America.

FLORES AND SANTA ELENA

Surrounded by the tranquil and expansive Lake Petén Itzá, the relaxed island city of Flores serves as a welcoming base for visitors who wish to explore sights and ruins throughout the Petén. Flores began life as the Itzá capital Tayasal. Cortés stopped by in 1524, just long enough to drop off a sick horse. It must have been quite a horse; almost a hundred years later the people were found worshipping a large idol they called "Thunder Horse" (Tzimin Chac). Something seems to have worked; Tayasal withstood the Spanish invasion, remaining an independent city until 1697. Today Flores is filled with colorful homes and cobblestone streets which are refreshingly cleaner than most of its neighbors. On the shore of the lake, Flores' neighbor Santa Elena takes care of Flores' dirty work, housing all the buses stations, banks, and airplanes that keep Flores working.

◪ TRANSPORTATION

GETTING THERE
There are several ways to get from Mexico to Flores. If you are in Chetumal, the easiest way to get to Flores is to take a direct bus (7hr., about 300 pesos) from the ADO station. San Juan Travel and Mundo Maya/Linea Dorada operate buses running from Flores to Chetumal; contact the bus station for schedules. If you are in **Palenque, Villahemosa,** or **Yaxhilán,** you must first travel to **Tenosique.** From Tenosique, catch a bus (2hr.) or a *colectivo* (1hr.) to the Mexican border post in **La Palma.** Once in La Palma, you can catch a ferry to the Guatemalan city of **El Naranjo** (5hr., 8am and irregular hours thereafter), and from there take a direct bus to Flores (4-5hr., several per day, Q20). There are a few basic hotels and restaurants in all of the border cities, but your best bet is to depart early. If you are in **Frontera Corozal,** take a boat to **Bethel** in Guatemala (30min., Q225 per group). After having your passport stamped by friendly Guatemalan authorities, a Transportes Pinita bus will take you from Bethel to **Flores** (5hr., several per day, Q30).

GETTING AWAY
Airport: The airport is 2km from Santa Elena along the highway toward Tikal; minibuses and local buses head into town. Minibuses to the airport generally leave from 4 Calle in Santa Elena (2min., Q10). Aerocaribe (☎926-0922) flies to **Palenque** (1hr., US$101). Both Aerocaribe and Grupo Taca fly to **Cancún** (1½hr., US$145).

Buses: To get to Flores from the bus drop-off, head east (right as you face the lake) on the main drag until the road signs point you left across the causeway. From Flores, it's possible to get most places in Guatemala and Belize. Buses go to: **Bethel** (5hr.; 5, 8am, 1pm; Q30); **El Naranjo** (5hr., 7 per day 5am-2:30pm, Q20); **El Remate** (1hr., every hr. 7-11am, Q5); **Sayaxché** (1½-2hr.; 5, 7, 8, 10am, 1, 3pm; Q10); and **Tikal** (1hr., 1pm, Q10), continuing on to **Uaxactún** (3hr., Q15). To get to **Guatemala City,** the best service is on Linea Dorada (☎926-0070), with an office in Mundo Maya on the southern Flores shore front road. Express luxury buses (8hr.; 8am, 8, 10pm; Q215). Also offers regular Pullman buses. Fuente del Norte (☎926-0517), on 4 Calle in Santa

Elena, has frequent departures (9-12hr., about every hr. 6:30am-7:30pm, Q60 and up). Most first-class buses leave from their company offices; buy tickets in advance. Tour Agencies in Flores and hotels at Tikal often offer tourist minibuses to Palenque, the Río Dulce, and Belize City; ask at the Jaguar in at Tikal for more information.

Tourist Minibuses: The most popular way of getting to **Tikal.** Purchase tickets most hotels or travel agencies in Flores or Santa Elena for hotel pick-up, or catch one on the southern shore road in Flores (5am-noon). They also run directly from the airport. **San Juan Travel** (☎926-0041) offers the most minibuses (1¼hr.; every hr. 5am-10am, returns every hr. noon-5pm; Q20 one way, Q30 round-trip). Most minibuses will stop in **El Remate** (30min., Q10-15). Minibuses operated by San Juan Travel and the preferable Mundo Maya/Linea Dorada (☎926-0070) go as far as **San Ignacio** and **Belize City, Belize** (US$15-20) and **Chetumal** (7½hr., US$30-35).

◢◪ ORIENTATION AND PRACTICAL INFORMATION

The island of Flores to the north and Santa Elena to the south are connected by a paved causeway across the lake. In Flores, the **parque central** (the Guatemalan equivalent of the *zócalo*) is on top of the hill at the center of town. Santa Elena's main street is **Calle 4,** three blocks south of the end of the causeway. Banks, stores, and buses are all along this street.

Tourist Information: INGUAT, in Flores' *parque central* (☎926-0669). Open M-F 8am-4pm. Also in the airport (☎926-0533). Open when planes arrive. More info, especially about treks to out-of-the-way ruins, at **CINCAP**—the Center of Information (☎926-0718), Culture, and Handicrafts of Petén, on the north side of the *parque* in Flores. Open M-F 9am-1pm, 2-6pm. Also useful is the **Destination Petén** magazine.

Tour Tours: Nakun (☎926-0587; nakun@guate.net), on Reforma off Centroamérica, and **Martsam** (☎926-3225), on Centroamérica. Tours at **Evolution Adventures** (☎926-0633) on Centroamérica. **Eco-Maya** (☎926-1363), on the west side of the main road, has tours and community projects.

Banks: Finding a good exchange rate in Flores is like finding an Enrique Iglesias song without the word *corazón* in it. It isn't likely. Instead, head to a bank in Santa Elena—there's an abundant supply along 4 Calle. **Corpobanco** has a **Western Union.** Open M-F 8:30am-7pm, Sa 9am-1pm. **Banco Industrial,** opposite the Hotel Posada Santander, has a Visa **ATM.** Open M-F 9am-7pm, Sa 10am-2pm.

Car Rental: San Juan Travel (☎926-0041), in Santa Elena right by the causeway. **Tabarini** (☎926-0272) and others at the airport.

Laundromat: Lavandería Petenchel, on Calle Centroamérica. Open M-Sa 8am-7pm.

Hospital: Hospital Privado (☎926-1140), in Santa Elena. Open 24hr.

Pharmacy: Farmacia Nueva, down from Restaurante Los Puertas. Open daily 8am-9pm.

Telephones: Telgua (☎926-1299), 2 blocks south of 4 Calle in Santa Elena. **Fax.** Open M-F 8am-8pm, Sa 8am-6pm, Su 8am-noon. Try also **Petén Internet.**

Internet Access: Tikal Net (☎926-0655; email tikalnet@guate.net), on Calle Centroamérica in Flores. Q14 per 30min. Open daily 8am-noon and 2-8pm. **Petén Internet** (☎926-3261) on the lakeside Calle Playa Sur, facing Santa Elena. Q14 per 30 min.

Post Office: In Flores, a half-block east of the *parque central.* Open daily 8am-noon. The one in Santa Elena, left of the causeway road on 4 Calle, has longer hours. Open M-F 8:30am-5:30pm, Sa 9am-1pm.

◤ ACCOMMODATIONS

Although accommodations in Santa Elena are closer to the bus station, Flores is safer and more enjoyable.

> **CHANGING CURRENCY.** The Guatemalan currency is the **quetzal** (as in the Quetzal bird), indicated by a capital Q. As of August, 2000, the exchange rate between the peso and the quetzal was approximately Q0.84 to 1 peso, and 1.18 pesos to Q1. The **money changers** on the Guatemalan side of the border generally give better rates for pesos than those on the Mexican side, but your best bet is to avoid small money changers and straight head for the **Banco de Quetzal** once in Guatemala.

Hospedaje Doña Goya, on the northern side of the island (☎926-3538). Spacious rooms are meticulously done, bright, comfortable, and come with or without bath. Lakeview rooftop. Breakfast served. Doubles Q50, with bath Q70.

Posada Santa Monica (☎926-1467), on the east side of the island. Rooms are bland but a good value. Communal baths are clean. Singles Q35; doubles Q60; triples Q90.

El Mirador de Lago, on the east side of the island. Bright, comfortable rooms and a dock great for swimming make this new hotel popular. Rooms have fans and private baths with hot water. Singles Q80; doubles Q90; triples Q100.

Hotel Mesa de los Maya (☎926-1240), on La Reforma, 1 block from Calle Centroamérica. An old-fashioned place with dark but elegant rooms that have cable TV and private bath. Many also have A/C at the cheapest rates in town. Pricey attached restaurant. Singles Q75, with A/C Q100; doubles Q112.50, with A/C Q150.

Hotel Santa Rita (☎926-3224), on the west side near Calle Centroamérica. Run by a friendly family, Santa Rita offers basic, clean rooms with private baths. Top floors offer lake views. Some rooms are stuffy—check for strong fan. Singles Q54; doubles Q72.

Hotel Posada Santander (☎926-0574), the best choice in Santa Elena. Near the bus terminal, on 4 Calle. The overgrown courtyard may not be charming, but rooms are well taken care of. Rooms in the new wing are slightly nicer. Singles Q30, with bath Q50; doubles Q40, with bath Q60.

FOOD

Flores has a surprising number of good restaurants. You won't get much in the way of regional specialties, but at least you'll eat well.

Pizzería Picasso, on the east end of Calle Centroamérica. Everybody knows how much the master artist loved a great pizza. At least he would have if he'd eaten here. Hawaiian pizza Q28, tortellini Q24. Open Tu-Su 10:30am-10:30pm.

Restaurante Las Puertas, on Santa Anna, off of Calle Centroamérica. A popular meeting place with the right amount of hip. Tasty sandwiches and pastas. Tuna sandwich Q22, spaghetti al pesto Q24. Occasional live evening performances. Open daily 8am-11pm.

La Canoa, on Calle Centroamérica. A good, inexpensive rendition of *comedor* food served in a cozy, family-run cafe. Omelettes Q15, tacos Q12. Open M-Sa 8am-10pm.

La Luna, on the west side of the island, by Eco Maya. The excellent food and warm ambiance justify higher prices. Chicken cordon bleu Q37. Open daily noon-11pm.

SIGHTS AND ENTERTAINMENT

Boatmen will take visitors out for tours of **Lago Petén Itzá**—the typical route includes a *mirador*, a small ruin, a swim, and the **Peténcito zoo.** Look for boats near the causeway or at the west end of the Calle Centroamérica by Hotel Santana; speak directly with the captain rather than with the commissioned agents roaming the streets. To go at it on your own, rent **kayaks** at La Casona de La Isla (Q12 per hr.) or Hotel Petén—both on the west side of the island. The **Aktun Kan cave,** also known as La Cueva de La Serpiente (Cave of the Snake), 2km south of Santa Elena, holds 300m of well-illuminated paths as well as several kilometers that are unlit (bring your own flashlight). To get to the cave, follow the causeway south; bear left at the fork and then turn right at the sign. (Open daily 8am-5pm. Q5.)

Laid-back Flores offers some appropriately laid-back **nightlife**. **El Balcón del Cielo,** on the town's hilltop plaza (opposite the church), is an open-air bar-cafe with a great view of the lake. (Open Tu-Su noon-1am.) Catch a movie at **Mayan Princess,** a *gringo*-run cafe on Reforma (screenings Th-Tu 4, 9pm) or a live performance at Restaurante Las Puertas (above). Especially hopping on weekend nights is **Discoteca Raices,** on the southwest corner of the island, with a lakefront deck.

EL REMATE

On the beautiful eastern shores of Lake Petén Itzá, the relaxed village of El Remate has long been known for its woodcarving. However, it's the location—halfway between Flores and Tikal and convenient to the Belizean border—that makes it a popular stop. El Remate also has a few interesting diversions, and a clean, swimmable lake.

⌶ TRANSPORTATION. Tourist minibuses going between Flores and Tikal stop in El Remate. Three daily public buses also make the trek. You can also take a Flores-Belize bus and get off at **El Cruce/Puente Ixlú,** 2km south of El Remate. To get to **Tikal** from El Remate, note that only **one minibus** stops at the hotels (5:30am); leave any later and you'll have to stand on the highway and flag it down yourself. Ticket sellers visit hotels in the evening; you can also buy them at La Casa de Don David. One **public bus** leaves for Tikal daily (2pm).

⌂⌂ ACCOMMODATIONS AND FOOD. Budget accommodations in El Remate are, for better or worse, more rustic than those in Flores. The town's standout is **⌶La Casa de Don David,** at the junction of the highway and the dirt road veering left along the lake. Owner David Kuhn and his staff provide plenty of tourist information, good cheer, and delicious food (dinner Q30). Rooms, though plain for the price, are comfortable and come with private baths. Bungalows, tiled and with kitchenettes, are great for families. Reservations requested. (Cell ☎306-2190. Singles and doubles Q125; triples Q140; Q20 per additional person.) **Mirador del Duende,** on a hill on the right side of the highway entering the village from Flores, does indeed have the best view in town, but the igloo-like bungalows are nothing more than cement shelters with mattresses. Hammock-slingers and campers are welcome, and the restaurant serves inexpensive vegetarian food. (Camping Q15; bungalows Q30 per person.) The friendly management at **John's Lodge,** on the highway just before the dirt road near La Casa de Don David, offers very basic dorms with mosquito net, plus a *comedor* and communal bath. (Q20 per person.)

⌖⌶ SIGHTS AND OUTDOOR ACTIVITIES. The **Biotopo Cerro Cahuí,** about 2km from the highway on the dirt road running along the lakeshore, contains 651 hectares of protected lands, including ponds and wonderfully undisturbed tropical forests. Monkeys, white-tailed deer, and numerous bird species make their home here. Two interconnecting loop trails—4km (2hr.) and 6km (4 3hr.)—traverse the reserve; just past the first turnaround lies a *mirador* with a wonderful view of the lake. (Open daily 6am-4pm, though visitors may stay later. Q25.) In the little village of **Puente Ixlú** (El Cruce), 2km south of El Remate, stand the largely unrestored ruins of **Ixlú.** Lake Tours runs a popular sunset boat trip to **Río Ixlú,** home to wildlife and great views. (Q40 per person; inquire at Don David's to reserve a place.) **Ervin Oliveros,** who lives in the house behind John's Lodge, offers walking tours to a nearby lake where crocodiles are the star attraction (2hr., Q20 per person).

TIKAL

Tikal attracts visitors from every corner of the globe. The ruins, 65km northeast of Flores, encompass more than 3000 Maya stone constructions. As impressive as the buildings themselves are, it is the surroundings—gloriously untouched tropical forest—that distinguish Tikal from other great Maya sites. It was this natural

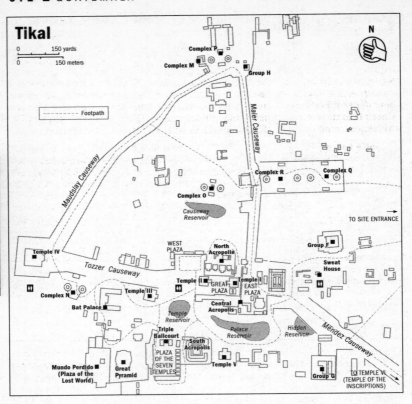

beauty that led movie executives to film part of *Return of the Jedi* here. Buses, airplanes, and many package tours are designed so that you can visit Tikal in a single day. While this is enough time to see the highlights, a longer visit will allow for a more leisurely pace and the opportunity to savor the ruins and the jungle as they change with the light. Sunrise at Tikal is particularly magical.

TRANSPORTATION

From Flores/Santa Elena, El Remate, or the airport, tourist **minibuses** are the easiest way to reach the ruins. Minibuses arrive in Tikal throughout the morning, and return in the afternoon and evening (1hr., departing when full, Q20). There's also a daily local bus from **Santa Elena** (1hr., 1pm, Q10).

ORIENTATION AND PRACTICAL INFORMATION

The ruins of Tikal sit in the middle of the expansive **Tikal National Park** (575 sq. km). The road from Flores crosses the national park boundary 15km south of the ruins; buses will stop so that you may pay the Q50 park entrance fee. (Tickets sold after 3pm are good for the next day as well.) The **visitors center** complex contains a post office, a restaurant, and one of the area's two museums. Three hotels are nearby, as well as a camping area, a few *comedores*, and the second museum. The entrance to the ruins is near the visitors center, but from the entrance it is a 20-minute walk to the Great Plaza.

ACCOMMODATIONS

Accommodations at Tikal are limited to one good campground and three expensive hotels; many budget travelers commute from El Remate or Flores. All three have restaurants and electricity until 9pm; during the night fans make for a lovely but motionless ceiling decoration. A grassy expanse across from the visitors center serves as a **camping ground.** Pitch a tent or sling a hammock (bring a mosquito net) under thatched-roof huts or try a small wooden cabin with sleeping pad. Check in at the restaurant inside the visitors center. (Q25 per person; singles Q50, with sheets and towels Q108; doubles Q100, with sheets and towels Q170.)

Jungle Lodge (☎476-8775; fax 476-0294), across from the visitors center by the site entrance. The best-looking property, with natural landscaping and attractive bungalows offering good beds and hot water with lackluster pressure. The rooms with shared bath are much less appealing but still clean and cool. Swimming pool. Singles US$25, with bath US$53; doubles US$30, with bath US$70.

Tikal Inn (☎/fax 926-0065), past the Jaguar Inn as you walk away from the ruins, is a slight step down but still pleasant, with reasonable rooms and slightly nicer bungalows set around an inviting pool. All rooms have baths with hot water (in the evenings). Singles US$25, US$45 bungalow; doubles US$35 room, US$55 bungalow.

Jaguar Inn (☎926-0002; solis@quetzal.net). The cheapest option. Simple, well-kept bungalow rooms come with cold-water private baths. Nice communal bathrooms are available for those who camp on the grounds or rent one of their hammocks with mosquito net. Dorm beds US$10; hammock/net rental Q40; camping Q25; singles US$20; doubles US$32; triples US$44; quads US$52. Prices rise Aug.-Mar.

FOOD

Prepare to be underwhelmed by the restaurant selection at Tikal. Though service is a bit slow, the restaurant at the **Jaguar Inn** serves the best food in the area. (Entrees Q26 and up. Open daily 6am-9pm). Four similar and unexciting *comedores* line the road in from Flores. (*Pollo frito* Q30. Open daily 6am-9pm.) **Café Restaurante del Parque Tikal,** in the visitors center, is overpriced but of reasonable quality. (Spaghetti Q35. Open daily 5am-4pm.)

THE ARCHAEOLOGICAL SITE OF TIKAL

A few explanatory signs are scattered throughout the ruins, but if you can spare the cash, hiring a tour guide makes for a more informed visit. Guides wait in the visitors center. Ask around, especially if you have a particular interest, since levels of specialization vary. Tours are available in Spanish or English (4hr., 1-5 people US$40, US$5 per additional person). Site open daily 6am to 6pm. Tickets (Q50) are typically purchased on the bus at the national park entrance, but may also be purchased at the site itself.

The Maya settled Tikal around 700 BC; they were likely attracted by its hilltop location and the abundance of flint for making weapons and tools. By the dawn of the Classic Period, AD 250, Tikal was major center. It was only after powerful city of **El Mirador** (65km to the north) fell into decline, that Tikal (along with **Uaxactún** p. 575) became the dominant city of the region. In AD 378, Tikal, aided by an alliance with the mighty highland center of **Kaminaljuyú**, on the modern site of Guatemala City, and the powerful **Teotihuacán**, handily defeated Uaxactún. From that moment, Tikal reigned over the Petén and grew in population and splendor. By the 6th century it spanned some 30 sq. km and supported a population of 100,000. The middle of the 6th century, however, saw Tikal's power overshadowed by that of **Caracol** (in Belize's Maya Mountains). For the next 150 years, Tikal seems to have languished. But in AD 700, the city embarked on a splendid renaissance. Led by the mighty **Ah Cacau (Lord Chocolate)**, Tikal regained its supremacy in the Petén. Ah Cacau and his successors built most of the temples seen on the Great Plaza today.

Around AD 900, Tikal—along with the entire Classic Maya civilization—mysteriously fell into decline. Theories explaining the downfall include earthquake, deforestation, or a massive popular uprising. While Post-Classic descendants of the original population continued to live and worship at Tikal, they did little of lasting significance other than pillage the ancient tombs. By AD 1000, the jungle had engulfed the city and it was not rediscovered until the Guatemalan government sponsored an expedition in 1848.

THE GREAT PLAZA. One kilometer west of the entrance lies Tikal's geographic and commercial heart, the Great Plaza. Towering above the plaza is **Temple I,** built by the son of the great Ah Cacau after his father's death in AD 721. Tikal's most recognizable symbol, the 44m-high temple is topped by a three-room structure and a roof comb that was originally painted in bright colors. Unfortunately, it's no longer possible to climb **Temple I.** You can, however, climb **Temple II** (38m), the **Temple of the Masks,** at the west end of the Great Plaza. The complicated **North Acropolis** also stands on the plaza. It was built and rebuilt on top of itself and contains the remains of around 100 structures—some of them dating back more than 2000 years. Don't miss the two huge stone masks near the base of the North Acropolis. One is displayed under thatched roof, and the other can be reached by following an adjacent dark passageway (you'll need a flashlight). To the south of the Great Plaza is the **Central Acropolis,** a complex of buildings probably used as a residential area for the elite. The configuration of rooms has changed repeatedly over time, perhaps to accommodate different families.

THE WEST PLAZA TO TEMPLE IV. The **West Plaza,** north of Temple II, features a large late Classic temple. Following the Tozzer Causeway to the north, you'll reach **Temple III,** still covered in jungle vegetation. Continuing on, you'll come upon **Complex N,** one Tikal's seven twin temples, all believed to have commemorated the completion of a Katun (a 20-year cycle in the Maya calendar). At the end of the Tozzer Causeway lies **Temple IV,** the tallest structure in Tikal (64m). Built in AD 741, possibly in honor of the ruler Coon Chac, the temple affords a stellar view from the top, especially at sunrise or sunset. Steep stairways facilitate the ascent.

MUNDO PERDIDO TO THE TEMPLE OF THE INSCRIPTIONS. The **Mundo Perdido,** a fairly recent 38-structure discovery, is capped by the 32m-high **Great Pyramid.** Not much is known about the buildings, but they appear to be from multiple historical periods. If you can handle the steep climb, the top of the Great Pyramid provides one of the park's nicest views. Just east is the **Plaza of the Seven Temples.** The visible structures date from the late Classic, but the hidden complex dates from the Pre-Classic Period. The north side of the plaza was once the site of a unique triple ball court. To the east of the Plaza of the Seven Temples are the unexcavated South Acropolis and **Temple V** (58m tall); the restoration is expected to be complete in 2004. The contrast between the temple's condition before and after restoration is striking. A 1.2km (20min.) walk along the Mendez Causeway from the Great Plaza leads to the **Temple of the Inscriptions (Temple VI),** noted for the hieroglyphic text on its 12m roof comb. The text, though badly eroded, is unique to Tikal and dates to AD 766.

OTHER STRUCTURES. Complexes Q and **R,** between the Great Plaza and the entrance, are late Classic twin pyramids. Complex Q has been well restored; to its left lies a replica of the beautiful Stela 22, which portrays Tikal's last known ruler, Chitam. The original is now in the visitors center. One kilometer north of the Great Plaza lie **Group H** and **Complex P,** additional examples of twin temples.

MUSEUMS. Museo Lítico, in the visitors center, holds a fine collection of stelae from the site, a scale model of Tikal, and photographs of the restoration process. (Open M-F 8am-4pm, Sa-Su 8am-3pm. Free.) **Museo Tikal,** between the Jungle Lodge and the Jaguar Inn, has a reconstructed tomb, carvings, ceramics, and other artifacts recovered from the ruins. (Open M-F 9am-5pm, Sa-Su 9am-4pm. Q10.)

🔢 DAYTRIPS FROM TIKAL

Hidden in the vast tropical forests north of Tikal are several other Maya sites. The important site of **Uaxactún** is the most accessible. **El Zotz, Río Azul,** and the splendid **El Mirador** are all largely unrestored and uncleared, and require quite a trek. For more information on these and other Petén sites, check out *Let's Go: Central America 2001*, a good read on any dull bus ride.

UAXACTÚN

The cheapest way to visit Uaxactún is to take the Transportes Pinita bus from Flores (3hr., 1pm, Q15) or Tikal (about 3pm), and then catch the return bus early the next morning (6am). Some travel agencies in Flores organize daytrips to Uaxactún, and the Jungle Lodge at Tikal offers a trip (departs 8am, returns 1pm; US$15 per person with 4-person minimum, US$60 for smaller groups). Site open 24hr. The road passes through the entrance to Tikal where you'll need to pay Q15 per person, Q50 per person if you plan to view Tikal that same day. Though Uaxactún is small, the roads are winding, and it may be wise to let one of the local kids show you around.

In the forest 23km north of Tikal hides Uaxactún (wah-shak-TOON), a small Petén village built around an airstrip and surrounded by Maya ruins. Uaxactún once rivaled Tikal in stature but was resoundingly defeated in AD 378. Tikal retains its edge to this day; the ruins in Uaxactún are underwhelming by comparison. Still, the ruins of Uaxactún are some of the best examples of early Maya architecture.

As you come into town and hit the disused airstrip, **Group E**—the most impressive site—is about a 10-minute walk to your right. Here, three side-by-side temples served as an observatory: viewed from atop a fourth temple, the sun rises behind the south temple on the shortest day of the year and behind the north temple on the longest day. Beneath these temples is **E-VII-Sub,** the oldest extant building in Petén, with foundations dating back to 2000 BC. On the other side of the old airstrip, a dirt road beginning at the far end of the field passes through unexcavated **Group B** and leads to the grander **Group A.** Mainly a series of temples and residential compounds, the area is topped off by **Temple A-18.** Climb up into the inside chambers to find a staircase leading to the top. Back on the ground, don't miss the stelae scattered about under thatched roofs.

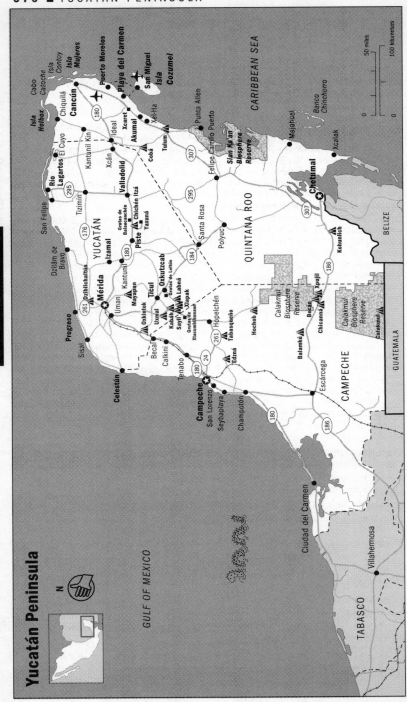

Yucatán Peninsula

YUCATÁN
PENINSULA

Francisco Hernández de Córdoba ran aground here in 1517; when he asked the native villagers where he was, the confused Maya replied something to the effect of, "We haven't a clue what you're talking about." Córdoba caught only the last few syllables of their reply, "tectetán," and erroneously named the region Yucatán. The peninsula today is divided into three parts, with interstate borders forming a "Y" shape through the center. The state of **Yucatán** sits on the north coast, drawing thousands of visitors who come to scramble up and down the incomparable Chichén Itzá. **Quintana Roo** borders the Caribbean on the east coast, full of luscious jungles, crystalline coastlines, and mega-resorts like Cancún and Playa del Carmen. Less touristed **Campeche,** facing the Gulf Coast to the west, is full of modest Maya ruins and reminders of Spanish colonial rule. The peninsula's flat limestone scrubland and tropical forest dotted with *cenotes* (places where freshwater can be accessed through a cave entrance) fill the landscape. Because of the porous limestone subsoil, rivers do not exist in the Yucatán.

The peninsula's culture remains essentially Maya, particularly in small towns, where the only form of capitalism evident is the weekly visit from the Coca-Cola truck. Mayan is still the first language of most inhabitants, and indigenous religious traditions persist within the boundaries of Spanish-instilled Catholicism. Yucatec women still carry bowls of corn flour on their heads and wear embroidered *huipiles* (woven dresses); fishing, farming, and hammock-weaving are all commercial and subsistence essentials for the Maya of today. Increasingly, however, workers drawn by the tourist industry are starting to flood big cities to work in *gringo*-friendly restaurants, weave hammocks for tourists, or act as guides at archaeological sites. The engineering of the pristine pleasure-world of Cancún has brought tourists in by the droves, and developers have earmarked most of the remaining Riviera Maya, as Mexico's Caribbean coast is called, for similar transformation. The result is a modern-day twist on the age-old tension between native and foreign, Maya world and outside world.

HIGHLIGHTS OF THE YUCATÁN PENINSULA

RUSH to visit the Maya ruins of **Chichén Itzá** (see p. 601) No trip to the Yucatán is complete without it. You've got to see 'em to believe 'em.

FLOCK with the rest of the foreign visitors to wild **Cancún** (see p. 613), Mexico's biggest resort. Ever popular, despite artificiality, congestion, and more pristine beaches nearby.

SHOP 'TIL YOU DROP in the bustling city of **Mérida** (see. p. 591); some of Mexico's best shopping awaits you.

CRUISE through the **Ruta Puuc** (see p. 585), an eclectic assemblage of relatively unknown jungle ruins.

THINK ruins can't exist on a beach? **Tulum** (see p. 637) is no joke—just look at our front cover.

SOAK up the sun in the laid-back island of **Isla Mujeres** (see p. 626), which draws a hip, international crew of backpackers.

SNORKEL and scuba-dive off the isle of **Cozumel** (see p. 631), among some of the best coral in the world.

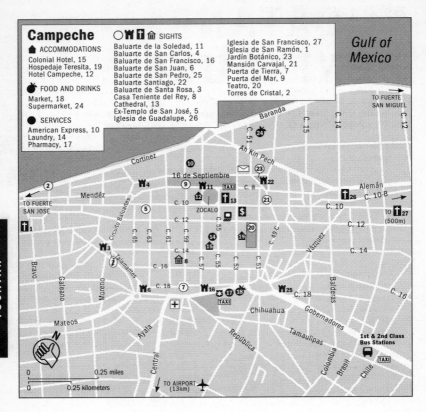

Campeche

🏠 **ACCOMMODATIONS**
Colonial Hotel, 15
Hospedaje Teresita, 19
Hotel Campeche, 12

🍎 **FOOD AND DRINKS**
Market, 18
Supermarket, 24

⬤ **SERVICES**
American Express, 10
Laundry, 14
Pharmacy, 17

○♍🛈🏛 SIGHTS
Baluarte de la Soledad, 11
Baluarte de San Carlos, 4
Baluarte de San Francisco, 16
Baluarte de San Juan, 6
Baluarte de San Pedro, 25
Baluarte Santiago, 22
Baluarte de Santa Rosa, 3
Casa Teniente del Rey, 8
Cathedral, 13
Ex-Templo de San José, 5
Iglesia de Guadalupe, 26

Iglesia de San Francisco, 27
Iglesia de San Ramón, 1
Jardín Botánico, 23
Mansión Carvajal, 21
Puerta de Tierra, 7
Puerta del Mar, 9
Teatro, 20
Torres de Cristal, 2

Gulf of Mexico

CAMPECHE

CAMPECHE ☎ 9

Once called "Ah Kin Pech"—Mayan for "Place of the Serpents and Ticks"—
Campeche (pop. 182,000) is, thankfully, much more pleasant than the original
name suggests. *Campechanos* today live up to their Spanish baptized name
"Campeche," which means friendship and hospitality. When Francisco Hernández de Córdoba arrived, he transliterated the name, and by 1540, when Francisco de Montejo conquered Ah Kin Pech, the small city had begun its
transformation into a booming port. As Campeche grew it battled buccaneers
and pirates, erecting stunning *baluartes* (bulwarks), fortified churches, and
forts, many of which still stand. The historic center, with its pastel facades,
hanging lanterns, and sidewalks raised over the flood-prone cobblestone
streets, is a sanctum of colonial architecture. With beaches, city-sponsored
entertainment, *haciendas* along the nearby Ruta Chenes and Ruta Río Bec,
and the biosphere reserves of Calakmul, Campeche is becoming less a stopover and more a destination for tourists who appreciate natural wonders and
old Spanish beauty.

TRANSPORTATION

GETTING AROUND

A confusing network of **buses** links Campeche's more distant sectors to the old city (2 pesos, daily 5am-11pm). The market, where Gobernadores becomes the Circuito, serves as the hub for local routes. Buses can be flagged down by waving. You'll have to get around the city center on foot; buses do not run there. **Taxis** (☎816 11 13 or 816 66 66) operate out of three stands: Calle 8 at 55, to left of the cathedral; Calle 55 at Circuito, near the market; and Gobernadores at Chile, near the bus terminal. Intra-city travel is 15-20 pesos, more after dark.

GETTING AWAY

Airport: (☎816 31 09) on Porfirio, 13km from the city center. **Aeroméxico** (☎816 56 76). Taxis from the airport to the *centro* cost 35 pesos.

Buses: First- and second-class terminals stand at Gobernadores and Chile, half a km from the old city. To reach the Parque Principal from the bus terminals, catch the "Gobernadores" bus (3 pesos) across the street from the station, and ask the driver to let you off at the Baluarte de San Francisco. Turn right into the old city and walk four blocks on Calle 57 to the park. Taxis run from bus station to *zócalo* (20 pesos). If you'd rather walk (15min.), head left on Gobernadores and turn left again when you reach the Circuito. Three blocks later, turn right on Calle 57 through the stone arch and walk four blocks to the park. ADO goes to: **Cancún** (7hr., 10 and 11:30pm, 201 pesos); **Chetumal** (7hr., noon, 159 pesos); **Mérida** (2½hr., 10 per day, 71 pesos); **Mexico City** (16hr.; 12:45, 7, 8:15, and 11:45pm; 544 pesos); **Palenque** (12:30, 2, and 10:30am, 138 pesos); **Veracruz** (12hr., 1:15 and 8pm, 350 pesos); **Villahermosa** (7hr., 6 per day, 169 pesos); and **Oaxaca** (9:55pm, 430 pesos). Altos goes to **San Cristóbal de Las Casas** (9:45pm, 210 pesos). From the second-class terminal (☎816 24 02 ext. 24 05), TRP goes to **Cancún** (7:30am, 178 pesos) and **Villahermosa** (1:45 and 11:55pm, 150 pesos). ATS goes to **Chetumal** (10pm, 124 pesos) and **Mérida** (4 per day, 59 pesos).

PRACTICAL INFORMATION

Tourist Office: (☎811 11 38) housed in the Baluarte de Santa Rosa, at the Circuito and Calle 14. Open M-F 9am-3pm and 6-9pm, Sa-Su 9am-1pm.

Currency Exchange: Banamex (☎816 52 52), at the corner of Calles 53 and 10. Open M-F 9am-5pm, Sa 9:30am-2pm. 24hr. **ATM.**

American Express: (☎811 10 00) Calle 59 between 16 de Septiembre and the shore. Open M-F 9am-2pm and 5-7pm, Sa 9am-1pm.

Car Rental: Maya Rent-a-Car (☎816 22 33), Cortines #51., in the Hotel del Mar lobby.

Market: On Circuito Baluartes, between Calles 53 and 55. Cheap fruits, vegetables, and meats. Open M-Sa sunrise-sunset, Su sunrise-3pm.

Supermarket: San Francisco de Asis (☎816 79 76), in the Pl. Comercial A-Kin-Pech, behind the post office. Open daily 7am-9:30pm.

Laundry: Lavandería y Tintorería Campeche, Calle 55 #22 (☎816 51 42), between Calles 12 and 14. Same-day service. 10 pesos per kg. Open M-F 8am-6pm, Sa 8am-4pm.

Police: (☎816 23 09) on Sierra, in front of El Balneario Popular. A more central station is at Calle 55 and the market.

Red Cross: (☎815 24 11), 1km up the coast from the old city. No English. Open 24hr.

Pharmacy: Farmacia Canto, Calle 18 #99 (☎816 31 65), at the market. Open 24hr.

Medical Assistance: IMSS (☎816 52 02), Central at Circuito Baluartes. **Hospital General** (☎816 09 20), across the street.

YUCATÁN

Fax: Telecomm (☎816 52 10) in the Palacio Federal, opposite MexPost. Open M-F 8am-7pm, Sa-Su 9am-noon.

Telephones: TelMex and **LADATEL** phones throughout the city.

Internet Access: The Password, Calle 12 #138B, between Calles 53 and 55 (☎811 19 84). 15 pesos for the first hr., 13 for each additional hr.

Post Office: (☎816 21 34) 16 de Septiembre at Calle 53 in the Palacio Federal. Open M-F 9am-5pm. **MexPost** (☎811 17 30) next door. Open M-F 9am-6pm, Sa 9am-1pm.

Postal Code: 24000.

■ ACCOMMODATIONS

Campeche has thus far avoided the price boom that has swept most of the Yucatán Peninsula. Budget accommodations abound in the historic center, and a good, inexpensive hostel is located on the edge of downtown.

Hospedaje Teresita, Calle 53 #31 (☎816 45 34) between Calles 12 and 14. The decor leaves something to be desired, but you'll be too busy taking advantage of the prime location to notice. Singles and doubles 40 pesos, with private bath 60 pesos.

Villa Deportiva Universitaria (☎816 18 02), on Melgár, 1½ blocks from the coastal highway. From outside the north walls of the city (Calle 49C), catch a bus marked "Lerma," "Playa Bonita," or "ISSTE" heading toward the water. Ask to get off at "Villa Deportiva" (15min.). A black iron gate across the street marks the spot. Single-sex dorm rooms with four bunks and communal baths. Often full July-Aug. and Dec. Call to reserve. Bunks 25 pesos; 25 pesos deposit.

Hotel Colonial, Calle 14 #122 (☎816 22 22 or 816 26 30), between Calles 55 and 57, 2½ blocks from the *zócalo*. A retro look saturates the tall rooms and tiny bathrooms. Singles 100 pesos; doubles 135 pesos; triples 164 pesos. 23 pesos per additional person. 50 pesos for A/C.

Hotel Campeche, Calle 57 #2 (☎816 51 83), between Calles 8 and 10. Overlooking Parque Principal, the hotel will bring joy to gazebo lovers. Rooms are sparse but serve their purpose. Singles 82 pesos; doubles 102 pesos; 20 pesos for additional person.

◖ FOOD

Campeche has developed cuisine that is as colorful as its streets. Sample *pan de cazón* (stacked tortillas filled with baby shark and refried beans and covered with an onion, tomato, and *chile* sauce). Other local specialties include *pámpano en escabeche* (pompano broiled in olive oil and flavored with onion, garlic, *chile*, and orange juice), Campechan caviar, and *chicozapote*, a regional fruit.

Restaurant La Parroquia, Calle 55 #8 (☎816 80 86), between Calles 10 and 12. Low prices and heaping portions. A cavernous all-night local eatery with TV on around the clock. Fat, steaming stacks of pancakes with honey (23 pesos). Open 24hr.

Nutrivida (☎816 12 21), on Calle 12 between 57 and 59. Vegetarians rejoice! Nutrivida packs a full house by dishing out all-natural foodstuffs such as apple yogurt (4.5 pesos) and meatless burgers (12 pesos). If you haven't had enough, buy a bottle of ginseng on your way out. Open M-F 8am-2pm and 5:30-8:30pm, Sa 8am-2pm.

Restaurante del Parque, Calle 57 #8 (☎816 02 40), at Calle 8. Tablecloths and cushioned chairs make this the height of budget elegance. Equally tasteful dishes, like *tortas al pastor* (18 pesos) and *pan de cazón* (29 pesos). Open daily 6:30am-11pm.

Restaurante Campeche, Calle 57 (☎816 21 28), between Calles 8 and 10. The A/C unit and futuristic blue lighting call the North Pole to mind. Complete the illusion with an ice cream dessert (11 pesos). Entrees 35 pesos. Open daily 6:30am-midnight.

Restaurant El Principal (☎811 12 11 or 816 22 48), in the gazebo in *El Parque Principal,* serves tropical ice cream (18 pesos), club sandwiches (30 pesos), and Campeche beer in a souvenir glass (15 pesos). Open Tu-Su 4:30-11pm; July-Aug. and Dec. 9am-11pm. The only place in town that rents **bikes** (25 pesos per hr.).

Cenaduría Portales (☎811 14 91), on Calle 10, 1km up the coast from downtown. Take any bus headed north on Alemán to the Iglesia de San Francisco. Cross the plaza in front of the church and head left to a smaller square; the restaurant is beneath the arches. An assembly line of highly trained sandwich makers leaps into action and nearly instantly produces not just a sandwich, but a work of art (12-15 pesos). Open daily 7pm-midnight.

◉ SIGHTS

Campeche's historical treasures are best seen at night. The city has eight *baluartes* (bulwarks), which can be seen by walking along Circuito Baluartes or taking the "Circuito Baluartes" bus. Perhaps the most convenient way to visit the city is to take the "Tranvia" red trolley that tours major sights. Catch it in the Parque Principal on Calle 10 in front of the gazebo. (1hr. M-F 9:30am, 6, and 8pm; Sa-Su 9:30am, 6, 7, and 8pm. 15 pesos. Tours in Spanish.) "El Guapo" (☎811 11 38), a handsome green trolley, also gives a guided tour on its way to Fuerte de San Miguel (Tu-Su 9am and 5pm) and Fuerte de San José El Alto (1¼hr.; Tu-Su 10:30am and 6:30pm; 15 pesos).

FUERTE DE SAN MIGUEL. This fort houses well-constructed exhibits on nearby ruins. On the top level, 19 cannons still protect the city. *(Take a "Lerma" or "Playa Bonita" bus from Circuito Baluartes, half a block toward the sea from the market. Ask the driver to drop you off at the Castillo stop, then walk up the steep hill on the left until you reach the fork in the road; the left turn leads to the fort. Open Tu-Su 8am-8pm. 17 pesos; free Su.)*

FUERTE DE SAN JOSÉ EL ALTO. Built in 1792, San Miguel's counterpart stands guard on the opposite side of the city. The path leading to the portcullis winds deliberately so that battering rams could not be used on the gate. Today, the ships and armaments have moved inside the fort to an impressive exhibit. *(The "Bellavista" or "San José El Alto" bus, caught at the same place as the bus for San Miguel, will drop you halfway up the hill, a 5min. walk from the fort. Open Tu-Su 8am-8pm. 17 pesos; free Su.)*

MUSEO DE LAS ESTELAS MAYA. Inside the **Baluarte de la Soledad,** the museum houses a small collection of well-preserved Maya stelae and reliefs taken from sites in Campeche state. *(Off Calle 8 near Calle 57 behind the Parque Principal. Open Su-M 8am-2pm, Tu-Sa 8am-8pm. 17 pesos.)*

JARDÍN BOTÁNICO XMUCH'HALTUN. Enclosed by the walls of the **Fuerte de Santiago,** the *jardín* is an inviting stop. Over 250 species of plant thrive in a tiny open-air courtyard shaded by trees and filled with benches, fountains, and frogs. *(On calles 8 and 51. Open M-F 8am-8pm, Sa 9am-2pm, Su 8am-2:30pm.)*

LA PURÍSIMA CONCEPCIÓN. The construction of Campeche's cathedral was initially ordered by Francisco de Montejo in 1540, but builders did not complete the massive structure until 1705. *(Open daily 7am-noon and 5-8pm. Free.)*

IGLESIA DE SAN FRANCISCO. This church, built in 1546, marks the place where the first Mesoamerican mass was held. It was the baptismal site of the grandson of Hernán Cortés. The three bells toll for humility, obedience, and chastity. *(About 1km from the center of town on Alemán. Open daily 8am-noon and 5-8pm.)*

IGLESIA DE SAN ROMÁN. The church houses the image of **El Cristo Negro** (The Black Christ), greatly venerated by *campechanos* in Mexico. *(A few blocks south of the centro on Calle 10. Open daily 6am-noon and 4-8pm.)*

BEACHES. The coast along downtown Campeche is not wonderful. For something prettier, catch a **Playa Bonita** bus to the beach of the same name.

🎵 🌿 ENTERTAINMENT AND FESTIVALS

Campeche's university is brimming with students. Students, of course, like to party. Unfortunately, however, that means that most clubs are by the university, a good distance from the *centro*. The swinging local crowd gets down at **Disco Dragon,** Resurgimiento 87. **KY8,** Calle 8 and 59, pumps the jams across Puerta de Mar. (Open F-Sa 10pm-3am. Cover 50 pesos.) **Millenium,** Resurgimiento 112, attracts the hottest Campeche salsa dancers on Friday nights and disco dancers on Saturday night. (☎816 45 55. Open F-Sa 10:30pm-3am. Cover 40 pesos.) *Campechanos* groove to a variety of rhythms on two different floors at **Platforma 21,** in *Loma Azul.* (☎812 61 78. Open F-Sa 10pm-3am. Cover 40 pesos.)

The city sponsors various outdoor events. Cheesy but interesting is the **sound and light show** at Puerta de Tierra, Calles 59 and 18, which tells the story of how the *campechanos* staved off the foolhardy pirates (Tu, F-Sa 8:30pm, 20 pesos). Weather permitting, a *ballet folklórico* performance follows the show. **Sabadito Alegre en La Plaza de la República,** at the Puerta de Mar, features *mariachi* and *danzones* (Sa 7-10pm). **Tradición y Folklore,** a celebration of *campechano* heritage, replete with music and dancing, takes place at the Ex-Templo de San José (Tu 7pm), and the state band strikes up *campechano* music from the kiosk in the Parque Principal (Su 8pm). During high season (July-Aug. and Dec.) more events are scheduled. Ask for the a program at the tourist information center. **San Román** is the city's patron saint, and *campechanos* celebrate his feast (Sept. 14-30).

🦶 DAYTRIPS FROM CAMPECHE

EDZNÁ

Catch a bus from the lot across the park from the market on República. The building at the entrance to the lot is marked "SUR" (7am, every hr. starting at 10am, 13 pesos). Be sure to ask the driver when he will return. Site open daily 8am-5pm. 25 pesos; free Su.

Edzná, meaning "House of the Itzáes," was named after Edzná's ruling family during its zenith in the late Classic Period (AD 600-900). The site covers 25 sq. km and had a unique rainwater distribution system, which was composed of an elaborate network of 29 canals, 27 reservoirs, and more than 70 *chultunes* (man-made water cisterns). The **Edificio de Cinco Pisos** (Building of the Five Floors) towers over the surrounding valley atop the **Gran Acrópolis.** Sixty-five stairs, some adorned with hieroglyphics over 1300 years old, lead to tiers of columns crowned by a five-room temple. The temple used to house a stela engraved with the image of the god of corn, illuminated twice yearly by the sun to signal planting and harvesting times. The east side of the Gran Acropolis faces the 15 steep stairs of **Nohoch-Ná** (Large House), resembling a stadium with four large rooms atop its last staircase. Be sure to see the remains of the **ballcourt** and its western stone ring, the **Small Acropolis** (the oldest building at the site), and the **Temple of Masks** with its two three-dimensional stucco masks representing the sunrise and sunset. On display near the entrance are some of the 19 stelae found at Edzná.

GRUTAS DE XTACUMBILXUNAAN

The caves lie on Rte. 261, 30km north of Hopelchen and 8km south of Bolonchen. Second-class buses between Campeche and Mérida (40 pesos) drop passengers at the access road. Open daily 8am-4pm. 15 pesos. Tours in Spanish only.

The **Grutas de Xtacumbilxunaan** (shta-koom-bill-shu-NAN, "Caves of the Sleeping Beauty") are 27km from the Yucatán-Campeche border. A guided tour leads down a stone stairway to several deep *cenotes,* a *ceiba* staff, and unusual rock formations. Spelunkers toting their own rock climbing equipment can take a two-day journey underground with the guides, and visit the seven connected *cenotes* 150m below ground. Bring camping gear and stay in the outdoor *palapa* for free.

RÍO BEC AND XPUJIL ☎ 7

Nestled in steamy southern Campeche, the dozen or so Río Bec archaeological sites are strewn over a stretch of **Rte. 186,** the Escárcega-Chetumal highway, occupying an area of 50 sq. km. The ruins have lain undisturbed for hundreds of years; it is only recently, with increasing interest in developing tourism in the state of Campeche, that the Mexican government has begun exploring and opening these Classic Maya ruins. The sites show great promise, and have already been found to contain the largest Maya structure ever built. Organized tours of the Río Bec sites are arranged in Campeche and Chetumal, but penny-pinchers will want to use the village of **Xpujil** (SHPOO-hil) as a base. The tiny town straddles Rte. 186 for about a kilometer, a few kilometers west of the Campeche-Quintana Roo border, and offers the most convenient access to the Río Bec sites.

▐▐ TRANSPORTATION AND PRACTICAL INFORMATION

The **ADO bus station** (☎871 60 27) is on the northern side of the highway, just east of the junction. Buses go to **Chetumal** (7am and 4:30pm, 46 pesos) and **Escárcega** (6 per day, 56 pesos). Buses are *de paso;* pray for room. Taxis can be found at the junction, and will take you to the ruins for hefty sums. *Combi*s are based in the same area and will cost less for the sites of Becán (5 pesos) and Chicanná (7 pesos). However, they only run on weekends (Sa-Su, every hr. 6am-4pm). The blue *combi* will take 8-10 people from the junction to and from Calakmul (550 pesos).

Xpujil is organized around the junction of Rte. 186 and the road to Dzibalchen. A **pharmacy** (which also offers **medical services**) can be found at the southeast corner of the junction. (Open M-Sa 8am-1pm and 3-8pm, Su 8am-1pm.) The **Telecomm** and **post office** are on the southwest corner of the junction. **Postal code:** 24640.

▐ ACCOMMODATIONS

There are two options, neither particularly cheap. **Hotel Calakmul,** in the pink building 600m west of the junction, has rustic *cabañas* with fans, mosquito nets, and shared bathrooms. (☎/fax 871 60 29. Singles 120-240 pesos; 60-120 per additional person.) Atop a hill 400m west, the **Bungalows El Mirador Maya** has *cabañas* with fancy private baths and porches. The owner, Moises, offers transportation to and from the ruins at reasonable prices. (☎871 60 05. Singles and doubles 200 pesos, with A/C 300 pesos; 50 pesos per additional person. Tours 200-300 pesos.)

▐ THE RÍO BEC RUINS

The Río Bec area was settled late in the Pre-Classic period, around 300 BC. The area reached its zenith some time later, in the middle of the Classic Period. Small and virtually ignored by tourists, the ruins are primarily known for the "Río Bec" architectural style, a mixture of the Petén style from the south and the Chenes style from the north. The result is distinctively rounded corners and false front stairways on flanking towers.

XPUJIL. Named after the cattail plant which grows there, Xpujil, across the street from the Mirador Maya, is the closest of the sites. Composed of 17 building groups, Xpujil most likely reached its peak in AD 500-750. The first ruin you will see is **Structure IV.** Note the holes in the interior walls, used to support curtain rods. Continue farther to **Structure I,** the centerpiece of the site. Atypical of Río Bec architecture, it has three towers instead of two. The center one is the best preserved. Enter the passage on the southeast side of the southern tower to climb the treacherous steps for a bird's-eye view of the site. *(Open daily 8am-5pm. 22 pesos, Su free.)*

BECÁN. Five kilometers west of town, Becán ("Trench") is named after the defensive moat built around it. Becán was the capital of the Río Bec region at its height (AD 600-800). As you enter the site, bear to the right after crossing

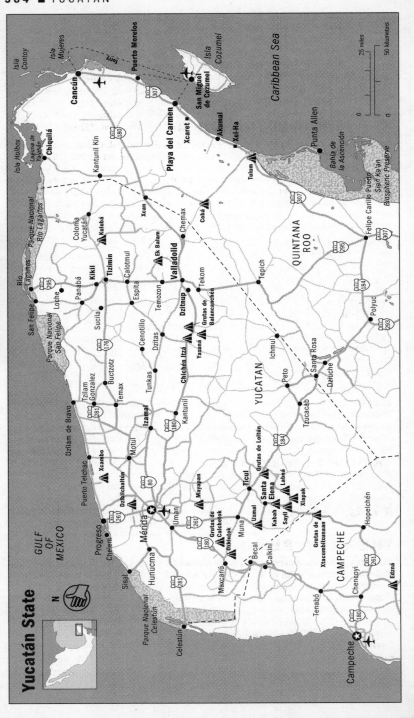

YUCATÁN

Yucatán State

N

Parque Nacional Celestún

GULF OF MEXICO

Caribbean Sea

QUINTANA ROO

YUCATAN

CAMPECHE

the bridge and enter the 66m passageway. You will emerge near **Structure VIII,** which can be climbed with the aid of a pair of ropes. The rooms here served as living quarters, storage facilities, and centers for religious ceremonies. Scramble around to the northern tower and try to find the secret staircase (unfortunately blocked off at the top). Continue on to **Structure X,** whose upper temple has representations of the god Itzamná, and to the **ballcourt** behind it. Just before you cross the bridge on your way out, take a short detour to the right to reach **Structures I-IV.** In this courtyard you will find steam baths, good examples of the Río Bec checkerboard motif, and a circular altar, erected AD 1100-1200 by the infiltrating cult of Kukulcán. *(Open daily 8am-5pm. 25 pesos, Su free.)*

CHICANNÁ. Named for the striking facade of its **Structure II,** Chicanná ("House of the Serpent's mouth") was a small elite center—if you will, a rich suburb of Becán. The ruins can be found 2km farther west and have their roots in the late Classic Period (300 BC-AD 250). The first building you will stumble upon is **Structure XX,** whose masks at all four corners are typical of the Chenes style. After passing the decrepit **Structure XI** you will arrive in the main plaza. **Structure I** is a fantastic example of Río Bec architecture, and, across from it, Structure II has the menacing facade mentioned above. *(Open daily 8am-5pm. 22 pesos, Su free.)*

■ CALAKMUL. Calakmul is an enormous site, covering 25 sq. km and containing 115 stelae. It was first inhabited between 900-300 BC, and reached its peak 400-800 AD. Population estimates range from 60,000-200,000 people, but there is no doubt that this was a site of great importance, most likely a regional capital. Calakmul's claim to fame is its **giant pyramid.** Rising 53m and covering an area of 5 acres, it is the largest Maya structure ever built. The first plaza you stumble upon was a center for astronomical observation. Three of the structures bordering it were used for recording the movements of the sun, moon, and stars. A path leading from the northwest corner of the plaza will bring you to the **grand acropolis, ballcourt,** and, father on, **wall remains.** *(The access road to Calakmul branches off from Rte. 186, 60km west of Xpujil. From there, it's a 65km ride on a paved, pot-holed road through the jungle. If you make the journey, leave early and spot some wildlife. Open daily 8am-5pm. 25 pesos, Su free. Toll for access road 50 pesos.)*

BALAMKÚ. If you make it all the way to Calakmul, you might as well stop by Balamkú, just 1km farther west on Rte. 186. Come here to see the remarkably detailed **frieze,** documenting the cycle of birth and death of the king. The king emerges from the mouth of a crocodile, which, in turn, emerges from an earth-monster, linking the underworld to the earth. To see the frieze, follow the arrows to the **Casa de Los Mascarones** and enter the building through the metal structure on its side. *(Open daily 8am-5pm. Free.)*

YUCATÁN

THE RUTA PUUC

The Ruta Puuc is an area between Mérida and Campeche that traverses the Puuc Hills and is dotted with dozens of Maya ruins. During the Classic period of Maya civilization (4th-10th centuries AD) it was home to about 25,000 people.

The ruins of **Uxmal** are 70km south of Mérida on Rte. 261, and 16km south of Muna. The sites of **Oxkintok** and **Las Grutas de Calcehtok,** not properly part of the Ruta, are 20km northwest of Muna, and the ruins of **Mayapán** are 30km northeast of Muna. Sixteen kilometers east of Uxmal is the town of Santa Elena. **Kabah** lies 8km south of Santa Elena. Five kilometers south of Kabah, the Sayil-Oxkutzcab road branches to the east to **Sayil, Xlapak, Labná, Hacienda Tabí, Las Grutas de Loltún,** and ends up in Oxkutzcab. From Oxkutzcab, Ticul is 19km to the west.

GETTING AROUND THE RUTA PUUC. The easiest way to get around is by renting a car in Mérida. Recently, though, more and more travel agencies in Mérida and Campeche are offering organized tours—inquire at a tourist office for the latest. Public transportation is the most difficult way to see the Ruta Puuc. Second-class **buses** traverse Rte. 261 frequently, and will stop when requested. None travel the Sayil-Oxkutzkub road with the exception of the **Autotransportes del Sur** "Ruta Puuc" bus that leaves Mérida at 8am and visits **Kabah, Sayil, Xlapac, Labná**, and **Uxmal**, returning to Mérida at about 4pm. If you don't mind a whirlwind tour of the sites, the bus is a bargain (25 pesos; admission to sites not included). The bus spends 30min. at each site and 90min. at Uxmal. *Combis* are most abundant in the mornings, and make frequent trips between **Oxkutzcab, Ticul, Santa Elena**, and **Muna**. They will make almost any trip if paid enough. It is easiest, though not easy, to get a *combi* to Uxmal, Kabah, and other sites from the *zócalo* in Muna. Unfortunately, with both *combis* and buses, return trips are by no means guaranteed. Travelers who make the Ruta Puuc more than a daytrip use **Ticul** as a base, or the even more convenient **Santa Elena**. From either of these places, two to three days should be ample time for exploration.

▧ UXMAL

Autotransportes del Sur (ATS) goes from Mérida to Uxmal (1½hr., 6 per day, 25 pesos). The "Ruta Puuc" bus also stops at Uxmal. From Campeche you'll have to take the Camioneros de Campeche bus to Mérida (3hr., 5 per day, 45 pesos). Ask the driver to stop at the access road to the ruins. To return, grab a passing bus at the crossing just outside the entrance to the ruins. The last bus passes at 8pm. Open daily 8am-6pm; light and sound show 7pm in winter, 8pm in summer. 75 pesos, includes show. Show only, 30 pesos; children under 13 enter free; Su and holidays free. Parking 10 pesos. Guides about 250 pesos for a group of 5.

Meaning "thrice built or occupied," Uxmal was once a capital with 25,000 inhabitants, reaching its most powerful in the last Classic and Post-Classic periods. The city was in union with Mayapán and Chichén Itzá in the Mayapán League, which dominated most of the Yucatán Peninsula until the arrival of the Spanish in the 1520s. While it is known that Uxmal was subordinate to the other two Mayapán League city-states, there is evidence that the city was the largest of the Puuc sites and dominated the neighboring cities of Kabah, Labná, and Sayil.

PYRAMID OF THE MAGICIAN. According to legend, the 35m pyramid was built overnight by a dwarf-magician who hatched from a witch's egg and grew to maturity in one year. The legend of the dwarf-magician's birth struck terror into the heart of the governing lord, who immediately challenged the dwarf to a contest of building skills. In reality, the pyramid was most likely built during the Classic Period, around AD 600-1000.

GREAT PYRAMID. The dwarf's pyramid easily out-classed the governor's Great Pyramid, visible to the right of the Governor's Palace. On top of the pyramid sits the **Macaw Temple,** named for its many engravings of that bird on its facade, inside of which sits a Chac-motif throne. The spiteful ruler tried to undermine the legitimacy of the dwarf-magician's pyramid by complaining that its base was neither square nor rectangular (standard shapes) but oval with massive rounded ends. The governor proposed that he and his adversary settle their quarrel by competing to see who could break a *cocoyol* (a small, hard-shelled fruit) on his head. The dwarf-magician slipped a turtle shell into his skull and easily cracked the *cocoyol*. The governor crushed his own unaltered skull.

QUADRANGLE OF THE BIRDS. Immediately to the west of the Grand Pyramid lies the Quadrangle of the Birds, named for the bird sculptures that adorn its western side. The pyramid forms the eastern barrier, the building to the north has a smooth facade, and the one to the south sports small columns.

CUADRÁNGULO OF THE NUNS. Continuing to the west is a large quadrangle—Uxmal's famed Nunnery, misnamed by the Spanish who thought its many rooms resembled a convent's. The four long buildings of this quad were each built on a different level, and each has a distinctive decor. The northern building is adorned with Chac masks; the eastern building has intricate lattice work and Venus symbols, the southern building contains a series of hut sculptures, and the western building shows kings and bound prisoners in high relief. The sizeable entryways of the southern building lead to the **ballcourt.** Only one of the glyph-engraved stone signs remains, through which well-padded players tried to knock a hardened rubber ball.

CEMETERY GROUP. Emerging from the ballcourt, head right along a narrow path to the Cemetery Group, a small, leafy plaza bounded by a modestly sized pyramid to the north and a temple to the west. Stones that once formed platforms bear haunting reliefs of skulls and crossbones. To the west the pyramid looks down on the fretworks of the **Pigeon House.** Behind this structure lie the jungle-shrouded remains of the **Chenes Temple.**

CASA DE LAS TORTUGAS (HOUSE OF THE TURTLES). The two-story house is on the northwest corner of the escarpment and is adorned along its upper frieze with a series of sculpted three dimensional turtles, which symbolized rain.

PALACIO DEL GOBERNADOR (GOVERNOR'S PALACE). The palace, replete with engravings and arches, is one of the last buildings constructed at the site, probably around AD 1000, and is considered by many to be an example of the finest architecture in the site—if not in the entirety of pre-Hispanic Mesoamerica.

KABAH

Kabah is bisected by Rte. 261, and lies 23km southeast of its cousin Uxmal. Because of its location on the Campeche-Mérida highway, it can easily be reached by any second-class bus running between Mérida and Campeche. Buses will stop at Kabah only if a passenger notifies the driver beforehand or if the driver sees a person wildly gesticulating on the shoulder of the highway. Things are easier with the "Ruta Puuc" bus. Open daily 8am-5pm. 17 pesos, Su free.

Once the second largest city in the northern Yucatán, **Kabah,** which means "Sir of the Strong Hand and Powerful," was built with the blood and sweat of many slaves. The name of the striking **Codz Poop Temple,** visible to the right of the entrance, refers to the curved nose of Chac, over 250 of which protrude from its facade. Unlike structures of the pure Puuc style, characterized by plain columns and a superior decorative frieze, Codz Poop is covered with ornamental stone carvings from top to bottom, more resembling the **Chenes style.** Continue east and you will come across **El Palacio,** a two-story structure containing 30 rooms. Follow a path from the left side of the Palacio for 200m and you'll find **Las Columnas.** The site is thought to have served as a court where justices settled disputes, with gods comprising the jury. Across the street by the parking lot, the short dirt road leads to rubble (right), more rubble (left), and the famous **Kabah Arch** (straight). The arch marks the beginning of the ancient *sacbé* (raised road) that ended with a twin arch in Uxmal. The perfect alignment of the archway with the north-south line is testimony to Maya astronomical wisdom.

◼ SAYIL

Sayil lies 5km off Rte. 261 on the Sayil-Oxkutzcab road, one of the stops of the "Ruta Puuc" bus. Buses between Mérida and Campeche stop here irregularly. Ask to be let off at the military checkpoint, then trek the 5km to the site. Buses returning to Mérida come by about 3 times daily. Site open daily 8am-5pm. 17 pesos, Su free.

The **Palace of Sayil** is an architectural standout among the region's ruins. The unique, three-story structure was constructed AD 800-1000. It harbors 90 rooms, which served as storage, administrative space, and housing for 350 people. Its foundation houses eight underground cisterns. The *sacbé* across from the Palace leads to **El Mirador,** a lofty pyramid-temple topped off by a peculiar roof-comb. Left of El Mirador, a 1km path leads through the jungle to the **Grupo Sun,** where the **Estela del Falo** (Stela of the Phallus) was a tribute to Yum Keep, a Maya god of fertility. A few nearby temples are visible through the undergrowth. Across the street, up a narrow dirt path, is **El Templo de las Cabezas** (The Temple of Heads/Masks). The masks may be scarce, but the view of Sayil's palace is splendid.

XLAPAC

The "Ruta Puuc" bus stops here for 20min. To stay for longer, hire a combi in nearby Oxkutzcab. Site open daily 8am-5pm. 12 pesos, Su free.

Xlapac, which means "old wall," lies between Labná and Sayil, and is the smallest and most often missed ruin on the Ruta Puuc. **El Palacio,** classic Puuc in style, pays homage to Chac with its impressive triple-decker masks of the Maya rain god. South of the palace 300m is a partially-excavated stone structure, with the remains of fallen columns and carved stones lying along its perimeter.

LABNÁ

Labná lies 14km east of Rte. 261, where buses between Mérida and Campeche pass. No buses, however, make the trip past Labná. Almost no combis come here, and hitching is reportedly tough. Your best bet is the "Ruta Puuc" bus or a private car. Open daily 8am-5pm. 17 pesos, Su free.

Labná was constructed toward the end of the Late Classic period (AD 700-1000), when the Puuc cities were connected by *sacbé* (paved, elevated roads). A short reconstructed section of the *sacbé* runs between Labná's two most impressive sights: the palace and the stone arch. On the northern side of the site, to the left as you enter, is the still-uncompleted palace, built over seven patios and two levels. Labná is famed for its picturesque stone arch, the **Arch of Labná,** 3m wide and 5m high. Archaeologists now believe that the arch served as a ceremonial point of entry for victorious returning warriors. Beyond the arch, at the base of a pyramid, is the observatory, known as **El Mirador.** Back toward the palace, **El Templo de las Columnas,** one of the best examples of the Puuc style, is off the *sacbé* to the right.

HACIENDA TABI

The Hacienda is accessible only with a reliable car. On the Sayil-Oxkutzcab road, take the road that branches off at the Grutas de Loltún. The now-dirt access road to the Hacienda, marked with a sign when approached from the east, goes straight (2km to the site) when the main road veers right. Open daily 8am-5pm. 15 pesos.

This *hacienda* was constructed as a sugar-producing facility in 1896. The site was abandoned, however, after a fire destroyed its church and sugar machinery. No one knows exactly when this occurred, lending an air of mystery to these "ruins." The most impressive sights are the *Palacio,* which greets you as you pass the gates, the gutted remnants of the church, and the two giant chimneys, used for burning the sugar.

GRUTAS DE LOLTÚN

To reach the Grutas, snag a combi to Oxkutzcab from Calle 25A between Calles 24 and 26 (every 10min., 6 pesos); you'll be let off at the intersection of Calles 23 and 26. Combis and pickup truck colectivos leave for Loltún from the lot across from Oxkutzcab's market, 20 de Noviembre. Tell the driver to let you off at the caves (10min., 3 pesos), as everyone else is probably headed for the agricultural cooperative 3km farther down the road. Entrance to the caves with tours only. Tours daily 9:30, 11am, 12:30, 2, 3, and 4pm; 42 pesos, Su 20 pesos. Restaurant open M-Sa 10am-6pm.

Below the dense jungle, kilometers of enormous caverns wind through the rock. The ancient Maya first settled this area in order to take advantage of the caves' water and clay. Hundreds of years later, Maya *campesinos* returned to the caves seeking refuge from the Caste War (1847-48). Important caverns include the **Room of Inscriptions,** full of handprints, the **Na Cab** (House of the Bees), where you can see the *ka'ob* (grindstones) left behind, the **Gallery of Fallen Rocks,** from which inhabitants broke off the stalactite tips to use as weapons, potion for strength and virility, and musical instruments. Several caves contain partially hollow stalactites and columns—strike each one with the heel of your hand and listen to the soft booming sound (*"loltún…loltún…"*) reverberate throughout the cave system. Archaeologists speculate that the Maya used these formations as a means of underground communication. Tours available in both Spanish and indecipherable English. Guides can be enticed to lengthen their tours with the promise of a fat tip.

OXKINTOK

By car, follow the signs for Oxkintok as you approach the village of Maxcanú from the east. Be forewarned: the road is badly potholed. Open daily 9am-6pm. 17 pesos, Su free.

Oxkintok lies 42km northwest of Uxmal, on the west end of the rolling Puuc hills. The ruins date from the Classic Period (AD 300-1050). If you have a car, Oxkintok might merit a visit, as it is a well-maintained and thoroughly excavated site. Climb atop the **Ah May Pyramid,** the tallest building, and the **Ah Canul Palace** for a good view of the site. A stroll through the labyrinth's narrow and dark corridors guarantees an eerie adventure, but watch for low ceilings and steep steps.

LAS GRUTAS DE CALCEHTOK

To get to the caves, follow the signs marked "Grutas" as you approach Oxkintok. A solitary guide mans the entrance. Take advantage of his services.

If you've made it all the way out to Oxkintok, you might as well swing by **Las Grutas de Calcehtok,** only 2km southwest of the ruins. At 4km, the cavern is the longest one in all of Yucatan, with four different entries, thousands of stalactites and stalagmites, and rock formations in comical shapes—Head of Frankenstein, a llama, Head of a Horse, etc. Bits of broken Maya ceramics abound, as well as man-made *chultunes* (water-holders). Ask the guide to lead you into the Maya ritual and sacrificial grounds, where 2000-year-old Maya bones dot the terrain.

MAYAPÁN

Mayapán is 50km southeast of Mérida on Rte. 18, and 26km northwest of Tekit on the same road. While officially not a part of the Ruta Puuc, Mayapán is only an hour drive from Ticul. Combis make the trip between Mérida and Tekit frequently. Open daily 8am-5pm. 12 pesos; Su free.

The ruins of Mayapán are not nearly as impressive as its history. From AD 1000-1200, the city was dominated by Chichén Itzá, which controlled the Mayapán League. After 1200, Mayapán overthrew Chichén Itzá and controlled the league until the arrival of the Spanish. The demise of Mayapán came in 1441, when Ah Xupan of Uxmal overthrew the Cocan dynasty. All that remains of the once-powerful city are the rubble of the main temple and the Caracol.

TICUL ☎9

A provincial town off the Campeche-Mérida highway, Ticul (pop. 40,000) is known for its excellent ceramics and cheap, durable shoes. It is also a convenient and inexpensive base from which to explore the Puuc sites of Labná, Kabah, Sayil, Uxmal, and Xlapak, as well as the Grutas de Loltún. For those with wheels, a number of *cenotes* and colonial buildings await exploration in the nearby towns of **Teabo,** 30km southeast of Ticul, and **Holcá,** 105km to the northeast. **Maní,** 15km east of Ticul, features a colonial monastery; **Tekax,** 35km to the southeast, a hermitage; and **Tipikal,** an impressive colonial church. Ticul itself is home to a 17th-century church, the **Templo de San Antonio** (open 8am-6pm), and pulls out all the stops for the week of its **Tobacco Fair** starting in early April.

TRANSPORTATION. Ticul's **bus station** (☎972 01 62) is on Calle 24, behind the church. Trips are made to **Mérida** (every hr., 26 pesos). *Combis* leave from across from the Hotel San Miguel for **Muna** (7 pesos); for **Santa Elena, Uxmal,** and **Kabah** (10 pesos) from Calle 30, between Calles 25 and 25A; and for **Oxkutzcab** from Calle 25A, between Calles 24 and 26 (every 15min., 6 pesos).

ORIENTATION AND PRACTICAL INFORMATION. Ticul's main thoroughfare, **Calle 23,** runs east-west, as do all odd-numbered streets, increasing to the south. Even-numbered streets run north-south and increase heading west. The *zócalo* is east of Calle 26, with most commercial activity taking place between the *zócalo* and Calle 30, three blocks to the west. Near the *zócalo*, on **Calle 25,** a strip of Maya statuettes pay tribute to ancient gods. **Bital,** Calle 23 #195, on the northwest corner of the *zócalo*, exchanges currency. (☎972 09 79. Open M-Sa 8am-7pm.) **Police:** on Calle 23, at the northeast corner of the *zócalo*. (☎972 02 10. Open 24hr.) **Farmacia Canto,** #202 Calle 23, at Calle 26. (☎972 05 81. Open M-Sa 8am-10pm, Su 8am-1pm and 5-9pm.) **Centro de Salud,** #226 Calle 27, between Calles 30 and 32. No English spoken. (☎972 00 86. Open 24hr.) **Telecomm office:** Calle 24A between Calles 21 and 23, northeast of the *zócalo*. (☎972 01 46. Open M-F 9am-3pm.) **Post office:** in the Palacio Municipal, on the northeast side of the *zócalo*. (☎972 00 40. Open M-F 8am-2:30pm.) **Postal code:** 97860.

ACCOMMODATIONS AND FOOD. The **Hotel San Miguel,** on Calle 28 half a block north of Calle 23, is inexpensive and it shows. (☎972 03 82. Singles 47 pesos; doubles 76 pesos; triples 112 pesos.) **Hotel Sierra Sosa,** on Calle 24, at the northwest corner of the *zócalo*, has firm beds, strong fans, and TVs loud enough to drown out the hot-rod mopeds outside. (☎972 00 08. Singles 85 pesos, with A/C 130 pesos; doubles 115 pesos, with A/C 160 pesos. 20 pesos per additional person.) After a hot day on the Ruta Puuc, Ticul is the place to refuel and rehydrate. **Los Almendros,** #207 Calle 23, between Calles 26A and 28, is known for its *poc-chuc* (pork served with onions, beans, tomatoes, and dangerous Habañero peppers). *Pollo pibil* and *pollo ticuleño* 36 pesos. (☎972 00 21. Open daily 9am-9pm.) **Restaurant Los Delfines,** Calle 27, between Calles 28 and 30, serves shrimp dishes, *chile relleno* (45 pesos), and jars of lemonade. (☎972 04 01. Open daily 11am-7pm.) **Pizzeria la Gondola** is a taste of Italy in the heart of the Yucatán. Spaghetti 20 pesos, pizza 45 pesos. Free delivery. (☎972 01 12. Open daily 8am-1pm and 5:30pm-midnight.) Ticul's **market** is off Calle 23 between Calles 28 and 30. (Open daily 6am-2pm.)

SANTA ELENA ☎9

This tiny town of 4000 Maya-speaking residents lies 8km north of Kabah and 15km east of Uxmal. It has a park, soda shops, one phone, and an 18th-century church, which affords magnificent views from its roof. Ask the "sacristan" to show you the way up. (Open Su-F 3-6pm.) Santa Elena even has its very own archaeological site of **Mulchic,** a small collection of platforms and substructures belonging to the late period. To get to the ruins, hike the 2km trail which branches off Rte. 261, 700m toward Mérida past the cemetery. Santa Elena's main attraction, however, is its prime location on the Ruta Puuc. The "Ruta Puuc" bus passes by the town on Rte. 261 at 9:30am and returns at 12:20pm. It then proceeds on to Uxmal, but doesn't return to Santa Elena. It is possible, however, to return by hitching a ride with the workers who live in Santa Elena, or by grabbing a *combi*. To go to the Grutas de Loltún from Santa Elena, hop on the 7:40am bus bound for Oxkutzcab, and from there take a *colectivo*.

Two budget accommodations lie along Rte. 261. The **Sacbé Camping-Bungalows** offers weary travelers pristine campgrounds with new shower and toilet facilities, outdoor grills and tables, and even a mosquito-netted thatched hut where the owners serve meals. (Campsites and hammock space 25 pesos per person; small bungalows with hot water, fans, and private baths 90-130 pesos. Breakfast and dinner 22-36 pesos.) Only 150m north toward Uxmal, on the opposite side of the road, lies the **Hotel/Restaurant El Chac-Mool.** Large helpings of eggs, tacos, sandwiches (35-40 pesos) and beer (10-12 pesos). Two large modern rooms adjacent to the dining area. (☎971 01 91. 130 pesos per room. Restaurant open daily 11am-8pm.)

MÉRIDA ☎9

Hub of the Yucatán Peninsula, Mérida (pop. 1.5 million) is a rich amalgamation of proud indigenous history, powerful colonial presence, and modern international flavor. The city was founded in 1542, by Francisco de Montejo atop what was once the Maya metropolis of **T'ho.** The Maya called the city "Place of the Fifth Point," to indicate that it was the center of the universe, the spot between the four points of north, south, east, and west. Modern Mérida continues to serve as a fifth point in the new Mexican cosmology of capitalism. The city's commercial centers burst with *jipis* (Panama hats) shipped from Campeche, hammocks (and plenty of them) from Tixcocób, and *henequén* (hemp) from all over the Yucatán Peninsula. The city serves as a magnet for people as well, drawing visitors and immigrants from all over the world. Yet while it is the largest city in the Yucatán Peninsula, it has yet to succumb to big-city indifference. Street cleaners struggle to maintain its reputation as "The White City," intimate conservations swirl about the *zócalo*, and every Sunday promenading families come out to enjoy Mérida at its best.

▐ TRANSPORTATION

GETTING AROUND

Mérida's **municipal buses** meander along idiosyncratic routes (daily 6am-midnight, 3 pesos.) The city is small enough that a bus headed in the right direction will usually drop you within a few blocks of your desired location. **Taxis** do not roam the streets soliciting riders; it is necessary to phone (**Radio Taxi;** ☎923 40 46) or go to one of the *sitios* (stands) along Paseo de Montejo, at the airport, or in the *zócalo.* Expect to pay at least 20-25 pesos for a trip within the *centro.* **Taxi-colectivos** (more commonly known as *combis*), charge only 3 pesos for any destination in the city; drop-offs are on a first-come, first-serve basis.

GETTING AWAY

Airport: 7km southwest on Rte. 180. Taxis to *centro* 50 pesos. **Aerocaribe,** Paseo Montejo 500B x 45 y 47 (☎928 67 90, or 946 13 35). **Aeroméxico,** Paseo Montejo 460 x 35 y 37 (☎920 12 99, or 946 13 05). **Aviateca,** Paseo de Montejo 475 x 37 y 39 (☎925 80 59, or 946 12 96). **Mexicana,** Paseo de Montejo 493 x 43 y 45 (☎924 66 33, or 946 13 32). **Continental,** (☎926 31 00, or 946 18 88).

Buses: Mérida's two main terminals are southwest of the *centro.* To reach the *zócalo* from either terminal, walk north to Calle 63 three blocks away, turn right and walk another three or four blocks.

First-class terminal, Calle 70 #555 x 71 (☎924 83 91). ADO goes to: **Cancún** (6 per day, 145 pesos); **Playa del Carmen** (1:15pm, 160 pesos); **Campeche** (9:45am, 7:15pm, 83 pesos); **Palenque** (8am, 10pm, and 11:30pm, 208 pesos); **Veracruz** (10:30am, 9pm, 421 pesos); **Mexico City** (12:05pm, 615 pesos); **Puebla** (6:30pm, 559 pesos); and **Villahermosa** (10 per day, 239 pesos). Premier goes to: **Tulum** (4 per day, 103 pesos); **Chichén Itzá** (8:45am and 1pm, 50 pesos); **Valladolid** (6 per day, 65 pesos). Cristóbal Colón goes to **San Cristóbal de las Casas** (7:15pm, 270 pesos).

Second-class terminal, Calle 69 #544 x 68 y 70 (☎923 33 87), goes to most of the same places for less: **Cancún** (15 per day, 93 pesos); **Cobá** and **Tulum** (11am, 67 and 80 pesos, respectively); **Chichén Itzá** (18 per day, 37 pesos); and **Playa del Carmen** (6, 11am, 11pm; 101 pesos). To go to **Progreso,** head to the Autoprogreso station at Calle 62 x 65 y 67 (extremely often, 9 pesos). Buses to **Tizimín** and **Izamal** can be found at the Oriente station (Calle 50 x 65 y 67). Buses to **Celestún** leave Occidente station, Calle 71 x 66 y 68 (every hr., 25 pesos).

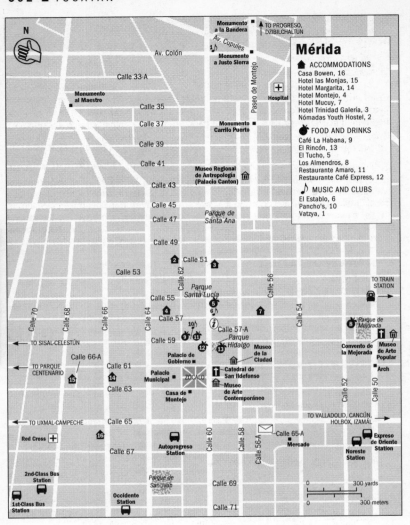

N

TO PROGRESO,
DZIBILCHALTUN

Monumento
a la Bandera

Av. Cupules

Av. Colón

Monumento
a Justo Sierra

Calle 33-A

Hospital

Monumento
al Maestro

Calle 35

Paseo de Montejo

Calle 37

Monumento
Carrillo Puerto

Calle 39

Calle 41

Museo Regional
de Antropología
(Palacio Canton)

Calle 43

Calle 45

Calle 47

Parque de
Santa Ana

Calle 49

Calle 51

Calle 53

Calle 62

Calle 55

Parque
Santa Lucia

Calle 56

TO TRAIN
STATION

Calle 70

Calle 68

Calle 66

Calle 64

Calle 57

Calle 54

Parque de
Mejorada

TO SISAL-CELESTÚN

Calle 59

Calle 57-A
Parque
Hidalgo

Convento de
la Mejorada

Museo
de Arte
Popular

Palacio de
Gobierno

Museo
de la
Ciudad

Arch

Calle 66-A

Calle 61

TO PARQUE
CENTENARIO

Palacio
Municipal

ZOCALO

Catedral de
San Ildefonso

Calle 52

Calle 50

Calle 63

Casa de
Montejo

Museo
de Arte
Contemporáneo

TO UXMAL-CAMPECHE

Calle 65

TO VALLADOLID, CANCÚN,
HOLBOX, IZAMAL

Red Cross

Calle 60

Calle 58

Calle 65-A

Expreso
de Oriente
Station

Calle 67

Autoprogreso
Station

Mercado

Calle 56-A

Noreste
Station

2nd-Class Bus
Station

Parque de
San Juan

Calle 69

0   300 yards

Occidente
Station

0   300 meters

1st-Class Bus
Station

Calle 71

Mérida

🏠 ACCOMMODATIONS
Casa Bowen, 16
Hotel las Monjas, 15
Hotel Margarita, 14
Hotel Montejo, 4
Hotel Mucuy, 7
Hotel Trinidad Galería, 3
Nómadas Youth Hostel, 2

🍎 FOOD AND DRINKS
Café La Habana, 9
El Rincón, 13
El Tucho, 5
Los Almendros, 8
Restaurante Amaro, 11
Restaurante Café Express, 12

♪ MUSIC AND CLUBS
El Establo, 6
Pancho's, 10
Vatzya, 1

■ 🚹 ORIENTATION AND PRACTICAL INFORMATION

Mérida sits on the west side of state of Yucatán, 30km south of the Gulf Coast. The city's gridded one-way streets have numbers instead of names. Even-numbered streets run north-south, with numbers increasing to the west; odd-numbered streets run east-west, increasing to the south. Addresses in Mérida are given using an "x" to separate the main street from the cross streets and "y" ("and" in Spanish) to separate the two cross streets if the address falls in the middle of the block. Thus "54 #509 x 61 y 63" reads "Calle 54 #509, between Calles 61 and 63."

TOURIST, FINANCIAL, AND LOCAL SERVICES

Tourist Information: Central Office (☎924 92 90), Calle 57A x 58 y 60, in the Teatro Peón Contreras. Distributes *Yucatán Today*. Open daily 8am-9pm. Also at the **Palacio del Gobierno** (☎928 22 58; open 8am-10pm) and in the **airport** (open 8am-9pm).

Travel Agencies: Yucatán Trails, Calle 62 #482 x 57 y 59 (☎928 25 82 or 928 59 13; fax 924 19 28). Canadian owner Denis Lafoy is a good source of information and hosts a party for travelers the first F of every month. Open M-F 8am-7pm, Sa 8am-2pm.

Consulates: UK, Calle 53 #498 x 58 y 56 (☎928 61 52; fax 928 39 62). Open M-F 9am-1pm. **US,** Paseo de Montejo 453 (☎925 50 11), at Colón. Open M-F 8am-1pm.

Currency Exchange: Banamex (☎924 10 11), in Casa de Montejo on the *zócalo*, has a 24hr. **ATM.** Walk through the courtyard. Open M-F 9am-5pm, Sa 9am-2pm.

American Express: Paseo de Montejo 492 x 41 y 43 (☎942 82 00 or 942 82 10). Open M-F 9am-2pm and 4-6pm, Sa 9am-1pm. Money exchange closes 1hr. earlier.

Car Rental: Mexico Rent-a-Car, Calle 57A #491 (El Callejón del Congreso) Dept. 12 x 58 y 60 or Calle 62 #483A x 57 y 59 (☎927 49 16 or 923 36 37). VW Beetles, including insurance, and unlimited kilometers 290 pesos per day (subject to increase during high season). Open M-Sa 8am-12:30pm and 6-8pm, Su 8am-12:30pm. **World Rent-a-Car,** Calle 60 #486A x 55 y 57 (☎924 05 87). Mr. Mohan offers attractive rates on cars with automatic transmission and A/C.

English-Language Bookstore: (☎923 33 19), Calle 53 #524 x 66 y 68.

Laundry: La Fe, Calle 61 #518 x 62 y 64 (☎924 45 31), one block west of the *zócalo*. 36 pesos per 3kg. Open M-F 8am-7pm, Sa 8am-5pm.

Market: Four square blocks extending south of Calle 65 and east of Calle 58. Open dawn to dusk.

Supermarket: San Francisco de Asís, Calles 65 x 50 y 52, across from the market in a huge gray building. Open daily 7am-9pm.

EMERGENCY AND COMMUNICATIONS

Emergency: ☎060

Police: (☎925 25 55) on Reforma (Calle 72) x 39 y 41, accessible by the "Reforma" bus. Some English spoken.

Red Cross: Calle 68 #533 x 65 y 67 (☎924 98 13). 24hr. emergency and ambulance services (☎060). Some English spoken.

Pharmacy: Farmacia Canto, Calle 60 #513 x 63 y 65 (☎924 14 90). Open 24hr.

Hospital: Centro Médico de las Américas, Calle 54 #365 (☎926 21 11 or 926 26 19), at Calle 33A. 24hr. service, including ambulances. **Clínica de Mérida,** Calle 32 #242 x 27 y 25 (☎920 04 11). English spoken in both.

Internet Access: Cybernet, Calle 57-A #491 (El Callejon de Congreso). 10 terminals. 15 pesos per 30min. Open Su-F 8am-9pm. **Cibercafé Sta. Luci@,** on the northwest corner of Calles 62 and 55. 12.5 pesos per 30min. Open daily 8am-11pm.

Fax: (☎928 59 97) in the same building as the post office. Entrance around the corner on Calle 56. Telegrams as well. Open M-F 8am-7pm, Sa 9am-4pm, Su 9am-noon.

Post Office: (☎924 35 90) on Calles 65 x 56 y 56A, 3 blocks from the *zócalo* in the Palacio Federal. Open M-F 8am-3pm, Sa 9am-1pm. **Mexpost** at Calle 58 x 53 y 55. Open M-F 9am-6pm, Sa 9am-1pm. **Postal Code:** 97000.

◢ ACCOMMODATIONS

Choosing budget accommodations in Mérida is like deciding in which bygone era to stay. What were once elaborate, private turn of the century mansions are now often affordable hotels, clustering near the main bus station and the *zócalo*.

YUCATÁN

⬛ **Nómadas Youth Hostel,** Calle 62 #433 x 51 (☎924 52 23; email nomadas1@prod-igy.net.mx). A haven for backpackers. Clean facilities include full kitchen, Internet access, a travel agency, bike rentals, and—most importantly—Direct TV. Beds 65 pesos; private doubles 158 pesos; 40 pesos each additional person.

Casa Bowen, Calle 66 #521B x 65 y 67 (☎928 61 09), halfway between the main bus station and the *zócalo*. Wicker-chaired lobby and dining room with TV and books. Large rooms have fans and firm beds. Reservations recommended in Aug. and Dec. Singles 130 pesos; doubles 140 pesos; 30 pesos per each additional person.

Hotel Montejo, Calle 57 #507 x 62 y 64 (☎928 02 77), 2 blocks north of the *zócalo*. Large wooden doors face maroon arches and a lush garden. Rooms have wooden ceiling beams, window porticos, and baths. A 10% discount with *Let's Go*. Singles 175 pesos; doubles 230 pesos, with A/C 275 pesos; 40 pesos per each additional person.

Hotel Trinidad Galería, Calle 60 #456 x 51 (☎923 24 63). The halls of this quirky colonial mansion are filled with artwork. Head past the art gallery and the fountain to find a masterpiece of a pool. Singles 200 pesos; doubles 250 pesos; triples 300 pesos. Rooms with A/C 500 pesos. Rooms with shared baths 150 pesos.

Hotel Mucuy, Calle 57 #481 x 56 y 58 (☎928 51 93), 2 blocks north and 2 blocks east of the *zócalo*. The sunny courtyard and blue rooms mask the hotel's central location, and elegant glass doors enclose the reading room and piano in the tiled lobby. Singles 140 pesos; doubles 160 pesos; triples 190 pesos.

Hotel Margarita, Calle 66 #506 x 61 y 63 (☎923 72 36). A mahogany doorway with bright-colored geometrical tiles leads to the cheap but characterless rooms. Singles 80 pesos; doubles 90 pesos; triples 100 pesos.

Hotel Las Monjas, Calle 66A #509 x 63 y 61 (☎928 66 32). Modern, with funky green curtains and spotless walls. Singles 95 pesos; doubles 115 pesos; quads 135 pesos.

◨ FOOD

Mérida's specialties make use of the fruits and grains that flourish in the Yucatán's hot, humid climate. Try *sopa de lima* (freshly squeezed lime soup with chicken and tortilla bits), *pollo pibil* (chicken with herbs baked in banana leaves), *poc-chuc* (pork steak with onions doused in sour orange juice), *papadzules* (chopped hard-boiled eggs wrapped in corn tortillas served with pumpkin sauce), and *huevos motuleños* (refried beans, fried egg, chopped ham, and cheese on a crispy tortilla, garnished with tomato sauce, peas, and fried banana). Some of the best meals can be found in the plastic-chair-and-table joints along the *zócalo*. The cheapest food in town is sold at the **market,** particularly on the second floor of the restaurant complex on Calle 56 at Calle 67 (*yucáteco* dishes 10-15 pesos; most stalls open M-Sa 8am-8pm, Su 8am-5pm).

Restaurante Amaro, Calle 59 #507 x 60 y 62 (☎928 24 51). Healthful and delicious, with lean and vegetarian options such as *crepes* (35-45 pesos). *Agua de horchata* (rice and almond milk, 12 pesos); avocado and cheese sandwich (22 pesos); fruit salads (34 pesos). Open July-Aug. M-Sa 8:30am-11pm; Sept.-June daily 8:30am-11pm.

Restaurante "Café" Express (☎928 16 91), Calle 60 x 59 y 61, across from Parque Hidalgo. One of the oldest places in town, the service lives up to the name. Breakfast and sandwiches 20 pesos, main entrees 35-50 pesos. Open daily 7am-11pm.

El Rincón (☎924 90 22), Calle 60 x 59 y 61, on the east side of Parque Hidalgo. Tables in the park. If in high spirits, the staff will sing and play the guitar. *Sopa de lima* 20 pesos, *arroz con plátanos* 15 pesos, and *pollo pibil* 45 pesos. Open daily 7am-11pm.

Los Almendros and **Los Gran Almendros,** Calle 50 #493 x 57 y 59 (☎928 54 59) on Parque Mejorada, and at Calle 57 #468 x 50 y 52 (☎923 81 35), respectively. The world-famous food has made it touristy. *Poc-chuc* 56 pesos, *pollo pibil* 35 pesos. Los Almendros open daily 10am-11pm. Less touristy Gran Almendros open daily 1:30-6pm.

El Tucho, Calle 60 #482 x 55 y 57 (☎ 924 23 23). Wildly entertains families, locals, and tourists. Comedy troupes and regional musicians perform while waiters ferry trays of free *botanas* (hors d'œuvres). Meals 45 pesos. Open daily 11:30am-late.

Café la Habana, Calle 59 #511 x 62 (☎ 928 65 02). After a meal in this place, you'll feel like a lifelong member of the Cuban Mafia. Yucatec dishes sizzle with Cuban spices. Daily breakfast and lunch specials 20-35 pesos. Open 24 hr.

👁 SIGHTS

Mérida stands alone as a testament to the fascinating history of the Yucatán. Surrounded on all sides by historic palaces and a towering cathedral, the *zócalo* is renowned as the capital's social center. The *zócalo* is busiest on Sundays, when the streets are closed to traffic and vendors cram in dozens of stalls. Yucatec folk dancers perform in front of the Palacio Municipal as crowds of people come from all over to enjoy *Mérida en Domingo.*

CATEDRAL DE SAN ILDEFONSO. Begun in 1563 and finished in 1598, the cathedral is the oldest cathedral and one of the oldest standing buildings on the American Continent. The stone blocks of the cathedral were stolen from the Maya temples of T'hó, and the unusually barren interior was looted during the Mexican Revolution in 1915. Features an immense 20m wooden crucified Christ, the largest indoor crucifix in the world. *(On the east side of the zócalo. Open daily 6am-7pm.)*

PALACIO DE GOBIERNO. Built from 1883 to 1892, the *palacio* fuses two architectural styles—Tuscan (main floor) and Dorian (upper floor). A jail until the 1700s, the building was rebuilt in 1735 with two stories of arches. From this building, the Yucatán declared its independence from Spain. Inside, murals painted by the Mérida native Fernando Castro Pacheco in the 1970s chronicle the history of the peninsula. *(Palacio de Gobierno on the north side of the zócalo. Open daily 8am-10pm.)*

CASA DE MONTEJO. Probably begun by Francisco de Montejo, governor of Yucatán in 1549, this house was occupied by his direct descendents until 1980, whereupon it was sold to Banamex. Built with stones from the Maya temple T'hó, the carved facade follows the Toltec tradition of representing warriors standing on their conquerors' heads. *(On the south side of the zócalo. Open M-F 9am-5pm.)*

MUSEO DE ARTE CONTEMPORÁNEO (MACAY). The collection of modern *yucáteco* art is displayed around a central courtyard. *(On the east side of the zócalo, just south of the church. Open W-M 10am-5pm. 20 pesos; Su free.)*

EL MUSEO DE LA CIUDAD. The small museum provides a concise historical background of the White City and its colonial structures. It houses visual layouts and models of Mérida's most famous sights and also includes a bit of pre-Hispanic history. *(Calle 58 x 61. Open T-F 10am-2pm and 4-8pm, Sa-Su 10am-2pm. Free.)*

▧ MUSEO REGIONAL DE ANTROPOLOGÍA E HISTORIA. Mérida's most impressive museum is housed in a magnificent Italian Renaissance-style building, the **Palacio Cantón,** on the corner of Paseo Montejo and Calle 43. The collection includes Maya head-flattening devices, jade tooth inserts, and a Chichén Itzá *chacmool*. The museum shop sells English-language guidebooks. *(☎ 923 05 57. Open Tu-Sa 8am-8pm, Su 8am-2pm. 20 pesos; Su free.)*

MUSEO DE ARTE POPULAR. The small museum has exhibits on modern-day Maya customs and handicrafts. Shares the building with a school of design, with a relaxing student lounge. *(6 blocks east of the zócalo on Calle 59 x 48 y 50, behind the Convento de la Mejorada. Open Tu-Sa 8am-6pm, 10 pesos; Su 9am-2pm. Free.)*

CENTENARY PARK AND ZOO. The zoo is home to lions, tigers, jaguars, and other animals. A miniature train makes circuits of the park, but don't expect a quiet ride or a glimpse of many of the dozing creatures. *(On the corner of Calle 61 and Calle 86 (Itzáces). Snag a bus at Calle 65 x 56 (3 pesos) and ask to be let off at "El Centenario." Park open Tu-Su 9am-6pm; zoo open Tu-Su 9am-5pm. Both free.)*

MUSEO DE HISTORIA NATURAL. Housed in a 19th-century *hacienda*, this small but ambitious collection chronicles the history of life from the origin of the universe through the emergence of species. *(Main entrance on Calle 61 x 84, one block east of Itzáes. Back entrance accessible from the park. Open Tu-Su 9am-4pm. 15 pesos; Su free.)*

TEATRO PEÓN CONTRERAS. Named for the Mérida poet, José Peón Contreras, the beautiful building was built around the turn of the century and is notable for its marble Rococo interior. Frequent concerts and shows visit *el teatro*; stop by the box office for more information. *(On the corner of Calles 60 and 57. ☎923 73 54.)*

UNIVERSIDAD AUTÓNOMA DE YUCATÁN. The headquarters of the state's national university is housed in a Hispano-Moorish complex built in 1938. The ground floor has a gallery exhibiting works by local artists, and a screening room for a variety of films. *(On Calle 57 x 60. Galería open M-F 9am-1pm and 5-9pm, Sa 10am-1pm, Su 10am-2pm. Movies Su 10:30am. Free.)*

PASEO DE MONTEJO. Aging French-style mansions and boutiques line the Paseo's brick sidewalks, culminating in the **Monumento a la Patria.** In faux-Maya style, the stone monument, built from 1945 to 1956, depicts major figures of Mexican history holding rifles and constitutions. On the other side of the monument, the *ceiba* (the Maya tree of life) stretches above a pool of water, enclosed by states' coats of arms. For an interesting detour from the Paseo, veer left (southwest) onto **Colón,** a street flanked by historic mansions in varying stages of decay.

OTHER SITES. The many churches, statues, and parks scattered throughout Mérida's *centro* invite exploration. The old **Arco,** Calle 50 x 61, is one of the three remaining arches in Mérida, built at the end of the 17th century to mark the extent of the *centro.* The **Iglesia Santiago,** on Calles 59 x 72, one of the oldest churches in Mexico, is worth a visit, as well as the **Iglesia de San Juan de Dios,** on Calle 64 x 67 y 71, and the Franciscan **Convento de la Mejorada,** at Calle 59 x 48 y 50.

🎵 ENTERTAINMENT

For a less culture-filled evening, drink a beer. Mérida has many good local beers, such as the distinctive **Montejo León** and the darker **Negra León,** both tough to find in other parts of the country. Local establishments give free snacks after the purchase of a few beers. Live music and dance abound at **Pancho's,** Calle 59 #509 x 60 y 62, where sombrero-wearing hosts serve you free popcorn. (☎923 09 42. Happy Hour 6-8pm. Open M-Sa 6pm-3am.) Or try **El Establo,** Calle 60 # 482A x 55 y 57, where young *merideños* and tourists shoot pool, play table hockey, and dance under sombrero lamp shades. (☎924 22 89. Cover 40 pesos men, 30 pesos women.) Another option is the salsa bar of **Tulipanes,** Calle 42 #462A x 45 y 47. Multi-colored discos with A/C are far from the center; taxi ride 50 pesos. **Vatzya** in Hotel Fiesta Americana, Colón x Calle 60, is where the young and trendy dance. (Cover 40-50 pesos. Open W-Sa 10pm-2am.)

❋ FESTIVALS

When in Mérida, do as *merideños* do—keep your eyes peeled for announcements of upcoming events glued to walls around the *zócalo* and in the local magazine *Yucatán Today,* available free in the tourist office. Mérida's municipal government provides a repeating series of music and dance events organized by day:

Monday: Outdoor concerts with *yucáteco* dancing in the Palacio Municipal (9pm).

Tuesday: 1940s big-band concerts in Santiago Park, Calles 59 x 72 (9pm).

Wednesday: Ballet Folklórico in the Teatro Peón Contreras (9pm, 35 pesos).

Thursday: The Serenade, the most historical event in Mérida, with music, poetry, and folklore, in Santa Lucia Park, Calles 60 x 55 (9pm).

Friday: University Serenade, in the main university building, Calle 60 x 57 (9pm).

Saturday: *Noche Mexicana,* a night of national dance performances and arts and crafts, on the south side of Paseo de Montejo near Calle 45 (7pm-midnight).

Sunday: *Mérida en Domingo,* when the *zócalo* and surrounding streets are crowded with vendors, strollers, food stalls, and live music (9am-9pm).

SHOPPING

The fact that Mérida offers the best shopping in the Yucatán is both a blessing and a curse—the good wares bring with them nagging vendors and high-pressure salespeople. The main **mercado** occupies the block southeast of the Palacio Federal, spreading outward from the corner of Calles 65 and 58. The ground floor of this behemoth center is occupied by the **food vendors.** Oodles of fruits, vegetables, and meats await you. (Open M-Sa 8am-6pm.) The pricier second-floor **artisans' market,** part of the modern building behind and to the right of the Palacio Federal, sells trinkets, regional clothing, and the omnipresent hammock. White *huipiles* 250-350 pesos, *rebozos* (woven shawls) 220 pesos, and *guayaberas* 150-250 pesos. Cheaper goods such as *huaraches* (hand-made leather sandals) are sold on the first floor of the market. Although jewelry stores line the streets, the best prices are at the smaller *prestas,* in the market, or at the *zócalo* every Sunday.

DAYTRIPS FROM MÉRIDA

DZIBILCHALTÚN

Combis *leave the Parque de San Juan in Mérida as soon as they fill up (about every 30min., 4 pesos). They will drop you off at the access road to the ruins, a 5min. walk from the entrance. To get back, walk back to the Conkal road and wait for one combis that run between Mérida and the villages past Conkal. Some travelers hitch the 5km to the highway. Autoprogreso buses and Mérida-bound combis abound on Rte. 261, passing by in both directions every 15min. Site open daily 8am-5pm; museum open Tu-Su 8am-4pm. 50 pesos, children under 13 free; Su free; parking 7 pesos.*

Saying the name is half the fun. Situated 20km north of Mérida en route to the Gulf coast, Dzibilchaltún (dzib-ill-shahl-TOON; Place Where There Is Writing on Stones) sprawls over 60 sq. km of jungle brush. The site flourished as a ceremonial and administrative center from approximately 300 BC until the arrival of the Spanish in the 1520s, making it one of the longest continuously-inhabited Maya settlements. The excavated site now houses a 300m "ecological path" with nearly 100 different species of birds and labeled plants. The site also houses **El Museo del Pueblo Maya** which displays carved columns from Dzibilchaltún and Maya ceramics. The museum is the first building to the left of the entrance. The path leading to the museum is lined with an all-star gallery of Maya *stelae* with original sculptures from Chichén Itzá and Uxmal.

From the museum, follow the path to *sacbé* No. 1, the central axis of the site, and turn left. At the end of this road lies Dzibilchaltún's showpiece, the fully restored **Templo de las Siete Muñecas (Temple of the Seven Dolls),** constructed in the 5th century. The seven clay "dolls" discovered in this temple are on display in the museum. Shortly after sunrise, a huge shadow mask of the rain god Chac appears as the sun's rays pierce the temple during the spring and autumn equinox. The other end of *sacbé* No. 1 leads to a Maya temple converted into a chapel for Franciscan missionaries. Just beyond the eastern edge of the quadrangle is the **Cenote Xlacah,** which served as a sacrificial well and a source of water. Divers have recovered ceremonial artifacts and human bones from the depths of the 44m-deep *cenote.* While the *cenote* is not the most striking, the water invites a non-sacrificial dip. A path to the south leads past several smaller structures to the site's exit.

CELESTÚN   ☎9

Celestún is an ideal vacation spot on the Gulf with seafood restaurants by the beach, inexpensive waterfront hotels, and pervasive *tranquilidad*. Many come for the warm shallow waters and refreshing breeze, but the main draw is the **Río Celestún Biosphere Reserve,** home to 200 species of birds, including pelicans, cormorants, flamingos, and the occasional stork. Mexican tourists and biologists flock here in July and August; call ahead to make sure there's room.

🖅🗐 TRANSPORTATION AND PRACTICAL INFORMATION. Celestún lies a good 150km west of Mérida on the Gulf Coast. Follow Rte. 281 into town and it becomes Calle 11, the main east-west street. Calle 11 passes the *zócalo* and hits the shore two blocks later after that. Odd numbers increase to the south, while even numbers decrease away from the sand. The *zócalo* is bounded by Calles 11, 13, 10, and 8. Autobuses de Occidente sends **buses** from a small booth at the corner of Calles 8 and 11, at the *zócalo*, to **Mérida** (2hr., 15 per day 5am-8:30pm, 25 pesos).

Police: (☎916 20 50) at the Calle 13 side of the *zócalo*. **Farmacia Don San Luis,** Calle 10 #108, between Calles 13 and 15. (☎916 20 02. Open daily 8am to 11pm.) **Health center** on Calle 5 between Calles 8 and 10. No English spoken, but wild gesticulations understood. (☎916 20 46. Open M-Tu 8am-9pm, W-Su open 24hr.) **Telecomm,** on Calle 11 at the *zócalo*. (Open M-F 9am-3pm.)

🖅🖾 ACCOMMODATIONS AND FOOD. All budget accommodations are on Calle 12. The **Hotel San Julio,** Calle 12 #93A between Calles 9 and 11, faces a sand patio that opens onto the beach. Rooms are very clean. (☎916 20 62. Singles 80 pesos. 20 pesos each additional person.) **Hotel María del Carmen,** Calle 12 #111 at Calle 15, has golden rooms with sea views, balconies, and immaculate baths. They also rent out bicycles. (☎916 20 51. Singles 170 pesos; doubles 200 pesos; 50 pesos each additional person; 10% student discount.) **Hotel Gutiérrez,** Calle 12 #127 at Calle 13, lets you fit as many as you like in the stucco rooms with aqua tiles. Ask for a room with a view. (☎916 20 41 or 6 20 42. 200 pesos.)

Restaurants line Calle 12 and the beach, and a few *loncherías* cluster in the *zócalo*. At **Restaurant La Playita,** Calle 12 #99, between Calles 9 and 11, sumptuous plates of *jaiba frita* (fried blue crab) go for 40 pesos. (☎916 20 52. Open daily 8am-8pm.) **Pelicano's,** Calle 12 #90 at Calle 9, has cheap fried fish (20 pesos) and crab claws (50 pesos), but sadly no pelicans. (Open 11am-7pm.) **La Boya,** Calle 12 #99 at Calle 11, has good seafood entrees (40 pesos), and a powerful sound system. (☎916 21 29. Open daily 10am-5pm.)

🔲 SIGHTS. Celestún's estuary is a major wintering sight on the central migratory bird flyway. One tour takes you north to **Isla de Pájaros** (Island of Birds), an avian playground. Another heads south through petrified forests and a river tunnel of intertwined tree branches before winding through the abandoned fishing village of **Real de Salinas,** with a breathtaking view of the salt fields. Both tours can be arranged with *lancheros* at the bridge ½km before the town (1½-2hr. tour for 5-8 people 400 pesos) or, if you're lucky, much more cheaply with local fishermen near the *lanchas*. **Celestún Expeditions,** (☎916 20 49) at Calle 10 between 9 and 11, offer "Eco-tours with a difference," as well as birding, shelling, jungle walks, and anything else you could possibly dream of doing in Celestún. Birdwatching US$150 for an all-day trip for 4 people. On Saturday nights, bands from Mérida perform in Celestún's *zócalo*.

PROGRESO   ☎9

If someone were to tabulate the prominent up-and-comers of the *yucáteca* coast, Progreso (pop. 25,000) would top the list. For decades, the port town, a popular weekend retreat for *merideños*, has busied itself with *henquén* (hemp) export, but today, a different type of cargo is being imported as well—tourists. Progreso now plays hosts to cruise ships that arrive weekly, and courts foreigners with its shell-lined beaches and fresh seafood. The sage travelers will catch the town mid-week, when it regains some measure of the tranquility it once had.

⧉ TRANSPORTATION. Autoprogreso Buses run to Mérida's Autoprogreso station (40min., every 12min. 5am-10pm, 9 pesos). From Progreso's station (Calle 29 between Calles 80 and 82) to the *zócalo*, go east on Calle 29 to the end of the block, turn right and walk one block on Calle 80. To reach the beach, follow Calle 80 in the opposite direction.

⊞⧉ ORIENTATION AND PRACTICAL INFORMATION. Calle 19, Progreso's turquoise *malecón* (boardwalk) runs east-west along the beach. Odd-numbered roads run parallel to the *malecón*, increasing to the south. Even-numbered go north-south and increase to the west. Progreso's *zócalo* is bounded by Calles 31 and 33 on the north and south, and bisected by Calle 80.

A **tourist office** is located in the northeastern corner of Progreso's **Casa de la Cultura,** which is situated just north of the lighthouse on Calle 80 between Calles 25 and 27. (☎935 01 04. Open M-F 8am-2pm and 4-8pm, Sa 8am-1pm). **Banamex:** Calle 80 #126, between Calles 27 and 29, has a 24hr. **ATM.** (☎935 08 99. Open M-F 9am-5pm and Sa 9am-2pm.) **Laundry:** Calle 29 #132, between Calles 76 and 78, offers next day service. (☎935 08 56. 6 pesos per kg; 3kg minimum. Open M-Sa 8am-6pm.) **Supermarket: San Francisco de Asís,** at Calle 80 #144 between Calles 29 and 31. (Open daily 7am-9pm.) **Police:** in the Palacio Municipal on the west side of the *zócalo* (☎935 00 26. Open 24hr.) **Farmacia Canto,** on the southwest corner of Calles 29 and 80. (☎935 15 49. Open daily 7am-midnight.) **Centro Médico Americano:** at Calles 33 and 82. Some English spoken. (☎935 09 51. Open 24hr.) **Telecomm** next door to the post office. (Open M-F 8am-7:30pm, Sa-Su 9am-noon.) **LADATELs:** found throughout town. **Post office:** Calle 31 #150, west of Calle 78, just off the *zócalo*. (☎935 05 65. Open M-F 8:30am-3pm.) **Postal code:** 97320.

⧉⧉ ACCOMMODATIONS AND FOOD. It's hard to go wrong at the **Hotel Miramar,** Calle 27 #124, between Calles 74 and 76. The hotel offers spacious, classy rooms with neat baths and skylights or cool, fiberglass spacecraft rooms with emergency escape pod-like baths. (☎935 05 52. Singles and doubles 110 pesos; 30 pesos for additional person.) The **Hotel Progreso,** in the center of town, Calle 78 #142, near Calle 29, has designer rooms with upside-down wine bottles. (☎935 00 39. Singles 140 pesos, with A/C 190 pesos; doubles 170 pesos, with A/C 220 pesos; 40 pesos each additional person.) **Hotel Real del Mar,** Malecón #144, entrance on Calle 70, is more touristy but right on the beach. (☎935 07 98. Singles 170 pesos; doubles 240 pesos; 50 pesos per each additional person.) It is a good idea to call all hotels in Progreso in advance.

The *pescado frito* signs on just about every corner are evidence for one fact: Progreso is all about cheap seafood. Like fish with a view? Just take a stroll down the *malecón*. At **Carabela,** east of Calle 70 on the *malecón*, you can rev up on the jukebox and watch the waves pound the shore as you down your fish. They have other dishes too. (☎935 33 07. Open daily 7am-1am). At **Restaurant Los Cocos,** on the *malecón* between Calles 76 and 78, fish are served, practically still flopping, for 35 pesos. (Open daily 24hr.) **El Cordobés,** Calle 80 #150 at Calle 31, doesn't offer a view of the sea but does lets you observe the peaceful *zócalo*, where uniformed children make their way to class. (Open daily 8:30am-6pm.)

⧉⧉ SIGHTS AND BEACHES. Progreso's shallow waters, beach boardwalks, and *palapas* attract hordes of visitors in August, but remain somewhat calm in other months. For a more placid spot, try the beach at **Chelém,** 8km west of town, or the wind-sheltered beach at **Yucalpetén,** just before Chelém. *Combis* leave for Chelém from the parking lot outside Supermarket San Francisco on Calle 80 (every 30min., 8 pesos). Head to the local bus terminal (bordered by

Calles 29, 31, 82, and 84) for an even cheaper ride. The custodian of **El Faro,** at Calle 80 near Calle 25, may let you climb the 120 steps to the top of the 19th-century lighthouse. The 6km *muelle* (pier), known as the **Puerto de Altura,** is a great spot to reel in fish in the early morning.

If sunbathing and fishing has you bored, a largely unexplored Maya site lies near **Xcambó,** at the end of a 2km access road that intersects the road to Telchac Puerto, 25km east of Progreso. *Combis* headed to Telchac Puerto from Progreso leave the Supermarket San Francisco and will drop you off at the access road (approx. every 30min., 10 pesos). The small, recently restored site has several small structures and two pyramids—one of which supports two large, unidentified stucco masks and offers a panoramic view of the coast. A peculiar, functional church is built into the side of one of the pyramids. Small paths branch from the site to unexcavated ruins and small villages; the caretaker may be coaxed into acting as a guide. (Open daily 9am-5pm. Free.)

IZAMAL ☎ 9

Izamal's many names are a window into the past millennia of Yucatán's history. "Izamal" itself means "City of the Hills" in Mayan. The city is also called *La Ciudad Amarilla* (The Yellow City) because of its main buildings, painted in colonial yellow with white trim. Yet another name, *La Ciudad de las Tres Culturas* (The City of the Three Cultures), begins to describe Izamal's harmonious blend of Maya, Spanish, and *mestizo* culture. The city's midday and evening tranquility is broken only by the occasional school-produced *ballet folklórico*, the clattering of *calesas victorianas* (horse-drawn carriages), and casual bicyclists.

TRANSPORTATION. The **bus station** is halfway between Calles 31 and 33 on Calle 32, right behind the municipal palace. ADO buses (☎954 01 97) leave from the terminal for: **Cancún** (6:30am and 1pm, 66 pesos); **Valladolid** (5pm, 27 pesos); and **Mérida** (every 30min., 5am-7:45pm, 20 pesos). Next door, the Autobuses de Centro del Estado sends buses to: **Cancún** (5½hr., every 2hr., 46 pesos); **Mérida** (1½hr., every 30min., 11 pesos); and **Valladolid** (2½hr., every 2hr., 17 pesos).

ORIENTATION AND PRACTICAL INFORMATION. The road from Hoctún, 24km to the southwest, turns into Calle 31, which runs east-west as do all odd-numbered streets, increasing to the south. This street runs past the Convent (on the right going east), passing north-south streets with decreasing even numbers. Calles 28, 31, 32, and 33 frame the town's *zócalo*, municipal palace, and market.

The **tourist office,** on the corner of Calles 32A and 31A, just southwest of the *zócalo* in the Palacio Municipal, will go out of its way to provide maps and pamphlets on the town, and all conceivable information on the Convent across the street. (☎954 00 09. Open Tu-Sa 9am-2pm and 7-11pm.) **Bank: BanCrecer,** on the corner of Calles 31 and 28 with 24hr. **ATM.** (Open M-F 9am-3pm; Sa 9am-2pm.) **Police:** across from the bus station in the Palacio Municipal. (☎954 00 09. Open 24hr.) **Market:** on the corner of Calles 30 and 33. **Farmacia Itzalana,** on the corner of Calles 31 and 32. Knock if closed. (☎954 00 32. Open 24hr.) **Medical Assistance: IMSS,** two blocks south and three blocks east of the *zócalo* on the corner of Calles 37 and 24. (☎954 02 41. Open 24hr.) **Fax: Telecomm,** on the corner of Calles 31A and 32. (☎954 02 63. Open M-F 9am-3pm.) **LADATELs** are scarce, but there is one in the post office. **Post office:** on the corner of 31 and 32A. (Open M-F 8am-2:30pm.)

ACCOMMODATIONS AND FOOD. The town's two budget options stand side by side on the northern side of the *zócalo;* nicer options lie further from the town center. The **Hotel Canto,** on Calle 31 between Calles 30 and 32, has old blue rooms with fans and very tall ceilings. (Singles 80-100 pesos; doubles 120-150.) The **Hotel Kabul,** next door, is nestled next to the Kabul pyramid and has fans and hammock hooks (☎954 00 20. 2 small beds 100 pesos; 2 big ones 120 pesos.)

Don't plan on too much late-night wining and dining in the Yellow City; most restaurants close by early evening. **Restaurant Kinich Kakmó,** Calle 27 #299, between Calles 28 and 30, serves regional dishes under a plant-heavy *palapa* (45 pesos) and makes an excellent end to an exhaustive inspection of the pyramid 50m away. (☎ 954 04 89. Open M-F 11:30am-6pm, Sa-Su 8:30am-noon.) **Los Portales,** on the corner of Calles 30 and 31A next door to the market, has the best view of the *zócalo* but it's the cheap, filling meals that are likely to hold your attention. (Full breakfasts and lunches 18-25 pesos. Open Th-Tu 7am-9pm.)

🄢 SIGHTS. The town's most impressive sight is **El Convento de San Antonio de Padua,** which is actually made of three parts: the **church,** built in 1554; the **convent,** built in 1561; and the **atrium,** built in 1618 with 75 arches and second in size only to the Vatican. When entering the church through the atrium, after passing a statue of the Pope, several original 16th-century frescoes can be seen on the church's facade. Inside the Baroque church is an ornate altar with a doorway at the top, through which Izamal's statue of the Immaculate Conception is wheeled out for every Mass. The room immediately behind the altar exhibits pictures and momentos of the Pope's August 1993 visit to Izamal. Continue up the stairs to arrive at Mexico's oldest *camarín*, where the statue of the Immaculate Conception rests when not in use. Fray Diego de Landa commissioned this statue in 1558 in Guatemala. There were originally two statues—called *Las Dos Hermanas*—one of which was sent to Mérida and the other to Izamal. In 1829, Izamal's statue was destroyed in a fire, and Mérida's copy was brought here. It is said, however, that the Izamal original was saved and taken to the nearby pyramid of Kinich Kakmó. Every December 8, at the climax of the town's week-long *fiesta*, the two switch places in *El Paso de las Dos Hermanas*. More legends can be learned at Izamal's small **museum,** on the north side of the Convent, on Calle 31. The museum details Izamal's three phases of history and has a model of the city as it was in 500 BC. (Open M-F 9am-1pm and 7-9pm. Free.)

It is not until they ascend the pyramid of **Kinich Kakmó** (Temple of the Fire Macaw) that visitors can truly appreciate Izamal's most dominating structure. This massive pyramid, measuring 200m by 180m, is the fifth-tallest in the Yucatán Peninsula. Yet even it was outclassed by the **Pap-hol-chac,** the largest pyramid in ancient Izamal, whose remains lie under the convent. Kinich Kakmó was built during the Early Classic period (AD 400-600) and was the northern border of the ancient city's central plaza. (Entrance on Calle 27 between 28 and 28A.) Other pyramids dot Izamal, blending seamlessly with the modern cityscape. **Itzamatul,** dedicated to the god Zamná, looms to the east and is accessible on Calle 26, between 29 and 31. **Habre** is the most removed, occupying the block encompassed by Calles 26, 28, 35, and 37. The most centrally-located pyramid, **Kabul,** or "working hand," is just north of the *zócalo*. Unfortunately it is almost impossible to reach, as it is surrounded by homes and businesses. (All pyramids open daily 8am-5pm.)

CHICHÉN ITZÁ ☎ 9

Gracing the cover of hundreds of glossy brochures and suffering under the footfall of thousands of tourists, the Post-Classic Maya ruins at Chichén Itzá seem almost an archaeological cliché. Once here, however, you will understand what the hype is about. The swarms of tourists do little to tarnish the history behind the magnificent, well-preserved site. The faultless architecture and the sheer size of this former Maya capital allow the ruins to serve as a window to the past on a grand scale. The structures inspire awe and endless questions about the skill and calculated creativity of Maya construction. A cliché it might be, but the site still merits a long, loving visit from all who cross the Yucatán Peninsula. Only 2.5km away, the town of **Piste** lacks charm, but may be worth a night's stay in order to enter Chichén Itzá at 8am and see the ruins at a comfortable pace. Avoid visiting around noon, when the sun scorches and the tourist wave crescendos.

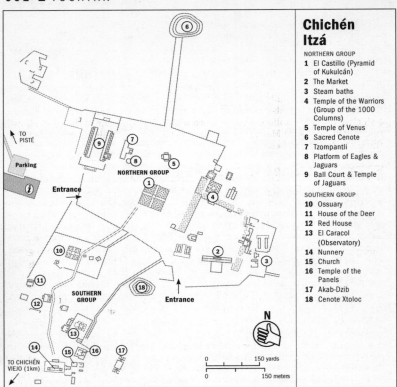

Chichén Itzá

NORTHERN GROUP

1 El Castillo (Pyramid of Kukulcán)
2 The Market
3 Steam baths
4 Temple of the Warriors (Group of the 1000 Columns)
5 Temple of Venus
6 Sacred Cenote
7 Tzompantli
8 Platform of Eagles & Jaguars
9 Ball Court & Temple of Jaguars

SOUTHERN GROUP

10 Ossuary
11 House of the Deer
12 Red House
13 El Caracol (Observatory)
14 Nunnery
15 Church
16 Temple of the Panels
17 Akab-Dzib
18 Cenote Xtoloc

▐▀ TRANSPORTATION

The ruins of Chichén Itzá lie 1.5km from **Rte. 180,** the highway running from Mérida (119km west) through Valladolid (42km east) to Cancún (200km east). The site can be reached via two access roads, one from the west (the main one) and one from the east. The roads used to be the main highway, which ran through the center of the site, but the highway has been rerouted north and Chichén Itzá is no longer a drive-through experience. Rte. 180 turns into **Calle 15** in **Piste,** the town's main drag. Piste's **bus station** (☎851 00 52) is between the Pirámide Inn and Posada Novelo on the eastern edge of town. ADO treks to **Cancún** (2½hr., 3:30pm, 95 pesos); **Mérida** (1½hr., 3pm and 5pm, 50 pesos); **Playa del Carmen** (2:45pm, 103 pesos; 4:30pm, 120 pesos); and **Valladolid** (1hr., 8, 11am, and 2:45pm, 21 pesos). Second-class buses are more frequent (and cheaper, of course).

Getting to the ruins is easy. If you would rather skip the 20min. walk from Piste, catch a taxi (25 pesos) or wait in the bus station for an eastbound bus (every 30min., 5 pesos). To get to Chichén Itzá from other towns, see bus listings for Mérida (see p. 591), Cancún (see p. 613), and Valladolid (see p. 607). To head back to Piste, wait in the bus parking lot until a taxi or bus swings by (every 45min.).

▚ PRACTICAL INFORMATION

A single **police** officer sits at a desk in the *comandancia* on the eastern side of Piste's *zócalo* (☎851 00 97). **Pharmacy: Farmacia Isis,** Calle 15 #53, a short way east of the *zócalo,* toward the ruins (open daily 7am-10pm). **Medical care: Clínica**

Promesa, Calle 14 #50 (☎851 00 05), in the blue-green building west of the *zócalo* and 100m north of Rte. 180 (open 24hr.). **Telephones: Centro Telefónico,** across from the bus station (☎851 00 88), lets you phone home (open daily 9am-9pm). **LADATELs** can be found all along Rte. 180.

Services in Chichén Itzá are located at the site's western entrance. Across from the ticket counter is a small **information booth.** The booth often provides free **luggage storage** (open daily 8am-5pm). The bus station offers free luggage storage 6am-6pm. There are also restrooms, a restaurant, an ice cream parlor, a gift shop (which accepts US dollars), a bookstore with guidebooks, an auditorium showing documentaries about Maya ruins, and a small museum. **Parking** is available right at the site. (Parking 10 pesos.)

ACCOMMODATIONS AND FOOD

Though some luxury hotels have invaded, plenty of economical lodging awaits in Piste. The places listed below can be found either on or just off Rte. 180/Calle 15. **Posada Olalde,** left off Calle 15 across from the Carousel Restaurant and two blocks down the dirt road. The large, decorated rooms in the main house and the four spotless rooms with *palapa* roofs off the intimate courtyard make the Posada a pleasant stay. (☎851 00 86. Singles 120 pesos; doubles 160 pesos.) **Hotel El Paso,** Calle 15 #48, across from El Carrousel, offers similar rooms. Bouncy beds make for good jumping and small windows ensure no one falls out. (☎851 01 94. Singles 100 pesos; doubles 160.)

Those too engrossed with the ruins to think about eating should consider themselves lucky—pickings are slim in Chichén Itzá. The on-site **restaurant** specializes in *comida non-típica:* high prices and small servings. (Dishes 45-60 pesos with a regional dance performance.) There are also a few *cantinas* scattered throughout the site, but, sadly, they offer food of little substance. Picnickers can save a few pesos by packing a lunch from one of the **small grocers** that line Calle 15 in Piste. **El Carrousel** serves three simple meals a day. Start a long, hot day right with eggs any style or 15-peso hotcakes. (☎851 00 78. Open daily 7am-10pm.) **Restaurant Poxil,** on the right just past the *zócalo,* is a bigger joint for bigger crowds with bigger dishes of *comida típica* (40 pesos). Comes with a dish of rice, a slice of avocado, a dessert of the day, and coffee. (☎851 01 16. Open 24hr.)

THE ARCHAEOLOGICAL SITE OF CHICHÉN ITZÁ

Open daily 8am-6pm. 75 pesos; Su and holidays free; children under 13 free. Documentary show times vary. Site museum and auditorium open daily 8am-6pm. Free. Light and sound show daily 7pm in Spanish, 8pm in English. 30 pesos. Guided tours begin at the entrance and cost upwards of 400 pesos.

Chichén Itzá was settled in roughly three periods; the first two are often grouped together and called the **Maya Phase** (or **Chichén Viejo**), and the third called the **Toltec-Maya Phase** (or **Chichén Nuevo**). The name Chichén Itzá means "by the mouth of Itzá's well," implying that the area's earliest inhabitants were drawn here by the two nearby freshwater *cenotes*. Settlers arrived in the first period around AD 700, during the Classic Era, when Maya strength was centered in Chiapas and Guatemala. These early settlers may have built the structures found today at Chichén Viejo, though scholars disagree. The second period, in the late Classic or early Post-Classic Era around AD 900, saw more central construction, including the inner pyramid of El Castillo, the original Temple of Chacmool (beneath the Temple de los Guerreros). The last period began in the 11th century with the arrival of the Itzá, a Maya group from Tabasco. A dwindling group of experts adheres to the traditional view (found on most markers) that sometime before 1000, the Toltec tribes of Tula infiltrated the Yucatán and overcame peaceful Maya settlements, bringing with them the cult of the plumed serpent Quetzalcóatl (Kukulcán in Mayan). The more widely accepted view, however, is that Chichén Itzá was a crossroads of trade and ideas, and eventually adopted many Toltec practices. Toltec influence is seen in the distinctive reclining portrayal of *chac-mool*, his head turned sideways, holding forth a plate to receive an offering or sacrifice. It was during this period that the Gran Plaza, El Castillo, the Templo de Guerreros, the Observatory, and the Juego de Pelota were constructed. In the 12th century, Chichén Itzá formed the powerful **Mayapán League,** through which it dominated the remaining Maya city-states in the Yucatán Peninsula. In 1461, Chichén Itzá was abandoned due to war with its rival city-state Mayapán, though religious pilgrimages to the site continued well after Spanish conquest.

For a more comprehensive (not to mention air-conditioned) understanding of Chichén and its people, visit the **Centro Cultural Cecijema,** Calle 15 #45, just west of the bus station in Piste. The gray building houses a small selection of Maya ceramic replicas, a modest library, and rotating exhibits. (☎851 00 04. Open M-Sa 8am-5pm. Free.) The **information center** and a few services can be found at the main entrance to Chichén Itzá, on the western side of the ruins. A small **museum** presents the site history and displays sculptures and objects removed from the Sacred Cenote. The **auditorium** screens documentaries about the ruins in Spanish and English. As if Chichén Itzá weren't already enough of a spectacle, those green panels (whose purpose you'll be contemplating all day) pop open for the evening **light and sound show.** If you trust your bug repellent, the nighttime stroll from Piste is quiet and well-lit; otherwise take a taxi (20 pesos).

EL CASTILLO (THE CASTLE). Chichén's trademark edifice, El Castillo (also known as the Pyramid of Kukulcán) stands as tangible evidence of the astrological understanding of the Maya. The 91 steps on each of the four faces, plus the upper platform, total 365; the 52 panels on the nine terraced levels equal the number of years in a Maya calendar cycle; and each face of the nine terraces is divided by a staircase, yielding 18 sections representing the 18 Maya *uinal* in each *tun* of the Maya Long Count dating system. Even more impressive is the precise alignment of El Castillo's axes, which produce a bi-annual optical illusion. At sunrise during the spring and fall equinoxes, the rounded terraces cast a serpentine shadow down the side of the northern staircase. A light-and-shadow lunar serpent-god, identical to that of the equinoxes, creeps down the pyramid at the dawn of the full moon following each of the equinoxes. El Castillo was built on top of an older, Classic-era temple, which can be can be entered at the western side of the base of the north staircase. After climbing the steps you'll be grimacing like the *chac-mool* in the ceremonial chamber. Behind the chamber is a fanged jaguar throne with jade eyes. *(The inner temple is open 11am-3pm and 4-5pm. Free.)*

JUEGO DE PELOTA (BALLCOURT). To the northwest of El Castillo is a playing field, bounded by high parallel walls, with a temple at the north and south ends. Measuring 146m by 37m, Chichén's ball court is the largest in Mesoamerica, and has amazing side-to-side echoes. The elaborate ball game once played here fascinated Cortés so much that he took two entire teams back to Europe in 1528 to perform before the royal court.

TZOMPANTLI (PLATFORM OF THE SKULLS). A short distance from the ballcourt in the direction of the grassy open area are eerie columns of bas-relief skulls decorating the lower platform walls.

PLATFORM OF THE JAGUARS AND EAGLES. Next to Tzompantli, these animals represented the warrior castes, who were ordered to kidnap members of other tribes for sacrifices to their gods. To either side of the feathered serpent heads on the balustrades, reliefs of jaguars and eagles clutch human hearts in their claws.

TUMBA DEL CHACMOOL (TEMPLE OF VENUS). Directly north of El Castillo is the Temple of Venus, a square platform decorated with a feathered serpent holding a human head in its mouth. The temple's reliefs symbolize the planet Venus and other stars and planets, and give information on their motions.

PLAY BALL! The great ballcourts found at Chichén Itzá and other Maya cities once witnessed an impressive game in which two contending teams endeavored to keep a heavy rubber ball (3-5kg) in constant motion by using only their hips, knees, shoulders, and elbows. A physically exhausting game, players scored by knocking the ball through small stone rings placed high on the court's side walls. The ball game was much more than a cultural pastime for the Maya; it was both symbolic of the battle between good and evil and a way to keep the celestial bodies in motion (the ball represented the sun; its constant motion symbolized the movement of the sun through the heavens). The game could also serve as gory religious ceremony; at certain festivals, teams competed for the honor of ritual decapitation and deification.

CENOTE DE LOS SACRIFICIOS (SACRED CENOTE). Three hundred meters north of El Castillo and connected via a *sacbé*, the 60m-wide subterranean pool was Chichén Itzá's most important religious symbol. The rain god Chac was believed to dwell beneath the surface, and would request frequent gifts to grant good rains. In 1907, numerous sacrificial offerings were dredged from the bottom by anthropologist Edward Thompson—included in these were skulls, teeth, shells, and jewelry. In the 1960s, scuba divers discovered even more remains, suggesting that children and young men were the sacrifices of choice.

TEMPLO DE LOS GUERREROS (TEMPLE OF THE WARRIORS). On the left as you return from the *cenote*, and northeast of El Castillo, the temple presents an array of carved columns that once supported a perishable roof. On the temple itself (not open to the public), in front of two great feathered serpents and several sculpted animal gods, is one of Chichén's best-preserved *chac-mools*, statues of the rain god Chac in a reclining position. The ornamentation of this building shows great Toltec influence; a nearly identical structure stands at Tula, the former Toltec capital to the west. The temple was built over the older Temple of Chac-mool.

GRUPO DE MIL COLUMNAS (GROUP OF A THOUSAND COLUMNS). Extending to the south and east of the Templo de los Guerreros, the group of columns, believed to have served as a civic or religious center, contains an elaborate water drainage system which channeled rainfall into a depression on the northeast side of the complex. The ruins extending to the southeast of the columns include several colonnades, a market, and a steam bath. The bath house is divided into a waiting room and an interior, where water was poured over hot rocks.

TUMBA DEL GRAN SACERDOTE. Also called the **Ossuary,** or **High Priest's Grave,** it is the first structure on the right on the path leading to the southern half of the site. Its distinctive serpent heads mimic El Castillo, and a natural cave extends from within the pyramid 15m into the earth. The human bones and votive offerings found in this cavern are thought to have belonged to an ancient high priest.

EL CARACOL (THE OBSERVATORY). One of the few circular structures built by the Maya, this ancient planetarium consists of two rectangular platforms with large, west-facing staircases, and two circular towers. It is the tower's spiral staircase that gave it the name El Caracol (The Snail). The slits in the dome can be aligned with the major celestial bodies and cardinal directions, and the red handprints on the walls were supposedly the hands of sun god Kinich Ahau.

TEMPLE DE LOS TABLEROS (TEMPLE OF THE PANELS). Just south of the Observatory, this small ruin has carved panels and rows of columns. Though difficult to decipher, the panels on the exterior walls contain emblems of warriors—jaguars, eagles, and serpents—in three rows. The upper part of the structure is believed to have been a site for fire-related ceremonies.

EDIFICIO DE LAS MONJAS (THE NUNNERY). At the southern extent of the South Group, this group of buildings was probably a royal palace. To the Spanish, however, the stone rooms looked suspiciously like a European convent—hence the ruins' name. Above the entrance on the right side of the building you can still see Maya glyphs. Also on the right side is the **annex** which predates the rest of the nunnery. Above the doorway facing the small courtyard is a spectacular bas-relief of a seated royal-divine figure. Many rooms in the nunnery have doorways that lead to dark corridors, home to bats and frogs.

LA IGLESIA (THE CHURCH). For similar reasons, the elaborate building diagonally across from the nunnery is misnamed the Church. One of the oldest buildings at the site, its top-heavy walls are encrusted with intricate masks of the hook-nosed Chac. The church is remarkable for its fusion of cultural styles: over the doorway are Maya stone lintels, while the use of wood and inclined edges is evidence of Toltec influence. Above the door are representations of the four *bacabs* that hold up the sky at four cardinal points, represented by a crab, a turtle, an armadillo, and a snail.

AKAB-DZIB. Sixty meters east of the Nunnery, the complex is named for the "dark writing" found in its 18 rooms. The oldest parts of this structure are believed to be Chichén's most ancient constructions; the two central rooms date to the 2nd or 3rd century, while the annexes on either side and to the east were added later. Inside, one can make out the small, red handprints of Kinich Ahau on the ceiling.

CENOTE XTOLOC. The overgrown Cenote Xtoloc hides behind the South Group ticket office. To reach it from the office, take the first left 20m into the site. The *cenote* is in the hollow, beyond the small, ruined temple of Xtoloc, dedicated to the lizard god of the same name. There is no path down the slope through the undergrowth, and swimming is prohibited because of the dangerous currents. Secular counterpart to the holy waters of the Sacred Cenote, this pool at one time provided all of Chichén with drinking water. Follow *sacbé* No. 5, which becomes a narrow, winding trail, to get to the back of the observatory.

CHICHÉN VIEJO

Not many visitors to Chichén Itzá know that there is another, adjacent site. Beginning about 1km south of the Nunnery and spreading southwest from the main site, Chichén Viejo is so named because it was originally thought to be the minor ruins of the first inhabitants of Chichén Itzá. Recent work done at the site, though, suggests that it was probably inhabited around the same time as the rest of the city. Most of the ruins are unrestored and scattered throughout the jungle. To get to the **Group of the Initial Series** and the **Phallic Cluster,** follow the dirt road (simply marked with arrows) to the right of the Nunnery past the intersection of other dirt paths to a deep well. Shortly beyond the well, a right at the T-junction brings you to the cluster, set in a clearing. Chichén Viejo carries the only dated inscriptions at Chichén Itzá, one of which can be clearly seen on the only remaining lintel of the **Temple of the Initial Series.** Upheld by two columns, **The Temple of the Four Lintels** features a hieroglyphic inscription corresponding to July 13, 878. The rest of the temple stands in ruin. The main features of the appropriately named Phallic Cluster protrude from the interior walls of the temple, while nine warriors stand watch in the courtyard. The remaining ruins at Chichén Viejo, reached by taking the path

---

WATER WATER NOWHERE, AND MANY DROPS TO DRINK
You may notice that in the Yucatán peninsula there are no bridges. That is because there is no surface water. The whole peninsula rests on a porous limestone shelf, so water seeps right through the bedrock. The water finds itself in a complex network of underground rivers, meticulously making its way to the ocean. Once in a while there will be a hole in the surface of the earth, revealing the water beneath. These are the *cenotes*, great places for swimming and diving. The ancient Maya, who relied heavily on the rains that fell from May to October, worshipped some *cenotes*, believing them to be the residences of the rain god Chac-mool.

CENTRAL AMERICA   MIDDLE AMERICA

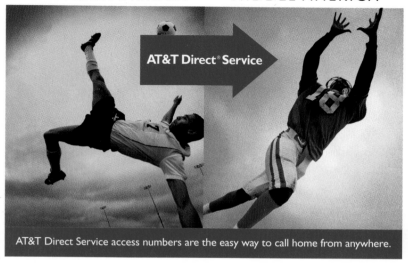

AT&T Direct® Service

AT&T Direct Service access numbers are the easy way to call home from anywhere.

Global
connection
with the AT&T
Network

AT&T
direct
service

AT&T

www.att.com/traveler

AT&T Direct® Service

The easy way to call
home from anywhere.

AT&T Access Numbers

Anguilla + ..1-800-USA-ATT1	British V.I. + 1-800-USA-ATT1
Antigua + ..1-800-USA-ATT1	Cayman Isl.+ 1-800-USA-ATT1
Argentina ...0-800-555-4288	**Chile 800-225-288**
Argentina ...0-800-222-1288	**Colombia......980-911-0010**
Aruba ▲ 800-8000	Costa Rica ...0-800-0-114-114
Bahamas ...1-800-USA-ATT1	Dominica + 1-800-USA-ATT1
Barbados+ 1-800-USA-ATT1	Dom. Rep. ..1-800-USA-ATT1
Belize ▲ ....811 or 555	**Ecuador ▲ 999-119**
Bermuda + 1-800-USA-ATT1	Grenada + .1-800-USA-ATT1
Brazil 000-8010	Guadaloupe▲ 0800-99-00-11

AT&T Direct® Service

The easy way to call
home from anywhere.

AT&T Access Numbers

Anguilla + ..1-800-USA-ATT1	British V.I. + 1-800-USA-ATT1
Antigua + ..1-800-USA-ATT1	Cayman Isl.+ 1-800-USA-ATT1
Argentina ...0-800-555-4288	**Chile 800-225-288**
Argentina ...0-800-222-1288	**Colombia......980-911-0010**
Aruba ▲ 800-8000	Costa Rica ...0-800-0-114-114
Bahamas ...1-800-USA-ATT1	Dominica + 1-800-USA-ATT1
Barbados+ 1-800-USA-ATT1	Dom. Rep. ..1-800-USA-ATT1
Belize ▲ ....811 or 555	**Ecuador ▲ 999-119**
Bermuda + 1-800-USA-ATT1	Grenada + .1-800-USA-ATT1
Brazil 000-8010	Guadaloupe▲ 0800-99-00-11

The best way to keep in touch when you're traveling overseas is with **AT&T Direct**® Service. It's the easy way to call your loved ones back home from just about anywhere in the world. Just cut out the wallet guide below and use it wherever your travels take you.

For a list of AT&T Access Numbers, tear out the attached wallet guide.

AT&T

Guatemala ● ▲ **99 99 190**	Peru ▲ 0-800-500-00
Guyana O 165	**Spain 900-99-00-11**
Honduras 800 0 123	St.Kitts/Nevis ✚ 1-800-USA-ATT1
Jamaica ● ..1-800-USA-ATT1	St.Lucia ✚ ..1-800-USA-ATT1
Mexico ● ..01-800-288-2872	**St.Pierre 0800-99-0011**
Mexico ● ▽ .001-800-462-4240	St.Vincent ✚ 1-800-USA-ATT1
Neth.Ant.▲⊕ 001-800-USA-ATT1	Trinidad/Tob. 0800-USA-ATT1
Nicaragua ● 174	Turks/Caicos ✚ 01-800-USA-ATT1
Panama 00-800-001-0109	**U.K. 0800-89-0011**
Paraguay ✚▲▶ ...008-11-800	Uruguay 000-410

Venezuela 800-11-120

FOR EASY CALLING WORLDWIDE

1. Just dial the AT&T Access Number for the country you are calling from.
2. Dial the phone number you're calling.   *3.* Dial your card number.

For access numbers not listed ask any operator for **AT&T Direct**® Service. In the U.S. call 1-800-331-1140 for a wallet guide listing all worldwide AT&T Access Numbers.

Visit our Web site at: **www.att.com/traveler**

Bold-faced countries permit country-to-country calling outside the U.S.
- ●   Public phones require coin or card deposit to place call.
- ✚   Public phones and select hotels.
- ▲   May not be available from every phone/payphone.
- O   Collect calling only.
- ▽   Includes "Ladatel" public phones.
- ⊕   From St. Maarten's or phones at Bobby's Marina, use 1-800-872-2881.
- ▶   City of Asuncion only.

When placing an international call *from* the U.S., dial 1 800 CALL ATT.

Guatemala ● ▲ **99 99 190**	Peru ▲ 0-800-500-00
Guyana O 165	**Spain 900-99-00-11**
Honduras 800 0 123	St.Kitts/Nevis ✚ 1-800-USA-ATT1
Jamaica ● ..1-800-USA-ATT1	St.Lucia ✚ ..1-800-USA-ATT1
Mexico ● ..01-800-288-2872	**St.Pierre 0800-99-0011**
Mexico ● ▽ .001-800-462-4240	St.Vincent ✚ 1-800-USA-ATT1
Neth.Ant.▲⊕ 001-800-USA-ATT1	Trinidad/Tob. 0800-USA-ATT1
Nicaragua ● 174	Turks/Caicos ✚ 01-800-USA-ATT1
Panama 00-800-001-0109	**U.K. 0800-89-0011**
Paraguay ✚▲▶ ...008-11-800	Uruguay 000-410

Venezuela 800-11-120

FOR EASY CALLING WORLDWIDE

1. Just dial the AT&T Access Number for the country you are calling from.
2. Dial the phone number you're calling.   *3.* Dial your card number.

For access numbers not listed ask any operator for **AT&T Direct**® Service. In the U.S. call 1-800-331-1140 for a wallet guide listing all worldwide AT&T Access Numbers.

Visit our Web site at: **www.att.com/traveler**

Bold-faced countries permit country-to-country calling outside the U.S.
- ●   Public phones require coin or card deposit to place call.
- ✚   Public phones and select hotels.
- ▲   May not be available from every phone/payphone.
- O   Collect calling only.
- ▽   Includes "Ladatel" public phones.
- ⊕   From St. Maarten's or phones at Bobby's Marina, use 1-800-872-2881.
- ▶   City of Asuncion only.

When placing an international call *from* the U.S., dial 1 800 CALL ATT.

CALA   © 8/00 AT&T

to the right of the **House of the Phalli,** following the rusted cart tracks, and cutting through the bushes, are best located with the help of a guide. In the **Principal Group of the Southwest,** glyphs depict the Maya practice of compressing children's foreheads with stone plates. The Principal Group contains a magnificently **ruined pyramid,** the restored **Temple of the Three Lintels** (dating to AD 879), and the **Jaguar Temple,** where a handful of columns salute the military order of the Jaguars.

⚑ DAYTRIPS FROM CHICHÉN ITZÁ

GRUTAS DE BALANCANCHÉN

5km east of Chichén Itzá and 2km past the Dolores Alba Hotel, the caves are easily reached from Chichén or Piste by hopping on any bus traveling east on Rte. 180 (3 pesos). When you board, be sure to ask the driver to stop there. To get back, catch any westbound vehicle, but be prepared to wait a while. Tours in Spanish, daily at 9am, noon, 2, and 4pm; in English at 11am, 1, and 3pm. 37 pesos. Two person minimum.

The inner caves of Balancanchén were only rediscovered in 1959 when a local noticed a passageway blocked with stones. Further exploration opened 300m of caves filled with stalactites carved to resemble leaves, and a huge treelike column representing the sacred *ceiba* tree. Archaeologists have come to believe that the cave was a center for Maya-Toltec worship of the gods Chac (Tlaloc) and Kukulcán (Quetzalcóatl) during the 10th and 11th centuries. For reasons unknown, subterranean worship in Balancanchén stopped at the end of this period, and the offerings of ceramic vessels and stone sculptures rested undisturbed for nine centuries. The impressive stalactites and ceramics merit a visit, but be prepared for an almost incomprehensible tour. Self-guided tours are not permitted.

YAXUNÁ

There is no public transportation to Yaxuná. Your options are either to hire a rent-a-car or to hire a taxi in Piste. There are two routes to Yaxuná. The better of the two takes you west on Rte. 180 to Libre Unión and then through Yaxcaba, a small town (300 pesos roundtrip). The poorer road cuts through the jungle, and taxistas charge more to cover possible damage to the car (450 pesos).

Thirty kilometers south of Chichén Itzá, Yaxuná is home to the ruins of yet another ancient Maya city. The temple was built by the Maya of Cobá, who were planning to declare war on the people of Chichén Itzá late in the Classic Period. To keep a close eye on their enemy, the Maya of Cobá aligned their temple with El Castillo. The most interesting feature of the site is the 100km *sacbé*, which connected Yaxuná to Cobá, making it the **longest in the peninsula.**

VALLADOLID ☎ 9

In the middle of the Mérida-Cancún route and only half an hour away from Chichén Itzá, Valladolid, (pop. 52,000) ought to be jammed with tourists. Strangely enough, most bypass the beautiful city, missing its colonial churches and natural *cenotes*. Formerly the Maya city of Zací, Valladolid was attacked in 1543 by the Spaniard Francisco de Montejo, and finally conquered several years later a man of the same name, his nephew. Eager to defeat the Maya spirit, the younger Montejo installed imposing churches and grid-like streets, reminders of Spanish control. The Maya were not so easily defeated, and in 1848 they rose up and held the city hostage for several months in what is now known as the War of the Castes. Today, the tension between Spanish and Maya is still visible. Grid-like streets and towering churches notwithstanding, Mayan can be heard among Indian women weaving *huipiles* (white dresses embroidered with colorful flowers), between vendors on street corners, and around the city's archaeological sites and *cenotes*.

YUCATÁN

TRANSPORTATION

Traversed by Rte. 180, Valladolid lies in the heart of Yucatán state, midway between Mérida and Cancún. The **ADO station** (☎856 34 49) is on the northwest corner of Calles 54 and 37. To get to the *zócalo*, walk south one block on Calle 54 to Calle 39. Turn left (east) and follow Calle 39 for six blocks. Better yet, you can get off before the bus station at the *zócalo* (look for a big twin-towered cathedral). ADO buses travel to: **Cancún** (2hr., 9 per day, 65 pesos); **Chichén Itzá** (1hr., every hr. 5am on, 13 pesos); **Mérida** (2½hr., every hr. 6:45am on, 65 pesos); **Playa del Carmen** (2½hr., 6 per day, 84 pesos); **Tizimín** (1hr., every hour. 5am on, 16 pesos); **Izamal** (1½hr., 8, 10am, and 7pm, 27 pesos) and **Chiquila** (2½hr., 2:30am, 47 pesos). The **Oriente station** sends buses to many of the same destinations, and is on the northwest corner of Calles 39 and 46.

ORIENTATION AND PRACTICAL INFORMATION

Even-numbered streets in Valladolid run north-south, increasing westward. Odd-numbered streets run east-west, increasing southward. Except for Cenote X'keken, in the nearby village of **Dzitnup**, everything lies within walking distance from the *zócalo* (circumscribed by Calles 39, 40, 41, and 42). Blocks are spaced out, so what appears a short jaunt might really be a long haul.

Tourist Information: The city hall (☎856 20 63), on the corner of Calles 40 and 41, provides information and pamphlets. Open M-Sa 9am-8pm, Su 9am-1pm.

Currency Exchange: Bancomer (☎856 21 50), on the Calle 40 side of the *zócalo* has a 24hr. **ATM** next door. Open M-F 9am-4:30pm, Sa 10am-2pm.

Bike Rental: Refaccionaria de Bicicletas Silva, on Calle 44 between Calles 39 and 41. 5 pesos per hr. Open daily 8am-8pm.

Luggage Storage: At the ADO bus terminal. 3 pesos per hr.

Market: Fresh and cheap fruits, meats, and vegetables in the market 5 blocks northeast of the *zócalo*, bordered by Calles 30, 32, 35, and 37. Open daily 6am-2pm.

Supermarket: Super Maz (☎856 37 74), three and a half blocks west of the *zócalo* on Calle 39. Open daily 7am-9:30pm.

Laundry: Lavandería Teresita (☎856 23 93), Calle 33 at 42, self-service 15 pesos per 3kg; full service 8 pesos per kg. Open daily 7am-7pm.

Emergency: ☎060.

Police: (☎856 21 00) Calle 41, 10 blocks east of the *zócalo*. Some English spoken.

Pharmacy: El Descuento, Calle 42 at 39, on the *zócalo*. Open 24hr.

Hospital: Hospital S.S.A. (☎856 28 83), on Calle 41, west of the *zócalo*. Open 24hr.

Fax: Telecomm, on Calle 41, west of the Museo San Roque, between Calles 38 and 40.

Internet Access: Cibercafé and Video Club (☎856 15 25), Calle 37 at 46. 10 pesos per 30min. Open daily 8:30am-11:30 pm.

Post Office: (☎856 26 23) on the Calle 40 side of the *zócalo*. Open M-F 9am-3pm.

Postal Code: 97780.

ACCOMMODATIONS

Penny-pinchers will want to stay away from the pricey hotels bordering the *zócalo*. Better bargains can be found one block west, especially on Calle 44.

Hotel Zací, Calle 44 #191 (☎856 21 67), between Calles 37 and 39, is a vacation from your vacation. Complete with restaurant, fountain, and glittering pool, colonial rooms with blue curtains, carved dressers, and cable TV are worth the extra pesos. Singles 156 pesos; doubles 205 pesos; triples 257 pesos. Add 50-60 pesos for A/C.

Hotel María Guadalupe, Calle 44 #198 (☎856 20 68), between Calles 39 and 41. The colorful bed covers and new ceiling fans enliven the dark wood furniture. They only have 8 rooms, so call in advance. Singles and doubles 100 pesos; triples 110 pesos.

Hotel Mendoza, Calle 39 #204 (☎856 20 02), 1½ blocks west of the *zócalo.* A cheap, basic option—as long as you don't mind ultra-soft beds. Singles 60 pesos; doubles 80 pesos; triples 120 pesos. With TV and A/C, 170 pesos.

Hotel Lily, Calle 44 #192 (☎856 21 63) between Calle 37 and 39, across from Hotel Zací. Hostel-like accommodations with shared bathrooms and hammock hooks in every room. Singles 70 pesos, with bath 85 pesos; doubles 100 pesos, with bath 135 pesos.

◗ FOOD

Comida yucateca is a mix of European and Mexican flavors, and in Valladolid, it tops every menu. Try the *poc-chuc* (tender slices of pork marinated in a Yucatec sauce, covered with pickled onions), *panuchos* (small tortillas filled with beans and topped with either chicken or pork, and lettuce, tomato, and hot sauce), or *escabeche oriental de pavo* (a hearty turkey soup). *Xtabentun* is a delectable drink of anise and honey.

Restaurante Cenote Zací, (☎856 21 07), on Calle 36 between Calles 37 and 39, underneath a large *palapa,* surrounded by jungle trees, atop a *cenote.* Excellent *comida yucateca* (entrees 40-50 pesos) and liquor selection, including *xtabentun* (8 pesos). Open daily 8:30am-6pm.

Bazar Municipal, Calle 39 at 40, right off the *zócalo,* is a narrow courtyard crowded with cafes and juice bars all serving *comida típica.* Prepare to be bombarded. Hours vary by restaurant, but generally open daily 6am-midnight.

Restaurante María de la Luz, (☎856 20 71), on the west side of the *zócalo,* in the Hotel María de la Luz. Eat *comida corrida* (35 pesos) in non-*comida corrida* surroundings as you observe the *zócalo* through French bay doors. Open daily 6am-10pm.

Restaurante del Parque, Calle 42 #199 (☎856 23 65), on the southwest corner of the *zócalo.* Situate yourself right and get an eyeful of the Franciscan Cathedral. *Comida yucateca* with sprinklings of US grub 30 pesos. Open daily 7:30am-10pm.

◉ SIGHTS

While most visitors take the next bus to Mérida or Chichén Itzá, those seeking a healthy dose of *cenotes* and cathedrals have come to the right place. The natural Yucatecan jungle makes a steamy backdrop that blends seamlessly into the colonial city, creating a mix of natural and man-made beauty.

CENOTE ZACÍ. In the middle of the city, Cenote Zací (pronounced sah-KEY) is a cavernous hollow full of plunging stalactites and daredevil divers doing their best to imitate their Acapulco counterparts. *(3 blocks east of the* zócalo, *on Calle 36 between Calles 37 and 39. Open daily 8am-8pm. 10 pesos, children 5 pesos. Free view from the palapa restaurant on the edge.)*

SAN BERNARDINO DE SIENA. Affiliated with the **Ex-Convento de Sisal,** the church was built over a *cenote* in 1552 with stones from the main Maya temple. It is the oldest ecclesiastical building in the Yucatán. On the altar at the rear of the church is a large image of the Virgin of Guadalupe. *(On Calle 41A, 4 blocks southwest of Las Cinco Calles. Open daily 8am-noon and 5-7pm. 5 pesos.)*

CATEDRAL DE SAN GERVASIO. According to legend, two criminals who took refuge in the church were discovered and murdered by an angry mob. When the bishop learned of the mob's actions, he had the church destroyed. It was rebuilt in 1720-1730 facing north instead of east, the only church in all of Yucatán be situated in this peculiar way. With its massive colonial twin towers it is an unmistakable landmark. *(Over the* zócalo *on Calle 41. Open daily 9am-1pm and 5-8pm. Free.)*

YUCATÁN

EL PASEO DE LOS FRAILES (THE STREET OF THE FRIARS). The picturesque, colonial street provides a backdrop for a beautiful stroll. Many residents leave their doors open, and you can catch peeks of interiors and courtyards—just don't be too nosy. *(Calle 41A between Las Cinco Calles and San Bernardino.)*

MUSEO DE SAN ROQUE. A relatively new addition to Valladolid's cultural scene, the museum features exhibits on the history of Valladolid, with particular emphasis on the pre-Hispanic Maya. The courtyard makes for a good place to relax and admire sculptures. *(On the northwest corner of Calles 41 and 38. ☎856 25 51. Open daily 9am-9pm. Donation suggested.)*

⚡ DAYTRIPS FROM VALLADOLID

▩ CENOTE DZITNUP (X'KEKÉN)

6km west of town. To get there by car or bike, take Calle 39 to the highway and go toward Mérida. Make a left at the sign for Dzitnup and continue to the entrance plaza on your left (20min.). Without wheels, catch a colectivo (5 pesos) in front of the Hotel María Guadalupe. Open daily 9am-7pm. 25 pesos, children free.

The beautiful *cenote* is mostly underground. Visit before midday, when a beam of light slices through a circular hole in the roof and bathes the cavern in blue. Bring a towel, warm clothes, and a swimsuit.

EK' BALAM

The ruins are 25km northeast of Valladolid and accessible only by car, taxi, or organized tour buses. Taxis run about 200 pesos round-trip; the driver will wait an hour. Open daily 8am-5pm. 12 pesos. Su and holidays free.

Ek' Balam ("Black Jaguar") was a Maya city that flourished in the late Classical period, around AD 700-1000. The site was discovered only 30 or so years ago. It contains temples, a ball court, and a magnificent pyramid, all organized around a main plaza. The pyramid itself is huge; it's not quite as tall as other Maya pyramids (30m), but its base is an astonishing 170m long. The unearthing of Ek' Balam is a work in progress. Note the two giant mounds flanking the pyramid—archaeologists believe they hide even more intriguing structures.

TIZIMÍN ☎9

Tizimín (pop. 80,000) has a prime location. Both the colonial Valladolid and the nature reserves of San Felipe and Río Lagartos lie within an hour's drive on Rte. 295. The archaeological sites of Ek' Balam and Kulubá are also nearby. Taking its cue from Valladolid, Tizimín is capitalizing on its colonial history with the ambitious restoration of the many buildings and pastel *portales* (arches) around its carefully manicured Parque Principal. Tizimín's mornings are big-city busy, but things quiet down to small-town proportion in the sultry afternoons.

▣ TRANSPORTATION. Tizimín is located in the heart of the eastern Yucatán. It is situated 55km north of Valladolid and 65km south of the Gulf Coast. Its **bus station** is on the northwest corner of Calles 46 and 47. To get to the *zócalo*, walk two blocks south and two blocks west. Don't confuse the *zócalo* with Parque Juárez, though, located one block northeast of the *zócalo*. ADO travels to **Valladolid** (1hr., 11 per day, 16 pesos); **Mérida** (3hr.; 6, 11:20am, 3:30pm; 59 pesos); and **Chichén Itzá** (6am, 28 pesos). Mayab goes to **Cancún** (3hr., 8 per day, 59 pesos); **Playa del Carmen** (8:30am, 85 pesos); and **Chetumál** (4:30am and 1:30pm, 107 pesos). Noreste goes to **Río Lagartos** (9:15am, 16 pesos).

◪▨ ORIENTATION AND PRACTICAL INFORMATION. Tizimín's even-numbered streets run north-south, decreasing to the east. Odd-numbered streets run east-west, increasing to the south. **Currency exchange: Bancomer,** on the corner of

Calles 48 and 51 across Parque Juárez, exchanges currency and has a 24hr. **ATM.** (☎ 863 23 81. Open M-F 8:30am-4pm, Sa 10am-2pm.) **Lavandería de los Tres Reyes,** three blocks south of the Parque Principal on Calle 57 between Calles 52 and 54. (6 pesos per kg. ☎ 863 38 83. Open daily 8am-1:30pm and 5-7:30pm.) **Police:** (☎ 863 21 13) in the Palacio Municipal on the corner of Calles 51 and 52. **Farmacia YZA,** on the corner of Calles 51 and 52. (☎ 863 44 62. Open 24hr.) **Hospital General San Carlos,** Calle 46 #461. (☎ 863 21 57. 24hr. ambulance service.) **Internet Access: Servidnet,** at the northeast corner of 52 and 43, one block north of the city's only basketball court (30 pesos for 1hr.; open M-Sa 8am-1pm and 5-9pm). **Post office:** Calle 53, south of the church. (☎ 863 32 10. Open M-F 8:30am-3pm.) **Postal code:** 97700.

▟▞ ACCOMMODATIONS AND FOOD. In Tizimín, going budget might be your only option. **Hotel San Jorge,** Calle 55 #412, on the southwest corner of the Parque Principal, sports a red and blue insignia. Outfit your large room with TV, A/C, or both. (☎ 863 20 37. Singles and doubles start at 100 pesos.) **Posada María Antonia,** Calle 50 #408, sits directly behind the statue of a woman breast feeding a baby on the south side of the church. Small rooms with two beds, a TV, and a fan. (☎ 863 28 57. Singles and doubles 130 pesos, with A/C 145 pesos.) **Hotel San Carlos,** Calle 54 #407, between Calles 51 and 53. Although the farthest from the *zócalo*, it's the most comfortable, with spotless rooms, private baths, and an inviting garden. (☎ 863 20 94. Singles 150 pesos, with A/C 175 pesos.)

When it comes to dining in Tizimín, options are limited, no matter what your budget. If you want to make your own meal, the *mercado*, on the southwest corner of Calles 47 and 48, sells fresh meats, fruits, and vegetables. The market's 21 booths also sell tacos and *tortas*. Willy Canto, the owner of **Restaurante Tres Reyes,** Calle 52 #395, on the southwest corner of the *zócalo*, has become the culinary and customer-service father of Tizimín. He advertises "La mejor comida del mundo." If nothing else, he gets credit for being friendly and funny. Generous meals (35 pesos), big enough for two, are accompanied by a stack of fresh tortillas. (☎ 863 21 06. Open daily 7am-midnight.)

▣ SIGHTS. Those curious about Tizimín can find out anything they want to from one man—Julio Caesar, a fountain of information about the region's Maya ruins. Having himself discovered the site of Kulubá, Caesar is eager to point tourists in its direction. If you can't reach him by phone, try finding him at his photography studio, Calle 47 #405, between Calles 50 and 52. (☎ 861 11 63. Studio open daily 8am-9pm.)

Tizimín's main attractions are the two relatively unexplored sites just outside the town proper, **Ek' Balam** and **Kulubá.** The ruins at Kulubá are somewhat hard to reach, and therefore extremely untouristed. To get to the ruins, take a taxi and have it wait while you explore the site (150 pesos). Dating from the late Classic period (AD 800-1000), Kulubá is the easternmost point of Puuc architectural influence. The *Edificio de Las Ues*, a structure 40m long, 8m high, and 7m wide, is carved with "U"s all along its facade. The original red stucco paint is still visible on the carved portions of the stone. The second partially restored building, the more impressive of the two, features two surprisingly well-preserved pairs of masks of the rain god Chac and other carved ornamentation.

The tiny town of **Kikil** (pop. 5000), 5km from Tizimín, has the remains of the first colonial church in the area, as well as the fresh waters of Nohock Dzonot de Kikil, a crystal clear *cenote*. To get there, take a taxi (85 pesos round-trip with wait) or get dropped off by one of the Río Lagartos-bound buses. The church, known to locals as **La Iglesia Kikil,** is just to the right of the highway as you enter Kikil from Tizimín. The church burned in the mid-19th century during the Caste War. Legend has it that years ago, residents threw a stone at a passing Catholic priest, who then predicted that the church would be laid to ruin. Just inside the gate of the small courtyard, to the left as you face the church, stands a carved stone baptismal font that rings like a bell when struck. To return to Tizimín, you will have to catch one of the southbound buses which come infrequently, about every two hours.

※ **FESTIVALS.** The most important of the town's religious processions is the **Festival of the Three Kings** (Dec. 30-Jan. 12), when over one million pilgrims pour into Tizimín from surrounding towns and the countryside. While the parades, dancing, bullfights, and banquets of *comida típica* last for two weeks, the most important day of the festival is January 6, when the pilgrims file through the church to touch the patrons with palm branches. In May and June, visitors to Kikil can enjoy several traditional Maya ceremonies such as the **Kaash Paach Bi,** a spiritual cleansing for the land, and the **Chaa-Chac,** a rain prayer. During January and June, the small indigenous town of Kikil participates in a **pig head dance ritual,** praising and giving thanks to Tsimin, a Maya deity.

RÍO LAGARTOS   ☎ 9

Known affectionately as *"La Ría,"* this 53km inlet of ocean water in the northeastern part of the Yucatán Peninsula is much the same today as it was when Hernán Cortés mistook it for a river. Now a 60,000-hectare wild animal refuge, *La Ría* is home to 30,000 long-legged pink flamingos and approximately 300 different bird species. The head of this inlet is commanded by the fishing village of Río Lagartos (pop. 3500), which is steadily adapting to its role as an ecotourist hotspot.

▐▌ TRANSPORTATION AND PRACTICAL INFORMATION. Perched on a tiny peninsula, standing guard over the entrance to *La Ría,* Río Lagartos lies on the northern shore of the eastern Yucatán, 65km north of Tizimín. Streets are numbered, but change names frequently and point in every possible direction. A good reference point is the flamingo fountain at the southern edge of the main park. One block east of the fountain is the **bus station.** Noreste offers service to **Tizimín** (10 per day, 16 pesos) and **Mérida** (4 per day, 82 pesos). **Tourist information:** at the Restaurante Isla Contoy (below). **Police station:** (☎862 00 02) just south of the basketball court, two blocks north of the fountain. Río Lagartos lacks most other services.

▐▌ ACCOMMODATIONS AND FOOD. Cabañas Los Dos Hermanos, two blocks east of the fountain on the waterfront. The *cabañas* may not be picturesque, but they include baths and fans. If you don't have your own hammock, the *hermanos* will provide one free of charge. (☎862 00 83. Singles 120 pesos.) **Restaurante Isla Conty,** Calle 19 #134, west of the fountain (follow the signs), provides seafood dishes on the shore in addition to complete tourist information and boat tours. (☎862 00 00. Open daily 8am-9pm.) **Las Gaviotas,** walk north from the fountain until you reach the water, then turn left. Relax on the waterfront while enjoying *ceviche* and *sopa de mariscos.* (☎861 14 55. Open daily 9am-7pm.)

▐▌ SIGHTS AND FESTIVALS. The town's main attraction is the multitude of flamingos, one of the largest concentrations in the western hemisphere. When choosing a tour guide, make sure the guide is certified. To be sure you'll get a professional, try the folks at **Isla Conty Tours,** Calle 19 #134, located in the restaurant. (☎862 00 00; email nunez@chichen.com.mx. 250 pesos per boat and up.) Another option is **Union de Lancheros** (☎862 00 42), offering flamingo tours (350 for 4 people per 2½hr.) and fishing trips (100 pesos per hr.). Besides flamingo-watching, not much happens during the day except a whole lot of fishing: it's not surprising, then, that even less goes on at night. The one exception is the **town fiesta,** which runs from July 20-30 in honor of Santiago Aposto, the younger brother of Spain's patron saint.

QUINTANA ROO

CANCÚN ☎9

Way back in the early 1970s, Mexican entrepreneurs scoured the entire nation looking for the perfect place to build their next cash cow resort. They fed their findings into a computer, which, after performing complex calculations, spit out a one-word answer: Cancún. Thirty years later, the computer's vision has erupted into a metropolis (pop. 500,000) whose alcohol-soaked, disco-shaken, sex-stirred insanity is carried out on a scale seen nowhere else in the Western Hemisphere. Ask any university student who's "done" Spring Break Cancún and their eyes will inevitably glass over and their heads shake in lingering disbelief as they recall night after night of drunken debauchery. Fear not, young party animal—this fishing village gone party town does not disappoint. However, budget travelers who seek culture and relaxation in Cancún will have to work a little harder and trek a little farther. Cancún's location serves as a great jump-off point for many budget-friendly excursions up and down the Turquoise Coast of the Caribbean, to spots such as the nature preserves at Río Lagartos and Xel-Ha, and the Maya ruins at Chichén Itzá and Tulum. Within Cancún proper, the party could leave you penniless. But who—except your liver and your peeling skin—can say no to the chance to get burned, hammered, and nailed again, and again, and again?

▨ TRANSPORTATION

GETTING AROUND

Getting around Cancún is a snap, as the city's public buses shuttle sunburned beachcombers to and fro with ease. Taxis (☎888 69 90) operate within the *Zona Hotelera* (25 pesos), within downtown (20 pesos), and between the two (as much as 80 pesos). **Buses** marked "Hoteles" run between the bus station downtown and the island's tip at Punta Nizuc around the clock (5 pesos) and can be caught at any blue sign along Tulum and Kukulcán; alternatively, you can stick out your hand and wave like a madman when you see one passing by. To get off the bus in the *Zona Hotelera*, push one of the little square red buttons on the ceiling when in sight of your stop—if you don't know where you need to get off, mention the name to the bus driver, with a *por favor*. While many places rent **mopeds** (useful for exploring the 18km of beaches from the CREA hostel to Punta Nizuc), buses are much cheaper and nearly as convenient.

GETTING AWAY

Airport: (☎886 00 28). The airport is located south of the city on Rte. 307. To reach either the downtown area or the *Zona Hotelera,* buy a ticket for the shuttle van **TTC** (75 pesos). **Taxis** will charge 150 pesos. Airlines include: **Aerocaribe** (☎884 20 00); **American** (☎883 44 60); **Continental** (☎886 00 06); **LACSA** (☎887 31 01); **Mexicana** (☎887 44 44); **Northwest** (☎886 00 46); **United** (☎886 00 25); **Lay Chile** (☎886 03 60); and **Martinair** (☎886 00 70).

Buses: (☎884 13 78). The **bus station** is downtown on the corner of Uxmal and Tulum, facing Plaza Caribe. Public buses are outside. ADO goes to: **Campeche** (6hr., 11:30am and 10:30pm, 170 pesos); **Valladolid** (2hr.; 11am, 1, and 10:30pm; 55 pesos) and **Palenque** (14hr., 3:45 and 5:45 pm, 325 pesos). Premier goes to: **Chichén Itzá** (2½hr., 9am, 50 pesos); **Playa del Carmen** (1 hr., every 15min., 20 pesos); and **Chiquilá** (3hr.; 6:15, 8:15am, and 4:30pm; 45 pesos). Second-class buses leave from the curb, and go to **Mérida, Tulum,** and **Chetumal.**

YUCATÁN

YUCATÁN

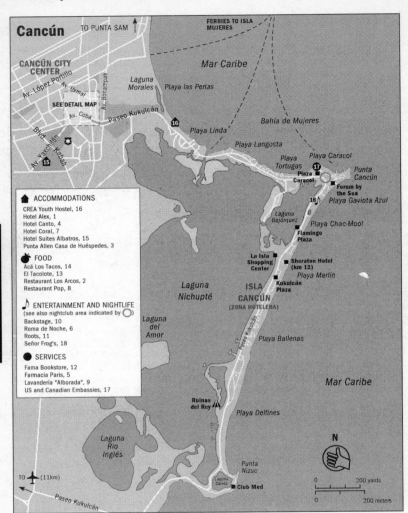

Cancún

ACCOMMODATIONS
CREA Youth Hostel, 16
Hotel Alex, 1
Hotel Canto, 4
Hotel Coral, 7
Hotel Suites Albatros, 15
Punta Allen Casa de Huéspedes, 3

FOOD
Acá Los Tacos, 14
El Tacolote, 13
Restaurant Los Arcos, 2
Restaurant Pop, 8

ENTERTAINMENT AND NIGHTLIFE
(see also nightclub area indicated by ⊙)
Backstage, 10
Roma de Noche, 6
Roots, 11
Señor Frog's, 18

SERVICES
Fama Bookstore, 12
Farmacia Paris, 5
Lavandería "Alborada", 9
US and Canadian Embassies, 17

Ferries: To get to **Isla Mujeres,** take a bus marked "Pto. Juárez" to the 2 ferry depots north of town (Punta Sam for car ferries, Puerto Juárez for passenger ferries, 15min.). Express service (15min., every 30min., 6am-8:30pm; every 15 min., 8:30am-8:30pm, 35 pesos) and normal service (45min., every 2hr. 8am-6pm, 18 pesos).

■ 🗲 ▐ ORIENTATION AND PRACTICAL INFORMATION

On the northeastern tip of the Yucatán Peninsula, Cancún lies 285km east of Mérida via Rte. 180 and 382km north of Chetumal and the Belizean border via Rte. 307. Cancún is divided into two areas: downtown Cancún, the *centro*, where you'll find more bargains but no beaches, and Isla Cancún, or the **Zona Hotelera,** with fewer bargains but oh-so-much beach and glam. The *Zona* is a slender "7"-shaped strip of land, and addresses along its one main road are given by kilometer number. Kilometer numbers increase from 1 to 20, roughly north to south.

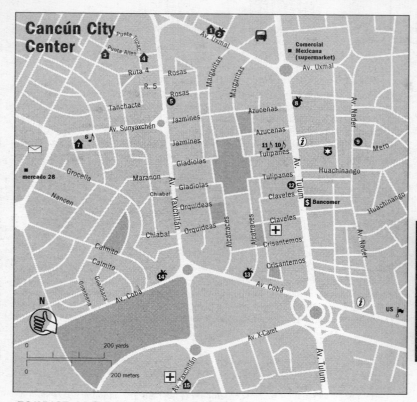

Cancún City Center

Comercial ■ Mexicana (supermarket)

mercado 28

Bancomer

YUCATÁN

N

0 — 200 yards

0 — 200 meters

US

TOURIST AND FINANCIAL SERVICES

Tourist Offices: Tulum 5 (☎887 43 29, ext. 114; email relacionespublicas@cancun.gob.mx), inside the Ayuntamiento Benito Juárez. Open M-F 9am-5pm. For national tourist assistance, call toll-free 91 800 9 03 92. **Visitor Office,** next door in the red building at Tulum 26 (☎884 65 31), offers similar paraphernalia and help. Open daily 9am-9pm. Ask for **Cancún Tips,** a free English-language magazine full of useful information and maps. Also available at the airport and at Plaza Caracol in the *Zona Hotelera*.

State Secretary of Tourism: Calle Pecari 23, S.M. 20 (☎881 90 00).

Consulates: Canada (☎883 33 60 or 883 33 61; fax 883 32 32), Plaza Caracol, 3rd fl. at km 8.5. Open M-F 10am-2pm. **UK** (☎881 01 00), in Hotel Royal Caribbean. Open M-F 8am-6pm. **US** (☎883 02 72), Plaza Caracol, 3rd fl. at km 8.5. Open M-F 9am-1pm.

Currency Exchange: Bancomer, Tulum 20 (☎884 44 00) at Calle Claveles. Open M-F 9am-4:30pm, Sa 10am-2pm. Both **Banamex,** Tulum 19 (☎881 64 02; open M-F 9am-5pm, Sa 9:30am-2pm), and **Banca Serfín,** Tulum at Cobá, give cash advances and have **ATMs** (☎881 48 5; available M-F 9am-5pm, Sa 10am-2pm).

American Express: Tulum 208 (☎884 19 99), 3 blocks south of Cobá. Open M-F 9am-6pm, Sa 9am-1pm.

LOCAL SERVICES

Luggage Storage: At the bus station. 2 pesos per hr., 10 pesos per day.

English Bookstore: Fama, Tulum 105 (☎884 65 86), between Claveles and Tulipanes. Newspapers, magazines, guidebooks, and more. Open daily 8am-10:30pm.

Supermarket: Comercial Mexicana (☎880 91 64), across from the bus station on Tulum. Open daily 7am-midnight. Smaller but more centrally located is **Super San Francisco** (☎884 11 55), Tulum next to Banamex. Open M-Sa 7am-10pm, Su 7am-9pm.

Laundry: Lavandería "Alborada," Náder 5 (☎884 15 84), behind the Ayuntamiento Benito Juárez. Self service 10 pesos. Open M-Sa 9am-8pm. **Tintorería Lavandería** (☎884 26 69) has dry cleaning. Open M-Sa 9am-8pm.

Car rental: Rental options are everywhere at the airport. Look for the booths on your right as you exit customs. Prices range from US$25-US$45 per day. **Alamo,** Uxmal No. 21 (☎886 01 68), in the lobby of Hotel Alux, has locations all along the *Zona Hotelera*. In the *centro*, **Ventura** (☎887 14 10) offers a rate of 400 pesos per day.

Moped Rental: Look for vendors between Hotel Aquamarine and Hotel Costa Real. 100 pesos per hr., 500 pesos per day. **Bicycles** and **in-line skates** also for rent. 70 pesos per hr., 160 pesos per day.

EMERGENCY AND COMMUNICATIONS

Emergency: ☎060.

Police:

21 (☎884 19 13), south of downtown.

Red Cross: Yaxchilán 2 (☎884 16 16). English spoken. Open 24hr.

Pharmacies: Several along Tulum and Yaxchilán. **Farmacia Paris,** Yaxchilán 32 (☎884 01 64), at the intersection with Rosas. Open 24hr.

Medical Assistance: Hospital Americano, Viento 15 (☎884 61 33, after hours 884 63 19), 5 blocks south on Tulum after its intersection with Cobá. For an **ambulance,** call **Total Assist** (☎884 80 82), at Claveles 5 near Tulum. English spoken.

Fax: (☎884 15 24) next to the post office. Open M-F 8am-6pm. Telegram service available as well.

Internet Access: Café Internet 20m west of Tulum, across from El Ayuntamiento Benito Juárez. 18 pesos per 30 min., 25 pesos per hr. **Sybcom Internet** (☎884 68 07), at Náder, behind Comercial Mexicana. 12 pesos per 15min., 22 pesos per 30min., 40 pesos per hr. Open M-Sa 9am-10pm. **Infonet** (☎887 95 16), in Plaza Bonita next to *Mercado 28*. 22 pesos per 30min. Open M-Sa 9am-9pm, Su 10am-3:30pm.

Post Office: (☎884 15 24), Xel-Ha at Sunyaxchén. From Tulum, cut through any side street to Yaxchilán and head up Sunyaxchén. The post office is 4 blocks farther. Open M-F 8am-6pm, Sa-Su 9am-12:30pm. **Postal Code:** 77500.

▟ ACCOMMODATIONS AND CAMPING

Trying to find cheap accommodations in Cancún is not for the faint of heart. The closest budget travelers will stay to the *Zona Hotelera* is the **CREA Youth Hostel,** located at the far end of the Paseo Kukulcán. All other budget options are located downtown, and, at about 250 pesos per person during the off season (spring and fall), are still far from "budget." Hotels are scattered throughout the *centro*, but many cluster around Yaxchilán. Keep in mind that prices generally rise during the summer and winter by about 25%. With Cancún regularly swamped in tourists, reservations are a good idea any time of the year.

▨ **Suites Albatros,** Yaxchilán 154 (☎884 22 42), 2 blocks south of Cobá and across the street from the Red Cross. It's easy to forgive the extra effort it takes to get here while walking through the shady courtyard and into one of the apartment-like rooms. Full kitchens, A/C, and large beds and closets. Each room upstairs has a balcony with laundry lines and sink. Make reservations at least 3 days in advance. Owner Pepe is the only man in town who doesn't raise prices during the high season. Doubles US$25.

Hotel Coral, Sunyaxchén 30 (☎884 20 97). Heading west from Yaxchilán, the hotel is 3 blocks down on the left; look for the red-and-white building with a garden inside. Charged fans make up for sparse furnishings. The attentive staff keeps the bathrooms clean and the *agua purificada* cold. Doubles 300 pesos, with A/C 300 pesos; triples 250 pesos, with A/C 400 pesos. For reservations, make payment 10 days in advance.

CREA Youth Hostel (HI), (☎849 43 60), Kukulcán at km 3. For those who plan to beach or club it, CREA is the cheapest place in the *Zona Hotelera*. Catch any *Hotelera* bus and ask to be let off at "CREA." 200 single-sex dorm rooms with 8 bunk-beds apiece and personal lockers (bring your own locks and use them). Sheets and pillows provided. No A/C; ask for a room with a working ceiling fan. Communal showers with no hot water. Beach volleyball, soccer field, ping-pong, and a small *cantina* in the lobby. Fifteen night maximum stay. No curfew. Bunks 100 pesos; cabins 350 pesos; pitch a tent on the back lawn for 50 pesos per person.

Hotel Canto (☎884 12 67), on Yaxchilán. As you turn off Uxmal onto Yaxchilán, look for the faded pink building, 2 blocks down on your right. Besides A/C, TV, and hot water, the only benefit Hotel Canto offers is its downtown location. Doubles 290 pesos; triples 320 pesos; quads 350 pesos.

Punta Allen Casa Huéspedes, Punta Allen 8 (☎884 10 01). Walk south from the intersection between Uxmal and Yaxchilán and turn right after 1 block. The hotel will be ahead on the left. Hot water, *agua purificada*, A/C, TV, and a free continental breakfast. Interior jungle theme decor. Rooms are small. Doubles 200 pesos.

Hotel Alux (☎884 66 13), located 1 block west of the bus station on the north side of the street. Its pink facade covers a well-maintained establishment, featuring A/C, TV, hot water, and phones in the rooms (3 pesos per local call). The cheapest bet downtown. Singles 240 pesos; doubles 270 pesos.

◖ FOOD

It's a good idea to stay away from the *Zona Hotelera*, where dining is both more expensive and of lesser quality than in downtown. However, a day of uninterrupted beachside frolicking may make it impossible to hop on the downtown bus every time hunger strikes. If trapped for the day in the *Zona Hotelera*, numerous small lunch counters offer cheap food. Be careful—it might be of dubious quality. Other options are the food courts in the massive air-conditioned *plazas* (shopping centers), which, however distasteful to the refined traveler, provide fast food at moderate prices. If downtown, breathe a little easier. The restaurants between Tulum and Yaxchilán, in **Mercado 28** (behind the post office and circumscribed by Xel-Ha), and in the center of *Parque de Las Palapas* serve more authentic, budget-friendly meals. All restaurants listed below are in downtown Cancún.

Acá Los Tacos, Cobá 43 (☎884 81 77), just west of Yaxchilán, in between Domino's Pizza and Los Chinos. Make your own *quesadillas* and tacos in this traditional Mexican joint. If it's your birthday everything you put down your throat, including drinks, is on the house. Don't forget to leave your mark by signing *El Mural de los Famosos. Quesadillas* and *gringas* 10 pesos, entrees 30-40 pesos. Open daily 6pm-1am.

Café México, Calle Grosella 2 (☎884 68 87), on the corner of Sunyaxchen, near Hotel Coral. A place to enjoy home-cooked breakfast, coffee, and desserts next to a *mariachi* silhouette or in the garden patio. Breakfast specials 17-20 pesos, sweet bread 5 pesos, coffee 7 pesos. Open M-Sa 7:30-11:30am and 1-4pm.

El Tacolote, Cobá 19 (☎887 30 45), 2 blocks east of Yaxchilán toward the *Zona Hotelera*. Look for the sombrero-sporting, taco-gobbling yellow chicken out front. Delicious grilled chicken and meat with an unlimited stack of tortillas and nachos and salsa start at 25 pesos. Mention *Let's Go* for a complimentary drink. Open daily 11am-2am.

YUCATÁN

Restaurante Río Nizuc, Paseo Kukulcán at km 22. Get on the "Hoteles" bus (4 pesos) and ask to be let off at Río Nizuc after passing most of the hotels. After crossing the bridge, take a left down a steep hill, then walk 3min. along a path on the right bank. Those who make the effort will be rewarded with shady *palapas* and a beautiful view of the river. Watch the cook prepare enormous servings of *tikin xic* (fresh barbequed fish, 60 pesos). Other entrees 50-60 pesos. Open daily 11am-6pm.

Restaurante Pop, Av. Tulum 25 (☎884 19 91), near the corner with Uxmal. About 1 block from the bus station, the air-conditioned interior and huge helpings provide the perfect recovery from a long bus ride. 3-course breakfast 39 pesos, lunch and dinner 30-60 pesos. Open daily 8am-11pm.

Restaurant Los Arcos, Uxmal 21 (☎887 80 71), 1 block west of the bus station. Grab one of the hanging sombreros and place it on your head as you dig into the seafood-heavy Mexican fare. You can't go wrong with all-you-can-eat. Buffet breakfast 39 pesos.

La Tortería, Kukulcán km 9.5 (☎883 46 97), in the Xtabenten liquor store and food cart. Sizeable *tortas* 25 pesos. Styles vary, from marinara to vegetarian. Watch bungee jumpers plunge to earth as you eat. Free delivery.

Roma de Noche, Sunyaxchen 30 (☎860 54 16), right under the Hotel Canal. Italian food at reasonable prices. Entrees average 50 pesos. Open noon-11pm.

Billy Jack's, Kukulcán km 9 (☎882 11 32). Breakfast is served all day and it's cheap (30 pesos). Beer 20 pesos, hard drinks 45 pesos. Open 7am-11pm.

SIGHTS

Cancún is not a town that obsesses about museums, history, or culture. About the only mildly educational thing around is the small archaeological site of **El Rey,** km 18, on the lagoon. The ruins were once a Maya fishing village (pop. 2500-3000), occupied during the Post-Classic Period (AD 1000-1500). When the Spanish arrived, bringing their lethal illnesses, the Maya buried their dead in the foundations of these houses, then moved out. The centerpiece of the site is now the king's pyramid, which rises above all other structures and is visible from the road. (Ruins open daily 8am-5pm. 17 pesos. Tours available in both English and Spanish.)

BEACHES

A visit to Cancún without frolicking on the beach is like a trip to Giza without seeing the Pyramids. The 22km of multi-hued turquoise water and white Caribbean coastline will leave you begging for just one more day on the beach. Don't fret about the wall of luxury hotels standing between you and the glorious surf. All beaches in Mexico are public property. Savvy travelers often pose as hotel guests to take advantage of such delicious amenities as fresh-water showers, pools, and lounge chairs. (Note that *Let's Go* does not condone such activity.) If you choose to avoid the resort scene, head for the peaceful **Playa Langosta,** east of the CREA, or for the shores south of the Sheraton Hotel, some of the most pleasant in Cancún. Boogie boards can be rented at the marina on the beach (40 pesos per 2hr.).

Cancún's surf is a whimper compared to the roar of the rest of the *costa turquesa* (turquoise coast). **Playa Chac-Mool,** just south of Punta Cancún, where waves are about 1m high, is as thrilling as it gets. Heading south from there, you will come across **Playas Marlín, Ballenas,** and **Delfines.** For some free, no-frills encounters with a surprising variety of tropical fish and coral, explore the rocks on the east side of **Playa Tortugas,** on the north coast of the island.

Water sport enthusiasts are in luck: Cancún offers opportunities to participate in nearly every aquatic sport known to mankind. Many organized recreational activities can be arranged through the luxury hotels lining the beaches, or through private companies and tour guides:

YUCATÁN

Aqua Sport, on Playa Las Perlas (km 1) offers wave runner rentals, parasailing (US$40), and banana boat rentals (US$15).

Big Game Fishing (☎884 16 17), at km 3.5, next to the Blue Bay Hotel, gives those interested a chance to kill their own dinner. Sunrise (6hr., US$99) and sunset (4hr., US$79) trips. Beer and bait included.

Aqua World (☎885 22 88) at km 15.1 and **El Embarcadero** (☎849 48 48) at km 4 are two popular choices for exploring Cancún's water paradise. Jungle tours and waterskiing in the oft-forgotten Laguna Nichuplé.

Scuba Cancún (☎883 50 46) at km 5, offers diving lessons (US$78), snorkeling (US$26), and other services at comparatively reasonable prices.

Mundo Marino (☎883 05 54), at km 5.5, gives certified divers a better bang for their buck. One-tank dive US$50. The dock to the right of the CREA hostel supports a dive shop that offers two hours of snorkeling, equipment included (US$30).

Scuba Staff (☎882 77 33) 10 Av., between Calle 1 and Juárez. Discover scuba program US$65, snorkeling trips US$25. Open daily 7am-9pm.

▓▓ ENTERTAINMENT AND NIGHTLIFE

As night descends, Cancún morphs from a beachgoer's playground into a hotspot for bars, clubs, and other forms of nocturnal diversion. Out on the *Zona*, expect to see drunken tourists parading down Kukulkán, drinks in hands and smiles on faces. In town, the locals gather at bars at the south end of Tulum near Cobá, where *mariachi* music can be heard floating through the night air. Most establishments open at 9pm and close when the crowds leave, around 5 or 6am. Crowds differ according to time and season—April is for US college students, June for high school and college graduates, and late night year-round belongs to the gamut of tourists from all across the world.

BARS

Bars in the downtown area cluster around Yaxchilán and Tulipanes. Out on the *Zona Hotelera*, you'll be out of luck finding local bars; expect instead larger US chains, such as T.G.I. Friday's and Señor Frog's.

▓ **Roots,** Tulipanes 26 (☎884 24 37; fax 884 55 47), between Palapas Park and Tulum. Caribbean-colored walls and eclectic artwork with a music motif set the stage in this jazz-n-blues joint. Get a table farther back to chat with the European and expat crowd. Live regional musicians Tu-Sa; shows start around 10pm. Cover F-Sa 30 pesos (most of the money goes to the local arts association). Open Tu-Su 7pm-2am. Menu until 1am.

CLUBS

Most clubs and discos are clustered at Punta Cancún, near **Playa Caracol** and the **Forum by the Sea.** Older travelers beware: Cancún's glam clubs are usually crowded with US teenagers eager to indulge in sinful pleasures. Dress code for the discos is simple; less is more, tight is just right. Bikini tops often get women in for free, use your judgment in the more laid-back clubs. Discos in the *Zona* prefer US dollars.

La Boom (☎883 11 52), near the CREA hostel, a 10min. walk toward the *Zona*. Two nightclubs, a bar, and a pizzeria under the same roof. Serious dancers groove with lasers and phone booths. Ladies night and open bar vary week to week. Cover US$20.

Dady'O (☎883 33 33), km 9, on Forum by the Sea. Its cave-like entrance lets you know you're heading for a disco inferno ("burn, baby, burn"). The cave-scape continues through to a stage and dance floor, surrounded by winding, layered walkways whose crevices sport tables and stools. A cafeteria in the club serves snacks (30 pesos). Laser show nightly at 11:30pm. Wristband-hawking staff outside will fill you in on the nightly special. Cover US$20. Open daily 10pm-late.

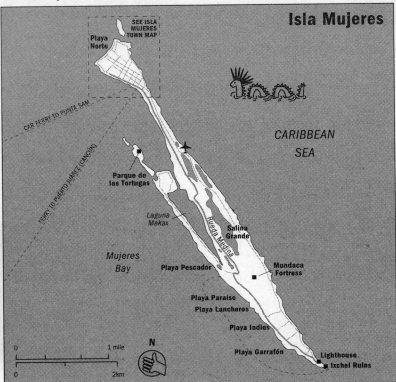

Isla Mujeres

SEE ISLA
MUJERES
TOWN MAP

Playa
Norte

CAR FERRY TO PUNTE SAM

FERRY TO PUERTO JUAREZ (CANCUN)

Parque de
las Tortugas

Laguna
Makax

Rueda Medina

Salina
Grande

Mujeres
Bay

Playa Pescador

Mundaca
Fortress

Playa Paraiso

Playa Lancheros

Playa Indios

Playa Garrafón

Lighthouse
Ixchel Ruins

CARIBBEAN

SEA

N

0 ——— 1 mile

0 ——— 2km

Dady Rock (☎ 883 33 33), next door to Dady'O. Provides the headbanging to complement Dady'O's hip-hopping. Hosts 2 live bands every night and has open bar deals
(US$15) several nights per week. Cover US$20. Open daily 6:45pm-late.

Coco Bongo (☎ 883 05 92), km 9, Forum By the Sea. Dance and drink to rock, pop, and
hip-hop. Partiers dance on stage, on the bar, on the tables, and yes, the dance floor.
Laser show and the flying mask nightly at 11:30pm. Cover US$20, includes open bar.

Batacha (☎ 883 17 55), km 10 in the Hotel Miramar Misión. Salsa and merengue bands
under refreshing *palapas*. A local favorite. Cover 30 pesos. Open Tu-Su 10pm-4am.

Backstage, Tulipanes 30 at Tulum (☎ 887 91 06). Nightly cabaret shows on a Broad-
way-like theater stage with scarlet curtains. Three nights no cover, otherwise 30 pesos
(drink included). Open 9pm-late.

Karamba, Tulipanes just off Tulum, in downtown Cancún. A gay disco with a spacious
multi-level floor, pop-art murals, and a colorful variety of dance music to complement
the wild lights. Tu-F 2-for-1 beers. Sa cover 25 pesos. Open Tu-Su 10pm-4am.

SPORTS

Beísbol (baseball) is played in Cancún just about every other night from April to
August. The Cancún Langosteros play in **El Estado Beto Avilo** (☎ 884 79 99), located
south of downtown, accessible by the R-2 bus. Get off at the WalMart and you will
see the lights. Cheaps seats 10 pesos.

FESTIVALS

El Parque de las Palapas, between Tulum and Yaxchilán in the very center of town, hosts free regional music and dance performances during the weekends. For slightly more intense entertainment, death occurs every Wednesday afternoon at 3:30pm in the **Plaza de Toros** (☎884 83 72; fax 884 82 48), on Bonampak at Sayil. Tickets for the bullfights are available at travel agencies on Tulum (300 pesos per person, group discounts, children free) or at the bullring on a fight day. The **Folkloric Ballet of Cancún** (☎881 04 00 ext. 193) is located in the convention center on the *Zona Hotelera* and performs occasionally at the Plaza de Toros.

Admirable foresight or lucky timing could mean enjoying Cancún's celebrated **Jazz Festival** (mid- to late-May) or the refreshing **Caribbean Festival** (November). Check with the tourist office for information.

ISLA MUJERES ☎9

In 1517, the Spaniard Francisco Hernández de Córdoba happened upon this tiny island while looking for slaves to work in Cuban mines. Instead of slaves, he found hundreds of small female statuettes scattered on the beaches and gave the island the name Isla Mujeres (Island of Women). Hernández had stumbled upon a Maya sanctuary for Ix Chel, the Maya goddess of fertility and the moon. For years Isla Mujeres was a small fishing village whose culture centered around the sea. In the 1950s, vacationing Mexicans discovered the pristine island, and were soon followed by Australians, Europeans, and North Americans who transformed the island into a hot spot for hippies and backpackers. While some present-day inhabitants of the island (pop. 14,500) still fish, most now sell souvenirs and cater to the daytrippers who arrive fresh from nearby Cancún every morning or who use the island as a jump-off point for exploring **Isla Contoy,** an island bird sanctuary 24km away. It's easy to lose track of time as *siestas* come and go under the shade of the tree-lined beaches. Here, time just slips away.

TRANSPORTATION

GETTING THERE AND AWAY

The only way to get to Isla Mujeres is by **ferry.** Catch a boat from **Puerto Juárez,** 3km north of downtown Cancún, accessible by a "Puerto Juárez" bus (15min., 5 pesos) or by taxi (20 pesos) from downtown Cancún. **Normal service** boats take much longer but sometimes have live music to pass the time (45min., every 2hr. 8am-6pm, 18 pesos). If you're in a hurry, there is also **express service** (20min., every 30min. 6am-9pm, 35 pesos). Arrive early—ferries are notorious for leaving ahead of schedule if they're full. A **car ferry** runs to Mujeres from Punta Sam, 5km north of Puerto Juárez (4 per day; 9 pesos per person, 50 pesos per car).

GETTING AROUND

Walking is the best way of navigating the island's lovely *centro.* For exploring the ends of the island, the best way to get around is by renting a moped, a bike, or a golf cart. Cars—with the exception of the occasional speeding taxi—are a rare sight on the island. Red **taxis** (☎877 00 66) line up at the stand directly to the right as you come off the passenger dock and zip to Playa Paraíso (10 pesos), Playa Lancheros (20 pesos), Garrafón (35 pesos), and the ruins (40 pesos). Taxis also roam the length of Isla Mujeres; you should have no problem catching one elsewhere. Public **buses,** on the other hand, go only as far as Playa Lancheros (3 pesos).

PRACTICAL INFORMATION

Isla Mujeres is a narrow landmass, 7.5km by 1km, 11km northeast of Cancún. The island's town—the *centro*—is located at the northwest corner of the island. The

Isla Mujeres Town

🏠 ACCOMMODATIONS

Hotel Caribe Maya, 4
Hotel Carmelina, 3
Hotel Isleño, 5
Hotel Xul-Ha, 1
Poc-Na Youth Hostel, 2

CARIBBEAN SEA

Playa Panchalo

Zazil-Ha

Playa Norte

Carlos Lazo

Guerrero

López Mateos

Hidalgo

Juárez

Matamoros

Abasolo

Madero

Sea Wall Walk

ZÓCALO

Morelos

Bravo

Mujeres Bay

Rueda Medina

Allende

0   200 yards
0   200 meters

FERRY TO PUERO JUÁREZ (CANCÚN)

CAR FERRY TO PUNTA SAM

TO PLAYA GARRAFÓN

Uribe

centro is laid out in a rough grid. Right in front and perpendicular to the dock is **Rueda Medina,** which runs the length of the island along the coastline, past the lagoon, Playa Paraíso, Playa Lancheros, and the Garrafón Reef.

TOURIST, FINANCIAL, AND LOCAL SERVICES

Tourist Office: (☎877 03 07) Rueda Medina, first left after exiting the port, on the right-hand side. Open M-F 8am-8pm, Sa-Su 10am-2pm.

Currency Exchange: Bital (☎877 00 05), on Rueda Medina to the right after exiting the port. Has a 24hr. **ATM.** Open M-Sa 8am-6pm.

Books: Cosmic Cosas, Matamoros 82 (☎877 08 06). Buy, sell, and exchange books in all different languages. Open daily 9am-2pm and 4-9pm.

Laundry Service: Lavandería Tim Phó, Juárez 94, at Abasolo. 35 pesos per 4kg. 2hr. turnaround. Open M-Sa 7am-9pm, Su 8am-2pm. **Lavandería Angel,** Juárez local A-3, near the beach. 5 pesos per kg. 4 kg minimum.

Rentals: Pepe's Moto Rent, Hidalgo 19 (☎/fax 877 00 19), between Matamores and Abasolo. Golf carts 100 pesos per hr.; mopeds 50 pesos per hr., 200 pesos per day. Open daily 8am-6pm.

Police: (☎877 00 98) on Hidalgo at Morelos, in the Palacio Municipal. Open 24hr.

Red Cross: (☎877 02 80) at the Colonia la Gloria, toward the south end of the island.

Pharmacy: La Mejor, Madero 17 (☎877 01 16), between Hidalgo and Juárez. Open daily 9am-10pm.

Medical Assistance: Centro de Salud, Guerrero 5 (☎877 01 17), at Morelos. The white building at the northwest corner of the *zócalo*. Open 24hr. Some doctors speak English, such as **Dr. Antonio E. Salas** (☎877 04 77 or beeper 91 98 88 78 68 code 1465), at Hidalgo near Madero, and will make house calls.

Fax: Telecomm, Guerrero 13 (☎877 02 45), next to the post office. Open M-F 9am-3pm.

Post Office: (☎877 00 85) Guerrero and López Mateos, at the northwest corner of town, 1 block from the Playa Norte. Open M-F 9am-4pm, Sa 9am-1pm.

Postal Code: 77400.

▌ ACCOMMODATIONS AND CAMPING

Prices increase by about 100 pesos during the high season (July-August and December-April). During those times, inquire ahead and consider making reservations. Most visitors stay in Cancún, where hotels are more plentiful.

Hotel Carmelina, Guerrero 4 (☎877 00 06), between Abasolo and Madero. Bright yellow baths liven up the well-kept rooms. A/C available. Singles 130 pesos; doubles 150 pesos; triples 200 pesos. Prices remain the same year-round.

Hotel Xul-Ha, Hidalgo 23 (☎877 00 75), between Matamoros and López Mateos. Large rooms have colorful blankets, ceiling fans, and wooden dressers and mirrors. The hotel has a color TV, coffee machines, refrigerator, and books in its lobby. Discounts for longer stays. Singles and doubles 150 pesos; 50 pesos more during high season.

Poc-Na Youth Hostel, Matamoros 15 (☎877 00 90), near *Playa Norte*. Whether staying in beds or hammocks, everyone comes together in the dining room *palapa*. Bring your own hammock, tent, and lock. Registration 6am-11pm. Cafeteria open 8am-11pm. Hammock space 25-29 pesos; dorm beds 39 pesos; private rooms 90-120 pesos.

Hotel Caribe Maya, Madero 9 (☎877 01 90), located between Hidalgo and Guerrero. Its greatest perk is the roof, which you can use to catch a few rays. Singles and doubles 160 pesos, 200 during the high season. With fans, private baths, and A/C, 200 pesos.

Hotel Isleño, Madero 8 (☎877 03 02), on the corner with Guerrero. The excruciatingly pink hotel offers rooms of all types. Singles 134 pesos, with private baths 168 pesos, with A/C 224 pesos; 56 pesos each additional person.

Last Resort Camping (cell phone ☎01 98 20 52 02), near the Garrafon National Park. Electricity, fresh water, restrooms, and "very special ambiance." 35 pesos per person.

◖ FOOD

Seafood abounds in Isla Mujeres. Try *pulpo* (octopus) or *ceviche* (seafood marinated in lime juice, cilantro, and other herbs). Be wary of the restaurants near the plaza as they are a bit pricier. Also plan ahead—many restaurant owners close between lunch and dinner to enjoy the afternoon life of Isla Mujeres.

Chen Huaye, Bravo 4, just off the plaza across from the playground. Unlike the wagon wheels in front, the service inside keeps the local dishes rolling. Try the zesty *pescado a la veracruzana* (50 pesos). W-M 8:30am-midnight.

French Bistro Francais, Matamoros 29, at Hidalgo. The most healthful menu on the island. Yogurt and crepe specials are popular morning picks, and the grilled seafood, cooked with a French flavor, satisfies the clientele. Open daily 8am-noon and 6-10pm.

Café Cito, Matamoros 42 (☎877 04 38), at Juárez. Patrons can pretend they haven't left the beach, with the sand and shells under the see-through tabletops. A visit here can replenish both body and soul with freshly made crepes, sandwiches, and orange juice. Open high season 8am-2pm and 5-10:30pm; off season 8am-2pm.

El Poc-Chuc Lonchería, Juárez 5, between Abasolo and Madero. The colorful murals of dolphins and butterflies will soothe the senses as you dine on traditional Mexican fare (20 pesos) or seafood (40 pesos).

SIGHTS AND BEACHES

While beaches in Cancún are packed with hungover American high school and college students, beaches in Isla Mujeres are peaceful and tranquil. The most popular and accessible beach is **Playa Norte** on the north shore, where tourists lounge and enjoy the shallow surf and gentle waves. On the west side of the island, **Playa Luncheros** and **Playa Paraíso** open onto Mujeres Bay. On the south end of the island, the **Faro Sur,** a lighthouse overlooking rocky bluffs, provides excellent views.

La Isleña travel agency, on Morelos, half a block from the dock, rents snorkeling gear (40 pesos) and mopeds (80 pesos per hr.) and organizes trips to nearby **Isla Contoy,** a wildlife sanctuary reef with over 100 bird species. (350 pesos. Equipment, breakfast, and lunch included. 6 person minimum. ☎877 05 78. Open daily 7:30am-9:30pm.) **Tarzan Watersports,** on the Playa Norte near Guerrero, offers an array of exploits and rents beach paraphernalia such as chairs and umbrellas. (☎877 06 79. Scuba diving lessons US$60, waterskiing US$40.)

To support a group of dedicated individuals helping to save the planet and have an unforgettable time while doing so, head over to **PESCA,** across the *laguna* from the populated northern half of the island. This biological research station breeds three species of sea turtles. Female turtles, captured by PESCA in May, lay their eggs in the safety of the station's beach throughout the summer and are returned to the wild in October. The young are reared for a year before they, too, are released. A guide will take you on a stroll through the center to see the giant turtles and their offspring (20 pesos; open daily 9am-5pm).

The Maya ruins of **Ixchel**—where women made pilgrimages to seek help from the goddess of fertility—are located on the south tip of the island, accessible by taxi (40 pesos). Unfortunately, the temple was reduced to rubble by Hurricane Gilbert in 1988. A partially reconstructed one-room building and an immense panorama of the Yucatán and the Caribbean Sea are about the only items worth visiting.

◪ NIGHTLIFE

The nightlife in Isla Mujeres pales in comparison to that in its flashier cousin, Cancún. Still, you never know when the **Superior Beer Truck** might roll up and unfurl its soundstage, complete with a salsa band. Locals gather and dancing ensues, while rival beer vendors covertly peddle their own suds to the throng. Look north of the dock on the western shore for this happening scene, which occasionally takes place in the afternoons.

Disco music often blares in the *zócalo*, well into the night. If you see workers setting up equipment during the day, you'll know you'll be in for a treat later. **La Palapa,** on Playa Norte to the right of Hidalgo, hosts a temporary dance floor on the sand, garnished in holiday lights and glow-in-the-dark artwork. **Bar Buho's** (☎877 03 01) right on shore, off Carlos Lazo, is the popular swing and hammock bar of *La Isla.* Tourists and locals swing from one bar to the next toasting with half-price Happy Hour bargains during sunset. (Beer 15 pesos; margaritas and cocktails 20 pesos. Flexible island hours.)

ISLA HOLBOX

Isla Holbox (EES-la ohl-BOSH) is a 33km finger-shaped fisherman's village whose sandy streets are surrounded by crystalline waters. The island is still blissfully unknown to many foreign tourists, and you'll want it to stay that way. Just off the northeastern tip of the Yucatán Peninsula, it is home to 3000 *holboxeños.* The pace of life here is unbelievably slow, the beaches and surrounding tiny islands are inspiring, and the people are welcoming. The fastest thing around is probably the chicken delivery man, making the morning rounds on his bicycle.

▣ ⚡ TRANSPORTATION AND PRACTICAL INFORMATION

Isla Holbox is just off the northern coast of Quintana Roo, in the Gulf of Mexico. Getting there requires planning. The easiest way is to take a **bus** from **Cancún** (8:15am, 50 pesos) to **Chiquilá,** then hop on a "Los 9 Hermanos" *lancha* (approx. every 2hr. 6am-5pm, returning 5am-4pm. 25 pesos). Take the bus from **Valladolid** (2:30am, 47 pesos). To return, Valladolid/Mérida buses meet the ferry (5am). The Cancún bus leaves Chiquilá at 1pm. If you miss the last ferry, Chiquilá's hotel **Puerta del Sol** (☎ 875 01 21) will welcome you for 100 pesos.

In Holbox, a 24hr. **police** trio may be found sitting on the benches of **La Alcaldía Municipal** (☎ 875 21 10), the light orange building on the corner of Juárez and Díaz. The **Centro de Salud** (☎ 875 21 63 or 875 21 64), a blue and white building 200m from the dock, on the right side of the Juárez, houses a 24hr. doctor. There is **no bank** on the island. **Fax** and **telegram** service on the corner of Juárez and Díaz. (☎ 875 20 53. Open M-F 9am-3pm.) **Telmex** phones scattered throughout the village and park.

▮ ACCOMMODATIONS AND CAMPING

Finding cheap places to stay in Isla Holbox isn't a problem. Many family-run *posadas* cluster around the *zócalo*. Prices increase during high season. Free camping is available on the beach; just get a permit from the mayor's office, the Alcaldía Municipal (☎ 875 21 10), on the south side of the *zócalo*.

Posada D'Ingrid (☎ 5 20 70), one block north of the *zócalo*, at Morelos and Joaquín. Gleaming pink rooms with sparkling baths and fans open up to a *palapa*-roofed patio with speakers and card tables. Singles and doubles 150 pesos; triples 175 pesos.

Posada La Raza (☎ 875 20 72), on the west side of Parque Juárez. The owners pride themselves in making their *posada* feel like home. Clean rooms and new fixtures. Singles 100 pesos, with A/C 250 pesos; during high season 50 pesos more. Discounts for longer stays.

Posada Los Arcos (☎ 875 20 43), next door to Posada La Raza. Rooms have 2 beds and fans. A large, flamingo-filled courtyard. The only place in town to rent bikes (15 pesos per hr., 60 pesos per day). Singles 100 pesos; doubles 150 pesos, with A/C 250 pesos.

Posada Don Joaquín (☎ 875 20 88), just east of Parque Juárez, on Igualidad, is the third house on the left, with a Coca-Cola sign on the upper doorway. The simplest and cheapest rooms on *La Isla*. Rooms 40 pesos.

◖ FOOD

Among the many budget seafood restaurants on Isla Holbox is **Zarabanda,** one block south of Parque Juárez on Palomino. Excellent fish and seafood dishes (30-50 pesos) are prepared in this *palapa*-covered restaurant, named after a Caribbean rhythm. (☎ 875 20 94. Open daily 8am-9pm.) **Restaurant Edelyn,** Palomino, east of the park, grills large fish (40 pesos) and flips pizza in its two-story *palapa*. (☎ 875 20 24. Open daily 8am-12am.) **Restaurant "El Parque,"** on Juárez, one door down from Posada La Raza, serves fresh and inexpensive seafood. Chicken and a frosty beer 40 pesos. (☎ 875 20 28. Open daily 9am-10pm.) **La Isla del Colibri** (☎ 875 20 00), Juárez and Díaz, blends natural juices and shakes (12-20 pesos) and prepares salads with tropical fruits (20 pesos with your choice of yogurt and granola).

◖ 🎵 BEACHES AND ENTERTAINMENT

The tranquil demeanor of the Isla demands a trip to the beach. **North Beach** is fairly crowded with fishing boats, so it's better to rent a bike for the 8km trek east to **Punta Mosquito,** where a 25km stretch of virgin beach begins. East of the Holbox is **Isla de Pájaros,** home to nearly 40 species of birds including flamingos and pelicans. Next stop is **Ojo de Agua** (Yalahau), an inlet on the mainland fed by a subter-

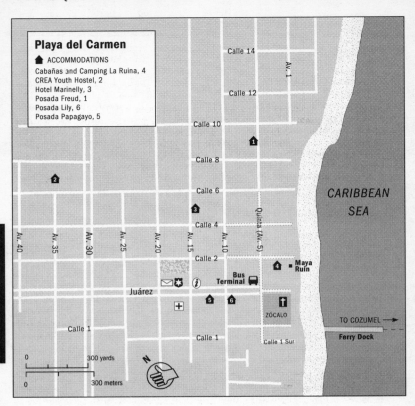

Playa del Carmen

♠ ACCOMMODATIONS

Cabañas and Camping La Ruina, 4
CREA Youth Hostel, 2
Hotel Marinelly, 3
Posada Freud, 1
Posada Lily, 6
Posada Papagayo, 5

ranean freshwater spring. Finally, across the lagoon that separates Isla Holbox from the mainland is **Isla Pasión,** named for the couples of birds and humans that "relax" there off-season. Tours of the islands can be arranged through private fishermen, or at the **Delfín Artículos de Pesca** house one block from the ocean on Juárez (4hr. tour 500 pesos. ☎875 20 18).

During the high season, Isla Holbox's restaurant/bar scene caters to tourists. To see *holboxeños* at their liveliest, cruise the brightly lit Parque Juárez at dusk, when friends and families gather to socialize, enjoy the playground, and watch the basketball games. Bob Marley fans will rejoice. A larger-than-life portrait of the man greets you as you cross the bridge/threshold into **Cariocas Restaurant and Disco,** on Igualdad, 1½ blocks east of the *zócalo.* For more natural entertainment, head to the north shore during the night. If conditions are right, you can witness *ardentía,* a rare and completely natural **phosphorescence.** Microorganisms respond to movement in the water by turning bright green; just kick the water or stir it with your hands to see the glow.

PLAYA DEL CARMEN   ☎9

Smack in the middle of Quintana Roo's legendary *Costa Turquesa* (Turquoise Coast), the inviting beach town of Playa del Carmen (pop. 20,000) serves as a convenient and pleasant crossroads for archaeologically inclined travelers en route to inland ruins, and for beach hunters heading to Cozumel and Cancún. Recently, however, "Playa" (as the locals call it) has become a destination in and of itself. Until recently a small fishing village, in the past decade its silky white sand and waters have made Playa a home-grown tourist paradise. The town's sidewalk shops, sunset happy hours, cafes, and breezy restaurants ideal for people-watching open onto the sunny pedestrian walkway, where jewelry artists and hammock vendors ply their trade.

⌐ TRANSPORTATION

Buses: From the station at the corner of Quinta and Juárez (☎873 01 09), ADO goes first-class to: **Chetumal** (4½hr., 5 per day 7:30am-midnight, 150 pesos); **Mexico City** (25hr.; 7am, noon, and 7pm; 610 pesos); **Orizaba** (14hr., noon and 7pm, 595 pesos); **Puebla** (23hr., 6pm, 654 pesos); **San Andrés** (9½hr., 3:30 and 10pm, 476 pesos); **Veracruz** (12hr., 3:30 and 10pm, 532 pesos); and **Villahermosa** (12hr., 6 per day noon-9pm, 370 pesos). Cristóbal Colón goes to: **Ocosingo** (13hr., 4:45pm, 350 pesos); **Palenque** (11hr., 4:45pm, 308 pesos); **San Cristóbal** (15hr., 4:45pm, 372 pesos); and **Tuxtla Gutiérrez** (16hr., 4:45pm, 410 pesos). ATS has second-class service to **Tulum** (1hr., 10 per day, 28 pesos). Premier goes to **Mérida** (5hr., 10 per day, 185 pesos), via **Ticul** (3½hr., 146 pesos).

⁊ PRACTICAL INFORMATION

Playa is located on the Maya Riviera, 34km south of Cancún and 90km north of Tulum. Two blocks south and one block east of the bus station, where Calle 3 hits the beach, are the docks for the ferry to Cozumel. **Juárez** and **Quinta** (Av. 5) intersect here. Juárez runs west from the beach to the Cancún-Chetumal road, **Highway 307**, 1.5km away. Quinta is a pedestrian walkway lined by popular shops and restaurants running perpendicular to Juárez and parallel to the beach. East-west *calles* increase by two in either direction; north-south *avenidas* increase by five.

Tourist Office: Information (☎872 28 04) located on the corner of Juárez and Av. 15. Open daily 8am-8pm.

Currency Exchange: Bital (☎873 02 72), on Juárez, 1 block west of the *zócalo*, exchanges currency and traveler's checks and has a 24hr. **ATM.** Open M-F 8am-7pm.

Laundry: Maya Laundry (☎873 02 61), on Quinta, 1 block north of the plaza, on the right. Wash and dry 13 pesos per kg. Dry cleaning. Open M-Sa 8am-8pm.

Emergency: ☎060.

Police: (☎873 02 91 or 873 02 42) on Juárez, 2 blocks west of the plaza. Open 24hr.

Pharmacy: Farmacia del Carmen (☎873 23 30), on Juárez, opposite the bus station. Open 24hr.

Medical Assistance: Centro de Salud (☎873 03 14), on the corner of Juárez, across from the post office. Some English spoken. Open 24hr.

Internet Access: Cibernet (☎873 21 65) on Quinta and Calle 8 in Plaza Rincón del Sol. 0.70 pesos per min. Open daily 7am-10:30pm.

Post Office: (☎873 03 00) on Juárez, 3 blocks from the plaza. Open M-F 8am-2:30pm, Sa 9am-1pm. **MexPost** in the same building. Open 9am-5pm.

Postal Code: 77710.

⌐ ACCOMMODATIONS AND CAMPING

With Playa's stunning recent growth, budget accommodations are becoming more scarce. During high season (Dec. 21-Apr. 15 and July 15-Sept. 15), prices shoot up especially high. Fortunately, as prices rise, so does quality. Most establishments lie along either **Quinta** or **Juárez,** close to the beach.

Posada Freud (☎873 06 01), on Quinta, between Calles 8 and 10. Palm trees and colorful hammocks persuade passersby to lounge in one of Freud's 11 pastel abodes, each one possessing its own personality and charm. Rooms 180 pesos and up; each additional person 50 pesos.

Posada Papagayo (☎873 24 97), Av. 15 between Calles 4 and 6. Spacious, nicely furnished rooms await the traveler who goes the extra mile to find Papagayo. Singles and doubles 150 pesos; triples 200 pesos. Prices rise 100 pesos in high season.

Posada Lily, the flaming pink building on Juárez, 1 block west of the plaza. Small, cushy beds in clean rooms with fans can be found at this noisy but convenient location near the bus stop. Singles 120 pesos; doubles 150 pesos; triples 200 pesos.

Hotel Marinelly (☎873 01 40), on Juárez, 1½ blocks west of the *zócalo*. Look for the yellow and blue building. Make sure to ask for one of their newly renovated rooms. Singles and doubles 150 pesos; triples 300 pesos; quads 350 pesos.

CREA Youth Hostel (☎873 15 08). On the corner of Av. 30 and Calle 8, about ½km northwest of the *zócalo*, CREA has a spacious lot with a soccer field and basketball courts. Single-sex dorms with bunk beds. 40 pesos per person. *Cabañas* with private bathrooms and A/C 200 pesos.

Cabañas and Camping La Ruina (☎873 04 05). Location, location, location! Beachfront *cabañas* and camping space on the beach, 200m north of the ferry dock, are a hop, skip, and jump away from Playa's main drag. Popular with Europeans, hostel-style *cabañas rústicas* have ceiling fans and tiny, stiff military beds, communal bathrooms, and cooking facilities. Lockers 5 pesos. Singles and doubles 150 pesos; triples 200 pesos. Hammock-space under the *palapa* 50 pesos; 15 pesos for a plastic hammock rental. Pitch a tent in the sand for 50 pesos; 15 pesos per extra camper.

FOOD

It can be hard to find a bargain in the glare of Quinta's flashy restaurants, although the occasional all-you-can-eat deal does come along. Cheaper fruit and *torta* experiences are found among the local hangouts along Juárez.

Media Luna (☎873 05 26), on Quinta between Calles 8 and 10. Whether you're digging into a healthful breakfast or simply sipping a frothy *frapuccino helado* (frozen frapuccino) sprinkled with cinnamon, you'll want to linger here in the padded corners. Tasty tropical fruit crepes (40 pesos) and luscious fruit platters topped with granola (25 pesos). Open daily 7am-11pm.

Sabor, 1½ blocks north of the *zócalo* on Quinta. Both locals and tourists enjoy *platillos vegetarianos* (vegetarian platters), coffee and pastry, and healthy breakfasts (15-30 pesos) under vines and a blossoming tree. Open daily 7am-11pm.

Café Tropical (☎873 21 11) on Quinta, across from Media Luna. Enjoy the generous portions served underneath a gigantic shady *palapa*. Smoothies 25 pesos; sandwiches 35 pesos; omelette on whole wheat bread 30 pesos. Open daily 7am-11pm.

Zas (☎873 05 20), on Quinta, between Calles 12 and 14. For a classy, jazzy dining experience, savor gourmet food with pizzazz at Zas. Although somewhat hidden and on the upscale side, it is well worth the one-time splurge. Entrees average 70 pesos. Open daily 7:30am-11:30pm.

SIGHTS AND BEACHES

Lined with palm trees and fringed by the turquoise waters of the Caribbean, Playa's beaches are sandy, white, and oh-so-relaxing. They are relatively free of seaweed and coral, covered instead with scantily (if at all) clad tourists. In search of an aquatic escape? Depending on your bargaining ability, 120-160 pesos will buy you an hour's worth of windsurfing. Windsurfing equipment and other gear can be rented from some of the fancier hotels just south of the pier, or from shacks a few hundred meters north. The **Abyss Dive Shop,** on the beach at Calle 12, will fulfill all your diving and snorkeling desires. It services 15-18 different dive sites and caters to all skill levels. ("Discover" scuba diving trips US$69. Open water courses US$345. Snorkeling equipment 50 pesos per day. ☎873 21 64. Open M-Sa, 8:30am-9pm, Su 8am-6pm.)

Come nightfall, the shops on Quinta close and the street is transformed from a busy thoroughfare of vendors into a glitzy nightlife hotspot. Sun-lovers recuperate from the day's rays by swaying in hammocks and jiving to guitar-strumming, flute-playing local musicians. At **Karen's Grill**, on Quinta, 1½ blocks north of the plaza, waiters start the party by making noise with trays, escorting women to the dance floor, and pouring *café flambe* in a waterfall style, all to the rhythm of salsa and merengue. Live South American music daily 6pm-midnight. (Cell ☎044 98 77 76 88. Happy Hour 10:30am-2am.) Swings replace the conventional bar stools at the **Blue Parrot Inn Palapa**, on the beach at Calle 12, voted one of the 10 best bars in the world by *Newsweek* magazine in 1996. Rock in your seats to the live music, which starts up every afternoon. (☎872 00 83. Open 11am-3am.) The techno beat pumps early in the afternoon and gets Europeans shakin' their thangs at **Kamikaze,** on the beach between Calles 4 and 6. Open bar US$19. Live music on weekends. (Cell ☎044 98 77 59 23. Open daily 8:30am-4am.) Check out **Capitan Tutix's**, Calle 4, a wooden ship on the beach where guests shake and groove to Latin and international dance hits (open daily 10pm-late). A hankering for Hollywood can be indulged at **Cinema Playa del Carmen,** four blocks west of the *zócalo* and one block north of Juárez (10-15 pesos).

AKUMAL ☎9

Akumal, "Place of the Turtles" in Maya, is a high-class, luxury resort catering to an older wealthier crowd, drawn to its older, wealthier activities. Don't let this deter you, fearless budget traveler, as there are some (well, at least one) deals to be had. The resort is a string of fancy, upscale hotels lining the bay but budget travelers should make a beeline for Ecocenter, the **Centro Ecólogico Akumal.**

⧉⧐ TRANSPORTATION AND PRACTICAL INFORMATION. Akumal is located on the Riviera Maya, 37km south of Playa del Carmen and 26km north of Tulum. The town proper is located to the west of Rte. 307, but the resort area is a short 5km walk toward the ocean. You can flag a bus down after you walk onto Rte. 307. Locals will usually be able to tell you when the next bus is due to pass.

Travel Agency TSA, right next to Ecocina, has it all: car and bike rental, telephone, fax and email, money exchange, airport transportation, and tours to nearly every sight. (Open M-Sa 9am-6pm, Su 8:30am-1:30pm. Exchange closes M-Sa 1-2pm.) The **supermarket Super Chomak,** on the right as you approach the main gates, stocks

XCARET: XCELLENT BUT XPENSIVE. Legend has it that the Maya bathed themselves in the clear sacred water of this *cenote* during their pilgrimage to Cozumel. Fifty kilometers south of Cancún and just a few kilometers south of Playa del Carmen, XCARET is a privately owned and operated theme park dedicated to Maya culture, the natural splendor of the Maya Riviera, and its own profit. A hefty 390-peso entrance fee will admit you to a massive seaside complex, complete with underground rivers, reconstructed Maya villages, archaeological ruins, an aviary, a museum, a beach, a lagoon, wading pools, dolphins, snorkeling and scuba diving tours, stables, botanical gardens, jungle cats, monkeys, and bats, and, yes, what you've been waiting for—a mushroom farm. It doesn't stop there. At night, XCARET puts on a variety of shows, from folkloric dances to ancient Maya rituals. (Buses to XCARET leave from the XCARET information center opposite Plaza Caracol in Cancún (9, 10, and 11am) or from Tulum (8:15am). Call ☎(98) 83 31 43 or (98) 83 31 44 for more information, or visit www.xcaretcancun.com.

YUCATÁN

DON'T HURT THE TURTLES Sea turtles are a natural attraction of the Riviera Maya. Unfortunately, the unfettered development and legions of tourists flooding the region haven't been as attractive to the sea turtles. The creatures nest through the summer, but, as of late, they haven't had much luck—encroaching hotels and beachfront properties have disturbed their nesting grounds. "What can I do to help?" you may ask. The best thing you can do is to give the turtles that are alive a greater chance of surviving. When you see a turtle while snorkeling, stay 5-6m away, or you may scare it from its food source. Also, do not litter on the beach; the turtles often mistake plastic bags for jellyfish and choke when they try to eat them.

all the essentials. (Open daily 7am-9pm.) **Laundry: Lavandería,** to your left 100m from the arch. (15 pesos per kg, 10kg minimum. Open M-Sa 7am-1pm and 5-7pm.) **Emergency:** ☎060. **Farmacia Tomy III,** on your left as you approach the gates, next to the basketball courts. (☎876 90 49. Open 9am-9pm.) **Postal Code:** 77760.

⬛⬜ FOOD AND ACCOMMODATIONS. The Centro Ecológico Akumal, or **Eco-center,** is the only budget option in Akumal. The center is a research facility where university students spend their summers earning credit by taking tropical marine science classes. Student rooms are sometimes available for rent. The large, well lit rooms (four beds in each) have private baths and some come with A/C. During university breaks, the Ecocenter gets busy; email or call ahead. There is a 50 peso deposit. (☎875 90 95; email ksr@caribe.net.mx. 100 pesos per night.)

Isla Cozumel

▲ CAMPING
Punta Morena, 1
Punta Chiqueros, 2

Like the hotels, most restaurants in Akumal go straight for the wallet. But a couple of places near the Ecocenter are great bargains. **Ecocina,** just outside the Ecocenter to the left of the welcoming arch, is a popular joint with students from the Ecocenter and workers from the resorts. *Torta McMaya* 35 pesos, milkshakes 20 pesos. (Open daily 8am-3pm.) Another good choice is **La Cueva del Pescador.** Grab a table outside, sliced from a giant tree trunk, or eat indoors and dig your toes into the sand (yup, sand indoors). Seafood is on everybody's plate here, and the entrees average a hefty 100 pesos. (☎875 92 00. Open 7am-9pm.)

⬛⬜ SIGHTS AND BEACHES. Step onto the beach of **Akumal Bay,** and you will see shores teeming with activity. Snorkelers, divers, and sunbathers all flock to the beach to take advantage of the tranquil waters, buffered by the offshore reef. The **Akumal Dive Shop** rents snorkeling equipment (US$8 per day), and organizes snorkeling and scuba trips to the ocean, caverns, and caves. Certification courses available. (US$30 for one tank dive, US$52 for two. ☎875 90 32. Open daily 8am-5pm.) In the mood to expand your environmental horizons? The Centro

Ecológico Akumal hosts lectures on a wide range of topics, from sea turtles to the modern Maya to theories of dinosaur extinction. (Tu-F 6:30pm. Free, but a modest donation accepted. ☎875 90 05; www.ceakumal.org.)

COZUMEL   ☎9

The calm diving mecca of Cozumel—"land of the swallows" in Mayan—has seen its share of history. The island was a key trading and ceremonial center for the Post-Classic Maya. In 1519, Hernán Cortés conquered Cozumel, the first in a series of conquests that would lead to the fall of the Aztec empire. After a period of desertion, the island became a 17th-century refuge for pirates such as Francis Drake and Jean Lafitte. The 1950s saw the island revitalized through the efforts of the French diver Jacques Cousteau, who called attention to the nearby **Palancar Reef,** the second largest barrier reef in the world. The initial diving craze has died down somewhat, and Cozumel today is a popular getaway for tourists wishing to explore Mexico's natural beauty without saying goodbye to the luxury resorts and eager service. Much of the island, however, remains undeveloped and ripe for exploration. Miles of empty white beach and dozens of Maya ruins greet the tourists who muster the energy to leave the town's city, San Miguel de Cozumel (pop. 75,000), and venture into the island itself.

▐ TRANSPORTATION

GETTING THERE

Most people reach the island via ferry from Playa del Carmen (to the west) or Puerto Morelos (to the north). Ferries from **Puerto Morelos** (☎872 09 50) transport cars to and from Cozumel (2½hr.; leaves at 5am and 2pm; 50 pesos, with a car 550 pesos). While tourist vehicles supposedly have priority, the car ferry is nevertheless inconvenient and unpredictable. If you're set on it, the tourist office recommends securing a spot in line 12 hours in advance. Ferries between **Playa del Carmen** and Cozumel run frequently. Tickets can be bought at the dock in Cozumel or from the booth on Playa's plaza (45min., 12 per day, round-trip 122 pesos). If you are coming from Cancún, an alternative to the bus-ferry ordeal is the 20-minute **air shuttle** operated by Aerocaribe (☎872 08 77).

GETTING AWAY

Airport: (☎872 04 85) 2km north of town. **Aerocaribe** (☎872 08 77), **Continental** (☎872 04 87), and **Mexicana** (☎872 29 45) serve Cozumel.

Ferries: Passenger ferries leave for **Playa del Carmen** from the dock at the end of Juárez (every hr. starting at 4am, one-way 61 pesos). Arrive early; ferries sell out several minutes before departure. Buy tickets at the corner of Melgar and the dock. Car ferries (☎872 08 27) leave from the dock south of the main dock bound for **Puerto Morelos.**

✦ ▐ ORIENTATION AND PRACTICAL INFORMATION

The island of Cozumel is 18km east of the Quintana Roo coast and 85km south of Isla Mujeres. At 53km long and 14km wide, Cozumel is Mexico's largest Caribbean island. The island's main town, **San Miguel de Cozumel** (home to the island's ferry docks), is located in the middle of the west coast. Downtown streets are clearly labeled and numbered with stubborn logic. Beaches are located both to the north and south of town, and the rest of the island is relatively untouristed and easily explored by bike, moped, or safari—if you don't mind occasionally spine-wrenching road conditions, that is. You can catch a **taxi** (☎872 02 36 or 872 00 41) easily as you come off the dock to the airport (34 pesos) or to Punta Moreno (100 pesos).

YUCATÁN

San Miguel de Cozumel

🏠 ACCOMMODATIONS
Hotel Flores, 4
Hotel Pepita, 3
Hotel Posada Edém, 1
Posada Letty, 2

TOURIST, FINANCIAL, AND LOCAL SERVICES

Tourist Office: (☎872 09 72), on the 2nd fl. of "Plaza del Sol," the building to the left of Bancomer, on the plaza. Open M-F 9am-2pm.

Consulates: While there are no consulates on Cozumel, **Bryan Wilson** (☎872 06 54; a Beach Boy of a different sort), who works closely with the Mérida US consulate, provides unofficial, free assistance to English-speaking travelers.

Currency Exchange: BanNorte (☎872 17 71), Av. 5 Norte, between Juárez and Calle 2, exchanges traveler's checks. Open M-F 9am-4pm. **Bancomer** (☎872 05 50), on the plaza, has the same rates but charges a flat fee of US$0.50 per check. Open M-F 9am-4:30pm, Sa 10am-2pm. **BITAL** (☎872 01 42), on the plaza, has a 24hr. **ATM.** Open M-F 9am-2:30pm, Sa 10am-1pm.

Car Rental: LE$$ Pay (☎872 47 44 or 872 19 47), on Melgar 628, about 1km south of town. VW Safaris (US$25 per day), jeeps, and mopeds available. Discounts for multiple-day rentals. Open daily 8am-8pm. **Executive** (☎872 13 08), Calle 1 Sur #19, between Av. 5 and 10. 15% off if you grab a coupon book from the ferry.

Moped Rental: Available in the lobby of Hotel Posada Edem (see **Accommodations**) from **Arrendadon Sol y Mar** (☎872 11 66). US$20 per day.

Bike Rental: Rentadora Cozumel (☎872 11 20 or 872 15 03) on Av. 10 at Calle 1 Sur. 172 pesos per day. 6pm return. US$25 deposit required. Open daily 8am-8pm.

Bookstore: Fama (☎872 50 20), on Av. 5, between Juaréz and Calle 2 Norte. CDs, books, magazines, and maps in English. Open daily 9am-10pm.

Supermarket: Sedenu (☎872 05 72), Av. Melgar and Calle 12 Norte, 6 blocks north of the dock.

Laundry: Express Lavandería (☎872 29 32), Salas, between Av. 5 and Av. 10. Open M-Sa 8am-9pm, Su 8:30am-3pm. Washer 15 pesos, dryer 11 pesos per 10 min.

EMERGENCY AND COMMUNICATIONS

Emergency: ☎060, or knock on Mr. Wilson's white house at Av. 15 and Calle 13 Sur.

Police: (☎872 04 09) on Calle 11 Sur near Rafael Melgar, in the Palacio Municipal. Some English spoken.

Red Cross: (☎872 10 58), on Av. 20 Sur at Salas. Open 24hr.

Pharmacy: Farmacia Kiosco (☎872 24 85), on the *zócalo* near Hotel López. Everything for the sun-happy or sun-sick tourist. Open M-Sa 8am-10pm, Su 9am-10pm.

Medical Assistance: General Hospital (☎872 51 82), Calle 11 Sur and Av. 20.

Fax: (☎872 00 56) next to the post office.

Internet Access: Internet Café, (☎872 00 76) Calle 1 Sur and Av. 10. Ten pesos per minute, minimum 10min.

Post Office: (☎872 01 06) off Melgar, just south of Calle 7 Sur along the sea. Open M-F 8am-5pm, Sa 9am-1pm.

Postal Code: 77600.

▟ ACCOMMODATIONS AND CAMPING

Since they cater primarily to foreign divers with cash to burn, hotels in Cozumel are generally more expensive than those on the mainland, and extra pesos do not guarantee higher-quality rooms. Resist being roped into a pricey package deal when stepping off the ferry. Try to secure a room before noon, especially during peak season. Camping, particularly on the secluded spots at **Punta Morena** and **Punta Chiqueros** on the east side of the island, might be the best option. Those thinking about camping should check in with the naval headquarters on Melgar near the post office, as a permit may be required.

Hotel Posada Edém, Calle 2 Nte. 124 (☎872 11 66), between Av. 10 and 5 Nte., across from the taxi station. From the dock, go left 1 block, turn right, and walk 2 blocks. Small, functional rooms with 2 beds, fans, and *agua purificada* in lobby. One of the cheapest places in town. Singles 140 pesos; doubles 160 pesos; extra person 40 pesos.

Posada Letty (☎872 02 57), Calle 1 Sur 272, between Av. 10 and 15. Their business card promises "Cleanliness-Order-Morality." We can only vouch for the first. Big green rooms have big windows with big beds and feel more like a house than a hotel. Singles 180 pesos; doubles 200 pesos; extra person 50 pesos. Prices rise 10% in high season.

Hotel Flores, Salas 72, (☎872 14 29) at Av. 5. Ask for a room with an ocean view. Singles and doubles 200 pesos; with A/C 250 pesos. Prices rise 10% in the high season.

Hotel Pepita, 15 Av. Sur 120 (☎872 00 98), just south of Calle 1 Sur. It might cost you a little extra, but private bath, refrigerator, A/C, and free coffee might be worth it. 220 pesos per person; 50 pesos per additional person. Prices remain the same year-round.

▟ FOOD

Food in Cozumel is expensive. Avoid places that advertise in English—they are probably pricier. Several moderately priced restaurants are located a few blocks from the *centro*, and small cafes are tucked away on side streets. The **market** at Salas between Av. 20 and 25 Sur, has fresh meat, fish, and fruit. The *loncherías* next door might be the most authentic and cheapest places in town. For a sweet treat, stroll into **Panificadora Cozumel,** on Calle 2 Nte. between Av. 5 Nte. and Melgar, where pastries and baked goods melt in your mouth for pocket change. (Open daily 6am-9:30pm.)

▨ **Casa Denis** (☎872 00 67), across from the flea market on the *zócalo.* Be a part of *La Familia Denis,* the first traditional restaurant in Cozumel. Home-cooked recipes complemented by photos of Che Guevara fishing with Fidel Castro. Breakfast (25 pesos); sandwiches (20-30 pesos); *comida regional,* (20-30 pesos). Open daily 7:30am-midnight.

El Abuelo Gerardo (☎872 10 12), on Av. 10, between Juárez and Calle 2 Nte. near the church is a mellow place to grab an ice-cold afternoon beer and enjoy generous portions of *antojitos* (20-40 pesos) and fish fillet (45 pesos). Or, if you prefer, sit down to a hearty breakfast (25 pesos). Open daily 7:30am-10pm.

San Francisco Restaurant, on the southwest coast of the island, km 15. Grab chilled drinks or freshly squeezed tropical drinks with chips, guacamole, and salsa. *Antojitos* (15-37 pesos); *pescado entero* (whole fish) is cooked in ten different styles.

Rock-n-Java Caribbean Café (☎8724 40 5), Melgar 602 near LE$$ Pay between Calle 9 and 11 Sur. Healthy breakfasts with fruit-topped multi-grain French toast (40 pesos), veggie salads (35 pesos), homemade soups (30 pesos), and flavored coffee (25-45 pesos) are all served with a view of the Caribbean, surrounded by black and white crusty sailor photos. Open Su-F 7am-11pm, Sa 7am-2pm.

The Coffee Bean, Calle 3 Sur, next to Pizza Hut and the shore. Freshly baked homemade desserts such as strawberry cheesecake, pecan pie, apple pie, and brownie. Espresso ice cream and coffee from Chiapas and Veracruz (15 pesos). Open 7:30am-11pm.

◆🌀 SIGHTS AND BEACHES

DIVING

Many visitors make the trek to Cozumel with one goal in mind: diving and snorkeling in the beautiful coral reefs around the island. If you arrive *sans* equipment, have no fear: dive shops proliferate like bunnies in Cozumel. Over one hundred shops operate out of the island with a concentration on the waterfront or along Calle 3 Sur, between Melgar and Av. 10. The standard rate for snorkeling equipment is US$4-8 per day. Scuba diving gear is, of course, more expensive (US$50-60 per day). Always consider safety before price; look for shops with **ANOAAT** (Asociación Nacional de Operadores de Actividades Aquaticas Turístico) affiliation.

Del Mar Aquatics (☎872 08 44), 200m north of La Ceiba Hotel, 7km south of town, rents snorkeling (US$6 per day) and scuba equipment (US$45 per day), and offers deep-sea fishing, night and day dives, and snorkeling trips. Open daily 7am-7:30pm.

Blue Bubble Divers (☎872 18 65; www.bluebubble.com), on Av. 5 at Calle 3 Sur, has a friendly, English-speaking staff and a choice of 20 reefs to visit. Snorkeling equipment US$6 per day; 1½hr. single-tank dive US$45. Open daily 7am-9pm.

Aqua Safari, (☎872 01 01) Melgar at Calle 5 Sur. Single-tank dive US$35; 2hr. snorkeling boat trip US$20. Open daily 7am-1pm and 4-6:30pm.

Once you have your equipment ready, mopeds or bikes are the best way of getting to the ideal spot. Otherwise, you might have to fork over money for an expensive taxi. Snorkelers will want to head toward south of town, toward **Playa La Ceiba** and **Chankanaab National Park.** Divers will want to head toward one of the reefs that hug the southeast side of the island. Note that some reefs (like the Colombia and Maracaibo Reefs) have strong currents and should only be attempted by more experienced divers. Be sure to ask before diving. Those looking to expend minimal effort might consider joining a pre-packaged excursion. (US$20-30 per day for snorkeling trips; US$60 and up for scuba dives, depending on skill level; US $300 for full certification courses.)

Don't touch the coral! We repeat: don't touch the coral! You will kill the coral. Then you'd feel pretty bad about yourself, wouldn't you.

BEACHES

Beachcombers should not be disheartened by the beach near San Miguel. The island's true treasures lie to the north, east, and south of town. Heading south will bring you to **Playa La Ceiba** near the Hotel La Ceiba. The beach has good snorkeling and a plane wreck from the film "Survive." Further south, **Playa Francisco** and **Playa Palancar** are some of the best beaches on the island, and are jump-off points for exploring the **Palancar Reef.** At the southern tip of the island, **Punta Celarain** has a lighthouse and sand dunes that buffer the beach. The top of the lighthouse offers a thrilling view of Cozumel's southern shores. The east coast of the island is lined with dozens of beautiful and less touristed beaches that make good picnic and camping spots. While the beaches offer tempting and magnificent turquoise waters, the water has a strong undertow and can be turbulent. Use caution.

SIGHTS

The **Chankanaab National Park,** 9km south of downtown, contains a beautiful bay circled by a botanical garden, museum, and a restaurant. The clear, oval lagoon nearby used to be open to swimmers, but the excessive traffic was found to be damaging to the coral; the lagoon has since been declared off limits. The real attractions are now the abundant fish and coral in the bay, which is open to snorkelers. The park's museum focuses on its natural resources, and houses photographs of the underwater caves in the lagoon. (Open daily 7am-6pm. 120 pesos.)

Cozumel, a former Maya trading center, is littered with dozens of ruins. None of them, unfortunately, are well preserved. **El Cedral,** the oldest ruins on the island, are just south of Playa San Francisco. The only excavated and reconstructed ruins are the ones at **San Gervasio,** which include the remains of an observatory and several arches. Take Juárez out of town. After 8km, a "San Gervasio" sign marks a gravel road branching to the left. Follow the road another 6km. (Open daily 8am-5pm. Admission 40 pesos, Su 20 pesos.) The small, air-conditioned **Museo de la Isla de Cozumel,** on the waterfront between Calles 4 and 6, is filled with photographs, poetry, coral, marine and jungle trivia, and sculptures. (☎872 14 75 or 872 14 34. Open daily 9am-6pm. US$3.)

 NIGHTLIFE

Most bars and clubs cluster around the *zócalo* in downtown San Miguel. Here, divers kick back after a day at the reefs, and tourists—fresh from cruise ships—unload their cash.

Carlos n' Charlie's (☎872 01 91), on Melgar, 1 block north of the dock. Entertains North Americans with drinks, slammer contests, and stupid rules of the house, the last of which is "there are no rules." Open daily 10am-1am.

SHOWDOWN OF THE NOT-SO-O.K. CORAL

The Palancar Reef of Cozumel, part of the second-largest reef system in the world, draws legions of scuba fanatics eager to explore its dramatically colorful depths. However, few visitors realize the biological importance of those majestic coral pillars. Coral is to a reef as topsoil is to a rainforest; if the coral is destroyed, the entire reef's ecosystem disintegrates. International law prohibits the harvesting of coral, but it does not forbid the purchase or exportation of coral-derived crafts. Several shops in Cozumel sell goods made from coral. By patronizing these establishments, tourists heighten the demand for coral, and contribute to the destruction of the splendorous reefs they have come to see. So no matter how cute a trinket they're selling, **don't buy coral.**

Joe's Restaurant and Reggae Bar (☎872 32 75), on Av. 10, between Salas and Calle 3 Sur. A live band starts it up at 10:30pm, and the place keeps kicking to island tunes until the wee hours of the morning. Beers 35 pesos. Open daily until 3am.

Neptuno (☎872 15 37), Calle 11 Sur, 5 blocks south of the plaza, has multi-level dance floors blasted by lasers and throbbing bass. Cover 75 pesos. Open daily 9pm-late.

Fat Tuesday, right off the dock, 50m in on Juaréz. Ever wonder where the tourists get their tall, fluorescent drinks? This is the place. The staff cracks jokes over the sound system and boozers belt it out on the karaoke machine. Open daily until late.

Coco Wook, (☎872 03 16) Melgar, right across from the dock. Get hypnotized by the non-stop techno and the jungle decor. No cover. Happy Hour Su-F. Open 9pm until late.

PUERTO MORELOS   ☎9

In Puerto Morelos (pop. 3000), the pace of life is comparable to service at a fine restaurant: interminably slow and well worth the wait. Here, life-long residents don't remember the street names, and location is measured relative to surroundings, not according to name and number. The pride of Puerto Morelos is its unspoiled coral reef, located 600m off shore; the townspeople do everything they can to preserve it. Waterskiing and parasailing are forbidden here, along with multi-million dollar resorts and other Cancún-style hedonistic activities. Puerto Morelos is a sleepy fishermen's town, and its residents intend to keep it that way.

⌷ TRANSPORTATION. Buses can be caught at Highway 307, 2km west of town, going to **Playa del Carmen** and **Cancún** (every 30min.). To get to the *centro*, take a taxi (13 pesos). A car-carrying **ferry** going to Cozumel leaves from the port half a kilometer south of the *zócalo* (5am and 2pm; 50 pesos, with car 550 pesos).

■⌷ ORIENTATION AND PRACTICAL INFORMATION. Puerto Morelos is located on the east coast of Quintana Roo, 30km south of Cancún and 30km north of Playa del Carmen. Highway 307 runs north-south, and passes 2km west of the town center. The town itself is laid out in a simple grid, organized around a central *zócalo*, which borders the beach.

The one-stop shop, **Marant Travel** (☎871 03 32), Tulum 1, on the southwest corner of the *zócalo*, offers **tourist information,** as well as bike rentals (10 pesos per hr., 50 pesos per day), car rentals (US$45-73 per day), and Internet access. **Mor Ex,** at the southwest corner of the *zócalo*, provides currency exchange. **Emergency:** ☎060. **Farmacia San José Obrero,** Rojo Gomez 2, is on the west side of the *zócalo*. (☎871 00 53. Open 8am-2pm and 4-10pm.) The police are located in the northwest corner of the *zócalo*. Punta Morelos has no post office; **mail** is handled by a friendly—if enigmatic—fellow called Sebastian. **Postal Code:** 77580.

⌷⌷ ACCOMMODATIONS AND FOOD. Budget accommodations are scarce in Puerto Morelos and the best option is probably camping on the beach. Request permission from the police and they might let you camp for a couple of nights. **Amar Inn,** between Mexicano and Cárdenas, north of the *zócalo*, holds prime real estate right on the beach. Run by the gracious Ana Luisa, the inn is comprised of three private cabins and three rooms. (☎871 00 26. US$30.) **Posada Amor,** on Rojo Gomez, south of the *zócalo*, is a maze of brightly colored courtyards. Some rooms have private baths. Common room contains a weight room and books. (☎871 00 33. Rooms 150 pesos and up.) Budget-friendly restaurants are also hard to come by in Puerto Morelos. It's best to stick to the *zócalo*, where prices tend to be more reasonable. **El Café de la Plaza** (☎871 05 13), on the southwest corner of the *zócalo* is a place where it's good to eat *au natural*. This cafe offers fresh fruits, salads, juices, and sandwiches (20-30 pesos).

🔲🔁 SIGHTS AND BEACHES. On June 5, 2000, Puerto Morelos was honored with a presidential visit and a dedication of its coral reef as a national park. Snorkeling and scuba diving are the best way to explore the beach. If you left your equipment at home, several dive shops dot the *zócalo*. **Secret Reef** (☎871 02 44) and **Twin Dolphin Marina** (☎871 01 53) both will gladly indulge your aquatic interests. Consider yourself more of a landlubber? Look no further than **Goyo** and his custom **Custom Jungle Adventures** (☎871 01 78), Rojo Gomez, just north of the *zócalo*. Goyo will guide you inland and show you Maya villages, trees with medicinal properties, and refreshing *cenotes*. Tours leave from his palapa (US$40-80).

Puerto Morelos' nightlife scene is not particularly thriving. If you are lucky enough to arrive during the **Marina Festival** (beginning Jun. 1), however, you can enjoy three days of fishing contests, amusement park rides, music, and dancing.

TULUM ☎9

On the edge of the Etaib (Black Bees) jungle, atop a rocky cliff, stands the walled Maya "City of the Dawn." While the ruins do not rival those of Uxmal or Chichén Itzá in terms of scale, many of the buildings are still intact, and their towering presence above the breaking waves of the Caribbean is unforgettable. First settled in the 4th century AD, Tulum was the oldest continuously inhabited city in the New World when the Spanish arrived. Today, sun worshippers of a different kind tramp to the ancient port, complementing their sightseeing with healthy doses of swimming. Tulum's temples and their natural backdrop, gracing book covers everywhere, are attracting a rising number of daytrippers from Cancún. There are two bases for exploring the ruins of Tulum: either the village of Tulum (pop. 16,000) or the numerous *cabañas* lining the beach south of the ruins are the perfect starting off points for an unforgettable experience in Tulum.

YUCATÁN

🔳 TRANSPORTATION

GETTING AROUND
Taxis are available at the crossing point, the *crucero*, in Pueblo Tulum, along Rte. 307, and at various *cabañas*, but they are quite expensive. The best budget option is to rent a bicycle and give your legs an old-fashioned workout. To get any of the sites near Tulum, wave down a *colectivo* as it passes by on Rte. 307. Some travelers wind up hitchhiking from site to site along the highway.

GETTING AWAY
Buses: There are two **ADO** bus stations. One is on the east side of Rte. 307, right in the middle of the Pueblo. The small waiting room is sandwiched between two currency exchange booths. ADO heads to: **Mexico City** (22hr., 1:10pm, 679 pesos), **Veracruz** (12hr., 4:30pm, 485 pesos). Second class buses go to **Cancún** (every hr., 40 pesos); **Playa del Carmen** (every hr., 18 pesos); **Chetumal** (8:10pm, 93 pesos); **San Andrés Tuxtla** (4:30pm, 427 pesos), **San Cristóbal de las Casas** (4:30pm, 302 pesos), **Mérida** (6:15am and 7am, 80 pesos), **Chichén Itzá** (11am and 6pm, 43 pesos), and **Palenque** (4:30pm, 260 pesos). There is also an ADO terminal located at the *crucero*, next to the Hotel Copal.

🔳🔁 ORIENTATION AND PRACTICAL INFORMATION

Located 42km southeast of Cobá, 63km south of Playa del Carmen, and 127km south of Cancún, Tulum is the southernmost link in a chain of tourist attractions on the Caribbean coast of Quintana Roo, known as the **Riviera Maya,** and the eastern extreme of the major Maya archaeological sites. Tulum sprawls over three separate areas: the **crucero** (the crossroads), the beach **cabañas,** and **Pueblo Tulum.** Arriving in Tulum from Cancún on Rte. 307, buses first stop at the *crucero*, a few km before town. Here, a couple of restaurants, hotels, and overpriced minimarts huddle 800m west of the ruins. The access road turns south at the ruins, leading to food and lodging at the *cabañas*, 2km farther down the road. Pueblo Tulum, 4km south of the *crucero*, also offers a handful of roadside restaurants and services.

Tourist Office: There is no tourist office, though a few stands at the ruins can provide sketchy maps. The hotel *cabañas* should also be able to provide information.

Currency Exchange: At the *crucero* in the Hotel Acuario or next to the bus office in Pueblo Tulum. There are currently **no banks** in Tulum; travelers should plan accordingly.

Police: (☎871 20 55), in the Delegación Municipal, 2 blocks past the post office.

Pharmacy: Farmacia, on the west side of 307, 3 blocks from the Pueblo (coming from the north). Open 24hr.

Supermarket: El Che, at the entrance to the Cabañas Cepal. Open 24hr.

Medical Assistance: Centro de Salud. Take the first left heading south from the bus station, and then another quick left. Open 24hr. for emergencies.

Internet Access: (☎871 20 00) in the same building as the post office. 30 pesos per hr. Open daily 9am-8pm.

Post Office: a few hundred meters into town on Rte. 307. Open M-F 9am-4pm. **Postal Code:** 77780.

▌ ACCOMMODATIONS AND CAMPING

Choosing accommodations in Tulum is a no-brainer. Head for the *cabañas* strung along the beach south of the ruins. They can't be beat in terms of price and location, a short walk to the ancient Maya ruins. Chill with the mellow international travelers, listen to local singers, and perfect your tan. Bring mosquito netting and repellent; bugs are nasty.

▓ **Cabañas Copal** (☎871 22 64). Perched atop cliffs overlooking crashing waves, these *cabañas* (located 5km south of the ruins on the beachfront road) make you feel like you're living in your own "city of the dawn." Common bath and shower. Restaurant and convenience store located on the property. Mention that *Let's Go* sent you and get a discount. *Cabañas* 100-150 pesos, high season 200-250 pesos.

Cabañas Santa Fe, off the paved road less than 1km south of the ruins. Follow the signs to Don Armando's and turn left. If you don't mind getting sand everywhere, you can shack up with backpackers from all over the world. No seasonal price changes, but be prepared to stand in line during high season; no reservations allowed. Hammocks 70 pesos and up; *cabaña económico* (i.e. an empty room) 100 pesos; beds 140 pesos.

Don Armando Cabañas (email don_Armando_mx@yahoo.com), on the access road ½km south of the ruins, is a humble paradise with a basketball court. The *cabañas* are generally solid and secure, and the communal facilities are more than outhouses. *Cabañas* 100-145 pesos; rooms with private baths 190 pesos. No seasonal price changes.

Hotel Copal (☎871 22 64), located 800m west of the ruins at the junction with Rte. 307. The sole non-*cabaña* option. Simple rooms with private baths won't dent your wallet. Call ahead in the high season. Double bed 100 pesos; queen size 150 pesos.

◖ FOOD

Although points of interest in Tulum tend to be rather spread out, hearty and inexpensive food is never too far away. The *pueblo*, the *crucero*, and the beachside *cabañas* have satisfying restaurants as well as *mini-supers;* the former are slightly cheaper and provide sustenance for daytrips.

▓ **Restaurante Santa Fe**, at the Cabañas Santa Fe. Reggae tunes, salsa rhythms, and local guitarists are the perfect compliment to the fresh fish (40-60 pesos) and *cabaña*-made breakfasts (30-40 pesos). Happy Hour 8-10pm. Open daily 7am-11pm.

El Gaucho Veloz (☎871 22 64), located in the Hotel Copal at the *crucero*. Listen to some well-chosen tunes as you dig into a giant, all-inclusive breakfast (45 pesos) or fresh seafood (50 pesos). Open daily 7am-7pm.

Crocodilos, under a red awning, half a block north of the bus station in town. The reggae jams as you chow down on seafood (65 pesos). Open daily 10am-midnight.

Don Cafeto (☎871 22 07), just north of Crocodilos. The green-checked table cloths and more-than-ample bar encourage guests to lounge. Shrimp cocktails 45 pesos, tacos 32 pesos. Open daily 7am-11pm.

◗ BEACHES

THE BEACH. Swimming, splashing, and tanning on the beach are popular ways to end a hot day in Tulum, and nude bathing is no longer a rare phenomenon. Offshore, waves crash over Tulum's **barrier reef,** the largest in the Americas; it runs the full length of the Yucatán Peninsula and Belize. Although the water is not as clear as at Xel-Ha (see p. 641) or Akumal (see p. 629), the fish are just as plentiful. To mingle with them, rent scuba and snorkeling equipment from the **dive shop** at Cabañas Santa Fe. (Snorkeling 60 pesos per day. ☎871 20 96. Open daily 8am-3:30pm.) The shop also plans trips to the reef and a nearby *cenote*. Another option is **Punta Piedra,** 5km south of the ruins, a bit past Cabañas Copal. They rent snorkeling equipment (50 pesos per day) and tanks (US$35 for one, US$60 for two). They also offer bike rental (60 pesos per day, 50 per day for two or more days) and a spectacular jungle tour (200 pesos), which includes visits to multiple *cenotes*. (Open daily 8am-8pm.)

CENOTES. The hidden treasures of Tulum are its numerous *cenotes*, sunk into the jungle throughout the area. *Cenotes* are places where the ground opens up to reveal a pool of fresh water below, actually part of a massive underground network of rivers. The rivers work their way through the limestone shelf on which the Yucatán Peninsula sits and out to the sea. **Cenote Escondido** and **Cenote Cristal** are both 3km south of the intersection of Rte. 307 and the road to Cobá (admission 10 pesos). Following the road to Cobá west out of town, you will come across the **Cenote Calaveras** after 1.6km (free). Look for a newly constructed house on your right, and follow the path through the roads behind it. Continue on the road to the **Grand Cenote,** 1.5km farther on and clearly marked with a sign (40 pesos). The *cenotes* are generally open from 8am to 5pm.

◉ THE ARCHAEOLOGICAL SITE OF TULUM

The ruins lie a brisk 10-minute walk east of Rte. 307 from the crucero; *the amusement park-style train (15 pesos) covers the distance in slightly less time. Admission tickets are sold at a booth to the left of the parking lot and at the entrance to the ruins. Open daily 8am-6pm. 25 pesos; Su free. Guided tours available; inquire at the crucero.*

Perhaps no other Maya ruins capture the imagination as do the beautiful ruins at Tulum ("Wall" or "Fortification" in Mayan). Perched on a cliff overlooking the calm, blue Caribbean, the ruins are a testament to the Maya aesthetic. It was precisely Tulum's position on the coast that the Maya valued. The city was first inhabited around AD 500, in the middle of the Maya Classic Period. It was not until well into the Post-Classic Period, however, that Tulum reached its zenith; all the buildings at the site date from this period. At its peak, the city was probably used as something of a fortification with dwellings inside for nobles and priests. The city thrived until its defeat at the hands of the Spanish in 1544, and, even after its defeat, was used to fend off English, Dutch, and French pirates. In 1847, Tulum provided refuge for Maya fleeing government forces during the Caste War.

YUCATÁN

THE WALL. The first thing visitors see in Tulum is the impressive dry-laid wall surrounding the city center's three landlocked sides. The wall, made of small rocks wedged together, was originally 3.6m thick and 3m high. It shielded the city from aggressive neighbors from other Maya city-states and prevented all but the 150 or so priests and governors of Tulum from entering the city for most of the year. Representations of the Maya "Descending God" cover the western walls and are illuminated every evening by the rays of the setting sun.

HOUSE OF THE HALACH UINIK AND THE PALACIO. Just inside and to the left of the entrance lie a grave and the remains of platforms that once supported huts. Behind these platforms are the **House of the Halach Uinik** (the House of the Ruler), characterized by a traditional Maya four-column entrance and the **Palacio,** the largest residential building in Tulum.

TEMPLO DE LOS FRESCOS (TEMPLE OF THE PAINTINGS). The temple is a stellar example of Postclassic Maya architecture and was most likely built in three separate stages. Well-preserved 600-year-old murals inside the temple depict deities intertwined with serpents, fruits, flowers, and corn offerings. Masks of Itzamná, the Maya Creator, occupy the northwest and southwest corners of the building.

EL CASTILLO (THE CASTLE). The most prominent structure in Tulum, El Castillo looms to the east over the rocky seaside cliff, commanding a view of the entire walled city. The pyramid was built in three separate stages, and was most likely not intended to be a pyramid after all. What is now visible was most likely built around the 12th or 13th centuries AD. A double-headed, feathered serpent is sprawled across the facade, and a diving god in the center. This diving god contains bee-like imagery, perhaps alluding to the importance of honey in Caribbean trade. In more recent times, El Castillo served as a lighthouse, aiding returning fishermen in finding the only gap in the barrier reef just off the shore. In front of the temple is the **sacrificial stone** where the Maya held battle ceremonies and warrior-prisoners were sacrificed.

TEMPLO DE LA SERIE INICIAL (TEMPLE OF THE INITIAL SERIES). On a plaza to the southwest of El Castillo is the Temple of the Initial Series. Named after a stela found here, the temple bears a date that corresponded to the beginning of the Maya religious calendar in the year AD 761.

TEMPLO DEL DIOS DESCENDENTE. The Temple of the Descending God, with a fading relief of a feathered, armed deity diving from the sky, stands on the opposite side of the plaza. Archaeologists believe that this figure, seen at various buildings in Tulum, symbolized the setting sun.

TEMPLO DE VIENTOS (TEMPLE OF THE WINDS). Perched on its own precipice on the northeast side of the beach, the Temple of the Winds was designed with special acoustics to act as a storm-warning system. Sure enough, before Hurricane Gilbert struck the site in 1988, the temple's airways dutifully whistled their alarm.

⚑ DAYTRIPS FROM TULUM

SIAN KA'AN BIOSPHERE RESERVE
Follow the coast road for 7km south of Tulum and you will come to the "Maya Arch," marking the entrance to the 1.5 million acre Sian Ka'an Biosphere reserve.

Sian Ka'an, comprising roughly 10% of the state of Quintana Roo, was set aside by a federal decree on January 20, 1988. It encompasses tropical forests, *cenotes*, savannas, mangroves, lagoons, and 70 mi. of coral reef. It is home to 1200 species of flora, 339 species of birds,103 species of mammals, and 23 Maya archaeological sites. The best way to see Sian Ka'an is by boat. You can drive a car along the coast for 57km before arriving in Punta Allen, but all you will see is a wall of dense jungle on either side. Also, the road is not carefully maintained; a sudden storm could spell danger. A variety of establishments offer tours of Sian Ka'an. Perhaps the first place you should check is the **Amigos de Sian Ka'an,** located in Cancún at Cobá (☎98 84 95 83; email sian@cancun.rce.com.mx). The main office for the reserve is also in Cancún, at Kukulcán km 4.5 (☎98 83 05 63). **Escape Tours** shuttles you from Playa del Carmen to the reserves and then into a boat for your final destination, the lagoons. (US$110. ☎98 71 3 18 42. Open 7am-6pm.) **Hidden Paradise,** out of Punta Allen, is cheaper, but the tour is shorter. (2hr., US$25 for 4 people. ☎871 20 81, 871 20 01, or 871 20 91.)

XEL-HA

Xel-Ha lies 15km north of Tulum. Get on any northbound bus and ask to be let off at Xel-Ha (5 pesos). Taxis charge exorbitant rates. Getting back to Tulum at the end of the day, when buses begin to come less and less frequently, can be challenging. Vigorously wave down a bus on its way to Tulum or Cancún. Locals will usually be able to tell you when the next one is due to pass. ☎98 84 94 22; www.xelha.com.mx. Open daily 8:30am-6pm. US$19.

Xel-Ha (SHELL-ha; "where the water is born") is famous for its natural aquarium, almost 2m deep, nestled amidst jungles, caves, and coves. Visitors can admire parrot fishes and meter-long barracudas and splash around all day in the nearby *caleta* (inlet). For relative peace during busy times, cross the inlet and explore the underwater caves, or stay dry and visit the sea turtle camp, where a ritual altar was discovered. Use caution and don't go diving under overhangs alone. Xel-Ha also contains two *cenotes,* a natural river, and underground sea caves. Try arriving before noon, when busloads of tourists from the resorts overrun the place. Lockers (10 pesos plus a 5-peso deposit) and towels (15 pesos plus a 50-peso deposit) are available at the shower area. Xel-Ha also maintains a small archaeological site on the highway, 100m south of the entrance to the inlet. **El Templo de Los Pájaros** and **El Palacio,** small Classic and Post-Classic ruins, were only recently opened to the public. The former (the ruin farthest into the jungle) overlooks a peaceful, shady *cenote* where swimming and rope swinging are permitted. The jungle at Xel-Ha is rife with mosquitoes, so bring insect repellent.

CENOTE DOS OJOS

Three trips depart daily from Dos Ojos Dive Center, several hundred meters south of the park entrance (9, 11am, and 1pm; ☎98 76 09 87). Trips also leave from the Cabañas Santa Fe (see p. 638). Getting to Dos Ojos requires the same patience as getting to Akumal or Xel-Ha. Hop on a combi or a colectivo after waving it down from the side of the road (every 10 min. or so).

Cenote Dos Ojos, 1km south of Xel-Ha, is the one of the longest and most extensive underwater caverns in the world, stretching 33,855m. It was originally a dry cave system with limestone formations in shades of amber as well as calcic stalactites, stalagmites, and natural wind-etchings. The system was flooded long ago, preserving the caves in their underwater condition. Snorkelers and divers find a haven in "the place of hidden waters," along with tetras, mollies, and swordfish. You must be an experienced certified open water diver to venture into Dos Ojos.

COBÁ

To get to Cobá, walk south on the main street in town as far as the T-junction at the lake. Here, take a left onto Voz Suave (Soft Voice); the ruins are a five-minute walk down this road. Regardless of when you arrive at the site, bring a water bottle and wear a hat. And unless you feel like being sacrificed to the mosquito, bring plenty of repellent as well. Ruins open daily 7am-7pm. 25 pesos; free Su.

Deep within the Yucatán jungle, guarded by shallow lakes, Cobá receives less attention than her big sisters, Chichén Itzá and Tulum. The government has poured less money into the site, leaving an estimated 6500 buildings unexcavated. The city flourished in the Classic Period, and construction reached a peak from AD 800-1100. Its population in the 8th century is believed to have been about 55,000 and it served as a major crossroad of the Yucatán Peninsula, connecting distant Maya cities through its vast network of *sacbéoob*, ancient Maya roadways. By the Post-Classic period, however, Cobá had lost its power to nearby cities such as Tulum (see p. 637) and Xcaret (see p. 629).

Once through the gate, the site's four main attractions are laid out before you in a "Y"-shaped formation, with the entrance and the ruins in **Groupo Cobá** at the base of the "Y." Past the entrance, and after an immediate right, looms the impressive **Temple of the Churches,** built over seven 52-year periods, each one associated with a new chief priest. Only the front face of the temple has been excavated, revealing a corbel-vaulted passageway that you can explore. Rising out of the jungle to the northeast are the gray steps of the ruins' centerpiece, **El Castillo.** In front of the structure is a stone **sacrificial table,** upon which animal offerings were made to Chac, the rain god. One stela (inscribed column) depicts Chac; another nearby features a kneeling Maya. Follow a second passageway farther south to the **Plaza del Templo,** where assemblies were once held. The red plant dye still visible on the walls of the passageway dates from the 5th century. A mortar here was used to prepare the staple food of the ancient (and contemporary) Maya, maize. Return to the main path for a look at the **ballcourt** with its intact stone arches.

A 1km walk up the "trunk" of the "Y" takes you to the other sites. Follow the right branch for another kilometer to reach a collection of eight stelae in the **Grupo Macanxoc.** On the way, a well-engineered Maya *sacbé* awaits your walk. This particular road is 20m wide and raised 4m from the jungle floor. The ornate stone slabs of the Grupo Macanxoc were erected as memorials above the tombs of Maya royals. Especially impressive and well preserved is the first, the **Retrato del Rey.** The king is shown standing on the heads of two slaves, bow and arrow in hand, wearing a *quetzal*-feather headdress.

Continue north to the left-hand branch of the "Y." After 200m, follow an unmarked trail on the right to the three stelae of **Chumuc Múl.** The first stela depicts a kneeling Maya ballplayer. Sure enough, this is the tomb of a victorious captain. You can make out the ball in the upper-left-hand corner. The second stela depicts a princess, while the third portrays a priest. His seal is stamped on top of the slab, along with a jaguar's head, a common Maya symbol of worship. Two hundred meters farther up this branch of the "Y," you'll run into **sacbé No. 1.** This thoroughfare ran from Cobá to Chichén Itzá, 101km to the west. Runners were posted every 5km so messages could be sent between settlements via a series of quick dashes. During the city's height (AD 800-1100), Cobá is believed to have been the major crossroads in a commercial region of 17 cities. Images of the honeybee god around the site are a reminder of this ancient economic hub. The Maya used honey (along with salt, coconuts, and jade) as a medium of exchange.

The tour climaxes with the breathtaking sight of the **Nohoch Múl,** the tallest Maya structure in the Yucatán. The pyramid's nine levels and 127 steps, where Maya priests once led processions, display carvings of the "diving god" similar to the ones in Tulum. On the top level, enjoy the view of Lake Cobá, Lake Macanxoc, and the rest of the ancient Maya commercial and religious city.

CHETUMAL ☎9

Residents of Quintana Roo are very proud of Chetumal (pop. 200,000), which snuggles against the Belize border, the relatively new capital of the youngest state in Mexico. The city was founded in 1898 to intercept shipments of arms to Maya insurgents and prevent illegal timber harvesting, and was subsequently leveled by a hurricane in 1955. The complete reconstruction explains the wide avenues, modern architecture, and waterfront boulevard. The city is also home to an extensive shopping district and world-class museum, and serves as a convenient rest stop between the Yucatán Peninsula and Guatemala or Belize.

▜ TRANSPORTATION

Airport: (☎832 04 65), 5km southwest of the city on Aquilar. **Aerocaribe** and **Mexicana,** Héroes 123 (☎832 66 75), at Plaza Baroudi. **Aviacsa** (☎832 76 76), Cárdenas at 5 de Mayo.

Buses: The bus station is at Insurgentes at Belice. To get to the *centro* from the station, your best option is a taxi (9 pesos); the walk is about 4km. From the station, ADO (☎832 51 10) offers first-class service to: **Campeche** (7hr., noon, 159 pesos); **Cancún** (5hr., 18 per day, 140 pesos); **Mexico City** (22hr., 4:30 and 9pm, 587 pesos); **Playa del Carmen** (4hr., 18 per day 12:30-11pm, 115 pesos); **Veracruz** (15hr., 6:30pm, 393 pesos); **Villahermosa** (9hr., 5 per day 9am-9pm, 212 pesos); and **Tulum** (4hr., 9 per day, 93 pesos). Cristóbal Colón leaves at 9:15pm for **Ocosingo** (218 pesos); **Palenque** (180 pesos); **San Cristóbal de las Casas** (266 pesos); and **Tuxtla Gutiérrez** (272 pesos). Batty's Bros. heads to **Belize City** 1st class (3hr., 11:45am, 3pm, and 6pm, 60 pesos) and 2nd class (5hr., 2 and 4pm, 50 pesos).

▗▙ ORIENTATION AND PRACTICAL INFORMATION

Tucked into the Yucatán's southeastern corner, Chetumal is just north of the Río Hondo, the natural border between Mexico and Belize. There are three principal approaches to the city: on Rte. 186 from Escárcega (273km), along the Caribbean coast from Cancún (379km), and from Mérida via Valladolid (458km). Chetumal's thriving shopping district lines **Héroes,** starting at the city's **Mercado Viejo** and extending 1km south to the bay. This compact commercial area encompasses most of Chetumal's hotels and restaurants. At the southern terminus of Héroes lies **Bahía,** a wide avenue flanked by statues, small plazas, and playgrounds that follows the bay for several kilometers. From here you can see part of Belize, the long, distant spit of land to the right as you face the sea.

Tourist Office: Secretaria de Turismo (☎835 08 60), on the northern extension of Héroes, 4km from the *centro*. If you take the 7-peso taxi, you will be rewarded with telephone book-like packets of information. Open M-F 8am-4pm.

Currency Exchange: Bancomer (☎832 53 00), on Juárez at Obregón, has good rates and a 24hr. **ATM.** Open M-F 8:30am-4pm, Sa 10am-2pm.

Consulates: Belize, Carranza 562 (cell ☎044 983 8 77 28). To enter Belize for 30 days, all that is needed for US, Canadian, and EU citizens is a valid passport and a bus ticket. Open M-F 9am-2pm and 5-8pm, Sa 9am-2pm. **Guatemala,** Chapultepec 354 (☎832 30 45), at Cecilio Chi. Again, US, Canadian, and EU citizens don't need a visa. For those who do, the process is quick (US$15). Open M-F 10am-2pm.

Market: Altamarino Market, also known as **El Mercado Viejo** at Aguilar and Héroes. Open daily 6am-6pm.

Supermarket: Súper San Francisco de Asis, next to the bus station.

Police: (☎832 15 00) on Insurgentes at Belice, next to the bus station. Open 24hr.

Red Cross: (☎832 05 71) on Chapultepec at Independencia, 2 blocks west of Héroes. Open 24hr.

Pharmacy: Farmacia Canto, Héroes 99 (☎832 04 83), at the north end of the market. Open M-Sa 7am-11pm, Su 7am-5pm.

Hospital: Hospital General, Quintana Roo 399 (☎832 19 32), at Sordio.

Fax: Telecomm, next to the post office. Open M-F 8am-6pm, Sa-Su 9am-12:30pm.

Internet Access: Eclipse, 5 de Mayo 83 (☎832 68 04), between Zaragoza and Calles, through a shopping plaza. 25 pesos per hr. **Ecosur,** Obregón 157 (☎832 39 60), at 16 de Septiembre. 30 pesos per hr. Open M-F 9am-6pm, Sa 9am-2pm.

Post Office: Calles 2 (☎832 25 78), 1 block east of Héroes. Open M-F 9am-4pm, Sa 9am-1pm. **Postal Code:** 77000.

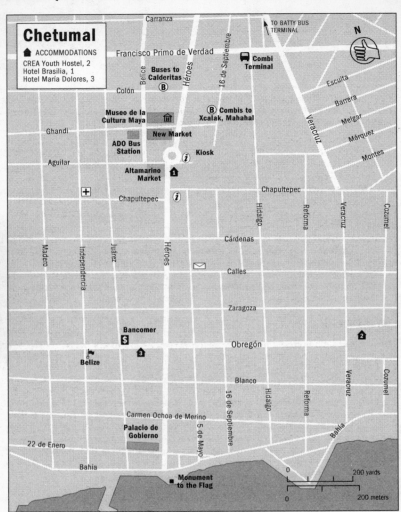

Chetumal

🏠 ACCOMMODATIONS
CREA Youth Hostel, 2
Hotel Brasilia, 1
Hotel María Dolores, 3

(map labels) Carranza, TO BATTY BUS TERMINAL, N, Francisco Primo de Verdad, Combi Terminal, Escuita, Belice, Buses to Calderitas, Héroes, Barrera, Colón, Melgar, Museo de la Cultura Maya, Combis to Xcalak, Mahahal, Márquez, Ghandi, New Market, Veracruz, Montes, ADO Bus Station, Kiosk, Aguilar, Altamarino Market, Chapultepec, Chapultepec, Cárdenas, Hidalgo, Reforma, Veracruz, Cozumel, Madero, Independencia, Juárez, Héroes, Calles, Zaragoza, Bancomer, Obregón, Belize, Blanco, Veracruz, Cozumel, 16 de Septiembre, Hidalgo, Reforma, Carmen Ochoa de Merino, Palacio de Gobierno, 5 de Mayo, Bahía, 22 de Enero, Bahía, Monument to the Flag, 200 yards, 200 meters, YUCATÁN

🏠 ACCOMMODATIONS

Chetumal's budget accommodations are far from fancy, but they score points for location. A stroll down Héroes, south of the market, will give you many options.

Hotel María Dolores, Obregón 206 (☎832 05 08), half a block west of Héroes. Look for the Donald Duck image pointing the way to aqua rooms with strong fans and private baths. Singles 100 pesos; doubles 110 pesos; triples 150 pesos.

CREA Youth Hostel (Villa Juvenil Chetumal; HI) (☎832 34 65). From Héroes, walk east on Obregón for 5 blocks until it ends. Take a left then a right and you're there. Heart-shaped pool in front and a lobby with *agua purificada* and TV. Fills July-Aug.; call to reserve. Small but clean single-sex rooms with 2 bunk beds each. Bed with sheets, pillows, and locker 30 pesos.

Hotel Brasilia, Héroes 157 (☎832 09 64), across from the market. Rooms are hit-or-miss; all are clean but some are cramped. Ask to see one first. Friendly management will store backpacks. Singles 80 pesos; doubles 105 pesos; triples 103 pesos; quads 152 pesos; TV 40 pesos extra.

☕ FOOD

Chetumal offers a spicy blend of Mexican and Belizean dishes, as well as several cafes. For cheap food, try the *loncherías* (small diners) at the market on Héroes and Aguilar, or the eateries on Obregón, west of Héroes.

Restaurante Pantoja, Gandhi 181 (☎832 39 57), past Hotel Ucum, just northeast of the market. An extremely popular family restaurant, and with good reason: *la comida casera* (homemade food) is very good and piping hot, delivered with your choice of soup (25 pesos). Drink options rotate daily. Open M-Sa 7am-9pm.

La Mansion Colonial, Bahía 8 (☎832 26 54), across from the Lázaro Cárdenas Monument at the south end of Calzada Veracruz, offers a romantic, rustic setting overlooking the bay. Try the never-ending *desayuno residencial* and eat like a king (48 pesos). Open daily 8am-midnight.

Espresso Café, Calle 22 de Enero 141 (☎833 30 13), at the southern tip of Hidalgo near the bay. Sip coffee from Chiapas and Veracruz while indulging in homemade desserts and admiring erotic art and apple trees. Open daily 8am-noon and 7pm-midnight.

Restaurant y Cocktelería Sosilmar (☎832 63 80), on Obregón, in the Hotel María Dolores. Straight from the sea to your plate. Fish filets start at 39 pesos. Open daily 8am-10:30pm.

👁 SIGHTS

At the northern end of the market is the **Museo de la Cultura Maya,** on Héroes between Ghandi and Colón. This high-tech, interactive museum is heralded as one of the best in the world devoted to Maya culture, and explores the Maya's three-leveled cosmos—the earth, underworld, and heavens—with glyphic text, sculptures, and see-through models of famous Maya temples. (Open Tu-Th 9am-7pm, F-Sa 9am-8pm, Su 9am-7pm. 50 pesos, Su free. Shows Sa 6pm and Su 11am.) A small but informative **Museo de la Ciudad** resides in the Centro Cultural de las Bellas Artes on Héroes 68, south of the market. (Open daily 9am-7pm. 10 pesos.) The nearest beach is the *balneario* at **Calderitas,** a bus ride from Chetumal. Buses leave from Colón, between Héroes and Belice. (15min., every 30min. 7am-9pm, 4 pesos.) Although the water is turbid and the shores rocky, the beach draws crowds during summer and school holidays.

↗ DAYTRIPS FROM CHETUMAL

BACALAR

Buses leave the station at the corner of Hidalgo and Verdad. (30min., every hr. 6am-9pm, 10 pesos.) The route passes Laguna Milagros and Cenote Azul before reaching Bacalar.

Much nicer than Calderitas, both for atmosphere and for swimming, are the *cenotes* near the town of Bacalar, 36km away. The bus route passes **Laguna Milagros** and **Cenote Azul** before reaching the town. Quieter than those at Bacalar, both have bathing areas, dressing rooms, and *cenote*-side restaurants. Past the **Fuerte de San Felipe** in Bacalar is the **Laguna de Siete Colores,** named for the seven hues reflected in its depths. The fresh water is warm, clear, and carpeted by powdery limestone, making it excellent for swimming. Nearby are bathrooms, dressing rooms, fruit vendors, expensive dockside restaurants, and a campground.

XCALAC

Buses (3hr., 45-65 pesos) to Xcalac, 254km from Chetumal, and the closer Mahahval, 154km from Chetumal, depart daily at 5:30am from 16 de Septiembre at Gandhi, 20m from the Restaurante Pantoja.

Much farther afield from Chetumal, the small seaside town of Xcalac, the southernmost center of population on the spit of land extending south from the **Sian Ka'an Biosphere Reserve,** provides mellow bungalows, restaurants, snorkeling, and boat rentals. Nearby off the coast is the enticing **Banco Chinchorro,** a collection of underwater shipwrecks comprising the second largest shipwreck site in the world, a deep-sea treasure-trove for experienced divers.

KOHUNLICH

Kohunlich is 67km west of Chetumal on Rte. 186. Hop on any combi from the terminal at Hidalgo and Verdad in Chetumal heading toward Villa or Bravo (1hr., every hr., 25 pesos). Ask to be let off at the crucero of Kohunlich. The entrance is 9km down a bumpy dirt road. Options are few: hitch, walk, or crawl.

Kohunlich, the ancient Maya ceremonial center of the early Classic Period famous for its stucco masks, is also a garden of palm trees and wild flowers. Its name originates from the English term Cohune Ridge, a tropical palm with copious foliage. More than 200 unexcavated Petén style and Río Bec style structures await excavation within the depths of the jungle. The **Pirámide de los Mascarones** (Pyramid of the Masks) is lined with several impressive 5th-century masks portraying the Maya sun god Kinich Ahau. The thick eyebrows and lips are similar to Olmec sculptures. To the west is the **Plaza de las Estelas** (Plaza of the Stelae), one of Quintana Roo's largest ceremonial centers. To the east of the plaza stands the **acropolis,** the largest building at the site, with 8m vaults, and the half-demolished rooms of the **residential complex** and the **palace.** To the south of the plaza a **ballcourt** lies stripped of stone arcs and markers. The farthest excavated structure is the **Building of the 27 Steps,** which served as a residence for the Maya elite AD 600-1200. Niches of all sizes line the walls, and were used to store incense canisters or home furnishings.

APPENDIX

NATIONAL HOLIDAYS

On national holidays, Mexican businesses are often closed and hotels and sights flood with vacationing Mexican families. It's a good idea to make reservations beforehand when planning to travel during these days. Official holidays are in **bold.**

January 1: Año Nuevo (New Year's Day)

January 6: Día de los Reyes (Day of the Maggi)

January 17: Día de San Antonio de Abad (Feast of the Blessing of the Animals)

February 2: Día de la Candelaria

February 5: Día de la Constitución (Constitution Day)

February 24: Día de la Bandera (Flag Day)

◪ Late February or Early March: Carnaval

March 21: Día del Nacimiento de Benito Juárez (Birthday of Benito Juárez, 1806)

Late March or Early April: Semana Santa (Holy Week)

May 1: Día del Trabajo (Labor Day)

May 5: Cinco de Mayo (Anniversary of the Battle of Puebla, 1862)

◪ May 10: Día de las Madres (Mother's Day)

August 15-16: Feast of the Assumption

September 1: Informe Presidencial (Presidential State of the Union Address)

September 16: Día de la Independencia (Anniversary of the Cry of Dolores, 1810)

October 12: Día de la Raza (Day of the Race, or Columbus Day)

November 1: Día de Todos Santos (All Saint's Day)

◪ November 2: Día de los Muertos (Day of the Dead)

November 20: Día de la Revolución (Anniversary of the Revolution, 1910)

December 12: Día de Nuestra Señora de Guadalupe

December 16: Posadas (Inns, celebrating the journey of Mary and Joseph to Bethlehem)

December 24-25: Christmas Eve and Christmas Day

SPANISH QUICK REFERENCE

PRONUNCIATION

Each vowel has only one pronunciation: A ("ah" in father); E ("eh" in pet); i ("ee" in eat); O ("oh" in oat); U ("oo" in boot); Y, by itself, is pronounced the same as Spanish I. Most consonants are pronounced the same as in English. Important exceptions are: J, pronounced like the English "h" in "hello"; LL, pronounced like the English "y" in "yes"; Ñ, pronounced like the "gn" in "cognac." R at the beginning of a word or RR anywhere in a word is trilled. H is always silent. G before E or I is pronounced like the "ch" in "chutzpah"; elsewhere it is pronounced like the "g" in "gate." X has a bewildering variety of pronunciations: depending on dialect and word position it can sound like English "h," "s," "sh," or "x." Spanish words receive stress on the syllable marked with an accent (´). In the absence of an accent mark, words that end in vowels, "n," or "s" receive stress on the second to last syllable. For words ending in all other consonants, stress falls on the last syllable. The Spanish language has masculine and feminine nouns, and gives a gender to all adjectives. Masculine words generally end with an "o": *él es un tonto* (he is a fool). Feminine words generally end with an "a": *ella es una tonta* (she is a fool). Pay close attention—slight changes in word ending can have drastic changes in meaning. For instance, when receiving directions, mind the distinction between *derecho* (straight) and *derecha* (right).

PHRASEBOOK

ENGLISH	SPANISH	ENGLISH	SPANISH
		ESSENTIAL PHRASES	
Yes/No.	Sí/No.	**Hello/Goodbye**	Hola/Adiós.
Please.	Por favor.	**I'm sick/fine.**	Estoy enfermo(a)/bien.
Thank you.	Gracias.	**Can you speak slower?**	¿Puede hablar más despacio?
You're welcome.	De nada.	**Can you repeat that?**	¿Lo puede repetir?
Do you speak English?	¿Habla inglés?	**How are you?**	¿Qué tal?/¿Cómo está?
I don't speak Spanish.	No hablo español.	**Where are (the ruins)?**	¿Dónde están (las ruinas)?
What?	¿Cómo?/¿Qué?/ ¿Mande?	**Where is (the center of town)?**	¿Dónde está (el centro)?
I don't understand.	No entiendo.	**Good morning. (Good afternoon/night.)**	Buenos días. (Buenas tardes/noches.)
What is your name?	¿Cómo se llama?	**My name is Inigo Montoya.**	Me llamo Inigo Montoya.
You killed my father...	Mató a mi padre...	**Prepare to die.**	Prepárese para morir.
How do you say (horse) in Spanish?	¿Cómo se dice (caballo) en español?	**Why (are you staring at me)?**	¿Por qué (está mirandome)?
How much does it cost?	¿Cuánto cuesta?	**That is cheap/expensive.**	Es muy caro (barato).
Excuse me.	Perdón.	**Sorry.**	Lo siento.
Closed/Open.	Cerrado(a)/Abierto(a).	**I like Let's Go.**	Me gusta Let's Go.
		YOUR ARRIVAL	
I am from the US/ Europe.	Soy de los Estados Unidos/Europa.	**What's the problem, sir?**	¿Cuál es el problema, señor?
Here is my passport/ papers.	Aquí está mi pasaporte (mis papeles).	**I have lost my passport.**	Perdí mi pasaporte.
I will be here for less than 6 months.	Estaré aquí por menos de seis meses.	**I do not know where these drugs came from.**	No sé de donde vinieron estas drogas.
I have nothing to declare.	No tengo nada para declarar.	**Please do not detain me.**	Por favor no me detenga.
		GETTING AROUND	
How do you get to (the bus station?	¿Cómo se va a (la terminal de autobúses)?	**Is there anything cheaper?**	¿Hay algo más barato/ económico?
Does this bus go to (Mérida)?	¿Este autobús va a (Mérida)?	**On foot.**	A pie.
Can I buy a ticket?	¿Puedo comprar un boleto?	**How can you get there?**	¿Cómo se puede llegar?
How long does it take?	¿Cuánto tiempo dura el viaje?	**Is it near/far?**	¿Está cerca/lejos de aquí?
Airport.	Aeropuerto.	**Turn right/left. Stay straight.**	Doble a la izquierda/ derecha. Continua al derecho.

ENGLISH	SPANISH	ENGLISH	SPANISH
The flight is delayed/cancelled.	El vuelo está retrasado/cancelado.	Hitchhike.	Pedir aventón.
I would like to rent (a car).	Quisiera rentar (un carro).	Please let me off at ...	Por favor, déjeme en...
How much does it cost per day/week?	¿Cuánto cuesta por día/semana?	I lost my baggage.	Perdí mi equipaje.

ACCOMMODATIONS			
Is there a cheap hotel around here?	¿Hay un hotel económico por aquí?	Are there rooms with air-conditioning?	¿Hay habitaciones con aire acondicionado?
Do you have rooms available?	¿Tiene habitaciones?	I am going to stay for (four) days.	Me voy a quedar (cuatro) días.
I would like to reserve a room.	Quisiera reservar una habitación.	Are there cheaper rooms?	¿Hay habitaciones más económicas?
Can I see a room?	¿Puedo ver una habitación?	Do they come with private bath?	¿Vienen con baño privado?
Do you have any single/doubles?	¿Tiene habitaciones sencillas/dobles?	I'll take it.	Lo tomo.
The bathroom is broken.	El baño está roto.	There are cockroaches in my room.	Hay cucarachas en mi habitación.

EATING OUT			
I am hungry/thirsty.	Tengo hambre/sed.	Do you have hot sauce?	¿Tiene salsa picante?
Where is a good restaurant?	¿Dónde hay un restaurante bueno?	This is too spicy.	Pica demasiado.
Can I see the menu?	¿Puedo ver el menú?	Disgusting!	¡Guácala!/¡Que asco!
Table for (one), please.	Mesa para (uno), por favor.	Check, please!	¡La cuenta, por favor!
Do you have anything vegetarian/without meat?	¿Hay algún plato vegetariano/sin carne?	Do you take credit cards?	¿Acepta tarjetas de crédito?
I would like to order (the shimp with peanut butter).	Quisiera (los camarones con manteca de cacahuete).	I am going to be sick.	Voy a vomitar.

EMERGENCY			
Help!	¡Auxilio!/¡Ayúdame!	Call the police!	Llame a la policía!
I am hurt.	Estoy herido(a).	Leave me alone!	¡Déjame en paz!
It's an emergency!	¡Es una emergencia!	I have been robbed!	¡Me han robado!
Fire!	¡Fuego!/¡Incendio!	They went that a-way!	¡Fueron en esa dirección!
Call a clinic/ambulance/doctor/priest!	¡Llame a una clínica/una ambulancia/un médico/un padre!	How can we solve this problem? [suggesting a bribe]	¿Cómo podemos resolverlo?
I need to contact my embassy.	Necesito contactar mi embajada.	I will only speak in the prescence of a lawyer.	Sólo hablaré en presencia de un abogado(a).

MEDICAL			
I feel bad/better/worse.	Me siento mal/mejor/peor.	I have a cold/a fever/diahrrea/nausea.	Tengo gripa/una calentura/diarrea/náusea.
I have a headache.	Tengo dolor de cabeza.	I have a stomach ache.	Tengo dolor de estómago.
I'm sick/ill.	Estoy enfermo(a).	It hurts here.	Me duele aquí.
I'm allergic to (cats).	Soy alérgico(a) a (los gatos).	Here is my prescription.	Aquí está mi receta médica.
What is this medicine for?	¿Para qué es esta medicina?	Where is the nearest hospital/doctor?	¿Donde está el hospital/doctor más cercano?
I think i'm going to vomit.	Pienso que voy a vomitar.	I haven't been able to go to the bathroom in (four) days.	No he podido ir al baño en (cuatro) días.

ENGLISH	SPANISH	ENGLISH	SPANISH
	(INFORMAL) PERSONAL RELATIONSHIPS		
What is your name?	¿Cómo te llamas?	Pleased to meet you.	Encantado(a)/Mucho gusto.
Where are you from?	¿De dónde eres?	I'm (twenty) years old.	Tengo (veinte) años.
This my first time in Mexico.	Este es mi primera vez en Mexico.	I have a boyfriend/girlfriend.	Tengo novio/novia.
What's your sign?	¿Cuál es tu signo?	I'm a communist.	Soy comunista.
I am gay/straight.	Soy gay/no soy gay.	Would you like to go out with me?	¿Quieres salir conmigo?
Do you have a light?	¿Tienes fuego?	It's true. Politicians can never be trusted.	De verdad. No se puede confiar en los políticos.
I had the very same dream!	¡Tenía el mismo sueño!	No thanks, I have diseases.	No gracias, tengo enfermedades.
Yes, I do believe in UFOs.	Sí, creo en los OVNIs.	Marrying me will not make you a US citizen.	Casarte conmigo no te hara automaticamente norteamericano(a).
I love you.	Te quiero.	What a shame: you bought Lonely Planet!	¡Qué lástima: compraste Lonely Planet!

	NUMBERS AND DAYS		
0	cero	21	veintiuno
1	uno	22	veintidos
2	dos	30	treinta
3	tres	40	cuarenta
4	cuatro	50	cincuenta
5	cinco	100	cien
6	seis	1000	mil
7	siete	1 million	un millón
8	ocho	Sunday	Domingo
9	nueve	Monday	Lunes
10	diez	Tuesday	Martes
11	once	Wednesday	Miércoles
12	doce	Thursday	Jueves
13	trece	Friday	Viernes
14	catorce	Saturday	Sábado
15	quince	today	hoy
16	dieciseis	tomorrow	mañana
17	diecisiete	day after tomorrow	pasado mañana
18	dieciocho	yesterday	ayer
19	diecinueve	day before yesterday	antes de ayer/anteayer
20	veinte	weekend	fin de semana

GLOSSARY OF TERMS

agua (purificada): water (purified)
almuerzo: lunch
andador: pedestrian walkway
antojitos: appetizers
artesanía: artisanry
avenida: avenue
bahía: bay
bandidos: bandits
baños: bathrooms
barrancas: canyons
batido: milkshake
basílica: basilica
buena suerte: good luck
buen provecho: bon appetit
café: coffee, cafe
calle: street
callejón: little street; alley
cascadas: waterfalls
camarones: shrimp
camión: bus
cantina: saloon-type bar (mostly-male clientele)
capilla: chapel
casa de cambio: currency exchange booth
caseta: phone stall
catedral: cathedral
cena: dinner
cenote: freshwater sinkhole
centro: center (of town)
cerveza: beer
colectivo: shared taxi
colonia: neighborhood
combi: small local bus
comida corrida: fixed menu
crucero: crossroads
cuarto: room
cucaracha: cockroach
cueva: cave

de paso: bus that picks up passengers by roadsides
desayuno: breakfast
dinero: money
dulces: sweets
embarcadero: dock
farmacia: pharmacy
faro: lighthouse
fiesta: party; holiday
frijoles: beans
fútbol: soccer
glorieta: traffic circle
gobierno: government
gratis: free
gringo: stupid white American
grutas: caves
güera: blond
helado: ice cream
iglesia: church
isla: island
lancha: boat
lavandería: laundromat
licuado: smoothie
lonchería: lunch place
malecón: promenade, boulevard
mar: ocean; sea
mariscos: seafood
menú del día: pre-set meal
mercado: market (often outdoor)
merienda: afternoon snack
microbús: minibus
mirador: viewpoint
norte (Nte.): north
oriente (Ote.): east
palapa: palm-thatched beach bungalow
panadería: bread shop
parque: park
paseo: promenade
pesero: local bus

pirámides: pyramids
playa: beach
plaza: square
pollo: chicken
poniente (Pte.): west
posada: inn
postre: sweet; dessert
poza: well; pool
primera clase: first-class
pueblo: village; community
queso: cheese
refrescos: refreshments
ruinas: ruins
ruta: local bus
sacbe (Maya): upraised, paved road
sacerdote: priest
salida: exit
salud: health
segunda clase: second-class
selva: jungle
servicio de lujo: luxury service
simpático: friendly/nice
stela: upright stone monument
supermercado: supermarket
sur: south
taquería: taco stand
tejano: Texan
telenovela: soap opera
templo: church; temple
típico: typical, traditional
torta: sandwich
turismo: tourism
turista: tourist; diarrhea
tranquilo: peaceful
vaquero: cowboy
valle: valley
zócalo: central square
zona: zone; region

APPENDIX

CLIMATE AND PRECIPITATION

	°C	°F	mm	°C	°F	mm	°C	°F	mm	°C	°F	mm
Acapulco	22/31	72/88	N/A	25/32	77/90	N/A	25/33	77/91	N/A	24/32	75/90	N/A
Guadalajara	7/23	45/73	15	14/31	57/88	8	15/26	59/79	257	10/25	50/77	54
La Paz	13/23	55/73	23	17/33	63/91	1	23/36	73/97	32	17/29	63/84	28
Mérida	18/28	64/82	60	21/34	70/93	148	23/33	73/91	122	19/29	66/84	269
Mexico City	6/22	43/72	8	13/27	5/81	19	13/24	55/75	129	9/23	48/73	44
Monterrey	9/20	48/68	18	20/31	68/88	29	22/34	72/93	62	12/23	54/73	78
Oaxaca	8/28	46/82	3	15/32	59/90	26	15/28	59/82	88	10/28	50/82	44
San Cristóbal	5/20	41/68	N/A	9/22	48/72	N/A	10/22	50/72	N/A	7/20	45/68	N/A
Tijuana	6/20	41/68	49	12/23	54/73	20	16/27	61/81	1	10/23	50/73	13
Veracruz	18/25	65/77	19	25/30	70/86	22	22/31	75/88	401	21/28	70/82	146

MEASUREMENT CONVERSIONS

1 inch (in.) = 25.4 millimeters (mm)	1 millimeter (mm) = 0.039 in.
1 foot (ft.) = 0.30 m	1 meter (m) = 3.28 ft.
1 yard (yd.) = 0.914m	1 meter (m) = 1.09 yd.
1 mile = 1.61km	1 kilometer (km) = 0.62 mi.
1 ounce (oz.) = 28.35g	1 gram (g) = 0.035 oz.
1 pound (lb.) = 0.454kg	1 kilogram (kg) = 2.202 lb.
1 fluid ounce (fl. oz.) = 29.57ml	1 milliliter (ml) = 0.034 fl. oz.
1 gallon (gal.) = 3.785L	1 liter (L) = 0.264 gal.
1 acre (ac.) = 0.405ha	1 hectare (ha) = 2.47 ac.
1 square mile (sq. mi.) = 2.59km^2	1 square kilometer (km^2) = 0.386 sq. mi.

APPENDIX

DISTANCES (KM) AND TRAVEL TIMES (BY BUS)

	Acapulco	Chihuahua	Cancún	El Paso	Guadalajara	La Paz	Mazatlán	Mérida	Mexico City	Monterrey	Oaxaca	Puebla	San Cristóbal	San Luis Potosí	Tijuana	Veracruz
Acapulco		2440	1938	2815	1028	4917	1429	1779	415	1402	700	544	1036	828	3228	847
Chihuahua	24hr.		3262	375	1552	3237	1031	2945	1496	834	2154	1625	2785	1195	1548	1841
Cancún	33hr.	47hr.		3637	2442	6499	2963	319	1766	2506	1693	1895	902	2267	4810	1421
El Paso	29hr.	5hr.	54hr.		1549	3009	1406	3320	1871	1209	2529	2000	3127	1569	1320	2216
Guadalajara	15hr.	17hr.	45hr.	25hr.		4159	521	2125	676	885	1222	805	1853	348	2340	1021
La Paz	60hr.	46hr.	96hr.	41hr.	60hr.		3508	6180	4733	4071	5279	4862	5883	4283	1689	5050
Mazatlán	21hr.	15½hr.	53hr.	25hr.	8hr.	50hr.		2646	1197	940	1743	1326	2374	799	1819	1542
Mérida	29hr.	42hr.	4hr.	47hr.	40½hr.	92hr.	40hr.		1449	2189	1374	1791	743	799	4491	1104
Mexico City	6hr.	20hr.	26hr.	25hr.	10hr.	68hr.	18hr.	22hr..		950	546	129	1177	413	3044	345
Monterrey	18hr.	12hr.	38hr.	17hr.	11hr.	60hr.	17hr.	32hr.	12hr.		1533	1116	1918	537	2382	1085
Oaxaca	9hr.	29hr.	29hr.	34hr.	17hr.	77hr.	27hr.	24½hr.	9hr.	21hr.		417	631	959	3590	450
Puebla	7hr.	22hr.	24hr.	27hr.	12hr.	71hr.	20hr.	20hr.	2hr.	14hr.	4hr.		1048	542	3285	303
San Cristóbal	16hr.	39hr.	17hr.	44hr.	28hr.	88hr.	19hr.	12½hr.	18hr.	30hr.	12hr.	16hr.		1590	4193	833
San Luis Potosí	10hr.	14hr.	31hr.	18hr.	6hr.	60hr.	12hr.	27hr.	5hr.	7hr.	20hr.	16hr.	23hr.		2743	846
Tijuana	46hr.	22hr.	72hr.	17hr.	36hr.	24hr.	26hr.	66hr.	44hr.	36hr.	53hr.	46hr.	62hr.	36hr.		3361
Veracruz	13hr.	28hr.	21hr.	33hr.	17hr.	76hr.	26hr.	13hr.	8hr.	17hr.	8hr.	4½hr.	13hr.	13hr.	52hr.	

APPENDIX

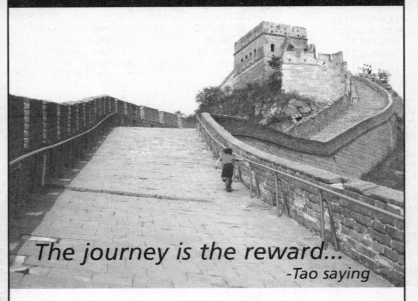

INDEX

INDEX

ABOUT LET'S GO

FORTY-ONE YEARS OF WISDOM

As a new millennium arrives, *Let's Go: Europe*, now in its 41st edition and translated into seven languages, reigns as the world's bestselling international travel guide. For over four decades, travelers criss-crossing the Continent have relied on *Let's Go* for inside information on the hippest backstreet cafes, the most pristine secluded beaches, and the best routes from border to border. In the last 20 years, our rugged researchers have stretched the frontiers of backpacking and expanded our coverage into Asia, Africa, Australia, and the Americas. This year, we've introduced a new city guide series with books on San Francisco and our hometown, Boston. Now, our seven city guides feature sharp photos, more maps, and an overall more user-friendly design. We've also returned to our roots with the inaugural edition of *Let's Go: Western Europe*.

It all started in 1960 when a handful of well-traveled students at Harvard University handed out a 20-page mimeographed pamphlet offering a collection of their tips on budget travel to passengers on student charter flights to Europe. The following year, in response to the instant popularity of the first volume, students traveling to Europe researched the first full-fledged edition of *Let's Go: Europe*, a pocket-sized book featuring honest, practical advice, witty writing, and a decidedly youthful slant on the world. Throughout the 60s and 70s, our guides reflected the times. In 1969 we taught travelers how to get from Paris to Prague on "no dollars a day" by singing in the street. In the 80s and 90s, we looked beyond Europe and North America and set off to all corners of the earth. Meanwhile, we focused in on the world's most exciting urban areas to produce in-depth, fold-out map guides. Our new guides bring the total number of titles to 51, each infused with the spirit of adventure and voice of opinion that travelers around the world have come to count on. But some things never change: our guides are still researched, written, and produced entirely by students who know first-hand how to see the world on the cheap.

HOW WE DO IT

Each guide is completely revised and thoroughly updated every year by a well-traveled set of nearly 300 students. Every spring, we recruit over 200 researchers and 90 editors to overhaul every book. After several months of training, researcher-writers hit the road for seven weeks of exploration, from Anchorage to Adelaide, Estonia to El Salvador, Iceland to Indonesia. Hired for their rare combination of budget travel sense, writing ability, stamina, and courage, these adventurous travelers know that train strikes, stolen luggage, food poisoning, and marriage proposals are all part of a day's work. Back at our offices, editors work from spring to fall, massaging copy written on Himalayan bus rides into witty, informative prose. A student staff of typesetters, cartographers, publicists, and managers keeps our lively team together. In September, the collected efforts of the summer are delivered to our printer, who turns them into books in record time, so that you have the most up-to-date information available for your vacation. Even as you read this, work on next year's editions is well underway.

WHY WE DO IT

We don't think of budget travel as the last recourse of the destitute; we believe that it's the only way to travel. Living cheaply and simply brings you closer to the people and places you've been saving up to visit. Our books will ease your anxieties and answer your questions about the basics—so you can get off the beaten track and explore. Once you learn the ropes, we encourage you to put *Let's Go* down now and then to strike out on your own. You know as well as we that the best discoveries are often those you make yourself. When you find something worth sharing, please drop us a line. We're Let's Go Publications, 67 Mount Auburn St., Cambridge, MA 02138, USA (email: feedback@letsgo.com). For more info, visit our website, www.letsgo.com.

If I had my life
to live over again,

I would relax. I would limber up. I would take more chances.

I would take more trips.

I would climb more mountains, swim more rivers, and watch more sunsets.

I would go places and do things and travel lighter than I have.

I would ride more
merry-go-rounds.

Excerpt from Nadine Stair, 85 years old / photo> John Norris

Lowe
alpine

technical packs & apparel

Find Yourself. Somewhere Else.

Don't just land there, do something. Away.com
is the Internet's preferred address for those
who like their travel with a little something
extra. Our team of travel enthusiasts and
experts can help you design your ultimate
adventure, nature or cultural escape. Make
Away.com your destination for extraordinary
travel. Then find yourself. Somewhere else.

away.com
1.877.769.2929

Will you have enough stories to tell your grandchildren?

Yahoo! Travel

Do You YAHOO!?